As the founder of sociology, positivism, and the history of science, Auguste Comte was arguably the most important nineteenth-century French philosopher. Yet he has been curiously neglected. Based upon ten years of research, including three years of archival work in Paris, Mary Pickering's projected two-volume study constitutes the first comprehensive intellectual biography of this thinker. This first volume covers the period from his birth to the completion of the seminal *Cours de philosophie positive* and places Comte's evolution within the context of postrevolutionary France. It shows that Comte, reacting to the cataclysmic upheavals of his time, developed sociology as a way to unify society. He conceived the new doctrine of positivism to serve as its basis and to eliminate the questionable abstractions of conventional philosophy.

The book examines the interplay between Comte's controversial intellectual development and the vicissitudes of his personal and professional life. It highlights his struggles with poverty and mental illness, his failed marriage to a so-called prostitute, and his violent confrontations with the government and the scientific community. At the same time, it investigates his volatile relationships with his family, friends, and disciples, as well as with such famous contemporaries as Saint-Simon, the Saint-Simonians, Guizot, and John Stuart Mill.

Pickering challenges the traditional view of Comte as an arid, simplistic thinker. According to her, he always emphasized the importance of the emotions and distrusted the scientistic approach that now is paradoxically associated with positivism. She thus demonstrates that his later religious direction did not constitute a break with his early beliefs but represented their logical outcome.

Auguste Comte

Auguste Comte

AUGUSTE COMTE

An Intellectual Biography, Volume I

MARY PICKERING

CAMBRIDGE
UNIVERSITY PRESS

Published by the Press Syndicate of the University of Cambridge
The Pitt Building, Trumpington Street, Cambridge CB2 IRP
40 West 20th Street, New York, NY 10011–4211, USA
10 Stamford Road, Oakleigh, Melbourne 3166, Australia

First published 1993

Printed in the United States of America

Library of Congress Cataloging-in-Publication Data
Pickering, Mary.
Auguste Comte: an intellectual biography / Mary Pickering.
v. <1>; cm.
Includes bibliographical references.
Contents: v. 1.
ISBN 0–521–43405–X
1. Comte, Auguste, 1798–1857. 2. Philosophers – France – Biography.
I. Title.
B2247. P53   1993
194 – dc20
[B]
                                                        92–44510
                                                             CIP

A catalog record for this book is available from the British Library.

ISBN 0–521–43405–X hardback

To My Father

Contents

Acknowledgments

I am grateful to many people who have helped me in the preparation of this book. I would like to thank Donald Fleming, whose encouragement and patience never faltered. His insights, criticisms, and humor made writing an intellectual biography a most rewarding experience. I also owe a great debt to Isabel Pratas-Frescata, the treasurer of the International Association of the Maison d'Auguste Comte. Radiating warmth and curiosity, she gave me complete access to the resources of the Maison d'Auguste Comte, the museum and research center in Paris devoted to Comte's memory, and she aided me in many ways both personally and professionally for three years. Included in my thanks is Trajano Bruno de Berrêdo Carneiro, president of the International Association of the Maison d'Auguste Comte. I am pleased to show my appreciation to Claudine Billoux, the archivist of the Ecole Polytechnique, who was ever ready to expend the greatest effort to find any document that I needed. My thanks go to the staffs of the Bibliothèque Nationale, the Bibliothèque de l'Arsenal, the Bibliothèque Thiers, the Archives Nationales, and the Archives de la Seine. The Comte scholars Henri Gouhier, the late Paul Arbousse-Bastide, Angèle Kremer-Marietti, and Barbara Skarga gave me valuable advice, for which I am most grateful.

Moreover, I am indebted to the French government and to the Institut Français de Washington for the fellowships that allowed me to do research in Paris during the academic year 1983–4. I owe a great deal to Harvard University for enabling me to attend the Institut d'Etudes Politiques in Paris, whose professors kindly encouraged my work on the relationship between Comte and Mill. I would also like to thank the Scholarly Research Committee of Pace University for giving me the time to finish this book.

In addition, I would like to thank the following people for their help and unflagging support throughout the years: Lilian and Oscar Handlin, Nancy Roelker, René Rémond, Londa Schiebinger, Lorenza Sebesta, Pascal Griset, and Kathleen Kete. Frank Smith, my editor at Cambridge University Press, was generous in sharing his wisdom with me. Mary Racine, my copyeditor, could not have been more careful, diligent, and good-humored. Donald Kelley kindly gave me permission to use material from my article on Comte and German philosophy that appeared in the *Journal of the History of Ideas* (1989). My thanks also go to James Farr and John Contreni for allowing me to use portions of my article on Comte and the Saint-Simonians that was published in *French Historical Studies* (1993).

Finally, those closest to me deserve recognition for their patience and sacrifice: my husband, Francis Lauricella; my children, Nicolas and Natalia Lauricella; my parents-in-law and "Auntie"; and my late mother, Helen Pickering, whose gift of determination I always sought to emulate. The book could not have been completed without the help of my brother John Pickering and his eagerness to share his computer expertise. Above all, I thank my father, Alexander Pickering, for reading and criticizing the manuscript several times, for offering his support at every opportunity, and especially for inspiring me with a deep love of history.

Abbreviations

AN	Archives Nationales
BA	Bibliothèque de l'Arsenal
BN	Bibliothèque Nationale
CG	*Auguste Comte: Correspondance générale et confessions,* edited by Paulo E. de Berrêdo Carneiro, Pierre Arnaud, Paul Arbousse-Bastide, and Angèle Kremer-Marietti, 8 vols. (Paris: Ecole des Hautes Etudes en Sciences Sociales, 1973–90)
EP	Archives of the Ecole Polytechnique
MAC	Archives of the Maison d'Auguste Comte, Paris
RO	*La Revue occidentale*

Introduction

At twenty-seven, Auguste Comte remarked to a friend, "The essence of my life is a novel, and an intense novel, which would appear truly extraordinary if I ever published it under some assumed names."[1] Although Comte never turned his attention to writing fiction, he remained thoroughly preoccupied by his own emotional development, which increasingly dominated his philosophy. In his letters and works, he set out to refashion his life to give the impression that he was a thoroughly original and creative genius, whose philosophy was unjustly neglected by his "metaphysical" contemporaries. Indifference to Comte's life and work has continued to be a problem. Although Comte is among the dozen most important intellectual figures in modern European history, he has never been the subject of an exhaustive or balanced book in any language. His story, however, is worth telling. This study in intellectual history seeks to fill this gap by deciphering the various strands of the myth consciously elaborated by Comte and further embellished by his disciples. It concentrates on Comte's so-called first career, which ended with the completion of his most influential work, the *Cours de philosophie positive*, in 1842, the year he turned forty-four. It was during this period that he made his main contribution to modern culture: the establishment of positivism and sociology.

This work seems particularly relevant because a new concern with Comte's thought has emerged in the past twenty years, due partly to a revived interest in the history of science and in the roots of sociology and modern positivism. It is reflected in new editions of his works, such as the *Traité philosophique d'astronomie populaire* and the *Cours de philosophie positive*, and in the publication for the first time of all of his early essays and his complete correspondence, primarily by the Ecole des Hautes Etudes en Sciences Sociales.[2]

---

[1] Comte to Valat, November 16, 1825, *Auguste Comte: Correspondance générale et confessions*, ed. Paulo E. de Berrêdo Carneiro, Pierre Arnaud, Paul Arbousse-Bastide, and Angèle Kremer-Marietti, 8 vols. (Paris: Ecole des Hautes Etudes en Sciences Sociales, 1973–90) (hereafter, *CG*), 1:163. Unless otherwise noted, the translations of all passages originally written in French are my own.

[2] Auguste Comte, *Traité philosophique d'astronomie populaire précédé du Discours sur l'esprit positif*, Corpus des oeuvres de philosophie en langue française (Paris: Fayard, 1985) (hereafter, *Traité*

Stanislav Andreski and Gertrud Lenzer have provided English translations of selections from Comte's works.[3] Other evidence of a
new interest in Comte is demonstrated by Angèle Kremer-Marietti's
and Sarah Kofman's semiotic analyses of his works, Pierre Arnaud's
study of his religion, the *Revue philosophique*'s two issues devoted to
his thought (published in 1985 and 1988), the *Revue de synthèse*'s
analysis of his politics in a 1991 issue, and Joan Landes's examination of his ideas on gender in *Women and the Public Sphere in the Age
of the French Revolution*.[4] Most of this work is being done by philosophers. This book seeks to complement their efforts. It explores
not only Comte's thought but his personal and familial life as well
as the cultural, intellectual, social, and political environment that
helped to shape his outlook. In this way, it sheds light on the interaction between Comte's ideas and their context.

The issue that was most important in the aftermath of the French
Revolution was that of the basis and ends of power. How could the
nation best be governed? How could it avoid the problem of mob
rule (i.e., a renewal of the Terror) as well as that of dictatorship (i.e.,
a new Napoleon)? Why should citizens obey a specific authority
or hold certain values? Was there even such a thing as truth any
more?[5] Such questions led to the ideological controversies of the

---

philosophique d'astronomie populaire); idem, *Philosophie première: Cours de philosophie positive,
leçons 1 à 45*, ed. Michel Serres, François Dagonet, Allal Sinaceur (Paris: Hermann, 1975)
(hereafter, *Cours*, 1); idem, *Physique sociale: Cours de philosophie positive, leçons 46 à 60*, ed.
Jean-Paul Enthoven (Paris: Hermann, 1975) (hereafter, *Cours*, 2); idem, *Ecrits de jeunesse,
1816–1828: Suivis du Mémoire sur la cosmogonie de Laplace, 1835*, ed. Paulo E. de Berrêdo
Carneiro and Pierre Arnaud (Paris: Ecole Pratique des Hautes Etudes, 1970) (hereafter, *Ecrits*);
CG, 1–8.

[3] Stanislav Andreski, ed., and Margaret Clarke, trans., *The Essential Comte: Selected from "Cours
de Philosophie Positive"* (New York: Harper & Row, Barnes & Noble, 1974); Gertrud Lenzer,
ed., *Auguste Comte and Positivism: The Essential Writings* (New York: Harper & Row, Harper
Torchbooks, 1975).

[4] Angèle Kremer-Marietti, *Le Concept de science positive: Ses Tenants et ses aboutissants dans
les structures anthropologiques du positivisme* (Paris: Klincksieck, 1983); idem, *Entre le Signe et
l'Histoire: L'Anthropologie positiviste d'Auguste Comte* (Paris: Klincksieck, 1982); idem, *Le Projet
anthropologique d'Auguste Comte* (Paris: Société d'Edition d'Enseignement Supérieur, 1980);
Sarah Kofman, *Aberrations: Le Devenir-femme d'Auguste Comte* (Paris: Aubier-Flammarion,
1978); Pierre Arnaud, *Le "Nouveau Dieu": Préliminaires à la politique positive* (Paris: J. Vrin,
1973); *Revue philosophique de la France et de l'étranger*, no. 4 (1985), no. 3 (1988); *Revue de
synthèse* 112 (January–March 1991); Joan B. Landes, *Women and the Public Sphere in the Age
of the French Revolution* (Ithaca, N.Y.: Cornell University Press, 1988).

[5] Isaiah Berlin, *The Crooked Timber of Humanity: Chapters in the History of Ideas*, ed. Henry
Hardy (London: John Murray, 1990; New York: Random House, Vintage Books, 1992),
97–8; Stephen Holmes, *Benjamin Constant and the Making of Modern Liberalism* (New Haven,
Conn.: Yale University Press, 1984), 15, 85, 96–99; Biancamaria Fontana, *Benjamin
Constant and the Post-Revolutionary Mind* (New Haven, Conn.: Yale University Press, 1991),
106.

Bourbon Restoration and July Monarchy. By revealing how these disputes helped to define the characteristics of Comte's system, I hope to contribute to the growing debate on the process by which postrevolutionary France modified and domesticated the explosive principles of 1789.[6]

I maintain that given the circumstances in which he developed his philosophy, Comte from the very beginning of his career distrusted the type of morally neutral, "positivist" or "scientistic" thinking that is now associated with his name. "Positivism" is indeed a problematical term. Reduced to extreme scientism, a strong faith in the ability of science to solve all problems, positivism is usually equated with empirical, experimental, and statistical methods of research applied to all areas of knowledge.[7] Irving Louis Horowitz provides one example of this interpretation: "By positivism is meant the development of a total portrait of man derived from the combination of discrete questionnaires, surveys, and other atomic facts."[8] Other social scientists call positivism a materialistic and antisubjective doctrine that delights in sterile formalism and disregards the emotional and moral side of human existence as well as the whole subject of values. They criticize Comte not only for promulgating such a philosophy, but for advocating the dictatorship of scientists.[9] But there is much evidence to demonstrate that Comte always gave his philosophical system a practical, political mission, one based on social justice.

As a boy, Comte was deeply affected by the chaos of ideas, uncertainties, and social and political divisions created by the French Revolution. Whereas his parents and the majority of townspeople in his native city of Montpellier tended to sympathize with the counterrevolution, Comte rebelled against their strong Catholicism and royalism and was attracted to the republican and secular ideals of the Revolution. Responding to the anarchy of his time, he committed himself at an early age to completing the work of the Revolution, which he came to realize had touched the entire Western world. Owing to his rebellious nature and the force of circumstances,

---

[6] Jack Hayward, *After the Revolution: Six Critics of Democracy and Nationalism* (New York: New York University Press, 1991), xi.

[7] Richard H. Brown, *A Poetic for Sociology: Toward a Logic of Discovery for the Human Sciences* (Cambridge: Cambridge University Press, 1977), 17, 33; Jack D. Douglas, "Understanding Everyday Life," in *Understanding Everyday Life: Toward the Reconstruction of Sociological Knowledge*, ed. Douglas (Chicago: Aldine, 1970), 23–4.

[8] Irving Louis Horowitz, *Professing Sociology: Studies in the Life Cycle of Social Science* (Chicago: Aldine, 1968), 200.

[9] See, e.g., William R. Catton, Jr., *From Animistic to Naturalistic Sociology* (New York: McGraw-Hill, 1966), 42; F. A. Hayek, *New Studies in Philosophy, Politics, Economics and the History of Ideas* (London: Routledge & Kegan Paul, 1978), 13–14, 20; idem, *The Counter-Revolution of Science: Studies on the Abuse of Reason* (Glencoe, Ill.: Free Press, 1952), 92, 183, 201–2.

his efforts to find a place for himself in postrevolutionary society failed. He became more and more marginal and increasingly disillusioned with his contemporaries' political experimentation. His association with Saint-Simon contributed to his growing awareness that he could rise above the Revolution by formulating an intellectual doctrine that would appeal to the traditionalism of the Right and the rationalism of the Left and thereby establish social harmony.

This doctrine, positivism, was all-encompassing, centering on a general understanding of the main sciences. Comte maintained that positivism systematized the whole range of human knowledge because of its keystone – a new science of society. Forged by Comte from different elements of the philosophies of the seventeenth, eighteenth, and early nineteenth centuries, this new science, which he called sociology in 1838, derived from the extension of the scientific method to society. It was based on his classification of the sciences and his law of the three stages of history. By making all ideas rest on the scientific method, which sought certain knowledge through the observation of facts, positivism would be able to establish irrefutable principles acceptable to each member of society. In this way, it would ensure social consensus.

Moreover, with a grasp of the laws of social progress acquired through the study of history, Comte contended that human conduct and development could be made more rational and predictable. Knowledge about the social world would give one control over the social world. No longer would there loom the threat of anarchy.

Comte never intended for sociology to be "objective" or purely empirical. Indeed, he felt pure empiricism was as dangerous as mysticism. Instead, he argued that induction must be complemented by deduction, for a person must first have a theory in order to observe. Comte's hierarchy of the sciences and his stress on the ruling power of ideas further demonstrate his idealistic, antimechanistic, and antireductionist inclinations. He denounced the statistical approach to scientific research that scholars, such as Horowitz, tend to equate with positivism. In fact, his abhorrence of the quantification of human experience led him to look favorably upon vitalism. Contrary to current assumptions, Comte was from the beginning of his career fully aware of the power of emotional and spiritual needs.

He maintained that positivism and its principal component, sociology, would profoundly change the way people think. This intellectual revolution would lead to a revival of moral order and then a political transformation that would usher in a new era of consensus. The people who would control the new society would not be scientists. Despite what is commonly believed about him, Comte distrusted scientific specialization, for he was convinced that the division of labor led to a narrowing of views and sentiments. His failed efforts to become a member of the Academy of Sciences and a professor at the Ecole Polytechnique reinforced his aversion to scientists. He argued that philosophers who had training in all of the sciences and thus had the most general knowledge possessed the widest possible views. They should replace the traditional clergy and guide the new positivist society, directing its energies toward a common goal, the improvement of humanity. As Comte's relationships with his friends and his wife foundered and he felt deprived of a rewarding emotional life, he found fulfillment in considering himself the savior of "humanity." And to save the species, he warned in particular against allowing his new spiritual power to have full authority over society; he feared the reign of the mind would stifle the progress he hoped to ensure.

In sum, although Comte's solution to the malaise of his era was an intellectual system that would give people new, homogeneous ideas and convictions, his central concerns were always political activism and social reform. He considered his goal to be "spiritual" because it involved the fundamental reorganization of people's ideas and sentiments. Society could function effectively only if based on a set of common opinions, ideas, and mores. Even before the blossoming of his love for Clotilde de Vaux in 1845, Comte was ready to proclaim that the belief system of positivism was a "religion" and that positive philosophers represented the new spiritual power. Thus there was no sudden change of direction from his "first" career to his "second."

Chapter 1 of this book sets the context and covers Comte's life up to 1817. After offering a glimpse of the chaos in France, especially in Montpellier, just before and during Comte's childhood, it reveals Comte's response to the challenges bequeathed by the French Revolution to the nineteenth century and his reaction to the Napoleonic regime and the Bourbon Restoration. In addition, this chapter explores his family life and his educational experience and explains his projects after his expulsion from the Ecole Polytechnique. It also discusses Comte's crucial reading of Montesquieu and Condorcet at this time.

Chapter 2 takes a long look at Saint-Simon, who had a significant impact on Comte's personal and intellectual development. Chapters 3, 4, and 5 deal with Comte's association with Saint-Simon and his journalistic endeavors. They also place Comte's efforts to establish a new doctrine within the context of the general search for a new foundation for liberal politics – a search that was partly inspired by the rejection of the discredited abstract language of the Revolution. After showing how Comte was beginning to combine his interest in politics and science and formulate positive philosophy, I analyze Comte's rupture with Saint-Simon in 1824.

Chapters 6, 7, and 8 concentrate on Comte's struggles to find personal and intellectual connections from 1824 to 1828. They cover his search for ideas and reassurance in the counterrevolutionary tradition, liberalism, the Scottish philosophy of the Enlightenment, phrenology, and the doctrines of Herder, Kant, and Hegel. I also examine Comte's work for the Saint-Simonian journal *Le Producteur*. Finally, I analyze his marriage to Caroline Massin and her role in his attack of insanity in 1826, which occurred after he finally began to give a course on positive philosophy.

Chapters 9 through 13 cover Comte's continuing efforts to find a stable source of livelihood and a place for himself in scientific circles from 1828 to 1842. They highlight his friendship with John Stuart Mill as well as his difficulties with the Academy of Sciences, the Ecole Polytechnique, his wife, his friends, and the Saint-Simonians. They also show Comte's problems in writing and publishing the *Cours de philosophie positive*. Chapters 14 and 15 offer a detailed analysis of the ideas contained in this masterpiece.

In the Conclusion, I reexamine the evidence refuting the contention that Comte was first an arid scientific thinker and then became a mad religious reformer in his so-called second career because of his sudden love for Clotilde de Vaux.[10] Comte's case is enlightening because his reversion to a traditional religious terminology exemplifies the nineteenth-century problem of dealing with spiritual longing in an age of growing skepticism. His authoritarian solution underscores the weakness of liberalism in nineteenth-century France.

---

[10] Raymond Aron calls Comte's religion a "biographical accident." Raymond Aron, *Main Currents in Sociological Thought*, trans. Richard Howard and Helen Weaver, 2 vols. (Garden City, N.Y.: Doubleday, Anchor Books, 1968), 1:124.

Chapter 1

The Early Years

The Revolution is still operative.
Alexis de Tocqueville, 1856

THE CONTEXT: THE FRENCH REVOLUTION

On 16 Nivôse Year VI, the Directory sent an ordinance to the administrators of Montpellier, the former center of the royal province of Languedoc and now the capital of the newly created department of Hérault. The decree asserted that order was impossible to maintain in the town in view of the fanaticism of the people and their violent, vengeful acts. As one of the nineteen cities having the most difficulty with royalist agitation, Montpellier was immediately placed in a state of siege.[1] It was amid such chaos that Isidore-Auguste-Marie-François-Xavier Comte was born on 30 Nivôse Year VI, more commonly known as January 19, 1798.[2]

Although Comte's life began in the waning years of the French Revolution, the turbulent decade of upheaval left its imprint upon him as upon several generations of Frenchmen. In his famous "Personal Preface" to volume 6 of his *Cours de philosophie positive*, the only childhood experience that he discussed at length had to do with the Revolution. He explained that by age fourteen, he had gone "through all the essential stages of the revolutionary spirit." Because of the

[1] J. Duval-Jouve, *Montpellier pendant la Révolution*, 2 vols. (Montpellier, 1879–81), 2:359–61; F. Saurel, *Histoire religieuse du département de l'Hérault pendant la Révolution, le Consulat, et les premières années de l'Empire*, 4 vols. (Paris, 1894–6), 3:188.
[2] The best biography of Comte for the period of his life up to age twenty-six is Henri Gouhier's *La Jeunesse d'Auguste Comte et la formation du positivisme*, 3 vols. (Paris: J. Vrin, 1933–41). For standard biographies that cover Comte's entire life, consult Henri Gouhier, *La Vie d'Auguste Comte*, 2d ed. (Paris: J. Vrin, 1965); Emile Littré, *Auguste Comte et la philosophie positive*, 2d ed. (Paris, 1864); Joseph Lonchampt, *Précis de la vie et des écrits d'Auguste Comte* (Paris, 1889; extract from the *Revue occidentale*), and [Jean-François Eugène] Robinet, *Notice sur l'oeuvre et la vie d'Auguste Comte*, 3d ed. (Paris, 1891). Two authors who evaluate his thought and also give biographical indications are Aron, "Auguste Comte," chap. in *Main Currents*, 1:73–143, and Frank E. Manuel, "Auguste Comte: Embodiment in the Great Being," chap. in *The Prophets of Paris* (New York: Harper Torchbooks, 1965), 249–96. A useful summary of Comte's thought can be found in D. G. Charlton, "From Positivism to Scientism (1) Auguste Comte," chap. in *Positivist Thought in France during the Second Empire, 1852–1870* (Oxford: Clarendon Press, 1959), 24–50.

Revolution – the "salutary crisis, whose principal phase [the Terror] had preceded my birth" – he "already felt the fundamental need for a universal regeneration" that would be both "political and philosophic."[3] The French Revolution was thus the point of departure for his thought. Throughout his life he was preoccupied with its accomplishments, its failures, and, most of all, the wide-ranging problems that it left to his generation.

Furthermore, he declared that the Revolution had a profound impact on him, since it "fully conformed to my own nature and was at that time repressed everywhere around me."[4] It had been "repressed" because in mid-1793 Hérault joined the federalist movement to resist the authoritarian, centralizing tendencies of the Convention, the new government in Paris. Suspecting Hérault of being disloyal to the Republic, the Convention denounced Montpellier as a potential source of civil war.[5] The Terror was beginning. As Comte's bourgeois family was very Catholic and royalist, it too opposed the Revolution.

The ensuing civil war, especially in Montpellier, stemmed partially from the Jacobins' attempt to exert control over the wealthy and powerful Church as a way of sweeping away the inequalities and abuses of the entire old order. Beginning in 1792, the revolutionaries permitted civil marriage and civil divorce, closed many churches and monasteries, eliminated the teaching and charity orders, and promulgated the revolutionary calendar. The de-Christianization campaign culminated in November 1793 with the abolition of Catholicism and its replacement by the Cult of Reason, which was supported by an elaborate ritual of festivals in honor of such entities as the Family and Nature. A placard in Montpellier's Temple of Reason (formerly the Cathedral of Saint-Pierre) appropriately read, "*The earth is destroying heaven.*"[6] Several months later Montpellier was subjected to yet another revolutionary religion – the Cult of the Supreme Being established by Robespierre. Influenced by the Enlightenment's dream of establishing a system of justice and fraternity on earth, the revolutionaries were trying, according to one historian, to create a "secular religion of humanity."[7] It would become the prototype of Comte's own Religion of

---

[3] *Cours*, 2:466.   [4] Ibid.

[5] Jacques Godechot, *The Counter-Revolution: Doctrine and Action, 1789–1804*, trans. Salvator Attanasio (New York: Fertig, 1971; Princeton, N.J.: Princeton University Press, 1981), 216–17; Duval-Jouve, *Montpellier*, 2:54–65, 116–20; Comte to Mill, March 4, 1842, *CG*, 2:37.

[6] Saurel, *Histoire religieuse*, 3:57.

[7] John Walsh, "Religion: Church and State in Europe and the Americas," in *The New Cambridge Modern History*, vol. 9, *War and Peace in an Age of Upheaval*, ed. C. W. Crawley (Cambridge: Cambridge University Press, 1965), 148. See also Saurel, *Histoire religieuse*,

Humanity, which he established in the 1850s. A great admirer of
the activism of the Convention, he would plan festivals, model the
Positivist Society on the Jacobin Club, devise his own sacraments,
and create a new calendar celebrating the great figures of the history
of humanity.

Resistance to the government's religious innovations spurred
counterrevolutionary and federalist activity in the Midi, especially in
Montpellier, whose inhabitants were intensely devout after centuries
of bitter religious wars. By late 1793, as a result of the revolutionary
army's terrorist activities and other means of repression, the Church
in Hérault had lost 354 priests, monks, and nuns from emigration,
deportation, or incarceration. In Montpellier alone, the bishop and
forty-four priests had been forced to leave France, and by the end of
the Terror, fifteen people had been guillotined and four hundred
imprisoned.[8] The issue of religion had clearly created profound social
agitation in the city and would later be foremost in Comte's mind
when he took up the task of regenerating France.

Although the French people in general and those of Montpellier
in particular were weary of revolution, the turmoil did not abate
after Robespierre's execution in July 1794. To eliminate the problems caused by the abolition of Catholicism, the new government,
that of the Directory, took additional punitive steps against the
Church and tried unsuccessfully to create a secular, humanistic religion with the *culte décadaire*. Challenged constantly by the Left and
Right, it resorted to unconstitutional measures, including rigged
elections, censorship, and arbitrary arrests, in order to stay in power.
Once people discovered the worthlessness and instability of their
new authoritarian government, they became politically apathetic,
refusing to vote or accept office.[9] This contempt for the political

3:28–61, Duval-Jouve, *Montpellier*, 2:135–6, 179–80; Alexis de Tocqueville, *The Old Regime and the French Revolution*, trans. Stuart Gilbert (Garden City, N.Y.: Doubleday, Anchor Books, 1955), 6–7, 151; George Lefebvre, *The French Revolution*, trans. Elizabeth Moss Evanson, 2 vols. (New York: Columbia University Press, 1962), 1:130, 159, 166–71, 241–7, 2:76–81.

[8] Emmanuel Le Roy Ladurie, *The Peasants of Languedoc*, trans. John Day (Urbana: University of Illinois Press, 1974), 269–86; Louis J. Thomas, *Montpellier: Ville marchande – Histoire économique et sociale de Montpellier des origines à 1870* (Montpellier: Valat, 1936), 209; Duval-Jouve, *Montpellier*, 2:145; Saurel, *Histoire religieuse*, 3:62–122; Richard Cobb, *Les Armées révolutionnaires des départements du Midi (automne et hiver de 1793, printemps de 1794)* (Toulouse: Soubiron, 1955), 14, 21–2, 78–80.

[9] Duval-Jouve, *Montpellier*, 2:191; Georges Lefebvre, *The Directory*, trans. Robert Baldick (New York: Random House, Vintage Books, 1967), 4–12, 16–17, 46, 170, 221; Denis Woronoff, *La République bourgeoise de Thermidor à Brumaire, 1794–1799* (Paris: Seuil, 1972), 7, 51–3, 222, 224; Lefebvre, *French Revolution*, 2:141, 162–4; Martyn Lyons, *France under the Directory* (Cambridge: Cambridge University Press, 1975), 5, 19, 36–7, 104, 106, 113, 165–7, 173, 215, 237.

process lingered for a long time and would later be evident in Comte's attitude.

In many ways, the Directory period – the period when Comte was born – was the low point of the Revolution, for the people suffered severely from cold winters, bad harvests, famine, poverty, and increasing conscriptions and requisitions for the war effort. As political and social divisions became exacerbated, no consensus was possible. Anger over the religious policies, still a leading cause of dissatisfaction, was largely responsible for the increased power of the royalists in Montpellier, who triumphed in the elections of 1797 but were unable to rout the Jacobins completely. The situation became so tense in France as a whole that on September 4, 1797, the republicans staged a coup d'état to prevent a royalist takeover. A new repressive dictatorship, the Second Directory, quickly inaugurated another reign of terror, which again was particularly harsh in Hérault, a stronghold of the royalist conspirators.[10]

Born in the midst of this civil war, Comte would spend most of his life grappling with the problems produced by the Revolution of 1789 – problems that troubled the nation throughout the first half of the nineteenth century. One of the principal challenges bequeathed by the Revolution to his generation was that of creating a social consensus for the modern era. Coming from an area shaken by the disunity of the civil war, Comte was particularly sensitive to the need to erect a social system that would give France the peace and stability it desired, especially in an age when the nobles and clergy would no longer dominate. This concern for social harmony and order would lead him to create the science of society. This science was a direct response to the vast problems stemming from the upheaval of his era.

The political reorganization of France was another problem addressed by Comte and his generation. Once rid of the traditional monarchy, the nation had to establish a new governmental system. Throughout the late eighteenth century and most of the nineteenth, it experimented unsuccessfully with different forms of government: constitutional monarchies, dictatorships, and republics. The role of the state and the problem of reconciling liberty and equality were constant subjects of dispute.[11] Despite the example of the Terror, a

---

[10] Saurel, *Histoire religieuse*, 3:143–226, 287–300; Duval-Jouve, *Montpellier*, 2:164, 203, 275, 284, 289–92, 305–7, 315, 331–3, 402–9; Colin Jones, *Charity and Bienfaisance: The Treatment of the Poor in the Montpellier Region, 1740–1815* (Cambridge: Cambridge University Press, 1982), 201; Lefebvre, *Directory*, 12, 106–7; Lyons, *France under the Directory*, 221–2.

[11] Stanley Hoffmann, "Paradoxes of the French Political Community," in *In Search of France: The Economy, Society, and Political System in the Twentieth Century*, by Stanley Hoffmann et al. (New York: Harper & Row, Harper Torchbooks, 1965), 13–14.

weak state did not attract much favor, for at least since the sixteenth century, the French had had a strong central authority.[12] Alexis de Tocqueville pointed out that "centralization was at once the Revolution's starting-off point and one of its guiding principles." Napoleon reinforced this tendency. The French people's inclination to favor a strong state derived at least in part from their ambivalence toward authority, for as Tocqueville also showed, the spirit of individualism and independence so vital to each French citizen made it hard to create a stable, effective government. Growing up in the authoritarian regimes of the Directory and Napoleon, Comte would reflect the general preferences of the French nation for a centralized government. His argument for a strong, dictatorial state was a response to an age of transition and divisiveness, when people felt frustrated with the plethora of political experiments, dreaded popular insurrections, and wanted a strong executive. Yet at the same time Comte held the equivocal French attitude toward authority in his own rebelliousness and desire to place certain restraints on the government. He disliked, for example, the personal dictatorships of Robespierre and Napoleon. Still, for both the French people and Comte himself, reconciling the authority of the centralized state and the freedom of the individual remained extremely problematic. By the mid-nineteenth century, Tocqueville feared that many French people had "lost their taste for freedom and come to think that, after all, an autocratic government . . . has something to be said for it."[13]

The Revolution also raised the paradoxical issue of religion. On the one hand, by making the Church the enemy of the Revolution, the revolutionaries strengthened the anticlerical tradition in France. Closely linked to monarchism, Catholicism was discredited as antipatriotic. Religious practices and religious education were severely hampered, and all classes experienced a loss of belief.[14] A new secularism or cynicism was particularly widespread in Comte's generation, which grew up during the period when the Catholic faith was most battered. Comte's lack of belief, indeed his pride in having lost his faith in his early youth, reflected this situation. On the other hand, the counterrevolution revealed the extent of the people's loyalty to the Catholic Church. Growing up in Montpellier, where the civil war was particularly bitter, Comte felt the immense strength of religion. And though an unbeliever, he was neither irreligious nor comfortable with atheism. His predicament was peculiarly "modern."

[12] Tony Judt, *Marxism and the French Left: Studies on Labour and Politics in France, 1830–1981* (Oxford: Oxford University Press, 1986), 4.

[13] Tocqueville, *Old Regime*, 60, 168. See also Hoffmann, *In Search*, 10.

[14] Lefebvre, *French Revolution*, 2:275.

In responding to his dilemma, Comte was influenced by the pattern set by the revolutionaries, who found changing the social and political order insufficient and demanded a corresponding transformation in the religious and moral order.[15] Faced with an antagonistic Church, which was both a spiritual community and a political institution, the revolutionaries adopted a policy of blending religion and politics, thereby accentuating the political character of religion. Their new cults demonstrated their awareness of the role religion could play in furnishing a government with moral support and in forging a social consensus. Since the revolutionaries failed to create a viable new religion for a new era, Comte inherited their problem. Recognizing that religion was a primary cause of the civil war and that it was intimately linked to politics, he would naturally stress the importance of religion when he set up his own political system. But since he did not believe in God, he was forced to create a new concept of religion, one that would suit the more secular age. In his efforts to accomplish such a task, his imagination was stimulated by the examples set by the revolutionary cults with their calendar, processions, hymns, and rites. At the same time, he was also burdened by one of the problems that most plagued the revolutionaries: the separation of church and state.

In conclusion, the developments and problems generated by the French Revolution created a fearsome confusion that engulfed Comte and his contemporaries. This chaotic feeling derived from a sense of kaleidoscopic change pervading every aspect of life. As Comte had first encountered the effects of the Revolution in a war-torn city, where unforeseen events had caused immense havoc, he became concerned with establishing order and predicting the future course of society. Condemning this period for its destructiveness, he sharply criticized the revolutionaries' intellectual principles. To him, the metaphysical doctrines of the Enlightenment were totally discredited, since they had provided the revolutionaries with a purely critical and unconstructive format. Positivism would surmount this negative phase of the Revolution.

Besides order, progress would be another of Comte's fundamental preoccupations, for the prevailing sense of change referred not only to severe dislocations, but to the potential for renovation. Unlike many people who dwelled exclusively on the horrors of the Revolution, Comte considered it a "salutary explosion," the culminating point of the whole process of decay that the old order had been undergoing for the past five hundred years.[16] Though lamentable,

---

[15] Albert Mathiez, *La Révolution et l'Eglise* (Paris: Armand Colin, 1910), 25.

[16] *Cours*, 2:584.

the social destruction was crucial to the triumph of the Revolution. Most important, it intensified the desire to reorganize the modern era. In emphasizing in his "Personal Preface" that by age fourteen he felt the "fundamental need for a universal regeneration," Comte deliberately suggested that he had adopted the revolutionary language of renewal at an early age. In fact, the revolutionaries who dominated the Montpellier government in the early years of the Revolution called themselves the "Régénérateurs."[17] The historian Mona Ozouf has pointed out that the Revolution was significant for opening up the "debate on the possible and the impossible." With the Revolution, it seemed that France had been given a clean slate to form a new political and social system. The Revolution's demonstration of rapid progress stimulated the desire for more progress. It now appeared that everything was possible – even creating the "new man," which became the "central dream" of the revolutionaries. This optimistic side of the feeling of transition was reinforced by the Enlightenment ideas of progress, reason, and the perfectibility of man and was reflected in the educational, legal, political, and religious experiments of the enthusiastic revolutionaries. Ozouf writes, "Regeneration, revolution: for certain of these men, the two terms are almost synonymous. . . . the revolution is itself the regeneration." Creation, not formation, was the key to the process of change. Thus the young Comte, in assimilating the discourse of regeneration, was from the beginning attracted, in Ozouf's words, to the "religious dimension of the revolutionary enterprise." And for him, as for the revolutionaries, the idea of regeneration was a global "program that was at the same time political, philosophical, physical and moral."[18] He looked forward to the day when there would be a new, more profound revolution, one instituting a regime that would ultimately create a new, purified society, not just in France but everywhere. By presenting humanity with a rational social theory, which the revolutionaries had lacked, positivism would preside over the second phase of the Revolution: the constructive phase.

COMTE'S FAMILY

Isidore Comte – as he was known throughout his youth – was born into a bourgeois family. A native of Jonquières in the countryside,

[17] Hubert C. Johnson, *The Midi in Revolution: A Study of Regional Political Diversity, 1789–1793* (Princeton, N.J.: Princeton University Press, 1986), 109.
[18] Mona Ozouf, "La Révolution française et l'idée de l'homme nouveau," in *The French Revolution and the Creation of Modern Political Culture,* vol. 2, *The Political Culture of the French Revolution,* ed. Colin Lucas (Oxford: Pergamon Press, 1988), 213–14, 218–19, 230n15.

his mother, Félicité-Rosalie Boyer (1764–1837), was the daughter of a merchant and came from a well-known family of doctors. Comte's father, Louis-Auguste (1776–1859), was from Saint-Hippolyte du Fort, a small town in the Gard, and was the son of a controller with property valued at four thousand francs, a modest sum. In 1796 Louis Comte went to Montpellier, where he became a merchant and married Rosalie Boyer, by whom he had three children: Isidore in 1798, Alix in 1800, and Adolphe in 1802. (A fourth child died in infancy in 1801.) After having already moved several times, the family finally settled down sometime between 1802 and 1805 at 103, rue Barallerie (now 2, impasse Périer), where Comte spent most of his childhood.[19]

The financial status of Louis Comte seems to be a matter of dispute. In 1799, when the family's finances were difficult, especially because Rosalie Boyer had no dowry, Louis Comte took a job as a minor civil servant in Hérault's new tax collection office. He worked his way up the bureaucratic ladder, becoming treasurer in 1814, the head clerk several years later, and the tax collector's official agent by the mid-1820s.[20] His daughter, Alix, maintained that he never earned more than six thousand francs a year, but Auguste claimed she understated his wealth to disinherit him.[21] It does appear that because the main tax collectors of the region were rich financiers who did nothing, Louis Comte assumed their duties, took care of all tax matters in the department, and even managed their money. He gradually amassed a great amount of power, which he used to enlarge his own fortune.[22]

[19] Albert Leenhardt, "La Maison natale d'Auguste Comte?" *Revue de l'Automobile-Club de l'Hérault et de l'Aveyron*, no. 62 (March–April 1940): 12–17; Robinet, *Notice*, 99–100. See also the five-part series on Comte's family and Montpellier in E. Montarroyos, "Voyage au pays natal d'Auguste Comte," *La Revue occidentale* (hereafter, *RO*), 3d ser., 6 (1914): 14–35, 37–56, 83–124, 155–74, 207–32.

[20] [Louis] Comte, *Mémoire justificatif* (Paris, 1846), 5nl; Statement by Louis Comte, notarized by Jacques Anduze, June 2, 1826, Montpellier, in affairs relating to the Justice de Paix, 2ᵉ arrondissement, the official minutes of the "Conseil Comte" (family meeting), June 23, 1826, D2 U1 142, Archives de Paris.

[21] Alix Comte to Auguste Comte, May 16, November 29, 1850, "Matériaux pour servir à la biographie d'Auguste Comte: Lettres d'Alix Comte à son frère Auguste Comte," ed. Pierre Laffitte, *RO*, 3d ser., 2 (January 1, July 1, September 1, 1910): 174, 190, 191; Comte to Audiffrent, October 21, 1852, *CG*, 6:409.

[22] Letter from Boyer to Pierre Laffitte, February 27, 1892. This letter is in the archives of the Maison d'Auguste Comte (henceforth, MAC). See also Alix Comte to Auguste Comte, April 21, 1850, "Lettres d'Alix Comte," ed. Laffitte, 172. There are other indications of Louis Comte's wealth. He was able in 1846 to invest 10,000 francs in a factory that made weighing instruments, his portfolio contained letters of credit totaling 22,000 francs, and the house that the family later occupied at 9, rue de la Vieille Intendance was considered prestigious. Alix Comte to Auguste Comte, May 16, 1850, "Lettres d'Alix Comte," ed.

Comte's family shared the bourgeois values that accompanied the acquisition of wealth: thrift, hard work, order, and even hypocrisy.[23] Much enamored of routine, Louis Comte seems to have been an honorable and devoted public servant throughout his forty-seven years in the French bureaucracy. Although he liked to think of himself as a family man, his whole life revolved around his work. Comte was not particularly fond of his father, who he said was "for forty years far more the treasurer of the general tax collector's office of Hérault than the father of the founder of positivism."[24] Yet Comte inherited his father's love of order, regularity, and asceticism. He also resembled him in his sense of duty, his rigid approach to life, his fondness for hierarchy and authority, and his feeling of self-importance.

Comte's mother was twelve years older than her husband. She was already thirty-two when they married. Her greater maturity and the father's austerity and devotion to his work meant that she was the major influence in the household.[25] Come described his mother as the "most passionate member of the family," and her letters to him reflect her very emotional, religious, and plaintive nature.[26] According to one of his childhood friends, she was also intelligent.[27] While reluctantly acknowledging that he physically resembled his father, Comte proudly stated that his "sympathetic nature" was similar to his mother's and that she was the "source" of all his essential qualities – qualities of the heart, mind, and character.[28] Since she adored him and always supported him, he was more affectionate with her than with his father, but even he admitted that he did not love her as much as she deserved. Feeling generally unappreciated at home, she therefore "spent her life in continual heart-

Laffitte, 173–4; Albert Leenhardt, *Vieux Hôtels Montpelliérains* (Ballegarde: SADAG, 1935), 202–5. Also consult "Les Maisons d'Auguste Comte," *La Vie Montpelliéraine* 35.1790 (December 15, 1928): 28.

[23] Georges Dupeux, *French Society, 1789–1970*, trans. Peter Wait (London: Methuen, 1976), 128.

[24] Comte to Audiffrent, October 1, 1852, *CG*, 6:399.

[25] Emile Corra, *La Naissance du génie d'Auguste Comte II: Sa Vie, son oeuvre en 1820* (Paris: Revue Positiviste Internationale, 1920), 8. Because of this odd age difference, she kept her date of birth a secret, even from her husband. Leenhardt, "La Maison natale," 15, 17; Alix Comte to Auguste Comte, December 31, 1848, "Lettres d'Alix Comte," ed. Laffitte, 122.

[26] Comte to Mme Auguste Comte, October 13, 1837, *CG*, 1:282.

[27] P. Valat, "Notes biographiques sur Aug. Comte," *Revue bordelaise* 2 (December 16, 1880): 432.

[28] Auguste Comte, *Système de politique positive ou Traité du sociologie instituant la religion de l'Humanité*, 5th ed., identical to the first, 4 vols. (Paris, 1851–4; Paris: Au Siège de la Société Positiviste, 1929) (hereafter, *Système*), 1:8, 12.

breaks."[29] In truth, there is no indication that Comte's relationship to either of his parents was ever close.

Suggesting that he found his upbringing unsatisfactory, Comte tersely remarked in his "Personal Preface" that he was born of an "eminently Catholic and monarchical family."[30] Evidently, he found his parents' political and religious affiliations to be the most telling fact about them. He was not pleased to have experienced the bitterness of the counterrevolution in his own home.

By all accounts, Comte's generation seemed more inclined than others to defy their parents because of their bitter memories of a childhood marred by the ordeals of the Revolution.[31] Like his comrades, Comte was eager to display his recalcitrance. He himself pointed out that one reason the Revolution made a profound impression on him was that it was rejected by his family.[32] At the precocious age of thirteen he therefore announced that he no longer believed in God or Catholicism.[33] Soon afterward, spurning his parents' royalism and following the example set by the revolutionaries, he became a republican.[34] (During the early nineteenth century, the republicans were distinguished mainly by their opposition to the prevailing government and by their vague desire for a nonmonarchical political regime formed by and devoted to the "people.")[35] Comte's extremely rebellious nature was a source of great conflict.

Nevertheless, Catholicism profoundly influenced Comte, who wrote toward the end of his life, "I have always congratulated myself on being born in Catholicism, without which my mission would have arisen with difficulty due to the intellectual and moral dangers inherent in Protestant or deist education."[36] His statement reflects the strength of anti-Protestant prejudices, which were very strong in Montpellier, as well as an enduring suspicion of the eighteenth century's challenge to traditional religion. Despite his radicalism in some areas, he could not completely abandon his Catholic roots. This aspect of his thought is so striking that Thomas Huxley once remarked that "Comte's ideal . . . is Catholic organization without

---

[29] Comte to Audiffrent, October 1, 1852, *CG*, 6:399.   [30] *Cours*, 2:466.
[31] Lefebvre, *French Revolution*, 2:315.   [32] *Cours*, 2:466.
[33] Auguste Comte, *Testament d'Auguste Comte avec les documents qui s'y rapportent: Pièces justificatives, prières quotidiennes, confessions annuelles, correspondance avec Mme de Vaux*, 2d ed. (Paris, 1896) (hereafter, *Testament*), 9.
[34] Lonchampt, *Précis*, 8.
[35] Claude Nicolet, *L'Idée républicaine en France (1789–1924): Essai d'histoire critique* (Paris: Gallimard, 1982), 26; Alan B. Spitzer, *The French Generation of 1820* (Princeton, N.J.: Princeton University Press, 1987), 66; Pierre Nora, "Republic," in *A Critical Dictionary of the French Revolution*, ed. François Furet and Mona Ozouf, trans. Arthur Goldhammer (Cambridge, Mass.: Harvard University Press, Belknap Press, 1989), 799.
[36] *Testament*, 9.

Catholic doctrine, or, in other words, Catholicism *minus* Christianity."[37]

There is no sign that Comte was ever on intimate terms with either of his siblings. His younger brother, Adolphe, was a rebel like Comte but manifested his defiance by avoiding his studies, going into debt, and leading a life of debauchery. Comte's sister, Alix, was sickly and prone to hysteria. Like her parents, she was intensely religious and politically conservative. Comte detested her. They seemed very jealous of each other, and the object of their sibling rivalry was usually their parents. The fact that Alix always stayed home with them and never married intensified his feeling of being an outsider.

In the light of his strained relations with his family, Comte's emotional and rebellious temperament becomes more understandable. The correspondence between him and his family members is characterized by constant feuding, demands, reproaches, and slights; the only subject neutral enough to be discussed calmly was health. The bulk of their letters consists of exaggerated and extremely elaborate accounts of illnesses – especially headaches, nervous disorders, and stomach problems – perhaps derived in part from a joyless, tense family life.

Although the details of his early family life are not known, it seems safe to say that Comte did not have a cheerful childhood. It was marked not only by the tensions of the Revolution but by the strains of constant relocations, the death of a baby sister, a difficult financial situation, illnesses, and family feuds. He did not blossom at the time. He was nicknamed "Comtou" because of his small size and feeble constitution, probably inherited from his mother.[38] He later admitted that he sought in "public life the noble but imperfect compensation of the unhappiness of his private life."[39]

EDUCATION

Comte's difficulties with his family, especially his sense that he was an outsider, derived to a certain extent from his education. The French Revolution severely disrupted the schools, which became the object of numerous experiments that reflected the renovating aims of each succeeding government.[40] In a way, Comte became a victim of the political vicissitudes plaguing the nation.

---

[37] Thomas Henry Huxley, "The Scientific Aspects of Positivism," chap. in *Lay Sermons, Addresses and Reviews* (New York, 1871), 153.

[38] P. Valat, "Auguste Comte," *Revue bordelaise* 3 (March 16, 1881): 54.

[39] Comte to Clotilde de Vaux, June 6, 1845, *CG*, 3:36.

[40] Antoine Prost, *Histoire de l'enseignement en France, 1800–1967* (Paris: Armand Colin, 1968), 22.

At first, he was taught reading, writing, and Latin by an elderly tutor hired by his parents. When Comte was six and a half, his gloating father described his achievements:

> He is beginning to learn to write, and the facility with which he does everything he wants, along with his astonishing memory, leads me to predict that he will repay me one day for the care that I ceaselessly lavish on him. He is lively and robust. All in all, he is a little devil.[41]

A few years later, at age nine, Isidore was sent to the local *lycée* in Montpellier, where due to the regulations of the school, he became a boarder.[42] At this early age, he witnessed the concrete results of government planning, for the *lycée* system had been recently created by Napoleon in the hope of forming a faithful body of supporters who would become his administrators and army officers. To gain the support of the Catholic Church, Napoleon revived the classical program of the *collèges* of the ancien régime with their religious instruction and heavy emphasis on Latin. He also demoted the sciences, which had been emphasized in the revolutionaries' pedagogical program and now were considered dangerous by people reacting against the principles of 1789. However, since mathematics was important for army officers, he retained that subject from the Ecoles Centrales, the science-oriented schools of the revolutionary era that he had abolished. Finally, he ruled that teachers must give the students fixed religious and political principles that would ensure the moral unity and stability of the new state.[43] Napoleon's pragmatic

---

[41] Letter from Louis Comte to Sébastien-François-Xavier Comte-Rochambeau, 29 Thermidor Year XII, excerpt in "La Jeunesse d'Auguste Comte d'après des lettres inédites," by Achille Ouy, *Mercure de France* 302.1014 (1948): 256.

[42] The state paid half the cost of his room and board since he was the son of a civil servant. "Minute du décret impérial," December 15, 1806, A. F. IV 232, Dossier 1548, Archives Nationales (hereafter, AN). See also F. J. Gould, *Auguste Comte* (London: Watts, 1920), 2; Emile Corra, *La Naissance du génie d'Auguste Comte: Sa Vie jusqu'en 1819* (Paris: Revue Positiviste Internationale, 1918), 12; Robinet, *Notice*, 100.

[43] Prost, *Histoire de l'enseignement*, 25, 55; Charles Coulston Gillispie, "Science in the French Revolution," in *The Sociology of Science*, ed. Bernard Barber and Walter Hirsch (New York: Free Press, 1962), 90, 96; Lefebvre, *French Revolution*, 2:292, 298; Georges Weill, *Histoire de l'enseignement secondaire en France, 1802–1920* (Paris: Payot, 1921), 14–16, 19, 34; H. C. Barnard, *Education and the French Revolution* (Cambridge: Cambridge University Press, 1969), 198; Frederick B. Artz, *The Development of Technical Education in France, 1500–1850* (Cambridge, Mass.: MIT Press, 1966), 180; Lyons, *France under the Directory*, 92–3; L. Pearce Williams, "Science, Education, and Napoleon I," in *The Rise of Science in Relation to Society*, ed. Leonard M. Marsak (New York: Macmillan, 1964), 81; Louis Liard, *L'Enseignement supérieur en France, 1789–1893*, 2 vols. (Paris, 1888–94), 2:10, 92; Louis Bergeron, *France under Napoleon*, trans. R. R. Palmer (Princeton, N.J.: Princeton University Press, 1981), 196; Charles Hunter van Duzer, *Contribution of the Ideologues to French Revolutionary Thought* (Baltimore, Md.: Johns Hopkins Press, 1935), 154–62; Michalina Vaughan and Margaret Scotford Archer, *Social Conflict and Educational Change in England and France, 1789–1848*

attitude toward religion, especially his careful manipulation of public opinion in matters of belief, would set an example for Comte.

At the Montpellier *lycée*, Comte studied Latin and French grammar, humanities, rhetoric, philosophy, and mathematics. He excelled in all his courses because he had an exceptional ability to concentrate, strong self-discipline, and an outstanding memory.[44] Not only could he remember several hundred lines of poetry after hearing them for the first time, but he could also recite backward a page of words that he had read just once. In 1813, after taking all the courses offered by the *lycée*, he passed the admissions examination for the Ecole Polytechnique, but at fifteen he was too young to attend. Instead, he was given permission to pursue special courses in mathematics with Daniel Encontre, a teacher at the *lycée* and also a professor at the local university. Because of Encontre's encouragement, his own abilities, and his eagerness to express his solidarity with the revolutionaries, Comte developed a strong and lasting interest in the sciences. He became so knowledgeable that, when Encontre was absent, he would enthusiastically take his place and stand on a chair to give a lecture to his classmates.[45]

Lycée life was extremely rigorous. With every hour of the day filled with planned activities and the minute details of life subject to regulation, the *lycées* resembled both military barracks and monasteries. To maximize their impact, Napoleon decreed that most, if not all, students had to be boarders. In a sense, each child was imprisoned and isolated so that he could be more easily fashioned into an ideal servant of the state. "Toughness" and "virility" were especially prized, since these were qualities that made good soldiers.[46]

Away from his family and separated from the world for seven important years, Comte was profoundly influenced by the school's

---

(Cambridge: Cambridge University Press, 1971), 184; Paul Gerbod, *La Vie quotidienne dans les lycées et collèges au XIX*ᵉ *siècle* (Paris: Hachette, 1968), 32; A. Aulard, *Napoléon et le monopole universitaire: Origines et fonctionnement de l'Université impériale* (Paris: Armand Colin, 1911), 273, 282.

[44] Comte won prizes in many subjects, including Latin, mathematics, and rhetoric. See the list of the prizes in Gouhier, *Jeunesse*, 1:260. See also ibid., 64; P. Valat, "Notes biographiques sur Aug. Comte (1)," *Revue bordelaise* 2 (October 1, 1880): 353; Weill, *Histoire de l'enseignement*, 34–5; Aulard, *Napoléon et le Monopole Universitaire*, 274–5.

[45] Lonchampt, *Précis*, 3; Joseph Bertrand, "Souvenirs académiques: Auguste Comte et l'Ecole Polytechnique," *Revue des deux mondes* 138 (December 1896): 529; P. Valat, "Notes biographiques sur Aug. Comte," *Revue bordelaise* 2 (December 1, 1880): 417; Robinet, *Notice*, 100–1; Gouhier, *Jeunesse*, 1:67–8; Corra, *La Naissance du génie d'Auguste Comte: Sa Vie jusqu'en 1819*, 13–15.

[46] Philippe Ariès, *Centuries of Childhood: A Social History of Family Life*, trans. Robert Baldick (New York: Knopf, 1962), 268, 413. See also H. C. Barnard, *Education*, 22, 222; Valat, "Notes biographiques sur Aug. Comte (1)," 354; Weill, *Histoire de l'enseignement*, 19.

spirit. In 1813, when Jacques Delpech, the famous surgeon from the Montpellier medical school, performed a long operation to remove a tumor from his neck, Comte showed that he had learned to be "tough" and courageous, for he did not flinch, complain, or allow his hands to be held. Besides the value of stoicism, he was taught that obedience and order were the highest values, hierarchy was necessary to reinforce subordination, and a regulated, disciplined life was most productive.[47] These lessons would not be lost on him, although he did not pay attention to them as a boy.

The very rigor of the *lycées* seemed to incite resistance, because the students were notorious for their lack of discipline and frequent revolts.[48] Comte was no exception. According to his friend and disciple Emile Littré, he was thoroughly rebellious, hating rules "to an extraordinary degree."[49] In 1812 or 1813, he caused a scandal when he persuaded his fellow students to put out the lamps in the study hall and throw all their books at a hated proctor.[50]

In addition, the schools were well known for their irreligion and promotion of free thought. Most of the scholarships went to sons of military officers, who were ardently anticlerical and Voltairian, while many of the teachers maintained the Enlightenment's questioning spirit. In this atmosphere, Comte found it easy to renounce his faith at thirteen.[51]

Shortly afterward, influenced at least partly by fellow students and teachers, Comte enthusiastically embraced the Revolution's ideals and republicanism. During breaks between classes, he would walk around the courtyard, lecturing his friends on Voltaire, Rousseau, and political economists. Always loyal to the Ecoles Centrales and their creator, the Convention, he hated Napoleon for trying to revive the ancien régime and developing a militaristic state. At one point he created quite a stir when he stood up in class to announce his hope that the Spaniards would defeat the French.[52]

Perhaps the aspect of school life that affected Comte the most was its isolation. The stress on Latin and the classics, the neglect of contemporary problems, and the school's physical seclusion created

---

[47] Lonchampt, *Précis*, 2; Robinet, *Notice*, 100; Gouhier, *Jeunesse*, 1:74; Félix Ponteil, *Histoire de l'enseignement en France: Les Grandes Étapes, 1789–1964* (Paris: Sirey, 1966), 103.

[48] Gerbod, *La Vie quotidienne*, 103–4; F. de Lamennais, "Education publique," in *Oeuvres complètes*, 12 vols. (Paris, 1836–7), 8:257; Valat, "Notes biographiques sur Aug. Comte (1)," 354.

[49] Littré, *Auguste Comte*, 7.   [50] Valat, "Auguste Comte," 55.

[51] Gerbod, *La Vie quotidienne*, 226; Lonchampt, *Précis*, 2.

[52] *Cours*, 2:466; Jean Poirier, "Lycéens impériaux (1814–1815)," *La Revue de Paris* 3 (1921): 400–1; idem, "Lycéens d'il y a cent ans: 1814–1815," *Revue internationale de l'enseignement* 67 (1914): 175–88; Valat, "Notes biographiques sur Aug. Comte," 432; Lonchampt, *Précis*, 2.

a hermetic and unreal atmosphere in which he felt too confined. Although his father rarely visited him, his sister and adoring mother came twice a week. During their visits, Comte remained very solemn, not daring to respond in a sensitive manner for fear of being labeled a sissy.[53] Reflecting on the bleakness of his early development, he later expressed deep regret that his "deadly scholastic imprisonment" had robbed him of his family's love at a crucial time in his life. He blamed it for having contributed to his sense of alienation from his family and to his late emotional development. It seemed to have only encouraged his tendency toward the "speculative life," which his own "nature" already favored "too much."[54] Curiously, his aloof father glimpsed his difficulties. Realizing that Isidore's years of being "imprisoned in the *lycée*" had left him with "no social graces," he decided to make Isidore stay at home the last year while he was being taught by Encontre. He hoped that in this way his son would acquire "a little savoir faire."[55] Even at an early age, Comte was apparently inept at handling social relations.

Most of Comte's energies at this time went into the sciences, and his relationship with Encontre was one of the most significant associations of his life. By all accounts, Encontre was an eminent man both intellectually and spiritually. A scholar and former Protestant minister, he became a prominent republican during the Revolution and helped found the Ecole Centrale of Montpellier, where he was offered a chair in literature. During the revolutionary festival of January 21, 1799, which celebrated the death of Louis XVI, his poem invoking the Supreme Being to help the republic was read aloud in all of the municipalities in Hérault. When the new *lycée* was established in 1804, Encontre was given a chair in mathematics, and in 1809 he was named dean of the Faculty of Sciences at the university, where he became professor of mathematics. Although known primarily as a brilliant mathematician, he was also one of the most important Protestants in all of France. One of his admirers, the future statesman François Guizot, called him the leader of the Calvinist revival, for he worked hard to reorganize the church and reconcile science and religion.[56] In 1814, the same year Comte left for the Ecole Polytechnique, Encontre sacrificed his interest in mathematics to take a post as professor of dogma at the Faculty of

[53] Prost, *Histoire de l'enseignement*, 50–3; Valat, "Auguste Comte," 54; *Système*, 1:12.

[54] *Système*, 1:8.

[55] Letter from Louis Comte to Comte-Rochambeau, July 12, 1813, in Ouy, "Jeunesse," 257.

[56] F. Guizot, *Méditations sur l'état actuel de la religion chrétienne* (Paris, 1866), 118, 123–9. See also Daniel Bourchenin, *Daniel Encontre* (Paris, 1877), 32, 36; Valat, "Notes biographiques sur Aug. Comte," 431; Duval-Jouve, *Montpellier*, 2:309, 383–4.

Protestant Theology in Montauban and then became the dean of this school.

Comte and Encontre were very close.[57] While Encontre recognized and encouraged Comte's brilliance, Comte venerated him in a manner that tempered his extreme self-confidence. Encontre's courses were the only ones that "really affected" his entire career, and they led to his interest in mathematics and teaching.[58] Moreover, because Encontre was a generalist, equally at home in the sciences, literature, and theology, Comte came to value a wide-ranging mind that delighted in all sorts of knowledge and shunned specialization. He would try to follow his teacher's example not only by studying a variety of subjects, including mathematics, biology, history, and literature, but by making sociology the science of generalities. Encontre's philosophical and encyclopedic approach to knowledge, his placement of mathematics in a more general perspective, and his stress on the rigors of the scientific method would later influence Comte's formulation of positivism.[59]

Furthermore, Comte inherited a concern for moral reform from Encontre, whom he considered to be as virtuous as he was talented. Encontre's insistence that the heart was more important than the mind led Comte later to proclaim the positivist principle of making the intellect serve "sociability."[60] He also first demonstrated to Comte the need to establish a universal religion and thereby initiated him into his mission.[61] Finally, Encontre may have persuaded Comte to become a republican, for Comte became one in 1812, the year they met. Recognizing his debt to Encontre, Comte dedicated his last book, the *Synthèse subjective*, to him in 1856, although he had died almost forty years before.

Besides Encontre, Comte had one other association that made a lasting impression on him. In 1813, when he was fifteen, he became infatuated with an attractive young woman, Ernestine de Goy, who used to play the harp and sing ballads to him. Although she looked upon him only as a brother, she introduced him to love, music, and Italian. The following year she crushed his "true love" for her when she suddenly married. As his "oldest memory of a woman,"

[57] In 1839 Comte received a letter from Encontre's son, who reminded him that he was "one of the most distinguished students" of his father. Encontre to Comte, October 4, 1839, MAC.

[58] Auguste Comte, *Synthèse subjective ou Système universel des conceptions propres à l'état normal de l'humanité*, vol. 1 (Paris, 1856) (hereafter, *Synthèse*), lvi. See also Comte to Mme Auguste Comte, September 4, 1839, *CG*, 1:316.

[59] Gouhier, *Jeunesse*, 1:92.   [60] *Synthèse*, lxv.

[61] Ibid., lviii, lxiii. Revealing his own religious bias, Comte carefully pointed out that Encontre never achieved his proper greatness because he embraced Protestantism and was thus unable to extricate himself totally from the theological-metaphysical stage of thought.

Ernestine was "linked to the most tender impressions" of Comte's adolescence.[62]

In 1814 Comte also had other things on his mind, for in August he again took the extremely rigorous admissions test for the Ecole Polytechnique. The examination covered French composition, Latin translation, drawing, mathematics, and statistics. In October he was admitted as the top student from the provinces and ranked fourth among all of the admitted candidates in the entire country. Despite his complaints about his national rank, his achievement was impressive. Because many of the best scientists in France were professors at the school and it ensured its graduates an excellent career, the Ecole Polytechnique was extremely prestigious and difficult to enter. In 1814 it admitted only seventy-five students.[63]

The Convention founded the Ecole Polytechnique in 1794 in the same spirit in which it established the Ecoles Centrales, for the revolutionaries were very interested not only in improving the military defense of France but in teaching, propagating, and advancing the sciences. The school's goal was to hire the best scientists to train civil and military engineers.[64] After a two-year course of study, its students applied to the more specialized and advanced Ecoles d'Application, which included the Ecole des Ponts et Chaussées and the Ecole des Mines. Most graduates ended by working for the government in such sectors as the army, navy, public works, and mining.[65]

When Napoleon came to power, the Ecole Polytechnique was the most famous school of science in the world. Generally disliked by the student body, he gave the school all the trappings of a military academy: barracks, uniforms, strict discipline, military training, and constant supervision. Many students were required to enter the artillery, and about twenty were wounded defending Paris several months before Comte's arrival. The school thus reinforced the

---

[62] Comte to Clotilde de Vaux, November 24, 1845, *CG*, 3:206; Comte to Alix Comte, June 10, 1848, *CG*, 4:154; Comte to Ernestine de Montfort, August 3, 1848, *CG*, 4:172. See also letter from Ernestine Ferdinand de Montfort to Comte, October 14, 1848, "Matériaux pour servir à la biographie d'Auguste Comte," ed. Pierre Laffitte, *RO*, 3d ser., 1 (January 1, 1909): 31.

[63] Artz, *Technical Education*, 232; Gouhier, *Jeunesse*, 1:94, 268–70; General Alvin, "Centenaire de l'institution de la philosophie positive par Auguste Comte," 2, in Dossier Auguste Comte, Archives of the Ecole Polytechnique (hereafter, EP); Comte to Roméo Pouzin, November 21, 1814, *CG*, 1:4.

[64] These scientists included Joseph Louis Lagrange and Pierre Simon de Laplace in mathematics; Nicolas Louis Vauquelin, Jean Antoine Chaptal, Antoine François de Fourcroy, Louis Bernard Guyton de Morveau, and Claude Louis Berthollet in chemistry; and Gaspard Monge and Jean Hachette in descriptive geometry.

[65] Artz, *Technical Education*, 155, 159, 239–40, 321.

militaristic and authoritarian mind-set that Comte had already encountered at his *lycée*. Nevertheless, the Ecole Polytechnique remained faithful to the founding ideals of the Convention. The fact,
for example, that most students were republicans pleased young
Isidore immensely.[66] Since both of his schools played a crucial part
in forming his political and religious beliefs, he would always stress
the critical role of education in establishing the *Weltanschauung* of the
entire society.

Comte arrived at the school, situated near the Panthéon, on November 2, 1814. His records show that he had blondish brown hair
and reddish brown eyes and that he was very small: at age sixteen,
he was only five feet, two inches. Given the rank of corporal and
paid a two-franc monthly salary, he delighted his parents several
months later by obtaining a reduction of four hundred francs on his
room and board thanks to his academic achievements and his family's connections. (The usual charge was eight hundred francs.)[67]

The atmosphere at the school was intense, with the boys awaking
at five a.m. to devote twelve hours of their day to their studies. The
scientific course of instruction was extremely rigorous. Physics was
Comte's most difficult course the first year because he thought Professor Alexis Petit went too fast.[68] Nevertheless, on the French scale

---

[66] L. Pearce Williams, "Science," 85; G. Pinet, *Histoire de l'Ecole Polytechnique* (Paris, 1887),
52, 59; A. Fourcy, *Histoire de l'Ecole Polytechnique* (Paris, 1828), 325, 327; Bergeron, *France
under Napoleon*, 36; Comte to Pouzin, November 26, 1814, *CG*, 1:4.

[67] Certificate of Comte's admission, October 7, 1814, MAC; Registre de matricule des élèves,
vol. 4, 1810–19, EP (part of this is reproduced in Gouhier, *Jeunesse*, 1:270); Comte Dejean,
"Etat de traitement des sous-officiers élèves de l'Ecole Polytechnique pendant octobre et
novembre 1814," November 14, 1814, F^{17} 1391, AN; Comte to Valat, April 29, 1815,
CG, 1:9–10; Gouhier, *Jeunesse*, 1:94.

[68] During his first year, 1814–15, Comte studied calculus with Louis Poinsot, descriptive
geometry with François Arago, chemistry with Louis Jacques Thenard, physics with Alexis
Petit, applied analysis with Jean Hachette, mechanics with Denis Poisson, and French
grammar with François Andrieux. He also followed courses in chemical experimentation,
stone cutting, topography, and drawing. The following academic year, he studied the
application of calculus to geometry with Arago, chemistry with Thenard, physics with
Petit, French literature with Andrieux, machines with Hachette, mechanics with Jacques
Binet, and infinitesimal calculus with Augustin Cauchy. Replacing Poinsot, who became
responsible for the final examinations of the second-year students, the young genius Cauchy
did not impress Comte, who found him a "deplorable professor." Comte's other courses
during this last year at the Ecole Polytechnique included chemical experimentation, mili-
tary art, architecture, and drawing. Comte to Pouzin, November 21, 1814, *CG*, 1:3; Comte
to Valat, January 2, 1815, *CG*, 1:5–6; Registre de l'instruction, 1814–16, EP; Letter from
Marielle to the Governor of the School, December 6, 1815, Dossier Louis Poinsot, EP.
Also see Comte's notebooks – replete with scribbles – in the Maison d'Auguste Comte:
*Cours d'analyse de Monsieur Poinsot, de Monsieur Reynaud, Cours d'analyse infinitésimale de
Monsieur Cauchy, Cours de mécanique de Monsieur Poisson, Cours d'analyse appliquée à la géométrie
de Monsieur Arago, Cours de physique de Monsieur Petit, Cours d'optique de Monsieur Petit, and
Cours de chimie de Monsieur Thenard*.

of 1 to 20, Comte received a perfect grade of 20 and attained top grades in most of his other courses, except descriptive geometry, where he did not get along with the teaching assistant, and drawing, which he considered a waste of time. Actually, part of his trouble in drawing stemmed from his extreme near-sightedness. The low grade in drawing, coupled with his poor marks for conduct, which was judged "mediocre" and "very reprehensible," lowered his grade-point average, and after the first year he was ranked eighth in the class.[69] Although he did not work hard, Comte had a very high reputation, as revealed by his professors' comments. François Arago called Comte "one of the most distinguished students of the Ecole Polytechnique," and Louis Poinsot considered him "one of the preeminent students" of the school.[70]

In the school's restrictive, closed environment, a strong esprit de corps developed, marking the Polytechnicien for life. At first Comte was depressed, especially by the routine, but once he made "several close" friends, he was "very happy" and compared the school to a "paradise," where the "most perfect union" existed among the students. He was particularly enchanted by a debate on whether to retain hazing rites for freshmen. In a letter to a friend, he described how the students, motivated by their "democratic idealism," appointed representatives to discuss the problem as if they were forming a "senate of a free people" and then arrived at decisions by voting. After the abolition of these rites, the second-year students began "proclaiming the most perfect equality between all the students and vowing union and fraternity." In several rooms, altars were erected to "*friendship*" and to "*Union and force*." Revealing his excitable nature, love of celebrations, and strong republicanism, Comte declared, "These ceremonies are very moving. . . . It is fine to hear people speaking in this way about liberty and equality in the same moment that our compatriots are running toward slavery and despotism."[71] He and his fellow students were trying to maintain what Lynn Hunt has called the "political culture" of the Revolution with its "gestures of equality and fraternity" and "rituals of republicanism."[72]

Back in their bedrooms, the students also participated in "very

---

[69] See the part of the Registre des Notes that Gouhier copied from the Archives de la Direction des Etudes, Ecole Polytechnique, and the document "Le Passage de la seconde à la première division," also reproduced in Gouhier, *Jeunesse*, 1:270–276. See also Littré, *Auguste Comte*, 8; Valat, "Notes biographiques sur Aug. Comte (1)," 353.

[70] See the professors' comments appended to the letter that Comte wrote to the Comte de Saint-Cricq, May 14, 1828, CG, 1:200–1.

[71] Comte to Valat, January 2, 1815, CG, 1:6–7.

[72] Lynn Hunt, *Politics, Culture, and Class in the French Revolution* (Berkeley and Los Angeles: University of California Press, 1984), 13, 15.

lively and very profound" debates on different issues of political economy. Comte impressed his friends by the speed with which he finished his homework so that he could concentrate on his political studies, especially his investigations into the French Revolution. In his desk he kept copies of the republican constitutions of the United States and France as well as speeches by French revolutionaries. He also began reading *Le Nain jaune* and its successor, *Le Nain jaune réfugié*, popular periodicals satirizing the Restoration and the ultras. After the Bourbon government insisted on introducing more Catholic practices into the *lycées*, Comte complained that it was making sure the new generation would be even more stupid (*abrutie*) than his own. This policy would leave the nation without hope or liberty.

> The royal despotism will be reborn just as it was before the sublime insurrection of 1789, and even worse!!! Poor France! Unhappy friends of liberty! The noble efforts that you made at the peril of your life to give to my fellow citizens the possession of their legitimate rights will be rendered useless, and maybe you will die, victims of your devotion to the cause of reason and Humanity! God! If only everyone shared the attitude that prevails at the School![73]

Forever devoted to the Ecole Polytechnique and its republican spirit, Comte was a child of the Revolution who had found a milieu in which he could thrive.[74] He became increasingly convinced that the elite of his generation were superior to the members of other age cohorts, who had betrayed or were betraying the ideal of the Revolution, "the cause of reason and Humanity." Like others of his generation, such as Honoré de Balzac, who prided themselves on their special destiny to regenerate France, Comte believed it was up to him and his friends to mold the future.[75]

Yet Comte's hatred of the new Bourbon monarchy unwisely led him to place his hopes on Napoleon, whom he had previously disliked. He experienced his "first political emotions" when he saw the "execrable adventurer" surrender in 1814.[76] A year later, however, Comte joined his fellow students at the Ecole Polytechnique in

---

[73] Comte to Valat, January 2, 1815, *CG*, 1:7–8. See also "Matériaux pour servir à la biographie d'Auguste Comte: Documents, 1816–1822," ed. Pierre Laffitte, *RO* 8 (1882), 321; [Hippolyte Philémon] Deroisin, *Notes sur Auguste Comte par un de ses disciples* (Paris, 1909), 19; Lonchampt, *Précis*, 4; Robinet, *Notice*, 101–2; Charles Ledré, "La Presse nationale sous la Restauration et la Monarchie de Juillet," in *Histoire générale de la presse française*, ed. Claude Bellanger et al., 5 vols. (Paris: Presses Universitaires de France, 1969), 2:38–40, 50, 55–6.

[74] Comte to Armand Marrast, January 7, 1832, *CG*, 1:233.

[75] Spitzer, *French Generation*, 4, 9, 11, 52.

[76] Comte to Audiffrent, June 7, 1851, *CG*: 6:108. See also Comte to de Tholouze, September 17, 1849, *CG*, 5:79; Comte to Alix Comte, December 7, 1848, *CG*, 4:210.

welcoming Napoleon back to France. Like many members of his generation, he was convinced that Napoleon had renounced his "ideas of gigantic ambition and despotism," which had caused "so many evils in the first part of his reign."[77] Comte's petition to allow the school to help defend the nation was approved by Lazare Carnot, the minister of the interior, but before the Polytechniciens could join the fight, the armistice was signed.[78] Yet by this time, Comte's faith in Napoleon had been shattered. Napoleon's militarism, his impoverishment of France, and his oppressive, reactionary policies in religion and politics made him one of the people Comte detested most throughout his life. He went so far as to say in the *Cours* that Napoleon was "more injurious to all of humanity than any other person in history."[79]

Nevertheless, Napoleon would always represent both a rival and an ideal to Comte, who spent most of his youth under his regime. To him, Napoleon ultimately failed to end the Revolution because he lacked a genuine political doctrine; he thus had neither a firm idea of social progress nor a concept of order that differed from that of the ancien régime.[80] Comte would later aim to provide this type of guiding policy, or ideology, which he considered essential to the effective use of power. By substituting ideas for wars, he, not Napoleon, would thus reap the glory of leading the Revolution to its triumphant conclusion. Despite his scorn for Napoleon, Comte resembled other great thinkers of the nineteenth century, such as Hegel, in being profoundly touched by his example; like the revolutionaries, Napoleon had demonstrated the possibility of transforming dreams into reality.[81]

While at the Ecole Polytechnique, Comte aspired to become a hero to his comrades. Though somewhat clumsy in his movements, he had strong leadership abilities and a sense of authority.[82] He was well liked and respected by his fellow students, who gave him two revealing nicknames: Sganarelle (a comic figure who appears in several of Molière's plays) because of his satiric flair, and "the philosophe" due to his seriousness.[83] Describing the influence that Comte exerted on his classmates, one person who disliked him wrote:

[77] Comte to Valat, April 29, 1815, *CG*, 1:9.

[78] Ibid., 10; Lonchampt, *Précis*, 10; Gouhier, *Jeunesse*, 1:276; Jean-Pierre Callot, *Histoire de l'Ecole Polytechnique* (Paris: Charles Lavauzelle, 1982), 54; Corra, *La Naissance du génie d'Auguste Comte: Sa Vie jusqu'en 1819*, 18; Robinet, *Notice*, 103.

[79] *Cours*, 2:603. See also Comte to Alix Comte, December 7, 1848, *CG*, 4:210; *Ecrits*, 429; *Système*, 3:607.

[80] *Cours*, 2:601–6; *Système*, 3:606–10.   [81] Gouhier, *Jeunesse*, 1:115.

[82] Valat, "Notes biographiques sur Aug. Comte (1)," 353.

[83] Lonchampt, *Précis*, 4; Comte to Blainville, April 15, 1826, *CG*, 1:195. The date of April 25 in *CG* is wrong. See the original letter in Maison d'Auguste Comte.

He was witty, deadpan . . . capable of a satiric and farcical eloquence and on the very same occasion of an infectious emotion. During the second year of studies, there was organized a distribution of prizes awarded by the seniors to the most well-behaved, virtuous freshmen. Comte presided over the ceremony, and from the beginning to the end – ten witnesses told me this was true – people roared with laughter.[84]

Comte evidently enjoyed having a good time and creating a ruckus.

Pierre Valat, one of Comte's best friends, described him in more sober terms as hard-working, dreamy, placid, reserved, and solitary. Yet he too said Comte quickly obtained ascendancy over his comrades, for "as soon as the occasion presented itself, he took first place because of the solidness and energy of his character as well as the superiority of his intelligence."[85] At least once, the students asked him to present their grievances to the administration.[86]

Comte's leadership abilities and his love of merrymaking were a dangerous combination from the moment he entered the school. Concerned about his "liberty," he complained a month after he arrived that he did not "go out enough," but he soon remedied that by breaking the curfew and other restrictive rules.[87] After committing twelve infractions in the spring semester and spending the whole night of June 18 roaming the streets, Comte was reported to be the "most reprehensible" of the five corporals in his class. On June 20, 1815, he was demoted.[88] His deteriorating reputation at the Ecole Polytechnique is revealed in a diary kept by General Jacques-David-Martin de Campredon, an old family friend and a member of one of the school's most important administrative councils, the Conseil de Perfectionnement. He became Comte's protector, for he already recognized his "talents." In the fall of 1815, Campredon wrote

[84] Bertrand, "Souvenirs académiques," 530. Perhaps it was this occasion that is described in a letter written in 1838 to Comte from an old classmate who was reminiscing about their school days: "I feel as if I am once again attending the examinations and the reception of the new students. I still see and hear you in Room 7, coming to the aid of our good friend Latour who, all disconcerted, could not respond to the discourse of [illegible]. He did not have, as you did, the brains of a president or the seriousness of the Great Priest. I still hear your voice, which made the freshman tremble, when you interrogated him on trivial, superficial subjects." Chavelet to Comte, September 8, 1838, MAC.

[85] Valat, "Notes biographiques sur Aug. Comte (1)," 353; idem, "Auguste Comte à l'Ecole Polytechnique," *Revue bordelaise* 3 (April 1, 1881): 104.

[86] "Un Billet inédit de Comte," in Dossier Auguste Comte, EP. Reproduced in Gouhier, *Jeunesse*, 1:272.

[87] Comte to Pouzin, November 21, 1814, CG, 1:3. See also Robinet, *Notice*, 102; Comte to Valat, January 2, 1815, CG, 1:7.

[88] L'Officier supérieur de la semaine, "Rapport à Monsieur le Gouverneur," June 19, 1825; Baron Greiner, "Ordre du jour," June 20, 1815, Dossier Auguste Comte, EP. Reproduced in Gouhier, *Jeunesse*, 1:272–3. (The date of June 20, 1813, in Gouhier is a mistake.)

in his diary that Comte was "very badly thought of" at the school
and that people pointed to him as a "very insubordinate seditionary."[89]
His lectures to Comte about changing his conduct were in vain.
Comte's insolent rejoinder to an administrator in November 1815
led to his condemnation to two weeks of prison. Talk of his expulsion
was in the air.[90]

In the spring of 1816 Comte became embroiled in a quarrel with
a mathematics tutor (*répétiteur*), Lefébure de Fourcy, who, though
popular with the professors, was notorious for being rude and con-
descending to students.[91] After the first-year students appealed to his
class for help, Comte decided to give Lefébure a lesson in manners.
He went to see the tutor for his routine oral examination and found
him stretched out as usual in a low chair with his feet on the table.
During the interrogation, Comte correctly answered the questions
but became very insolent. Extremely annoyed, Lefébure exclaimed,
"My child, you are behaving very badly." Comte responded, "Sir,
I thought I was doing well by following your example."[92] Lefébure
threw him out of the room and demanded that he be punished with
detention. After several more confrontations between Lefébure and
students, Comte drafted a letter to the tutor, which bluntly stated,
"Sir, although it pains us to take such action against a former student of the school, we enjoin you never to set foot here again."[93]
Comte was the first to sign this petition and was able to gain much
support. Not at all pleased by this movement, the administration
abruptly dismissed him and the whole student body on April 13,
1816. It seems that this trivial incident of insubordination served as
a pretext for the royalists to eliminate the hostile republican spirit
that pervaded the school.[94] As Alan Spitzer has shown, animosity
toward the regime was "chronic" in the schools at this time; the

---

[89] Général de Campredon, "Extrait d'un cahier de notes du général de Campredon," in
"Matériaux pour servir à la biographie d'Auguste Comte: Correspondants, amis et
protecteurs d'Auguste Comte: Le Général Campredon. Pièces justificatives," ed. Pierre
Laffitte, *RO*, 2d ser., 34 (September 1906): 165. Campredon had helped Comte obtain a
reduction on his room and board. See also C. Auriol, *Le Lieutenant Général de Campredon*
(Montpellier, 1894), 12–13; P. de Saint-Paul, *La Vie du Général Campredon* (Montpellier,
1837), 13–15, 80.

[90] See l'Officier de semaine, "Conseil d'ordre: Rapport particulier sur M. Comte," November
14, 1815, in Dossier Auguste Comte, EP.

[91] Lefébure de Fourcy was originally called Louis Lefebvre, but when the monarchy was
restored, he changed his name to have the cachet of nobility. Alvin, "Centenaire," 3, Dossier
Comte, EP. See also Dossier Lefébure de Fourcy, EP, and the comments made by Siméon
Poisson about Lefebvre, Letter from Poisson, October 14, 1815, in Dossier Poisson, EP.

[92] Bertrand, "Souvenirs académiques," 530.

[93] The petition to Lefébure, quoted in Robinet, *Notice*, 103.

[94] Pinet, *Histoire de l'Ecole Polytechnique*, 95–7; Artz, *Technical Education*, 240; Terry Shinn,
L'Ecole Polytechnique: 1794–1914 (Paris: Presses de la Fondation Nationale des Sciences
Politiques, 1980), 35.

students' "militant hostility toward the authorities . . . was indistinguishable in its consequences from hostility to the political regime." Once the ultraroyalists triumphed, they purged the University in the same way they had the Ecole Polytechnique. The result was that Comte and his generation became even more committed to liberating themselves from all authority and seeking their own solution to the problems of the period.[95]

With his promising career ruined, Comte left for Montpellier a week later.[96] But before departing, he took an active role in founding an association to provide the students with assistance and a sense of unity. Comte was the secretary of the association's headquarters in Montpellier and had under him at least twenty-five students.[97] Since the government was engaged in a "legal White Terror," the subversive undertones of this Polytechnical association alarmed Elie Decazes, the minister of police and future prime minister, who placed Comte under police surveillance and had his correspondence censored. Although government agents were unable to determine whether this secret society ever met at his home, Comte's experiment in preserving the feeling of solidarity in a tightly knit organization was aborted.[98]

Comte's desire to found such an association reveals, however, his loyalty to the Ecole Polytechnique, which had deeply colored his

[95] Spitzer, *French Generation*, 41; see also 50.

[96] Callot, *Histoire de l'Ecole Polytechnique*, 55–6; Littré, *Auguste Comte*, 8; Lonchampt *Précis*, 11; Corra, *La Naissance du génie d'Auguste Comte: Sa Vie jusqu'en 1819*, 19; General Louis-Pierre-Jean-Mammès Cosseron de Villenoisy, "Auguste Comte," in Ecole Polytechnique, *Livre du centenaire, 1794–1894*, 3 vols. (Paris, 1894–7), 3:450; Letter from Comte Dejean to the Minister of the Interior, April 12, 1816, F¹⁷ 6817, Dossier 2076, AN; "Compte des frais de transport du bagage des élèves de l'Ecole Polytechnique, partis par les diligences de l'exploitation généralᵉ des messageries royales," F¹⁷ 1391, AN; Registre de matricule des élèves, vol. 4. 1810–19, EP. In his letter of April 12, 1816, to the minister of the interior, Dejean blamed six corporals from the first-year class for causing most of the trouble. Yet he did mention that there were "dangerous leaders, especially in the second-year class." Comte was eighth on the list of students recommended for expulsion. This letter is reproduced in Gouhier, *Jeunesse*, 1:277–9. Valat's version is close to Dejean's. See Valat, "Auguste Comte à l'Ecole Polytechnique," 104.

[97] See the copy of the original proposal, "Association des élèves de l'Ecole," in "Matériaux pour servir à la biographie d'Auguste Comte: Documents d'Auguste Comte relatifs à l'Ecole Polytechnique," ed. Pierre Laffitte, *RO*, 2d ser., 16 (July 1892): 151–3. The original proposal exists in the Maison d'Auguste Comte.

[98] Guillaume de Bertier de Sauvigny, *The Bourbon Restoration*, trans. Lynn M. Case (Philadelphia: University of Pennsylvania Press, 1966), 134. See also the letter from the Préfet de l'Hérault to Comte Decazes, June 14, 1816, F⁷ 6817, Dossier 2076, AN; letter from the Préfet de l'Hérault to the Ministre Secrétaire d'Etat au Département de la Police Générale du Royaume, July 12, 1816, F⁷ 6817, Dossier 2076, AN. These letters are reproduced in Gouhier, *Jeunesse*, 1:288–9. See also Valat, "Auguste Comte (Suite et fin)," *Revue bordelaise* 3 (1881): 181; Gouhier, *Jeunesse*, 1:171–2.

outlook. Above all, he retained the idealism that the school instilled in its student body. Its concern for human progress and social welfare inspired many of its graduates to become reformers. Among the more famous were Prosper Enfantin, Frédéric Le Play, Victor Considérant, and Georges Sorel, all of whom believed that social engineering involved the same process of applying laws to social structures that they had learned in their civil engineering classes. Although French scientists were in disfavor because of their allegiance to the Revolution and their leadership role in society was being taken over by literary men, they were still the most outstanding scientists in the world, and their achievements had convinced Comte that the sciences held the key to improving the human condition.[99]

Moreover, he became fascinated by the philosophy of science thanks in part to the mathematician Louis Poinsot, the professor who perhaps had had the greatest impact on him at the Ecole Polytechnique.[100] Like Encontre, Poinsot also encouraged Comte's interest in teaching as a vocation. He was one of the few who put mathematical "analysis in its proper place" by making the students concentrate on content instead of form.[101]

Mathematics was the field that most fascinated Comte. Characterizing mathematics as a "science of pure relations," the philosopher Ernst Cassirer explained that a mathematician was not at all interested in whether figures existed:

> Indeed in so far as mathematical thought is concerned their existence does not matter. The single elements receive their roles, and hence their significance, only as they fit together into a connected system;

[99] David Knight, *The Age of Science: The Scientific World-view in the Nineteenth Century* (Oxford: Basil Blackwell, 1986), 5, 11; Artz, *Technical Education*, 161, 241–3, 266; Gouhier, *Jeunesse*, 146–7; Lewis A. Coser, *Masters of Sociological Thought: Ideas in Historical and Social Context* (New York: Harcourt Brace Jovanovich, 1971), 33–4; L. Pearce Williams, "Science," 89; Hayek, *Counter-Revolution*, 105–6. On the changing role of writers, see Paul Bénichou, *Le Sacre de l'écrivain, 1750–1830: Essai sur l'avènement d'un pouvoir spirituel laïque dans la France moderne*, 2d ed. (Paris: José Corti, 1973; Paris: José Corti, 1985).

[100] In early 1815 Comte recommended two books by Sylvestre-François Lacroix and Lazare Carnot to Valat and told him that if he meditated on them, he would learn the "metaphysics" of calculus, that is, its basic principles. Comte to Valat, February 14, 1815, *CG*, 1:8. See also Comte to Valat, January 2, 1815, *CG*, 1:6. When Comte later wrote an outline of a work on the philosophy of mathematics, he showed it to Poinsot, whom he considered an "excellent judge in this matter." Comte to Valat, September 24, 1819, *CG*, 1:58. In the *Cours* Comte declared that among all the French geometers of their day, Poinsot was the closest to the "true philosophic state." *Cours*, 2:632. Information on Poinsot, who enjoyed moving in fashionable circles and actually taught very little, can be found in "Matériaux pour servir à la biographie d'Auguste Comte: Relations d'Auguste Comte avec L. Poinsot," ed. Pierre Laffitte, *RO* 16 (March 1, 1886): 147; *Cours d'analyse de Monsieur Poinsot, de Monsieur Reynaud*, MAC.

[101] Comte to Louis Poinsot, September 18, 1836, *CG*, 1:262.

thus they are defined through one another, not independently of one another.[102]

The systematic approach to knowledge, together with the emphasis on relations and the whole, would emerge in the positivist outlook. This mind-set may also help to account for Comte's tendency to disregard the problems of epistemology. His philosophy would reflect one other concern of the mathematician: the reconciliation of abstract thought and concrete objects.[103] The relationship between the abstract and the concrete would be as important to Comte as the connection between theory and practice was to Marx.

Comte adopted other scientific attitudes that affected his perception of politics and society. He learned the value of the "objective" observation of facts, classifying and categorizing data, and making general scientific laws to explain and predict the operations of the world. Regularity, reliability, and certitude developed into major preoccupations. Finally, he shared the scientific assumption of the existence of a natural order. To various degrees, these scientific perspectives would become the basis of social science, which would assume that the collectivity behaved according to natural laws and was a more important object of research than the individual.[104]

In his famous study, *La Jeunesse d'Auguste Comte*, Henri Gouhier pointed out that this scientific outlook was the only one that was taught to the young Comte and it thus naturally dictated his approach to social regeneration. Moreover, since Comte never really grappled with any problems in theology or metaphysics, he assumed that such subjects would no longer be discussed.[105] Frederick Hayek in *The Counter-Revolution of Science* went further than Gouhier in demonstrating Comte's narrowness. Labeling him a scientistic thinker, Hayek contended that Comte corrupted the study of society by his "engineering type of mind," which led him to apply blueprints organizing the world according to certain preconceived goals. According to Hayek, the Ecole Polytechnique was responsible for breeding generations of men who believed that scientific reasoning held the solution to all religious, social, and political

---

[102] Ernst Cassirer, *The Problem of Knowledge: Philosophy, Science, and History since Hegel*, trans. William H. Woglom and Charles W. Hendel (New Haven, Conn.: Yale University Press, 1950), 26.

[103] Pierre Ducassé, *Auguste Comte et Gaspard Monge* (Paris, Extract from *Revue positiviste internationale*, 1937), 15.

[104] Ian G. Barbour, *Issues in Science and Religion* (New York: Harper & Row, Harper Torchbooks, 1971), 137–50; Cynthia Eagle Russett, *Sexual Science: The Victorian Construction of Womanhood* (Cambridge, Mass.: Harvard University Press, 1989), 193.

[105] Gouhier, *Jeunesse*, 1:230–47.

questions. Comte's schemes for large-scale social remodeling reflected the technological mentality that he learned there.[106]

Comte himself admitted that his approach to social reform incorporated the scientific idealism of his period and especially of his
school. Yet he was not the narrow-minded technician that Hayek
in particular found him to be. Comte realized that his education had
been too abstract and one-sidedly academic and had disregarded
emotional development.[107] He therefore always resisted the temptation to quantify human experience. Moreover, he was an antireductionist who rejected his contemporaries' efforts to find one
general, unifying scientific law or one body of knowledge that would
explain everything. Most significantly, he combated throughout
his life the nineteenth-century trend toward specialization, which
was, in fact, the basis of his education and represents the mark of a
technological culture.[108] Commenting precisely on the encyclopedic
aspect of Comte's thought, Ernst Cassirer called Comte "perhaps
the last thinker to grasp the problem of philosophy and the general
theory of knowledge in its universal extent." Fearful of the "increasing fragmentation of knowledge," caused especially by "'specialization,'" Comte established positivism and proposed educational
reforms "to oppose the intellectual division of labor, *no matter how
useful and even indispensable it may be to the progress of science.*"[109]

Gouhier and especially Hayek thus seem to have underestimated
the more fundamental philosophical tenor of Comte's thought. Interested in the larger questions that make up philosophy, Comte
himself recognized "immediately" the "extreme insufficiency" of
his education at the Ecole Polytechnique and sought to remedy it by
studying biology and history.[110] After his expulsion and return to
Montpellier, he pursued courses in biology at the Ecole de Médecine,
which, unlike its rival in Paris, had a strong vitalist tradition, stressing the differences between the animate and inanimate worlds.[111]

---

[106] Hayek, *Counter-Revolution*, 16; see also, 94–113, 168–88.

[107] *Cours*, 2:466; *Système*, 1:8.

[108] Vaughan and Archer, *Social Conflict*, 186–91; William Barrett, *The Illusion of Technique: The Search for Meaning in a Technological Civilization* (Garden City, N.Y.: Doubleday, Anchor Books, 1979), 26.

[109] Cassirer, *Knowledge*, 8–9 (my emphasis). As Cassirer pointed out, Comte's stress on the universal aspect of philosophy embodied the "classical, rationalistic ideal" inherent in Cartesianism.

[110] *Cours*, 2:466. See also Barrett, *Illusion*, 27–8.

[111] Perhaps Comte was spurred in this direction by his friend Roméo Pouzin, who had already given up his studies at the Ecole Polytechnique and was enrolled in 1816 in the Ecole de Médecine. In 1820 Pouzin received his doctorate in medicine and several years later became a professor at the Ecole de Pharmacie in Montpellier. At the Ecole de Médecine,

Comte's continuing fascination with political economy and a new concern with history are also evident because several weeks after his arrival in his hometown, he wrote his first essay, a discussion of the past twenty-five years in France. Surely this indicates that Comte had some awareness of subjects other than the sciences and was trying to be less specialized than Hayek and Gouhier claimed him to be.

Finally, it is important to recognize that many of the characteristics that Hayek stated are inherent in the technological mind-set may not be part of scientific activity at all. Various philosophers of science refute the notion that there exists an essential scientific mentality unconnected with the culture at large.[112] Thus some of the tendencies Comte displayed may not have come from a specifically technological training, but from political, social, cultural, and familial influences as well as from his own temperament.[113]

COMTE'S FIRST ESSAY

Comte first displayed his wide-ranging interests in the aforementioned essay, which he wrote in June 1816: "Mes Réflexions: Humanité, vérité, justice, liberté, patrie. Rapprochements entre le régime de 1793 et celui de 1816, adressés au peuple français."[114] Comte wrote it to express his feelings of horror regarding the royalists' recent series of vengeful massacres in the Midi. Although the essay resembled a journalistic article, it was never published.

In this essay, Comte lamented that the French people were unable

Comte may have come into contact with such celebrated professors as Jacques Lordat, J. Delpech, Clément-Victor-François-Gabriel Prunelle, and Augustin Pyrame de Candolle. The great exponent of vitalism, Paul-Joseph Barthez, had died there only ten years before, in 1806. Henri Mazet, Introduction to *Six Lettres inédites à Roméo Pouzin* (Paris: Crès, 1914), 6; *Almanach royal pour l'an 1816* (Paris, 1816), 389; Erwin Ackerknecht, *Medicine at the Paris Hospital, 1794–1848* (Baltimore, Md.: Johns Hopkins University Press, 1967), 25, 54.

[112] See Barry Barnes, *Scientific Knowledge and Sociological Theory* (London: Routledge & Kegan Paul, 1974), 48-9, 164-5n2.

[113] At one point, Comte explained that he "naturally ceased to believe in God" as a young boy and that his later studies *confirmed* this "necessary emancipation." Comte to Louis Comte, January 26, 1857, *CG*, 8:391. Authoritarian inclinations could have been reinforced by his life in the Napoleonic school system, where he learned the importance of authority, submission, devotion, centralized hierarchy, planning, administrative detail, efficiency, and, above all, order. Also, his dislike of theology may have derived from the revolutionaries' animus against the Church and thus may have preceded his scientific education.

[114] This essay is published in *Ecrits*, 417–31. Obviously proud of his educational background, Comte added under his name the words "élève de l'ex-Ecole Polytechnique." Throughout his life, Comte referred to himself as a former student of the school.

to see that the government of Louis XVIII was at least as despotic as the regimes of the Terror and Napoleon. In fact, Comte argued that the current monarchy was the worst government of all because it was the most Machiavellian and hypocritical. Louis XVIII was insincere in that he pretended to espouse liberal principles but secretly undermined them in defiance of the will of the people. He could wield his power easily because Napoleon had already removed the biggest possible obstacle to tyranny: "the spirit of reason, liberty, and philosophy."[115]

This phrase, "the spirit of reason, liberty, and philosophy," and the title of the essay itself, which used the words "humanity," "truth," "justice," "liberty," and "homeland," show the extent to which Comte's language was formed by the discourse of the Enlightenment and Revolution. Like the radical revolutionaries inspired by the ideas of Rousseau, he longed for a republic founded on the "national will"[116] and condemned its enemies as despots and tyrants.[117] He seemed to echo the words of Encontre's hymn to the Supreme Being: "We all come to swear hatred of tyranny . . . and love of the homeland [*la Patrie*]."[118]

Although Comte was intent on criticizing the Bourbon Restoration, his attention was focused on the Revolution. Like other liberals of this period, especially Madame de Staël and Benjamin Constant, Comte was confronted with the difficult task of explaining the Terror. At this time, the Right was denying the positive aspects of the Revolution by reducing it to the events of 1793–4. Challenged in this way, liberals were debating the problem of how to condemn the Terror and still remain loyal to the Revolution.[119] What Comte did in this essay was to attribute the Terror to false revolutionaries, like Robespierre and Marat, who pretended to love the Republic but were really "vile instruments of royalism," intent on satisfying their own ambitions. These "villains" were not even loyal Frenchmen; in destroying true republicans and liberty, they sought to fulfill the "horrible conditions of their treaty with the foreigners."[120] Thus like other republicans of his period, Comte excluded Robespierre's reign from the heritage of the Revolution. In Comte's history, which reflected the essential creed of the liberal doctrine that was evolving at the time, Robespierre, Marat, and other extremists functioned as scapegoats and were used to explain why the Revolution of 1789 went out of control. In this way, Comte hoped to save the

---

[115] Ibid., 428.   [116] Ibid., 421.   [117] Hubert C. Johnson, *The Midi*, 81.
[118] Daniel Encontre, quoted in Duval-Jouve, *Montpellier*, 2:383.
[119] Alice Gérard, *La Révolution française: Mythes et interprétations (1789–1970)* (Paris: Flammarion, 1970), 27, 30.
[120] *Ecrits*, 418.

Revolution, and condemned the king and his supporters for betraying it.

Moreover, Comte sought in a sense to mitigate the horrors of the Terror of 1793 by insisting that the White Terror, carried out by the royalists and condoned by the monarch and Church, was even worse. Again reflecting the mentality of the revolutionary period, he seemed to feel that there was an "immense conspiracy" against liberal principles and institutions; it was evident during the Terror but was even more dangerous now: "Everywhere the tyrant is commanding in a despotic manner. . . . He is always striding toward the ancien régime, which he has practically reached and beyond which he will try to go. . . . Who could defend . . . [liberty] against the appalling league of Kings and Priests?"[121]

Comte maintained that Louis XVIII, Napoleon, and the terrorists of 1793 easily created despotic governments because they received support from the majority of the people, who at the time did not recognize what their rulers were doing. Most people even favored the ancien régime until the "absurdity" of the government was revealed to them by "some wise and courageous men." Reflecting the influence of the philosophers and the revolutionaries who had created his school, the Ecole Polytechnique, with a regenerative mission in mind, Comte was sure that the "progress of knowledge" and the spread of education could eliminate the French people's blindness.[122] Here Comte was implicitly attacking the Right, which blamed philosophy and reason for the disasters of the Revolution.[123] He argued to the contrary that the government's attempt to halt the "progress of the sciences and philosophy" by censorship, the banishment of scholars, and other means was most dangerous; it effectively silenced criticism, strengthened the beliefs upholding the ancien régime, and opened the door to tyranny. "Enlightened men moan and are silent: they are almost losing the hope of ever seeing the rebirth of liberty, for who could make it triumph from terror and prejudices?"[124]

Since Comte considered himself a member of the small elite of "enlightened men, accustomed to thinking on their own, distrusting appearance, and examining [events] with sang-froid," he felt it was his duty to show the French people the evils of the Bourbon government and spur them to action. He sought to teach – "to enlighten" – the French people about the great threats to their liberty by making eleven systematic comparisons between the Bourbon

---

[121] Ibid., 431. On the revolutionaries' preoccupation with conspiracy, see Hunt, *Politics, Culture, and Class*, 39–40.

[122] *Ecrits*, 417–18.   [123] Gérard, *La Révolution française*, 27.

[124] *Ecrits*, 423–4, 431.

regime and that of the Terror. His scientific training is evident, for these comparisons, using the "fact of history," were similar to evidence used to "prove" a mathematical theorem.[125] Nevertheless, he was most interested in disseminating the lessons of history, not science.

This essay thus encapsulates the essence of positivism, for Comte's philosophy both inherited the didacticism of the Revolution and shared his contemporaries' fascination with the past.[126] As Linda Orr has demonstrated, history in the early nineteenth century became for romantic historians, such as Lamartine, Michelet, and Louis Blanc, an "act of social bonding" and "social action."[127] Like these historians, Comte became increasingly interested in using the past to create social harmony in the present. He believed that the correct interpretation of history held the key to action, to solving the problems of his time. History would thus become the basis of sociology, the science of social consensus, and would become central to positivism's educational mission.

Moreover, this essay already foreshadows the tension that would exist in positivism between its concern for the people and its elitist tendencies. Comte accepted the Montagnards' definition of a "legitimate" government as one "created or accepted by the nation" or the "national will." He believed that the government should rest on popular consent. But he exhibited a fundamental ambivalence toward the people. On the one hand, he distrusted their judgment, for he believed that their support of the government was all too often passive and blind. On the other hand, he shared the rationalist, Enlightenment faith that if they were freed from the priests, kings, and false revolutionaries who stifled their reason, they could create a republic that would ensure justice and liberty. The key to this process was the creation of an intellectual elite composed of "scientists and philosophers" who would enlighten the people. The knowledge that the elite would impart, not the people's independent action, would save the members of society from arbitrary authority. What is most revealing about the text is what is suppressed. Comte did not refer to the concepts of equality or individual rights. Although he condemned the monarchical version of legitimacy as well as the Charter, which was "hardly liberal," he did not offer any solutions to the problem of representation.[128] The revolutionaries and Napoleon had sought to avoid this problem by using symbols and rhetoric. Their authoritarian solutions had prevented the emergence

[125] Ibid., 417–19.   [126] Hunt, *Politics, Culture, and Class*, 214.

[127] Linda Orr, *Headless History: Nineteenth-Century French Historiography of the Revolution* (Ithaca, N.Y.: Cornell University Press, 1990), 18.

[128] *Ecrits*, 421, 424, 429.

of liberal politics. But with a new, parliamentary government, the problem of representation was at the center of the political debates. Preoccupied by the Terror and the danger of popular insurrection, liberals sought to determine the relations between liberalism and democracy; they wanted the people to participate in public life in such a way as not to threaten liberty.[129] Comte's adoption of the revolutionary rhetoric of "national will" and "the people" without any analysis of the means to translate these concepts into political reality points to the central difficulty he would have in formulating his political philosophy: his poor understanding of power. He was in a sense committed to what Jean-Paul Frick has called the "democratic invention of society," but he inclined toward the rule of an elite.[130] As positivism developed, Comte would abandon a liberal vision of politics, which had trouble implanting itself in France, and would embrace an increasingly complex concept of elitism.

This essay also reveals Comte's formidable self-confidence and sense of authority at age eighteen. Passionate about nascent liberalism, he did not hesitate to lash out at the oppression that reigned in his country. Instead of feeling shame at his dismissal from school, he was proud of having been a victim of the royalist regime. His rage against the government encouraged the feeling that he had a special calling, for he seemed to be searching in this essay for his own self-identity. With his career plans in disarray, he wanted to play an idealistic part in French politics, one that would save "the Revolution and philosophy."[131] The essay foreshadows two of the roles that he assumed in later life: the savior of the people and the perennial victim of a conspiracy against enlightened thought.

THE RETURN TO PARIS

During the two and a half months he spent in Montpellier, Comte had difficulty deciding whether the tedium of provincial life or the reactionary and religious atmosphere was worse. Paris beckoned with its intellectual and political excitement and cultural offerings, especially the theater, which he loved to attend. He finally left for

[129] Hunt, *Politics, Culture, and Class*, 48–9, 229; François Furet, *Interpreting the French Revolution*, trans. Elborg Forster (Cambridge: Cambridge University Press, 1981), 27; Pierre Rosanvallon, "Les Doctrinaires et la question du gouvernement représentatif," in *The French Revolution and the Creation of Modern Political Culture*, vol. 3, *The Transformation of Political Culture, 1789–1848*, ed. François Furet and Mona Ozouf (Oxford: Pergamon Press, 1989), 412–13; Pierre Rosanvallon, *Le Moment Guizot* (Paris: Gallimard, 1985), 13.

[130] Jean-Paul Frick, "Le Problème du pouvoir chez A. Comte et la signification de sa philosophie positive," *Revue philosophique de la France et de l'étranger*, no. 3 (1988): 301; see also 277.

[131] *Ecrits*, 429.

the capital in July 1816. On his way, he made a stop in Lyons, where he scribbled a note to a friend, revealing that he was at least in some respects a typical eighteen-year-old:

> Last Sunday I was invited to a picnic which greatly amused me; there were some young girls who were very pretty and especially very amiable, one could even say very accommodating; ... I had a delightful day. I must admit to you that I would not be able to console myself for leaving Lyons if I were not going to Paris, where the women are generally less pretty but even more amiable and ... life offers so many pleasures that one does not find here.[132]

When Comte arrived in Paris, the city was just entering a period of intense revival. With the fall of Napoleon's dictatorship, there was a new sense of stability and liberation as well as a resurgence of creative energies. Paris retained its leadership in the sciences and was soon able to resume its position as the center of the arts and letters. Eugène Delacroix, Hector Berlioz, Alexandre Dumas, Victor Hugo, Alfred de Vigny, Prosper Merimée, Honoré de Balzac, and Charles Augustin Saint-Beuve were members of Comte's generation (born between 1792 and 1803) who were preparing their careers.[133]

Politics dominated discussions in Paris, for the nation was engaged in yet another experiment in government – the restoration of the Bourbon monarchy. Representing a compromise between the ancien régime and the Revolution, the Bourbon government allowed for a very limited representative government and the continuation of some newly won civil rights, but it also brought back the king, the aristocrats, and the Church. With the establishment of a new alliance between throne and altar, spiritual and worldly affairs seemed as intertwined as before. The Church, in addition, grew stronger as a result of an intense religious revival, which centered on appeals to feelings and on the emotive power of beauty as reflected in cults and ceremonies – a far cry from the rationalism of the Enlightenment. The efforts of the clergy and the nobles to obliterate the past twenty-five years of French history were reflected in the policies of the ultra party. Ultracism was opposed by the heirs of the Enlightenment and revolutionary tradition – the middle-class liberals, who wanted a constitutional monarchy and a more effective parliament. Like the ultras, the liberals sought to rejuvenate the spiritual power but preferred it to be held by philosophers, not priests. The period was characterized by the struggles between the ultras and liberals over such issues as civil rights, political participation, religion, and

---

[132] Comte to Pouzin, July 9, 1816, *CG*, 1:11–12.
[133] Spitzer, *French Generation*, 6, 283–6.

education. One party was constantly looking for solutions in the seventeenth and eighteenth centuries, while the other was seeking to promote the new industrial society that was emerging in these years. In short, the nation was witnessing the last blossoming of the old order at the same time that it was experiencing the pleasures and the pains of the new. This period of ambiguity and uncertainty would prove to be a fertile ground for the intellectual growth of Comte, who was experiencing his own problems of transition and self-definition.[134]

Like many other students and provincials who were flocking to Paris at this time, Comte decided to settle in the Latin Quarter and rented a room on the rue Neuve de Richelieu, near the place de la Sorbonne. Having failed to get a job as a chemical engineer, he hoped to gain financial independence by tutoring students in mathematics at three francs an hour. Meanwhile, he remained dependent upon his parents, who had reluctantly permitted his return to Paris in the hope that he would accept the Ecole Polytechnique's offer to redeem himself.

Reorganized along religious lines, the school had decided to allow the dismissed students who could prove their good behavior and the continuation of their studies to take the examination for the Ecoles d'Application, the pathway to fine jobs in the public sector. Comte rejected the school's offer but could persuade his parents to support him only by misleading them into believing that he was preparing for this test, scheduled for June 1817.[135] He was convinced that his own prominent role in the spring revolt and his position of secretary of the student association would prevent his success. Although he was certain that few students would apply or be allowed by the government to take the examination, eighty-two of his classmates accepted the offer and seventy-two were finally admitted.[136] It is

---

[134] Bénichou, *Le Sacre de l'écrivain*, 193–263; Spitzer, *French Generation*, 3, 283–6; Henri Peyre, *What Is Romanticism?* trans. by Roda Roberts (University: University of Alabama Press, 1977), 51–3; John Hall Stewart, *The Restoration Era in France, 1814–1830* (Princeton, N.J.: Van Nostrand, 1968), 9–10, 37, 39, 69, 74–82, 93–4; Bertier de Sauvigny, *Bourbon Restoration*, 235, 288–324, 330–6, 338–49, 357, 362, 460, 457–59; idem, *Nouvelle Histoire de Paris: La Restauration, 1815–1830* (Paris: Hachette, 1977), 331, 415–17, 457–9; John Plamenatz, *The Revolutionary Movement in France, 1815–1871* (London: Longmans, Green, 1952), 21; Gordon Wright, *France in Modern Times: From the Enlightenment to the Present*, 4th ed. (New York: Norton, 1987), 95–111.

[135] Thenard, Letter of Recommendation, July 25, 1816, MAC; Comte to Valat, October 13, October 29, 1816, *CG*, 1:12–14, 17; Comte to G. d'Eichthal, December 10, 1824, *CG*, 1:142; Bertrand, "Souvenirs académiques," 531; Alvin, "Centenaire," 4, Dossier Comte, EP; Callot, *Histoire de l'Ecole Polytechnique*, 57.

[136] Comte to Valat, October 13, 1816, *CG*, 1:13; Gouhier, *Jeunesse*, 1:197; Callot, *Histoire de l'Ecole Polytechnique*, 57.

difficult to escape the impression that Comte's arguments were used simply to justify his own inaction, for he seemed pleased to have found an excuse to exchange the drab rigors of an engineering student's existence for the bohemian life in Paris.

A POSSIBLE ESCAPE TO THE UNITED STATES

In truth, Comte was already immersed in other projects. His protector was General Campredon, who besides aiding him financially introduced him in September to General Simon Bernard, a Bonapartist about to be exiled. Heading for the United States to direct the Army Corps of Engineers, Bernard promised to suggest Comte as a geometry teacher at an engineering school that was supposed to be established by Congress on the model of the Ecole Polytechnique.[137]

This job appealed to Comte for several reasons. It greatly encouraged his interest in teaching, a profession he had chosen not only because his teachers and friends had repeatedly pointed out his "special aptitude" for it, but because it could sustain his more significant "vocation" – that of a thinker.[138] Moreover, he was struck by how much the French seemed to "esteem highly the sciences and those who teach them."[139] To be a nonbelieving teacher was a way of carrying on the work of the philosophes and revolutionaries, who had promoted secular education as a powerful instrument of regeneration. Comte was also excited about the job because there were few opportunities in France for men with his education. By teaching ignorant U.S. engineers, he could make a name for himself, earn a sizable income, and contribute to the building of the new republic.[140]

For the next six months, he prepared himself by studying English and geometry and investigating American life. As the establishment of peace in 1815 normalized relations between the two countries, a vast amount of information about the United States was being

---

[137] Having graduated from the Ecole Polytechnique during the Directory in 1796, Bernard had gone on to serve Napoleon as a lieutenant general in the corps of engineers and had devotedly fought for him during the Hundred Days. He was condemned to death by the Restoration government. Edith Philips, *Les Réfugiés bonapartistes en Amérique (1815–1830)* (Paris, n.d.), 26, 73; René Rémond, *Les Etats-Unis devant l'opinion française, 1815–1852*, 2 vols. (Paris: Armand Colin, 1962), 1:35; Auriol, *Campredon*, 13; Comte to Valat, October 13, 1816, *CG*, 1:35.

[138] *Cours*, 2:468.   [139] Comte to Valat, October 29, 1816, *CG*, 1:15.

[140] Ibid, 15–17; Comte to Valat, October 13, 1816, *CG*, 1:13–14; Lenore O'Boyle, "The Problem of an Excess of Educated Men in Western Europe, 1800–1850," *Journal of Modern History* 42 (December 1970): 471–95; Rémond, *Les Etats-Unis*, 1:39, 74, 76.

published, fed no doubt by frustration over the situation in France. Like many of his contemporaries, Comte idealized the United States as a simple, virtuous, primitive land and contrasted it with aging, decadent Europe: "I would rather live in a mediocre fashion in America than swim in opulence in Anglo-Germano-Latino-Hispanic-Gaul."[141] A country devoid of nobles, kings, and priests, the very groups that were creating havoc in France, seemed the only home of liberty in the world. As he watched Bernard and several thousand other Bonapartists fleeing to the United States to seek political asylum, Comte, an outcast from the Ecole Polytechnique, was likewise attracted to that country as a land of refuge and liberty.[142] There, he could escape the fiery nationalism, empty slogans, and feeling of uncertainty creating much malaise in France.

Comte sought to acquire an "exact idea" of this "promised land" by reading book after book.[143] One work that impressed him was the *Constitution des treize Etats de l'Amérique*, a compilation of the different state constitutions. It revealed how citizens of each state used the emergent science of politics to create independent republics and a free government. As the French liberals struggled against the Right's attempts to undo the French Revolution, Comte shared their growing fascination with U.S. politicians, who had used this science successfully. Washington, with his love of peace and disinterested service to the state he founded, seemed in particular to offer a marked contrast to Napoleon. Comte decided that creating a new government was not only an intellectual operation that required a systematic, scientific approach, but also a moral process. It was the American people's "genius" and "virtue" that had enabled them to build their fine institutions on the basis of "liberty and equality."[144]

The United States was, in short, Comte's first utopia. It was simple, stable, and uncorrupted, while at the same time interested in development, science, industrial genius, comfort, and the rational

---

[141] Comte to Valat, October 29, 1816, *CG*, 1:17. See also Rémond, *Les Etats-Unis*, 1:76, 169, 242, 258, 315–412, 2:445, 477, 483, 489–96, 511–15.

[142] *Ecrits*, 420; Comte to Valat, October 29, 1816, *CG*, 1:17; Rémond, *Les Etats-Unis*, 1:36–8, 44, 58, 343, 365, 2:532.

[143] Comte to Valat, October, 13, October 29, 1816, *CG*, 1:14, 17. Some books that he bought or was given include *Recherches historiques et politiques sur les Etats-Unis de l'Amérique septentrionale*, written by a "Citizen of Virginia" in 1788; Volney's *Tableau du climat et du sol des Etats-Unis d'Amérique* (1803); and a 1794 edition of *La Crise américaine*, a series of articles written by Thomas Paine for *Common Sense*. Comte did not read the last; its pages remain uncut, and he put it with other untouched material in his least important bookcase, called the "Bibliothèque Superflue." An incomplete list of the books in Comte's library can be found in "Matériaux pour servir à la biographie d'Auguste Comte: Bibliothèque d'Auguste Comte," ed. Pierre Laffitte, *RO*, 2d ser., 14 (January 1897): 105–42.

[144] Comte to Valat, October 29, 1816, *CG*, 1:17. See also Gordon S. Wood, *The Creation of the American Republic, 1776–1787* (New York: Norton, 1972), 53–70, 129–34, 271, 594; Rémond, *Les Droites*, 1:358, 2:554–60, 570, 640–1.

construction of government.[145] The idea of an earthly paradise that was both primitive and "modern" was now firmly set in Comte's mind, despite the conflicting elements that it entailed.

SOURCES OF CONSOLATION: BENJAMIN FRANKLIN AND FRANÇOIS ANDRIEUX

Preoccupied by his preparations, Comte lived in "solitude," hardly ever leaving his apartment except for quick meals and seeing no one besides his students and, occasionally, Campredon. His chief companion seems to have been Benjamin Franklin, the hero of the French revolutionaries and now the symbol of American progress to the liberals. Comte, like other opponents of the Bourbons, found political inspiration in Franklin's stress on merit instead of birth and his faith in improvements through perseverance and willpower. But he most admired Franklin for having been a self-made man who overcame his early misfortunes to become a successful publicist, scientist, philosopher, and politician. Just as he had earlier sought to follow Encontre's example, Comte now chose Franklin to be his "model of conduct."[146]

Franklin represented a model because owing to his skepticism, belief in progress and freedom, and interest in the sciences, he epitomized the more "modern" spirit of the Enlightenment philosophes.[147] As his school nickname and first essay demonstrated, Comte too thought of himself as a philosopher with a mission to liberate humanity. Yet he wondered about the suitability of his behavior. If, as liberals asserted, philosophers were to replace priests, then the philosophers would have to be as morally upright as the priests claimed to be. One of the key words of the discourse of the radical revolutionaries had been "virtue." Inspired by Rousseau, Robespierre had written, "In order to form our political institutions, we would have to have the morals that those institutions must someday give us."[148] Comte's studies of the United States had also convinced him that

---

[145] Rémond, *Les Etats-Unis*, 2:509–11.

[146] Comte to Valat, October 29, 1816, *CG*, 1:16–17. See also Rémond, *Les Etats-Unis*, 1:358, 372–4, 2:570–91. Because Comte recounted in detail Franklin's life, it appears that he was reading his autobiography, first published in France in 1791. (Comte also owned the two volumes of the *Correspondance inédite et secrète du docteur Benjamin Franklin*, which appeared in 1817.)

[147] Rémond, *Les Etats-Unis*, 2:586, 649; Peter Gay, *The Enlightenment: An Interpretation*, 2 vols. (New York: Norton, 1977), 2:557–8.

[148] Maximilien Robespierre, *Lettres à ses commettans*, ed. G. Laurent (Gap: Louis Jean, 1961), vol. 5 of the *Oeuvres complètes*, 20; quoted in Carol Blum, *Rousseau and the Republic of Virtue: The Language of Politics in the French Revolution* (Ithaca, N.Y.: Cornell University Press, 1986), 161.

the success of a republic depended on its citizens' morality.[149] And his 1816 essay showed that he believed that the dishonesty and hypocrisy of the "tyrants of 93" and Louis XVIII prevented the creation of a good government.[150] As a proud nonbeliever, Comte could not turn to religion for moral guidance. Instead, he chose Franklin, who at age fifteen had abandoned religion but retained his interest in moral principles. What particularly inspired Comte was Franklin's code of secular and practical morality, which was grounded in scientific deductions from human nature and was supposed to lead to "moral perfection."[151] Like other Frenchmen of the period, Comte considered Franklin the "modern Socrates" because he aimed to create a terrestrial morality, emphasizing virtuous simplicity and moderation.[152] This morality would unite humanity by transcending divisive dogmas.[153]

Increasingly interested in the science of morality, Comte focused more on observing human nature. He closely examined his friends, and because of his absorption in questions of behavior and his own loneliness, he became more introspective. "I am obliged to observe myself." Reading about Franklin's life every day for encouragement, Comte claimed he was learning to use his reason to vanquish certain possibly "fatal" inclinations, including his "strong" ardor for women. In describing the war within him, Comte revealed himself to be a very passionate man. When he told Valat that his senses had "gradually disappeared" and that he felt, consequently, "much happier," he did not seem entirely convincing.[154] Nevertheless, he did have an optimistic faith in reason and in himself; he even insinuated that he was superior to his mentor because he was attempting to follow his code at a younger age.

Comte's interest in Franklin contributed to his concern with morality as *the* key factor in human existence. Franklin taught that such virtues as chastity, order, thrift, foresight, plainness, and hard work led to moral and material success. A product of the American spirit and the Enlightenment, he was Janus-faced, combining the

---

[149] Gay, *The Enlightenment*, 1:3, 10, 13–16; Comte to Valat, October 29, 1816, *CG*, 1:16; Bénichou, *Le Sacre de l'écrivain*, 116, 193; Hunt, *Politics, Culture, and Class*, 21; Wood, *American Republic*, 68–9.

[150] *Ecrits*, 419.

[151] Benjamin Franklin, *Autobiography of Benjamin Franklin*, ed. Leonard W. Labaree et al. (New Haven, Conn.: Yale University Press, 1964), 148. See also Rémond, *Les Etats-Unis*, 2:575–6, 581; Comte to Valat, October 29, 1816, *CG*, 1:16.

[152] Comte to Valat, October 29, 1816, *CG*, 1:16.

[153] Franklin reinforced the archaic picture that Comte and many other Frenchmen had of the United States. Rémond, *Les Etats-Unis*, 2:494, 498, 503–7, 579, 581, 586, 651; Wood, *American Republic*, 50–3.

[154] Comte to Valat, October 29, 1816, *CG*, 1:15–17.

primitive morality of austere simplicity with the modern utilitarian morality of material wealth. Comte to some extent inherited this same tension.[155] While his formal education had trained him to master the outer world of nature, his inner self remained confused and chaotic. He turned for help to Socrates' and Franklin's precept, "Know thyself," and in this way began to associate discipline and order with happiness. His preoccupation with radical self-reformation suggests that Comte was more attracted in some ways to the simplicity and austerity of the past than to the materialism and indulgence of the modern period.

In early 1817 Comte also sought to follow the example of François Andrieux, a famous neoclassical playwright and former professor at the Ecole Polytechnique, where he had taught Comte grammar, composition, and literature.[156] They renewed their relationship when Comte attended his popular course at the Collège de France. Though doubtless impressed by Andrieux's skills as a teacher and playwright, he seemed attracted to him most of all for political reasons. Andrieux had occupied several important positions under the revolutionary government and had been an active member of the deistic cult, Theophilanthropy. He had also belonged to the group of Idéologues surrounding Madame Helvétius and Cabanis, all of whom had been devoted to maintaining the ideas of the philosophes. Andrieux's grammar course at the Ecole Polytechnique was directly inspired by the Idéologues, who, instead of encouraging the search for first causes, advocated scientific observation, analysis, and classification. During the Empire, Andrieux had become president of the Tribunal, where he opposed the emergent despotism of Napoleon, who had him removed from office. During the Restoration, Andrieux remained loyal to the revolutionary idealism of his youth and was idolized by young people.[157] At the time of the students' rebellion at the Ecole Polytechnique, he was suspected by the royalists of being their

[155] Franklin, *Autobiography*, 13, 144; Rémond, *Les Etats-Unis*, 2:583, 587; Gay, *The Enlightenment*, 1:8.

[156] Information on Andrieux's courses can be found in Registre de l'Instruction, 1814–16, EP.

[157] Andrieux had also helped found the Idéologue periodical *La Décade philosophique*. The Idéologue philosophy was suppressed in the Institut and the Ecoles Centrales by Napoleon in 1803. When Andrieux later fought against the philosophy of Cousin, he reiterated the Idéologues' position that "there is some extravagance in wanting to resolve insoluble questions." Andrieux, quoted in François-Joseph Picavet, *Les Idéologues: Essai sur l'histoire des idées et des théories scientifiques, philosophiques, religieuses, etc. en France depuis 1789* (Paris, 1891), 413. See also ibid., 68, 411–12, 573; Prosper Alfaric, *Laromiguière et son école* (Paris: Les Belles Lettres, 1929), 41, 49; Martin S. Staum, *Cabanis: Enlightenment and Medical Philosophy in the French Revolution* (Princeton, N.J.: Princeton University Press, 1980), 150; Lyons, *France under the Directory*, 120; Maurice Tourneux, "Andrieux," in *La Grande Encyclopédie*, 31 vols. (Paris, 1885–1902), 2:1046.

accomplice, and he too was expelled. In 1817 he lamented to Comte that he even feared dismissal from the Collège de France.[158] Thus because of the similarity of their plights, Comte in his loneliness sought support and sympathy from Andrieux, who represented a direct link to the revolutionary past – a past Comte worried was being betrayed.

THE CONTINUATION OF HIS STUDIES

Preparing for the courses he was about to give in the United States, Comte read works by Joseph Louis Lagrange (1736–1813) and Gaspard Monge (1746–1818), two famous mathematicians who had been associated with the Idéologues and had taught at the Ecole Polytechnique. Lagrange dealt with the methodology, philosophy, and history of science.[159] Monge was interested primarily in the practical and social applications of science, and his works reinforced Comte's belief that technological advances led to social progress and the happiness of the human race.[160]

To his investigation of the exact sciences, Comte in early 1817 added another area of exploration: "the study of the moral and political sciences." Possibly inspired by his readings on the U.S. government and Franklin, he now began to "meditate on Condorcet and Montesquieu," two very influential philosophes who would play a significant role in his development.[161]

Like many of the other philosophes, Montesquieu was fascinated by the natural sciences and hoped to use scientific investigations to improve the human condition. Comte was familiar with Montesquieu's major works: the *Lettres persanes*, *Considérations sur les causes de la grandeur des Romains et de leur décadence*, and *De l'esprit des lois*.[162] It was mainly the last that introduced Comte to the idea that society

---

[158] Comte to Valat, February 12, 1817, *CG*, 1:21. See also Tourneux, "Andrieux," 1047.

[159] Three of Lagrange's books are in Comte's library: *Théories des fonctions analytiques*, *Traité de la résolution des équations numériques de tous les degrés* (which was written with Joseph Fourier), and *Mécanique analytique*. On Lagrange, see Jean Itard, "Lagrange, Joseph Louis," in *Dictionary of Scientific Biography*, ed. Charles Coulston Gillispie, 16 vols. (New York: Scribners, 1970–1980), 7:559–73.

[160] Comte owned Monge's *Géométrie descriptive* and his *Application de l'analyse à la géométrie*. At one point in the 1820s Comte praised Monge's conception of descriptive geometry as a model theory of a practical operation (the art of construction). Monge's approach may have inspired Comte's future plan of establishing a class of engineers who would mediate between the theoretical and practical domains. See *Système*, vol. 4, "Appendice," 174n2; Ducassé, *Comte et Monge*, passim.

[161] Comte to Valat, February 12, 1817, *CG*, 1:19.

[162] Comte owned the *Lettres persanes* ar ' *De l'esprit des lois*. Also see *Système*, vol. 4, "Appendice," 156.

could be examined scientifically. Montesquieu was one of the first thinkers to go beyond the examination of purely political questions and to consider the problems of social relationships and the connection between the individual and society. Moreover, unlike previous thinkers who sought to construct ideal societies that would provide them with norms enabling them to change reality, Montesquieu made no use of transcendent moral and religious principles or social contract theories. He wanted to observe and explain concrete social facts, not to judge them.[163] His efforts to establish the method, subject matter, and general goals of the science of society greatly influenced Comte.

Montesquieu asserted that underlying the diversity of social and political forms throughout history, there was a rational, intelligible order, similar to the natural order and thus governed by natural laws. He therefore rejected previous efforts, such as those of Hobbes and Locke, to grasp the essence of society and focused instead on understanding society by discovering the laws ruling social phenomena. In keeping with Newtonian principles, these social laws were to be descriptive, not prescriptive as they had been in the past, and were to refer to the necessity inherent in the relations between social and political phenomena. Montesquieu sought in particular to discover the laws explaining the variations and development of social phenomena because he was convinced that "each diversity is *uniformity*, each change is *constancy*."[164] This search for regularity is evident in his use of classification; he explained that there were three main types of government and by extension three forms of society – a republic (aristocracy, democracy), monarchy, and despotism. Thus Montesquieu taught Comte a scientific approach to social reality by stressing an empirical search for laws of both social variation and social development; such laws were to be based on concrete facts culled from all areas of the globe and all periods.[165] In addition,

---

[163] Robert Shackleton, *Montesquieu: A Critical Biography* (Oxford: Oxford University Press, 1961), 340; Emile Durkheim, *Montesquieu and Rousseau: Forerunners of Sociology*, trans. Ralph Manheim (Ann Arbor: University of Michigan, Ann Arbor Paperbacks, 1965), 2, 4, 13, 17; Louis Althusser, *Montesquieu, Rousseau, Marx: Politics and History*, trans. Ben Brewster (London: Verso, 1982), 20, 29–31, 37; John Plamenatz, *Man and Society: Political and Social Theory*, 2 vols. (New York: McGraw-Hill, 1963), 2:298.

[164] Montesquieu, *De l'esprit des lois*, 2 vols. (Paris: Garnier, 1973), 1:7–8. The first lines of the first book of the *De l'esprit des lois* read, "Laws, in their most general signification, are the necessary relations which derive from the nature of things, and in this sense all beings have their laws." Ibid., 1:7. See also Durkheim, *Montesquieu and Rousseau*, 13; Aron, *Main Currents*, 1:14; Althusser, *Montesquieu*, 20, 31–4; Shackleton, *Montesquieu*, 244–64.

[165] Montesquieu, *De l'esprit des lois*, 1:6, 14, 25–35. See also Durkheim, *Montesquieu and Rousseau*, 24; Aron, *Main Currents*, 1:21–2; Althusser, *Montesquieu*, 47–8; Ernst Cassirer, *The Philosophy of the Enlightenment*, trans. Fritz C. A. Koelln and James P. Pettegrove

Comte learned to regard the comparative method and classification by types as crucial aspects of this nascent social science.

Equally important to Comte was Montesquieu's depiction of society as an integrated cultural whole endowed with a nature of its own. All social forces – religious, political, moral, social, physical, psychological, cultural – were so interrelated that none could be understood apart from the whole. Since social institutions and all modes of feeling and thought were closely connected, even religion was merely a social product dependent on "les moeurs." Comte learned that society itself was a reality and that each individual was shaped by his social environment. At the same time, he was influenced by Montesquieu's cultural relativism, which derived from his belief that each country was unique because it had its own particular configuration of social phenomena. The search for universal solutions to the problems of freedom and coercion was invalid.[166]

From reading Montesquieu, Comte also became aware that progress consisted of the growing impact of moral factors (such as religion, laws, tradition, customs, opinions, and manners) at the expense of the physical ones (such as climate) on the nature of society.[167] Since change was restricted by the complexity of social and political relationships, the key to improving society lay in the general spirit, that is, the manners and morals, of the people. Opposed to autocratic government, prejudice, superstition, and formal religion, Montesquieu advocated a doctrine of toleration, which he hoped would make people more concerned with morality than with dogma.[168] Like Franklin, Montesquieu therefore underscored for Comte the fundamental importance of a moral system.

Condorcet had an even greater impact on Comte because of his

(Boston: Beacon Press, 1955), 210; Robert Bierstedt, "Sociological Thought in the Eighteenth Century," in *A History of Sociological Analysis*, ed. Tom Bottomore and Robert Nisbet (New York: Basic Books, 1978), 12.

[166] Montesquieu, *De l'esprit des lois*, 1:12–13. See also Althusser, *Montesquieu*, 23; Plamenatz, *Man and Society*, 1:294; Shackleton, *Montesquieu*, 338; Ronald Fletcher, *The Making of Sociology: A Study of Sociological Theory*, 2 vols. (London: Michael Joseph, 1971), 1:119; Gay, *The Enlightenment*, 2:326–27.

[167] Montesquieu, *De l'esprit des lois*, 1:329. Although some commentators, such as Emile Durkheim and Raymond Aron, criticize Montesquieu for his lack of interest in social and political development, Robert Shackleton persuasively demonstrates that he did have a theory of progress based on empirical historical and scientific evidence. Durkheim, *Montesquieu and Rousseau*, 59; Aron, *Main Currents*, 1:45–6; Shackleton, *Montesquieu*, 316–19.

[168] Althusser, *Montesquieu*, 56–7; Nannerl O. Keohane, *Philosophy and the State in France: The Renaissance to the Enlightenment* (Princeton, N.J.: Princeton University Press, 1980), 396–8. See Frick's compelling argument that Montesquieu's concept of the separation of powers did *not* influence Comte's approach to the spiritual and temporal authorities. Frick, "Problème du pouvoir," 288.

rich and influential life. A brilliant mathematician and permanent secretary of the Academy of Sciences, Condorcet was the only philosophe actively engaged in the French Revolution. As an ardent republican with anticlerical views, he was an important member of both the Legislative Assembly and the Convention. He was also an active journalist who not only campaigned for a system of public instruction that would emphasize scientific thinking but also popularized the moral and political sciences, which he felt were necessary for a strong representative government. His proposals, which influenced the Idéologues, left a lasting imprint on French schools, including the Ecole Polytechnique. Excelling both in the intellectual sphere and in the public arena, Condorcet was, in short, an inspiring role model who showed Comte how to combine an interest in scientific enlightenment with a concern for social reform.[169]

In 1817 Comte bought the five-volume set of Condorcet's *Eloges des Académiciens de L'Académie royale des sciences, morts depuis l'an 1666 jusqu'en 1790, suivis de ceux de l'Hôpital et de Pascal.*[170] By celebrating the achievements of prominent scientists, Condorcet wrote a history of the sciences, which he hoped would clarify the progress of the human mind and inspire others.[171] His eulogy of Benjamin Franklin no doubt also sparked Comte's interest.[172]

In all likelihood, Comte was reading in early 1817 the *Esquisse d'un tableau historique des progrès de l'esprit humain* (1793), Condorcet's main contribution to the "moral and political sciences," which Comte was studying at this time.[173] Like Montesquieu and many other philosophes, Condorcet wanted to extend the spirit, method, and general aims of the natural sciences to other areas of human endeavor in order to improve all aspects of existence. His optimism was tempered, however, by his realization of the inherent limitations of human nature. Since Newton had shown that the ultimate nature of the universe was unknowable, Condorcet, along with Montesquieu and other eighteenth-century thinkers, derided metaphysics and system making and stressed that knowledge was limited to what

---

[169] Keith Michael Baker, Introduction to *Condorcet: Selected Writings*, ed. and trans. Baker (Indianapolis, Ind.: Bobbs-Merrill, 1976), viii, ix, xxvii; idem, *Condorcet: From Natural Philosophy to Social Mathematics* (Chicago: University of Chicago Press, 1975), viii–ix, 304–5, 320–42; Michelangelo Ghio, "Condorcet," *Filosofia* 6.1 (1955): 227, 229; Alexander Koyré, "Condorcet," *Journal of the History of Ideas* 9.2 (1948): 131; Manuel, *Prophets of Paris*, 58; Picavet, *Les Idéologues*, 68; Stuart Hampshire, Introduction to *Sketch for a Historical Picture of the Progress of the Human Mind*, by Antoine-Nicolas de Condorcet, trans. June Barraclough (New York: Noonday, 1955), vii.

[170] See Comte's library at the Maison d'Auguste Comte.

[171] [Marie-Jean-Antoine-Nicolas Caritat de] Condorcet, *Oeuvres complètes de Condorcet*, ed. Mme Condorcet et al., 21 vols. (Paris, 1804), 1:12–13.

[172] Ibid., 4:91–165.   [173] Comte to Valat, February 12, 1817, *CG*, 1:19.

could be observed. Thus man himself should become the object of knowledge.[174] If the sciences became anthropocentric, they would become less a source of ultimate truth than a tool useful to the human condition. The acceptance of the limitations of the mind, the relationship of all knowledge to man, and the utility of science to the human condition were aspects of Enlightenment humanism that were fervently embraced by Condorcet.[175] These ideas would also have a great impact on Comte.

Condorcet was most interested in applying the scientific method to the study of man. He employed various expressions to describe this study, such as "moral sciences," "political sciences," and "moral and political sciences." Once in his *Esquisse* he used the term "social science."[176] Though of unknown origin, the term appeared from time to time in the writings of the Idéologues. Referring to the science of politics, it had been employed, for example, by Condorcet's colleague Sieyès in the first edition of *Qu'est-ce que le tiers-état?*, the famous revolutionary pamphlet published in January 1789. In fact, scholars have been unable to find any prior use of the term.[177] Both Sieyès and Condorcet worked in the early 1790s to create a rational science of society that would close the Revolution in a peaceful, orderly fashion and create a stable social system. Comte would become attracted to this science for the same reasons. From the beginning, then, the science of society was closely associated with the French Revolution and politics.[178]

As the scholar Keith Baker has explained, Condorcet adumbrated the concept of social science "in the sense of a general science of social

---

[174] If a thinker used the word "man" or "mankind" in a sense that does not seem also to refer to "woman," I have for the sake of precision and context kept the original term.

[175] [Marie-Jean-Antoine-Nicolas Caritat de] Condorcet, *Esquisse d'un tableau historique des progrès de l'esprit humain* (Paris, 1797), 314–15. See also Baker, *Condorcet*, 81–2, 88–95, 189; Gay, *The Enlightenment*, 2:177.

[176] In discussing the absence of any Roman book on politics, Condorcet wrote: "It was not in the midst of convulsions of expiring liberty that *social science* could be naturalized and improved. Under the despotism of the Caesars, the study could only have seemed a conspiracy against their power." Condorcet, *Esquisse*, 127 (my emphasis). According to Keith Baker, the term "social science," based perhaps on the Physiocrats' expression "social art," appeared in a letter written to Condorcet by a member of his intellectual circle; no one knows, however, who actually coined it. Baker, *Condorcet*, 39, 197–8, 391–5.

[177] Emmanuel Sieyès, *Qu'est-ce que le tiers-état?* ed. Roberto Zapperi (Geneva: Droz, 1970), 151. See Brian W. Head, "The Origins of 'La Science Sociale' in France, 1770–1800," *Australian Journal of French Studies* 9 (January–April 1982): 124; Keith Michael Baker, "Closing the French Revolution: Saint-Simon and Comte," in *The Transformation of Political Culture*, ed. Furet and Ozouf, 324; Robert Wokler, "Saint-Simon and the Passage from Political to Social Science," in *The Languages of Political Theory in Early-Modern Europe*, ed. Anthony Pagden (Cambridge: Cambridge University Press, 1987), 327–31.

[178] Baker, "Closing the French Revolution," 323–6; Wolker, "Saint-Simon," 329.

action and organization susceptible of the methods and procedures of the natural sciences."[179] Condorcet believed that the moral and political sciences could be established because the French Revolution had created the liberty that such reform-oriented sciences required. They could attain the same level of certainty as the natural sciences, provided that they too were based on the observation of facts as well as on laws, analytical reasoning, and precise language. And just as the natural sciences had helped to liberate humanity from the constraints of the natural world, social science could enable people to construct a more rational, freer society. To Condorcet, the primary vehicle of progress was scientific knowledge, which freed the mind from absurd, debilitating beliefs, especially religious dogmas.[180]

He was one of the first philosophers to present a secular, organic history of continuous progress and argue that it was the foundation of social science. The law of progress consisted of the growth of human reason and its concomitant, freedom, defined as the power to change and control the secular world.[181] Condorcet divided history into ten epochs and traced in each the progress of the sciences, the arts, economics, politics, morality, and society. These realms of human experience were closely interconnected, so that a change in one affected all of the others.[182] This was the essence of his organic approach to history – an approach Comte later adopted along with his important theory of progress.

Notwithstanding his emphasis on scientific geniuses, whom he called the "eternal benefactors of humanity," Condorcet rejected a great-man approach to history and favored the study of "the most obscure, the most neglected" part of humanity, that is, the people, who constituted "the most important part" of history.[183] He pointed out that each generation depended on the achievements of past generations and in turn contributed to civilization, the ever-increasing endowment that belonged to humanity; this process was, in fact, the essence of progress. In the *Cours*, Comte praised Condorcet for

---

[179] Baker, *Condorcet*, 198.

[180] Condorcet, *Esquisse*, 335, 364, 371–2, 388–9. See also Baker, *Condorcet*, 87, 118, 346; Gay, *The Enlightenment*, 2:122; Manuel, *Prophets of Paris*, 64–5.

[181] Not until the eighteenth century did the notion of continual progress become at all prevalent, but even then most philosophes did not confidently believe it could be realized. Turgot, who was Condorcet's mentor, first declared progress to be a law of history in a famous speech that he gave at the Sorbonne in 1750. See Henry Vyverberg, *Historical Pessimism in the French Enlightenment* (Cambridge, Mass.: Harvard University Press, 1958), 1–6, 229–31; Gay, *The Enlightenment*, 2:99–108; Robert Nisbet, *History of the Idea of Progress* (New York: Basic Books, 1980), 180, 207; Baker, *Condorcet*, 348–9, 352–3.

[182] Condorcet, *Esquisse*, 391–2. See also Manuel, *Prophets of Paris*, 63; Hampshire, Introduction to *Sketch*, x.

[183] Condorcet, *Esquisse*, 9, 328.

having provided him with the example of constructing the hypothetical history of a single, abstract people – "humanity" – in order
to portray human evolution.[184]

Condorcet assumed that the laws of the moral and intellectual
progress of society, which were ultimately based on the growth of
the faculties of the individual, were constant. Because of this regularity, knowledge of the past enabled one to predict the future and
thereby accelerate and ensure the progress of society. This principle
was one of the most important lessons that Comte learned from the
Esquisse. He discovered that social science had a corresponding social
art, which put into practice the truths garnered from the historical
observation of societies. Grounded in an understanding of human
nature, social science would provide clear, rational principles of
private and public morality and of social organization. The science
of morality and politics would be the basis of the system of education, which instead of teaching religious dogmas would help to instill
general principles of justice as well as the habit of benevolence. Thus
social science would make conduct more rational, leading to a new
morality, which would emphasize "humanity," that is, compassion,
and provide politics with a new basis.[185] As people's conduct improved – as it became more rational and scientific, due to the social
sciences – their self-interest and concern for society as a whole would
begin to coincide, for the whole point of the "social art" was to
create social harmony.[186] Thanks to the advance of the sciences and
mass education, which would ensure intellectual progress, there were
no limits to the improvements that the human race could expect. As
shown in the description of the future tenth epoch, Condorcet believed that when people became rational, free individuals in control
of their own destiny and not subject to the manipulation of priests
and tyrannical rulers, social ills and ignorance would disappear, social
relationships would improve, and inequality would decrease. There
would be infinite progress toward truth, virtue, and happiness, all of
which were linked.[187] Condorcet's description of the future reinforced Comte's growing preoccupation with education, the science
of society, history, political reforms, and moral conduct. It also

[184] *Cours*, 2:123.
[185] "Humanity" referred to "a tender, active compassion for all the ills that afflict the human species, a horror for whatever in the public institutions, in the acts of government, and in private actions added new sorrows to the inevitable sorrows of nature." Condorcet, *Esquisse*, 268–9. See also ibid., 1–3, 17–19, 120, 323, 365–72; Ghio, "Condorcet," 230, 259; Baker, *Condorcet*, 198–9, 371, 392.
[186] Condorcet, *Esquisse*, 371.
[187] Ibid., 28–9, 48, 69–70, 100, 167, 185, 333–6, 345–59, 362, 364, 371–92. Gay argues that "perfectibility" to Condorcet meant only "capacity for growth," not perfection. Gay, *The Enlightenment*, 2:121. See also Baker, *Condorcet*, 348–9, 352–3.

encouraged Comte's utopian inclinations, which prevailed especially in the *Système de politique positive*, the four-volume work published between 1851 and 1854.

Although Condorcet emphasized the free, inherently rational individual, he was at the same time concerned with the way in which each person was formed by external authorities. Revealing a tension in his thought between democratic liberalism and intellectual elitism, he implied that those who controlled the educational system and shaped public opinion possessed the real power in the state.[188] This concept would later be taken up by Comte in his formulation of the spiritual power, which would exhibit a similar tension.

More dynamic than Montesquieu's view of development, Condorcet's picture of history affirmed the possibility as well as the desirability of change. He believed progress could be accelerated by the philosophers, who had a unique ability to propagate truth. Just as they had been crucial in instigating the French Revolution, so too they would be in the vanguard of the inevitable revolution that was to embrace all of humanity once the moral and political sciences were established. Comte could hardly have failed to be profoundly struck by Condorcet's description of the role of the philosopher and his assertion that "everything tells us that we are approaching the epoch of one of the greatest revolutions of the human species."[189]

THE FAILURE OF HIS EMIGRATION PROJECT

Depressed by the situation at home, Comte in mid-February 1817 was "more than ever" eagerly anticipating his "project of expatriation," for he believed that he could never do anything in France if the government did not adopt a more liberal direction. Extremely critical of the "tyranny" of the royal government, he claimed that it corrupted the postal service by its censorship, turned his beloved

---

[188] Condorcet's elitist inclinations are evident in his theory that to prevent wasting time and effort, it was necessary to unite scientists under a common direction. This plan seems to make the scientists a very powerful authority free of all controls. Frank Manuel states that Condorcet's plan was particularly evident in the 1804 edition of the *Esquisse*. Appended to this edition were extra sections on the scientific organization of society as well as Condorcet's commentary on Francis Bacon's *New Atlantis*, which concentrated on the need for scientific authority. Manuel asserts that Comte was deeply influenced by this edition. But Comte's library contains the 1797 edition, which was more concerned with the freedom of the individual than with scientific power. Condorcet, *Esquisse*, 76–7, 138; Manuel, *Prophets of Paris*, 62, 84–5; Robert Nisbet, *Idea of Progress*, 209; Baker, *Condorcet*, 340–2; Eric Voegelin, *From Enlightenment to Revolution*, ed. John H. Hallowell (Durham, N.C.: Duke University Press, 1975), 126–33.

[189] Condorcet, *Esquisse*, 19.

Ecole Polytechnique into a vapid "convent" complete with a "plaster Christ," and gave engineering jobs only to royalist sycophants. At one point, he expressed surprise that a letter Valat had written to him was not opened by postal officials although it was addressed "to a poor devil more than suspected of philosophy and liberalism." The only encouraging sign he saw was that the works of the "two great men" Voltaire and Rousseau were being published in a new inexpensive edition and that when the Catholic vicars threatened to excommunicate anyone who read them, the number of buyers more than doubled.[190]

In April 1817 Comte received news that Congress had decided to postpone indefinitely the establishment of a polytechnic school. Lamenting the fact that he would be unable to emigrate to a "country freer than our old Europe," he consoled himself with the thought that although Paris had less "political liberty" than Washington, it did have at least more "civil liberty," which he found more important for his happiness.[191]

In adopting this distinction between the two types of liberty, Comte showed that he was familiar with current political discourse. Liberal writers, such as Madame de Staël and Benjamin Constant, were trying to find safeguards against authoritarianism and warned that political liberty might threaten, not guarantee, civil liberty. In his famous *De l'esprit de conquête et de l'usurpation* of 1814, Constant had maintained that ancient liberty (political liberty), which allowed citizens to participate actively in politics through deliberation and lawmaking, often resulted in the subjugation of the individual to the whole in the interest of national sovereignty. In contrast, modern liberty (civil liberty) was more concerned with the private independence of the individual, who had more means to achieve happiness than the ancients. Constant was implicitly criticizing the Jacobins and Napoleon for reviving the kind of liberty espoused by the ancient republics and dismissing the possibility of realizing the rewards of private liberty. To him, political power, even if legitimate, had to be restrained.[192]

Preoccupied like Staël and Constant with preserving the individual

---

[190] Comte to Valat, February 12, February 25, 1817, *CG*, 1:20–4.
[191] Comte to Valat, April 17, 1818, *CG*, 1:26. See also Campredon, "Extrait d'un cahier de notes:" ed. Laffitte, 166–7.
[192] Benjamin Constant, *De l'esprit de conquête et de l'usurpation*, in *Oeuvres*, ed. Alfred Roulin (Paris: Gallimard, 1957), 1010–14. See also Dominique Bagge, *Le Conflit des idées politiques en France sous la Restauration* (Paris: Presses Universitaires de France, 1952), 49–52; Pierre Arnaud, Note XI, *CG*, 1:374; Fontana, *Benjamin Constant*, 20, 25; George Armstrong Kelly, *The Humane Comedy: Constant, Tocqueville and French Liberalism* (Cambridge: Cambridge University Press, 1992), 56–7.

from arbitrary authority, Comte declared that civil liberty, or what he called "bourgeois liberty," was "the liberty of behaving and living as one wants . . . at all moments." He echoed the views of other nineteenth-century Frenchmen, such as Constant, who feared that democracy led to dull uniformity, when he implied that Americans were basically conformists, constrained in their daily thoughts and actions. In contrast, Paris was a very "agreeable" place to live, for at least "one could do at home all that one likes without fearing the despotism of the gossips . . . and live, in short, according to one's fancy."[193] Yet like other liberals, he made it clear that he still prized political liberty, which as a rule defended civil liberty, the most important freedom of all.

OBSERVATIONS ON MORALITY

Comte's personal problems increased his sensitivity to the social and economic conditions of the people. In late 1816 and 1817, a ruined harvest, coupled with an economic slump, caused a severe famine, which was aggravated by inadequate housing and public services. Struck by the contrast between the rich and poor, he wrote angrily:

> One cannot take a step in the city without having his heart broken by the distressing picture of mendicancy; every moment one meets workers without bread and without work, and nevertheless, [there is so much] luxury! Luxury! Ah! How revolting it is when so many individuals lack absolute necessities.[194]

When Comte thought he was on the point of leaving France forever, he decided to attend the Mardi Gras ball at the opera to find out if it was as debauched as Jean-Baptiste Louvet de Couvray's description of it suggested. Louvet had been a well-known republican writer and member of the Convention during the Revolution. Comte had read his *Mémoires* while he was at the Ecole Polytechnique, and in 1817 he took up an earlier work, *Les Amours du chevalier de Faublas*, which was shaping the French image of the United States because of its allusions to virtuous European heroes fighting in a noble republic's struggle for independence. In describing the

---

[193] Comte to Valat, April 17, 1818, *CG*, 1:26. See also Rémond, *Les Etats-Unis*, 2:681; Constant, "Fragments sur la France du 14 juillet 1789 au 31 mars 1814," in *Oeuvres*, 817. Alexis de Tocqueville later voiced similar fears of democracy. See his *Democracy in America*, ed. and trans. Philips Bradley, 2 vols. (New York: Random House, Vintage Books, 1945), 1:273.

[194] Comte to Valat, February 12, 1817, *CG*, 1:21. See also Bertier de Sauvigny, *Bourbon Restoration*, 218–19, 333; idem, *Nouvelle Histoire de Paris*, 22.

adventures of the young libertine Faublas, Louvet at one point made
a brilliant portrayal of the Mardi Gras ball at the opera to illustrate
the corruption of the ancien régime.[195] When Comte attended the
real ball, he found himself bored and lonely during his four hours of
"philosophical observation" and was painfully reminded of what an
unimportant person he was. Reflecting his preoccupation with codes
of conduct, he was, however, surprised by the "decency" that marked
people's behavior, which contrasted sharply with Louvet's description of their licentiousness. He concluded that "morals must have
improved" since the Revolution.[196]

Despite his interest in the "moral sciences," Comte did not succeed in fulfilling his own "projects of retreat and sobriety." He spent
money to go to the Théâtre Français to see Talma and Mademoiselle
Mars. He also often sought the services of a prostitute. As if re-
counting his sins in confession, Comte told Valat that he had committed "this little foolishness . . . only three times" in the past four
months.[197]

While seeking to create his own unconventional way of life, he
fell madly in love in August 1817. No longer did he need to seek
"physical pleasures" from the "disgusting beauties of the gallery of
Valois" in the Palais Royal. Now that he had met Pauline, he was
in "ecstasy."[198] This was his first romantic affair.

Older than Comte, Pauline was an Italian pianist who, according
to him, had a wonderful sense of humor, a "highly finished education," a "very good heart," and an "agreeable figure." Appealing to
Comte's fondness for music and the Italian language, which his friend
Ernestine had instilled in him at an early age, she provided him with
a diversion from his lonely, unhappy existence:

> I teach her English, she rewards me with Italian; we deliver ourselves
> to the charm of a delicious and varied conversation; we indulge our
> sentiments and sometimes our sensations; and I forget completely
> during all this time the anxieties of my monetary position, my pains,
> my torments, my uncertainty about the future. Oh! What a beautiful
> invention love is! Without it, what a hell on earth human life is!

---

[195] The *Mémoires* may have influenced Comte's image of the Terror, especially when he wrote
his 1816 essay. Deroisin, *Notes sur Auguste Comte*, 19; Rémond, *Les Etats-Unis*, 1:408–9;
John Rivers, *Louvet: Revolutionist and Romance Writer* (New York: Brentano's, 1911), 8, 19–
20, 26; F. A. Aulard, Preface to *Mémoires de Louvet de Couvrai sur la Révolution française*,
by [Jean-Baptiste] Louvet de Couvrai, 2 vols. (Paris, 1889), 1:iii, x, xx, xiii–xv; [Jean-
Baptiste] Louvet de Couvray, *Les Amours du chevalier de Faublas*, with an introduction by
Michael Crouzet (Paris: Bibliothèque 1018, 1966), 10, 60, 267–8; Crouzet, Introduction
to ibid., 8, 16, 18, 20–38.

[196] Comte to Valat, February 25, 1817, *CG*, 1:23.

[197] Comte to Valat, February 12, 1817, *CG*, 1:19–20.

[198] Comte to Valat, April 17, 1818, *CG*, 1:30.

The fact that she was married and had a young daughter delighted Comte even more, for he thought of himself as a young rebel. He was thrilled when he learned that he had made her pregnant, exclaiming that his position was assuming a "far more grave and interesting character."[199] With his new paternal responsibility, he was pleased to find another reason for disobeying his parents' entreaties to return home, where he believed there was neither political liberty nor civil liberty. To become financially independent, he began to search for a stable teaching position, which he hoped would lead eventually to a chair at the Ecole Polytechnique, the Ecole Normale, or the Ecole de Médecine.

OTHER CAREER OPTIONS: TRANSLATION AND JOURNALISM

While maintaining his tutoring schedule, Comte agreed to translate into French a treatise written in 1811 by a Scottish mathematician. The project was given to him by J. N. Hachette, one of his former professors, who found himself in a situation similar to that of Comte and Andrieux. As a friend and collaborator of Monge, he had been teaching geometry at the Ecole Polytechnique since its establishment, but because of his revolutionary ideals the royalists did not ask him back when the school reopened in 1817. Hachette then decided to publish a supplement to Monge's series of geometry lectures, which he had first collected and published in 1799 in order to disseminate the knowledge of the new branch of mathematics called descriptive geometry.[200] To give readers a better understanding of more basic plane geometry, he included John Leslie's *Geometrical Analysis* in the book.[201] To help Comte earn some money and recognition, he gave him the task of translating this work.[202] By the summer of 1817, Comte had finished translating the 120-page book,

---

[199] Ibid., 30, 32. Pauline's age remains mysterious. In this letter written to Valat in April 1818, Comte declared that she was twenty-five, which made her five years older than he was, but he later admitted to Clotilde de Vaux that Pauline was old enough to be his mother. See Comte to Clotilde de Vaux, March 1, 1846, *CG*, 3:339.

[200] In 1812 Hachette had published a first supplement to these lectures. On Hachette, consult René Taton, "Hachette, Jean Nicolas Pierre," in *Dictionary of Scientific Biography*, ed. Gillispie, 6:1–3; idem, "Monge, Gaspard," in *Dictionary of Scientific Biography*, ed. Gillispie, 9:469–78; Gouhier, *Jeunesse*, 1:192–6; Gouhier, *Vie*, 63.

[201] [Jean-Nicolas-Pierre] Hachette, *Second Supplément de la Géométrie descriptive suivi de l'Analyse géométrique de M. John Leslie* (Paris, 1818), xiv. In his library, Comte had this book as well as three other works by Hachette: *Traité élémentaire des machines*, *Traité de géométrie descriptive*, and *Eléments de géométrie à trois dimensions* (which was autographed by Hachette).

[202] Since May 1817 Hachette had been advising Comte on his studies and trying to persuade him to work on a new edition of his work on machines. He had also been consulting General Campredon about how to help Comte. Campredon, "Extrait d'un cahier de notes," ed. Laffitte, 167.

which consisted primarily of mathematical propositions and problems, and the entire work was published in early 1818.

Although commended by Hachette, Comte found it to be a "bad book," complained about its unprofitability, and refused all other offers from him.[203] This experiment appears to have been a fiasco. Nevertheless, Comte began another writing venture, which would have a significant impact on his development: in August 1817 he followed the example of Franklin, Condorcet, and Louvet and proudly became a political journalist.

During the French Revolution, when the Declaration of the Rights of Man affirmed the freedom of the press, journalism began to play a major role in politics. But because it had been instrumental in the downfall of the monarchy, the Restoration government sought to limit freedom of the press. The regime's efforts were soon frustrated, however, because it needed to compromise with the liberals, who forced it to relax censorship for the first time in twenty years. The result was a flood of new periodicals. By 1818, 190 periodicals of all types were being published in Paris, and many talented writers wrote for them. All over the country, newspapers, especially liberal ones, became increasingly popular as the demands for political, economic, and social changes grew ever more strident.[204]

Comte revealed his awareness of this reemergence of liberal journalism when he informed Valat that he had become a "political writer in the latest style, that is, as you well know, in the liberal genre." In devoting himself to journalism, which was generally considered a dangerous, subversive activity, he was taking political action in the only way open to him. He was also making a moral statement, for the government, by its repressive measures, had inadvertently made journalists a well-respected power, the conscience of the nation. Finding his new employment "very interesting," Comte

---

[203] Comte to Valat, April 17, 1818, *CG*, 1:27. Hachette introduced Comte's section with this tribute: "I confided the translation of the text to M. Comte, former student of the Ecole Polytechnique, who wanted to make himself known by a work useful to mathematical studies; he has fulfilled this task with the greatest zeal. I have made hardly any changes in the translation." Hachette, *Second Supplément*, xv. See also R. Teixeira Mendes, ed. *Auguste Comte: Evolution originale*, vol. 1, *1798–1820* (Rio de Janeiro: Au Siège Central de l'Eglise Positiviste de Brésil, 1913), 228.

[204] John Roach, "Education and Public Opinion," in *The New Cambridge Modern History*, vol. 9, *War and Peace in an Age of Upheaval, 1793–1830*, ed. C. W. Crawley (Cambridge: Cambridge University Press, 1965), 179–80, 183, 187–8, 193; Fernand Terrou, "Le Cadre juridique," in *Histoire générale de la presse française*, ed. Claude Bellanger et al., vol. 2, *De 1815–1871* (Paris: Presses Universitaires de France, 1969), 3–7, 10; Bertier de Sauvigny, *Bourbon Restoration*, 66–7, 443–5, 450–1; idem, *Nouvelle Histoire de Paris*, 344, 349–50; Charles Ledré, "La Presse nationale," 2:29–30; Irene Collins, *The Government and the Newspaper Press in France, 1814–1881* (Oxford: Oxford University Press, 1959), ix, 28–9, 58.

relished his new career, which allied him with the revolutionary tradition and put him at the center of political life. Yet he asked Valat not to tell his parents the name of his employer, for if they knew that he was working with a "man whose liberalism was so well known," they would certainly believe that their son "had been handed over to the terrible tribunal of the correctional police."[205] The man for whom Comte began to work in August 1817 was Claude Henri de Rouvroy, Comte de Saint-Simon.

[205] Comte to Valat, April 17, 1818, *CG*, 1:27. See also Ledré, "La Presse nationale," 30; Collins, *Newspaper Press*, x.

Chapter 2

The Life and Works of Saint-Simon up to 1817

The philosopher places himself at the summit of thought; from there he views what the world has been and what it must become. He is not just an observer, he is an actor; he is an actor of the highest kind in a moral world because it is his opinions of what the world must become that regulate society.

Saint-Simon, *Mémoire sur la science de l'homme*

THE PROBLEM OF SAINT-SIMON'S INFLUENCE ON COMTE

The seven-year association of Comte and Saint-Simon, from 1817 to 1824, profoundly changed each man's intellectual development. Although the different strands of their thought seem tied together inextricably, an effort to disentangle them is required to understand Comte's evolution and the origins of positivism and sociology. Before these subjects can be addressed, however, it is necessary to review the life and thought of Saint-Simon up to the time of his first meeting with Comte in 1817. This examination will provide a closer look at the political, intellectual, and psychological world in which Comte found himself during his period of maturation. As a synthesizer of ideas, Saint-Simon not only introduced him to recent late-eighteenth- and early-nineteenth-century developments, but also gave him a certain perspective on more general, long-range movements throughout history.

SAINT-SIMON'S EARLY LIFE

Saint-Simon was born in 1760 of a poor, obscure noble family that claimed descent from Charlemagne and was distantly related to the Duc de Saint-Simon, the famous memorialist of the court of Louis XIV. Indifferently educated by private tutors, he studied classical literature and the writings of Enlightenment philosophes, especially the Encyclopedists, whose ideal was to unify knowledge. Prompted by Enlightenment ideas, he rejected Catholicism at thirteen and later embraced republicanism. In 1779 he went to the United States, where he fought as an officer in the Revolution and was twice wounded. From that point on, he considered himself one of the heroic "founders of the liberty of the United States."[1] At the outbreak of the French Revolution, he quickly shed his title of count and supported the sans-culottes. But he devoted most of his energy to making a fortune on the sale of national property in partnership with a Prussian diplomat, J. Sigismund Ehrenreich, count de Redern. After being briefly jailed during the Terror in a case of mistaken identity, he bought a mansion near the Palais Royal, where he entertained in grand style. Monge and Lagrange, scientists much admired by Comte, were regular guests and became his close friends. When Redern dissolved their partnership for fear of bankruptcy, Saint-Simon decided to begin a "new career [devoted] to human intelligence, the *physico-political* career."[2]

SAINT-SIMON'S NEW CAREER:
THE INFLUENCE OF THE IDÉOLOGUES

The term "physico-political career" reflects Saint-Simon's goal of using the physical sciences to effect social change. To study the sciences and thus prepare for his new mission, he moved in 1798 across the street from the Ecole Polytechnique, where he took courses and became friends with various professors. Three years later, he broadened his interests and moved next door to the Ecole de Médecine, which was maintaining Paris's reputation as the center of European medicine. He basically bought his knowledge of biology by providing the professors with "great food," "good wine," and financial assistance.[3]

Saint-Simon was especially generous in his support of young

[1] *Lettres de Henri Saint-Simon à un Américain*, in *Oeuvres de Claude-Henri de Saint-Simon*, 6 vols. (Paris: Anthropos, 1966) (hereafter, *Oeuvres*), 1.2:140. See also Gouhier, *Jeunesse*, 2:62, 64; Frank Manuel, *The New World of Henri Saint-Simon* (Cambridge, Mass.: Harvard University Press, 1956), 13–14; Paul Janet, "Les Origines de la philosophie d'Auguste Comte," *Revue des deux mondes* 82.3 (1887): 607–9.

[2] Saint-Simon, "Préface: Histoire de ma vie," *Lettres au Bureau de Longitudes*, in *Oeuvres*, 1.1:68n2. On Saint-Simon's life after his return from the United States, see Saint-Simon, *Oeuvres*, 1.1:64–8; Manuel, *Saint-Simon*, 24–47; Gouhier, *Jeunesse*, 2:xii–xiii, 74–100; Emile Durkheim, *Socialism and Saint-Simon*, ed. Alvin Gouldner, trans. Charlotte Sattler (Yellow Springs, Ohio: Antioch Press, 1958), 83.

[3] Saint-Simon, "Préface: Histoire de ma vie," 69n5. See also Georges Gusdorf, *Introduction aux sciences humaines: Essai critique sur leurs origines et leur développement* (Paris: Les Belles Lettres, 1960), 308.

scientists and doctors, such as Jean Burdin.[4] A friend of the Idéologues, Burdin was the first to acquaint him with their program and show him the importance of physiology.[5] Around this time, two important Idéologues became Saint-Simon's friends: the doctors Marie-François-Xavier Bichat and Pierre-Jean-Georges Cabanis.[6]

The Idéologues exerted a great influence on both Saint-Simon and Comte. Andrieux, for example, was an important member of their circle.[7] In the aftermath of the Terror, when philosophy was blamed for much of the destruction, these philosophers, publicists, physicians, and scientists sought to maintain the Enlightenment spirit – especially the rationalism, utilitarianism, and scientific concerns of the *Encyclopédie*. Influenced by the sensationalism of Condillac, they called for a new science of ideas, which Destutt de Tracy dubbed "Idéologie." It stemmed from their animus not only against theologians, who dealt with questions beyond the scope of reason, but also against metaphysicians, who studied first causes and essences. Repeating the position of the English empiricists Locke and Hume and the French thinkers d'Alembert, Turgot, and Condorcet, Destutt de Tracy wrote that practitioners of his new science would "observe facts with the greatest scruple . . . and prefer absolute ignorance to any assertion that is only plausible."[8] Idéologie – "the science of methods," as Cabanis called it – would unify the sciences by making sure they were limited to observing and describing phenomena.[9]

---

[4] Among the people whom Saint-Simon helped were the geometer Denis Poisson, the biologist Henri Ducrotay de Blainville, and the doctor Prunelle. G. Hubbard, *Saint-Simon: Sa Vie et ses travaux* (Paris, 1857), 33; Gouhier, *Jeunesse*, 2:104–5; Henri Gouhier, "Lettres inédites de Saint-Simon à Blainville," *Revue philosophique de la France et de l'étranger* 131.1–2 (1941): 70–80; Picavet, *Les Idéologues*, 99.

[5] Saint-Simon, *Mémoire sur la science de l'homme*, in *Oeuvres*, 5.2:45–6; Picavet, *Les Idéologues*, 454; Gouhier, *Jeunesse*, 2:190.

[6] For information concerning Saint-Simon's new life, consult Saint-Simon, "Préface: Histoire de ma vie," 68–71; Manuel, *Saint-Simon*, 50–8; Gouhier, *Jeunesse*, 2:100–5; Felix Markham, Introduction to *Social Organization, the Science of Man and Other Writings*, by Henri de Saint-Simon, ed. and trans. Markham (New York: Harper Torchbooks, 1964), xiv–xv; Durkheim, *Socialism and Saint-Simon*, 83.

[7] Besides Bichat, Cabanis, and Andrieux, other members or auxiliaries of the Idéologue circle included Joseph Lakanal, the Abbé Sieyès, Anthelme Richerand, Charles-François Dupuis, Pierre Laplace, Philippe Pinel, Joseph-François de Saint-Lambert, Pierre-Claude-François Daunou, Maine de Biran, Madame de Staël, J. B. Say, Benjamin Constant, Dominique-Joseph Garat, Joseph-Marie Degérando, Pierre Sue, Pierre-Louis Roederer, François Broussais, Constantin-François de Chasseboeuf, comte de Volney, and Antoine-Louis Claude, comte de Destutt de Tracy.

[8] [Antoine-Louis Claude de] Destutt de Tracy, "De la métaphysique de Kant," in *Mémoires de l'Institut National des Sciences et Arts: Sciences morales et politiques*, 5 vols. (Paris, Year VI–Year XII), 4:550–1.

[9] Pierre-Jean-Georges Cabanis, "Lettre sur un passage de la 'Décade philosophique' et en général sur la perfectibilité de l'esprit humain" (Year VII), in *Oeuvres philosophiques de Cabanis*, ed. Claude Lehec and Jean Cazeneuve, 2 vols. (Paris: Presses Universitaires de France, 1956), 2:515.

Derived from the Idéologues' interest in medicine and physiology, it was to focus on the physical, animal nature of man to see how his ideas were formed from his sensations. Knowledge of the physiological generation of ideas would become the foundation of the science of morality and politics, that is, the science of society, which held the key to rational social reorganization. With a greater understanding of the human intellect, Idéologie would make moral and political ideas as valid, precise, and clear as concepts of physical phenomena and would thus eliminate the dangerous errors of perception and judgment that had caused the upheaval of the revolutionary period. The Idéologues hoped in this way to fulfill Condorcet's dream of creating a social science that would derive the laws of social organization from the study of human nature.[10] They believed that because the basis of morality and human institutions was physical, the study of man and society had to become a branch of physiology.[11]

The Idéologues played a key role during the French Revolution, especially in the years 1794–1803, when their doctrines became the official philosophy of the moderate republican government. As members of the liberal bourgeoisie, they upheld the ideals of 1789 but shied away from radical political reforms. Their main goal was to create an educational system that would impart a secular, scientific system of morality akin to Helvétius's ethical humanism and transform the intellectual and moral life of the people. They hoped eventually to set up a new aristocracy of enlightened men to lead government and society. To further this end, they established in 1795 the Institut National, which was divided into three classes of scholars. The second was the Classe des Sciences Morales et Politiques, composed mainly of the most important Idéologues. It

---

[10] The Idéologues were also influenced by Bacon's scientific method, Locke's and Condillac's sensationalism, Helvétius's theory of the impact of the environment on behavior, Voltaire's anti-Catholic animus, and Kant's critique of metaphysics.

[11] Picavet, *Les Idéologues*, 21, 572–6, 579, 580, 625–7; Thomas E. Kaiser, "Politics and Political Economy in the Thought of the Idéologues," *History of Political Economy* 12.2 (1980): 142; van Duzer, *Contribution*, 5–6, 16–19, 24, 43, 58–9, 77–8, 43; Lyons, *France under the Directory*, 117–20; Baker, *Condorcet*, 371; Keith Baker, "Politics and Social Science in Eighteenth-Century France: The Société de 1789," in *French Government and Society, 1500–1850*, ed. J. F. Bosher (London: University of London, Athlone Press, 1973), 238; Markham, Introduction to *Social Organization*, xxix; Staum, *Cabanis*, 168; Bergeron, *France Under Napoleon*, 93; L. G. Crocker, "Cabanis, Pierre-Jean Georges," in *The Encyclopedia of Philosophy*, ed. Paul Edwards, 8 vols. (1967; reprint, New York: Macmillan, 1972), 2:3–4; Alvin W. Gouldner, *The Dialectic of Ideology and Technology: The Origins, Grammar, and Future of Ideology* (New York: Oxford University Press, 1982), 6, 11–14; Sergio Moravia, *Il pensiero degli idéologues: Scienza e filosofia in Francia (1780–1815)* (Florence: La Nuova Italia, 1974), 723; George Boas, *French Philosophies of the Romantic Period* (Baltimore, Md.: Johns Hopkins Press, 1925), 241; Maxime Leroy, *Histoire des idées sociales en France*, 2d ed., 3 vols. (Paris: Gallimard, 1950), 2:153; Gusdorf, *Introduction*, 282, 288, 290.

comprised the various sciences of man: history, geography, political economy, social science and legislation, morality, and the analysis of sensations and ideas. Concerned with improving the human condition, the Idéologues thus kept alive the idea of a social science by institutionalizing their interdisciplinary effort to make man and his relationships the subject of scientific knowledge. Napoleon, however, abolished this second class in 1803 because of the Idéologues' opposition to his authority. Nevertheless, their lofty picture of man, their anticlericalism, and their ideas about progress, the power of education, enlightened self-interest, and the empirical basis of the social sciences became part of nineteenth-century liberalism. Moreover, by their reforms of hospitals, museums, and the educational system, they presented an example of philosophers, or more accurately, scientists of society, actively involved in government.[12]

Saint-Simon reached intellectual maturity during the time of the Idéologues' dominance and remained in contact with them for the rest of his life. Emphasizing the need for a "general metaphysics" that would unite all realms of knowledge, his first writing, *A la Société du Lycée*, which appeared in 1802, showed that the ideals of the Encyclopedists and their successors, the Idéologues, were fixed in his mind.[13]

His interest in the Idéologues was reinforced when, on a trip to Geneva in late 1802, he supposedly met and unsuccessfully proposed to the recently widowed Madame Germaine de Staël. Dominating French liberal thought in the early nineteenth century, she was personally close to many of the Idéologues and is considered by some

---

[12] Wokler, "St.-Simon," 330; Lyons, *France under the Directory*, 117, 121; van Duzer, *Contribution*, 6–7, 43, 80, 83, 108, 111, 116–17, 163, 165; Kaiser, "Politics and Political Economy," 145–7; Baker, *Condorcet*, 371; Gusdorf, *Introduction*, 271–4, 278; idem, *La Conscience révolutionnaire: Les Idéologues* (Paris: Payot, 1978), 354; Baker, "Politics and Social Science," 230; Bergeron, *France under Napoleon*, 92–3; Picavet, *Les Idéologues*, 7, 69–70; Leroy, *Idées sociales*, 2:157, 166–7; Martin S. Staum, "The Class of Moral and Political Sciences, 1795–1803," *French Historical Studies* 11.3 (1980): 371–2; C. C. Gillispie, "Science and Technology," in *The New Cambridge Modern History*, Vol. 9, *War and Peace in an Age of Upheaval, 1793–1830*, ed. C. W. Crawley (Cambridge: Cambridge University Press, 1965), 118–21.

[13] Saint-Simon, *A la Société du Lycée*, in Jean Dautry, "Sur un imprimé retrouvé du Comte de Saint-Simon," *Annales historiques de la Révolution française* 20 (1948): 291. Associated with the Idéologue-dominated Institut and transformed into the celebrated Athénée in late 1802, the Lycée Républicain had several professors who were Idéologues: the anatomist Sue, the moral philosopher Degérando, and the political economist Roederer. Comte's professor Poinsot (along with Reynaud) was also teaching mathematics there in 1802. See Manuel, *Saint-Simon*, 62–3; van Duzer, *Contribution*, 116; Picavet, *Les Idéologues*, 505–15; Dautry, "Imprimé retrouvé," 297–9; Kaiser, "Politics and Political Economy," 148–9; Moravia, "Il pensiero," 717–23; Michael James, "Pierre-Louis Roederer, Jean-Baptiste Say, and the Concept of *Industrie*," *History of Political Economy* 9.4 (1977): 456.

historians to have been an Idéologue herself.[14] Saint-Simon read her recently published *De la littérature considérée dans ses rapports avec les institutions sociales*, which defended Enlightenment thought against the counterrevolutionaries. Since men of letters offered an especially strong shield against tyranny, she hoped they would become the "ministry" of a lay spirituality to guide the people.[15]

Worried about the chaos generated by party passions, she believed that political and moral errors were more glaring than ever because the data of the physical sciences were becoming increasingly accurate and reliable. She was so impressed by the progress of the "exact sciences" that she called them the "positive sciences," echoing Buffon's use of the word "positive" to refer to the precise and scientific. She explained that the "positive sciences" dealt chiefly with phenomena that could be demonstrated mathematically and regarded anything that could not be quantified as "illusory." By providing real, objective knowledge, instead of abstract, metaphysical nonsense, they showed the correct way to seek truth and protected the mind from fallacies caused by the "party spirit."[16]

Inspired by Condorcet, Staël called for the creation of moral and political sciences – the social sciences – based on the "philosophy of the positive sciences," which was the scientific methodology that unified and guided knowledge.[17] Although others such as Condorcet

[14] Kaiser, "Politics and Political Economy," 142n4; Maxime Leroy, *La Vie véritable du Comte Henri de Saint-Simon (1760–1825)* (Paris: Bernard Grasset, 1925), 215; Dautry, "Imprimé retrouvé," 299; Georges Weill, *Un Précurseur du socialisme: Saint-Simon et son oeuvre* (Paris, 1894), 18.

[15] Madame Germaine de Staël, *De la littérature considérée dans ses rapports avec les institutions sociales, suivi de L'Influence des passions sur le bonheur, des individus et des nations* (Paris, 1842), 232, 233n1, 234, 238. See also Weill, *Saint-Simon*, 17; Roland Mortier, "Madame de Staël et l'héritage des Lumières," in *Madame de Staël et l'Europe: Colloque de Coppet (18–24 juillet 1966)* (Paris: Klincksieck, 1970), 128, 135, 138; Bénichou, *Sacre de l'écrivain*, 228–45; Leroy, *Idées sociales*, 2:153, 169, 172.

[16] Staël, *De la littérature*, 219, 232–3, 425, 483. See also Emmet Kennedy, *A Philosophe in the Age of Revolution: Destutt de Tracy and the Origins of "Ideology"* (Philadelphia: American Philosophical Society, 1978), 47. According to T. R. Wright, the word "positive" came from *ponere* and had been employed since the fourteenth century to mean "laid down." In the sixteenth century, it began to refer to knowledge that was based on facts and was thus presumably certain. Eighteenth-century thinkers used the word "positive" to oppose the "metaphysical." Angèle Kremer-Marietti has discovered the first use of the word "positive science" in the first volume of a work by Juvenel de Carlencas, *Essais sur l'histoire des belles-lettres, des sciences et des arts*, published in 1740. See T. R. Wright, *The Religion of Humanity: The Impact of Comtean Positivism on Victorian Britain* (Cambridge: Cambridge University Press, 1986), 18; Kremer-Marietti, *Le Concept*, 22–3.

[17] She wrote: "It is then by applying as much as possible the philosophy of the positive sciences to the philosophy of intellectual ideas that one will be able to make useful progress in this moral and political course, whose direction is always being obstructed by the passions." Staël, *De la littérature*, 483.

had used the term "positive" in relation to the sciences, she may have been the first to refer explicitly to the "philosophy of the positive sciences" and to connect it with social science. And she agreed with Condorcet that the science of society would come from the application of mathematics – especially the calculus of probabilities – to all human ideas. However, because of her spiritual inclinations, she maintained that morality had more to do with the spontaneous love of virtue than with rational calculations. Like Turgot, with whom she shared an interest in rehabilitating the Middle Ages, Staël believed that religion and enlightenment need not be enemies; both were necessary for the grandeur of man. Religion could be made rational. As a result, philosophy had to rest not only on the sciences but on morality, which was superior to them.[18] Staël's desire to rehabilitate philosophy, her argument in favor of a lay ministry of thinkers, her conviction that the scientific method would lead to certainty in politics and morality, her discussion of a philosophy of positive sciences, and her deep concern with spirituality – all are reflected in the important book that Saint-Simon wrote while he was in contact with her in 1802: *Lettres d'un habitant de Genève à ses contemporains*.

LETTRES D'UN HABITANT DE GENÈVE À SES CONTEMPORAINS

Like Madame de Staël and the Idéologues, all of whom were influenced by Condorcet, Saint-Simon contended that the public good was best served when those who dominated society were its most enlightened members. To help men of genius, who were frequently impoverished and persecuted, he proposed that a subscription fund be raised to allow twenty-one elected scientists, artists, writers, and musicians to work freely and independently. Called the "ELECT OF HUMANITY" and led by the mathematicians, they would be responsible for both the progress of humanity and the formation of public opinion.[19] They held the key to resolving the crisis brought about by the French Revolution. This concept of a directing elite became one of the main themes of Saint-Simon's works.

In an unpublished manuscript written in 1804, Saint-Simon admitted that Condorcet had profoundly influenced him. Adopting the term "positive science" used by Madame de Staël in *De la littérature*, he maintained that the "science of social organization" would "become a positive science" based on Condorcet's theories.

---

[18] Ibid., 484–96; Boas, *French Philosophies*, 105; Mortier, "Madame de Staël," 132–4, 137; Bénichou, *Sacre de l'écrivain*, 232–3.

[19] Saint-Simon, *Lettres d'un habitant de Genève*, in *Oeuvres*, 1.1:14.

The philosophe's most important idea was that control over society must be given to "men of genius," especially scientists, who should be led by mathematicians.[20]

Revealing Condorcet's influence and the utilitarianism of the time, Saint-Simon argued that the progress of the sciences would benefit all of humanity, especially because of the growing ability of scientists to make predictions. By using mathematical calculations, scientists would even be able to apply Newton's law of gravity to foresee "all the successive changes" that would occur in the world.[21] Like many of the philosophes, such as Voltaire, Saint-Simon was fascinated by Newton, and he hoped the law of gravity would become the unifying principle of the universe.

At this point, Saint-Simon abruptly changed topics. "In spite of the efforts that I am going to make to express myself clearly, I am not perfectly sure that you will understand me at the first reading; but in reflecting a bit upon it, you will master it." In the disjointed style that characterized all of his work, Saint-Simon then outlined the history of the sciences to elucidate the "progress of the human mind." Astronomical phenomena were the first to be observed because they were the simplest, but astronomy could not develop fully until the astrologers were expelled and facts established by observation were the only ones admitted. After a time, chemistry, whose phenomena were more complex than astronomical ones, went through a similar process, eliminating alchemists. Physiology, whose phenomena were the most complex of all, was still basically undeveloped and needed to rid itself of the imaginative work of "the philosophers, moralists, and metaphysicians," who did not understand that moral and physical phenomena had the same character.[22] (Saint-Simon was using "moral" in the way the Idéologues did, that is, as relating to ideas and passions.)[23] After physiology became a science, a general system would have to be found through mathematics to link all the observed facts of these sciences. Besides reflecting the influence of Condorcet, Saint-Simon's approach to progress was indebted to the materialist concepts of Diderot, Helvétius, and Holbach, as well as those of the Idéologues, especially Cabanis, who highlighted the importance of physiology.

---

[20] Saint-Simon, *Essai sur l'organisation sociale*, in *Henri Saint-Simon (1760–1825): Selected Writings on Science, Industry and Social Organisation*, ed. and trans. Keith Taylor (London: Croom Helm, 1975), 84–5. Condorcet's ideas about the scientific elite were influenced by the *New Atlantis* of Bacon, whose works were very popular when Saint-Simon wrote this essay. See Manuel, *Saint-Simon*, 71–80.

[21] Saint-Simon, *Lettres d'un habitant de Genève*, 59. [22] Ibid., 38, 39.

[23] Jan Goldstein, *Console and Classify: The French Psychiatric Profession in the Nineteenth Century* (Cambridge: Cambridge University Press, 1987), 94.

But perhaps recalling Madame de Staël's insistence on the importance of reconciling spiritualism and the scientific spirit, Saint-Simon
claimed that God had commanded him to establish a new religion
devoted to Newton. It would embrace all of humanity and ensure
that priests were once again scholars, freed from the domination of
the temporal power. With the twenty-one elected officials acting
as God's representatives and committed to making the earth a paradise, this religion bore some resemblance to the various cults that
flourished during the French Revolution. Although Saint-Simon
admitted that he was portraying "religion as a human invention"
and as the "only kind of political institution" that could organize
"humanity," his careful reference to his vision of God made it possible for him to avoid giving the dangerous impression that he was
an atheist.[24]

The underlying morality of Saint-Simon's religion expressed the
industrialist ethos that Idéologues such as J. B. Say and Pierre-Louis
Roederer were beginning to advocate. Like his early idol, d'Alembert,
Saint-Simon regarded men who did not help humanity as "useless."
His "God" announced: "ALL MEN WILL WORK; they will consider each
other workers attached to a workshop."[25] In this religious system,
science would advance because there would be respect for talent
instead of such "insignificant virtues" as continence and chastity.[26]
In a sense, Saint-Simon was using religious language to promote the
secular march of science and industry. At this point in the early
nineteenth century, industrial development was embryonic in France
and seemed full of promise to many progressives who sought to
give their country a new identity based on the common good.

Like the Idéologues, Saint-Simon hoped to restore order through
the rule of a predominantly scientific elite, but he worried about
the possibility of his elect's creating another upheaval. Thus he
gave political power only to the proprietors, who were more akin

---

[24] Saint-Simon, *Lettres d'un habitant de Genève*, 58. During the Directory, republican intellectuals who believed that religion was necessary for society created Theophilanthropy,
which was characterized by similar abstract ideas. Saint-Simon may also have been cognizant of the work of Chateaubriand, whose *Essai sur les révolutions* (1797) described the decay
of Christianity and the need for another religion to prevent the demise of society. [François
René, vicomte de] Chateaubriand, *Essai sur les révolutions; Génie du christianisme*, ed. Maurice
Regard (Gallimard, 1978), 428–31. See also Manuel, *Saint-Simon*, 70–1; Leroy, *Saint-Simon*,
221, 223; Lyons, *France under the Directory*, 110; Yves Le Febvre, *Le Génie du christianisme*
(Paris: Edgar Mayère, 1929), 28–33.

[25] Saint-Simon, *Lettres d'un habitant de Genève*, 55, 58. The principle "All men will work" was
reminiscent of the slogan of Gracchus Babeuf, who came from Saint-Simon's native Picardy
and conspired against the government in 1796. Markham, Introduction to *Social Organization*, xxxii.

[26] Saint-Simon, *Lettres d'un habitant de Genève*, 56.

to businessmen than to an idle nobility. In effect, he was stressing a new idea of central planning, that is, government as administration.[27] To ensure social harmony, he placed "the spiritual power . . . in the hands of the scientists . . . [and] the temporal power in the hands of the property owners." Maintaining the "line of demarcation" between the two powers was also crucial, because men of speculation and men of action possessed incompatible capacities.[28] Nevertheless, he suggested that once the scientists replaced the priests as the spiritual elite, they would eventually become more important than the temporal power and assume the role of the lords of the universe.[29] Their natural allies against the bourgeois property owners would be the masses, especially the workers or those who had no property.

Gouhier is correct in pointing out that Saint-Simon was at heart a philanthropic aristocrat who was trying to adapt to a new age. Although the privileges of birth were an anachronism, he did not aim to reorganize society on the basis of equality or a representative government. In his eyes, the new France would still be a hierarchy with a division between governors and governed. But its values would be those of the new scientific and industrial period that he saw emerging: predictability, utilitarianism, and rationalism. France would be a meritocracy in which the nobility and clergy would be replaced by a temporal power and spiritual power consisting of men qualified by their superior talents.[30]

Although written in an incoherent and inelegant style, Saint-Simon's *Lettres d'un habitant de Genève* contains the germs of much of his later thought. Throughout his life, he sought a radical solution to the political and social crisis stemming from the French Revolution. Traditional society was outworn and had to be replaced by a new one that would resemble a workshop where the highest value was placed on activity benefiting humanity. Moreover, he believed social stability and harmony could not be established without an understanding of the intellectual roots of the existing crisis. To him, the sciences held the key to intellectual order and therefore to social reorganization, especially because their progress improved social conditions. He was so entranced by the sciences that he reduced all

---

[27] Manuel, *Saint-Simon*, 76.

[28] Saint-Simon, *Lettres d'un habitant de Genève*, 47, 56. See also idem, *Lettres aux Européens*, in Comte Henri de Saint-Simon, *Lettres d'un habitant de Genève à ses contemporains [1803]*, *réimprimées conformément à l'édition originale et suivies de deux documents inédits – Lettres aux Européens [Essai sur l'organisation sociale]*, ed. Alfred Pereire (Paris: Félix Alcan, 1925), 87–93. Saint-Simon used the word *savant* to denote scientist. The word *scientiste* came into use in 1898. See *Le Grand Robert*, s.v. "scientiste."

[29] Saint-Simon, *Lettres d'un habitant de Genève*, 59n1.

[30] Gouhier, *Jeunesse*, 2:149–67; Manuel, *Saint-Simon*, 69.

social phenomena to physical facts. His interest in the philosophy and history of science led him not only to classify the sciences according to their increasing complexity but also to attempt to unify knowledge through universal gravitation and mathematics. He pointed out, however, that before such unity could be achieved, physiology would have to become scientific. Although his concerns with prediction and the principle of gravitation as the sole universal law gave his thought a deterministic and mechanistic character, he showed an interest in creating a scientific religion when he supported Madame de Staël's belief that enlightenment and faith need not be incompatible. In fact, he felt that religion was necessary for social reorganization and that there should be a spiritual power, separate from the temporal power. Freed from the control of the government, this scientific elite would ultimately be supreme. The philosophes – and their successors, the Idéologues – would be vindicated and back in control. Although none of these ideas was fully developed, they were to prove seminal.[31]

INTRODUCTION AUX TRAVAUX SCIENTIFIQUES DU XIXE SIÈCLE

By 1805 Saint-Simon was financially ruined and was being supported by a wealthy former servant, Diard, who two years later paid for the publication of his next major work, the *Introduction aux travaux scientifiques du XIXe siècle*.[32] Extending the line of thought of the *Lettres d'un habitant de Genève*, this new work was basically a hodgepodge of insights set down in a style somewhat akin to stream of consciousness:

> I am writing because I have new things to say; I will present my ideas as they have been forged by my mind; I am leaving to the professional writers the trouble of polishing them; I am writing as a nobleman, as a descendant of the counts of Vermandois, as an inheritor of the pen of the Duke of Saint-Simon. Whatever has been the greatest thing to do, the greatest thing to say, has been done, has been said by noblemen: Copernicus, Galileo, Bacon, Descartes, Newton, and Leibnitz were noblemen.[33]

---

[31] Pierre Ansart, *Sociologie de Saint-Simon* (Paris: Presses Universitaires de France, 1970), 16–17; idem, *Marx et l'anarchisme: Essai sur les sociologies de Saint-Simon, Proudhon et Marx* (Paris: Presses Universitaires de France, 1969), 21, 25; Weill, *Saint-Simon*, 38; Manuel, *Saint-Simon*, 64–71; Boas, *French Philosophies*, 270; Gouhier, *Jeunesse*, 2:227–31; Leroy, *Saint-Simon*, 218–24; Taylor, Introduction to *Henri Saint-Simon*, 20.

[32] Saint-Simon, "Préface: Histoire de ma vie," 73–4.

[33] Saint-Simon, *Introduction aux travaux scientifiques du XIXe siècle*, in *Oeuvres*, 6:16.

Falling back on his aristocratic heritage for support, Saint-Simon was trying to formulate a scientific and religious program, which he felt unqualified to implement himself owing to his inadequate education. The essay indeed suffered from great confusion. In trying to come up with the laws of history, for example, he asserted that each year of the life of the individual corresponded to two hundred years of the development of the species and that humanity was in its forties.

The main point of the work was to show that the moral crisis threatening European civilization could be resolved by the immediate construction of a theoretical system unifying all knowledge. Saint-Simon supported his argument with a philosophy of history showing that the past consisted of alternating periods of analysis and synthesis. During the periods of analysis, such as the seventeenth century, the particular sciences were most important because the mind was ascending from particular to more general facts. During the periods of synthesis, such as the eighteenth century, general science dominated since the mind was descending from general to particular facts.

Saint-Simon highlighted the achievements of the natural and social sciences during the eighteenth century.[34] One of the works he most respected was Condorcet's *Esquisse*, which he called "one of the most beautiful productions of the human mind," especially because of its attempt to decipher the progress of the mind.[35] Yet Saint-Simon wanted to show that his own version of history of the progress of the mind was superior. Critical of Condorcet's concept of human perfectibility, he contended that the contemporary period was making great scientific advances but was still inferior to the Greeks in the arts.[36] Moreover, in his view, Condorcet's history was not objective because he had not confined himself to intellectual work. His involvement in government contradicted Bichat's con-

---

[34] Two of the works that Saint-Simon analyzed were influenced by Locke: Condillac's *Traité des sensations* and Condorcet's *Esquisse*. Another two, Lagrange's *Théorie des fonctions* and Laplace's *Mécanique celeste*, developed Newton's ideas and reflected Saint-Simon's interest in reducing all principles to the single law of gravity. See also Gouhier, *Jeunesse*, 2:13; Markham, Introduction to *Social Organization*, xxiiin1; Picavet, *Les Idéologues*, 169–72.

[35] Saint-Simon, *Introduction aux travaux scientifiques*, 64. Saint-Simon had carefully read and annotated the *Esquisse*. See Saint-Simon, "Nottes [sic] sur Condorcet," Fonds Pereire, N.a.fr. 24605, fols. 100–16, Bibliothèque Nationale (hereafter, BN). See also Francesco Gentile, "La trasformazione dell'idea di progresso da Condorcet a Saint-Simon," *Revue internationale de philosophie* 14 (1960): 418.

[36] Saint-Simon's view was not unique; many eighteenth-century thinkers and even Madame de Staël had frequently referred to the demise of the "poetic spirit" accompanying the progress of the sciences. Turgot had also pointed out that the Greeks remained unsurpassed in the arts. Frank E. Manuel, *The Eighteenth Century Confronts the Gods* (Cambridge, Mass.: Harvard University Press, 1959), 306; idem, *Saint-Simon*, 158.

cept of mutually exclusive capacities, the foundation of Saint-Simon's idea of the strict separation between temporal and spiritual powers.[37] A mere "diatribe against kings and priests," Condorcet's history of the mind failed to provide the basis of a general theory of society.[38]

The inability to link facts into a general theory was, according to Saint-Simon, a major flaw of eighteenth-century thinkers, including Newton, who failed to make the law of gravity the principle of an all-encompassing philosophical system. Conscious that he was making a significant, "new" judgment, Saint-Simon also condemned the Encyclopedists, such as Diderot and d'Alembert. Although they had presented a "general system of human knowledge," they had been exclusively critical and destructive; they did not invent or construct anything to replace what they despised.[39] In short, the eighteenth-century analytical method had become unproductive, and now it was time to revive Descartes's synthetic approach. Saint-Simon astutely intuited that the nineteenth century would be characterized by the construction of systems. Pointing out that construction was far more difficult than demolition, he wrote elsewhere in a famous passage, "The philosophy of the eighteenth century was critical and revolutionary, that of the nineteenth century will be inventive and organizing."[40]

Saint-Simon urged scholars to develop an encyclopedia organizing the scientific system proposed by Descartes, who had understood that "positive philosophy" included the two equally important divisions of science – the physics of inorganic matter and that of organic matter – but had failed to base them on the same physical law. Convinced that man and the universe were run by the same mechanism because man was like a watch and the universe resembled a clock, Saint-Simon argued that it was possible to connect everything in the universe by means of a single law, the law of gravity, which would replace God as the "sole cause of all physical and moral phenomena."[41] Once the new encyclopedia organized

---

[37] Manuel, *Prophets of Paris*, 121.   [38] Saint-Simon, *Introduction aux travaux scientifiques*, 65.

[39] Ibid., 102, 104. Despite these fundamental reservations, the Encyclopedists had an enormous impact on Saint-Simon's thought. In fact, at the end of the first volume of the *Introduction aux travaux scientifiques*, he inserted a copy of the *Encyclopédie's* tree of knowledge as well as its preliminary discourse. Ibid., 106.

[40] Saint-Simon, *Esquisse d'une nouvelle encyclopédie, ou Introduction à la philosophie du XIXᵉ siècle*, in *Oeuvres*, 1.1:92; see also 93.

[41] Saint-Simon, *Introduction aux travaux scientifiques*, 121n1, 154. Influenced by Mesmer and eighteenth-century mechanists, such as Boerhaave, Saint-Simon further maintained that everything in the universe derived from fluids and solids in motion because they were materials subject to the pull of gravity. Ibid., 126, 131, 175. Staum, *Cabanis*, 57–58; Robert Darnton, *Mesmerism and the End of the Enlightenment in France* (New York: Schocken Books, 1970), 3, 148–9.

his scientific system, which he called "physicism," he believed new general principles built upon reason and observation would emerge to guide humanity.[42] Based on the general idea of universal gravitation, physicism would serve as the foundation for a new religion.

Saint-Simon's view of the scientific nature of religion was shaped by another Idéologue, Charles Dupuis, who published in the mid-1790s *De l'origine de tous les cultes*, a work that became immensely popular among liberals.[43] Saint-Simon was primarily impressed by Dupuis's assertion that religion consisted of scientific explanations of the physical world clothed in a sacred form. Therefore, as the sciences improved, so did religion. Saint-Simon agreed with Dupuis on the need to abolish the idea that man was the center of the universe. But whereas Dupuis criticized the priests' use of religion as a tool of oppression and wanted the common people to abandon religion in favor of reason, Saint-Simon argued to the contrary that religion must be a "SET OF APPLICATIONS OF GENERAL SCIENCE BY MEANS OF WHICH ENLIGHTENED MEN GOVERN IGNORANT MEN."[44]

This need to use religion as a political tool seems to have come from adversaries of the Idéologues, the Catholic counterrevolutionaries headed by Louis de Bonald, Joseph de Maistre, François René de Chateaubriand, and, later, Félicité Robert de Lamennais. Although Saint-Simon quarreled with these conservative monarchists, who were reviving religious ideas and deriding scientific trends, he did not altogether escape their influence.[45] He greatly admired Chateaubriand, who had just published *Le Génie du christianisme* (1802), which made Catholicism and the Middle Ages intellectually respectable by demonstrating the ennobling aesthetic aspects of

---

[42] Saint-Simon, *Introduction aux travaux scientifiques*, 199.

[43] Dupuis served on the Committee of Public Instruction when he was a member of the Convention. Under the Directory, as part of the Council of Five Hundred, he supported Louvet's project for the liberty of the press and helped establish the Ecoles Centrales. He then joined his fellow Idéologues in the Institut. Along with Volney's *Ruines*, *De l'origine de tous les cultes* was the primary tract used in the fight against Catholicism during the Restoration. Picavet, *Les Idéologues*, 141–3; Burton Feldman and Robert D. Richardson, eds., *The Rise of Modern Mythology, 1680–1860* (Bloomington: Indiana University Press, 1972), 276.

[44] Saint-Simon, *Introduction aux travaux scientifiques*, 169. See also Charles Dupuis, *Abrégé de l'Origine de tous les cultes* (Paris, 1836), 12, 20–1, 251, 255, 340, 357–65, 377, 390–1; Weill, *Saint-Simon*, 46; Saint-Simon, *Mémoire sur la science de l'homme*, 30; Manuel, *Saint-Simon*, 125.

[45] Chateaubriand particularly derided the so-called certainty of scientific knowledge: "Well, my God, what is there less positive than the sciences, whose systems change several times every century." François Chateaubriand, *Le Génie du christianisme* (Paris: Garnier-Flammarion, 1966), 411–12. See also Leroy, *Idées sociales*, 2:116; Robert Nisbet, "Conservatism," in *A History of Sociological Analysis*, ed. Tom Bottomore and Robert Nisbet (New York: Basic Books, 1978), 84.

medieval religion. Most of all, Saint-Simon was struck by Bonald's views on the political and social utility of religion.[46]

In reacting against the Enlightenment, which he blamed for the anarchy of the Revolution, Bonald condemned individualism and any type of liberal, representative system. To him, the individual was nothing, while the social order was supreme. Man had significance or reality only insofar as he was a social being and had a function in society.[47] Stressing that society was greater than the sum of its parts, Bonald even maintained the extreme position that society was an organic, "*necessary* being," whereas man was a "contingent being, who may or may not exist."[48] Since man was a creation of society, he had no rights, but only duties to serve it and follow its traditions. Just as man had to bow to the power of society, society itself had to obey a higher authority, God. The divine origin of all social and political institutions, traditions, laws, truths, and human faculties was the simple unifying principle that Bonald insisted would solve the current anarchical situation. And like Hegel, Bonald implied that God, or the absolute, worked through society and history and had to be the reference point of all human activity. Favoring uniformity of beliefs and opinions as the foundation of social stability, Bonald thus argued that the period of greatest unity was the Middle Ages, when all Europeans had the same religion. Because religion bonded people together and compelled them to perform their duties, it made the existence of society possible and provided it with a moral basis. The more religious a society was, the more perfect it was.[49]

Bonald's works impressed Saint-Simon, who proclaimed them to be the "most estimable productions that have been brought to light in several years." Since he too believed that his era was one of disintegration, he favored Bonald's perception of the "utility of systematic unity." He agreed that scientific and literary works needed a unifying principle, which gave society definition, guidance, and stability. Without objecting to the authoritarianism implied by

---

[46] Saint-Simon, *Introduction aux travaux scientifiques*, 158, 161; Yves Le Febvre, *Le Génie du christianisme*, 72.

[47] *Oeuvres complètes de M. de Bonald*, ed. Migne, 3 vols. (Paris, 1859–64), 1:123–4, 132–3, 358, 623–8, 844–851, 994. See also Henri Mouliné, *De Bonald* (Paris: Felix Alcan, 1916), 22–3; Leroy, *Idées sociales*, 2:140; Robert Nisbet, "Conservatism," 83–4; Paul Bénichou, *Le Temps des prophètes: Doctrines de l'âge romantique* (Paris: Gallimard, 1977), 122; Irving Zeitlin, *Rethinking Sociology: A Critique of Contemporary Theory* (Englewood Cliffs, N.J.; Prentice-Hall, 1973), 43.

[48] *Oeuvres complètes de M. de Bonald*, 1:138.

[49] Ibid., 1:163–8, 613, 838, 1260; Zeitlin, *Rethinking Sociology*, 44; Robert Nisbet, "De Bonald and the Concept of the Social Group," *Journal of the History of Ideas* 5 (1944): 315–31.

Bonald's stance, Saint-Simon criticized him only for maintaining that Christianity could satisfy contemporary demands for unity. Saint-Simon felt that because Christianity and all other religions had decayed beyond repair, only the idea of universal gravitation had the requisite strong, "unitary character." It should "serve as the basis of the new scientific system and *thus of the new religious system.*"[50]

Saint-Simon briefly discussed the evolution of humanity in terms of interrelated scientific and religious changes. He showed that because people tended to think in terms of cause and effect, religion had always existed. Its history involved an evolution from a belief in particular causes to a faith in one general cause. Modern history began when Socrates linked ideas into a general explanatory system and first showed that there was one ruling intelligence called God. This belief in one God triumphed with Christianity, which Saint-Simon thought was designed by Paul, not Jesus.[51] Thanks to the works of Madame de Staël and especially Bonald and Chateaubriand, Saint-Simon greatly respected the Middle Ages. Implicitly arguing against Condorcet, he contended that the medieval period was not barbarous but broke the ground for the scientific revolution. Yet, like Condorcet, he showed that toward the end of this time, the clergy declined, ceding their authority to lay scholars, their intellectual and thus moral superiors. The sciences began to make significant advances when Galileo dealt the Church a mortal blow. The demolition of the old structure was completed by Bacon, Descartes, Locke, Newton, and the Encyclopedists, who showed the importance of reason and experiment. By the eighteenth century, gravity seemed to be the sole cause of all phenomena, and the deity completely disappeared from scientific consideration. At the same time, the clergy were being replaced by lay mathematicians and scientists, who would become the new spiritual power. The principle that every man must work was transforming morality, displacing the golden rule, which was too negative, only indirectly obligatory, and wholly neglectful of the individual's obligation toward himself. As soon as rentiers and other idlers who burdened society disappeared, humanity would attain the greatest possible happiness, which simply derived from the pleasure of working, whether in government, the arts and sciences, manufacturing, or agriculture.

Saint-Simon insisted that this earthly paradise was not ready to be established, for civilization was in an age of transition marked by

---

[50] Saint-Simon, *Introduction aux travaux scientifiques*, 167–8.
[51] Saint-Simon argued that Jesus was too ignorant to have been the mastermind of Christianity. Paul was able to use his Socratic training to organize a coherent creed and a corps of teachers.

two competing belief systems, a worn-out deism (or Christianity) and an ill-formed theory of physicism.[52] He argued that the formulation of the theory must precede the practical work of setting up a religious organization. Contrary to Condorcet's abhorrence of such a ploy, he wanted the ignorant masses to continue to believe in one God but the educated elite to adopt physicism secretly while proclaiming publicly their faith in deism. He was evidently heeding Bonald's warning that every society needed a religion for stability.[53]

SAINT-SIMON'S SEARCH FOR SUPPORT: 1808–1813

When the *Introduction aux travaux scientifiques* failed to persuade mathematicians and other scientists to work with him, Saint-Simon wrote in great frustration *Lettres au Bureau des Longitudes* (1808), which appealed to the patriotism of French scientists. Echoing the admiration of many of the philosophes for Cartesian materialism, Saint-Simon asserted that Descartes was superior to English thinkers because he was the first and only scientist to conceive of the "positive system." He had founded modern " positive science" when he established the scientific method of synthesis, an a priori method consisting of the descent "from mathematical ideas to ideas of physics."[54] Saint-Simon reiterated that it was time to take up again this synthetic method, which he suggested should be founded on Descartes's theory of vortices, a general idea that could connect the separate theories of solids with those of fluids if it were improved by Newton's law of gravity. When Saint-Simon used the term "positive system," he was thus referring to a system of scientific knowledge that was unified by a single explanatory principle formulated in mathematical terms. In his mind, the new positive system would represent the nineteenth-century version of the *Encyclopédie*.

In the rest of his book, he offered to help scientists improve their discipline and presented them with many of his amateurish, eccentric ideas about the equal quantities of fluids and solids in the universe. Fearful that they were disregarding his ideas because of his reputation,

---

[52] He felt his present age was comparable to the period between Socrates and Paul, the last time there existed two competing belief systems. During those five hundred years of transition, scholars believed in one divinity, whereas the people believed in numerous gods.

[53] Later in the *Nouvelle Encyclopédie* of 1810, he reiterated this odd double standard and argued that scientists were forbidden to believe in God when they were involved in research, but once they published their discoveries, they had to profess their faith.

[54] Saint-Simon, *Lettres au Bureau des Longitudes*, 261, 262. See also Markham, Introduction to *Social Organization*, xxii; Aram Vartanian, *Diderot and Descartes: A Study of Scientific Naturalism in the Enlightenment* (Princeton N.J.: Princeton University Press, 1953).

he inserted odd autobiographical information justifying his fortune hunting and general debauchery during the Revolution. Here and in other works, Saint-Simon appeared very defensive about his personal behavior. He admitted that he lacked the clarity and precision necessary for success in intellectual matters, but because he had failed in business and social relationships, he felt that the only way left for the descendant of Charlemagne to achieve greatness was through philosophy. His haughty defense of his ancestry and his insistence that Charlemagne appeared in person to tell him he would be a great philosopher could not have helped to legitimize his philosophy.[55]

Saint-Simon produced the following works in the next couple of years: *Projet d'encyclopédie* (1809), *Nouvelle Encyclopédie* (1810), *Esquisse d'une nouvelle encyclopédie, ou Introduction à la philosophie du XIXe siècle* (1810), and *Histoire de l'homme* (1810). All of these were repetitive, fragmentary, and unorganized pieces of larger works that never came close to being completed. Increasingly insecure about achieving his goals, he blamed his problems on his late start in philosophy, his "passionate" and extravagant nature, his clumsy style, and his "insane actions."[56] Nevertheless, like others during this period of romanticism, he argued in favor of spontaneity and the passions and maintained that idiosyncratic behavior and madness generated brilliant ideas.[57]

In the *Projet d'encyclopédie* and the other works written during Napoleon's regime, Saint-Simon further analyzed the interrelationship between intellectual and political developments, for he assumed that politics was "nothing other than the principal philosophy." Opposing the position of the Right, he put the French Revolution in a long-term perspective to defend its significance as well as the value of philosophy. To him, the Revolution was not a response to some minor problem, but was deeply rooted in the history of the past one thousand years, when theology was declining and the positive system was emerging. In the eighteenth century, the Encyclopedists, who incompletely organized the "positive doctrine," destroyed the "superstitious doctrine" and prepared the way for the Revolution.[58] The Revolution had to take place because the intellectual atmosphere was far more advanced than the social, political, and religious institutions, which were not based on reason. Since the

---

[55] Saint-Simon, "Préface: Histoire de ma vie," 64, 66n2, 67, 77–86; idem, "Epître dédicatoire à mon neveu, Victor de Saint-Simon," *Nouvelle Encyclopédie,* in *Oeuvres,* 1.1:96–102; idem, *Histoire de l'homme,* in *Oeuvres,* 6:337, 345.

[56] Saint-Simon, *Projet d'encyclopédie,* in *Oeuvres,* 6:287, 312.

[57] J. L. Talmon, *Romanticism and Revolt: Europe, 1815–1848* (1967; New York: Harcourt, Brace & World, 1970), 145.

[58] Saint-Simon, *Projet d'encyclopédie,* 303, 310.

cause of the Revolution was a change in scientific and thus religious attitudes, so was the remedy. Saint-Simon was reiterating the position of the liberal Idéologues, such as Madame de Staël, who wrote, "It is the philosophers who made the Revolution, [and] it is they who will terminate it."[59] He particularly wanted to underscore the necessity and inevitability of the French Revolution to demonstrate the necessity and inevitability of his own theoretical system. Both the Revolution and his system had to be accepted as legitimate because they were part of progress. As many of the romantic historians were to do because of the opprobrium attached to the sacred political and religious principles of the ancien régime and the Revolution, he looked to history as a source of legitimization.

Saint-Simon's view of progress was, however, confused in these works, because he often changed his periodization both in the number of eras and in their dates. At one point, he said that there were five epochs, characterized by mankind's progress to a new religion, which he defined as a system of common general ideas and moral precepts. This fifth era would be that of physicism.[60] But he failed to explain satisfactorily the interconnections between intellectual and religious changes. At another point, he claimed there were three historical epochs; in each, two men worked in tandem to advance knowledge. The first era was marked by Plato and Aristotle, the second by Descartes and Bacon, and the third by Kant and presumably Saint-Simon himself. Whereas Plato, Descartes, and Kant made vague, useless speculations, Aristotle and Bacon led the way in scientific progress by founding the philosophy of general science – "positive philosophy." By means of the law of gravitation, Saint-Simon believed he could link all ideas into a "systematic whole" and complete Aristotle's and Bacon's project of establishing positive philosophy.[61] Instead of developing the new concept of "positive philosophy," he celebrated his own role in history.

Preoccupied by his problems in realizing this role, Saint-Simon tried in these works to ingratiate himself with Napoleon in order to gain his support. Besides praising him for being the only man capable of organizing a new political system, Saint-Simon adopted a more conservative stance. For example, when he turned his attention to the Revolution, he condemned the royalists, who had cared only about maintaining their privileges, as well as the republicans,

---

[59] Madame de Staël, *Des circonstances actuelles qui peuvent terminer la Révolution et des principes qui doivent fonder la république en France*, ed. Lucia Omacini (Paris: Droz, 1979), 273.

[60] Saint-Simon, *Esquisse d'une nouvelle encyclopédie*, 93. See also idem, *Nouvelle Encyclopédie*, 317–20; idem, *Travail sur la gravitation universelle: Moyen de forcer les anglais à reconnaître l'indépendance des pavillons*, in *Oeuvres* 5.2:244; Nisbet, *Idea of Progress*, 250.

[61] Saint-Simon, *Esquisse d'une nouvelle encyclopédie*, 90; idem, *Nouvelle Encyclopédie*, 324.

who had created ineffective institutions. He even criticized the Encyclopedists for having erroneously attacked the king. As an enlightened aristocrat, he thus favored the position of the moderates, the constitutional monarchists, inspired by Montesquieu. Saint-Simon's attitude toward religion was also opportunistic. He professed his faith in God in a strained manner and boasted that his own constructive approach to social reform respected the "throne and altar."[62]

In the *Projet d'encyclopédie*, Saint-Simon emphasized that the "positive doctrine" itself would be a religion because it would establish a general science linking all knowledge. Taking up the idea that he had expressed in his *Lettres d'un habitant de Genève à ses contemporains*, he declared that all scientists should unite to form a permanent body of "clergy" who would create a new "church."[63] They would not only discover natural laws but also establish moral principles emphasizing everybody's duty to work, preferably in the sciences or industry, for mankind's happiness on this earth. To teach the scientific and moral principles appropriate for the nineteenth century, they would be in charge of education just as the clergy used to be.

Saint-Simon's efforts to gain Napoleon's support did not succeed. In 1810 he suddenly became destitute after Diard, his protector, died and the nearly bankrupt Redern ceased paying him his annuity. Desperate, he pursued his dispute with Redern about his rightful share of the liquidation of their business. This became a public battle, with the two men publishing summaries of their cases and their letters. Saint-Simon sought to defend his behavior by depicting himself as an ignorant, highly imaginative philosopher.[64] Becoming increasingly deranged, he collapsed in late 1812, whereupon Burdin and the great psychologist and Idéologue Pinel sent him to a sanitorium. By mid-1813 he had recovered his mental balance and was even able to obtain financial assistance from relatives.

MÉMOIRE SUR LA SCIENCE DE L'HOMME

At this time, he wrote the *Mémoire sur la science de l'homme*. Perhaps because of the "moral revolution" brought on by his "physical crisis," he became increasingly absorbed by man and his relationship to society.[65] In this work, he asserted that the crisis facing Europe

---

[62] Saint-Simon, *Nouvelle Encyclopédie*, 330.   [63] Saint-Simon, *Projet d'encyclopédie*, 297.
[64] Saint-Simon, *Correspondance avec M. de Redern*, in *Oeuvres*, 1.1:110. See also Manuel, "The Climacteric," chap. in *Saint-Simon*, 95–113.
[65] Saint-Simon, *Correspondance avec M. de Redern*, 136.

made it imperative for humanity to rebuild its entire structure. Thinkers had to devote themselves to reorganizing not only the scientific system but also the religious, political, and moral systems, that is, "the system of IDEAS under whatever aspect one envisages them." Reflecting the influence of Bonald, he added, "The religious institution . . . is the principal political institution."[66] Thus the *Mémoire sur la science de l'homme* seems to mark Saint-Simon's passage from an interest in the physical sciences to a preoccupation with the science of society.[67] Whereas previously he had sought to connect the physical sciences, now he concentrated more on moral and political principles.

In the *Mémoire*, he also shifted his attention from the inorganic sciences to physiology, which he thought could illuminate these principles.[68] Disappointed by the indifference of mathematicians and inorganic scientists to the bloodiness of the Napoleonic wars and to his ideas, he announced that physiologists would become the new vanguard of the scientific establishment. Adopting the position of the Idéologues, he maintained that physiology was related to the science of man, whose development was the main subject of his work. Involving the study of the human body, physiology was synonymous with biology, which did not emerge as an independent science until later in the nineteenth century.[69] Yet Saint-Simon's science of man was not just biological, but evolutionary; it encompassed physiology, psychology, history, and forecasts of the future.[70]

Before examining the two main divisions of the science of man – the study of the individual man and that of the human species – Saint-Simon explained how his ideas had been influenced by the physician Jean Burdin, whom he had supported many years before.[71] He reproduced an alleged conversation of theirs in 1798 to show that he had learned from him the theory of scientific progress.[72] This theory, which Saint-Simon had vaguely expressed in his *Lettres d'un habitant de Genève* and had more clearly outlined in a letter to Redern during their dispute, was that each science began by basing its theories on very few observed, examined facts and was therefore

---

[66] Saint-Simon, *Mémoire sur la science de l'homme*, 11, 158.
[67] Weill, *Saint-Simon*, 74.   [68] Ansart, *Sociologie de Saint-Simon*, 18, 25.
[69] William Coleman, *Biology in the Nineteenth Century: Problems of Form, Function, and Transformation* (New York: Wiley, 1971), 2–3.
[70] Manuel, *Saint-Simon*, 137.
[71] Saint-Simon helped Burdin publish a medical textbook, *Cours d'études médicales*, in 1803. Burdin was a friend of Bichat and was greatly influenced by Vicq d'Azyr's pedagogy and Chaussier's vitalism. Gouhier, *Jeunesse*, 2:187–90, 195–8, 326; Manuel, *Saint-Simon*, 133.
[72] Saint-Simon, *Mémoire sur la science de l'homme*, 66.

conjectural.[73] With more experience and new facts, the science be-came half conjectural and half positive. Finally, it became wholly positive. In addition, Burdin showed that the sciences become posi-tive according to the complexity of their facts and the number of relations between them; astronomy was therefore the first science, followed by chemistry. His thoughts on this matter had a certain affinity with eighteenth-century concepts of the chain of being and contemporary evolutionary schemes; both of these sets of ideas pro-ceeded from the simple to the complex.[74]

Moreover, according to Saint-Simon, Burdin explained that physiology would become positive as soon as a general theory was formulated from principles established by Vicq d'Azyr, Bichat, Cabanis, and Condorcet. Saint-Simon believed their ideas had to be synthesized, for they had done more than anyone to advance the science of man by establishing their theories on a "positive basis," that is, on "observed facts."[75] Already, astronomy, physics, and chemistry had been established on such a positive foundation. Pol-itics and morality would become sciences once their basis, physiol-ogy, was established by systematizing the work of these four scientists. As soon as all these sciences became positive, the general science, that is, the philosophy encompassing them, would become positive as well. Saint-Simon wrote, "We are at the point that the first good summary of the particular [positive] sciences will constitute positive philosophy."[76]

Saint-Simon also claimed to have adopted Burdin's view of the implications of the establishment of the positive philosophy. Along with mathematics, the positive sciences of astronomy, physics, and chemistry had already infiltrated the schools. Once physiology and psychology became positive, the science of man would become the "principal object of education."[77] The erudite man of the future would be the scientist of man. Referring directly to Dupuis, Burdin alleg-edly maintained that changes in the scientific system would lead to the reorganization of religion and scientists would replace the clergy.

Saint-Simon's citation of Burdin might reflect his own opportun-ism more than Burdin's actual influence, the extent of which re-mains unclear. Besides seeking reassurance and support, Saint-Simon

---

[73] In the letter to Redern, Saint-Simon explained that the sciences were at first conjectural, then half conjectural and half positive, and now positive because they rested on observed facts. Since all phenomena belonged to one of the four sciences, the entire body of human knowledge had become positive, and a positive philosophy could be constructed. Saint-Simon, *Correspondance avec M. de Redern*, 108–9.

[74] Manuel, *Saint-Simon*, 134.   [75] Saint-Simon, *Mémoire sur la science de l'homme*, 17.

[76] Saint-Simon, *Correspondance avec M. de Redern*, 109.

[77] Saint-Simon, *Mémoire sur la science de l'homme*, 187.

was trying to gain scientific respectability. To bolster his case, he may, therefore, have attributed to a doctor the important outline of the law of three stages as well as the key ideas of a general scientific philosophy, the scientific basis of a religion, and a scientific clergy.[78]

The first section of Saint-Simon's *Mémoire* dealt with the study of the individual, to which Bichat, Cabanis, and especially Vicq d'Azyr had made the most important contributions. Saint-Simon agreed not only with Bichat's insistence on the independence of the life sciences but with his division of animal functions, which led to the conclusion that there were three categories of human skills: motor, rational, and emotive. Theorizing that people had a given amount of energy and that if one organ became strong others became weak, Bichat was the source of Saint-Simon's principle that scientific advancement meant the atrophy of the artistic faculties and that a person could excel in only one capacity.[79]

Saint-Simon was also influenced by Cabanis, whose *Rapports du physique et du moral de l'homme* (1802) proposed a physiological foundation for the subject embraced by the Encyclopedists and Idéologues: the science of man. By providing a better understanding of man and his behavior, physiology would lead to moral, political, and social progress. The science of man was thus necessarily a science of society. Influenced by Helvétius, Holbach, and Condillac, Cabanis justified his physiological approach by arguing that morality was basically physical and that all morals and ideas could be traced to physical sensations. As the fundamental principle characterizing all vital phenomena, physical sensitivity was a manifestation of the force of affinity, which included gravitation. This force was universal and united all of nature. Convinced that the moral spirit of man was inseparable from his physical body, he opposed Descartes's dualism

---

[78] To detract from Saint-Simon's originality, Gouhier argues that Burdin urged him to embrace a scientific career in 1798 and decisively shaped the next fifteen years of his life. Yet in the past, Saint-Simon had used the same eccentric procedure of reproducing imaginary conversations and ascribing ideas haphazardly to different thinkers. He may have attributed some ideas to Burdin merely because they logically followed from Burdin's original insistence on the importance of physiology and made a neater whole. Instead of Burdin, d'Alembert, who was Saint-Simon's early mentor, may have been the source of the important idea of the opposition between the conjectural and observational sciences. Also, the preface to the *Mémoire* suggests that Saint-Simon's conception of the science of man was really formed by the ideas of Cabanis, Bichat, Vicq d'Azyr, and Condorcet. Gouhier, *Jeunesse*, 2:182, 187, 324; Manuel, *Saint-Simon*, 133; Saint-Simon, *Mémoire sur la science de l'homme*, 21.

[79] Canguilhem, "Bichat, Marie-François-Xavier," in *Dictionary of Scientific Biography*, ed. Gillispie, 2:122–3; Staum, *Cabanis*, 255–571; Manuel, *Saint-Simon*, 159. For more information regarding Bichat's influence on Saint-Simon, see Barbara Haines, "The Inter-Relations between Social, Biological, and Medical Thought, 1750–1850: Saint-Simon and Comte," *British Journal for the History of Science* 11 (March 1978): 19–35.

and declared that physiologists should observe man as an animal species. Yet because he believed that scientific laws became increasingly complex as their phenomena became more complicated and the science of life dealt with the most complex phenomena, he maintained that its method had to be different from that of the sciences concerned with more simple, inorganic matter.[80] Cabanis was thus at the origin of ideas that supposedly belonged to Burdin: the connection of the intellect with biological organization, the view of the sciences of morality and politics as applications of physiology, and the concept of the increasing complexity of the sciences.[81] Like Cabanis, Saint-Simon also wished to unite all of knowledge and nature with a single, universal force.

The person whom Saint-Simon hailed for founding the "positive bases of the science of man" was the anatomist Vicq d'Azyr. He was famous for having demonstrated the interdependence of the organs, which made a living being a totality, and for having insisted on extending the scientific method to the organic sciences.[82] In the second installment of the *Mémoire*, also written in 1813, Saint-Simon was more critical of Vicq d'Azyr, whom he faulted for rejecting the idea that vital phenomena could be explained by the same force that accounted for chemical and astronomical occurrences. He feared that Vicq d'Azyr and all physiologists, who had adopted his ideas, were dangerously close to vitalism, which kept physiology in its conjectural state. In seeking another cause of the phenomena of life, they were creating an "insurmountable obstacle to the organization of the positive scientific system, because this system can have no other base than one single and unique law regulating the universe."[83] Thus although Saint-Simon approved of Bichat's and Vicq d'Azyr's call for the establishment of physiology as a separate science, his enthusiasm for the principle of gravitation tended to make him reduce

---

[80] Except for Martin Staum, who argues that the principle of sensitivity was a vitalist element, most historians consider Cabanis a mechanist and a materialist because he reduced all moral, intellectual, and social forces to the physical. On Cabanis, see P. J. G. Cabanis, *Rapports du physique et du moral de l'homme*, 3d ed. (Paris, 1815), xxv, xxxvii; Martin S. Staum, "Cabanis and the Science of Man," *Journal of the Behavioral Sciences* 10.1 (1974): 135–7; Staum, *Cabanis*, 3, 5, 16–17, 19, 37–40, 49, 71, 86–90, 103–7, 161–2, 178–9, 190, 237, 253, 309–10; Crocker, "Cabanis," 3–4; Lyons, *France under the Directory*, 118; Leroy, *Idées sociales*, 2:158; Gusdorf, *Introduction*, 237; Picavet, *Les Idéologues*, 226, 292; Moravia, *Il pensiero*, 27–8, 288; van Duzer, *Contribution*, 38–40; Ansart, *Sociologie de Saint-Simon*, 43; Fletcher, *Making of Sociology*, 1:149; Gouhier, *Jeunesse*, 2:47.

[81] Gouhier, *Jeunesse*, 2:324.

[82] Saint-Simon, *Mémoire sur la science de l'homme*, 71. See also ibid., 73; Gusdorf, *Introduction*, 133; Pierre Huard and M. J. Imbault-Huart, "Vicq d'Azyr, Félix," in *Dictionary of Scientific Biography*, ed. Gillispie, 14:14–17; Gouhier, *Jeunesse*, 2:195–7.

[83] Saint-Simon, *Mémoire sur la science de l'homme*, 210.

biology to physics and revealed the greater impact of Cabanis's materialism on his thought.[84]

As for the fourth significant thinker, Condorcet, Saint-Simon was growing increasingly critical of his disregard for the value of religion and the clergy.[85] After commending him for being the pioneer in the study of the human species, he expressed disapproval of his joining Rousseau, d'Alembert, and other philosophes not only in nostalgically depicting the happy "noble savage" but also in condemning religious, civil, and political institutions as producers of the world's sorrows and evils. He believed the recent discoveries of explorers, such as Cook, Bougainville, and La Pérouse, invalidated Condorcet's historical conjectures and filled in the gaps in the chain of being to create a "noninterrupted series of observed facts" from primitive savages to contemporary Europeans.[86] Besides medicine, cultural anthropology thus had its place in the development of the science of man.

The "primitive man" who most engaged Saint-Simon's attention was the celebrated Wild Boy of Aveyron, who was discovered in January 1800.[87] Saint-Simon claimed that the boy's limited reason and inability to speak proved that primitive man – Condorcet's "noble savage" – was only slightly superior to the animals. By the Wild Boy's example, Saint-Simon was able to show the crucial importance of society in creating, that is, civilizing, the individual – a view that came remarkably close to Bonald's. The collective effort of society, not the individual man, was the motor of progress.

Saint-Simon then presented a twelve-stage history of the human intellect. In the twelfth and future stage, the whole system of knowledge would be based on one general, immutable law. This change would lead to the reorganization of religion, politics, civil law, morals, and education because these always reflected the general system of ideas, that is, the scientific system. Once the sciences, and therefore all of philosophy, became positive, politics would also become positive, for it was merely an "application of general science," that is, positive philosophy. When the science of man became part of education, everybody would be able to deal with political questions in a scientific, rational manner and would thus seek to reorganize society instead of destroying it as the revolutionaries did. Scientific

---

[84] Gouhier, *Jeunesse*, 2:264, 298.

[85] Saint-Simon, *Correspondance avec M. de Redern*, 113–16.

[86] Saint-Simon, *Mémoire sur la science de l'homme*, 115.

[87] Pinel, the doctor who diagnosed Saint-Simon when he went mad and frequented his asylum in Paris, was one of the scientists who examined the Wild Boy. Roger Shattuck, *The Forbidden Experiment: The Story of the Wild Boy of Aveyron* (New York: Farrar, Straus, & Giroux, 1980), 24, 181.

expertise would become the salvation of society by preserving it from "moral insurrection."[88]

While still impoverished, Saint-Simon published in 1813 a second installment of the *Mémoire*, which contained the important *Travail sur la gravitation universelle*. Reacting to the physiologists' indifference to his work, Saint-Simon wrote the *Travail* to convince them that they needed his help to show them the way to construct the science of man on the basis of the universal law of gravity.

The deterioration of the political situation in Europe gave Saint-Simon a sense of urgency. He addressed the *Travail* to the emperor with an introductory letter begging him to stop his wars and attacks on the Church and to accept a plan for peace based on the sciences. Church and state had to be separated again as they had been during the Middle Ages. This separation had been weakening since the fifteenth century, when Christianity began to decline under the impact of the scientific enlightenment. But now the sciences were ready to assume the functions of Christianity. By uniting all people, they could reorganize European society and bring about tranquillity and stability. Yet it was not a propitious time to approach Napoleon, for he had just decided to blame his problems on philosophers, especially the Idéologues.[89]

Saint-Simon's work was confused and full of contradictions, made worse by the new method of exposition that he adopted to give more "life" to his ideas. He avoided using the impersonal third-person pronoun *on*, which he felt was too "cold," and he multiplied his interlocutors, who would give speeches expressing his ideas, even if these ideas were not wholly consistent with their own positions.[90] He believed that "the most admired work" was "one where there are the least number of phrases intended to create connections."[91] The muddle that resulted made his discussions of history almost nonsensical. Obsessed with creating a symmetrical historical schema, he argued, for example, that for the first 1,000 to 1,100 years after Socrates, a priori ideas, which related to the science of man, made the most progress. For the next 1,000 to 1,200 years, a posteriori ideas advanced the most. Yet he was contradicting his own theory that scientific development had been initiated by the simple, inorganic sciences.

[88] Saint-Simon, *Mémoire sur la science de l'homme*, 19, 194.   [89] Leroy, *Idées sociales*, 2:256.
[90] Saint-Simon, *Mémoire sur la science de l'homme*, 47; see also 48.
[91] Saint-Simon, *Mémoire sur la science de l'homme: Deuxième Livraison*, in *Oeuvres*, 5.2:221.

In another historical schema, which consisted of three stages, the first great epoch involved all the preliminary work accomplished before Socrates. The second era began with the inauguration of the conjectural system by Socrates, the ultimate general theorist who combined a priori and a posteriori approaches and first stated that the world was regulated by one animated cause. Finally, 2,000 to 2,500 years later, the third era was to begin with the appearance of a man similar to Socrates – obviously, Saint-Simon – who would establish the positive system. In what was basically the positive era, all phenomena, even so-called moral phenomena, would be considered physical and would be explained by means of Newton's gravitational law.

In making forecasts about the future, positive stage of history, Saint-Simon followed Condorcet's theory that "it is always on the past that one must base arguments about the future."[92] Not only were the events of the present too unstable a foundation for prediction, but the person who made the forecasts could not be suitably objective or dispassionate. It was important to discuss the development of the mind first in terms of the past, then the future, and finally the present. Saint-Simon claimed that this order or division was completely original and would improve political thought.

Trying to satisfy his contemporaries' spiritual yearnings, Saint-Simon ended the *Travail* with a strikingly religious appeal. Still fearful of popular atheism, he carefully pointed out that his principle of gravitation was not opposed to the divine because it was only the "idea of the immutable law by which God governs the universe." By implication, the positive system was inherently spiritual. Combining the language of Hobbes with the fears of the Catholic counterrevolutionaries, Saint-Simon maintained that the destruction of religion had caused the twenty-year-old general war and was about to "plunge the human species back into the state of nature, which is a state of continuous war." Scholars had to form immediately a new clerical body united by a common belief in the law of gravity. Their first step would be to elect a new pope in Rome. Because they would be able to limit national ambitions as the old clergy once did, they would have the power to reorganize Europe and stop wars. The need for this new scholarly clergy was so urgent that it was "necessary to make practice advance before theory."[93] This statement represents a significant reversal of Saint-Simon's principle that theory had to precede practice. Although the positive philosophy was not ready to be implemented, the scientists should immediately make themselves the spiritual power. Henceforth,

[92] Saint-Simon, *Travail sur la gravitation universelle*, 254. [93] Ibid., 286, 312–13.

Saint-Simon would increasingly focus his attention on the practical and political aspects of his philosophy.

The *Mémoire sur la science de l'homme* proved to be Saint-Simon's first successful book, easing his financial problems to such a degree that he could begin to search in earnest for a collaborator to help him complete the works he had outlined in the *Mémoire*. But Redern was out of the question, and Saint-Simon's good friends Burdin and the scientist Henri Ducrotay de Blainville proved unresponsive to his entreaties.[94] Finally, out of desperation, he tried to buy himself a collaborator. In late 1812 or 1813, after leaving his sanitarium, he had established himself near the Ecole Normale to meet some of its students. Because of his seductive charm, grand ideas, and love of youth, he soon attracted a group of admirers, one of whom may have introduced him to Augustin Thierry, a brilliant student and enthusiast of Rousseau and history.[95] At first, Thierry refused to have anything to do with Saint-Simon, especially because he found the *Mémoire sur la science de l'homme* too elitist and presumptuous. But in early 1814, when he found himself without a teaching position, he accepted Saint-Simon's offer of a secretarial position at two hundred francs a month.[96]

Hoping to influence the outcome of the Congress of Vienna, they published in October 1814 *De la réorganisation de la société européenne ou De la nécessité et des moyens de rassembler les peuples de l'Europe en un seul corps politique en conservant à chacun son indépendance nationale*. Thierry was listed as a coauthor and Saint-Simon's "student." Pressing for the reestablishment of Europe on the basis of a constitution, *De la réorganisation de la société européenne* did not follow the plan Saint-Simon had outlined in the *Mémoire*, where his future works were to be primarily physiological.[97] Instead of discussing the natural

---

[94] Gouhier, *Jeunesse*, 3:73.

[95] One member of Saint-Simon's circle of admirers in this period was the geometer Hachette, who was one of Thierry's good friends. Saint-Simon probably knew Hachette when he first became interested in supporting Poisson, one of Hachette's students at the Ecole Polytechnique. Gouhier argues that Saint-Simon and Thierry did not meet at this time. Gouhier, *Jeunesse*, 3:77, 106–7.

[96] A. Augustin-Thierry, *Augustin Thierry (1795–1856) d'après sa correspondance et ses papiers de famille* (Paris: Plon, 1922), 5, 17, 20, 24; Kiernan Joseph Carroll, *Some Aspects of the Historical Thought of Augustin Thierry* (Washington, D.C.: Catholic University of America, 1971), 4; C. P. Gooch, *History and Historians in the Nineteenth Century* (New York: Longmans, Green, 1913), 169; Leroy, *Saint-Simon*, 256.

[97] Saint-Simon, *Mémoire sur la science de l'homme*, 187–90.

sciences or the law of universal gravitation, the work focused directly on the science of politics and was infused with a new vocabulary relating to parliaments and constitutions. Perhaps this shift was due to Thierry's influence or to the virulent contemporary debates over the proper form of government for the new Bourbon state. The source of one change is undeniable; thanks to Thierry, *De la réorganisation de la société européenne* was superior in precision, clarity, style, and organization to anything that Saint-Simon had ever written before.

Instead of vaguely delineating different historical epochs as Saint-Simon's previous books had done, this work began with a far more detailed and dramatic account of the way each century assumed a distinct identity owing to its intellectual climate. Thus the character of the sixteenth century was theological, that of the seventeenth was artistic and literary, and that of the eighteenth was critical and revolutionary. The nineteenth century would be constructive if political questions were submitted to the rigors of the scientific method. Yet Saint-Simon feared the recurrence of another revolution. Parliament seemed to be floating dangerously "between an order of destroyed things, one that cannot come back, and another [order] toward which we are advancing, one that is not yet assured." It was impossible to be constructive when the government was an unstable, "bizarre mixture" of two irreconcilable systems, an absolutist regime and a representative government.[98]

Saint-Simon shared the philosophes' belief that men of letters had to take charge of events by their control over opinion, which ruled the world. Even more important than scientists at the moment, writers, with their ability to spread ideas, could show the way out of the current, painful transitional period by creating general institutions, such as a European parliament. Independent of national governments, this parliament would derive its power from public opinion and have a "constitution." Saint-Simon's concept of a "constitution" had nothing to do with a written document but pertained vaguely to "any system of social order tending to the common good."[99]

Influenced by Chateaubriand's romantic image of the Middle Ages, Saint-Simon and Thierry proposed that this parliament be based on the unifying principles of the medieval papacy, which had made Europe into one peaceful political body. Because the popes had their own laws, government, territory, and public support during the Middle Ages, they had been stronger than the kings, and they had

---

[98] Saint-Simon, *De la réorganisation de la société européenne*, in *Oeuvres*, 1.1:230.
[99] Ibid., 183.

been able to restrain national ambitions, the leading cause of conflict and violence. Yet since the Reformation had shattered the common government represented by the papacy, European society had been chronically troubled.

Either because of Thierry's more democratic inclinations or his own opportunistic nature, Saint-Simon abandoned some of his more elitist pronouncements. He adopted the liberal principles that identified self-interest with the interest of the community and emphasized the freedom of the individual, especially liberty of expression. Moreover, he argued that because France and England were the most politically advanced countries, with established representative governments devoted to the common good, they should spread liberal concepts throughout the Continent and take the lead in creating a general European parliament, which each nation would join once it became a parliamentary state.

Though enthusiastic about liberalism, Saint-Simon was by no means a democrat. In his new unified Europe, there would be a hereditary king, and the vast majority of the delegates to the European parliament would be scholars, businessmen, magistrates, and administrators, elected only by their colleagues. Moreover, except for twenty unusually talented individuals, these delegates would be required to be members of a wealthy, property-owning elite. Saint-Simon's preferred government was thus a cross between a plutocracy and a meritocracy.

Once under a European parliament, Europeans would be united on the basis of "conformity of institutions, union of interests, harmony of maxims, and community of morality and public instruction."[100] In a famous passage, he wrote that "the golden age of the human species is not behind us, it is before us. It lies in the perfection of the social order."[101] Saint-Simon seemed to value above all else the tranquillity that came from eliminating the inconvenience and dangers of conflict and difference. His vision was profoundly marked by fears of the anarchy of the Terror and the horrors of the revolutionary and Napoleonic wars.

De la réorganisation de la société européenne was trimmed so well by Thierry of all apparitions, anachronistic speeches, and scientific babble that Saint-Simon at last gained some success and respectability as a political writer. He became associated with the Idéologues and joined the liberal party headed by such Idéologues as Benjamin Constant and Jean-Baptiste Say.[102] Yet claiming that the liberals had

---

[100] Ibid., 205.   [101] Ibid., 248.
[102] Augustin-Thierry, *Augustin Thierry*, 26; Picavet, *Les Idéologues*, 573; Manuel, *Saint-Simon*, 180.

destroyed feudal and theological institutions without having furnished a substitute, he assigned himself the task of formulating the general doctrine that would serve as the basis of the new social and political structure.

After the leading liberal periodical, *Le Censeur*, gave Saint-Simon's book a highly favorable review in 1814, he met its editors, Charles Comte and Charles Dunoyer. Influenced by J. B. Say, who later became Charles Comte's father-in-law, these two leaders of the liberal party shared Saint-Simon's hope of creating a science of politics to help resolve contemporary problems. They grew very close to Saint-Simon, and all three men participated in formulating the liberal philosophy of the early Restoration.[103] In *Le Censeur* and in the *Journal de la librairie*, Saint-Simon published articles supporting the recently established Charter, a strong parliament, and the creation of an effective two-party system.[104]

During the Hundred Days, he denounced the hypocritical liberal promises of Napoleon, whose military despotism he accused of having brutally despoiled France.[105] In spite of his criticisms, Saint-Simon accepted the position of librarian at the Bibliothèque de l'Arsenal – a post procured for him by his old friend and new minister of the interior, Lazare Carnot.[106] He also wrote a letter to Carnot, urging him to encourage Napoleon to create a political code. For liberal institutions to flourish, it was necessary to create a science of politics that would unite the new, but incoherent political ideas. Since politics was a moral science that was more complex than chemistry or physics, it would undeniably take longer to become a positive science consisting of simple, clear theories based on observed facts. New moral precepts also had to be codified to replace the old Christian moral code. Going back to Dupuis's idea, Saint-Simon wrote, "For religions are essentially no more than different ways of representing the philosophical and moral principles useful to society, of popularizing them, and of authorizing them in accordance with manners and enlightenment."[107]

During the early Restoration, Saint-Simon outlined another plan for unifying Europe in *Aux Anglais et aux Français qui sont zélés pour le bien public*. However, it was never published, because Say objected,

[103] Ledré, "La Presse nationale," 38–9; Augustin-Thierry, *Augustin Thierry*, 22–3, 26, 29.
[104] See e.g., his "Lettre sur l'établissement du parti de l'opposition," which was published in January 1815 in *Le Censeur*. It can be found in *Henri Saint-Simon*, ed. Taylor, 137, 139–40. See also Saint-Simon, *Oeuvres*, 1.2:7–9.
[105] Saint-Simon, "Profession de foi du comte de Saint-Simon au sujet de l'invasion du territoire français par Napoléon Bonaparte," *Oeuvres*, 6:349.
[106] Saint-Simon held this post until the return of the Bourbons. Manuel, *Saint-Simon*, 181.
[107] Saint-Simon, "Lettre au Ministre de l'Intérieur," in *Henri Saint-Simon*, ed. Taylor, 144.

proclaiming it too difficult for the public.[108] This episode reflects the growing influence of Say on Saint-Simon and his colleagues Charles Comte and Dunoyer, all of whom began to spread his ideas in their writings.

An avid supporter of the Revolution and critic of Napoleon, Say founded and edited the important Idéologue periodical *La Décade philosophique, littéraire, et politique*. Much of his importance lay in popularizing Adam Smith's ideas in France. In contrast to the eighteenth-century Physiocrats, who were among the first economists to conceive of a unified social science, Smith had argued that political economy should be founded on the interests not just of the agriculturalists but of the whole community; that labor, not agriculture, was the true source of wealth; and that the division of labor, which bound all workers together, was the origin of the well-being and progress of society. Say took up these ideas. He was very important in nineteenth-century thought for emphasizing the productivity of industry instead of agriculture and the value of all kinds of useful labor instead of nature. He argued that "industry" referred to all productive work, whether practical or theoretical. Men of industry included laborers, managers, entrepreneurs, and scientists or scholars. They formed one social class because they were the only productive people in society. The enemies of society were idle, unproductive men, such as rich property owners and capitalists who lived off the labor of others. Disappointed with the results of the Revolution, Say shifted attention away from politics, for, like Marx, he contended that economic phenomena exerted the dominant influence in society and that government was of secondary importance. To Say as well as to many other Idéologues, who sought to eliminate the dangers of anarchy, industrialism held the key to moral rejuvenation and social stability because it led to social cooperation. The coming industrial state, based on maximizing production, would be characterized by a social consensus, where each person would have a function in the economic order. Since the essence of society lay in industry, political economy was the sole science of society. Say's famous *Traité d'économie politique* (1803) and *Catéchisme d'économie politique* (1815) expressed his conception of this new science, and in 1816 he taught at the Athénée probably the first course on political economy ever given in France.[109] Perhaps Auguste Comte first

---

[108] Taylor, Introduction to *Henri Saint-Simon*, 24.

[109] Jean-Baptiste Say, *Traité d'économie politique*, 3d ed., 2 vols. (Paris, 1817), 1:52; Charles Gide and Charles Rist, *A History of Economic Doctrines from the Time of the Physiocrats to the Present Day*, trans. R. Richards, 2d English ed. (London: George G. Harrap, 1948), 22, 73–8, 87, 102–3, 122–7, 145–60; Gaston Leduc, "Say, Jean Baptiste," in *International Encyclopedia of the Social Sciences*, ed. David Sills (New York: Macmillan, 1968); Mark

became familiar with Say's thought as early as 1815, when he and his friends at the Ecole Polytechnique engaged in long discussions about political economy. Andrieux also contributed to La Décade.[110]

Many of Say's themes appear in Saint-Simon's Aux Anglais et aux Français qui sont zélés pour le bien public. To unify Europe, Saint-Simon proposed an Anglo-French organization, the "Baconian Society," which would be composed of the most important artists, scientists, and industriels, who would base their work on observed facts, not on "metaphysics."[111] This was the first time Saint-Simon used the term industriel, which, along with the word industrielisme, he claimed, perhaps wrongly, to have coined.[112] His new language indicates the changes that were occurring in the French socioeconomic system as well as his growing interest in creating the new science of political economy. Reflecting Say's influence, the term industriel did not refer only to a person involved in manufacturing but to anyone engaged in productive work, including banking, commerce, and farming. Around this time, Saint-Simon also defined "society" for the first time as the "mass and union of men devoted to useful works."[113] Reifying society in this fashion, Saint-Simon's language confirms William Sewell's theory that "the Revolution transformed France from a hierarchical spiritual body with the king at its head into a voluntary association of productive citizens." Joining the movement revaluing work, Saint-Simon was concerned with portraying the needs of this new "industrial society." This society was industrial in two ways. Not only was industrial production growing but citizens were industrious, working together for the benefit of the nation, not for the glory of the king.[114] The three main groups mentioned by Saint-Simon – the artists, scientists, and industriels – corresponded to Bichat's three types of human skills – emotive, rational, and motor – and would henceforth form the heart of his schemes for constructing the industrial society. Besides analyzing the contemporary political situation, the Baconian Society was to give a historical account

Weinburg, "The Social Analyses of Three Early Nineteenth-Century French Liberals: Say, Comte, and Dunoyer," Journal of Libertarian Studies 2.1 (1978): 53–9; Kaiser, "Politics and Political Economy," 144–9, 154, 157–160; James, "Pierre-Louis Roederer," 466, 470–5; Edgard Allix, "La Méthode et la conception de l'économie politique dans l'oeuvre de J.-B. Say," Revue d'histoire des doctrines économiques et sociales 4 (1911): 336, 342, 350, 352–9; Picavet, Les Idéologues, 86–8.

[110] Comte to Valat, January 2, 1815, CG, 1:7.

[111] Saint-Simon, Aux Anglais et aux Français qui sont zélés pour le bien public, in Henri Saint-Simon, ed. Taylor, 155.

[112] Ibid., 145, 307n44; Manuel, Saint-Simon, 188.

[113] Saint-Simon, "Déclaration de principes," L'Industrie, in Oeuvres, 1.2:128.

[114] William H. Sewell, Jr., Work and Revolution in France: The Language of Labor from the Old Regime to 1848 (Cambridge: Cambridge University Press, 1980), 145.

of the advance of civilization from the fifteenth century, a traumatic period that marked the beginning of the revolution that had been unfolding ever since. Because of Saint-Simon's new interest in the economy, his ideas on the transformations of the spiritual and temporal spheres throughout history had changed significantly. The new language of industrialism had colored his interpretation of history. For example, he praised the Arabs for having introduced not only the scientific "capacity" into the spiritual sphere of Europe, but also the industrial "capacity" into the temporal sphere.[115] Moreover, he explained that the scientists were antagonistic to the clergy, and the *industriels*, who used contracts instead of commands to regulate their affairs, were opposed to military men. To him, the development of these two capacities, the scientific and the industrial, was the source of the crisis of the fifteenth century. No longer was social conflict connected in his mind only with intellectual clashes. Besides his new interest in industry and its contractual style of administration, his greater stress on "capacity" reflects his growing concern with productive power. He hoped to guide the political transition of the Restoration period so that science and industry would triumph over the obsolete theological and feudal powers and establish tranquillity and order.

The Baconian Society's work would result in an Anglo-French union that would be administered by two powers – the temporal and the spiritual. Each country would retain its own temporal government with a legislative council composed of *industriels* and an executive council composed of the wealthiest farmers, manufacturers, merchants, and bankers. The spiritual power would have an executive council of rich men and a legislative council of scientists committed to finding a replacement for Christianity. The scientists' social doctrine would prescribe work useful to society, the acquisition of knowledge, and a strict moral code. They would base public instruction on this social doctrine as well as on positive knowledge, which Saint-Simon now opposed to "metaphysical" knowledge even more directly than before.[116]

Although he tried to placate the rich by giving them control of the executive councils of both the spiritual and temporal realms, Saint-Simon basically embraced the utilitarianism of Say, condemning "talkers" and giving a great deal of control to the "doers," mainly scientists and industrialists.[117] His plan was meant to appeal to the industrialists, bankers, and other men who were trying to acquire a powerful position in the new society that was emerging in

[115] Saint-Simon, *Aux Anglais et aux Français*, 145.
[116] Ibid., 154.   [117] Ibid.

the early Restoration. Champion of the industrial cause, Saint-Simon was providing them with a liberal doctrine that justified their goal of administering society and their hostility to the aristocracy and clergy. His conversation, which was far more logical than his writings, especially charmed and captivated these businessmen as well as the intellectuals, artists, and scientists of the period.[118] For the first time in his life, Saint-Simon was achieving an alliance with a powerful sector of society. As many of them began to back his views financially, he gave them more attention in his writings and grew increasingly enthusiastic about their role in reconstructing society.

Saint-Simon devised a plan whereby liberal bankers, merchants, deputies, scientists, owners of national property, and industrialists would pay him ten thousand francs a month to issue a periodical called *L'Industrie*, which eventually began publication in 1816.[119] Among the approximately 150 subscribers were some of France's most illustrious men: Say; the scientists Cuvier, Berthollet, and Arago; the actor Talma; the peers the Duc de Broglie and the Duc de la Rochefoucauld; the businessmen Ternaux, Perregaux, Ardouin, Hottinguer, and Delessert; the minister of finance, Antoine Roy; the governor of the Bank of France, Jacques Laffitte; and almost twenty-five deputies, including Lafayette and Casimir Périer.[120] Many of these people joined the celebrated painter Arie Scheffer and the famous printer Firmin Didot to spend long evenings with Saint-Simon, who was re-creating the life he had led during the Directory, though on a less extravagant level.[121] Never before had he enjoyed such influence.

In the "Déclaration de principes" of volume 2 of *L'Industrie*, which appeared in May 1817, Saint-Simon argued that industry, which

---

[118] One man who was seduced by Saint-Simon's charm and "exquisite" politeness wrote that the "great master" used to sit for two hours every night at the Café Procope, where he invariably attracted a large group of listeners because "his discourses seemed rational and refuted the opinion that people formed of him in reading his works, whose exaltation went as far as madness." Letter from A. De Vauseine [?] to M. Nichet, November 27, 1830, Fonds Pereire, N.a.fr. 24605, item 83, BN.

[119] Manuel, *Saint-Simon*, 189–92. The first volume was called *L'Industrie littéraire et scientifique liguée avec l'industrie commerciale et manufacturière, ou Opinions sur les finances, la politique, la morale, et la philosophie dans l'intérêt de tous les hommes livrés à des travaux utiles et indépendants.* It was mainly written by his friend, the economist Saint-Aubin, who analyzed banking procedures and public finance. Saint-Simon changed the title of the second volume to *L'Industrie, ou Discussions politiques, morales et philosophiques, dans l'intérêt de tous les hommes livrés à des travaux utiles et indépendants.*

[120] See list in Alfred Pereire, *Autour de Saint-Simon: Documents originaux* (Paris: Honoré Champion, 1912), 4–9; Manuel, *Saint-Simon*, 181; Leroy, *Saint-Simon*, 265–6.

[121] Leroy, *Saint-Simon*, 267.

guaranteed the existence of society, was about to triumph along with its ally, liberalism. For this victory to occur, the productive members of society needed liberty to produce and consume without being hampered by the government, whose power should be limited to protecting them from nobles, clergy, and other idlers. *L'Industrie* sought to associate the *"commercial and manufacturing industry"* with the *"literary and scientific industry"* to achieve this new industrial state.[122] The true heads of this state would be the political writers, because they worked most effectively for the common good. Saint-Simon's conception of the industrial community, which stressed the interdependence of its members, resembled Say's organic, almost vitalistic model of society, in which there was no social conflict. Bonald's vision of an organic society was also not forgotten. In the aftermath of the Revolution, thinkers on both the Left and Right were trying to avoid the dangers of social dissolution and approached society from a biological standpoint instead of the eighteenth-century mechanistic one, which tended to highlight the importance of the individual.[123]

In this second volume of May 1817 also appeared *Lettres de Henri Saint-Simon à un Américain*. Boasting of his own role in the foundation of liberty at the Battle of Yorktown, Saint-Simon argued that unlike the Americans, the French had not been able to construct a liberal regime because of their ignorance of political science, the "science of liberty." They did not realize that true liberty could be developed only by means of industry. Just as he had previously sought a general unifying idea in physics and physiology, he now was certain that the study of political economy would yield the fundamental principle of production needed by the liberals to reorganize politics and society. The production of useful things should be the criterion for judging all political institutions and social affairs. Convinced that the economic structure was inseparable from the political and social system, Saint-Simon was certain that political economy would soon become the basis of political science. The tenet of production would make political science a true positive science, the *"science of production."*[124]

Finally, Saint-Simon called on philosophers, political writers, and others to make the nineteenth century the "industrial century."[125] His emphasis on the triumph of industry in the temporal sphere corresponded to his previous stress on the victory of synthesis in the spiritual realm. But as he himself pointed out in the *Mémoire*, it was

---

[122] Saint-Simon, "Déclaration de principes," 137.   [123] Rosanvallon, *Le Moment Guizot*, 18.
[124] Saint-Simon, *Lettres de Henri Saint-Simon à un Américain*, 188, 213.
[125] Ibid., 214.

time to concentrate on practice instead of theory. Thus he gave the spiritual realm far less attention in this work.

Thierry wrote an article on the development of European civilization toward a more moral, industrial, and liberal order in the May 1817 issue of *L'Industrie*.[126] Although his collaboration with Saint-Simon in creating the liberal doctrine of industrialism seemed fruitful and he was even referred to as the "adoptive son of Henri Saint-Simon," he left his mentor sometime in the first half of 1817 for obscure reasons.[127] It seems clear that Thierry leaned more toward democracy than the aristocratic Saint-Simon, who always seemed to distrust the people despite his so-called love of the common good.[128] Also, Thierry could no longer abide his authoritarianism. According to legend, Saint-Simon told him, "I cannot conceive of any association without the government of someone." Thierry angrily responded, "As for me, I cannot conceive of any association without liberty."[129] An anonymous secretary who worked for Saint-Simon described the philosopher as a very difficult employer. He worked constantly, and if inspired in the middle of the night, he did not hesitate to ring, several times if necessary, for the secretary to write down his ideas. The secretary left a good account of other frustrations of working for Saint-Simon in 1817:

> M. de Saint-Simon had not yet given nor even conceived any particular system of social or even *scientific* organization. . . . Up to this point, he had only presented several aperçus, or raised detached questions; but he had not connected his materials nor elevated the edifice. His plan was not settled; his ideas were so vague, so confused, that it was impossible for him to explain them clearly and to make known what he himself only glimpsed very imperfectly. Also, almost every time that we resumed the work, after he had me read what he had dictated the preceding session, he tore it up or threw it into the fire while telling me to get another piece of paper.

[126] Thierry, "Politique," *L'Industrie*, part 2, in Saint-Simon, *Oeuvres*, 1.2:19–127.

[127] Title page of *L'Industrie*, in Saint-Simon, *Oeuvres*, 1.2:17. See also Rulon Nephi Smithson, *Augustin Thierry: Social and Political Consciousness in the Evolution of a Historical Method* (Geneva: Droz, 1972), 16.

[128] For example, Saint-Simon helped some bourgeois industrialists found the Société de Paris pour l'Instruction Elémentaire based on the Bell and Lancaster concept of "mutual education," which Charles Comte, Say, and Blainville all ardently supported. Though this school was directed primarily at working-class children, Saint-Simon felt the lower class was not yet ready for enlightenment, and he would have preferred that it direct its efforts at children of artisans and the middle class. Manuel, *Saint-Simon*, 182–3. See also Saint-Simon's comment that the liberals learned during the Revolution that the government of "ignorant proletarians" was worse than that of the ancien régime. Saint-Simon, *Lettres de Henri Saint-Simon à un Américain*, 178.

[129] Augustin-Thierry, *Augustin Thierry*, 36.

The secretary further suggested that Saint-Simon's obscure ideas and uncertain principles upset Thierry. Already tormented by his master's "continual insistence" on "his collaboration," Thierry preferred in the end " to leave rather than work at something he could not understand."[130] He would, in fact, go on to become one of the greatest historians of the period.[131] The break was not, however, a bitter or angry one, for Thierry always retained some affection for Saint-Simon.[132]

THE NATURE OF SAINT-SIMON'S THOUGHT IN THE SUMMER OF 1817

When Thierry left Saint-Simon, the philosopher was strikingly bereft of any scientific or social system, for his talent did not lie in formulating a consistent philosophy. At one moment, Socrates was the most eminent thinker in Western civilization; at another, it was Bacon or Descartes. Some of his historical schemes had twelve epochs, others five, and still others three. In one essay, he embraced an a priori method; in the next, he praised an empirical approach. At one time, it was the mathematicians who were the scientific vanguard; at another, it was the physiologists. He admired Newton's law of gravity until Say's political economy became more attractive.

These vacillations suggest, however, that Saint-Simon's genius derived from his impressionable nature. Although Gouhier accuses him of not being original, Saint-Simon excelled at absorbing ideas, which he used inventively.[133] With a sense of living in a new era opened up by the French Revolution, he perceived the need for a radical change in the intellectual, social, and political structures of

---

[130] Unknown secretary of Saint-Simon, "Notice sur Saint-Simon et sa doctrine et sur quelques autres ouvrages qui en seraient le développement," in Pereire, *Autour de Saint-Simon*, 188–90.

[131] On Thierry, see Stanley Mellon, *The Political Uses of History: A Study of Historians in the French Restoration* (Stanford, Calif.: Stanford University Press, 1958), 9–10; Augustin Thierry, Preface to *Dix Ans d'études historiques*, 5th ed. (Paris: 1846), 1–24; Charles Rearick, *Beyond the Enlightenment: Historians and Folklore in Nineteenth-Century France* (Bloomington: Indiana University Press, 1974), 26–7, 81; Carroll, *Historical Thought of Augustin Thierry*, 37, 59; Hayek, *Counter-Revolution*, 125; Gooch, *History and Historians*, 169–73.

[132] Thierry later visited Saint-Simon after his suicide attempt and attended his funeral. Because Comte was also involved in these events and the two men had a common friend, Hachette, it seems probable that they met. It is interesting that the one work by Chateaubriand that Comte included in the Positivist Library was *Les Martyrs* – the book that inspired Thierry to become a historian. Augustin-Thierry, *Augustin Thierry*, 39; Smithson, *Augustin Thierry*, 308; Carroll, *Historical Thought of Augustin Thierry*, 6, 17–18; Picavet, *Les Idéologues*, 484.

[133] Gouhier, *Jeunesse*, 2:331, 334, 348–9, 3:1–3.

Europe. To define the new age, he not only revived the ideas of the seventeenth century (those of Locke, Bacon, Descartes, and Newton) and the theories of the Enlightenment thinkers (especially Condillac, Condorcet, Montesquieu, and the Encyclopedists) but borrowed from his contemporaries (such as Constant, Staël, the Idéologues, Chateaubriand, Bonald, and Say). In many ways, his thought epitomizes the transitional nature of his period.

Saint-Simon sensed that the nineteenth century would be one of reconstruction, whose mission would be to create a new social structure based on industry and a new philosophical system or synthesis. He called this synthesis a "positive system" and a "positive philosophy," but the labels were not particularly significant to him; he did not make them the object of great fanfare. Nor did he methodically describe this philosophy. Nevertheless, from 1802 to 1813, he gave vague indications of its composition. The positive philosophy was a scientific system uniting all knowledge, including that of man and society. It was a science of classification based on the increasing complexity of knowledge. This knowledge had to be scientific in that it had to be established on facts, experiments, observation, reason, and discussion. Banned would be theological ideas, investigations into first causes, and examinations of the origin and end of the universe. Although based on empirical, scientific facts, the positive system was primarily an a priori synthesis founded on one explanatory universal law – Newton's principle of gravitation.

Ultimately, this philosophy was spiritual, as Saint-Simon himself pointed out. Because he held that all religions reflect the reigning philosophy of their time, he called his encyclopedic system a religion. Moreover, he argued that every society was a reflection and application of its intellectual system. As a "community of ideas," every society was therefore religious in nature.[134] Because ideas effect change and religious and scientific transformations led to the social and political turmoil of the French Revolution, a new intellectual structure was needed to replace Catholicism and to create social and political stability. His positive system would be the new religion fulfilling this need. The new society, which would reflect this system, would have to be directed by a new spiritual power consisting of the most enlightened members of society, the scientists. Devoted to progress and the improvement of the human condition, they would create the new general theory that would unite people as Catholicism once did in the Middle Ages. Like the Catholic clergy, they would also control education, the key to intellectual and social progress.

---

[134] Emile Durkheim, "Saint-Simon, fondateur du positivisme et de la sociologie: Extrait d'un cours d'histoire du socialisme." *Revue philosophique* 99 (1925): 322–3.

From the start, Saint-Simon intended to make man and society the object of scientific knowledge. Since man was a part of nature, the human science would have to be similar to the natural sciences.[135] At first, he made the science of man, which included a science of morality and politics, part of physiology. But his physiology seemed to reduce vital phenomena to physical facts. In addition, he insisted that physiology had to become positive before the whole scientific system could become positive. Then, beginning with the *Travail sur la gravitation universelle*, he tended increasingly to equate his science of man with practical politics, which, along with morality, he claimed was the application of his positive system. With the advent of a less repressive regime and the help of Thierry, he turned from physical science to political economy, which then became his science of society. The primary, collective activity of society became the main object of his study. He believed that the new, emerging society would be basically organic, for it would be shaped by industrial relations, which he thought were characterized by interdependence.[136] Economic factors grew more significant in his theory as industry came to dominate his vision of society and he began to consider political regimes irrelevant to community life. The temporal power, which was to be in a state of equilibrium with the spiritual power, was to be held by the industrialists. And the new morality would uphold the industrial system because it would emphasize working productively for the happiness of man on earth.

In sum, Saint-Simon's study of man and society involved an interdisciplinary approach including the physical sciences (especially physics), medicine and biology, anthropology, sensationalist psychology, history, morality, politics, and political economy. The first task of the scientists of society was to study man in an almost animalistic state and then trace his evolution through the centuries.[137] Throughout Saint-Simon's writings, the history of progress had the privileged position in the science of society because it held the key to understanding the direction of intellectual and thus social change.

Saint-Simon's passionate involvement with his own volatile era tended to make him hasty, anxious, and unscientific. The man who called for coherence in ideas as the key to social and political reconstruction was painfully aware that he himself was unable to construct a comprehensible general philosophy. He therefore constantly called for a collaborator. At various times, he appealed to Madame de Staël, Redern, Blainville, Burdin, Napoleon, Thierry, the math-

[135] Durkheim, *Socialism and Saint-Simon*, 98.
[136] Ansart, *Sociologie de Saint-Simon*, 19, 59, 187, 193.   [137] Durkheim, "Saint-Simon," 336.

ematicians, the physiologists, and the publicists. But for one reason or another, they all rejected him either immediately or after a short while. Finally, he came across a young man who was always searching for a mentor – Auguste Comte. Their association would make them both immortal figures in the history of ideas.

Chapter 3

Comte's First Works for Saint-Simon

I worked with Saint-Simon, an excellent man and a man of great merit. . . .
He is over fifty years old; well, I can tell you that I have never known any
young man as ardent or as generous as he: he is an original being in all
respects.

Auguste Comte, 1818

Just before meeting Saint-Simon, Comte was in a "state of full negativity."[1] Condorcet had impressed him, but he was frustrated by the
"inadequacy" of his "great effort" and did not know where to turn.[2]
He had learned the revolutionary discourse of the eighteenth century
but was groping for a way to apply its critique to the new circumstances of the Restoration. Demoralized by his failures during the
past year and intensely critical of material and intellectual conditions
in France, Comte had turned for help largely to thinkers from the
past, like Franklin. He felt, however, the youthful need to venerate
a living figure, one capable of providing more active guidance. Saint-
Simon would satisfy this need but would also make more demands
on his mind and spirit.

It is not clear how they first made contact. One of Comte's friends
or former professors may have introduced them when he noticed
the similarity between their opinions.[3] It is important to realize that,
before meeting Saint-Simon, Comte had already begun to form a
distinct perception of the world that made him a suitable collaborator.[4] Like Saint-Simon, he was tormented by the problem of the
French Revolution, felt betrayed by Napoleon's tyranny, and saw
himself as a liberal philosopher carrying on eighteenth-century traditions, especially in opposition to the regressive Bourbon regime.
In fact, his desire to resolve the crisis afflicting France was probably
one of the main factors that led him to Saint-Simon in the first

[1] Comte to George Frederick Holmes, September 18, 1852, CG, 6:377.
[2] Cours, 2:466.
[3] Lonchampt, Précis, 16; Lonchampt to Laffitte, 11 Charlemagne 100, MAC.
[4] Gouhier, Jeunesse, 3:168–70.

place.[5] They also shared a high regard for the United States, Montesquieu and Condorcet, and the moral and political sciences, particularly political economy. Both had renounced Catholicism in their early teens. Comte's adoption of Franklin's moral code of hard work harmonized with Saint-Simon's stress on productivity and industry. In addition to these political and moral concerns, Comte shared Saint-Simon's enthusiasm for the natural sciences, especially for the new science of physiology, which they had studied at different medical schools. They also embraced the progressive and technological ideals of the Ecole Polytechnique, with which they both had been connected. Moreover, in his letters and his translation of Leslie's work, Comte had revealed an interest in the philosophy of science and in the extension of the scientific method to all areas of knowledge, also subjects of concern to Saint-Simon. Finally, Comte's dedication to education coincided with Saint-Simon's beliefs about the ability of public instruction to effect social change. They even shared personal similarities. Considering themselves individualists and outcasts from the mainstream, they were anxious to forge an identity for themselves in the new age that they saw emerging from the revolutionary turmoil. Presently at the pinnacle of his influence, Saint-Simon was already enjoying his novel role and would soon help his new student create one for himself.

THE PROBLEM OF THE PROSPECTUS OF JUNE 1817

Comte's association with the aging philosopher coincided with the new approach that Saint-Simon was developing in the third volume of *L'Industrie*. On the basis of evidence supplied by the Saint-Simonian bibliographer Henri Fournel, most scholars agree that Comte wrote all four of the *cahiers*, or issues, of volume 3 and the first *cahier* of volume 4, which appeared in September and October 1817 under Saint-Simon's name.[6] Some scholars maintain that Comte also wrote the June circular announcing the new volume.[7] Fournel suggested this

---

[5] Angèle Kremer-Marietti, Introduction to *Comte: Plan des travaux scientifiques nécessaires pour réorganiser la société* (Paris: Aubier, 1970), 15–16.

[6] Henri Fournel, *Bibliographie Saint-Simonienne: De 1802 au 31 décembre 1832* (Paris, 1833), 17. This date is confirmed by Comte's statement in a letter to Valat that he began writing as a publicist for Saint-Simon in August of that year. Comte to Valat, April 17, 1818, *CG*, 1:28.

[7] Pereire, *Autour de Saint-Simon*, 67; Teixeira Mendes, *Auguste Comte*, v–xiii, 88–91; *Ecrits*, 33–41; Paul Arbousse-Bastide, *La Doctrine d'éducation universelle dans la philosophie d'Auguste Comte*, 2 vols. (Paris: Presses Universitaires de France, 1957), 1:9. Gouhier seems skeptical about Comte's authorship of the prospectus of June 1817. See Gouhier, *Jeunesse*, 3:173; idem, *Vie*, 72.

possibility when he stated that Comte wrote the third volume "in totality," which would include the circular.[8] The association of Comte and Saint-Simon does seem to date from late May or early June 1817, although it was not until August that Comte was installed as the official successor of Thierry and paid a salary.[9]

This early date for the beginning of their association is credible because Saint-Simon's orientation suddenly changed in June, when he announced that he had discovered a "new idea," which he was "eager to communicate."[10] The prospectus that he included in the announcement was entitled "Opinion qui sera émise dans le troisième volume de *L'Industrie*." This was the essay probably written by Comte.

Instead of extending the principles of production that had recently preoccupied Saint-Simon, the prospectus reverted to his earlier concerns about the spiritual power. Like the writings he had composed seven to eight years before, such as the *Projet d'encyclopédie, Nouvelle Encyclopédie*, and the *Esquisse d'une nouvelle encyclopédie*, it praised eighteenth-century writers for having come together in a "single philosophical workshop" to compose the *Encyclopédie*, which had successfully attacked the theological system. The "good idea" that the nineteenth century should realize was the need to organize a "system of terrestrial morality."[11] Never before had Saint-Simon gone so far in advocating the eradication of the divine. Recently inspired by the secular moral code of Franklin, Comte probably encouraged this new direction. His youth gave him a certain audacity that Saint-Simon had lost as a result of his various difficulties.

The prospectus also proposed that "writers of all types, from the philosophers themselves to the song writers," work together, supported by the wealthy, first to make their ideas "positive" and then to construct the "*encyclopedia of positive ideas*."[12] In his works written during the Empire, Saint-Simon had frequently referred to the need for a new positive encyclopedia and subsidies for thinkers, but the odd allusion to "song writers" seems to derive from Comte, whose enthusiasm for music had been inspired by Ernestine de Goy and Pauline.

Moreover, whereas Saint-Simon previously had been wary about

[8] Fournel, *Bibliographie Saint-Simonienne*, 17.

[9] Arbousse-Bastide, *Doctrine d'éducation*, 1:9. In a letter to Valat on May 15, 1818, Comte said that he abandoned his bad political direction "hardly a year ago." Also, on June 15, 1818, Comte wrote that it was "barely more than one year ago" that he had abandoned his absolute ideas. Comte to Valat, May 15, June 15, 1818, *CG*, 1:37, 42; Teixeira Mendes, *Auguste Comte*, xii.

[10] See the original *Lettre de Henri Saint-Simon à Messieurs les Publicistes*, a short pamphlet available in the Maison d'Auguste Comte; see also Saint-Simon, *Oeuvres*, 1.2:214. The copy of this prospectus in the *Ecrits de jeunesse* is incomplete. *Ecrits*, 39–41.

[11] *Ecrits*, 40.   [12] Ibid.

teaching non-Christian moral beliefs, here he seemed urged by an impatient Comte to recommend imposing a single *secular* moral code upon children because the "similarity of positive moral ideas" was the "sole bond" that could unite members of society and improving "positive morality" was equivalent to improving the "social state."[13] In keeping with his studies of the United States, Franklin, and Montesquieu, Comte reaffirmed Saint-Simon's belief that society was characterized by its moral spirit, the element that kept people together. Thus as early as 1817, Comte maintained that the renovation of morality was the way to effect social change even if at the expense of liberty of conscience.

At the end, the prospectus announced that the next volume of *L'Industrie* would demonstrate the necessity of first reorganizing the intellectual system before a "truly positive, industrial, and liberal regime" could be established.[14] Comte's influence is evident from the fact that Saint-Simon was not only reverting to his old idea that theory should precede practice but abandoning all references to the unity of knowledge based on one principle.[15]

The sudden change in emphasis in the prospectus raised an outcry among many journalists who did not care for Saint-Simon's proposal for a new atheistic morality. One writer for *Le Constitutionnel* derided Saint-Simon's relativism and reminded him that God was the "only truly positive idea."[16] He found the notion of creating a *"morality of the nineteenth century"* to be as shocking as that of devising a *"geometry of the nineteenth century."*[17] In the *Journal des débats*, another journalist was even more sarcastic about Saint-Simon's discovery:

> Previously, he had Charlemagne appear, descending from Heaven to speak. . . . At that time M. de Saint-Simon had the pretension . . . of being from a rather good family; but now he no longer wants anything to do with nobles or with kings or especially with Heaven.[18]

COMTE'S ARTICLES IN *L'INDUSTRIE*:
THE GERMS OF THE POSITIVE SYSTEM

In the third volume of *L'Industrie*, Comte further developed Saint-Simon's philosophical and moral ideas and then connected them

---

[13] Ibid., 40n1.   [14] Ibid., 41.   [15] Gouhier, *Jeunesse*, 3:159.

[16] "B," Review of *L'Industrie*, vol. 2, *Le Constitutionnel*, June 24, 1817, 3–4. "B" stands for Benaben. See Saint-Simon, *Oeuvres*, 1.2:223.

[17] Benaben, Letter, *Le Constitutionnel*, July 2, 1817, quoted in Saint-Simon, *Oeuvres*, 1.2:222–3.

[18] "Z," "France," *Journal des débats*, June 7, 1817, 4.

with his master's recent writings on political economy. He was, in effect, constructing a kind of synthesis of his employer's thought. He assimilated Saint-Simon's ideas about the *Encyclopédie* as a model of knowledge, the destructive mission of the eighteenth century and the constructive task of the nineteenth century, the dominant role of industry in the new society and its responsibility to aid philosophers financially, the need to render all ideas positive and to devise a new intellectual system, and finally the importance of replacing theology with a new morality marked by common sense. Yet unlike Saint-Simon's treatment of these ideas, Comte's work was notable for its clarity, precision, and systematization.

The first article of the first *cahier* was entitled "Programme d'un concours pour une nouvelle encyclopédie."[19] Expanding the idea mentioned in the June prospectus, Comte stated that the intellectual and moral system that had been dominant for 2,200 years was obsolete and had to be replaced by a new system before social reconstruction could take place: "Today, for the first time since the existence of societies, it is a question of organizing a totally new system; of replacing the celestial by the terrestrial, the vague by the positive, and the poetic by the real."[20] This emphasis on the "terrestrial" and "real" and on beginning anew would be the essence of positivism.

Here Comte fully endorsed the idealist and Baconian creed so dominant in Saint-Simon's early works: theory must precede practice. Thinking like an engineer, Comte insisted that one must have a conception, that is, a blueprint, of the type of social system that was needed before building it. Yet at the same time, he warned against pure rationalism because he felt that one's conception had to be formed with the help of experience as well as reason. This distrust both of pure empiricism and of pure rationalism would recur throughout Comte's writings and echoed Saint-Simon's call to combine a priori and a posteriori ideas.

Following Condorcet and Saint-Simon, Comte maintained that observing human experiences in the past was the way to approach the reorganization of the future. The belief that one had to study history to understand the future and to grasp what action was needed in the present to prepare for it would appear in all of Comte's writings. He wanted to be sure his plans for social reforms, unlike those of the revolutionaries, were timely and thus likely to succeed. History would be the basis of sociology.

Comte selected two periods of transition, each of which resulted in a monumental intellectual transformation effected by a group of

[19] "Programme d'un concours pour une nouvelle encyclopédie," *Ecrits*, 43–9.
[20] Ibid., 47.

"enlightened men" working together on a philosophical synthesis. In the first period, Socrates challenged the old system of polytheism and promoted theism, which finally triumphed with the Bible. The second period, from Bacon to Diderot, witnessed attacks on the old theistic system, that is, theology, which culminated in another work of synthesis, the *Encyclopédie*. Like Saint-Simon, Comte criticized the eighteenth-century philosophes for being too destructive, yet praised them for having laid the groundwork for the organization of a new intellectual system: the "positive system."[21] He also believed that the nineteenth century had to be an age of organization in which scientists would work together to create another encyclopedia and thus complete Bacon's project. This work would represent a third philosophical synthesis, unifying the general ideas of all the sciences, that is, the "positive truths" that already existed.[22] Without such a common philosophy connecting them, these truths could not effectively combat theology. This encyclopedic philosophy was, in fact, Saint-Simon's positive system, the "general metaphysics" announced in *A la Société du Lycée* and developed in the *Introduction aux travaux scientifiques*. Furthermore, Comte adopted Saint-Simon's argument that the science of society had to be incorporated into the system of positive sciences; the encyclopedia needed a new system of moral and political ideas for the emergent industrial society.[23] Thus Comte was already interested in the battle between theology and positive philosophy, considered the antitheological phase a transitional period, and foresaw the advent of a third historical period. Yet at this point, his three main stages of history were polytheistic, theological, and positive.

Remembering perhaps Encontre's stress on the importance of general knowledge, Comte was concerned that contemporary scientists were incapable of working together. During the Empire, Saint-Simon had also referred to the indifference of scientists to general ideas.[24] In his *Mémoire sur la science de l'homme*, he had attacked the mathematicians – "these sad calculators, enclosed behind a rampart of X and Z" – for their neglect of the study of man, which alone could reconcile human interests.[25] In much the same fashion, Comte took the scientists to task for lacking a common general philosophy and immersing themselves so completely in their specialties that they could not converse with scholars outside their own field.[26] The

---

[21] *Ecrits*, 45. See also Saint-Simon, *Introduction aux travaux scientifiques*, 100–5.
[22] *Ecrits*, 45.
[23] Steven Lukes, "Saint-Simon," in *The Founding Fathers of Social Science*, ed. Timothy Raison (Harmondsworth: Penguin Books, 1969), 31.
[24] Saint-Simon, *Projet d'encyclopédie*, 282–85.
[25] Saint-Simon, *Mémoire sur la science de l'homme*, 39.   [26] *Ecrits*, 45.

Academy of Sciences was especially delinquent. The idea that all the scientists could be united once their common scientific principles were systematized held the germ of the positive philosophy.

It is important to realize that Comte was repelled by scientific specialization even before he had his own problems with the Academy of Sciences. In other works written around this time, he frequently ridiculed scientists, especially mathematicians, whom he accused of cowardice, egoism, and coldness.[27] His later difficulties with scientists only intensified his distaste for their narrowness and reinforced his belief in the necessity of establishing a philosophy of the sciences. Thus from the beginning, he tended to equate scientific specialization with moral egoism and general philosophy with strong social feelings.[28]

Furthermore, he argued that once scientists had a philosophy and organized an association, they would wrest control of education from the decadent theological system. Echoing Saint-Simon's idea, expressed in the *Mémoire sur la science de l'homme*, that positive philosophy must be taught in schools, Comte was already linking the reorganization of the intellectual system with a revolution in education.

Reflecting Saint-Simon's naive tendency to resolve intellectual questions by means of a contest, Comte tried to persuade scientists to compete to make the best encyclopedia. Scholars, he said, would be motivated partly by their desire for glory and monetary rewards and partly by their "love of Humanity." Equally "passionate about the good of Humanity," many of the producers would establish a general prize because of their interest in the industrial regime that would emerge from the positive synthesis.[29] This idea of industrial support for scientific thinkers foreshadowed the positivist subsidy of the 1840s and dated back to Saint-Simon's *Lettres d'un habitant de Genève à ses contemporains*, which proposed setting up a fund to support the "Elect of Humanity." Comte's references to the well-being and love of humanity would be later central to his philosophy. Such expressions had been employed by Saint-Simon.[30] It is doubtful, however, that Saint-Simon introduced the idea to him, for allusions

---

[27] Comte, "Lettre à M. H. Saint-Simon par une personne qui se nommera plus tard," *Ecrits*, 440.

[28] Antimo Negri, *Augusto Comte et l'umanesimo positivistico* (Rome: Armando, 1971), 37; Maurice Boudot, "De l'usurpation géométrique," *Revue philosophique de la France et de l'étranger*, no. 4 (October–December 1985): 391–2, 399–402.

[29] *Ecrits*, 48, 49.

[30] Saint-Simon had, for example, referred to the "love of humanity" as at least as powerful a stimulus of human action as "personal interest." Saint-Simon, *Lettres d'un habitant de Genève*, 14.

to humanity were frequent at that time, appearing throughout the writings of the philosophes, the revolutionaries, and Condorcet. In fact, before meeting Saint-Simon, Comte had already used the term "Humanity" in his letters[31] and in the title of his essay of 1816.

In sum, the first article that Comte wrote for *L'Industrie* brought together many themes that Saint-Simon had vaguely mentioned before and that Comte was in the process of adopting. At nineteen, he was already defining his lifework, although he did not yet see that he alone would have to devote his energies to constructing a new encyclopedic philosophy and a new moral and political system. The germs of positivism and sociology were definitely planted in his mind.

Resembling the trend of Saint-Simon's own intellectual development, Comte's eight other articles in the third and fourth volumes became increasingly practical and focused on contemporary problems.[32] Impatient with pure theorizing, he praised primitive man's interest in the "concrete." Man's faculty of abstraction, he said, only increased his egotism and his disdain for the material, natural world:

> It is time today to take a more reasonable course, to admire, to esteem, [and] to pay for only what is useful, that which can contribute to the well-being of the individual and the species. Let us leave the beautiful; let us seek the good, let us return to nature, never to leave it again. May the faculty of abstraction be employed only to facilitate the combination of concrete ideas; in short, may it no longer be the abstract which dominates, but the positive.[33]

This passage shows that, for Comte, the positive represented not only the terrestrial and the real, but also the useful and the concrete. This interest in the primitive and a return to nature reflects the continuity of Enlightenment thought and his earlier admiration for

---

[31] Comte to Valat, January 2, 1815, and October 29, 1816, *CG*, 1:8, 15.

[32] The other three articles in the first *cahier* of the third volume of *L'Industrie* are "Programme d'un concours pour un plan général des finances," *Ecrits*, 49–54; "Programme d'un travail sur les rapports des sciences théoriques avec les sciences d'application," *Ecrits*, 55–61; and "Entreprise des Intérêts Généraux de l'Industrie, ou Société de l'Opinion Industrielle," *Ecrits*, 62–8. The article in the second *cahier* is "Premier aperçu d'un travail sur le gouvernement parlementaire, considéré comme régime transitoire," *Ecrits*, 68–74. The article in the third *cahier* is "Programme d'un travail sur le gouvernement parlementaire," *Ecrits*, 74–84. The article in the fourth *cahier* is "Considérations à l'appui des idées présentées dans les article précédents," *Ecrits*, 84–96. The first *cahier* of the fourth volume of *L'Industrie*, which was published in October 1817, contains two articles by Comte, entitled "Comparison entre l'état politique de l'industrie en France et l'état politique de l'industrie en Angleterre," *Ecrits*, 97–107. Because the *Ecrits* does not clearly show the placement of the articles in the various *cahiers*, it is useful to consult the original issues of *L'Industrie*, which can be found in Réserve R 1529, BN.

[33] *Ecrits*, 61.

Rousseau.[34] It would blossom at the end of his life, when he empha-sized that positivism would mark a return to fetishism.

When he referred to utility, the concrete, the "science of the happiness of men," the importance of experts, and a future "era of felicity," Comte showed his awareness of utilitarianism.[35] In fact, in the last article for volume 3 of *L'Industrie*, he commended Jeremy Bentham's recently published *Plan of Parliamentary Reform in the Form of a Catechism*.[36] Acknowledging that utilitarianism was similar to his own philosophy, especially because of its support of the positive method, he suggested, nevertheless, that he had not become a pro-ponent of the movement, because Bentham had misunderstood this method. Yet he still found Bentham's doctrine to be the "most eminent derivation of what one calls political economy" and an ex-cellent preparation for his science of society.[37]

Throughout the volume, one of the main themes of Saint-Simon and Comte was that of social cooperation, which they considered the concomitant of intellectual progress. The "progress of the hu-man mind" made people see the importance of uniting their inter-ests. Moreover, reflecting Say's and Saint-Simon's program of industrialism, Comte argued that social consensus could take place only in an industrial age when the two classes that represented "all the real forces of society" – the scientists and the *industriels* – ended their rivalry and came together to work for an identical goal, the "production of useful things." Although the two classes had different capacities, they should support each other, working to increase the dominance of industry and thus the happiness of society. The theor-etical class, that is, the scientists, should enlighten the practical class, that is, the men involved in industry, especially because theory without practice led only to empty, useless abstractions. The *industriels* had to subsidize the scientists, for practice without theory consisted solely of "blind routine."[38] Always searching for a middle way, Comte disliked pure theory and pure practice as much as he did pure rationalism and pure empiricism. He insisted that knowledge be useful and productive, enhance human power over nature, and improve the material aspect of social existence – an indication of the

[34] See Comte's praise of Rousseau for insisting that a mother breast-feed her child. Comte to Valat, June 15, 1818, *CG*, 1:44.

[35] *Ecrits*, 73. See also Taylor, Introduction to *Henri Saint-Simon*, 37.

[36] Comte approved of the reforms proposed by Bentham in this book to make the House of Commons more representative. *Ecrits*, 84, 86–7; Jeremy Bentham, *Plan of Parliamentary Reform*, in *The Works of Jeremy Bentham*, ed. John Bowring, 11 vols. (Edinburgh, 1843), 5:435–552.

[37] Comte to John Stuart Mill, November 20, 1841, *CG*, 2:22. In the *Cours*, Comte called utilitarians the "most advanced portion of the revolutionary school in England." *Cours*, 2:445.

[38] *Ecrits*, 56, 57, 60.

impact of Bacon, Say, and the political economists on his development.[39] At one point, he went so far as to imply that scientists were
inferior to producers because they merely discovered the natural
laws, which the producers applied to create objects. Comte wanted
to emphasize the point that scientists and producers needed each
other and were united by the goal of production.

In discussing the need for social cooperation, Comte extended
the critique of political economy that Saint-Simon had begun in a
far more confused manner in volume 2 of *L'Industrie*. Since the
departure of Thierry, Saint-Simon's faith in liberalism and political
economy had diminished. Whether Comte encouraged Saint-Simon's
disillusionment or whether, on the contrary, Saint-Simon's disenchantment influenced Comte is not clear.[40] In any case, Comte
maintained that political economy adequately explained the mech-
anisms of production, especially the division of labor, but erred in
being exclusively descriptive and empirical; it was a "science of facts
without an end."[41] His criticism reflects the fact that Say, unlike
Adam Smith, did not connect his principles to a larger theory of
government. In the *Traité d'économie politique*, Say had written that
political economy must limit itself to teaching "how wealth is formed,
distributed, and consumed" and must not be concerned about organizing society as politics was.[42] This attitude struck Comte as too timid
and passive. In their efforts to avoid challenging the government,
political economists seemed interested in increasing production only
to help the governing classes make more money. Thus they failed to
present any goals or reforms that would help society as a whole and
did not even show how to produce the best goods at the lowest
cost. Comte's criticism of political economy for being indifferent to
questions of justice was leading him to a deeper understanding of
the essence of social science.

His approach to social science was now ambiguous. He wanted
politics to be a science, but he seemed ambivalent about the objective, value-free model that this adoption of the scientific method
entailed. Although this neutralism was part of the definition of the
scientific spirit, he wanted social science to be normative.[43] It had to

---

[39] Benjamin Farrington, *Francis Bacon: Philosopher of Industrial Science* (New York: Henry
Schuman, 1949), 3, 45; Kremer-Marietti, *Le Concept*, 53.

[40] Bénichou, *Temps des prophètes*, 261; Ansart, *Sociologie de Saint-Simon*, 12–13, 22.

[41] *Ecrits*, 51. See also Rosanvallon, *Le Moment Guizot*, 15.

[42] Say, *Traité d'économie politique*, 1:vii.

[43] Pierre Arnaud shows that Comte did not completely abandon political economy until
lesson 47 of the *Cours*, written in 1839. Arnaud, *Le "Nouveau Dieu,"* 19–30. See also Angèle
Kremer-Marietti, "L'Accomplissement du positivisme: A propos de la thèse de P. Arnaud,"
Les Etudes philosophiques, no. 3 (July–September 1974): 395–403.

fulfill the moral aim of the radical revolutionaries, that of improving the welfare of humanity. In particular, it had to favor work, punish laziness, and honor production. In this way, it would extend the aspect of the new doctrine of industrialism that seemed to stress moral rejuvenation through social cooperation.

Although critical of the science that he had once embraced enthu-siastically, Comte still believed political economy held the key to establishing the science of society because it recognized the new predominance of the economic element in modern human existence. Like Say and Saint-Simon, Comte asserted that "in our language *society, industrial society,* [and] *industry* are exactly synonymous words." Reflecting the fact that the Revolution had devalued the nobility and clergy, Comte asserted that anyone not involved in industrial or scientific production was the "enemy" of society.[44] Thus political economy, which dealt with industrial issues, could alone ensure human happiness. It needed simply to be refounded on "more vast, more daring, and more general views." Comte endorsed economic principles of production that could benefit all classes and lead to greater social harmony and tranquillity. Revealing the influence of Say, who first discussed the important role of the "entrepreneur" in modern industrial society, Comte asserted that "the great entrepre-neurs of industry" should produce cheap necessities rather than luxury items to improve the "people's lot" and increase their own profits.[45] Protective tariffs should be eliminated to ease the tensions in inter-national relations.

Like Saint-Simon, Comte maintained that the goal of politics must be to prevent interference in production. The state itself should not intervene excessively in the economy. Although this distrust of the government indicates that he was still a liberal, Comte seemed to reproach liberalism for its passivity and social indifference. Implicit in his articles was a criticism of the "great capitalists" for not making the people's interests – their material comfort and their happiness – paramount.[46] His proposal for a financial plan demonstrated his skepticism of the liberals' faith in laissez-faire and the "natural or-der." He wanted some economic organization but did not think it should come from the state.

Comte was no more blind to the faults of liberalism than he was to those of political economy.[47] He worried that at least at their

[44] *Ecrits,* 62. See also Arnaud, *Le "Nouveau Dieu,"* 31–6; Sewell, *Work and Revolution,* 145.
[45] *Ecrits,* 51, 53.   [46] Ibid., 52–3.
[47] Roger Mauduit errs when he claims that Comte's reading of the theocrats caused him to become critical of liberalism and political economy later, around 1820. Roger Mauduit, *Auguste Comte et la science économique* (Paris: Félix Alcan, 1929), 15, 22, 27, 186–7; Kremer-Marietti, *Le Concept,* 48, 52, 58.

present stage of development in France, liberalism and political economy were not sufficiently aware of the "community of interest." So far, the French "did not yet know how to connect closely enough the interest of the individual with the interest of everyone." Comte's preoccupation with this dilemma would grow, especially as industrialization came increasingly to aggravate economic and social problems. Eventually, creating this connection would become central to the positivist mission. Already in 1817 he believed the key to this connection was philosophy, whose "most important effect" was "to change struggle into coalition."[48] Comte's positive system privileged the social from the very beginning in that it emphasized the importance of making individuals think about and work for the good of the whole society instead of themselves.[49]

Comte was concerned about the way the reactionary government was dominating the producing classes. He believed they needed to assert themselves, first by deciding what their own general interests were and then shaping public opinion so that it favored industry.[50] He had been taught very well by Saint-Simon, who in his *De la réorganisation de la société européenne* had declared that publicists (journalists and political writers) held the key to nineteenth-century reconstruction because they ruled opinion, which reigned over the world. As Keith Baker has shown, the term "public opinion" emerged in the late eighteenth century as a "central rhetorical figure in a new kind of politics" and a "new source of authority."[51] And although Comte himself was trying to mold public opinion, he wrote paradoxically that he would submit himself "entirely to its empire" because with the disappearance of absolute standards, it was the only judge of the "truth" of political theory.[52] It was, Baker pointed out, the "supreme tribunal" to which all thinkers felt obliged to appeal in a period when other sources of legitimation were lacking.[53]

In seeking to legitimize his theories by referring to the opinion of the people, Comte would also try to show throughout his writings that his scientific theories accorded perfectly with common sense.[54] His assumption that the positive or scientific spirit was simply the

[48] *Ecrits*, 57, 100.   [49] Kremer-Marietti, *Le Concept*, 43.

[50] Comte encouraged the *industriels* to join the Société de l'Opinion Industrielle, whose members already included Lafayette, Guillaume Louis Ternaux, Gabriel Delessert, Jean Antoine Chaptal (fils), J. J. Bérard, A. Ardouin, the Périer brothers, the Duc de Broglie, and the Duc de la Rochefoucauld. *Ecrits*, 66.

[51] Keith Michael Baker, *Inventing the French Revolution: Essays on French Political Culture in the Eighteenth Century* (Cambridge: Cambridge University Press, 1990), 168; see also 116.

[52] *Ecrits*, 64.   [53] Baker, *Inventing the French Revolution*, 168.

[54] In the prospectus announcing the third volume of *L'Industrie*, Comte had also alluded to imprinting each moral idea with the "seal of common sense," which would replace the stamp of theology. *Ecrits*, 40.

extension of common sense – the "prolongation of universal reason and experience" – derived from the Cartesian tradition, which exerted a strong influence on him.[55] More specifically, it reflected his intense interest in the concrete that came from his engineering education with its dislike of the obscure and its emphasis on utility. He always wanted to demystify the thought process by seeking the tangible point of departure – the immediate or common experience – that was at the source of all abstractions. In this way, he hoped to demonstrate that the positive spirit was ultimately the normal state of the human mind. The scientific mind-set could therefore become that of every person.[56]

When he turned his attention to contemporary political problems, Comte demonstrated his belief in relativism. He maintained that because public opinion was being molded in favor of the positive regime, moderation was advisable:

> It is no longer a question of expounding interminably in order to know what is the best government; speaking in an absolute sense, there is nothing good, there is nothing bad; the only absolute is that everything is relative; everything is relative especially when social institutions are concerned.[57]

Comte was proud of the boldness of this statement.[58] However, he did not understand the ramifications of relativism; his own faith in progress subsumed a belief in certain standards of judgment, which demanded the improvement of the human condition. He clearly sought in relativism the attributes of absolutism.[59]

Comte had a deterministic and optimistic picture of the regime of the future. In his view, progress was leading from the absolute monarchy of the old system to the free, representative government of the positive regime. All efforts would then be directed at social improvement and at realizing the Declaration of the Rights of Man, which caused chaos during the French Revolution only because it appeared prematurely. Despite his espousal of relativism, Comte had no doubt that this positive, "purely liberal" regime would be absolutely the best.[60]

Comte's plea for relativism was part of his argument for political moderation. Although driven by ennui, people should seek to

---

[55] *Cours,* 1:523.

[56] Serres, ed., in *Cours,* 1:523n7; Pierre Arnaud, *Pour connaître la pensée de A. Comte* (Paris: Bordas, 1969), 58; Pierre Ducassé, *Méthode et intuition chez Auguste Comte* (Paris: Félix Alcan, 1939), 28–42; Kremer-Marietti, *Le Concept,* 17.

[57] *Ecrits,* 71.   [58] *Système,* vol. 4, "Appendice," ii.

[59] Jean Delvolvé, *Réflexions sur la pensée Comtienne* (Paris, Félix Alcan, 1932), 58.

[60] *Ecrits,* 76.

establish only what was appropriate for their period. They should remember that what might seem suitable for one era was not necessarily good for another and that progress was always slow: "The human spirit does not make sudden leaps." Comte no longer discussed immediate radical change and the need to do away with the Charter as he did in 1816. Instead, he recommended that people confine themselves to creating the transitional period that would lead to a new era. The most that could be done at the moment was to improve and spread to other countries the current parliamentary government, which was admittedly imperfect but could, nevertheless, "guarantee liberty" and put an end to arbitrary measures.[61] It was the best government for the transitional period because it combined and therefore linked the two opposite regimes of the past and future: the old monarchical order and the new representative system. Comte's idea that a transitional period was characterized by the blend of the old and the new, which were completely contrary, would be a leading principle of the law of three stages.

According to Comte, the political party that was most appropriate for the transitional period and thus the least impractical was the moderate, pro-Charter party of the center. This was the liberal "Constitutional" party backed by the doctrinaires Royer-Collard, Guizot, and the Duc de Broglie. (The last-named had contributed to *L'Industrie*.) Yet Comte's support for it was halfhearted. He accused it of inertia, weakness, and "deadly prudence." He also condemned the theocrats on the Right, the ultras, who foolishly attempted to establish order by rebuilding the past and ignoring progress. To him, there was no question that the old philosophy of theism, the foundation of the monarchical system, had been almost destroyed and that it was time to improve life on earth. "Heaven no longer monopolizes all our thoughts, the ministers of heaven are no longer our arbiters in all things nor our masters; [and] work is no longer considered an original sin to which the mass of men are condemned for the glory of God."[62] Yet he also criticized the disparate group of liberals on the Left, despite the fact that he had been directly or indirectly influenced by men connected with it – Benjamin Constant, Charles Comte, Dunoyer, Say, and Destutt de Tracy. The leaders of this party, Casimir Périer, Gabriel Delessert, Jacques Laffitte, and Lafayette, had also contributed to *L'Industrie*. Nevertheless, Comte argued that they were trying to eliminate the monarchy and create a completely representative system too quickly, without first creating a clear principle of liberty. Their desire for limitless freedom was making them repeat the errors of 1789. Here

---

[61] Ibid., 69, 74, 85.   [62] Ibid., 66, 77–9.

Comte seemed to have been influenced by what Saint-Simon had said in *Lettres de Henri Saint-Simon à un Américain:* "Love of liberty did not suffice for a people to be free; they need above all the science of liberty."[63]

What emerges most clearly in Comte's discussion of contemporary politics is his disdain for political change and all political parties, which remained constant throughout his life. He was deeply affected by the political apathy that afflicted his contemporaries, who had been numbed by the constant changes during the revolutionary period. He was already looking beyond politics for a way to unify society. His attitude indicates the extent to which social questions were displacing political matters in postrevolutionary discourse.

To Comte, the main advantage of the mixed government was that it allowed people to devote themselves freely to the more crucial "preliminary" work, that of organizing a new philosophical system for a new society.[64] Much like Saint-Simon, who in his writings during the Empire had pointed out that "general politics" was "nothing other than the principal philosophy," Comte argued that politics was only an application of philosophy, that is, the "science of general ideas and their influence."[65] He thus reiterated Saint-Simon's view that a philosophical revolution, which changed people's opinions, was most crucial and had to precede the political revolution. "Every social regime is founded on a philosophical system. . . . The new regime cannot be established until a new system of moral and political ideas has been conceived, produced, and adopted." A liberal regime required a clear "philosophy of liberty" founded on positive grounds.[66]

In sum, Comte believed that a united and liberal society had to be based on a unified, "homogeneous," common philosophical system, which he significantly called a "universal faith."[67] He did not understand that a liberal society was characterized by conflicts and differences of opinion. To him, as to Benjamin Constant, liberty was the absence of arbitrary measures.[68] But Constant went further, defining liberty as the "triumph of individuality."[69] Although attached to his own independence, Comte did not concentrate on this aspect of liberty, the development of the individual. He did not often refer to the concept of individual rights or dwell on the individual's ability to attain happiness and personal fulfillment. He did not embrace

[63] Saint-Simon, *Lettres de Henri Saint-Simon à un Américain*, 213.   [64] *Ecrits*, 72.

[65] Saint-Simon, *Projet d'encyclopédie*, 310; *Ecrits*, 77.   [66] *Ecrits*, 72, 78.

[67] Ibid., 78, 80.

[68] Constant denounced the "arbitrary" throughout *De l'esprit de conquête*. See Constant, *Oeuvres*, 1058–77.

[69] Benjamin Constant, *Mélanges de littérature et de politique* (Paris, 1829), vi.

pluralism, as Constant did. Comte's attitude toward liberalism was thus ambivalent at the beginning of his career. He wanted the positive regime to be liberal in that it should be loyal to the ideals of the French Revolution and critical of the ancien régime, Terror, and Napoleon. It should eliminate privileges of birth and wealth, severely limit state intervention and the role of the Church, allow for freedom of expression, promote progress and an industrial society, and encourage entrepreneurs. But he already feared a free market economy and a society of bickering, self-interested individuals. He doubted whether an autoregulated economy could solve social problems. And he did not share many of the liberals' faith in political reforms and constitution making as a way of regenerating society.

One reason Comte's liberalism was confused was that, during the Restoration, French liberalism itself was confused. Up to this point, it had been a politics of opposition. With the installation of a parliamentary monarchy, it was only beginning to create its own culture. It still lacked intellectual coherence. Rejecting bourgeois economic liberalism, Comte, in effect, believed that a true "liberal" regime was one that aimed at improving the welfare of the people instead of defending the interests of the most powerful members of society, With his concern for social justice and the importance of a unified society, Comte seemed to reflect the fact that the French radical (or Jacobin) tradition was less committed to the rights of the individual than was the English democratic one.[70]

Extending the argument of his essay of 1816, Comte was sure that future calamities could be avoided and a new philosophy formulated now that people understood more clearly how to proceed in a transitional period: "Being conscious of our condition, we are conscious of what it is appropriate for us to do."[71] Thus like Marx, Comte thought that people's increasing consciousness allowed them to have some influence on their social development.[72] Yet whereas Marx stressed the complex role of labor, alienation, and revolutionary *praxis* in the creation of human consciousness, Comte simply looked to the study of history as the instrument for increasing this consciousness.

Comte asserted that the new philosophical system that would replace theism would consist chiefly of morality, that is, the "knowledge of the rules that must preside over the relations between the

---

[70] *Ecrits*, 470–1; Bénichou, *Temps des prophètes*, 15; Rosanvallon, *Le Moment Guizot*, 25; Albert S. Lindemann, *A History of European Socialism* (New Haven, Conn.: Yale University Press, 1983), 33.

[71] *Ecrits*, 90.

[72] Shlomo Avineri, *The Social and Political Thought of Karl Marx* (Cambridge: Cambridge University Press, 1968), 68, 78, 148.

individual and the society so that the one and the other are as happy as possible." He believed with Bonald and Saint-Simon that the origins of morality and society were inseparable, because there had to be "common moral ideas" for society to exist.[73] Insisting on the moral aspect of social development, Comte, moreover, repudiated social contract theory with its stress on utility as the source of human association. This stance reflects the fact that he had entered a new discursive world. According to William Sewell, nineteenth-century thinkers on both the Left and the Right no longer considered society a "contract arrived at by a collection of individual wills, but a *sui generis* and determinative object with its own suprapersonal laws."[74] Society was a far more complex entity than a political association of individuals who combined their efforts out of self-interest.

To Comte, politics was the second part of social science, but it corresponded to and derived from the first part, morality. The science of politics was, in effect, the science of universal moral rules. Both morality and politics were relative and in a stage of transition, but because morality was the basis of politics, it had to be restructured first, before political reform could be attempted. Thus morality was at the center of Comte's reconstructive plans.

Modifying Saint-Simon's ideas, especially those regarding historical development based on religious change, Comte wrote that Christianity had once performed a valuable service. Unlike Greek morality, it was able to unite more peoples into a larger society "by the belief in a single God and by the dogma of universal fraternity." But he criticized it for remaining stagnant and creating unscientific and supernatural ideas. It neglected present life, condemned work as sinful, made priests too dominant, failed to create international fraternity, terrorized people with visions of hell, and treated them like children with promises of heavenly rewards. Christian morality also had political liabilities, for it failed to make the government serve the governed.

In sum, Comte called for the reformation of contemporary morality to make it "terrestrial" and positive: "The era of positive ideas is beginning: one cannot give to morality any other motives except those that involve palpable, certain, and present interests." Morality, like politics and, in fact, all ideas, had to be based on the principles of industry, especially production, in order to fulfill its goal of ensuring the "greatest possible happiness of the human species."[75]

---

[73] *Ecrits*, 78, 91, 92.

[74] William H. Sewell, Jr., "Beyond 1793: Babeuf, Louis Blanc and the Genealogy of 'Social Revolution,'" in *The Transformation of Political Culture*, ed. Furet and Ozouf, 520.

[75] *Ecrits*, 93–4.

The lessons of Bentham, political economists (especially Say), and Saint-Simon were not lost on the young Comte, who sought to improve upon the program of the revolutionaries.

Reflecting the fact that current political discourse had adopted a historicized terminology, one that respected evolution, Comte argued that changing morality should be as gradual as transforming the political structure.[76] To replace Christian institutions immediately with new ones corresponding to the new moral system would be premature and indeed impossible. The efforts to destroy Christian institutions during the Revolution were as disastrous as the attempts to eliminate the monarchy. Just as the philosophy of liberty had to be completed first, so the science of morality had to be established before institutional change could be effected.

In the meantime, the clergy, like the monarchy, could be improved. Comte recommended that priests be compelled by law to pass an examination verifying their knowledge of the positive sciences – mathematics, physics, chemistry, and physiology. Instead of remaining "idiots," they would "almost" become philosophers.[77] Because moral education was inseparable from scientific instruction, the priests' students would then learn not only the positive sciences but also positive morality. Establishing the scientific, that is, positive, foundation for moral ideas was important so that society would have as much confidence in moral educators as it already had in scientists. Comte's conviction that a teacher of morality must have a scientific background would lead him later to write the *Cours de philosophie positive*. Moreover, for Comte, as for Saint-Simon, education was crucial during the transitional period, because by introducing people to the positive sciences, morality, and politics, it made the passage to the new regime less painful and more peaceful. Education was the key to the transition from theory to practice.[78]

COMTE'S ASSIMILATION OF SAINT-SIMON'S IDEAS

The articles that Comte wrote for *L'Industrie* are significant in that they reflect the way he was absorbing the main outlines of Saint-Simon's philosophy. Because of his education, his recent studies of the United States and the philosophes, and current political and social discourse, many of the elements of this philosophy were probably already familiar to him before he met Saint-Simon: the belief in progress based on the efficacy of the sciences; the lessons offered by

[76] Sewell, "Beyond 1793," 525.   [77] *Ecrits*, 96.
[78] Arbousse-Bastide, *Doctrine d'éducation*, 1:14, 28.

history in understanding the present; the obsolescence of the divine; the importance of philosophy, political economy, and secular morality; the key role of education and political writing in producing changes in public opinion and *les moeurs*; the need to work for the common good; the ideals of liberty and fraternity; and the requirement that the government stem from the governed in a representative system.[79] Yet Saint-Simon showed him the manner in which these discrete elements could be blended into a trenchant critique of the crisis wreaking havoc in Europe. Although Comte had angrily rejected the reactionary tendencies of the Bourbon regime and had hoped that the ideals of the Revolution would one day be realized, his analysis in his 1816 essay and letters had not been particularly profound. Saint-Simon not only put the decadence of the moral and political structures into historical perspective, but showed more clearly its relationship to the decrepitude of the entire intellectual system. He also demonstrated to Comte the critical role of political science (political economy), which affected his approach to the other sciences. Besides giving him a deeper understanding of the present situation and its derivation from the past, Saint-Simon presented him with a *constructive* vision of a future that would be inevitably liberal, industrial, and positive. In a later letter to Valat, Comte himself summarized what he learned from Saint-Simon:

> In the first place, by this bond of work and friendship with one of the men who see the furthest in political philosophy, I have learned a mass of things that I would have vainly searched for in books, and my mind has made more headway in the six months of our association than it would have in three years if I had been alone. Thus this job has formed my judgment on the political sciences, and, as a consequence, it has enlarged my ideas on all the other sciences to such an extent that I find that I have learned more philosophy and a more correct, lofty view.[80]

When Comte later republished many of his early works, he called his articles in *L'Industrie* "premature" and "artificial" and refused to reprint them, perhaps because they showed so clearly his intellectual debt to Saint-Simon. After all, in his work for *L'Industrie*, he displayed his adoption of Saint-Simon's historical schema and many of his themes: the need for a positive system of knowledge and a new science of society based on morality and politics, especially political economy; the requirement that theory precede practice; and the vision of a future industrial regime governed by scientists and producers. Furthermore, the ideas of making philosophers out of the clergy

---

[79] Gouhier, *Jeunesse*, 3:178.   [80] Comte to Valat, April 17, 1818, *CG*, 1:28.

and creating a new intellectual system to replace Christianity suggest the concept of an intellectual, spiritual power preaching a new religion – a principle that was also originally Saint-Simon's. But Comte did take pride in one element of this work that he believed showed his own originality, the idea that "everything is relative; that is the only absolute principle."[81] This, he said, showed that from the first he was interested in a positive religion. Yet the political and moral relativism that Comte claimed to be his special contribution was also inherent in Saint-Simon's writings, though never so boldly stated by him.

THE REACTION TO *L'INDUSTRIE*

In general, these two volumes of *L'Industrie* were a strange mixture of boldness and conservatism, perhaps reflecting the difference in the experiences of the two collaborators and the political climate. Whereas Saint-Simon previously had complained about the instability of the mixed government of France, these articles urged readers to support it. They advocated working through the existing parliamentary and religious system in order to effect gradual transformations by means of a more fundamental intellectual revolution. With no hint of his revolutionary fervor of 1816, Comte even went so far as to criticize Bentham for his radicalism, especially for frightening the English *industriels* by not ensuring the monarchy's position. Comte was trying to allay the fears of the wealthy French *industriels* to whom his articles were addressed. Talk about further immediate and profound change might estrange them. Insisting upon the moderation of his approach, Comte seemed to have been encouraged by Saint-Simon to flatter these men to obtain their continued financial support.

Although his arguments seemed to maintain the status quo, Comte's goals were radical, so much so that they appeared dangerous. Already in late September, Hachette told General Campredon that he was worried and thought Comte should go to Russia, presumably to escape the French authorities.[82] His ideas certainly caused havoc among the readers of *L'Industrie*. Many of its subscribers disavowed their allegiance to Saint-Simon. They were disturbed by the principle of relativism: they did not consider the current parliamentary regime simply a stopgap and disliked the veiled attacks on the king. What concerned them most, however, was the fourth *cahier's* blatant denunciation of Christian morality. While many anticlericals advocated at most the separation of church and state, Saint-Simon

---

[81] *Système*, "Appendice," ii.
[82] Campredon, Diary entry for September 22, 1817, "Extrait d'un cahier de notes," 168.

and Comte went further, attacking the basic principles of Catholicism and calling for a re-creation of the moral system that was at the heart of European civilization. In the atmosphere of the Catholic reaction, reflected in the White Terror, such effrontery seemed alarming, even to those on the Left.[83] On October 30, 1817, some of the eminent subscribers to *L'Industrie*, such as Casimir Périer, Vital-Roux, Hottinguer, and Gabriel Delessert, wrote a letter to the minister of police in which they insisted upon their ignorance of Saint-Simon's intentions. Afraid of being accused of treason, they denied having given him money to support his projects, especially the recent volume, which represented a threat to order.[84]

Comte was surprised that so few "commercial and manufacturing" *industriels* had read the volume. He resented the fact that the majority of them were so concerned about the "profit of their private interests" that they did not think about the "general interest." And he criticized the few *industriels* who did approve of his ideas for fearing to compromise themselves by actively supporting the journal. The "egoism" of both the *industriels* and the scientists, who seemed equally oblivious to the problems of social reconstruction, began to bother him.[85]

COMTE'S SEARCH FOR STUDENTS AND WORK FOR CASIMIR PÉRIER

The failure of the volume caused Saint-Simon a "terrible pecuniary crisis." He could no longer afford to pay his secretary the considerable sum of three hundred francs a month. Nevertheless, Comte misled General Campredon and his parents when he told them he had ended his association with Saint-Simon. In April 1818 he wrote to Valat, "I have kept with this excellent man very active relations of friendship and even of work."[86]

However, without a salary, Comte was left again to try to make ends meet. Besides reluctantly turning to his parents, he attempted to find a teaching position, a difficult endeavor. Poinsot had already

---

[83] Hubbard, *Saint-Simon*, 80; Manuel, *Saint-Simon*, 203–5.

[84] Vital Roux et al. to the Ministre, Secrétaire d'Etat du Roi au Département de la Police Générale, October 30, 1817, in Saint-Simon, *Oeuvres*, 2.1:9. La Rouchefoucauld-Liancourt said the volume's "principles" affronted "friends" of the government and could give rise to "dangerous interpretations." La Rouchefoucauld-Liancourt to Saint-Simon, October 20, 1817, in Pereire, *Autour de Saint-Simon*, 27–8n3. Two of Saint-Simon's supporters did not repudiate him: Ternaux and Jacques Laffitte. See Hubbard, *Saint-Simon*, 80.

[85] *Ecrits*, 441.

[86] Comte to Valat, April 17, 1818, *CG*, 1:27. See also Campredon, "Extrait d'un cahier de notes," 168.

arranged for him to teach the Prince de Carignan.[87] And thanks partly to Campredon's help, he was preparing General Chasseloup's son for the Ecole Polytechnique. In December 1817 Campredon also got him a job tutoring the children of Casimir Périer, a big supporter of Saint-Simon. He was one of France's richest bankers and an important deputy in the Chamber.[88]

Besides teaching in a "great house of Paris," Comte was given the task of writing Périer's speeches.[89] At that moment, Périer and the banker Jacques Laffitte, another supporter of Saint-Simon, were reorganizing the new antigovernment party on the Left – that of the Independents – which supported individual rights and popular sovereignty.[90] Despite the financial and political rewards involved in his position, Comte worked for Périer for only three weeks before they had some sort of intellectual disagreement.[91] Embarrassed, Comte gave Valat the impression that Périer had changed his mind about hiring him and that, in any case, he found it repugnant to become "first slave to Monsieur, Madame, and their progeny." Being a preceptor would only have "compromised" his "character."[92] This would not be the only time Comte would break with someone who he believed threatened his freedom.[93]

Before leaving, Comte wrote several speeches for Périer, one of which defended freedom of the press against a proposed law on censorship.[94] Just as he was anxious about his own personal liberty, he was concerned about the "slavery" of the French people when their freedom of thought and discussion was hampered. To him,

---

[87] Lonchampt, *Précis*, 13. Elio Pépin maintains, however, that the Prince de Carignan was probably not in Paris at the time. Elio Pépin, "Matériaux pour servir à la biographie d'Auguste Comte: Le Prince de Carignan," *Revue positiviste internationale* 9 (May 15, 1914): 439–42.

[88] Périer had given Saint-Simon one thousand francs to launch *L'Industrie*, and some extracts from his pamphlets on the budget had appeared in volume 2 of *L'Industrie*. See the list of subscribers, Pereire, *Autour de Saint-Simon*, 7.

[89] Comte to Valat, April 17, 1818, *CG*, 1:29; Emile Corra, *La Naissance du génie d'Auguste Comte: Sa Vie jusqu'en 1819*, 24; Campredon, "Extrait d'un cahier de notes," 169.

[90] Bertier de Sauvigny, *Bourbon Restoration*, 145. Thierry also seems to have been writing speeches for Laffitte at this time. Augustin-Thierry, *Augustin Thierry*, 58.

[91] Périer had already signed the letter objecting to Comte's daring concepts in *L'Industrie*. See Deroisin, *Notes sur Auguste Comte*, 21; Gouhier, *Jeunesse*, 3:338–40; "Matériaux pour servir à la biographie d'Auguste Comte [Documents, 1816–1822]," ed. Pierre Laffitte, *RO* 8 (May 1, 1882): 326–8.

[92] Comte to Valat, April 17, 1818, *CG*, 1:29.

[93] "Matériaux pour servir à la biographie d'Auguste Comte [Documents, 1816-1822]," ed. Laffitte, *RO* 8 (1882): 328.

[94] A sketch of Comte's thoughts on the subject was found among his unpublished papers. Casimir Périer gave the speech on December 13, 1817. See "Opinion sur le projet de loi relatif à la presse," *Ecrits*, 433–6.

"the vague, the arbitrary, and despotism" were equivalent. "Free discussion," which included criticism of "everything" (including laws), was "good for society" because it enlightened both the government and the people about current issues and their interests. Rejecting the conservative argument that freedom of thought led to social upheaval, he pointed out that the French Revolution had proved the contrary, that "the most terrible insurrections took place precisely in times when thought was enslaved." If the government were really interested in preventing revolutions, it would improve the lot of the proletarians and provide them with education. The key to education was the system of mutual education, which Comte, unlike Saint-Simon, wanted to extend to the "last class of society."[95] Yet like Saint-Simon and his liberal industrial supporters, he believed that respect for property, which would derive from education, was the "basis of society" and happiness and a bulwark against revolution.[96]

At this point (in 1817–18) Comte still embraced the liberal tenets of representative government and free speech – "the sweet liberty of saying everything that passes through one's head."[97] Although he later changed his opinion about other aspects of liberalism, he would continue to value freedom of discussion not only because it led to the growth of reason and thus progress but because, without it, his ideas could not be disseminated. However, in the prospectus of the third volume of *L'Industrie*, where he had proclaimed the need for a single moral code to make people's ideas similar, he had displayed his true attitude toward freedom of thought in the positive state.

AN ATTACK OF DEPRESSION

After he lost his job with Périer, Comte became deeply depressed. By mid-1818, he had only two students, and his monthly income

---

[95] *Ecrits*, 433–6. See also Saint-Simon, *Quelques idées soumises par M. de Saint-Simon à l'Assemblée Générale de la Société d'Instruction Primaire*, 7, 8. In June 1818, Comte expected to be commissioned to write a book on mutual education by one of the people he was tutoring, Alexandre de Laborde, who was the director of the Ponts et Chaussées and an important participant in the Société d'Instruction Elémentaire, to which Hachette and Saint-Simon belonged. Perhaps Comte became acquainted with Laborde through Saint-Simon, who greatly admired him. The project for the book never materialized, much to Comte's disappointment. Comte to Valat, June 15, 1818, *CG*, 1:42–3; Saint-Simon, *Catéchisme des industriels*, 2d *cahier*, *Oeuvres*, 4.1:171; Louis Comte to Comte-Rochambeau, September 20, 1818, excerpt in Ouy, "Jeunesse," 258.
[96] *Ecrits*, 435. See also the original circular for the third volume of *L'Industrie*, in which Comte wrote, "The preservation of property is the great object of politics."
[97] Comte to Valat, November 17, 1818, *CG*, 1:45.

from teaching was 120 francs, supplemented by another 40 or 50 francs from his parents. His mother did not raise his spirits; she complained about the unhealthy conditions of Paris, urged him to find consolation in religion, and ordered him to get a stable position to ease the strain on the family's finances. Back in Montpellier, Campredon received distressing letters from Comte and promised to find him an "honorable" means of existence.[98] Like his parents, Campredon insisted that he return to Montpellier. Although Comte refused, he began to regret not having taken the examination for the Ecoles d'Application, because if he had become a geographical engineer, he would have appeased his parents and solved his monetary troubles. But then he remembered that he did not like engineering and was not suited for a "sad career" as a government employee.[99]

Comte survived in Paris on his small income by reducing his expenses. His relationship with Pauline lessened his visits to prostitutes, and he lost interest in going to the theater. In an attempt to stop buying books, he subscribed to a reading room and began to follow Saint-Simon's example of thinking more and reading less.

Throughout this difficult period, Comte was changing both emotionally and intellectually. Because of his love for Pauline, he became "sentimental": "I have need of that [sentimentality] in order to develop entirely within myself tender affections, which are, as Destutt-Tracy has so well said, and as all other sensitive hearts have recognized, the source of the greatest happiness."[100] When in June 1818 Pauline bore him a daughter named Louise, he enjoyed "conjugal and paternal affections" and even reproached Pauline for not following Rousseau's "good arguments" in favor of breast feeding.[101] In somewhat bittersweet tones that reflected his frustration with life, he wrote, "The gentle and tender affections are the happiest, the source of the only true happiness that one can get hold of on this miserable planet, and one could never have enough of them."[102] Already Comte recognized the primacy of the emotions.

[98] Campredon to Comte, March 24, 1818, "Correspondants, amis et protecteurs: Le Général Campredon," ed. Laffitte, 171. See also Comte to Valat, June 15, 1818, *CG*, 1:39; Rosalie Boyer to Comte, March 18, 1818, "Lettres de la Mère d'Aug. Comte, Rosalie Boyer, à son fils (1)," ed. Pierre Laffitte, *RO*, 3d ser., 1 (May 1, 1909): 87.

[99] Comte to Valat, April 17, 1818, *CG*, 1:28. See also Alix Comte to Auguste Comte, June 25, 1818, "Lettres d'Alix Comte," ed. Laffitte, 56.

[100] Comte to Valat, May 15, 1818, *CG*, 1:33.

[101] Comte to Valat, June 15, November 17, 1818, *CG*, 1:44, 46.

[102] Comte to Valat, November 17, 1818, *CG*, 1:46. Comte later told Clotilde de Vaux that he suspected that Louise was not his daughter. Comte to Clotilde de Vaux, March 1, 1846, *CG*: 3:339.

COMTE'S CHANGING VIEWS OF POLITICS AND MORALITY

Although he had a mistress and a child, Comte was lonely. He seemed desperate for companionship, for his comrades were dispersed and his three "true friends" – Cabanes, Conrot, and Valat – were not in Paris. The person whom Comte missed most was Valat, who had been with him at the *lycée* in Montpellier and one year behind him at the Ecole Polytechnique. Comte was very sentimental about their relationship and would often expatiate on the pleasures of their friendship or rebuke Valat for neglecting to write: "I need your letters. I need this delightful commerce of friendship. I need this outpouring of emotion, this absolute abandon: don't deprive me of it anymore, I beg of you, it would be very cruel."[103] As he grew increasingly melancholy, Comte's letters to Valat became even more maudlin.

Valat provided Comte not only with an emotional outlet, but with an audience for his jeremiads. Continually scolding him for stagnating in the provinces, where he was a teacher at the Collège de Béziers, Comte corrected his opinions and tried to convert him to his own beliefs. His association with Saint-Simon had given him confidence, and he was eager to impart his new vision to others.

Comte was in the process of redefining his views on politics and morality. In May 1818 he criticized Valat's "political direction," though he admitted that he himself had followed the same direction the year before. Comte now rejected the idea of basing politics on "the theory of the rights of man, on the idea of the *Social Contract*, in short on the systems of philosophy of the last century." He had learned the "key of good philosophy," which was "that *all* human knowledge grows from century to century, and that the political institutions and ideas of each epoch of a people must be relative to the state of enlightenment of this people in this epoch." Referring to his belief that "everything is relative," he argued that eighteenth-century philosophy was appropriate for that time but now was unsuitable.[104] Valat should abandon Rousseau's *Social Contract*, read historical works, such as Hume's *History of England* and Robertson's *History of Charles V*, and study political economy, especially the writings of Smith and Say.

Comte's remarks confirm the impression that Saint-Simon had taught him a new way of approaching politics in the past year. But Saint-Simon was not the only influence on Comte. The entire discursive world of early-nineteenth-century Paris was marked by a

[103] Comte to Valat, May 15, 1818, *CG*, 1:33.   [104] Ibid., 37.

greater appreciation of historical context and a preoccupation with the problem of social reconstruction. Thinkers generally felt the need for new general theories of society, politics, and morality.[105] To take one example, Victor Cousin, who perhaps most enraptured the members of Comte's generation, considered the work of the eighteenth century necessary but destructive and obsolete, promulgated the doctrine of historical relativism, regarded the current period as one of transition, and called for a new philosophical synthesis based on a "solid terrain, accessible to observation," in order to create a unifying doctrine for the nineteenth century. He sought "opinions" that could "govern the world" and fill the "void" left by the eighteenth century.[106] Comte was familiar with the very popular lectures given by Cousin between 1815 and 1820, and although he preferred the far less metaphysical way in which Saint-Simon played with these same ideas, he shared his resolution to search for a new general doctrine that would save society.

Comte's own readings in history and political economy had shown him the interplay between political institutions and ideas. They had also reinforced his conviction that to be a science like the other natural sciences, politics had to be based on concrete facts. Like other liberals, such as the English utilitarians and the Idéologues, he criticized Rousseau's social contract for being "hypothetical." Moreover, he shared their ambivalence toward natural rights; whereas in his writings he expressed the hope that the Declaration of the Rights of Man would soon be realized, he suggested in a letter to Valat that the notion of "right" was too absolutist and vague.[107] He commented later, in one of Saint-Simon's works, that the "theory of the rights of man" was "nothing other than an application of high metaphysics to high jurisprudence."[108] It was legalistic nonsense that could be dangerously abused. To many liberals, such as Guizot and, to a lesser extent, Destutt de Tracy and the Idéologues, the language

---

[105] Rosanvallon, *Le Moment Guizot*, 76.

[106] Victor Cousin, *Cours de philosophie professé à la Faculté des lettres pendant l'année 1818* (Paris, 1836), 8, 388. See also idem, "Programme des leçons données à l'Ecole Normale et à la Faculté des Lettres pendant le premier semestre de 1818," in idem, *Fragmens philosophiques*, 2d. ed. (Paris, 1833), 284–312; Spitzer, *French Generation*, 71–96; W. M. Simon, "The 'Two Cultures' in Nineteenth-Century France: Victor Cousin and Auguste Comte," *Journal of the History of Ideas* 26 (January–March 1965): 45–51.

[107] Comte to Valat, May 15, 1818, *CG*, 1:37. See also D. H. Monro, "Bentham, Jeremy," in *The Encyclopedia of Philosophy*, ed. Edwards; Cheryl B. Welch, "French and English Utilitarians," chap. in *Liberty and Utility: The French Idéologues and the Transformation of Liberalism* (New York: Columbia University Press, 1984), 135–53.

[108] Comte's section in Saint-Simon, *Considérations sur les mesures à prendre pour terminer la Révolution, Du système industriel*, Part 1, in *Oeuvres*, 3.1:83.

of natural rights, popular sovereignty, and the social contract seemed demagogic, opened the door to anarchy, and should be used as little as possible.[109] Even Constant was wary of Rousseau's concept of popular sovereignty because of its misuse by the Jacobins.[110] Though still a liberal, Comte was in the process of formulating a systematic critique of some aspects of liberal philosophy. He already appeared to be searching for a new basis for politics. Besides industrialism, historical relativism seemed to be a good candidate.

Comte appeared to overlook the fact that relativism was well known to eighteenth-century philosophers. Montesquieu, for example, seemed to have a better understanding of its implications. In fact, Comte's criticisms of the great philosophes reveal his own insecurity about the best way to contribute to intellectual progress. Although he considered eighteenth-century theories obsolete, he was not sure how to formulate a substitute. He still seemed to favor such Enlightenment ideas as liberty, education, fraternity, a just society, and a rational, more "scientific" study of society and politics. His continuing fascination with this tradition is revealed by his purchase in 1819 of a new edition of Rousseau's *Confessions*, which he read most carefully.[111]

While reconsidering his own political concepts, Comte was also reevaluating his moral philosophy because of his new appreciation of relativism and his new understanding of love and the importance of the emotions for one's happiness. In the past, he and "other modern youths" had adopted Franklin's stoicism because it was "decisive and absolute" and aroused "enthusiasm and exaltation," but for the same reasons, he now spurned it. Rejecting stoicism for denying "all the sentiments that form the sole charm of human nature," he decided that the sensations of love, or more accurately sex, had to be procured now in his youth, when they could be fully enjoyed.[112] He deplored, however, hedonism and resolved to opt for Horace's philosophy of moderation. Yet this decision did not mark the end of Comte's search for the proper code of conduct.

---

[109] Welch, *Liberty and Utility*, 23, 30–3; Rosanvallon, *Le Moment Guizot*, 76–7, 91. See Guizot's critique of representation, popular sovereignty, and equality, in F. Guizot, *Des moyens de gouvernement et d'opposition dans l'état actuel de la France*, 2d ed. (Paris, 1821), 135–80.

[110] Holmes, *Benjamin Constant*, 85, 96–9.

[111] Comte's copy of Rousseau's *Confessions* is in his Bibliothèque Superflue, Maison d'Auguste Comte. Its cut pages suggest that Comte read the two-volume set thoroughly. Though he usually did not mark his books, he valued this one to such an extent that he wrote on the inside cover of volume 1: "M. Comte, rue St. Germain des Prés #8, Faubourg St. Germain près de la rue des Petits Augustins." This seems to be the only book in which he wrote his address.

[112] Comte to Valat, May 15, 1818, *CG*, 1:34.

A NEW FOURTH VOLUME OF *L'INDUSTRIE*

Besides his relationship with Pauline, Comte's main source of satisfaction in 1818 was his new "career" in politics. Saint-Simon helped
him not only by teaching him political philosophy, but also by
increasing his self-confidence. Comte boasted to Valat about how
happy Saint-Simon was with his work:

> This work has revealed to me a political capacity that I would never
> have believed myself endowed with, and it is always useful to know
> precisely what one is good at. Old Simon and several publicists whom
> I have had the occasion to know at his house have rhapsodized often
> about my great capacity for philosophical and social sciences, and
> they tell me that my talent would be wasted elsewhere. . . . now, if
> this is his opinion of me, there must be something to it.[113]

Saint-Simon gave Comte the calling to become a social scientist and
philosopher, a position that involved joining the publicists, who
were as much members of the "thinking class" as scientists were.[114]
   A year after meeting Saint-Simon, Comte could still use only
superlatives to describe him. He was the "most estimable and lov-
able man whom I have ever known in my life." He was struck by
Saint-Simon's energy, the harmony between his personal and intellectual life, and his strong convictions. Above all, he believed
Saint-Simon was "pure, totally pure."[115] Comte admired his mentor
for having supposedly helped the Americans establish their liberty,
renounced his noble heritage, abstained from criminal activities during
the Revolution, and avoided flattering Napoleon. He was apparently
unaware that Saint-Simon was proud of his noble birth, had profited
from the Revolution, and had made continual appeals to Napoleon.
Comte obviously loved Saint-Simon in these early years of their
association and needed to believe in his unwavering views, goodness, and integrity. This affection appears to have been reciprocated,
for Comte said Saint-Simon loved him like a son. Comte had finally
met a man who could fulfill the role of an approving father.
   Despite Saint-Simon's inability to pay him, Comte continued
in 1818 to "do" political economy for him.[116] He studied Malthus's
theory of population, Adam Smith's *Wealth of Nations*, the works of
the French Physiocrats, and Say's *Traité d'économie politique* and
other writings.[117] Although he still believed political economy could

[113] Comte to Valat, April 17, 1818, *CG*, 1:28.   [114] *Ecrits*, 440.
[115] Comte to Valat, May 15, 1818, *CG*, 1:36–7.
[116] Comte to Valat, April 17, 1818, *CG*, 1:27.
[117] Reflecting the popularity of Say, Campredon in March had urged Comte to study his

become the basis of positive politics and morality, he criticized it for
being a mass of unconnected facts. Preoccupied like Saint-Simon
and the Encyclopedists with the ideal of unifying knowledge, he
hoped to make political economy a true science by finding a principle that would unify the discrete "positive truths" established by
the French Physiocrats, Smith, Malthus, and Say.[118]

In 1818 Comte was helping Saint-Simon launch a new issue of
L'Industrie, which would incorporate some of the research he had
been doing. The fourth volume was supposed to have a second part,
but instead Saint-Simon decided to publish a whole new volume in
the hope of erasing the memory of the previous year's fiasco. Appearing in May or early June 1818, the new first *cahier* of volume 4
contained a single, long article entitled "Moyen constitutionnel
d'accroître la force politique de l'industrie et d'augmenter les
richesses de la France." Comte probably helped Saint-Simon draft
it.[119]

Acknowledging the criticisms of the previous work, the article
expressed the hope that the readers would be more indulgent once
they read this new issue. Saint-Simon seemed to repudiate the approach of radical moral reform that Comte had persuaded him to
adopt. Instead, he stressed the primacy of economic and political
reconstruction, which had been the main theme of his work immediately before he met Comte. Saint-Simon argued that the producers, the only "useful" class, should dominate the Chamber of Deputies
to gain control of the nation and make the government direct its
attention solely to production.[120] All of society would benefit, for
the interests of the industrial class coincided with those of the
nation. Throughout history, the producers had fought for freedom,
in contrast to the lawyers, who wanted only power. Although the
purpose of the new volume was to flatter the wealthy *industriels*

"excellent works," especially his *Traité d'économie politique*. Comte then recommended it
to Valat because he felt that it showed most clearly the distinction between political economy
and what was commonly known as "politics." Perhaps Comte also met Say through Saint-
Simon. In 1818 Say sent Comte an autographed copy of a book entitled *Petit Volume
contentant quelques aperçus des hommes et de la société*. In his "Bibliothèque Usuel," Comte
kept an 1809 copy of Malthus's *Essai sur le principe de population* and an 1800–1 copy of
Smith's *La Richesse des nations*. See Campredon to Comte, March 24, 1818, "Correspondants, amis et protecteurs: Le Général Campredon," ed. Pierre Laffitte, 172; Comte
to Valat, May 15, June 15, 1818, *CG*, 1:38, 42; the undated note of Pierre Laffitte at
MAC.

[118] *Ecrits*, 447–8.

[119] In a letter to Valat, Comte explained that "we" – he and Saint-Simon – had just launched
the journal. Comte to Valat, May 15, 1818, *CG*, 1:35.

[120] Saint-Simon, "Moyen constitutionnel d'accroître la force politique de l'industrie et
d'augmenter les richesses de la France," in *Oeuvres*, 2.1:74. See also Pereire, *Autour de Saint-
Simon*, 29; Corra, *La Naissance du génie d'Auguste Comte: Sa Vie jusqu'en 1819*, 33.

sufficiently for them to forget their disenchantment with the previous work, it failed to regain their support. This issue of *L'Industrie* was the last. Comte was disappointed, because he had already written a "great devil of an article" for the next one.[121]

TWO "ANONYMOUS" LETTERS TO SAINT-SIMON

The article to which Comte referred has disappeared, but the tenor of his thought can be inferred from two letters that he wrote to Saint-Simon.[122] In the first one, he warned Saint-Simon that the fourth volume of *L'Industrie* would fail because every social group, from the lawyers to the scientists, would have some reason to neglect or repudiate its views. Even the *industriels* would once again decline to support him energetically; they were so devoted to their own private interests that they had no time for intellectual matters or questions relating to the common good.

In the second letter, Comte gave Saint-Simon advice on how to rectify his "bad direction."[123] He accused him of concentrating excessively on the practical, political means to realize his significant idea that property should be reorganized to favor production. Saint-Simon should have confined himself to the theoretical aspects of his idea and made it a fundamental truth of both components of social science, politics and morality. Once recognized as a true theoretical principle, it would influence the practical realm.

Instead of addressing himself to the general public and becoming involved in a "game of passions," Saint-Simon should also have had his theories evaluated rationally and objectively by the political economists, his "natural judges." In this way, the idea of property would have become the fundamental, unifying concept of the new science of political economy.[124]

Finally, Saint-Simon failed to point out that morality could become a science only if it too were established on the idea of the importance of property and its relationship to production. Comte asserted that "moral rules, like political institutions, must be judged according to the influence they exercise or can exercise on *production*." Christian morality was insufficient. Its main injunction to love thy neighbor was only the "expression of a sentiment and not a rule of conduct." Even the best sentiments did not lead to the "happiness of society" unless they were "guided by positive knowledge."[125]

---

[121] Comte to Valat, May 15, 1818, *CG*, 1:35.
[122] The letters are reproduced in *Ecrits*, 439–49.   [123] Ibid., 445.
[124] Ibid., 445–6.   [125] Ibid., 447–8.

Naturally loving, people had to be taught different ways to be useful to others. The same conflict between objectivity and subjectivity that characterized Comte's critique of political economy appears here in his discussion of morality. He was aware of the richness and importance of the inner life, but in wanting to base morality on knowledge and production, he reflected his attraction to the objective and concrete, which seemed more certain than feelings.

Written in Comte's handwriting, these letters were found among Saint-Simon's papers after his death.[126] The first was entitled "Lettre à M. H. Saint-Simon par une personne qui se nommera plus tard" and is signed "J."[127] The second was untitled and unsigned but ended with the statement "I will make myself known in addressing this article to you."[128] Some scholars think these were real letters sent anonymously by Comte to show his complete disagreement with Saint-Simon.[129] But because the letters are covered with scratch marks and corrections and are not creased, it seems more likely that they were never meant to be final copies and were not sent through the mail.[130] In any case, Saint-Simon would probably have recognized Comte's handwriting. Furthermore, in May 1818 Comte had just proclaimed his eternal friendship to Saint-Simon and was certainly not on the verge of ending their association as these scholars assert.

Other critics, such as Gustave d'Eichthal, Alfred Pereire, and Henri Gouhier, feel that Comte and Saint-Simon wrote the letters together with the intention of publishing them as anonymous letters in a daily paper to stimulate debate on the issues touched upon in the recent *cahier* of *L'Industrie*. Such a debate would supposedly lead to more publicity and support for their enterprise.[131] But this view is untenable because Saint-Simon would not have wanted to bring up again the problematic issue of a new morality and would have refused to allow himself to be so severely criticized.

The probable explanation is that Comte in a playful manner was stating his position on the direction that Saint-Simon should be taking. Known for his humor at the Ecole Polytechnique, he could have pretended to write these letters anonymously partly as a joke, since Saint-Simon knew the young man was afraid of signing anything for fear his parents would find out.[132] The letters do not reveal any

---

[126] Pereire, *Autour de Saint-Simon*, 31.
[127] Ibid., 35. The signature "Y" in the *Ecrits* is wrong. *Ecrits*, 444.   [128] *Ecrits*, 449.
[129] Weill, *Saint-Simon*, 199; Georges Dumas, *Psychologie de deux messies positivistes* (Paris: Félix Alcan, 1905), 261; Paul Dubuisson, Comte et Saint-Simon: *Comte n'est-il que le disciple de Saint-Simon?* (Paris: Au Siège de la Société Positiviste Internationale, 1906), 16–19; Robinet, *Notice*, 369–70.
[130] Pereire, *Autour de Saint-Simon*, 33–8.   [131] Ibid., 33–69; Gouhier, *Jeunesse*, 3:193–8.
[132] Comte to Valat, May 15, 1818, *CG*, 1:35.

fundamental conflict, but rather a difference over tactics. After the problems with the prospectus and the third volume, Saint-Simon did not want to bring up subjects that might alienate his wealthy supporters. Comte, however, was younger, more impatient, and more uncompromising. He wanted to take Saint-Simon's original position to its logical conclusion.

The two letters are important for showing that Comte was beginning to have his own views. He was not at all disillusioned with his work with Saint-Simon and even decided in mid-1818 to devote his life to it.[133] At this time, less than a year after they had first met, Comte considered himself more than Saint-Simon's secretary or even friend; he saw himself as his collaborator. For the moment, he was willing to forgo his plan for a social science and concentrate instead on the practical, political sphere. Yet these questions of tactics – whether to concentrate on theory or practice, whether to address a wide, nontechnical audience or a certain elite, and whether to challenge Christianity directly or indirectly – would later cause tension in their relationship. By straddling both sides of these issues, Saint-Simon planted the seeds of this controversy himself. As Comte grew in self-confidence, he would demand more consistency.

COMTE'S SHORT CAREER AS A TUTOR AT
A BOARDING SCHOOL

In October 1818, several months after the curious affair with the letters, Comte became an instructor at a boarding school run by Baron Antoine Reynaud, his old tutor who used to teach calculus at the Ecole Polytechnique when Poinsot was absent. With his 1,200-franc salary, Comte developed a pleasurable routine, teaching at school, giving private lessons, working on his own, visiting Pauline, reading at home, having philosophical talks with Saint-Simon, and going to bed early "in a bourgeois fashion [*bourgeoisement*]." But at the end of the month, his tranquillity disappeared when he insisted on following his own ideas about teaching mathematics instead of using the "rotten" and "boring" teaching manuals that Reynaud had written. Finding Reynaud full of "self-love," Comte finally left him in January. He explained to Valat that "the pleasure of doing as I please has always been and will always be for me the most delightful of all pleasures."[134] But at the same time he claimed to be a "victim"

---

[133] Ibid.
[134] Comte to Valat, November 17, 1818, *CG*, 1:45, 46, 48. See also Comte to Valat, June 15, 1818, *CG*, 1:40; Comte's notebook: *Cours d'analyse de Monsieur Poinsot, de Monsieur Reynaud*, MAC.

of Reynaud's more powerful position.[135] Comte's difficulty obeying others, which was already apparent in his break with Périer, and his sense of being a victim would be recurring themes in his future quarrels.

LE POLITIQUE

Comte quickly forgot about the pain of losing his teaching position because he had been working since December 1818 on Saint-Simon's new journal, *Le Politique ou Essais sur la politique qui convient aux hommes du XIXe siècle.* After the first four issues, Saint-Simon had to seek financial help and in February 1819 signed a contract with two friends, dividing the ownership of the journal into twenty-four shares.[136] Saint-Simon, the largest shareholder with ten shares, arranged for Comte to have two shares, making him a shareholder in his enterprises for the first time. The other two shareholders esteemed Comte's talents sufficiently to allow him to become an owner with no capital contribution. Yet as a precautionary measure, the director of the journal retained the right to prevent the publication of any article that he judged potentially troublesome.

Intended to be a more popular, less philosophical journal than *L'Industrie*, the new periodical was to concentrate on current affairs, which were being hotly debated under the new, more liberal ministry of Elie Decazes. The articles generally supported the views of the liberals. Saint-Simon rejected the position Comte took in his anonymous letters, for instead of treating political theory first, he gave priority to practical issues. He still hoped that by supporting the position of the *industriels*, especially bankers, on the key issues of the day, he would win back their support.[137] Those persons still worried about his previous references to "terrestrial morality" would find reassurance in his argument that the *industriels* (who included artisans, scientists, and artists) were the most moral of all men because they adhered to the golden rule established by Jesus Christ. And to avoid being accused of republicanism, which was considered

[135] Comte to Valat, September 24, 1819, *CG*, 1:54.
[136] The two friends were Daniel Coutte and Auguste-Louis Lachevardière. Coutte was a property owner and notary in Peronne who had been a close associate of Saint-Simon during the Revolution and saved him from total derangement in 1812. Lachevardière was also a rich property owner. He became the director of the journal. See the contract between Saint-Simon, Comte, Daniel Coutte, and Auguste-Louis Lachevardière, February 22, 1819, MAC; Teixeira Mendes, *Auguste Comte*, 401; Manuel, *Saint-Simon*, 36, 108.
[137] Bertier de Sauvigny, *Bourbon Restoration*, 158–62; Gouhier, *Jeunesse*, 3:205; Manuel, *Saint-Simon*, 209–10; Weill, *Saint-Simon*, 116; Arbousse-Bastide, *Doctrine d'éducation*, 1:16.

dangerous because of its connection with the Terror, he cautiously explained that he aimed to show the "utility of the monarchy in social organization."[138]

Although Saint-Simon was clearly going against his recommendations, Comte was excited by a new adventure that demanded his "sublime functions" as a publicist. Growing in self-confidence, he finally decided to take responsibility for his own work.[139] But he was still fearful of the authorities and signed "B., ancien élève de l'Ecole Polytechnique," instead of using his own name. "B" referred to the first letter of his mother's name, Boyer.[140]

Comte's first article, entitled "Lettre d'un ancien élève de l'Ecole Polytechnique à MM. les auteurs du *Politique*," was inspired by his study of Madame de Staël's *Considérations sur les principaux événements de la Révolution française*. Published posthumously in 1818, Staël's work unleashed a virulent debate in France on the significance of the Revolution and was an important contribution to liberal historiography.[141] Perhaps influenced by Saint-Simon's stories about her, Comte called her a "truly extraordinary woman" who was "far superior" to her lover Benjamin Constant. And Comte found her book, which argued that the French Revolution was an inevitable result of intellectual and political progress, "infinitely superior" to any other on the subject.[142] Like Madame de Staël, Comte maintained in his article that the "state of enlightenment" led to the overthrow of the government, which ruled solely by force in order to benefit the privileged. The Revolution was an effort to make politics "liberal and moral" by establishing a regime devoted to the "interests of the greatest number." The horrors that occurred were not the fault of revolutionaries but were due to the necessity of fighting foreign invading armies. Comte still believed that "liberal"

---

[138] Saint-Simon, Introduction to the "Prospectus," in *Oeuvres*, 2.1:189.
[139] Comte seems to have made this decision to sign his name in late November or December 1818, because on November 17 he wrote to Valat that he was not the "*ostensible author*" of any articles and thus was not the "*responsible author*." Comte to Valat, November 17, 1818, *CG*, 1:45.
[140] Besides the six articles that are included in the *Ecrits de jeunesse*, there are two other articles, merely signed "B," which probably came from Comte's pen: "Sur la Proposition de changer la loi des élections," *Le Politique* (1819): 175–82; "Sur l'effet produit par la Proposition de M. Barthélemy," *Le Politique* (1819): 213–19. These were analyses of an electoral law proposed by Barthélemy, the spokesman of the ultras. See also Gouhier, *Jeunesse*, 3:202–4.
[141] The article was written on December 27, 1818, and was published in the first issue of *Le Politique*, which appeared in January 1819. It is reproduced in *Ecrits*, 109–12. See also Comte to Valat, May 15, 1818, *CG*, 1:36; Gérard, *La Révolution française*, 32.
[142] Comte to Valat, June 15, 1818, *CG*, 1:43. See also Madame de Staël, *Considérations sur les principaux événements de la Révolution française*, 3 vols. (Paris, 1818), 1:1–15.

and "enlightened" thinkers like himself had a duty to explain the current situation. They must show that the European crisis would not end until the Revolution was completed. Comte saluted the launching of Le Politique as a way of creating a "uniform and common system" among liberal, enlightened publicists.[143] As in the past, he believed intellectual unity was crucial for political efficacy.

Thus in this article Comte was announcing the need to complete the work of the Revolution and his continued loyalty to its social goals. Out of fear of offending his readers, he did not, however, describe in detail the way to realize its aims. He merely suggested that physical force, strengthened by money and the army, upheld the control of a minority, privileged class and had to be "dethroned" before the people could make the moral force – the "law of common interests" – dominant and thereby create a liberal regime.[144] He seemed to be following Saint-Simon's advice in suggesting that the immediate political situation had to be addressed before a total moral reformation could occur. His other articles therefore dealt with specific political issues of the day.

Comte wrote two articles on the budget. In the early years of the Restoration, the liberals and political economists used the issue of the Chamber's control over the budget to push not only for a stronger parliamentary regime but also for a more economical and thus limited government.[145] Comte argued that the political power of the people rested on the Chamber's right to pass financial laws, especially those relating to taxes and their uses. The government had to be accountable to the people, who increasingly in this industrial age supplied it with its main material basis. Comte criticized liberals, including Benjamin Constant, for not going far enough in ensuring that the budget would be trimmed of all excess and designed wholly for the benefit of the people rather than for the well-being of the governing classes, who used taxes for their own self-interested ends. He also reproached publicists for continuing to concentrate on the political form of government instead of the financial system, which was the essential problem of the modern age. Thus he still had an economic vision of politics; in an industrial age, politics should be subordinate to the economy and the interests of society and industry should be the same.[146]

---

[143] Ecrits, 109–10.   [144] Ibid., 110–11.
[145] Rosanvallon, "Les Doctrinaires," 411; idem, Le Moment Guizot, 48.
[146] Kremer-Marietti, Le Concept, 71. Comte's articles, called "Du budget," are reproduced in Ecrits, 113–39. Saint-Simon wrote an article demanding the dismissal of the permanent army – a position that Comte was explaining to Valat at the same time in his letters. Weill, Saint-Simon, 116; Comte to Valat, November 17, 1818, CG, 1:46–8; Saint-Simon, Oeuvres, 2.1:195–234.

Comte also wrote three articles defending the liberty of the press at a time when censorship laws were being hotly debated.[147] To him, a liberal regime was a "regime of public opinion," which found expression in both the parliamentary system and a free press. Since journalists kept an eye on government, especially on wasteful public expenditures, freedom of the press was the foundation of all rights and liberties. It was, in fact, the "basis of the representative system" because the Chamber of Deputies itself had to serve public opinion – the "queen of the world." Thus it was more than a "civil right"; it was a "political institution." Furthermore, as the voice of public opinion, a free press better represented the people because the Legislative Assembly represented only a tiny minority of the population and at the moment was made up mainly of paid government officials who were interested only in increasing their own power and wealth. Although a system of parliamentary representation was a "very useful intermediary" between the people and their rulers, its role was exaggerated, for the people could influence their rulers' decisions directly through journalists, who surveyed the governing classes and made them serve the "common interest." He wrote, "With freedom of the press, the majority of citizens can participate in the formation of the law, not by a deliberative voice, which would be absurd, but by a consultative voice."[148] In effect, a parliamentary system needed a press, but a free press did not need a parliament.

Although he still favored the basic concept underlying the rhetoric of popular sovereignty, Comte, like most liberals of his time, was by no means committed to democracy. Like many of them, he believed that with a large population, France could never give everyone a role in the formation of law. (The demand for universal suffrage would not become prevalent until the 1840s.) Instead, the voice of the people could be heard through a free press, which could be used especially by educated citizens. With such freedom and the problems with the Chamber, it did not really matter that the people's electoral rights – their "natural rights" – were restricted. Reflecting his despair with the dangers and corruption of the political realm, Comte appeared to be arguing for the rule by an elite of publicists, for even he admitted that only "enlightened," that is, literate, men could really voice their opinions in the press. Although in a previous article he had asserted that the ideas and prejudices of political writers, including himself, often diverted them from serving the general interest, he now argued that publicists could

---

[147] The articles are entitled "Lettre servant d'introduction à un article sur la liberté de la presse," "De la liberté de la presse envisagée comme institution politique," and "Des lois sur la liberté de la presse." They can be found in *Ecrits*, 141–59.

[148] Ibid., 142, 143, 149–51.

adequately represent the people.[149] In a sense, public opinion, to Comte, seemed to be the opinion of enlightened thinkers who corrected the ideas of blind individuals. Thus liberty of the press also served an educational purpose.

There was a tension in Comte's thought between serving and creating, that is, manipulating, public opinion. He boasted that he always obeyed the "voice" of his "mistress," public opinion, but at the same time he had been trying since 1816 to enlighten it.[150] This tension had been inherent in the discourse of the revolutionaries and was also being discussed by his liberal contemporaries, Constant and Guizot. Constant upheld the traditional liberal view that government should serve public opinion. Liberty of the press was a natural extension of the faculty of expression and a right that protected the interests of the people, especially by ensuring the surveillance of government institutions. "All civil, political, [and] judicial barriers become illusory without liberty of the press."[151] Guizot, however, argued that liberty of the press was not "only the exercise of an individual right," as Constant maintained.[152] Instead, it was a public institution, an "institution of reason" that served the general interest.[153] To avoid repeating the horrors of the Revolution, he dissociated representation from the principle of election and connected it with publicity, which allowed for communication in politics. But to him, a free press was not a vehicle for the expression of individuals' desires or criticism of the government, as it was to Constant. Instead, its function was "to develop and manifest public reason, which . . . is not any less favorable to the reasonable needs of the power than to the legitimate rights of the citizens."[154] And since he believed that reason stood above parties, classes, and individuals, he declared public opinion to be an objective, rational amalgam of the judgments of enlightened men.[155]

---

[149] Ibid., 150, 159. See also ibid., 64; Gouhier, Jeunesse, 3:211.   [150] Ecrits, 64.

[151] Benjamin Constant, Réflexions sur les constitutions et les garanties (1814), in Constant, Collection complètes des ouvrages, 4 vols. (Paris, 1818), 1:155. See also idem, Opinion sur la nouvelle législation de la presse prononcée à la Chambre des députés le 14 avril 1819, in ibid., 4:236–67; idem, Observations sur le discours prononcé par S. E. le Ministre de l'Intérieur en faveur du projet de loi sur la liberté de la presse (1814), in Oeuvres, 1249, 1260; idem, De la liberté des brochures, des pamphlets et des journaux considérée sous le rapport de l'intérêt du gouvernement (1814), in ibid., 1219–43; Mona Ozouf, "Public Spirit," in A Critical Dictionary, ed. Furet and Ozouf, 772–7.

[152] [François Guizot], Review of Annales de la session de 1817 à 1818, by Benjamin Constant, Archives philosophiques, politiques, et littéraires 2 (1817): 265.

[153] [François Guizot], "Politique spéciale: Des garanties légales de la liberté de la presse," Archives philosophiques, politiques, et littéraires 5 (1818): 186, 195.

[154] Guizot, Review of Annales de la session, 262.

[155] Rosanvallon, "Les Doctrinaires," 421–8.

Comte was undoubtedly influenced by Constant's view of a free press as a safeguard against government corruption. Yet his position that liberty of the press was an institution allowing for representation was similar to Guizot's. At heart, Comte adopted the position of Guizot and the doctrinaires, who like the Idéologues, believed that social power should be in the hands of the most capable, rational members of society. All were concerned with creating a new elite to avoid the dangers of democracy.

But Comte's rhetoric differed substantially from Guizot's. It betrayed an elitism of another sort and his greater loyalty to the social goals of the Revolution, when the "political point of view" was "more general and elevated" and took into account common interests. Comte never, for example, used the term "new aristocracy" to designate his elite as Guizot did, because it was too reminiscent of the hated upper class of the ancien régime.[156] Comte's elite, the "spiritual power," was not to be a new social class in the same fashion. Moreover, one reason Comte tended to be dismissive of parliamentary government was that, unlike Guizot, he had little faith in the political system, whose electoral laws made the Chamber unrepresentative. He was very critical of the *gouvernants*, including the deputies, because they were so driven by self-interest that they lacked a vision of the whole nation. Terrified of revolutions, they looked upon the people as "turbulent" and "inept" instead of recognizing the fact that they were more capable and advanced than they themselves were.[157] Thus he distrusted the idea of a separate, superior political class, whereas Guizot sought to create one, especially because of his own political aspirations.

Comte wanted the government to serve the people, a position Guizot rejected owing to his preference for the rule of the bourgeoisie and his greater fear of the excesses of the Revolution.[158] As Pierre Rosanvallon has pointed out, Guizot always emphasized the gulf between capable men and the masses – the governors and the governed – in order to ensure that the "social power" was a "reasonable power."[159] In *Du gouvernement représentatif et de l'état actuel de la France* of 1816, Guizot wrote, "It is not to govern themselves, [but] to be well-governed that nations elect deputies . . . ; it is thus necessary that all the important means of government be placed between the hands of the power that governs."[160] But Comte looked forward to the day when the "mass of men" would be literate and capable of enjoying the consultative voice given to them by a free

---

[156] Guizot, *Des moyens de gouvernement*, 157.   [157] *Ecrits*, 144, 155.
[158] Guizot, *Des moyens de gouvernement*, 26, 142, 162–75.
[159] Rosanvallon, *Le Moment Guizot*, 72; see also 48–9, 98, 107–19.
[160] F. Guizot, *Du gouvernement représentatif et de l'état actuel de la France* (Paris, 1816), 51.

press. Even "poorly instructed" citizens could thus give their advice on political issues. Using for his own purposes Saint-Simon's and Guizot's key term, "capacity," he insisted that the "nation," that is, "the governed," had the "principal political capacity."[161] Although Comte seemed unsupportive of Constant's view that "no liberty can exist . . . without representative assemblies,"[162] he followed the new direction that Constant had taken in arguing that public opinion and political authority had to derive from the same source, the people.[163] It did not occur to him that their representatives and his elite, the publicists, could misrepresent them.

Many years later, Comte disavowed all his articles in *Le Politique* except those on the liberty of the press. He said they indicated that his thought was always moving in the direction of the positive religion because they showed that a free press gave every citizen a "consultative authority."[164] The idea that the press should be an overseer of the government and "serve" the citizens' interests contained the essence of his theory of the spiritual power. When Comte later became disillusioned with journalists, he replaced them with the priests of the Religion of Humanity, who became the new "champions" of the people.

---

[161] *Ecrits*, 149, 150n1, 158.   [162] Constant, *Réflexions sur les constitutions*, 29.

[163] Fontana, *Benjamin Constant*, 88.

[164] *Système*, vol. 4, "Apendice," ii. Comte was mistaken when he said that he wrote these articles in 1818.

Chapter 4

Comte's Growing Independence,
1819–1821

I will be careful to indicate to you exactly what is my work and what is
Saint-Simon's.

Comte to Valat, 1820

COMTE'S FIRST SIGNED ARTICLES: *LE CENSEUR EUROPÉEN*

In mid-1819 Saint-Simon and his friends were unable to fulfill the
requirement of a new law that they deposit "caution money" at the
Treasury in case they incurred a fine. Consequently, the government forced *Le Politique* to close.[1] Comte's work for it must have
been well regarded because in June he began to write articles and
book reviews for *Le Censeur européen*, which had replaced *Le Censeur*
and was just beginning its daily publication. Besides being pleased
with the pay, Comte was happy to work for a well-respected periodical with strong ties to the Independents.[2]

In the second issue, which appeared on June 16, 1819, Comte
contributed an article in which he again called for a less wasteful
administration. He condemned the proliferation of useless function-
aries since Napoleon's regime because they made the government
more expensive and more powerful. The government should be
based on the "noble passion of equality," which had been so "grand"
and "pure" in 1789. Comte defined equality as the "horror of
privileges," which entailed the elimination of sinecures and the
limitation of state power. But he did not feel that everyone, regardless
of their abilities, should have equal access to government jobs.

---

[1] Collins, *Newspaper Press*, 22; Comte to Valat, September 24, 1819, *CG*, 1:55. *Le Politique*
had appeared only twelve times.

[2] Ephraim Harpaz, "*Le Censeur européen*: Histoire d'un journal industrialiste," *Revue d'histoire
économique et sociale* 37 (1959): 357; C. M. Des Granges, *La Presse littéraire sous la Restauration,
1815–1830* (Paris: Société du Mercure de France, 1907), 55; Louis Girard, *Les Libéraux
français, 1814–1875* (Paris: Aubier, 1985), 85. Perhaps at this point Comte met Augustin
Thierry, who was contributing many articles on history and philosophy to the journal.

Reflecting his own meritocratic inclinations, he insisted that "only capable men" be given such positions.[3] Thus he supported the revolutionary principle of the career open to talents but rejected the egalitarianism of the extreme Left. Moreover, in keeping with the pro-industrial bias of the journal, he maintained that people engaged in productive work should be honored and paid more than those involved in politics. In this way, political positions would not be considered more lucrative and honorable. As a rule, politicians and bureaucrats used their offices to exploit the public for their own gain. Comte again showed his distrust of the governing classes and the political realm.

Although he later considered his articles in *Le Censeur européen* "secondary," Comte was very proud of them in 1819.[4] They were the first that he ever really signed, perhaps because the more lenient press laws of 1819 made such boldness less dangerous. Also, he was working for the first time independently of Saint-Simon, who did not overshadow him. Comte signed the article of June 16 with the initials A.C., instead of I.C. (Isidore Comte).[5] He may have decided to mark the beginning of a new era in his own development by using "Auguste" for his first name. In July, when he wrote a book review in which he proposed that the role of the government be limited to the maintenance of law and order and the protection of industry, he signed the article for the first time with "all the letters" of his new name – Auguste Comte.[6] His only worry was that his parents might find out that he was still working as a journalist.

---

[3] *Ecrits*, 162, 164. The article, entitled "Sur une doctrine singulière professée récemment à la Chambre des Députés," can be found in *Le Censeur européen*, no. 2 (June 16, 1819): 2–3.

[4] Comte to George Frederick Holmes, April 19, 1852, *CG*, 6:268. See also Comte to Valat, September 24, 1819, *CG*, 1:55. In these two letters, Comte gave the impression that he wrote more articles for the journal. But since he did not sign any of them, it is impossible to tell which ones are his.

[5] See the original article in *Le Censeur européen*, no. 2 (June 16, 1819): 3. The initials are not reproduced in *Ecrits*, 164.

[6] Comte to Valat, September 24, 1819, *CG*, 1:55. See also Lonchampt, *Précis*, 13. Comte signed "Auguste Comte, Ancien Elève de l'Ecole Polytechnique" to his review of a book on the history of navigation, *Histoire de la navigation intérieure et particulièrement de celle de l'Angleterre et de la France*, by J. Cordier. See *Le Censeur européen*, no. 33 (July 17, 1819): 3–4. This review is reproduced in *Ecrits*, 165–9. However, the editors of the *Ecrits de jeunesse* did not reprint the signature, and the editors of the *Correspondance générale* were incorrect when they added "A. Comte" to the end of the letters that Comte wrote before May 1, 1824. The letter of May 1, 1824, to d'Eichthal is the first one signed "Auguste Comte" that still exists. See Comte to d'Eichthal, May 1, 1824, in "Matériaux pour servir à la biographie d'Auguste Comte: Correspondance d'Auguste Comte et Gustave d'Eichthal," ed. Pierre Laffitte, *RO*, 2d. ser., 12 (March 1, 1896): 203.

THE FIRST OPUSCULE: "SÉPARATION GÉNÉRALE ENTRE LES OPINIONS ET LES DÉSIRS"

Comte took the most pride in an article entitled "Séparation générale entre les opinions et les désirs." Written in July 1819, it was intended for *Le Censeur* but was never published. Three years before he died, he republished six works of his youth at the end of the *Système* to demonstrate the continuity of his thought. This article was the first of these six "primitive opuscules on social philosophy" and revealed, in Comte's words, "how much I inclined at twenty-one years of age toward the division of two powers."[7] The opuscule, in effect, makes 1819 the year of Comte's philosophical debut.[8]

Echoing Bichat's conception of mutually exclusive capacities, one of Saint-Simon's principles, Comte maintained in this article that a person could not be both an actor and a spectator.[9] The governing classes' claim that they alone had correct political views was "absurd" because they were too involved in day-to-day practical operations to be capable theoreticians.[10] Only publicists could form appropriate political opinions, but they had to avoid political practice by rejecting any public employment or function. This clearly points to Comte's future theory of the separation of powers, where there would always be a sharp distinction between the spiritual and temporal authorities.

The first opuscule marked a change in Comte's attitude toward the people. In his articles for *Le Politique*, he had looked forward to the day when each "enlightened" Frenchman could contribute to the press and adopt the "character of a legislator perfectly analogous to that of a deputy."[11] Now he maintained that "enlightened" meant trained in political science, not merely literate as it did before, and he dismissed as foolish the idea that every man could "set himself up as a legislator."[12] He referred to Condorcet's argument that people did not dare to feign knowledge of the physical sciences without having first studied them and they should apply the same logic to the political world.

---

[7] *Système*, vol. 4, "Appendice," i, iii. At the top of the original manuscript Comte wrote, "Reserved Sunday 20 Aristote 62 while burning several other old manuscripts." MAC. This statement, written in 1850, also gives the impression that Comte was embarrassed about other articles that he wrote for *Le Censeur européen* and perhaps for other journals and burned them.

[8] Corra, *La Naissance du génie d'Auguste Comte: Sa Vie jusqu'en 1819*, 34.

[9] Manuel, *Prophets of Paris*, 121. Comte mentioned the *Recherches sur la vie et sur la mort*, where Bichat outlined this theory, in "Essais sur quelques points de la philosophie des mathématiques," *Ecrits*, 494.

[10] *Système*, vol. 4, "Appendice," 1.   [11] *Ecrits*, 153, 154.   [12] *Système*, vol. 4, "Appendice," 1.

Realizing, however, that he sounded as indifferent to the people as the governing classes did, Comte sought a role for them. Though incapable of forming trustworthy opinions because of their lack of training, they did have political desires, including a longing for "liberty, peace, industrial prosperity, economical public expenditures, and the good use of taxes."[13] Therefore, they should indicate the goals of society and leave the means of achieving it, which they were not able to construe, to the publicists, the future scientists of society. Like other liberals of his time, Comte seemed torn by his political cause and political realities, for many of the people were peasants, nostalgic for the past and supportive of the conservatives, while most publicists were liberal.[14] Despite his ambivalence toward popular opinion, he still subscribed to the leftist position that liberty of the press should permit the people to formulate their desires.

Strikingly elitist and authoritarian, this opuscule extends the arguments Comte made in his 1816 essay and foreshadows his belief that politics must be based on expertise.[15] Since neither the governing class nor the governed class was competent in the new science of society, they had to trust the experts. Comte changed his view of these experts, that is, the publicists. Previously, he had portrayed them simply as the representatives of the people. Now he maintained that they would become the scientists of society once politics became a positive science. Although his view of the scientists of society was still vague, he was already advocating their rule and restricting the freedom of the other members of society.

COMTE'S ATTITUDE TOWARD WORKERS AND WOMEN

Comte was generally impassioned by the possibilities of reform in 1819 because of the developing power of the press and the growing strength of the Independents in the Chamber. A letter written to Valat in September 1819 reveals more about his political and social attitudes. His "profound observation of cities" had made him "profoundly revolted by the insolence, hardness, dullness, fatuity, and egoism" of the "upper classes," who represented the "scum of the human species." The "lower classes" had, in fact, more virtues.

---

[13] Ibid, 2. In the fifth paragraph of the original manuscript in the archives at the Maison d'Auguste Comte, Comte wrote: "It seems to me that it would be good to distinguish more than one has done up to now political opinions from their political desires." When he reprinted the manuscript, he left out the word "political" before "opinions" and before "desires."

[14] For information about the press at this time, consult Ledré, "La Press nationale," 29; Collins, *Newspaper Press*, 28–9.

[15] Angèle Kremer-Marietti, Introduction to *Plan des travaux*, 10.

Their vices, such as "avidity," "servility," and a "stupid admiration for luxury and grandeur" were due primarily to their "ignorance" and their "dependence" on the upper classes' influence. Like Marx, Comte believed that the vices of the lower classes were the "inevitable" result of their oppressed socioeconomic position.[16]

Comte halfheartedly admitted that he was most respectful of the urban middle class ("la classe moyenne des villes"), the members of which had "many qualities," such as productivity. But even "men of merit" were seduced by the desire for wealth and power or remained indifferent spectators of the class struggle.[17]

It is clear that although he came from a bourgeois background, Comte sympathized most with the workers. He was frustrated by his lack of success and felt oppressed by the same social system that was persecuting them. He resisted the temptation to live "apart from men," for he realized that he had to "live a little" for others to be happy. He asked Valat to join the "small number of enlightened men" devoted to reorganizing the social order for the benefit of the majority of people, the truly "useful people." He wanted to stop the domination of the workers by their idle masters, who were stealing the products of their labors. In this class "struggle," he would be forever on the "side of the weak." This deep, sincere concern for the "little man," which is reflected in this "apostolic epistle" to Valat, is sometimes lost in the elitist tones of his first opuscule and later writings.[18]

Comte's sympathy for the weak extended to women. At the height of his relationship with Pauline, he declared that "this delicious half of the human species was worth . . . infinitely more than the other [half]."[19] Even when love had grown "very old" and he felt his "liberty" threatened, he helped her take care of their sick daughter. He wanted to continue to be nice to Pauline because he recognized that "women in general and collectively have suffered so much from the males of their species, that I believe that I am particularly obliged to compensate as much as I can for the general offenses of my sex." Men, he claimed, used the "horrible law of the strongest" to lord it over women, whom they regarded as a "piece of furniture" or a

[16] Comte to Valat, September 24, 1819, *CG*, 1:52.   [17] Ibid., 52–3.
[18] Ibid., 52–4. Comte's sympathies for the common people are also evident in another unpublished article he wrote for *Le Censeur européen*. It was a review of Jacques-Guillaume Thouret's *Abrégé des révolutions de l'ancien gouvernement français, ouvrage élémentaire extrait de l'abbé Dubos et de l'abbé Mably*. Because the book's publisher, Aimé Comte, felt that Comte's review was too critical, her brother, Charles, refused to publish it in *Le Censeur européen*. The book review is reproduced in *Ecrits*, 453–8. See also Gouhier, *Jeunesse*, 3:264; Arbousse-Bastide, *Doctrine d'éducation*, 1:19.
[19] Comte to Valat, June 15, 1818, *CG*, 1:39.

"toy destined for all eternity for the good pleasure and usage of his Majesty *Man*." A woman was like a "domestic animal" owned by the physically stronger man; she was scarcely more than his serf or slave. If she had no money, she had only two choices: either she sold her body or worked in the hardest, worst paid jobs imaginable – if she could find employment. Men, after all, left women only "the very smallest number of professions and the least lucrative ones." Comte argued that all women should be liberals interested in progress, for as civilization advanced, their social and political conditions improved. Thus at this point, he believed that reforming society included overturning the law of the strongest to better the condition of women.[20]

His views reveal the influence of the wave of feminist thinking that surged during the Revolution, when revolutionary women used their male colleagues' arguments about equal rights to advance their own cause. One of the leading proponents of women's political rights at the time was Condorcet, the only philosophe who argued that women were not inferior to men and should have the same education. Comte had, of course, carefully read the *Esquisse*, in which Condorcet called for equal rights for women and blamed men for abusing their greater physical strength – a position echoed by Comte. Condorcet was perhaps influenced by Mary Wollstonecraft, who lived in Paris during part of the Revolution.[21] Arguing in favor of education as a means to ensure women's independence and equality, her *Vindication of the Rights of Woman* was directed against Rousseau's influential theory that a woman was made to be a "coquetish [*sic*] slave" to a man.[22] Although translated into French in 1792, this book was considered scandalous and was not well known in nineteenth-century France.[23] Yet Comte owned a copy and later admitted to Mill that this "strange work" had made a "strong impact" on him in his youth.[24] Wollstonecraft's views were reflected in his desire to

[20] Comte to Valat, September 24, 1819, *CG*, 1:56–8. Comte even sent his daughter out to the country for three months to escape the polluted Parisian air and often went to visit her there. When Louise was nine, she died of croup. In 1846 Comte told Clotilde de Vaux that he still cried over this loss. Comte to Clotilde de Vaux, March 1, 1846, *CG*, 3:339.
[21] Claire Goldberg Moses, *French Feminism in the Nineteenth Century* (Albany: State University of New York, 1984), 9–13; Landes, *Women and the Public Sphere*, 112–17; Susan Groag Bell and Karen M. Offen, *Women, the Family, and Freedom: The Debate in Documents*, 2 vols. (Stanford, Calif.: Stanford University Press, 1983), 1:51, 72, 79–83.
[22] Mary Wollstonecraft, *A Vindication of the Rights of Woman*, ed. Carol H. Poston, 2d ed. (New York: Norton, 1988), 25.
[23] Landes, *Women and the Public Sphere*, 196–7.
[24] Comte to Mill, October 4, 1843, *CG*, 2:198. Madame de Staël expressed feminist ideas in her novel *Delphine*. Comte owned an 1839 edition of this book. It is thus not clear whether he read it before he made these statements criticizing women's inferior position in society.

liberate women from men's domination and improve their economic independence.

When Valat accused him of working only for his own glory, Comte vehemently denied it. He admitted that he hoped to establish his reputation and become a member of the Institut, or more specifically, the Academy of Sciences, "as soon as possible," but he claimed that this was only to acquire a "comfortable and secure existence," especially so that he would never have to implore "some titled ass [*sot*]" to help him. Besides the desire for financial security, he was stimulated by intellectual pleasure and the idea of helping his "poor fellow men." Recognizing already in 1819 that science and politics were the two areas to which he would be forever devoted, he explained that even though his scientific studies gave him the greatest enjoyment, pure intellectual speculation was not enough: "I have a sovereign aversion to scientific works in which I do not clearly perceive utility, whether it be direct or remote." In a sense, he preferred his political studies because they not only engaged him intellectually because of their great difficulty, but contributed to the "amelioration of the fate of the poor human species." Almost as an afterthought, Comte adduced a fourth motive for his activity. He maintained that if he could acquire a "scientific reputation," his "political sermons" would have more value and weight.[25] He remembered this idea of using the sciences to acquire prestige and respect when he wrote the *Cours de philosophie positive*, whose first volumes were devoted to establishing the scientific background of the philosopher.

Various scholars have commented on Comte's analysis of his motives. To Jean Delvolvé, Comte demonstrated that he lacked "true scientific curiosity" and the "thirst for knowledge for knowledge's sake." His system was characterized by a desire to influence human action through the force of ideas. Agreeing with Delvolvé, Antimo Negri points out that Comte's interest in the sciences was inspired not only by this utilitarian or practical principle but by an ethical or humanistic spirit; the sciences cultivated egoism if human obligations were overlooked. Convinced that the sciences could not be separated from social concerns, Comte imbued his pursuit of the sciences with a political passion. And Kremer-Marietti argues that Comte was expressing his conviction that a positive science could not be founded

[25] Comte to Valat, September 28, 1819, *CG*, 1:63–5.

merely on facts but had to relate to social reality. A positive science had to study this reality in order to change it. This letter also underscores the conflict that Barbara Skarga shows to have existed within Comte: that between his naturalistic perspective and his more human point of view.[26] All four scholars suggest that he was basically an activist whose concerns were ultimately moral.

The human side of Comte emerges in a story he later told about himself. He said that one day in 1820, while supposedly watching a solar eclipse from the garden of the Palais Royal, he learned more from watching the other onlookers, who struck him as sadly ignorant of what was happening, than from observing the scientific phenomenon itself. He admitted that by nature he was always "far more engaged by the . . . spectators than by the spectacle itself." His scientific curiosity was, indeed, limited by his humanism and interest in the social world.[27]

THE BEGINNING OF COMTE'S FORMULATION OF THE SCIENCE OF SOCIETY

Although most of his published articles for *Le Politique* and *Le Censeur européen* involved practical matters, other unpublished material reveals that Comte, convinced of his own intellectual stature and the moral purity of his goals, was working hard to create a science of society. Later he said that it was around this time, that is, around 1819–20, that he stopped learning from Saint-Simon and no longer considered himself his "student" in the strict sense of the word.[28]

In 1819 Comte wrote at least five and perhaps as many as eight incomplete fragments on political science. A manuscript that I discovered at the Bibliothèque Nationale reveals that at least some of them were intended to be part of a long essay for the fourth *cahier* of volume 3 of *Le Politique*, which Saint-Simon never published.[29] Perhaps he lacked the funds or Comte could not finish his work.

[26] Delvolvé, *Réflexions*, 38–40; Negri, *Augusto Comte*, 23–30; Kremer-Marietti, *Le Concept*, 22; Barbara Skarga, "Le Coeur et la raison, ou Les Antinomies du système de Comte," *Les Etudes philosophiques*, no. 3 (July–September 1974): 389.

[27] *Traité philosophique d'astronomie populaire*, 366n1.

[28] Comte to d'Eichthal, May 1, 1824, *CG*, 1:80. Comte gave his family the impression that he was working on an important, original work independently of Saint-Simon. See Alix Comte to Auguste Comte, August 23, November 20, 1820, "*Lettres d'Alix Comte*," ed. Laffitte, 70–1, 73–4.

[29] Five fragments, whose original manuscripts can be found in the Maison d'Auguste Comte, are entitled "Ce que c'est que la politique positive"; "De la division qui a existé jusqu'à présent entre la morale et politique [*sic*]"; "Considérations sur les tentatives qui ont été faites pour fonder la science sociale sur la physiologie et sur quelques autres sciences";

In these unpublished fragments, Comte addressed the question of what made politics positive. He asserted that political theory reflected developments that had already taken place in political practice. But at the same time theory also influenced practice in a "more or less important" fashion.[30] Reflecting his tendency to take a middle position, which took into account the complexity of the problem, he stressed the mutual relationship in politics between theory and practice. But he did not clarify the extent to which theory influenced practice. Nevertheless, like Staël, Constant, Dunoyer, Guizot, and other liberals, he assumed that once political theory became scientific, it would remove government from the dangerous realm of the passions and make political practice more rational.[31]

To illustrate his argument, Comte claimed that throughout history the basic principle of society was the law of the strongest, which divided people into masters and slaves. His idea that political theory merely fortified the dominant social power is strikingly similar to the Marxist concept of hegemony. But with greater optimism than Marx, he believed that since the abolition of slavery, people treated others increasingly as equals. Now that the law of common interest was becoming the underlying social principle, political science had to adopt a new goal, the improvement of the public good. He urged society to shift its attention from the domination of men to the "action of *men* over *things*."[32] As an engineer, he upheld the Baconian dictum that man should act on nature to harness it

"Considérations sur les tentatives qui ont été faites pour rendre positive la science sociale, en la fesant [*sic*] dériver de quelqu'autre science"; and "Sur les travaux politiques de Condorcet." These are reproduced, although in a misleading fashion, in *Ecrits*, 467–89. The manuscript of what appear to be the final copies of the unpublished issues of *Le Politique* is in the Fonds Pereire, N.a.fr. 24606, BN. The fourth *cahier* in this collection reproduces almost exactly two fragments that are known to have been written by Comte. The first fragment, "Considérations générales sur la possibilité de rendre actuellement la politique une science positive," represents the introduction in the manuscript of *Le Politique* and reproduces almost exactly the rough copy at the Maison d'Auguste Comte entitled "Ce que c'est que la politique positive." The second fragment, "De la division qui a existé jusqu'à présent entre la morale et politique [*sic*]," is the third chapter of the manuscript and is nearly the same as the rough copy at the Maison d'Auguste Comte. Three other fragments in the manuscript of *Le Politique* that Comte probably wrote are entitled "Chapitre Premier – Origine de la politique positive"; "Chapitre Second – Pourquoi la politique n'a pas pu être jusqu'à ce jour une science positive"; and "Chapitre Quatrième – De la nouvelle division qui doit s'établir dans la politique." As for Comte's inability to finish his work, see the fifth and final article in the fourth *cahier*, called "Chapitre Quatrième – De la nouvelle division qui doit s'établir dans la politique." It is also interesting that in the first article he explained that his work was just a "first try" and that his ideas were "necessarily incomplete," especially since the materials were so "new" and "difficult." For information regarding the subject of volume 3 of *Le Politique* and Saint-Simon's misgivings, see *Le Politique* 1 (1819): 54, 165.

[30] *Ecrits*, 467.   [31] Rosanvallon, *Le Moment Guizot*, 20–1.   [32] *Ecrits*, 468.

productively for his own purposes and that the "empire of man over things" depended on the sciences.[33]

He felt that the time was already ripe for politics to become a positive science.[34] One reason was that people's activities were far less regulated by the government. Repeating Constant's argument in *De l'esprit de conquête et de l'usurpation*, Comte declared, "A great number of operations which had first been considered public or political . . . have become private, or free." As a liberal, he considered the public sphere to signify "the arbitrary." He agreed with Adam Smith and his successors, who had developed political economy after noticing that individuals benefited from personal liberty, that is, freedom from government interference. Political economy was still for Comte the "germ of positive politics."[35]

Another important reason for the timeliness of politics as a positive science had to do with its position in the scientific hierarchy.[36] Comte showed that "since all superstitious beliefs have man as their object, the sciences that first escaped from their influence had to be those whose subject matter was the farthest away from man."[37] Thus astronomy became positive first, followed by physics, mechanics, chemistry, and physiology. Because politics studied the most complicated phenomena and man himself, it was the last to free itself from theological superstitions and become a positive science. Thus already in 1819 Comte was basing the progress of the sciences on the complexity of their data and the closeness of their subject matter to man. Used to prove that the establishment of positive politics was inevitable, these ideas provided the basis of his law of three stages and the classification of the sciences. The only difference between this order of sciences and the one he described in 1822 was that in 1822 he deleted mechanics and made mathematics the first science.

Despite Comte's denials, some of Saint-Simon's old writings probably influenced him. Comte may have been familiar with the *Mémoire sur la science de l'homme* and *Lettres d'un habitant de Genève à*

---

[33] Francis Bacon, *Novum Organum*, in *The Works of Francis Bacon*, ed. James Spedding, Robert Leslie Ellis, and Douglas Denon Heath, 14 vols. (London, 1857–74), 2:222; Farrington, *Francis Bacon*, 3, 7.

[34] Comte made this argument in the second essay in the manuscript at the Bibliothèque Nationale: "Chapitre Premier – Origine de la politique positive." This chapter seems to have been written by Comte because it refers to the first, introductory chapter and follows logically from it. Manuscript of *Le Politique*, [1819], Fonds Pereire, N.a.fr. 24606, fols. 85–8, BN.

[35] Ibid., fol. 89v, 90r, 91r.

[36] See the third article in the fourth *cahier* called "Chapitre Second – Pourquoi la politique n'a pas pu être jusqu'à ce jour une science positive." Ibid., fols. 92–6.

[37] Ibid., fol. 93r.

ses contemporains. In both of these, Saint-Simon claimed that a scientific theory consisted of observed facts, referred to the positive sciences of mathematics, astronomy, physics, and chemistry, and revealed his expectation that physiology would become positive soon. (At that point, Saint-Simon viewed the science of man as part of physiology.) In fact, the idea that the sciences became positive according to the complexity of their data was attributed by Saint-Simon to Burdin. Therefore, it seems that some of the essential features of Comte's positivism derived from Saint-Simon.

Comte also inherited Saint-Simon's respect for Christianity and the Middle Ages, which in turn could be traced to Chateaubriand and Bonald. But Comte was also affected by what Edward Berenson has called a new "left-wing Christian discourse" inspired by a populist image of Jesus. After the French Revolution, many leftists took up the egalitarian and fraternal values preached by Jesus to criticize economic liberalism and the market society. They wished to point the way to a true spiritual regeneration, one that would touch the individual and society more deeply and effectively than political reform.[38] Appropriating their language, Comte praised Jesus for refining morality and maintained that he was basically "liberal" because he had tried to improve the general well-being.[39] Killed by the "ultras of their time," Christ and his apostles should be admired for having championed the oppressed and having preached "equality and philanthropy." Comte revealed his own sympathies when he declared that the French revolutionaries – presumably the extreme leftists Jacques Roux and Jacques Hébert – were correct in calling Christ the "first sans-culotte of the universe."[40]

It is clear that in 1819 Comte was beginning to consider Christ a model for founding a religion. He suggested, moreover, that he himself was a convert to a new religion that would consist of positive politics and morality or, more precisely, of social science. He wanted to disseminate its truths just as Christ had preached his religious principles. Yet he would be more effective than Christ and his followers, who had been able to make themselves only an

[38] Edward Berenson, "A New Religion of the Left: Christianity and Social Radicalism in France, 1815–1848," in *The Transformation of Political Culture*, ed. Furet and Ozouf, 543; see also 544.

[39] See the fourth article in the manuscript of *Le Politique* at the Bibliothèque Nationale entitled "Chapitre Troisième – De la division qui a existé jusqu'à présent entre la morale et la politique," fols. 97–100. In the rough copy at the Maison d'Auguste Comte, the article is called "De la division qui a existé jusqu'à présent entre la morale et politique [*sic*]." The manuscript copy at the Bibliothèque Nationale and the rough copy at the Masion d'Auguste Comte are nearly the same. The article is reproduced in *Ecrits*, 469–71.

[40] Comte to Valat, September 24, September 28, 1819, *CG*, 1:54, 65. See also the comment by Pierre Arnaud, Note XVI, *CG*, 1:377.

inferior power outside of and opposed to the state and thus could not change the "vicious and illiberal" political system, which always supported the interests of the strongest members of society. Comte believed that once politics became scientific, it would at last share the aim of morality, that of improving the happiness of society as a whole. "Politics," "morality," and "moral and political sciences" would then become synonymous.[41] Convinced of the overriding importance of morality, Comte intended from the beginning to make politics a normative moral system that would protect the people. Like Saint-Simon, he believed that politics reflected the reigning moral system.

Thus despite his previous criticism of Christian morality for being sentimental and ineffective, the goal of Comte's system – the creation of a "moral," "liberal" regime where men treated one another as "equals" and "brothers" – appeared to be the same as that of the Christian system.[42] Although he despised its theological dogmas, which went against his scientific education, he evidently still admired its moral principles, which had been a central part of his religious upbringing. In a highly ambivalent manner, he was implying that positive political theory would make Christian morality effective because it would preserve its essence while ridding it of the trappings that made it lose credibility.

Comte was very critical of other thinkers' approach to "positive science." He claimed that Cabanis and other recent French philosophers who attempted to base the science of man on physiology had made a tremendous error. Here Comte seemed to be criticizing the direction taken by Saint-Simon in his early writings.[43] Comte argued that physiology and social science were two separate sciences, for the former examined man as an individual, while the latter considered him as a member of society. Social science rested on physiology only to the extent that its precepts could not contradict those of biology. But, he added, social science must also rest on all the other sciences in the same fashion. Foreshadowing his theory of the classification of the sciences, he declared that the sciences had to give each other help, but at the same time they must remain *distinct*, concerned only with observations proper to their respective fields of investigation. The science of society could be founded only on the data provided by political economy. Although Comte would change his mind about the value of political economy, his argument against

---

[41] *Ecrits*, 469, 471.   [42] Ibid., 471.
[43] Instead of praising Cabanis as his mentor had, he called his *Des rapports du physique et du moral de l'homme* "radically vicious." Ibid., 474. Comte had an 1815 copy of this book in his library.

reductionism would remain one of the most constant and important themes of his writings.

Like Saint-Simon, who had written a critique of the *Esquisse* in the *Introduction aux travaux scientifiques* and *Mémoire sur la science de l'homme*, Comte was impressed by Condorcet's attempt to establish the science of society on the basis of history, especially the law of progress of the mind, which the philosophe had discovered to be the "immediate cause of the improvement of civilization." Comte believed that because political advances reflected and coincided with intellectual developments, one must study the state of enlightenment in order to effect social reform at the correct moment. Otherwise, one would not know whether one's efforts were impractical or premature or whether one was fighting against a development that "had to be executed necessarily by the imperious force of things." Comte therefore praised Condorcet for showing that civilization was a governing power far above men. The most that even the governing class and publicists could hope to do was to reinforce, clarify, and hasten the effects of the power of civilization and to lessen the friction it could cause in the "political machine."[44]

Repeating many of Saint-Simon's objections, Comte also criticized Condorcet. According to him, Condorcet's effort to derive social science from mathematics, particularly the calculus of probabilities, was untenable. This hatred of statistics would reappear throughout Comte's writings. Furthermore, Condorcet did not concentrate enough on developing his own law of progress, for he used different criteria to mark the change from one epoch to another. Instead, he should have based the transformations on the most important set of ideas, that of politics and morality, which led to changes in the other areas of human existence. Moreover, Condorcet shared the philosophes' general habit of judging other eras by the more enlightened standards of their own time. His work failed to be scientific because instead of observing the past, he criticized it. Intoxicated by an "absurd idea of the absolute," he did not appreciate the useful function of seemingly unprogressive ideas and institutions in previous stages of civilization or the way in which they corresponded to the state of enlightenment at that time. Rather than claiming that Christianity was inferior to the ancient religion or that it was a dangerous enemy of enlightenment, he should have realized that it provided scholars with the means to civilize humanity. At the time of its establishment, Christianity was the "most liberal work" possible.[45]

These incomplete fragments are important because they reveal that, at twenty-one, Comte was already seizing the law of progress

[44] Ibid., 485–6.   [45] Ibid., 488.

as the basic idea of the science of society. Its significance had been pointed out by Saint-Simon, but even he had had some doubts about the indefinite perfectibility of the human species. Unlike Saint-Simon, who at one point complained that Condorcet had overemphasized humanity's intellectual achievements, Comte criticized Condorcet for not having been more systematic about them, and he made the law of progress far more deterministic than its originator had intended. Comte emphasized the similarity between social and natural phenomena; the "natural laws" of history were as "determined" as those of the "fall of a stone."[46] Condorcet, however, had used history to show how people could free themselves from restrictive conditions, for he found the real principles of social science in the statistical study of man in society. Rejecting this reduction of one science (social science) to another (mathematics), Comte made Condorcet's law of the progress of reason the centerpiece of his study of society, especially because he took a more relativistic approach to historical development.[47] Whereas Condorcet at times seemed overwhelmed by the barbarism of previous ages, Comte was more optimistic about the advance of civilization; he claimed to find something beneficial in every idea and institution of the past.

Though an advocate of relativism, Comte himself seemed to take an absolutist position when he reified civilization and made the law of progress the cause of all intellectual, social, and political change. To him, people were but puppets of the law of progress, whose dictates they unknowingly had to follow. Unlike Condorcet, who believed people could control their future, Comte severely restricted the scope of the human will, especially to effect change.[48] He hoped that with a greater grasp of history, people would no longer have to be "pushed blindly" by the law of progress, but he still argued that the most they could do was to obey this law with full consciousness of the "direction that it prescribes for us."[49] Even the influence of theory on practice seemed limited. Like Marx, Comte sought to escape this determinism by arguing that the enlightened could accelerate inevitable developments. He seemed to be saying that men who interpret the law of progress ultimately controlled society.

After reviewing Condorcet's contributions to the science of society, Comte examined the philosophy of Destutt de Tracy, a friend of Cabanis and Condorcet and founder of the new science of ideas, "Idéologie." To eliminate the barrier between mind and body created by Christianity and to make knowledge more reliable, this science sought to discover the physical laws regulating the functioning

---

[46] Comte to Buchholz, November 18, 1825, *CG*, 1:170; Comte to Valat, September 8, 1824, *CG*, 1:127.

[47] Baker, *Condorcet*, 371–82.   [48] Baker, "Closing the Revolution," 334.

[49] *Système*, vol. 4, "Appendice," 24.

of reason. Destutt de Tracy sought to make it the method of a new science of society that would provide a more solid basis for political and social reform than the abstract, unscientific concept of natural political rights.[50] Whereas Cabanis worked on its physiological basis, Destutt de Tracy elucidated the principles of "rational Idéologie" in the *Elémens d'idéologie*, published in four volumes from 1801 to 1815. Stating that Idéologie was "a part of Zoology," he began with the first certain principle, that a person is a sensate being.[51] To feel is to think. Since we are sure of what we feel, all our perceptions are incontrovertible. Although he argued that knowledge is relative since each person can know only his own perceptions, he sought to escape a purely idealist position by arguing that our sensory perceptions are accurate and thus the same for everyone. He called the general model of reality shared by all people *"reason, good sense, common sense."*[52]

Working from his concept of the will, the intellectual faculty that was the source of the sensations of movement and resistance, Destutt de Tracy hoped to expose the principles of the moral and political sciences. In the fourth volume of the *Elémens*, which concentrated on political economy, he showed that the will gave rise to the sense of personality and property, was the origin of one's needs, and provided the means to satisfy these needs. The power to exercise one's will without undue constraint was the essence of liberty, whose growth should be the first goal of society. He criticized social contract theory for claiming that man renounced part of his liberty upon entering society. To Destutt de Tracy, man could never live apart from society; nor would he ever wish to sacrifice his freedom. Influenced by Smith and Say, he argued that the social state provided man with the advantages of exchanges – especially economic ones – that helped him to fulfill his needs. He denounced idlers and lauded laborers for their productivity. With a strong dislike for inequalities of power and wealth, he asserted that the interests of the poor were the same as those of society as a whole and that the general interest should be supreme.[53]

Like Condorcet, Destutt de Tracy believed in the power of public

---

[50] On Destutt de Tracy, consult Picavet, *Les Idéologues*, 328–31; Moravia, *Il pensiero*, 212–13; Ducassé, *Méthode et intuition*, 60; Weill, *Saint-Simon*, 60; Kennedy, *Philosophe*, 16–48, 59; Brian Head, *Ideology and Social Science: Destutt de Tracy and French Liberalism* (Dordrecht: Martinus Nijhoff, 1985), vii; Welch, *Liberty and Utility*, 33, 35.

[51] [Antoine Louis Claude de] Destutt de Tracy, *Elémens d'idéologie*, 4 vols., 2d and 3d eds. (Paris, 1817–18), 1:xiii.

[52] Ibid., 3:280. See also Kennedy, *Philosophe*, 143–4.

[53] Destutt de Tracy, *Elémens*, 4:60–106, 128–9, 148–56, 294–6, 333; Picavet, *Les Idéologues*, 315–16, 340, 386–7; Kennedy, *Philosophe*, 58, 112–16, 132, 152, 180, 203, 206–7, 336; Moravia, *Il pensiero*, 407–12.

education to disseminate scientifically based ideas, which would supplant theology. During the Directory, he recommended that Idéologie be taught in schools to inculcate the secular and republican values necessary for good citizenship and social integration. His *Elémens d'idéologie* was in fact originally intended to be a textbook, and his guidelines were followed by many professors, including François Andrieux in his grammar courses at the Ecole Polytechnique. In fact, Andrieux probably first introduced Comte to the principal tenets of Idéologie.[54]

Comte's interest in this philosophy remained high during the early years of the Restoration, when Destutt de Tracy's prestige rose. Seeking to justify his new concern with sentiments, Comte wrote to Valat in 1818 that Destutt de Tracy was an authority who considered affections to be the source of happiness.[55] And Comte was no doubt familiar with the articles Thierry wrote in September 1819 for *Le Censeur européen*, which praised Destutt de Tracy's recently published works and proposed Idéologie as the basis of a new morality.[56] During this period, Comte probably read Destutt de Tracy's *Elémens d'idéologie*; the volumes he owned were from the second and third editions of this work, published in 1817 and 1818, and his comments to Valat show his familiarity with the last chapter, "On Our Sentiments and Our Passions, or Morality."

Many of Destutt de Tracy's ideas appealed to Comte, who asserted that his "rational ideology" was the "only one that intelligent minds acknowledge."[57] He particularly favored Destutt de Tracy's effort to make social science "positive" by basing it on a philosophy that would ensure certain knowledge, escape the twin evils of theology and metaphysics, and avoid the dangerous rhetoric of 1789. He also seemed influenced by Destutt de Tracy's rejection of Condorcet's use of mathematics to ascertain the legitimacy of principles on the grounds that mental functions were too complicated to be reduced to mathematical equations.[58] Destutt de Tracy's criticisms increased Comte's wariness of the use of probability theory in social science.[59]

---

[54] See Comte's comment about his "first adolescence" in *Cours*, 1:855. See also Kennedy, *Philosophe*, 86, 174, 232–6; Picavet, *Les Idéologues*, 87, 232, 320, 327–8; Head, *Ideology*, 99–104.

[55] Comte to Valat, May 15, 1818, *CG*, 1:33.

[56] A.-L. C. Destutt de Tracy, *Quels sont les moyens de fonder la morale chez un peuple?* (Paris, Year VI), 19; Kennedy, *Philosophe*, 64, 235–6.

[57] *Ecrits*, 479.

[58] Destutt de Tracy, *Elémens*, 4:31–5. See also Picavet, *Les Idéologues*, 375; Kennedy, *Philosophe*, 49–50; Moravia, *Il pensiero*, 351–7.

[59] *Ecrits*, 481. Mauduit is thus mistaken when he suggests that Comte was appropriating Bonald's criticisms of Condorcet. Mauduit, *Auguste Comte*, 56.

However, Comte criticized Idéologie for being only a "science of the processes that the human mind follows in its operations and of the methods that it uses to render its course prompter, easier, and more sure." He could not see how this general science of method could be the basis of any science, especially the science of society. Idéologie seemed to remain "outside of the scientific trunk."[60]

Comte's opinion of Idéologie is clearer in a letter he wrote to Valat in 1819, where he condemned the principles of psychology, the science of man that was the basis of Victor Cousin's philosophy. In fact, Destutt de Tracy's criticism of psychology for studying an unknown entity, the soul, may very well have inspired Comte's own rejection of it. But Comte's comments were directed not only at Cousin, but also at Destutt de Tracy. In his *Principes logiques ou Receuil de faits relatifs à l'intelligence humaine*, a copy of which Comte owned, Destutt de Tracy had declared, "It is easy for us to see, in looking at ourselves, that all our ideas are easily formed within us, by the operations of feeling and judging alone."[61] Comte countered by stating that metaphysical philosophies (such as Cousin's), Idéologie, and studies of logic erred when they pretended to observe the human mind. In a famous passage he stated:

> The human mind . . . cannot be a subject of observation because someone obviously cannot observe the mind of others; and on the other hand, he cannot observe his own mind. In effect, we observe phenomena with our mind; but with what do we observe the mind itself, its operations, its way of proceeding? We cannot divide our mind, that is to say, our brain, into two parts, one that acts, while the other watches it to see the way it goes to work.[62]

Comte prided himself on recognizing that the introspective study of purely intellectual processes was too speculative and metaphysical to be the basis of a science: "Fine thinkers have for a long time . . . agreed on this point; but I do not think that anyone has realized this

---

[60] *Ecrits*, 479, 480. In the *Cours*, Comte was even more critical of Destutt de Tracy's attempt to make this "basic science" independent of all the other sciences and at the same time their director. *Cours*, 1:855.

[61] [Antoine Louis Claude de] Destutt de Tracy, *Principes logiques ou Recueil de faits relatifs à l'intelligence humaine* (Paris, 1817), 24.

[62] Comte to Valat, September 24, 1819, *CG*, 1:58. Robert Scharff makes the important point that Comte was not opposed to all types of psychology. According to Scharff, Comte was really arguing against the "pre-scientific, metaphysically driven 'rational' psychology" that was inspired by Descartes's meditation because it had "for centuries spawned hopelessly conflicting doctrines of the self, or soul." Robert C. Scharff, "Positivism, Philosophy of Science, and Self-Understanding in Comte and Mill," *American Philosophical Quarterly* 26 (October 1989): 260. See also idem, "Monitoring Self-Activity: The Status of Reflection before and after Comte," *Metaphilosophy* 22 (October 1991): 333–48.

result in this way."[63] However, Pierre Macherey has recently suggested that Comte's argument against psychology was influenced by Bonald. In his *Recherches sur les premiers objets des connaissances morales* (1818), Bonald asserted that the mind could not know itself and must be understood in action, that is, through its works.[64] Comte took the same position. Although he never mentioned Bonald by name at this early date, it is possible that he was familiar with this book, especially because Saint-Simon was a great admirer of Bonald.

According to Comte, the falseness of Destutt de Tracy's approach was most evident in his work on political economy – the fourth volume of the *Elémens d'idéologie* – where he began executing his idea of basing social science on Idéologie. Although he praised Destutt de Tracy's economic doctrines, Comte felt he had fallen into "pure metaphysics" when he tried to deduce political principles relating to property, misery, wealth, and even the existence of external reality simply from an analysis of the will, a "purely nominal" entity.[65] His analysis was too "removed from the facts" and reductionist in its attempt to deduce all truths from the fundamental principle of sensibility. Such monism was a throwback to theology.[66]

In sum, Destutt de Tracy resembled Cabanis and Condorcet in that he had repeated the same mistakes he had criticized others for making and his doctrine ended by being metaphysical, if not theological. In fact, Comte considered his effort to make social science positive ultimately less important than the attempts of Cabanis and Condorcet.[67] (At this point, Comte felt Cabanis's approach was the least erroneous.) Consequently, Destutt de Tracy's name was omitted from the original edition of the Positivist Calendar, which Comte created after the Revolution of 1848 to encourage a "respectful appreciation of the diverse services of all our predecessors."[68]

Nevertheless, Comte considered Destutt de Tracy one of the metaphysicians "closest to the positivist state."[69] His interest in simple, concrete reality and his desire to limit knowledge to the observable had a deep impact on Comte's intellectual development.

---

[63] Comte to Valat, September 24, 1819, *CG*, 1:59. See also Gouhier, *Jeunesse*, 3:244n4.
[64] Pierre Macherey, *Comte: La Philosophie et les sciences* (Paris: Presses Universitaires de France, 1989), 52–5.
[65] *Ecrits*, 480; *Cours*, 1:855. See Destutt de Tracy, *Elémens*, 60–98.
[66] *Ecrits*, 480. See also *Cours*, 2:93.   [67] *Ecrits*, 479n1.
[68] Auguste Comte, *Calendrier positiviste ou Système générale de commémoration publique . . . .* (Paris, 1849), 12. Destutt de Tracy's name does appear, however, in a later version of the calendar, published in Auguste Comte, *Catéchisme positiviste, ou Sommaire exposition de la religion universelle en treize entretiens systématiques entre une femme et un prêtre de l'humanité* (Paris: Garnier-Flammarion, 1966) (hereafter, *Catéchisme positiviste*), 270.
[69] *Cours*, 1:855.

Like Stendhal, who was deeply influenced by Destutt de Tracy's attack on dualism, Comte was attracted to his concept that feeling and thinking were related and that the mind and the heart were essentially one.[70] Destutt de Tracy fostered Comte's concern with the emotions, particularly the natural feeling of "sympathy," which he regarded as crucial to social life.[71] The phrenologist Gall and the Scottish philosophers Hume and Smith, all of whom influenced Destutt de Tracy, would later encourage Comte's inclination toward this point of view.[72] Destutt de Tracy's ideas appear not only in Comte's denunciation of theology, metaphysics, psychology, social statistics, and social contract theory, but in his belief that liberty was the absence of constraints (impediments to action), his emphasis on productivity and the general interest, his desire to establish a secular morality, his frequent allusions to common sense as the basis of epistemology, and his belief that the growth of knowledge depends on methodological improvements.

In conclusion, Comte maintained that the efforts of the Idéologues Cabanis, Condorcet, and Destutt de Tracy to found the science of society on another positive science, whether on physiology, mathematics, or Idéologie, reflected the "general need felt by the best minds to make politics a positive science."[73] By taking up their idea of creating a scientific study of society, he was proclaiming himself the inheritor of the Idéologue tradition.[74]

At the same time, he was searching for a new approach to the problems posed by the Idéologues. He agreed with Adam Smith that politics, like the other sciences, could become positive only if it were based on the "observation of facts that are proper to it."[75] His idea that the reduction of one science to another was a step backward in intellectual progress was an important concept that could not be ascribed to Saint-Simon, who had especially in his early writings endeavored to found social science on mathematics or physiology.

COMTE'S DEVELOPMENT OF HIS PHILOSOPHY OF
THE SCIENCES

Comte's critique of Destutt de Tracy's Idéologie and Cousin's psychology led him to reflect more on the problem of knowledge. He decided that the way to uncover the rules and operations of the mind

---

[70] Kennedy, *Philosophe*, 252–5.   [71] Destutt de Tracy, *Elémens*, 4:72–3, 515–16.
[72] Head, *Ideology*, 82–3; Kennedy, *Philosophe*, 218, 336; Welch, *Liberty and Utility*, 215n57.
[73] *Ecrits*, 482.   [74] Ducassé, *Méthode et intuition*, 59.   [75] *Ecrits*, 481.

was not by using pure logic and introspection but by observing the mind's works, its concrete products. Thus like Bonald, Comte sought to deflect attention away from the individual mind in order to concentrate on the exterior, collective facts of society. Yet unlike Bonald, who advocated the study of religion, politics, the arts, morality, and the sciences, Comte concentrated only on the sciences as the key to understanding mental functions.[76] And he was less interested in the content of the sciences than in observing the *method* used by the mind in each science to make discoveries. Reflecting the operations of the mind, the methods or rules of each science were equivalent to the *"philosophy"* of that particular science. By gathering what was common to the separate philosophies of each science, one obtained the "general philosophy of all of the sciences," which was the "only reasonable logic."[77]

In reaction against Idéologie and psychology, Comte was sketching for the first time the characteristics of positive philosophy. Already in September 1819 he believed that the distinctive philosophy of each science as well as the general philosophy of all the sciences would become positive and certain. In addition, he felt that there should be specialists developing the methods and philosophy of each science and, above them, a class of general philosophers of science devoted to "observing these different philosophies, comparing them, bringing them into general use, and perfecting them by their mutual relationships."[78] If such an interdisciplinary approach were taken and the methods of one science were applied to other sciences, all of the sciences would progress more rapidly and would be more usefully applied to human needs. This *general*, methodological approach contained the essence of positive philosophy.

Despite Comte's rejection of Destutt de Tracy's concept of method as the key to the unity of the sciences, he adopted a similar approach. Comte's philosophy, like Destutt de Tracy's, was a philosophy of the mind, but it rejected reducing mental life to the process of combining physical sensations. Instead, it dealt with the creations of the mind as seen through the methods invented by the mind to increase its power in scientific research.

In many respects, Comte was adopting Saint-Simon's early effort to unify the sciences into one system. But he rejected his promotion of a single philosophy synthesizing all knowledge of nature and his deduction of all ideas from one general principle, whether it be universal gravity or the necessity of production. Moreover, Comte went further than Saint-Simon in arguing that each science had its own

---

[76] Macherey, *Comte: La Philosophie*, 53–5.
[77] Comte to Valat, September 24, 1819, *CG*, 1:59.   [78] Ibid., 59–60.

philosophy and that a general philosophy must aspire to coordinate them all.[79] At least in the beginning of his career, the unity of Comte's system would come more from the scientific method common to all sciences than from a single positive principle.

THOUGHTS ON THE PHILOSOPHY OF MATHEMATICS

To implement his idea, Comte resolved in 1819 to write a "significant work" on the philosophy of mathematics, which would include an introduction on the history of the sciences.[80] He chose to write on mathematics because he knew it best. Also, as the most advanced branch of human knowledge, it had the greatest need for a philosophy. Besides hoping to make mathematical research itself more philosophical, he sought to outline the correct way to teach and study mathematics. Ever since his dismissal from Reynaud's boarding school, he had been bitter about mathematicians.[81] Some of his complaints about them – their lack of agreement, their inability to rise above details, their indifference to the relationship between mathematics and the other sciences, and their "almost mechanical" use of mathematical methods – resurfaced in this essay on mathematics.[82]

In spite of encouragement from several scientists, including Poinsot, Comte was daunted by the task. Afraid his essay would be "bad" and full of mistakes, he had difficulty setting down his ideas systematically.[83] In 1820, when he heard that the Institut had established a prize for the best essay on mathematics, he redoubled his efforts and hoped that this work (together with another on the calculus of variations) would win, thereby assuring him a chair in geometry at the Academy of Sciences.[84] But it remained a series of incomplete fragments like those he wrote for *Le Politique* around the same time. Although later a very prolific writer, Comte lacked the necessary self-confidence at the start of his career.

---

[79] Gouhier, *Jeunesse*, 3:179–80.
[80] Comte to Valat, September 24, 1819, *CG*, 1:58. Mathematics was also on Comte's mind because one of his good friends, Gabriel Lamé, had just published *Examen des différentes méthodes pour résoudre les problèmes de géométrie*, and Comte was trying to help him promote it. See copies of letters from Comte to Lamé, October 6, 1816, and January 13, 1819, at the Maison Charavay on the rue de Furstemburg, Paris.
[81] Some fragments of this essay were written in late 1818, when he had his fight with Reynaud. *Ecrits*, 492, 502–5, 520.
[82] Comte to Valat, September 24, 1819, *CG*, 1:60–1.
[83] Ibid., 58. See also Poinsot to Comte, [January 1, 1819], in "Relations d'Auguste Comte avec Poinsot," ed. Laffitte, 150; *Ecrits*, 495.
[84] Comte to Valat, September 6, 1820, *CG*, 1:69–70.

The fragments that he wrote from late 1818 to early 1820 give us an idea of his concept of the philosophy of science.[85] He began by asserting that philosophy was the "view of the whole" and that philosophers of the whole had different "capacities" than scientists cultivating details.[86] Echoing Saint-Simon's denunciation of mathematicians as "sad calculators," he hoped that students would be preserved from becoming narrow-minded "calculating machines" if they were taught a philosophical view of mathematics.[87] Positive philosophy grew out of his horror of excessive specialization, which hindered the achievement of general views.

Recognizing from his studies at the Ecole Polytechnique that it was impossible to understand the philosophy of any science without studying its relationship to the other sciences, Comte declared that the philosophy of mathematics could not be conceived without first acquiring a "general knowledge of the other positive sciences – astronomy, physics, chemistry, and physiology."[88] In effect, he expanded his curriculum at the Ecole Polytechnique by including physiology and then made this new program the training ground for every philosopher of science.

Yet at this stage, he could not decide whether mathematics should be studied first or last. On the one hand, he contended that one must know the other sciences before approaching mathematics. On the other hand, the fact that he began his investigation of the philosophy of the sciences with mathematics suggests that he felt it was the fundamental science, the one to be studied first. Thus in 1819–20 he had not yet settled the problem of whether to begin his intellectual reformation with mathematics or social science.

As for questions of method, he followed Saint-Simon's recommendation to discover new truths by using both an a priori approach founded on reasoning and an a posteriori approach based on observations. Each could also be used to verify the truths uncovered by the other. Later he would develop his principle that a scientist should employ both empiricism and rationalism without embracing either one exclusively.[89]

Comte also discussed the relationship between signs and ideas, a subject that had been taken up in the past by Condillac, Destutt

---

[85] The first fragment is called "Essais sur quelques points de la philosophie des mathématiques," *Ecrits*, 491–505. The second fragment is entitled "Essais sur la philosophie des mathématiques," *Ecrits*, 507–41. There is a one-page undated outline of the work Comte intended to write. See "Quelques réflexions sur la composition et sur la rédaction des ouvrages élémentaires de mathématiques," MAC.

[86] *Ecrits*, 494.   [87] Saint-Simon, *Mémoire sur la science de l'homme*, 39; *Ecrits*, 502.

[88] *Ecrits*, 495.

[89] Ibid., 496, 539. See also Saint-Simon, *Introduction aux travaux scientifiques*, 22.

de Tracy, and Saint-Simon. He maintained that both algebra and arithmetic were languages that were superior to ordinary language because they used signs – letters or numbers – to represent ideas, thereby simplifying the reasoning process. This discussion of signs is important because, as Pierre Ducassé shows, positive philosophy grew partly out of Comte's preoccupation with the reciprocal relationship between the abstract and the concrete in mathematics – a concern that he inherited from Descartes through Leibniz, Lagrange, d'Alembert, and the Idéologues.[90] He wanted to link knowledge and social reality in the same way that mathematics connected "logic and things."[91] A training in mathematics was essential for developing the power of abstraction, a fruitful way of thinking that should be generalized to the social sphere.

Moreover, Comte believed that the history of mathematical language showed that the key to the advancement of the sciences lay in methodological, not technical, improvements.[92] The history of a science should thus be a history of its method rather than its discoveries, which simply derived from the technical applications of its principles. Studying changes in a science's method, which reflected the progress of philosophy, produced new reflections, and these led to new methods and principles. Comte believed the nineteenth century would be an age of pure methodology like the seventeenth century, whereas the eighteenth century had been concerned with technical applications.

The seventeenth-century sources of positive philosophy are, in fact, evident, and it is not surprising that Comte would later call Bacon and Descartes two of his main "predecessors." Bacon was at the origin of his empirical idea that all scientific principles must be based on observed facts, and Descartes helped form Comte's rationalism, that is, his tendency to go from principles to facts. Descartes was responsible for the even more important idea that the unity of the sciences came from unity of method.[93]

Although Comte was probably familiar with Bacon and Descartes before meeting Saint-Simon, his mentor's influence cannot be overlooked. Saint-Simon had always admired Bacon's encyclopedic, synthetic approach and his insistence on "observed facts."[94] He had also praised Descartes for having founded modern "positive science"

[90] Ducassé, *Méthode et intuition*, 5.
[91] Pierre Ducassé, *Essai sur les origines intuitives du positivisme* (Paris: Félix Alcan, 1939), 75.
[92] *Ecrits*, 534.
[93] Lucien Lévy-Bruhl, *La Philosophie d'Auguste Comte* (Paris: Lacan, 1900), 66; Kremer-Marietti, *Le Concept*, 13.
[94] Saint-Simon, *Catéchisme des industriels*, 2d *cahier*, in *Oeuvres*, 4.1:169.

by means of the scientific method of synthesis.[95] In a way, Comte was modifying the ideas of his mentor, who had expressed the hope that the nineteenth century would revive the synthetic, a posteriori techniques of the seventeenth century.[96] Yet Destutt de Tracy gave Comte a deeper understanding of methodology, which led to his approaching the problem of creating a synthesis in an altogether different manner. As Pierre Ducassé has noted, Comte, unlike Saint-Simon, insisted that the sciences reform themselves and achieve a certain "rigor" and "lucidity" before undertaking the task of re-generating society.[97]

While discussing the history of the mind as reflected in the growth of the sciences, Comte stated that epochs changed according to which science progressed the most. The new science of politics would blossom in the current period and would change the nature of general philosophy, itself in the process of becoming a science. The general philosophy would then affect the particular philosophies of each science, causing them to advance further. Then the "truly scientific era" would commence.[98] Comte was reflecting once again the influence of Saint-Simon, who had voiced similar ideas in his *Mémoire sur la science de l'homme;* he had shown that once all of the sciences became positive, the general science or philosophy encompassing them would become positive as well. Then politics would also become positive. It would become, in Saint-Simon's words, an "application of general science."[99]

Thus in these fragments on the philosophy of mathematics, Comte appeared to be forging some links between his two interests, politics and science. For the first time, he announced that the science of politics would be the *sixth* science, coming after mathematics, astronomy, physics, chemistry, and physiology, and that it would have such an extensive impact on intellectual progress that it would advance philosophy as a whole.

It is clear that 1819 was a most productive year for Comte. He had dealt with practical political matters in articles in *Le Politique* and *Le Censeur européen*, developed his concept of positive politics in his first opuscule and his unpublished fragments, and concentrated on

---

[95] Saint-Simon, *Lettres au Bureau des Longitudes*, 261.
[96] Saint-Simon had referred to the history of the human mind as consisting of alternations between eras of synthesis (in which the general science was important) and those of analysis (in which particular sciences attracted all the attention). This is the closest he came to the theory of alternations between critical and organic periods that is often wrongly ascribed to him.
[97] Ducassé, *Essai sur les origines intuitives*, 77.   [98] *Ecrits*, 540.
[99] Saint-Simon, *Mémoire sur la science de l'homme*, 19.

the relationship between politics and morality and their connection with the other sciences. In addition, scientific methodology and its link with changes in history had become a fundamental concern, as had the significance of mathematics. In 1819 Comte thus seemed to be working feverishly, thinking more on his own in regard to the science of society. His scientific investigations, which often echoed the early interests of Saint-Simon, were leading him to conceptions that his untrained mentor could never have originated.

L'ORGANISATEUR

Although Comte was beginning to establish himself independently of Saint-Simon, he was till closely tied to his mentor. In late 1819 he helped Saint-Simon launch a new journal called *L'Organisateur*, which appeared from November 1819 to February 1820 and consisted of fourteen letters addressed to Frenchmen. Since all the articles were signed by Saint-Simon, the extent of Comte's participation is not clear.[100]

L'Organisateur started with Saint-Simon's famous article in which he showed that the death of all aristocrats, clergymen, wealthy bourgeois proprietors, government officials, and civil servants would not harm France, whereas the death of its leading scientists, artists, and artisans (who included farmers, workers, manufacturers, bankers, and other producers) would be very detrimental. The aim of *L'Organisateur* was to turn the current immoral society upside down. The most capable, thrifty, and hardworking men, the producers, who were the "soul" and "flower" of society, should no longer be subjected to the direction of the most incompetent and useless idlers.[101] Though supposedly "scientific," Saint-Simon's political plans for this future society included a fanciful design of a government composed of three chambers, whereby the spiritual power (embodied in the first two chambers, the Chamber of Invention and the Chamber of Examination) would work with the temporal power (the Chamber of Execution). These chambers would represent the scientific, artistic, and industrial elites of the nation. The general outlines of this future society – the separation of powers and a government of three elites – would be preserved by Comte.

To counter possible charges that his plan was utopian, Saint-Simon inserted in the seventh letter a section reviewing historical evidence,

---

[100] For an example of the way in which Comte and Saint-Simon worked together, see the manuscripts of *Le Politique* and *L'Organisateur* (1819), Fonds Pereire, N.a.fr. 24606, BN. See especially fol. 150.

[101] Saint-Simon, *L'Organisateur*, in *Oeuvres*, 2.2:19–20.

which was a revision of a book review Comte had had no success publishing in *Le Censeur européen* in 1819.[102] This book review is highly significant because it shows that Comte was at the forefront of the movement calling for a "new history," one that would not be considered simply a form of literature or a review of salient political events from the conqueror's perspective. Comte was directly inspired by Condorcet, who, he said, wisely rejected traditional history as a mere "biography of the *gouvernants*," in which the common people "appeared solely as instruments or victims." Instead, in his *Esquisse* he had tried, though unsuccessfully, to present the first "really philosophical history." Comte called on new historians to realize his project by determining with greater precision the "general law of progress of the human mind and civilization." If they considered "the whole," that is, "all the facets of the social state," and did away with the old division of history into dynasties and reigns, history would become a "true science" with the same predictive power as the other sciences.[103] It would offer politics as the key to action because it would predict the unmodifiable future so that society need not march blindly toward it. Thanks to his reading of David Hume and other British historians (such as Robertson), Comte now realized that the principle of the progress of civilization would be the basic law of his science of society and that all people, including great men, were mere "instruments" of this law. Resolved to find a replacement for God, Comte went so far as to call this law of progress "our true providence."[104] He was increasingly looking to history, instead of political economy, for the concrete facts that were proper to social science. And for history to become the basis of social science, it needed to become a science itself.

The seventh letter of *L'Organisateur* also summarized the part of Comte's book review in which he showed his deepening appreciation of the value of the Middle Ages.[105] By belittling the past, Condorcet and other philosophes had denied all gradual progress

---

[102] The "Compte rendu de *L'Abrégé des révolutions de l'ancien gouvernement français*" (the second edition of Jacques-Guillaume Thouret's book based on excerpts from the works of Jean-Baptiste Dubos and Gabriel Bonnot de Mably) is reproduced in *Ecrits*, 453–8. Comte's first five paragraphs relating to historical method were inserted in *L'Organisateur* as the scientific underpinning of Saint-Simon's practical reforms leading to the three Chambers. The first two paragraphs of Comte's text were reproduced with very few changes. Parts of the next three paragraphs were inserted both before and after Saint-Simon's first two paragraphs. Ibid., 553–4; Saint-Simon, *L'Organisateur*, 69–74. See the very incomplete comparison of texts in "Matériaux pour servir à la biographie d'Auguste Comte: Considérations sur la période de sa vie qui s'étend de 1816 à 1822," ed. Pierre Laffitte, *RO* 9 (July 1882): 44–7.

[103] *Ecrits*, 453–4.   [104] *Système*, vol. 4, "Appendice," 24.

[105] See the seventh and ninth paragraphs of Comte's article on Thouret, *Ecrits*, 455–7.

and had therefore been unable to show the evolution of their own superior civilization. To Comte, the Middle Ages were the point of departure for "modern civilization" because during this time Christianity was completely organized, serfdom was abolished, the communes were freed, and the separation of powers (temporal and spiritual) was instituted.[106]

Later, positivists seized upon this seventh letter to show how Saint-Simon appropriated Comte's ideas. In the *Nouveau Dieu*, published in 1973, Pierre Arnaud maintained that Comte was responsible for the entrance of history into Saint-Simon's politics.[107] But Saint-Simon, following Condorcet, had also stated in his early writings that history should not be the story of great men, the key to the future was in the study of the past, the law of progress was of primary importance in politics, new divisions of history had to be devised, and eighteenth-century historians were too critical, especially of the Middle Ages. Yet it is true that Comte gave Saint-Simon's ideas a sophistication and scientific cast that they had lacked. Saint-Simon did not, however, feel altogether comfortable with Comte's approach, and acting as the prudent member of their team, he disavowed any implied criticism of current historians, whom he did not wish to alienate.[108]

THE SECOND OPUSCULE: "SOMMAIRE APPRÉCIATION DE L'ENSEMBLE DU PASSÉ MODERNE"

Comte attempted to realize his own project to reform history in the eighth and ninth letters of *L'Organisateur*, which were actually signed by Saint-Simon. Comte first claimed authorship in 1838 to emphasize the consistency and integrity of his thought.[109] Later, in the appendix of the fourth volume of the *Système de politique positive*, he reprinted them as his second opuscule, which he called the "Sommaire appréciation de l'ensemble du passé moderne."[110] According to him, it revealed "the first sketch of my general conception of the modern past, which I already separated into two movements, positive and negative, whose rivalry characterizes the Occidental revolution."[111]

---

[106] Ibid., 455.   [107] Arnaud, Le "*Nouveau Dieu*," 33.   [108] Saint-Simon, *L'Organisateur*, 75.
[109] *Cours*, 2:7. Saint-Simon just added a few introductory and concluding remarks and made minor revisions of the text itself. The letters are reproduced in Saint-Simon, *L'Organisateur*, 77–166.
[110] The "Sommaire appréciation de l'ensemble du passé moderne" is reproduced in *Système*, vol. 4, "Appendice," 4–46. Comte also claimed that his historical contrast between France and England, which looked at the two countries according to the domination of the central or local power, had influenced many writers. Again, he did not give their names.
[111] Ibid., iii.

In fact, however, it was not the first sketch, because in the first *cahier* of *L'Industrie*, which he had written for Saint-Simon three years previously, he had demonstrated that destruction and organization were parts of the same process. Even Saint-Simon, in such works as *De la réorganisation de la société européenne*, showed a familiarity with these ideas. But Comte wanted to prove that his ideas, unlike those of Saint-Simon, remained the same.

The "Sommaire appréciation" reflected the historicist approach that was becoming widespread in nineteenth-century thought. Turning to his advantage the conservatives' approach of founding legitimacy on tradition, Comte sought to justify a new kind of social organization by demonstrating its roots in the past. Saint-Simon had expressed this view when he declared in his introduction to the essay:

> But we must observe that, for eight centuries, the system from which we want to extricate ourselves has always been losing, while that whose establishment I am proposing has always gained in men's minds. This last system is an immense vault, on which our fathers have worked for 800 years, and to which the present generation is destined to put in the key.

Thus the radical changes Saint-Simon and Comte envisioned were supposedly firmly established in historical tradition. They claimed not to desire to construct something new, which could be construed as dangerous in the conservative political climate of the Restoration. Instead, they aimed to show, in Saint-Simon's words, that the social system was already in existence, hidden from view by the "frontispiece of the old edifice."[112] The drama of the essay derived from the removal of the frontispiece to offer a glimpse of this new system.

Comte demonstrated that the spiritual and temporal powers that were about to be overturned had been established in the third and fourth centuries. As soon as they were fully realized in the papal and feudal structure in the eleventh and twelfth centuries, they began to decline in the face of the new system that was growing to replace it. Adopting ideas from Saint-Simon and Thierry, he showed how the emancipation of the communes and the development of the positive "industrial capacity," whose property was based on labor, caused the deterioration of the feudal, military power, whose territories derived from force. The new industrial activity proved to be superior because it was characterized by peaceful enterprises for the general good and an almost total absence of commands, whereas the temporal power remained militaristic and arbitrary. Likewise, the spiritual

---

[112] Saint-Simon, *L'Organisateur*, 77, 180.

power was weakened by the Arabs' introduction of the positive sciences into Europe in the eleventh century. Whereas the old papal and theological power was based on conjectures and demanded total submission, the growing new spiritual power was the "scientific capacity," which rested on demonstration. Belonging to the communal classes, who had no part in the old system, these new temporal and spiritual capacities supported each other against the two older powers. They contained not only the "principle of the destruction of the old system" but the "germ of the new system."[113] Their development characterized all of history since the eleventh century.

Unlike other historians, who neglected the medieval period and viewed the past in terms of sudden changes, Comte showed the roots of the Reformation and of all subsequent explosions in the "period of splendor of the feudal and theological system," that is, the eleventh to the sixteenth centuries. His view of history was dialectical. Beginning in the eleventh century, the old system began to decline, while the new one, based on a different foundation, grew increasingly powerful. Yet the two systems were able to coexist until the sixteenth century, when the new one became strong enough to challenge the old one. Comte called the disorganization of the old social system the "negative" movement of history, and the organization of the new society, the "positive" movement of history.[114] He was evidently coming closer to formulating the law of the three stages; the "negative" movement would become the "metaphysical" stage of history, and the "positive" movement would become the "positive" stage.

In the section on the negative movement, Comte asserted that the first open attack on the spiritual power was made by Luther with his principle of the "right of examination," which destroyed blind beliefs.[115] In some countries, the temporal power took up the Protestant cause against the pope, whose influence was further reduced. This split between the monarchy and the papacy was one indication of the deterioration of the old system. Once the spiritual reformation was completed in the early seventeenth century, the temporal power was attacked in France and England, especially by the communes, consisting of artisans, scientists, and artists (Saint-Simon's favorite triad). Comte emphasized that the communes took the initiative, allying themselves with one part of the temporal power against the other to acquire what they wanted. In England the nobles and communes allied against the king and provoked the Revolution of 1688. In France the communes associated with the king and seriously hurt the nobles during the reign of Louis XIV. Thus the

---

[113] *Système*, vol. 4, "Appendice," 23.   [114] Ibid., iii, 10.   [115] Ibid., 10.

growing scientific capacity of the communes weakened the spiritual power, while their rising industrial capacity challenged the temporal power. Though often regarded as the philosopher of consensus, Comte, like Marx, stressed the crucial role of conflict in historical evolution as well as the vital part played by the bourgeoisie in creating the modern system.[116]

What especially helped the middle class was the invention of the printing press. It led to the importance of public opinion, whose force Comte again emphasized. The printing press also spread the discoveries of Copernicus and Galileo, who destroyed the foundation of theology, the idea that the earth and all of nature were made for man. Comte's aversion to the principle that man was the center of the universe reflects the sentiments of Dupuis and Saint-Simon.

The sixteenth-century attack on the spiritual power and the seventeenth-century assault on the temporal power were united in the eighteenth century in an all-out war on the old system, whose destruction was thus assured. The accomplishments of the eighteenth century were the culminating point of all history since the eleventh century. Echoing Saint-Simon's belief that the eighteenth century was primarily destructive, Comte criticized the men of this period for acting too hastily, neglecting the past, and proposing only vague plans for the future. But to a greater extent than his mentor, he also stressed the period's constructive aspects, as he had done in *L'Industrie*. Besides celebrating its scientific discoveries, he praised the political reforms of the French Revolution. The abolition of privileges destroyed the remaining authority of the nobles. The establishment of a constitution limited the temporal power of the monarchy. The creation of a legislative assembly allowing the public to voice its opinion was the "true means of transition" to the positive system.[117] Most important, the French Revolution's proclamation of freedom of conscience demolished the political and moral bases of both the spiritual and temporal powers.

Comte then turned to the positive movement in modern history and showed how it derived from the development of scientific and industrial capacities, represented by scientists, artists, and artisans. Foreshadowing Freud's theory of repression, he argued that the medieval communes were instrumental in the positive movement because they transferred the object of man's innate desire for domination from human beings to nature. By tempering this instinct and making it useful, civilization made people more intelligent as well as

---

[116] Angèle Kremer-Marietti, Introduction to *Auguste Comte: Sommaire appréciation de l'ensemble du passé moderne* (Paris: Aubier Montaigne, 1971), 25, 35.

[117] *Système*, vol. 4, "Appendice," 18.

more moral. Comte believed that because man preferred to act on nature instead of people, the transition from the feudal to the bourgeois world had brought him closer to his real self. Comte thus shared with Marx a concern with human alienation and saw man as a creator, remaking the natural world outside himself according to his will. The difference was that Marx denied that human emancipation had taken place during the transition to capitalism, and he put greater emphasis on the sense of alienation in the labor process itself.[118]

Comte described how the communes took over the temporal direction of society. By pitting one temporal and spiritual power against the other and by exploiting nature more effectively, they grew so rich and powerful that all of society came to depend on them. Their increasing political and fiscal power gave them the means to proceed directly and legally to the new system.

In the spiritual, or intellectual, realm, scientists, such as Bacon, Galileo, and Descartes, began to base the sciences on observation and experiment and in this way disengaged them one by one from the reigning theological and metaphysical beliefs. Comte referred for the first time to the growth of the natural sciences in the historical progression that would make him famous. Dropping mechanics, which figured in the fourth *cahier* of *Le Politique*, he said the sciences became successively positive according to their distance from man. First astronomy became positive, followed by physics, chemistry, and physiology. Once founded on observation, philosophy, morality, and politics would join them. As soon as the sciences became positive, they were adopted by the educational system, where they began to triumph over theology and metaphysics. But until morality became a science taught by scientists, education – and society as a whole – would remain in the control of the priests.

To Comte, the history of the people was the story of how they acquired education and important habits of thrift, hard work, and order, enabling them to conduct their own affairs and live freely under the new system, which evolved more rapidly after the liberation of the communes and serfs. The "three greatest causes of disorder," ignorance, misery, and idleness, began to disappear. Once the people had property, a stake in society, and some "capacity," they would no longer need to be governed; they would cooperate as associates, not subjects, of their industrial chiefs, whom they would choose to lead them. These chiefs would not need to issue many commands, for "in a society of workers, everything tends naturally

[118] David McLellan, *Karl Marx: His Life and Thought* (New York: Harper Colophon Books, 1973), 83, 110.

to order." Thus in the industrial society, one of association and labor, the main scourges of Comte's own existence would disappear: arbitrary authority and chaos.[119]

As William Sewell has pointed out, "The corporate idiom became a language of opposition" after the Revolution to counter "competitive individualism."[120] Comte's discussion of association points to this trend, which became more pronounced with the proliferation of plans for associated production in the 1830s. Comte assumed, however, that each man would acquire as much importance and profit as his capacity and his investment warranted: "This constitutes the highest degree of equality that is possible and desirable."[121] His faith in a peaceful association based on hierarchy and obedience, instead of equality, would have little appeal to workers.

Comte believed that just as the people grew closer to the industrial chiefs, so they were drawn to the scientists, who provided them with information helpful to their work. The people abandoned the old theological ideas whenever the scientists presented a new theory because of their faith in these men who had proved their qualifications. (Even scientists from other specialties had to take the word of their colleagues on matters outside their own competence.) Although scientific beliefs still kept the people subordinated to a spiritual power and these beliefs were accepted without proofs, the individual did not have to renounce his use of reason or submit blindly to the spiritual power as he did before. Unlike theological beliefs, scientific truths could be proved if necessary. Thus in the future, the individual would never be humiliated; he could always examine and refute "received opinions."[122] Moreover, scientific "truths" were always provisional because they could be proved wrong at any time.

Comte displayed, however, as in the third *cahier* of *L'Industrie*, an ambivalent attitude toward freedom of thought. Perhaps because of his experience of change in his own period, he viewed people and society as basically unstable: "Once beliefs are left to the discretion of each individual, there will not be perhaps even two professions of faith that are entirely uniform, and that of each person could change from morning to evening." He attributed these variations in man's beliefs to "the perpetually mobile state of his moral and physical affections, as well as [to] the equally mobile circumstances in which he finds himself successively placed." Unlimited freedom of conscience had the same political consequence as "absolute theological indifference": the elimination of supernatural beliefs as the foundation of morality. Consequently, morality, which was "the base, or

---

[119] *Système*, vol. 4, "Appendice," 36, 39.   [120] Sewell, *Work and Revolution*, 162.
[121] *Système*, vol. 4, "Appendice," 39.   [122] Ibid., 41.

rather the general link, of social organization," had to be refounded on new positive principles derived from observation.[123] Convinced that one moral code was necessary for the maintenance of society, Comte did not say whether freedom of conscience would be permitted in the future. The fact that he confined these remarks on freedom of conscience to a small footnote indicates that he knew his views would not be popular, particularly with Saint-Simon, who feared any reference to a new secular morality.

Reflecting his fear of a recurrence of the type of despotism that occurred during the ancien régime, the Terror, and Napoleon, Comte sought in this essay to emphasize the people's gradual emancipation from arbitrary authority in both the temporal and spiritual realms. To him, the march of history was leading to a new type of social order in which commands would be kept to a minimum. Yet his vision was based on the assumption that when a person obeyed authorities because of their superior industrial or intellectual competence, his submission was voluntary, natural, and spontaneous. Comte subverted his own text when he dismissed as "ridiculous" the idea that future scientists would abuse the confidence of the people and set up a dictatorship.[124] He seems to have foreseen the reproach that would be most often leveled against him.

Besides fearing the despotism of authority, Comte distrusted the unlimited power of the common people. He declared that they were ready to enter the new system because their relations with their new temporal and spiritual leaders were well established. However, the people must let their leaders act for them. The "industrial capacity" had to perfect its hold over the Chamber, while the scientists had to gain control over the instruction of morality by turning this subject into a science. Comte made it clear that although the new regime would be most interested in the people, the people themselves must remain "exterior and passive" during the last phases of the transition to it.[125] Again, there is a tension in Comte's thought between his deep moral concern for popular welfare and his elitism.

SAINT-SIMON'S AND COMTE'S VIEWS ON HISTORY

Henri Gouhier denies that Comte was profoundly influenced by Saint-Simon in this essay on history, for "there was a common fund of information and hypotheses from which the two constructors drew their materials."[126] However, since many of Comte's views

---

[123] Ibid., 18n1.   [124] Ibid., 42.   [125] Ibid.   [126] Gouhier, *Jeunesse*, 3:275.

can be found scattered throughout Saint-Simon's early writings, it is hard to dispute that he adopted many of his mentor's ideas.[127]

He embraced Saint-Simon's idea of looking at progress in terms of the fundamental dichotomy in mankind: men – or at least useful men – were involved in either theoretical or practical matters. There must, therefore, always be a spiritual power and a temporal power, although their characteristics changed throughout history. Ever since the *Lettres d'un habitant de Genève à ses contemporains*, Saint-Simon had called for a new social reorganization based on the division between the temporal and spiritual powers. Comte maintained the importance of this division, for to him it represented the separation of theory and practice in the social sphere. If theory were not kept distinct from practice, a science such as that of politics could not be created.

Saint-Simon had shown Comte that the spiritual and temporal powers had functioned well together during the Middle Ages, an organic period marked by unity. Following Condorcet, Saint-Simon had also demonstrated that the Arabs' introduction of the sciences into Europe had marked the beginning of a new system, when scientists would forge ahead to become the new elite. Thus Saint-Simon had taught Comte to appreciate the Middle Ages as the period during which the theological power began to deteriorate and the positive intellectual system started to rise. In fact, Comte had borrowed Saint-Simon's term "conjectural" to describe theological ideas, and he opposed it to "positive" in the same way that his mentor had done. Both men saw that open intellectual and social conflicts had developed during the Reformation, but Comte had a better understanding of the significance of Luther's proclamation of freedom of conscience and the effects of its adoption by the Revolution.

Both Comte and Saint-Simon admired Bacon and Descartes for organizing the positive system and reviewed the historical progression of the natural sciences, beginning with astronomy and extending to physiology and the science of politics. And both agreed that the key to the new order resided in the scientists' control of the teaching of morality.

Moreover, Saint-Simon and Thierry had described the way the industrial power had been gaining in strength and wealth ever since the freeing of the communes. Working from the assumption of man's urge to dominate, which Comte adopted, Saint-Simon explained the fundamental opposition between the old military temporal

---

[127] The writings to which I refer are *Introduction aux travaux scientifiques, Projet d'enyclopédie, Mémoire sur la science de l'homme, Aux Anglais et aux Français qui sont zélés pour le bien public, De la réorganisation de la société européenne,* and *Lettres à un Américain.*

system and the pacific industrial one, especially in terms of the different ways they exerted authority. But Saint-Simon, along with Thierry, was not working in a vacuum; many other thinkers were trying to characterize the new society that was emerging, one they hoped would be free of violence and marked by the harmony that came from peaceful exchange. Saint-Simon himself admitted that he took this idea of opposing the two systems from the first article that Charles Comte wrote for *Le Censeur européen*.[128] The idea was also prominent in another work that influenced him and Thierry, Constant's *De l'esprit de conquête et de l'usurpation*, which contrasted two great ages, one imbued with the oppressive spirit of conquest and the other with the peaceful spirit of industry.[129]

Saint-Simon had suggested that there were connections between intellectual, religious, economic, and political developments. But his insights were spread throughout his writings and were never developed. He had never approached Comte's very systematic account of how these various trends worked together in destroying the old order through a series of discrete and then coordinated attacks. Assuming that an organic society once existed in the early Middle Ages, Comte dramatized his narrative by showing how this society fragmented: "Every schism between the elements of a system is an evident sign of decadence."[130] In his eyes, disunity, or division, always led to dissolution. When Saint-Simon tried to arrive at a definitive history of civilization, the unsystematic nature of his thought became apparent. Sometimes, he stressed alternative periods of synthesis and analysis. At other times, he made the transition from idolatry to physicism or the Socratic period the watershed of intellectual development. More recently, he concentrated on the rise of the industrial class, especially to flatter the new bourgeoisie. In short, he seemed incapable of methodically describing how the new system evolved as a whole from the old. He had suggested the link between the new temporal and the spiritual capacities, but he had never so adroitly demonstrated their connection and their collaboration to place society on a new foundation – control over nature, not men – as Comte did.

Adopting Saint-Simon's concept of "capacity," Comte insisted more strongly that throughout history scientific and industrial competence had led to the right to govern. The modern social system was based on "capacity," not on force or old notions of power.[131]

---

[128] Saint-Simon, *Catéchisme des industriels*, 170.

[129] Constant, *De l'esprit de conquête*, 992–5. See Thierry's acknowledgment of Constant's influence: Saint-Simon, *L'Industrie*, 94n1. Saint-Simon mentions Constant's "excellent work" in *Catéchisme des industriels*, 190.

[130] *Système*, vol. 4, "Appendice," 12.   [131] Ibid., 7–8. See also Gouhier, *Jeunesse*, 3:275–6.

Whereas Saint-Simon tended to scorn the people and advocated their manipulation by the elite, Comte merely said they would display the same faith in the sciences that the intellectual community itself did.[132] In discussing the process by which their allegiances were transferred from the old to the new system, he showed more astutely than his mentor how social relationships changed owing to economic and intellectual transformations. He undeniably took many of Saint-Simon's ideas, but he gave them a new and more extensive interpretation. He was justified in later life for feeling frustrated that the letters in *L'Organisateur* had not been properly attributed to him; historians even today base much of their exposition of Saint-Simon's theory of history on Comte's "Sommaire appréciation de l'ensemble du passé moderne."[133]

Comte's essay is pivotal in modern historiography because he was one of the first thinkers to use history to legitimize the Revolution. He placed the Revolution within an evolutionary context and tied it to the long process of emancipation of what was basically the Third Estate. The Revolution was thus the apex of all of history since the early Middle Ages, when the bourgeoisie first started to assert themselves by their labor in the cities. Comte's view reflects the typical Manichean attitude of the consciousness of the revolutionaries. According to François Furet, this logic, which was used to justify revolutionary events, centered upon "single-cause explanations at every level of argument: victory of the Enlightenment over obscurantism, of liberty over oppression, of equality over privilege; or the advent of capitalism on the ruins of feudalism."[134] Yet, like Tocqueville, who would also stress the continuity of history, Comte did not believe the process was over. More changes were necessary to complete the transformation of France.

Comte's interpretation of the Revolution as a part of the long rise of the bourgeoisie and the inevitable culmination of European history was directed against conservatives, who believed the Revolution was an aberration, a disastrous break with the orderly past.[135] His explanation became central to the liberal historiography of the Restoration. His emphasis on the bourgeoisie's struggle for liberty appears, for example, in the later works of Guizot and Thierry. They all ultimately reflected the influence of Saint-Simon, who often spoke of the emancipation of the communes. In fact, Saint-Simon

---

[132] Gouhier, *Jeunesse*, 3:281–2.

[133] Manuel, *Saint-Simon*, 219–36; Jean Walch, *Les Maîtres de l'histoire, 1815–1850: Augustin Thierry, Mignet, Guizot, Thiers, Michelet, Edgard Quinet* (Paris: Editions Slatkine, 1986), 50; Ansart, *Sociologie de Saint-Simon*, 61–105; Weill, *Saint-Simon*, 126n2. Weill at least added a footnote explaining that Comte wrote this part.

[134] Furet, *Interpreting the French Revolution*, 21.   [135] Mellon, *Political Uses of History*, 7–8.

accused Guizot of borrowing ideas of history from *L'Organisateur*. Having read Thierry and Guizot, Marx would incorporate this interpretation into his doctrine of the "bourgeois revolution."[136] Comte's essay demonstrates the extent to which history in the early nineteenth century was at an important watershed. The changes it underwent reflect the discredit cast upon political institutions by the Idéologues, Say, and others, who in the aftermath of the Revolution no longer believed political changes alone could lead to social order.[137] Guizot and the doctrinaires had also insisted that one could not understand modern political institutions without first studying the structure of modern society. The Revolution had thus made people more cognizant of the impact of social change, and liberals in particular insisted that a theory of social change, instead of a hypothesis about an immutable human nature, had to constitute the basis of political theory.[138] Comte's disgust at the futile attempt by the revolutionaries and Bonapartists to tamper with political institutions and his preoccupation with the social realm affected the way he viewed history. He did not think about the past in traditional terms as a series of political events dominated by great individuals. He turned his attention to the social question, which he felt was more crucial than the political.[139] And as Boris Réizov has shown, during the Restoration the "development of society" was no longer considered a "mechanical process" but, "above all, a creation and a struggle."[140]

Comte's essay is also significant because it used the new doctrine of industrialism to interpret history. According to Say, there was one fundamental reality, that of society, which was equivalent to the *gouvernés*. Their *industrie*, that is, their productive labor, not the maneuvers of the government, was most important, especially for national prosperity.[141] Reflecting Say's antistatism, which was shared by Saint-Simon, Charles Comte, and Dunoyer, Comte asserted that the history of the French nation was that of the people. Thus he emphasized the importance of socioeconomic factors throughout history and connected them to the changing intellectual forces. He

[136] Furet, *Interpreting the French Revolution*, 13, 21, 120, 135–6; Boris Réizov, *L'Historiographie romantique française, 1815–1830* (Moscow: Editions en Langues Etrangères, n.d.), 6–7; Mellon, *Political Uses of History*, 29; Douglas Johnson, *Guizot: Aspects of French History, 1787–1874* (London: Routledge & Kegan Paul, 1963), 338–9. On Saint-Simon's comments on Guizot, see *Du système industriel*, 192.

[137] Kaiser, "Politics and Political Economy," 145.

[138] Larry Siedentop, "Two Liberal Traditions," in *The Idea of Freedom: Essays in Honour of Isaiah Berlin*, ed. Alan Ryan (Oxford: Oxford University Press, 1979), 156–9.

[139] Donald R. Kelley, *Historians and the Law in Postrevolutionary France* (Princeton, N.J.: Princeton University Press, 1984), 24–5.

[140] Réizov, *L'Historiographie romantique*, 795.   [141] Allix, "La Méthode," 347.

integrated politics into his narrative so that all aspects of the evolutionary process fit together in a continuous, seamless fashion. But he shifted interest from the study of powerful men to the examination of the people's struggle for freedom and enlightenment. By giving the people, that is, the nonprivileged Third Estate, a history, he sought to empower them. "It was not the communes that were instruments in the hands of the old powers; it was rather these powers themselves that should be seen as having served as instruments of the communes."[142] He particularly wished to give a sense of their own history to the three groups in industrial society that Say had highlighted in his works: the scientists, the entrepreneurs, and the workers, who obeyed the first two groups.[143]

Comte showed that the class struggle was a motor force in history. Since "the people" had played such a crucial role against the aristocracy and monarchy, it was time for the state to act in their interest. Like other thinkers of the Restoration and July Monarchy, Comte used history to justify his own politics and to discover guides for action in the present.[144] He assumed that once "the people" came into power, the class struggle would disappear and there would be no more need for violence; the economic and intellectual leaders of the bourgeoisie could adequately represent the interests of the different elements of the Third Estate. Only with the advance of industrialization would Comte become more aware of the struggle within the ranks of "the people," the conflict between the proletariat and the bourgeoisie.

Thus the "Sommaire appréciation" is a crucial text in modern intellectual history because it was one of the first to offer a global perspective on the Revolution, to present an evolutionary instead of a mechanical model of interpretation, and to emphasize the power of nonpolitical forces in the past. It preceded by several months the crucial series of articles that Thierry wrote in the summer of 1820 for the *Courrier français*, which have usually been considered a decisive turning point in modern historiography.[145] In this "manifesto," Thierry called for the "renovation of the history of France."[146] Criticizing historians for concentrating exclusively on wars and great men, especially kings, he insisted that the true history of France was "the history of the subjects, the history of the people." The "progress of the popular masses toward liberty" – a struggle that began with the emancipation of the medieval communes – was far more import-

---

[142] *Système*, vol. 4, "Appendice," 13–14.   [143] Say, *Traité d'économie politique*, 1:41–2.
[144] Mellon, *Political Uses of History*, 1.
[145] Kelley, *Historians*, 20–1; Rearick, *Beyond the Enlightenment*, 23–31.
[146] Thierry, Preface to *Dix ans*, 11.

ant than the "fortune of the magnates and the princes." The history
of the past thirty years made no sense unless one realized that "our
ancestors" had been preparing for it for seven centuries. These people
were the true "heroes" of the past. It was up to the new generation
of historians to show that the common people could, like the nobility, find signs of their "glory" in the past. This glory was "that of
industry and talent."[147] These were precisely the same themes that
appeared in the "Sommaire appréciation."

Comte's essay seems to have inaugurated a decade of prolific
writing on French history. Some of the important works that were
published in part or as a whole during this period include Sismondi's
Histoire des Français (1821–44), Guizot's *Essais sur l'histoire de France*
(1823), Thiers's *Histoire de la Révolution française* (1823–7), Mignet's
Histoire de la Révolution française (1824), Thierry's *Lettres sur l'histoire
de France* (1827), and Michelet's *Précis d'histoire moderne* (1827). Many
of these historians took up theories similar to those expressed by
Comte. Jean Walch dismisses Comte's influence on them because
he mistakenly asserts that his works were published too late to have
affected them.[148] Walch completely passes over the "Sommaire
appréciation." Yet Comte complained in 1838 and 1854 that the
"Sommaire appréciation" had influenced "diverse distinguished"
historians who never acknowledged their debt to him.[149]

Whether Comte directly influenced these historians is impossible
to determine. What is clear, however, is that he, along with Saint-
Simon, Thierry, Guizot, Constant, Thiers, Mignet, Michelet, and
others of the Restoration, was participating in the creation of the
"new history," a history that would reflect the new power relationships of postrevolutionary Europe and concern itself with the social
questions of the day, those relating to the class struggle and the
changing economy. Written by men who were commoners themselves, these histories, which sought the origins of the nation in
the Middle Ages, were part of the *classe industrieuse*'s struggle for
power and a sense of identity. In their industrial, liberal dream of the
new world, they assumed, as Lionel Gossman has pointed out, that
there would ultimately be harmony between "the parts and the whole,
the individual and the State, spontaneity and reason, [and] individual
enterprise and general well-being."[150]

---

[147] Thierry, "Première Lettre sur l'histoire de France" (July 13, 1820), in *Dix Ans*, 258–62.
See idem, "Sur l'affranchissement des communes" (October 13, 1820), in ibid., 275–80;
Lionel Gossman, "Augustin Thierry and Liberal Historiography," *History and Theory* 15,
no. 4 (1976): 11, 12, 15, 21.
[148] Walch, *Les Maîtres de l'histoire*, 23.
[149] *Cours*, 2:7. See also *Système*, vol. 4, "Appendice," iii.
[150] Gossman, "Augustin Thierry," 60.

THE ELEVENTH LETTER: "LA DIRECTION DE PROSPÉRITÉ
QUE LA SOCIÉTÉ DOIT PRENDRE"

In addition to the seventh, eighth, and ninth letters, Comte wrote
a great deal of the eleventh letter for *L'Organisateur*. The title on the
manuscript of this section is "La Direction de prospérité que la société
doit prendre." Although the editors of Comte's *Ecrits de jeunesse* included it among his unpublished works, the fragment was used by
Saint-Simon, who incorporated it in a slightly revised form in his
"Deuxième extrait de mon ouvrage sur la théorie de l'organisation
sociale."[151] Reflecting Comte's interest in social welfare, the main
point of his fragment was that even though the progress of knowledge had reduced the power of the governing classes, they still
exploited the people. The new, generally recognized political principle that government should be solely involved in administering
society for the happiness of the governed was too vague; the
governing classes simply assumed that their own interests coincided
with those of the governed. They ruled arbitrarily, deciding the
direction society should take to ensure its well-being. Thus the basic
nature of government had not changed.

Comte expanded the main thesis of his first opuscule ("Séparation
entre les opinions et les désirs"). The people should set the general
goal of society, that of happiness. The publicists should propose the
means of arriving at that goal. Still subscribing to the doctrine of
industrialism, Comte assumed that the happiness of society came
from economic growth. Thus the publicists had "to fix the ideas on
the direction of prosperity that society must take, and make it take
this direction." The *gouvernants* should be limited to realizing the
publicists' plan. Their "natural function" was simply "to guide society in a given direction."[152] Comte continued to give the key role
to the publicists, who were, in a sense, the intermediaries between
the *gouvernants* and the *gouvernés*. In his mind, they could fulfill their
function no matter what the form of government was, because their
expertise in matters of society and economics made them superior to
pure politicians.

THE TRIAL

When the Duc de Berry was assassinated in February 1820, Saint-
Simon was accused of moral complicity, for the duke had been

---

[151] "La Direction de prospérité que la société doit prendre" is reproduced in *Ecrits*, 463–5.
Comte's fragment corresponds to Saint-Simon, *L'Organisateur*, 186–91.

[152] *Ecrits*, 464–5. Under what must have been Comte's influence, Saint-Simon in one part of
the essay used the example of the original Ecole Polytechnique to characterize the new
social system. Saint-Simon, *L'Organisateur*, 203.

included in his parable as one of the aristocrats whose death would not affect France. During the trial, Comte took an active part in preparing the defense and was delighted with the publicity when they "emerged victoriously."[153]

Although he had contributed to almost half of the *L'Organisateur*, Comte had escaped prosecution because he had taken the "precaution" of not signing his articles out of fear his parents would be displeased to learn that he was writing on politics.[154] His worries were well founded, for in April 1820 his father wrote to congratulate him on being free of danger and exhorted him "to leave politics aside, and not to get mixed up in anything."[155]

Although he claimed that he did not sign his articles out of deference to his parents, in reality he seemed genuinely afraid of the repercussions. Because of the prestige of *Le Censeur européen*, signing articles for that journal was relatively risk-free, but working for Saint-Simon was different. Comte said he would come out into the open as soon as "there is no longer the least fear of danger in this respect."[156]

Yet it is clear that his own precautions were beginning to frustrate him. He was convinced that he had much to contribute to the construction of the new system and that he was not getting proper credit for his work.

COMTE'S STATE OF MIND IN 1820

Except for the improvement in his daughter's health, Comte had little to rejoice over at this time. His inability to complete many of his works during this period reflected not only his intellectual difficulties, but his frustration with his social life, personal finances, and family.

He still mourned the death of his friend Cabanes the year before, which left him with but one childhood friend – Valat.[157] And even with Valat, a whole year passed without any exchange of letters. Becoming something of a solitary, Comte felt very lonely.

---

[153] Comte to Valat, September 6, 1820, *CG*, 1:69. See also Manuel, *Saint-Simon*, 212–14; Hubbard, *Saint-Simon*, 85.

[154] Comte to Valat, September 6, 1820, *CG*, 1:69.

[155] Louis Comte to Auguste Comte, April 20, 1820, in "Matériaux pour servir à la biographie d'Auguste Comte (Suite): Dix-huit lettres de Louis Comte à son fils," ed. Pierre Laffitte, *RO*, 3d ser., 2 (January 1, 1910): 7. In June, Louis Comte reiterated his warnings. Louis Comte to Auguste Comte, June 16, 1820, in ibid., 11.

[156] Comte to Valat, September 6, 1820, *CG*, 1:69.

[157] Comte was pleased that Cabanes died as a "true philosopher," with no "unworthy priests" present to insult him. Comte to Valat, September 24, 1819, *CG*, 1:61.

Also, he still had trouble supporting himself, for his journalistic endeavors paid nothing and his lessons had diminished. Hopeful that a prestigious connection would further his career, he and his parents were pleased when Hachette arranged for him to teach the grandson of Jean-Antoine Chaptal, a former professor at the Montpellier medical school, a member of the Institut, and a successful manufacturer.[158] Yet Chaptal turned out to be disappointingly stingy.[159] Nevertheless, Comte refused to follow Valat's example and seek a post in a *collège* (a kind of secondary school) because it was part of the reactionary University, whose curriculum he criticized as too traditional and literary.[160] (In France, the University comprised the faculties and secondary schools.)

Comte found the poverty and uncertainty of his life hard to bear, especially when he saw old schoolmates from the Ecole Polytechnique, who had been mediocre students, earning twenty to twenty-five francs a day. But he had an "insurmountable aversion" to making connections or fawning over "some stupid and important moneybags" to get a student.[161] As usual, he refused to compromise himself. Yet when Poisson, one of his former professors, was appointed to the Committee of Public Instruction, Comte hoped he would get him a suitable job in mathematics. Nothing came of it, however.[162]

Comte grew more despondent when he realized he did not have enough money to go to Montpellier to visit his parents, whom he had not seen for four years. Yet in truth his contact with them had been fitful. His mother and sister sent him one letter after another full of emotional pleas, caveats, and recriminations, and his father claimed that his indifference was threatening their emotional and physical well-being. His mother, always covering his letters to her with "kisses and tears," was constantly "devoured by anxiety" regarding his well-being.[163] Comte was even reproached for insensi-

---

[158] Comte and Chaptal had many friends in common, for Chaptal knew Campredon and had supported Saint-Simon. See Alix Comte to Auguste Comte, January 20, 1820, "Lettres d'Alix Comte," ed. Laffitte, 57–8; Campredon, "Extrait d'un cahier denotes," ed. Laffitte, 167. Chaptal had written an article, "Histoire des progrès de l'industrie," for the second volume of *L'Industrie* in 1817. See Saint-Simon, *Oeuvres*, 1.2:127.

[159] Rosalie Boyer to Comte, February 4, 1820, "Lettres de Rosalie Boyer (1)," ed. Laffitte, 91; Louis Comte to Auguste Comte, April 2, 1820, "Lettres de Louis Comte," ed. Laffitte, 7; Alix Comte to Auguste Comte, May 9, 1820, "Lettres d'Alix Comte," ed. Laffitte, 63.

[160] Comte to Valat, April 17, May 15, 1818, and September 24, 1819, *CG*, 1:25, 38, 55.

[161] Comte to Valat, September 6, 1820, *CG*, 1:70.

[162] Alix Comte to Auguste Comte, August 2, 1820, "Lettres d'Alix Comte," ed. Laffitte, 69; Comte to Valat, September 6, 1820, *CG*, 1:71. In his early career, Poisson had been greatly aided by Saint-Simon.

[163] Rosalie Boyer to Comte, January 20, 1819, September 11, 1820, "Lettres de Rosalie Boyer (1)," ed. Laffitte, 88, 92.

tivity by his profligate brother, who spent his parents' money on questionable activities instead of concentrating on his studies at the Montpellier medical school.[164]

His family's possessiveness, pettiness, and hypocrisy undoubtedly dampened his enthusiasm for writing home. Their insistence on seeing him succeed in a respectable career alienated him, especially since he was already frustrated. They were furious when they discovered from one of his friends that he was still working for Saint-Simon, after he had denied it. Alix's remark was typical: "This [news] has greatly pained our parents because while seeking to establish yourself, you must not do it with a man who has such a bad reputation; that could be prejudicial to you."[165] Nevertheless, his mother did not hesitate to ask Comte to get Saint-Simon's help in getting his father the coveted post of tax collector for the second *arrondissement* in Montpellier.[166] Because Comte disliked such political ploys, nothing came of her plans.

Comte's financial dependence on his parents further aggravated them. He finally promised his father that he would stop asking for money after January 1820, and that he would tell him the names of all his creditors so that they could be repaid. Comte was indebted particularly to Jean-François Bérard de Favas, a justice of the peace who was his father's financial agent in Paris. Bérard de Favas was helping Louis Comte collect money he inherited from his recently deceased mother, and he occasionally received instructions to give some of it to Auguste.[167] Although Auguste's dealings with Bérard de Favas were clear, he could not tell his father the names of the

---

[164] Rosalie Boyer to Comte, February 4, September 11, 1820, and December 11, 1823, "Lettres de Rosalie Boyer (1)," ed. Laffitte, 90, 92, 93, 95; Alix Comte to Auguste Comte, March 4, March 11, June 28, July 17, August 2, 1820, "Lettres d'Alix Comte," ed. Laffitte, 59, 60, 64, 67-9; Louis Comte to Auguste Comte, June 16, 1820, "Lettres de Louis Comte," ed. Laffitte, 11; Adolphe Comte to Auguste Comte, July 1, September 8, 1820, in "Matériaux pour servir à la biographie d'Auguste Comte: Trois Lettres d'Adolphe, frère d'Auguste Comte," ed. Pierre Laffitte, *RO*, 3d. ser., 1 (November 1, 1909): 146-7.

[165] Alix Comte to Auguste Comte, October 7, 1820, "Lettres d'Alix Comte," ed. Laffitte, 72-3. The next month Alix repeated her warning to Comte that his collaboration with Saint-Simon could hurt his own career. Alix Comte to Auguste Comte, November 2, 1820, ibid., 74.

[166] See the original letter of Rosalie Boyer to Auguste Comte, January 20, 1819, MAC. The letter reprinted in the *Revue occidentale* is full of mistakes: the Baron "Nouis" is Baron Louis, and the "illisible" is Laborde. "Lettres de Rosalie Boyer (1)," ed. Laffitte, 89.

[167] Alix Comte to Auguste Comte, March 11, 1820, "Lettres d'Alix Comte," ed. Laffitte, 61; Rosalie Boyer to Auguste Comte, February 4, 1820, "Lettres de Rosalie Boyer (1)," ed. Laffitte, 91; *Almanach royal pour l'an 1820*, 764; Alix Comte to Robinet, January 26, 1861, in Teixeira Mendes, *Auguste Comte*, 63-4; Louis Comte to Auguste Comte, April 2, May 2, May 27, 1820, "Lettres de Louis Comte," ed. Laffitte, 7, 9-10. Alix Comte's original letter is in Papiers Emile Corra 17AS (4), AN.

other people who had lent him money. His parents' displeasure increased when they discovered that Comte had secretly borrowed more money in February from Bérard de Favas, whom he had ordered to continue to support him.[168]

Perhaps motivated by jealousy, Alix was by far the most vocal in her reproaches about money:

> People have told us that you would have had a place a long time ago if you had really wanted it, but that you preferred to be independent; so this is the result of all your fine promises, of all your fine phrases. Adolphe gives us enough pain without your adding to it by your lack of concern about finding a job. How can you come to Papa's aid as long as you remain what you are? Instead of helping him, you are ruining him.[169]

To make him feel guilty, she claimed his debts had even caused their father to sell his beloved horse. She finally warned him that if he did not get a stable job, their father would force him to return home, where he would "vegetate" for the rest of his life.[170]

Comte's situation was not unique. Historians have long noted that his generation had an unusually difficult time finding careers. Apparently thanks to the new schools founded by the revolutionaries and Napoleon, there were simply too many educated men for the few important posts available.[171] Government administration and the professions were also congested, for relatively young men controlled the higher positions, blocking the path to those below them.[172] The situation was particularly difficult in the sciences because scientific community doubled between 1775 and 1825 and Comte's generation was both gifted and ambitious.[173] Moreover, as we have seen, the Bourbon government in its educational policies put up obstacles to hinder the advancement of potentially subversive young people. Thus Comte, along with other members of his cohort, struggled with problems of unemployment and underemployment for his entire life.[174] Although the new meritocracy encouraged his

---

[168] Louis Comte to Auguste Comte, May 27, 1820, "Lettres de Louis Comte," ed. Laffitte, 9–10; Rosalie Comte to Auguste Comte, March 11, 1820, "Lettres de Rosalie Boyer (1)," ed. Laffitte, 61–2.

[169] Alix Comte to Auguste Comte, November 2, 1820, "Lettres d'Alix Comte," ed. Laffitte, 73–4.

[170] Alix Comte to Auguste Comte, March 11, 1820, "Lettres d'Alix Comte," ed. Laffitte, 62.

[171] O'Boyle, "Educated Men," 471–95.

[172] Bertier de Sauvigny, *Bourbon Restoration*, 238–9.

[173] Nicole Dhombres and Jean Dhombres, *Naissance d'un pouvoir: Sciences et savants en France (1793–1824)* (Paris: Payot, 1989), 170–1, 185, 214–17.

[174] Spitzer, *French Generation*, 228–58.

ambitions, he found the crowded market impossible to penetrate, especially because his qualifications were not impeccable in the first place owing to his expulsion from the Ecole Polytechnique.

COMTE'S SCIENTIFIC INVESTIGATIONS

Because there are no existing letters from Comte between September 1820 and April 1824, it is difficult to reconstruct his life during these four years. There are few indications of what he was doing and even fewer of what he was feeling and thinking. Found among Comte's papers after his death, however, were some pages relating to the philosophy of mathematics, which reveal that in early 1821 he was continuing his work on the subject he had begun writing about three years before.[175] Evidently he still hoped to win the Institut's prize for the best essay on mathematics in order to advance his career.

Comte aimed to consider mathematics in relation to the whole system of knowledge and to fix its "encyclopedic rank." He argued that the various divisions of this science (as well as those of the other sciences) should be defined by their objectives, not by their historical development, methods, or instruments. A true "positive philosophy" would be created by making sure that these definitions showed the interrelationships of the various divisions.[176] A philosophy course in mathematics would divide the study of calculus into arithmetic and algebra and then would delineate them according to their aims, the source of the differences. For example, algebra sought to envisage quantities according to their relationships, whereas arithmetic looked at them according to their values.

Besides foreshadowing lesson 4 of the *Cours* on mathematical analysis, this fragment is important in Comte's intellectual development because it set his approach to the entire philosophy of the sciences. Throughout the *Cours*, whenever Comte began to discuss a science (or one of its divisions), he first defined it and then examined its relationship with the other sciences (or other divisions).

The increasing importance that Comte attributed to the philosophy of science also emerges in another incomplete manuscript that Comte worked on in early 1821.[177] It was the first part of the essay

---

[175] "Essais de philosophie mathématique," *Ecrits*, 543–7.   [176] Ibid., 544–5.
[177] "Mémoire sur le calcul des variations," *Ecrits*, 563–9. The dates on this original manuscript show that he worked on it on January 6 and 13, 1821. See the original manuscript of the "Mémoire sur le calcul des variations," MAC.

on the calculus of variations – the second work that Comte planned to submit to the Institut.[178] Here he criticized mathematicians for being so absorbed in the applications of their science that they were neglectful of its philosophy and therefore unable to generalize or compare concepts. By comparing the calculus of variations with that of partial differentials and finding their interrelationships, Comte intended to show that their methods were similar so that the calculus of variations would become more generalized and important. He hoped this would be the first example of an improvement in method that derived from the method itself instead of from the demands of application. This essay reveals Comte's continued interest in methodology and his dislike of specialization.

Both incomplete essays demonstrate the way Comte's mind always sought the underlying relationships among phenomena. This search for interrelationships was inspired by his training in mathematics. Biology and history also attracted his attention because they too were based on filiations.[179] To Comte, nothing could be studied in isolation; everything had to be related to the whole. This intellectual practice would eventually lead him to consider everything in relation to humanity.

In addition to working on the philosophy of mathematics, he displayed an interest in expanding his knowledge of the sciences in other ways. Sometime between 1818 and 1822, he began to perform experiments relating to the compression of air. His findings sufficiently impressed his former professor Arago for him to urge Comte to construct a machine to demonstrate them.[180] As in the summer of 1817, when Comte frequented the courses given by Arago and Gay-Lussac at the Observatory, he decided in 1821 to attend lectures on astronomy given at the Collège de France by Jean-Baptiste Delambre, the permanent secretary of the Academy of Sciences and a onetime supporter of Saint-Simon.[181] After several lessons, Comte was the only auditor, a fact that so touched the elderly astronomer that he invited him home for the rest of the course.[182] Ten years later, Comte's own decision to give a public course in astronomy was at

[178] Comte to Valat, September 6, 1820, *CG*, 1:69.

[179] Ducassé, *Méthode et intuition*, 63.

[180] See the notes that Comte wrote on the back of an envelope addressed to him at rue Saint-Germain-des-Prés No.8. It is possible that Comte was working with a friend named Pillet, an industrial chemist. See Langlade to Tabarié, September 3, 1824, MAC.

[181] "Notes des cours suivis par Auguste Comte à la cours d'astronomie à l'Observatoire," MAC. Delambre gave one hundred francs as his subscription to *L'Industrie* in 1816. See the list of subscribers in Pereire, *Autour de Saint-Simon*, 5.

[182] Lonchampt, *Précis*, 30.

least partly inspired by the example of Delambre, whom he always called his "illustrious master in astronomy."[183]

DU SYSTÈME INDUSTRIEL: SIGNS OF DIVERGENCE

After the trial, Comte continued to work closely with Saint-Simon. Exhilarated by all the publicity, his mentor began publishing in September 1820 a number of brochures, which formed the first volume of *Du système industriel*. Underwritten by important scholars, businessmen, and liberal members of the Chamber, two more volumes were published before it collapsed in June 1822.[184] The main purpose of this journal was to counter Bonald's strong defense of the nobility by showing the need for the king and the bourgeoisie to unite to make France an industrial society.[185]

Although no sketches or articles were found among Comte's papers, differences in style provide some clues of the extent of his participation. Comte's writing was clear and systematic. Saint-Simon was more emotional and repetitive; he wrote in the first person and emphasized his points with exclamation marks and underlined words. There were also variations in content, especially in the sections on history.

It seems fairly certain that in the brochure *Considérations sur les mesures à prendre pour terminer la Révolution*, Comte wrote the section called "Au Roi" because the first footnote alluded to the view of history that he had elaborated in the eight and ninth letters of *L'Organisateur*.[186] When the *Considérations* was enlarged and republished as the first part of *Du système industriel* in February 1821, he

---

[183] *Cours*, 1:314; see also 325–6, 342. Comte owned many of Delambre's books: *Histoire d'astronomie ancienne, Histoire d'astronomie du moyen âge*, and *Histoire d'astronomie moderne, Abrégé d'astronomie, Rapport historique sur les progrès des sciences mathématiques depuis 1789*, and *Méthodes analytiques pour la détermination d'un arc du méridien*. One of the few magazines that Comte kept was the issue of *Le Mercure* of June 7, 1823, describing Joseph Fourier's eulogy of Delambre. "Académie des Sciences," *Le Mercure*, June 7, 1823, 414–20.

[184] The scholars included Claude Louis Berthollet, Georges Cuvier, François Arago, and J. B. Say. The businessmen and bankers were Schlumberger and Richard-Lenoir. Among the men of the Left were Lafayette and Jean Denis Lanjuinais. The actor Talma even gave one hundred francs. Gouhier, *Jeunesse*, 3:218–21; Manuel, *Saint-Simon*, 215. Both Gouhier and Manuel assert that *Du système industriel* began publication in September 1820, but Fournel in his bibliography of Saint-Simonian literature and the editors of the *Oeuvres de Saint-Simon* claim that it began in June 1820. However, the first brochure, *Considérations sur les mesures à prendre pour terminer la Révolution*, appeared, according to Comte, on September 5, 1820. Fournel, *Bibliographie Saint-Simonienne*, 22–30; Saint-Simon, *Oeuvres*, 3.1:vii; Comte to Valat, September 6, 1820, *CG*, 1:69.

[185] Saint-Simon, "Les Communes ou Essais sur la politique pacifique," in *Oeuvres*, 6:394.

[186] Saint-Simon, *Considérations sur les mesures*, 70.

probably also drafted the new preface, which pertains mainly to the subject matter of "Au Roi." Both of these sections show that Comte was significantly developing his conception of the past.[187]
   While repeating his idea that the origins of the French Revolution lay in the transfer of temporal and spiritual power from the military-theological system to the industrial-scientific system, he formulated a new so-called natural law to explain the revolutionaries' "false direction": "It is in the nature of man not to be able to pass without an intermediary from one doctrine whatsoever to another." This law applied not only "to the different political systems that the natural march of civilization obliges the human species to follow" but also to the development of the sciences. Each scientist was well aware that "before passing in each branch from purely theological ideas to positive ideas, the human spirit uses metaphysics for a long time." This "intermediate," metaphysical stage was "useful" and "even absolutely indispensable in order to make the transition."[188] Thus in early 1821 Comte was ready to assert not only that politics went through three stages but that *each* science experienced this same development as well.
   Comte's concept of the three stages of theological, metaphysical, and positive ideas resembles the theory that Saint-Simon purportedly borrowed from Burdin many years before but had not mentioned for some time. According to the *Mémoire sur la science de l'homme*, Burdin had explained that each science went through a conjectural stage, a half conjectural and half positive stage, and a positive stage. In the preface, Comte referred to the passage of politics "from the conjectural to the positive, from the metaphysical to the physical."[189] He seemed to equate "conjectural" with "theological" because both referred to the condition of the sciences at their origin. Metaphysics appeared to coincide with Burdin's half conjectural and half positive state. Positive, of course, meant purely scientific and certain. But so far Comte had not really defined theological or metaphysical. In fact, since he slipped his new theory about scientific advancement into a footnote, he obviously did not yet realize its significance. Nevertheless, it seems clear that Burdin's and

---

[187] Evidence for Comte's collaboration also comes from Alix's letter of reproach written after she and the family discovered that he was not working alone on an original work as he had said. Alix Comte to Auguste Comte, October 7, 1820, "Lettres d'Alix Comte," ed. Laffitte, 73. Also, in a letter to Valat, Comte wrote, "We have just put out yesterday a brochure of about 100 pages, entitled *Considérations sur les mesures à prendre pour terminer la Révolution*." Claiming that he had recently labored a great deal on this essay, he sent a copy to Valat as part of a parcel of his political works that he had written in the past year. See Comte to Valat, September 6, 1820, CG, 1:69.
[188] Saint-Simon, *Considérations sur les mesures*, 79.   [189] Ibid., 6.

Saint-Simon's earlier formulations played a role in the development of his law of three stages.

In "Au Roi," Comte described how this law applied to the social and political realm. Progress gave rise to "a temporal power and a spiritual power of an intermediate, bastard, and transitory nature, whose unique role was to operate the transition from one social system to another."[190] In the temporal sphere, lawyers helped to destroy military despotism and create a new temporal power. Although Comte agreed with Saint-Simon that lawyers first arose as agents of the military power and could not be considered *industriels*, he did not support his view that they were always hateful enemies of the *industriels*.[191] He argued instead that they restrained the old temporal power through laws, which they directed in the interest of the *industriels*.

In the spiritual realm, Comte explained that a new class of metaphysicians arose to effect the transition from the theological to the scientific power. They were "men of letters" who recognized the superiority of certain basic religious beliefs but demanded the "right of examination in all secondary articles," which they used to modify the influence of the theological power. In blaming the Encyclopedists for the destruction of the Revolution, Saint-Simon seemed to have foreshadowed Comte's position, but he had not called them "metaphysicians" or seen them as part of a long-range intellectual movement. To Saint-Simon, the negative philosophy of the men of letters was confined to the eighteenth century. But Comte maintained that their action began during the Reformation and ended with the proclamation of unlimited liberty of conscience in the eighteenth century. And whereas Saint-Simon praised their antitheological bias, Comte maintained that they had never ceased to "found their arguments on a religious basis."[192] They were thus closer to the old spiritual power than Saint-Simon had made them.

Comte seemed to synthesize the ideas on lawyers and on philosophes that Saint-Simon had scattered through his books and had sometimes even abandoned. Developing these ideas in a coherent manner, Comte gave them a significant place in his system of history. In all his writings, the lawyers and metaphysicians would remain the temporal and spiritual representatives of the intermediate, transitional stage of civilization.

In addition, Comte placed the lawyers and metaphysicians in the historical context that he had previously described in his articles for

[190] Ibid., 80.
[191] Saint-Simon, *Aux Anglais et aux Français qui sont zélés pour le bien public*, in *Henri Saint-Simon*, ed. Taylor, 152.
[192] Saint-Simon, *Considérations sur les mesures*, 81.

L'Organisateur (the "Sommaire appréciation de l'ensemble du passé moderne"). They became involved in politics in the sixteenth century, when they defended the interests of the communes. Although by the time of the Revolution they had fulfilled their transitional role of modifying the old regime, the communes made the mistake of calling on them to establish the new regime. These lawyers and metaphysicians were actually expert only at establishing guarantees for the governed and setting up barriers against the governing class. When they tried to form a new government, they fell into the trap of imagining the best government possible and basing it on empty formulas from jurisprudence and metaphysics. Instead of changing society by devoting it to work instead of conquest, they created new political systems based on the metaphysical doctrine of the rights of man. These systems represented only superficial changes.

The fault lay not with the lawyers and metaphysicians, who could not have done any better, but with the *industriels*, who should have "chosen their leaders among themselves."[193] The Revolution would not be completed until the *industriels* directly formed the new political system instead of leaving it to the transitional forces. Comte's view was radically different from that of Saint-Simon, who always portrayed the *industriels* in the best light to get their support. Saint-Simon had praised the *industriels* for refusing to take an active part in the Revolution, insisted on their political neutrality and quietism, and blamed the horrors of the period on the lawyers, who became convenient scapegoats.[194] Comte gave both the lawyers and *industriels* more complex roles.

It appears that Saint-Simon had not read or perhaps understood what Comte had written. In "Deuxième Correspondance avec Messieurs les Industriels," a section added in February 1821 to the *Considérations sur les mesures à prendre*, Saint-Simon claimed to offer proof of the opinion set forth in the first section. In discussing the progress of the sciences, he wrote:

> The epoch in which astronomers constituted astronomy by disengaging the basis of this science from imagined facts . . . was not marked by any great discussion; there was established a line of demarcation between the astronomers and the astrologists; the former were classed among the scientists, and the others among the charlatans. . . . The passage from alchemy to chemistry did not find any opponents whose resistance left a trace in history either; it did not occasion memorable discussion.[195]

---

[193] Ibid.   [194] Saint-Simon, *Oeuvres*, 2.2:167–8.
[195] Saint-Simon, *Considérations sur les mesures*, 144.

Suggesting that a science went directly from an imaginative to a positive state, this passage takes no notice of Comte's idea of a science struggling through three stages.

This same neglect or misunderstanding of Comte's theories is also apparent in Saint-Simon's claim in the next paragraph that "positive politics" emerged directly from the theological stage and that the *industriels* would soon apply its principles to free themselves from feudal and theological doctrines. "Just as theology was the foundation of the feudal regime, one will see that the lawyers will no longer set the end toward which society must direct itself."[196] He considered lawyers, along with the clergy and nobles, to be part of the old system. These views contradicted those of Comte, who reproached lawyers for *not* establishing a new goal for society. He considered them a necessary transitional force, not a nuisance.

There were other differences between the two men. Saint-Simon called the philosophes "littérateurs" (literary hacks), although Comte in "Au Roi" had just forbidden the use of this word and insisted they be called "metaphysicians."[197] Furthermore, Saint-Simon criticized the philosophes for their unconstructive attacks on the lawyers. In fact, he blamed the Encyclopedists for the Revolution, contradicting the position he had taken in "Moyen constitutionnel d'accroître la force politique de l'industrie," in which the lawyers were his scapegoats. He now suggested that the Revolution was directed against the lawyers, whereas before he said it had been led by them. Comte, in contrast, argued that the metaphysicians and lawyers united against the old regime; the lawyers headed the Revolution, which they directed with the help of the doctrines of the metaphysicians.[198] These examples show that Comte was indeed thinking on his own and developing new ideas.[199] Although he and Saint-Simon were working together, it seems that already in 1821 they did not seem to be communicating very well, and their theories were beginning to diverge.

In addition, Saint-Simon embarked in 1821 on a new tack that was appropriate to the religious revival of the Restoration but could not have pleased Comte. Since the fiasco of 1817, when Saint-Simon, probably prompted by Comte, had suddenly proclaimed the need

---

[196] Ibid., 145.
[197] Comte wrote, "But because all their principles [the principles of the men of letters] were essentially metaphysical, I believed it necessary to adopt the denomination of *metaphysicians* in preference to that of *littérateurs*, as being both more general and more characteristic." Ibid., 81n1.
[198] Ibid., 10.
[199] Sometimes in later articles Saint-Simon did take up Comte's ideas about the transition, but he did not use them consistently. Ibid., 92.

for a positive terrestrial morality and then watched his bourgeois supporters abandon him, he had carefully avoided the issue of religion. Now he declared that the positive, industrial, scientific society would incorporate a purified form of Christianity. In his article "Adresse aux Philanthropes" in the 1821 edition of *Du système industriel*, Saint-Simon, who previously had embraced the doctrine of self-interest of Hume, Adam Smith, and Bentham, now proclaimed that self-interest was egotism and that "insatiable avidity" was ruining civilization. The solution was to return to the "primitive catechism" of brotherly love given by God to the first Christians. Concerned with the public good, especially the welfare of the workers, the positive society would be the definitive Christian society that God wanted to see established: "God has traced the route that we must follow; we have only to march."[200] In effect, Saint-Simon now made the positive system part of the divine plan; Bossuet's God had reentered history. The remaining issues of *Du système industriel* concentrated on working out the details of this "new Christianity" and appeared with the religious epigraph "God has said: Love and help each other."[201]

Apparently bowing to the pressure to make his system seem more Christian, or at least deistic, Comte in his "Au Roi" maintained that superficial eighteenth-century philosophes were correctly reprimanded by the "strongest minds of the last century, such as Montesquieu and Rousseau" for wantonly attacking religious ideas. Reflecting the atmosphere – and pressure – of the Catholic revival as well as the increased emphasis on Christian values by many on the Left, he stated that the "present generation" no longer tolerated "this tone of frivolity and joking about religious beliefs that the preceding generation paraded."[202] Yet although he admired Christ and the founders of Christianity as models, he still did not believe in God. Contemptuous of the nostalgia of current theological and metaphysical politics for antiquity and early Christendom, he continued to uphold in the "Sommaire appréciation de l'ensemble du passé moderne" the principle of one positive moral doctrine for all of society. It is therefore hard to believe that he would have enthusiastically supported Saint-Simon's reversion to primitive Christianity. In effect, Saint-Simon was going back to the position he had held before he met Comte: that public respect for the prevailing religion must be maintained to secure social order.

[200] Saint-Simon, *Du système industriel*, 255.
[201] Saint-Simon, "Adresse aux Philanthropes," in *Oeuvres*, 3.2:102, 105, 124, 132; idem, *Du système industriel*, xv. See also Manuel, *Saint-Simon*, 349–53.
[202] Saint-Simon, *Oeuvres*, 3.1:95, 96.

Chapter 5

The Fundamental Opuscule and Comte's Rupture with Saint-Simon

The fact is that I foresaw the result for a rather long time, and I should have foreseen it earlier. M. de Saint-Simon had, like fathers vis-à-vis their children and like mother countries with regard to their colonies, the small inconvenience, which physiology shows to be almost inevitable, of believing that having been his student, I must continue to be so indefinitely, even after my beard grew.

Comte, 1824

THE COMPOSITION OF THE OPUSCULE

Throughout *Du système industriel*, Saint-Simon had been appealing to the scientists, the "positive *intellectuals*" who should lead France to the industrial regime.[1] Suddenly, in the article "VIᵉ Lettre: Résumé des lettres sur les Bourbons," Saint-Simon called for "positive philosophers" – "men busy with observing and coordinating positive generalities" – to develop a "general idea" to help the scientists form an "industrial doctrine." He was willing to accept this "great mission," but would be happier if it were taken up by a "more capable positive philosopher."[2] Saint-Simon obviously had Comte in mind. The essay that eventually emerged from Comte's pen was the *Prospectus des travaux scientifiques nécessaires pour réorganiser la société*. Because, as he himself said, it marked his philosophical debut and "irrevocably" determined the direction of his life, it has always been called the "fundamental opuscule."[3]

The first sign of the *Prospectus* appeared in April 1821, two months after Comte had contributed to the preface of the first volume of *Du système industriel*. On April 9 he began to sketch an article called "Première Série de travaux."[4] He probably meant to include it in the second part of *Du système industriel*, which consisted of six pamphlets

[1] Saint-Simon, *Du système industriel*, 190; see also 161, 191.
[2] Saint-Simon, "VIᵉ Lettre: Résumé des lettres sur les Bourbons," in *Oeuvres*, 3.2:58–9.
[3] *Système*, vol. 4., "Appendice," iii. It was the third opuscule published in the *Système*.
[4] See the original manuscript, "Première Série de travaux," 1821, MAC. The editors of the *Ecrits de jeunesse* gave it the title "Fragment: Le Rôle de l'observation et de celui de l'imagination dans la politique. Première série de travaux," *Ecrits*, 573.

published from April to November. But unable to finish it in time, he expanded it and made it the beginning of the fundamental opuscule's third and last part, also entitled "Première Série de travaux."[5] The central argument was that politics could not become positive until it was based on observation and relativism. In theological and metaphysical political theories, where imagination reigned supreme, absolutist judgments were reflected in the view that certain institutions represented the "best social order" and could be established anywhere at any time. Looking to earlier, less civilized societies for "models of social organization" and a "sort of universal panacea," both types of political theory were nostalgic and reactionary.[6] Comte clearly opposed the ultras' project to revive the ancien régime. But like many of his contemporaries, such as Benjamin Constant, who attributed the failure of the Revolution to anachronistic thinking, he was also wary of looking to antiquity as a political model; the revolutionaries' error in this regard had led to their downfall.[7] Above all, Comte wished to establish the science of politics in order to discover the action that would be most appropriate for social reconstruction and thus most likely to succeed.

The next sign of Comte's work on the fundamental opuscule was a series of fragments called "Du système industriel (2ᵉ partie): Prospectus."[8] As he did with his "Première Série de travaux," Comte kept an exact log of his work. It indicates that he worked intermittently and late at night in July and August, experiencing great frustration in trying to characterize the present crisis as a product of the tension between society's desire for reorganization and the incoherence of the guiding doctrines.[9] Despite his efforts, he could not finish

[5] The first paragraph of the fragment is the same as the "Première Série de travaux" of the opuscule. The second paragraph of the fragment is spread throughout the next two pages. *Système*, vol. 4, "Appendice," 82–4.

[6] *Ecrits*, 573.

[7] Marcel Gauchet, "Constant," in *A Critical Dictionary*, ed. Furet and Ozouf, 928–30.

[8] See fragments in "Matériaux pour servir à la biographie d'Auguste Comte [Documents, 1816–1822]," ed. Laffitte, *RO* 8 (1882): 410–12. These are not published in the *Ecrits*.

[9] The first fragment was written on July 23, 1821, from 9:00 to 10:00 p.m. and the second on July 26 from 9:30 p.m. to 2:00 a.m. In frustration, Comte crossed out the first two paragraphs of the second fragment, both of which dealt with the contemporary crisis. Comte worked on the third fragment on August 14 (9:30 p.m.), August 15, (8:30 p.m.), and August 16 (10:45 p.m.) and ended with the following one line, which he actually crossed out: "A social system that is dying, a new system that is tending to establish itself – this is the double fundamental character of the present epoch." The fourth time Comte tried to write this *Prospectus* was on August 22 between 9:45 p.m. and 2:00 a.m. It now consisted of two paragraphs, each of which repeated the crossed-out line of August 14–16 and tried to develop the idea that his contemporaries were neglecting the fact that a new social order was emerging. See ibid., 410–12; the original manuscript of the fragment "Du système industriel (2ᵐᵉ partie): Prospectus" in MAC.

the *Prospectus* in time for it to be included in the second volume of *Du système industriel*.

One possible reason for his inability to complete it was that he had to return home to Montpellier after his nineteen-year-old brother died of yellow fever in Martinique on September 23, 1821.[10] Earlier that year or in late 1820, Adolphe had quit medical school and left Montpellier after having played on Alix's obsessions in some fashion that led to a clash with their father.[11] Comte blamed her for having induced their father to run him out of the house in the hope that Adolphe would die and she would inherit more money. But when Louis Comte heard of this accusation in 1843, he called it an "odious" and "revolting" lie.[12] The only time Comte truly seemed to regret his brother's passing was when he became close to John Stuart Mill and realized that his death had deprived him of "fraternal life."[13]

Although he returned from Montpellier in October 1821, Comte did not resume work on the opuscule again until January 1822, the date he cited later as marking the real beginning of its "direct composition."[14] Writing more slowly than he anticipated, he did not finish it until May 6, more than a year after he had started it. The meticulous log of his work is testimony to the immense effort that went into it; at times, he would write no more than three paragraphs in a day, only to cross them out later.[15] The essay was printed in May 1822 in circumstances that will be described later.

---

[10] Rosalie Boyer to Auguste Comte, October 20, 1821, "Lettres de Rosalie Boyer (1)," ed. Laffitte, 94; Louis Comte to Comte-Rochambeau, January 13, 1822 [1821], excerpt in Ouy, "Jeunesse," 259; Montarroyos, "Voyage au pays natal," 54. Yellow fever was mentioned as the cause of death in the letter from Louis Comte to Comte-Rochambeau, February 17, 1822, cited in Ouy, "Jeunesse," 259n1.

[11] "Trois lettres d'Adolphe Comte," ed. Pierre Laffitte, *RO* (1909): 1n1. See also Comte to Audiffrent, October 21, 1852, *CG*, 6:409.

[12] Louis Comte's Statement, June 4, 1843, N.a.fr. 10794, page 276, BN. In at least one of his 1820 letters to Comte, Adolphe had insinuated that he had been unjustly represented: "I know that I have faults and even very big ones, but I am not the type of person that someone has wished to depict to our good parents. . . . I am leaving it to our good parents, who have been duped as I was, to exonerate me and to rehabilitate me in your eyes." In the letters that Comte received from his family, it was Alix who complained the most about their brother, alleging that his debauchery was causing their father to go increasingly into debt. Adolphe Comte to Auguste Comte, September 8, 1820, "Trois Lettres d'Adolphe Comte," ed. Laffitte, 148; Alix Comte to Auguste Comte, November 25, 1820, "Lettres d'Alix Comte," ed. Laffitte, 76–7; Louis Comte to Comte-Rochambeau, January 13, 1822 [1821], excerpt in Ouy, "Jeunesse," 259.

[13] Comte to John Stuart Mill, February 27, 1843, *CG*, 2:141.

[14] Comte to Valat, May 21, 1824, *CG*, 1:87.

[15] The fact that he had to work so intensely during the final sessions shows that he was hard put to finish it. The manuscript was only slightly changed before the final printing. See the rough draft of the "Première Série de travaux," 1822, N.a.fr. 17901, fols. 1–27, BN. See also the final manuscript of the *Prospectus des travaux scientifiques nécessaires pour réorganiser*

A CRITIQUE OF THE REACTIONARY AND
REVOLUTIONARY DOCTRINES

Taking up the theme of his "Sommaire appréciation de l'ensemble du passé moderne," Comte began his essay by maintaining that the coexistence of the opposing movements of disorganization and of reorganization accounted for the "great crisis experienced by the most civilized nations." The crisis began with the disorganization of the old system. But as the new system emerged, the critical tendencies, which had fulfilled their destructive function, only prolonged the anarchical situation. Comte hoped to stop the trend toward revolution by demonstrating a more effective, "organic approach" to reconstruction.[16]

First, he showed that the efforts of the kings and people throughout the West to reorganize society had been "vague and imperfect." Supported by the reactionaries, the kings' project of reestablishing the feudal and theological system by reviving the concept of divine right was "monstrous" because it tried to deny progress. In effect, reactionaries aimed to destroy all the advances of civilization that caused the decay of the old system. But the Enlightenment philosophy – "the direct cause of the fall of the old system viewed in its spiritual aspect" – could not be eliminated without also obliterating Reformation thought and the sciences. Similarly, in the secular order, because the cause of the destruction of the old system was the freedom of the communes, the kings would have to put the industrial classes back into serfdom. And in truth, the kings themselves, in encouraging the sciences, the beaux arts, and industry, were unconsciously working to undermine the old system. Asserting that the "principle of progressive civilization" was "inherent in the nature of the human species" and ridiculing the illogical behavior of the Right, Comte showed he was far from being a simple exponent of conservative thought.[17]

Nevertheless, increasingly doubtful about liberal, laissez-faire

la société, N.a.fr. 17902, BN. Originally thirty-three pages long, this manuscript is missing five folios: folios 6 and 7, which correspond to pages 60–4 of the essay printed in the *Système*, and folios 11v–14v, which correspond to pages 75–81 in the *Système*. See also "Opuscule fondamental d'Auguste Comte, publié en mai 1822," ed. Pierre Laffitte, RO, 2d. ser., 10 (January 1, 1895): 4. This article is full of mistakes. A more accurate article is Henri Gouhier, "L'Opuscule fondamental," *Les Etudes philosophiques*, no. 3 (July–September, 1974): 329–30.
[16] *Système*, vol. 4, "Appendice," 47, 48.
[17] Ibid., 48–50. See also Antimo Negri, "A. Comte, cent cinquante ans après," *Les Etudes philosophiques*, no. 3 (July–September 1974): 370–1. Like Byron and many young liberals throughout Europe, Comte condemned the pope's support of the Muslim Turks against the Greeks, who were fighting for their freedom.

doctrine, he criticized the people for trying to build an organic system on the basis of critical principles, which limited the state's ability to act. Instead of viewing the government as a "natural enemy" and restricting its role to maintaining order, the people should make it the "head of society, destined to unite it into a network and to direct all individual activities toward a common aim."[18] However, Comte himself wavered on the appropriate role for the state. Sometimes he gave it the active direction of society, while at other times he returned to his original idea of restricting it.

There were two aspects of the antigovernment doctrine advocated by the people that he particularly condemned. In the spiritual realm, the concept of unlimited freedom of conscience, which had destroyed theology, now was preventing the "uniform establishment of any system of general ideas without which . . . there is no society." To demonstrate the absurdity of this freedom, Comte wrote in a celebrated passage, "There is no liberty of conscience in astronomy, physics, chemistry, [and] physiology, in the sense that everyone would find it absurd not to believe with confidence in the principles established in these sciences by competent men."[19] Although in his "Sommaire appréciation de l'ensemble du passé moderne," Comte had sustained the right of each individual to question scientifically established concepts, this right disappeared in the fundamental opuscule. After the recent electoral triumph of the Right, Comte seemed more anxious to create immediately the general doctrine necessary to reunite and reconstruct society, even if achieving this goal meant sacrificing private, or civil, liberty.

The counterpart in the secular sphere to the doctrine of freedom of conscience was the concept of the sovereignty of the people, which destroyed the principle of divine right on which the feudal system rested. But neither this doctrine nor that of freedom of conscience offered any organic principle that could serve as the basis of reorganization: "If the one . . . presents nothing else except individual infallibility substituted for papal infallibility, the other does only the same by replacing the arbitrariness of kings by the arbitrariness of people, or rather, by that of individuals."[20] In addition to failing to give direction to society, these two revolutionary dogmas led to political upheaval by placing power in the hands of the least civilized and least educated people.

Comte's criticism of the theory of popular sovereignty, like his denunciation of the principle of freedom of conscience, was directed against the revolutionaries, who had used these doctrines to justify their radical measures. Inspired by Rousseau's idea of inalienable

[18] *Système*, vol. 4, "Appendice," 52.   [19] Ibid., 53.   [20] Ibid., 53–4.

popular sovereignty, they identified the nation with the general will. Comte had subscribed to this theory in his 1816 essay, when he said that government had to obey the national will. In the aftermath of the Terror, while many liberals continued to support this idea of basing the government on the consent of the people to counter the monarchy, they voiced their concerns about the people's unlimited sovereignty. Comte too was worried about the abuse of power, the key problem of the period. He denounced the arbitrary authority of the legislator, who, he said, could take the form of an elected or hereditary man or an elected or hereditary assembly. Thinking of Rousseau, he even criticized the idea of society making itself the legislator, because the "arbitrary" would then "be exercised by all of society on itself."[21]

Comte was basically repeating Benjamin Constant's famous argument that individuals should never be completely at the mercy of an arbitrary, concentrated sovereign power, whether that power resided in a monarch or a collectivity of which they were a part. But he gave Constant's argument more of an antidemocratic slant. Comte worried about popular sovereignty because it tended to give power to the wrong people, those unfit intellectually and morally to rule, and worked against the rule of an elite. Constant, who was no democrat either, was, however, far more concerned about preserving a private sphere, where the individual could enjoy his independence without any interference whatsoever.[22] One guarantee of this sphere was the doctrine of individual rights, such as freedom of conscience, which Comte denied.

THE CREATION OF CONSENSUS BY MEANS OF A NEW THEORY

To Comte, the only difference between the monarchical and popular doctrines was that the former tried to create a strong government in opposition to society, while the latter insisted that society must be on guard against the government. Each tried to limit or cancel the other. The only escape from "this deplorable vicious circle," the source of revolutions, was a new organic doctrine. It would be supported by the kings, who feared social disintegration, and by the people, who were becoming aware of the anarchical nature of the critical doctrine. This new organic doctrine would thus satisfy his contemporaries' two great, seemingly contradictory desires: "the

[21] Ibid., 102.
[22] Keith Baker, "Sovereignty," in *A Critical Dictionary*, ed. Furet and Ozouf, 856–8.

abandonment of the old system and the establishment of a regular and stable order."[23]

Any plan of social reorganization had two parts, first theoretical and then practical. Taking up the idea he had expressed in one of his first works for Saint-Simon ("Programme d'un concours pour une nouvelle encyclopédie") as well as in his "anonymous" letters to him, Comte proclaimed that the theoretical (or spiritual) task consisted of establishing the "new principle" of social relations as well as the general system of ideas that would guide society. Like Rousseau, Comte argued that society was not a mere agglomeration of individuals: "There is only a *society* where a general and combined action is exercised."[24] To conceive of a social system, one must first determine the primary aim of its activity, which fixed its social relationships. And as Saint-Simon, inspired by Constant, maintained, society had only two possible goals: conquest ("the violent action on the rest of the human species") and production ("the action on nature to modify it to man's advantage").[25] Once the theoreticians had chosen one of these goals and thereby established the principle of society, the men in charge of practical matters would distribute power and coordinate administrative institutions so that they harmonized with the new spirit of the social system. Making use of his own background as an engineer, Comte was suggesting the idea of a blueprint, where work was divided into conception and execution. One of his main principles was that practical action had to be guided by informed thought.

He made this distinction between theory and practice into a scientific law. The people flagrantly disobeyed it when they tried to change the whole social system "at one stroke in several months" by means of practical reforms alone. Led by "incompetent" lawyers, they had proclaimed ten different "eternal and irrevocable" constitutions in the space of thirty years. Yet it was an "extravagant chimera" to think that society could be made to advance by means of a mere constitution.[26] It took hundreds of years to establish a new social system. Thus the source of the people's errors was their *unscientific approach* to social reconstruction.

The people also mistakenly believed they could change the direction of society simply by altering the character of the temporal power. Their constitutions were filled with superficial, detailed rules relating to the division of power between the legislature and the executive – an insignificant division compared with that between the

---

[23] *Système*, vol. 4, "Appendice," 56.
[24] Ibid., 63. See also Angèle Kremer-Marietti, Introduction to *Plan*, 21.
[25] *Système*, vol. 4, "Appendice," 64.   [26] Ibid., 61, 69.

temporal and spiritual power. In fact, the constitutions completely omitted the spiritual power, which had been the old system's source of strength and stability. Thus instead of concentrating on the practical and immediate reforms of the temporal power, the people needed to organize society around its new industrial goal and reorganize the spiritual power. Comte devoted the rest of this essay to outlining the characteristics of this new power.

THE LAW OF THREE STAGES

According to Comte, the classes that would become the new powers would be in charge of bringing about the new system. The *industriels* would transform the temporal administrative system. The scientists would create a spiritual organic doctrine because they alone had the "two fundamental elements of moral government": an incontestable authority in all theoretical matters and the capacity of reason.[27] And since the crisis was European rather than national, they alone could resolve it because they were the only supranational social group. They could help create a new union of European countries, which would be superior to the old system's because it would be not only spiritual but temporal.

To establish a new organic doctrine, the scientists would have to raise politics to the "rank of the sciences of observation."[28] Comte was certain that they could do this now because he had just grasped the "law of three stages." Later he explained to his disciple Pierre Laffitte that this law had come to him early one morning in 1822 after two long nights of continuous meditation stretching from 7:00 p.m. to 10:00 a.m. Almost immediately afterward, he perceived the law of scientific hierarchy, which was inseparable from it.[29] To Comte, the law of three stages was a scientific discovery. He was not *creating* a theory but uncovering a *scientific* law. Thus he described his recognition of this law in terms of a revelation that occurred after an intense physical experience. To him, coming across this law was almost a religious experience because it became the keystone of his philosophy. It would enable him to "*discover* what others *invent.*"[30]

---

[27] Ibid., 73.   [28] Ibid., 77.

[29] Presumably these discoveries took place sometime between January and early April 1822, when he wrote the section describing them. For information on them, see Robinet, *Notice*, 151nl. There is a slightly different version according to which Comte claimed to have discovered the law of three stages after one sleepless night. "Opuscule fondamental," ed. Laffitte, 4.

[30] *Système*, vol. 4, "Appendice," 101.

In reality, he did not discover this law in the abrupt, dramatic manner that he depicted. His unpublished articles in *Le Politique* and his "Sommaire appréciation de l'ensemble du passé moderne" prove that he had vague impressions of it before 1822. Moreover, the unmethodical, diffuse exposition of the law in the fundamental opuscule suggests that he was developing and refining his ideas during the writing of the opuscule itself.[31] The story he told Pierre Laffitte was intended to make his "discovery" seem brilliant and, above all, original. In this way, the influence of Saint-Simon and Burdin was obliterated.[32]

---

[31] In the section entitled "Exposé général," Comte discussed the "spiritual" aspect of it; later when criticizing Condorcet in the part called "Première Série de travaux," he examined its temporal application and added crucial introductory material regarding classification. Ibid., 111.

[32] There has been much controversy over Turgot's possible influence on Comte. In his *Tableau philosophique des progrès successifs de l'esprit humain*, a discourse given at the Sorbonne in 1750, Turgot discussed the progress of the human mind in terms of its emancipation from anthropomorphic concepts. In the first stage, people assumed that physical effects were produced by intelligent beings who resembled men. In the second stage, they explained the causes of phenomena by abstract expressions, such as faculties or essences, which were treated in much the same manner as the old divinities were. In the third stage, people began to observe the mechanical action of bodies and created hypotheses that could be developed by mathematics and verified by experiments. Harry Elmer Barnes declared that Turgot's ideas represented the origins of Comte's law of the three stages. Turgot's theory is, indeed, very close to Comte's view of the advancement of the mind, though as Littré pointed out, it was not meant to be a law of general evolution as Comte's was. It is difficult, however, to determine if Comte was influenced by Turgot's *Discours*. His library contains none of Turgot's books. However, Comte did own Condorcet's *Vie de Monsieur Turgot* (1787). His copy shows the wear of much use; Comte even wrote his name in it, which was quite rare. Yet although Condorcet gave a one-paragraph summary of Turgot's famous discourse, he did not mention this particular theory of intellectual development. He discussed, instead, Turgot's idea of infinite human perfectibility. In the *Cours*, Comte mentioned Turgot several times, but usually it was to praise him for having prepared the way for Condorcet with this idea of human perfectibility. Because of this idea, Turgot earned a day in his honor in the Positivist Calendar. Thus it seems that one can trust Robinet's statement that Comte became familiar with Turgot's *Discours* only in 1852 or 1853. Robinet's view is based on a letter that Laffitte wrote to him on June 10, 1875. As Littré and Emile Corra also pointed out, if Comte knew of Turgot's theory of a three-stage development, he would probably have mentioned him as one of his predecessors. As will be shown later on, Comte was very eager to gather eighteenth-century ancestors once he broke up with Saint-Simon. [Anne Robert Jacques] Turgot, "Tableau philosophique des progrès successifs de l'esprit humain," in *Oeuvres de Turgot et documents le concernant*, ed. Gustave Schelle, 5 vols. (Paris: Félix Alcan, 1913–23), 1:214–35; Nicholas S. Timasheff and George A. Theodorson, *Sociological Theory: Its Nature and Growth*, 4th ed. (New York: Random House, 1976), 72; Harry Elmer Barnes, "Social Thought in Early Modern Times," in *An Introduction to the History of Sociology*, abridged ed., ed. by Barnes (Chicago: University of Chicago Press, 1948), 72; Littré *Auguste Comte*, 38–52, 74; [Marie-Jean-Antoine-Nicolas Caritat de] Condorcet, *Vie de Monsieur Turgot* (Paris, 1787), 11–12, 244–9; *Cours*, 2:89, 577, 586; "Positivist Calendar," *Système*, vol. 4, table "B'"; Robinet, *Notice*, 141–2; Emile Corra,

Although positivists later claimed that there was no evidence that Burdin's ideas were still circulating in Saint-Simon's circles around 1822, Comte seemed familiar with the *Mémoire sur la science de l'homme*, in which Saint-Simon outlined Burdin's theory that each seience went through a conjectural stage, a half conjectural and a half positive stage, and a positive stage.[33] It seems even likely that Comte knew Burdin personally, for Burdin was Saint-Simon's neighbor and was one of his doctors when he became ill in 1825.[34] Comte also included him on a very short list of people to whom he sent a copy of his opuscule in 1824.[35]

In the opuscule Comte described the law of three stages in these terms:

> Because of the nature of the human mind, each branch of our knowledge is necessarily obliged in its advancement to pass successively through three different theoretical stages: the theological or fictive stage; the metaphysical or abstract stage; and finally the scientific or positive stage.[36]

Although Comte had referred to theology, metaphysics, and positive philosophy before, he had not defined them in the very particular manner that he did now.

Theology meant more to Comte than a body of religious dogmas. During this first stage, he declared that supernatural ideas were created to link the small number of isolated observations of primitive knowledge. Imagination dominated observation. Observed facts were explained in an a priori manner according to invented "facts." Though imperfect, this way of connecting facts was the only one possible in the beginning and at least allowed some reasoning about them. This stage of thought was thus indispensable to the progress of the mind.

Previously Comte had alluded to the middle stage in the passage of the sciences from the theological to the positive, but he had failed to name it. Now in calling it metaphysical, he wanted it to connote more than the usual meaning of metaphysics – the study of the

---

La Naissance du génie d'Auguste Comte III: L'Eclosion définitive – *L'Opuscule de 1822* (Paris: Revue Positiviste Internationale, 1922), 26. See also Manuel, *Prophets of Paris*, 321n24.

[33] Corra, *La Naissance du génie d'Auguste Comte III: L'Eclosion définitive*, 31.

[34] Saint-Simon lived at 34, rue de Richelieu, while Burdin had an apartment at 15, rue de Richelieu. See "Burdin," *L'Annuaire: L'Académie Royale de Médecine*, vol. 1 (Paris, 1824); Manuel, *Saint-Simon*, 328; Leroy, *Saint-Simon*, 325.

[35] The list of people to whom Comte sent the fundamental opuscule is in the Maison d'Auguste Comte. The list is reproduced, with some problems, however, in "Matériaux pour servir à la biographie d'Auguste Comte: De la circulation des ouvrages d'Auguste Comte: De l'opuscule fondamental," ed. Pierre Laffitte, *RO*, 2d ser., 8 (September 1, 1893): 326–7.

[36] *Système*, vol. 4, "Appendice," 77.

nature of phenomena – and more than Saint-Simon's definition of metaphysics as "idle and impractical contemplation."[37] To Comte, metaphysics was an intermediary, or transitional, stage of thought, which employed more and more extensive analogies, especially personified abstractions, to bring together an increasing number of facts. Describing the bastard character of metaphysics, he wrote: "It links facts according to ideas that are no longer totally supernatural and not yet entirely natural." These ideas were "personified abstractions" that, according to whether they were closer to theology or to science, called to mind "the mystical name of a supernatural cause or the abstract statement of a simple series of phenomena."[38] With some limitations finally imposed on the use of the imagination, observation gained in importance throughout this epoch and eventually acquired the right of examination. The character of this era was therefore one of argument and criticism.

In the final, third stage of thought, facts were linked "according to the general ideas or laws of an entirely positive order," and they were "suggested or confirmed by the facts themselves."[39] Regarded as a way to express phenomena, these basic connecting laws should be reduced in number as much as possible without, however, admitting hypotheses unverifiable by observation. Comte wanted to avoid the reductionism of Saint-Simon.

Without minimizing the influence of Burdin and Saint-Simon, one cannot deny that Comte did define these three stages – especially the middle one – far more clearly than they had ever done. In Saint-Simon's *Mémoire sur la science de l'homme*, the middle stage had been vaguely defined as merely half conjectural and half positive. In covering progress in general, Saint-Simon never consistently used a three-stage schema; he often pictured history in terms of five or even twelve epochs. Moreover, when Saint-Simon (and Burdin) had discussed a three-stage development, it was mainly in reference to the sciences. In contrast, Comte introduced his law by means of the sciences but then applied it to religious, political, and social progress, in fact to all of human evolution. It became for him the key to social science, something it never was for Saint-Simon.

Comte used this law to demonstrate that despite the impetus arising from man's need to act on nature, the intellectual development of the mind derived basically from the nature of the human mind itself.[40] As the mind progressed from one mode of thinking to another, it gave birth to a different theoretical system, which in turn affected the social order. Due to the law of three stages, Comte

---

[37] Saint-Simon, "Prospectus," *L'Industrie*, 13.
[38] *Système*, vol. 4, "Appendice," 77.   [39] Ibid., 78.
[40] Christian Rutten, *Essai sur la morale d'Auguste Comte* (Paris: Les Belles Lettres, 1972) 47.

claimed he could understand the changes that had occurred and would occur in the human mind and thus in the social system. It was this greater understanding that made the science of society possible.[41]

THE CLASSIFICATION OF THE SCIENCES

From his law of three stages, Comte proceeded to the classification of the sciences, which illustrated and complemented it. While the law of three stages expressed the progress of the intellect in the constitution of the sciences (and philosophy), the classification showed the order in which the sciences were established. As Lucien Lévy-Bruhl pointed out, the law of the three stages represented the *dynamic* point of view, while the classification of the sciences reflected the *static* point of view.[42] Both were expressions of the same basic idea: the inevitability of the triumph of positive ways of thinking in politics.[43]

According to Comte's principle of classification, each science went through the first two stages and then became positive according to the simplicity of its phenomena, which was equivalent to its distance from man. Astronomy became a positive science followed by physics, chemistry, and physiology in that order. The implication was that the science of society, which was the most complex science and the one closest to man, would be established last.

The seeds of Comte's theory are evident in Saint-Simon's *Lettres d'un habitant de Genève à ses contemporains*, which stated that because astronomical phenomena were the simplest, astronomy was the first science in which observation triumphed over imagination. Saint-Simon did not mention physics, but he did say that chemistry became based on observed facts after astronomy because its phenomena were more complex. Physiology, which was even more complex, was just beginning to rid itself of metaphysics.[44] Comte himself in the unpublished fourth *cahier* of *Le Politique* and the "Sommaire appréciation de l'ensemble du passé moderne" had already discussed the sciences as developing according to their distance from man and had referred to their development in exactly the same order. The classification of the sciences was therefore not a sudden revelation that came after the discovery of the law of three stages.

[41] Paul Arbousse-Bastide, *Auguste Comte* (Paris: Presses Universitaires de France, 1968), 21.
[42] Lévy-Bruhl, *Philosophie d'Auguste Comte*, 69.
[43] Raymond Aron, *Les Grandes Doctrines de sociologie historique: Les Cours de Sorbonne* (Paris: Centre de Documentation Universitaire, 1965), 59.
[44] Saint-Simon, *Lettres d'un habitant de Genève*, 38–9.

One novel, important aspect of Comte's theory in the *Plan* was his argument that these three stages could exist contemporaneously. He gave the example of physiology, in which some scientists attributed moral phenomena to supernatural action, others to an abstract being, and still others to "organic conditions susceptible of being demonstrated."[45] Thus to Comte, progress was a complex, continuous process in which the breaks between the main periods were not clear-cut or abrupt.

THE STAGES OF POLITICAL THEORY

Taking up the theme of his recent writings, Comte stated that since the natural sciences had become positive, politics, which depended on all of them, was ready to enter its third stage. To emphasize its inevitability, he declared that political science was a doctrine dictated by history, not something that he concocted.

For the first time, Comte described the theological and metaphysical stages of politics. The theological stage was reflected in the doctrine of the kings. In this stage, politics revolved around theology: the supernatural idea of divine right was the foundation of all social relations, while historical change was viewed as part of a divine plan.

The metaphysical stage of politics was embodied in the doctrine of the people. As the theoretical foundation of their natural rights, the concept of a primitive social contract was systematized primarily by Rousseau, who gave metaphysical politics its "definitive form" and helped make social contract theory its basis.[46] Comte felt that Rousseau, carried away by his imagination, had mistakenly equated the growth of civilization with the degeneration of society. To Comte, the state of nature was an early, flawed phase of civilization and could never coincide with a perfect social order. Praising primitive virtue and simplicity not only encouraged civilization's "universal regression" to a "primordial and invariable type" of society but also denied progress.[47] Although he himself was not wholly free of Rousseau's influence, Comte wanted people to create new forms for the future rather than adopt outdated models of the past.

In the scientific stage of politics, society would be in harmony with human nature. Since man tended to modify the world for his own advantage, political science would give society the goal of developing "this natural tendency" to maximize useful activity.[48] Here

---

[45] *Système*, vol. 4, "Appendice," 78.
[46] Ibid., 107; see also 79.   [47] *Cours*, 2:34–5.   [48] *Système*, vol. 4, "Appendice," 79.

Comte was grafting his science of society onto physiology in a much more intelligible way than Saint-Simon did in his *Mémoire sur la science de l'homme*, which made social science part of physiology.

To Comte, the triumph of the positive doctrine was assured not only intellectually by the development of the other positive sciences, but also morally and socially. Since the theological system was dead and the metaphysical system, which had been created to combat it, had fulfilled its transitional function, it now was possible for society to be reorganized around the modification of nature. He believed that the profound change in the intellectual study of politics would effect a radical "moral revolution," which would, in turn, produce a fundamental political and social reorganization – the most complete revolution in all of history.[49] Thus it was the moral and not only the purely intellectual aspect of this scientific change that interested Comte.

THE ROLE OF OBSERVATION IN THE CREATION OF POLITICAL SCIENCE

Besides the introduction and general exposition, the *Prospectus* was supposed to have three more sections, one on history, a second on positive education, and a third on society's action on nature. Comte finished only the first section, demonstrating that political science was a "particular physics, founded on the direct observation of phenomena relating to the collective development of the human species."[50] He sought to demonstrate that history represented the scientific basis of political science.

The section began by developing the sketch on observation and imagination that Comte had written on April 9, 1821. (This was the manuscript entitled "Première Série de travaux.") To emphasize the importance of observation in politics, he declared that the reign of imagination during the first two stages of history had led men to believe they had unlimited control over all phenomena. Astrology, alchemy, medical panaceas, and claims to have found the best type of government not only indicated man's imaginative search for absolutes but reflected his view of his own unrestricted importance and power over nature. As the growth of the first four positive sciences required that observation be more important than imagination, man was gradually displaced as the center of the universe, and his sense of dominance over nature was severely reduced. He found that he could modify only certain phenomena that he could observe and that the number of possible modifications was very restricted.

[49] Ibid., 80. [50] Ibid., 130.

Although Comte emphasized that the new society had to be built on the conquest of nature, he did not share some scientists' view of man's unlimited power. Indeed, he worried about man's lack of respect for nature.

Politics could not be based on observation unless it fulfilled two conditions: it had to consider social organization to be dependent on the state of civilization, and it had to subject the progress of civilization to a scientific law founded on the laws of human nature. Thus to become a science, it had to adopt a relativistic and concrete view of society and civilization.

Society was the product of civilization because its character derived from its members' activities in the three main aspects of civilization – the sciences, the beaux arts, and industry. Since the state of civilization created the temporal and spiritual forces that directed general activity, it established the aim, nature, and form of society. Society, in turn, had a limited effect on civilization.

In many respects, Comte's analysis of society was similar to Marx's. Like Comte, Marx not only sought a "scientific" approach to society and a natural law of development, but argued that society could not be considered apart from civilization. Likewise, Comte and Marx shared a view of civilization that was both materialistic and idealistic. Although Marx is remembered for his economic determinism, his doctrine was idealistic in its stress on the growth of consciousness. But Comte's idealism went further because he saw civilization as consisting primarily of the "development of the human mind." Comte did not, however, overlook the materialistic side of human evolution, for he insisted that civilization also included the "development of the action of man on nature," which was the consequence of intellectual progress.[51] (These two aspects of the advance of civilization – intellectual and material progress – were embodied in the arts, the sciences, and industry.) Friedrich Hayek exaggerated the materialistic aspect of Comte's view of history because he overlooked his point that man's action on nature was the *consequence* of his intellectual progress.[52] As mentioned before, Comte also seemed to foreshadow aspects of Marx's doctrine of hegemony, for he believed that a political system always gave "supreme power [to] the preponderant social forces, whose nature is invariably determined by the state of civilization."[53] To both men, the political system reflected the civil order, which in turn reflected the state of civilization. Thus the political system was directed by the dominant forces in society. To Marx, these forces were represented by the economic ruling class; to Comte, they included the intellectual elite as well.

---

[51] Ibid., 86.   [52] Hayek, *Counter-Revolution*, 139.   [53] *Système*, vol. 4, "Appendice," 87.

Comte was so sure of the harmonious relationship between a political state and the corresponding stage of civilization that he claimed that society was usually as well directed as the "nature of things allowed." Rejecting criticisms of past institutions and practices, he admitted that his approach to history was very similar to the "famous theological and metaphysical dogma of optimism," which stated that "everything is as good as it could ever be."[54] Presumably he was referring to Leibniz's doctrine, the target of Voltaire's *Candide*. Although Comte acknowledged that this doctrine was mystical and absolutist, he maintained that it was a useful way of reasoning, one that would be developed by positive philosophy. Whereas the traditional optimistic doctrine obstructed progress, his philosophy would demonstrate that society was only as good as the corresponding stage of civilization permitted. It thus encouraged action to advance civilization, which was the only way to reform society. To work directly to improve society was futile. Besides showing a lack of faith in political voluntarism, Comte's optimistic attitude betrays an old-fashioned belief in providence.

THE BASIS OF CIVILIZATION: THE LAWS OF
HUMAN NATURE

Because the law of three stages, the "supreme law of all political phenomena," would shed light on what type of action was appropriate for the present, Comte sought to validate it by arguing that it derived from the laws of human nature.[55] His social theory, like that of Saint-Simon, was inspired by the example of physiology. Yet as a result of his medical studies at Montpellier, Comte had a better understanding of biology than did his mentor, and it became a more crucial part of his theory of society. By giving history a motor in human nature, he made it part of the natural order. Since human nature was the same everywhere, the three invariable stages of the development of civilization were universalized.[56]

Comte argued that because the human species resembled man in its instinct to perfect itself, nothing could hinder the inexorable march of civilization. In fact, civilization, with its basis in science and industry, had never ceased to progress. Like Saint-Simon, Comte suggested that the only element of civilization that may not have always

---

[54] Ibid., 116. [55] Ibid., 89.
[56] G. Canguilhem, "Histoire de l'homme et nature des choses selon Auguste Comte dans le *Plan des travaux scientifiques nécessaires pour réorganiser la société 1822*," *Les Etudes Philosophiques*, no. 3 (July–September 1974): 294, 295, 297; *Système*, vol. 4, "Appendice," 88–91.

advanced was the beaux arts, but he felt this did not detract from his concept of all-embracing progress.

In addition, he declared that even misguided politicians could not slow the movement of progress. Here Comte relied once again on his medical studies, arguing that civilization, like the human body, could overcome "evidently vicious treatments" because every living organism spontaneously acted "to repair accidental disturbances of its structure." Earlier political theory tried to invent remedies without considering the illness, but it was as foolish to seek the "best government possible" without considering the state of civilization as it was to search for a "general treatment applicable to all illnesses and all temperaments." Opposed to this approach, scientific politics held that the "principal cause of recovery is the vital force of the patient." Comte's belief in the inherent strength of the vital force reflects the vitalist tendencies of the Montpellier medical school, especially its famous professor Barthez. The role of positive politics was therefore to foresee and facilitate the "natural outcome" of crises so that inappropriate political solutions, akin to bad medical remedies, could be avoided.[57]

Moreover, like the human body, civilization was subject to the scientific law that living forces needed a certain amount of resistance in order to develop fully. Political (or intellectual) trends that seemed to be obstacles to progress often favored it in the long run. By claiming that civilization made social improvements in each epoch whether or not statesmen or philosophers consciously aided it, Comte seemed to be paralleling Hegel's concept of the cunning of reason.

To support his points, Comte used many facile biological analogies because he wished to show that the positive society was a *natural* development. It derived not only from history but from human nature. It was not an artificial construct imposed by human beings acting as legislators. Disillusioned by the political maneuvers that he had witnessed since his youth, Comte was skeptical about large-scale human action and became convinced that what was "natural" was best. In spite of his suggestion that human nature was inherently progressive because people were inclined to self-improvement, the laws of human nature, the basis of his theory, remained extremely vague. For example, he tried to escape the similarity between scientific determinism and historical determinism by asserting that even though his law of three stages was as "necessary" as the law of gravity, it was "more modifiable."[58] However, he offered no reasons to support his faith in a "modifiable determinism"[59] and seemed to stress the limits rather than the possibilities of human action.[60] In

[57] *Système*, vol. 44, "Appendice," 85, 90, 101.   [58] Ibid., 95.
[59] Ducassé, *Méthode et intuition*, 34.   [60] Arnaud, *Le "Nouveau Dieu,"* 95–6.

fact, Comte rejected Turgot's call for more men of genius to help progress, for he claimed they were not needed. Just as nothing could hinder progress, so nothing could propel it. Humanity just followed a prescribed course.

THE ROLE OF MAN IN HISTORY

Comte again used a biological analogy – that of instinct – to illustrate the extent of the human ability to modify his historical law. According to Comte, an individual's instincts could not be changed but their development could be accelerated or retarded "up to a certain limited point."[61] This applied also to the human species. The most mankind could do to affect its own development was to modify within limits the *speed*, not the basic character, of civilization's advance by physical, moral, and political means. Comte criticized historians for exaggerating the importance of the power of individuals and disregarding the latent currents that actually commanded them to act. Recognizing that the human species obeyed its own impulses, creative individuals who sought to influence human affairs first had to notice the changes dictated by the stage of civilization and then proclaim the corresponding doctrines or institutions. As one scholar aptly points out, the only liberty that Comte allowed man was "to regularize a spontaneous evolution."[62] The reorganization of society consisted solely of this regularization. As seen already in his belief that scientists had to be directed by common sense, Comte was convinced that the spontaneous had to precede and found the systematic.[63]

He admitted that finding the law of history was difficult. Political scientists, like biologists, should avoid the idiosyncrasies of human development, which might obscure general behavior. Another problem was that the march of civilization did not follow a straight line but was "composed of a series of progressive oscillations" around a "middle line." The institutions and doctrines in their years of vigor were progressive, while others were old and in decline. Scholars would have to concentrate on the "middle movement that always tends to predominate" in progress.[64] They could verify the laws of

---

[61] *Système*, vol. 4, "Appendice," 93.
[62] Gérard Buis, "Le Projet de réorganisation sociale dans les oeuvres de jeunesse d'Auguste Comte," chap. in *Régénération et reconstruction sociale entre 1780 et 1848*, by A. Amiot et al. (Paris: J. Vrin, 1978), 145.
[63] Ducassé, *Méthode et intuition*, 44.
[64] *Système*, vol. 4, "Appendice," 97–8. The idea of a middle line or mean perhaps derived from Comte's mathematical background, while his concept of the oscillatory march of civilization may have come from the Idéologue physiologist Anthelme Richerand, who

history by observing the different stages of civilization that still existed around the globe. They could also perform experiments, studying pathological, that is, apparently abnormal, cases of social and political development.

Avoiding violent revolutions was one of the most important goals of positive politics. With a firm grasp of the law of progress, the new science of politics would enable people to obey the dictates of history and devise political schemes accelerating the "progressive oscillations." The "inevitable crises" would be shorter and more peaceful; turbulent upheavals would be avoided; and chimerical plans would be discarded. People would be less inclined to revolt against what they learned was in the "nature of things."[65]

Fearful of the political commotions of his own time, Comte sought to convince his readers and perhaps himself that violent change did not have to be part of progress. Unlike Marx, who claimed that revolutions were the inevitable result of the class struggle, Comte held that violent upheavals came from ignoring historical laws. A firm grasp of the scientific method could easily eliminate such ignorance along with most social clashes. In effect, Comte was straddling two positions. On the one hand, man was a very passive tool of a higher law; on the other, because of his intelligence, he could act effectively to avoid such horrifying events as the French Revolution. Although up to now a story of social conflict, history could become a tale of harmony.

THE APPLICATION OF THE LAW OF THREE STAGES IN POSITIVE POLITICS

Just as physiology had to study man in relation to the animals and to all organic bodies, political science had to observe other epochs in order to understand the present, whose constitution was not altogether clear. To discover the law of history, it needed at least three terms. Here Comte was inspired by his mathematical training, which stressed discovering the value of unknown variables in equations.

depicted bodily movement in much the same terms. Comte owned an 1820 edition of Richerand's *Eléments de physiologie* and later found it valuable enough to be included in the "Positivist Library of the Nineteenth Century." In this book Richerand spoke of the "movements of *locomotion*" by which the human body changed positions in the same way as Comte referred to the "mechanism of locomotion" in describing the march of civilization. Anthelme Richerand, *Nouveaux élémens de physiologie*, 2d ed. (Paris, 1802), 2:195, 293; *Système*, 4:97. On Comte's intellectual debts, see also Canguilhem, "Histoire de l'homme," 296; Kremer-Marietti, Introduction to *Plan*, 27.

[65] *Système*, vol. 4, "Appendice," 96–8.

Comte liked to study the two extremes of a problem and to find the continuity between antitheses. His predilection reflects his taste for the dialectic and for synthesis.[66] Again the similarity to Hegel is striking.

Comte adopted Saint-Simon's idea of the appropriate sequence of study. By first studying the past and then the future, one would be able to see the political action appropriate to the present. In this fashion, political science could fulfill its practical goal of finding the political and social system that best conformed to the state of civilization. When it did so, Comte assumed that all rational people would automatically agree that this system was the most appropriate. Arguments as to the best type of government would be avoided.

The law of three stages thus represented an escape from the arbitrary, from the absolute power of legislators, who sought to impose their ideal of the best government on society. With his belief that scientific laws could solve all political problems, Comte clearly did not subscribe to the view that government represented an accommodation of interest groups, each jockeying for position to shape policy in its favor. The positive government would be a scientific product, not a game of power. Everyone would agree on a political course of action as much as they did on the movement of the earth.

Maintaining that the same institution or doctrine could be bad in one era and good in another, Comte revealed his relativistic view of freedom:

> Liberty . . . in a reasonable proportion is . . . useful to an individual and to a people who have attained a certain degree of instruction and have acquired some habits of foresight because it permits the development of their faculties, [but it] is very harmful to those who have not yet fulfilled these two conditions and have the indispensable need, for themselves as much as for others, to be kept in tutelage.[67]

Freedom was thus a right that could be enjoyed only by an educated elite concerned about self-development.

Since Comte believed that the arbitrary in practice corresponded to the absolute in theory, it would seem that freedom in practice should correspond to relativism in theory. When he declared that positive politics eliminated the absolute and the vague, the source of the arbitrary, he implied that the civilized nations that adopted positive politics would always be free. Adopting Saint-Simon's terminology, he explained that in these free nations "the government of things replaces those of men" and "there is truly *law* in politics in the real and philosophical sense attached to this expression by the

[66] Ducassé, *Méthode et intuition*, 44, 46.   [67] *Système*, vol. 4, "Appendice," 101.

illustrious Montesquieu." Determining everything in the political sphere, this law – the law of three stages – was as sovereign as the law of gravity but could not be considered despotic any more than any other natural law.[68] Yet Comte found himself in the same position as Montesquieu, for they both were attracted by relativism and fixed standards. The absolute standards seemed to contradict his relativistic stance. Using his relativistic doctrine, Comte tried to escape from this dilemma by saying that his standard – freedom – was part of progress and was not always desirable. But it seemed paradoxical to use relativism – the doctrine of the antiarbitrary – to support the advantages of limiting freedom.

Comte declared that in order to understand the past, political science had to adopt the system of classification recently developed by botany and zoology. His interest in classification may have been piqued by Saint-Simon's friend, the naturalist Henri Ducrotay de Blainville.[69] Comte owned Blainville's *De l'organisation des animaux* of 1822 and adopted his view that the order of generality of the different divisions of the classification had to correspond to the real relationships between the phenomena that were being observed. The hierarchy of different families of genres should consist of a series of general facts that were divided into more and more particular orders. In this hierarchy, the complex had priority over the simple. To Comte, classification was the philosophical expression of a science: "To know the classification is to know the science, at least in its most important aspect."[70] By implication, the essence of political science was its method of classification, that is, its distribution of epochs according to their natural relationships. The core of this science, the law of three stages, derived from relating and coordinating political facts.

Whereas in the preceding section of the opuscule, Comte had discussed this law mainly in terms of scientific and intellectual developments, now he connected these developments with the social and economic world. Elaborating on the position that he had taken in the "Sommaire appréciation de l'ensemble du passé moderne," he

[68] Ibid., 102–3.
[69] Comte's enthusiasm for classification may have also been inspired by the botanist Augustin Pyrame de Candolle, a friend of Daniel Encontre and professor at the Montpellier medical school. In Comte's library one can still find an 1819 copy of the *Théorie élémentaire de la botanique* by Candolle. It is not clear whether Comte knew him, but he did send him a copy of the opuscule in 1824 and was pleased to discover that the scientist seemed to approve of it. See the list of people to whom Comte sent his opuscule at the Maison d'Auguste Comte. Comte mentioned Candolle in a letter to Tabarié, July 17, 1824, *CG*, 1:101. Also see Gouhier, *Jeunesse*, 1:179.
[70] *Système*, vol. 4, "Appendice," 110. See also Allal Sinaceur, ed., "Introduction aux leçons 40 à 45," *Cours*, 1:652.

explained that the first stage of civilization, the theological epoch, was militaristic. Its primary institution was slavery of the producers. In the second epoch, the metaphysical and legal one, society was no longer totally militaristic because industry began to develop and production joined conquest as a goal of social action. Slavery eventually disappeared, although producers were still subject to the arbitrariness of rulers. In the third stage, the positive one, social relations were to be based entirely on industry and all of society was to be directed toward production. Because the separate elements of the temporal and spiritual spheres had reached this third stage, it now was time for society as a whole to advance to this epoch. This discussion of social and economic progress was basically an elucidation of the temporal, that is, secular, side of the law of three stages. In this fashion, Comte gave his law a new global or all-encompassing character, one that the Burdin–Saint-Simonian theory never had.

THE PROPAGATION OF THE NEW SCIENCE: THE ROLE OF
IMAGINATION AND ARTISTS

Up to this point, Comte had stressed the importance of observation in the formation of the theories of political science. Now he affirmed that imagination also played a role, although a secondary one, for it had to fill in the details of the new social system, whose general outline was provided by observation. Above all, it had to invent theories to link secondary facts temporarily until more definitive connections could emerge from the facts themselves. This novel theory of hypotheses would become more important to him later.

He also gave imagination the dominant role in the *propagation* of the new science among the people, whose consent to its ideas was crucial. Realizing that scientific proofs of the inevitability of the new society would not arouse popular enthusiasm, he argued that imagination must persuade the people to support it by showing them how it would improve their lives. The people would then undergo a "moral revolution," shedding the egoism and apathy that had developed within them during the dissolution of the old system. Like Marx, Comte looked forward to the day when everyone's faculties would be "in continual action."[71] Thus already in 1822, Comte envisioned the positive society as characterized by a new burst of activity and by an unselfish interest in the welfare of others.

The social force corresponding to the imagination consisted of

[71] *Système*, vol. 4, "Appendice," 105.

the experts in the beaux arts. They alone could judge the value of phenomena and would become the main moral force in the new society. The scientists would determine the plan of the new system, the artists would make sure it was propagated and adopted, and the *industriels* (the practical, producing classes) would establish practical institutions to implement it.[72] This division of labor was similar to the one Saint-Simon was advocating at the time.[73]

Because the king and the aristocrats had lost their power as the sole patrons and focus of culture and new forms of wealth were emerging, the purpose of art had indeed become a key question. Comte's idea of the need for propaganda in an age when popular consent was crucial had already been recognized by the revolutionaries, who believed art should serve the new republic, and by Napoleon, who also considered culture an influential social force. All were concerned with using art to educate the masses and to mold public opinion in favor of their regimes. The moral and regenerative function of cultural education had long ago been touted by the Encyclopedists, who believed art should inculcate virtue. The idea that culture could shape morality and politics in a particular direction reappeared in Saint-Simon's works and was taken up by Comte. In fact, most early-nineteenth-century doctrines, including liberalism, neo-Catholicism, and romanticism, gave a special regenerative role to the artist.[74]

Comte's discussion of the role of imagination, the human being's inherent need for moral exaltation, and the importance of a moral revolution revealed his understanding of the emotional requirements of mankind. From the outset, he was aware that reason alone could not adequately meet all of a person's needs. Objective, rational demonstrations of the appropriateness of a new society could never move the people to work to bring about that society. Even scientists needed the emotional stimulus provided by the imagination so that they would become passionate about the new system. Thus appeals to the imaginative and subjective side of a person were vital, especially if a new society characterized by a spirit of love was proposed. It seemed that Comte was already coming close to espousing a new religion. Yet his ideas in this regard were still hazy. Whereas he had previously accused political economy of being indifferent to values, now he insisted on the objectivity of the social scientists and gave artists the role of creating norms.

---

[72] Ibid., 106.
[73] See Saint-Simon, "Travaux philosophiques, scientifiques, et poétiques ayant pour objet de faciliter la réorganisation de la société européenne," Extract from *Du système industriel*, 3d part, in *Oeuvres*, 6:470.
[74] F. W. J. Hemmings, *Culture and Society in France, 1789–1848* (Leicester: Leicester University Press, 1987), 2–3, 55, 63, 249; Bénichou, *Temps des prophètes*, 11–12, 67–8.

A CRITIQUE OF HIS PREDECESSORS

To stress that the moment had come to create a positive social science, Comte ended his fundamental opuscule with a long survey of his predecessors' attempts to make politics a science. This section grew out of the fragmentary essays that he had written in 1819.[75] He again considered Condorcet and Cabanis. But instead of reviewing Destutt de Tracy's works as he did before, he examined Montesquieu's ideas. Although partly inspired by political economy, Comte failed to mention Adam Smith or J. B. Say. Perhaps his opinion of these thinkers was undergoing a change and he was losing his enthusiasm for political economy. The "objective" laws of history were beginning to seem more promising as a basis of the science of society.[76]

Although he had omitted Montesquieu in previous essays, Comte now described him as having been the first to "treat politics as a science of facts, not dogmas" and to treat law in a philosophical manner.[77] He praised *De l'esprit des lois*, especially the first section, which defined laws as the "necessary relations arising from the nature of things."[78] He explained that Montesquieu's originality lay in demonstrating that political phenomena, like all other phenomena, were subject to natural laws and were not regulated arbitrarily by all-powerful legislators, as his contemporaries liked to think.[79] Furthermore, because Montesquieu perceived the "emptiness of metaphysical and absolute politics," his work was not marred by the critical tendencies of his contemporaries.[80] Though still essentially metaphysical, his philosophy was closer to the positive state than any previous one. Comte clearly considered himself to be Montesquieu's successor.

Yet he did criticize him for not having successfully raised politics to a science because of his ignorance of progress. In the *Cours*, he explained that Montesquieu's classification of social and political systems into three types – republic, monarchy, and despotism – was ahistorical and exaggerated the importance of governmental forms.[81] He did not share Montesquieu's enthusiasm for the English parliamentary system as a model government or his interest in the influ-

---

[75] These essays were "Considérations sur les tentatives qui ont été faites pour fonder la science sociale sur la physiologie et sur quelques autres sciences," "Considérations sur les tentatives qui ont été faites pour rendre positive la science sociale, en la faisant dériver de quelques autres sciences," et "Sur les travaux politiques de Condorcet."
[76] Arnaud, Le *"Nouveau Dieu,"* 79–80.   [77] *Système*, vol. 4, "Appendice," 106.
[78] Montesquieu, *De l'esprit des lois*, 1:7. In the *Cours*, Comte praised the "admirable" preliminary chapter of *De l'esprit des lois*, which he felt defined the general idea of law for the "first time since the original blossoming of human reason." *Cours*, 2:85.
[79] *Cours*, 2:85.   [80] *Système*, vol. 4, "Appendice," 107.   [81] *Cours*, 2:84.

ence of climate on society, which threatened the law of three stages, whereby all countries had to follow the same course of civilization.[82]

Finally, Comte criticized Montesquieu for lacking a radical social theory and thus suggesting only slight modifications of the old theological and feudal system.[83] In Comte's mind, a political theory was not truly positive unless it had a vision of a reformed society and therefore an immediate bearing on practical politics. In truth, he was more of a moral philosopher than an objective scientist interested in a purely descriptive theory of the functions of society. From the very beginning, his thought revealed a fundamental tension that derived from the contradiction between the objective ends implied in his epistemology and his faith in teleology.[84]

As he had done in his essays of 1819, Comte praised Condorcet for having shown that political science must rest on a theory of progress and that prediction was an essential part of the science of history, but he condemned his philosophy for being "sterile." Too critical of the past, Condorcet failed to understand that the eighteenth century was not a miraculous anomaly, but merely the "sum of the partial advances made by civilization in all the preceding intermediary stages."[85] Having misjudged the past, Condorcet was untrustworthy in his forecasts about the future. By rectifying Condorcet's errors, Comte believed he would develop the correct theory of progress and become his worthy successor.

To a far greater extent than he had done in his essays of 1819, Comte also criticized Condorcet's effort to apply mathematical analysis to social phenomena. Condemning any attempt to reduce the science of politics to other positive sciences, he asserted that the use of probabilities in social analysis led to self-evident, trivial results and was mere scientific affectation. Furthermore, inspired by Bichat and other physiologists, he declared that the science of society resembled physiology because social phenomena, like biological phenomena, were too complex and variable to be subject to "calculable and precise laws," that is, laws of quantity. Though a

---

[82] Ibid., 87; *Système*, vol. 4, "Appendice," 107–8.

[83] Comte's criticisms of Montesquieu were not altogether valid. Montesquieu did have some concept of development, for he felt that the growing importance of such factors as public opinion, customs, and religion reflected progress. Moreover, he did not stress the importance of climate as much as Comte said he did. Nor was he as socially indifferent as Comte pretended, for he formulated one famous prescription for society: the theory of the separation of powers. Comte's critique resulted either from a superficial reading of *De l'esprit des lois* or from a deliberate misinterpretation of the text in order to make his own achievement seem more salient. He was really rebuking Montesquieu for not achieving what he, Comte, prided himself on having established: a theory that showed the historical inevitability of the new system. For Montesquieu's concept of progress, see Shackleton, *Montesquieu*, 316–19.

[84] Delvolvé, *Méthode et intuition*, 54, 68.   [85] *Système*, vol. 4, "Appendice," 109, 115.

mathematician himself, he strongly objected to the "metaphysical prejudice that outside of mathematics there can exist no true certitude." Mathematics was at most only an *instrumental science*, that is, a science of method. Used alone, it could teach nothing about reality. Because it was not at all involved in observing nature and thus had a "metaphysical character," mathematics *never* was the key to making any science positive.[86]

Although positivism today is often closely associated with statistical analysis, the fundamental opuscule demonstrates that Comte was always very much opposed to the quantification of social phenomena, which he thought would remain "impossible" no matter how exact human knowledge became.[87] He never equated the positive method with mathematical analysis. Instead, he was convinced that each science became positive from the observation of its own data. To become positive, political science had to avoid mathematical procedures, which were unproductive, and directly observe its own phenomena, that is, political phenomena. By rejecting mathematics as a means to connect the physical and moral sciences, Comte was implicitly striking a blow at the Cartesian tradition in France. This critique of Descartes, one of his "predecessors," would become more developed in the *Cours*.

Finally, Comte reviewed once again Cabanis's efforts to raise politics to a science by making it a product of physiology. He gave credit to Cabanis for the "great revolution" whereby the study of the affective and intellectual functions became part of physiology and thus advanced from the metaphysical to the positive state.[88] Henceforth, all types of human phenomena, especially moral and physical ones, were considered interrelated and were no longer studied in isolation.

Comte agreed with Cabanis that in some respects the study of society – the study of the "collective development of the human species" – was part of the science of man.[89] After all, the law of three stages was based on the laws of human nature. However, he criticized Cabanis and consequently the whole Idéologue program for exaggerating the scope of physiology by making it encompass the entire study of social phenomena. To reduce the science of society to that of the individual was as erroneous as the effort to make the science of living matter a part of that of inert matter.

Moreover, Comte believed the study of society no longer had to rely on physiology to become positive, for it now could use history for this purpose. Physiology was an inappropriate model precisely because it did not study the past. The history of the individual was very different from that of social phenomena. For example, when

---

[86] Ibid., 123–4.   [87] Ibid., 121.   [88] Ibid., 129.   [89] Ibid., 125.

physiologists examined beavers, a very intelligent, sociable species, they directly connected the study of the history of beaver societies with the study of the development of the individual beaver. However, since the human species, unlike beavers, progressed from generation to generation, it needed a special science – social physics – to deal with the history of its civilization. Although the progress of mankind was ultimately related to the structure of the human being, society was a collectivity of individuals with a character of its own.[90] For this reason, it would be impossible to deduce its whole history from a departure point established by human nature. Social physics was, in short, a mixture of physiology and history and could never be reduced to either one.

The same twofold division – the science of the individual man, which included physiology, and the science of the human species, which encompassed history – appeared in Saint-Simon's *Mémoire sur la science de l'homme*. In this book, Saint-Simon also discussed at length Cabanis and Condorcet and referred to the beaver example. Thus Comte may have been referring to the *Mémoire* when he wrote the fundamental opuscule.

COMTE'S ADDITIONS TO THE OPUSCULE

Little is known about Comte's life during the two years after he finished his fundamental opuscule. Yet his political and scientific observations led him to make several additions when he republished it in 1824.[91] Despite the fact that he called these additions "secondary," they were very significant.[92]

Several of them involved further thoughts on the "social malaise" gripping his contemporaries, which he attributed to the spiritual anarchy that had preceded and engendered the temporal chaos.[93] He was more than ever convinced that this malaise was more spiritual than temporal in character and that therefore the reorganization of the spiritual power was most important and would lead to the restructuring of the temporal power.[94]

---

[90] Kremer-Marietti, Introduction to *Plan*, 162.

[91] Pierre Laffitte displayed these changes in "Opuscule fondamental," 1–124. See also Gouhier, "L'Opuscule fondamental," 325–37. The 1822 edition is in Henri Saint-Simon, *Suite des travaux ayant pour objet de fonder le système industriel: Du contrat social* (Paris, April 1822). The 1824 edition is in Saint-Simon, *Catéchisme des industriels: Troisième cahier* (Paris, 1824).

[92] *Système*, vol. 4, "Appendice," iii.

[93] Ibid., 69. Compare page 54 in the 1822 edition, page 45 in the 1824 edition, and pages 68–9 in the 1854 edition.

[94] To the tenth paragraph of the "Introduction," Comte added that the kings' (or governing classes') desire to reestablish the old system was understandable because they grasped more

Comte also added six pages that reveal a deeper appreciation of the political situation of the time.[95] As France drifted more to the Right between 1822 and 1824, he seemed increasingly anxious to find a "provisional" solution. In this addition, he stressed that neither the party of the kings nor that of the people had made any social improvements because they both were intellectually bankrupt. Politics was in a state of constant oscillation between these two opposing doctrines. The party that epitomized this oscillation was the center party, which he had not mentioned in 1822. Lacking character and decisiveness, this moderate ("doctrinaire") party of Guizot and Royer-Collard was a contradictory blend of reactionary and critical opinions and contributed to the sense that society was lurching back and forth between its feeling of the absurdity of the old system and its fear of anarchy. Yet Comte argued that until an organic party emerged, he and other "sensible men" should support this center party, for at least it prevented the violent disorders that would erupt from the triumph of either one of the extremes.[96] In another addition, he softened his stand on lawyers, whom he encouraged to support the direction that "others" were going to give to society.[97]

Evidently, Comte perceived more clearly the useful role that metaphysicians, such as the lawyers and the doctrinaires, could assume in the present situation and did not want to alienate them, especially at a time when the Left was becoming increasingly unpopular. The Left was disunited and in a state of crisis, for it encompassed not only constitutional monarchists and Bonapartists, but republicans. Many leftists were also engaged in subversive activity, reflected in the proliferation of conspiratorial groups, such as the Carbonari. Comte's essay reflects the widespread fear of violence and disgust their extremism was causing. It thus may have been politically expedient for him to favor the liberal center. Although its support of the Charter could not have pleased him, he was clearly attracted to the elitism of Guizot and his colleagues, who spoke of the "sovereignty of reason," instead of popular sovereignty.[98] Thus at this point he sacrificed his own republicanism to his desire for

than anyone else the "anarchical state of society" and the need to remedy it. Ibid., 49. Compare page 19 in the 1822 edition, page 5 in the 1824 edition, and page 49 in the 1854 edition (in *Système*).

[95] Compare page 35 in the 1822 edition, pages 20–6 in the 1824 edition, and pages 56–8 in the 1854 edition.

[96] *Système*, vol. 4, "Appendice," 58nl.

[97] See footnote in the "Exposé général," ibid., 71n1, and pages 50–51n1 in the 1824 edition. Compare with page 59 in the 1822 edition.

[98] François Guizot, *Du gouvernement de la France depuis la Restauration et du ministère actuel*, 3d ed. (Paris, 1820), 201.

stability, which he thought was crucial to create a suitable climate for his own doctrines. He seemed convinced that his ideas were novel and offered more constructive possibilities for the post-revolutionary society than those of the Left, whose empty slogans had proved dangerous and had been discredited.

In an important footnote, Comte clarified his position as to which scientists would be most actively involved in creating the new social or "organic doctrine."[99] He explained that these scientists would *not* be specialists in any one particular science, for they were too preoccupied with their own work. Rather, they would be generalists, that is, men who "possess the scientific capacity and have made a sufficiently profound study of all of positive knowledge to be imbued with its spirit and familiar with the principal laws of natural phenomena."[100] This was very different from the idea he had expressed five years before, when in his first opuscule, "Séparation générale entre les opinions et les désirs," he had explained that the publicists would be the scientists of society.[101] It is true that in his private correspondence, he had advocated the creation of a class of philosophers of science who would help advance all of the sciences, but he had not connected them specifically with the science of society.[102] Only in his unpublished fragments on the philosophy of mathematics in 1820 did he begin to connect the sciences and politics. He had explained that the new science of politics would help make the general philosophical system more scientific.[103] But even this concept was far from the new notion that generalists, trained and educated in all of the sciences, would become social scientists. Although Comte confined his idea to a footnote in his fundamental opuscule, it would later become one of the leading themes of his work. In fact, the need to supply philosophers with the necessary general knowledge of the sciences would lead him to write the *Cours*. Comte was correct when he boasted in the forty-sixth lesson of the *Cours* that he had developed the concept of "positive philosophy" in the fundamental opuscule.[104]

Comte's most significant addition occurred at the end of the opuscule, where in nine pages he explained the reason for his insistence on establishing the general march of the human species before examining national diversities.[105] He maintained that the laws of society had to be discovered in the same manner as those of the

[99] *Système*, vol. 4, "Appendice," 72n1; page 52n1 in the 1824 version. Compare with page 60 in the 1822 version.

[100] Ibid., 72n1.   [101] Ibid., 3.   [102] Comte to Valat, September 24, 1819, *CG*, 1:59.

[103] *Ecrits*, 549.   [104] *Cours*, 2:15.

[105] Compare page 191 in the 1822 edition with pages 180–9 in the 1824 edition. See also *Système*, vol. 4, "Appendice," 131–6.

human body and that the procedure for discovering both sets of laws differed from that of uncovering the laws of the inorganic world. In the inorganic world, where man was an insignificant part of many phenomena, which he could never grasp as a whole, he first had to consider the details with which he was familiar and proceed from the study of particular facts to the discovery of general laws. In the disciplines of organic matter, he still went from the known to the unknown, but there was an inversion. Because "man himself is the most complete type of the whole of all phenomena," the correct scientific procedure was to begin with the "most general facts," which could then shed light on the study of the details.[106] In other words, because man knew more about the whole than the parts in physiological and social research, he went from the general to the particular. Comte was at least partly indebted to Saint-Simon for this idea of going from the particular to the general and from the general to the particular, but unlike his former mentor, he gave specific reasons to prove its validity.[107]

One reason had to do with his increasing interest in the "science" of history. Comte criticized conventional historians for writing biographies, chronicles, and descriptions of particular events, which failed to connect isolated facts and create historical laws. To write scientific history, it was impossible to go from the study of particular facts to the discovery of general laws, because all social phenomena were interrelated. One could never discover the laws of any particular branch of society without first knowing the laws of all the other branches to which it was attached. Instead, one must first connect the most important advances achieved by the human species in its main spheres of activity and in this way establish the general lines of historical development of society as a whole. One's view of the past or future could never be perfect, but it could be made more precise by considering smaller and smaller intervals of time and by observing different categories of phenomena. This way of proceeding from the general to the particular was, to Comte, the "method strictly dictated by the nature of social physics."[108]

This last addition of 1824 on the scientific method is critical because it brought out more clearly the originality of the organic sciences – especially the science of society. Although throughout the opuscule Comte referred to this science as "social physics" and used

---

[106] Ibid., 132.
[107] In *Travail sur la gravitation universelle*, Saint-Simon expanded one of Blainville's principles, stating that a posteriori (analytical) ideas were dominant in the inorganic sciences, whereas a priori (synthetic) ideas were most prevalent in the organic sciences. See Allal Sinaceur, ed., in *Cours*, 1:745n98.
[108] *Système*, vol. 4, "Appendice," 136.

mechanistic expressions, such as "reconstruction," to describe its functions, he seemed ambivalent about its true nature, for he also alluded to it in physiological terms, such as "regeneration."[109] At one point, he even called political science the "physiology of the species." There seemed, therefore, to be a tension between an organic development of positive society and an intentional, human construction of this system. The pages he added in 1824 underlined the close relationship between the science of society and physiology. He went so far as to say that social physics was "only a branch of physiology" – the position Saint-Simon had taken in the *Mémoire*.[110] For the first time, Comte wished to stress the break between inorganic and organic nature.[111] Although the study of society had to be based on the sciences, it did not have to limit itself to the method of the inorganic sciences. Instead, Comte was sure that the science of the human body had a method that was equally legitimate and positive and even more fruitful for political science.[112] Henceforth, Comte would be much more concerned with discovering the interrelationships of the parts of the social body. Although it remained undeveloped for many years to come, the germ of the idea of the "subjective method," that is, the domination of the human point of view, was already planted in 1824.[113]

THE SIGNIFICANCE OF THE FUNDAMENTAL OPUSCULE

Comte's opuscule marked a watershed in his development. It was the outcome of his ruminations during the past seven years of association with Saint-Simon. The opuscule particularly reflected his intellectual development from 1819 to 1822, when he tried to work out his own position on political science vis-à-vis the philosophes, the Idéologues, the political economists, and Saint-Simon himself. Once he had enunciated the law of three stages in this opuscule, he felt that he himself had passed from the metaphysical to the positive stage and was ready to establish the science of society that other thinkers had failed to accomplish.[114] Representing the crowning achievement of his thought up to 1824, the opuscule was therefore

---

[109] Ibid., 127, 130, 136; Buis, "Projet de réorganisation," 134.
[110] *Système*, vol. 4, "Appendice," 127, 134.   [111] Arnaud, *Le "Nouveau Dieu,"* 119.
[112] Gouhier, "L'Opuscule fondamental," 336.   [113] Arnaud, *Le "Nouveau Dieu,"* 121.
[114] Comte later told Pierre Laffitte, "Up to the moment when I found the law of three stages in my fundamental opuscule, I was in the metaphysical stage, and that can be seen in the opuscule itself because I still use the regime of entities." Comte, quoted in "Opuscule Fondamental," ed. Laffitte, 10. It could be argued, however, that Comte's law of three stages never lost its metaphysical, that is, mechanistic, character.

the point of departure for his future work. He would devote his life to developing the essential tenets of the positive philosophy contained in this early essay: the need for a new science of society to terminate the revolutionary era by making all minds converge in one doctrine, the law of three stages, the classification of the sciences, the vision of a new social and political system, the importance of creating a new spiritual power to replace the clergy and to regenerate Europe through education, and the condemnation of practical and purely governmental reforms. Unlike Saint-Simon, who tended to waver in his allegiances, Comte remained faithful throughout his life to the concepts of his youth. Moreover, Comte liked to stress this continuity in order to differentiate himself from Saint-Simon. To demonstrate the invariability of his thought, Comte included the fundamental opuscule in 1854 in the appendix of the fourth volume of the *Système*. However, although he assigned it the date of May 1822, he actually republished the 1824 version with some minor revisions.[115] (Thus there were three editions of the fundamental opuscule – 1822, 1824, and 1854.) He also gave it what he called its "proper" title: *Plan des travaux scientifiques nécessaires pour réorganiser la société*.[116] This title was that of the 1824 edition, not that of the original version of 1822, which began with the word "*Prospectus.*"

In the *Cours* and the *Système*, Comte often explained the significance of this essay in his own development. Before writing the opuscule, he had been pulled in two directions because he had pursued his works in science and politics separately even if they did parallel each other.[117] But as early as his years at the Ecole Polytechnique, he had felt the need to apply the new way he was learning to think about the inorganic sciences to man and society. After having left the school and studied biology and history, he gradually felt the "growing instinct of a final harmony" between his "intellectual tendencies" and his "political tendencies." "This decisive equilibrium" was realized in his 1822 essay, when he achieved "at the age of twenty-four a true mental and even social unity, [which was] afterwards more and more developed and consolidated under the continual inspiration of my great law relating to the whole of human evolution."[118] Thanks then to the law of three stages, which was both a scientific and a political law, Comte felt he had achieved a "true cerebral unity."[119]

Unity had always been a characteristic that Comte greatly admired. He had respected Saint-Simon for what he felt was the unity

---

[115] The revisions involved changing every *nous* to *je* and omitting several unimportant footnotes.

[116] *Système*, vol. 4, "Appendice," iii.   [117] Ibid.   [118] *Cours*, 2:466–7.   [119] *Système*, 1:2.

of his life. He had also looked to the Middle Ages as a model of harmony and stability. Throughout his life, he aspired to resolve the contradictions that he saw within himself and within society. This yearning for unity and synthesis was echoed by others of his time, such as Hegel, Fichte, and Schelling.[120] Under Saint-Simon's guidance, Comte learned that he could join his disparate interests by creating a science that would be social and a politics that would be scientific.[121] His fundamental opuscule was therefore important not only for marking the point at which he felt he had achieved inner unity, but also for showing the way in which he would always work to establish such harmony within society itself; he would try to ensure that its political and scientific tendencies were as closely intertwined as he felt they were within himself.

THE LIMITED PUBLICATION OF THE OPUSCULE IN 1822

Comte's opuscule was "fundamental" in another way: it led to the end of his collaboration and friendship with Saint-Simon. The apparent cause of this breakup was a series of quarrels relating to the publication of the opuscule. Since Comte's opinion is the only view that is known, it is difficult to state precisely what occurred between the two men. At least according to Comte, the problem began in 1822 when his essay was not given wide distribution.

Entitled *Prospectus des travaux nécessaires pour réorganiser la société*, the opuscule was signed by Comte and first printed in April 1822 as one of the brochures probably intended to make up the second part of *Du système industriel*.[122] The cover page of Comte's brochure read "*Suite des travaux ayant pour objet de fonder le système industriel: Du contrat social*, par Henri Saint-Simon." Comte's name did not appear there or on the title page, which read "*Du contrat social.*"[123]

The first part of the title of the cover page of Comte's brochure – *Suite des travaux ayant pour objet de fonder le système industriel* – shows that the essay was meant to be a sequel to the first brochure of the third part of *Du système industriel*, which was called *Travaux philosophiques, scientifiques, et poétiques ayant pour objet de faciliter la réorganisation de la société européenne*. Published in January 1822, this

---

[120] Skarga, "Le Coeur et la raison," 385, 390.

[121] Lévy-Bruhl, *Philosophie d'Auguste Comte*, 8.

[122] See fragments in "Matériaux pour servir à la biographie d'Auguste Comte [Documents, 1816–1822]," ed. Laffitte, *RO* 8 (1882), 410–12.

[123] Saint-Simon, *Suite des travaux ayant pour objet de fonder le système industriel: Du contrat social* (Paris, 1822). This original brochure can be found in a collection of Saint-Simon's pamphlets put together by his disciple Henri Fournel: *Oeuvres de Saint-Simon: Lettres, brochures, articles de journaux, pièces diverses, 1802–1822*, 8°Z 8086 (16), Réserve, BN.

first brochure announced the imminent publication of a "scientific work" describing the new social organization that would improve the "fate of the last class of society."[124] Saint-Simon was referring to Comte's *Prospectus*.

The second part of the title – *Du Contrat social* – corresponded to another brochure, *Suite à la brochure "Des Bourbons et des Stuarts,"* also published in January 1822.[125] Adapting Rousseau's famous title to his own purposes, Saint-Simon explained that a social contract, that is, a "contract of union," between the producing classes was necessary to create a new system of social organization. The contract had to stipulate the goal of this new society and the means by which its desires would be satisfied. He promised that his next work on the "Social Contract" would clarify his position and propose the founding of a new party – "THE PARTY OF THE PRODUCERS." Limiting governmental powers to favor production, this party would "preserve the King and the Nation from the calamities menacing them."[126]

Preceded by this enthusiastic brochure, *Du contrat social* contained solely Comte's opuscule and a short ten-page introduction by Saint-Simon entitled "A Messieurs les Chefs des travaux de culture, de fabrication, et de commerce." Saint-Simon must have devised the brochure's title, for Comte thought that the theory of a social contract was false and that Rousseau's *Du contrat social* was the epitome of eighteenth-century metaphysical philosophy with its overemphasis on governmental forms.[127] In addition, Saint-Simon's notion of a new act of association was contrary to the opuscule's main principle that society developed according to certain necessary laws and that social physics must observe rather than invent.[128] The idea of a contract seemed to disregard Comte's aversion to documents purporting to arrange social life.[129] Moreover, Comte's opuscule did

---

[124] Saint-Simon, *Travaux philosophiques, scientifiques, et poétiques ayant pour objet de faciliter la réorganisation de la société européenne*, in *Oeuvres*, 6:461, 474.

[125] It did not seem to be a part of *Du système industriel*. See *Oeuvres choisies de C. H. de Saint-Simon, précédées d'un essai sur sa doctrine*, by [Charles] Lemonnier, 3 vols. (Brussels, 1859), 1:cxi–cxxx.

[126] Saint-Simon, *Suite à la brochure "Des Bourbons et des Stuarts,"* in *Oeuvres*, 6:514, 525.

[127] Comte to Valat, May 15, 1818, *CG*, 1:37. See also Comte's essay "Fragment d'un article sur la Révolution française," *Ecrits*, 459–61. This essay was never published during his lifetime.

[128] "Opuscule fondamental," ed. Laffitte, 5.

[129] In the 1822 edition of the opuscule, Comte referred to a "contract" only one time. He said that the first condition of a "contract of association" was setting the goal of the organization. As if repudiating the use of "contract" and its voluntaristic implications, he changed the expression "contract of association" to "social order" in the edition of 1824. Comte, *Prospectus*, in *Suite des travaux*, 44; idem, *Plan*, in Saint-Simon, *Catéchisme des industriels: Troisième cahier*, 35; *Système*, vol. 4, "Appendice," 64.

not deal with the points that Saint-Simon suggested it was going to make. Although it mentioned the need for a new party, it devoted little attention to the rich *industriels*, criticized Saint-Simon's concept of a limited government, and failed to praise the monarchy.[130] Again, there seems to have been a breakdown in communication between Comte and Saint-Simon.

Interested in submitting Comte's work to influential *industriels* and sensing they might be apprehensive of its contents, Saint-Simon tried to mollify them in advance in his introduction.[131] He reassured them of his support for the hereditary monarchy, flattered them by calling them the "most useful class of society," and declared that the scientists, to whom Comte gave a large role, would never become their superiors.[132]

In order to persuade the scientists to commit themselves to recon-struction, Saint-Simon explained that "it was necessary that my system be presented to them in its scientific form. One of my collaborators and friends has taken charge of this important operation. Here is his work, which corresponds to the preliminary discourse of the *Encyclopédie* by d'Alembert."[133] This passage is significant. It shows that he considered this system his own creation, since he called it "my" system, instead of "our system," a position that could not have pleased Comte. Perhaps too there is a hint of exasperation that Comte decided on his own to explain the scientific, theoretical aspects of the positive system.

This passage also demonstrates that Comte was fulfilling the task that Saint-Simon had originally assigned him in the third volume of *L'Industrie* in 1817 – the drafting of the nineteenth-century version of the *Encyclopédie*. Yet despite the importance of Comte's work, only one hundred copies of the opuscule were printed in April 1822. Each was distributed free of charge, with the word "Proof" (*Epreuve*) handwritten on the cover page and on twelve of the pages of the text.[134]

---

[130] Comte to Armand Marrast, January 7, 1832, *CG*, 1:233.

[131] In discussing the tensions between Comte and Saint-Simon, Gustave d'Eichthal remarked to his brother that it was "unreasonable" for Saint-Simon "to want to submit this work to the judgment of the *industriels*. There are many scholars who would not be capable of understanding it." Gustave d'Eichthal to Adolphe d'Eichthal, Fonds d'Eichthal, 14396, item 2, Bibliothèque de l'Arsenal (hereafter, BA).

[132] Saint-Simon, Preface ("A Messieurs les Chefs des travaux de culture, de fabrication, et de commerce") to *Suite des travaux ayant pour objet de fonder le système industriel: Du contrat social*, 7. The full text is not reproduced in the *Oeuvres*.

[133] Ibid., 12.

[134] See the copy of the *Prospectus* in the *Suite des travaux*. The editors of Saint-Simon's *Oeuvres* said fifty copies of Comte's *Prospectus* were made, but Comte declared in his preface to the appendix of the *Système* that there were one hundred copies. Saint-Simon, *Oeuvres*, 3.3:6; *Système*, vol. 4, "Appendice," iii.

REASONS FOR THE POSTPONEMENT OF THE
OPUSCULE'S PUBLICATION

Not until two years later, in April 1824, was the work properly published and distributed in the usual fashion. It formed the third *cahier*
of the *Catéchisme des industriels*, a journal that Saint-Simon had begun
publishing in December 1823. The important question is, Why was
the publication of Comte's great work – the first one that he had
signed while working for Saint-Simon – postponed for two years?
There are several possible explanations. One is Saint-Simon's
fear of government reprisals. On October 26, 1821, the prefect of
the Seine informed the head of the police that several liberals had
received a "rather large quantity" of brochures written by Saint-
Simon.[135] The police chief assured the prefect that the brochure in
question was "more ridiculous than dangerous, like all of those by
the same author."[136] Nevertheless, in early 1822 the authorities seized
Saint-Simon's *Des Bourbons et des Stuarts* and *Suite à la Brochure "Des
Bourbons et des Stuarts."*[137] Given that he was being watched carefully
by the police, he might have decided that publishing the *Prospectus*
was too dangerous.
Because of the expenses incurred by his publications, Saint-Simon
was also in severe financial straits. His deep worries about his
mounting debts were a cause of his attempted suicide on March 9,
1823.[138] He probably did not have the money to publish Comte's
brochure of almost two hundred pages until late 1823, when he
attracted some wealthy new disciples, such as Olinde Rodrigues.[139]

---

[135] Préfet de la Seine-Inférieur to Monsieur le Directeur Générale de l'Adminstration
Départemental de la Police, October 26, 1821, F[7] 4333, dossier 29, AN. The brochure
in question is *Première Opinion politique des industriels*, the fifth pamphlet making up the
second part of *Du système industriel*.

[136] Monsieur le Directeur Générale de l'Adminstration Départemental de la Police to the
Préfet de la Seine-Inférieur, November 2, 1821, F[7] 4333, dossier 29. AN. The prefect
responded that some liberals were distributing the brochure to the manufacturers of
the Pays de Caux. Préfet de la Seine-Inférieur to Monsieur le Directeur Générale de
l'Adminstration Départemental de la Police, November 13, 1821, F[7] 4333, dossier 29, AN.

[137] Saint-Simon, *Oeuvres*, 3.3:5. Comte's friend Langlade wrote to Emile Tabarié on January
29, 1822: "The direction of matters is turning directly to the right; where is this leading
us? They seized two brochures of Saint-Simon two days ago. The day before, I had seen
Comte, who did not suspect anything. They made some searches of his place without any
result. This is truly a disagreeable process." Langlade to Tabarié, January 29, 1822, MAC.

[138] Saint-Simon was apparently trying to limit his costs, for each of the two essays that he did
manage to publish in mid-1822 contained only about a dozen pages. Saint-Simon, "Deux
Lettres à Messieurs les Electeurs de la Seine qui sont producteurs," and "Les Intérêts
politiques des producteurs," Extracts from *Du système industriel*, part 3, in *Oeuvres*, 6:475–
95. See also *Oeuvres*, 3.3:7; "Souscription," March 1, 1823, Fonds Pereire, N.a.fr. 24606,
fol. 258, BN; Hubbard, *Saint-Simon*, 92–3; Bertrand, "Souvenirs académiques," 533.

[139] Hubbard, *Saint-Simon*, 95–6.

Remembering the fiasco caused by Comte's ideas in the past, Saint-Simon in his precarious financial condition may simply have printed proofs of Comte's work to show it to people whom it might interest rather than risk a larger distribution that might offend his patrons, the wealthy *industriels*. In other brochures published at the time, he concentrated on more mundane and timely issues, which were safer than topics covered by Comte.[140] Even the first two *cahiers* of the *Catéchisme des industriels* appealed to the practical interests of the producers. Abandoning his theory about the necessary coexistence of the spiritual and temporal powers, Saint-Simon told the industrial class – cultivators, manufacturers, and merchants – that the scientists and other classes had to work for them. They should take complete control over the movement of reorganization and over society itself, especially by managing the budget and forming a new party in the interests of all members of society, including the workers. The liberal party was too vague; it was composed of revolutionaries and Bonapartists, who had opposite ideas and wanted power chiefly for themselves. Referring to the party's repeated defeats throughout Europe and in France, Saint-Simon urged the industrial class to replace liberalism with a new slogan that he had just coined, "industrialism," and to call themselves "industrialists" to differentiate themselves from the unpopular liberals.[141] In this context, Comte's piece on the science of society must have seemed incongruous, for it did not cater to the cultivators, manufacturers, and merchants. Whereas Saint-Simon stressed their role in bringing about the new order, Comte tended to belittle them because he was intent on proving that the new society was philosophically inevitable and that the scientists had merely to uncover its natural evolution. Furthermore, in contrast to Saint-Simon's simple question-and-answer style of popularizing his industrial doctrine, Comte's style was straightforward, academic, perhaps even somewhat pedantic.

It is clear that Saint-Simon was expecting something different from his collaborator. He seemed aware that Comte was having difficulties writing, for when he thought he was dying after his attempted suicide, he told Comte, who rushed to his side, "Come on, let's use these hours well that remain to us and let's discuss your work."[142] Nine months later, in the first *cahier* of the *Catéchisme des industriels*, Saint-Simon announced that he had confided the third *cahier* to his "student" Auguste Comte, who was to write on science

[140] See the brochures making up the third part of *Du système industriel*, published in June 1822: "Deux Lettres à Messieurs les Electeurs de la Seine qui sont producteurs" and "Les Intérêts politiques des producteurs." Saint-Simon, *Oeuvres*, 3.3:7, 6:475–95.

[141] Saint-Simon, *Catéchisme des industriels: Deuxième Cahier*, in *Oeuvres*, 4.1:178.

[142] Hubbard, *Saint-Simon*, 95.

and education.[143] In the first section of his opuscule, Comte also claimed he would cover education, but he never did.[144]

Instead of working on education, he decided to enlarge the first section, which he separated into two parts, one on the method and the other on the application of social physics. The latter would discuss not only the history of civilization according to the laws of progress but the new social system.[145] In fact, an undated and unsigned copy of the contract between Comte and Saint-Simon reveals that Saint-Simon agreed to pay Comte twenty-four hundred francs for a volume composed of these two parts, which were called "Plan des travaux scientifiques nécessaires pour réorganiser la société" and "L'Esquisse d'un tableau historique du progrès de la civilisation."[146] Having completed the first part, Comte told Saint-Simon that he was working on this second part, but he had not yet written a single line. In April 1824 Comte admitted to a friend that the delays were at least partly his fault:

> The latter [the second part] originally was to go first, but, while working [on it], I recognized that it should follow, and as this change caused a new delay in its execution (in the same way as many other causes, about which it would take too long to talk to you), we agreed that the part executed two years ago would appear first by itself.[147]

The next month he told another friend that partly because he detested revising his work, he could not write a word until he knew exactly what he was going to say. In great frustration, he described his situation:

> I ask your pardon for having hidden from you the truth in this matter; but the fact is that there has not yet been one line of writing on this subject [the second part of the opuscule]. Up to now I have spent almost all my time pondering this work, and many different types of harassments and annoyances have prevented me from writing earlier. To put an end to the very importunate entreaties of M. de Saint-

---

[143] Saint-Simon, *Catéchisme des industriels: Premier Cahier*, in *Oeuvres*, 4.1:50.

[144] *Système*, vol. 4, "Appendice," 81.

[145] Comte, "Avertissement" to the *Plan*, in Saint-Simon, *Catéchisme des industriels: Troisième Cahier*, 7.

[146] Contract between Comte and Saint-Simon, n.d., MAC. Two copies of the contract were drafted. Thus this unsigned one may be Comte's copy. The contract must have been written after May 1823 since it refers to Olinde Rodrigues as the arbiter of any disputes between the two men. Saint-Simon did not meet Rodrigues until May 1823 at the banker Ardouin's house. According to this contract, Comte would begin receiving installments of two hundred francs a month after the volume was printed. On Rodrigues, see Leroy, *Saint-Simon*, 317.

[147] Comte to Tabarié, April 5, 1824, *CG*, 1:77.

Simon in this regard and the more flattering, but less fatiguing, overattentiveness of Mr. Rodrigues and several other people, I said several times that I was busy writing and even rewriting it although I was only thinking about it because nothing ever came to me to write.[148]

In short, Comte had failed to begin not only the section on education that Saint-Simon was anxiously awaiting, but the historical part that was to follow and complete the first section. Thus besides the political dangers, the financial difficulties, the problem of alienating readers, and the incongruity of the subject matter, the opuscule was delayed by Comte's inability to complete his work.

These delays exasperated Saint-Simon, who expected to gain financial support from the wealthy industrialist Guillaume-Louis Ternaux when Comte finished the entire essay.[149] However, it is difficult to assess just how strained their relations were between 1822 and 1824, for despite apparent problems in understanding what each was doing, they seemed to have remained on fairly good terms. Saint-Simon thought well enough of Comte to introduce him to the scientist Blainville, who was to become a close friend.[150] After Blainville received a copy of the opuscule, he wrote to Saint-Simon, praising "this excellent work" and congratulating him on having found such an appropriate collaborator.[151] Saint-Simon also knew that he needed Comte's scientific abilities and often spoke highly of Comte's work to others. Ternaux came to visit him and pointing to Comte, who was sitting in the same room, said, "This is the gentleman who wrote this remarkable work." Saint-Simon responded proudly, "Wrote! Oh! better than that."[152] Comte's mistress, Caroline Massin, likewise reported that Saint-Simon showed noticeable "consideration and even respect" for her future husband: "Nothing was more affectionate than the relations between these two men and . . . they truly loved each other."[153]

Comte's feelings for Saint-Simon can be inferred from the fact that he insisted on watching over him all night when he found him

[148] Comte to G. d'Eichthal, May 1, 1824, *CG*, 1:83.
[149] Bertrand, "Souvenirs académiques," 533; Hubbard, *Saint-Simon*, 93; Robinet, *Notice*, 129. Laffitte also recalled that Comte told him that Ternaux had sent Saint-Simon three thousand francs to continue the work that Comte had begun. "Opuscule fondamental," ed. Laffitte, 7. See Gouhier's approach to these different positions. Gouhier, *Jeunesse*, 3:353–70.
[150] "De la circulation des ouvrages d'Auguste Comte: De l'opuscule fondamental," ed. Laffitte, 324–6.
[151] Blainville to Saint-Simon, [1822?], in ibid., 325. This letter is also in the Maison d'Auguste Comte.
[152] This story is recounted by Laffitte, ed., "Opuscule fondamental," 7.
[153] Littré, *Auguste Comte*, 13–14.

bleeding on his bed after his suicide attempt.[154] Two days later, on March 11, 1823, he wrote to Blainville, expressing relief that "there is every hope that we will keep him."[155] There is strong evidence that Comte may actually have been living with Saint-Simon. In 1823 his family addressed their letters to Comte at 34, rue de Richelieu, which was Saint-Simon's address.[156] The fact is confirmed by a letter of February 9 from Comte's friend Adolphe d'Eichthal to his brother: "I believe I have already written to you that he [Comte] is no longer living at M. St. Simon's but in his household [*ménage*] on rue de l'Oratoire N° 6."[157] Comte moved there in February 1824 to live with Massin, and in the spring when the problems with Saint-Simon arose, he exclaimed that it was "lucky" that he had already changed his "lodging."[158] It seems then that Comte may have lived with Saint-Simon for as long as a year. Despite the tensions arising from financial problems and his incomplete and diverging work, they had a stable and "intimate relationship," as Comte put it.[159] Such closeness made the break that came later far more painful.

THE END OF THE RELATIONSHIP

The break seems to have occurred in March 1824, when they had a dispute over the opuscule. Saint-Simon wanted to publish it, for he had already announced it. But Comte refused because he had only finished the first part.[160] He reluctantly yielded but then objected to Saint-Simon's insistence on omitting his name, giving his

---

[154] Hubbard, *Saint-Simon*, 95; Gouhier, *Jeunesse*, 3:365.

[155] Comte to Blainville, March 11, 1823, *CG*, 1:162. The date April 11, 1825, in *CG* is wrong. The original letter in the Maison d'Auguste Comte reads only "mardi soir 11." Since Saint-Simon tried to commit suicide on March 9, 1823, the correct date of this letter is March 11, 1823.

[156] Rosalie Boyer to Comte, December 11, 1823, "Lettres de Rosalie Boyer (1)," ed. Laffitte, 95; Alix Comte to Auguste Comte, September 2, 1823, "Lettres d'Alix Comte," ed. Laffitte 78. On Saint-Simon's address, see Manuel, *Saint-Simon*, 328. In July 1818, Comte had moved from 5, rue Neuve Richelieu near the Sorbonne to 8, rue St.-Germain-des-Prés (now 36, rue Bonaparte), where he had lived until late 1822 or early 1823. Comte to Valat, October 16, April 17, July 22, 1818, *CG*, 1:14, 33, 45.

[157] Adolphe d'Eichthal to Gustave d'Eichthal, February 9, 1823, Fonds d'Eichthal 13746, item 68, BA.

[158] Comte to Tabarié, April 5, 1824, *CG*, 1:78. In this letter, Comte said that his mistress was the one who had the furniture, which suggests that he had previously lived with a person who owned some – Saint-Simon.

[159] *Cours*, 2:467.

[160] Comte to G. d'Eichthal, May 1, 1824, *CG*, 1:81. See also Comte to Valat, May 21, 1824, *CG*, 1:91.

essay the same title as his own journal (*Catéchisme des industriels*), and writing an introduction to it. A bitter argument ensued, when all of Comte's rancor exploded.

Comte angrily accused Saint-Simon of being jealous of his talent and trying to keep him in a subordinate position in the hope of taking all the glory. He claimed that, seven years before, people had warned him not to work for Saint-Simon, a man who would use any means to make a "sensation in the world."[161] It now was clear, he thought, that Saint-Simon had not wanted him to become known. That is why he had dissuaded him from signing his articles in the past.

Supported by his friends, who congratulated him for having written an essay "destined to be epoch-making,"[162] Comte decided his opuscule was his first "major work."[163] It would not only serve as the foundation for his future writings but mark the beginning of his independence and his public career. Since he felt that the work was his own – "entirely unsullied by the influence previously exercised on me by Saint-Simon" – he insisted on getting full credit for it.[164]

In effect, Comte's complaints reflect the end of his apprenticeship and of his youth. At twenty-six, he had reached his maturity, and his problems with Saint-Simon derived from his growing pains. Now he wished to sign his articles and shake off the "guardianship" of his parents and that of Saint-Simon, which was "no less annoying."[165] The conflict between his love for Saint-Simon and his desire for independence is revealed in the almost Freudian account of their painful breakup, in which he complained that his mentor was like a father who could not let his child go.[166]

Though admitting that at the beginning Saint-Simon's direction of his work had been useful because of his need for "philosophical education," he claimed that since 1819–20, when he began to write his own essays on the science of society, Saint-Simon "had nothing more to teach me, and . . . in fact he taught me nothing."[167] As their

---

[161] Comte to G. d'Eichthal, May 1, 1824, *CG*, 1:81.
[162] Desjardins to Comte, May 11, 1822, MAC. See also Desjardins to Clément, October 27, 1892, MAC. Desjardins was a graduate of the Ecole Polytechnique. His letter to Comte is reproduced in "De la circulation des ouvrages d'Auguste Comte: De l'opuscule fondamental," ed. Laffitte, 322.
[163] Comte to Valat, May 21, 1824, *CG*, 1:88. See also Comte to Tabarié, April 5, 1824, *CG*, 1:77.
[164] Comte to Valat, May 21, 1824, *CG*, 1:88.   [165] Ibid.
[166] Comte to Tabarié, April 5, 1824, *CG*, 1:76.
[167] Comte to Valat, May 21, 1824, *CG*, 1:88; Comte to Tabarié, April 5, 1824, *CG*, 1:76. In the letter to Tabarié, Comte said that he had learned nothing in the past four years. In another letter to d'Eichthal, Comte wrote that he had learned nothing in the past four or five years. Comte to G. d'Eichthal, May 1, 1824, *CG*, 1:80.

opinions diverged, Comte found Saint-Simon's control increasingly "ridiculous" and "intolerable."[168] Thierry, too, had suffered under the weight of Saint-Simon's authoritarian ways and had felt compelled to go off on his own. Perhaps Comte developed the self-confidence and fortitude to confront Saint-Simon because Massin had moved in with him several weeks before and he had never felt happier in his life. Always jealous of his reputation, she may have encouraged his rebellion.

Comte finally succeeded in wringing some concessions from Saint-Simon:

> In short, as he absolutely wanted to print and as I was truly the master of my work, he was forced to submit to what I wanted, that is, that the work be printed at this moment with the general title: Système de politique positive par A. Comte, etc., l[er] vol., l[re] partie, without any extraneous introduction.

Delighted that he had not compromised his "intellectual" self, Comte was genuinely surprised to discover soon afterward that Saint-Simon harbored a "grudge" and no longer wanted anything to do with him. Sure that Saint-Simon needed him more than he needed Saint-Simon, Comte was crushed by this rupture. He had wanted to preserve their relationship in spite of their quarrels. Now he was convinced that Saint-Simon was taking revenge by abandoning him without any financial resources whatsoever, although his work had been just as "useful" as his and had cost him a stable position.[169] He blamed Saint-Simon both for balking at the prospect of no longer being his "director" and for forcing him to seek out influential men on his own – a task Saint-Simon knew he had always disliked.[170] Comte thus felt betrayed by the man who had been his friend, educator, and father substitute. It apparently never occurred to him that his mentor may have been so disappointed by his behavior – especially by his having broken their contract – that he saw no future in their continued association. According to Prosper Barthélemy Enfantin, the future leader of the Saint-Simonian sect, Saint-Simon's heart was "broken" by Comte's conduct.[171]

Regretting the turn of events and wanting to heal the rupture, Comte probably wrote at this time the foreword to his opuscule. Just as Saint-Simon in his introduction fawned on the industrialists out of financial insecurity, Comte flattered Saint-Simon to get his

[168] Comte to Tabarié, April 5, 1824, *CG*, 1:76.
[169] Ibid., 77–78. [170] Comte to G. d'Eichthal, May 1, 1824, *CG*, 1:82.
[171] Père Enfantin to Fournel, March 9, 1833, Fonds d'Eichthal, Manuscrits, Carton IIA, fol. 344, Bibliothèque Thiers.

continued support. Yet he hoped to absolve himself of the "least wrong" in the quarrel.[172] In submissive tones, he declared in this foreword, "Although being, I like to declare it, the student of M. Saint-Simon, I have been led to adopt a general title [that is] distinct from that of the works of my master." He claimed that in calling his work *Système de politique positive*, he did not mean to indicate any fundamental disagreement over their goals. He had, in fact, "adopted completely" Saint-Simon's idea that the reorganization of society required two equally important types of spiritual work. The scientific capacity must establish general ideas, while the literary and beaux arts capacity – the imaginative capacity – must renew "social sentiments." Comte explained that after thinking about Saint-Simon's ideas "for a long time," he had decided to devote himself "exclusively" to developing the "insights of this philosopher" regarding the scientific capacity. The result was the "formation of the system of positive politics." If his work received praise, this acclaim, he said, must be directed to the "founder of the philosophical school of which I am honored to be a part."[173] The pathetic character of this foreword, which was so contrary to Comte's noncompromising nature, reveals how desperate he was to revive their association. He must have felt some guilt about his behavior or had second thoughts about being able to make it on his own to have abased himself in this fashion.[174]

This sycophantic foreword, however, did not repair the breach. His demands were met only in the hundred copies that he received in accordance with the terms of the business contract. The title page of these copies read "*Système de politique positive* par Auguste Comte, ancien élève de l'Ecole Polytechnique, élève de Henri Saint-Simon. Tome Premier (Première partie)." This first part was called *Plan des travaux scientifiques nécessaires pour réorganiser la société*. (Comte had substituted "Plan" for "Prospectus.") But Saint-Simon printed another thousand copies bearing an additional title page that came before Comte's and read *Catéchisme des industriels, troisième cahier*. Comte felt that in doing this Saint-Simon broke the agreement they had made not to include the opuscule as part of the *Catéchisme des industriels*. He further irritated Comte by sending all of the copies to his subscribers and others so that not a single one could be purchased at bookstores. Comte was forced to send his own hundred copies to friends and important men with whom he wished to establish relationships. This was a professional task that greatly annoyed him.

---

[172] Comte to Valat, May 21, 1824, *CG*, 1:90. See also Gouhier, *Jeunesse*, 3:372–3.
[173] Comte, "Avertissement" to the *Plan*, in Saint-Simon, *Oeuvres*, 4.2:8–9.
[174] Weill, *Saint-Simon*, 206.

Comte did not have much right to object to some of Saint-Simon's actions. The contract gave his mentor the privilege of publishing the opuscule until 1825. Furthermore, when Saint-Simon had announced in December 1823 that the third *cahier* of the *Catéchisme des industriels* would be written by Comte, he raised no objection at that time to his essay's inclusion in the journal.[175]

Comte was more justified when he claimed that Saint-Simon deceived him by going against their agreement and adding an introduction, which underscored his subordinate position. Saint-Simon referred to Comte as his "student" and spoke disparagingly of his work:

> He does not achieve exactly the goal that we had in mind. He does not expose the generalities of our system, that is, he discusses only one part, and he gives the preponderant role to some generalities that we consider only secondary.[176]

Saint-Simon said that Comte failed to recognize the superiority of the industrial capacity and was wrong in setting the physical and mathematical sciences over it as well as over the philosophical capacity and spiritualism ("the study of moral man").[177] By being too scientific, he neglected the emotional and religious aspect of social reorganization. Many of these criticisms were unjust and suggest that Saint-Simon did not understand much of what Comte had written. To say that the opuscule was too scientific was odd, since Saint-Simon knew at the outset that it was to have this character.

A FINAL ANALYSIS OF THE TENSIONS IN
THEIR ASSOCIATION

Saint-Simon's comments may not have been fair, but they point to the different paths that he and Comte had chosen. Saint-Simon was increasingly taken with the power of the wealthy industrial class because of their financial status, which made them the dominant force in the community as well as his chief supporters. Comte, however, had remained faithful to Saint-Simon's original idea that the authority of the scientists should be comparable to, if not superior to, that of the *industriels*. To Comte, before the *industriels* could organize society around the practical needs of production, the scientists of society had to discover the regime that the march of civilization had destined for the contemporary epoch. The advantages or the utility of the system were not as crucial as its opportuneness,

---

[175] Dumas, *Psychologie de deux messies*, 276.
[176] Saint-Simon, Introduction to *Catéchisme des industriels: Troisième Cahier*, 3–4.
[177] Saint-Simon, *Catéchisme des industriels: Quatrième Cahier*, in *Oeuvres*, 5.1:43n1.

necessity, and ineluctability. Although social scientists responded to the needs of society, they were concerned mainly with satisfying the demands of the mind for intellectual unity and convictions.[178] Their responsibility for drawing up the blueprint of the new society in such a way as to avoid false starts and unnecessary upheaval made them the most powerful class. Control over ideas was ultimately more important than economic power. Thus Comte still maintained that theory was more crucial than practice, whereas to Saint-Simon, practical reforms were to take precedence.

Comte was no doubt correct when he pointed to Saint-Simon's different age, personality, and position as one cause of their problems. It is clear that Saint-Simon had already spent fifteen years working on the preparatory, scientific material and now felt ready to go on to the next step. Comte therefore accused him of increasingly displaying the disposition "to change institutions before doctrines are redone, a revolutionary disposition to which I am and must be in absolute opposition."[179] Having just started outlining the theoretical work of reconstruction, Comte was convinced this preparatory work was far from complete.

Saint-Simon's reproach that Comte had neglected the sentimental and religious part of the system marked another difference between them. Comte believed artists had to propagate the new system originally conceived by the social scientists, and he only vaguely mentioned that they would be responsible for a moral revolution. Saint-Simon gave them a more important role, especially in reviving social sentiments.[180]

In his old age, Saint-Simon also wanted to revive deism, but Comte was still determined to establish a terrestrial morality. Some scholars have gone so far as to claim that this disagreement was the cause of their breakup.[181] But in 1824 Comte did not complain about Saint-Simon's religious views. As he himself pointed out, Saint-Simon had not yet adopted the "theological color." It was not until 1832, seven years after Saint-Simon had announced his new Christianity, that Comte wrote that "our rupture must even be attributed in part to my beginning to perceive in him a religious tendency that was profoundly incompatible with my own philosophical direction."[182]

[178] Rutten, *Essai sur la morale*, 46–8, 58.
[179] Comte to G. d'Eichthal, May 1, 1824, *CG*, 1:82n1.
[180] Saint-Simon, "Travaux philosophiques, scientifiques, et poétiques," 470. See also Rutten, *Essai sur la morale*, 56–7.
[181] Hayek, *Counter-Revolution*, 139; Lonchampt, *Précis*, 24; Boris Sokoloff, *The "Mad" Philosopher Auguste Comte* (New York: Vantage Press, 1961), 45.
[182] Comte to Michel Chevalier, January 5, 1832, *CG*, 1:227–8. See also Comte to Armand Marrast, January 7, 1832, *CG*, 1:231–2.

Yet here Comte was defending himself in a letter to Michel Chevalier, the editor of the Saint-Simonian journal *Le Globe*, to distance himself from the disreputable religious practices of the Saint-Simonians. His feelings about their cult affected his memory of what had happened in 1824. If religion had been one of the key points of their dispute at that time, Comte would have mentioned it in one of the long letters he wrote in 1824 to his friends. Probably the most accurate statement is in the *Cours*, where he denounced the Saint-Simonians for perverting Saint-Simon's ideas and declared that even after the suicide attempt, Saint-Simon's religious inclinations were "banal" and "vague."[183] In sum, while Saint-Simon may very well have disliked his student's lack of religious enthusiasm and boldness regarding a new moral system, Comte was frustrated mainly by his mentor's tendency to give priority to practice and his neglect of theory. This disagreement had been a growing source of tension between them ever since his anonymous letters of 1818.

Intellectual differences were exacerbated by their clash of personalities. Saint-Simon was an unschooled, imaginative, unsystematic, and fickle thinker who was, as Comte noted, highly motivated by publicity. He did not mind pandering to whomever was in power, whether to Napoleon or to the king. An opportunist, he grew increasingly interested in advancing the cause of the influential *industriels* as he came to rely on their financial support. After he broke with Comte, his concern with the science of society waned as he became caught up in the religious revivalism of the period. Comte, in contrast, had been trained as a scientist and could present, develop, and argue ideas well. Unlike Saint-Simon, who wanted to popularize his ideas quickly, Comte demanded the time to work out his theories and to write logical pieces that sustained a certain argument. Above all, he insisted on maintaining his integrity and detested toadying to others. At the beginning, the two men probably complemented each other, but as Saint-Simon grew more enamored of his role as a messiah and as Comte developed from adolescence to manhood, their differences were bound to create conflicts.

The similarities between the two men also made a break inevitable. As demonstrated by his relationships with Redern and Thierry, Saint-Simon insisted on being in control. Comte's letters to Valat reveal that he too had to have the final word. Fearful of being used and wary of arbitrary actions, he stressed in this breakup the importance of maintaining his own independence and integrity. His reasoning followed a certain pattern that was repeated in all of his quarrels with those close to him – his parents, his wife, and his

---

[183] *Cours*, 2:467.

friends. It even appeared in his problems with Casimir Périer and at the Ecole Polytechnique. Thus both Comte and Saint-Simon found a relationship between equals unbearable. Comte would replay Saint-Simon's dictatorial role several times as he grew older. What would never change was the note of paranoia that always underlay his arguments.

Once his opuscule appeared as part of Saint-Simon's *Catéchisme des industriels*, Comte declared that their rupture was "decisive."[184] He consoled himself with the thought that it came at least at a good time because he was now launching himself into the scientific world and wanted to be free to express his views without worrying about irritating Saint-Simon. Their rupture marked the "opening of my career as a man."[185]

However, the experience left him with a bitter taste. Comte was not a forgiving person. He sought and found faults in Saint-Simon wherever possible. Whereas he had once found him generous and amiable, Comte now called him egotistical. Though previously much impressed by his youthful energy, Comte now hinted that he was becoming senile.[186] Overlooking the fact that he himself had not finished the opuscule, he even accused Saint-Simon of having deliberately – and maliciously – delayed printing it for two years when he found he could not sign it and started to fear that his student would outshine him.[187] Yet Saint-Simon was obviously proud of Comte. Instead of hiding his identity, he had mentioned him by name in the third *cahier* of the *Catéchisme des industriels*. The reason Comte had not signed his name to his works was that he did not want to take responsibility for them. After all, Thierry had signed his.

Comte's memory of slights, real or imaginary, did not fade with years. If anything, they became more vivid. Eighteen years after the rupture, in his "Personal Preface" to volume 6 of the *Cours*, Comte went so far as to assert that his early development had been fundamentally disturbed by a "catastrophic relationship with a very ingenious, but very superficial writer," motivated by an "immense personal ambition."[188] He derided Saint-Simon for his lack of "true convictions," his weak education, and his hunger for "immediate resounding success."[189] Accusing Saint-Simon of having taken advantage of his "extreme youth," Comte felt he had exerted a "disastrous influence" on him by making him waste his time on "vain

184 Comte to G. d'Eichthal, May 1, 1824, *CG*, 1:82.
185 Comte to Tabarié, August 22, 1824, *CG*, 1:112.
186 Comte to G. d'Eichthal, May 1, 1824, *CG*, 1:80.
187 Comte to Valat, May 21, 1824, *CG*, 1:89.   188 *Cours*, 2:466.
189 Comte to Valat, May 15, 1818, *CG*, 1:35; *Cours*, 2:466–7.

attempts at direct political action."[190] As Comte's interest in moral-ity increased, he began to attack Saint-Simon for being a sly and unscrupulous person – a "depraved juggler"; his mentor became as immoral as he was shallow.[191] The main point of Comte's descrip-tion of him in the *Système de politique positive* was to show that Saint-Simon's success reflected the moral and mental anarchy of the nineteenth century because it was due solely to "unbridled char-latanism."[192] As John Stuart Mill astutely remarked: "Comte was unjust to Saint-Simon as he was in general to all those who ceased to please him."[193]

THE PROBLEM OF INFLUENCE

There was one other source of tension between the two men. Both were immensely preoccupied by their originality. Already in May 1824, Comte was aware that their intellectual relationship was so close that it would be difficult to disentangle his ideas from those of Saint-Simon and his contribution would be overlooked. He com-plained to Valat that Saint-Simon had been trying since 1822 "to arrange things in such a way" as to present him "to the public as a sort of literary hack at his orders and on his payroll." He feared his ideas would then appear as "only an emanation and a simple devel-opment" of Saint-Simon's.[194]

Later he tried to deny that Saint-Simon had influenced him at all. Some of Comte's disciples and correspondents noticed basic simil-arities between his ideas and those of Saint-Simon.[195] One American insulted Comte by suggesting that he was influenced by Saint-Simon

---

[190] *Cours*, 2:466–7.

[191] *Système*, 3:xv. In 1853, Comte also declared that the only reason Saint-Simon differed from other "literary hacks" (*littérateurs*) was that he was "less well read." Ibid., xvi. Ac-cording to Comte, Saint-Simon spent the "major part of his day reading bad novels." Comte to George Frederick Holmes, September 18, 1852, *CG*, 6:377. This view is verified by the Saint-Simonian Léon Halévy, "Souvenirs de Saint-Simon," *La France littéraire*, 1st ser., 1. 3 (1832): 535.

[192] *Système*, 3:xvi.

[193] Mill to Gustave d'Eichthal, March 30, 1864, in John Stuart Mill, *The Later Letters: 1849–1873*, ed. Francis E. Mineka and Dwight N. Lindley, 4 vols. (Vols. 14–17 of *The Collected Works*) (hereafter, *Later Letters*) (Toronto: University of Toronto Press and Routledge & Kegan Paul, 1972), 15: 931. Even in his lectures, Comte treated Saint-Simon "harshly," according to one of his disciples. Deroisin, *Notes sur Auguste Comte*, 21.

[194] Comte to Valat, May 21, 1824, *CG*, 1:89.

[195] Littré, *Auguste Comte*, 13n1. Having begun to read a biography of Saint-Simon and the first volume of his works, Robinet said that the similarities between this thinker and Comte left him with feelings of a "singular perplexity." He begged Laffitte to explain these surprising resemblances. Robinet to Laffitte, 5 Saint Paul 70, MAC.

without his knowledge.[196] It did not help matters when it was discovered that Comte had described himself as Saint-Simon's "student" in his foreword to the *Plan*.[197] To counter the suggestion that he was indebted to his former mentor, Comte claimed that he had been guided by Condorcet before he met Saint-Simon and that this eighteenth-century philosophe was his "essential precursor" in the endeavor to base politics on science and history.[198] He even called Condorcet his "spiritual father" as if to block out the memory of "*le père* Simon."[199] Furthermore, Comte alleged that he had not needed Saint-Simon because he had studied the economic doctrines on which Saint-Simon's system was based before he met him and was therefore already aware of the impact of industrial development on society.[200] In 1853 he stated categorically, "I owed nothing to this personage, not even the slightest instruction."[201] Although Comte had found Saint-Simon in 1818 to be an "original being in all respects," he had quite a different impression of him thirty-five years later:

> Always incapable of creating anything, he [Saint-Simon] limited himself to reflecting external inspirations. . . . The heart and mind of this personage are precisely depicted in the cynical summary that he liked to make of his own life, whose two halves he represented as consecrated respectively to the buying and selling of ideas.[202]

Henri Gouhier takes Comte at his word in his three-volume study of his youth and describes Saint-Simon in much the same terms as Comte – a parasite on other thinkers' ideas. According to Gouhier, Comte was imbibing the "prepositivist" atmosphere of the times even before he met Saint-Simon; his ideas reflected the "scientific

---

[196] Comte to George Frederick Holmes, November 28, 1852, *CG*, 6:430. See the argument between Comte and George Frederick Holmes on the impact of Saint-Simon. Comte to George Frederick Holmes, September 18, 1852, *CG*, 6:377–8; Comte to George Frederick Holmes, November 28, 1852, *CG*, 6:430–1; Holmes to Comte, October 30, 1852, in Richard Laurin Hawkins, *Auguste Comte and the United States (1816–1853)* (Cambridge, Mass.: Harvard University Press, 1936), 118–19.

[197] Comte explained his description of himself by claiming to have been carried away by his own "generosity" and youthful enthusiasm. *Cours*, 2:466. The date "1835" in this Hermann edition is wrong. The date in the original edition is 1824. See Auguste Comte, *Cours de philosophie positive*, 6 vols. (Paris, 1830–42) (hereafter, *Cours de philosophie* [1830–42]), 6:viii-n1. See also Comte to George Frederick Holmes, November 28, 1852, *CG*, 6:431.

[198] *Catéchisme positiviste*, 32. See also *Cours*, 2:466; *Système*, 3:xv; Comte to J. M'Clintock, August 7, 1852, *CG*, 6:325; Comte to George Frederick Holmes, September 18, 1852, *CG*, 6:378.

[199] *Système*, 3:xv.   [200] *Cours*, 2:466.   [201] *Système*, 3:xvi.

[202] Ibid., xvi–xvii. In a letter to J. M'Clintock, Comte referred to a similar summary that Saint-Simon had made of his life: "During the first part of my life, I made ideas with money; during the second, I want to make money with ideas." Comte to J. M'Clintock, August 7, 1852, *CG*, 6:324.

consciousness of a republican Polytechnicien."[203] Comte would surely have discovered his theories elsewhere if he had never met this eccentric philosopher.[204] Also denying Saint-Simon's influence, the positivists went so far as to suggest that Comte affected Saint-Simon.[205]

It is evident that Comte had absorbed the ideas of Montesquieu and Condorcet and was influenced by Constant, Staël, Say, Cabanis, and Destutt de Tracy. His doctrine would reflect the Idéologue program to which most of these thinkers subscribed. It stressed a secular, educated elite leading a republic, not according to vague, potentially dangerous political principles, such as inalienable natural rights, but according to the findings of a rational, all-encompassing "science of man."[206] Nevertheless, the decisive impact that Saint-Simon had on Comte's life and his thought is also irrefutable. He particularly helped him to assimilate the Idéologues' doctrine and also pointed out to him its narrowness and neglect of moral issues.[207]

Comte acknowledged that Saint-Simon had made him pay far more attention to the social ramifications of industrial development.[208] Extending the Idéologues' industrialist model of society, Saint-Simon had taught him that economic phenomena were vital to modern civilization and that the growth of industry would transform social relationships and lead to a new moral society. The problem of social dissolution would be solved when people became united and interdependent through their productive work for humanity.[209] Implicit in Saint-Simon's vision of a harmonious society was the counterrevolutionaries' stress on organicism and solidarity, achieved through unifying principles.

---

[203] Gouhier, *Jeunesse*, 1:237; 3:387; see also 1:17.

[204] See the provocative interpretation of Gouhier's stance by L. Zsigmond, "Le Sort de l'heritage de Saint-Simon: La Manifestation de l'école saint-simonienne sous la direction d'Enfantin et Bazard, l'engagement de Comte pour élaborer le système scientifique du positivisme et de la sociologie: 1825–1826," trans. by A. Rényi, in *Acta Historica* 24 (1978): 245–46. Zsigmond argues that, writing in the 1930s and early 1940s, Gouhier was trying to seek an ideological basis for his conservatism and thus aimed to separate Comte from the Saint-Simonian tradition, which was considered a variation of socialism.

[205] Pierre Laffitte called the fundamental opuscule a "truly sacred work" owing nothing to Saint-Simon. Laffitte believed that Comte had a "very big" influence on Saint-Simon. "Opuscule fondamental," ed. Laffitte, 2, 7; "Considérations sur la période de sa vie qui s'étend de 1816 à 1822," ed. Laffitte, 35. In a similar fashion, Robinet mocked the mediocre, unoriginal, and parasitic mind of Saint-Simon. Robinet, *Notice*, 114. Even Littré, who admitted that Comte took up many of Saint-Simon's ideas, denied that Saint-Simon was ever his "philosophical master" and asserted that "more than once Auguste Comte acted upon the floating thought of Saint-Simon." Littré, *Auguste Comte*, 92. See also Charles Jeannolle, "Bibliographie," *RO*, 2d ser., 12 (November 1, 1896): 412.

[206] Welch, *Liberty and Utility*, 28–9, 33, 137; Head, *Ideology*, 78.

[207] Kaiser, "Politics and Political Economy," 158, 160.   [208] *Cours*, 2:466.

[209] Kaiser, "Politics and Political Economy," 155, 157, 160.

Comte often credited Saint-Simon with having saved him from the "state of pure negativity" and "demoralization" in which he found himself in 1817.[210] At that time, he was dissatisfied with his own atheism and overall skepticism. Saint-Simon taught him that critical ideas, particularly many of the stock phrases of the eighteenth century that Comte respected, could be harmful and that it was more fulfilling to devote oneself to the task of construction. These lessons applied to both Comte's personal life and political life, which became increasingly intertwined.

Just after the rupture, while explaining to Valat that his foreword was merely an act of "complaisance" that went "beyond reality," he stated:

> I certainly owe a great deal intellectually to Saint-Simon, that is to say, he has powerfully contributed to launching me in the philosophical direction that I have clearly created for myself today and that I will follow without hesitation all my life.[211]

This certain "direction" was Saint-Simon's great contribution to Comte's development. His mentor had shown him that each social system was an application of a system of ideas, especially moral ideas, because people were linked by a common way of thinking. Politics and morality reflected the reigning philosophy; they needed to be reorganized as the philosophy changed. As Pierre Ansart noted, the originality of Saint-Simon lay in his acute awareness of the intellectual break that was taking place in his era and of the need to create a new *unified* system of knowledge focusing on the human species and society.[212] Deriving from both a priori and a posteriori methods, this system had to be based on "positive" ideas, which were certain and definitive because they were established by observation. Only by such a unified, positive system could society be saved from anarchy. The mission that Comte inherited from Saint-Simon consisted of constructing this philosophy. It satisfied his longings for "spiritual discipline."[213]

In addition to showing Comte the general outline of the positive system, Saint-Simon provided him with insights into the nature of the science of society that would help regenerate philosophy, morality, and politics. Influenced by Condorcet, Saint-Simon gave this study a method – historical observation – which Comte fully adopted. Comte learned from him the predictive power of history as well as the *progressive* role that the Middle Ages and even the Catholic clergy had played in the development of Western civilization. Both of these

[210] Comte to M'Clintock, August 7, 1852, *CG*, 6:324.
[211] Comte to Valat, May 21, 1824, *CG*, 1:90.   [212] Ansart, *Sociologie de Saint-Simon*, 9.
[213] Comte to Louis Comte, January 26, 1857, *CG*, 8:391.

ideas were essential to the law of three stages. Saint-Simon also taught him that the study of society must share the same spirit as the other sciences, including physiology. To connect social science with the other sciences and create a synthesis of knowledge, Comte formulated the classification of the sciences, which owed a great deal to Saint-Simon's (or Burdin's) view of each science passing through three stages – a conjectural stage, a half conjectural and half positive stage, and a positive stage – according to its degree of complexity. Finally, despite its problems, the other discipline that was a fruitful source of information about the new industrial society was political economy.

Social science was not, however, just an intellectual mixture of history, the physical sciences, physiology, and political economy. It had a practical vocation: to regenerate society and thus close the Revolution. This regeneration could come about only if society were administered in a scientific fashion by an educated elite of technocrats who would create a rational system of central planning based on social utility. "Politics" in the usual sense of the term was anachronistic. Impassioned discussions of political regimes, marked especially by appeals to popular sovereignty, could lead only to more upheaval. Along with Montesquieu, Saint-Simon taught Comte to concentrate on the importance of social relationships. This change of focus from politics to social relationships broke with the tradition of political philosophy.[214]

Influenced by the counterrevolutionary thinkers, Saint-Simon also demonstrated to Comte that there must be a separation between the temporal and spiritual powers; the industrialists had to replace the military leaders as the temporal power and the scientists had to take over from the clergy as the spiritual power. These new powers would lead the transition from the old military and arbitrary rule to the liberal, pacific, and industrial regime of modern times. Even the ideas that Saint-Simon developed in his last years influenced Comte later on – the concept that a coherent and certain system of scientific beliefs could be substituted for theology, the view that mankind had a religious future, and the theory that the artists had to play a large role in creating moral unity.[215]

Most of Saint-Simon's ideas that influenced Comte were developed during the Empire. After 1816, perhaps because he did not feel equipped for the task, Saint-Simon grew less and less interested in developing the theoretical basis of the reorganization of society – a task taken up by Comte with increasing enthusiasm. Comte felt it

[214] Ibid., 26, 185–87; Baker, "Closing the Revolution," 329.
[215] Markham, Introduction to *Social Organization*, xxiii.

was still too early to define the industrial reorganization of society as Saint-Simon was doing. He was able to build on his mentor's legacy by developing the ideas that the capricious man had left by the wayside. Although Saint-Simon may have thought of the essence of positivism and sociology, he did *not* establish them as Emile Durkheim, Georges Dumas, Steven Lukes, and others have asserted.[216] Comte would make a far more systematic exposition of history and would define the scientific spirit much more clearly. To him, the scientific method, not a single natural law like that of gravity, was the key to unifying the sciences. Most of all, he was aware that the social and economic revolution generated by industrialism would be incomplete without a far-reaching intellectual transformation; establishing sociology as a separate discipline entailed a total revision of human knowledge. Because of his rebellious nature, his sense of integrity, and his philosophical nature, Comte managed to sever himself from Saint-Simon and would acquire an originality of his own. In devoting his life to the creation of a new intellectual clergy who would be responsible for the indirect reform of society, he would prove to be even more "spiritual" than Saint-Simon.[217]

[216] Georges Dumas, "Saint-Simon, père du positivisme," parts 1, 2, *Revue philosophique* 57 (1904): 136–57, 263–87; idem, *Psychologie de deux messies*, 266; Emile Durkheim, "Saint-Simon, fondateur du positivisme," 321–41; Lukes, "Saint-Simon," 34.

[217] For information regarding Saint-Simon's influence on Comte, see Ducassé, *Essai sur les Origines intuitives*, 53; Markham, Introduction to *Social Organization*, xxiii, xxvii; Taylor, Introduction to *Henri Saint-Simon*, 31, 33, 36; Dumas, "Saint-Simon, père du positivisme," 277–8; idem, *Psychologie de deux messies*, 268–70, 278; Durkheim, "Saint-Simon, fondateur du positivisme," 322–3; Rutten, *Essai sur la morale*, 30, 41; Ansart, *Sociologie de Saint-Simon*, 7–13, 22–6, 56, 184–7, 190–1, 203–4; Weill, *Saint-Simon*, 208–9, 223; Harry Elmer Barnes, "Social Thought," 74; Zeitlin, *Rethinking Sociology*, 62; Delvolvé, *Réflections*, 37, 42–3; Dubuisson, *Comte et Saint-Simon*, 30n; Robinet, *Notice*, 116–39; Littré, *Auguste Comte*, 73–97; Bénichou, *Temps des prophètes*, 253–5, 260; Coser, *Masters of Sociological Thought*, 27–8; Elie Halévy, *The Era of Tyrannies*, trans. R. K. Webb (Garden City, N.Y.: Doubleday, Anchor Books, 1965), 30; Janet, "Origines de la philosophie d'Auguste Comte," 615.

Chapter 6

The Aftermath of the Rupture:
The Search for Connections

You are watching the number of your predecessors augment each day.
Gustave d'Eichthal to Comte, 1824

THE RECEPTION OF THE FUNDAMENTAL OPUSCULE

When Comte left Saint-Simon, he felt an immediate sense of liberation. Eager as always to analyze and dramatize his own development, he called his "rupture" a "moral revolution."[1] He was proud that he had achieved the same sort of transformation within himself that he hoped to effect within humanity. Just as humanity would be able to proceed to the final stage of maturity after its moral revolution, Comte felt that he was about to enter his adulthood and age of glory, when his "intellectual existence" could develop in a "purer and more complete manner." But he remained anxious about his intellectual debts and his unsettled and financially insecure existence. Therefore, from 1824 to 1828, he devoted himself to establishing his "perfect independence" from both Saint-Simon and his parents.[2]

His first step was to distribute his hundred copies of the *Plan des travaux nécessaires pour réorganiser la société*, the ones without Saint-Simon's offensive introduction and extraneous title (*Catéchisme des industriels*). Worried, however, about damaging his reputation, he first angrily crossed out his own flattering foreword along with his references to being the "student of Saint-Simon."[3] He then sent copies to his parents, friends, acquaintances, teachers, and former employers (including Comte and Dunoyer), whom he wanted to impress with his achievement.[4] He also delivered his essay to important

[1] Comte to Tabarié, August 22, 1824, *CG*, I:112.
[2] Comte to G. d'Eichthal, May 1, 1824, *CG*, I:82.
[3] Comte crossed out the phrase following his name – "élève de Henri Saint-Simon" – on the cover and the title page and on the first page of the opuscule itself. See the *Système de politique positive* dedicated by Comte to a Monsieur Gilbert, Res. p.r. 753, BN. See also Fournel, *Bibliographie Saint-Simonienne*, 41.
[4] People on Comte's list included Olinde Rodrigues (Saint-Simon's associate), Gustave and Adolphe d'Eichthal, Cerclet, Bailly, Valat, Tabarié, Duvergier, Burdin, Bérard de Favas, Lachevardière (his associate in *Le Politique*), Cordier (the engineer whose book he had reviewed for *Le Censeur européen*), J. Delpech (the surgeon who removed his tumor when he

scientists, such as Blainville, Poinsot, Fourier, Arago, Poisson, Humboldt, Cuvier, Flourens, Gay-Lussac, Ampère, and Laplace; the Idéologues Daunou and Laromiguière; the political economists Say, Sismondi, and Rossi; the liberal politicians Constant, F. Guizot, the Duc de Broglie, Ternaux, Benjamin Delessert (also a rich banker and industrialist), Comte Pierre Daru, and Comte Alexandre de Laborde; the powerful royalist minister Joseph de Villèle; and the bankers André, Cottier, Ardouin, Baron Rothschild, and Vassal. Other influential figures who received the opuscule included Jean-Antoine Chaptal, Baron de Staël, General François-Alexandre Desprez, General Louis Tirlet, Talleyrand, and Baron André de Férussac.[5] Comte's carefully selected list of recipients indicates that despite his distaste for lobbying, he sought to form relations with "men in power or in an eminent social position" as a means of ensuring his career. He hoped especially to woo some of the former supporters of Saint-Simon's enterprises.[6] He could not forgive Saint-Simon for having reaped the financial gain from the success of his opuscule and cut him off from the journals that had formerly offered him a source of income.[7]

In the first few months after the break with Saint-Simon, Comte was delighted with the praise his essay received. The general impression it created can be gathered from comments later made by John Stuart Mill:

> It is the performance of a highly philosophical mind: it is far superior to the two first cahiers. Allowing to Saint-Simon the merit of having first conceived the outline of the work which Comte has executed, it must be admitted that the master has been surpassed by the pupil. In the hands of Saint-Simon the "doctrine Industrielle" appears sometimes vague and unintelligible, almost always "trenchant and dogmatical" and the "système industriel" (à établir) absolutely absurd. But in the hands of Comte the doctrine assumes a form in which it is fit

was a little boy), Caizergues (the family doctor in Montpellier), Jourdan (Comte's nurse when he was an infant), Baron Reynaud (the teacher who had given him the job in the pension), General Bernard, General Campredon, and friends from the Ecole Polytechnique – Savary, Duhamel, Gondinet, Servier, and Menjaud.

[5] Ternaux to Comte, April 27, 1824, MAC; see list of people to whom Comte sent his opuscule, MAC; "De la circulation des ouvrages d'Auguste Comte: De l'opuscule fondamental," ed. Laffitte, 315–34. This list is reproduced on pages 326–7 of this article. Other scientists on Comte's list were Candolle, Hachette, Pictet, Nicolas Clément, Bérard (a famous doctor from Montpellier who upheld vitalism), and Lordat (who had taught at the medical school in Montpellier).

[6] Comte to Valat, September 8, 1824, *CG*, 1:121. The supporters of Saint-Simon were Chaptal, Cuvier, Arago, Say, Ternaux, Delessert, André, Cottier, Ardouin, Vassal, the Duc de Broglie, and Lachevardière.

[7] Comte to Tabarié, April 5, 1824, *CG*, 1:77.

either to produce conviction or to become matter of instructive discussion.[8]

The scientific community also praised Comte's work. Lazare Carnot, the exiled mathematician and revolutionary who had helped Saint-Simon during the Hundred Days, had already encouraged Comte in 1823.[9] Others who complimented him included Poinsot, Cuvier, and Alexander von Humboldt. The last was so impressed that he met with Comte to discuss his ideas.[10] Pierre Flourens, a famous physiologist, also requested an interview because he was struck by the "loftiness" and "depth" of Comte's views and the way he was founding the "moral and political sciences" on "observation and experimentation, the bases of every positive science."[11]

In addition, important figures in business and politics such as Ternaux, Delessert, Laborde, and Philippe Panon Desbassayns de Richemont approved of Comte's ideas.[12] Despite Comte's criticisms of the party of "the people," Say joined the liberals Guizot and Broglie in welcoming his scientific approach to the crisis that France faced. During a meeting with Comte to discuss politics, Say declared his support for positive philosophy and stated that he recognized the impact his ideas on political economy had had on Comte's conception of social science.[13] Comte was most excited, however,

---

[8] Mill to G. d'Eichthal, October 29, 1829, Fonds d'Eichthal 13756, fol. 6, BN. This letter was copied by Adolphe d'Eichthal. It is not included in the collected letters of Mill. See *The Earlier Letters of John Stuart Mill, 1812–1848*, ed. Francis E. Mineka, 2 vols. (vols. 12 and 13 of *The Collected Works*, ed. John M. Robson) (hereafter *Earlier Letters*) (Toronto: University of Toronto Press and Routledge & Kegan Paul, 1963).

[9] *Système*, 1:22. Also see letter from Laffitte to Senator Carnot, August 1, 1882, MAC; Auguste Comte, *Appel aux Conservateurs* (Paris, 1855), ix. According to Lonchampt, Charles Bonnin transmitted Carnot's congratulations to Comte. Lonchampt, *Précis*, 30–1.

[10] Comte to G. Cuvier, May 9, 1824, *CG*, 1:86; Comte to Valat, May 21, 1824, *CG*, 1:92; Comte to G. d'Eichthal, May 1, May 21, June 6, 1824, *CG*, 1:83–4, 92, 94; Comte to Humboldt, December 27, 1855, *CG*, 8:162–3; Cuvier to Comte, May 10, 1824, MAC. Also, Comte was very pleased that Candolle was impressed with his essay. Comte to Tabarié, July 17, 1824, *CG*, 1:101.

[11] Flourens to Comte, n.d., MAC. This letter is reproduced in "De la circulation des ouvrages d'Auguste Comte: De l'opuscule fondamental," ed. Laffitte, 333. Flourens seems to have remained an admirer of Comte. See his addition to the form letter sent by the Académie des Sciences acknowledging the receipt of a volume of the *Cours*, August 5, 1839, MAC.

[12] Comte to Valat, May 21, 1824, *CG*, 1:92; Comte to Tabarié, August 22, 1824, *CG*, 1:114; Campredon to Comte, June 30, 1824, "Correspondants, amis et protecteurs: Le Général Campredon," ed. Laffitte, 173; Ternaux to Comte, April 27, May 18, 1824, MAC. Comte Alexandre de Laborde claimed that he was a "true admirer" of Comte. Laborde to Comte, May 2, 1824, MAC. Laborde's letter is reproduced in "De la circulation des ouvrages d'Auguste Comte: De l'opuscule fondamental," ed. Laffitte, 333.

[13] H. Say wrote a letter on his father's behalf to Comte on April 19, 1824, MAC. It is reproduced in "De la circulation des ouvrages d'Auguste Comte: De l'opuscule fonda-

when he learned that Guizot wanted to "place himself" under his "banner."[14] Some members of Guizot's party, the "doctrinaires," asked him to join a new organization devoted to the moral and political sciences and to help launch a monthly journal, but nothing ever came of these projects.[15]

Generals Bernard and Campredon also complimented him. The former expressed his pleasure that Comte was trying to prevent future revolutions. The latter voiced his admiration for Comte's "moderation" and congratulated him on his break with Saint-Simon, which he hoped was "irrevocable."[16]

Because his book had received widespread approval, Comte hoped it would "profoundly influence minds of the first order."[17] In July he sent copies to James Monroe and Thomas Jefferson and planned to send one to Canning too.[18]

Comte was disappointed, however, by Valat's reaction to his chef d'oeuvre. After not having written to him for more than two years, Comte sent him a copy of the *Plan*.[19] Valat's response was full of praise. But he suggested that Comte had exaggerated the certainty of positive knowledge and the possibility of establishing political principles acceptable to all classes. He also objected to Comte's belief that physiology was already a positive science, his search for laws of social development, his denial of the efficacy of political reforms, and his use of a dry scientific style.[20] Comte found Valat's response "so metaphysically silly and ridiculous" that he was "thunderstruck."[21] He was especially angry that Valat believed his philosophy was similar to Cousin's, for he felt that Cousin was a "sophist" whose ideas were breeding fanaticism and endangering the

mental," ed. Laffitte, 334. See also Pierre Laffitte, "L'Athénée," *RO* 22 (January 1, 1889): 19; Comte to Mill, July 22, 1844, *CG*, 2:270–1.

14 Comte to Valat, May 21, 1824, *CG*, 1:92. See also Comte to G. d'Eichthal, May 1, 1824, *CG*, 1:83.

15 Comte to G. d'Eichthal, May 1, June 6, 1824, *CG*, 1:84, 97.

16 Campredon to Comte, June 30, 1824, "Correspondants, amis et protecteurs: Le Général Campedron," ed. Laffitte, 173–4. Responding in all likelihood to Comte's display of remorse and pity for his master, Campredon added that Saint-Simon was "undoubtedly very much a man to feel sorry for, but who can blame himself for almost all his misfortunes." See also Bernard to Comte, February 8, 1825, MAC.

17 Comte to Valat, May 21, 1824, *CG*, 1:92.

18 Comte to G. d'Eichthal, August 5, 1824, *CG*, 1:108; Comte to Tabarié, August 22, 1824, *CG*, 1:113; Comte to Jefferson, July 16, 1824, *CG*, 1:99; Comte's list of people to whom he sent his opuscule, MAC. Jefferson never read Comte's very flattering letter. Nicholas Philip Trist to Comte, January 11, 1853, MAC.

19 See Valat's comments on the original letter from Comte to Valat, May 21, 1824, MAC.

20 Comte to Valat, September 8, November 3, December 25, 1824, *CG*, 1:123–32, 147.

21 Comte to Tabarié, August 22, 1824, *CG*, 1:119.

public peace.[22] In truth, Comte was very jealous of Cousin's strong following among the members of their generation.

Valat was irritated. Although the two men continued to correspond intermittently throughout the period from 1824 to 1826, they then lost contact with each other for eleven years.[23]

Comte's only other major disappointment was that the *Plan* was not reviewed in any French journal in 1824 or 1825.[24] Despite this setback, he was pleased with his growing reputation and felt sure that once he completed the second part of the essay, his relations with scientists and thinkers would improve. He dreamed of being admitted promptly to the Academy of Sciences.[25] Even his family was convinced he would be rich and famous.[26]

FEAR OF SAINT-SIMON

In trying to establish his own identity, Comte faced more than financial difficulties; he also had to situate himself philosophically vis-à-vis his former mentor. His first worry was that Saint-Simon would try to damage his budding "relationship with the public" by publishing a fourth *cahier* of the *Catéchisme des industriels*, which would be "intellectually inconvenient and perfectly ridiculous."[27] And, indeed, the fourth *cahier*, which appeared in June 1824, did seem to be directed at him. At one point in the *cahier*, an interlocutor, modeled on Comte, upbraids Saint-Simon for not first addressing himself to the scientists, which would have been "more natural" and "methodical." Saint-Simon retorts that although scientists do render crucial services, the industrial class provides them with much more, namely, the very means of their existence: "The industrial class is the fundamental class, the nourishing class of all society; no other class could subsist without it."[28] Saint-Simon's rupture with his

[22] Comte to Armand Marrast, January 7, 1832, *CG*, 1:231. See also Comte to Valat, November 3, 1824, *CG*, 1:132.

[23] In November 1824 Comte complained that Valat neglected to write to him. Comte to Valat, November 28, 1824, *CG*, 1:139. See also Comte to Valat, September 28, 1837, *CG*, 1:279; Valat's comments on the back of the original letter of September 1837, MAC.

[24] Comte to G. d'Eichthal, August 5, 1824, *CG*, 1:108; Comte to Tabarié, August 22, 1824, *CG*, 1:117. Comte had sent his essay to the prestigious *Journal des débats* and also expected the *Revue encyclopédique* and Férussac's *Bulletin des sciences* to publish reviews of the *Plan*.

[25] Comte to Valat, September 8, 1824, *CG*, 1:121. On the importance of the Academy of Sciences in the careers of young men, see Roger Hahn, *The Anatomy of a Scientific Institution: The Paris Academy of Sciences, 1666–1803* (Berkeley and Los Angeles: University of California Press, 1971).

[26] Comte to Tabarié, July 17, 1824, *CG*, 1:100.

[27] Comte to G. d'Eichthal, June 6, 1824, *CG*, 1:93–4.

[28] Saint-Simon, *Catéchisme des industriels: Quatrième Cahier*, 25.

disciple apparently made him even more convinced of the vital role of the *industriels*.

Moreover, to reorganize society, he urged the establishment of three professorships – in political and industrial conduct, morality, and positive sciences – and two academies, which would formulate a general doctrine based on the sciences and a code of sentiments. With these institutions in place and the industrial class in control of the budget, society would finally be in harmony with the state of civilization. Such simplistic plans could only have reconfirmed Comte's conviction that Saint-Simon had a "revolutionary disposition" to make practical, institutional reforms precede important doctrinal changes.[29]

Moreover, when Saint-Simon turned to the history of civilization, the very subject that Comte was working on for the second part of the *Plan*, he returned to his old idea that there were two main eras, each consisting of 1,200 years. The first era was Platonic and focused on the moral study of man, while the second was Aristotelian and dealt with the physical study of man. The omission of any reference to Comte's law of three stages indicates that Saint-Simon did not think highly of it.

Saint-Simon had intended to fill the lacuna created in the third *cahier* by Comte's so-called neglect of the religious aspect of human existence, but he failed to address this issue. The only part of Saint-Simon's work that was vaguely religious was his banal statement that moralists must find new applications for the principle of divine morality – the golden rule.

Comte's reaction to the fourth *cahier* is not known. Before its appearance, he had vowed not to become embroiled in a public dispute with Saint-Simon. He hoped to avoid all contact with him and to work without distraction on his own material. Yet his attention was diverted in December when Saint-Simon published his next volume, *Opinions littéraires, philosophiques et industrielles*.

Without Comte to help him, Saint-Simon had sought assistance to put this book together. The *Opinions* contained articles written not only by himself and his new disciple Olinde Rodrigues but by three young collaborators: Léon Halévy, a poet; J. B. Duvergier, a lawyer; and E. M. Bailly, a physiologist.[30] Except for Halévy, they

---

[29] Comte to G. d'Eichthal, May 1, 1824, *CG*, 1:82.

[30] Despite the rupture with Saint-Simon, Rodrigues and Comte continued to be very good friends. Comte had known Bailly since 1816 or 1817. Both Bailly and Duvergier had received a copy of the fundamental opuscule. See list of people to whom Comte sent his fundamental opuscule, MAC; Comte to Bénard, January 22, 1825, *CG*, 1:153; Comte to G. d'Eichthal, June 6, December 10, 1824, *CG*, 1:97, 145. For information regarding the authorship of the articles in the *Opinions*, see Saint-Simon, *Oeuvres*, 3.3:11. In the *Opinions*, the articles were unsigned.

were also friends of Comte. The *Opinions* immediately received a favorable review from the *Revue encyclopédique*.[31] But Comte commented that the articles were "very weak" and "pitiful" and blamed Saint-Simon for the entire "mess."[32] In his essays, Saint-Simon claimed that the recently formed Holy Alliance facilitated the transition to the new industrial and scientific regime; urged philosophers, the scientists of "generalities," to form a new encyclopedia: stressed the need to make proletarians the administrators of property; and talked vaguely about establishing a "truly universal religion."[33] Comte chafed at the "ridiculously audacious" schemes and the "eternal and tiresome drivel of the same ideas and the same expressions." He scorned Saint-Simon's attempt to organize society "brusquely" by means of a "little constitution." To him, the fact that bankers and manufacturers were wasting their money on such "revolutionary extravagance" was laughable.[34] Saint-Simon's successful writings and his growing coterie of disciples had clearly aroused Comte's jealousy.

The disorderly ideas contained in the fourth *cahier* and *Opinions* reaffirmed Comte's sense of superiority but they alarmed him nonetheless. He worried, with justification, that the public was associating him with the eccentric philosopher.[35] Thus when Saint-Simon's disciples tried to take advantage of Comte's growing prestige by asking him in late 1824 to contribute to the second volume of the *Opinions* as well as to a new journal, he gave them his "absolute refusal."[36]

Nevertheless, Comte's effort to distance himself from the Saint-Simonians was not entirely successful. In March 1825 Comte suddenly alienated the director of the Ecole d'Etat-Major, General Desprez, whom Campredon was trying to persuade to help Comte.[37]

---

[31] "F.," review of *Opinions littéraires, philosophiques et industrielles, Revue encyclopédique*, 2d ser., 24 (December 1824): 760–2. "F" wrote a review of the *Catéchisme des industriels*, but he referred only to Saint-Simon, not Comte. "F.," review of *Catéchisme des industriels*, by Saint-Simon, *Revue encyclopédique*, 2d ser., 22 (April 1824): 183–5.

[32] Comte to G. d'Eichthal, December 10, 1824, *CG*, 1:145.

[33] [Henri de] Saint-Simon, "Quelques opinions philosophiques à l'usage du dix-neuvième siècle" and "De l'organisation sociale: Fragments d'un ouvrage inédit," in [Henri de] Saint-Simon et al., *Opinions littéraires, philosophiques et industrielles* (Paris, 1825), 25, 148.

[34] Comte to G. d'Eichthal, December 10, 1824, *CG*, 1:145.

[35] Comte to G. d'Eichthal, November 6, 1824, *CG*, 1:135; Deroisin, *Notes sur Auguste Comte*, 20.

[36] Comte to G. d'Eichthal, December 10, 1824, *CG*, 1:145.

[37] Desprez had received a copy of Comte's fundamental opuscule. On Desprez, see A. Rabbe, Vieilh de Boisjoslin, and Saint Preuve, eds., *Biographie universelle et portative des contemporains ou Dictionnaire historique des hommes vivants et des hommes morts depuis 1788 jusqu'à nos jours*, 2d ed., 5 vols. (Paris, 1834), 2:1350; Georges Six, *Dictionnaire biographique des généraux et amiraux français de la Révolution et de l'Empire (1792–1824)*, 2 vols. (Paris: Georges Saffroy, 1934), 1:344.

Campredon suspected that Comte's "amour-propre" had deeply offended Desprez and his colleagues, but Comte denied this. After hearing Comte's side, Campredon agreed that he had been probably harmed by the "former comrade that you suspect." He lamented that Comte's "perfidious comrade" had "secret designs" to hurt him and feared that their "troublesome relations" had estranged Comte "all too long from the career of the Sciences."[38]

A NEW TACTIC: AN APPEAL TO THE RIGHT

As if to encourage Comte's independence from Saint-Simon and his disciples, Campredon urged him to develop a relationship with one of his relatives, Baron Desbassayns de Richemont. When Comte had planned to emigrate to the United States, Desbassayns had written a letter on his behalf to the U.S. secretary of war.[39] As the brother-in-law of Comte Joseph de Villèle, the ultraroyalist minister of finance, who headed the government, Desbassayns was in a position to help him again. And in 1824, with only twenty liberal deputies in the newly elected Chamber, the ultras were stronger than ever.[40]

Comte genuinely admired Villèle, who he said possessed more than any other statesman the "political character that is particularly appropriate to the second quarter of the nineteenth century."[41] Comte respected his moderate use of power, willingness to compromise, and distaste for ultrafanaticism.[42] Above all, Comte believed the new period of "political inactivity" was "indispensable" to the gradual establishment of the positive doctrine, which would take "two or

---

[38] Campredon to Comte, March 30, 1825, "Correspondants, amis et protecteurs: Le Général Campredon," ed. Laffitte, 175.

[39] Baron Desbassayns de Richemont to William Crawford, December 31, 1816, "Correspondants, amis et protecteurs d'Auguste Comte: Le Général Campredon," ed. Laffitte, 169–70.

[40] Campredon to Comte, March 30, 1825, "Correspondants, amis et protecteurs: Le Général Campredon," ed. Laffitte, 175; Campredon, "Extrait d'un cahier de notes," ed. Laffitte, 166, 169–70; Baron Desbassayns de Richemont to W. Crawford, December 31, 1816, "Correspondants, amis et protecteurs: Le Général Campredon," ed. Laffitte, 169–70 (the original letter exists in the Maison d'Auguste Comte); René Rémond, *Les Droites en France*, 4th ed. (Paris: Aubier Montaigne, 1982), 67; Gordon Wright, *France in Modern Times*, 108, 110.

[41] Comte to G. d'Eichthal, August 5, 1824, *CG*, 1:105.

[42] Comte praised in particular the measure indemnifying the émigrés for their lost property, which put an end to one of the most bothersome problems of the regime. Comte to Tabarié, April, 5, 1824, *CG*, 1:78; Comte to G. d'Eichthal, June 6, 1824, *CG*, 1:97. On Villèle, see A. Jardin and A. J. Tudesq, *La France des notables*, 2 vols. (Paris: Seuil, 1973), 1:106–11; Rémond, *Les Droites*, 67; Gordon Wright, *France in Modern Times*, 106–11.

three generations."[43] Despite his contempt for the ultras, he felt the peace they could ensure was more likely to lead to the renewal of political doctrines than the distracting political activity of the liberals. Direct practical reforms would be the work of future generations. This need for political calm even led Comte to praise the Holy Alliance's repression of the liberal uprising in Spain.[44] He was already showing his political quietism and his willingness to accept an authoritarian solution if it ensured the peace required for intellectual work.

Comte dreamed of inducing Villèle to get him a prestigious teaching position and protect him not only from the Jesuits and other religious forces that might hinder his success, but also from government officials who might arrest him.[45] For months, he hoped that Desbassayns would persuade Villèle to read the fundamental opuscule as well as an "adroit" letter in which he explained the "points of contact" between the minister's "practical politics" and the positive theory of politics.[46] Desperate to get Villèle's attention, Comte even told him in his letter that he felt that corruption was an "indispensable" manner of governing in the anarchical times in which they lived.[47] He wanted to tell him personally that the positive philosophy would "ruin liberalism and ultraism without being obliged to borrow arguments from each of them as the fools of the center do."[48] As a nonpartisan doctrine, the positive philosophy would attract people tired of all the political parties. By encouraging people to think rather than act, it would provide a new source of support for the government. After months of delays, Villèle finally received Comte's materials, but he never read them.[49] Comte's first appeal to the conservatives was a complete failure.

Given this episode, it is clear that Comte was willing to stomach almost any form of governmental behavior in return for financial assistance. Although he had criticized Saint-Simon for supporting

[43] Comte to G. d'Eichthal, August 5, 1824, *CG*, 1:104; Comte to Valat, December 25, 1824, *CG*, 1:149.

[44] Comte to G. d'Eichthal, May 1, 1824, *CG*, 1:84; Comte to Valat, May 21, 1824, *CG*, 1:91. Comte believed that the Holy Alliance represented "one of the real and capital needs of the epoch." Comte to G. d'Eichthal, April 6, 1825, *CG*, 1:160.

[45] Comte to Valat, September 8, 1824, *CG*, 1:120–2.

[46] Comte to G. d'Eichthal, November 6, 1824, *CG*, 1:134; Comte to Tabarié, August 22, 1824, *CG*, 1:114. See also Comte to G. d'Eichthal, August 5, 1824, *CG*, 1:108.

[47] Comte to G. d'Eichthal, November 6, 1824, *CG*, 1:134.

[48] Comte to Valat, September 8, 1824, *CG*, 1:122.

[49] Campredon to Comte, March 30, 1825, "Correspondants, amis et protecteurs: Le Général Campredon," ed. Laffitte, 175; Comte to G. d'Eichthal, December 10, 1824, *CG*, 1:142; Comte to Valat, May 21, December 25, 1824, *CG*, 1:92, 151; Comte to G. d'Eichthal, April 6, 1825, *CG*, 1:160.

advantages for the *industriels* to get their help, he was not above doing the same for the ultras. Despite his pride in his republicanism and antiroyalism, he appeared to have no scruples about advocating the "fall of liberalism" or allying himself with the ultra party in power, especially because this group was not linked to Saint-Simon.[50] Yet whereas Saint-Simon was useful to the *industriels*, Comte could be of no value to the ultras. He was not well known and moreover did not seem trustworthy since he had severely criticized reactionaries in the fundamental opuscule. His political naïveté is revealed by his expectation that Villèle would risk coming to his aid.

FROM DESPAIR TO A SENSE OF VOCATION

Comte had placed so much confidence in Villèle's help that he had not developed any other plan, and therefore when nothing materialized his financial position became desperate. His numerous social and intellectual connections had not led anywhere, especially not to a stable teaching job. Even his "precarious profession as an itinerant teacher" was not going well. And his worries increased when he decided to marry Caroline Massin, the woman with whom he was living. Resentful of the risky and "cruel circumstances" in which he found himself at the end of his twenties, he bemoaned his lack of skill in intrigue and his inattention to his own interests. By Christmas of 1824 he was threatening to take almost any job offered to him. He was sure that without the "deadly influence" of Saint-Simon working against him, he would have had at least ten chances to create a successful career for himself.[51]

As Comte's frustrations mounted throughout the mid-1820s, his feelings both about his own situation and that of France turned to despair. Increasingly sensitive to the growing wealth of the middle classes during this period of economic expansion, he wrote:

> It is even only too true that in the anarchical and material era that still exists and perhaps will bury us, ideas are so confused that money is an indispensable means of esteem even in the spiritual order; the tendency to wealth is evident in our scholars, who believe themselves to be inferior as long as they are not able to give a dinner as the bankers do.

He was no longer sure that his scholarly works would bring him success, for it seemed to him that philosophical work ran "against

---

[50] Comte to G. d'Eichthal, May 1, 1824, *CG*, 1:84.
[51] Comte to Valat, December 25, 1824, *CG*, 1:150–2.

the grain" of his century. In "this age of anarchy," when people were motivated only by their personal interests, no one was really concerned with ideas. Like other young men of his generation stricken by the "mal de siècle," Comte cursed his century and lamented that the entire political system was being reduced to a "government of money," poisoning all aspects of social life.[52] The iniquities of capitalism seemed more glaring than ever. He still hoped his new generation could effect the moral regeneration of society.

Comte felt trapped by the turn of events with Saint-Simon, the materialism of his era, and his own character, which made him uninterested in business and unskillful at making money. Increasingly aware of his own marginal status in the postrevolutionary environment, he attached himself more and more to the vocation he had taken up with Saint-Simon:

> I will work all my life and with all my forces for the establishment of the positive philosophy . . . because it is my irresistible vocation and the source of my principal happiness. I will never claim any other recompense than the esteem of the chief thinkers of Europe.[53]

Comte's growing dislike of the commercialism of his period, which was also of grave concern to the romantics, led him to depict his vocation as a special calling with spiritual characteristics, including a vow of poverty. The language he used to describe it took on a religious tone, reflecting the way in which the critique of economic liberalism in France at this time was infused with Christian terminology.[54] He said that he had a "pronounced philosophical predestination" to assume the role of an intellectual and moral reformer, that is, a spiritual leader.[55] His mission was to end the "spiritual struggle" enveloping Europe by means of an "intellectual revolution," which would bring about a "completely new era for the human spirit."[56] In his view, his crusade to rally people around "certain political ideas" and to regenerate the social world secretly by acting outside of it recalled the original impetus behind Christianity: "I do not say entirely: *my kingdom is not of this world*, but the equivalent adjusted to our epoch."[57] He shared the desire felt by many opponents of the regime to ground his criticisms in what Edward Berenson

[52] Comte to G. d'Eichthal, December 10, 1824, *CG*, 1:141, 146. See also Comte to Tabarié, August 22, 1824, *CG*, 1:112; Comte to Valat, September 8, 1824, *CG*, 1:119.
[53] Comte to Valat, September 8, 1824, *CG*, 1:120. See also Comte to Tabarié, August 22, 1824, *CG*, 1:112–13.
[54] Berenson, "A New Religion," 547.
[55] Comte to G. d'Eichthal, December 10, 1824, *CG*, 1:141.
[56] Comte to Jefferson, July 16, 1824, *CG*, 1:99.
[57] Comte to Valat, December 25, 1824, *CG*, 1:149.

has called the "culture of moral and spiritual solidarity."[58] Christianity offered a strong spiritual basis for anticapitalist doctrines on the Left.

As Comte's sense of alienation deepened and his concern with moral issues increased, he saw the industrial developments promoted by Saint-Simon in a different light. Temporal progress was misleading, for as material conditions improved, people became blind to the "inconveniences of the spiritual anarchy."[59] Men devoted to making money were mediocre, avaricious, and "indifferent" to the human condition.[60]

In an effort to create "something spiritual" in order to "counterbalance" the rampant materialism of his era, Comte began to make his feeling of isolation a virtue and a necessity.[61] His own moral virtue became an obsession, as it had been during the time of his interest in Franklin. He now told his friends about the "enormous difficulty" he was having preserving his "spiritual character in all its purity in the middle of a completely temporal society." He shuddered at the thought of the future "persecutions" he would experience.[62] But these future trials were an indispensable part of the battle for truth because of their cathartic effect, which would set him apart from his contemporaries. It was as if he had experienced a religious calling without the requisite belief in God. He even expressed a desire to be a member of a distinct organization – the clergy: "I feel that . . . I am much more suited to be part of a regularly organized spiritual power than to contribute to founding one."[63] Although doubtful of his abilities in this regard, he realized that he would have to create a new clergy, one that would preach and spread his doctrine. The difference between his doctrine and the Gospel was that his ideas were intended at the moment only for "enlightened men"; the masses must not "be involved until later."[64]

Already in 1824 Comte envisaged a scientific society that would develop the type of "spiritual supremacy" imperfectly represented by the Academy of Sciences.[65] The members, young people with

---

[58] Berenson, "A New Religion," 557.

[59] Comte to G. d'Eichthal, December 10, 1824, *CG*, 1:146.

[60] Comte to Valat, December 25, 1824, *CG*, 1:152; Comte to Tabarié, August 22, 1824, *CG*, 1:112.

[61] Comte to Valat, March 30, 1825, *CG*, 1:156.

[62] Comte to G. d'Eichthal, December 10, 1824, *CG*, 1:141; Comte to Tabarié, August 22, 1824, *CG*, 1:112.

[63] Comte to G. d'Eichthal, November 6, 1824, *CG*, 1:134n1. See also Comte to Valat, March 30, 1825, *CG*, 1:158.

[64] Comte to Valat, May 21, 1824, *CG*, 1:92.

[65] Comte to G. Cuvier, May 9, 1824, *CG*, 1:86.

a scientific education, would have a secret understanding among themselves so that they would never have to meet. They would be Comte's avant-garde. He modeled them on two groups, one religious and one political, who prided themselves on their superior virtue and considered themselves missionaries of a new order: the Jesuits and the Jacobins. Unlike the Academicians, who came together out of a belief that specific ideas were scientific, the Jesuits and Jacobins, according to Comte, formed true societies because they were inspired and united by an entire system of thought. He realized that setting up his own elitist society would be the "great practical affair" of his life, and he vowed to be "constantly" devoted to this task.[66] This concept of a scientific elite reflected his growing interest in establishing a new spiritual power devoted to disseminating the positive philosophy. But before this elite could be formed, he would have to develop the doctrine that would serve as its basis.

The contradictory impulses represented by the Jacobins and the Jesuits reflect the divergent trends in Comte's thought. Although the actions of many of the Jacobins, especially Robespierre, had degenerated into the Terror, Comte, like many members of the republican secret societies of the Restoration, still respected them as a whole and considered them the representatives of the Revolution. He took up their call for a radical revolution on behalf of the people and their search for a substitute for Catholicism. His claim to be the heir of the Jacobin tradition would become particularly apparent in the 1840s, when social problems in France became more acute and he became more outspoken in his advocacy of an authoritarian, centralized republic.[67] Besides seeking to imitate the Jacobin Club's campaign to control ideas, Comte shared the preoccupations of the Jesuits. They were theoretically outlawed in France but were infiltrating the educational system, raising an outcry among the liberals, who associated them with rigid ultramontanism.[68] Though fearful of their influence, Comte resembled them in his stress on the need for a strong spiritual power and an intellectually respectable spiritual doctrine that could be taught in the schools and regenerate morality.[69] Of course, the Jacobins too believed in the regenerative potential of education. In short, Comte's desire for a "revolution in the

---

[66] Comte to G. d'Eichthal, June 6, 1824, *CG*, 1:97–8.
[67] On the history of Jacobinism, see François Furet, "Jacobinism," in *A Critical Dictionary*, ed. Furet and Ozouf, 710–15; Lucien Jaume, *Le Discours Jacobin et la démocratie* (Paris: Fayard, 1989), 18.
[68] A. Latreille and René Rémond, *Histoire du catholicisme en France: La Période contemporaine*, 2d ed. (Paris; Spes, 1962), 241–50; Roger Henry Soltau, *French Political Thought in the Nineteenth Century* (New York: Russell & Russell, 1959), 69–78.
[69] Comte to G. d'Eichthal, December 10, 1824, *CG*, 1:146. See also *Système*, 3:553–7.

minds" that would have moral, purifying consequences combined
both radical and conservative tendencies.[70]

Comte's sense of vocation was encouraged by Gustave d'Eichthal,
the man to whom he turned for friendship and support after Valat
refused to embrace wholeheartedly the positive science of society.[71]
D'Eichthal was six years Comte's junior and had been a brilliant
student at the Lycée Henri IV. He came from a Jewish banking
family, originally from Munich, but in 1817 he had followed his
mother's example and converted to Catholicism.[72] He and Comte
had become acquainted in late 1822, when Olinde Rodrigues, his
old childhood friend and a disciple of Saint-Simon, advised him to
hire Comte to give mathematics lessons to his younger brother
Adolphe. D'Eichthal described his first meeting with Comte:

> I will never forget this disorderly dwelling, this nearsighted man
> sitting up to answer me, and so absorbed in his own ideas and speech
> that he appeared not to perceive the real presence of his interlocutor.
> Yet Comte's reputation as a professor made me go beyond this
> impression.[73]

D'Eichthal decided to attend the lessons that Comte gave his
brother. Within a few months, positive philosophy displaced mathematics, and d'Eichthal said that he became "perhaps the first disciple of Comte, one of those whom he loved the most and who
devoted to him in return the most passionate affection."[74] He
became attracted to Comte's creed because he "admired the new
light that it shed on the history of humanity" and "quivered" at its

---

[70] Comte to G. d'Eichthal, November 24, 1824, *CG*, 1:137.
[71] The letters between Comte and d'Eichthal are reproduced in "Correspondance d'Auguste Comte et Gustave d'Eichthal," ed. Laffitte, 186–276; "Matériaux pour servir à la biographie d'Auguste Comte: Correspondance d'Auguste Comte et Gustave d'Eichthal (Suite)," ed. Pierre Laffitte, *RO*, 2d ser., 12 (May 1, 1896): 345–88. Volume "12" of the *RO* should be volume "13."
[72] Barrie M. Ratcliffe and W. H. Chalone, eds. and trans., *A French Sociologist Looks at Britain: Gustave d'Eichthal and British Society in 1828* (Manchester: University of Manchester, 1977), 109; G. d'Eichthal, "Notes sur ma vie," July 1868, Fonds d'Eichthal 14408, item 10, BA; Marquis de Queux de Saint-Hilaire, "Notice sur les services rendus à la Grèce par M. G. d'Eichthal," in Gustave d'Eichthal, *La Langue grecque* (Paris, 1887), 3; "Correspondance de Comte et d'Eichthal," ed. Laffitte, 187.
[73] Letter from d'Eichthal, no date or name of the person to whom he was addressing, reproduced in "Correspondance de Comte et d'Eichthal," ed. Laffitte, 190.
[74] Ibid.

"brilliant perspective of the future."[75] Thus in 1823 d'Eichthal switched his allegiance to the atheistic positive philosophy, which freed him from the constraints of religion. He had been worried about the possible ill effects that Catholic sexual proscriptions might have on him; his new faith, he hoped, would not hinder his relations with women.[76]

In March 1824 d'Eichthal went to Germany and in his first letter to Comte presented himself as his disciple, telling him that he had such a "decisive" influence on his life that he could not erase the traces even if he wanted to.[77] Comte eagerly adopted the role of counsellor and told him to study the areas in which he himself felt weakest: philosophy, physiology, and industry. He saw in d'Eichthal a collaborator who could provide him with knowledge he did not have time to acquire.[78]

Comte felt a great affinity with d'Eichthal. Like Louis Comte, d'Eichthal's father disapproved of his philosophical inclinations and insisted that he seek a traditional and lucrative profession. He also highly objected to his relationship with Comte, just as Comte's father had disliked Comte's association with Saint-Simon.[79] Comte encouraged d'Eichthal to get away from the "tutelage" of his father so that he could "become a man."[80]

Comte was sure that d'Eichthal had a true philosophical bent, and after consulting with Blainville, who confirmed his impression, he decided that d'Eichthal should no longer consider himself his student, but his colleague and friend.[81] He repeatedly told d'Eichthal with great warmth that he was the "only man" with whom he felt in such "perfect harmony."[82] Comte's delight in feeling close to this new friend, which was reminiscent of his previous friendship with Valat, reflected his deep sense of isolation and need to believe there was someone who understood him.

Despite claims about their equal relationship, Comte did not seem any more receptive to d'Eichthal's differing opinions than he was to Valat's. When d'Eichthal objected that Comte's ideas about political science in his fundamental opuscule were too "abstract" and would

[75] G. d'Eichthal to Resseguier, February 26, 1830, Fonds Enfantin 7644, fol. 163, BA.
[76] Ibid.; G. d'Eichthal, "Notice sur ma vie," 1869, Fonds d'Eichthal 14408, item 9, BA; G. d'Eichthal, "Notes sur ma vie."
[77] G. d'Eichthal to Comte, March 23, 1824, "Correspondance de Comte et d'Eichthal," ed. Laffitte, 191.
[78] Comte to G. d'Eichthal, May 1, June 6, December 10, 1824, *CG*, 1:79–80, 97, 140.
[79] Comte to G. d'Eichthal, May 1, 1824, *CG*, 1:85; G. d'Eichthal to Comte, April 19, 1824, and January 12, 1825, "Correspondance de Comte et d'Eichthal," ed. Laffitte, 195, 269.
[80] Comte to G. d'Eichthal, November 6, 1824, *CG*, 1:135.
[81] Comte to G. d'Eichthal, May 1, 1824, *CG*, 1:79.
[82] Comte to G. d'Eichthal, May 1, June 6, 1824, *CG*, 1:84–5, 93.

strike most people as metaphysical,[83] Comte retorted that his work was not meant for the common reader and he expected even the erudite to read it twice.[84] Although this time d'Eichthal retreated and admitted his mistake,[85] several months later, after he had read Kant's *Idea for a Universal History*, he criticized Comte again, this time for failing to make his objectives more explicit in the beginning of his work. He advised him to drop his introduction describing the present crisis and to state almost immediately that politics must become a positive science.[86] Comte argued that this approach would be too deductive and a priori.[87] Dismissing the warnings of both d'Eichthal and Valat, Comte showed that he did not care if his readers had difficulty reading his work, which he knew was obscure. His position contradicted his alleged aim of enlightenment and would end by alienating him from mainstream intellectual life.

Despite d'Eichthal's gratitude to Comte for having invited him to join him in the "career of positive philosophy," where he expected to find his "happiness," he yielded at the end of 1824 to his father's demands to lead a more practical life and accepted a position as a banking apprentice.[88] This was a real blow to Comte, who was genuinely astonished that d'Eichthal had repudiated his "mission." He urged him repeatedly to reconsider: "Your real vocation is incontestably for the scientific, or rather philosophic, career, whatever you say about it; I do not like your defiance in this regard."[89]

Comte's evident disappointment served only to alienate d'Eichthal further. In January 1825 he sent Comte three hundred francs in a letter warning him to find a way to support himself. In addition to telling him that success in the temporal world required more assiduity than Comte imagined, d'Eichthal announced that he was completely abandoning his philosophical studies in order to pursue his new career.[90] Yet despite his annoyance, d'Eichthal never lost his admiration for Comte. He wrote his brother in mid-1826, "I felt it was necessary to alienate myself from him [Comte] for the time

---

[83] G. d'Eichthal to Comte, May 11, 1824, "Correspondance de Comte et d'Eichthal," ed. Laffitte, 205.
[84] Comte to G. d'Eichthal, June 6, 1824, *CG*, 1:95.
[85] G. d'Eichthal to Comte, June 18, 1824, "Correspondance de Comte et d'Eichthal," ed. Laffitte, 226.
[86] G. d'Eichthal to Comte, August 22, 1824, "Correspondance de Comte et d'Eichthal," ed. Laffitte, 246–7.
[87] Comte to G. d'Eichthal, November 6, 1824, *CG*, 1:137.
[88] G. d'Eichthal to Comte, June 4 and 18, 1824, and January 12, 1825, "Correspondance de Comte et d'Eichthal," ed. Laffitte, 217, 270.
[89] Comte to G. d'Eichthal, December 10, 1824, *CG*, 1:140.
[90] G. d'Eichthal to Comte, January 12, 1835, "Correspondance de Comte et d'Eichthal," ed. Laffitte, 269–71.

being in order to avoid speculative ideas and to train myself for work, but I cannot stop admiring his talent and pitying the hardships that his superiority causes."[91] Even though the two remained friends, the excitement of constructing a new philosophy together had disappeared. Thus within the space of little more than a year, Comte had gained and lost his first close associate.

As Comte's appreciation of the extent of the spiritual crisis of his era deepened, he began referring directly to the philosophers of the "reactionary" school, namely, Maistre, Bonald, and Lamennais.[92] In the ferment of ideas after the Revolution, these theocrats were important for laying the basis of antiliberal thought in France.[93] Comte probably first became conversant with their doctrines when he worked for Saint-Simon, who always acknowledged his great debt to their ideas, particularly their stress on the value of the Middle Ages and the need to base social reorganization on a "systematic conception."[94] Yet it was only after his rupture with Saint-Simon that he turned to these writers to situate his thought philosophically. He sought to obliterate any trace of his mentor's influence by acknowledging his intellectual debt to Saint-Simon's sources rather than to Saint-Simon himself. Thus at this time he began to emphasize that Condorcet was his "immediate predecessor" and claimed that the main nineteenth-century figure who influenced him was Maistre.[95] This strategy can be glimpsed in a statement he later made to a friend in which he admitted that he had "absorbed" what was valuable in Maistre's works "spontaneously," that is, through Saint-Simon and other thinkers, and thus did not really need to read them.[96]

[91] Letter from G. d'Eichthal to A. d'Eichthal, April 20, 1826, Fonds d'Eichthal 14396, item 30, BA. See also a letter from d'Eichthal with no date and no name of the addressee, reproduced in "Correspondance de Comte et d'Eichthal," ed. Laffitte, 190.

[92] *Système*, vol. 4, "Appendice," 185. Comte also sometimes mentioned a minor figure, Baron d'Eckstein. See Auguste Comte, "Considérations philosophiques sur les sciences et sur les savants," *Le Producteur: Journal de l'industrie, des sciences et des beaux arts* 2 (1826): 459n1. In reproducing this article in the *Système*, Comte omitted the reference to d'Eckstein. See *Système*, vol. 4, "Appendice," 168.

[93] Holmes, *Benjamin Constant*, 222.

[94] For the impact of these writers on Saint-Simon, see Saint-Simon, *Catéchisme des industriels: Deuxième Cahier*, 172. Comte claimed to have been influenced by the reactionary school from the beginning of his career. *Catéchisme positiviste*, 32. Yet Roger Mauduit's statement that Comte and Saint-Simon definitely read Maistre around 1820 seems too categorical. Mauduit, *Auguste Comte*, 22, 27–8.

[95] Comte to G. d'Eichthal, August 5, 1824, *CG*, 1:106.

[96] Comte to M'Clintock, August 7, 1852, *CG*, 6:325.

Besides using the reactionary thinkers to deny the influence of his former mentor, Comte was reflecting the prevailing political mood of the mid-1820s. In 1824, with the ultras' electoral victory and the accession of the intensely religious Charles X to the throne, there was a vigorous Catholic revival, which Comte tried to use to his own advantage. We have seen how he curried favor with Villèle, the ultra minister, and wanted to demonstrate that his doctrine would fulfill the essential demands of the reactionaries' program.[97] Hoping to effect a synthesis that would transcend stale ideological debates and appeal to people tired of party politics, he had already staked his claim to the liberal tradition by linking his philosophy to that of Condorcet and the Idéologues (especially Cabanis and Destutt de Tracy). Now, he said, "from the political point of view, Condorcet had to be complemented for me by de Maistre."[98] He even placed Maistre's *Du pape* right next to Condorcet's *Esquisse* in his main library.[99] Moreover, he, like Saint-Simon, was inclined to join forces with the theocrats against the capitalist ethic underlying liberalism, which made him feel increasingly uncomfortable. Thus owing to socioeconomic tensions, the religious revival, and his split with Saint-Simon, which made him more open to other influences, he developed from 1825 a "growing respect for Catholicism."[100]

The idea of the reactionaries (particularly Maistre and Lamennnais) that most impressed Comte was that "moral anarchy" was the "great scourge" of the nineteenth century and derived from the absence of a general unifying doctrine.[101] According to him, the reactionaries were "perfectly correct" to point out that the "universal decadence of religious doctrines" had led to the most "abject" individualism, that is, egoism.[102] Inspired by their romanticization of the Middle Ages, he declared that the "fixed principles" and "regular spiritual order," which were the basis of medieval social unity, had been destroyed by the Protestant Revolution, with its stress on the individual. The result was that Europeans lived in an increasingly disorderly, materialistic, and corrupt world. Thus the Catholic reactionaries helped make Protestantism and its concomitant, individualism, his bêtes noires. Their critique of individualism and interest in uniformity reinforced Comte's animus against liberalism. He, like the theocrats, came to see liberalism as an antisocial doctrine, one that led to the atomization of society.[103] Most important of all, they taught him that the current violent crisis in Europe was *not* a regular or normal state. "Fixed, positive, and unanimous principles" could

[97] Comte to Valat, May 21, 1824, CG, 1:92.   [98] *Catéchisme positiviste*, 32.
[99] See "Bibliothèque Usuel I," in the Maison d'Auguste Comte.   [100] *Testament*, 9.
[101] Comte to Valat, December 25, 1824, CG, 1:147.
[102] Comte to Valat, March 30, 1825, CG, 1:156.   [103] Holmes, *Benjamin Constant*, 222.

be reestablished and in fact had to be to fulfill the "spiritual condition" for the continued existence of human society.[104] Maistre was the Catholic reactionary writer whom Comte most respected. He considered him the only distinguished nineteenth-century thinker – the "only thinker" after Condorcet and Gall to whom he owed "something important."[105] Three of Maistre's works impressed him: *Considérations sur la France*, *Les Soirées de Saint-Pétersbourg*, and especially *Du pape*, which he later included among the one hundred and fifty books in the "Positivist Library of the Nineteenth Century," the complement to the Positivist Calendar.[106] (These were the great books of civilization that he recommended should be read during the transition to positivism.) Given the dates of the editions of Maistre's works that Comte owned, he may have read them in 1821–2, while writing the fundamental opuscule.[107]

Comte found Maistre's arguments against "revolutionary dogmas" most valuable.[108] According to Maistre, anything that threatened social unity was pernicious. The Enlightenment philosophers' concept of the individual was dangerous because man could not be understood apart from the organic society in which he lived. The philosophes' promotion of the social contract, individual rights, and liberty had led to a harmful growth of egoism and pride. Moreover, their affirmation of the sovereignty of reason had destroyed social bonds and left people to suffer in an agitated state of unbelief.[109] Stressing man's basic spiritual need for a "vast and important theory," Maistre was convinced that a "great moral revolution" leading to a new religious age was about to begin.[110]

He considered human nature inherently weak and corrupt and insisted that people needed to be governed by a strong authority ruling a hierarchical society. Social solidarity and stability could

---

[104] Comte to Valat, December 25, 1824, *CG*, 1:147. See also Comte to G. d'Eichthal, December 10, 1824, *CG*, 1:146.

[105] Comte to M'Clintock, August 7, 1852, *CG*, 1:325. See also *Cours*, 1:852, 2:20; *Système*, vol. 4, "Appendice," 184–5.

[106] See Comte's library at the Maison d'Auguste Comte; "Bibliothèque Positiviste au dix-neuvième siècle," *Système*, 4:557–61. See also his explanation of the library, ibid., 405–6.

[107] Comte owned the 1821 edition of *Du pape* and the 1822 edition of the *Considérations sur la France*. Comte's personal library does not include a copy of Maistre's *Les Soirées de Saint-Pétersbourg*, published in 1821, but he was familiar with its arguments. See Comte's comments on the book's discussion of the destructive impact of the sciences on theology and metaphysics in *Système*, vol. 4, "Appendice," 154.

[108] Comte to M'Clintock, August 7, 1852, *CG*, 6:325.

[109] Joseph de Maistre, *Considérations sur la France*, 2d ed. (Paris, 1814), 59, 70; idem, *Du pape*, 2d ed., 2 vols. (Paris, 1821), 1:xl, 2:37; idem, *Soirées de Saint-Pétersbourg (les six premiers entretiens)*, vol. 4 of *Oeuvres complètes de J. de Maistre*, new ed., 14 vols. (1884–6), 108.

[110] Maistre, *Du pape*, xvii; idem, *Considérations*, 65–6.

certainly not be achieved without the unlimited power of the pope, the very embodiment of Catholicism and the source of all valid authority. Deprived of this strong spiritual ruler, Catholicism was "nothing more than a system, a human belief, incapable of entering into hearts and modifying them."[111] In fact, Maistre was less concerned with doctrine than with politics, that is, the way religion worked as an institution supportive of the social order.[112] Appreciative of his having demonstrated the importance of the institutional aspects of Catholicism, Comte most often referred to him as a political philosopher, not as a religious reformer, and strongly endorsed his ultramontanism as the only way to ensure the independence of papal authority from temporal government. He even approved of Maistre's support for the doctrine of papal infallibility because the concept of infallibility put an end to controversies, always a source of trouble to society.[113]

Furthermore, Comte believed Maistre was superior to Condorcet in his appreciation of the past, especially the Middle Ages. Maistre valued the intellectual and moral unity of that period and the way in which the pope had acted as a strong independent force, enlightening and counterbalancing the temporal power, ensuring order, and making political life more moral.[114]

In sum, Comte's system demonstrated Maistre's belief that a unifying spiritual doctrine and structure represented the key to social cohesion. Like Maistre, Comte believed that a strong spiritual power was not a loose intellectual body, but rather a tightly organized institution endowed with the mission of ensuring political and social existence.[115] Moreover, Maistre's concepts of the weakness of individual reason and the importance of faith were reflected in Comte's argument that it was possible to create unified opinions and a new "spiritual organization of society" only if "individuals" were not allowed "to apply their reason magisterially, as they do today, to

[111] Maistre, *Du pape*, 2:153.
[112] Richard Allen Lebrun, *Throne and Altar: The Political and Religious Thought of Joseph de Maistre* (Ottawa: University of Ottawa Press, 1965), 61, 123; Bernard Reardon, *Liberalism and Tradition: Aspects of Catholic Thought in Nineteenth-Century France* (Cambridge: Cambridge University Press, 1975), 20-2, 42; Emile Faguet, *Politiques et moralistes du dix-neuvième siècle*, 3 vols. (Paris, 1891-9), 1:4-5, 67; Berlin, "Joseph de Maistre and the Origins of Fascism," chap. in *The Crooked Timber of Humanity*, 91-174.
[113] Comte to Mill, April 5, 1842, *CG*, 2:44; *Cours*, 2:339-40.
[114] Comte to M'Clintock, August 7, 1852, *CG*, 6:325; *Système*, vol. 4, "Appendix," 154. See also *Cours*, 2:66-7.
[115] Comte's appreciation of Maistre's depiction of a strong spiritual power, or clergy, is particularly evident when he contrasts Maistre with Benjamin Constant. See Comte to G. d'Eichthal, November 6, 1824, *CG*, 1:137-8.

their beliefs"; they must believe in their natural superiors.[116] To both thinkers, individualism had worked against social order by destroying obedience.[117] Maistre thus reinforced Comte's emphasis on the limits of freedom of thought and discussion and his dislike of individual rights, popular sovereignty, the social contract, and political reforms.[118] Both believed that moral regeneration would come from an all-encompassing theory supported by a powerful spiritual authority. Though strong, the influence of Maistre on Comte should not be exaggerated, for he said that, before reading *Du pape*, he "had already produced . . . the essential equivalent from the progressive point of view" and thus could have "easily managed without it."[119]

Another counterrevolutionary thinker highly esteemed by Comte, at least between 1824 and 1826, was Lamennais.[120] Although he could never forgive him for later joining the leftists, Comte called Lamennais in December 1825 the "most rational philosopher" of the reactionary position.[121] At that time, Lamennais was still one of the most vigorous champions of the ultramontane cause.[122]

Between 1817 and 1823, Lamennais published *Essai sur l'indifférence en matière de religion*, which appeared in four volumes. Comte was familiar with this work, which he said was the "only book" of Lamennais that was "worthy to survive." He particularly prized Lamennais's characterization of the prevailing spiritual apathy – the "Western illness."[123] Denouncing Protestantism and the Enlightenment for promoting individualism and liberty of conscience, Lamennais pointed out that no one recognized authority any more: "The world is the prey of opinions: everyone wants to believe only himself and consequently obeys only himself. No more dependence, no more duties, no more ties." Religious indifference was as unnatural and destructive as moral and political apathy. To save the "social edifice"

---

[116] Comte to Valat, December 25, 1824, *CG*, 1:148. See also Berlin, "Maistre," 127, 134.
[117] Massimo Boffa, "La Contre-Révolution, Joseph de Maistre," in *The Transformation of Political Culture*, ed. Furet and Ozouf, 304.
[118] *Cours*, 2:613; Maistre, *Considérations*, 79.
[119] Comte to M'Clintock, August 7, 1852, *CG*, 6:325. Macherey also argues that Maistre's impact on Comte has been overstated. See Pierre Macherey, "Le Positivisme entre la Révolution et la Contre-Révolution: Comte et Maistre," *Revue de synthèse* 112 (January–March 1991): 41–7.
[120] Comte first mentions Lamennais in December 1824. Comte to Valat, December 25, 1824, *CG*, 1:147.
[121] *Système*, vol. 4, "Appendice," 186. See also Comte's comments on Lamennais, ibid., iv.
[122] Alec Vidler, *Prophecy and Papacy: A Study of Lamennais, the Church and the Revolution*, The Birkbeck Lectures 1952–3 (New York: Scribners', 1954), 44–58.
[123] The "P.S." in the letter from Comte to Audiffrent, 26 Charlemagne 67, N.a.fr. 10794, fol. 150v, BN.

from this widespread "uncertainty," or "anarchy of opinions," it was necessary to "reestablish authority," which would put "truth . . . back on its immutable base" and restore "order."[124] The health of society – its conduct and culture – thus depended on the stability of its doctrines and beliefs, which had to be set by a strong spiritual power. Church authority, particularly in education, had to be strengthened, and the independence of the clergy from the state guaranteed.[125] Like Lamennais, Comte denounced the isolation, confusion, and skepticism that arose from freedom of conscience. He too claimed that dogmatism was the natural state of man and that people needed an independent spiritual power.

To combat the allegedly destructive rationalism of his era, Lamennais also pointed out that truth in any area could not be determined by individuals, who were unable to verify everything they believed by rational demonstration. People had to believe simply on the basis of their faith, that is, on their willingness to accept the testimony of others. Not only theology but philosophy and science were necessarily authoritarian in their demand for passive obedience.[126] Perhaps reflecting Lamennais's influence, Comte in the mid-1820s expressed similar views. He took an increasingly authoritarian approach to scientific truth, emphasizing faith and the limited impact of rational demonstration. In fact, Comte's theocratic tendencies became so blatant that they would receive the approbation of Lamennais himself.

In spite of Comte's support for some of the ideas of the counterrevolutionaries, it is an exaggeration to number him among the founders of Christian politics.[127] His attitude toward them was far more ambivalent than some scholars claim.[128] While he strategically

---

[124] F. de Lamennais, *Essai sur l'indifférence en matière de religion*, vols. 1–4 in *Oeuvres complètes*, 12 vols. (Paris, 1836–7), 2:1v–lvi.

[125] Christian Maréchal, *La Jeunesse de Lamennais: Contribution à l'étude des origines du romantisme religieux en France au XIXe siècle* (Paris: Perrin, 1913), 672, 678, 694; Bénichou, *Temps des prophètes*, 122–3, 132–5; Vidler, *Prophecy and Papacy*, 45–57, 101; Jean-René Derré, *Le Renouvellement de la pensée religieuse en France de 1824 à 1834: Essai sur les origines et la signification du Mennaisisme* (Paris: C. Klincksieck, 1962), 724; Louis Le Guillou, *L'Evolution de la pensée religieuse de Félicité Lamennais* (Paris: Armand Colin, 1966), 38.

[126] Lamennais, *Essai*, 2:78, 89–97. See also Vidler, *Prophecy and Papacy*, 68, 70–4, 81, 85–9, 92–3; Derré, *Renouvellement*, 56–60; Douglas Johnson, *Guizot*, 36–7; Boas, *French Philosophies*, 128.

[127] Boas, *French Philosophies*, 92.

[128] Soltau, *French Political Thought*, 22; Mauduit, *Auguste Comte*, 32; Robert A. Nisbet, *The Sociological Tradition* (New York: Basic Books, 1966), 57–8. Robert Nisbet argues that Comte was instrumental in making the conservative ideas of this period an integral part of the discipline of sociology. See Robert Nisbet, "Conservatism and Sociology," *American Journal of Sociology* 58 (1952): 167, 172–3; idem, "The French Revolution and the Rise of Sociology in France," *American Journal of Sociology* 49 (1943): 156, 160–2. For a rejoinder

allied his thought to theirs to strengthen his appeal to all parties and was undoubtedly influenced by many of their ideas, he was very critical of their approach. He found that their doctrines shared the anarchical individualism of the age because they were so divergent and contradictory that they would cause chaos if put into practice.[129] Even their individual doctrines had inconsistencies. Lamennais, for example, supported liberty of worship, which contradicted his authoritarianism, and Maistre used "positive considerations," such as references to reason and natural law, to support his antiquated theological and metaphysical arguments.[130] Although Comte agreed with their call for a general doctrine and a strong spiritual power, he differed from them in envisioning a totally new spiritual order that recognized the achievements of progress and the needs of the future industrial-scientific society. In short, Comte did not approve of the reactionaries' revival of Catholicism, their disrespect for the achievements of the sciences, their return to the past and tradition, their establishment of a government of "throne and altar," their providential and degenerative views of history, and their absolutist judgments, which showed they were in "total disharmony" with their century. In fact, he worried that their efforts to restore the ancien régime would discredit his own plan to recreate a spiritual power.[131] Consequently, he declared that the reactionary solution to the problem of European reconstruction was "absolutely false" and futile.[132]

Furthermore, some of the concerns he shared with the reactionaries were also those of the liberals. They too criticized eighteenth-century revolutionary doctrines, worried about maintaining social order, warned about the possible "tyranny of the individual," and

to Nisbet's argument, see Siedentop, who points out that the counterrevolutionaries had no concept of social change and that the liberals made a greater contribution to sociology. Siedentop, "Two Liberal Traditions," 159–60. Another rejoinder can be found in Macherey, "Comte et Maistre," 47.

[129] *Système*, vol. 4, "Appendice," 186.   [130] Ibid., 157n1, 2, 185n1; *Cours*, 2:21.

[131] *Système*, vol. 4, "Appendice," 196–7n1.

[132] Comte to Valat, December 25, 1824, *CG*, 1:148. For more of Comte's criticisms of this school, see *Cours*, 2:20–4. For more information regarding the reactionaries (especially Maistre) and Comte, see Reardon, *Liberalism and Tradition*, 20–42; Soltau, *French Political Thought*, 15–24; Mauduit, *Auguste Comte*, 22–36; Faguet, *Politiques*, 1:1–67; Lebrun, *Throne and Altar*, 41–5, 49, 61, 64, 123, 156–8; Lévy-Bruhl, *Philosophie d'Auguste Comte*, 345–6; Zeitlin, *Rethinking Sociology*, 43–4, 50–3; Boas, *French Philosophies*, 85–93; Georges Goyau, *La Pensée religieuse de Joseph de Maistre* (Paris: Perrin, 1921), 195–210; Jean Lacroix, *La Sociologie d'Auguste Comte*, 2d ed. (Paris: Presses Universitaires de France, 1961), 20–5; Don Martindale, *The Nature and Types of Sociological Theory* (Boston: Houghton Mifflin, 1960), 61–2. Robert Nisbet is mistaken when he suggests that Bonald was Comte's favorite French conservative. Nisbet, "Conservatism," 89.

held a limited view of liberty, whose excesses they had witnessed during the Revolution. And some, such as Théodore Jouffroy, longed for a unitary social creed.[133]

THE LIBERALS

In his search for intellectual allies with no connections to Saint-Simon, Comte sought an association with someone his mentor disliked, François Guizot, who was the leader of the Constitutionals.[134] He had been recently dismissed from the government for his Protestantism and mildly liberal views, which made the triumphant ultras bristle. When Comte first came into contact with him, he was actively participating in the Protestant movement, writing articles for various journals, such as *Le Globe*, and working on histories of the Middle Ages and the English Revolution.[135]

The two men became acquainted because of Guizot's enthusiasm for the *Plan des travaux scientifiques*.[136] On April 19, 1824, Guizot wrote to Comte that while he usually found his contemporaries' books "empty," Comte's essay impressed him because it was so "full." Comte had left the "squalid ruts" where most people crawled and with a "single leap" had acquired "many truths."[137] Few works, Guizot said, had ever affected him so strongly, and he insisted on meeting Comte to advise him on additions to the *Plan*.[138]

During the latter part of 1824, Guizot and Comte became good friends. They met often to discuss current events, philosophical

[133] Soltau, *French Political Thought*, 32–8; Bénichou, *Temps des prophètes*, 33–4, 56–7.

[134] Saint-Simon accused him of vulgarizing his ideas. See Saint-Simon, *Du système industriel*, 192. Comte and Guizot may have first made contact through General Campredon, for in 1816, when the general became director of the Ecole Polytechnique, he sought to appoint Guizot professor of history and belles lettres, the post previously held by Andrieux. Yet like Campredon himself, Guizot was eventually disqualified because he was a Protestant. Campredon may have given Guizot a copy of the *Plan*. "Correspondants, amis et protecteurs d'Auguste Comte: Le Général Campredon," ed. Laffitte, 155.

[135] Douglas Johnson, *Guizot*, 1, 4, 6, 30–8, 121–2; Gordon Wright, *France in Modern Times*, 106; Charles H. Pouthas, *Essai critique sur les sources et la bibliographie de Guizot pendant la Restauration* (Paris: Plon, 1923), 4–5; idem, *Guizot pendant la Restauration: Préparation de l'homme d'état (1814–1830)* (Paris: Plon, 1923), 15–16, 102, 219, 335–63.

[136] Comte to Valat, May 21, 1824, CG, 1:92.

[137] Guizot to Comte, April 19, 1824, in [Pierre] Valat, "Document historique sur Guizot et Aug. Comte," *Actes de l'Académie Nationale des Sciences, Belles-Lettres et Arts de Bordeaux*: 1874, 3d ser. (Paris, 1875): 21. This letter is also reproduced in "De la circulation des ouvrages d'Auguste Comte: De l'opuscule fondamental," ed. Laffitte, 332.

[138] Guizot was so excited by Comte's *Plan* that he sent a copy to a friend in Leipzig. Gustave d'Eichthal to Comte, May 1, 1824, in "Correspondance de Comte et d'Eichthal," ed. Laffitte, 206.

matters, educational reforms, and their respective historical works.[139] Even in 1842, after their friendship had long ceased, Comte thought that Guizot's "philosophical conversations" of 1824 were far superior to anything he had written since.[140] Familiar with the German historical school, Guizot may have acquainted him with the thought of several of its members, such as Savigny, Heeren, Meyer, and Herder.[141] While Guizot gave Comte advice on his search for financial stability, Comte in turn sympathized with Guizot, who was feeling frustrated because his course at the Sorbonne had been closed in 1822 by the government in the wake of the Duc de Berry's assassination. The ultras were engaged in a campaign to purge the doctrinaires and to take control of education. Although Guizot was associated with Cousin, whose popular courses had also been suspended, Comte was sure that his "positive instruction" in history had served as a useful counterweight to Cousin's metaphysical philosophy.[142]

What drew Comte and Guizot together was their common interest in the regeneration of society and their conviction that contemporary political thought was stale and inappropriate. Comte commended Guizot in the *Cours* for his solid understanding that their era was one of "half convictions" and weak wills.[143] Concerned, like the counterrevolutionaries, about the rapid disintegration of beliefs, Guizot argued that the reorganization of society depended on the formulation of a philosophy elucidating the necessary principles of action. This philosophy had to be based on a new theory of society and morality and a sound knowledge of history.[144] Perhaps what initially appealed to Guizot in the *Plan* was Comte's insistence that history played an important role in the regeneration of society.[145]

---

[139] Comte to Tabarié, July 17, 1824, *CG*, 1:102; Comte to G. d'Eichthal, June 6, 1824, *CG*, 1:95; Douglas Johnson, *Guizot*, 88–154; Comte to Guizot, March 30, 1833, *CG*, 1:245. Comte's enthusiasm regarding his old teacher Encontre may have led Guizot to write about his achievements in a book on religion many years later: Guizot, *Méditations sur l'état actuel de la religion chrétienne*, 118, 123–9.

[140] Comte to Mill, June 19, 1842, *CG*, 2:52.

[141] Comte owned Savigny's *Histoire du droit romain au moyen-âge* and Heeren's *Manuel de l'histoire ancienne* and *Système politique de l'Europe*. He valued these three books enough to place them in his most important library. In the *Cours*, he praised this school for recognizing the importance of linking "in each historical epoch the entire legislation to the corresponding state of society." *Cours* 2:98. On Guizot's praises of Herder, see Comte to G. d'Eichthal, August 5, 1824, *CG*, 1:105–6.

[142] Comte to Valat, November 3, 1824, *CG*, 1:132. See also Comte to Valat, September 8, 1824, *CG*, 1:120.

[143] *Cours*, 2:60; see also 61n.

[144] Guizot, *Des moyens de gouvernement*, 44–5.

[145] Some of Guizot's books on history were familiar to Comte, who had in his library the 1819 edition of Guizot's translation of Gibbon's *Decline and Fall of the Roman Empire*, his

Likewise, Guizot's "historical erudition" impressed Comte, who believed it reflected a "rather pronounced positive intention."[146] Thus both Comte and Guizot sought to establish a new general doctrine that would go beyond the unacceptable theories of the counter-revolutionaries and the revolutionaries. They wanted to establish a politics and society of consensus, where moral duties would take precedence over individual rights and the social contract. The government, they agreed, should be in the hands of the experts, that is, an elite of rational men.[147]

At first, Comte aimed to convert Guizot to the positive system and cultivated him because he was an important figure. But he soon concluded that Guizot could not understand his system owing to his inadequate scientific education and his Protestantism; Guizot believed that each age required a religion and people had a profound need for God. Comte also attributed this religious attitude to Guizot's scientific ignorance, which made it impossible for him to grasp the distinction between theory and practice and therefore the importance of the separation of spiritual and temporal powers – the social application of this scientific principle.[148] Guizot wanted a strong temporal government, controlled by a new "legitimate aristocracy" consisting of members of the "middle class," whereas Comte felt the elite should include the scientists, who could check bourgeois greed and egoism.[149] In fact, he suspected that Guizot paid no heed to his social theories because he, Comte, had never been in government. Moreover, Comte was not as compromising as Guizot. He never followed Guizot in supporting the principle of heredity, especially the heredity of peers, or a constitutional monarchy.[150] Guizot did not share Comte's social conscience; he was basically a practical politician – one "corrupted" by power, according to Comte – who became well known for supporting the new status quo.[151] To Guizot, unlike Comte. "France [had] obtained from . . . [the Revolution] all that it needed."[152]

1822 *De Shakespeare à la poésie dramatique*, the 1824 edition of his *Essais sur l'histoire de France*, and his 1826 *Histoire de la Révolution d'Angleterre*. See Comte's library at the Maison d'Auguste Comte.

[146] Comte was referring to Guizot's *Essais sur l'histoire de France*, which he said was "probably his best production." Comte to Mill, April 5, 1842, *CG*, 2:42.

[147] Douglas Johnson, *Guizot*, 35–7, 51–60, 73–4, 77, 80–6, 438; Pouthas, *Guizot*, 323–4, 359–60; Guizot, *Des moyens de gouvernement*, 45; idem, *Histoire des origines du gouvernement représentatif en Europe*, 2 vols. (Paris, 1851), 2:139; idem, *Mémoires pour servir à l'histoire de mon temps*, 8 vols. (Paris, 1858–67), 1:158–9, 2:237–8.

[148] Comte to G. d'Eichthal, May 1, June 6, 1824, *CG*, 1:83–4, 96.

[149] Guizot, *Des moyens de gouvernement*, 217–18.　　[150] *Cours*, 2:156.

[151] Comte to G. d'Eichthal, June 6, 1824, *CG*, 1:96.

[152] Guizot, Review of *Annales de la session*, 275.

As so often happened when Comte was at odds with someone who resisted his proselytizing, he began to think that Guizot was acting contemptuously toward him. According to those who knew him, Guizot tended to impose his authority and his ideas on others, especially young writers, whom he liked to patronize.[153] Irritated by his sense of superiority and meddling, Comte felt Guizot was trying to become his protector "at a cheap price." He insisted on maintaining his independence. "I am very excited by fraternity, but I cannot bear paternity, especially in a philosopher."[154] After the problems with his father and Saint-Simon, Comte was leery of any attempts to dominate or exploit him, especially since he himself liked to be the dominant figure in relationships. The intellectual differences between Comte and Guizot and their personality clashes soon put an end to their relationship.

Nevertheless, Comte boasted to Valat in late 1824 that despite the fact that they were far from having the same doctrine, Guizot was the contemporary thinker with whom he shared the "most numerous and most important points of contact."[155] The fact that Comte felt closest to this conservative "liberal" thinker undermines the argument that associates him only with the Catholic thinkers.

Comte's statement to Valat suggests that he felt alienated from thinkers on the extreme Left. But in fact this was not entirely the case. He later told Mill that Charles Dunoyer had always been "one of my immediate predecessors," the one "who most merited all my sympathies." Although not as intelligent as Guizot, he was, according to Comte, more just and more conscientious. Of all the writers of the Restoration, he was the closest to the "true positive state."[156]

A classical liberal economist, Dunoyer had been the editor of *Le Censeur* and *Le Censeur européen* and had influenced Saint-Simon's views of industrial development.[157] While working for Saint-Simon, Comte became friends with Dunoyer and wrote at least one article for *Le Censeur européen* in 1819.[158] In 1825 Dunoyer published *L'Industrie et la morale considérées dans leurs rapports avec la liberté*, which

---

[153] Pouthas, *Guizot*, 165, 351.

[154] Comte to G. d'Eichthal, December 10, 1824, *CG*, 1:143. See also G. d'Eichthal to Comte, May 11, 1824, "Correspondance de Comte et d'Eichthal," ed. Laffitte, 206.

[155] Comte to Valat, November 3, 1824, *CG*, 1:132. Even after he became embittered by Guizot's behavior toward him, Comte had a fond memory of their early conversations. See Comte to Mill, June 19, 1842, *CG*, 2:52.

[156] Comte to Mill, February 28, 1845, *CG*, 2:333.

[157] Saint-Simon gave credit to Dunoyer for having pointed out that the industrial class should manifest its opinion. Saint-Simon, *Catéchisme des industriels: Deuxième Cahier*, 171.

[158] Anatole Dunoyer – Charles Dunoyer's son – had found a few letters from Comte to his father as well as some from his father to Comte. Laffitte copied them, but for some reason he never published them. All are now missing from the Maison d'Auguste Comte except

presented a history of the industrial regime to prove that "we become free only by becoming industrial and moral."[159] He sent Comte the first volume, signed with his "affectionate regards."[160] Although he found Comte authoritarian and too skeptical of the common person's ability to think critically and freely, he respected him and liked to exchange ideas with him.[161] They remained good friends until at least 1845, when Dunoyer sent him an autographed copy of his new book, *De la liberté du travail*.[162]

"Very impressed" by Dunoyer's works, Comte acknowledged that he owed to him "several useful" but "secondary" concepts.[163] He valued Dunoyer's laws of temporal progress, which showed the growth and superiority of industrial over military life and the close connection between the economy and moral and intellectual conditions. Most of all, Comte appreciated his demonstration that the liberal, industrial regime could never completely eliminate social inequalities because it depended on them for its development. Although disparities would decrease, there would always be a small number of free, rich, enlightened, and virtuous people and a great number of enslaved, poor, ignorant, and immoral persons.[164] Congratulating Dunoyer for disproving the doctrine of indefinite perfectibility and showing that the industrial regime would have as many "causes of disorder" as the military regime, Comte maintained that the temporal system would have to have recourse to a spiritual power to contain them.[165] His interest in this aspect of Dunoyer's thought reflected his own growing disenchantment with the reign of the industrialists whom Saint-Simon had once showered with praise.

---

for one Comte wrote in 1845 to Dunoyer. See A. Dunoyer to Laffitte, June 6, March 14, 1884, MAC.

[159] Charles-Barthélemy Dunoyer, *L'Industrie et la morale considérées dans leurs rapports avec la liberté* (Paris, 1825), 1. The book contained the series of successful lectures that Dunoyer had just given at the Athénée. Laffitte, "L'Athénée," 20.

[160] See the copy in Comte's library at the Maison d'Auguste Comte.

[161] See Dunoyer's annotations of Comte's *Plan* in "De la circulation des ouvrages d'Auguste Comte: De l'opuscule fondamental," ed. Laffitte, 329–32.

[162] Comte to Dunoyer, March 12, 1845, *CG*, 2:338–9. Dunoyer mentioned Comte several times in *De la liberté du travail*. At one point, he criticized Comte for not giving more weight to race in the development of civilization. See *De la liberté du travail ou Simple Exposé des conditions dans lesquelles les forces humaines s'exercent avec le plus de puissance*, 3 vols. (Paris, 1845), 1:75, 79, 81, 87–8, 91, 93.

[163] Comte to Dunoyer, March 12, 1845, *CG*, 2:339; Comte to M'Clintock, August 7, 1852, *CG*, 6:324; Comte to George Frederick Holmes, September 18, 1852, *CG*, 6:377. See also *Système*, 3:62, vol. 4, "Appendice," 208n1.

[164] Dunoyer, *L'Industrie et la morale*, 375. See Comte's reference to Dunoyer, *Cours*, 2:352; Comte to Dunoyer, March 12, 1845, *CG*, 2:339.

[165] *Système*, vol. 4, "Appendice," 207.

Although he considered Dunoyer a metaphysician whose conception of the government's role in regulating the economy was too negative, Comte showed his high regard for him when he placed him in the Positivist Calendar as an alternate for the great Adam Smith himself.[166] Like his tributes to Condorcet and Maistre, Comte's commendation of Dunoyer may have reflected his preference for conceding the influence of a respectable, nonmenacing thinker who had inspired Saint-Simon rather than acknowledging the impact of his former mentor himself.

One other liberal thinker to the left of Guizot impressed Comte: Benjamin Constant. Constant had influenced Saint-Simon, who was indebted to his political analyses, especially his examination of the Chamber's inability to make a budget in the national interest.[167] Comte called him a "philosopher full of wisdom."[168] It is evident that Constant's contrast between ancient and modern life and his denunciations of arbitrary government and censorship had an impact on Comte's early writings.

In the mid-1820s, Comte was interested primarily in Constant's arguments against the Catholic Church and his own evolution toward spiritualism.[169] Constant had begun his career as an atheistic disciple of the Encyclopedists, but owing to the influence of Herder, Schelling, and Schleiermacher and his own distressing breakup with Madame de Staël, he became a participant in the religious regeneration of the time. Comte owned the first two volumes of his history of religion, *De la religion considérée dans sa source, ses formes, et ses développements*, which appeared in 1824 and 1825.[170] Its anticlericalism made it a frequent target of attack by the theocrats Bonald, Maistre, and Lamennais.[171] Constant argued that religions changed in accordance with each generation's needs, and that after the dramatic social changes caused by the French Revolution, there had to be a corresponding transformation in the realm of beliefs.[172] Comte was not convinced by Constant's definition of religion as a vague sentiment common to all individuals, for it struck him as a typically Protestant concept. He preferred Maistre's theory that the power of religion came from its institutional, sacerdotal aspects.[173]

---

[166] Comte to G. d'Eichthal, November 24, 1825, *CG*, 1:175; Comte to Mill, February 28, 1845, *CG*, 2:333–4; *Système*, 4: Table B'.
[167] Saint-Simon, *Catéchisme des industriels: Deuxième Cahier*, 170.
[168] Comte to Armand Marrast, January 7, 1832, *CG*, 1:232.
[169] Comte to G. d'Eichthal, November 6, 1824, *CG*, 1:137.
[170] Comte also owned a copy of Constant's novel, *Adolphe*.
[171] Fontana, *Benjamin Constant*, 105.
[172] Benjamin Constant, *De la religion considérée dans sa source, see formes, et ses développements*, 5 vols. (Paris, 1824–31), 1:3; Derré, *Renouvellement*, 67–8, 74, 85, 91, 93, 96.
[173] Comte to G. d'Eichthal, November 6, 1824, *CG*, 1:137.

Nevertheless, Constant's theory of religious development proved to be as important to Comte as Dunoyer's description of temporal development.[174] Constant employed a new term that was almost never used at this time: "fetishism." Derived from Portuguese, it had been invented by Charles de Brosses in his *Du culte des dieux fétiches* (1760) to denote a universal stage of mental consciousness, that of primitive man.[175] Probably influenced by Brosses, Constant used the term "fetishes" to refer to the "material divinities" worshiped by primitive people during the infancy of humanity.[176] In adoring concrete objects and animals, primitive man believed that he could persuade the power animating them to act for him. This system gradually improved morality.[177] The Greeks then transformed fetishism into the next, more abstract stage of religion, polytheism, which reflected the development of society. Religion's third and most abstract stage was theism. *De la religion* was important because it considered fetishism and polytheism to be historical antecedents of monotheism instead of later, degenerate forms of the worship of one god.[178]

Although Comte may have heard of fetishism from a work he had read in his youth, the Grimm–Diderot correspondence, which discussed Brosses's work, it seems more likely that his theory of religious development was influenced by Constant.[179] In the same month that he said he was going to read Constant, he wrote "Considérations philosophiques sur les sciences et les savants," in which he mentioned for the first time "fetishism" as the original stage of development before polytheism.[180] Neither he nor Saint-Simon had

---

[174] Comte to G. d'Eichthal, November 24, 1825, *CG*, 1:174. Comte heard that the erudition of Constant's second volume was as impressive as that of the book recently published by George Friedrich Creuzer, the famous German scholar of myths. Comte assumed that it would in fact be superior because it would be free from "metaphysical and theological hotchpotch." Ibid.

[175] The neologism "fetishism" does not seem to have been used very often in the late eighteenth and early nineteenth centuries; its usage was not accepted by the French Academy until 1835. Manuel, *Eighteenth Century Confronts the Gods*, 186–7.

[176] Constant, *De la religion*, 2:237.   [177] Ibid., 237, 282.

[178] Warren Schmaus, "A Reappraisal of Comte's Three-State Law," *History and Theory* 21 (1982): 249.

[179] Comte to Armand Marrast, January 7, 1832, *CG*, 1:232. See also Emile Bréhier, *The Nineteenth Century: Period of Systems, 1800–1850*, vol. 6 of *The History of Philosophy*, trans. Wade Baskin (Chicago: University of Chicago Press, 1968), 18–19. Comte mentions the Grimm correspondence in the essay that he wrote in 1816 – "Mes Réflexions: Humanité, vérité, justice, liberté, patrie," *Ecrits*, 425. Manuel, in his *Eighteenth Century Confronts the Gods*, suggests that Comte derived the term directly from Brosses and used it in the *Système* of the 1850s. But it seems that Comte borrowed it from Constant. He also used it earlier than in the *Système*, since it appears in his opuscule of 1825. See Manuel, *Eighteenth Century Confronts the Gods*, 186–7, 208.

[180] *Système*, vol. 4, "Appendice," 139.

ever used the term before. Thus Comte was beginning to integrate the ideas of liberal thinkers – not just those of the theocrats – into his own system.

GERMAN PHILOSOPHERS

Comte's search for philosophers with whom he could ally himself went beyond the confines of France. In March 1824 he began to receive letters from Gustave d'Eichthal, who was occupied with business matters in Munich but soon afterward moved to Berlin to make contact with German intellectuals.[181] He sent Comte reports not only on German political and intellectual life but also on his progress in stimulating interest in positive philosophy.

In circulating the fundamental opuscule, d'Eichthal gave one copy to Friedrich Buchholz, an acclaimed political essayist, who was a professor at the military school of Brandenburg. Buchholz published two-thirds of it in the July, August, and September issues of his political journal, *Hermès*. But Comte and d'Eichthal were disappointed that he did not review it, and they soon decided he was not a suitable German contact.[182]

Comte's work did, however, receive a review in the September 21, 1824, issue of the *Leipziger Literatur-Zeitung*. The only review of the *Plan* that ever appeared, it was written by Wilhelm Krug, who had held Kant's chair at the University of Königsberg and was now professor of philosophy at Leipzig. He criticized Comte for failing to go beyond empiricism and neglecting to establish a more solid basis for the new science of politics.[183] Since both d'Eichthal and Comte had a low opinion of Krug's works, they were not particularly disturbed by his remarks.[184]

---

[181] Ratcliffe and Chalone, eds. and trans., *French Sociologist*, 131.

[182] G. d'Eichthal to Comte, March 23, April 19, May 11, July 2, August 22, November 18, 1824, "Correspondance de Comte et d'Eichthal," ed. Laffitte, 192, 193–4, 206, 228, 245, 258–9; Comte to G. d'Eichthal, June 6, 1824, *CG*, 1:96; Fréderic Bucholz [*sic*] to Comte, September 28, 1825, in "Relations d'Auguste Comte avec l'Allemagne," ed. Laffitte, *RO* 8 (1882): 228; Hayek, *Counter-Revolution*, 159, 236n280.

[183] [Wilhelm Krug], Review of *Système de politique positive*, by Auguste Comte, in *Leipziger Literatur-Zeitung*, no. 231 (September 21, 1824): 1846–8. The French translation of this article can be found in "Relations d'Auguste Comte avec l'Allemagne," ed. Laffitte, 233–6. Laffitte was mistaken in dating the article September 27. See also G. d'Eichthal to Comte, November 18, 1824, "Correspondance de Comte et d'Eichthal," ed. Laffitte, 257; Comte to d'Eichthal, December 10, 1824, *CG*, 1:145; "Relations d'Auguste Comte avec l'Allemagne," ed. Laffitte, 228.

[184] Comte already knew of Krug because Guizot had given him a copy of Krug's book on political science several months before. Comte to G. d'Eichthal, June 6, 1824, *CG*, 1:95–6; G. d'Eichthal to Comte, May 11, 1824, "Correspondance de Comte et d'Eichthal," ed. Laffitte, 206.

According to his letters, d'Eichthal was principally excited about his discovery of German philosophy and its relation to the positive system. Before his departure, Comte had shown an interest in learning about German philosophy, a subject much discussed at the time. Many French thinkers during and after the Revolution were looking to Germany for new ideas. Some were seeking to correct the skepticism and rationalism that seemed to have led to the destruction of the revolutionary period.[185] Madame de Staël, Pierre Cabanis, Benjamin Constant, and Victor Cousin were just some of the French thinkers who helped to awaken interest in German philosophy.[186] Comte was familiar with Cousin's lectures on Kant at the Sorbonne, though he thought Cousin had misunderstood him, and he had read with d'Eichthal in late 1823 passages from Fichte's works, which he considered disappointingly metaphysical.[187] He was also learning about German philosophy from Guizot, who was particularly knowledgeable about Kant and Herder.[188] But it was d'Eichthal who most encouraged his interest in German philosophy. At a crucial turning point in his development, Comte was eager to evaluate another philosophical system with no connections to Saint-Simon.[189] And d'Eichthal was delighted to help his master, the genius who was going to redeem society.

In his letters, d'Eichthal told Comte that the German philosophers were very knowledgeable about the sciences and had eliminated all theological ideas from their philosophy. In fact, they resembled Comte in trying to "place the existing philosophy in harmony with the progress of the sciences." Their philosophy, which he called "Kantism," represented the best "metaphysical" preparation for the

---

[185] Comte to G. d'Eichthal, August 5, 1824, *CG*, 1:106; Rearick, *Beyond the Enlightenment*, 12; Spitzer, *French Generation*, 84.

[186] Boas, *French Philosophies*, 171–96; F. M. Barnard, *Herder's Social and Political Thought* (Oxford: Clarendon Press, 1965), 170.

[187] Nevertheless, Fichte earned a position as a substitute for Kant in the Positivist Calendar. *Système*, 4: Table B′. See also F. Sartiaux, "Kant et la philosophie française du XVIIIᵉ siècle: Kant et la Révolution," *La Revue positiviste internationale* 21.6 (November 1, 1918): 153; Maximilien Vallois, *La Formation de l'influence Kantienne en France* (Paris: Félix Alcan, 1932), 286–320; Comte to Valat, November 3, 1824, *CG*, 1:132; Comte to G. d'Eichthal, November 6, 1824, *CG*, 1:135–6.

[188] D'Eichthal even jokingly referred to Guizot as "German" and encouraged Comte to consult him. G. d'Eichthal to Comte, May 11, 1824, "Correspondance de Comte et d'Eichthal," ed. Laffitte, 206. In his *Tableau philosophique et littéraire de l'an 1807*, Guizot had developed the principles of Herder's *Ideen zur Philosophie der Geschichte der Menschheit*, and he frequently praised Herder in Comte's presence. Comte to G. d'Eichthal, August 5, 1824, *CG*, 1:105. See also Douglas Johnson, *Guizot*, 334; Pouthas, *Guizot*, 13–14.

[189] Comte to G. d'Eichthal, May 1, 1824, *CG*, 1:81–2.

triumph of positive philosophy.[190] It was not as advanced or original because it was too abstract, speculative, and indifferent to politics. Addicted to pure philosophy, German philosophers sought the "source of the development of all natural phenomena" in the "development of what they call 'the Spirit,'" which was nothing other than a "metaphysical personification of the laws of nature."[191]

Despite their neglect of politics, d'Eichthal claimed that some German philosophers had tried to apply scientific ideas, such as the concept of natural laws, to social phenomena. Fichte was one example he cited, but the two thinkers he admired most were Herder and Kant.

HERDER

In June 1824 d'Eichthal informed Comte of his new "discovery" – Herder's *Ideen zur Philosophie der Geschichte der Menschheit*.[192] Although d'Eichthal found his work as a whole too theological, he regarded Herder's "scientific philosophy" as "extremely positive" and commended his efforts to establish a "positive science."[193] Herder not only had seen the "connection between the physical and physiological sciences and social science" but had been able to demonstrate this connection as much as was possible "in his time."[194]

Originally published in four volumes in 1784–91, Herder's masterpiece was not well known in France until it was translated into French by Edgar Quinet in 1827.[195] To give Comte an idea of Herder's work, d'Eichthal sent him extracts of Heinrich Luden's famous introduction to an 1821 edition of the *Ideen*, which discussed Herder's philosophy of history and nature and his concept of

---

[190] G. d'Eichthal to Comte, June 6, 1824, June 4 and 18, 1824 (one letter), "Correspondance de Comte et d'Eichthal," ed. Laffitte, 216, 219.

[191] G. d'Eichthal to Comte, July 24, 1824, "Correspondance de Comte et d'Eichthal," ed. Laffitte, 231.

[192] D'Eichthal to Comte, June 18, 1824, "Correspondance de Comte et d'Eichthal," ed. Laffitte, 223.

[193] D'Eichthal to Comte, June 6, June 18, 1824, "Correspondance de Comte et d'Eichthal," ed. Laffitte, 216, 223.

[194] D'Eichthal to Comte, June 18, 1824, "Correspondance de Comte et d'Eichthal," ed. Laffitte, 223.

[195] Actually Benjamin Constant was one of the few Frenchmen familiar with Herder's philosophy. He even referred to Herder in his *De la religion* to support his principle that enlightenment brings about religious improvements. G. A. Wells, *Herder and After: A Study in the Development of Sociology* (The Hague: Mouton, 1959), 248. On the influence of Herder in France, see Henri Tronchon, *La Fortune intellectuelle de Herder en France* (Paris, 1920).

the unity of humanity.[196] Yet Comte had an opportunity to take a closer look at the *Ideen,* for during the summer of 1824 d'Eichthal sent him two different packets containing forty-three pages of his own translations of passages he had selected from Herder's work.[197] Later, he would also send him translated passages from the works of Kant and Hegel.

Pierre Laffitte, the head of the positivist movement after Comte's death, mentioned at least twice in the *Revue occidentale,* the organization's journal, that d'Eichthal's translations of passages from the works of Hegel, Kant, and Herder existed in the Positivist Archives, but he never discussed their contents.[198] Although he scrupulously published most of the other important material in the Positivist Archives, he was not interested in making d'Eichthal's translations available to the public for fear they would rival Comte's thought and detract from his originality.[199] After Laffitte's death, the manuscripts of these translations were lost. As a result, biographers of Comte have always relied on his own statement in the *Cours* that he had never read the works of Herder, Kant, or Hegel "in any language," and they dismissed the possible impact of German philosophy on his development.[200]

One day while going through a closet full of unclassified, dusty papers in the museum located in Comte's former apartment, I discovered the faded pages that d'Eichthal had appended to a letter written to Comte on November 18, 1824.[201] The letters between Comte and d'Eichthal had supposedly been reproduced by Laffitte in the *Revue occidentale* in 1896, but these attached pages had been omitted. They were translations of some sketches of a course that Hegel had given at the University of Berlin on the philosophy of history in 1822–3. In a black box containing Laffitte's sundry notes, I then found the translations that d'Eichthal had made of passages

---

[196] D'Eichthal to Comte, July 24, 1824, "Correspondance de Comte et d'Eichthal," ed. Laffitte, 231; Wells, *Herder,* 155.

[197] Containing twenty-six pages, the first packet, which will be called "Manuscript 1," was sent June 18, 1824, and was received by Comte in late July 1824. The second packet, of seventeen pages, which will be designated "Manuscript 2," was sent July 23 and was received August 2. The packets contained the table of contents and passages from the preface; book 1, chaps. 1, 3, and 4; book 2, chap. 4; book 4, chap. 7; book 12, chap. 6; book 14, chap. 6; book 15, chap. 1; and book 20, chap. 6. See also d'Eichthal to Comte, June 18, July 24, 1824, "Correspondance de Comte et d'Eichthal," ed. Laffitte, 223, 230, 231, 233; Comte to d'Eichthal, August 5, 1824, *CG,* 1:104.

[198] "Relations d'Auguste Comte avec l'Allemagne," ed. Laffitte, 227. See also Pierre Laffitte, "Nécrologie: M. Gustave d'Eichthal," *RO* 16 (May 1, 1886): 385–6.

[199] "Relations d'Auguste Comte avec l'Allemagne," ed. Laffitte, 224.   [200] *Cours,* 2:479.

[201] See the packet entitled "Lettres de d'Eichthal à A. Comte: Copies faites par d'Eichthal," MAC.

from Herder's *Ideen* and Kant's *Kritik der Reinen Vernunft* (the 1787 edition).[202] Refuting Comte's famous statement, they help to establish the extent of his knowledge of German philosophy.

D'Eichthal's passages from Herder's work were the most extensive.[203] They showed that the history of mankind should have its own philosophy and science because everything else in the world did. Herder sought to establish the scientific approach to the philosophy of history, for, like Comte, he believed that the scientific method could produce social consensus. His criticism of metaphysical statements as nonsense led d'Eichthal to exclaim that he was a great "antimetaphysician."[204]

Yet the *Ideen* was infused with a religious fervor that was at odds with this enthusiasm for a scientific history grounded on concrete experience. Herder believed in a divine plan and sought to discern God's intentions in nature and in the development of the species. He explained that when he personified nature in his book, he was alluding to God, and when he discussed the "organic forces of creation," he did not want his readers to imagine that he was referring to "occult qualities."[205] D'Eichthal did not elaborate, but these "organic forces" were an allusion to Herder's famous concept of *Kraft*, which represented the unifying principles of growth in nature. Its significance seems to have escaped d'Eichthal's notice, for despite Herder's insistence on empiricism, this concept was completely metaphysical.[206]

D'Eichthal avoided as much as possible the religious aspects of the *Ideen*, which he knew would repel Comte, and instead concentrated on Herder's belief that history and nature formed an organic, harmonious whole because man was an integral part of nature.[207] To illustrate Herder's conviction that an understanding of man's total environment was crucial for grasping the history of his actions, d'Eichthal included passages relating to astronomy and physiology.

---

[202] I also found excerpts of Buchholz's *Darstellung eines neuen Gravitations Gesetzes* (1802) and *Über die Natur des Gesellschaft* (1810), which d'Eichthal had also sent to Comte.

[203] A more detailed description of the Herder manuscripts can be found in Mary Pickering, "New Evidence of the Link between Comte and German Philosophy," *Journal of the History of Ideas* 50 (July–September 1989): 443–63.

[204] D'Eichthal to Comte, June 6, 1824, "Correspondance de Comte et d'Eichthal," ed. Laffitte, 216.

[205] Herder, Preface, "Manuscript 1," 3.

[206] F. M. Barnard, *Herder's Social and Political Thought*, 38, 52.

[207] Robert T. Clark, Jr., *Herder: His Life and Thought* (Berkeley and Los Angeles: University of California Press, 1969), 303; Emile Bréhier, *The Eighteenth Century*, vol. 5 of *The History of Philosophy*, trans. Wade Baskin (Chicago: University of Chicago Press, 1967), 183; Max Rouché, Introduction to Johann Gottfried Herder, *Idées pour la philosophie de l'histoire de l'humanité* (Paris: Aubier-Montaigne, 1962), 7.

As we have seen, Comte had studied these two subjects in depth at the Ecole de Médecine in Montpellier, the Paris Observatory, and the Collège de France, and he felt they had the greatest impact on intellectual development because questions about the world and man had always attracted the most attention.[208] Both he and Herder emphasized the continuity between man and his physical and organic environments.[209]

Herder maintained that the "philosophical history of the human race" had to begin with astronomy because it was from "celestial forces" that the earth derived "its properties, its form, and its power to organize and preserve creatures."[210] Herder's theory coincided with Comte's classification of the sciences, which began with astronomy because "the general laws of celestial phenomena are the first foundation of . . . knowledge."[211] Society could not be understood unless its celestial environment was taken into account.

In emphasizing that the earth was only a "star among the stars" and was nothing without its connections to the rest of the universe, Herder was also arguing that man should feel a sense of modesty: "Thus the scene and the sphere of activity of my race are as well determined and circumscribed as the mass and course of the earth on which I must pass my life."[212] D'Eichthal underlined this passage, remembering that in the "Sommaire appréciation" Comte had explained that astronomy proved that man was not the center of the universe.[213]

As for physiology, Herder believed that just as one had to examine the earth's position among the stars, so one had to determine man's place among the animals. A creationist in the tradition of Leibniz, he believed in the continuity of forms beginning with a single, original prototype.[214] Because all beings had a similar structure, one could learn about the traits of the human species by studying them in the other species. Comparative anatomy gave to man the "guiding thread that leads him *to himself* through the vast labyrinth of organic creation."[215]

---

[208] *Cours*, 1:453.

[209] Frederick Copleston, *A History of Philosophy*, vol. 6, part 1, *Modern Philosophy: The French Enlightenment to Kant* (1960; Garden City, N.Y.: Doubleday, Image Books, 1964), 200–1.

[210] Herder, Book 1, chap. 1, "Manucript 1," 5.   [211] *Cours*, 1:309.

[212] Herder, Book 1, chap. 1, "Manuscript 1," 5, 9. See also Rouché, Introduction to Herder, *Idées*, 9.

[213] *Système*, vol. 4, "Appendice," 15. See also *Cours*, 1:666.

[214] Herder, Book 2, chap. 4, "Manuscript 1," 1; Bréhier, *Eighteenth Century*, 183; Clark, *Herder*, 305–6.

[215] Herder, Book 2, chap. 4, "Manuscript 1," 15.

Comparative anatomy also played a crucial role in Comte's philosophy because it was a key part of physiology, the basis of social physics. Sharing Herder's conviction that the human being could not be understood in isolation, he emphasized that every organism had a similar anatomic structure, that it was "indispensable to envisage man as a term of the animal series," and that the "comparison of the different classes of living beings" should be "regularly employed in the study of man."[216] Unaffected by Lamarckian transformism, which he considered too anarchical, Comte therefore supported the old theories of continuous linear development and the chain of being that strongly resembled Herder's.[217]

The two men's common interest in physiology led them to stress the interdependence of phenomena in both nature and history. A passage sent by d'Eichthal clearly shows Herder's opposition to the mechanistic theories of the Enlightenment: "In the physical world, everything holds together that exercises a common or reciprocal action in order to produce, preserve, or destroy. It is not different in the physical world of history."[218] He was convinced that the natural and historical worlds were marked not only by interrelationships but by change. Moreover, like natural phenomena, historical occurrences did not take place by chance, for accidental events seemed meaningless and arbitrary. In keeping with his belief in a divine plan, his vision of historical development was both teleological and deterministic: "There happens everywhere on our earth everything that must happen there."[219]

Without clarifying this fundamental law of history, the *Ideen* celebrated the "prodigious diversity" that marked life on earth.[220] Struck by the differences between peoples and between historical periods, Herder scorned those who refused to recognize the value of change and variety and who dreamed of converting the earth to one philosophy or one religion:

> We must consider as the will of nature not what man is among us or even less what he must be according to the conceptions of some dreamer; but what he is everywhere on the earth and at the same time what he is particularly in each climate. We do not want to seek or find for him a favorite form or country.[221]

[216] *Système*, vol. 4, "Appendice," 98. See also *Cours*, 1:699.
[217] *Cours*, 1:775–7; J. Lessertisseur and F. K. Jouffroy, "L'Idée de série chez Blainville," *Revue d'histoire des sciences* 32.1 (1979): 25–42; Allal Sinaceur, ed., Introduction to lessons 40 to 45, in *Cours* 1: 658–9.
[218] Herder, Book 4, chap. 6, "Manuscript 1," 21.
[219] Herder, Book 12, chap. 6, "Manuscript 1," 18–19.
[220] Herder, Book 1, chap. 4, "Manuscript 2," 9.   [221] Ibid., 10.

Repudiating the French philosophes' characterization of previous periods as times of darkness, Herder felt that each event had its own meaning and value. He was thus a firm believer in relativism.

Comte's philosophy of history had much in common with Herder's. It had the same emphasis on organicism that made the *Ideen* a significant landmark in intellectual history. In discussing interrelationships, Comte stated at one point in the fundamental opuscule:

> In effect . . . all the classes of social phenomena develop simultaneously and under each other's influence in such a manner that it is absolutely impossible to explain the development of any of them without having previously conceived in a general manner the progression of the whole.[222]

As reflected in the law of three stages, all of society represented an organic being in the process of development. In addition, Comte's necessitarianism resembled Herder's. Sharing Herder's admiration for Leibniz, he had declared in his fundamental opuscule that society had usually been as well directed as the "nature of things permitted."[223] Like Herder's, his system was both deterministic and teleological. The law of three stages described the evolution that every civilization inevitably went through as well as a future positive age of splendor, which was definitive. Finally, Comte's philosophy resembled Herder's in its relativism and historicism. Comte too criticized the philosophes' disparagement of previous ages and believed social science should become relativistic to end disputes about the perfect government.[224]

Comte was unaware that Herder's relativism actually went further than his own. D'Eichthal failed to convey the degree to which Herder was an innovator on this issue. Herder had written the *Ideen* partly to discredit complacent eighteenth-century theories of progress – especially Condorcet's. He went beyond Comte by rejecting the philosophes' theory that progress represented a development from religion and superstition to secular morality. D'Eichthal also did not translate the passages where Herder seemed to have Condorcet in mind when he rebutted the hypothesis that destined man to an "indefinite growth of his faculties" and activities and viewed much of history as a preparation for a goal that only the last generation could realize.[225] In a further effort to adjust Herder's ideas to please Comte, d'Eichthal omitted from his translation of parts of book 14, chapter

---

[222] *Système*, vol. 4, "Appendice," 135.

[223] Isaiah Berlin, *Vico and Herder: Two Studies in the History of Ideas* (New York: Random House, Vintage Books, 1977), 174.

[224] *Ecrits*, 454, 483–9; *Système*, vol. 4, "Appendice," 109–19.

[225] Herder, *Idées*, 141; Rouché Introduction to Herder, *Idées*, 16.

6, the section in which Herder renounced the view that "the Romans existed . . . to form above the Greeks a more perfect link in the chain of civilization."[226] Instead of discussing the stages of progress in terms of a linear growth of scientific knowledge and material improvement, Herder examined the particular way each culture developed as a whole, struggled to achieve its own standard of improvement, and manifested a distinct form of humanity that was valuable in itself. He had a much more relativistic concept of progress, which was, in F. M. Barnard's words, an "'operative ideal' related to a specific social setting at a given time."[227]

D'Eichthal did not stress Herder's approach, because it would have challenged Comte's idea that since man was naturally inclined to self-improvement, all peoples necessarily went through similar, all-embracing stages of development. The political differences among countries could be attributed to the fact that they were temporarily in different stages of civilization.[228] Whereas Herder believed that each period of time and each people should be respected for the uniqueness of its path of development and its different achievements, Comte thought one could discover the general laws of history only by disregarding the idiosyncrasies of human evolution and the "diversities observed from people to people."[229] Sharing the philosophes' belief in France's special civilizing mission, he was enthusiastic about the *uninterrupted* march of the whole human species toward *one* final, universal, and uniform regime, which would increase the happiness of everyone by applying all the means possible to obtain prosperity.[230] Comte's teleology was more limited than Herder's because it posited a universal goal for all of mankind and failed to appreciate the blossoming of specific cultures.

Despite Herder's relativism, his philosophy of history did have certain progressive aspects, which were exaggerated by the passages that d'Eichthal sent to Comte. D'Eichthal's interpretation would in fact seem unorthodox to some historians, who would argue that Herder was not at all a fervent believer in progress.[231] Nevertheless,

---

[226] Herder, *Idées*, 266.

[227] F. M. Barnard, *Herder's Social and Political Thought*, 129–34, 148. See also Copleston, *French Enlightenment*, 165–6, 199; Berlin, *Vico and Herder*, 190–1; Bréhier, *Eighteenth Century*, 182; Kenneth Bock, "Theories of Progress, Development, Evolution," in *A History of Sociological Analysis*, ed. Tom Bottomore and Robert Nisbet, 55; Robert Nisbet, *Idea of Progress*, 352.

[228] *Système*, vol. 4, "Appendice," 91, 97, 126.   [229] Ibid., 131.   [230] Ibid., 47, 90.

[231] Franklin L. Baumer, *Modern European Thought: Continuity and Change in Ideas, 1600–1950* (New York: Macmillan, 1977), 296–7; Berlin, *Vico and Herder*, 209. On the problem of reconciling Herder's progressive approach and his belief in relativism and pluralism, see ibid., 208–9; Copleston, *French Enlightenment*, 205–6; Frank E. Manuel and Fritzie P. Manuel, *Utopian Thought in the Western World* (Cambridge, Mass.: Harvard University Press, Belknap Press, 1979), 523.

instead of emphasizing Herder's interest in nationhood, the *Volk*, or primitive cultures, d'Eichthal translated the last parts of the *Ideen* that embraced the older ideas of progress, looked forward to the future harmony of nations united by education and a common constitution, and praised the leadership and civilization of Europe. The material sent by d'Eichthal concentrated on the rise since the Middle Ages of a new social class busy in the sciences, arts, and useful activity and prone to challenging the anachronistic clerics and knights. He underlined the passage in which Herder attributed European "excellence" to "*the activity and spirit of invention, the sciences, and the community and emulation of efforts.*"[232] In this way, d'Eichthal gave Comte the impression that Herder depicted in his particular fashion the development of the positive age from the medieval communes' battle for freedom. Most important, he suggested that Herder's relativism was as narrow as Comte's with similar absolute standards of judgment. As a result, he reinforced Comte's already strong feelings of Eurocentrism and his esteem for the sciences and industry as two sources of the progress of civilization.

The culminating part of Herder's *Ideen* was that every man had to work for the improvement of "humanity." D'Eichthal was so entranced by this emphasis on humanity that he underlined the word every time it appeared in his translation of book 15, chapter 1. It has been notoriously difficult to determine what Herder meant by "humanity."[233] D'Eichthal tried to explain to Comte in the margin of the manuscript that "humanity" referred to "all of the functions of human nature" and was equivalent to what Condorcet called the "perfection of the species."[234] Ignoring Herder's animus against Condorcet, d'Eichthal sought to lure Comte into seeing a line of continuity between Condorcet's thought and Herder's.

According to Herder, God made man a "god on earth" and placed his destiny – the improvement of humanity – in his own hands. "Humanity" was a product of history and was also innate in man. Every person at all times, impelled by the "interior and exterior needs of his nature," aimed to realize the potential, ideal constitution of his species – *Humanität* – by a better use of his human characteristics and institutions.[235] In this way, he extracted "from his own nature all that can produce what is noble and excellent." The vaguely progressive, enlightened tendency of Herder's work was evident when he described the "law of human destiny" in the following way: "Nature . . . has given man as a goal not the maintenance of despots

---

[232] Herder, Book 20, chap. 6, "Manuscript 1," 25.   [233] Berlin, *Vico and Herder*, 193.
[234] Herder, Book 15, chap. 1, "Manuscript 2," 14.
[235] Herder, Book 15, chap. 1, "Manuscript 2," 16, 17. See also Copleston, *French Enlightenment*, 167, 201.

Herder

285

and traditions but the perfection of humanity."[236] As already noted, it is doubtful that Herder always believed in the future perfection of mankind, but at least some passages of the *Ideen* gave the impression that because the desire for advancement was deeply rooted in human nature, the species marched toward some overall goal of *Humanität*, a product of all societies in all periods of time.[237]

The concept that later resonated throughout positive philosophy was this idea of humanity. Condorcet had frequently alluded to "humanity" in terms of the mass of the human species, and Comte later acknowledged in the *Cours* that his "necessary hypothesis" of a single people experiencing the three stages of history was based on Condorcet's use of this "rational fiction."[238] Yet Herder gave the idea of humanity a new significance by redefining it in two ways, whose originality was underlined by Professor Heinrich Luden in his introduction to the *Ideen*.[239] First, it connoted the unity of all peoples throughout the world. Second, it referred to the continuity of history, whereby each generation transmitted its contributions to an enduring and growing civilization.[240] The twin concepts of the unity and continuity of humanity would play key roles in Comte's system, which began in the *Cours* to center on the idea of humanity as the supreme reality. In this work, Comte equated the study of humanity with sociology, which he said would represent

the mass of the human species, whether in the present, the past, or even the future, as increasingly constituting in every respect, both in space and in time, an immense and eternal social unity, whose diverse individual or national organs, which are continually united by a close and universal solidarity, inevitably cooperate . . . in the fundamental evolution of humanity.[241]

Like Herder's approach to *Humanität*, Comte's view of humanity fused the past, present, and future and involved the contributions of each generation to the improvement of society.[242] Comte called this idea of humanity a "truly capital and very modern conception," one that would be the "basis of positive morality."[243] It is therefore

[236] Herder, Book 15, chap. 1, "Manuscript 2," 16, 17.
[237] Berlin, *Vico and Herder*, 190–1. [238] *Cours*, 2:123.
[239] D'Eichthal to Comte, July 24, 1824, "Correspondance de Comte et d'Eichthal," ed. Laffitte, 232.
[240] On Herder, see F. M. Barnard, *Herder's Social and Political Thought*, xviii–xx, 37, 83, 98, 109, 123, 129, 143, 148, 171. Barnard's statement that Comte was not influenced by Herder is not so evident. Also see Berlin, *Vico and Herder*, 145–213.
[241] *Cours*, 2:136; see also 109–10, 123.
[242] F. M. Barnard, *Herder's Social and Political Thought*, 108; *Système*, vol. 4, "Appendice," 30.
[243] *Cours*, 2:136.

possible that Herder's conviction that "what is most noble for man is humanity" was one source of inspiration for Comte's creation of the Religion of Humanity.[244]

In his portrayal of Herder's thought to Comte, d'Eichthal did not concern himself with its complexities or ambiguities.[245] He was most eager to highlight Herder's idea of the perfection of humanity without discussing his doubts about the eighteenth-century doctrine of perfectibility. D'Eichthal did not engage in any subtle analyses of the *Ideen* or even introduce Comte to many of the concepts that made Herder a key figure in intellectual history. As a consequence, Comte was not familiar with Herder's stress on *Kraft*, the uniqueness and intrinsic value of primitive cultures, kinship, pluralism, localism, decentralization, nationhood, language development, or the feeling of belonging. He had only a slight sense of Herder's celebration of unity in diversity, his hatred of uniformity, and his dislike of general laws and facile, rationalist abstractions masking the individuality of each culture and each era.[246]

In sum, as d'Eichthal was deeply honored to be Comte's colleague, he seems to have chosen his extracts from Herder to reassure his mentor of the validity of the positive philosophy that they were going to develop together. Mainly interested in giving Comte a picture of Herder that would confirm and reinforce his own point of view, he avoided the delicate problem of reconciling Herder's progressive tendencies with his emphasis on relativism, his Eurocentrism with his pluralism, his depiction of the future brotherhood of nations with his strong feelings of nationalism, his determinism with his endorsement of voluntarism, and his attraction to the scientific method with his belief in an unverifiable plan of history. D'Eichthal could not bring up these contradictions because they were also present in Comte's philosophy. The fundamental problem with both Herder and Comte is the limited place they left in their systems for human initiative in shaping the advance of society. Advocating a resignation to the laws of the universe and history, both philosophers skirted the border of fatalism.[247] Yet the weakness of Comte's and Herder's philosophies did not interest d'Eichthal.

[244] Herder, Book 15, chap. 1, "Manuscript 2," 26.
[245] On the difficulties involved in interpreting Herder, see Copleston, *French Enlightenment*, 206; Berlin, *Vico and Herder*, 153, 208, 213; F. M. Barnard, *Herder's Social and Political Thought*, xix; H. B. Nisbet, *Herder and the Philosophy and History of Science* (Cambridge: Modern Humanities Research Association, 1970), 1–3.
[246] H. B. Nisbet, *Herder*, 8–16; Rouché, Introduction to Herder, *Idées*, 10, 15; Clark, *Herder*, 315–16; Robert Nisbet, *The Idea of Progress*, 270; Berlin, *Vico and Herder*, 145, 153, 175–6, 195, 213–16.
[247] Herder, Book 1, chap. 1, "Manuscript 1," 8; F. M. Barnard, *Herder's Social and Political Thought*, 126, 147, 171; A. Gillies, *Herder* (Oxford: Basil Blackwell, 1945), 92.

Since Comte made most of his comments about Herder after receiving only the first packet, his reaction to Herder's philosophy as a whole is not clear. What is certain, however, is that Comte was not fooled by d'Eichthal's interpretation of Herder as a scientific thinker.[248] He warned him that he had exaggerated the elements of positive philosophy in the *Ideen*.[249] After all, Herder's trust in a divine plan was theological, while his tendency to personify nature and to substitute *Kraft* for first causes represented the essence of the Comtean definition of metaphysics.

Taking the cues that d'Eichthal had already given him in evaluating German philosophy, Comte interpreted the Herder manuscripts in such a way as to affirm his sense of superiority. He declared that his great advantage over Herder was that he had united the practical and theoretical points of view.[250] Herder could not attain this perspective because of three deficiencies. First, his education had not been "*completely and exclusively*" scientific.[251] After his experience with Saint-Simon, whose formal education had been almost nonexistent, Comte was convinced that the instruction that he had received at the Ecole Polytechnique had given him a matchless edge in clear, scientific thinking. For the rest of his life, whenever he disagreed with someone, he was quick to blame his opponent's deficient, that is, nonscientific, education.[252] Second, Herder had lived in Germany, a country too enamored of theory, whereas he, Comte, lived in France, which was concerned with both speculation and immediate utility.[253] Third, Herder had died before the French Revolution (or so Comte mistakenly believed) and thus had not been forced to think about the practical realm. Experiencing the anarchy created by the Revolution, theorists since 1789, according to Comte, had more "complete" conceptions because they were forced to reflect for the first time in a scientific and extremely urgent manner on the progressive reorganization of the social and political realm.[254]

Comte used Herder to flatter himself at a moment in his life when he feared he would be accused of being an unoriginal parasite of Saint-Simon's doctrine. He was convinced that only he could solve the "crisis" stemming from the French Revolution because only his social science offered a scientific and *constructive* solution.[255] It alone

---

[248] Comte to d'Eichthal, November 6, 1824, *CG*, 1:136.
[249] Comte to d'Eichthal, August 5, 1824, *CG*, 1:105. [250] Ibid., 107.
[251] Comte to d'Eichthal, August 5, 1824, *CG*, 1:107.
[252] See Comte's comments on Guizot, Comte to d'Eichthal, June 6, 1824, *CG*, 1:96–7.
[253] Comte to d'Eichthal, December 9, 1828, *CG*, 1:202.
[254] Comte to d'Eichthal, August 5, 1824, *CG*, 1:107; see also *Système*, 1: 11, 336; vol. 4, "Appendice," 108–9.
[255] *Système*, vol. 4, "Appendice," 48.

was "complete" because it had the "practical goal" of conceiving the new social system that best conformed to the state of civilization.[256]

Despite his judgment that Herder was too metaphysical, abstract, and removed from political reality, Comte was excited to have discovered him. He immediately defended him against Luden, who criticized the *Ideen* for being unclear and superficial.[257] Comte called Herder "distinguished" and unique among German philosophers, for their ideas, he said, were generally not nearly as close as his to positive philosophy.[258] Eager to read all of the volumes of the *Ideen*, he urged d'Eichthal to translate it in its entirety so that he could use Herder's details and insights as "material" for his own philosophy. Moreover, if Herder's philosophy were better known in France, it could lay the groundwork for the acceptance of the more advanced positive system.[259]

Comte's desire to appropriate Herder's ideas was motivated partly by the fact that he was completely swayed by d'Eichthal's perception of Herder as a keen believer in progress. D'Eichthal criticized Herder only for failing to establish in specific terms the "chain of the different degrees of civilization," even though he demonstrated the existence of stages of history "almost in the same way that Condorcet did."[260] As a result, Comte called Herder the "predecessor of Condorcet, my immediate predecessor."[261] To a certain extent, he was again altering his own intellectual development to obscure his indebtedness to Saint-Simon. Appearing in d'Eichthal's picture as a generalist with a wide knowledge of the sciences and history and a belief in progress, Herder fulfilled in many respects Comte's requirements for the positive philosopher. Consequently, Herder offered him the opportunity of having another "spiritual father."[262] Thus Comte gave him a position in the Positivist Calendar.

Because of the human being's mysterious reactions to his or her emotional and intellectual environment, questions of influence are extremely complex, if not insolvable. Nevertheless, the incorporation of Herder into the "Positivist Pantheon" in the Calendar indicates the impact that Herder may have had on the evolution of Comte's thoughts.[263] Herder's espousal of the scientific method in social studies, his interest in studying the life of the community

[256] Ibid., 108.   [257] Comte to d'Eichthal, August 5, 1824, *CG*, 1:105.
[258] Comte to d'Eichthal, November 6, 1824, *CG*, 1:136.
[259] Comte to d'Eichthal, August 5, 1824, *CG*, 1:105–6.
[260] D'Eichthal to Comte, July 24, 1824, "Correspondance de Comte et d'Eichthal," ed. Laffitte, 231n1.
[261] Comte to d'Eichthal, August 5, 1824, *CG*, 1:106.
[262] Comte, *Système*, 3:xv; vol. 4, "Appendice," 72n1.
[263] Comte, *Calendrier positiviste*, 12, 18, 33.

rather than that of the individual, his concept of the vaguely pro-gressive, organic development of humanity, his relativistic and determinist approach to history, his concern with showing the inter-relations of natural phenomena and the interaction of natural and social phenomena, his conviction that nothing could be understood apart from the whole, his emphasis on the continuity between man and both his physical and organic environments, and his desire to synthesize the study of the past and that of nature combined to strengthen Comte's own tendencies.[264] In his future works, Comte would develop Herder's concept of *Humanität*. In short, Herder rein-forced the approach to the philosophy of history that Comte had already adopted from Condorcet and Saint-Simon.

KANT

D'Eichthal's revelations about Herder and German philosophy in general were a source of wonder to Comte. Basing his judgment largely on what d'Eichthal told him, Comte believed German meta-physics was the most advanced philosophy to have appeared in the past hundred years. Germany seemed, moreover, to be the only country where "positive scientists" were clearly inclined toward philosophy.[265] He was so sure of being well received there that he wanted to have his own work translated and published in Berlin.

Nevertheless, he suspected that "Kantism" was not as free of the-ology as it claimed to be. The triumph of the positive system might be hindered by the German neglect of practice, concepts like the Absolute and the a priori, the notion of a logical method that was "independent of all application," vague moral obligations, and the stress on abstract social systems not grounded in any particular civilization.[266]

D'Eichthal sought to allay Comte's fears by claiming that Kant's ideas were very close to his own and, indeed, often reflected the "highest degree of positive philosophy."[267] In his effort to dissuade Comte from dividing German philosophy between a historical sec-tion (consisting of the works of Herder, Heeren, Savigny, and Meyer) that was close to positive philosophy and a metaphysical section (comprising the ideas of Kant and Fichte) that was antagonistic to it, he summarized Kant's works and sent him translations of the *Idea for a Universal History* and parts of the *Critique of Pure Reason*. These,

---

[264] F. M. Barnard, *Herder's Social and Political Thought*, 371; Arnaud, *Le "Nouveau Dieu,"* 133.
[265] Comte to G. d'Eichthal, August 5, 1824, *CG*, 1:105.   [266] Ibid., 106.
[267] G. d'Eichthal to Comte, November 18, 1824, "Correspondance de Comte et d'Eichthal," ed. Laffitte, 259.

together with Cousin's lectures and some extracts from the two *Critiques* that he had read previously, appear to have been the main source of Comte's knowledge of Kant.[268]

D'Eichthal claimed that Kant's smaller works were the least metaphysical. His *Perpetual Peace* stated that general peace had to be established before the "revolution of the human species" could begin.[269] His *Idea for a Universal History* demonstrated the need for a "scientific history of Humanity." It was "exactly the sketch" of Comte's opuscule of 1824 and was in some respects clearer because, according to d'Eichthal, it immediately got to the main point, which was that human phenomena, including civilization, could be reduced to natural laws. Having proved this, it showed that the establishment of a science consisting of these laws was essential to the progress of society.[270]

Comte was eager to learn more about Kant's two smaller treatises and asked d'Eichthal to translate them.[271] In late November, he received d'Eichthal's translation of Kant's *Idea for a Universal History from a Cosmopolitan Point of View*.[272] Calling for a deterministic, teleological approach to the past to make history scientific, Kant argued that although man seemed to have a free will, his actions were ultimately determined by universal laws because nature never worked without a plan. A great philosopher should discover within the seemingly chaotic course of human affairs a design of nature that people *unconsciously* realized throughout history. Moreover, since each organic being was destined to develop its natural capacities to the fullest and man was a naturally rational being with a short life, his full development could be achieved only in the species. Therefore, the historian's subject matter had to be mankind, not the individual. Kant urged the writing of this "philosophical" and "universal" history to illustrate the ever-growing rationality, enlightenment, cosmopolitanism, and morality of the human species. It would help predict

---

[268] *Cours*, 2:479; Comte to G. d'Eichthal, November 6, 1824, *CG*, 1:136. Comte begged d'Eichthal to translate the entire two *Critiques*, but d'Eichthal said that it would be an enormous task and that it was in any case being undertaken by Cousin. G. d'Eichthal to Comte, November 18, 1824, "Correspondance de Comte et d'Eichthal," ed. Laffitte, 259.

[269] G. d'Eichthal to Comte, November 18, 1824, "Correspondance de Comte et d'Eichthal," ed. Laffitte, 259.

[270] G. d'Eichthal to Comte, August 22, 1824, "Correspondance de Comte et d'Eichthal," ed. Laffitte, 244, 248.

[271] Comte to G. d'Eichthal, November 6, 1824, *CG*, 1:136.

[272] D'Eichthal's translation does not exist at the Maison d'Auguste Comte. Kant's *Idea for a Universal History from a Cosmopolitan Point of View* can be found in Immanuel Kant, *On History*, ed. Lewis White Beck, trans. Beck, Robert E. Anchor, and Emil L. Fackenheim (Indianapolis, Ind.: Bobbs-Merrill, 1963), 11–26.

the future and console the present generation about its own woes. Most important, it would stimulate the realization of nature's plan for the "civic union of the human race" and thus its design for the fulfillment of mankind.[273]

Comte was astounded by Kant's *Idea for a Universal History*, which he read and reread "with infinite pleasure," concluding that its "details" reflected the "positive spirit."[274] Kant's philosophical approach to the history of the human species, his insistence on scientific laws of progress, and his interest in the unity of humanity bolstered Comte's convictions.

In fact, his reading of Kant was almost a humiliating experience. Never had he lavished or would he lavish so much praise on another thinker. He could not get over the fact that Kant excelled not only as a philosopher but also as a historian. The originality and merit of Condorcet began to diminish immediately, for Kant's conception of development was "just as strong and even in some respects clearer." Even Comte's own achievement seemed less striking. He admitted to d'Eichthal:

If I had known it [the essay] six or seven years earlier, it would have spared me the effort [of writing my own]. . . . Today I thank my lack of erudition, for if my work, such as it is now, had been preceded . . . by the study of Kant's treatise, it would have lost much of its value in my eyes.

He added, "After reading this [treatise of Kant], I hardly find . . . any value [in my own work] other than that of having systematized and fixed the conception sketched out by Kant without my knowledge." Comte believed his own "most distinct" achievement was simply to have discovered the law of three stages. Since it showed the chain of historical facts and stressed the growth of man's reason, he asserted that it seemed to be the "basis of the work whose execution Kant had recommended."[275] In a way, then, Comte was admitting that his history was just as determined, teleological, and providential as the one that Kant wanted written.[276] Moreover, d'Eichthal's warning to him to make his own history even more deterministic would not be lost on him.[277] Despite its scientific and objective airs, Comte's

[273] Ibid., 23–6. See also William A. Galston, *Kant and the Problem of History* (Chicago: University of Chicago Press, 1975), 209–61; Lewis White Beck, Introduction to Kant, *On History*, vii–xxvi.
[274] Comte to G. d'Eichthal, December 10, 1824, *CG*, 1:143.
[275] Ibid. [276] Delvolvé, *Réflexions*, 53–4.
[277] In an article that he wrote in 1825, Comte praised Kant's "very remarkable" work for having "formally established that social phenomena must be regarded as being as reducible to natural laws as all the other phenomena of the universe." *Système*, vol. 4, "Appendice," 157.

system would increasingly become, as one critic said, a "vast poem of human destiny" whose "finalistic faith" was undeniable.[278]

Comte and d'Eichthal also discussed Kant's *Critique of Pure Reason*. D'Eichthal explained that Kant wanted the moral sciences to follow the example of the physical sciences and not surpass the limits of experience.[279] Kant argued, in d'Eichthal's words, that we could never have any "*absolute* knowledge of things" and that "all that there was of the Absolute, of the a priori in ourselves was only our modes of perception of phenomena, the processes of our mind." Because all of our knowledge came from experience through the "intermediary of these constant processes," we could not reason about anything that was not an "object of the senses."[280] There could be no rational demonstration of such dogmas as the existence of God, the immortality of the soul, and the freedom of the will. But in the *Critique of Practical Reason* Kant declared that these dogmas must be allowed as "simple *postulata*" in order for moral and social laws to be conceived.[281] Comte later agreed with d'Eichthal that Kant's use of inaccessible absolutes to ensure morality on the grounds of social necessity was hypocritical.[282]

At some point, d'Eichthal sent Comte his own translations of parts of the *Critique of Pure Reason*.[283] As mentioned before, I found them scattered among the pages of the Herder manuscript that I discovered in a box of Laffitte's notes.[284] Like the Herder manuscript, the newly discovered translations of Kant's masterpiece offer a glimpse of the possible influence of German philosophy on Comte's development. They reveal that Comte was not telling the truth when he told John Stuart Mill that he had never read Kant but only guessed "his general conception from some very imperfect bits of information."[285]

Dealing with Kant's epistemology, these selections covered his

---

[278] Delvolvé, *Réflexions*, 54.

[279] G. d'Eichthal to Comte, August 22, 1824, "Correspondance de Comte et d'Eichthal," ed. Laffitte, 244.

[280] G. d'Eichthal to Comte, November 18, 1824, "Correspondance de Comte et d'Eichthal," ed. Laffitte, 258.

[281] G. d'Eichthal to Comte, August 22, 1824, "Correspondance de Comte et d'Eichthal," ed. Laffitte, 244.

[282] G. d'Eichthal to Comte, November 18, 1824, "Correspondance de Comte et d'Eichthal," ed. Laffitte, 259; *Système*, 3:606. See also Comte to G. d'Eichthal, December 10, 1824, *CG*, 1:144.

[283] "Relations d'Auguste Comte avec l'Allemagne," ed. Laffitte, 227.

[284] See the original manuscript of the selections from Kant's *Critique*, MAC. In the manuscript, the "*Einleitung ch. VII*" that follows "*Einleitung IV*" is a mistake. It is really *Einleitung V*. These passages correspond to Immanuel Kant, *Kritik der Reinen Vernunft*, 2d ed., with an introduction by Benno Erdmann (Leipzig, 1880), 5–13, 34, 37–48, 69–76.

[285] Comte to Mill, December 23, 1843, *CG*, 2:223.

distinction between theoretical reason and practical reason, his discussion of analytical and synthetic judgments, and his theory of the
two sources of knowledge – the *Sinnlichkeit* (sensibility) and the
understanding.[286] Basically they showed that Kant wanted to formulate a critique of reason, which would enumerate the fundamental
a priori concepts of pure knowledge and thereby show in what sense
a science of metaphysics was possible. Convinced that objects were
subordinated to the human way of knowing, that is, to the human
mind, he stated that he was not concerned with the things-in-them-
selves, which were real but remained unknown to us because they
could never be objects of experience. (Even the Absolute could not
be known because it went beyond human sense experience.) Instead,
he was interested in our mode of perception of these objects insofar as it was possible in an a priori manner. Space and time were, for
example, a priori forms of perception. Disregarding to some extent
the subtlety of Kant's arguments about the *phenomena* and *noumena*,
d'Eichthal wrote, "Thus what we have wanted to show is this: that
all our perceptions are only perceptions of *phenomena*; that the things
in themselves have no relationship with what we perceive."[287]
    With these pages in front of him, Comte had a fairly good intro-
duction to Kant's theory of the senses, but because he did not have
an opportunity to read the next sections of the *Critique*, he was less
familiar with Kant's theories of the Categories and the Ideas, especially his important conception of causality. He had, however, some
idea of the latter, for he referred to it in the *Système*.[288]
    Though at the outset delighted with Kant's historical approach,
Comte was ambivalent about his philosophy, especially because of
the way it had been popularized in France. When Valat pointed out
similarities between the positive system and Cousin's "Kantism,"
Comte angrily replied that there was an "absolute opposition" between the "general spirit" and "method" of his own positive philosophy and that of Kant. Yet he did concede that there was "in some
respects, a certain analogy between the tendency of my works and
that of the most general ideas of Kant."[289]
    Although at first he liked to stress the differences between himself

---

[286] D'Eichthal sent Comte passages from Kant's preface in the second edition and chapters
4–7 of the Introduction as well as certain paragraphs from "General Observations on
Transcendental Aesthetic," which was heading 8, section 1, part 1 of the first portion of
the *Critique*, entitled "Transcendental Doctrine of Elements."

[287] See the page with the title "Transcendental Aesthetik." The pages in the manuscript are
not numbered.

[288] Comte merely said that Kant had summed up Hume's dissertation against causality. *Système*,
3:588.

[289] Comte to Valat, November 3, 1824, *CG*, 1:132.

and Kant, later he referred frequently to him to support his ideas. And it was not the *Idea for a Universal History* but the *Critique of Pure Reason* that always emerged in his discussions.[290] Despite the gaps in his knowledge of Kantian thought, Comte apparently wanted to profit from the prestige of his philosophy.

What most affected Comte was Kant's theory of the limits of knowledge. Echoing Kant, Comte wrote that conceptions were the result of a "continual commerce between the world that furnished the matter and man who determined the form."[291] Thus Kant's *Critique of Pure Reason* helped Comte to understand that scientific laws were only "hypotheses" constructed by man with "external materials" and confirmed by observation; they amounted to no more than "approximations of a reality that could never be rigorously understood."[292] Comte went so far as to note the positive advantages of the mind's limitations, arguing that it had a "certain speculative liberty," which it could use to satisfy "its own inclinations – whether they be scientific or aesthetic – by rendering our conceptions more regular and even more beautiful, without being any less true."[293] Thus inspired by Kant, Comte gave the mind considerable creative powers and acknowledged the role of aesthetics in its deliberations.

Recognizing the "fundamental dualism between the spectator and the spectacle," Kant also deepened Comte's understanding of relativity and the subjective side of human existence.[294] Comte credited Kant with the "great logical notion" that our opinions are both subjective and objective because our mind is active and passive at the same time.[295] Kant destroyed the artificial, "metaphysical" division between observation and reasoning by showing that these two functions worked together simultaneously.[296] This was one step toward Comte's theory that the emotions influenced intellectual activity. In short, Kant's theories helped Comte to wend his way between a purely idealistic position and a thoroughly empirical one.

Comte later prided himself on realizing Kant's effort "to escape directly from the philosophic Absolute."[297] He felt he improved Kant's notion of an "objective and subjective" reality by grounding it in a biological theory showing that man's ideas were affected, on

---

[290] Comte referred to Kant's *Critique* especially in lesson 58 of the *Cours*, the "Second Conversation" of the *Catéchisme*, and the first and third volumes of the *Système de politique positive*.

[291] *Catéchisme positiviste*, 85.

[292] *Système*, 2:32, 33; *Cours*, 2: 729. Delvolvé exaggerated when he suggested that Comte was not preoccupied by the limits of science. Delvolvé, *Réflexions*, 47.

[293] *Catéchisme positiviste*, 86.   [294] *Système*, 3:588.

[295] Ibid., 1:441, 712. See also *Traité philosophique d'astronomie populaire*, 34.

[296] *Système*, 1:712.   [297] *Cours*, 2:727.

the one hand, by his milieu, that is, the physical and social environment, which acted on him, and, on the other hand, by his organism, that is, his own living body, which was sensitive to this action. Thus besides man's innate mental dispositions, internal and external variations, which were reminiscent of sensationalist theories, influenced his ideas and made them relative.[298] Knowledge came from this interplay between sensory perceptions and innate faculties.[299] Kant's problem was that he had considered the mind too much in isolation. Our conceptions were not only "human phenomena" but "social phenomena" resulting from "collective evolution."[300] According to Comte, positive philosophy had a better picture of the relativity of knowledge because it showed how the "collective intelligence of humanity" changed throughout time, whereas Kant had focused on the *individual* intellect, which he believed was immutable.[301] Thus Comte recognized that our conceptions were always affected by changing social forces and could never be considered fixed or definitive.

As seen in his references to Kant's desire to contain the Absolute and to establish an "objective reality" and "internal laws" (instead of categories), Comte's understanding of Kant was superficial. In fact, it is doubtful that Comte thoroughly understood Kant's antirealist position. Although Comte was against extreme empiricism, which gave excessive priority to the object, and extreme rationalism, which gave too much prominence to the subject, he often appeared close to maintaining that the thing that is perceived exists just as the spectator perceives it, whereas Kant would never suggest that the relations between two bodies exist outside the observer's mind.[302] To him, such relations derived from the "Categories" of the mind. Finding any hint of subjective "idealism" in this matter repugnant since it threatened "collective life," Comte seemed far more eager for the exterior world to regulate the subjective processes of the mind than Kant was.[303] In the *Catéchisme positiviste*, he wrote, "Our principal theoretical merit consists of improving sufficiently this natural subordination of man to the world so that our mind becomes the faithful mirror of the exterior order whose future results can henceforth be foreseen according to our interior operations.[304]

---

[298] *Catéchisme positiviste*, 85.

[299] M. J. Hawkins, "Reason and Sense Perception in Comte's Theory of Mind," *History of European Ideas* 5 (1984): 153.

[300] Comte, *Traité philosophique d'astronomie populaire*, 25. [301] *Cours*, 2:728.

[302] See *Système*, 1:439, 441. On Comte's comprehension of Kant, see Arnaud, *Le "Nouveau Dieu,"* 218–19, 261–7. On his arguments against empiricism and rationalism, see M. J. Hawkins, "Reason and Sense Perception," 159.

[303] *Catéchisme positiviste*, 85; *Système*, 2:32. [304] *Catéchisme positiviste*, 85.

Although Comte admitted that we could never fully know external reality, he assumed that scientific theories were getting closer to representing it "exactly."[305]

Another example of Comte's misunderstanding was his statement that Kant completed the fundamental law, which had been developed by Leibniz, that "subjective constructions" had to be subordinated to "objective materials."[306] In the passages sent by d'Eichthal, Kant had argued against Leibniz and had said the exact opposite of what Comte attributed to him. Kant had said that objects had to conform to the human mind.

As already mentioned, Comte later claimed that he brought Kant's thought to its completion.[307] The law of three stages, he said, was the type of deterministic principle of intellectual and social development that Kant had sought in order to formulate a providential interpretation of history. Positivism embodied their shared assumption that science could not refer to what lies beyond experience. And Comte used the Kantian idea of the dynamic, creative power of the mind to create his theory of the "subjective synthesis."[308] It is therefore not surprising that Comte considered Kant one of his principal predecessors – in fact, the "last eminent thinker" who had preceded him.[309] He called him the "greatest modern metaphysician," the one "closest to the positive philosophy," and he gave him a highly prominent place in his Positivist Calendar.[310]

HEGEL

Besides furnishing Comte with information on Herder and Kant, d'Eichthal told him about Hegel, "one of the most celebrated philosophers today in Germany."[311] Fully aware of Comte's biases, d'Eichthal hastened to inform him that he was strong in mathematics and the sciences and opposed "all these poetic philosophies that are too common in Germany."[312] D'Eichthal's inability to understand

---

[305] *Traité philosophique d'astronomie populaire*, 26.   [306] *Système*, 4:176; see also 3:18.

[307] *Catéchisme positiviste*, 32. See also Arnaud, *Le "Nouveau Dieu,"* 218–22, 261–5; *Système*, 3:541–2.

[308] *Système*, 3:542.

[309] Comte to Mill, December 23, 1843, *CG*, 2:223. See also *Catéchisme positiviste*, 32.

[310] *Cours*, 2:727; Comte to G. d'Eichthal, December 10, 1824, *CG*, 1:143. One day was devoted to Kant in the Positivist Calendar. *Système*, 4: Table B'.

[311] In addition, d'Eichthal briefly alluded to Schelling and Schleiermacher. G. d'Eichthal to Comte, June 18, 1824, "Correspondance de Comte et d'Eichthal," ed. Laffitte, 224. See also d'Eichthal to Comte, June 4 and 18, 1824, and January 12, 1825, "Correspondance de Comte et d'Eichthal," ed. Laffitte, 221, 271.

[312] G. d'Eichthal to Comte, January 12, 1825, "Correspondance de Comte et d'Eichthal," ed. Laffitte, 271.

Hegel prevented him from following his courses at the University of Berlin. But he did have the chance to read some sketches of the course that Hegel had given on the philosophy of history in 1822 and 1823.[313]

D'Eichthal considered Hegel's "abstract view of history" superior to Herder's in discerning the connections among phenomena.[314] In his view, Comte and Hegel, despite their apparent differences, had a "veritable identity" at least in the "essential points." He told Comte:

> You will say that the Spirit of unity of an individual or a people is the abstract expression of the series of his or their actions. Hegel has absolutely the same idea; but he says that the essence of the Spirit of a people or of an individual is to pass into their or his acts, to transform itself into facts, to objectify itself; that it is only Spirit inasmuch as it realizes itself.[315]

In addition, according to d'Eichthal, Comte and Hegel were similar in their defense of the government, opposition to liberalism, and rejection of the idea of a "religion of sentiment" such as Constant advocated. In short, d'Eichthal urged Comte to ally himself with Hegel, who, as the head of German philosophy in their day, had "great influence."[316]

On June 30, 1824, d'Eichthal had a copy of Comte's recent opuscule delivered to Hegel and later also personally gave him a copy in homage. He met with Hegel to discuss Comte's ideas on two occasions, in November 1824 and in December 1824 or January 1825. D'Eichthal claimed that Hegel warmly welcomed Comte's essay and admired the way in which French thinkers like Comte were able to analyze the contemporary scene in a penetrating fashion. In fact, however, Hegel's opinion of Comte does not seem to have been as favorable as d'Eichthal suggested, for although he approved of the "details" of the *Plan* and praised the first section, he "attacked

---

[313] The compilation of students' notes on this course later evolved into the *Lectures on the Philosophy of History*, which was published posthumously in 1837. For information on Hegel's lectures, see D. Eduard Gans, Preface to *Vorlesungen über die Philosophie der Geschichte*, by Georg Wilhelm Friedrich Hegel, vol. 9 of *Werke: Vollständige Ausgabe durch einen Verein von Freunden des Verewigten*, ed. D. P. Marheineke et al. (Berlin, 1837), xviii–xxii. F. A. Hayek points out similarities between the thought of Comte and that of Hegel in *Counter-Revolution*, 189–206. Also see G. d'Eichthal to Comte, June 18, July 2, November 18, 1824, "Correspondance de Comte et d'Eichthal," ed. Laffitte, 224, 228, 260.

[314] G. d'Eichthal to Comte, August 22, 1824, "Correspondance de Comte et d'Eichthal," ed. Laffitte, 245.

[315] G. d'Eichthal to Comte, November 18, 1824, "Correspondance de Comte et d'Eichthal," ed. Laffitte, 259.

[316] Ibid., 260.

the general conception."³¹⁷ In the second section, where Comte suggested the use of observation in political science, Hegel felt the term "observation" was far too vague because it could not be the same type of observation that a scientist uses in studying electricity or magnetism.³¹⁸ He did not share d'Eichthal's belief that his own doctrine was similar to positive philosophy and rejected the idea of an alliance on the grounds that he disliked the pettiness involved in practical affairs. Since there is no mention of Comte in Hegel's letters, he probably gave him little thought.³¹⁹

In November 1824, d'Eichthal sent Comte translations from Hegel's lectures on the philosophy of history, which had been lost until I found copies of them at the Maison d'Auguste Comte in a packet of material labeled "Lettres de d'Eichthal à A. Comte: Copies faites par d'Eichthal." The selections covered Hegel's views of the state and the individual. In the first section, Hegel explained that the usual definition of the state was too limited for his purposes because it considered politics in isolation. To him, politics was related to industry, military life, the arts, religion, and so forth, because they all were various objectifications of the Spirit of a people. This Spirit embodied what was ultimately true and substantial.³²⁰

D'Eichthal was most interested in religion because it encapsulated the very nature of the Spirit. In the extracts he sent to Comte, Hegel argued that religion was the "system of spiritual *knowledge* of the Spirit of the people." Reduced to a simple system of thought, it represented what the people considered to be the truth and was, in fact, closely related to the sciences, the "source of the people's notion of truth." Since religion determined the character of all aspects of social existence, including the arts and sciences, it was the "general basis" of society and the state. A new religion took a long time to be established because society had to be "reworked" around the new principles.³²¹ For example, the world had not become truly Christian until the eleventh century.

In his second section, Hegel asserted that general principles were realized and became alive through individuals, who took part in the various activities of a society. Thus the individual became power-

---

³¹⁷ Ibid., 257. See also G. d'Eichthal to Comte, July 2, 1824, January 12, 1825, "Correspondance de Comte et d'Eichthal," ed. Laffitte, 228, 271.

³¹⁸ G. d'Eichthal to Comte, January 12, 1825, "Correspondance de Comte et d'Eichthal," ed. Laffitte, 271.

³¹⁹ [Georg Wilhelm Friedrich] Hegel, *Briefe von und an Hegel*, ed. Johannes Hoffmeister, 4 vols. (Hamburg: Felix Meinen, 1969–81).

³²⁰ See d'Eichthal's translation of Hegel manuscript, 464, MAC. The pages correspond to a block of note paper and the numbering is faulty.

³²¹ Ibid., 465, 466, 469.

ful by identifying with the General, that is, with generalities, such as laws and customs, which made up the substance of the state and activated the "masses." Although state constitutions tried to balance the influence of the General and the freedom of the individual, individuals could "never" act in an "assertive" or "decisive" manner in matters of general interest. Their value came from representing the Spirit of the people, especially by fulfilling the "duties" of their vocation. This theory echoed Hegel's view of international relations, which stressed the "law of the general Spirit of Humanity" and underplayed the independence of the state: "In history there is a higher law, a law in virtue of which a people exercises its action on another in the interest of Humanity in general. It is the position of a civilized people with regard to a barbarous people."[322]

Hegel's interest in history centered upon the "continual movement of organization, to which is joined a movement of disorganization." These movements were carried out by individuals since it was in them that ideas became real. Great men were those individuals who glimpsed the truth of their era and sought to achieve a goal that conformed to a "higher notion of the Spirit" than existed at the time.[323] They did not look within themselves to formulate their goal but sought to ascertain the will of the Spirit, which reflected ultimately the desire of the people, who then obeyed them.

The discovery of this manuscript reveals that d'Eichthal gave Comte a fairly good introduction to Hegel's concept of the Spirit and its manner of realizing itself through history. Pleased to have become acquainted with Hegel's philosophy, Comte called him "without doubt a man of merit." He did not, however, think Hegel's doctrine was as impressive as Kant's. To Comte, Hegel was "still too metaphysical," especially in his conception of the "Spirit," which he felt played a very "singular role."[324] Comte seemed to have Hegel in mind when he complained in the *Cours* that the Absolute, which had been contained by Kant, had reappeared in the writings of his successors, who formulated its supremacy even more "dogmatically."[325]

Although Comte did not think the Hegelian philosophy was as similar to the positive philosophy as d'Eichthal did, he thought that its details were "positive" and that there were a "great number of points of contact" between them.[326] He especially appreciated Hegel's recognition that Christianity was not established until the eleventh century, an idea that Comte had formulated as early as 1820.[327]

[322] Ibid., 467–8.   [323] Ibid., 468.
[324] Comte to G. d'Eichthal, December 10, 1824, *CG*, 1:144.
[325] *Cours*, 2:727.
[326] Comte to G. d'Eichthal, December 10, 1824, *CG*, 1:144.
[327] *Système*, vol. 4, "Appendice," 4; see also 191.

This idea supported his thesis that Christianity would span a short, transitory period and that it was normal for the acceptance of new ideas to take a long time.[328]

Comte made no mention of other points of contact, but there are other similarities between him and Hegel. Hegel's theory that history contained two connected movements – one of organization and one of disorganization – was close to Comte's idea in the fundamental opuscule that the character of his era could be ascertained from the fact that "two different movements are at work today in society: one of disorganization, the other of reorganization."[329] In subscribing to the concept that antagonism was the source of progress and that progress was the development of what was latent, Comte was enunciating the same concepts that lay at the heart of the Hegelian dialectic – a subject that d'Eichthal neglected to explain more fully.[330]

Both thinkers also agreed that producing a philosophy of history with laws relating to the "necessary development of humanity" was the key to understanding the present state of affairs and the predetermined endpoint of human evolution.[331] The growth of mankind's self-conscious control over its destiny was the focal point of their philosophies. Hegel's famous theory that "all is rational and all that is rational is also real" was not far from Comte's faith in moral relativism.[332]

Another "point of contact" was the recognition given by Comte and Hegel to the interrelationships of all aspects of social life – religion, science, military life, industry, and the arts. Comte would agree with Hegel that an intellectual system was the determining factor in society and that the different stages in the development of the mind incurred corresponding changes in civilization.[333] Moreover, he shared Hegel's view that religion was closely related to science and that it was above all an *intellectual* system. Although at this time, Comte did not think his system needed to be strictly religious, Hegel's viewpoint would be reflected twenty years later in the Religion of Humanity.

Comte also agreed with Hegel's organic approach to social theory and his view of the limited freedom of the individual.[334] Society was far more than a group of individuals and should be considered as a

---

[328] Alexandre J.-L. Delamarre, "Le Pouvoir spirituel et la ruine de la constitution catholique chez Joseph de Maistre et Auguste Comte," *Revue philosophique de la France et de l'étranger*, no. 4 (October–December 1985): 434.

[329] *Système*, vol. 4, "Appendice," 47.

[330] G. Salomon-Delatour, "Comte ou Hegel?" *La Revue positiviste internationale* 52.3 (May 25, 1936): 116.

[331] Hayek, *Counter-Revolution*, 196, 200.   [332] Ibid., 201; see also 198.

[333] Ibid., 197.   [334] Ibid., 197–8.

whole. While Hegel thought that the individual expressed the drive of the Spirit, Comte would later subordinate him to humanity. The law of the "Spirit of Humanity" would be as supreme for Comte as it was already for Hegel. In addition, both thinkers believed that great men simply identified themselves with the spirit of the times and were essentially tools of a greater force. Comte would come close to adopting Hegel's view of freedom as a fulfillment of one's duties regarding the vocation imposed by the state of civilization.[335]

Despite his ambivalent comments, Comte concluded that Hegel was the "most capable man to promote the positive philosophy" in Germany.[336] Although their relationship never developed and he did not extend his knowledge of the Hegelian system, he thought highly enough of Hegel to devote one day to him in the Positivist Calendar.[337]

THE SIGNIFICANCE OF COMTE'S ENCOUNTER WITH GERMAN PHILOSOPHY

One of the oddest aspects of Comte's reaction to German philosophy was that it was virtually devoid of intellectual curiosity, for he showed no interest in learning new concepts. In the midst of breaking with Saint-Simon, he was using German philosophy mainly to confirm his own system.[338] At one point, in explaining his enthusiasm for German philosophy, he even admitted that he was seeking "help in the details of a few positive generalities scattered in this metaphysical obscurity."[339] Thus Comte was anxiously looking abroad for reassurance, looking for ways to bolster his self-confidence.

Comte and d'Eichthal were apparently engaged in a game of seeking antecedents in order to appear to be on firmer ground. After mentioning that Buchholz had borrowed ideas on political science from a minor French writer (Charles His), d'Eichthal proudly told Comte, "You are watching the number of your predecessors augment every day."[340] Finding nonthreatening predecessors was a way to demonstrate that the science of society was a doctrine dictated by history – not by Saint-Simon. This strategy explains why Comte claimed Herder, Kant, and Hegel as his antecedents and

---

[335] On Hegel's view of freedom, see H. B. Acton, "Hegel, George Wilhelm Friedrich," in *The Encyclopedia of Philosophy*, ed. Edwards.
[336] Comte to G. d'Eichthal, April 6, 1825, *CG*, 160.   [337] *Système*, 4: Table B'.
[338] Comte to d'Eichthal, May 1, 1824, *CG*, 1:81–2.
[339] Comte to d'Eichthal, August 5, 1824, *CG*, 1:107.
[340] D'Eichthal to Comte, June 18, 1824, "Correspondance de Comte et d'Eichthal," ed. Laffitte, 225.

incorporated them in the Positivist Calendar. Comte, however, did not want to give the impression that he was merely mimicking other thinkers. To maintain his own originality, and to add to his sense of superiority, he criticized Herder, Kant, and Hegel for not being sufficiently scientific and practical. Later he openly boasted about not having read his predecessors in any depth.[341] In the *Cours*, Comte solemnly proclaimed his own creativity:

> I have never read in any language . . . Kant, Herder, or Hegel, etc; I know their different works only by several indirect reports and certain very insufficient extracts. Whatever may be the real inconveniences of this *voluntary negligence*, I am convinced that it has contributed a great deal to the purity and harmony of my social philosophy.[342]

Yet the extracts recently uncovered at the Maison d'Auguste Comte reveal that Comte in fact knew more than he suggested.

Herder, Kant, and Hegel reinforced the abstract, deterministic approach to the philosophy of history that Comte had already found in Condorcet and Saint-Simon. In fact, Saint-Simon had frequently complimented German idealists on their a priori approach and their emphasis on general theories.[343] Comte's concentration on the development of humanity as a whole instead of on acts of individuals, his organicism, his belief in the supreme power of reason and ideas, and his search for the interrelationships of historical phenomena – all were confirmed by his contact with Germany.[344] He even sought to form an alliance with German philosophers, for he wanted to join his French "clarity" to the German "genius" for systematizing and generalizing.[345] He was convinced that he had the greatest affinity with the German school – a sentiment that indicates his profound alienation from the prevailing ideas in France, including those of the reactionaries, who he implied were not true philosophers.[346] This attachment to a foreign philosophy added to his sense of mar-

[341] Comte's pride in this matter was common knowledge. See Odysse-Barot, "Auguste Comte," Fonds Enfantin 7803, BA.
[342] *Cours*, 2: 479–80 (my emphasis).
[343] On Saint-Simon's attitude toward German philosophy, see Saint-Simon, *Lettres au Bureau des Longitudes*, 69–70; *Esquisse d'une nouvelle encyclopédie*, 90; *Travail sur la gravitation universelle*, 299–300.
[344] Arnaud, *Le "Nouveau Dieu,"* 133.
[345] Comte to G. d'Eichthal, November 6, 1824, *CG*, 1:136; *Cours*, 2:593. Comte later told Mill that once he finished the *Cours*, he would learn German in order to grasp the "necessary points of contact" between the positive philosophy and German philosophers despite the latter's "metaphysical nebulosities." But he never did learn the language. Comte to Mill, August 24, 1842, *CG*, 2:73; *Cours*, 2:480.
[346] Comte to G. d'Eichthal, November 6, 1824, *CG*, 1:135.

ginality and isolation vis-à-vis his own country. For example, his appreciation of the organicism of Herder's philosophy and of that of the German school in general gave him an even dimmer opinion of French metaphysicians, whom he regarded as too specialized, critical, and unconstructive.[347] At the same time, however, because of the advantages he felt the French Revolution and his scientific education gave him, he was able to maintain his conviction that positive philosophy was superior to "German mysticism."[348]

GALL AND PHRENOLOGY

Another German thinker who had an impact on Comte was Franz Joseph Gall, the leading promoter of phrenology. Increasingly influential in Paris since his arrival in 1807, Gall had a very good relationship with the Saint-Simonians and with Blainville, who discussed him in the course he gave in 1824 at the Athénée – a course that Comte probably attended.[349] Encouraged by Blainville, Comte renewed his friendship with one of Gall's students, Etienne-Marie Bailly, who was also a disciple of Saint-Simon.[350] With the support of Blainville and Bailly, Comte participated in the phrenology movement that swept France in the nineteenth century and left its mark on the works of such writers as Balzac, Vigny, George Sand, Baudelaire, and Flaubert.[351] When criticized for succumbing to this pseudoscience, he defended himself by claiming that every "enlightened physiologist" supported Gall's doctrines.[352] However, many

[347] Comte to d'Eichthal, August 5, 1824, CG, 1:105. [348] *Cours*, 2:585.
[349] Gall examined Saint-Simon on his deathbed and then performed an autopsy on his skull, which revealed signs of an "untiring perseverance" as well as a "complete absence of circumspection." In addition, Gall's course, "Philosophy of the Intellectual Faculties," at the Athénée, was given a favorable review in the Saint-Simonian journal, *Le Producteur*. See Hubbard, *Saint-Simon*, 109–10; Leroy, *Saint-Simon*, 325; Laffitte, "L'Athénée," 48; "Physiologie du cerveau: Analyse du cours de M. Gall à l'Athénée," *Le Producteur* 2: (1825): 464–70; Ackerknecht, *Medicine*, 172; Comte to Mill, June 19, 1842, CG, 2:54; Rosalie Boyer to Comte, December 11, 1823, "Lettres de Rosalie Boyer (1)," ed. Laffitte, 95.
[350] Bailly had also been a classmate of Augustin Thierry at the *lycée* in Blois. Many years before, he had given Comte his 1817 medical thesis, *Quelques Réflexions sur le traitement des phlegmasies*. Though disappointed by his work, especially his article in Saint-Simon's *Opinions littéraires, philosophiques et industrielles*, Comte was sure that Bailly would "do very important things" to advance Gall's doctrines. Bailly seems to have convinced Comte that Flourens's famous criticisms of Gall's philosophy were wrong. Comte to G. d'Eichthal, August 5, 1824, CG, 1:109. See also Comte to G. d'Eichthal, May 1, June 6, December 10, 1824, CG, 1:79, 97, 145; G. d'Eichthal to Comte, May 11, 1824, "Correspondance de Comte et d'Eichthal," ed. Laffitte (1896): 208; Comte to Tabarié, July 17, 1824, CG, 1:101; Augustin-Thierry, *Augustin Thierry*, 11; Ackerknecht, *Medicine*, 172.
[351] Ackerknecht, *Medicine*, 172. [352] Comte to Valat, September 8, 1824, CG, 1:125.

famous doctors and scientists remained doubtful. In fact, the Academy of Sciences refused to admit Gall in 1821.[353]

For Comte, Gall was important for having completed the revolution begun by Cabanis, that of combating metaphysical theories of human nature and making physiology a positive science. Gall fulfilled Cabanis's goal of looking at moral phenomena in the same way as physical phenomena by demonstrating that moral functions corresponded to a physical organ. The "seat of the intellectual and affective functions" was the cerebral nervous system, and each organ in this system (the brain) corresponded to one intellectual or affective faculty.[354] If one had a particularly strong moral faculty, the corresponding cerebral organ had to be more developed as well. Comte felt that this theory of the brain was the essential part of Gall's doctrine and that it was perfectly reasonable. He also agreed that the form of the cranium reflected that of the brain. The size of a brain organ could be discovered by examining the shape of the skull, particularly cranial bumps.[355]

Thus Comte adopted the theory that Gall had established in opposition to sensationalism; according to phrenology, each person had "innate dispositions, independent of education and of exterior circumstances."[356] These innate intellectual and emotional dispositions were very powerful. But at least at this point, Comte believed they could be modified and did not in themselves rigorously determine all of an individual's actions.

Gall's theory did not gain the complete approval of Comte, who found his effort so far to assign specific organs to particular functions "absurd." But he argued that this error was of secondary importance and should not discredit the entire doctrine. He was sure that in several decades scientists would arrive at a valid list of organs and their corresponding functions, which would finally enable one to determine "up to a certain point" a person's intellectual and emotional "dispositions" by the form of his cranium.[357]

Although Comte was not a blind follower of phrenology, he seemed to find reinforcement for his own philosophy in its organic, functional doctrine. Its so-called biological basis seemed to him much less speculative than the introspective, epistemological foundations

---

[353] Robert Young, "Gall, Franz Joseph," in Dictionary of Scientific Biography, ed. Gillispie; Ackerknecht, Medicine, 172.

[354] Comte to Valat, September, 8, 1824, CG, 1:125.

[355] For a clear discussion of Gall's doctrines, see Goldstein, Console and Classify, 254-5.

[356] Comte to Valat, September 8, 1824, CG, 1:126.

[357] Ibid. See also Robert M. Young, Mind, Brain, and Adaptation in the Nineteenth Century (Oxford: Clarendon Press, 1970), 253.

of Cousin's psychology and the Idéologues' sensationalism.[358] Gall's materialism, with its denial of original sin and the immortality of the soul, also offered a replacement for the religious explanation of the world and human existence. Progressives throughout Europe were excited by the support that phrenology gave to their reformist doctrines of secular morality and social improvement. And in France phrenology became a sign of liberal animosity toward the government; the ultras tried to repress its spread in the early 1820s. Thus Comte joined the movement because phrenology not only gave his social investigations a scientific cast, but offered him another way to express his opposition to the government.[359] Later he called Gall his main scientific predecessor (along with Bichat) and gave him a prominent place in the Positivist Calendar.[360] He claimed to owe more to Gall than to any other thinker except Condorcet. Maistre, he said, represented the third greatest influence.[361]

SCOTLAND

In his letters to d'Eichthal, Comte also indicated his appreciation of the philosophers of the Scottish Enlightenment, who had sought to establish moral principles on a secular, empirical basis.[362] Years later, he hailed the Scottish school as the "most advanced of all [the philosophical schools] of the last century."[363] Enthusiasm for the Scottish philosophy had always been widespread in France, starting with the eighteenth-century Idéologues. In the early nineteenth century, its doctrines figured prominently in courses given by Pierre Paul Royer-Collard, Victor Cousin, and Théodore Jouffroy. But Cousin and his colleagues mainly employed the commonsense theories of Thomas Reid for the same reason they used the critical

[358] Angus McLaren, "A Prehistory of the Social Sciences: Phrenology in France," *Comparative Studies in Society and History* 23.1 (1981): 3–22.
[359] For information on the significance of phrenology, see Goldstein, *Console and Classify*, 240–5, 255; Angus McLaren, "Phrenology: Medium and Message," *Journal of Modern History* 46.1 (1974): 86–97; idem, "A Prehistory"; R. J. Cotter, "Phrenology: The Provocation of Progress," *History of Science* 14 (1976): 211–34; Anne Harrington, *Medicine, Mind and the Double Brain: A Study in Nineteenth-Century Thought* (Princeton, N.J.: Princeton University Press, 1987), 10; Richard Vernon, "The Political Self: Auguste Comte and Phrenology," *History of European Ideas* 7 (1986): 271–86.
[360] *Système*, 4: Table B'. [361] Comte to M'Clintock, August 7, 1852, *CG*, 1:325.
[362] Albert Salomon, "Adam Smith as Sociologist," *Social Research* 2 (February 1945): 22; Alan William Swingewood, "Origins of Sociology: The Case of the Scottish Enlightenment," *British Journal of Sociology* 21.2 (1970): 165–80.
[363] Comte to Mill, February 27, 1843, *CG*, 2:141.

idealism of Kant, namely, to destroy the sensationalism of the Idéologues.[364] Scarcely interested in the battle between Cousin's "eclecticism" and the Idéologues' sensationalism, both of which struck him as metaphysical philosophies of the mind, Comte had a different agenda. He was more interested in the theories of Hume, Robertson, Smith, and Ferguson, for he hoped they would enrich his new science of society. By 1818 he had read Smith's *Wealth of Nations*, and at some point he read his *Essays on Philosophical Subjects* with its preface by Dugald Stewart.[365] In the latter, the essay entitled "The History of Astronomy" so impressed Comte that he said it had a "more positive character than the other productions of the Scottish philosophy, if one excludes the works of Hume."[366] By 1825 he was familiar with Hume's philosophy and owned a 1764, five-volume edition of Hume's *Oeuvres philosophiques*, which contained *An Enquiry Concerning Human Understanding*. He would include this set, along with Smith's essay, in the standard Positivist Library.[367] In 1818, he called Hume's *History of England* and Robertson's *History of Charles V* the best works of history in existence and later also added them to the Positivist Library.[368] Furthermore, in 1824, he mentioned that Ferguson's *Essay on the History of Civil Society* had "very shrewd" insights into the history of civilization.[369] Besides this work, Comte owned Ferguson's *Principles of Moral and Political Science* and *History of the Progress and Fall of the Roman Republic*.

Perhaps the main reason for Comte's attraction to the Scottish Enlightenment can be inferred from an article written in 1819 by Augustin Thierry for *Le Censeur européen*. Thierry praised Cousin for having shown that the Scottish philosophers, unlike the French, had made social man the focus of their moral philosophy and had been able to derive the "most positive consequences" from their research.[370] Comte was also interested in the way the Scots had turned their attention from the study of the individual to that of society. Ferguson had written:

---

[364] Spitzer, *French Generation*, 84–8; Boas, *French Philosophies*, 156–8, 164; Picavet, *Les Idéologues*, 572; Grave, *Scottish Philosophy*, 3–4; Emile Boutroux, *Etudes d'histoire de la philosophie* (Paris, 1897), 414–15, 421–9. See also idem, *De l'influence de la philosophie écossaise sur la philosophie moderne*, extract from the *Revue française d'Edimbourg* (Edinburgh, 1897).

[365] Comte to Valat, May 15, 1818, *CG*, 1:38. Comte's library at the Maison d'Auguste Comte contains a four-volume edition of *La Richesse des nations*, published in 1800–1, and a 1797 edition of Smith's *Essais philosophiques*.

[366] *Système*, vol. 4, "Appendice," 139n1.   [367] *Système*, 4:560.

[368] Comte to Valat, May 15, 1818, *CG*, 1:37.

[369] Comte to G. d'Eichthal, November 6, 1824, *CG*, 1:136.

[370] Augustin Thierry, Review of Cousin's course entitled "Histoire de la philosophie morale pendant le dix-huitième siècle" at the Faculté des Lettres and the Académie de Paris, *Le Censeur européen*, August 4, 1819, 2–4.

Mankind are to be taken in groups, as they have always subsisted. The history of the individual is but a detail of the sentiments and thoughts he has entertained in the view of his species; and every experiment relative to this subject should be made with entire societies, not with single men.[371]

Along with Hume, Ferguson argued that government and society developed gradually from man's inherently social nature and were never deliberately established by a contract among strong individualists.[372] Although Comte's stance against the social contract is usually traced to Bonald and Maistre, it seems that the Scottish philosophers, who removed all trace of the divine from their considerations, played a more important role. They had already influenced the position of the Idéologues and Destutt de Tracy on this issue. When Comte voiced his opposition to the theory of an original state of nature, it was often in the context of an exposition of the Scottish point of view.[373]

The Scottish philosophers studied society mainly through its history. Like Condorcet, they sought to demonstrate the natural laws of progress, but they were more scientific, using a great deal of documentation and comparative analysis. In addition, they concentrated not only on political changes but on social, economic, and cultural developments.[374] Recognizing these innovations, Comte praised their work as part of the eighteenth-century effort to establish a political science.[375]

He especially admired Robertson and Hume for developing the idea of continual progress and the contrast between the ancient and modern worlds, especially in terms of social customs.[376] Comte favored Robertson's definition of progress as the development of peace, order, and refinement, which included the improved social state of women, and agreed with his view that science and commerce had played a large role in this softening of manners.[377] Hume too judged history in terms of the growth of a "more cultivated

---

[371] Adam Ferguson, *An Essay on the History of Civil Society* (Basel, 1789), 6.

[372] Adam Ferguson, *Principles of Moral and Political Science*, 2 vols. (Edinburgh, 1792), 1:24. See also Gladys Bryson, *Man and Society: The Scottish Inquiry of the Eighteenth Century* (Princeton, N.J.: Princeton University Press, 1945), 162–4.

[373] *Cours*, 2:192–3, 575. See also Swingewood, "Origins of Sociology," 166.

[374] Swingewood, "Origins of Sociology," 165, 168; Fletcher, *The Making of Sociology*, 1:645–6; Donald G. MacRae, "Adam Ferguson," in *The Founding Fathers of Social Science*, ed. Timothy Raison (Harmondsworth: Penguin Books, 1969), 18–26; Bryson, *Man and Society*, 12–29.

[375] *Système*, vol. 4, "Appendice," 157. See also *Cours*, 2:575.

[376] *Système*, 3:589–90; *Cours*, 2:493.

[377] William Robertson, *The History of Charles V* (Paris, 1828), 7, 18, 49–50; *Cours*, 2:300.

life."[378] Comte praised him for being the first to describe the "irrevocable supremacy of industrial life" over the old military regime.[379] Hume was the "best organ of the critical doctrine" and the "founder of the law of temporal evolution" later elaborated by Dunoyer.[380]

Ferguson also dealt with the progress of the human species "from rudeness to civilization" in a manner that impressed Comte.[381] Ferguson was most interested in social conflict. Comte admired his theory that social change often derived from the interaction of various social groups but that even the "action of one people on another," such as conquest, could not by itself alter the basic direction taken by society.[382] Group behavior could at most accelerate or extend natural developments. Thus, like Ferguson, Comte would stress the limited influence of all types of human action and the ineluctable nature of social advancement.[383]

Comte took a great interest in Adam Smith's historical skills. The *Wealth of Nations* offered Comte a description of the growth of industry, especially during the Middle Ages; an analysis of the military's reliance on industrial growth to finance wars; and an explanation of the communes' influence on industrial and agricultural development – an explanation that Comte pointed out was inspired by Hume.[384] Like Smith, Comte viewed industrial development in terms of the growth and freedom of the manufacturing and commercial classes and their inevitable domination of the military classes.

Smith's essay on astronomy provided Comte with a model of the history of science, showing how men first became philosophers when they began seeking "those hidden chains of events that bind together the seemingly disjointed appearance of nature."[385] Religious superstitions emerged when people attributed irregular events (such as thunder and lightning), which they could not understand, to supernatural beings, who behaved like humans. Smith's anthropomorphic depiction of gods reappeared in Comte's account of the theological stage. Comte was also influenced by his view that people

[378] David Hume, *The History of England from the Invasion of Julius Caesar to the Accession of Henry VII*, 2 vols. (London, 1762), 1:154. For Hume's theory of history, see Duncan Forbes, *Hume's Philosophical Politics* (Cambridge: Cambridge University Press, 1975), 296.
[379] *Système*, 3:62.   [380] Ibid., 3:62, 590. For other comments on Hume, see *Cours*, 2:437.
[381] Ferguson, *Essay on Civil Society*, 2. See also *Cours*, 2:193.   [382] *Cours*, 2:134.
[383] *Système*, 2:453; Bierstedt, "Sociological Thought," 27; Ronald Meek, *Economics, Ideology and Other Essays: Studies in the Development of Economic Thought* (London: Chapman & Hall, 1967), 38; Donald G. MacRae, *Ideology and Sociology: Papers in Sociology and Politics* (London: Heinemann, 1961), 140–2; Fletcher, *The Making of Sociology*, 1:649.
[384] *Cours*, 2:496, 499, 514. Comte also referred to the Scots for having shown the positive effects of colonialization on industrial development. Ibid., 520.
[385] Adam Smith, *Essays on Philosophical Subjects*, with an introduction by Dugald Stewart (London, 1795), 23. See also *Cours*, 2:575.

were never totally theological; even in the most primitive eras they sought to discover the natural laws of certain simple, regular phenomena, mainly those of the heavens, which made astronomy the first science to develop.[386] Besides Delambre, Smith thus also convinced Comte of the significance of astronomy and played a role in his later decision to give courses in it to workers.[387]

Smith was also the political economist whom Comte respected the most, especially as his enthusiasm for Say and Charles Comte diminished.[388] Smith's view that economic phenomena were part of social philosophy was adopted by Comte as he tried to make political economy the heart of the science of society.[389] Like Saint-Simon, he also embraced Smith's idea of the crucial role that banks and money played in industrial development. Although often critical of economic liberalism, Comte seemed to endorse Adam Smith's arguments in favor of free trade. In 1825 he applauded English plans to reduce trade restrictions as a way of lessening the power of the House of Lords.[390] Comte was mainly interested in Smith's concept of the division of labor as an important source of progress and a means of reconciling self-interest and the interest of the community.[391] Comte applied it not only to economic activities, but also to intellectual, social, political, and moral life. Like Marx, whom Smith also influenced, Comte was struck by the debilitating and alienating effects of the specialization that the division of labor – and progress – entailed. To combat these adverse consequences, Smith had prescribed education and religion, the very same remedies Comte would offer.[392]

---

[386] *Système*, vol. 4, "Appendice," 139. See also *Cours*, 2:222.

[387] *Cours*, 2: 575; see also 193, 222.

[388] Comte had liked Charles Comte for many years, until he decreed that all theories that could not be immediately applied to industrial practice must be disdained and abandoned. Say initially appealed to Comte, but when he grouped together scientists, artists, lawyers, priests, and policemen and called them "immaterial producers," Comte found this a "metaphysical mess" because it made the concept of producer insignificant. Comte to G. d'Eichthal, November 24, 1825, *CG*, 1:173–5. Comte also admired Dunoyer, but not to the same extent as he admired Smith.

[389] Adam Smith, *An Inquiry into the Nature and Causes of the Wealth of Nations*, 4th ed. (Edinburgh, 1870), 187; *Cours*, 2:93.

[390] Comte to G. d'Eichthal, April 6, 1825, *CG*, 1:161.

[391] On the theory of the division of labor, see Smith, *Wealth of Nations*, 2–10. Comte also seemed aware of Ferguson's extensive use of the division of labor, for he alluded to a passage from his *Principles of Moral and Political Sciences* to demonstrate that the uniqueness of the human species lay in this "cooperating of many, to some common purpose or end." Ferguson, *Principles of Moral and Political Science*, 1:21; see also *Cours*, 2:93, 193.

[392] On Smith, see Meek, *Economics, Ideology, and other Essays*, 48–50; Swingewood, "Origins of Sociology," 176; Harry Elmer Barnes, "Social Thought," 54, 63; Gide and Rist, *History of Economic Doctrines*, 74–125.

The Scottish philosophers did not confine their analysis of society to history and the economy but were interested in psychology as well. Comte called their psychological doctrines the "least absurd" of all those embraced by the different schools of thought.[393] To the Scots, human nature was the mainspring of social development, and since they felt that reason was an inadequate basis for a code of ethics, they stressed that man was by nature a sentient, social being. Moved more by his feelings and beliefs than by reason and composed of a mixture of selfish and unselfish inclinations, man was usually guided by enlightened self-interest and was therefore inherently good.[394]

In his introduction to Smith's *Essays on Philosophical Subjects*, Dugald Stewart compared Smith's concept of human nature (as outlined in his *Theory of Moral Sentiments*) to that of Hutcheson and Hume. Hutcheson had claimed that man is naturally endowed with "moral sense," which makes him feel pleasure when he experiences virtue and pain when he encounters vice.[395] Hume and Smith extended this view when they stated that man has a natural feeling of "sympathy" for his fellow beings. Hume defined sympathy in terms of mutual interest and mutual dependence; we perform virtuous actions because they are useful to ourselves or to others. Smith went further when he maintained that sympathy was the ability to enter into other people's situations and to understand their feelings. If we find a person's sentiments agreeable, then we approve of them and call them virtuous. Applying these same standards to ourselves, we present our actions in the light of how they appear to mankind in general in the hope of attaining approval. As a result of this morality based on approbation and disapprobation, the individual can be happy only if his actions are approved of by society and are thus in harmony with social interests. As a fundamental characteristic of human nature, sympathy, then, was the basic unifying force in society. To Smith, as well as to Hume and Ferguson, morality was therefore fundamentally secular and social; it reflected the constant interaction and interdependence of people in society.[396]

Although Comte was probably familiar with this view of morality as early as 1825, when he alluded to the book in which Stewart added his introduction, he left no record of his reaction.[397] Later,

---

[393] *Cours*, 2:853.   [394] Bryson, *Man and Society*, 172, 243.

[395] Dugald Stewart, Introduction to Smith, *Essays on Philosophical Subjects*, xxiii.

[396] Ibid., xxiii–xxxvi; Salomon, "Adam Smith," 27–9; Swingewood, "Origins of Sociology," 169–70.

[397] *Système*, vol. 4, "Appendice," 139n1. At one point Comte also praised Hume, who in his *Enquiry Concerning the Principles of Morals* had shown that the primary passion of man was "disinterested benevolence." David Hume, *An Enquiry Concerning the Principles of Morals*,

however, when he turned his attention to human nature, the Scottish philosophy of man's natural sociability had an important impact on his ideas.[398] He praised Hume's recognition of the "natural existence of altruistic penchants," that is, concern for others, and Ferguson's suggestion that one could gain an idea of the "sympathetic instinct" by comparing human societies to animal societies.[399] He also deplored the fact that the Scots' picture of human nature as both egoistic and sympathetic had not had more influence:

> The philosophical works of Hume, Adam Smith, and Ferguson show a tendency that is far more pronounced toward the true positive state, and they present elements of a theory of man that is much less erroneous than those of all the other metaphysical schools. One always notes with interest in these works the best refutation that was possible to make – before the foundation of cerebral physiology [phrenology] – of the principal aberrations of the French school on the moral nature of man.[400]

As a means of combating "egoistic metaphysics," that is, doctrines of individualism, the theory of the Scots, along with Gall's phrenology, would contribute to Comte's own doctrine of "altruism" and to the establishment of morality as a seventh science based on the social psychology of man.[401]

Perhaps the most significant of Comte's acquisitions from the Scottish school of philosophy was Hume's concept of causality. Hume argued that it was a waste of time debating questions that could not be verified by the scientific observation of facts and experimentation.[402] Written to determine the limitations of knowledge, his *Enquiry Concerning the Human Understanding* showed that ideas derive solely from corresponding sensations or impressions and are connected with three principles: resemblance, contiguity, and cause and effect. Hume questioned the legitimacy of the principle of cause and effect, because it went beyond sensory evidence. There was no reason to assume that because objects or events followed each other in time, they were necessarily connected.[403] The search for general, or

in *Enquiries Concerning the Human Understanding and Concerning the Principles of Morals*, 2d ed., ed. L. A. Selby-Bigge (Oxford: Clarendon Press, 1902), 301.

[398] *Cours*, 2:180. [399] *Système*, 3:589; *Cours*, 2:145, 193. [400] *Cours*, 1:863.

[401] *Système*, 3:589.

[402] Leszek Kolakowski, *The Alienation of Reason: A History of Positivist Thought*, trans. Norbert Guterman (Garden City, N.Y.: Doubleday, Anchor Books, 1969), 43.

[403] In *A Treatise of Human Nature*, Hume discussed contiguity of space as well as that of time, but this book was not in the set of Hume's works that Comte owned. Thus it is difficult to determine if Comte knew this aspect of Hume's famous argument. David Hume, *A Treatise of Human Nature*, 2d ed., ed. L. A. Selby-Bigge, revised by P. H. Nidditch (Oxford: Clarendon Press, 1978), 73–8, 170–2.

first, causes, which led people outside the realm of human experience, was ultimately vain. Instead of building theological and metaphysical theories, people should learn to accept their ignorance, blindness, and weakness.[404]

Although Comte claimed to have known Hume's doctrine before he formulated the law of the three stages, he did not allude to it in his fundamental opuscule, where the search for first causes did not characterize the theological stage. Only in 1825 did he mention that Hume revealed that the illusory pursuit of first causes lay at the heart of religion.[405] From then on, Comte frequently referred to Hume's scientific method, which he said was important for having replaced the search for causes with the study of descriptive laws.[406] Like his great successor Kant, who Comte felt had extended Hume's conclusions, Hume had discovered the "fundamental dualism between the spectator and spectacle" and had brought mankind closer to the triumph of relativism and nominalism.[407] By showing that an "artificial logic" is the "provisional link" of our thoughts, both Hume and Kant had demonstrated that people could never know more than what appeared to them through their senses and categories, and they thus contributed to Comte's theory of the "subjective synthesis."[408] Yet in spite of his praise of Hume, one could argue that Comte in his dogmatism about his own laws and in his optimism about predictability did not seem to grasp the depth of Hume's skepticism and relativism.[409] Comte seemed merely to substitute laws for causes and, in fact, continued to discuss causes themselves.[410]

Although few scholars emphasize the influence of the Scottish Enlightenment on positivism, Comte clearly traced the roots of his thought to the Scottish school, explicitly expressing his gratitude to Hume and Smith, whose influence had been "very useful" in his "first philosophical education," before the discovery of the law of three stages.[411] Yet he criticized them for not offering a more coherent theory of society and hoped to surpass them in establishing a more systematic philosophy.[412] Nevertheless, Comte remained loyal to many of their leading concepts: the division of labor, continual

[404] Hume, *An Enquiry Concerning Human Understanding*, in *Enquiries*, 13–47, 73–6; Kolakowski, *Alienation of Reason*, 43–59; Georges Gusdorf, *L'Avènement des sciences humaines au siècle des lumières* (Paris: Payot, 1973), 53–8; Fernand Papillon, "David Hume, précurseur d'Auguste Comte," *La Philosophie positive* 3 (September–October 1868): 292–308.

[405] *Cours*, 2:575; *Système*, vol. 4, "Appendice," 77, 138.   [406] *Cours*, 2:575.

[407] *Système*, 3:588.   [408] Ibid., 342. See also Fletcher, *The Making of Sociology*, 1:152.

[409] *Cours*, 2:575.   [410] Arnaud, *Le "Nouveau Dieu,"* 87.

[411] *Cours*, 2:575. See the different approaches of the following: Salomon, "Adam Smith," 22; Jerzy Szacki, *History of Sociological Thought* (Westport, Conn.: Greenwood Press, 1979), 71; Swingewood, "Origins of Sociology," 175–7.

[412] *Cours*, 1:863, 2:575; Comte to Mill, February 27, 1843, *CG*, 2:14.

progress, the gradual domination of industry over the military, the importance of studying society instead of the individual, the relativism and the limits of human knowledge, and the view of man as mainly "sympathetic." He too embraced an interdisciplinary approach to the study of society, one that combined political economy, psychology, moral philosophy, and history. To underscore the link between the Scots' ideas and the establishment of positivism and sociology, Comte called Hume his "principal philosophical predecessor" and gave him as well as Ferguson, Smith, and Robertson prominent positions in the Positivist Calendar.[413]

CONCLUSION

After his break with Saint-Simon in early 1824, Comte began to seek intellectual alliances. Previously he had visualized himself as perfecting the work of Montesquieu and the Idéologues Condorcet, Cabanis, Destutt de Tracy, and Say. He had praised Adam Smith as a political economist and Hume and Robertson as historians. But after his rupture, he began to make more explicit the influence of these and other thinkers on his development. As his disenchantment with the liberals grew, the appeal of the reactionaries Maistre, Bonald, and Lamennais increased, but not to the extent that is sometimes claimed.

   Above all, Comte seemed eager to enrich his ideas and confirm his philosophical tendencies by contact with France's neighbors, Germany and Scotland, whose systems of thought represented to him the only true philosophy since Bossuet and Leibniz. German and Scottish thinkers seemed to be far more serious about constructing something truly new than the French philosophers.[414] Moreover, Comte wanted his system to be not only the completion of the French Enlightenment but the endpoint of a more wide-ranging, European intellectual evolution as well. In his eyes, this greater comprehensiveness made his work even more serious and significant.[415] In allying himself with Herder, Kant, and Hegel on the one hand and with Robertson, Ferguson, Hume, and Smith on the other, he gave himself a wealth of important predecessors. By showing the convergence between his thought and that of many great European thinkers, he could demonstrate the appropriateness and inevitability of the triumph of the positive philosophy.

   Comte did not subject any of these thinkers to an extended,

---

[413] *Système*, 4: Table B'. Kolakowski calls Hume the "real father of positivist philosophy." Kolakowski, *Alienation of Reason*, 43.
[414] Comte to d'Eichthal, August 5, 1824, *CG*, 1:105.   [415] *Cours*, 2:467.

systematic analysis. The nuances of their various approaches to the study of man and society did not seem to preoccupy him, even though the differences between German idealism and Scottish empiricism were as great in many respects as those between the French liberal and the reactionary Catholic positions. He rightly pointed out the significance of his two main philosophical predecessors, Kant and Hume, who were both engaged in subjecting knowledge to new rigorous standards, but he never analyzed their opposite approaches to a priori knowledge. Thus there was a certain eclecticism, simplicity, and even superficiality in his embrace of all these traditions. He appeared anxious to synthesize philosophical movements no matter how different they might be. Like his contemporary Guizot, Comte was trying to find a "juste milieu" that would accommodate all opinions. Rejecting the liberal, parliamentary approach to reaching a compromise, he would seek to achieve this harmony through his philosophy.

Most of all, Comte used this strategy of intellectual alliances to efface the influence of Saint-Simon. In August 1824 Comte announced to d'Eichthal that "the more precedents we have, the more we will be worth; we must appear to be old in order to be firmly fixed in people's minds."[416] Later in the *Cours*, he explained that he liked to mention the "roots" of an idea in order to give "more force" to his own thoughts.[417] Thus already as a young man, he was beginning to reconstruct his own past, an effort that would culminate in the Positivist Calendar of great men where the name of his most important predecessor was conspicuously absent: Saint-Simon.

[416] Comte to d'Eichthal, August 5, 1824, *CG*, 1:106.   [417] *Cours*, 2:467.

Chapter 7

Comte's Efforts to Establish Himself

I have no friends at all around me, nobody but indifferent or almost [indifferent] persons. Many people take a great interest in my head . . . but no one takes a true interest in my heart, where in intimate relations such sweet compensation is found for deep inner pains, pains of which I have a good number, especially right now.

Comte, 1824

COMTE'S MARRIAGE TO CAROLINE MASSIN

Disappointed by many of his friends, Comte decided in July 1824 to marry Caroline Massin, the woman with whom he had been living since early February. He later lamented that this was the "sole irreparable mistake" of his life.[1] The question, then, is, Who was she and why did he marry her?

Throughout his life, Comte tried to keep the background of his wife a mystery, even portraying her as a young widow.[2] Yet the year before he died, he wrote a five-page description of their relationship, which he sealed in an envelope and called the "Secret Addition" to his testament.[3] It was to be opened by his executors at his death.

In this "Secret Addition," Comte described his wife's background and the circumstances surrounding their meeting.[4] He explained that on May 3, 1821, he took advantage of a public holiday to wander about his neighborhood. After dining in a modest restaurant, he decided to do what he usually did when he was lonely in Paris, that is, visit the Galeries de Bois of the Palais Royal. The bookstores and boutiques always attracted a throng of people, including *filles publiques*, seeking their own special clients. It was there, he said, that he

---

[1] Comte to Littré, April 28, 1851, *CG*, 6:62.
[2] Comte to Tabarié, August 22, 1824, *CG*, 1:115.
[3] The "Secret Addition" was first published in the second edition of Comte's *Testament*, 36a–36g.
[4] For a full account of Caroline Massin and the circumstances of her marriage to Comte, see Mary Barbara Pickering, "Auguste Comte: His Life and Works (1798–1842)" (Ph.D. diss., Harvard University, 1988), 1214–44.

met Caroline Massin, who led him to a nearby house reserved for her type of business.[5]

Born on July 2, 1802, in Châtillon-sur-Seine, Anne Caroline Massin was the illegitimate daughter of two provincial actors, Louis Hilaire Massin and Marie Anne Baudelot, who separated soon after her birth.[6] She was raised in an upright, loving manner in Paris by her maternal grandmother. But when her grandfather, a tailor, died in 1813, her grandmother could no longer support her and returned her to her mother.[7] According to Comte, Anne Baudelot was so "depraved" that she taught Massin to consider men solely as "objects of exploitation" and took advantage of her beauty to sell her as a virgin to a young leftist lawyer named Antoine Cerclet.[8] When Cerclet left her several months later and her beloved grandmother died, she inscribed her name in the police registry of prostitutes. It was in that capacity that she met Comte two years later.[9]

For six months, they saw each other whenever he could afford it at her apartment on the rue St. Honoré near the Eglise St. Roch.[10] But in November 1821, the sudden reappearance of Antoine Cerclet put an end to this affair. A year later, Comte was walking on the boulevard du Temple in the Marais and decided to rest in a reading room (*cabinet de lecture*). He was astonished when he saw that the woman running the establishment was Caroline Massin, whom he had not seen since their break. Cerclet, the political activist, had

[5] *Testament*, 36d; Lonchampt, *Précis*, 25–6; Françoise Parent-Lardeur, *Les Cabinets de lecture: La Lecture publique à Paris sous la Restauration* (Paris: Payot, 1982), 140. Littré, who was very friendly with Caroline Massin, maintained that she originally met Comte through Cerclet and that she was a bookseller. Littré, *Auguste Comte*, 33.

[6] See Caroline Massin and Comte's marriage certificate, Louis Massin's birth certificate, and Anne Baudelot's death certificate, all of which can be found at the Archives de Paris. See also the two slightly different versions of Caroline Massin's birth certificate, one at the Mairie at Châtillon-sur-Seine and the other in the Archives Générales du Département de la Côte d'Or et de l'Ancienne Province de Bourgogne in Dijon. Caroline Massin's birth certificate confirms Comte's information.

[7] *Testament*, 36c, 36d; "Matériaux pour servir à la biographie d'Auguste Comte: Acte de Mariage d'Auguste Comte," ed. Pierre Laffitte, *RO*, 2d ser., 7 (January 1, 1893): 94.

[8] *Testament*, 36d, 36e. In his youth, Cerclet was linked with Philippe Buonarotti, the professional revolutionary and associate of François-Noël Babeuf. Later, under the July Monarchy, he became a respected figure in liberal circles. He was secretary of the Présidence de la Chambre des Députés and Maître des Requêtes at the Conseil d'Etat. Littré, *Auguste Comte*, 33; Sébastien Charléty, *Histoire du Saint-Simonisme, 1825–1864* (Paris, 1896), 371n1.

[9] *Testament*, 36c, 36d; Lonchampt, *Précis*, 26. See also Caroline Massin to Comte, February 28, 1846, MAC, and the marriage certificate "Comte et Massin" at the Archives de Paris. This certificate is reprinted in "Acte de Mariage," ed. Laffitte, 92–4.

[10] *Testament*, 36d. It seems likely that the address of their meetings was 193, rue Saint-Honoré, which was the apartment of Massin's mother. See the Marriage Certificate of Caroline Massin and Auguste Comte, Archives de Paris; Death Certificate of Marie Anne Baudelot, Archives de Paris.

bought it for her, perhaps not only to give her financial assistance but also to help him propagate his ideas.[11]

Without engaging in any intimacy, Comte and Massin saw each other from time to time, always in public. But in the fall of 1823, when Massin asked Comte to give her mathematics lessons to improve her bookkeeping, they began meeting more often at her place on the rue de Tracy in the Sentier, where, as Comte said, the lessons "bore fruit" and the instruction became "mutual."[12] In early 1824 Massin sold her reading room and intended to live off of the proceeds until forced to work again. She found a wealthy new lover, the director of a business establishment in the Palais Royal, who promised to help her but then changed his mind, leaving her penniless. Massin used the horrible prospect of returning to prostitution to persuade Comte to let her live with him, which they began doing on February 10, 1824. She contributed her furniture, and he borrowed some money so that they could set up an apartment at 6, rue de l'Oratoire, just off the rue St. Honoré.

At this point, Comte confided the secret of his new living arrangements only to his friend Emile Tabarié, to whom he complained:

> I am really a little tormented by my Caroline to realize the matrimonial fiction that we have established, but I hope she will calm down, and I am, moreover, very determined, just between us, not to go any further in this regard because . . . I believe that in this special circumstance the thing is hardly suitable.[13]

Yet Comte became accustomed to his new way of life, claiming that in many ways he was the happiest he had ever been. He and Massin led a regular life, eating at home, going to bed at 9:00 p.m., and rarely seeing visitors. Even his health improved. To accentuate his new austere existence, he took to wearing black like a clergyman.[14]

In July 1824, during a rare Sunday dinner at a restaurant, he and Massin were disturbed by a policeman, who threatened to arrest her for failing to submit to her mandatory biweekly medical

[11] Littré, *Auguste Comte*, 33n. According to Littré, Caroline Massin received the required license to open the reading room on October 2, 1822, which would have been right after the triumph of the ultras.

[12] Comte to Tabarié, April 5, 1824, *CG*, 1:75.

[13] Ibid., 75–6. For information on this period, see also Lonchampt, *Précis*, 26–7; *Testament*, 36d–36e. There are some slight discrepancies regarding dates in the accounts given by Comte in his 1824 letter to Tabarié and the *Testament*. Massin mentions in her letters that Comte taught her mathematics in 1823. See Massin to Comte, March 29, June 21, 1843, MAC.

[14] Comte to Tabarié, August 22, 1824, *CG*, 1:117; Lonchampt, *Précis*, 33.

examination.[15] Facing a two-week prison sentence, Massin began to cry and persuaded him to let her go. The next day, at the police station, the chief pardoned her but explained that the only way she could get her name erased from the registry of prostitutes was by marriage. Comte was so angry at the authorities and at the same time touched by her trust in his being able to find a solution that he agreed to marry her and wrote to his parents for their permission.[16]

Comte had many reasons for marrying Massin. Lonely in Paris, he longed for a close relationship, especially because he felt that he had suffered too long from the rigors of his intellectual life. Furthermore, he was convinced that he was so unsociable that he would never meet other women, and that even if he did, his "lack of charm and beauty" would put them off.[17] He also found it unseemly for a moral philosopher with a rising reputation to be living secretly with a woman. And to improve his approach to the "moral reorganization" of society, he sought to develop his own feelings.[18] Thus in a sense, he married Massin out of insecurity and convenience, hoping she would develop a "suitable culture." He thought that by saving her he would win her eternal gratitude, which would "certainly survive pure and simple love."[19] Referring with pride to his "extraordinary sacrifice," he enjoyed the role of savior: "It is unfortunately certain that in this century it is necessary to have courage to dare to let oneself be directed by anything other than base egoism."[20] Comte was attracted to the idea of rehabilitating a fallen woman, which was one of the leading themes of the literature of his epoch.[21] He himself seemed to sense the fantastical aspect of his action when he told Valat that his life resembled a "novel."[22]

---

[15] Although ever since the Consulate, prostitution had been treated with tolerance and was no longer strictly illegal, an administrative system of surveillance and sanitary control had been instituted. See N. M. Boiron, *La Prostitution dans l'histoire, devant le droit, devant l'opinion* (Paris: Berger-Levrault, 1926), 79; A. Corbin, *Les Filles de noce: Misère sexuelle et prostitution (19ᵉ siècle)* (Paris: Flammarion, 1982), 13; Jill Harsin, *Policing Prostitution in Nineteenth-Century Paris* (Princeton, N.J.: Princeton University Press, 1985), 6–7.

[16] This account was omitted in the edition of Lonchampt that was published by the Positivists in France, but it is in the Portuguese edition. J. Lonchampt, *Epitome da vida e dos escritos de Auguste Comte*, 2d ed., ed. and trans. Miguel Lemos (Rio de Janeiro: Sede Central da Igreja Positivista do Brazil, Templo da Humanidade, 1959), 136–7. See also Comte to Clotilde de Vaux, September 9, 1845, *CG*, 3:117.

[17] *Testament*, 36e.   [18] Comte to Clotilde de Vaux, August 5, 1845, *CG*, 3:81.

[19] Comte to Tabarié, August 22, 1824, *CG*, 1:114–15.

[20] *Testament*, 36e; Comte to Valat, March 30, 1825, *CG*, 1:156.

[21] General letter to the reader, signed J. S. Florez et al., December 1896, *Testament*, green insert, 3.

[22] Comte to Valat, November 16, 1825, *CG*, 1:163.

Despite later denials, one important reason Comte married Massin was that he loved her. In his letters, he described her "as very witty, very kind, and pretty."[23] He liked "her good heart, graces, . . . amiability, happy disposition, and good habits."[24] Her mind was "of a hardly common quality," while her character was the same as that of Madame de Staël and perfectly suited to his.[25] His feeling toward Massin is confirmed by Valat, who wrote that she had great charm and the "intelligence of a member of the elite" and was "passionately loved" by her husband.[26] Even later, in 1843, after Comte had come to hate her, he acknowledged that she was morally and intellectually exceptional: "My own wife . . . possesses really more mental force, depth, and . . . soundness than the majority of the most justly vaunted personages of her sex."[27]

Another reason for Comte's marriage was his desire to outrage his parents and break away from them. He complained that only money and success moved them, in spite of their pretended devotion to God. By presenting them with a woman who had lived in sin with him for several months and had "o franc o centime," he enjoyed defying them once again.[28] But his parents angrily refused to permit the marriage. They did not want him to marry a woman without resources when he could not even support himself.[29] Furious that his parents were treating him "like a child" and trying to make his marriage into an "affair of money," Comte threatened to go to court. They finally relented in November.[30]

Pleased to have won a new victory over his parents, Comte told his friend Emile Tabarié that he was happy Massin had no family that would have to be "humored and cultivated."[31] Although he may not have had to pay them much attention, Massin did have a mother

---

[23] Comte to Valat, November 3, 1824, *CG*, 1:133.

[24] Comte to Valat, December 25, 1824, *CG*, 1:152.

[25] Ibid; Comte to G. d'Eichthal, November 6, 1824, *CG*, 1:133. See also Comte to Tabarié, August 22, 1824, *CG*, 1:116.

[26] P. Valat, "Auguste Comte et ses disciples," *Revue bordelaise* 2 (August 16, 1880): 304. See also Valat to Robinet, May 10, 1860, Papiers Emile Corra, 17 AS (4), AN.

[27] Comte to Mill, October 5, 1843, *CG*, 2:200. See also Comte to Mill, August 24, 1842, *CG*, 2:76.

[28] Comte to Tabarié, August 22, 1824, *CG*, 1:116. See also Comte to Tabarié, July 27, 1824, *CG*, 1:100–1.

[29] Alix Comte to Robinet, January 26, 1861, in Teixeira Mendes, *Auguste Comte*, 63–4. See the more complete original letter in Papiers Emile Corra 17AS (4), AN. At the end of the original letter, Alix tells Robinet to omit this family quarrel from his biography of Comte. See also Littré, *Auguste Comte*, 33; Lonchampt, *Précis*, 33.

[30] Comte to Tabarié, August 22, 1824, *CG*, 1:116–17. See also *Testament*, 36e; "Acte de Mariage," ed. Laffitte, 93.

[31] Comte to Tabarié, August 22, 1824, *CG*, 1:115.

in Paris as well as an aunt and two uncles on her mother's side.[32] Comte did not seem to have wanted the complications involved in having a family. According to d'Eichthal, Massin had already told him that she was unable to have children.[33]

Comte's marriage is another indication of his deep sense of alienation from society. The legalization of his union displayed a certain desire to conform to the "present state of civilization."[34] But at the same time, his marriage reflected an effort to distance himself further from the society that he scorned. As Gustave d'Eichthal wrote Comte:

> Bear in mind . . . that there are two ways of being a useful member of society: one is to identify with it as much as possible, and it is this [way] that leads to comfort; the other, on the contrary, is to remove oneself as much as possible from its present spirit . . . which leads to glory.[35]

Expelled from the Ecole Polytechnique, affiliated with the subversive thought of Saint-Simon, and repelled by the new society of the Restoration, Comte had already chosen the latter route. Now by going against his parents' wishes and marrying a prostitute in a civil ceremony during the fanatically Catholic regime of Charles X, he had found one more way to challenge generally accepted ideas and social norms. His marriage was, as one positivist later said, the "most revolutionary action" that he could have possibly committed at the time.[36]

At one point, Comte referred to his married life as a period of "sad personal experimentation."[37] In a way, he was following Saint-Simon's recommendation that scientists of society lead an "experimental life" by coming in contact with all types of people.[38] But this experiment reinforced Comte's marginality. Many of his friends, such as Tabarié, disapproved of his action.[39] Although Comte's disciple Lonchampt, one of the executors of his will, claimed that Massin had elegant manners and the "natural grace" of Parisian women, Adolphe d'Eichthal did not find her a "lady of good breed-

---

[32] Comte knew his mother-in-law, for she appeared at the wedding, and he must have seen at least one uncle, because in his address book appears the name Auguste Baudelot. See Comte's address book, MAC; Caroline Massin to Comte, February 27, 1846, MAC.

[33] Deroisin, *Notes sur Auguste Comte,* 22n1.

[34] Comte to Tabarié, August 22, 1824, *CG,* 1:116.

[35] G. d'Eichthal to Comte, January 12, 1825, "Correspondance de Comte et d'Eichthal," ed. Laffitte, 269.

[36] Deroisin, *Notes sur Auguste Comte,* 22.   [37] Comte to Mill, August 24, 1842, *CG,* 2:77.

[38] Saint-Simon, "Préface: Histoire de ma vie," 81.

[39] "Correspondants, amis et protecteurs d'Auguste Comte: Tabarié," ed. Pierre Laffitte, *RO,* 2d ser., 11 (September 1, 1895): 88.

ing" even if she did sparkle with wit.[40] Gustave told his brother that he should not be so "shocked," for Comte's action represented a "very common example among persons who find themselves in the same position as he. They are forced to seek real assistance in a woman, and not a cultivated mind [*bel esprit*]."[41] Reflecting his own disapproval, Gustave advised his brother to keep a certain distance from Comte, advice that he himself was soon to follow.

Notwithstanding the special circumstances surrounding the marriage, Comte acceded to bourgeois custom by signing a marriage contract, which may have been necessary to have Massin's name erased from the registry of prostitutes.[42] He and Massin went to see a notary on February 18, the day before their marriage.[43] They agreed to a community of goods according to the Napoleonic Code with some modifications.

One part of the contract would become controversial. It involved the amount of money brought to the marriage. According to the contract, Comte's household items and personal effects amounted to two thousand francs, whereas Massin had twenty thousand francs, equally divided between goods and cash, which supposedly stemmed from her earnings and savings. Yet in the *Testament*, Comte refers to this dowry as an "invention" that was "twenty times" larger than the sum she actually contributed.[44] Indeed, her family had no money,[45] and whether she was an *ouvrière en linge*, as the marriage certificate states, or a prostitute, she could not have saved such a

---

[40] Lonchampt, *Précis*, 34; Adolphe d'Eichthal to Gustave d'Eichthal, April 21, 1824, Fonds d'Eichthal 13746, item 72, BA.

[41] Gustave d'Eichthal to Adolphe d'Eichthal, April 4, 1824, Fonds d'Eichthal 14396, item 1, BA.

[42] Presenting a marriage contract in order to have one's name erased was necessary at least in the second half of the nineteenth century. Corbin, *Les Filles de noce*, 60. Louis Comte did not know about the contract until after his son's death. See Louis Comte to Laffitte, September 28, 1857, in a packet entitled "Testament d'Auguste Comte," which can be found at the house of the former curator of the Maison d'Auguste Comte, Sybil de Acevedo. I thank her for kindly allowing me to consult her private archives. See also Adeline Daumard, *Les Bourgeois de Paris au XIXe siècle* (Paris: Flammarion, 1970), 170–1.

[43] Caroline Massin to Comte, February 28, 1846, MAC. According to the inventory of Comte's apartment, the marriage contract was in his possession at the time of his death ("Inventaire après le décès de M. Auguste Comte, October 14, 1857, MAC). But it disappeared from the archives and was never mentioned by his biographers. However, a copy of this marriage contract, signed by two witnesses, can still be found in the official papers of the notary, Didier Nicolas Riant. See Etudes 48, number 612, Minutier Central des Notaires Parisiens, AN.

[44] *Testament*, 6.

[45] Her mother died penniless, and when one uncle died, leaving ten thousand francs, Massin received nothing because she was considered a "poor bastard" without rights. Caroline Massin to Comte, February 28, 1846, MAC. See also Caroline Massin to Comte, February 27, 1846, MAC.

large fortune. (A worker at this time earned approximately five or six hundred francs per year.)[46] In fact, Comte supposedly married her because she was totally destitute, and his letters make clear that the couple's financial problems were severe. It is fair then to assume that the dowry was a fiction invented to give the marriage social respectability. Perhaps too Massin hoped it would provide her with some financial security in the future. Later in life, Comte felt victimized by the "generous lie" of his youth, knowing full well that he could not write a will bequeathing his belongings to anyone but Massin.[47] He wrote the *Testament* to counter her legal claims to his estate.[48]

After some delays, the marriage finally took place in a civil ceremony on February 19, 1825, in the town hall of what is now the first arrondissement. The atmosphere must have been tense. Massin's delinquent mother put in an appearance to give her consent. She listed her occupation as washerwoman (*ouvrière en linge*), and her daughter did likewise.[49] The only other guests were the four witnesses. Massin asked her previous lover and protector Antoine Cerclet, whom Comte had met on several occasions. He had even agreed to give Cerclet mathematics lessons, but once he decided to marry Massin, he stopped them.[50] Massin's other witness was a fifty-five-year-old merchant named Louis Oudan.[51] One of Comte's witnesses was Jean-Marie Duhamel, who had been his classmate at the Ecole Polytechnique and was now a teacher at the Collège Louis-le-Grand.[52] The other was Olinde Rodrigues, who had been a tutor

[46] Parent-Lardeur, *Les Cabinets de lecture*, 146.   [47] *Testament*, 5.

[48] Montègre to Laffitte, April 2, 1858, MAC. At Comte's death, when Caroline Massin insisted on her rights under the contract, Comte's executors thought about challenging this sum, but then decided not to do so for fear the judges might favor her since she was in such dire straits. Foucart to Laffitte, October 17, 1857, MAC; Audiffrent to Laffitte, 15 Frédéric 69, 23 Frédéric 69, MAC; Laffitte to Audiffrent, December 1, 1857, fols. 320–1, N.a.fr. 10794, BN; *Tribunal de Première Instance de la Seine. Audience du 11 février 1870. Affaire Auguste Comte. Nullité du Testament. Plaidoirie de Me Allou pour les Exécuteurs Testamentaires* (Paris, 1870), 23.

[49] "Acte de Mariage," ed. Laffitte, 92–4; Lonchampt, *Précis*, 33. Despite Littré's pains later to show that Caroline Massin was a bookseller, she did not list this as her profession on the marriage certificate.

[50] Comte to Cerclet, August 4, 1824, *CG*, 1:103.

[51] Oudan may have been the father of one of Comte's comrades from the Ecole Polytechnique. Louis-Marie Oudan was dismissed from the school at the same time that Comte was. Louis Oudan, the father, was listed in the school records as a landlord who lived at 9, rue du faubourg Montmartre. Several months later Comte and his wife moved almost next door at 13, rue du faubourg Montmartre. "Louis-Marie Oudan," *Registre de matricule des élèves*, vol. 4, *1810–1819*, p. 136, EP; Lonchampt, *Précis*, 34.

[52] Duhamel later became a member of the Academy of Sciences and director of studies at the Ecole Polytechnique. See "Matériaux pour servir à la biographie d'Auguste Comte: Carrière

(*répétiteur*) at the Ecole Polytechnique, where he may have first met Comte. He now was Saint-Simon's main disciple.[53]

Three of the four witnesses to this wedding probably knew one another and reflect the political and academic network in which Comte worked. Duhamel and Cerclet had been co-conspirators in the Carbonari. Duhamel and Rodrigues had attended the Collège Henri IV, met again at the Ecole Polytechnique, and were mathematicians.[54] Cerclet would soon become editor of Rodrigues's Saint-Simonian journal. Judging by the political inclinations of these three men, Comte's ties were still with the Left, despite the fact that his views were becoming increasingly idiosyncratic.

After the wedding, Comte claimed that Massin's name was finally erased from the police registry of prostitutes.[55] Although this problem was resolved, the couple's financial situation was not. Around the time of their marriage, Comte fell heavily into debt, having borrowed more than five hundred francs from the d'Eichthal brothers and a stockbroker, Charles Bénard.[56] He seemed to have no luck finding students, for at this time he had only one – Léon de Lamoricière, the future general, who was introduced to him by Gustave d'Eichthal.[57] His financial worries were so terrible that they prevented him from working.[58]

Polytechnique d'Auguste Comte," ed. Pierre Laffitte, *RO* 19 (November 1, 1887): 315. See also Sigalia Dostrovsky, "Duhamel, Jean-Marie Constant," in *Dictionary of Scientific Biography*, ed. Gillispie.

[53] Although Comte had criticized Rodrigues's article on the political importance of industry that appeared in Saint-Simon's *Opinions littéraires, philosophiques, et industrielles*, he considered him a good friend. Comte to G. d'Eichthal, December 10, 1824, *CG*, 1:145; Comte to Valat, December 25, 1824, *CG*, 1:145; Comte to Bénard, January 22, 1825, *CG*, 1:153. See also Charléty, *Saint-Simonisme*, 32.

[54] Spitzer, *French Generation*, 23, 294.

[55] *Testament*, 36e. Comte says in his *Testament* that on officer of the peace who was one of Massin's witnesses was able to effect this deletion. However, no such person is listed as a witness in the official marriage certificate.

[56] Adolphe d'Eichthal to Gustave d'Eichthal, February 25, 1825, Fonds d'Eichthal 13746, item 69, BA; G. d'Eichthal to Comte, December 10, 1824, "Correspondance de Comte et d'Eichthal," ed. Laffitte, 269; Comte to G. d'Eichthal, April 6, 1825, *CG*, 1:159. Comte repaid part of Bénard's loan by giving lessons to his son in early 1826. He repaid the remainder in 1843. Comte to Bénard, January 22, January 25, January 29, 1825, *CG*, 1:153–5; the envelope of the original letter and the note added in 1843 at the bottom of the receipt at the MAC.

[57] Gustave d'Eichthal had been Lamoricière's classmate at the Pension Lecomte – later Pension Jubé – which was a preparatory school for the Ecole Polytechnique. E. Keller, *Le Général de Lamoricière: Sa vie militaire, politique, et religieuse*, 2 vols. (Paris: Librairie Militaire de J. Dumaine, 1974), 1:13–14; Comte to Valat, December 25, 1824, *CG*, 1:152; Littré, *Auguste Comte*, 34–5.

[58] Adolphe d'Eichthal to Gustave d'Eichthal, February 25, 1825, Fonds d'Eichthal 13746, item 69, BA.

Campredon prevailed upon Reynaud to help Comte. Overlooking his differences with Comte over teaching methods, Reynaud found him a job at the Ecole de Sorèze. Yet Comte delayed his acceptance because he thought it absurd that he should teach at a Benedictine high school, and the position fell to another.[59] As mentioned before, Comte also failed to win an appointment at the Ecole d'Etat-Major despite Campredon's support.[60] Undaunted, Campredon and Reynaud then tried to get Comte a post at the Ecole des Pages, which trained people to serve the king.[61] Here Comte could have at least made some connections if, in Campredon's words, Massin had been able to transform him into an "amiable courtier."[62] Nothing came of these efforts either. Comte's father had already sadly noted in the past to his cousin that Auguste "was not very gifted in making visits and in anything that had to do with etiquette."[63]

Nevertheless, Comte's financial situation mysteriously improved in the spring. Either he borrowed some more money, or Massin unexpectedly received some money.[64] Perhaps Cerclet offered to help her again.

At this juncture, Monsieur de Narbonne, who had received a copy of the fundamental opuscule, proposed to Comte that he take his son as a boarder-student. Comte accepted, and in the hope of enticing more such great families to entrust the care of their offspring to his care, he and Massin moved to a larger apartment at 35, rue de l'Arcade at the corner of rue St. Lazare. But the students never came, and Comte sent Narbonne's son back to him.[65]

At the end of July, Comte decided to take his new wife to Montpellier to introduce her to his parents, to whom he still felt "gratitude and affection," despite their differences.[66] On the way

[59] Campredon to Comte, March 30, 1825, "Correspondants, amis et protecteurs: Le Général Campredon," ed. Laffitte, 175–6; Comte to Valat, March 30, 1825, *CG*, 1:157; Comte to G. d'Eichthal, April 6, 1825, *CG*, 1:159.

[60] Comte to G. d'Eichthal, April 6, 1825, *CG*, 1:159; Campredon to Comte, March 30, 1825, "Correspondants, amis et protecteurs: Le Général Campredon," ed. Laffitte, 175.

[61] Reynaud was "inspector and examiner of studies" at the school. *Almanach royal pour l'an 1826*, 61–2.

[62] Campredon to Comte, March 30, 1825, "Correspondants, amis et protecteurs: Le Général Campredon," ed. Laffitte, 176.

[63] Louis Comte to Comte-Rochambeau, January 13, 1822 [1821], in Ouy, "Jeunesse," 259.

[64] Comte to Valat, March 30, 1825, *CG*, 1:157; Comte to G. d'Eichthal, April 6, 1825, *CG*, 1:158.

[65] Comte to Mme Auguste Comte, August 23, 1839, *CG*, 1:313; Littré, *Auguste Comte*, 34–5. For the precise address, see Adolphe d'Eichthal to Comte, September 6, 1825, in "Correspondance de Comte et d'Eichthal (Suite)," 345.

[66] Comte to Tabarié, July 17, 1824, *CG*, 1:101. See also Comte to Valat, November 16, 1825, *CG*, 1:162. In 1826 Comte even gave his father a token of his affection – a tortoise shell snuffbox. Alix Comte to Laffitte, December 12, 1859, MAC.

south, they spared no expenses, passing a wonderful twenty-four hours in a hotel room in Avignon, where they achieved a "mutual satisfaction."[67] But once they arrived, Massin did not make a good impression on Comte's family. She despised the provincial town and unrefined people and refused ever to return. She also found her father-in-law's attitude toward his son appalling. She told Comte: "In the moments when he revealed his emotions, he always complained about you (to me), only calling you the scholar. You insulted him from the moment that you refused to follow his career."[68] Sadly aware that the differences in character, "manners, [and] habits" between his family and wife could not be bridged, Comte was unable to decide which side had demonstrated the "greatest inflexibility of disposition" or the "greatest rivalry for power."[69]

Because of his hopes of creating a warm and friendly family environment, the failure of his "fatal" voyage was disheartening. Since about 1822, he had toyed with the idea of settling in Montpellier. Paris, having served its function of providing stimulation, was now a constant source of torment, materially, intellectually, and personally. It was a "desert," filled with "indifferent people" whose egoism and corruption had become increasingly unbearable. Because they were so "dissipated," scheming, and "superficial," it was impossible to make any real attachments. He denied the accusations of acquaintances that he himself was too rigid and distrustful and claimed, on the contrary, that he was too eager to seek "sincere and profound affections." Nevertheless, he had not made a single friend during the eleven years he had lived there:

> Now sufficiently stocked with supplies against the needs of the mind, it is those of the heart that I especially need to worry about in order to complete the state of my moral life. . . . For the heart, mutuality [and] human contacts are indispensable in a continual manner. . . . [M]y heart has needs that are as strong as those of my mind.

After all those years, he recognized that he felt affection only for his family and childhood friends. Painting an idyllic picture of these relations, he wrote:

> I am sadly convinced that nothing in the world could replace the pure affections, so sublimely stripped of all egoism, that one finds in one's family and in friendships formed in the first years of life, before the

---

[67] Comte to Mᵐᵉ Auguste Comte, September 26, 1838, *CG*, 1:301. See also Littré, *Auguste Comte*, 34.

[68] Caroline Massin to Comte, August 30, 1838, MAC.

[69] Comte to Valat, November 16, 1825, *CG*, 1:163–4. Again Littré is mistaken in implying that everything went smoothly in Montpellier. Littré, *Auguste Comte*, 34. See Louis Comte to Comte-Rochambeau, July 19, 1826, in Ouy, "Jeunesse," 260.

development of self-love, rivalry, and opposition of interests and positions have made all deep attachments impossible.

Desperately unhappy in Paris, Comte thought he might be able to rediscover these "pure affections" at home in Montpellier, and therefore Massin's refusal ever to go back, even for a visit, was a "cruel and profound blow."[70]

Comte had to resign himself to the coldness of life in Paris. He decided that although he would be denying himself the "sweetest part of happiness," the joy coming from the affections, he would withdraw increasingly from society and devote himself exclusively to his intellectual work. It is clear that years before creating his religion, Comte considered the feelings the most vital aspect of human existence. But when personal relationships did not live up to his expectations, he would retreat into his work, despite his realization that it offered "insufficient compensation."[71]

COMTE'S CHANGING VIEWS ON WOMEN

Comte's reflections indicate that life with Massin was what mainly disappointed him. Already in November he said he would not wish upon "his cruelest enemy" the pains he was experiencing. Relations among men offered "the only complete, the only truly durable" attachments. Comte's personal experience and his increasingly conservative views of society led him to change his attitude toward women. For peace to exist in a household, as in society at large, he said there had to be "unity of direction." While it was true that the basis of this unity could be provided by superior women in marriages involving "ordinary" men, who needed guidance, different standards applied to "men of merit" like Comte. In a woman, characteristics such as intelligence and good taste – qualities that he ascribed with much praise to Massin – were not at all important because they were not the foundation of a happy marriage. Even the most intelligent and refined woman amounted to a "rather secondary man, only with many more pretensions." A man of merit should therefore choose a woman with a "certain intellectual mediocrity" and a "decent character" who would voluntarily submit to him and respect his "moral superiority." The main qualities to look for were "attachment, devotion of heart, and sweetness of character." Most of all, he should avoid a woman who was his equal because she could become "his most direct rival."[72]

[70] Comte to Valat, November 16, 1825, *CG*, 1:163–6.   [71] Ibid., 166.
[72] Ibid., 163, 165–7.

These comments suggest that Massin, clearly a woman of intelligence, threatened Comte. Following his earlier, more feminist principles, he had married a strong woman. But he was disturbed by the fact that she was not in awe of his abilities and tried to assert herself. He could never tolerate a relationship based on equality, for he always suspected the other person of trying to dominate him. No longer did he compare Massin happily to Madame de Staël, whose superiority he now felt was an anomaly and full of "inconveniences."[73]

Thus besides changing his attitude toward family life, which he now valued far more than previously, Comte in 1825 adopted a new, more traditional position with regard to gender roles – a position in keeping with the contemporary, conservative ideology of the separation of spheres. Angry at his unruly wife, he now seemed closer to those men (such as Rousseau) whom he had previously denounced for maintaining the "horrible law of the strongest" and making women submit to "his Majesty *Man*." Like other nineteenth-century Frenchmen on both the Left and Right who reacted against the movement in favor of women's emancipation, Comte denigrated independent, outspoken women by attacking their morality and implying that they were in some way demonic. Thinking about his wife, who had no religious upbringing, he complained that intellectually "distinguished" women often adopted atheism, had poor moral and domestic habits, and reveled in argumentation.[74] In the imagery of French patriarchal society, the opposites of such unprincipled, disorderly women were angels.[75] From this point on, he developed an angelic ideal of women as primarily adoring, dependent, self-sacrificing creatures whose ability to discuss intelligently the "merit of such and such a play" or "such and such a novel" was fundamentally immaterial.[76] A woman's individuality did not count; what mattered was her nurturing role and especially the support she gave to a man.

It is clear that the "woman question" contributed to Comte's growing reaction against liberalism. As reflected in the comments that he made during his pro-Wollstonecraft phase, he sensed that the logic of liberal principles led to a greater emphasis on woman's individuality and her rights. But now he decided that sexual equality would destroy the family and society. When he congratulated Valat for wisely choosing an obedient, conventional wife, he

---

[73] Comte to Valat, November 16, 1825, *CG*, 1:166.   [74] Ibid., 166–7.
[75] On the reaction against feminism, see Moses, *French Feminism*, 17–18, 38; Nina Auerbach, *Woman and the Demon: The Life of a Victorian Myth* (Cambridge, Mass.: Harvard University Press, 1982), 63; Bell and Offen, *Women*, 133–41; Bonnie G. Smith, *Changing Lives: Women in European History since 1700* (Lexington, Mass.: Heath, 1989), 129–31, 183–8, 204–7.
[76] Comte to Valat, November 16, 1825, *CG*, 1:167.

specifically denounced the general trend of his "philosophic century" that allowed each person, even the most superficial and intellectually limited, "to reason freely . . . on the most important and difficult questions of life," those relating to morality. Thus individualism, especially in a woman, who was intellectually inferior, was morally dangerous. No longer did Comte promote women's material and moral independence. After witnessing the discordant effects of his wife's atheism, he was more than ever convinced of the need for people to share a single uniform moral system:

> Now people who are intelligent enough not to believe in God are not lacking, . . . [but] hardly any of them are sufficiently intelligent to reconstruct . . . on other bases a fixed and positive morality, capable of influencing life in a useful direction and producing something other than argumentations.[77]

The creation of a uniform "code of political and moral opinions admitted without contest by all classes" and both sexes became of utmost importance in order to stifle individualism and create social harmony.[78] Marriage, like society itself, could not work if it was not based on a hierarchical relationship, where one sex, or class, voluntarily submitted to the other, which was intellectually and morally superior.

PROBLEMS WITH PART 2 OF THE *SYSTÈME DE POLITIQUE POSITIVE*

One of the reasons Comte needed peace in his life was to complete the *Système de politique positive*, of which the *Plan* was the first part.[79] The second part was supposed to be a detailed account of the history of civilization. To make his doctrine more understandable, Comte intended to publish this second part with a modified version of the first part in one volume. The addition of a new preface, minimizing his "intellectual obligations" to Saint-Simon, would erase "all traces" of their relationship, which he worried were discrediting his work.[80]

Comte had a mental block about this second part. It contributed to his rupture with his mentor, led to tensions with Valat and d'Eichthal, and caused him to lie to friends to hide his embarrass-

---

[77] Ibid.   [78] Comte to Valat, December 25, 1824, *CG*, 1:148.
[79] The *Système de politique positive* was never completed in the 1820s. In the 1850s, Comte called his four-volume work on sociology the *Système de politique positive*.
[80] Comte to Tabarié, July 17, 1824, *CG*, 1:101–3. See also Comte to G. d'Eichthal, November 6, 1824, *CG*, 1:135.

ment.[81] Throughout 1824 he used one excuse after another to put off writing it, although he believed people were impatient to read it. His incapacity even interfered with his plans to teach at the Athénée, a private institution that invited famous scholars or rising young stars to give courses to adults. Blainville was instrumental in arranging for Comte to teach a course in politics there. But to complete the second part, Comte twice postponed his course, in January and November 1825.[82] However, by January 1826 he still had not written a single line. Two months later, he decided that his ideas were in such disorder that he had to start all over again.[83] Thus for at least two years, from 1824 to 1826, Comte remained "horribly tormented" by his project. He ascribed his problems to the lack of tranquility required for "long and unrelenting meditations."[84]

Besides financial and marital troubles, Comte faced another obstacle, the great scientific and personal importance he attached to the second part. While the first part had described the positive method of social physics, the second would deal with the basis of the science of society, that is, with the "invariable natural laws" of history, which showed the connections among social phenomena throughout time and determined "with certitude" the future of society.[85] This part of the *Système* would establish the positive science of society, destroy theological and metaphysical thinking, and lead to a vast intellectual revolution. Comte believed he would then be recognized as a prominent intellectual figure and would make important contacts with powerful men throughout Europe.[86] At that point, he could concentrate on the next and most important part of his life's work, the creation of the positive code of morality. He was

---

[81] Comte to Tabarié, April 5, 1824, *CG*, 1:78; Comte to G. d'Eichthal, May 1, 1824, *CG*, 1:83.

[82] Comte began thinking about lecturing at the Athénée as early as the summer of 1824, not in 1825, as Laffitte declared. Comte to Tabarié, July 17, August 22, 1824, *CG*, 1:102, 117; Laffitte, "L'Athénée," 2, 11, 21. See also Comte to G. d'Eichthal, May 1, November 6, 1824, and April 6, November 24, 1825, *CG*, 1:83, 135, 159, 175–76; Comte to Valat, March 30, November 16, 1825, and January 18, 1826, *CG*, 1:158, 167, 182; Letter from Blainville to Comte, January 21, 1825 at MAC; Comte, "Considérations philosophiques sur les sciences et sur les savants," *Le Producteur* 1 (1825): 289n1 (this footnote was suppressed in the *Système*).

[83] Comte to Valat, January 18, 1826, *CG*, 1:182; Comte to Blainville, February 27, 1826; Auguste Comte, *Correspondance inédite d'Auguste Comte*, 4 vols. (Paris: Au Siège de la Société Positiviste, 1903) (hereafter, *Corr. inédite*), 1:24–5. The very important letter of February 27, 1826, that Comte wrote to Blainville is accurately reproduced in *Corr. inédite*, 17–26, not in *CG*, 1:185–90. See the original letter, MAC.

[84] Comte to Valat, December 25, 1824, and January 18, 1826, *CG*, 1:152, 182.

[85] Comte to Buchholz, November 18, 1825, *CG*, 1:170.

[86] Ibid.; Comte to G. d'Eichthal, May 1, November 6, 1824, *CG*, 1:83, 135; Comte to Tabarié, July 17, 1824, *CG*, 1:102; Comte to Valat, September 8, 1824, *CG*, 1:121.

afraid, however, that his abilities might not be up to this series of tasks. The pressure on him was all the greater when Campredon and d'Eichthal insisted that, without the second part, his volume would not be as clear or successful.[87]

Although he preferred to mention nonintellectual problems, such as his wife's health, as the source of his troubles, he occasionally admitted that he had difficulty conceptualizing the work as a whole and wondered whether he had the necessary "erudition" to connect historical facts to general laws.[88] Part of his complaint was that the language of politics was polluted by "literary pedantry." In trying to establish a totally "new order of ideas," he felt "opposed at every moment by language, by the need for new expressions, freed from the theological and metaphysical character under whose influence our languages are formed."[89] At the same time, he remembered Campredon's warning that his excessive use of scientific expressions had already alienated many readers.[90] Like the revolutionaries of 1789, Comte was very conscious of the need to create the correct terms to communicate his new ideas. "Language, . . . examined historically, presents a faithful picture of the revolutions of the human mind."[91]

Another source of discouragement for Comte was that d'Eichthal, Campredon, and Valat had convinced him that many of his ideas in the first part, especially his concept of the scientific class, were too obscure.[92] But what shocked him the most was Blainville's blunt remark that, despite its title, the *Système de politique positive* was not at all systematic.[93] Since Comte looked upon him as an adviser, the tremendous anxiety caused by this comment threatened his mental health.

---

[87] Campredon to Comte, June 30, 1824, "Correspondants, amis et protecteurs: Le Général Campredon," ed. Laffitte, 174; G. d'Eichthal to Comte, September 4, 1824, "Correspondance de Comte et d'Eichthal," ed. Laffitte, 250; Adolphe d'Eichthal to Gustave d'Eichthal, January 23, 1825, Fonds d'Eichthal 13746, item 82, BA.

[88] Comte to G. d'Eichthal, May 1, August 5, 1824, *CG*, 1:83, 108; Comte to Tabarié, July 17, 1824, *CG*, 1:101. D'Eichthal suggested Bossuet's *Discours sur l'histoire universelle* as a model, which did not seem to inspire Comte at the moment. Later, however, he included it in the Positivist Library. G. d'Eichthal to Comte, May 11, 1824, "Correspondance de Comte et d'Eichthal," ed. Laffitte, 206; *Système*, 4:560.

[89] Comte to Valat, December 25, 1824, *CG*, 1:150.

[90] Campredon to Comte, June 30, 1824, "Correspondants, amis et protecteurs: Le Général Campredon," ed. Laffitte, 174.

[91] *Système*, vol. 4, "Appendice," 146n1. On the revolutionaries' creation of a new language, see Hunt, *Politics, Culture, and Class*, 19–28.

[92] Comte to Valat, September 8, 1824, *CG*, 1:127; Comte to G. d'Eichthal, November 6, 1824, *CG*, 1:137; G. d'Eichthal to Comte, September 4, November 18, 1824, *RO* (1896): 250, 257; Gouhier, *Jeunesse*, 3:304.

[93] Comte to Blainville, February 27, 1826, *Corr. inédite*, 1:19–20.

In late 1825 Comte received an opportunity to direct his energies elsewhere. Antoine Cerclet, his wife's friend, sought to persuade him to write for a new publication to which he had just been named editor. The weekly journal, called *Le Producteur: Journal de l'industrie, des sciences et des beaux-arts*, had been founded by Olinde Rodrigues and his colleague Enfantin on June 1, 1825, twelve days after the death of Saint-Simon. Comte had attended the funeral at Père Lachaise, where he undoubtedly made contact again with the Saint-Simonians.[94]

At first, Comte was loath to accept the offer. Besides worrying about being diverted from his own work, he feared the new journal might be too "revolutionary," thereby hindering his appeal to all parties.[95] Its goals also struck him as too vague and ambitious. By covering industrial and political issues as well as philosophical ones, it risked repeating Saint-Simon's error of giving priority to temporal reorganization.[96]

Despite these reservations, Comte in the end accepted the job. His inability to find students had already forced him in October to move to a smaller apartment at 13, rue du Faubourg-Montmartre.[97] Though aware that he had to "bend" his character to the "damned century" in which he lived, he found it impossible to cultivate people like Reynaud who could help his teaching career.[98] Considering the fact that he had run out of money, the job at *Le Producteur* could not have come at a better time. In addition, Comte accepted the position because he did not want to alienate his friend Rodrigues or the Saint-Simonians, many of whose supporters, such as Ternaux, Ardouin, and Lachevardière, he was trying to woo.[99] He also trusted Cerclet, who was not a devoted member of the Saint-Simonian "coterie" and could act as a moderating influence. Comte was happy to see that the first issues were not as "revolutionary" as he had feared and did not publicize their affiliation with Saint-Simonian ideas.[100]

[94] Littré, *Auguste Comte*, 35; Fournel, *Bibliographie Saint-Simonienne*, 34; Hubbard, *Saint-Simon*, 110.
[95] Comte to G. d'Eichthal, November 24, 1825, *CG*, 1:172.
[96] Comte to Valat, December 25, 1824, *CG*, 1:149.
[97] Littré, *Auguste Comte*, 35; Comte to Valat, November 16, 1825, and January 18, 1826, *CG*, 1:168, 182; Comte to G. d'Eichthal, November 24, 1825, *CG*, 1:171–2.
[98] Comte to Valat, March 30, 1825, and January 18, 1826, *CG*, 1:157, 182.
[99] Comte to G. d'Eichthal, November 24, 1825, *CG*, 1:172; "Copie de l'acte de société du journal *Le Producteur*," June 1, 1825, Fonds Enfantin 7643, fols. 36–9. See also Henri de Saint-Simon and Prosper Enfantin, *Oeuvres de Saint-Simon et d'Enfantin*, 47 vols. (Paris, 1865–78), 1:150.
[100] Comte to G. d'Eichthal, November 24, 1825, *CG*, 1:172.

Moreover, after the death of Saint-Simon, Comte saw himself as the master of the new industrial and scientific philosophy and thought *Le Producteur* could be a useful vehicle for propagating his own ideas. Already, he boasted that a letter from Buchholz was able to reach him despite the fact that it had only the following address: "To Mr. Auguste Comte, author of the système de politique positive [*sic*], in Paris."[101] He was equally pleased to tell Valat that the founders of *Le Producteur* had "urged me so much to write for it in order to make the journal's reputation that I could not refuse."[102]

In fact, *Le Producteur* did address many of Comte's concerns. In the first issue, of October 1825, Cerclet explained that the publication aimed to spread the principles of a "new philosophy," which would make production the common goal of society and thus provide the basis for political and moral reorganization. The articles would examine the scientific, economic, and literary productions that were leading to the growth of the new social system, which Cerclet emphasized was becoming "more and more positive." The journal stressed the creation of a science of politics and political economy; the laws of progress; the role of an elite of scientists, industrialists, and artists; the establishment of a future industrial and scientific society marked by peaceful associations; and the importance of a solid foundation for people's opinions. These were the same themes that Comte and Saint-Simon had been espousing in *L'Organisateur* and *Le Catéchisme industriel*. Comte was in a sense asked to join *Le Producteur* in order to continue his work as a theorist of the "new philosophy."[103]

Cerclet and his associates made no effort to build upon the ideas launched by Saint-Simon in his last book, *Nouveau Christianisme: Dialogues entre un conservateur et un novateur*, which had appeared in April 1825. Imbued with a "divine mission," Saint-Simon announced in this book the religious future of mankind and called for the renewal of the original, true spirit of Christianity – brotherly love – in order to reform society.[104] Thus, unlike Comte, Saint-Simon advocated establishing a general moral code that would be formulated in terms of traditional religion. Although the *Nouveau Christianisme* has often been considered one of Saint-Simon's most significant works, it was not regarded as such when it first appeared. *Le*

---

[101] Comte to Valat, November 16, 1825, *CG*, 1:168.

[102] Comte to Valat, January 18, 1826, *CG*, 1:182.

[103] Cerclet, "Introduction," *Le Producteur* 1 (1825): 5–10. See also Enfantin to Thérèse Nugues, August 18, 1825, Fonds Enfantin 7643, folio 69, BA.

[104] Saint-Simon, *Nouveau Christianisme*, in *Oeuvres*, 3.3:188. See also ibid., 101, 108, 110, 112, 125–6; Saint-Simon's dying words, Henri-René d'Allemagne, *Les Saint-Simoniens, 1827–1837* (Paris: Gründ, 1930), 13; Fournel, *Bibliographie Saint-Simonienne*, 33.

Producteur made no mention of this revival of the Christian religion, at least in its early issues. In fact, Enfantin, Comte's fellow alumnus of the Ecole Polytechnique, was completely puzzled by Saint-Simon's last work. Therefore, at this time Comte had no reason to complain about any religious tendencies among his mentor's disciples because such inclinations did not exist. The Saint-Simonians were most interested in studying industrial and scientific developments. Consisting solely of Olinde Rodrigues, Prosper Enfantin, Saint-Armand Bazard, Léon Halévy, Bailly, and Charles Duveyrier, the disciples of Saint-Simon had not yet even formed a school, much less a new church, and they welcomed outsiders, such as Adolphe Blanqui, to their journalistic enterprise.[105] Comte was correct in his judgment that the new journal lacked a clear plan, for the subjects of the articles were indeed very far ranging.[106]

In sum, by participating in this journal, Comte was not proclaiming his allegiance to any Saint-Simonian doctrine. He maintained his distance, attended no meetings, and dealt directly with Cerclet, to whom he submitted his articles. His relations to *Le Producteur* were, in his words, strictly "literary."[107]

THE FOURTH OPUSCULE: "CONSIDÉRATIONS PHILOSOPHIQUES SUR LES SCIENCES ET LES SAVANTS"

Comte's first essay, "Considérations philosophiques sur les sciences et les savants," was published as a series of three articles, which appeared in November and December 1825.[108] Comte thought well enough of them to republish them as his fourth opuscule at the end of his *Système* in 1854. They show the evolution of his philosophy as well as his problems in formulating it.

Comte chose to discuss in these articles the spiritual power. With the liberals engaged in an anticlerical campaign opposing the ultras' bid for control of education, the question of power and its relationship to knowledge had been a subject of intense debate for many years, especially after the accession to the throne of Charles X, who wanted to do more to favor the state religion.[109] Comte himself had

---

[105] D'Allemagne, *Les Saint-Simoniens*, 30–34; Charléty, *Saint-Simonism*, 57; Hubbard, *Saint-Simon*, 102.

[106] Comte to Valat, January 18, 1826, *CG*, 1:181.

[107] Comte to Michel Chevalier, January 5, 1832, *CG*, 1:228.

[108] The articles appeared in the seventh, eighth, and tenth issues of *Le Producteur*, published respectively on November 12, November 19, and December 3, 1825. Fournel, *Bibliographie Saint-Simonienne*, 39–40. Arnaud's note xlviii is erroneous. *CG*, 1:397.

[109] Holmes, *Benjamin Constant*, 15.

been preoccupied by this subject for several years. He had often expressed his regret that a new spiritual power did not yet exist, and in the *Plan* he had promised that his future works would deal with the "spiritual reorganization of society" and the "great question of the division of spiritual power and temporal power."[110] Furthermore, he had realized, thanks to d'Eichthal and Valat, that he had not clarified the role of the scientists, who represented the spiritual power, and he had not sufficiently focused on the new class of scholars who were to develop the science of society.[111] The *Plan* had failed to specify that the scientists of society had to be experts in the positive method, an omission he now intended to rectify.[112] Also, in the *Plan* he had relegated his thoughts on this new class of scholars to a mere footnote, which stated that the distinction between specialized and general scientists was only of "secondary" importance.[113] Henceforth, this distinction would be of primary importance.

Finally, Comte probably chose this topic because he wanted to emphasize a point of difference between himself and Saint-Simon. He wanted to remind the founders of *Le Producteur* and others that the general scientists, not the industrialists or artists, were primarily responsible for the reorganization of society.[114] To him, the industrialists were too megalomaniacal, utilitarian, and materialistic; their insistence on having absolute power made them just as "impertinent" as the nobles, if not more so. Industrialists thought social reform involved merely improving the food, clothing, and housing of the people. They would convert scientists into "pure engineers whom they would put on bread and water" if they did not create something new every week.[115] Hoping to guarantee an important role for scholars in the new society being promoted by *Le Producteur*, Comte thus did not share Saint-Simon's and his disciples' trust in the industrialists and criticized his period's growing obsession with material, practical values.[116]

When he wrote the "Considérations philosophiques sur les sciences et sur les savants," Comte heeded d'Eichthal's advice to follow

[110] Comte, "Avertissement" to the *Plan* in Saint-Simon, *Oeuvres*, 4.2:6; *Système*, vol. 4, "Appendice," 67n1.

[111] Comte also felt he had been wrong in the *Plan* to speak of the intervention of the scientists before having first demonstrated that the establishment of the new science of politics was historically inevitable. Comte to G. d'Eichthal, November 6, 1824, and April 6, 1825, *CG*, 1:137, 160; G. d'Eichthal to Comte, August 22, November 18, 1824, "Correspondance de Comte et d'Eichthal," ed. Laffitte, 248, 257; Comte to Valat, September 8, 1824, *CG*, 1:127. See also Gouhier, *Jeunesse*, 3:306.

[112] Gouhier, *Jeunesse*, 306.   [113] *Système*, vol. 4, "Appendice," 72n1.

[114] Comte to Blainville, February 27, 1826, *Corr. inédite*, 1:22.

[115] Comte to G. d'Eichthal, November 24, 1825, *CG*, 1:174.

[116] Manuel, *Saint-Simon*, 339.

Kant's example in the *Idea for a Universal History*. Therefore, instead of giving an account of the current French political situation as he had done in the *Plan*, he immediately set forth the law of three stages and gave it the clearest and longest exposition he had attempted so far. It was now the "point of departure for all philosophical research on man and society."[117]

Inspired by Kant, d'Eichthal had also encouraged Comte to begin by showing that *"the life of society is determined like that of every organic being."*[118] Ferguson, Condorcet, and Saint-Simon had frequently used this argument by analogy, but Comte had rejected it for fear of reducing the science of society to physiology. Now, however, basing his new science on a physiological or, more precisely, a psychological argument, he argued for the first time that the mind of the individual and that of the species developed according to the same principles. By observing himself, any enlightened man could see that he had been "a theologian in his childhood, a metaphysician in his youth, and a natural philosopher [*physicien*] in his maturity."[119] Comte thus contradicted his previous position that it was impossible for a man to observe himself. By embracing the deterministic position recommended by d'Eichthal, he was trying above all to remove all doubts about the validity of his law of three stages.

Comte adopted another suggestion of d'Eichthal, who asserted that Kant had shown not only that there could be a science of human phenomena based on natural laws but that this science was necessary for social progress.[120] Comte repeated this formula when he announced in his essay:

> One must envisage this law [of three stages], like all social facts, according to a double point of view: according to the physical [or scientific] point of view of necessity, that is, as deriving from the natural laws of human nature, and according to the moral point of view of its indispensability, that is, as being the sole mode suitable to the development of the human spirit.[121]

Like Kant, Comte now regarded the law of civilization as a scientific description of human phenomena and a social imperative.

Comte had developed his view of the theological stage in several respects. Influenced by Hume, he said this stage was marked by man's search for first and final causes. Moreover, he divided it into

[117] *Système*, vol. 4, "Appendice," 146.
[118] G. d'Eichthal to Comte, August 22, 1824, "Correspondance de Comte et d'Eichthal," ed. Laffitte, 248.
[119] *Système*, vol. 4, "Appendice," 138.
[120] G. d'Eichthal to Comte, August 22, 1824, "Correspondance de Comte et d'Eichthal," ed. Laffitte, 246.
[121] *Système*, vol. 4, "Appendice," 138.

three periods: fetishism, polytheism, and theism. This was a new concept. Saint-Simon had talked vaguely about idolatry, polytheism, and deism, but had not defined them or joined them into one theological period. In Comte's essay, the theological period also took on a more anthropocentric flavor. Early man believed phenomena were inhabited by supernatural agents, who acted like human beings, that is, erratically and arbitrarily. But as Smith had shown, primitive man, even at this early fetishist stage, began to see that some phenomena acted in a regular manner and were regulated by natural laws.[122] Thus positive philosophy was at least as old as theology. Gradually, as a result of more extensive observations, early man developed the doctrine of polytheism. No longer alive with spirits, nature was supposedly controlled by a certain number of independent, invisible superhuman agents whose authority was based on the type and extent of phenomena they ruled. Progress in observation led finally to the last stage of theology, that of theism, which attributed to one supernatural being the functions previously belonging to many gods. The three theological stages reflected the gradual limitation of supernatural intervention to areas whose positive laws remained unknown. As soon as people had a scientific explanation for a natural occurrence, they immediately adopted it because they found that it satisfied their needs of prediction and effective action. The power of theology therefore declined as the positive method started directing the intellect.

Comte had not changed his view that the second stage, that of metaphysics, was a transitional period that reflected the influence of science on theology and substituted abstract forces for supernatural causes. He did, however, clarify his definition of the positive stage. In the *Plan*, he had described the third stage as one limiting human knowledge to the establishment of general laws confirmed by the observation of facts. Now he extended this definition, explaining that a scientific law expressed the "constant relations of similitude and of succession that facts have among themselves."[123] Therefore, one had to observe phenomena in their development in order to grasp their relationships. Comte's stress on the need to discover this type of scientific law instead of causes again reflects Hume's influence. Although he believed that if a proposition did not express a fact, it was meaningless, he insisted at the same time that positive philosophy could not be reduced to pure empiricism. Maintaining the importance of imagination and theory, he wrote:

---

[122] Comte referred to Smith's "Essai philosophique sur l'histoire de l'astronomie" to support his theory. Also see *Cours*, 2:222.

[123] *Système*, vol. 4, "Appendice," 144.

Man is incapable by his nature not only of combining facts and deducing from them several consequences, but of even simply observing them with attention and retaining them with certainty if he does not attach them immediately to some explanation. He cannot have connected observations without some theory any more than [he can have] a positive theory without regular observations.

In fact, because Comte thought "absolute empiricism" was impossible and man must have a theory in order to observe, he considered theological theories an appropriate and indispensable beginning to human history; they allowed early man the ability to unify facts, which led to progress.[124] He wanted positive philosophy to employ the methods of both empiricism and rationalism. Either method could be used, for example, to establish the law of three stages. He did not address himself to the ambiguities in his position.

Having shown that the mind developed according to these three stages, Comte claimed that its progress was also determined by social or moral conditions because the mind evolved only "in society and by society."[125] Ideas could grow only in a complex society where some people had the leisure to study nature properly and to form a philosophical system. Just as Comte tried to avoid giving priority to either rationalism or empiricism, he attempted to make idealism and materialism equally important. On the one hand, the growth of the mind depended on the economic and social division of labor, but on the other hand, ideas played a crucial role in social life. Comte still had not solved the problem of showing the interplay of the spiritual and temporal realms – a problem that also plagued him in writing the second part of the *Système* in the mid-1820s.

Much of this opuscule covered the development of positive knowledge since the seventeenth century. In the *Plan*, each science became positive according to the proximity of its corresponding phenomena to man and their degree of complexity. Comte now added two new conditions: the independence of the phenomena and their degree of specialization.[126] Astronomy became positive first not only because its phenomena were the farthest away from man and the simplest but also because they were the most independent: they affected all other phenomena without ever being changed by them. They were also the most general (or least specialized) because they obeyed one universal law, that of gravitation. These two new

---

[124] Ibid., 141. [125] Ibid., 143.

[126] The biological roots of his thought are revealed in a footnote in the original article, which Comte later eliminated. There he explained that this principle of classification had already been developed by physiologists, notably by Candolle in his *Théorie de la botanique*. Comte owned an 1819 edition of this book. Comte, "Considérations philosophiques," 350–1n.

factors of independence and specialization demonstrated more clearly the relationships among the sciences themselves. On the one hand, even though a science might not be positive, its predecessors in the scientific hierarchy could be, because each science was independent of the sciences that followed it. On the other hand, each science was dependent on the knowledge achieved by its predecessors because it dealt with increasingly complex phenomena, and it could not become positive until its predecessors became positive. Comte also added these conditions to emphasize the point that his science of society was the last science to develop because it depended on the other sciences. Whereas in the *Plan*, Comte referred to the science of society as the science of politics, political science, scientific politics, positive politics, and social physics, he now tended to call it simply "*social physics*" to emphasize its scientific nature.[127]

Since social physics dealt with the phenomena that were the most complicated, the most specialized, the closest to man, and the most dependent on all the others, it had to wait for the other sciences to become positive, especially physiology, which provided it with the laws of human nature. Astronomy, physics, and chemistry were now positive, and thanks to Gall, the last section of physiology, which concerned the moral, that is, intellectual and affective, realm, was finally becoming positive too. For the first time, Comte distinguished between moral phenomena that were organic and thus belonged to physiology and those that were social and hence formed part of "social physics." Because the human mind required its doctrines to harmonize with its methods, it would naturally apply the same scientific principles used in all the other areas of knowledge to social phenomena. Positive philosophy, encompassing all of man's knowledge of natural phenomena, would be complete when all phenomena were regarded in a scientific fashion. Perhaps inspired by his recent encounter with German idealism, Comte suggested that the positive philosophy, in addition to fulfilling the practical goal of ensuring social unity and development, corresponded to the intellectual need for coherence.[128] Since scientific principles and social theories were always closely related, changes in the former effected transformations in the latter. Having already vanquished almost all of the strongholds of theology and metaphysics, the positive method would inevitably triumph in all spheres, for reason always prevailed over faith. To give substance to his theory, Comte claimed such distinguished thinkers as Bacon, Galileo, and Descartes as the originators of his new intellectual system, and he also discussed the

---

[127] Ibid., 150.   [128] Arnaud, *Le "Nouveau Dieu,"* 141.

works of Montesquieu, Condorcet, Maistre, Kant, Herder, and the eighteenth-century Scottish philosophers.

In this essay, Comte became much more precise about the philosophical ramifications of social physics. Whereas previously he had discussed the classification of knowledge in terms of the growth of the positive method and the development of individual positive sciences, now he suggested that as the sciences became positive, they were simultaneously creating a positive philosophy. He seemed to be developing ideas that he had sketched out in 1818–21 and expressed in his first articles for *L'Industrie*, where, under Saint-Simon's inspiration, he called for a new common philosophy or "encyclopedia" of positive truths.[129] Still preoccupied by the model of the eighteenth-century *Encyclopédie*, he said that it had failed to achieve "order and unity" in human knowledge because it combined theological, metaphysical, and positive elements that were ultimately mutually exclusive. The establishment of social physics would lead to homogeneity in human knowledge and permit philosophers to construct the desired complete intellectual system, the positive philosophy. He did not discuss the rise of positive philosophy in terms of scientific methodology as he had before, but stated vaguely that it would emerge from the discovery of the "natural chain" linking all of our knowledge of natural phenomena. Using the Encyclopedists' metaphor of a tree, he explained that this philosophy would be the "sole and same trunk" linking all the "diverse branches" of science.[130]

In addition to being indispensable from an intellectual point of view, positive philosophy was necessary socially and politically. Here Comte's interest in education as the solution to the "great social question" reemerged. Education, which reflected the state of philosophy, was the key to social change; it was the crucial link between theory and practice. Yet he felt it was presently ineffective because theological, metaphysical, and positive methods were being used simultaneously. The establishment of positive philosophy would, however, give people a complete and homogeneous doctrine and unite them in a "single communion of ideas." By providing them with the spiritual doctrine and direction they desperately needed and creating a "fixed and regular hierarchy," positive philosophy would eliminate the corruption, materialism, and "unrestrained individualism" that were impeding the founding of a stable society and a moral order.[131]

It was the moral aspect of the positive philosophy that already most preoccupied Comte. Disagreeing with *Le Producteur* and

---

[129] *Ecrits*, 81. [130] *Système*, vol. 4, "Appendice," 158–9. [131] Ibid., 159–60.

statements he had made in his youth, he argued that the sciences' influence on man's action on nature was only "indirect and secondary." Their primary importance lay not in their practical, material function, which had been grossly exaggerated, but in their ability to effect man's "moral revolution." Having already freed society from theology and metaphysics, they were about to provide it with a new *spiritual* basis. The scientists were people's spiritual advisers, not industry's hirelings. To preserve scientists' independence and purity, he envisioned creating a special class of engineers to serve as intermediaries between them and the industrialists. These engineers would fulfill the functions that the excessively practical spirit of the new industrial age demanded.[132] As a result, the sciences would be judged solely by "their philosophical importance" and would remain uncorrupted.[133]

Nevertheless, scientific theories would have a great bearing on the political world. As he had already pointed out in his *Plan*, Comte explained that social physics would offer statesmen a certain amount of foresight and control. With knowledge of the "diverse tendencies" of their period, they could establish the appropriate "practical forms" and thus avoid "crises" caused by unforeseen, spontaneous developments and futile direct political actions.[134] Politicians, in Comte's view, were similar to doctors, for both could only alleviate the pain caused by natural afflictions they could not prevent. Showing how institutions reflected the social state, social physics was thus characterized by limited, humble goals. People might be witnesses to radical changes, but they could not bring them about themselves if such transformations did not accord with the spirit of the times.

Comte's position was not, however, entirely conservative, because he insisted that men accept and adapt to the inevitable changes generated by progress. As he pointed out in his next series of articles, "I repeat, everything that happened had to happen, and I am certainly as far away as anyone from any sterile regrets for the past."[135] His approach to the political world was to a certain extent marked by realism, relativism, and pragmatism. Rejecting utopian schemes of immediate social reconstruction, Comte believed the new positive era would come about only through slow, gradual change. But in a sense, he did not have to call for special action, because he had the faith of a believer; to him, history proved that it was only a matter of time before all of Europe would be "converted" to the positive system.[136]

[132] Comte explained that the engineers' doctrine would develop ideas touched on in Monge's book on descriptive geometry, the work he had translated for Hachette.
[133] *Système*, vol. 4, "Appendice," 173.   [134] Ibid., 151.   [135] Ibid., 184.   [136] Ibid., 175n1.

In reviewing the history of the world in the "Considérations philosophiques," Comte concentrated on the development of the spiritual power instead of the intellectual system itself. He divided the history of the spiritual power, that is, the scientists, into three eras corresponding to the theological, metaphysical, and positive stages, whose dates he changed. According to his "Sommaire appréciation de l'ensemble du passé moderne," the theological and feudal system emerged in Europe in the third and fourth centuries and reached its fullest development in the eleventh and twelfth centuries.[137] Armed with knowledge acquired not only from Herder, Smith, and Constant but from Friedrich Creuzer, the German authority on mythology, Comte now asserted that the theological system began in primitive societies and triumphed particularly in the non-European societies of Egypt, Chaldea, India, Tibet, China, Japan, Peru, and Mexico.[138] In those societies, there was no clear division of labor, and absolute authority was held by the spiritual power, a caste of scholars who controlled the theological system. Since knowledge was limited, they were experts in all fields and were regarded not only as priests but as philosophers and scientists. In fact, the credit they gained as scientists served as the basis of their political power, which gave them the freedom to develop their theories. Because of this theocracy, some limited intellectual progress was possible.

It is clear that Comte greatly admired the "vigor," order, and coherence given to these early social systems by the spiritual corporation. He even went so far as to assert that the "absolute systematization" and "unity" of their homogeneous intellectual systems, the source of their social order, could be reproduced only by positive philosophy. In fact, he said that if the reactionary philosophers like Maistre were truly loyal to their principles, they would try to revive primitive society's fully developed theocracy instead of Christianity, which represented a very decadent theological form. Thus it appears that the primitive era had joined the Middle Ages as one of the primary objects of Comte's deep respect. However, his nostalgia was limited because he realized that a theocracy's strong social organization, which allowed for no division of labor, was the very cause of its "almost stationary" position. To resolve the "necessary incompatibility" between order and progress, he sought to establish a strong spiritual organization in which priests would be scientists and philosophers, as they were in the

---

[137] Ibid., 4.
[138] For Comte's knowledge of Creuzer, see his letter to d'Eichthal, November 24, 1825, *CG*, 1:174.

theocracies, but would also be supporters of the division of labor essential to the development of human faculties and thus to progress.[139]

The first country to show signs of real development was Greece. The origins of science, especially its non-Western roots, have recently become a subject of much controversy. To a certain extent, Comte had a typically Eurocentric view of the evolution of civilization – a view that underestimated the contributions of other cultures. Nevertheless, it is important to note that he recognized that valuable scientific knowledge came to Greece from Egypt and the Orient and, moreover, played a liberating role. Because of its foreign provenance, this knowledge helped distance and free the Greek intellectual system from the prevailing political and social order. Yet as many other nineteenth-century historians of science, such as William Whewell, were to do later, Comte concentrated on Greece, instead of these Eastern cultures, as the birthplace of formal "science." It was there that scientific "progress" began to take off.[140] What made Greece stand out for Comte was that it developed the institutional basis for scientific advancement.

Motivated especially by his anticlericalism, Comte tied the growth of science in Greece to the development of the division of labor, that is, specialization, which was made possible by the absence of a theocracy. Because of its numerous wars, Greece had a strong temporal power. Its weaker spiritual power was uninvolved in politics and could pursue research without material worries or interference. Thus there developed almost immediately a beneficial division between theory and practice. Moreover, among the theorists, a division of labor arose between the priests, who dealt with theology, and philosophers, who concentrated on philosophy and the sciences. This distinction heralded the beginning of the metaphysical age in the intellectual sphere.

Previously, in the "Sommaire appréciation de l'ensemble du passé moderne," Comte had placed the beginning of this change in the eleventh century, when the Arabs introduced the sciences to Europe. As he did with the theological stage, he now pushed the origins of the metaphysical stage further back in time. Like Saint-Simon, he traced the beginnings of modern history to ancient Greece.[141]

---

[139] Système, vol. 4, "Appendice," 163–4.

[140] The controversy over the origins of science raises the questions of how to define "science" and whether there is linear scientific "progress." See F. Rochberg, Introduction to the special section entitled "The Culture of Ancient Science: Some Historical Reflections," Isis 83 (December 1992): 547–53. This section contains important articles by David Pingree, G. E. R. Lloyd, Heinrich von Staden, and Martin Bernal.

[141] In his Travail sur la gravitation universelle, Saint-Simon had divided history into three epochs: the pre-Socratic, the Socratic, and the reappearance of Socrates.

A new spiritual organization developed when moral and social philosophy split off from the physical sciences, which were developing more rapidly. Plato's disciples concentrated on moral and social theories, which were linked to the theological system, and they led people from polytheism to theism. Following Aristotle, scientists created metaphysical theories that began to approach the positive stage. Separated from the dynamic fields of knowledge, theology ultimately decayed. At the time of Alexander, scientists and philosophers finally became enemies and had remained antagonistic ever since.

These intellectual changes were later complemented by temporal modifications. Once Rome united the civilized world, the old system of conquest decayed, and a new social organization suitable to theism began to appear: the medieval system. But as soon as this new social system was established, theology began to lose its intellectual authority to the emerging spiritual power of the scientists.

After having focused on the Egyptian and Asiatic organizations in the theological stage and the Greek organization in the metaphysical stage, Comte urged the scientists to create a new spiritual corporation for the positive stage now that they were creating the positive philosophy. This third corporation would consist of a new, distinct class of scientists devoted to social physics. Because social phenomena depended on the laws of other phenomena and man could not be studied in isolation, these scientists would have a firm grasp of the main principles and methods of each science. Their concern with all of the sciences would lead them "inevitably" to finish constructing the positive philosophy, which would "make up for the impotence of theology in the moral government of society."[142] Possessing general knowledge, these scientists would thus form a new sacerdotal caste; the words "priest," "philosopher," and "scientist" would again be synonymous. Because they would refrain from practical affairs, positive society would retain the division of labor of the metaphysical stage and avoid the dangers of theocracy. But Comte never explained what would prevent these scientists who formed the new spiritual power from rejecting theories that threatened their position. Would they not eventually prove to be as conservative as their theocratic predecessors and make the positive social regime as stationary as primitive societies?

THE FIFTH OPUSCULE: "CONSIDÉRATIONS SUR
LE POUVOIR SPIRITUEL"

Comte discussed more extensively the spiritual power's function in the "Considérations sur le pouvoir spirituel," the second series of

---

[142] Ibid., 171–2.

three articles that he wrote for *Le Producteur*. He completed them in February 1826, and they later formed his fifth opuscule.[143] Whereas the fourth opuscule looked at the spiritual power from a philosophical and scientific point of view, this series of articles considered it from a more concrete, political and social perspective.[144] Comte wanted to shed light on the moral state of contemporary society and to emphasize the intellectual and moral authority of the spiritual power.

He started by praising the medieval Catholic and feudal system, which he had ignored in the previous essay because of its alleged theological weakness. Yet in terms of politics, the Catholic division of the spiritual and temporal powers remained his ideal of social organization because it allowed people to appeal to a legitimate moral power instead of submitting slavishly to the wishes of their government. It also permitted countries to unite on a different plane, as happened, for example, during the Crusades.[145]

The decay of the medieval system was inevitable, however, because it did not allow the human species to mature. The three centuries of anarchy – the sixteenth, seventeenth, and eighteenth centuries – were typical eras of transition marked by the need for a new system and the removal of obstacles to its creation. The dogma of unlimited liberty of conscience destroyed the theological power; the dogma of the sovereignty of the people threatened the temporal power; and the dogma of equality challenged social classification. Though necessary and legitimate, these critical doctrines could not serve to construct a new system.

Comte liked to say that he appreciated as much as anyone else "all that was of real value in the critical doctrine," but there was one new revolutionary idea that he could not tolerate: the widespread and popular notion that a spiritual power was no longer necessary. Even the kings and lawyers who talked of subordinating the spiritual power to the temporal power secretly hoped the former would disappear. But if it were suppressed, an immense, deadly lacuna would result. As indicated already by his comments on Massin's lack of religion, Comte, though himself an atheist, was profoundly alarmed by the increasing secularization of society.

To illustrate the damage caused by the dissolution of the spiritual authority, Comte cited many examples. Without standards, no one could agree on even the simplest social questions. Personal

---

[143] The three articles were published on December 24, 1825, and February 11 and 18, 1826. Comte was mistaken when he dated the fifth opuscule March 1826.

[144] Comte to Blainville, February 27, 1826, *Corr. inédite*, 1:21.

[145] Comte complimented Maistre for having demonstrated the power of the "European monarchy." *Système*, vol. 4, "Appendice," 183.

ambition, egoism, and materialism had no check. People lacked a sense of duty and paid too much attention to political assemblies and other institutions. International relations had also regressed to a "savage state," where each nation regarded the other as an enemy.[146] Though he had once admired the United States for its moral purity, now he found that the materialism and spiritual disorganization there were worse than anywhere else.

Comte also expressed a new concern about the growth of "administrative despotism."[147] He believed governments were becoming more centralized to stem the social dissolution caused by a lack of moral authority. Like Herder, he objected to this artificial method of creating social unity. He feared that a completely new type of autocracy was emerging since there was no spiritual power to check the material power. The bureaucracy was even more dangerous because it operated by corruption, which was replacing violence as the means of ensuring social harmony. Owing to industrialization, wealth had replaced military force as the main source of social influence. Comte was, therefore, very conscious of some of the disadvantages and dangers of "progress." His advocacy of a fixed hierarchy, denunciation of individualism, and dislike of centralization indicated a decided estrangement from the principles of the Revolution. He seemed to have abandoned the language of both liberty and equality. This tendency was also evident in his praise of the Holy Alliance, lukewarm support for the Greeks' struggle for independence, and elation over the liberals' defeat in Spain and in the elections of 1824 in France.[148] Yet Comte's new position against centralization also proved that he was becoming frustrated with Charles X's government, which sought to enlarge the power of the state in order to enforce the ultra program, instead of following Bonald's advice to resurrect local communities.[149] His disgust with the scandals and corruption of the regime echoed the discontent of the people. Though disturbed by the anarchy of the transitional period, Comte warned that it should not be checked by "arbitrary

---

[146] Ibid. Comte praised Lamennais's argument that the Holy Alliance was ineffective because it ultimately represented only the temporal power and could not therefore exercise a spiritual influence. Nevertheless, having approved of its repression of the liberal revolution in Spain, Comte felt that the alliance was necessary to maintain order. Comte to G. d'Eichthal, May 1, 1824, *CG*, 1:84. Lamennais had expressed his opinion about the Holy Alliance in an essay that he wrote in 1822: "De la Sainte Alliance." It was later reprinted in F. de Lamennais, *Nouveaux mélanges*, vol. 1 (Paris, 1826), 279–90.

[147] Ibid., 187.

[148] Adolphe d'Eichthal to Gustave d'Eichthal, February 9, 1824, Fonds d'Eichthal, 13746, item 68, BA; Comte to G. d'Eichthal, May 1, 1824, and April 6, 1825, *CG*, 1:84, 160–1; Comte to Valat, May 21, 1824, *CG*, 1:92.

[149] Yann Fauchois, "Centralization," in *Critical Dictionary*, ed. Furet and Ozouf, 638–39.

means," including the new government's muzzling of the press.[150] But Comte's stance against the regime was also partly a result of his own bitterness that his advances to Minister Villèle had been repulsed and he was forced to make his way outside of the University, which he felt was being ruined by the government's Catholic policies.[151]

Comte argued that a new spiritual power was most essential because it was in accord with the dignity and distinctiveness of man, which derived not solely from his material interests, as political economists claimed, but from his speculative abilities. Given the nature of society, which reflected man's dual character, government had to consist of two parts. The material, temporal part controlled actions, while the spiritual part regulated opinions, inclinations, and ideas. The basis of the spiritual government was its moral authority, which derived from its superior intellect and knowledge. Thus every society rested on material and intellectual inequalities.

As the governor of opinion, the spiritual power was in charge of learning. Reflecting the battle between the ultras and liberals over the school system, Comte began to develop his theory of education, for he believed that it was crucial for his new spiritual power to take control of the schools. If this power monopolized education, it would be able to regulate social relations.[152] To Comte, education signified the "entire system of ideas and habits necessary to prepare individuals for the social order in which they live." In the new society marked by social mobility and achievement by merit, people would need a good education to develop their abilities and to learn the same doctrine, the basis of social unity and international harmony. This stress on developing every person's potential seemed to reflect the typical liberal point of view inherited from the revolutionaries, who were committed to a national system of public instruction. But Comte also insisted that education had to make each individual "adapt as much as possible to the special destination he must fulfill." He did not address the question of how this "special destination" was to be determined. He merely assumed that every person would have a "precise type of activity to which he is most suited, whether by his natural dispositions, his antecedents, or the special circumstances in which he finds himself placed." It seems clear that in Comte's mind, education reinforced the social hierarchy by teaching people to resign themselves to their assigned niches in society. The spiritual power would have considerable authority in this regard, for it would

[150] *Système*, vol. 4, "Appendice," 191; Jardin and Tudesq, *Notables*, 1:78–82.
[151] Comte to Valat, November 27, 1825, *CG*, 1:178–9.
[152] Arbousse-Bastide, *Doctrine d'éducation*, 1:47.

not only preside over the school system but remind people continually of moral principles. He explicitly praised its "conservative influence."[153]

Moreover, because most people were called to a life of action and had neither the time nor capacity to create moral principles, they would have to rely on the spiritual power to create rules of conduct for them. These rules were crucial because "dogmatism" was the "normal state of human intelligence" and the basis of action. Reflecting his increasing alienation from liberal principles and his own authoritarianism, Comte asserted that the only role for skepticism was that it permitted the individual or the species to move from "one dogmatism to another." The spiritual power would thus provide the moral guidelines countering antisocial and pleasure-seeking impulses, which were the "most energetic impulses of human nature."[154] It would exert this socializing, repressive influence in all aspects of community life, including international relations.

From this discussion of the different functions of the spiritual and temporal powers, it is clear that Comte took a far wider view of the division of labor than had the political economists. He asserted that it not only was the "general cause" and the end product of progress but could be applied to all types of theoretical and practical activities on the individual and national levels. In a world with a perfect division of labor, each nation and person would be specialized. Everyone would devote himself "exclusively"[155] to the task which most suited him. Comte's view that a person had limited potential to branch off in many directions seemed to echo Bichat's theory of mutually exclusive capacities and contrasted strongly with the vision of Charles Fourier, who urged people to realize themselves through a variety of tasks.[156]

Comte maintained that increasing specialization led ideally to greater cooperation and harmony among individuals and among nations. Because of the development of industry, the human species should be coming closer to organizing this perfect division of labor, which would be finally realized during the positive stage. Yet he did not want to give the impression that he was a utopian thinker who thought absolute perfection was possible. Apologizing for his imprecise language, he explained that when he spoke of the "perfection" and the "development" of society, he meant merely to designate a "certain succession of stages that the human species attains according to determined laws." Again referring to the biological model, he

---

[153] *Système*, vol. 4, "Appendice," 193, 198, 207.   [154] Ibid., 202–3.   [155] Ibid., 198.
[156] On Fourier's concept of work, see Jonathan Beecher, *Charles Fourier: The Visionary and His World* (Berkeley and Los Angeles: University of California Press, 1986), 274–96.

asserted that he was using the two words in the same way physiologists employed them in the study of the individual: "to indicate a series of transformations to which no idea of necessary continual amelioration or deterioration is . . . attached."[157]

In this essay, Comte was, in fact, critical of progress. His reflections on the harmful effects of industrial growth led him to make his first systematic critique of political economy. In an unpublished article of 1819, Comte had written that only political economy could "lift politics to the rank of the positive sciences," but since then, his attitude had become increasingly ambivalent, reaching the point that he omitted any reference to it at all in the fundamental opuscule.[158] Now he became far more outspoken in his criticism, subtly distancing himself from *Le Producteur*, which aspired to be the "herald of the economic science."[159]

One of political economy's many failures as a social doctrine was that it wrongly assumed that people, classes, and nations were motivated primarily by material considerations. Comte argued that nineteenth-century physiology, especially Gall's phrenology, had discredited all metaphysical theories, such as utilitarianism and Idéologie, that focused on self-interest as the primary stimulus of people's actions. Because happiness did not derive from such antisocial behavior, the political economists' liberal morality would be ineffective in the modern, industrial era. Moreover, they wrongly imagined that as soon as the industrial class was in control, national (and international) order would arise from the inevitable, spontaneous convergence of different interests. In Comte's view, such laissez-faire doctrines were absurd. The industrial era would create its own type of problems and would require a new moral system.[160] Above

---

[157] Ibid., 198n1.

[158] "Considérations sur les tentatives qui ont été faites pour rendre positive la science sociale, en la faisant dériver de quelque autre science," *Ecrits*, 476. See also Arnaud, *Le "Nouveau Dieu,"* 19–78. In trying to make lesson 47 of the *Cours* a big turning point in Comte's idea of political economy, Pierre Arnaud seems to underestimate the importance of this fifth opuscule.

[159] A. Blanqui, "Esquisse historique de l'origine et des progrès de l'économie politique," *Le Producteur* 1 (1826): 348.

[160] Here Comte praised Dunoyer for having been the only one to perceive the problems generated by the industrial age. Comte, who was less naive about industrialization than the Saint-Simonians, was apparently criticizing one of them, P. J. Rouen, who wrote two articles rebuking Dunoyer for having exaggerated the problems inherent in industrial society. See Auguste Comte, "Considérations sur le pouvoir spirituel," *Le Producteur* 2 (1826): 366n1. Comte's regret that Dunoyer's work was not better known was suppressed at the end of the footnote in the reprinted version of the opuscule in the *Système*, vol. 4, "Appendice," 208. See also P. J. Rouen, "Examen d'un nouvel ouvrage de M. Dunoyer, ancien rédacteur du *Censeur européen*," parts 1, 2, 3, *Le Producteur* 2 (1826): 158–79, 451–64, 3:134–58.

all, Comte sought a moral system that would not stress the individual's self-interest, for such egoism would work against the social harmony he wished to establish.

Comte felt his concept of the division of labor was superior to that of the political economists, although it was based largely on Adam Smith's work. He made this division of labor the keystone of his social philosophy; it was the ultimate proof of the need for a spiritual power in modern society – a power that would be different from the Catholic type, which was suitable only for the Middle Ages. Expanding again on Smith's ideas, Comte argued that as people (and nations) became more specialized, their points of view narrowed to such a degree that they became preoccupied with their own interests, could no longer see the common good, and had even less intellectual capacity to create rules of general conduct. Moreover, as people became more isolated and had less intense relationships, their community seemed to dissolve. Comte's portrayal of modern society foreshadowed Durkheim's concept of *anomie*. To prevent the spread of alienation and the collapse of the social structure, a government composed of both a moral and a physical force was necessary. No longer a simple guardian of order, the government would actively intervene in society to ensure that individuals worked for a common goal and that the general good prevailed. Only in this coercive way would the division of labor lead to greater social cooperation.

For the first time, Comte announced that the new spiritual force – the specialists in the general point of view – would be far more powerful than in the past because they would have to combat the anarchy caused by the division of labor. Using terminology borrowed from phrenology, he called the new moral government the "organ" of the common good; its "function" was to ensure the triumph of the general point of view.[161] In opposition to the exponents of laissez-faire doctrines, he emphasized that the spiritual power would make sure that each individual worked for the good of society and each country's actions were useful to the international community.

Comte did not have a hedonistic view of progress, for he felt that as people's pleasures and desires increased, a moral government would necessarily have to impose more sacrifices as a corrective. Moreover, although more people were beginning to perform functions that suited them, the spiritual power would have to show those who were disgruntled how to contain their desires in the interest of society. Comte believed that each person should be satisfied

---

[161] *Système*, vol. 4, "Appendice," 206n1.

to stay in his proper niche – a reflection of his medieval view of society.

In his view, the jurisdiction of the temporal government would wane, although it would never disappear because a society with only a spiritual power would be unstable and incomplete. Influenced by the Scottish philosophers, he assumed that with the progress of civilization, people would become far more "sensitive to moral interests" and "much more disposed to the amiable reconciliation of [their personal] interests." As government became a matter of directing opinion, the temporal authority, which ruled by force, would control areas only where the spiritual power was ineffective. Eventually, the temporal authority would be reduced almost completely to a bureaucracy of civil servants, who would exercise much less political authority in their "natural sphere of activity" than spiritual governors would in theirs.[162] In showing how the jurisdiction of the spiritual power would grow at the expense of the temporal power's, Comte could not have made his preference for a theocratic type of government plainer.

Still preoccupied with "terrestrial morality," which had concerned him ever since his first article in *L'Industrie*, Comte asserted that the spiritual power's doctrine would be composed of concepts of *"good"* and *"evil"* equivalent to what was *"prescribed"* and *"prohibited"* by "positive precepts." These concepts were to be accepted on faith as their Christian counterparts had been. Previously in the "Sommaire appréciation de l'ensemble du passé moderne" and the *Plan*, he had stressed the importance of trust in science. Now he made trust more explicitly a religious phenomenon. He defined faith as the "disposition to believe spontaneously, without previous demonstration, in the dogmas proclaimed by a competent authority." Catholicism had shown that faith was essential to happiness and "true intellectual and moral communion."[163] Therefore, in the positive era, individuals would obey the spiritual power on the basis of their faith in positive precepts. Forbidden to change the reigning social doctrine, they could at most ask the spiritual power to correct a part of it if it did not seem to fulfill its purpose. Comte clearly did not consider freedom of conscience important.

In fact, he argued that in the positive era "spiritual repression" would grow as "temporal repression" lessened. He even admitted at one point that he was stressing the repressive rather than the directive function of positive morality. Referring to Malthus's conservative theory of population, Comte claimed that, in industrial society, moral authority had to bring about a "certain permanent repression"

---

[162] Ibid., 201.   [163] Ibid., 205–6.

of man's "vicious" sexual urges; otherwise the industrial population would continue to surpass the means of subsistence.[164] Already in 1826 Comte was advocating sexual abstinence as a cure for social ills.

In addition, he was convinced that a spiritual power was necessary to exercise "preventive or repressive action" in the event of class strife, which would intensify in the industrial era. The political economists' plans were ill-conceived because they would only substitute "the despotism founded on the right of the most wealthy for the despotism founded on the right of the strongest."[165] The industrial leaders would inevitably abuse their position, while the workers would resort to violence. Only an impartial spiritual power could solve the problem of class conflict by making each class fulfill its duties to the other. It would also moderate the hostile relations between farmers and manufacturers, between both of these and merchants, and between everyone and bankers. Comte's analysis of the alienating and exploitative aspects of the industrial revolution was strikingly similar to Marx's but did not bring him to the same radical conclusions.

In sum, Comte supported his case for the spiritual power by employing the arguments of both the liberals and ultras, although he had criticized the center party for this practice. He agreed with the liberals' idea of progress, "true liberty," and "civilization," but he feared that their means to achieve these goals would lead to the "most degrading despotism, that of force deprived of all moral authority." At the same time, he disagreed with the ultras' regressive goal but praised them for recognizing that "moral superiority" was the "corrective and regulator of force or wealth."[166] Thus, like them, he concluded that the way to end the revolutionary period was to institute a spiritual order. Although the new moral authority would be scientific to ensure progress, it would have the same function as the medieval Catholic Church. But it would be more powerful.

THE SIGNIFICANCE OF COMTE'S TWO OPUSCULES

These two series of articles absorbed almost all of Comte's attention during the winter of 1825–6 and proved to be significant landmarks in the history of his system. He had addressed the question of the reorganization of the spiritual power and had begun creating its

---

[164] Ibid., 205, 210. Later, Comte would criticize Malthus's "irrational exaggerations" about population growth. *Cours*, 2:208.
[165] Ibid., 210, 211.   [166] Ibid., 190.

doctrine. He had also developed his concept of the law of three stages and applied it for the first time to political reorganization. However, unresolved problems still plagued him. In his description of the law of three stages, his contention that the theological, metaphysical, and positive methods were sometimes used simultaneously raised the most serious objection. His answer that they were not used for the same order of ideas contradicted what he had said in the *Plan*, where he had pointed to physiology as a field where all three methods were still employed.[167] As for his spiritual power, Comte was not clear as to how it would escape the stationary fate of theocracies in the past or create a superior moral system. In fact, his moral system was very vague. While criticizing both the utilitarianism of the political economists and liberals and the philanthropy of Saint-Simon, he offered no substitute. His conception of human nature was also inconsistent. On the one hand, he said that people were inherently individualistic and antisocial and were becoming even more egotistical. Yet on the other, he agreed with the Scots and Gall that they were naturally moral and were, in addition, growing more sensitive to moral issues.

These essays also reflect the influence of the German idealists in that Comte adopted a more philosophical approach to the sciences, including social physics.[168] It is true that he had previously mentioned the Encyclopedists' and Saint-Simon's idea of a general philosophy linking all knowledge, but he had never before devoted as much attention to it as in these works. The idea of positive philosophy became inseparable from his concept of social physics. He even told d'Eichthal in a letter written during the period of their exploration of German thought that the "true title" of his works should not be *Politique positive*, but *Philosophie positive*.[169] Later, in the 1850s, he explained that the fourth opuscule signaled his "more direct tendency toward the establishment of a new spiritual authority according to a *philosophy* founded on science."[170] This philosophy would *not* be a profound study of each science but a compendium of knowledge suitable for the generalist. It would clarify the relationship between each science and the most important science of all, that of social physics. The science of society was therefore no longer merely a doctrine of production for the benefit of the industrialists, who were hardly ever mentioned in these opuscules except as objects of scorn. Comprising a *scientific* morality and politics, social

---

[167] Ibid., 78, 154n2.
[168] Comte to G. d'Eichthal, November 6, 1824, *CG*, 1:136; Arnaud, *Le "Nouveau Dieu*," 129–33.
[169] Comte to G. d'Eichthal, August 5, 1824, *CG*, 1:110.
[170] *Système*, vol. 4, "Appendice," iii (my emphasis).

physics was presented as an intellectual necessity in itself: it completed the positive philosophy and fulfilled the need for coherence and unity in people's ideas.

As Comte came to object increasingly to the materialism that seemed to deny the spiritual (the intellectual and moral) side of human nature, he started to present the sciences from a purely philosophical point of view. He now stressed their intellectual value instead of their social role or utility, as he had in the past.[171] Disillusioned with the precepts of political economy, he worried that men were too attached to the material world, did not appreciate the abstractions of theoretical thought, and tried to reduce scientists to pure technicians. When writing the *Plan*, he had felt that the distinction between scientists as specialists and as general philosophers was so insignificant that he confined this idea to a mere footnote. But a year later in his articles for *Le Producteur*, he was more outspoken in his belief that the positive clergy must consist of moral and social philosophers. Therefore, the widespread idea that Comte advocated the rule of an elite of scientists is misleading. Instead, he favored the rule of men who had a general knowledge of the natural sciences as well as of the science of society (which included history, political economy, and morality). Because these men possessed general knowledge and therefore had the widest views, they were in a position to speak for the whole community.

The organization of this special class of natural and social scientists now became the object of his attention. Though still without a unifying doctrine, Comte stressed the crucial need for a class of men to implement it. He had clearly been impressed by the privileged position of the scientific class in Germany, swayed by the ultramontanism of Catholic writers like Maistre and Lamennais, and exasperated by the liberals and political economists, who disapproved of a clergy and promoted a moral system based on man's self-interest. Applying Gall's functional theory of organs to social physics, he argued that the spiritual power was the organ of the social doctrine and that its function was to interpret it. Without the spiritual power, the social doctrine was, in effect, meaningless.

In these opuscules, the role of this spiritual power underwent a change because of Comte's more complex view of progress. Although he still believed that progress entailed better social conditions,

---

[171] In 1817 Comte had suggested that he admired the usefulness and concreteness of the sciences, especially because they were an antidote to man's intellectual faculty of abstraction, which made him too egotistic and contemptuous of the material world. Two years later he wrote to Valat that the sciences attracted him intellectually in themselves but that he had a "sovereign aversion" to devoting himself to them if he did not see their "utility." Comte to Valat, September 28, 1819, *CG*, 1:64.

improvements in private morality, and a greater degree of association, he now recognized that it did not mean absolute perfection or
even improvement in all areas. His recent study of ancient peoples,
for example, led him to the belief that they were superior in their
"generality of spirit" and "political energy."[172] He also became more
aware of the problems of specialization and class relations. No
longer were all producers cooperative friends with the same interests
as they had been in *L'Industrie*. And he took a dimmer view of
government. Instead of praising positive philosophy as a "philosophy of liberty" as he had earlier, he now favored a fixed social
hierarchy and repression. Gone were the revolutionary ideals of
individual liberty, the rights of man, and equality. Authoritarianism
had taken their place. Yet oddly enough, he continued to share at
least one idea of the political economists – the idea that the scope of
the temporal government would diminish in the future. In his system,
it would give way to a regime resembling the theocracy of the
primitive societies. Comte was prescient in recognizing that the
control of opinions, or ideas, would represent the key to power in
the modern state. By taking over education, the spiritual power
would finally be in control. Thus another reason Comte was concerned with the organization of the scientific class was that he was
projecting his own desire for a powerful position in the state educational system.

REACTIONS TO LE PRODUCTEUR

Comte was pleased with the articles he wrote for *Le Producteur*.
Although he later sought to give the impression that he had decided
at this time to make a break with the Saint-Simonians, the truth is
that he intended to continue working for the journal. In fact, he
attached great importance to completing his work on the spiritual
power with two or three articles clarifying this concept.[173]

Despite their later quarrel with Comte, the editors and writers of
Le Producteur considered him the principal theoretician of the journal
as well as its most important writer.[174] Enfantin, the future leader of

---

[172] *Système*, vol. 4, "Appendice," 199.

[173] Comte to Valat, January 18, 1826, *CG*, 1:181; Comte to Blainville, February 27, 1826,
Corr. inédite, 1:20–2; Comte to Chevalier, January 5, 1832, *CG*, 1:288; Comte, "Considérations sur le pouvoir spirituel," 376. At the end of his last article, Comte begged his
readers to suspend their criticisms until they had read his next two articles on the spiritual
power. He deleted this paragraph when he republished his opuscule in the *Système* in order
to avoid giving the impression that his association with *Le Producteur* had been satisfactory.
Charléty is thus mistaken when he states that Comte quit *Le Producteur* when, like Saint-
Simon, the editors became too religious. Charléty, *Saint-Simonisme*, 148.

[174] Georges Weill, *L'Ecole Saint-Simonienne: Son histoire, son influence jusqu'à nos jours* (Paris,
1896), 291.

the Saint-Simonians, openly spoke of Comte's having assisted the journal by his "strong intelligence."[175] The writers often even quoted whole sections from his works, and his ideas were a source of inspiration for other articles in the journal, especially those of Saint-Amand Bazard, who was to become one of the main propagators of Saint-Simonianism.[176]

Comte was essential primarily because he helped his colleagues understand Saint-Simon's doctrine, which they found too dispersed and muddled.[177] Enfantin in particular complained that Saint-Simon's principles were often "confused" and that his presentation was so "bizarre" that it could only "disgust" his readers.[178] According to him, Comte's articles best explained the scientific method, although they were "perhaps a bit hard to digest for the common herd."[179] When Lazare Carnot's son came to Paris to meet the disciples of Saint-Simon, they advised him "to follow the course that Auguste Comte was just beginning at his house."[180]

Comte also seemed to consider himself the most important exponent of the antiliberal doctrine of *Le Producteur*. He was pleased when he attracted the notice of such important figures as Benjamin Constant, for he felt that Constant's criticisms were really directed at him.[181] In his course at the Athénée and in a letter written to the *Journal de l'opinion*, Constant attacked *Le Producteur* for neglecting liberty and political guarantees and denouncing freedom of conscience. He charged the journal and especially Comte with advocating a theocracy and reviving the spirit of the Inquisition.[182] Comte's picture of the positive era certainly went against Constant's principle that "variety is life; uniformity is death."[183]

---

[175] Enfantin to Resseguier, May 20, 1827, Fonds Enfantin 7643, fol. 119v. This letter also suggests that Comte intended to continue working for *Le Producteur*.

[176] "Physiologie du cerveau: Analyse du cours de M. Gall à l'Athénée," *Le Producteur* 2:464–6; J. Allier, "Prédominance de la doctrine positive sur les doctrines théologiques et métaphysiques," ibid., 2:588n1; P. Enfantin, "Le Temps, l'opinion publique," ibid., 3:12n1; Saint-Amand Bazard, "Considération sur l'histoire," ibid., 4:414n1; M. Laurent, "Considérations sur le système théologique et féodal et sur sa désorganisation," ibid., 4:473–5; P. M. Laurent, "Coup d'oeil historique sur le pouvoir spirituel," ibid., 5:64n1.

[177] P. J. Rouen, "Examen d'un nouvel ouvrage de M. Dunoyer," part 3, 3:143n1.

[178] Enfantin to Pichard, August 23, 1825, Fonds Enfantin 7643, fol. 10v, BA.

[179] Enfantin to Pichard, November 26, 1825, Fonds Enfantin 7643, 14v, BA. See also Enfantin to Pichard, February 2, 1826, Fonds Enfantin 7643, fol. 86, BA.

[180] Senator Carnot to Pierre Laffitte, August 3, 1882, MAC.

[181] *Système*, vol. 4, "Appendice," iii.

[182] Constant's letter is reproduced in *Le Producteur* 1 (1825): 536–8. See also "Lettre de M. Benjamin Constant au Rédacteur de L'Opinion," *Le Producteur* 1 (1825): 482–4; Cerclet's response to Constant, *Le Producteur* 1 (1825): 540. In fact, in 1825–6 the liberal press often criticized *Le Producteur* for its dogmatism and desire to create an absolute authority in politics and morality. Charléty, *Saint-Simonisme*, 52.

[183] Constant, *De l'esprit de conquête*, 984.

Comte blamed the incompleteness of his exposition for having led Constant, whom he greatly respected, to make "painful and false interpretations."[184] Having made a point of giving power to the scientists of society, not to all scientists, he was genuinely surprised by the reproach that he was trying to create a "sort of scientific theocracy," a characterization that he recognized would completely "discredit" his new philosophy from the beginning. He resolved from then on to reassure his readers that he did *not* seek to establish a scientific form of "despotism," which they (his readers) tended "to fear *with reason* more than any other type." To avoid this accusation, he intended to appeal more to the "revolutionary school," whose adherents, he felt, would be more "sincere and complete" than those of the reactionary school.[185] In his later works Comte took pains to emphasize the balance that had to exist between the spiritual and temporal powers, but he never succeeded in erasing the impression that his system was theocratic. In a biographical dictionary published in 1834, the author of an entry praised Comte for having written some of the most brilliant essays of the epoch but added that his articles in *Le Producteur* led to his being accused of "theocratism" and "papism" in the "philosophical world."[186]

One person on the Right who read the journal carefully and considered Comte its most important writer was Lamennais. He congratulated *Le Producteur* for recognizing the importance of religion and the authority of the spiritual power in maintaining social life: "It is thus proved by . . . the formal avowals of all the enemies of Catholicism that, without the Pope, there is no Church; without the Church, there is no Christianity; without Christianity, there is no religion and no society."[187] Bazard too was struck by the similarity between *Le Producteur*'s analysis of the "moral and intellectual character" of their period and that of Lamennais.[188]

Six months before Comte began writing for the journal, Lamennais had published the first part of his *De la religion considérée dans ses rapports avec l'ordre politique et civil*, which Comte bought and read.[189] The second volume of Lamennais's work appeared in February 1826, the same month Comte completed his "Considérations sur le pouvoir

---

184 Comte to Armand Marrast, January 7, 1832, *CG*, 1:232.
185 Comte to Mill, December 25, 1844, *CG*, 2:308 (my emphasis).
186 "Comte, Auguste," in *Biographie universelle et portative des contemporains*, ed. Rabbe, Boisjoslin, and Saint Preuve.
187 F. de Lamennais, *De la religion considerée dans ses rapports avec l'ordre politique et civil*, 2 vols. (Paris, 1825–6), 2:80; see also 76.
188 [Saint-Amand] Bazard, "Sur un ouvrage de M. de Lamennais et sur un article du *Mémorial Catholique*," *Le Producteur* 3 (1826): 320–1.
189 See Comte, "Considérations sur le pouvoir spirituel," 609n1. The wording of this footnote was changed in the *Système*. *Système*, vol. 4, "Appendice," 185n1.

spirituel." In this volume, Lamennais quoted at length from an article by Bazard, which repeated Comte's ideas on the destructiveness of the sovereignty of individual reason and the need to suppress freedom of conscience in order to reorganize society.[190] It is impossible to resolve the question of whether Comte influenced Lamennais or whether Lamennais's treatment of the relationship between the spiritual and temporal prompted Comte to examine the same subject from a different perspective.[191] What is evident is that they were thinking along the same lines. Lamennais criticized Gallicanism, which contributed to the despotism of the temporal power; the atheistic, materialistic, and corrupt Bourbon regime; and contemporary tendencies toward democracy and popular sovereignty. He stressed not only the urgency of establishing common beliefs but, especially in the second part of his book, the need for the spiritual power to be independent of the temporal power; these ideas were strongly endorsed by Comte.[192]

COMTE'S MEETING WITH LAMENNAIS

In March 1826 their common interests brought Comte and Lamennais together. Lamennais had read and liked all of Comte's articles for *Le Producteur*, especially the last one on faith and the spiritual power, which he called "very remarkable."[193] He told a friend: "Comte seems to me more powerful than Jouffroy. I sought an occasion to talk to him out of curiosity."[194] He then arranged for an interview with Comte. The intermediary between the two men was Camille Menjaud, a friend of Lamennais who had been a class

---

[190] Bazard, "Des partisans du passé et de ceux de la liberté du conscience," *Le Producteur* 1 (1825): 399–413.

[191] Derré, *Renouvellement*, 385; Charles Boutard, *Lamennais: Sa vie et ses doctrines*, vol. 2, *Le Catholicisme libéral* (Paris, 1908), 138. Laffitte shows that when Lamennais summarized human knowledge in *Des progrès de la révolution et de la guerre contre l'Eglise* (1829), he adopted Comte's series of mathematics, astronomy, physics, chemistry, and physiology and justified this classification of the sciences by alluding to Comte's notion of the growing complication of relationships. "Variétés: Relations d'Auguste Comte avec l'abbé de Lamennais," ed. Pierre Laffitte, *RO* 5 (September 1, 1880): 248–9.

[192] Lamennais, *De la religion*, 1:34–48, 62, 89, 102–3, 105, 2:80, 104, 231, 236, 250, 261; Derré, *Renouvellement*, 268–71, 385; Bénichou, *Temps des prophètes*, 136–7; Latreille and Rémond, *Histoire du catholicisme*, 274–6; Vidler, *Prophecy and Papacy*, 105–15. See also *Cours*, 2:22.

[193] Menjaud to Comte, February 27, 1826, in "Relations d'Auguste Comte avec M. de Lamennais," ed. Pierre Laffitte, *RO* 16 (January 1, 1886): 52.

[194] Lamennais, Conversation recorded by Théophile Foisset, who is quoted in Henri Boissard, *Théophile Foisset* (Paris, 1891), 21.

ahead of Comte at the Ecole Polytechnique.[195] After hearing from
Menjaud how much Lamennais respected him, Comte immediately
accepted with the "greatest pleasure" the invitation and told Menjaud
to inform Lamennais how "profoundly moved" he was by his expression of esteem, which he valued "even more from a moral point
of view than from an intellectual one":

> In the midst of the injustices and persecutions that I already have
> good reason to foresee will thwart my career because of the egoism
> and mediocrity of my contemporaries (and most especially a certain
> class of them), it will always be a personal and precious consolation
> to have been perceived and appreciated by a man of this merit and
> caliber, who has, moreover, all the qualities required for being abso-
> lutely impartial.[196]

Although Comte did not expect Lamennais to agree completely with
him, he was heartened by his reassuring words and perhaps hoped
for some support against his critics.[197]

The meeting took place on March 2 and lasted four hours. It left
both men "very satisfied" and eager to see each other often.[198] Yet
little is known of what transpired, for Comte wanted to keep it
secret. Perhaps he felt an encounter with this reactionary theologian
might compromise him.[199] Nevertheless, the meeting must have been
marked by an atmosphere of great respect and seriousness because
Comte considered Lamennais the "veritable head of the Catholic
party," while Lamennais regarded Comte as the "strongest mind of

195 Adolphe d'Eichthal to Gustave d'Eichthal, April 18, 1826, Fonds d'Eichthal 13746, item
    136, BA. Comte later confirmed that Lamennais "initiated" their meetings. Comte to
    Sabatier, April 2, 1857, *CG*, 8:430. See also Menjaud to Comte, February 27, 1826, in
    "Relations d'Auguste Comte avec M. de Lamennais," ed. Laffitte, 52; "Matériaux pour
    servir à la biographie d'Auguste Comte: Relations d'Auguste Comte avec M. de La
    Mennais," ed. Pierre Laffitte, *RO*, 2d ser., 6 (July 1892): 154; Comte to Valat, April 29,
    1815, *CG*, 1:10; Association Polytechnique, *Documents pour servir à l'histoire de cette asso-
    ciation, 1830–1855* (Paris, n.d), 9; Dossier of Menjaud, EP; "Menjaud," Registre de
    matricule des élèves, vol. 4, 1810–19, EP. There was also some question as to whether
    Menjaud was the person who had introduced Comte to Saint-Simon. Lonchampt to Laffitte,
    11 Charlemagne 100, MAC.
196 Comte to Menjaud, February 28, 1826, *CG*, 1:190–1.
197 Charles Calippe, "Les Relations d'Auguste Comte avec Lamennais," *Revue du clergé français*
    96 (1918): 19.
198 Comte to Blainville, March 31, 1826, *CG*, 1:193. The date "March 11" in *CG* is in-
    correct. See the original letter in the Maison d'Auguste Comte. Adolphe d'Eichthal also
    referred to the "great satisfaction" experienced by Comte and Lamennais. Adolphe d'Eichthal
    to Gustave d'Eichthal, April 18, 1826, Fonds d'Eichthal 13746, item 136, BA.
199 Adolphe d'Eichthal to Gustave d'Eichthal, April 18, 1826, Fonds d'Eichthal 13746, item
    136, BA.

the liberal party."[200] Finding Comte to be a "man of good faith," Lamennais later boasted that he "very nearly converted him."[201] Comte claimed, however, that neither tried to convert the other, although he implied that the priest favored his ideas.[202]

In some ways, the two men were very similar. Both were deeply troubled by the spiritual aridity and intellectual anarchy of their times. Lamennais suffered from severe bouts of depression, which finally led him to consult the analyst Philippe Pinel in 1806. Comte was shortly to visit Pinel's disciple. Lamennais found much comfort in *The Imitation of Christ*, a work that became one of Comte's favorites.[203]

Disturbed by the egoism and corruption of the period, they were also kindred spirits in their effort to create "doctrines" that could rally their contemporaries and in their campaign to strengthen the moral and intellectual power so that it could enlighten the temporal power.[204] Although Comte differed from Lamennais in that he sought a religion outside of Catholicism to regenerate society, Lamennais was impressed by his approach to the spiritual power, which he felt resembled Maistre's; he believed the young man could become an important associate. For his part, Comte approved of Lamennais's ultramontane position because he found it consistent with his (Lamennais's) principles.[205] During their meetings, these two men, both endowed with a prophetic streak, discussed the spiritual power and the possibility of establishing an alliance. At the end of his life, Comte would return to their original idea of creating a "great religious league" between Catholics and positivists to eliminate Protestant and deist metaphysics.[206]

---

[200] Comte to Sabatier, April 2, 1857, *CG*, 8:430; Lamennais, quoted in "Variétés: Relations d'Auguste Comte avec l'abbé de Lamennais," ed. Laffitte, 244.

[201] Lamennais, Conversation recorded by Foisset, in Boissard, *Théophile Foisset*, 21.

[202] Comte to Sabatier, April 2, 1857, *CG*, 8:430; Comte to Lamennais, March 31, 1826, *CG*, 1:191; *Système*, vol. 4, "Appendice," iv.

[203] Georges Hourdin, *Lamennais: Prophète et combattant pour la liberté* (Paris: Perrin, 1982), 43–5, 60, 66–8; Jean Lebrun, *Lamennais*, 22, 27, 37, 40; H. G. Schenk, *The Mind of the European Romantics* (Oxford: Oxford University Press, 1979), 120; Vidler, *Prophecy and Papacy*, 41, 65–7, 95, 114. On Lamennais and *The Imitation*, which he translated into French in 1824, see Hourdin, *Lamennais*, 61; Derré, *Renouvellement*, 344. Comte preferred Corneille's translation of *The Imitation of Christ* and made it part of the Positivist Library. *Système*, 4:560.

[204] Comte to Valat, March 30, 1825, *CG*, 1:156. See also Lamennais to Comte, April 1, [1826], in "Relations d'Auguste Comte avec M. de Lamennais," ed. Laffitte, 56; Vidler, *Prophecy and Papacy*, 151; Paul Lazerges, *Lamennais: Essais sur l'unité de sa pensée* (Montauban, 1895), 53.

[205] Comte to Mill, April 5, 1842, and May 15, 1845, *CG*, 2:44, 3:10.

[206] Comte to Sabatier, April 2, 1857, *CG*, 8:430. See also Comte to Audiffrent, June 22, 1857, *CG*, 8:487.

The meeting went so well that several weeks later, on March 31, Comte wrote to Lamennais to express his emotional and intellectual affinity with him.[207] Lamennais responded immediately:

> I congratulate myself a great deal, Sir, for having met you, and I feel very honored by your esteem and attachment. These are the feelings that I felt for you before I had the honor of knowing you personally and that have grown further since then.

He hoped to tighten the "bonds" between them.[208]

In the same letter of late March, Comte thanked Lamennais for having written an article on him in the latest issue of *Le Mémorial catholique*.[209] This new journal was directed by Lamennais and two of his disciples, Gerbet and Salinis. For the rest of his life, Comte boasted that Lamennais himself had written the article, and most of his biographers have accepted this claim.[210] In fact, however, Lamennais's biographers have pointed out that the author was actually Abbé Gerbet, who had met Comte when he visited Lamennais.[211]

The article declared that among the ever-growing number of new philosophical schools, one of the few deserving attention was *Le Producteur*. Gerbet particularly praised its theory of the foundation of the social order, which he ascribed to Comte, who correctly realized that the "great question of the century" was "spiritual authority." Gerbet then reproduced a number of passages from Comte's two series of "remarkable" articles. Yet he thought the concept of a spiritual power based on the agreement of a few scholars was unconvincing. Nevertheless, because Comte seemed to have a "character

---

[207] Comte to Lamennais, March 31, 1826, CG, 1:192.

[208] Lamennais to Comte, April 1, [1826], in "Relations d'Auguste Comte avec M. de Lamennais," ed. Laffitte, 56. Although Comte claimed that Lamennais "initiated" three conferences, it seems that he included his later intimate discussions with the priest in these three meetings. Comte to Sabatier, April 2, 1857, CG, 8:430.

[209] Comte to Lamennais, March 31, 1826, CG, 1:192; "X," "D'une nouvelle école philosophique," *Le Mémorial catholique*, 5 (February 1826): 113–19. On pages 130–1 appears a letter to the editor that was written on February 23; thus the issue must have been published after this date. In fact, it must have appeared in March, because Comte thanked Lamennais for the first time at the end of the month. Calippe errs when he says that Comte's articles on the spiritual power appeared in March after his interview with Lamennais. Calippe, "Relations d'Auguste Comte avec Lamennais," 20–3.

[210] *Système*, vol. 4, "Appendice," iii, iv; "Relations d'Auguste Comte avec M. de Lamennais," ed. Laffitte, 49; F. Gould, *Auguste Comte*, 25; Gouhier, *Vie*, 122–3.

[211] Le Guillon in Lamennais, *Correspondance*, 3:177n1; Derré, *Renouvellement*, 387n8; Calippe, "Relations d'Auguste Comte avec Lamennais," 22. Comte had thought highly enough of him to include in his library Gerbet's *Des doctrines philosophiques sur la certitude*, which was published in 1826 and quoted from various *Le Producteur* articles. See P. Gerbet, *Des doctrines philosophiques sur la certitude dans leurs rapports avec les fondements de la théologie* (Paris, 1826), 191–2.

of good faith rare in our days," Gerbet declared that *Le Mémorial catholique* was eager to open a discussion with him. Perhaps prompted by Lamennais, Gerbet sensed that Comte was fundamentally a very religious person who was undergoing a painful spiritual struggle and seeking a dialogue with others:

> Several of the opinions that Mr. Comte professes are fundamentally incompatible with religion; but it will be difficult for a naturally righteous mind to be able to escape for a long time the truths to which several of his principles directly lead him.[212]

Just as Comte was watching Lamennais turn more and more to liberalism, the Mennaisian camp was ready to survey Comte's adoption of a more overtly religious stance and sought to make him an ally.[213]

---

[212] "X," "D'une nouvelle école philosophique," 113–14, 118. Laffitte did not include this last quotation when he reproduced most of the other significant passages from this article in the *Revue occidentale*. "Variétés: Relations d'Auguste Comte avec l'abbé de Lamennais," ed. Laffitte, 246–7. See also Derré, *Renouvellement*, 388.

[213] *Système*, vol. 4, "Appendice," 185n1.

Chapter 8

Intellectual and Mental Crises

Madame Comte does not at all fear this revelation; she has quite provoked it. . . . We must believe that he [Comte] brought against his wife an accusation that he knew was false [and] that he succeeded in believing in the existence of an imaginary fact. . . . One must not doubt, then, that Auguste Comte was ill. He invented the fatal secret just as he had imagined the utopia of the Virgin Mother, and he believed in the reality of the one just as he believed in the certain realization of the other. His hatred for his wife grew with his love for Clotilde de Vaulx [sic]; he pictured his wife capable of everything. From this to believing that she had committed everything that he imagined, there was only one step.

Griolet, Massin's lawyer, 1870

THE CRISIS OF FEBRUARY 1826

Comte's articles on the spiritual power not only enhanced his reputation but reoriented his life. He began to understand more clearly the intellectual task that lay ahead of him. But in developing the new direction that he believed his thought had to take, he experienced a severe intellectual and physical crisis.

On February 20, 1826, two days after the appearance of the third article of "Considérations sur le pouvoir spirituel," Comte started his next article. He wanted to finish it as soon as possible, for he feared his readers might misunderstand his insistence on a powerful moral government and raise "serious objections."[1] Yet once again a mental block seemed to threaten his plans. He meditated upon the problem of a strong spiritual power for eighty hours without a break. He barely slept at all. During these three to four days, his head was "in the highest degree" of "excitation," and he began to experience a "true nervous *crisis*." Its severity is reflected in a letter he wrote to Blainville, where he maniacally underlined such words as "the whole," "crisis," "system," and "systematic."[2]

In this letter, Comte was asking for advice from the friend he hoped would become a sort of mentor to replace Saint-Simon. Ever

[1] Comte, "Considérations sur le pouvoir spirituel," 376n1.
[2] Comte to Blainville, February 27, 1826, *Corr. inédite*, 1:17–26.

362

since Blainville had read the opuscule of 1822, which had been sent to him by Saint-Simon, he had admired Comte. A proud, irascible Norman noble, the forty-nine-year-old biologist had broken with his teacher, Cuvier, and kept his distance from his colleagues, whom he scorned. Comte liked in him not only his candor but his wide knowledge of both the sciences and the arts and his systematic and synthetic mind – the "most coordinating" since Aristotle.[3] Seeking to reproduce Blainville's method of linking details and subordinating them to the whole, he was desperate for his guidance. He met personally with Blainville for a talk about his crisis on February 24 and then sent him this revealing letter three days later.[4]

In accordance with the Idéologues' theory, Comte tried in this letter to uncover the "moral" aspect of his physical condition. Using almost religious language to express himself, he suggested that he had received some kind of revelation:

[The crisis] made me see in a far more complete and clearer light than ever before the whole of my life. . . . [T]his *view* had a bearing on both my intellectual life and my social life, a combination to which I had never raised myself until then. . . . [T]his sensation . . . of the *whole* will leave profound traces on me and will give my whole future a strong direction.[5]

He now felt he had a firmer grasp on his mission and could combine his personal and intellectual life into one whole. This sense of a special calling had been growing in him since 1824. Recently, in the last part of the fifth opuscule, he had declared that the "greatest social perfection imaginable" would occur if each individual fulfilled the "special function to which he was the most suited" and there were no "missed vocations."[6] Having repeatedly argued that only a spiritual power could resolve current social conflicts, he now seemed to realize that he himself had to construct the new moral government. Years later, he emphasized that the fifth opuscule of 1826 marked a turning point in his life:

My whole mission was spontaneously announced in the decisive opuscule of 1826, where I dedicated my life to the foundation of the

---

[3] Auguste Comte, "Discours prononcé aux funérailles de Blainville," *Système* 1:739.
[4] Comte to Blainville, February 27, 1826, *Corr. inédite*, 1:18. On Blainville, see William Coleman, "Blainville, Henri Marie Ducrotay de," in *Dictionary of Scientific Biography*, ed. Gillispie; Pol Nicard, *Etude sur la vie et les travaux de M. Ducrotay Blainville* (Paris, 1890), clviii, 7; Sinaceur, Introduction to *Cours* 1:652–3; Henri Gouhier, "La Philosophie 'positiviste' et 'chrétienne' de D. de Blainville," *Revue philosophique de la France et de l'étranger* 131.1–2 (1941): 41–5.
[5] Comte to Blainville, February 27, 1826, *Corr. inédite*, 1:18.
[6] *Système*, vol. 4, "Appendice," 204, 211.

new spiritual power. . . . One must regard as a pure chimera the hope
of rallying and regulating men according to a faith – no matter how
complete and demonstrable it may be – that does not lead to the
installation of the true clergy.[7]

While the fundamental opuscule of 1824 was a synthesis of his scientific and political interests, which gave him "true cerebral unity,"
the opuscule of 1826 thus went further by uniting his personal and
intellectual lives.[8] He now achieved the same kind of unity that he
had admired in Franklin and Saint-Simon.

Comte's intellectual revolution led him to reflect on his recent
articles, which he came to realize were as unsystematic as his fundamental opuscule.[9] To solve this problem, he decided he had to use
the law of three stages to elucidate the political nature of the modern
spiritual power. In this manner, he believed he would unite the
"abstract" viewpoint of the fourth opuscule, which demonstrated
the intellectual necessity of social physics, with the "concrete" perspective of the fifth opuscule, which showed the political necessity
of social physics' organ, the spiritual power.[10] The union of these
two points of view would satisfy people's practical and theoretical needs. At the same time, Comte saw more clearly that social
physics would create both the unifying scientific doctrine and spiritual
reorganization.

Comte's new sense of the harmony between his life and work was
related to his feeling of the unity of his political and scientific work;
he saw he had to be the founder of both social physics and the
spiritual power. The one could not exist without the other. Thus the
new synthesis of theory and practice that he would achieve in his
work would unite his intellectual and social life.[11]

In reflecting on the new stage of his life, Comte decided that
all his preceding works, including his articles for *Le Producteur*,
were "simple *studies*" or "*preparations*" that made up his "sort of
general *novitiate*." He had to return to his *Système de politique positive*.
But before undertaking the second part, which had already eluded
him for two years, he decided to rework the first part, that is,
the fundamental opuscule. Thanks to his February crisis, he now
understood for the first time Blainville's criticism that the fundamental opuscule was unsystematic. With a new appreciation of its

---

[7] Comte to Henry Edger, 9 *Archimède* 69 (April 3, 1857), *CG*, 8:434.   [8] *Système*, 1:2.
[9] In the rough copy of this February 27, 1826, letter in the Maison d'Auguste Comte, Comte
explained that he did not call the first series of articles for *Le Producteur* a "system" because
he did not want to "prejudge anything."
[10] Comte to Blainville, February 27, 1826, *Corr. inédite*, 1:22.
[11] For a fine discussion of this complex problem, see Gouhier, *Jeunesse*, 3:314–19.

organizational and conceptual problems, he asked Blainville if it would be systematic if he combined the "abstract and the concrete points of view." So desperate was he for Blainville's approval that he told him his response would have a "powerful influence" on the rest of his life.[12]

A COURSE ON POSITIVE PHILOSOPHY

Another result of Comte's crisis was that it made him take more seriously the course that he was supposed to begin two days later. After having twice postponed his lectures on politics at the Athénée, he had decided in January 1826 to offer instead a course on positive philosophy at home. He did not want to lecture first on politics, because he worried that his political ideas would not be taken seriously unless he had first acquired a solid reputation in the sciences.[13] Furthermore, besides sharpening his own ideas, he wanted to regenerate French education by offering sound scientific instruction outside the decrepit University. Most of all, the course offered a way out of his financial troubles. He hoped to attract enough subscribers to allow him to devote his full time to finishing the *Système de politique positive*.[14] D'Eichthal, who had helped Comte often in the past, appears to have originated the scheme. When he later asked his brother if Comte's course brought him "enough to shelter him from need," Adolphe answered that it must because "I am not the only one to have paid him 200 francs, which was its price."[15] Thus like the important articles written for *Le Producteur*, the future *Cours de philosophie positive* was stimulated by financial needs and at first struck Comte as a serious distraction from what he still considered his primary task, the immediate establishment of the science of society.

Once he decided to give his course on positive philosophy more importance after his February crisis, he realized that he was contradicting the position he had taken in "Considérations philosophiques sur les sciences et les savants." In that work he had said that positive philosophy could not be founded until the last science, social physics, had been established. And to create social physics, he still needed

---

[12] Comte to Blainville, February 27, 1826, *Corr. inédite*, 1:24.

[13] Comte to Valat, September 28, 1819, *CG*, 1:64. See also Comte to Valat, January 18, 1826, *CG*, 1:182; Comte to Audiffrent, February 12, 1857, *CG*, 8:400–1.

[14] Comte to Valat, November 27, 1825, and January 18, 1826, *CG*, 1:177–8, 183. See also Lamoricière to Comte, February, 1826, MAC; Gouhier, *Jeunesse*, 3:311.

[15] Gustave d'Eichthal to Adolphe d'Eichthal, April 20, 1826, Fonds d'Eichthal 14396, item 30, BA; Adolphe d'Eichthal to Gustave d'Eichthal, May 9, 1826, Fonds d'Eichthal 13746, item 137, BA. See also Adolphe d'Eichthal to Gustave d'Eichthal, March 4 1826, Fonds d'Eichthal 13746, item 132, BA.

to write a history of civilization showing the development of social phenomena – the subject of the unwritten second part of the *Système*. Up to this point, Comte had not seriously considered the possibility that he would establish positive philosophy, for he believed its construction would take many years.[16]

Yet at the same time, in the "Considérations sur les sciences et les savants," he had stressed the importance of a "preliminary" scientific education. Since social phenomena were intricately linked to other phenomena, scientists of society first had to know the principal methods and concepts of the other sciences. In the past two years, Comte had increasingly come to value his scientific education, which he thought gave him insights that escaped Saint-Simon, Guizot, and the German philosophers. He felt that scientific training provided a certain viewpoint based on "facts" that led inevitably to consensus – or at least to agreement with him. Nevertheless, he did not yet equate this "preliminary education" with positive philosophy, which he reaffirmed had to be created by social physicians *after* they had sufficiently established their specialty.[17] He certainly had no intention of providing this preliminary education. Years later, he explained, "I felt . . . that the new faith demanded among all systematic minds a scientific foundation equivalent to the one which I had painfully acquired and from which I had at first hoped to be able to dispense the public."[18]

In sum, Comte had a hard time deciding whether social science should precede or follow positive philosophy. In terms of the system of the sciences, it seemed to come before positive philosophy and serve as its foundation. Yet in terms of the education of the spiritual power, social physics seemed to be the last section or pinnacle of positive philosophy. Social physicians would have to know all five previous sciences and would in short be positive philosophers themselves. Their preparation would have to replicate Comte's pedagogical history.[19]

The course on positive philosophy gradually became more important to Comte because while writing the fifth opuscule, he realized that by controlling education and morality, the spiritual power united both the theoretical and practical aspects of social reconstruction.[20] Organizing this clergy was as crucial as creating the doctrine it was to profess; in fact, the doctrine was unenforceable without it. Since

---

[16] Comte to G. d'Eichthal, August 5, 1824, *CG*, 1:109–10; *Système*, vol. 4, "Appendice," 150, 151ni, 158.

[17] *Système*, vol. 4, "Appendice," 172–3.   [18] Ibid., 1:2.

[19] Arbousse-Bastide, *Doctrine d'éducation*, 1:59; Arnaud, Le "*Nouveau Dieu*," 146; Gouhier, *Jeunesse*, 308, 319–20.

[20] Gouhier, *Jeunesse*, 314, 319; Arbousse-Bastide, *Doctrine d'éducation*, 62–4.

Comte now aimed at founding the spiritual power, he recognized that he himself had to furnish his clergy with the requisite education, equivalent to the Catholic novitiate. It would provide them with the same authority that the old system of universal knowledge had given priests.[21] This education was also important because Comte was more aware that he needed to clarify his idea of the new spiritual power; it did not include all scientists but only the generalists who had studied the applications of the positive method in other sciences as well as the natural laws of all phenomena – in short, the encyclopedia of positive knowledge.[22] He now understood that the formation of the social scientist and that of the positive philosopher were exactly the same, and he realized that he himself would have to establish not only social physics but positive philosophy because they were inseparable.

Comte wrote the letter to Blainville to ask his advice about how to proceed. He realized that giving the course was a "great task" and deserved his full attention, but he still wanted first to write the *Système de politique positive* to establish the historical foundation of social physics.[23] He was not sure he had the energy to do both jobs well, especially since they were so different. He had obviously not resolved the problem of the vicious circle.

It is not clear whether Comte temporarily abandoned the project of the *Système* between February 27 and mid-April or during the years of his illness. Pierre Arnaud suggests that the *Cours de philosophie positive* was an "accidental" product of Comte's madness, but Comte suggested that he conceived this project before he fell ill.[24] He told Clotilde de Vaux that once he realized that all of his efforts to effect the "spiritual reorganization of modern societies" had been "premature," he had abandoned his "great political elaboration almost from its debut" to devote himself to the "foundation of a true philosophy." His "crisis" of 1826 led him to conceptualize the new philosophy.[25] Unfortunately, as Henri Gouhier pointed out, one does not know whether by "crisis" Comte was referring to the problems of February or his period of madness later in the year.[26] Usually, however, Comte used the word *folie* to describe his madness. And there is an indication that he had some idea of the *Cours* before he became sick, for he explained in 1851:

[21] *Système*, 1:2, vol. 4, "Appendice," 163, 203–4.
[22] Comte to Valat, September 8, 1824, *CG*, 1:127.
[23] Comte to Blainville, February 27, 1826, *Corr. inédite*, 1:18. See also ibid., 1:24–5, and Comte to G. d'Eichthal, August 5, 1824, *CG*, 1:110; Gouhier, *Jeunesse*, 3:302, 313.
[24] Arnaud, *Le "Nouveau Dieu,"* 156.
[25] Comte to Clotilde de Vaux, August 5, 1845, *CG*, 3:79–80.
[26] Gouhier, *Jeunesse*, 3:319n42.

This direct reconstruction of the spiritual power promptly stimulated in me a continuous meditation of eighty hours, which led me to conceive, as an indispensable preamble, the total systematization of positive philosophy, whose oral exposition I began in the spring of the same year 1826.[27]

This "meditation of eighty hours" probably refers to the crisis of February 20. Although Comte had not resolved the problem of the vicious circle by late February when he wrote to Blainville, he seemed completely committed to writing first on positive philosophy by the time he began his course in early April. It seem likely that Blainville – "absolutely the only man in the world" whom Comte trusted intellectually – had advised him first to give a solid scientific basis to politics. A staunch Catholic and ultraroyalist, Blainville, according to Comte, worried about the "rarity" of "true ideas of *government*" in France. He no doubt reaffirmed Comte's feeling that without a sound theoretical basis, social physics would be as empirical and unsteady as political economy and liberalism.[28]

The *Cours* is thus paradoxical in that it appears to be an antireligious, scientistic work, but actually derived from Comte's moral and political preoccupations, especially from his desire to establish a strong spiritual power. The *Cours* represented the first part of his newly conceived project for terminating the French Revolution: the "full abstract systematization of all our real conceptions." It would be followed by the spiritual reorganization and then the immense political regeneration of society.[29]

Though disappointed that he did not get enough subscribers to clear his debt, Comte decided near the end of March that his course was so fundamental that he would go ahead with it anyway.[30] He was partly helped by a gift of five hundred francs from Lamoricière, a former student who had just finished the Ecole Polytechnique and borrowed the money from his mother.[31] Adolphe d'Eichthal

---

[27] *Système*, 1:2.

[28] Comte to Blainville, February 27, 1826, *Corr. inédite*, 1:18, 22. See also Gouhier, *Jeunesse*, 3:319.

[29] Comte to Clotilde de Vaux, August 5, 1845, *CG*, 3:79.

[30] Comte to A. d'Eichthal, March 29, 1826, *CG*, 1:191; Adolphe d'Eichthal to Gustave d'Eichthal, April 18, 1826, Fonds d'Eichthal 13746, item 132, BA.

[31] Comte had helped Lamoricière get into the Ecole Polytechnique in 1824 and then gave him lessons to clarify the theories of the mathematician Cauchy, which were being taught there. It appears that Lamoricière also lived with Comte at one point. Comte would turn to him again later, when he became minister of war. See Lamoricière to Comte, February, 1826, MAC, and Laffitte's notes written on a copy of this letter at the house of the former curator of the Maison d'Auguste Comte, Sybil de Acevedo; Comte to Lamoricière, July 16, 1848, *CG*, 4:169; C. P. Marielle, *Répertoire de l'Ecole Impériale Polytechnique ou Reseignements sur*

lamented that he could not help Comte again without incurring the wrath of his father.[32]

By January Comte had already determined the course's general outline. He decided to give lectures twice a week at noon in his apartment at 13, rue du faubourg-Montmartre with a long break from July to November. Although an important objective was to reveal the new science of social physics, he did not intend at first to devote any more time to it than to the other five sciences of positive philosophy. In fact, he decided to give six extra lectures to his specialty, the science of mathematics, which he considered the foundation of all of the other sciences. Thus the plan was to devote two lectures to the goals of the course, sixteen to mathematics, and ten each to astronomy, physics, chemistry, physiology, and social physics. Later, when he postponed the opening of his course from March to April in an effort to get more subscribers, he altered his strategy and decided to give fourteen lectures on social physics.[33] This switch reveals that in Comte's mind social physics was beginning to rival mathematics in importance.

Comte hoped to attract prominent individuals, especially scientists, who would recognize his contribution. He invited Guizot, although he had not seen him for some time. Guizot replied that he could not make the opening lecture but would attend the course later. He seized the occasion to compliment Comte on the "very remarkable" articles in *Le Producteur* and to voice his regret that differences of opinion had estranged them. "You are, Sir, among the small number of men of intellect with whom one always sympathizes; and I would far rather have the pleasure of arguing with you than of being fully approved of by so many others."[34] Ten days later he sent Comte a copy of the recently published first volume of his *Histoire de la Révolution d'Angleterre* in the hope of a good review in *Le Producteur*. Evidently he felt Comte could help his career just as Comte hoped Guizot would advance his own. Yet Comte never did read the book, nor did Guizot ever come to his course.[35]

les élèves qui ont fait partie de l'institution depuis l'époque de sa création en 1794 jusqu'en 1853 inclusivement (Paris, 1855), part one, 118; Keller, *Lamoricière*, 15–18.

[32] Adolphe d'Eichthal to Gustave d'Eichthal, May 9, 1826, Fonds d'Eichthal 13746, item 137, BA.

[33] Comte to A. d'Eichthal, January 27, March 29, 1826, *CG*, 1:185, 191; Comte to Lamennais, March 31, 1826, *CG*, 1:192; Parent-Lardeur, *Cabinets de lecture*, 51; Comte, "Cours de philosophie positive en 72 séances du 1er avril 1826 au 1er avril 1827," MAC. Comte wrote on the back of this handwritten table of contents, "Retrouvé dans un ancien agenda le samedi 16 mai 1846."

[34] Guizot to Comte, April 1, 1826, in Valat, "Document historique," 22.

[35] Comte to Mill, April 5, 1842, *CG*, 2:42.

Comte did not hesitate to use other connections. Sure of the attendance of Poinsot, he wanted him to induce Joseph Fourier, his colleague at the Academy of Sciences, to come. Poinsot also encouraged the Prince de Beauveau to attend. Blainville, as Comte's new mentor, agreed to hear the lectures, and he tried to persuade his colleagues and students to accompany him. He urged Comte to write to his friend Alexander von Humboldt, whose work in physical geography and meteorology had brought him great fame. Humboldt's favorable answer was followed by a meeting that left both men pleased. Later, when Comte applied for a job, he cited with pride Humboldt's presence at his course as sufficient proof that he was well respected. Comte also wrote to Lamennais, who, however, could not attend because he was involved in legal problems arising from his attacks on Gallicanism and the king.[36]

Despite his excitement or perhaps because of it, Comte could not write a single word. Evidently, he had not recovered from the instability and confusion that had caused his crisis the month before. On Friday, March 31, two days before he was to begin his course, he wrote Blainville the following enigmatic lines, which reveal his state of mind:

> I fear a great deal that I will not be sufficiently prepared [for the opening of the course] because I have experienced and still experience violent derangements. . . . For an occasion that is so decisive for me in so many respects, I needed to concentrate all my forces; but the same causes that have impeded them have, on the other hand, stimulated them; you will judge if there has been compensation.[37]

After much difficulty, Comte's course began as planned on April 2. The twenty-eight-year-old philosopher of science was honored by the presence of several key members of the scientific elite: Blainville, Arago, Fourier, Humboldt, and François Broussais.[38] Although Poinsot was too ill to attend, Comte's former employer at *Le Censeur* was there: the famous economist Dunoyer. And Cerclet, his present employer at *Le Producteur*, appeared too. Adolphe

[36] Poinsot to Comte, April 5, 1826, in "Relations d'Auguste Comte avec Poinsot," ed. Laffitte, 150; Comte to Blainville, February 27, 1826, *Corr. inédite*, 1:19, 26; Comte to Blainville, March 31, April 3, 1826, *CG*, 1:192–4; Rough copy of a letter from Blainville to Caroline Massin, [1826], MAC; Adolphe d'Eichthal to Gustave d'Eichthal, April 18, 1826, Fonds d'Eichthal 13746, item 132, BA; Unsigned letter from an "Abonné de l'Athénée" to Comte, [February 28, 1826?], MAC; Comte to the Comte de Saint-Cricq, May 14, 1828, *CG*, 1:199; Comte to Lamennais, March 31, 1826, *CG*, 1:191.

[37] Comte to Blainville, March 31, *CG*, 1:193.

[38] Gouhier is wrong when he says that Poinsot came to Comte's opening lecture. Gouhier, *Vie*, 125. See Poinsot to Comte, April 5, 1826, in "Relations d'Auguste Comte avec L. Poinsot," ed. Laffitte, 150.

Gondinet and François Mellet, two classmates from the Ecole Polytechnique, were there as well. Gondinet also contributed to *Le Producteur*. He was joined by Joseph Allier, another writer for *Le Producteur* and a great admirer of Comte. Other young men in the audience included Hippolyte Carnot, Adolphe d'Eichthal, and Napoléon de Montebello, a duke who had recently attended the Ecole Polytechnique. The Prince de Beauveau may also have been there since he told Poinsot that he was going to recommend it to his friends. General Jean-Pierre Maransin, Jacques-Philippe Mérigon de Montgéry (a famous military technologist), several doctors, and a few simply curious people completed the audience.[39] Thus the opening of Comte's course was by any standards a "very remarkable" success, as Adolphe d'Eichthal put it.[40] Yet Comte hoped for an even greater triumph, for the day afterward he begged Blainville to persuade more of his colleagues, such as Ampère, to come.[41]

Unfortunately no record exists of the contents of Comte's lectures. The course must have been difficult, for Adolphe d'Eichthal feared "few people" would be "capable of following it."[42] What is certain is that after having given the two introductory lectures and the first lecture on mathematics, Comte simply did not appear for the fourth on April 12.[43] He had quite literally gone mad.

CAUSES OF THE ATTACK OF MADNESS

No doubt partly to avoid giving his enemies ammunition that they could use against him, Comte was surprisingly open – up to a certain point – about his attack of insanity. Like Rousseau in his *Confessions* – a book Comte had carefully read – he seemed to take an odd sort of pleasure in publicly analyzing his mental and emotional difficulties. Even in a work as serious as the *Cours*, he discussed his mental problems. Such publicity seemed warranted to him, for he had made it a principle that his personal and intellectual

---

[39] Marielle, *Répertoire de l'Ecole Impériale Polytechnique*, part 1, 126; Gouhier, *Vie*, 125; Littré, *Auguste Comte*, 36; Robinet, *Notice*, 169; Comte to G. d'Eichthal, December 9, 1828, *CG*, 1:204; Lonchampt, *Précis*, 35; Poinsot to Comte, April 5, 1826, "Relations d'Auguste Comte avec Poinsot," ed. Laffitte, 150. Gouhier erred in saying that Poinsot attended and Montgéry graduated from the Ecole Polytechnique.

[40] Adolphe d'Eichthal to Gustave d'Eichthal, April 18, 1826, Fonds d'Eichthal 13746, item 136, BA.

[41] Comte to Blainville, April 3, 1826, *CG*, 1:193–4.

[42] Adolphe d'Eichthal to Gustave d'Eichthal, March 4, 1826, Fonds d'Eichthal 13746, item 132, BA.

[43] Lonchampt, *Précis*, 36.

lives were one. Moreover, divulging private matters seemed to re-
instate the revolutionaries' theory of authenticity or "transparency,"
whereby members of the community were to communicate openly
with one another to create a sense of real solidarity and avoid the
manipulations of politicians. In revolutionary discourse, inspired by
Rousseau, the truly virtuous republican was free of guile and had
nothing to conceal. Like Rousseau's admirer, Robespierre, Comte
accepted the challenge of showing that the future republic would be
morally correct because he himself was a model of virtue.[44]

To display his honesty, Comte explained in the *Cours* that his
"cerebral crisis" had resulted from the "fatal coincidence of great
moral pains and violent excesses of work."[45] He was unquestionably
working too hard, trying to revise his work on positive politics,
finish his articles on the spiritual power for *Le Producteur*, and prepare a course on positive philosophy, which he felt was crucial to his
career, both professionally and philosophically. As the weeks passed,
the pressure mounted. But he produced nothing. The impression
that he was personally falling apart made him further despair about
the unity and consistency of his work.

Signs of the second reason to which Comte alluded – his "great
moral pains" – had been evident to his friends for quite some time.
Adolphe d'Eichthal often referred to Comte's unhappiness – especially his financial difficulties and his enduring bitterness regarding
Saint-Simon.[46] Apparently Comte owed fifteen hundred francs to
the banker Ardouin, who had received a copy of the fundamental
opuscule and had helped finance *L'Industrie* (Saint-Simon's old
journal) and *Le Producteur*. Comte also owed a thousand francs to
Rodrigues. According to Comte's friend Emile Tabarié, Comte was
worried about being "obligated" to these two men and to others, all
of whom were "hardly refined."[47] Owing a large sum of money to
people connected with the Saint-Simonian movement – a movement
he wished to maintain his distance from – was undoubtedly a source
of grave concern.[48] And the extent of his other debts is not even
known.

Another source of Comte's unhappiness was his wife. Since

[44] Hunt, *Politics, Culture, and Class*, 44–6; Blum, *Rousseau*, 35, 150–4, 161.

[45] *Cours*, 2:467.

[46] Adolphe d'Eichthal to Gustave d'Eichthal, March 4, 1826, Fonds d'Eichthal 13746, item
132, BA.

[47] Information about Comte's debts can be found in a letter from Emile Tabarié to Blainville,
May 8, 1826, *Collection des lettres autographes* (letters written to Blainville), MAC. On
Ardouin, see list of subscribers in Pereire, *Autour de Saint-Simon*, 4–9; d'Allemagne, *Les
Saint-Simoniens*, 32; list of people to whom Comte sent opuscule, MAC.

[48] Bertier de Sauvigny, *Nouvelle Histoire de Paris*, 227.

November 1825 – nine months after his marriage and five months before his mental crisis – Comte had often written to Valat about his "internal sorrows," alluding to the fact that he found his allegedly domineering and opinionated wife difficult to bear. But the precise cause of his "bizarre and disastrous position" vis-à-vis Massin so disgusted and shamed him that he would not describe it on paper, even to Valat.[49]

Many years after his bitter separation from Massin, Comte did reveal the "domestic secret" in the "Secret Addition" to his *Testament*.[50] This information was to be used by his executors if they were in any way challenged by Massin. He seemed to have foreseen that his wife, backed by Littré, would demand the possession of his manuscripts. Fearing that she would spoil his reputation when he could no longer defend himself, he decided out of desperation to discredit her first.[51]

In the "Secret Addition," Comte accused Massin of never appreciating the fact that he had rescued her from her previous profession: "Her ingratitude was the principal source of my unhappiness."[52] He complained that she made fun of his devotion to her and disdained him as a weakling. What further disturbed him was that though he sought her love by providing her with security, he could not support her. She annoyed him by seeking to transform him "into an academic machine, earning money, titles, and posts for her."[53] Her discontent was confirmed by Adolphe d'Eichthal, who always dreaded seeing her because he knew he would have to "suffer" a "torrent of words and complaints."[54] Comte claimed that whenever they had financial troubles, she threatened to support him by reverting to her former profession, but his "feelings formed an invincible barrier against her shameful expedients, which she perhaps practiced secretly."[55] Thus he jealously hinted that she had returned to prostitution. Perhaps she sought lovers partly out of sexual frustration with Comte, or at least he thought she did.

These problems with money and sex apparently were the source of intense marital strife. Shortly after their marriage, Comte claimed that Massin even wanted to bring Cerclet to their apartment to make more money; she would thus have broken her promise to sever all relationships with her former lover. In a letter to Littré, he explained

---

[49] Comte to Valat, November 27, 1825, *CG*, 1:177. [50] *Cours*, 2:467; *Testament*, 36².

[51] Mecca M. Varney, *L'Influence des femmes sur Auguste Comte* (Paris: Presses Universitaires de France, 1931), 57.

[52] *Testament*, 36ᶠ. [53] Comte to Littré, April 28, 1851, *CG*, 6:63.

[54] Adolphe d'Eichthal to Gustave d'Eichthal, May 9, 1826, Fonds d'Eichthal 13746, item 137, BA.

[55] *Testament*, 36ᶠ.

that from the beginning of their marriage she was "very licentious" and enjoyed "almost innumerable" "secondary escapades" where she would stay "several weeks in a lodging house [*hôtel garni*] under the slightest pretext."[56] Comte chose his words carefully, for lodging houses were notorious haunts of prostitutes.[57] Besides making him feel inadequate and jealous, her "turpitudes" enraged him because they seemed to mock his commitment to the regeneration of morality.[58] By January 1826 he realized that to "get the upper hand" and find some peace, he would have to sacrifice the "most precious part of happiness."[59] Their separation began in March 1826, a year after their marriage, with the argument over Cerclet or with the act of betrayal itself.[60] This separation was undoubtedly an important source of the "profound agitations" that hindered his work and caused him to delay the opening of his course from March to April.[61] His solitude, bitterness, and intense jealousy, together with his intellectual exhaustion, led soon afterward to his "cerebral explosion."[62]

Comte's disciples stressed Massin's role in causing his insanity. They disliked her not only for the pain she caused their master but for her challenge to his will. Among themselves, they referred to her as the "unworthy or shameful [*indigne*] wife."[63] Lonchampt and Robinet were particularly virulent in their attacks on her and dramatized Comte's attack of madness by linking it directly with his discovery of his wife's sexual betrayal.[64]

Although the version condemning Massin has been always accepted, there is another side that deserves to be explored. It does seem possible that Comte, naturally paranoid and unable to forget his wife's past, simply imagined that she was returning to her former lover.[65] Massin always denied that she had ever contributed to Comte's illness, and her version of the story was defended by Littré, Comte's most famous disciple.[66] Littré was, in fact, so concerned about her that he incurred Comte's wrath and eventually broke with

---

[56] Comte to Littré, April 28, 1851, CG, 6:62–3.   [57] Harsin, *Policing Prostitution*, 33.

[58] *Testament*, 36[f].   [59] Comte to Valat, January 18, 1826, CG, 1:181.

[60] *Testament*, 36[f]; Comte to Littré, April 28, 1851, CG, 6:63; Lonchampt, *Précis*, 37.

[61] Comte to Valat, January 18, 1826, CG, 1:183.   [62] *Testament*, 36[f].

[63] Dr. Montègre to Laffitte, April 2, 1858, MAC; Bazalgette to Laffitte, September 27, 1857, MAC; Florez to Laffitte, 9 Frédéric 69, MAC; Laffitte to Audiffrent, October 30, 1857, N.a.fr. 10794, fol. 317, BN. Other words used to describe Caroline Massin were "abominable" (Audiffrent to Laffitte, 15 Frédéric 69), "miserable" (Hadery to Laffitte, November 30, 1857), and "horrible" (Hadery to Laffitte, February 1, 1858, and Laffitte to Henry Edger, February 1, 1858). All these letters are in MAC. Florez called her an "evil crawling viper." Florez to Laffitte, 9 Frédéric 69, BA.

[64] Lonchampt, *Précis*, 37; Robinet, *Notice*, 168, 395–6.

[65] Sokoloff, *"Mad" Philosopher*, 73–5.

[66] *Testament*, 36[f]; Comte to Littré, April 28, 1851, CG, 6:63.

him.[67] In his book on Comte, Littré admitted that Massin had problems with Comte in March, but he said they derived from her husband's illness, not from her infidelity. Unaware that he was mentally ill, she wrongly blamed his violent actions on meanness.[68] Littré's version is confirmed in a letter that Massin wrote in 1839 to Blainville: "When in 1826 Mr. Comte fell ill, for two months everything pointed to it. But I did not understand anything, I was very young and had no idea about this type of malady."[69] Littré argued that during Comte's illness, his family spread lies about Massin's unfaithfulness in order to acquire his "interdiction." His mental breakdown, according to Littré, was really due to three other factors: intellectual strain, his terrible problem with indigestion, which disturbed his sleep and made him depressed, and his "violent quarrel" with the Saint-Simonians.[70] As we have seen, there is evidence to support the first factor. The second factor also seems possible, since Comte did have severe stomach disorders. In 1823 they had been so severe that they had required Saint-Simon's care.[71] But the third factor seems invalid. Littré claimed that after Comte read Bazard's article, "Des partisans du passé et de ceux de la liberté de conscience," he accused him of having stolen his idea that there was no liberty of conscience in the positive sciences. Bazard refused to cite his fundamental opuscule, where it first appeared, and challenged Comte to a duel. Yet Bazard's essay appeared in late 1825, right before the publication of Comte's third article. Why would Comte have waited four or five months to make his accusation if he were truly offended? Moreover, according to Laffitte, Comte did not resent Bazard and indeed felt he had explained his idea "very well."[72]

Despite this problem in Littré's story, it is by no means certain that Massin had extramarital affairs or, more important, was even a prostitute in the first place. Her relations with Cerclet and later with Littré may have cast her in the role of prostitute in Comte's mind, especially as his love for the deceased Clotilde de Vaux became abnormal at the end of his life, when he made this secret accusation against his wife. As Nina Auerbach has shown, the angel–demon dichotomy was common in the mid-nineteenth-century cultural imagination.[73] The Catholic tradition in which Comte was brought

---

[67] Comte to Littré, July 15, 1850, *CG*, 5:173; Comte to Littré, April 28, 1851, *CG*, 6:60–6.

[68] Littré, *Auguste Comte*, 114.   [69] Caroline Massin to Blainville, December 20, 1839, MAC.

[70] Littré, *Auguste Comte*, 112–13.

[71] Rosalie Boyer to Comte, December 11, 1823, "Lettres de Rosalie Boyer (1)," ed. Laffitte, 95.

[72] Laffitte's words, "Variétés: Relations d'Auguste Comte avec l'abbé de La Mennais," 248.

[73] Auerbach, *Women and the Demon*, 1.

up displayed a similar ambivalence toward women, with the Virgin Mary as the symbol of absolute purity and Eve as the source of evil. Comte partook of the "binary logic" of his era.[74] After Clotilde, who refused to have sex with him, became his angel in the Religion of Humanity, he expressed his hatred for his unruly, atheistic wife by portraying her as the antipode, the fallen woman who, as a threat to the family and patriarchal society, represented the ultimate symbol of evil in the positive system. Moreover, the image of the prostitute was readily available to him. Besides appearing everywhere in nineteenth-century French novels and paintings, she was the topic of a much discussed book, Alexandre Parent-Duchâtelet's *De la prostitution dans la ville de Paris* (1836), which for the first time presented prostitution as a social problem in need of regulation.[75] Comte owned both volumes of this massive study, which perhaps fueled his imagination.

His accusations against his wife were not easy to challenge. During the trial of 1870 that pitted Massin against the executors of Comte's will, she maintained he was insane at the end of his life in order to nullify his final testament, which among other provisions, effectively deprived her of her proper inheritance and left his papers to his disciples. They feared that she and Littré, intent on preserving Comte's reputation as a *scientific* positivist, would destroy the documents celebrating Clotilde de Vaux and the Religion of Humanity.[76] They also worried that she would tear up the envelope containing the "Secret Addition" and prevent the executors from publishing the *Testament* as Comte wished.[77] Massin's lawyer argued that Comte hated her and simply invented the fatal secret to force her to follow his wishes in the *Testament*, which went against the rights given to her by their marriage contract.[78] The contents of the "Secret Addition" were not revealed during the trial, and therefore no one could directly challenge them. Although the judge ordered

[74] Mary Poovey, *Uneven Developments: The Ideological Work of Gender in Mid-Victorian England* (Chicago: University of Chicago Press, 1988), 12.

[75] Charles Bernheimer, *Figures of Ill Repute: Representing Prostitution in Nineteenth-Century France* (Cambridge, Mass.: Harvard University Press, 1989), 2; Harsin, *Policing Prostitution*, 97.

[76] Laffitte to Audiffrent, February 23, 1870, MAC.

[77] General letter to the reader, signed J. S. Florez et. al., December 1896, *Testament*; *Tribunal de Première Instance de la Seine, Audience du 11 février* 1870. Also see the handwritten, rough copy "Affaire Comte: Réplique de Mᵉ Allou" in a packet of documents relating to the succession, MAC; the summary of the trial: "Tribunal Civil de la Seine. Présidence de M. Benoît-Champy. Audiences des 4, 11, 18 et 25 février," *Gazette des Tribunaux: Journal de jurisprudence et des débats judiciaires*, March 2, 1870: 207–9; March 3, 1870: 211–12; March 4, 1870: 215–16.

[78] Griolet's statement, quoted in "Tribunal Civil de la Seine," *Gazette des Tribunaux*, March 2, 1870: 208.

the envelope containing the information destroyed, his instructions for some reason were not followed, and the "Secret Addition" was published in the second edition of the *Testament* in 1896.[79] Since this was nineteen years after Massin's death and she had no heirs, there was no one left to defend her.[80] Positivists later made sure that Comte's version of the events would be the only one that survived when they destroyed letters that might have shed light on Massin's story.[81]

Eugène Deullin, one executor of Comte's will, was astounded that no one had done the "essential research" to verify Comte's assertions after the envelope was opened.[82] Since the registry of prostitutes for this period no longer exists at the Archives de la Préfecture de Police or at the Archives Nationales, Comte's accusation is now impossible to document. In any case, Comte cleverly maintained that Massin's name was erased from the books by an officer of the peace, her co-witness along with Cerclet at their wedding. But here Comte's superb memory failed him, for the marriage certificate in the Archives de Paris states that the co-witness was not a peace officer, but Louis Oudan, a merchant.

Other evidence also casts doubt on Comte's allegation. When Massin alluded to the origins of their marriage in a letter to him written in 1843, she said that despite her knowledge that he was stubborn, she "took" him because she admired him for being "incorruptible and in our epoch that is not common."[83] There is no hint of her being coerced into marriage to escape a life of prostitution.

Moreover, Massin did seem to have other, legitimate ways of supporting herself. Littré, however, was not completely correct when he said that Massin was a bookseller by trade, for she had run the *cabinet de lecture* for only a short time. She herself claimed on her marriage certificate that she was an *ouvrière en linge*, that is, a laundry woman or seamstress. In her letters to Comte, she often mentioned sewing something for him, and his old laundry bills at the Maison d'Auguste Comte reveal that many of his socks and underwear

[79] Foucart to Laffitte, n.d. (postmark May 31, 1868), MAC; Laffitte to Audiffrent, February 28, 1870, N.a.fr. 10794, fol. 421, BN; "Tribunal Civil de la Seine," *Gazette des Tribunaux*, March 4, 1870: 216.

[80] Information about Caroline Massin's death is in the Table de *l'état civil des actes de décès du 1er janvier 1873 au 31 décembre 1882* for the seventeenth arrondissement, fol. 61v, Archives de Paris. Her date of death is listed as January 27, 1877. A copy of her death certificate is in *Département de la Seine. Ville de Paris. 17ᵉ Arrondissement Municipal. Registre double des actes de décès*, V.⁴ E 4794, fol. 22, entry no. 176, Archives de Paris.

[81] Littré's lettres in support of Massin, such as the one referred to in a letter of September 20, 1857, from Laffitte to Deullin, cannot be found in the Maison d'Auguste Comte.

[82] Deullin to Laffitte, April 29, 1868, MAC.

[83] Caroline Massin to Comte, November 18, 1843, MAC.

were sewn with the initials "CM."[84] Furthermore, when she grew old, she complained that rheumatism prevented her from using her "needle," the only profession she claimed suited her character.[85]

Even more telling are her statements about her shyness. In a letter of August 1849 in which she complained about Comte's not having acknowledged her when she went to his course, she wrote:

> I have never been alone in a public place, and to find myself there like a stranger makes my position very embarrassing. Believe me, I had to have a very great desire to see you and hear you in order to overcome the habits of reserve and timidity, which age has not eliminated.[86]

If, in fact, she had been a prostitute and her husband knew it, it would have been absurd to write these lines. In the obituary he wrote for her, Littré confirmed this impression of shyness when he stated that she loved to "hide herself" and hated to appear very often in public.[87]

It could be argued, of course, that as a seamstress Massin had a weak, precarious position in the economy and occasionally may have had to overcome her shyness to sell herself and make ends meet. But because she was intelligent and somewhat educated, she probably had more options than most marginal people. For example, when she finally separated from Comte years later, she was immediately offered a job as a governess.[88]

Although Comte's allegations against Massin cannot be proved conclusively one way or the other, there seems little doubt that she was at least partly involved in the onset of Comte's problems. On April 18, Adolphe d'Eichthal informed his brother of Comte's madness in these terms:

> I told you that I was following Mr. Comte's course. It appears that he is very distressed about his wife. People are talking about a separation. All I can tell you is that he is becoming mad because of it. At least his excitation is extreme.[89]

[84] Caroline Massin to Comte, August 30, 1838, MAC. She mentions mending Comte's shirts in her letter to Comte, October 28, 1842, MAC. See also a packet entitled "Factures de blanchissage," MAC.

[85] Caroline Massin to Comte, October 28, 1842, MAC.

[86] Caroline Massin to Comte, [August] 1849, MAC.

[87] Emile Littré, "Mme Comte," *La Philosophie positive*, 2d ser., 18 (January–June 1876): 293.

[88] Caroline Massin to Comte, October 25, 1842, MAC.

[89] Adolphe d'Eichthal to Gustave d'Eichthal, April 18, 1826, Fonds d'Eichthal 13746, item 136, BA.

Also, on March 31, 1826, Cerclet suddenly announced in *Le Producteur* that he was resigning from his post as editor in chief.[90] No reason was given. Comte gave Adolphe d'Eichthal the excuse that Cerclet was leaving because he did not share the "democratic opinions" that were "invading" the journal.[91] On April 12, Cerclet wrote to Enfantin thanking him for advising him to leave the journal.[92] Six years later, Enfantin added a note to this letter that explains its circumstances:

> I gave myself the responsibility of notifying him [Cerclet] of the necessity [of the resignation]: the cause was his conduct with regard to M. and Mme. Comte (Augte), the very shady role that he played in the madness of Comte, a role that almost made him figure in a criminal case that the public prosecutor wanted to bring against him because of Comte's madness. I was the only one who could enter into peaceful negotiations with Cerclet.

Enfantin went on to describe how Cerclet's questionable relationship with Massin caused an uproar among the Saint-Simonians, who took Comte's side:

> Rouen and Buchez wanted to hit him [Cerclet] in the face. Cerclet wanted to fight a duel with Rodrigues, whom he accused of gossiping. And finally the idle remarks that he expressed about Bazard and the opinion that he had of him prevented any natural conversation. Cerclet's challenging Rodrigues to a fight had no sequel.[93]

Thus Littré was right in saying that a duel and Bazard's character were involved in the altercation, but wrong in describing the circumstances.

The triangle of Comte, Cerclet, and Massin is problematic. Littré seems correct in maintaining that Massin met Comte through Cerclet, for Comte and Cerclet belonged to the same liberal circle and both were involved in journalism.[94] They seemed to be friends, for Comte gave Cerclet mathematics lessons and had a close relationship with him when he was editor of *Le Producteur*.[95] It seems likely that Comte

---

[90] A. Cerclet, "Lettre du Rédacteur Général aux Propriétaires du Journal," March 31, 1826, *Le Producteur* 2 (1826): 627.

[91] Adolphe d'Eichthal to Gustave d'Eichthal, May 9, 1826, Fonds d'Eichthal 13746, item 137, BA.

[92] Cerclet to Enfantin, [April 12, 1826], Fonds Enfantin 7643, fol. 42–3. The letter does not say precisely April, but at the top are the words "Mercredi, 12 courant," which would correspond to April 12.

[93] Enfantin's comment, 1832, inserted as a footnote in Cerclet to Enfantin, [April 12, 1826], Fonds Enfantin 7643, fol. 43.

[94] Littré, *Auguste Comte*, 33.

[95] Comte even told Adolphe d'Eichthal how much he valued Cerclet as an editor. Adolphe d'Eichthal to Gustave d'Eichthal, May 9, 1826, Fonds d'Eichthal 13746, item 137, BA.

met Massin when she was Cerclet's mistress or the manager of the *cabinet de lecture* purchased for her by Cerclet. Shortly after she sold it, she may have moved in with Comte. But if she had resumed her relationship with Cerclet, it seems logical that the association between the two men would have ended. Yet Cerclet went to the opening of Comte's course in 1826 and 1829, helped Massin hospitalize him when he went mad, and sent him in 1830 a copy of his new book (*Du ministère nouveau*) with a personal inscription. Nevertheless, the impression remains that the closeness of the relationship between Massin and Cerclet gave rise to ugly rumors and that she at least threatened to return to Cerclet when she and Comte needed money. In sum, Comte's accusation that Massin had resumed her relationship with Cerclet and that this was a contributing cause of his madness is possible, although it would be speculative and hazardous to make a definite judgment at this distance in time.

COMTE'S "FOLIE"

The events surrounding Comte's attack reveal the depths of his despair. Immediately after his breakdown began on April 13 or April 14, Comte left his building in an agitated state and accidentally passed Lamennais's apartment on the rue de l'Arbalète in the fifth arrondissement. He burst in and found the priest talking to Gerbet. In front of these two priests, Comte knelt down and made his confession with streams of tears running down his face. He supposedly confided to Lamennais what he could not tell Valat or his other close friends: the secret about Massin's past, his reasons for marrying her, and her recent betrayal. Until he told his housekeeper just before he died, this was the only disclosure of these matters that he made throughout his whole life.[96]

Thus Comte's desperation drove him back to the institution he despised – the Church. He referred to Lamennais not only as his "friend" but also as his "confessor."[97] Sometime after hearing this act of confession, Lamennais described Comte as a young man with a "beautiful soul that does not know where to cling."[98] To the priest, Comte's plight was far more complex than that of an overworked,

---

[96] *Testament*, 31–2; Lonchampt, *Précis*, 37.

[97] Comte to Blainville, April 15, 1826, *Corr. inédite*, 1:30. This letter to Blainville is inaccurately reproduced in *CG*, 1:125–6. (The date April 15 in *CG* is also wrong.) Yet even in the *Corr. inédite*, there are omissions. For example, on page 31 under Comte's second signature, the letters "D.M." are absent though they are in the original letter, which is in the Maison d'Auguste Comte.

[98] Lamennais, quoted in Comte to Clotilde de Vaux, August 5, 1845, *CG*, 3:85.

slighted husband; his grief represented a spiritual crisis – one of belief.

After making his confession, Comte fled to St. Denis, where he registered at a hotel on the morning of Saturday, April 15. Perhaps it was there that he wrote an "extravagant letter" reflecting his "extreme" despair to Ternaux in the hope that he would help him once again.[99] He also wrote a frantic letter to Blainville, a doctor and the only person to whom he felt close. The letter is full of incoherent statements, phrases written in the margins, and multiple underlinings of words. Comte's mental trouble is revealed in the first paragraph: "Here is *the effect*. Yesterday morning (from 10:00–11:00), I *believed* I was dead and, certainly, it was related to nothing? that I became suddenly worse than a dead person." If Blainville could not guess the *"cause"* (underlined twice), Comte told him to ask Lamennais; if he wanted more details, he should then visit Comte in Montmorency at the Cheval Blanc Hotel, where he intended to stay from Sunday to Tuesday. But Comte was so disoriented that he wrote a note in the margin saying he would be asleep at night. The letter also describes his efforts to treat himself and reflects not only his excessive pride in doing so, but also his delusions, doubts, fears, and especially deep loneliness:

I *treated* myself by myself, *seeing* [underlined twice] that I was absolutely *isolated*; it is to this fortunate and inflexible *necessity* that I attribute my *recovery*. . . . Today I just made my *plan* of convalescence. Tomorrow, or this evening (or even presently) the execution commences. Wednesday at 3:00 [the time of his course] you will *judge* my medical capacity. . . . Having found myself *obliged* [underlined three times] here *to be* and even *to appear* a *true* [underlined twice] *doctor in spite of himself*, that suggested to me this morning a very *original fantasy* that I cannot prevent myself from letting you *see* at the risk of hearing you *laugh* like a god of Homer. My *nickname* at the Ecole Polytechnique was *Sganarelle*. . . . Would my comrades then have been *prophets* since I was a *doctor* yesterday? If my *fantasy* makes you simply *laugh* (*after your dinner*) you should fix *arbitrarily* the time and manner of the *ceremony*.

"Ceremony" refers to the formal reception of new doctors. Trying to be a medical doctor as well as a doctor of society, Comte signed his letter with the initials "D.M.," standing for Doctor of Medicine (*Doctor Medicus*).[100] Yet his ironic use of the words "Sganarelle" and

---

[99] Gustave d'Eichthal to Adolphe d'Eichthal, April 20, 1826, Fonds d'Eichthal 14396, item 30, BA.

[100] Comte to Blainville, April 15, 1826, MAC. Also see the inexact reproduction, *Corr. inédite,* 1:30; Dumas, *Psychologie de deux messies,* 139; Gouhier, *Vie,* 127.

a "doctor in spite of himself," which allude to Molière's plays by the same name, reflects a moment of deep self-awareness. In these plays, Molière ridicules people's obsession with cuckoldry and medicine, which suggests that Comte recognized the absurdity of his jealousy and his efforts to treat himself. When Blainville read the letter, he understandably found it "rather singular."[101]

After returning to Paris and trying unsuccessfully to see Blainville, Comte went back to Lamennais to give him a letter. Lamennais was so alarmed by Comte's growing "mental alienation" that he hurried to Blainville to discuss it with him. Not finding him at home, he left the letter there for him to read.[102] Blainville, an admirer of Lamennais, later wrote him back to inform him of Comte's condition.[103]

The same day Comte also wrote another confused letter, this time to Adolphe d'Eichthal. It was signed with the same initials "D.M.": "You know *the cause*, you perceive the effect. No anxiety until Wednesday at 3:00. *Silence*. . . . I am in a hurry, if you *do not understand*, go to my course tomorrow."[104] But Comte had told Blainville that he would be in Montmorency, a suburb of Paris, the next day. In any case, when Adolphe met him soon afterward, he was frightened by Comte's "extreme" exaltation.[105] Comte's ranting about his perfect comprehension of physiology convinced Adolphe that he had indeed gone mad.

Comte wrote a fourth letter – to his wife. Yet by the time she received it on Monday, he had left St. Denis. She remembered that before they were married, he had liked to roam around Montmorency, and it was there that she found him, just as he was setting fire to his room.[106] Shocked, she quickly wrote to Blainville and enlisted the help of the local doctor, who was so struck by her "grief" that he abandoned his other patients to watch over Comte.[107] Once Comte calmed down, he decided to go for a walk, accompanied by

[101] Rough copy of a letter from Blainville to Caroline Massin, [July 9, 1826], MAC. Littré reproduced this letter in his book (pp. 121–6), but it does not always accord with the rough draft in the Maison d'Auguste Comte. In general, he is fairly careless in his reproductions.

[102] Rough copy of a letter from Blainville to Caroline Massin, [July 9, 1826], MAC; Littré, *Auguste Comte*, 122–3.

[103] Blainville to Lamennais, April 19, 1826, "Variétés: Relations d'Auguste Comte avec l'abbé de Lamennais," ed. Laffitte, 249.

[104] Comte to Adolphe d'Eichthal, April 15, 1826, CG, 1:195.

[105] Adolphe d'Eichthal to Gustave d'Eichthal, April 18, 1826, Fonds d'Eichthal 13746, item 136, BA.

[106] Littré, *Auguste Comte*, 114; Deroisin, *Notes sur Auguste Comte*, 23. Lonchampt says that Comte was arrested, but the police records of the Val d'Oise at this time show no such arrest. See Lonchampt, *Précis*, 38; "Rapports de la Gendarmerie," April, May 1826, F⁷ 4107, F⁷ 4108, AN.

[107] Dr. Allion to Blainville, n.d., *Collection de lettres autographes*, MAC.

Massin. Arriving at the lac d'Enghien, he threw himself into it to prove that despite his inability to swim, he would not drown. In doing so, he tried to drag Massin in with him, but she was able to hold onto some roots and thus save them both. At this point, Comte was in a state of rage with eyes afire and froth pouring from his mouth. Massin ran for help and found two policemen, whom she paid to guard Comte while she returned to Paris to get Blainville. Arriving in the city around midnight, she went to Blainville's apartment on the rue Jacob with Cerclet, whom she introduced as a "friend of Mr. Comte."[108] The scientist agreed to go to Montmorency the next morning. Meanwhile, Cerclet was to secure a place for Comte at the asylum run by the famous psychiatrist Jean-Etienne Dominique Esquirol, who continued Pinel's path-breaking approach of treating the mentally ill as human beings with emotional problems.[109]

Massin returned to Montmorency that night. When Blainville arrived the next morning, Comte gave him a detailed, incoherent report of his illness, which convinced him that he was "in a state of cerebral surexcitation very close to a true mental alienation." Cerclet appeared at this point with the news that Esquirol had no place for Comte but had sent an orderly to take him to the national asylum at Charenton, of which he was director. Blainville preferred, however, that Comte go home, a suggestion that Massin refused on the grounds that she could not handle his violence alone. Thereupon Blainville decided that they should all go directly to Esquirol's private clinic, for he was sure he could persuade the doctor to take Comte. However, when Comte found out about the plan to put him in a mental institution, he became furious. Continuing to confuse times and places, he shouted in a paranoid fashion that "people wanted to separate him from his wife; that he knew perfectly well that it was the scheme of the Prince de Carignan, etc.; but that they would not succeed."[110] (The Prince de Carignan was one of the

---

[108] Rough copy of a letter from Blainville to Caroline Massin, [July 9, 1826], MAC. See also Littré, *Auguste Comte*, 114–15, 122–3; Lonchampt, *Précis*, 38.

[109] Curiously, two of Pinel's most famous patients had been Saint-Simon and Lamennais. Pierre Chabert, "Pinel, Philippe," in *Dictionary of Scientific Biography*, ed. Gillispie; Goldstein, *Console and Classify*, 65–119; Ackerknecht, *Medicine*, 48, 169; Michel Foucault, *Histoire de la folie à l'âge classique* (Paris: Gallimard, 1972), 146; Louis Timbal, *Un Grand Médecin français: Etienne Esquirol (1772–1840)* (Extract from the *Toulouse Médical*, July 1 and 15, 1938), 20; P. Dheur, *La Maison de santé d'Esquirol* (Paris, 1898), 10, 35; Monique Dumas, "*Etienne Esquirol: Sa famille, ses origines, ses années de formation*" (Ph.D. diss., University of Paul Sabatier-Toulouse, 1971), 15, 92; Marcel Gauchet and Gladys Swain, Preface to Etienne Esquirol, *Des passions considerées comme causes, symptômes, et moyens curatifs de l'aliénation mentale* (Paris: Librairie des Deux Mondes, 1980), vii–viii.

[110] Rough copy of a letter from Blainville to Caroline Massin, [July 9, 1826], MAC; Littré, *Auguste Comte*, 123–4.

students that Poinsot had found for Comte in 1817.) He insisted that his cure depended on his being able to stay home with his wife. Blainville pretended to agree with his wishes to placate him and make him enter the carriage. Comte insisted Massin get in first. Trembling with fright, she obeyed. He sat next to her, leaning on her shoulder to sleep. Yet when he discovered that their carriage was not heading to his apartment, he became so violent that he had to be restrained by a policeman.

Shortly afterward, when examined by Esquirol at his famous clinic on the rue Buffon, Comte was diagnosed as having "mania."[111] According to Esquirol, mania was characterized by a "general delirium," an "overexcitement of all functions," and an inability to concentrate:

> Because the natural relationships of maniacs with the exterior world are broken, all the impressions that the patient receives are painful; they irritate him, exasperate him, and push him to violence and fury, especially if one resists his desires, which are as transient as they are energetic. The disorder of the intelligence involves the perversion of moral affections, whence is born the defiance, distance, and hatred for anybody approaching the maniac.[112]

In sum, the patient, who no longer understands what is transpiring around him, concludes that everyone – even those he loves the most – is conspiring against him and persecuting him.[113]

In dealing with the insane, Esquirol advocated a mixture of moral and physical treatments.[114] Isolation was particularly necessary for maniacs "to vanquish their resistance against curative methods," "to make them again adopt intellectual and moral habits," and to remove them from their regular environment and the people at the source of their illness. New stimuli could then be given to them to promote the formation of new ideas.[115] So Comte, whose paranoia had been evident for years, was isolated and given sedatives. To cure his excitability, he also received two baths a day, cold showers, and bleedings by means of leeches.[116]

Massin had frequent discussions with Esquirol and the assistant doctors, Jean-Etienne Mitivié and Etienne-Jean Georget, concerning

---

[111] See the extract from Esquirol's registry in Dumas, *Psychologie de deux messies*, 144n1.
[112] Esquirol in *Notice sur les ouvrages du Docteur Esquirol* (Paris, 1832), 4.
[113] [Jean-Etienne Dominique] Esquirol, *Aliénation mentale* (Paris, 1832), 38–9.
[114] Goldstein, *Console and Classify*, 265.
[115] *Notice sur les ouvrages du Docteur Esquirol*, 67. See also Dheur, *Maison de santé* 20; Goldstein, *Console and Classify*, 289.
[116] Littré, *Auguste Comte*, 116; Caroline Massin to Blainville, [April] 25, 1826, MAC; Jean-Etienne Dominique Esquirol, *Des maladies mentales considerées sous les rapports médical, hygiénique, et médico-légal*, 2 vols. (Paris, 1838), 1:144.

the character of her husband. Comte proved to be a difficult patient, driving a fork into the cheek of his servant and maliciously criticizing Dr. Georget, especially his book on the nervous system.[117] In spite of Esquirol's assurances, Massin found little improvement and complained that "there is still the same wandering, the same volubility, the same petulance; there is even less presence of mind."[118] Her concern for her husband is evident in a letter she wrote to Blainville on June 1:

> Mr. Comte had been a little better the last week, but unfortunately it did not last, and since Monday he has not been well. When I had the honor of seeing Mr. Esquirol, he told me that he could not specify the time of recovery. But he guaranteed it would occur. . . . I would be pleased to know if he gave you the same assurance when you saw him.[119]

Convinced that Comte's recovery was imminent and would be impeded by contact with his family, Esquirol and Blainville commanded that no one be told about Comte's illness. Already he was showing some improvement by asking for his wife.[120] There thus seemed to be no reason to worry his parents or to risk scandal.

Massin did, however, confide in a person close to the family – a man named Fisher, the Comtes' neighbor in Montpellier. He too advised her to tell them nothing.[121] Tabarié, who still lived in Montpellier, somehow found out that Comte was ill and wrote to Blainville, offering to help pay his debts. Above all, he hoped to spare Comte's parents the news, which would give them "such a severe shock."[122] Thus notwithstanding Alix Comte's later charges,

---

[117] Later Comte changed his mind and placed Georget's book, *De la physiologie du système nerveux et spécialement du cerveau*, in his main library. This work was influenced by Gall's phrenology.

[118] Massin to Blainville, [April] 25, 1826, MAC.

[119] Caroline Massin to Blainville, June 1, 1826, MAC. Although the letter is dated May 1, 1826, Massin made a mistake because the postmark says June 2.

[120] Letter from Caroline Massin to Tabarié, May 18, 1826, in "Correspondants, amis et protecteurs d'Auguste Comte: Tabarié," ed. Laffitte, *RO* (1895): 113.

[121] Rosalie Boyer to Comte, December 11, 1823, *RO* (1909): 96. The space marked "illisible" in the letter from Rosalie Boyer to Comte, October 20, 1821, printed on page 95, should be filled by two names, "Marsal, Ficher." See the original letter of Rosalie to Comte, October 20, 1821, MAC. The "Ficher" mentioned by Rosalie Boyer seems to be the same Fisher who wrote to Comte. See also Fisher to Caroline Massin, April 5, 1827, MAC. Fisher was a good friend of Madame Goy, the mother of Comte's childhood sweetheart, Ernestine. Comte to Ernestine de Montfort, October 18, 1848, *CG*, 4:200.

[122] Tabarié to Blainville, May 8, 1826, in *Collection de lettres autographes*, MAC. See also, "Correspondants, amis et protecteurs d'Auguste Comte: Tabarié," ed. Laffitte, *RO* (1895): 86.

Massin was not the only one who was trying to hide Comte's illness from his parents.

Despite all these efforts at secrecy, on May 17, 1826, Comte's family heard about his madness from an unlikely source: Massin's father. When Comte was married, he told his parents that her father was dead, for a man who had abandoned his daughter as an infant was scarcely a man to be acknowledged. Trying to earn a living from speech lessons, Louis Massin emerged shortly before Comte's illness to ask his daughter for money. When she refused, Louis Massin decided to seek revenge by visiting her husband's very Catholic and bourgeois family. To shock the Comtes, he told them that he had married another woman, although his first wife (Caroline's mother) was still alive, and that he had had children by this other woman. Then on May 17, he wrote to Louis Comte, informing him that Caroline had abandoned his son, who had gone mad because of her infidelities. He also presumably told him about her having been a prostitute or perhaps invented this story, which Auguste Comte later adopted to threaten her. In any case, Louis Comte was so upset that he gave M. Massin money to leave him alone and warned him that if he ever troubled him again, he would have him arrested for bigamy. In spite of the threat, M. Massin then wrote him another letter against his daughter, which arrived after Rosalie Boyer, Comte's sickly mother, had left for Paris.[123]

Comte's family was profoundly shocked by M. Massin's "vile" revelations and was sure that their son had married into a family belonging "to the pure scum of the populace [*la pure canaille*]."[124] Despite their efforts to suppress the rumors, all of Montpellier was soon discussing Caroline Massin and her sordid past. Comte's friend Fisher said he heard so many "disagreeable things from one side and the other" that he did not know what to believe.[125]

---

[123] The letters from Louis Massin were probably burned in the 1850s by Louis Comte when he destroyed a number of precious documents, including many letters from his son. "Déclaration de Mademoiselle Alix Comte, soeur d'Auguste Comte," May 19, 1868, in "De quelques documents relatifs à la crise cérébrale d'Auguste Comte en 1826," ed. Pierre Laffitte, *RO*, 2d ser., 11 (May 1895): 439; Rosalie Boyer to Comte, July 13, 1830, "Lettres de Rosalie Boyer (1)," ed. Laffitte 107; Caroline Massin to Tabarié, May 18, 1826, "Correspondants, amis et protecteurs d'Auguste Comte: Tabarié," ed. Laffitte, 114; Alix Comte to Robinet, March 25, 1860, MAC. Alix Comte may have fabricated some information, for she wrote to Robinet, "I have been completely silent about the information that you asked me. . . . [I]f . . . someone asks me if I remember how we learned of the . . . illness that my brother had, I will say by a letter from Mr. Massin, describing the behavior of his daughter in a letter written to my father and I will talk about it as if it were something inscribed in my memory." Alix Comte to Robinet, May 29, 1860, Papiers Emile Corra, 17 AS (4), AN.

[124] Alix Comte to Robinet, March 25, 1860, MAC.

[125] Fisher to Comte, April 5, 1827, MAC.

In the meantime, Caroline Massin, seeing no improvement in her husband's condition, informed his parents that their son had been ill for some time and was resting in the country. She added that she was coming to visit them, no doubt to tell them the alarming news in person.[126] But her letter arrived Sunday, May 21, three days after Rosalie Boyer had left. With her father gone on business, Alix Comte opened it and was dumbfounded by what she "dared to say."[127] Fearful that Caroline would arrive in Montpellier before Louis Comte's return, she responded immediately, telling her that "it was vile of her to leave her husband" and generally reproaching her severely for everything that Louis Massin had revealed.[128] She threatened to enter a convent if Caroline ever set foot in Montpellier.[129] This letter caused such a severe reaction in Caroline that when she received another letter from Alix seventeen years later, she wrote, "The sight of this handwriting truly upset me by putting under my eyes again and in all the most horrible details the wrong that I pardon but that I can never forget."[130] Comte himself, even after separating from his wife, refused to visit his family until Alix asked Caroline's forgiveness and showed her some respect. This Alix would not do.[131]

Meanwhile in Paris, Rosalie Boyer went to the clinic every day, but Esquirol would not allow her to see her delirious son until September 15. Alix unfairly blamed Massin – a "vile woman" – for persuading Esquirol to delay her mother's meeting with Comte until then. In truth, the doctor was following his own rules of therapy.[132] He also would not agree to Rosalie Boyer's plan to separate Comte from Massin by taking him back to Montpellier. Since Massin was the person who had admitted him to the clinic, she was the responsible party.

Rosalie Boyer then decided to find Massin. When they met, she immediately tried to convince her that Comte should be moved. According to one of Comte's disciples, Lamennais and Gerbet obtained Rosalie Boyer's authorization to have him taken to a "religious house," which apparently belonged to the congregation directed by Lamennais's brother, Jean-Marie. They wanted to "get him away from the influence of Paris, by using the pretext that a stay in the

[126] Littré, *Auguste Comte*, 117; Caroline Massin to Tabarié, May 18, 1826, in Laffitte, "Correspondants, amis et protecteurs d'Auguste Comte: Tabarié," ed. Laffitte, *RO* (1895): 113.
[127] Alix Comte to Robinet, March 25, 1860, MAC.
[128] "Déclaration de Mademoiselle Alix Comte," in "De quelques documents relatifs à la crise cérébrale," ed. Laffitte, 439. See also Alix Comte to Robinet, May 25, 1860, MAC.
[129] Rosalie Boyer to Comte, July 13, 1830, "Lettres de Rosalie Boyer (1)," ed. Laffitte, 106.
[130] Caroline Massin to Comte, August 18, 1843, MAC.
[131] Alix Comte to Robinet, March 25, 1860, MAC.   [132] Ibid.

country . . . could help a great deal in bringing him back to health."[133]
Lamennais probably felt that Comte's illness was brought about by
a crisis of belief and, with the right religious environment, he would
return to the faith. Rosalie Boyer strongly favored this plan because
she thought her son was being punished by God for having married
a prostitute outside of the Church. She hoped prayers and a pious
atmosphere would bring about his recovery.[134] Massin, however,
rejected the idea.[135]

Hoping to separate Comte from his sinful wife and take over his
care, his family resorted to a legal procedure called an "interdiction." It would deprive Comte of his legal rights and make his father
his guardian. Since the story of the interdiction casts an unfavorable
light on the Comtes, it is omitted by most of Comte's biographers,
except Littré. Alix Comte positively denied it and claimed that it
was a story invented by Massin to gain her husband's gratitude.[136]
But Littré's version is true because a rough draft of the letter that
Blainville wrote to Massin mentioning the family's desire for an
interdiction still exists, as do all the legal documents.[137]

Rosalie Boyer worked throughout June trying to convoke a meeting of family and friends, who, she hoped, would persuade the
justice of the peace in Comte's second arrondissement to declare an
interdiction.[138] She eventually found six people who agreed to claim
to be friends of Comte and not mention his wife. Only two were
close enough to him to figure in his letters. One was Blainville,
whose help she obtained by appealing to his royalist and Catholic
sentiments, and the other was Bérard de Favas, Louis Comte's financial agent, who had often lent Comte money.[139] These six people

[133] Declaration of Audiffrent, January 18, 1870, MAC. See also Deroisin, *Notes sur Auguste Comte*, 26.

[134] Littré, *Auguste Comte*, 118, 120.

[135] The positivist Audiffrent asserted that Massin feared that the two priests were trying to "sequester the young thinker whose merit and revolutionary ardor they recognized would be opposed energetically to the realization of their project." This interpretation seems exaggerated and reflects the positivists' anticlericalism. See Declaration of Audiffrent, January 18, 1870, MAC.

[136] Alix Comte, to Audiffrent, July 8, 1859, MAC.

[137] Rough copy of a letter from Blainville to Caroline Massin, [July 9, 1826], MAC; Registre, Justice de Paix, 2ᵉ arrondissement, June 1826, D2 U1 171, fol. 11, article of registration no. 1006, Archives de Paris; Procès-Verbal, Justice de Paix, 2ᵉ arrondissement, D2 U1 142, the official minutes of the "Conseil Comte" (family meeting), June 23, 1826, Archives de Paris. See also Littré, *Auguste Comte*, 118, 126–7.

[138] Statement by Louis Comte, notarized by Jacques Anduze, June 2, 1826, Montpellier, D2 U1 142, Archives de Paris.

[139] Two cloth manufacturers – Guillaume Captier and François Didier – who lived at 29, rue de Richelieu, were part of this council as well. Perhaps they were Comte's neighbors when he lived with Saint-Simon. The last two people – Joseph Arthaud of the rue du faubourg

and Rosalie Boyer, appearing before the justice of the peace of the second arrondissement on June 23, 1826, swore that there existed no one in Paris or its environs closer to Comte than themselves. They not only failed to mention that he had a wife, but insinuated that he had a mistress whose depravity had led to his madness. Implying that she had made no effort to find Comte, Blainville declared that he had found him wandering alone in the forests of Montmorency and brought him home for two days before taking him to Esquirol's asylum.[140] The judge, Rosalie Boyer, and the "friends" then agreed upon an act of interdiction.

This act of interdiction had to be read to Comte twice before it could be enforced. Although Massin knew nothing about it the first time, Esquirol discovered the scheme and warned her right before the second reading. Accompanied by her lawyer, Massin went to Blainville's apartment to demand that he tell the justice of the peace the truth. Blainville agreed to do what she wanted to clear her name, conceding that the interdiction arose from an effort to hurt her reputation and thus destroy her relation with Comte. Considering that Comte had never alluded to any infidelity on her part, he agreed that he had been "extremely wrong to sign, that it was because of domestic woes that Mr. Comte experienced the illness for which one solicits his interdiction."[141]

With Blainville's support, Massin was able to stop the interdiction on the obvious grounds that she was Comte's wife and did not agree to its terms. Comte remained at Esquirol's and was not subjected to potentially damaging publicity. Even in his *Testament*, Comte said his wife's conduct during his "medical incarceration" was the "sole honorable phase of her whole life."[142]

Boyer remained in Paris for six months. When she moved from rue Saint-Denis to the boulevard Poissonnière, she was practically Massin's neighbor, and even after Massin rented a new, small, and inexpensive apartment on 36, rue du faubourg Saint-Denis, they were still close.[143] Meeting by chance on the street one day, they decided

Saint-Denis and Antoine Brun of the boulevard Poissonnière – were possibly friends from his new *quartier* or recent allies of Rosalie Boyer, who lived on the rue Saint-Denis and the boulevard Poissonnière during her stay in Paris.

[140] The official minutes of the family meeting – "Conseil Comte" – in D2 U1 142, Archives de Paris. See also the rough copy of a letter from Blainville to Caroline Massin, [July 9, 1826], MAC.

[141] Rough copy of a letter from Blainville to Caroline Massin, [July 9, 1826], MAC; Littré, *Auguste Comte*, 122.

[142] *Testament*, 36[f].

[143] Minutes, D2 U1 142, Archives de Paris; the note added to the letter from Mme Auguste Comte to G. d'Eichthal, November 29, 1826, "Correspondance d'Auguste Comte et Gustave d'Eichthal (Suite)," ed. Laffitte, 354; Littré, *Auguste Comte*, 127.

to end their feud for Comte's sake. They then saw each other so often that Massin could remind Comte twelve years later that she had lived with his mother for six months.[144]

Although religious tensions existed between the two women and there were some violent scenes, even Alix admitted that her mother began to see Massin's point of view and understood that she was "very unhappy and very slandered."[145] When Boyer checked the registry of prostitutes to confirm what she had heard, she could not find Massin's name.[146] Then she let Caroline read Louis Massin's letter. Caroline was so shocked that she showed it to her own mother.[147] Boyer decided she no longer believed the "horrors" that Louis Massin had written.[148] She partly blamed her son for the couple's problems and even criticized Alix's behavior.

In letter after letter and later in person, Alix sought unsuccessfully to change her mother's opinion about Massin, a "sordid woman."[149] In Alix's unrelenting campaign against her, it is hard to escape the suspicion that she was a bitter spinster who spent a very virtuous life at home with the family in the hope of being able to get more than her fair share of the inheritance. Envious of her beautiful, charming sister-in-law, she tried to slander her and thus alienate her parents from her brother. But Boyer believed Alix was "wrong," although her daughter's attitude was understandable because she had read Louis Massin's "two foul letters . . . against Caroline."[150] Massin always retained a grudging respect for her mother-in-law, as this statement to Comte in 1838 reveals: "I have been convinced for a long time that except for your great aptitudes, your direction toward academics came from the influence of your mother, whom one could certainly not accuse of mediocrity."[151]

By late November, Esquirol had still failed to win Comte's confidence, which he considered the key to his recovery, and feared he was "almost lost."[152] Boyer wanted to bring him back to Montpellier, since she and her husband could no longer afford the clinic, which catered to a wealthy clientele. Louis Comte, however, refused to let

---

[144] Caroline Massin to Comte, August 30, 1838, MAC.

[145] Alix Comte to Audiffrent, July 8, 1859, MAC.

[146] *Testament*, 36ᵉ.

[147] Rosalie Boyer to Comte, July 13, 1830, "Lettres de Rosalie Boyer (1)," ed. Laffitte, 107.

[148] Alix Comte to Audiffrent, July 8, 1859, MAC. The fourth page is misplaced and can be found in her letters to Robinet.

[149] Alix Comte to Robinet, March 25, 1860, MAC. See also Alix Comte to Audiffrent, July 8, 1859, MAC.

[150] Rosalie Boyer to Comte, July 13, 1830, "Lettres de Rosalie Boyer (1)," ed. Laffitte, 107.

[151] Caroline Massin to Comte, August 30, 1838, MAC.

[152] Caroline Massin to Blainville, December 20, 1839, MAC. Also see Littré, *Auguste Comte*, 128–29; Dheur, *Maison de santé*, 28.

Massin into the house.[153] Since Massin lacked the money to pay for further treatment, she had to consent to Comte's release.[154] She did insist, however, that Comte spend two weeks with her to see whether he was strong enough for the trip and to find out if she could help him.[155]

On December 2, Esquirol pronounced Comte incurable and released him in about the same condition in which he had been in when he was admitted.[156] Massin went to get him, accompanied by two of their friends: François Mellet, an engineer and classmate of Comte at the Montpellier *lycée* and the Ecole Polytechnique, and Adolphe Issalène, a merchant from Montpellier whose wife she had befriended.[157] During the ride to Massin's apartment, Comte mistook the Austerlitz Bridge for the Golden Horn in Istanbul, and when Mellet contradicted him, Comte hit him.[158]

Upon his return home, he was immediately forced to go through a Catholic wedding ceremony, which Boyer had arranged. With Lamennais's assistance, she obtained the archbishop of Paris's authorization to have the ceremony performed in the apartment.[159] The parish priest, refusing to officiate since the groom was too ill to consent, sent a substitute. Comte's witnesses were Mellet and an employee of the Church. Massin's witnesses were Issalène and the person sent by Esquirol to help her.[160] As the weak, sick

---

153 Caroline Massin to Comte, August 1838, April 20, 1843, and late October 1843, MAC; Louis Comte to Comte-Rochambeau, September 20, 1826, excerpt in Ouy, "La Jeunesse," 260; Goldstein, *Console and Classify*, 141.

154 Mme Auguste Comte to G. d'Eichthal, November 29, 1826, "Correspondance d'Auguste Comte et Gustave d'Eichthal (Suite)," ed. Laffitte, 354.

155 Lonchampt was wrong when he said that it was originally Comte's mother's idea to bring him back to his apartment. This is one of many examples of how the positivists sought to prevent Massin from having any credit. Lonchampt, *Précis*, 40.

156 Littré, *Auguste Comte*, 116; *Cours*, 2:468; Extract from Esquirol's registry with "NG" – "*Non Guérit*" – written on it. Dumas, *Psychologie de deux messies*, 144n1.

157 Littré, *Auguste Comte*, 116, 128, 135; Dumas, *Psychologie de deux messies*, 144; Marielle, *Répertoire de l'Ecole Impériale Polytechnique*, part 2, 13; *Ecrits*, 187; Valat, "Auguste Comte," 2:354. Comte had seen a great deal of Mellet in 1818, when the latter was studying law in Paris. Comte to Valat, April 17, 1818, *CG*, 1:33.

158 Deroisin, *Notes sur Auguste Comte*, 24–5.

159 Another person who helped Rosalie was the vicar of the Church of the Petits-Pères, who was the confessor of Madame Issalène, Massin's friend. A fanatical anti-Catholic, Littré claimed that Lamennais was eager to "conquer" his opponent Comte and took advantage of the situation in order to "stimulate such an important conversion." But as Gouhier has pointed out, Rosalie might have told Lamennais that her son was coming home because he was cured. Littré, *Auguste Comte*, 130–1; Gouhier, *Vie*, 133; Registre de Mariage de l'Eglise de Saint Laurent, Registre no. 664 in the archives deposited by the archdiocese, Archives de Paris.

160 Registre de Mariage de l'Eglise de Saint Laurent, Registre no. 664, Archives de Paris; Littré, 135; Dumas, *Psychologie de deux messies*, 144.

philosopher recited the prayers, he began to ramble. The priest's long sermon caused Comte suddenly to suffer a severe attack of "cerebral excitation," and he began to give an antireligious harangue.[161] Rosalie Boyer burst into tears, called for God's blessing, and finally gave the kiss of peace to Massin, now her legitimate daughter-in-law. With no religious education or faith in God, Massin was so nervous and disoriented that she signed "AC Massin" twice on the marriage registry.[162] For the rest of her life, she shuddered in horror whenever she remembered that scene.[163]

RECOVERY

During the first week at home, Comte made no improvement. Somber and uncommunicative, he would often crouch behind doors and act more like an animal than a human. He still had many fantasies. Every lunch and dinner, he would announce he was a Scottish Highlander from one of Walter Scott's novels, stick his knife into the table, demand a juicy piece of pork, and recite verses of Homer. He often tried to scare Massin by throwing his knife at her. Once he even grazed her arm. One day, when his mother joined them for a meal, an argument broke out at the table, and Comte took a knife and slit his throat. The scars were visible for the rest of his life.[164]

The second week, Massin decided to remove all reminders of his illness from the apartment. She took off the bars on the windows that she had ordered installed and dismissed Esquirol's attendant. It was only then that Comte began to make an "almost miraculous recovery."[165] Giving him baths and purges, Massin treated him

---

[161] Littré, *Auguste Comte*, 131. According to legend, Comte signed the marriage registry "Brutus Bonaparte Comte," which combined the names of two historical figures he despised. Despite Georges Dumas's assurance about the legibility of the signature, one cannot make out the supposedly erased words "Brutus Bonaparte" on the marriage registry. Comte signed "Ate Comte." Dumas, *Psychologie de deux messies*, 144–5; Gouhier, *Vie*, 133; Registre de Mariage de l'Eglise de Saint Laurent, Registre no. 664, Archives de Paris.

[162] Registre de Mariage de l'Eglise de Saint Laurent, Registre no. 664, Archives de Paris. In a letter to one of Comte's disciples, she stated her "abstention from all religious practice" and mentioned her lack of religious education. Caroline Massin to Charles Robin, April 14, 1876, MAC. See also letter of Caroline Massin to Littré, January 20, 1868, in Emile Littré, "Mme Comte," *La Philosophie positive*, 2d ser., 18 (January–June 1876): 293; Lonchampt, *Précis*, 41.

[163] Littré, *Auguste Comte*, 131.

[164] Deroisin, *Notes sur Auguste Comte*, 25; Littré, *Auguste Comte*, 131; Caroline Massin to Blainville, December 20, 1839, MAC; Alix Comte to Robinet, April 3, 1860, MAC.

[165] Mme Auguste Comte to G. d'Eichthal, December 22, 1826, "Correspondants, amis et protecteurs d'Auguste Comte (suite)," ed. Pierre Laffitte, *RO* (1898): 355.

according to Esquirol's recommendations, though she dared not say so to her husband, who hated doctors and medicine. Since he could not stand contradiction, it required great sensitivity and tact to persuade him to do what was necessary. She even took his medicine when he did so that he would not feel he was being treated differently. Within six weeks, she claimed that Comte's "recovery" was "complete" partly because of her devotion to him: "Only in his affection did I find the way to act on him. I repeat, his total confidence [in me] was the way and the cause of the almost miraculous success that I obtained."[166] Seeing her son improve from day to day, Rosalie Boyer decided to leave Paris on December 18. About a week later, Adolphe d'Eichthal testified to his recovery in a letter to his brother:

> I just left Monsieur Comte's, my dear friend, and am very satisfied with the state in which I found him; during the three-quarters of an hour in which we talked together, he was perfectly calm and did not let me perceive any trace of his illness. . . . He has a perfectly fresh memory and talked well on all subjects. Yet according to what Monsieur Blainville told me in the morning, I avoided politics – the only issue on which he appears still to wander a bit.[167]

Since Comte was unable to work during his recovery, his financial situation continued to be very precarious. The four hundred francs left by Boyer were soon gone, and though she occasionally sent some of her savings, Louis Comte was not eager to send a substantial amount of money. Rosalie Boyer's visit and his son's stay at Esquirol's expensive clinic had already cost him almost four thousand francs.[168] Desperate, Massin turned to anyone she could find for help. Having already been aided by Blainville and Tabarié, she accepted Gustave d'Eichthal's offer of assistance but asked him not

---

[166] Caroline Massin to Blainville, December 20, 1839, MAC.

[167] Adolphe d'Eichthal to Gustave d'Eichthal, December 26, 1826, Fonds d'Eichthal 13746, item 140, BA.

[168] On November 30, 1826, Rosalie Boyer paid Esquirol fifteen hundred francs, the charge for her son's stay in the hospital. This did not count the first month's bill for five hundred francs paid by Comte's friend Tabarié. "Déclaration de Mademoiselle Alix Comte," in "De quelques documents relatifs à la crise cérébrale," ed. Laffitte, 439; Mme Auguste Comte to G. d'Eichthal, December 22, 1826, "Correspondants, amis et protecteurs d'Auguste Comte: Tabarié" ed. Laffitte, *RO* (1896): 355; Receipt signed by Mitivié for Esquirol, November 30, 1826, in "De quelques documents relatifs à la crise cérébrale," ed. Laffitte, 440; Caroline Massin to Tabarié, May 18, 1826, "Correspondants, amis et protecteurs d'Auguste Comte: Tabarié," ed. Laffitte, *RO* (1895): 113; "Note de Louis Comte: Dépenses faites par sa femme à Paris pour le traitement de leur fils," MAC; Louis Comte, "Note des avances faites pour mon fils, pendant ou après la maladie dont il fut atteint en 1826," MAC. The latter is reproduced inaccurately in "De quelques documents relatifs à la crise cérébrale," ed. Laffitte, 441–2.

to tell Comte for fear of worrying him. Duc Napoléon de Montebello and Hippolyte Carnot, auditors of Comte's course, also appear to have helped.[169] And Massin had another source – Cerclet, who lent her twelve hundred francs. Comte was heavily indebted to Cerclet for fourteen years, because the sum was repaid only in 1840.[170] Whether she performed some services for this loan is not known, but Comte probably thought so, at least later when he imagined she was a prostitute.

In early 1827 Comte began to consider giving his course again, but he grew very depressed and questioned whether he would ever recover his mental abilities. As he became sadder, his paranoia increased. He saw signs of betrayal in all of Massin's words and actions and accused her repeatedly of preferring someone else.[171] As he faced the anniversary of his attack, he became so depressed that he tried in March to commit suicide by throwing himself into the Seine from the Pont des Arts. A royal guard, passing by, saved him. After visiting Comte, Gustave d'Eichthal feared his rambling discourse signaled a recurrence of his illness – a fear Comte shared.[172] Adolphe sadly noted that "vexations . . . continued to beset Auguste," and he lost hope of ever seeing him recover.[173] From the context, it is not clear whether Adolphe was referring to problems with money or

---

[169] Lonchampt, *Précis*, 42; Louis Comte, "Note des avances faites pour mon fils, pendant ou après la maladie dont il fut atteint en 1826," MAC; Adolphe d'Eichthal to Gustave d'Eichthal, December 26, 1826, Fonds d'Eichthal 13746, item 140, BA; Adolphe d'Eichthal to Gustave d'Eichthal, January 4, 1827, Fonds d'Eichthal 13746, item 141, BA; Emile Littré, "Procès de Mme Auguste Comte contre les Exécuteurs testamentaires de son mari," *La Philosophie positive* 3 (March–April 1870): 351n1.

[170] In the late 1830s and early 1840s, Massin and Comte kept notebooks recording their expenses. In Comte's notebook, which is called "Recettes et dépenses courantes," he wrote down for May 19, 1840: "Delivered to my wife to give back to M. Cerclet a sum lent by him during my illness of 1826." Caroline Massin kept two notebooks. The one labeled "Recettes et dépenses janvier 1837 à juillet 1842" is an informal, rough-draft version of the other, which is called "Recettes et dépenses janvier 1837 à décembre 1841." In the informal notebook, she marked down for May 1840, "Rendu à M. Cerclet 1200," whereas in the second notebook, which is done in regular accounting style, she marked this down for June 1840.

[171] Concerned about Comte's health, d'Eichthal and Montebello offered to pay for him to convalesce in the country for two to three months. Massin thanked d'Eichthal for the offer but said that her husband refused out of pride. She added bitterly that it was his parents who should be making such an offer. Mme Auguste Comte to G. d'Eichthal, March 6, March 8, 1827, "Correspondance d'Auguste Comte et Gustave d'Eichthal (Suite)," ed. Laffitte, 356–7. See also letter from Adolphe to Gustave d'Eichthal, November 25, 1827, Fonds d'Eichthal 13746, item 154, BA.

[172] Gustave d'Eichthal to Adolphe d'Eichthal, March 14, 1827, Fonds d'Eichthal 14396, item 35, BA.

[173] Adolphe d'Eichthal to Gustave d'Eichthal, March 29, 1827, Fonds d'Eichthal, 13746, item 146, BA.

with Massin. In any case, Comte, deeply ashamed of his cowardly, suicidal action, resolved to overcome his despair.[174] Louis Comte now realized he had to help the couple financially.[175]

When Comte received three hundred francs from his father on June 7, he decided to leave the countryside where he was convalescing and visit his parents.[176] Whether due to lack of money, Louis Comte's refusal to see her, or Alix's threat to enter a convent, Massin did not go with her husband but found someone to accompany him.[177] En route, Comte changed his mind and started to return to Paris and his wife, until he thought better of his decision. He finally arrived in Montpellier in late June, his tardiness having caused his wife "deadly worries."[178] These worries were not groundless, for Comte later admitted that he was still in a "state of quasi-vegetation" during the summer of 1827.[179] While in Montpellier, he refused to read the letters that Louis Massin had sent to his parents, who had hoped to use them to justify their behavior during his illness.[180] By the end of July, he was as eager to see Massin as she was to see him, and after only six weeks in Montpellier, he rejoined his wife in the countryside. At his departure, his father gave him 325 francs. From September 1827 to November 1828, he sent him at irregular intervals another seventeen hundred francs.[181]

When Comte returned to Paris, he moved to the Latin Quarter to be closer to students. Yet after settling at 159, rue Saint-Jacques,

[174] Lonchampt, *Précis*, 41–2. Alix Comte also declared that this incident marked a turning point in his recovery. She could not remember if the suicide attempt took place in March or April, but she believed it was in April. All of Comte's biographers say the incident occurred in April. But the letter from Gustave to Adolphe d'Eichthal, which was written on March 14, 1827, mentions Comte's suicide attempt. Alix Comte to Robinet, April 3, 1860, MAC; Gustave d'Eichthal to Adolphe d'Eichthal, March 14, 1827, Fonds d'Eichthal 14396, item 35, BA.

[175] Receipt, Auguste Comte to Reboul, April 25, 1827, in "De quelques documents relatifs à la crise cérébrale," ed. Laffitte, 440.

[176] Louis Comte's "Note des avances faites pour mon fils," MAC.

[177] Rosalie Boyer to Comte, July 13, 1830, "Lettres de Rosalie Boyer (1)," ed. Laffitte, 107; Caroline Massin to Comte, August 30, 1838, MAC.

[178] Mme Auguste Comte to G. d'Eichthal, August 3, 1827, "Correspondance d'Auguste Comte et Gustave d'Eichthal (Suite)," ed. Laffitte, 357. See also Louis Comte, "Note des avances faites pour mon fils," MAC; Receipt, Comte to Mme de la Salle (and Louis Comte's note that is written on it), June 17, 1827, in "De quelques documents relatifs à la crise cérébrale," ed. Laffitte, 440. The original note is in the Maison d'Auguste Comte.

[179] Comte to Mme Auguste Comte, October 6, 1837, *CG*, 1:281.

[180] Rosalie Boyer to Comte, July 13, 1830, *RO* (1909): 107.

[181] Mme Auguste Comte to G. d'Eichthal, August 3, 1827, "Correspondance d'Auguste Comte et Gustave d'Eichthal," ed. Laffitte, 357; Louis Comte, "Note des avances faites pour mon fils, MAC." Littré errs in claiming that Louis Comte was very generous with his son, while Lonchampt is mistaken in saying that he did not help him at all. See Littré, *Auguste Comte*, 134; Lonchampt, *Précis*, 42.

he still had difficulties finding work as a teacher. He was especially disappointed that he failed to get a job tutoring Montalivet's son. With no prospects in sight, he turned to the industrialist Ternaux for help. Early in 1827 Ternaux had given him twice the money he had requested, but this time he refused. Although resentful at first, Comte later felt Ternaux had wisely forced him to make his own way, and he intended to dedicate to him the last volume of the *Synthèse*, which was to deal with industry.[182]

Comte finally started giving mathematics lessons again. D'Eichthal put him in contact with Mr. Jubé, who ran a boarding school that prepared students for the Ecole Polytechnique. D'Eichthal and Lamoricière had once attended it. Since Comte's reputation as a teacher was excellent, the students finally came to him.[183]

Comte also helped Mellet translate Thomas Tredgold's book into French: *Traité des machines à vapeur et de leur application à la navigation, aux mines, aux manufactures, etc.* The book was published in two volumes in 1828, with a second edition in 1838. Perhaps because he found the work demeaning, he did not want his contribution publicized.[184]

Although Comte at this time began to consider giving his course again, he was dissuaded by his friends, such as Issalène, who warned him not to "meditate too much" and rightly feared that all was not perfect in the Comte household.[185] In November 1827 Comte asked his father for four hundred francs, but Louis Comte, irritated by the sacrifices he had already made for his son, refused to send him the whole sum until Auguste pleaded with him.[186]

Shortly afterward, on January 13, 1828, Louis Comte wrote a will, leaving a third of his estate to Alix. He told his executors that in calculating her share, they had to keep in mind the advances he had made to his son Auguste during his illness and recovery – advances that he said totalled 4,067.40 francs. (This amount did not include the 1,890 francs spent on his wife's stay in Paris.) This sum plus any future advances he made to his son had to be considered part of his estate when Auguste came to collect.[187] These provisions may well have been prompted by the rapacious Alix, for Louis Comte did not consider that he had been supporting her all her life. Also, the fact

[182] Littré, *Auguste Comte*, 128; Gondinet to Comte, [May 1827], MAC; Lonchampt, *Précis*, 42–3; Robinet, *Notice*, 129.

[183] Littré, *Auguste Comte*, 228; Keller, *Lamoricière*, 1:14.

[184] Littré, *Auguste Comte*, 36; Georges Audiffrent, *Réponse à M. J. Bertrand* (Paris, 1897), 50.

[185] Issalène to Comte, December 11, 1827, MAC.

[186] Alix Comte to Robinet, March 25, 1860, MAC.

[187] "Testament olographe de Louis Comte," signed by Louis Comte, January 13, 1828, N.a.fr. 10794, fol. 274, BN.

that he was writing a holographic will suggests that he may have been trying to prevent his wife from learning that he was reducing their son's inheritance.

In spite of all his troubles, Comte appears to have regained his sanity eighteen to twenty-four months after the onset of his attack thanks to what he called the "intrinsic power of my organization assisted by affectionate domestic care."[188] To demonstrate his recovery, he invited Esquirol to his course in 1829 and then the following year sent him an inscribed copy of the brochure containing the first two lessons of his published *Cours*.[189] In a sense, Comte was mocking Esquirol, who had proclaimed his patient incurable.

THE CONSEQUENCES OF COMTE'S ILLNESS

Comte always retained a poor opinion of Esquirol and psychiatrists in general, whose work he found not only unscientific but dangerous. Reflecting his own hatred of being dominated, he pointed out in the *Cours* that instead of studying mental illness, psychiatrists were "usually busier lording it over their patients in a vulgar fashion."[190] Esquirol had been particularly irresponsible for promising to treat him but instead abandoning him to his assistants.[191] Comte felt that being incarcerated and forced to depend for all of his needs on the "most subaltern" attendants, who were half-crazy themselves, was an unbearable humiliation.[192] After Esquirol's death, Comte stated bluntly that his mental condition would have "undoubtedly" soon become normal again but the "disastrous intervention of an empiric medication . . . led me rapidly to a very marked alienation." To Comte, Esquirol's "absurd treatment" hampered his recovery; it was not until the winter of 1827–8 that his body triumphed "naturally" not only over the illness but "especially over the remedies."[193] Although Comte praised medical advances and eventually attracted many doctors as disciples, he had no faith in medicine when it came to his own health.

Comte's view of Esquirol's approach was consistent with the principle already enunciated in the fundamental opuscule that positive philosophy would respect the spontaneous efforts of living bodies to cure themselves. Taking into account the "vital force of the ill person," the true scientific approach to sickness was to "foresee by

---

[188] *Cours*, 2:468. Comte implies that he recovered approximately a year and a half after he became ill. Also see Robinet, *Notice*, 169.

[189] See Comte's note on the first brochure of the *Cours*, MAC.

[190] *Cours*, 1:877. See also Robin to Littré, June 18, 1861, in Littré, *Auguste Comte*, 143.

[191] *Système*, vol. 4, "Appendice," 227.

[192] Comte to Mme Auguste Comte, October 2, 1838, *CG*, 1:304.   [193] *Cours*, 2:467–8.

observation the natural outcome of the crisis in order to facilitate it by putting aside the obstacles created by empiricism."[194] As Georges Canguilhem has pointed out, "This is Hippocrates taken up again by the School of Montpellier."[195] Both vitalism and Hippocratism shared an appreciation of the uniqueness of life. Comte's attitude toward medicine also helps to explain why he was so insistent in his letter to Blainville about observing and curing himself and why he resisted Esquirol's "empiric," that is, haphazard and unsystematic, treatment.[196] Esquirol held views of sensationalism that resembled those of the Idéologues,[197] and as we have seen, Comte regarded their studies of the brain as too speculative. To him, the sensationalists gave too much importance to the outside world and thereby made man too passive. He knew that his own approach would be appreciated by Blainville, who once told Saint-Simon, "We do not treat a crisis; we direct it, favor it, or divert it."[198]

His statements to the contrary, most of the positivists, such as Laffitte, Lonchampt, and Robinet, ascribed Comte's recovery to the devotion of Rosalie Boyer.[199] Their hatred of Massin made them unwilling to accept Comte's gratitude toward his wife, whom they accused of trying to estrange him from his family in order to augment her power over him.[200] But even after his separation, Comte told one of his disciples: "In spite of all the wrongs that Madame Comte committed toward me and in the midst of our most lively fights, I never forgot a very important service that she rendered to me and to which I owe my liberty and perhaps my life."[201] He thanked her not only for blocking the plans of Lamennais and Gerbet, but for saving him from Esquirol by bringing him home and taking good care of him.[202] Gustave d'Eichthal, who was closely involved in the crisis, agreed with Comte that Massin had "truly saved him."[203]

---

[194] *Système*, vol. 4, "Appendice," 101.

[195] Canguilhem, "Histoire de l'homme," 296.

[196] Jean-François Braunstein, *Broussais et le matérialisme: Médecine et philosophie au XIXe siècle* (Paris: Meridiens Klincksieck, 1986), 36.

[197] Goldstein, *Console and Classify*, 246–9.

[198] Blainville to Saint-Simon, [1822?], in "De la circulation des ouvrages d'Auguste Comte: 'De l'opuscule fondamental,'" ed. Laffitte, 325.

[199] "De quelques documents relatifs à la crise cérébrale," ed. Laffitte, 437; Lonchampt, *Précis*, 60; Robinet, *Notice*, 170n1.

[200] "Tribunal de première instance de la Seine. Audience du 11 février 1870. Affaire Auguste Comte," 5; Robinet, *Notice*, 399.

[201] Comte, quoted in Declaration of Audiffrent, January 18, 1870, MAC.

[202] Ibid. See also his praises of Massin in *Testament*, 36^f; Robin to Littré, June 18, 1861, in Littré, *Auguste Comte*, 143; Comte to Mme Comte, October 2, 1838, *CG*, 1:301–2.

[203] Gustave d'Eichthal, "Notes Préparatoires," Fonds d'Eichthal, Manuscripts, Carton IV^H, Institut Thiers, which is connected with the Institut and is located on the Place Saint Georges in Paris.

Whatever judgment Comte himself may have made about Massin's character, he would not permit others to criticize her. Alix lamented that her brother died "with a poor opinion of his family," for he never fully forgave them for their treatment of his wife.[204] In spite of Fisher's efforts to redeem himself, Comte also broke off relations with him because of his critical comments about Massin.[205]

The impression that Comte was distressed by the rumors about her and wished to quell them is confirmed by the letters exchanged between Massin and Tabarié, who had met during her trip to Montpellier. After thanking Tabarié for having given her five hundred francs to help pay Esquirol, Massin berated him for having misjudged her. She declared that her husband's accusations against her were motivated by jealousy and were absolutely without foundation:

> Far from harm and danger, you have judged a woman who finds herself in the middle, absolutely alone. . . . I am, I admit, unreasonably astonished that you have not made the reflection, although a very simple one, that it was without my knowledge that you were informed of my quarrels with my husband, that his position prevented me from defending myself and that this last circumstance *obliged* you to be considerate. Your procedures, Sir, make me fear that while in loving me a great deal, Auguste has ruined my future by taking away from me the esteem of decent people to which I have a right. . . . I am certainly very unhappy, but this is not a reason to renounce my character, which has never permitted flattery.[206]

As with Fisher, Comte again took his wife's side and paid no heed to his friend. In February 1827 Tabarié expressed the worry that their friendship was ending because of the "person who appears to be the dearest thing to you in the world." Tabarié unwisely explained that although he had never believed the "vulgar and calumnious lies" used to "tarnish" Caroline's reputation, he was still convinced that Comte's marriage was "one of the greatest mistakes" he had ever committed.[207] This letter marked the end of their close friendship, and Tabarié remained forever shocked by the "absolute oblivion" to which Comte relegated him.[208] Thus during the 1820s,

[204] Alix Comte to Audiffrent, July 8, 1859, MAC.
[205] Littré, *Auguste Comte*, 117; Fisher to Comte, April 5, June 4, 1827, MAC.
[206] Caroline Massin to Tabarié, May 18, 1826, "Correspondants, amis et protecteurs d'Auguste Comte: Tabarié," ed. Laffitte, 114.
[207] Tabarié to Comte, February 18, 1827, in ibid., 118.
[208] Tabarié to Comte, February 20, 1844, MAC. Significantly, this letter was *not* republished in the *Revue occidentale*. Tabarié was asking Comte to repay him the five hundred francs he had lent to Massin in 1826. Comte's rude response shocked him.

Comte broke his relationships not only with Saint-Simon, Guizot, d'Eichthal, and Valat, but also with his family, Fisher, and Tabarié.

THE MEANING OF HIS MADNESS

Various scholars have attempted to go beyond Esquirol's limited analysis of Comte's illness. Georges Dumas, a professor of psychology, declared in 1905 that Comte was a megalomaniac, for "ideas of grandeur" stimulated many of his illusions, such as posing as a doctor, showing that he could survive in a lake though he could not swim, and being the object of a prince's plot. Dumas shows that Comte himself was aware of his susceptibility to mental illness because afterward he organized his life to avoid all stimulation. He ate simple meals, slept seven to eight hours a night, gave up coffee and other stimulants, and took long walks every day to tire himself physically; intense intellectual effort and violent emotion remained a constant threat. In fact, he had at least two more mental crises, though not of a serious nature, in 1838 and 1845. Dumas argued that although Comte was no longer strictly insane after 1826, he never surmounted his mental trouble because he had a "psychopathic temperament."[209]

In 1911 Dr. Joseph Grasset went further than Dumas. Noting Comte's inappropriate treatment of his wife, his excessive pride, and his unbalanced notion of himself, Grasset proclaimed that he was "half-crazy." After his first attack, Comte was not totally insane, but he was never perfectly normal either.[210]

Agreeing with Grasset, another Comte scholar, Jean Delvolvé, pointed out that the philosopher suffered from a "constant congenital abnormality."[211] From his earliest days, his inability to carry on normal human relationships demonstrated that the emotional part of his being remained undeveloped in comparison with the intellectual part. Comte was so preoccupied with *his* vision that he could never understand the point of view or personal feelings of others. Despite his passionate nature, he was an emotional cripple.

In more modern psychological terms, Dr. Louis Timbal was possibly the most accurate when he noted that Comte suffered from "manic depressive psychosis . . . or paranoia, characterized by alternations of periods of manic excitation and periods of melancholy

---

[209] Dumas, *Psychologie de deux messies*, 152. See also ibid., 140, 157, 159; Lonchampt, *Précis*, 90.

[210] Joseph Grasset, *Un Demifou de génie: Auguste Comte, déséquilibré constant et fou intermittent* (Montpellier: Roumégous et Déhan, 1911), 12; see also 18, 21, 30, 42.

[211] Delvolvé, *Réflexions*, 4.

depression."[212] Comte himself noticed just before his attack of 1826 that his "interior climate" was marked by short periods of calm and long bouts of depression and frustration.[213] Evidently in his melancholy moments, he had great difficulty motivating himself to teach or to write, while in his agitated, manic phase, he was apprehensive and overworked. His thoughts raced and wandered, which made producing anything systematic impossible. Throughout his life, he exhibited similar violent tendencies, suicidal thoughts,[214] grandiose ideas, an inflated sense of self-esteem, demands for affection, and paranoid notions – all of which are typical of manic-depressives. It is no wonder that Caroline Massin found him moody and difficult to live with. Yet Comte's condition not only was associated with creativity but was characterized by complete recovery between episodes. Thus he had long periods of normal, fruitful work.[215]

In the early nineteenth century, the scientific approach to mental illness was in its infancy. For hundreds of years, madness had often been considered a sign of moral corruption. According to Michel Foucault, it now was especially marked by "the ethic of unreason and the scandal of animality"; the French term for madness, *aliénation*, indicates that the mad were considered strangers to society.[216] Their confinement was necessary not just for medical reasons but also for social reasons because they could harm others. Society wanted to be spared the scandalous sight of someone deprived of reason. Thus for Comte, the founder of positivism, which aspired to be both a moral and a scientific system, his attack of madness was a serious failure. It signified his rupture with the entity that was his object of study – society.[217] The credibility of his mission to uphold a reasoned, scientific approach to society therefore seemed undermined by his susceptibility to attacks of unreason. His enemies used the sickness to detract from his philosophy.[218] Even Littré and Mill, his former

---

[212] Timbal, *Grand Médecin*, 31.

[213] Comte to Valat, November 27, 1825, *CG*, 1:177. See also Comte to Valat, January 18, 1826, *CG*, 1:181.

[214] Comte said he often thought about suicide during the seventeen years of his marriage. Comte to Littré, April 28, 1851, *CG*, 6:64.

[215] S. Ivano Arieti, "Psychoses," in *The New Encyclopaedia Britannica: Macropaedia*, 15th ed. (Chicago: Encyclopedia Britannica, 1981); B. Brooker, "Mania" and "Manic-Depressive Psychosis," in *Encyclopedia of Psychology*, ed. H. J. Eysenck, W. Arnold, and R. Meili (New York: Herder & Herder, 1972), 2:224; J. Marès, "Maniaque dépressive ou maniaco-dépressive (psychose)," in *Dictionnaire encyclopédique de psychologie* (Paris: Bordas, 1980), 703–4; Frederick K. Goodwin and Kay Redfield Jamison, *Manic-Depressive Illness* (New York: Oxford University Press, 1990), 3, 337; Deroisin, *Notes sur Auguste Comte*, 26.

[216] Michel Foucault, *Histoire de la folie à l'âge classique* (Paris: Gallimard, 1972), 148.

[217] Gauchet and Swain, Preface to Esquirol, *Des passions*, x.   [218] Robinet, *Notice*, 169–72.

disciples, implied that Comte was slightly mad in order to explain the bizarre nature of his later works. In addition, his wife upheld this judgment to invalidate Comte's testament, which did not favor her.[219] Comte never rid himself of the reputation that he was a "dangerous crazy man."[220]

Comte's madness influenced his philosophical development in *both* negative and positive ways. He himself tried to emphasize what he had learned from his crisis. He came away from it with a deeper feeling of the dangerous effects of complete negation, that is, skepticism, and with an even greater sense of the urgency to bring society back to health, as he had done for himself.[221] His experience with extreme disorder and a sharp rupture with unity improved his understanding of the "normal" state of individual or social existence. He was doubly convinced by his illness that "normal," sane living had to include a certain prescribed harmony and a rather rigid order since these were the elements that helped his recovery.[222]

Comte claimed that this "sad experience" also gave him "personal illuminations" that confirmed the law of three stages.[223] Although contradicting his belief that personal observation was psychologically invalid, he maintained that during his attack he went through the three phases of progress in an inverse and then direct sense. During the first three months, as his illness grew worse at Esquirol's, he descended from positivism to monotheism, then to polytheism, and finally to fetishism. This would partially explain his recourse to Lamennais and the Catholic Church. He claimed that in the next five months, from July to December 1826, he was recovering and went "slowly" forward again from fetishism to polytheism to monotheism and then to positivism:

> In procuring immediately for myself a decisive confirmation of my law of three stages, and in making me better understand the necessary relativity of all our conceptions, this terrible episode then permitted me to identify myself further with any one of the human phases, according to my own experience. The continual profit that I have attained for all my historical meditations gives me reason to hope that my suitably prepared readers will also be able to utilize this brief indication of a memorable anomaly.[224]

[219] Grasset, *Demifou*, 11.   [220] Robinet, *Notice*, 171.   [221] Ibid., 169–72.

[222] Paul Arbousse-Bastide, "Auguste Comte et la Folie," in *Les Sciences de la folie* (Paris: Mouton, 1972), 72.

[223] *Cours*, 2:468; see also *Système*, 3:75.

[224] *Système*, 3:75–6. In a letter to G. d'Eichthal in 1829, Comte also seemed to have himself in mind when he wrote, "I will only tell you that when a mind that has already reached the positive state drops again into infancy and comes back, through a true mental indisposition, to the theological state, it is not at the outset and by a single leap that it stuffs

Thus, like many of the other experiences of Comte's life, his attack of madness found a place in his system.

itself with all the vulgar theological stupidities. It holds itself usually for a certain time in a vague pantheism. . . . But if the illness persists, this state cannot be prolonged, and the mind again involuntarily falls back into ordinary theology." Comte to G. d'Eichthal, December 11, 1829, *CG*, 1:214.

Chapter 9

The Road to Recovery, 1828–1830

Who more than we could thus appreciate all its [the *Plan*'s] value?
Olinde Rodrigues, 1829

BACK TO JOURNALISM

Although his "precarious" way of life had "powerfully contributed" to his edification, Comte now sought a financially secure position, one that would guarantee a calm, peaceful environment in which to develop his ideas and preserve his mental health.[1] He resumed his work as a journalist and collaborated in founding the *Journal du génie civil, des sciences et des arts*, which first appeared on September 1, 1828. It aimed to review "all the new discoveries and all the developments that will tend to improve and simplify civil constructions."[2] The journal was attractive to engineers and therefore to former students of the Ecole Polytechnique. Many of Comte's friends and acquaintances were listed as collaborators.[3] Since most of the articles are unsigned, it is difficult to gauge the extent of Comte's contribution. But in the October and November issues, he signed articles reviewing two books on docks and canals written by J. Cordier, whose *Histoire de la navigation intérieure* he had discussed in *Le Censeur européen* in 1819.[4] Though pedestrian, his articles helped him to make ends meet.

Comte also began writing in March 1828 for *Le Nouveau Journal de Paris*, a liberal daily newspaper founded the year before. With a

---

[1] Comte to Guizot, March 30, 1833, *CG*, 1:245.

[2] "Prospectus," *Journal du génie civil, des sciences et des arts* 1 (September 1, 1828), 2. Comte subscribed to the journal from 1828 to 1831 and from 1846 to early 1847. The issues are in Comte's library at the Maison d'Auguste Comte.

[3] Comte knew the following people: Dupin, Cordier, Navier, Montgéry, Mellet, Meissas, Lamé, and Margerin. See list of collaborators, *Journal du génie civil, des sciences et des arts* 1 (September 1, 1828).

[4] Auguste Comte, Review of *Mémoire sur le canal de jonction de la Saône à la Moselle, de Châlons à Toul, de la Mer Méditerranée à celle du Nord*, by Cordier, *Journal du génie civil, des sciences et des arts* 1 (October 1, 1828): 340–52; idem, review of *Mémoire sur les projets présentés pour la jonction de la Marne à la Seine . . .*, by Cordier, *Journal du génie civil, des sciences et des arts* 1 (November 1, 1828): 537–56.

circulation of about 1,300, it covered various aspects of Parisian life and became openly radical and republican a few months after Comte joined it.[5] From March to September 1828, Comte contributed eight articles, most of which he carefully signed.[6]

Although Comte rejected his mother's requests to discuss books by her friends, he did use some of the articles to praise several of the people who had helped him recently, including Amboise Tourasse (the owner of the journal), Mellet, and Ternaux.[7] Mellet, who was building a railway line along the Loire, repeatedly offered Comte a good job. But Comte stubbornly refused because he preferred to devote himself to the sciences.[8]

These articles served chiefly as a way for Comte to develop larger ideas. Four of them were book reviews, but Comte treated the books in an offhand manner, hardly mentioning them at all. He insulted at least one author, who objected to his severe tone and criticism.[9] Although neglected by Gouhier and other biographers, the articles are important, for they show that Comte did not return immediately to philosophy after his recovery, but to a subject that he knew well from his years with Saint-Simon – political economy. As in his contributions to the *Journal du génie civil*, he concentrated primarily

---

[5] The journal was founded by Léon Pillet, the liberal drama critic for the *Journal de Paris*, which had just ceased publication. Two years later, he joined other journalists protesting the new repressive press laws – a protest that helped to bring about the Revolution of 1830. Letter from Ministère de l'Intérieur, April 21, 1828, F[18] (366), AN; "Prospectus," *Le Nouveau Journal de Paris et des départements: Feuille administrative, commerciale, industrielle, et littéraire*, July 1827; Daniel L. Rader, *The Journalists and the July Revolution in France: The Role of the Political Press in the Overthrow of the Bourbon Restoration, 1827–1830* (The Hague: Martinus Nijhoff, 1973), 52, 110, 190, 214, 274; Collins, *Newspaper Press*, 53; Charles de Rémusat, *Mémoires de ma vie*, vol. 2, *1820–1832*, ed. Charles H. Pouthas (Paris: Plon, 1959), 313n2; Deschiens, *Collection de matériaux pour l'histoire de la Révolution de France depuis 1787 jusqu'à ce jour: Bibliographie des journaux* (Paris, 1829), 220; René de Livois, *Histoire de la presse française*, vol. 1, *Des origines à 1881* (Lausanne: Spes, 1965), 203; Ledré, "La Presse nationale," 75n5; idem, *La Presse à l'assaut de la monarchie, 1815–1848* (Paris: Armand Colin, 1960), 294.

[6] Comte's articles are reproduced in *Ecrits*, 171–93. The date "August 28" on page 186 should read "August 18."

[7] Rosalie Boyer to Comte, December 27, 1828, "Lettres de Rosalie Boyer," ed. Laffitte, 98; *Ecrits*, 176, 184, 186–93. On Tourasse, see Declaration of Léon Pillet, Amboise Théodore Tourasse, and Joseph Raymond Plassan, F[18] (366), AN.

[8] Mellet to Comte, September 22, 1828, in "De la publication du *Cours de philosophie positive*," ed. Pierre Laffitte, *RO* 20 (January 1, 1888): 25–7; Issalène to Comte, October 17, 1828, and September 6, 1832; Gondinet to Comte, November 14, 1832, MAC.

[9] On May 27, Comte reviewed *Courtes observations sur l'état actuel du commerce et des finances de l'Europe et sur celui de l'agriculture en France et les moyens de l'améliorer*, by Colonel Swan. Swan wrote an angry letter to the editor, which was published in *Le Nouveau Journal de Paris* on June 9, 1828. In his response, Comte did not hesitate to tell Swan that his ideas of political economy were contrary to "generally accepted principles." See Comte, Letter to the editor, June 2, 1828, *Le Nouveau Journal de Paris*, June 9, 1828, 3.

on questions relating to industrialization. Although he saved himself from intense mental efforts that could prove dangerous to him, he violated his rule that theoretical reforms had to take precedence over practical issues.[10]

The articles thus give us a good idea of Comte's political and social views in the late 1820s, a difficult period marked by economic crises, unemployment, and bad harvests.[11] He clearly aligned himself with the "progressives," those who favored the introduction of machines and the creation of new jobs. In his articles for the column "Political Economy," he urged other journalists to follow his example of encouraging the development of sound industrial inventions and enterprises.

Yet his progressivism was limited by a growing concern for the working class and a greater distrust of the liberal views of political economists and capitalists. In his view, the relationship between workers and owners was now "one of the most fundamental questions of the social order." Although liberty in business affairs was required to break the ancien régime's chains on the economy, social measures were necessary to counteract the abuses of this freedom. The cupidity and ignorance of the "capitalists" had to be controlled if their ruinous speculations and extravagant projects were to be eliminated. For industry to advance, the growing hostility between the "two great classes of producers" had to give way to a new spirit of association.[12] To this end, Comte favored more central planning by the government, profit-sharing schemes, industrial training for workers, business education for owners, the creation of a special corps of engineers, and a system of public works, which would provide jobs for workers who had been laid off through the introduction of machinery. Some of these ideas were not far from the nascent socialism of the Saint-Simonians. To him, such measures were a supplement to the natural order, not an evil artifice opposed to nature. But his faith in the inherent goodness of nature, also apparent in his views on his illness, was not entirely consistent with his ideas of social planning and seemed to be a remnant of his liberal past.

THE SIXTH OPUSCULE: "EXAMEN DU TRAITÉ DE BROUSSAIS SUR L'IRRITATION"

Comte's two articles of August 4 and August 11 were a critique of François-Joseph-Victor Broussais's *De l'irritation et de la folie*. They

---

[10] Comte to G. d'Eichthal, December 9, 1828, *CG*, 1:202.
[11] *Ecrits*, 176; Bertier de Sauvigny, *Bourbon Restoration*, 233–4. [12] *Ecrits*, 176, 180.

were his last contributions to a periodical. Although he hesitated, he finally decided to call them the sixth and final opuscule of his youth and have them reprinted at the end of his *Système de politique positive*.[13] In this opuscule, Comte returned to one of his favorite topics, physiology. Although this was the first time that he wrote at length about it, he knew the subject well and was able to use the "insights" gained from his own bout of madness. In fact, he explained that the essay reflected the "passage from my social beginning to my intellectual career."[14] Unlike his work for Saint-Simon or *Le Producteur*, it was strictly academic, making no mention of the spiritual power or social problems. Having decided that his plans for the "immediate moral reorganization of society" had been premature, Comte was preparing to launch himself into the *Cours* with its purely theoretical discussion of the sciences.[15]

Broussais was a dissident student of Pinel and Bichat and taught medicine at the Val de Grâce, where his courses attracted a large number of enthusiastic students. His "physiological medicine" made him a leader of the Parisian medical community in the 1820s.[16] Comte owned a medical school thesis that his childhood friend Roméo Pouzin had written on Broussais in 1820.[17] Perhaps thanks to Saint-Simon, whom Broussais treated shortly before he died, Comte even knew him personally. Broussais attended the opening of Comte's course in 1826.[18] A clear indication of Broussais's influence on Comte is that the scientist earned a prominent place in the Positivist Calendar and three of his books were included in the Positivist Library.[19]

Like Gall's doctrines, the materialistic theories of Broussais appealed to liberals. In fact, *De l'irritation et de la folie* was the subject of a heated debate in French intellectual circles. Three weeks before

[13] For evidence of Comte's problems in deciding to reprint these articles, see the end of his copy of the fifth opuscule and his manuscript of the sixth opuscule, MAC; "P.S.," manuscript of vol. 4 of the *Système*, N.a.fr. 17914, fol. 183, BN. Comte's sixth opuscule is reproduced in *Système*, vol. 4, "Appendice," 216–28.

[14] *Système*, vol. 4, "Appendice," iv.

[15] Comte to Clotilde de Vaux, August 5, 1845, *CG*, 3:81.

[16] Ackerknecht, *Medicine*, 61–2.

[17] See the autographed copy of Roméo Pouzin's *Réflexions sur la doctrine de Monsieur le Docteur Broussais* in Comte's bookcase called the "Bibliothèque Superflue" at the Maison d'Auguste Comte. Adolphe Comte sent it to Comte in late 1820. Adolphe Comte to Auguste Comte, "Trois Lettres d'Adolphe Comte," ed. Laffitte, September 8, 1820, 148.

[18] Ackerknecht, *Medicine*, 63, 197; Bertier de Sauvigny, *Bourbon Restoration*, 342; Hubbard, *Saint-Simon*, 106–7. Comte also sent his two articles reviewing the book to Broussais, who thanked him. See Broussais to Comte, August 12, 1828, MAC.

[19] *Système*, 4:559; Table B'. The three books in the Positivist Library were *De l'irritation et de la folie*, *L'Histoire des phlegmasies chroniques*, and *Propositions de médecine*. Comte also owned Broussais's *Examen des doctrines médicales et des systèmes des nosologies*.

Comte wrote his article, *Le Globe* – a new iconoclastic newspaper with ties to Cousin and the doctrinaires – began a series of articles criticizing Broussais's book for denouncing eclecticism (or spiritualism) as unscientific.[20] The first issue, still in Comte's library, ridiculed Broussais for trying to "include everything in his physiology, moral man as well as physical man, the facts of the soul as well as those of the body, the conscience as well as the organs."[21] It may have been this review that prompted Comte to discuss Broussais's book in the first place. The debate was intensely political because Cousin, the philosopher of eclecticism, was hated by republicans and leftist liberals for his support of the constitutional monarchy. By this time, "spiritualism" was also closely associated with the doctrinaires' antirevolutionary political philosophy. Cousin's conservatism seemed particularly threatening since he had just finished giving a very successful course on his philosophy in 1828. To supporters of the Revolution like Comte, Broussais's work was the first serious philosophical and political challenge to the Restoration. Comte may have chosen to write a favorable review of it as an indirect way of aligning himself with the antigovernment faction without risking a direct attack.[22] After its publication, Broussais hailed the adherence of "so vigorous an athlete" and sent Comte his response to the first article of *Le Globe*.[23]

In his review, Comte praised Broussais for having helped raise physiology to a positive science by furthering the revolution started by Cabanis and advanced by Gall and Spurzheim. This revolution consisted of extending the positive method to emotional and intellectual phenomena and including them in physiology. Broussais claimed that maladies derived from the "excess or absence of excitation of diverse tissues, above or below the degree that constituted the normal state." The pathological state was therefore different from the normal only because of the intensity of the stimulants acting on the organs. Comte valued the controversial part of Broussais's doctrine, which declared that gastrointestinal irritation, a material

---

[20] P. [Damiron], Review of *De l'irritation et de la folie*, by François Broussais, *Le Globe*, 6 (July 9, August 9, November 8, 1828): 533–6, 606–8, 812–15. Damiron was a great admirer of Cousin. On *Le Globe*, see Spitzer, *French Generation*, 21n41, 97–128.

[21] [Damiron], Review of *De l'irritation*, July 9, 1828, 534.

[22] Boas, *French Philosophies*, 197, 203–10; Braunstein, *Broussais*, 9, 19, 96–103, 110–11, 120; Goldstein, *Console and Classify*, 245.

[23] Broussais to Comte, August 12, 1828, MAC. His *Réponses aux critiques de l'ouvrage du Docteur Broussais sur l'irritation et la folie* is in Comte's "Bibliothèque Auxiliaire" no. 2 in the Maison d'Auguste Comte. One can also find there J. J. Virey's autographed copy of the *Examen de la doctrine médico-philosophique du matérialisme*, which he wrote against Broussais's response to the article in *Le Globe*.

phenomenon, was the source of illness owing to the fact that the digestive intestines exerted a "great sympathetic influence" on all other organs. By eliminating the metaphysical or "ontological" approach whereby sicknesses were independent entities that assailed the body, Broussais attacked not only Pinel's "six pretended fevers," but the vitalist philosophy of Bichat and the medical school of Montpellier.[24] Thus Comte was attracted to Broussais for the same reason that he was drawn to Gall, that is, because of his attempt to assign specific, concrete organs to ailments. Whereas Gall claimed the cerebral nervous system to be the seat of intellectual and affective problems, Broussais said the stomach tended to be the source of many illnesses.

Comte also declared that in replacing the so-called vital force by the property of irritability, which existed only in living tissues, Broussais had clarified the distinction between inorganic and organic phenomena. Without subscribing to vitalism, he had given physiology a more solid basis as a separate science irreducible to the inorganic sciences. Yet he was also able to keep himself free of the more offensive features of medical materialism by retaining the useful vitalist idea of the sympathies.[25] In fact, Broussais's concept of the sympathy that exists among organs and his notion of their interdependence may have encouraged Comte's idea of social consensus.

Taking sides in the recent debate, Comte particularly commended Broussais for demonstrating the "emptiness and nothingness" of the psychological method upheld by Victor Cousin and Jouffroy, the leading opponents of sensationalism.[26] The memory of his recent illness made Comte even more contemptuous of this school's effort to base philosophy on the study of the active Ego (the *moi*). Without naming Cousin directly, Comte denounced "some men" who were trying to popularize German metaphysics among the French youth by creating a separate science of psychology, a science that studied the soul, or the mind, independently from the body and thus considered itself superior to physiology. Broussais was right to criticize these "Kanto-Platonists" for regarding interior sensations as "revelations of the divinity that they name consciousness." Such ideas were "reactionary" and "chimerical."[27] To Broussais and Comte, interior sensations were caused solely by physiological phenomena, and mental life was part of the physical world of the body. Reacting against Cousin's dualism and defense of religion, Comte feared that

[24] *Système*, vol. 4, "Appendice," 223, 226. See also *Braunstein, Broussais*, 52.
[25] Braunstein, *Broussais*, 221.   [26] *Système*, vol. 4, "Appendice," 218; see also iv.
[27] *Système*, vol. 4, "Appendice," 217–18, 220; Broussais, quoted in Comte, *Système*, vol. 4, "Appendice," 219; F. J. V. Broussais, *De l'irritation et de la folie* (Paris, 1828), xx, 134.

his vague notion of consciousness reflected a "mystical spirit" that would lead science back to "theological conceptions."[28]

In fact, Comte criticized Broussais for not going far enough in his attack on psychologists. Comte felt that because they limited their studies to healthy adults and thus neglected children, animals, and deranged persons, psychologists had an incomplete, unscientific view of human nature. Their introspective method was also unscientific because individuals could not observe their own intellectual operations. In Comte's view, one could arrive at an understanding of intellectual phenomena by observing the *organs* involved in intellectual operations, which were in the domain of physiology, as well as the results of these operations, which were seen in the sciences. But one could not study the *intellectual functions* themselves because they were in the "thinking organ," which was doing the observing and could not study itself. Comte, however, did make one concession to the concept of self-observation. He said that moral phenomena, such as the passions, could be observed because, though cerebral, they were not located in the "thinking organ."[29] He may have come to this position because it was held by the phrenologists and he himself had studied the storm of his own emotions in 1826.[30]

Comte also felt Broussais should have emphasized that his criticism of Cousin and the other psychologists did not ally him with the sensationalists. Comte agreed with Cousin's and the other psychologists' rejection of the sensationalism of Helvétius and Condillac, but he argued that the physiologists, particularly the phrenologists, were more effective in combating this doctrine. Cabanis, Gall, and Spurzheim had successfully shown the importance of *interior* physical sensations, which ran counter to the sensationalists' theory that internal cerebral organs had no predispositions and that intelligence derived solely from the action of the external senses. Clearly Comte was becoming increasingly attached to the aspects of phrenological epistemology that could support his conservative doctrine of people filling suitable social niches.[31]

Comte concluded by praising Broussais's active approach to the treatment of madness. He applauded him for underlining the "importance of moral treatment," which referred to the attention given to the affective faculties advocated by Pinel. Yet he did not miss the

[28] *Système*, vol. 4, "Appendice," 222. See also Goldstein, *Console and Classify*, 242–5.

[29] *Système*, vol. 4, "Appendice," 219.   [30] Braunstein, *Broussais*, 134; *Cours*, 1:34.

[31] Comte later claimed that his sixth opuscule – the review of *De l'irritation et de la folie* – made Broussais appreciate Gall's doctrine. *Système*, vol. 4, "Appendice," iv. Although previously not a fervent advocate of Gall, Broussais became so entranced by his theory that he gave a course on phrenology, the published version of which can still be found in Comte's library today. See Broussais, *Cours de phrénologie*, published in 1836.

opportunity to criticize Broussais's colleague Esquirol, who also favored the physiological approach to mental illness.[32] Without referring to Esquirol by name, Comte said he was astonished that Broussais had not bothered to observe mental hospitals, whose directors neglected the practice of medicine and left the moral treatment of their patients to the incompetent, "arbitrary action of subordinate and coarse assistants."[33] It is clear that like most manic-depressive individuals, Comte felt angry about his disorder and treatment, which threatened his exaggerated self-importance.[34]

Comte approved of Broussais's principle that madness was merely a state of irritation in the brain caused by stomach trouble instead of a metaphysical war between opposing forces within a person.[35] In the future, Comte did what he could to avoid stomach trouble. Moreover, Broussais's theory that two causes of irritation were "passions that are too exalted . . . and intellectual work that is pushed too far" was repeated by Comte in the *Cours*, where he explained that his insanity was due to "great moral pains" and a "violent excess of work."[36]

While reading Broussais's book in 1828, Comte came to a better understanding of his own crisis and that of society. He immediately recognized the significance of Broussais's principle that the normal and pathological states were basically the same except for a difference of intensity. In fact, Comte helped to make it a popular doctrine in the nineteenth century.[37] The idea that madness was not inherently different from sanity comforted Comte on a personal level. Henceforth, for him, the "natural" became even more the "normal." In the preface to the sixth volume of the *Cours*, he illustrated this idea when he claimed that his crisis would have "reestablished the normal condition" had it not been for Esquirol's unscientific and unsystematic intervention.[38] In a sense, Esquirol should have let nature run its course. Thus Comte's concept of therapy increasingly stressed the development of natural order, which was equivalent to progress. Later Broussais's principle became the scientific basis of Comte's theory of "social statics." In the *Système de politique positive*, he wrote:

---

[32] Goldstein, *Console and Classify*, 248.   [33] *Système*, vol. 4, "Appendice," 227.

[34] Goodwin and Jamison, *Manic-Depressive Illness*, 741.

[35] Georges Canguilhem, *Le Normal et le pathologique*, 5th ed. (1966; Paris: Quadrige-Presses Universitaires de France, 1984), 13.

[36] Broussais, *De l'irritation*, 333; *Cours*, 2:467.

[37] Canguilhem, *Le Normal et le pathologique*, 9, 14, 18–31; Michel Foucault, *Naissance de la clinique* (Paris: Presses Universitaires de France, 1963), 186–94.

[38] *Cours*, 2:467.

Now, I have demonstrated that this theory [of social statics] is summarized entirely in this universal principle, which comes from the
systematic extension of the great aphorism of Broussais: every
modification . . . of the real order concerns only the intensity of the
corresponding phenomena. . . . [P]henomena always keep the same
arrangement; every change of *nature*, strictly speaking, . . . is, moreover, seen to be contradictory.

In limiting how much phenomena could change, Comte guaranteed
the "invariability" of natural laws and believed he could make correct forecasts of the future, which were necessary for "guiding intervention."[39] Broussais's philosophy made Comte's thought more
deterministic, normative, and optimistic.

Since the pathological was practically identical with the normal,
Comte also concluded that the study of disease could lead to insights
into what constituted health. He felt his bout of madness had given
him insights into his own health as well as that of society. Again
using biological theories as a source of information for social physics, Comte would later extend Broussais's approach to society.[40]
Observation of a sick society would help decide which therapy would
lead it back *systematically*, instead of empirically, to its "normal" state.
A prime example of social illness was revolution.

One difficulty with the idea of the continuity between the pathological state and the normal one was that it was hard to define convincingly the difference between a diseased condition and a natural
one. After all, the pathological became in a sense normal and natural
itself.[41] Defining the "normal" became difficult. Yet Comte would
later try to demonstrate that the key to normalcy and thus health lay
in the condition that he had always admired and tried to achieve –
that of social unity.[42]

RENEWED EFFORTS TO FIND A POSITION

By mid-May 1828, with his health restored and his finances still
precarious, Comte applied for the job of inspector of commerce in
the newly created Department of Commerce and Manufactures. He
had applauded its formation in *Le Nouveau Journal de Paris* as the first

[39] *Système*, 3:71–2.
[40] Ibid., 1:652–3. On the subtle changes in Comte's attitude toward Broussais's theory, see
    Wolf Lepenies, *Das Ende der Naturgeschichte: Wandel kultureller Selbstverständlichkeiten in den
    Wissenschaften des 18. und 19. Jahrhunderts* (Munich: C. Hanser, 1976), 171–96.
[41] Canguilhem, *Le Normal et le pathologique*, 22, 24, 155.
[42] Paul Arbousse-Bastide, "Auguste Comte et la folie," 59.

step toward industrial planning.[43] J. Allier, a former auditor of his course and a friend of Cerclet, told Comte about the position.[44] In addition to Allier, who was the secretary to the new minister, Comte had other friends in the department who could exert influence on his behalf. One was Baron André de Férussac, the editor of the *Bulletin universel pour la propagation des connaissances scientifiques et industrielles*, on which Comte collaborated from time to time.[45] To gather more support for his case, Comte obtained nine very flattering recommendations from important people, including Alexandre de Laborde, a nobleman, who had admired Comte's fundamental opuscule;[46] Guizot; Ternaux; and six members of the Academy of Sciences: Baron Louis Thenard, Louis Poinsot, François Arago, Baron Joseph Fourier, Baron Charles Dupin, and Comte Jean-Antoine Chaptal.[47] Dupin, Thenard, Laborde, and Ternaux were also at various times liberal members of the Chamber of Deputies. Arago, Thenard, and Poinsot had been Comte's professors at the Ecole Polytechnique. The chemist Chaptal had hired Comte to give his grandson lessons in 1820. Fourier, the powerful secretary of the Academy of Sciences, had been favorably impressed by Comte's course in 1826, while Dupin, a disciple of Monge, had given a course in 1826 at the Consérvatoire des Arts et Métiers, which Comte had attended.[48] These nine letters reflect the high esteem in which Comte was held by some of the most eminent scientific, political, and industrial figures of the Restoration. Although Comte received a formal promise from the minister that he would be awarded the post, the Chamber of Deputies refused to allocate the necessary funds for its establishment.[49]

Encouraged by his friends, especially d'Eichthal, Comte then decided in late 1828 to present himself for the competition for the *agrégation*, the degree that was necessary to teach in the University. Comte went through all the necessary steps only to be thwarted by a condition instituted in December 1827 that a candidate had to have been a *maître d'études* in a royal *collège* (a secondary school) for three

---

[43] Comte to the Comte de Saint-Cricq, May 14, 1828, *CG*, 1:199; *Ecrits*, 175, 181.
[44] Littré, *Auguste Comte*, 36; Allier to Comte, March 1829, MAC.
[45] *Almanach royal pour l'an 1828*, 185. Another friend who could help him was Jules Azévédo, who, like Férussac, had received a copy of Comte's fundamental opuscule.
[46] Comte A. de la Borde to Comte, May 2, 1824, MAC.
[47] See the letters of recommendation attached to Comte's letter to the Comte de Saint-Cricq, May 14, *CG*, 1:200–1.
[48] Alix Comte to Auguste Comte, January 20, 1820, "Lettres d'Alix Comte," ed. Laffitte, 58; Comte to Valat, January 18, 1816, *CG*, 1:184.
[49] Comte to G. d'Eichthal, December 9, 1828, *CG*, 1:204; Rosalie Boyer to Comte, December 27, 1828, "Lettres de Rosalie Boyer," ed. Laffitte, 97; Allier to Comte, March 1829, MAC.

years.[50] (A *maître d'études* occupied the rank below teacher.) Given the fact that *collèges* were generally supervised by bishops, the reactionaries hoped to fill the University with clerics or laymen favorable to conservative Catholicism.[51] When Comte complained to the minister about the "absurdity" of recruiting teachers from such a poorly qualified group, he replied, "We do not care about having the brightest people in the University."[52]

Soon afterward, Comte was offered a position as a mathematics teacher in a new industrial school that was to be established in January 1829.[53] However, d'Eichthal, who wanted to teach there too, decided that they had been "duped," and nothing came of this project either.[54]

During the 1828–9 school year, Comte increased the number of his private students, so much so that he was able to hire a servant. Lamoricière even sent his younger brother to be a boarder in Comte's apartment. But after three months, Comte found that he could not adjust to having a stranger in the house and sent him away. By March 1829 Comte had to ask his father for financial help, and when summer vacation started and his lessons stopped, he and Caroline were compelled to let the servant go, pawn most of their belongings, and again turn to his father, who this time gave him only part of the requested amount.[55]

REJECTION BY THE SAINT-SIMONIANS

In 1828 Comte was also rebuffed by the Saint-Simonians. After *Le Producteur* had gone bankrupt in December 1826, the group had scattered and devoted themselves to their personal matters. When Comte finally reemerged in 1828 to continue basically along the same

[50] Comte to G. d'Eichthal, December 9, 1828, *CG*, 1:202–3; "Certificat d'Entrée de Classement," signed Marielle, September 24, 1828, MAC.
[51] Bertier de Sauvigny, *Bourbon Restoration*, 318.
[52] Vatisménil, quoted in Comte to G. d'Eichthal, December 9, 1828, *CG*, 1:203.
[53] B. Sainte-Preuve, a professor of physical sciences, obtained from the government the authorization to found the Ecole d'Industrie Manufacturière. Prospectus, Ecole d'Industrie Manufacturière, n.d., Fonds d'Eichthal 13747, item 1, BA. See also Comte to G. d'Eichthal, December 9, 1828, *CG*, 1:203.
[54] G. d'Eichthal to Comte, December 18, December 20, 1828, and letter no. 35, n.d. [late December 1828 or early 1829], "Correspondance de Comte et d'Eichthal (Suite)," ed. Laffitte, 367–9.
[55] L. de Lamoricière to G. d'Eichthal, September 23, 1828, Fonds d'Eichthal 14379, item 76, BA; Keller, 1:19; Comte to Mill, June 27, 1845, *CG*, 3:44; Comte to Louis Comte, September 20, 1829, *CG*, 1:207–9; Louis Comte, "Note des avances faites pour mon fils," MAC.

path that he had been following two years before, the Saint-Simonians were beginning a radical transformation of their doctrine.

Up to this point, Saint-Simonianism had adopted a primarily industrial and scientific posture; henceforth, it became increasingly religious and dogmatic.[56] Eugène Rodrigues, the younger brother of Olinde, persuaded Enfantin that religion was superior to philosophy and science in addressing basic questions about life and supplying the foundation of social unity.[57] Enfantin reread Saint-Simon's *Nouveau Christianisme* several times, and by exaggerating its general concepts about religion, he made it the basis of the doctrine that he and his closest colleagues, Bazard and Olinde Rodrigues, developed between 1828 and 1830.[58]

One of the Saint-Simonians' motivations in adopting a more religious orientation was precisely to differentiate themselves from Comte, who had become a negative example in their eyes. They were aware that the *Plan* and his articles in *Le Producteur* had attracted important people to their cause, including Count Jules Resseguier – the future head of the Saint-Simonian church in the Midi.[59] Since the Saint-Simonians maintained an interest in the science of society and shared Comte's desire to create a new industrial age marked by association, they were eager to exploit his ideas, especially his concept of the positive method, which, according to d'Eichthal, they used "constantly" in their historical works.[60] Yet Comte was an aloof master, who threatened them. Not wanting to join them or succumb to the charms of "le père" Enfantin, he appeared to be a "difficult person" (*mauvais coucheur*) who had to be

---

[56] Enfantin to Bailly, April, 1830, Fonds Enfantin 7644, fol. 101v, BA; *Doctrine de Saint-Simon: Exposition, première année, 1829*, 2d ed. (Paris, 1830), 5–28.

[57] Comte knew Eugène Rodrigues, whom he had found "intelligent enough" to translate some German essays for him. Comte to G. d'Eichthal, June 6, 1824, *CG*, 1:96. Like Comte, Eugène Rodrigues was profoundly impressed by the works of Maistre and Lamennais and by the essays of Kant that d'Eichthal had introduced to him and to the other Saint-Simonians. Through the writings of Madame de Staël, he also became interested in the aspects of German philosophy that emphasized pantheism and the feelings. These different writers inspired his call for the regeneration of religion. G. d'Eichthal to Coiesin, September 22, 1863, Fonds d'Eichthal 14406, item 4, BA; A. Cerclet to Père Enfantin, [April] 12, [1826], Fonds Enfantin 7643, fol. 42, BA. On Enfantin's initial dislike of Saint-Simon's religious doctrines, see Papers of Ch. Lambert, Fonds Enfantin 7804, BA. On Eugène Rodrigues, see Robert B. Carlisle, *The Proffered Crown: Saint-Simonianism and the Doctrine of Hope* (Baltimore, Md.: Johns Hopkins University Press, 1987), 62–3, 87–90.

[58] Record of a conversation between Gustave d'Eichthal and Enfantin, March 2, 1832, Fonds Enfantin 7646, fol. 16, BA.

[59] Saint-Simon and Enfantin, *Oeuvres de Saint-Simon et d'Enfantin*, 1:174n1; Enfantin to Resseguier, May 20, 1827, Fonds Enfantin 7643, fol. 19, BA.

[60] G. d'Eichthal to Comte, December 8, 1828, "Correspondance de Comte et d'Eichthal (Suite)," ed. Laffitte, 371.

exorcised.[61] To this end, they seized upon Saint-Simon's statement in his introduction to the *Plan* that Comte was too scientific and too indifferent to the religious and emotional aspects of social re-organization. D'Eichthal confirmed this verdict when he told them that once when he met Saint-Simon at Comte's apartment, the master had told him that religion and sentiment were more important than science.[62] In the presence of Comte, Saint-Simon had given him the following warning:

> M. d'Eichthal, people tell me that you are devoting yourself to the Doctrine; that is very good; but you are dealing with a terrible man. M. Comte wants everything for science; and if we are not wary of him, these scientists will become as intractable as the Catholic theologians.

This story circulated among the Saint-Simonians, who felt that they had confirmation that Saint-Simon had more of a "soul" than his famous student.[63]

This judgment especially suited the head of the Saint-Simonians, Enfantin, who had met Saint-Simon only once briefly in December 1824 but nevertheless desired to oust Comte as the master's fore-most disciple.[64] Though a former Polytechnicien like Comte, he did not care for the "sublime indifference," coldness, and lack of spon-taneity exhibited by "positive" scientists.[65] He admitted that Comte was a "profound *reasoner*," but he found his intelligence threatening and accused him of immodesty and pretentiousness.[66] Overlooking or perhaps unaware that Saint-Simon, like Comte, had tried to kill him-self, Enfantin declared that he liked Comte "very little" because he "preached and practiced suicide, disgust, indifference, [and] *doubt*."[67]

In August 1829 Enfantin circulated among his friends a long ar-gument against Comte's *Plan*, a work that he highly respected but felt the need to destroy in order to establish his own position.[68] He

[61] Enfantin to Fournel, March 13, 1833, Fonds d'Eichthal, Manuscript, Carton IIᴬ, Bibliothèque Thiers.

[62] Gustave d'Eichthal, "Notice sur ma vie," 1869, Fonds d'Eichthal 14408, BA.

[63] G. d'Eichthal to Resseguier, February 26, 1830, Fonds Enfantin 7644, fol. 163, BA.

[64] Halévy, "Souvenirs de Saint-Simon," 545. Halévy declared that Enfantin never met Saint-Simon, but Enfantin said that he believed he met him in December 1824. See letter from Enfantin to Fournel, March 13, 1833, Fonds d'Eichthal, Carton IIᴬ, Bibliothèque Thiers.

[65] Enfantin, "Note d'Enfantin sur la science positive," 1829, Fonds Enfantin 7655(2), BA.

[66] Enfantin to Picard, August 15, 1829, Fonds Enfantin 7643, fols. 361–4, BA.

[67] Enfantin to Margerin, May 1831, in Saint-Simon and Enfantin, *Oeuvres de Saint-Simon et d'Enfantin*, 27:188.

[68] Olinde Rodrigues to Enfantin, September 4, 1829, Fonds Enfantin 7643, fol. 454, BA. Even four years later, the *Plan* continued to obsess d'Eichthal. In 1833 the Saint-Simonian Alexis Petit told Comte how much it was valued by "*Le Père*" (underlined twice) and begged him for one or two copies. Alexis Petit to Comte, May 29, 1833, MAC.

deplored Comte's picture of man as a "mechanism without life, without passion, without *love*, and consequently without beliefs." To him, Comte was also a fraud and a hypocrite, for while asserting that the scientist should be a "calculating automaton" without feeling or imagination, he himself began with certain "revelations of genius" – Saint-Simon's imaginative ideas – which he *then* developed in a rational fashion. Although he pretended to be in the "positive" stage, he could be doing theology: "In the place of these words, *nature of things, invariable law* (which he employs so often)," he should put "*God* and *providential plan*." Thus Comte himself was motivated by "beliefs" and "faith," not reason.[69] In sum, partly because he felt intellectually inferior to Comte, Enfantin stressed increasingly the one area where he felt superior, that of the feelings. Comte represented the "glacial" scientism that he and the Saint-Simonians rejected as inadequate.[70] The ideological differences between Comte and the Saint-Simonians masked an intense power struggle.

The Saint-Simonians immediately attracted a number of young people disappointed by the liberals' apathetic and compromising spirit. Enfantin made a special effort to appeal to Comte's close friends and accomplished his purpose with Gustave d'Eichthal and Gabriel Lamé. He seemed to be the only Saint-Simonian who stayed on friendly terms with Cerclet after his dispute with Comte.[71]

The activities of the Saint-Simonians were reflected in the launching of a new *Le Producteur* in October 1828. Its supporters included people whom Comte knew well or would come to know: the Rodrigues brothers, Montgéry, Vieillard, Hippolyte Carnot, Margerin, Talabot, and Mellet. A month later, there was a religious meeting for the installation of the new church hierarchy, at whose head were Bazard, Enfantin, and Olinde Rodrigues.[72] Comte's reaction was one of surprise and then pleasure that he was not asked to join them. He felt sure their efforts to create a new religion involving a "sort of incarnation of the divinity in Saint-Simon" would bring them "ridicule" and "public disrepute." Because of their lack of intellectual rigor, "general speculations" had wreaked "havoc" in their minds. Just as he appeared to the Saint-Simonians to be the

[69] Enfantin to Picard, August 15, 1829, Fonds Enfantin 7643, fols. 361–3, BA.

[70] Enfantin to Bailly, April 1830, Fonds Enfantin 7644, fol. 105 bis verso, BA.

[71] Enfantin to Picard, August 15, 1829, Fonds Enfantin 7643, fols. 361–4; G. d'Eichthal to Resseguier, February 26, 1830, Fonds Enfantin 7644, fols. 162–4; Enfantin's comment, 1832, inserted as a footnote in Cerclet to Enfantin, [April 12, 1826], Fonds Enfantin 7643, fol. 43; Enfantin to Bailly, April 1830, Fonds Enfantin 7644, fols. 101–7, BA.

[72] Saint-Simon and Enfantin, *Oeuvres de Saint-Simon et d'Enfantin*, 2:11; Fournel to Enfantin, February 4, 1833, Fonds d'Eichthal, Manuscripts, Carton II^A, Bibliothèque Thiers; G. d'Eichthal to Comte, February 1, 1829, "Correspondance de Comte et d'Eichthal (Suite)," ed. Laffitte, 369; Georges Weill, *L'Ecole Saint-Simonienne*, 17.

archetype of a cold scientistic thinker, they struck him as the epitome of fuzzy thinkers because of their "sentimentalism," which led them to rely exclusively on the feelings.[73] Whereas his approach spurred them to religiosity, their example reinforced his belief that a firm grounding in the sciences was essential to proper reasoning.

THE PRESENTATION OF THE COURSE ON POSITIVE PHILOSOPHY

Although he still hoped to finish the second part of the *Système de politique positive* before 1831, Comte began preparing to resume his lessons on positive philosophy at his apartment in the Latin Quarter on December 1, 1828.[74] Perhaps he was prompted by the news that the Saint-Simonians were planning to give a course themselves. But he had trouble getting the ten subscribers he needed. Some former auditors, such as the Duc de Montebello, Alexander von Humboldt, and Hippolyte Carnot, were away; Arago promised to come but apparently changed his mind; and Guizot said he was too busy.[75] Another problem was that once again Comte could not meet his deadline. Finally, he began a month late, on January 4, 1829. In the audience were Cerclet, Allier, Captain Montgéry, Esquirol, Broussais, and four members of the Academy of Sciences: Blainville, Fourier, Poinsot, and Navier. Another auditor was Jacques Binet, professor of astronomy at the Collège de France and the Ecole Polytechnique.[76] When Gustave d'Eichthal returned from England on December 29, he too joined the course and commented happily to his brother that Comte was "decidedly perfectly recovered."[77]

---

[73] Comte to G. d'Eichthal, December 9, 1828, CG, 1:204–5.

[74] Auguste Comte, "Avertissement de l'auteur pour la première édition," in original edition of the *Cours de philosophie positive* (Paris, 1830–42), 1:vi. This foreword is omitted in the Hermann edition.

[75] Though unable to come, Guizot did say, "I know how much your ideas are worth, even those that I do not share." Guizot to Comte, December 11, 1828, in Valat, "Document historique sur Guizot et Aug. Comte," 23. The date of 1826 in the article is wrong. See the original letter, MAC. See also Guizot to Comte, January 4, 1829, in Valat, "Document historique sur Guizot et Aug. Comte," 24. The date of January 24 in the article is also wrong. The original letter in the Maison d'Auguste Comte is postmarked January 4, 1829.

[76] Littré, *Auguste Comte*, 37; *Almanach royal pour l'an 1829*, 850; Dossier of Jacques Binet at the Archives of the Collège de France; Comte to G. d'Eichthal, December 9, 1828, CG, 1:204; Comte, "Avertissement de l'auteur," 1:v.

[77] G. d'Eichthal to A. d'Eichthal, February 26, 1829, Fonds d'Eichthal 14396, item 45, BA. See also G. d'Eichthal to A. d'Eichthal, January 1, 1829, Fonds d'Eichthal 14396, item 44; G. d'Eichthal to Comte, December 20, 1828, "Correspondance de Comte et d'Eichthal (Suite)," ed. Laffitte, 367.

Demonstrating his recovery and showing the "perfect continuity" of his work were Comte's primary objectives, for to him, the "grave perturbation" of 1826 amounted to only a "simple oscillation" in his "total evolution."[78]

Although Comte and his biographers insist that all seventy-two lectures of the course were given without incident, there is some evidence to the contrary.[79] In the fall of 1829, he complained that the preparation of his course was giving him violent headaches and stomach problems, which caused him to vomit if he worked too hard. In June he found himself "incapable of all work demanding great and continual mental application, that is to say, just about every other labor besides giving my [mathematics] lessons."[80] Narcisse Vieillard, an auditor who was to become one of his most loyal friends, received in late June a note from Comte announcing the "necessity" of "terminating" his course, just when he was about to begin the difficult exposition of the new science of social physics.[81] His mental strain probably resulted in physical troubles and another bout of depression, which forced him at least to consider closing his course for the second time. Yet he seems to have successfully overcome his problems and finished his lectures.[82]

Since he spoke from memory, there is no record of their contents.[83] He did, however, print a general program in December 1828 as well as a final summary of the lectures in November 1829 after the course's completion.[84] In spite of his claim that there was "perfect continuity" between his two courses, Comte had, in fact, changed his ideas between 1826 and 1829. The various programs of 1826, 1828, and 1829 show that he added a series of concluding lectures, increased the number of lectures on the organic sciences, and reduced the number of lectures on the inorganic sciences. While the series of lectures on chemistry was shortened the most, from ten lessons in 1826 to eight in 1828 and then six in 1829, the lessons devoted to physiology increased from ten to twelve. Physiology had

---

[78] *Système*, 3:76. In the *Cours* Comte also insisted upon the "perfect continuity" of his "mental development." *Cours*, 2:468.

[79] Lonchampt, *Précis*, 44; Gouhier, *Vie*, 141.

[80] Comte to Louis Comte, September 20, 1829, CG, 1:207.

[81] Vieillard to Comte, June 29, 1829, MAC. A friend of Vieillard, B. Dufresne, also was sad about the closing of Comte's course. B. Dufresne to Comte, June 22, 1829, MAC.

[82] Comte, "Avertissement de l'auteur," 1:v.

[83] Comte to Pouzin, December 23, 1829, CG, 1:215.

[84] Comte to G. d'Eichthal, December 9, 1828, CG, 1:205–6; "Discours d'ouverture du Cours du philosophie positive de M. Auguste Comte, ancien élève de l'Ecole Polytechnique: Exposition du but de ce Cours: ou Considérations générales sur la philosophie positive," *Revue encyclopédique* 44 (November 1829): 274. For the program of 1826, see *Système*, vol. 4, "Appendice," iv, and the original outline of the course, MAC.

become a far more central part of his thought, as already reflected in his article on Broussais. In preparing his lectures, he realized that his studies at the Ecole de Médecine in Montpellier in 1816 had left him with serious gaps in his knowledge. To fill this void, he followed Blainville's course on general and comparative physiology at the faculty of sciences from 1829 to 1832. It would provide the basis for the biological sections of the *Cours*.[85] His program also shows that he gave four lectures on the "intellectual and affective" part of physiology, which indicates how important phrenology had become to him. In fact, in early 1831 he became one of the founding members of the Société Phrénologique de Paris.[86] Most important, Comte's new conception of his course demonstrates that social physics was now more clearly the key science, for he increased the number of sessions devoted to it from ten to fourteen.

COMTE'S PERSONAL LIFE

Little is known of Comte's personal life during this period. He later admitted that his illness and long convalescence had deeply perturbed all his relationships – "even the oldest and the most intimate."[87] No longer did he write rich, expansive letters, as he had in his earlier years. Instead, he focused entirely on his intellectual work, finding no need to develop his affections as he had in the past, when he was concentrating directly on social problems. Now he isolated himself more and more.[88]

During these years of intense concentration, Comte became increasingly detached, forgetful, and scatterbrained. Friends complained about his indifference and his air of "coldness and distraction."[89]

---

[85] *Cours*, 1:665.

[86] Members of the Société Phrénologique de Paris included Comte's friends Broussais, Bailly, Lenoir, the Duc de Montebello, Ternaux, and Pinel-Grandchamp (his doctor). Yet a rift between Comte and the society occurred because of some disagreements. Comte did not approve of the way in which Broussais was losing himself in "vain and ridiculous quests" for localization, and he quarreled with Harel, the treasurer. See Braunstein, *Broussais*, 19–20; Société Phrénologique de Paris, signed by its secretary Casimir Broussais, the son of F. Broussais, to Comte, March 22, 1831, MAC; Harel (the treasurer of the Société) to Comte, December 6, 1831, MAC. See also *Société Phrénologique de Paris: Prospectus*, [1831?], 22; *Journal de la Société Phrénologique de Paris* 1 (1832): 21–6. Also, in early 1831 Jean-Baptiste Bouillaud, a medical professor and leftist politician, had asked Comte to come to the meetings of the "Société de la Doctrine de Gall." Jean-Baptiste Bouillaud to Comte, January 9, 1831, MAC. See also McLaren, "A Prehistory of the Social Sciences," 7, 10, 17, 21–2.

[87] Comte to Valat, October 22, 1839, *CG*, 1:323.

[88] Comte to Clotilde de Vaux, August 5, 1845, *CG*, 3:81–2.

[89] Issalène to Comte, December 18, 1830, MAC. See also Issalène to Comte, April 20, 1829, MAC; Rosalie Boyer to Comte, January 25, 1830, "Lettres de Rosalie Boyer," ed. Laffitte, 101.

Even Valat tried vainly to renew his correspondence with his "best friend."[90]

His family fared no better. His mother begged him to be a little more friendly after she received an angry letter saying he would not tolerate any more complaints about his failure to write. Then, after sending his parents information about the course he was giving at the Athénée, he accused them of not taking any pleasure in his achievements. His mother denied it and said she would no longer allow him to take out his bad temper on the family.[91] To make him feel guilty, she told him that his father was about to lose his job owing to his failing eyesight and that they would soon be reduced to selling off their furniture piece by piece to avoid the poorhouse. She wanted to know what they had received for all the sacrifices they had made for Auguste, who, she lamented, had cost them twenty thousand francs. Had he at least made some "advantageous arrangements" with a publisher? If he was going to publish his work, he had better not write "anything against our sacred Religion."[92] Another subject of discord was Comte's "indifference" toward Alix, whom he refused to forgive for her poor treatment of Massin.[93] Rosalie Boyer's appeals to the "goodness of Caroline's heart" and her commands to Comte to stop sulking were all in vain.[94]

As for Caroline, she seemed frustrated by her husband's absorption in his work and found life in the Latin Quarter boring. Not feeling well herself, she became increasingly depressed.[95] No doubt her misery was compounded by their impoverished state and Comte's frail condition. According to Comte's "Secret Addition" to his *Testament*, she even tried to invite for the last time a "rich gallant" to their apartment as soon as he finished his course in late 1829.[96] Whether true or not, the statement indicates that either their marital problems had not ceased or Comte's jealousy and paranoia were as intense as ever. In 1831 Comte chose to go on a vacation without

[90] Valat to Comte, July 30, 1830, MAC.
[91] Rosalie Boyer to Comte, December 27, 1828, and January 31, 1830, "Lettres de Rosalie Boyer," ed. Laffitte, 98, 102–3. In the original of the January letter in the Maison d'Auguste Comte one can read the word "prospectus," which is the word that is "illisible" in the *Revue Occidentale*.
[92] Rosalie Boyer to Comte, January 31, 1830, "Lettres de Rosalie Boyer," ed. Laffitte, 104–5. See also Rosalie Boyer to Comte, July 13, 1830, ibid., 107.
[93] Rosalie Boyer to Comte, January 25, 1830, "Lettres de Rosalie Boyer," ed. Laffitte, 102.
[94] Rosalie Boyer to Comte, July 13, 1830, "Lettres de Rosalie Boyer," ed. Laffitte, 107–8.
[95] Hearing of Caroline's state of mind, Issalène wrote, "Madame Comte is very bored in the Latin Quarter but she has too much good sense not to sacrifice a little of the agreeable to the useful." Issalène to Comte, December 11, 1827, MAC. See also the comments about Caroline's "melancholy" and "disgust with life" in Issalène to Comte, June 22, 1828, MAC.
[96] *Testament*, 36[f].

her. Answering his first letter, Caroline wrote in her witty, caustic style:

> You ask me not to respond to the letter that I just received, and judging by the manner in which you scribbled your address, it does not appear that you care much. Yet the feminine spirit intervenes, and by contradiction I hasten to tell you that I have been much happier than you and that I have not lacked distractions. . . . I am very disturbed to know that you are alone, and I need a lot of fortitude not to go join you.[97]

THE ATTACKS BY THE SAINT-SIMONIANS

Besides devoting himself to his work and watching over his wife, Comte was very concerned in 1829 by the progress of the Saint-Simonians. While he was giving his course in his apartment, the Saint-Simonians were developing their doctrine in a series of public lectures attended by fifty people.[98] Again the parallel between the development of Saint-Simonianism and positivism is noteworthy.

To keep track of what they were professing, Comte obtained a copy of the book that contained their lectures.[99] In them the Saint-Simonians proclaimed sympathy, rather than reason, to be the root of progress and called woman the "model of this sympathetic power." They sought to develop three sources of feeling: the family, the nation, and the human species, or humanity, which was a "collective being" equivalent to society at large.[100] Since humanity developed in three directions – scientific, industrial, and artistic – all men were to be considered scientists, industrialists, or artists. Calling for the abolition of privileges and inheritance, the Saint-Simonians demanded that each person work and be rewarded according to his "capacity." Yet industry and science were not ends in themselves, for they had to serve as the basis of religion and help develop the "social sentiments." In this way, the "critical state" of present society would give way to a new organic era characterized by close social associations as well as a strong religion. This religion would represent the "collective thought of humanity" and glorify a "GOD of *love*."[101]

---

[97] Caroline Massin to Comte, September 16, 1831, MAC.

[98] Fournel, *Bibliographie Saint-Simonienne*, 63.

[99] In Comte's Bibliothèque Superflue at the Maison d'Auguste Comte, there is a copy of the second edition of *Doctrine de Saint-Simon, première année, 1829*, published in 1830.

[100] *Doctrine de Saint-Simon, première année*, 28; Eugène Rodrigues, "Avis du Traducteur," *L'Education du genre humain de Lessing* (Paris, 1830), 2.

[101] *Doctrine de Saint-Simon, première année*, 23, 38–40, 79–81, 355, 408.

These lectures reveal an ambivalent attitude toward Comte. Olinde Rodrigues admitted that Comte's *Plan* had introduced many of the Saint-Simonians to the doctrine of their master. In establishing the study of society on a sound scientific basis, the fundamental opuscule remained unsurpassed. Yet the whole thrust of the Saint-Simonians' lectures was to oppose scientific arguments, especially those that tried to undermine religion. Bazard ridiculed the term "positive," which he claimed was fashionable but unintelligible. Consisting of an "inventory of facts," the positive method could be used only to verify scientific discoveries, which were essentially intuitive. Rodrigues also accused Comte of not wanting to recognize that imagination and sentiment were the key to the creative process even in the sciences. Despite the pretensions of scientists, their hypotheses resembled theological dogmas in that they too were ultimately based on "invented facts." Comte did not seem to realize that scientists in many fields were already going beyond immediate experience, and that even if the facts themselves could be observed, their laws could not be. Comte's positive method thus could never verify the movement of the earth or the laws of history. He could never even confirm his law of three stages, for it was based on his own faith in progress and was essentially *"THE WILL OF GOD."*[102] Like Lamennais, the Saint-Simonians saw through Comte; behind his scientific proclamations, they detected a fundamentally religious spirit.

Because of his enthusiasm for science, Comte was also accused of underestimating the role of artists, that is, poets and priests, in the creation of a new society. He mistakenly limited their role to propagating the social plans already "coldly" worked out by the scientists.[103] Comte had inverted their roles. Because of their love for humanity, the artists were actually the masters of society, and the scientists merely justified the artists' revelations about social destiny.

The Saint-Simonians concluded that Comte misunderstood Saint-Simon's intention when he pretended to use the master's method to portray a positive, scientific era freed from religion. He overlooked the "positive" fact that man is an "eminently religious being."[104] Science was only now atheistic because mankind was in a critical, purely transitory period. Comte did not understand that in the new organic age the sciences themselves would fortify religion by giving people a greater idea of God. In a lecture given during the summer of 1829, Bazard specifically condemned the antireligious habits inculcated by *"positivism."* This seems to have been the first time the

---

[102] Ibid., 125, 374, 377, 388. Enfantin also pointed out that Comte was acting on "faith" alone. Enfantin to Picard, August 15, 1829, Fonds Enfantin 7643, fol. 362v, BA.
[103] *Doctrine de Saint-Simon, première année*, 385.   [104] Ibid., 363.

word "positivism" appeared in print. Heretofore, Comte had referred to his system as "positive philosophy." Thus perhaps it was Bazard who coined the term that Comte would adopt six years later.[105]

In celebrating irrationalism, love, and a deistic religion, these lectures of 1829 were, in effect, the Saint-Simonian manifesto of independence from the most famous of Saint-Simon's disciples, Auguste Comte. Just as he looked upon them as pure sentimentalists, they exaggerated his defining characteristic and helped spread the view that he was a frigid scientistic thinker. Their attacks on Comte culminated in the fifteenth session of their lectures, on July 15, 1829; in discussing the fundamental opuscule, Rodrigues summarized their opinion of him: "The man who is absorbed in his love for *science* and who, in outlining the history of humanity, almost forgets to speak about the progress of its *sympathies* . . . , we say: this man is an heresiarch, he has denied his master."[106] Rodrigues's statement amounted to a formal excommunication of the friend who had chosen him to be his best man only four years before. Henceforth, Comte was not only the Saint-Simonians' rival but their enemy.

Undoubtedly rattled, Comte grew jealous of the immediate success of the Saint-Simonians. Eager to make the Ecole Polytechnique the "channel by which these [Saint-Simonian] ideas spread throughout society," Enfantin launched a very successful campaign to win adherents among its graduates, the very group Comte had targeted.[107] They would constitute one of the main forces of this new sect, much to Comte's despair.[108] The Saint-Simonians also attracted many

---

[105] Ibid., 416. In a letter written June 6, 1824, to Gustave d'Eichthal that is published in the *Correspondance générale*, Comte wrote that scientists agreed on "particular ideas, the only ones that are yet positivist." *CG*, 1:98. This is the only time that Comte wrote "positivist" until the later volumes of the *Cours*. He always wrote "positive" and referred to his doctrine as the "positive philosophy." In fact, one may well suspect that the word "positivist" in this letter is a misprint. The original letter is, unfortunately, missing. Comte to G. d'Eichthal, June 6, 1824, *CG*, 1:98, and "Correspondance de Comte et d'Eichthal," ed. Laffitte, 214. It was in lesson 28 that Comte appeared to use the term "positivism" for the first time when he wrote: "In astronomy the discussion [between people supporting the positive spirit and those maintaining metaphysics] was less marked, and positivism triumphed almost spontaneously, except on the subject of the earth's movement." *Cours*, 1:453.

[106] *Doctrine de Saint-Simon, première année*, 374.

[107] Enfantin to Picard, February 2, 1826, in Saint-Simon and Enfantin, *Oeuvres de Saint-Simon et d'Enfantin*, 1:165.

[108] In the *Cours de philosophie positive*, Comte lamented that "antisocial utopias" had succeeded in attracting many students of the Ecole Polytechnique. *Cours*, 2:744. Indeed, almost seventy graduates of the school took an interest in Saint-Simonianism. See James Bland Briscoe, "Saint-Simonism and the Origins of Socialism in France, 1816–1832" (Ph.D. diss., Columbia University, 1980), 348; Saint-Simon and Enfantin, *Oeuvres de Saint-Simon et d'Enfantin*, 3:237; Hayek, *Counter-Revolution*, 152–4; Weill, *L'Ecole Saint-Simonienne*, 33.

disciples in the Midi, especially in Comte's native town of Montpellier, where Enfantin hoped to make a "very beautiful cathedral in ten years."[109]

What most upset Comte was that several of his friends, such as Mellet, Lamé, and Joseph-Léon Talabot, all graduates of the Ecole Polytechnique, were sympathetic to the new church.[110] The most bitter setback occurred when his former disciple Gustave d'Eichthal decided to join the Saint-Simonians in July 1829, immediately after hearing Rodrigues's lecture on Comte's *Plan des travaux scientifiques*.[111] The man most instrumental in his conversion was Comte's chief rival, Enfantin. He knew how to take advantage of d'Eichthal's feeling of resentment against Comte for having criticized his decision to enter the business world. D'Eichthal found Enfantin to be a "man of the finest talent."[112] With a "touching tenderness," Enfantin explained to him that the valuable parts of Comte's doctrine derived from the "genius of Saint-Simon."[113] Enfantin then carefully gave d'Eichthal the impression that he was the "only man" who understood him and persuaded him to accept the Saint-Simonians' "joys of love," which better suited d'Eichthal's nature than his "tiring" intellectual activities.[114] (By this, perhaps d'Eichthal was referring to the Saint-Simonians' championship of greater sexual liberty; after all, one reason he had switched earlier from Catholicism to positivism was his desire to fulfill his sexual needs.) Enfantin could not help gloating as he described his triumph to Bailly: "D'Eichthal . . . was for a long time a student of Comte, who, if this had been possible, would have reduced his heart to the frozen state in which his own is to be found, We have pulled him from the abyss."[115] Playing an important part in the sect, d'Eichthal later humiliated

---

[109] Enfantin to Resseguier, July 1830, in Saint-Simon and Enfantin, *Oeuvres de Saint-Simon et d'Enfantin*, 27:113. See also Weill, *L'Ecole Saint-Simonienne*, 57.

[110] Talabot had been in Enfantin and Menjaud's class at the Ecole Polytechnique, which had entered in 1813. He had been very interested in Comte's doctrine but would soon give his allegiance to the Saint-Simonians. Eventually he would become one of Enfantin's strongest supporters. Registre de matricule des élèves, vol. 4, 1810–19, EP; Talabot to Comte, December 28, 1829, MAC; Talabot to Comte, n.d., MAC; G. d'Eichthal, note, in Manuscrits Carton II A, fol. 320, Bibliothèque Thiers; Enfantin to Picard, August 15, 1829, Fonds Enfantin 7643, fols. 361, BA; Carlisle, *Proffered Crown*, 68.

[111] G. d'Eichthal to Adolphe d'Eichthal, July 23, 1829, Fonds d'Eichthal 14407, item 10, BA.

[112] G. d'Eichthal to Adolphe d'Eichthal, July 23, 1829, Fond d'Eichthal 14407, item 10, BA.

[113] G. d'Eichthal to Resseguier, February 26, 1830, Fonds Enfantin 7644, fol. 163, BA.

[114] Gustave d'Eichthal, remarks in "Les Enseignements," in Saint-Simon and Enfantin, *Oeuvres de Saint-Simon et d'Enfantin*, 16:194; G. d'Eichthal to Resseguier, February 26, 1830, Fonds Enfantin 7644, fol. 163v, BA.

[115] Enfantin to Bailly, April, 1830, Fonds Enfantin 7644, fol. 105 bis verso, BA.

Comte when he not only converted his former student and boarder Lamoricière to Saint-Simonianism but denounced Comte in the Saint-Simonian meetings for *"atheism"* and *"materialism."*[116]

Profoundly shaken by d'Eichthal's new allegiance, Comte wrote to him sarcastically in late 1829:

> Ever since the change in the direction that your mind just underwent, I admit that I no longer count on you in any manner. Here you are placed at a point of sublimity, which must lead you . . . to pity our unhappy positive research, of which you now no longer have any need and which would, on the contrary, trouble your theological works.[117]

Insulted, d'Eichthal tried to explain to him that the Saint-Simonians felt he (Comte) had not carried his positive method "far enough" and had misinterpreted the law of three stages. The third, positive stage had to "reunite *materialism* and *spiritualism* into one whole."[118] Positive philosophy had to demonstrate that the entire universe was a reflection of God.

Comte was plainly shocked and pained by "*the vulgar drivel*" and "vague pantheism" that d'Eichthal's "present masters" had inspired in him. In answer to d'Eichthal's claim that he did not know the Saint-Simonians well enough to judge them, Comte angrily retorted: "How could you write that when you know very well that I saw them born, if I did not form them myself." He accused them of stealing and deforming his ideas and denigrating him. They could never have surpassed him, as d'Eichthal implied, because he had had a ten-year head start and the "little Messieurs" were intellectually inferior, especially his archrival Enfantin, who was "generally regarded at the Ecole Polytechnique by all his comrades as one of the most mediocre students." Although their theology might have at most an "ephemeral success," it would eventually "extinguish itself under the blows of universal ridicule." If d'Eichthal had to embrace a theological position, he might at least have returned to a more respectable Catholicism.[119]

D'Eichthal, hurt by this "torrent of insults," secretly thought that Comte considered himself a "Divinity" who was angry that the Saint-Simonians had committed the "crime of high treason" against

---

[116] Gustave d'Eichthal, remarks in "Les Enseignements," 16:193. See also Gustave d'Eichthal to Duveyrier, April 30, 1830, Fonds Pereire, N.a.fr. 24609, BN; Weill, *L'Ecole Saint-Simonienne,* 59; G. d'Eichthal, Note, October 12, 1868, Fonds d'Eichthal 14394, BA.

[117] Comte to G. d'Eichthal, December 7, 1829, *CG,* 1:210.

[118] G. d'Eichthal to Comte, December 8, 1829, "Correspondance de Comte et d'Eichthal (Suite)," ed. Laffitte, 372–3.

[119] Comte to G. d'Eichthal, December 11, 1829, *CG,* 1:211–14.

him. The crime was that they "dared believe that there was something other than . . . [Comte] in the world."[120]

THE ATHÉNÉE

Despite his quarrels, Comte was able in late 1829 to achieve the greater level of respectability he felt he deserved and fulfill a desire he had expressed five years previously. He was given permission to teach his course on positive philosophy at the Athénée, thanks to the help of Ternaux, a former president.[121] The Athénée was well regarded not only because of the number of famous men who had taught there, but because of its unusual loyalty to the scientific philosophy of the eighteenth century.[122] Since its "antireligious and antimonarchical doctrines" were considered "pernicious" by the royal government, the Ministry of the Interior kept a constant watch over its activities.[123] Recently, the Athénée had attacked romanticism and Cousin's eclecticism, and so its slightly subversive atmosphere suited Comte, who felt a great affinity with its former professors, especially Condorcet.[124] He was particularly eager to give his course there because the Saint-Simonians were preparing to begin a second series of lectures on their doctrine on November 18, and he wanted a more effective way of disseminating his ideas.[125]

By November 4, 1829, Comte had written his opening discourse, although as usual he had trouble finishing it and as usual claimed it was not his fault. As soon as he completed it, he asked his friend Gondinet, who was writing for the prestigious *Revue encyclopédique*, to persuade Marc-Antoine Jullien, its editor, to print this first lesson. But he told Gondinet and d'Eichthal not to mention to the Saint-Simonians that he was planning to offer a course at the Athénée.[126] He was apparently worried that some of them might

[120] G. d'Eichthal to Comte, [December 8, 1828?], rough draft of a letter that was never sent, "Correspondance de Comte et d'Eichthal (Suite)," ed. Laffitte, 379.

[121] Ternaux to Comte, October 22, 1829, MAC. The letter is reproduced with the wrong date in Laffitte, "L'Athénée," 50.

[122] Some of the people who taught at the Athénée were Condorcet, Monge, Cuvier, Thenard, Gall, Blainville, Say, Constant, Joseph Fourier, Dunoyer, and Adolphe Blanqui. See Laffitte, "L'Athénée," 16–47; *Programme pour l'an 1829* (Paris, 1829), 2; Charles Dejob, *De l'établissement connu sous le nom de Lycée et d'Athénée et de quelques établissements analogues*, Extract from the *Revue internationale de l'enseignement* (Paris, 1889), 33.

[123] Ministère de l'Intérieur, Direction de la Police, Note, January 29, 1825, F⁷ 6915, AN.

[124] Dejob, *De l'établissement connu sous le nom de Lycée et d'Athénée*, 32.

[125] Fournel, *Bibliographie Saint-Simonienne*, 74; Issalène to Comte, December 8, 1829, MAC.

[126] Comte to Gondinet, November 4, 1829, CG, 1: 209–11; Charléty, *Saint-Simonisme*, 37n1; Association Polytechnique, *Documents pour servir à l'histoire de cette association, 1830–1855* (Paris, n.d.), 4–8; Comte to G. d'Eichthal, December 11, 1829, CG, 1:211. See also Gondinet's favorable review of *Le Producteur* in the *Revue encyclopédique*, 30 (May 1826): 543–4.

try to hurt his reputation and prevent him from getting a good publisher.

Jullien, a former Jacobin who had founded the journal in 1819, was happy to comply with Comte's wishes.[127] Not only did he advertise the opening of the course, but he also inserted at the beginning of the November issue a thirty-six-page article entitled "Discours d'ouverture du Cours de philosophie positive de M. Auguste Comte, ancien élève de l'Ecole Polytechnique: Exposition du but de ce cours, ou Considérations générales sur la philosophie positive."[128] Proud of the article and hopeful that it would attract a large audience to his lectures, Comte sent copies of it to all sorts of people.[129]

Comte's course met on Wednesday and Saturday evenings from December 1829 until November 1830. The program followed the plan of the course that he had given the year before, but because of time constraints, he had to reduce the number of lectures from seventy-two to fifty.[130] Yet he still had difficulties conveying the material within the time allotted to him; in his opening discourse, for example, he rambled on to such an extent that an usher had to remind him three times that another professor was waiting for the lecture hall.[131]

Although Comte may have taxed his audience's attention span, he achieved great success. More than two hundred people came to hear him outline his new system of thought.[132] The Saint-Simonians were sufficiently impressed to encourage d'Eichthal to follow the course because of its "scientific" value.[133] Thus after years of disillusionment, Comte began to attract a following of his own.

---

[127] Ledré, "La Presse nationale," 79; Rémond, *Les Etats-Unis,* 1:421; Des Granges, "Presse littéraire," 53–4, 81–3; Jullien to Comte, November 17, 1829, MAC.

[128] "Discours d'ouverture du Cours de philosophie positive de M. Auguste Comte," *Revue encyclopédique* 44 (November 1829): 273–309.

[129] Guizot again declined to attend Comte's opening lecture but promised to come later. Guizot to Comte, December 12, 1829, in Valat, "Document historique sur Guizot et Aug. Comte," 23. Valat does not date the letter, but it is December 12, 1829. See the original letter, MAC. See also Comte to Pouzin, December 23, 1829, *CG,* 1:215.

[130] "Discours d'ouverture du Cours du philosophie positive de M. Auguste Comte," 274; Contract between Comte and Rouen frères, December 16, 1829, MAC; "Programme du Cours de philosophie positive" in brochure called "Cours de philosophie positive de Mr. Auguste Comte, ancien élève de l'Ecole Polytechnique. Annonce." This undated brochure is in MAC and is reprinted with the wrong date of 1828 in *Ecrits,* 577–9. This brochure must relate to the course at the Athénée since fifty lectures are listed instead of seventy-two.

[131] Laffitte, "L'Athénée," 22; G. d'Eichthal, footnote, in G. d'Eichthal to Comte, [December 8, 1828?], "Correspondance de Comte et d'Eichthal (Suite)," ed. Laffitte, 379n1.

[132] Comte to Pouzin, December 23, 1829, *CG,* 1:215.

[133] G. d'Eichthal to Comte, December 8, 1829, "Correspondance de Comte et d'Eichthal (Suite)," ed. Laffitte, 371. Also see G. d'Eichthal to Comte, [December 8, 1828?], ibid., 379; Comte to G. d'Eichthal, December 7, 1829, *CG,* 1:210; Talabot to Comte, December 28, 1829, and January 17, no year, MAC.

Years of Success and Confrontation, *1830–1838*

Ever since [your separation from Saint-Simon], tell me, have you been happy? . . . There is no joy for the isolated man; there is for him only hatred and bitterness. . . . Everything is hollow to him; the universe is an immense emptiness. To fill it, he vainly inflates his personality; the pride with which he fills himself oppresses and suffocates him. An acrid disdain blends into his words and runs under his pen. . . . Because he separates himself from every-one, he believes that everyone rejects him, that everyone is his enemy. Your enemy, Sir, we [the Saint-Simonians] are not, and we would like to be your friends because we know that there is in you a power to do great things for the progress of humanity.

Michel Chevalier to Comte, 1832

PUBLICATION OF THE *COURS DE PHILOSOPHIE POSITIVE*

At the end of 1829, Comte decided he needed to expand his ideas and spread them more effectively.[1] On December 16, 1829, less than two weeks after beginning his course at the Athénée, he made an agreement with Rouen frères to publish the original seventy-two lessons. (Rouen frères put out the *Journal des sciences et institutions médicales*.)[2] According to the contract, two lessons would appear each week in the form of a *cahier*; when bound together, the *cahiers* were to constitute four volumes. Although he had not written a single line, Comte was sure he would complete the project by the end of 1830. One thousand copies of each volume would be printed, and a subscription to all four would cost thirty-two francs. Rouen would pay Comte three thousand francs for his efforts, half to be paid immediately, the other half to be paid as the volumes were sold.[3]

---

[1] "Discours d'ouverture du Cours du philosophie positive de M. Auguste Comte," *Revue encyclopédique* 44 (November 1829): 274; Comte to G. d'Eichthal, December 7, 1829, *CG*, 1:210–11.

[2] Comte to Pouzin, December 23, 1829, *CG*, 1:215; Nicole Felkay, "Les Libraires de l'époque romantique d'après des documents inédits," *Revue française d'histoire du livre*, n.s. 5.9 (1975): 31–87.

[3] Contract between Comte and Rouen frères, December 16, 1829, MAC; "Annonces Biblio-graphiques," *Revue française* 15 (May 1830): 310; "De la publication du *Cours de philosophie positive*," ed. Laffitte, 262.

Among the people who subscribed between 1830 and 1833 to receive one or more volumes of the *Cours* were a number of Comte's friends and acquaintances, including Esquirol, Valat, and Menjaud. The notable physicist Nicolas-Léonard-Sadi Carnot also subscribed. In addition, many Saint-Simonians or their sympathizers took an interest in Comte's work: Olinde Rodrigues, Buchez, Talabot, Resseguier, Dugied, Dufresne, Lechevalier, Boulland, Lamé, Mesnier, Jules Alisse, Adolphe Alisse, Simon, Mellet, Montgéry, Zédé, Bertrand, Lamoricière, and Veilliard.[4] Altogether 103 persons or establishments signed up to receive the *Cours*.

From the very beginning, Comte was unable to follow his publication schedule. The two first lessons appeared in December 1829, but by February 1830 only seven more had been published.[5] It was not until July that he completed the first volume, which consisted of eleven brochures covering eighteen lessons. But at least he was beginning to realize the project that he had conceived four years before.

One of the results of the publication of the *Cours* was that Comte began to be invited to fashionable soirées given by prominent scientists, such as Henri Navier, Baron Fourier, and Baron de Férussac (the director of the important *Bulletin universel pour la propagation des connaissances scientifiques et industrielles*). Later Blainville invited him regularly to his famous monthly dinners. Comte's sense of importance further increased when he received a highly congratulatory message from Dr. Jacques Lordat, the dean of the medical school in Montpellier.[6]

Though undoubtedly gratified by the reception of the *Cours* in scientific circles, Comte was disappointed by the press's reaction. He was unjustified, however, in complaining later that his work had not had the "honor of the smallest review."[7] Some journals did ask

---

[4] List of subscribers, packet on Rouen frères, MAC.
[5] "Livres français: Sciences physiques et naturelles," *Revue encyclopédique*, 45 (February 1830): 384.
[6] Fourier to Comte, March 1, April 21, 1830, MAC; Navier to Comte, February 9, 1830, February 21, 1831, January 19, 1832, and January 30, 1833, MAC; Férussac to Comte, November 30, 1830, MAC; "Soirée scientifique chez le Baron de Férussac," *Revue de Paris*, 13 (April, 1830): 252; Nicard, *Blainville*, clviii; "Variétés: Relations d'Auguste Comte avec l'Abbé de Lamennais," ed. Laffitte, 245; Lordat to Comte, January 5, 1831, MAC; Rosalie Boyer to Comte, January 29, 1831, "Lettres de la mère d'Aug. Comte, Rosalie Boyer, à son fils (Suite)," ed. Pierre Laffitte, *RO*, 3rd ser., 2 (July, 1909), 47. In one of the offshoots of Férussac's *Bulletin universel*, Comte was listed as a collaborator from April 1825 to May 1826 and in March 1829, but as the articles are unsigned, the extent of his contributions is unknown. His distinguished colleagues included Fourier, Comte de Laborde, Delambre, and Augustin Thierry. See *Bulletin universel des sciences géographiques, etc. économie publique, voyages* for this period.
[7] Comte to Valat, January 5, 1840, *CG*, 1:333; see also *Cours*, 2:473.

him to write a review of his work, but he refused, criticizing journalists for being lazy and unwilling to read difficult books. Yet their request is understandable. Since Comte was publishing his lessons and his volumes in separate installments, many journals, such as the *Revue encyclopédique*, did not know how to approach his work and were waiting for him to finish the entire *Cours* before making their evaluations.[8]

Moreover, Comte overlooked the reviews that were less than favorable. The *Revue française* and *Le Lycée*, which were connected to the reigning doctrinaire philosophy, found Comte competent but obscure and unoriginal. Constructing a totally new philosophy based on Cousin's eclecticism, they "combated" him for merely repeating the obsolete antimetaphysical ideas of the eighteenth-century sensationalists and for belittling the study of psychology and "moral and intellectual phenomena" in general.[9] His work suffered from two principal errors, materialism and atheism – exactly the vices that d'Eichthal had imputed to Comte. They would soon become the terms customarily associated with positivism. Comte's continued discussion of the natural sciences in several more volumes and the unanticipated nine-year delay of his exposition of social physics, the key to his system of thought, helped to give the impression that the positive philosophy was too narrow, arid, and scientistic. Whatever initial interest many of the reviewers might have had in his system would be dissipated in the intervening period. Historical circumstances did not work in Comte's favor either. Less than a month after the appearance of the first volume, the July Revolution broke out in France, distracting attention from the *Cours* and financially ruining his publisher.

THE REVOLUTION OF 1830 AND COMTE'S REPUBLICANISM

Comte warmly welcomed the "great" revolution of 1830. Despite his cultivation of Villèle, he had always disliked the Bourbon government because it sought to reestablish the ancien régime and destroy such "guarantees of progress" as liberty of the press.[10] Its "reactionary velleities" had, moreover, prevented him from teaching

[8] "Livres français: Sciences physiques et naturelles," 384-5.
[9] Review of *Cours de philosophie positive*, by Auguste Comte, *Revue française* 15 (January 1830): 256; Review of *Cours de philosophie positive*, by Auguste Comte, part 1, *Le Lycée: Journal de l'instruction publique de la littérature, des sciences, et des arts* 7 (January 6, 1831): 395; see also part 2, ibid. (January 13, 1831): 403-5.
[10] *Système*, 1:68.

in the public school system.[11] Although he included himself among the republicans and many people he knew participated in it, Comte's own role in this revolution is not clear.[12] A man who subsequently became a police sergeant later swore that he and Comte had mounted guard together on July 29, 1830, and had faced oncoming troops.[13] Alexandre Dumas père wrote in his *Mémoires* that when the Duc de Chartres, the eldest son of the Duc d'Orléans, was arrested south of Paris, General Lafayette had Comte deliver the crucial note that prevented his murder and obtained his release.[14] Since one of Comte's friends intimated that he participated in a dangerous mission and Dumas's account contains numerous details, the story is probably valid, though it seems out of character and efforts to substantiate it have proved fruitless.[15] If true, it indicates that Comte was one of the many moderate republicans who turned to Lafayette, in the hope that he would create a new provisional government. Instead, Lafayette was pressured into becoming an early supporter of the Orleanist solution, which damaged the republican cause.[16]

After the Revolution of 1830, Comte continued to work to modify the government. When the Chamber of Peers failed to condemn the former ministers of Charles X to death, the people staged a demonstration against the government on December 21, 1830. The next day Comte wrote a letter to Louis-Philippe urging him to establish a "truly durable order" and imprint a "progressive direction" on the government.[17] This letter shows that Comte, like many of his compatriots, had already become disillusioned with the results of the revolution.[18] He argued that the constitutional monarchy represented a betrayal of the revolutionaries' goals because it

---

[11] *Cours*, 2:469.

[12] Deroisin, *Notes sur Auguste Comte*, 30; Eloi Pépin, "Matériaux pour servir à la biographie d'Auguste Comte: Aux journées de Juillet, 1830," *Revue positiviste internationale* 12 (May 15, 1912): 445–8; Jardin and Tudesq, *Notables*, 1:118–24; Issalène to Comte, August 31, 1830, MAC.

[13] Statement of sergeant of the gendarmerie at rue Saint-Jacques, August 17, 1833, in the medical certificate relating to Comte's myopia, MAC.

[14] Alexandre Dumas, père *Mes Mémoires*, 2 vols. (Poissy, 1866), 2:112.

[15] Lellvyn to Comte, August 3, 1830, MAC; Pépin, "Matériaux," 445–8.

[16] David H. Pinkney, *The French Revolution of 1830* (Princeton, N.J.: Princeton University Press, 1972), 144, 294; Welch, *Liberty and Utility*, 168–9.

[17] The letter was signed by members of the Association Polytechnique, which Comte had just helped to establish. At four o'clock in the afternoon of December 22, Comte gave it to the liberal Comte Bachasson de Montalivet to deliver to the king. Robinet, *Notice*, 190n1.

[18] See the brochure in Comte's library entitled *A Messieurs les députés des départements*. It is a letter signed July 25, 1831, by the "Commission des condamnés pour délits politiques," which complained that the people who had prepared the Revolution of 1830 had not reaped the fruits of their efforts. Comte's friend Charles Bonnin was one of the signers of this letter.

was based on the parliamentary system – a "vain" foreign import – and was controlled by narrow interest groups.[19] Thus instead of effecting social, political, and educational improvements for the people, the revolution had brought about only a "simple displacement of power."[20] Comte's impression that France was a "bourgeois monarchy" run by a narrow oligarchy was widely shared by thinkers on both the Left and Right, including Stendhal, Balzac, Tocqueville, and Marx.[21] He became increasingly convinced that the abolition of the monarchy was the first step in completing the "great revolution" of 1789.[22]

In the early nineteenth century, the radical republican opposition to the government took inspiration in the expanding legend of the Convention.[23] Inspired by Voltaire's concept of the enlightened dictator and by the example of the "glorious" Convention, when "men of action" dominated, Comte himself began to move toward advocating a republic ruled by progressive, strong leadership.[24] He was tired of anarchy and corruption, discouraged by the parliamentary system, and fearful of the Right; a "republican dictatorship" that was provisional and worked to improve public welfare seemed a possible solution to the problem of the exercise of power – a solution that would, moreover, avoid the horrors of despotism.[25]

The expression "dictatorship," which went back to the Romans and had become widespread since the early days of the Revolution of 1789, had two definitions in the first half of the nineteenth century. Comte took up the positive meaning of the term, referring to a virtuous savior who rescues society from danger by temporarily suspending normal political rules. He did not endorse the other, pejorative sense of dictatorship as violent tyranny without limits.[26] To emphasize the first meaning of the term, Comte took his distance from Robespierre, who fell after being called a dictator, and made Danton the model leader. According to Comte's myth-making account, Danton prevailed during the ten-month period between the expulsion of the Girondins and his own execution – a period when he directed the defense of the republic and finished dismantling the monarchy. Danton, in Comte's mind, best understood the need for

---

[19] *Système*, 1:70; see also 69.
[20] "Adresse du Comité permanent de l'Association polytechnique au Roi des Français," December 22, 1830, in Robinet, *Notice*, 414–15.
[21] Roger Magraw, *France: 1815–1914* (New York: Oxford University Press, 1986), 51.
[22] Comte to Armand Marrast, January 7, 1832, *CG*, 1:233.
[23] Welch, *Liberty and Utility*, 164.
[24] Comte to Mill, March 4, 1842, *CG*, 2:36–7. See also Robinet, *Notice*, 189–90.
[25] *Cours*, 2:596.
[26] Nicolet, *L'Idée républicaine*, 102–3; Frick, "Problème du pouvoir," 287n11.

temporary strong leadership in a time of transition in order to provide stability.[27] Comte would develop his idea of progressive dictatorship mainly after the Revolution of 1848, around the time Marx originated his concept of the dictatorship of the proletariat as his answer to the liberal *malaise*. As Claude Nicolet and Mona Ozouf have pointed out, Comte's use of the word "dictator" turned out to be idiosyncratic, infelicitous, and confusing; it would cost him and his disciples much support.[28]

This authoritarian streak in Comte's politics certainly tended to set him apart from other republicans in France in the 1830s. He probably did not become actively involved in any republican organizations, which proliferated from 1830 to 1833 and became the most important source of opposition to the July Monarchy. He not only feared harassment from the government but disagreed with the republicans' deist and pantheistic inclinations, their support of violence, and their passion for equality, universal suffrage, popular sovereignty, and democratic institutions. They seemed to be abandoning the moderate, scientific spirit of the Idéologues, which had inspired them before.[29] Nevertheless, he claimed that he was a republican and kept himself informed of the doctrines and travails of the influential elite republican group, the Société des Amis du Peuple.[30] Like them, he was concerned with working-class conditions and was determined to overthrow the monarchy and destroy the system of privilege upheld by the bourgeoisie and the aristocracy. He shared their commitment to the Convention and their scorn for Napoleon, the man who had destroyed the glorious Republic.[31]

Comte also expressed his solidarity with the republican movement by refusing in November 1831 to serve in the repressive National Guard, which was aggressively pursuing the Société des

---

[27] *Système*, 3:599–600; Mona Ozouf, "Danton," in *A Critical Dictionary*, ed. Furet and Ozouf, 216–17. Ozouf argues forcefully against Comte's interpretation of Danton.

[28] Nicolet, *L'Idée républicaine*, 101–5, 240–2; Ozouf, "Danton," 216–18.

[29] Gabriel Perreux, *Au temps des sociétés secrètes* (Paris: Hachette, 1931), 2; Welch, *Liberty and Utility*, 169–71; Robinet, *Notice*, 188–93.

[30] Comte received the first fourteen brochures of propaganda that the Société des Amis du Peuple published from July 1831 to January 1832. See Comte's library at the Maison d'Auguste Comte. Also see Littré, *Auguste Comte*, 251; Perreux, *Sociétés secrètes*, 8–9, 15, 38–42; Lucien de la Hodde, *Histoire des sociétés secrètes et du parti républicain de 1830 à 1848* (Paris, 1850), 35, 38.

[31] La Société des Amis du Peuple, brochure of August 18, 1831, p. 9. On their desire for a regime based on meritocracy, see La Société des Amis du Peuple, *L'Eclaireur*, brochure 10, October 1831: 5–6. On their social ideas, see Bernard H. Moss, "Parisian Workers and the Origins of Republican Socialism, 1830–1833," in John M. Merriman, ed., *1830 in France* (New York: Franklin Watts, New Viewpoints, 1975), 205–10; I. Tchernoff, *Le Parti républicain sous la Monarchie de Juillet* (Paris: A. Pedone, 1901), 263–70.

Amis du Peuple. Called to appear before the disciplinary council of the Third Legion, Comte explained, "Being a republican in heart and mind, I cannot swear to defend at the peril of my life and that of others a government that I would combat if I were a man of action." Taking part in "purely political struggles" was out of the question for a man who prided himself on being "exclusively contemplative" and engaged in spiritual reform.[32] The disciplinary council had him incarcerated, however, for three days in March.[33] Bringing paper, ink, and enough books for three months and greeting his wife and students, he served his term in a handsome room in the National Guard's prison, overlooking the Seine. The following year he tried a different tactic: he carefully established his ineligibility for the National Guard by persuading Blainville, Esquirol, Poinsot, and others to sign a medical certificate attesting to his extreme shortsightedness.[34]

Shortly after the Revolution of 1830, Comte expressed his social concerns and his desire for an intellectual revolution in another way. Beginning in mid-August, he worked hard to form the Association Polytechnique, an organization dedicated to reviving the "generous sentiments" stifled by the Bourbon and Orleanist regimes.[35] Its political leanings were evident in the fact that it was founded by five hundred alumni of the Ecole Polytechnique at a banquet in honor of the students who had fought against the government in July. Comte was vice-president of the association, a post he held until 1834, when he resigned. His friends Menjaud and Gondinet were the secretaries. Besides creating ties and a spirit of confraternity among the former students of the school, the association set up free courses on the sciences for workers.[36] Inspired by Delambre and Adam Smith and

---

[32] Comte, quoted in Littré, *Auguste Comte*, 252; Comte to Blainville, June 21, 1832, *CG*, 1:238. See also Tchernoff, *Parti républicain*, 237; de la Hodde, *Histoire des sociétés secrètes*, 43, 53.

[33] "Certificat d'Ecrou," March 15, 1832, MAC; Littré, *Auguste Comte*, 252–3.

[34] Medical certificate attesting to Comte's myopia, July–August, 1833, MAC; Document from Conseil de Recensement for the twelfth arrondissement, January 27, February 2, 1839, MAC.

[35] Colonel Raucourt, "Note relative au projet d'association à fonder entre tous les anciens élèves de l'Ecole Polytechnique," *Journal du génie civil, des sciences et des arts* 9 (September 1, 1830): 186.

[36] Other members of its board of directors were the Duc de Choiseul Praslin, who was president, the Marquis Victor de Tracy (Destutt de Tracy's son), Vauvilliers, and Larabit, who were also vice-presidents, Thurninger, who was treasurer, and Perdonnet and Meissas, who were secretaries. Comte may have resigned from the vice-presidency because the Association decided not to help him establish a journal propagating his ideas. Mellet's apparent opposition to Comte's project seems to have led to a rupture in their friendship. Mellet later became an Owenite. See Gondinet to Comte, November 14, 1832; Vieillard to Comte, November 1, 1832; Mellet to Comte, November 20, 1832; Issalène to Comte, December 7, 1833, MAC; Comte to Hadery, December 14, 1855, *CG*, 8:160. On the

prompted by the belief that every educated person had a duty to enlighten those who wished to learn, Comte began in late January 1831 to lecture on elementary astronomy, which he felt was easier to understand than mathematics. Almost two hundred people came to his course as well as to two other series given by the Association.[37]

Comte also chose to teach astronomy because he believed that it was the only science freed from all theological and metaphysical influences and it offered the best introduction to positive philosophy.[38] If he could stimulate the workers' interest, correct their fallacious concepts, and spread "positive ideas" among them, they might see the need to study all the branches of natural philosophy. In sum, disillusioned by the results of July 1830, Comte endeavored to instigate an intellectual "revolution" among the people, with whom he felt a sense of solidarity. Well aware of the social effects of his enterprise, he maintained that a theoretical course "exclusively destined up to now to the use of the *messieurs*" would awaken in the workers a "just sentiment of their dignity."[39]

The revolutionary implications of his and other professors' lectures to the working class did not escape the government. When an insurrection occurred in June 1832, the government suspended all courses for workers.[40] Comte angrily protested that he would never compromise the "dignity" of science by bringing into his talks anything "heterogeneous," such as politics.[41] Yet the prefect refused to bend the rules for him.[42] In late October Comte pleaded personally with Guizot, who had just become minister of public instruction.[43]

Association Polytechnique, see material in F[17] 12529 in AN, especially the brochure published by the Association Polytechnique, *Documents pour servir à l'histoire de cette association, 1830–1835* (Paris, n.d.).

[37] Louis de Troismonts to Comte, September 16, 1833, MAC; Alexandre Meissas, "Rapport sur les cours de l'Association Polytechnique," *Association Polytechnique, Compte rendu trimestriel: Janvier 1833* (Paris, 1833), 11.

[38] *Cours*, 1:300; see also 307.

[39] Comte to the President of the Association Polytechnique, December 14, 1830, *CG*, 1:218–19.

[40] Association Polytechnique, *Documents pour servir à l'histoire de cette association, 1830–1855*, 1, 7; de la Hodde, *Histoire des sociétés secrètes*, 94; Meissas, "Rapport," 13; Préfet de la Seine au Mairie du IIIe arrondissement to Comte, June 29, 1832, MAC.

[41] Comte to the Maire du 3e arrondissement, June 22, 1832, *CG*, 1:239. He also tried to deny that his course on astronomy had ever been attached to an association. Yet only in mid-1831, after the government had expressed its disfavor with the Association Polytechnique, did Comte begin to give the course in his own name. Even in its 1832 bulletin, however, the Association mentioned Comte's course in astronomy. Association Polytechnique, *Compte rendu trimestriel: July 1832* (Paris, 1832), 5; Meissas, "Rapport," 11.

[42] Préfet de la Seine au Mairie du IIIe to Comte, June 29, 1832, MAC.

[43] Guizot had, moreover, turned down three of his requests to come to the courses at the Athénée. Guizot to Comte, December 11, 1828, and January 4, December 12, 1829, in

He had shown no interest in Comte since 1828 but seemed willing to help. After making inquiries and hearing that Comte's course was successful and innocuous, Guizot enthusiastically authorized the Association Polytechnique to continue its courses to the workers.[44] For some reason, perhaps bureaucratic, Comte was not informed. Writing Guizot a very angry letter, he accused him of indifference to social problems, criticized the government's "brutality," and defended his course by arguing that the workers were too unprepared to understand his social doctrines.[45] Only in mid-January, six months after its suspension, was Comte's course allowed to resume.[46] Henceforth, he made sure to give it in his own name, not that of the Association Polytechnique.

For seventeen consecutive years, Comte found satisfaction in greeting "numerous" workers every Sunday afternoon in the city hall of the third arrondissement, located on the rue des Petits-Pères.[47] He was disappointed, however, that only about a quarter of the audience belonged, in fact, to the proletariat.[48] Nevertheless, this experiment in public education was one of the most successful enterprises of his life. Over the years, he received many letters from auditors expressing their gratitude on behalf of the "working class."[49]

DISAPPOINTMENTS AT THE ECOLE POLYTECHNIQUE AND THE ATHÉNÉE

Like his fellow teachers connected with the Association Polytechnique, Comte was not paid for his work.[50] He therefore had to

Valat, "Document historique sur Guizot et Aug. Comte," 22–4. The dates on the original letters in the Maison d'Auguste Comte are clearer than those in the article by Valat.

[44] Comte to Guizot, October 26, 1832, F[17] 6688, AN (this letter is not published in *CG*); Guizot to Inspecteur Générale Rousselle, November 2, 1832, F[17] 6688, AN; Guizot to Comte, November 2, 1832, F[17] 6688, AN and MAC; Report from Bourdon to Rousselle, November 8, 1832, F[17] 6688, AN; Rousselle to Guizot, November 10, 1832, F[17] 6688, AN; Minister of Public Instruction to Mayor of 6ᵉ arrondissement, November 21, 1832, VD4 5829, Archives de Paris.

[45] Comte to Guizot, November 27, 1832, *CG*, 1:241. This letter can also be found in F[17] 6688, AN.

[46] Guizot to Delebecque, note written on Comte's letter to Guizot, November 27, 1832, F[17] 6688, AN; Delebecque, Ministry of Public Instruction to Comte, December 29, 1832, MAC; Mairie du 3ᵉ arrondissement to Comte, January 2, January 14, 1833, MAC.

[47] Comte to Guizot, November 27, 1832, *CG*, 1:241; Littré, *Auguste Comte*, 253.

[48] Comte to Mill, May 1, 1844, *CG*, 2:248.

[49] Milcent to Comte, January 29, 1831; Vaudoux to Comte, n.d.; A. Grasset to Comte, May 19, 1842; Auguste Nougarède to Comte, May 12, 1839, MAC.

[50] Comte accused one friend of lying to Massin by telling her that he was being paid for this course. The friend promised to squelch the rumor, which he realized had "acutely hurt" Comte. See letter called "Illisible," MAC.

continue his search for a stable source of income. After his former professor Cauchy died, Comte applied in February 1831 to the Academy of Sciences for his chair of analysis and general mechanics at the Ecole Polytechnique.[51] (There were two chairs in this subject at the school.) According to the new regulations of 1830, the Academy of Sciences and the Conseil d'Instruction (composed of the professors of the Ecole Polytechnique) had to present separate lists of desirable candidates for jobs at the school to the minister of war, who made the final decision.[52] Comte had already been trying to attract the Academy's attention; in 1830 he had sent the first volume of the *Cours* to the Academy. But he then refused to make the usual summary of it when Poinsot, who was supposed to do it, fell ill.[53] Despite the fact that his attempt to win the Academy's favor had been halfhearted, he was shocked to learn that the "geometry section" (the usual term for the pure mathematics section) did not even mention him in its list of recommended candidates.[54] He wrote an insulting letter to the Academy in which he condemned its "contemptuous" and "thoughtless" silence. Admitting that he had not made any special contribution to the field, he tactlessly asserted that eminent specialists were often mediocre teachers. He claimed that he could have developed one of the "new mathematic views" in his *Cours* but felt that his teaching experience and general knowledge of the sciences more than qualified him for the position.[55] Nevertheless, the Academy decided to nominate one of its own members who had applied for the post – Comte's friend Henri Navier.[56]

[51] Comte to the President of the Academy of Sciences, February 21, 1831, CG, 1:221.
[52] Comte had joined his comrades in the Association Polytechnique to object to these new regulations, which seemed to them opposed to the wishes of the founders of the Ecole Polytechnique. See letter of December 1, 1830, written to Comte by a member of this association whose name is illegible. It is in a packet called "Administration de l'Ecole Polytechnique," MAC.
[53] Comte was indignant because he felt Poinsot had simply not wanted to bother with this task. Comte to the President of the Academy of Sciences, February 21, 1831, CG, 1:221. Comte also sent his opening discourse to Cuvier. See Comte to Cuvier, January 2, 1830, CG, 1:217. Accusé de réception, Academy of Sciences to Comte, August 23, 1830, MAC; Comte to Cuvier, February 21, 1831, CG, 1:221; Comte to the President of the Academy of Sciences, March 7, 1831, CG, 1:223; Comte to Valat, January 5, 1840, CG, 1:334; "Matériaux pour servir à la biographie d'Auguste Comte: Candidature d'Auguste Comte à la Chaire d'analyse et de mécanique à l'Ecole Polytechnique," ed. Pierre Laffitte, RO 22 (January 1, 1889): 124–5.
[54] See the summary of the meeting of March 7, 1831, in Académie Royale des Sciences, *Registre des Procès-Verbaux et Rapports des Séances de l'Académie Royale des Sciences. Institut* (Paris, 1921), 9:583. This can be found in the archives of the Academy of Sciences.
[55] Comte to the President of the Academy of Sciences, March 7, 1831, CG, 1:222–3.
[56] Navier to Comte, February 21, 1831, MAC; Carrière Polytechnique d'Auguste Comte," ed. Laffitte, 310. The commission of the Conseil d'Instruction that was in charge of presenting the Academy with candidates for the chair submitted on March 4, 1831, five names

This was not his only sharp disappointment in 1831. Comte had repeated his course on positive philosophy at the Athénée during 1831, even though he was allotted only one evening a week. Yet in November 1831 he was informed by the administrator, a friend and admirer, that his course was not given approval for the following year since the "damned audience at the Athénée likes variety."[57] Comte's course was particularly unpopular because it seemed too similar to the outmoded sensationalist philosophy of the eighteenth century.[58]

Again, within the context of the philosophical debates of the period, Comte's doctrine struck many as unoriginal and uninteresting. Cousin, reinstated in his post after the defeat of the ultras in the election of 1828, was again giving an enormously popular series of lectures and definitely had the upper hand. But Comte, who was exasperated by Cousin's triumph, criticized his doctrines for lacking all substance, for bringing together the "most incompatible systems," and for being "out of season" as well.[59] Comte wished to rival Cousin but was frustrated because although he, like Cousin, opposed the theocrats and sensationalists and sought to create a new general doctrine, his scientific exposition connected him with the Enlightenment philosophy of materialism that was considered passé. He had not managed to excite enthusiasm for his science of society.

OPEN BATTLE WITH THE SAINT-SIMONIANS

Deprived of the possibility of expounding his ideas, Comte became increasingly aware of and embittered by the obvious success of his other rivals, the Saint-Simonians, who had seventy-eight members in their Parisian hierarchy alone.[60] With their journal, missions, and

in the following order of preference: Navier, Gustave Gaspard Coriolis, Paul Binet, Duhamel, and finally Comte. (Coriolis, Binet, and Duhamel were *répétiteurs* at the school.) On March 18, the majority of the members of the Conseil d'Instruction followed the Academy in voting to present Navier as their nominee for the post. See minutes of the meetings of March 4, March 18, 1831, Registre: Procès-Verbal du Conseil d'Instruction, vol. 7, EP.

[57] Lenoir to Comte, November 22, 1831, MAC. See also Comte to the President of the Association Polytechnique, December 14, 1830, CG, 1:218; Lonchampt, *Précis*, 30; Program of the Athénée for 1830–1 in Dejob, *De l'établissement connu sous le nom de Lycée et d'Athénée*, 44. Laffitte is incorrect when he says that Comte taught for one year – 1829–30 – at the Athénée. Laffitte, "L'Athénée," 1.

[58] Dejob, *De l'établissement connu sous le nom de Lycée et d'Athénée*, 32.

[59] Comte to Barbot de Chement, December 26, 1846, CG, 4:87; Comte to Valat, November 3, 1824, CG, 1:132.

[60] D'Allemagne, 106, 123; Vieillard to Comte, November 1, 1832, MAC; Mellet to Comte, November 20, 1832, MAC; Gondinet to Comte, November 14, 1832, MAC.

well-attended lectures, they were creating a much bigger name for themselves and stealing some of his disciples. One historian estimates that they attracted the attention of as many as 25,000 people throughout France.[61] Like Cousin, but unlike Comte, they excelled in theatricality and appealed to people prone to sentimentalism, enthusiastic about metaphysical problems, and desirous of some type of spiritualism. To stay abreast of their activities, Comte attended one of the Saint-Simonian lectures at the Salle Taitbout, where he had a fierce altercation with another member of the audience.[62] The Saint-Simonian religious ceremonies and doctrines of universal love were becoming more extravagant and controversial. One of the disaffected Saint-Simonians sent Comte a book describing the scandal and schism that occurred in November 1831, after "le Père Suprême" Enfantin called for the rehabilitation of the flesh and sexual equality.[63] The government began proceedings against the group for anarchy and swindling around this time.[64]

With the Saint-Simonians becoming the object of ridicule just as he had predicted, Comte feared that their efforts to associate him with their visionary doctrine were causing him to lose credibility as a scientific thinker.[65] An opportunity to separate himself from the Saint-Simonians in a decisive manner arose in January 1832, when Armand Marrast, editor of one of the most outspoken republican journals, *La Tribune politique et littéraire*, published an article criticizing Saint-Simonianism. He included Comte among Saint-Simon's enthusiastic and devoted "young collaborators" who had worked together on the "materialistic" journal *Le Producteur*, and he claimed that when "rival talents each claimed to have superiority" and schisms occurred, Comte was the "first to escape."[66] The following day Michel Chevalier, a graduate of the Ecole Polytechnique and editor

[61] Briscoe, "Saint-Simonism," 344.

[62] Claudel to Comte, July 19, 1847, MAC; Lellvyn to Comte, August 3, 1830, MAC.

[63] Jules Lechevalier, who had been a member and had also subscribed to the *Cours*, sent him an autographed copy of his *Lettres sur la division survenue dans l'Association Saint-Simonienne*, which described the schism that occurred on November 19, 1831. See Comte's library at the Maison d'Auguste Comte.

[64] Rapports de la Haute Police to the Président du Conseil des Ministres, August 24, August 26, August 29, September 2, 1831, F^{1a} 353–361^3, AN. On the Saint-Simonians at this time, see Moses, *French Feminism*, 45–50; Manuel, *Prophets of Paris*, 151–93; Charléty, *Saint-Simonisme*, 85–202; Weill, *L'Ecole Saint-Simonienne*, 42–118; d'Allemagne, *Les Saint-Simoniens*, 93–260; Jean Walch, *Michel Chevalier: Economiste Saint-Simonien, 1806–1879* (Paris: J. Vrin, 1975), 6–24.

[65] An example of the enduring ill effects of a Saint-Simonian reputation can be found in the defensive letter written by Michel Chevalier to Guizot, November 17, 1850, Guizot Papers, 42 AP 151, item 12, AN.

[66] Armand Marrast, "Le Saint-Simonisme," *La Tribune politique et littéraire*, January 2, 1832, 4.

of the well-respected *Le Globe: Journal de la religion Saint-Simonienne,*[67] wrote an article ridiculing Marrast for failing to understand the Saint-Simonian conception of history. He repeated d'Eichthal's argument that Comte had simply remained "behind" the group owing to his "inability to follow the march of progress."[68] In his response, published in *Le Globe*, Marrast angrily explained that the concept of history developed by Enfantin, Bazard, and Comte was an incomprehensible "patchwork" because each man had a different way of formulating it.[69]

No longer able to bear being associated with a group whose intellectual capabilities he and others scorned, Comte decided to join in the debate. With great bitterness, he wrote letters to both Marrast and Chevalier, which were published in their respective periodicals.[70] He insisted that he had never belonged to the Saint-Simonian sect and that he had broken completely with Saint-Simon and his disciples because they had grown increasingly religious. This simplistic, not completely forthright explanation arose from his desire to stress that from the beginning of his career, he had considered religious ideas to be the "chief obstacles" to intellectual and social progress. Moreover, he maintained that although he had influenced their "philosophical and political education," the Saint-Simonians – the "supreme priests" – were the ones who had remained behind, especially because of their intellectual inferiority and their refusal to devote themselves to the "long and difficult preliminary studies" of the sciences: "It is much simpler and quicker to give oneself up to vague utopias in which no scientific condition intervenes to halt the growth of an unchained imagination."[71] Under their "pope-king" Enfantin, they had abdicated their "intellectual and moral

---

[67] *Le Globe* had become the organ of the Saint-Simonians in October 1830.

[68] Michel Chevalier, "France," *Le Globe: Journal de la religion Saint-Simonienne*, January 3, 1832, 3.

[69] Marrast to Chevalier, *Le Globe*, January 5, 1832, 18.

[70] Comte to Marrast, January 7, 1832, *La Tribune*, January 10, 1832, 2; Comte to Chevalier, January 5, 1832, *Le Globe*, January 13, 1832, 49–50. Comte was very aware of Marrast's activities as a prominent leftist because he was an important member of the Société des Amis du Peuple and his name was frequently mentioned in the brochures that Comte received. Marrast had also taught in late 1828 at the Athénée, where he denounced romanticism and eclecticism. Thus in his letter to him, Comte was careful to flatter him for his republicanism and his attack on the "sophist" Cousin. Marrast responded favorably. When he published Comte's letter to him in *La Tribune*, he appended a note threatening to publish Comte's letter to Chevalier if it was not printed by *Le Globe*. See Comte to Marrast, January 7, 1832, *CG*, 1:231; "Relations d'Auguste Comte avec Armand Marrast," ed. Pierre Laffitte, *RO* 10 (March 1, 1883): 168. In his Bibliothèque Superflue, Comte had a brochure entitled *Procès des Fusils. Gisquet. Plaintes en Diffamation de MM Casimir Périer et Soult, Ministres du Roi contre M. Armand Marrast. Rédacteur en Chef de la Tribune* (Paris, 1831).

[71] Comte to Chevalier, January 5, 1832, *CG*, 1:228–30.

individuality" and set up the "most complete despotism" imaginable.[72] Sarcastically alluding to Enfantin, Comte added that writing "three or four sacramental epigraphs" and "some verbose homily" was certainly a "very attractive" way to become a "great man" and a "model of virtue" venerated by a "rather numerous circle." Comte jealously claimed to prefer the esteem of a "very small number of eminent minds" even if it meant that he had to live in "misery."[73] In effect, he was proclaiming his own martyrdom to the lonely cause of science.

Angered by Comte's "sarcasms," Chevalier published a caustic reply in *Le Globe*, reminding him that he was tied to the Saint-Simonians because they were all disciples of the same great thinker. Again, Comte was attacked for not being innovative. Just as Comte had blamed the Saint-Simonians for stealing his positive ideas, Chevalier reproached him for appropriating the principles of Saint-Simon, the man who had "loved" him "like a son." Even the *Plan* was only the development of Saint-Simon's *Lettre d'un habitant de Genève à ses contemporains*. Hoping to shame him into glorifying Saint-Simon, Chevalier appended a note from d'Eichthal, who declared that despite his new allegiance to the Saint-Simonians, he was still very attached to his former master Comte. In Chevalier's eyes, Comte's scientific capacities were twisted by a "dream of irreligion and pride." Declaring that Comte could never appreciate the Saint-Simonian religion because he loved no one but himself and was in turn loved by no one, Chevalier goaded him about his solitary, unhappy life and painted a strikingly accurate description of his psychological state. Unable to carry on normal human relationships, Comte was disdainful, bored, unjust, and paranoid. He offended the very people whom he had hoped to make his disciples. The Saint-Simonians had desired his association because they knew he could help "humanity." But keeping himself closed to the fellowship of men, Comte had refused to deal with them. Consequently, he remained ineffectual.[74]

Chevalier's letter only increased Comte's hatred for Saint-Simon and the Saint-Simonians. Preoccupied by their success, he carefully noted their activities and acquired their main works for his library.[75]

---

[72] Comte to Marrast, January 7, 1832, *CG*, 1:232, 234.

[73] Comte to Chevalier, January 5, 1832, *CG*, 1:230.

[74] Réponse de Chevalier, *Le Globe*, January 13, 1832, 50.

[75] Comte's library at the Maison d'Auguste Comte contains not only the 1830 edition of the *Doctrines de Saint-Simon: Exposition, première année 1829* but also two other key documents that were published in 1832: *Religion Saint-Simonienne. Morale. Réunion générale de la famille. Enseignements du père suprème. Les Trois Familles* (which included the teachings of Enfantin) and the two volumes of *Religion Saint-Simonienne. Receuil de prédications*. In the 1840s or

In fact, the Saint-Simonians perhaps influenced Comte more than they ever thought possible. He would not forget their having criticized him for not paying enough attention to the sentiments and to the role of the beaux arts in developing the affections. Although he claimed that he would "never" become involved in the "fabrication of a new religion, and especially a miserable parody of Catholicism," he would eventually take the same direction they had.[76] He too would recognize that throughout the ages mankind had become increasingly religious. Their concept of a future religion of love directed by a supreme priest and based on the family, the nation, and humanity would also not be lost on him.[77] The Saint-Simonians had already even referred to this religion as the *"religion of humanity."*[78] Other Saint-Simonian ideas that later found their place in Comte's system were the need to liberate both women and workers and the picture of woman as primarily a sympathetic creature who complemented the priest.[79] In a way, then, the Saint-Simonians proved to be right: Comte had remained "behind"; it would take him almost twenty years to realize the full importance of religion in the organization of society. However, he always remained faithful to his original idea of the separation of powers, which the Saint-Simonians felt was only a provisional, medieval institution that had to be eliminated to allow for the triumph of spiritual authority.[80] Most important, he never wavered in his initial principle that God had to be eliminated in the new society.

JOB APPLICATIONS AT LEADING INSTITUTIONS

The jealousy and bitterness that characterized Comte's state of mind in the early 1830s was nourished not only by the success of Cousin and the Saint-Simonians but by that of his friends from the Ecole Polytechnique, Félix Savary and Gabriel Lamé, who were appointed

---

1850s, Comte bought a book called *Littérateurs français* and carefully marked the passages referring to Saint-Simon's *Introduction aux travaux scientifiques du XIXe siècle* as an "enormous *bottle of ink* whose purely scientific part is worth nothing." This part, the author said, was abandoned by Saint-Simon, who did not feel that he was "mature" enough to complete it. Even after twenty years, Comte still evidently derived satisfaction from the thought that he had surpassed his old mentor. See Un Homme de Rien, *Galerie des contemporains illustres: Littérateurs français* (Paris, n.d.), 50.

[76] Comte to Marrast, January 7, 1832, *CG*, 1:233.

[77] *Doctrine de Saint-Simon, première année 1829*, 27, 358.

[78] *Religion Saint-Simonienne. Receuil de prédications*, 2 vols. (Paris, 1832), 2:64.

[79] Ibid., 1:123–54, 2:325–30.

[80] *Religion Saint-Simonienne. Morale. Réunion générale de la famille. Enseignements du père suprême. Les Trois Familles* (Paris, 1832), 76.

professors there respectively in 1831 and 1832.[81] When Comte heard that Savary was going to apply for one of the most prestigious posts in the Academy of Sciences, that of permanent secretary, he was dumbfounded. Now thirty-four and increasingly fearful of the financial consequences of his way of life, Comte lamented to Blainville in June 1832 that it was "cruelly sad for me to watch a crowd of my comrades, who are generally regarded (and even by themselves) as my inferiors, reach brilliant scientific positions." He could not "in conscience" silently consent to let himself be ranked as their inferior nor could he bear being "condemned to the sterile condition of a sort of scientific worker hired by entrepreneurs of instruction."[82] Undaunted by the Academy's cool reception the year before and convinced that he had as much right to the secretarial post as his friend, Comte decided to apply for it and asked Blainville to support him. Since the secretary was almost always a famous Academician or at least an eminent scientist, Comte's desire must have appeared extremely presumptuous. The post went, in fact, to Flourens, who had once told Comte that he admired his fundamental opuscule.

Despite this failure, Comte did have some success six months later. In the winter of 1832, the administration of the Ecole Polytechnique was seeking an assistant for Gustave-Gaspard Coriolis, the répétiteur for Navier's course in analysis and mechanics.[83] A répétiteur was the teaching assistant who tutored students needing help; he explained the professor's lessons and gave them weekly and annual oral examinations on their work. The post often led to a professorship at the school.[84] With some difficulty, Gondinet persuaded Comte to ask Navier to present his candidacy.[85] Navier agreed but, knowing Comte well, begged him not to feel demoralized by this "subordinate position."[86]

On December 24, Comte was given official notification of his

[81] After Arago replaced Fourier as perpetual secretary of the Academy of Sciences, Savary, who had been in the class behind Comte at the Ecole Polytechnique, took Arago's place as professor of geodesy at the school in March 1831. A year later, Comte's good friend Lamé was named professor of physics. See Dossier of Arago in the Archives of the Academy of Sciences; Roger Hahn, "Arago, Dominique François Jean," in *Dictionary of Scientific Biography*, ed. Gillispie; Dossiers of Lamé, Savary, and Arago, EP; Meeting of March 25, 1831, Registre: Procès-Verbal du Conseil d'Instruction, vol. 7, EP.

[82] Comte to Blainville, June 21, 1832, *CG*, 1:238.

[83] See the minutes of the meeting of November 30, 1832, Registre: Procès-Verbal du Conseil d'Instruction, vol. 7, EP; Dossier of Coriolis, EP.

[84] M. P. Crosland, "The Development of a Professional Career in Science in France," in *The Emergence of Science in Western Europe*, ed. Crosland (London: Macmillan Press, 1975), 150–1.

[85] Gondinet to Comte, n.d., written to Comte at rue des Francs-Bourgeois, MAC.

[86] Navier to Comte, December 11, 1832, MAC.

appointment as adjunct *répétiteur*; he was to tutor some of Navier's second-year students three mornings a week. Despite the modesty of the position, he was now attached to the institution that had profoundly marked his existence and philosophy and had never ceased to be the object of his loyalty, if not his affections. Moreover, in a regime that admired titles and positions, being on the Ecole Polytechnique's teaching staff could only help his chances to propagate his philosophy and enhance his scholarly reputation.

Although the salary was only twelve hundred francs a year, Comte was happy that at least his material life had changed for the better.[87] But confirming Navier's intuition, he generally abhorred this "most subaltern" position, which he insisted he should have obtained sixteen years before.[88] Not satisfied with being a mere assistant to an assistant and tired of giving five or six lessons a day, he continued to pursue his campaign for a "fixed and suitable position" that his ambitious wife had encouraged him to undertake several months before.[89]

Comte wanted to have an impact on the development of academic disciplines. He contended that the time had come to conceptualize and teach the philosophy and history of the sciences as "true knowledge." Since he believed that he, the generalist, was most suited to realize this new idea, he asked Guizot in late October 1832 to establish a chair for him in the history of sciences at the prestigious Collège de France.[90] For months, Guizot evaded Comte, who wrote him increasingly angry letters reminding him of his "legal duty" to see him.[91] Finally, Guizot tersely answered that he had discussed Comte's case with several respectable persons and had decided to adjourn "all measures on that account."[92]

[87] Navier to Comte, December 11, 1832, MAC; Dulong to Comte, December 24, 1832, MAC; Perronier to Comte, September 8, 1837, MAC; Lonchampt, *Précis*, 52–3; "Auguste Comte: Répétiteur d'Analyse et de Mécanique à l'Ecole Polytechnique," ed. Pierre Laffitte, *RO*, n.s., 1 (1890): 272. Laffitte's article contains some of Comte's notes on the examinations that he gave. Gouhier is mistaken when he suggests that Comte became a full *répétiteur* in 1832. Gouhier, *Vie*, 145. Comte did not obtain the post of *répétiteur titulaire* until November 1838. See Comte's dossier, EP. The dossier adds that Comte was named "adjoint aux répétiteurs d'analyse et de mécanique" by the minister of war on December 22, 1832. The minutes of the meetings of the Conseil d'Instruction are missing from December 1832 to March 1833.

[88] *Cours*, 2:471.

[89] Comte to Guizot, March 30, 1833, *CG*, 1:245. See also Lonchampt, *Précis*, 54.

[90] Comte to Guizot, October 29, 1832, *CG*, 1:407; Anatole France, "Le Positivisme au Collège de France," *Le Temps*, February 7, 1892.

[91] Comte to Guizot, May 6, 1833, *CG*, 1:248. The original can be found in Guizot Papers, 42 AP 277, AN.

[92] Guizot to Comte, May 3, 9, 1833, in "De la fondation de la Chaire d'Histoire générale des sciences au Collège de France," ed. Pierre Laffitte, *RO*, 2d. ser., 16 (September 1, 1892):

Comte sought to avenge his humiliation by airing the subject publicly.[93] In the fall of 1833, his letter to Guizot of October 29, 1832, was published in Armand Marrast's *Le Tribune* and in Armand Carrel's *Le National*.[94] (A vociferous opponent of the government and the editor of the most influential Parisian newspaper at the time, Carrel had been Thierry's secretary and a writer for *Le Producteur*.)[95] In the explanatory note accompanying his letter, Comte denounced Guizot for not challenging the traditional domination of the history of philosophy – "the minute study of the reveries and aberrations of man throughout the centuries." A tool of the "sophists and rhetoricians" surrounding him, Guizot had merely consolidated the theological regime in public education and resurrected a "legal congregation of political metaphysicians" – the Academy of Moral and Political Sciences.[96]

Guizot took his revenge in his memoirs. He said that when he was creating new chairs at the Collège de France and elsewhere, numerous "ambitious scholars," including Auguste Comte, came to see him. Guizot sought to deny that they had been friends: "I did not know him at all and had never even heard anyone talk about

197–9. See also Guizot to Comte, October 30, 1832, MAC; Comte to Guizot, April 16, 1833, Guizot Papers, 42 AP 277, AN (this letter is not published in *CG*). In addition, see the rough draft of the latter and the note attached to it, Guizot Papers, 42 AP 277, AN. Guizot was actually busy forcing through the nomination of Pellegrino Rossi to replace J. B. Say as professor of political economy at the Collège de France. On Rossi, see the Administrateur du Collège Royal de France to the Ministre de l'Instruction Publique, July 22, 1833; Charles Comte to the Ministre de l'Instruction Publique, August 10, 1833, F[17] 13556, AN; Rosanvallon, *Le Moment Guizot*, 45n1.

[93] *Cours*, 2:472.

[94] See "Note sur la création d'une chaire D'HISTOIRE GENERALE DES SCIENCES PHYSIQUES ET MATHEMATIQUES au Collège de France," *La Tribune*, October 7, 1833, 3; Comte, "L'Observation de l'auteur de cette note," attached to his letter to Guizot of October 29, 1832, *Le National*, October 8, 1833, 3–4. The article is published in *CG*, 1:406–9. Comte also tried unsuccessfully to have his article published by *Le Temps*, an opposition journal. See Nestor Urbain to Comte, May 3, 1833, September 24 and 26, 1833, MAC. For background on *Le Temps* and *Le National*, see Pinkney, *Revolution of 1830*, 88, 93; Ledré, "La Presse nationale," 97–8; Angus McLaren, "Culture and Politics during the July Monarchy: The case of the *National*," *Journal of European Studies* 10, part 2 (June 1980): 93.

[95] Des Granges, *Presse littéraire*, 169; Perreux, *Sociétés secretes*, 15; Louis Blanc, *Revolution française: Histoire de dix ans, 1830–1840*, 5 vols. (Paris, 1841–4), 3:111–12, 161–2.

[96] Comte, "L'Observation de l'auteur de cette note," 4. In the *Cours*, Comte denounced the Academy for excluding him. (His comments on the "Société de l'Histoire de France," which had been established by Guizot to publish historical works, were no less acerbic.) Curiously, however, Comte sent the Academy of Moral and Political Sciences volumes of his *Cours* in 1839 and 1842. See *Cours*, 2:638, and the letters acknowledging their receipt sent by the Académie des Sciences Morales et Politiques to Comte, August 10, 1839, and September 10, 1842, MAC.

him."[97] Neglecting to point out that he had been very interested in Comte's doctrine approximately ten years before, Guizot added:

He [Comte] explained to me in a heavy and confused manner his views on man, society, civilization, religion, philosophy, and history. He was a simple, honest man, who was profoundly convinced of his ideas and devoted to them; modest in appearance, although prodigiously proud, . . . [he] sincerely believed himself called to open a new era for the human mind and for human societies. In listening to him, I had some trouble not expressing aloud my astonishment that such a vigorous mind was limited to the point of not even glimpsing the nature or the significance of the facts that he manipulated or the questions that he settled . . . his sincerity, his devotion, and his blindness inspired in me this sad respect that hides itself in silence.

Although Guizot found Comte to be a moral man "in spite of himself," he felt that Comte's ideas were "immoral" and reflected the "condition of mathematical materialism." Even if he had judged it "appropriate" to create the chair, he "would certainly not have thought one moment about giving it to him."[98] In sum, Guizot was loath to admit any embarrassing connection with such a dangerous man.

After Littré challenged him, Guizot rectified his account in volume 6 of his memoirs, published in 1864. He claimed that he had involuntarily forgotten that Comte had visited him several times before 1830. This was Guizot's only concession to the offended positivists. He went on to complain that Comte wished to replace "God-made man" by "man-made God," that he mutilated "humanity and history" in the strangest manner, and that he was a narrow-minded egotist who had no appreciation of the "great problems" or doubts preoccupying the human mind.[99] Aghast at his idea of founding morality on the sciences, Guizot, like many of their contemporaries, considered Comte a materialist and a danger to society.

FRICTION WITH HIS FAMILY AND WIFE

In the early 1830s, reports of the difficulty of Comte's character came from other sources besides Guizot.[100] Comte's problems with

---

[97] Guizot, *Mémoires*, 3:126. Also see Littré's and Valat's objections to this omission. Littré, *Auguste Comte*, 201–2; Valat, "Auguste Comte," 2:241–3; Valat, "Document historique sur Guizot et Aug. Comte," 15–17.

[98] Guizot, *Mémoires*, 3:126.   [99] Ibid., 6:350, esp. 350n1.

[100] See "Illisible" (signed "Comrade") to Comte, March 1831, MAC; Harel (treasurer of the Société Phrénologique) to Comte, December 31, 1831, MAC.

his family and his wife also reemerged. Although praise for his attacks on the Saint-Simonians had pleased Rosalie Boyer, she became more insistent about his defending "with the same zeal our holy Religion."[101] When a cholera epidemic struck Paris and almost thirteen thousand people died in the month of April alone, she again insulted him by inviting him to escape to Montpellier without Massin.[102] She may have been reluctant to welcome Caroline because Louis Massin, "covered with scabies," had reappeared several times since 1830 in Montpellier and "everywhere" in the area, boasting about being Louis Comte's brother-in-law, sullying his name, harassing him in his office, and perhaps seeking to blackmail him. Exasperated, Boyer begged her son to do all he could to "have him shut away."[103] Louis Massin's demented behavior makes his accusations about his daughter even more dubious.

Comte was more shocked, however, by his own mother's "scandalous" conduct. Complaining bitterly to his father, he said that he could not imagine "how a person as *religious* as my mother" could be so "*immoral*" as to invite him to Montpellier without Caroline. "I especially congratulate myself on not being in the least religious, if it is to such a *morality* that religion must lead in practice. . . . Am I finally a married man for you or not?" Tired of writing letters that were only superficial "sanitary bulletins," Comte threatened to cut off all relations with his family if they continued to treat his wife with such "blind" hatred and "stubborn animosity." After all, he said, she had never hurt him and meant to him more than "any other being in the world."[104]

Despite this implication of marital bliss, the problems between Comte and Massin grew worse. In March 1833 Comte told Blainville that his "interior affairs" were "still in the same sad state" and that the most he could hope for was the "sad tranquillity of isolation."[105] Hearing rumors of a "complete disunion," Issalène, who had alienated Comte's mother when he refused to support her plans for a separation in 1826, analyzed the tension in their relationship:

---

[101] Rosalie Boyer to Comte, March 5, 1832, "Lettres de Rosalie Boyer (Suite)," ed. Laffitte, 62.

[102] Jardin and Tudesq, *Notables*, 1:131; Rosalie Boyer to Comte, April 3 and 24, 1832, "Lettres de Rosalie Boyer (Suite)," ed. Laffitte, 64–66. Comte was concerned enough to procure a copy of Broussais's *Le Choléra morbus épidémique, observé et traité selon la méthode physiologique*.

[103] Rosalie Boyer to Comte, December 5, 1831, "Lettres de Rosalie Boyer (Suite)," ed. Laffitte, 58. Curiously, the words "with all my soul" are in the original letter in the MAC but are omitted in the *Revue occidentale*. See also Rosalie Boyer to Comte, October 16, 1830, "Lettres de Rosalie Boyer (Suite)," ed. Laffitte, 111.

[104] Comte to Louis Comte, May 17, 1832, *CG*, 1:235–7.

[105] Comte to Blainville, March 17, 1833, *CG*, 1:244.

You both make each other unhappy by jealousy, animosity, and violent flare-ups of anger. . . . I do not understand very well how you, a philosopher, a scholar, and [a man] absorbed by occupations of an altogether serious type, have the time to be jealous and quarrel with your wife. I scarcely understand any better how she, whose frail and delicate health demands attention and caution, could torment herself gratuitously and make herself unhappy morally and physically while aggravating her sufferings and getting excited about vain fancies. . . . I would like to see you united since I gave myself a lot of trouble for that [end] with your family. . . . You wanted it, both of you.[106]

Yet Issalène's wish for their reconciliation was not to be granted. Apparently, Massin had suffered a severe attack of smallpox in late 1832.[107] Her poor physical condition made her more demanding and querulous at a time when Comte wanted nothing more than to work in peace. As a result, he was not very sympathetic to her needs. According to Comte, she demanded a separation, which seems to have started in mid-March and ended in early August.[108] Finding no fault with himself, he maintained that the cause of their separation was simply his wife's "unrestrained need for liberty" and her "vexation," which arose from "not being able to command arbitrarily." Despite the fact that he said he was much less affected by this separation than by the first one in 1826, Comte boasted later that he was "good enough" to ask her to come back.[109]

Massin went to Valence for ten days in July, and the letters she wrote to him make one wonder if there was a complete estrangement at all. Despite the fact that she addressed Comte with the formal *vous* and goaded him by telling him stories of handsome soldiers, she was affectionate. She began her first letter with these words: "Having arrived today in Lyons, I was concerned first about writing you a note since I did not doubt that you were worried and I feared that you were sad. . . . You must admit that it is fine on my part to write to you without hope that you will do as much in return."[110] All she could discuss was her loneliness, "ennui," and unhappiness: "I feel always in arriving (wherever it may be) the same pang of anguish, the same sadness, the same disgust at what I

---

[106] Issalène to Comte, December 7, 1833, MAC.

[107] Although Comte told Issalène that his wife's illness left her unscarred, he contradicted himself in the *Testament*, stating that it left her disfigured for life. He insinuated with some relish that her physical deformity prevented her from ever inviting rich lovers to their house again. Issalène to Comte, January 5, 1833, MAC; *Testament*, 36^f.

[108] Caroline Massin to Comte, August 3, 1833, MAC.

[109] Comte to Littré, April 28, 1851, *CG*, 6:63.

[110] Caroline Massin to Comte, July 22, 1833, MAC.

find.''[111] These signs of deep melancholy, which Issalène reproached her for in 1828, indicate that she may have had the same tendencies toward depression as Comte himself.[112] In fact, her letters suggest that she made the voyage to improve her mental and physical health, not to break away definitively from her husband.[113] This was not the first time that one of them took a separate vacation. She went south alone again in 1834.[114] Several years before, Comte had left by himself for Normandy, where he spent some time with Blainville.[115] She evidently expected that Comte was repeating this trip: "If I had not been persuaded that you would make the trip to Normandy, I would not have left." Although Comte maintained that she "disdainfully" granted his request that she return, it actually seems that Massin was still responsive to his needs and decided to go back to him of her own accord because she wanted to be "close" to him, worried about his sitting all alone in Paris, and knew that he could not join her because of the expense.[116]

Comte was not completely indifferent to her either. Shortly after her return, her mother died on August 29, 1833, and Massin was the one who needed help. She began to experience severe nervous crises, which terrified and worried everyone. So as not to aggravate her weak condition, Comte took care of everything and even asked his friends, such as Menjaud, for advice on how to handle the situation.[117] Again one cannot help noticing a sincere concern on the part of Comte and his friends for a woman who was supposedly evil.

COMTE'S PAPER ON THE COSMOGONY OF LAPLACE

A continuing source of marital strain during these years was financial problems, which were particularly severe in 1834. For various

---

[111] Caroline Massin to Comte, July 26, 1833, MAC.

[112] Issalène to Comte, June 22, 1828, MAC. When in May 1834 she was again traveling alone to this area, memories of the state in which she found herself in 1833 haunted her. Caroline Massin to Comte, May 20, 1834, MAC.

[113] Caroline Massin to Comte, August 2, 1833, MAC.

[114] Caroline Massin to Comte, May 8, May 20, 1834, MAC.

[115] Comte to Blainville, September 11 and 15, 1831, CG, 1:224–5.

[116] Caroline Massin to Comte, August 2, 1833, MAC. See also Comte to Littré, April 28, 1851, CG, 6:63.

[117] Death certificate of Marie Anne Baudelot, August 29, 1833, Archives de Paris. See also the death announcement of Marie-Anne Massin in a packet entitled "Faire-Part de Décès," MAC; Menjaud to Comte, September 8, 1833, MAC; Mme Vourran to Comte, October 30, 1833, MAC; *Testament*, 36^f; funeral bill of August 1833, signed Zome (?), packet of "Factures-P," MAC.

reasons, the Comtes were forced to change apartments twice, which cost a great deal of money.[118] After Vieillard and Issalène refused to lend Comte any money, he was finally reduced to asking a favorite student for a thousand francs.[119]

Recognizing the superiority of her husband, Massin urged him to try once more to become an Academician.[120] It was clear that Comte needed to improve his standing among scholars by presenting more recent material, especially because he was known mainly for the articles he had composed before the *Cours*.[121] Moreover, his works were not sufficiently specialized to meet the approval of the French Academy. According to Maurice Crosland, the Academy of Sciences in the early nineteenth century was forming a new image of a true scientist as a person who advanced the frontiers of a narrow field of knowledge and publicized his contributions through research publications.[122] Recognizing the new criteria, Massin thus had Blainville persuade Comte to present the Academy with a scientific essay, which he completed in October 1834.

After some angry exchanges with Gay-Lussac and Blainville over the long delay, Comte was allowed to present his "Premier Mémoire sur la cosmogénie positive" during the Academy's meetings of January 19 and 26, 1835.[123] The essay sought to present mathematical evidence verifying the imprecise hypothesis about the formation of the solar system that was first proposed by William Herschel and

---

[118] The Comtes moved from 159, rue Saint-Jacques to 9, rue d'Enfer in the spring. (The rue d'Enfer is now the avenue Denfert-Rochereau.) Some problems forced them to give notice of their departure only several months later. See Quittances de Loyer, MAC.

[119] Vieillard to Comte, August 29, 1834; Issalène to Comte, September 16, 1834, MAC; Comte to Blainville, October 29, 1835, *CG*, 1:254. Because the student, Louis de Troismonts, was at a loss as to how to proceed, his mother, who had carried on a two-year correspondence with Comte on the love life and mathematical progress of her son, was pleased "to be useful" to Comte and paid him the sum in November. Madame de Troismonts to Comte, November 15, 1834, MAC. See also Louis de Troismonts to Comte, September 5, 1834, MAC.

[120] Lonchampt, *Précis*, 53.

[121] The *Biographie universelle et portative des contemporains* had included him among the eminent personages of the period in its editions of 1830 and 1834. However, the article on Comte did not mention the *Cours* but praised his earlier writings, such as his *Plan des travaux scientifiques nécessaires pour réorganiser la société* and his articles for *Le Producteur*. See A. Rabbe and Vieilh de Boisjoslin, eds., *Biographie universelle et portative des contemporains ou Dictionnaire historique des hommes vivants et des hommes morts depuis 1788 jusqu'à nos jours*, 4 vols. (Paris, 1830), 1:1052; Rabbe, Vieihl de Boisjoslin, and Saint Preuve, *Biographie universelle*, 1:1052.

[122] Maurice Crosland, *Science under Control: The French Academy of Sciences, 1795–1914* (Cambridge: Cambridge University Press, 1992), 30.

[123] Académie Royale des Sciences, *Procès-Verbaux et rapports des séances de l'Académie Royale des Sciences* (Paris, 1922), 10.1: 649, 653. This can be found in the Archives of the Academy of Sciences. See also Gay-Lussac to Comte, December 19, 1834, MAC; Comte to Blainville, January 17, 1835, *CG*, 1:249.

then developed by Laplace.[124] The "nebular hypothesis" was very controversial because it offered a scientific explanation of creation and thus seemed to deny that the universe came about through a sudden, complete act of God.[125] What is most remarkable about this paper is that it plainly embarrassed Comte, who even announced that he had decided only after a "long hesitation" to present his premature and "incomplete" ideas.[126] He appeared to anticipate the criticisms that would follow by declaring that he was not, after all, a specialist.

The indifference of the Academy to Comte's essay is suggested by the fact that Arago, Savary, and Libri, who were assigned to examine the paper formally, never bothered to make their report.[127] Comte later accused them of negligence.[128] In the provinces, Charles Person, a member of the Académie Royale des Sciences, Belles-Lettres, et Arts of Rouen, reviewed Comte's work for his colleagues. Pointing out that Comte's theory rested on a vicious circle, or "paralogism," Person maintained that it was as if Comte had said, *"I assume, in my formula, that the sun turns like a planet, and I find, after having done the calculation, that it turns like a planet."*[129] Similar criticisms were later voiced by British astronomers: John Pringle Nichol, Adam Sedgwick (in the *Edinburgh Review*), and William Herschel's illustrious son John (in the *Athenaeum*).[130] When Mill offered to make a rebuttal, Comte deterred him, confirming that his paper was full of "logical vices" and "scientific weaknesses."[131] Nevertheless, he

---

[124] Comte's "Premier Mémoire sur la cosmogénie positive" is reproduced in *Ecrits*, 585–608.

[125] Silvan S. Schweber, "Auguste Comte and the Nebular Hypothesis," in *In the Presence of the Past: Essays in Honor of Frank Manuel*, ed. Richard T. Bienvenu and Mordechai Feingold (Dordrecht: Kluwer, 1991), 145.

[126] *Ecrits*, 586, 607.

[127] Arago was the head of this committee. Académie des Sciences, *Procès-Verbaux*, 10: 653, Archives of the Academy of Sciences. On the first page of Comte's manuscript of his "Mémoire" is a written statement regarding the examination by Savary, Arago, and Libri: "Il n'y a pas lieu à rapport." The manuscript is in the dossier on Comte, Archives of the Academy of Sciences.

[128] Comte to Mill, August 8, 1845, *CG*, 3:89.

[129] Person, quoted in "Classe des Sciences. Rapport fait par M. Des Alleurs, Secrétaire Perpétuel de la Classe des Sciences," in *Précis analytique des travaux de l'Académie Royale des Sciences, Belles-Lettres, et Arts de Rouen pendant l'année 1835* (Rouen, 1835), 51, 52. This book can be found in the Bibliothèque de l'Institut de France. In his article on Comte, Joseph Bertrand also said that Comte's work rested on a "paralogism." Bertrand, "Souvenirs académiques," 537.

[130] See comments by the astronomer J. P. Nichol, *The Positive Philosophy of Auguste Comte*, ed. and trans. Harriet Martineau, 2 vols. (London: J. Chapman, 1853), 1:212–213n. See also Mill to Comte, July 18, 1845, *CG*, 3:399.

[131] Comte to Mill, August 8, 1845, *CG*, 3:87–8. Comte had already suppressed the mathematical demonstration of Laplace's hypothesis in his astronomy course in 1839 or 1840 and intended to eliminate it in the second edition of his *Cours*. He never asked the Academy for his original manuscript, which remained in its archives.

again reacted to the criticisms as if they were personal attacks. After this halfhearted attempt to present his own research, Comte never even began the second paper that he had announced he would write. By 1836 he had resigned himself to the "impossibility" of his ever being admitted to the Academy.[132]

SUCCESS AT THE ATHÉNÉE AND WITH VOLUME 2 OF THE *COURS*

Around the time that Comte decided to write the essay, he was invited by the Athénée to give another course in 1835. Perhaps acceding to their demands for variety, he did not lecture on positive philosophy but on the subject that was most on his mind at the moment – astronomy. He discussed the "true spirit" of astronomical research and showed the philosophical, that is, antitheological, implications of cosmological laws.[133] He was giving, in effect, an enlarged version of what was the first part of the second volume of the *Cours*.

The most salient fact of Comte's life in the early 1830s was that he apparently did not devote any attention at all to his great work. Personal problems and other activities, such as the foundation of the Association Polytechnique, the preparation of his lectures on astronomy, the organization of his course for the Athénée, and his various efforts to acquire a position at the Academy and Ecole Polytechnique, took up a great deal of energy and exhausted him. The events of 1830 also destroyed his momentum. More important, they hurt the publishing trade, which had already been experiencing severe financial difficulties since the economic depression of 1828. Its market seemed to disappear as people became more interested in politics than in reading and had less money to spend on books. One of the publishing houses financially ruined by the Revolution of 1830 was Rouen frères, which annulled its contract with Comte on February 20, 1833. His frustration was matched by that of his readers.[134]

---

[132] Comte to Paul Dubois, September 25, 1835, *CG*, 1:273.

[133] Athénée, *Programme pour l'an 1835* (Paris, 1835), 4–5; Laffitte seemed ignorant of this course because he made no mention of it in his articles on Comte and the Athénée. Laffitte, "L'Athénée"; "Documents pour servir à l'histoire de l'Athénée," ed. Pierre Laffitte, *RO*, 2d ser., 9 (September 1894), 261–74.

[134] "De la publication du *Cours de philosophie positive*," ed. Laffitte, 259; Second contract between Comte and Rouen frères, February 20, 1833, MAC; James Smith Allen, *Popular French Romanticism: Authors, Readers, and Books in the Nineteenth Century* (Syracuse, N.Y.: Syracuse University Press, 1981), 191–4; idem, "Le Commerce du livre romantique à Paris (1820–1843)," *Revue française d'histoire du livre*, n.s., 26 (1980): 72–3; Paul Dupont, *Histoire de l'imprimerie*, 2 vols. (Paris, 1854), 1:322; Felkay, "Libraire de l'époque

To find another publisher in this period of crisis was particularly difficult, since the *Cours* had been anything but a financial success. Of the first volume, only 170 copies out of a 1,000 had been sold by 1833.[135] However, in November 1832, almost two years after the first volume's appearance, Comte's old friend Mellet persuaded his own publisher, the eminent Bachelier, to undertake the task.[136] Bachelier had strong ties to the scientific community and published the works of Lacroix, Lamé, Charles Dupin, Poinsot, Poisson, and Arago as well as the journals, yearbooks, and textbooks of the Ecole Polytechnique.[137] In fact, Bachelier decided to publish the *Cours* because Comte was a former student of the Ecole Polytechnique and Mellet had convinced him that "several hundred" graduates would buy it.[138] After persuading Bachelier to publish three more volumes, each containing eighteen lessons, and to send them free of charge to his subscribers of 1830, Comte signed the contract with him on March 3, 1833.[139]

Although Comte was pleased that he had acquired another publisher, Bachelier did not find time to print the *Cours* until more than a year later. Finally, in July 1834, Bachelier requested the whole manuscript, or at least a good part of it.[140] Comte, however, had not written one word, despite the fact that four years had passed since he had composed the first volume. He liked to believe that he was unable to motivate himself to write if he knew his material would not be published immediately.[141] Nevertheless, he waited another two months after Bachelier's request before he resumed his task. He still had enormous difficulties finding the necessary "energy."[142]

romantique," 44–63; Charles Fournerat (Judge at the Tribunal de la Seine) to Comte, October 1, 1833, in "Relations d'Auguste Comte avec Charles Fournerat," ed. Pierre Laffitte, *RO* 14 (May 1, 1885): 328.

[135] Second Contract between Comte and Rouen frères, February 20, 1833, MAC.

[136] Bachelier was publishing Mellet's brochure on railroads. See Dossier on Bachelier, F[18] 44, AN; Mellet to Comte, November 20, [1832], in "De la publication du *Cours de philosophie positive*," ed. Laffitte, 261.

[137] Dossier on Bachelier, F[18] 44, AN.

[138] Mellet to Comte, November 30, [1832], in "De la publication du *Cours de philosophie positive: M. Mellet*," ed. Pierre Laffitte, *RO* 20 (January 1, 1888): 25; Statement of Bachelier, n.d., MAC.

[139] Bachelier declared that he would print a thousand copies of each volume together with an additional fifty for Comte and the journals. Moreover, Comte would be paid three thousand francs, half of which he would receive by October 1833 and the rest as the volumes were sold. Comte received his first fifteen hundred francs on April 5, 1833. Contract between Comte and Bachelier, March 3, 1833, MAC. See Comte's note of April 5, 1833, on ibid.

[140] Bachelier to Comte, July 9, 1834, MAC.   [141] *Cours*, 2:465.

[142] Comte to Valat, May 10,1840, *CG*, 1:337.

Finally prodded by Bachelier's deadline, he began on September 1, 1834, to write the lessons of the *Cours* that dealt with astronomy. As he knew this subject extremely well and could always write quickly once he started, it took him only five weeks to complete it.[143] Bachelier must have thought that the volume was finished at this point because he declared to the government on October 21 that he was printing the second volume. Undaunted by Bachelier's demands, Comte took a two-month vacation from the *Cours* before beginning to compose the part on physics, which he apparently found more difficult because he did not know physics as well as mathematics and astronomy.[144] After another two-month interruption, he finally completed the section in late March – a week after Bachelier's final ultimatum.[145] Instead of the nine lessons that he had originally planned to devote to physics, he was able after four months to write only seven.[146] With sixteen lessons instead of eighteen, the second volume appeared in April 1835.[147] Comte planned to publish the third volume a year later.[148]

THE TRIAL OF 1835

Like the first volume, the second appeared in the midst of a political crisis, which involved Comte and proved to be a distracting factor both for him and for his potential audience. In April 1834 Paris and other cities experienced a series of revolts directed largely by the Société des Droits de l'Homme. With more than three thousand members in Paris alone, this republican organization continued the work of the earlier Société des Amis du Peuple but laid more emphasis on social programs and tended to be more radical and Jacobin.

[143] Writing almost every day, Comte finished lessons 19 through 27 on October 5, approximately two months before he began giving his course on the same subject at the Athénée. Lesson 27 was enlarged on October 10 into the paper he presented to the Academy.

[144] When various people encouraged Comte several years before to try to acquire the chair of physics at the Ecole Polytechnique, he had declined since he did not feel he could fulfill his functions "with a high distinction." Comte to Navier, July 23, 1835, *CG*, 1:252.

[145] "Tableau du nombre de jours et de feuilles employées par Aug. Comte, dans la rédaction de ses ouvrages," in "Matériaux pour servir à la biographie d'Auguste Comte: Du temps dans le travail intellectuel," ed. Pierre Laffitte, *RO*, 2d ser., 16 (November 1, 1892): 436–7. Comte's original record concerning the hours that he worked can be found in the Maison d'Auguste Comte. See also Bachelier to Comte, March 17, 1835, MAC.

[146] See the "Tableau synoptique du *Cours de philosophie positive* de M. Auguste Comte," *Cours de philosophie positive* (1830–42), 1:ix.

[147] Arnaud, "Chronologie," in Introduction to Comte, *Catéchisme*, 9.

[148] Comte to Barbot de Chement, January 15, 1836, *CG*, 1:255.

Comte knew two of its most active leaders: Armand Marrast, who favored open resistance to the state, and Armand Carrel, a more moderate member who tried to attract the bourgeoisie.[149]

After arresting about two thousand people for their part in the April riots, the government decided in February 1835 to bring 121 of them to trial. Among these *accusés d'avril* was Armand Marrast, who was arrested for having used the *Tribune* to incite revolution. Marrast and his colleagues decided that since their trial by the Chamber of Peers would put them in the limelight, they should use the opportunity to publicize their cause. Therefore, instead of using lawyers, the *accusés* called on more than a hundred prominent republicans to defend them. This defense committee consisted of some of France's most eminent men, such as Philippe Buonarotti, Adolphe Blanqui, François-Vincent Raspail, Lamennais, and Armand Barbès. Among their number were also former Saint-Simonian sympathizers, including Hippolyte Carnot, Jean Reynaud, Henri Baud, Edouard Charton, Laurent d'Ardèche, and Pierre Leroux.[150]

Marrast asked Carrel and Comte to defend him. Encouraged by Massin, who dreamed of his playing an important role in the republican movement, Comte accepted. He and Marrast had become close friends since the 1832 dispute with the Saint-Simonians, when Comte's letter proclaiming his republicanism had increased the famous journalist's respect for him. Also, Comte liked him because he had written a scathing critique of Cousin in 1828.[151]

Comte and the other members of the defense committee met for weeks to prepare their case for republicanism. The sessions were stormy, marked by personality clashes and grave political disagreements.[152] After one such session, Comte turned sadly to Lamennais

---

[149] H. A. C. Collingham, *The July Monarchy: A Political History of France, 1830–1848*, ed. R. S. Alexander (London: Longman Group, 1988), 137–9, 157–61; Tchernoff, *Parti républicain*, 150–6, 272–3, 292, 296, 301, 304.

[150] Jean Reynaud, who had taken sides against Enfantin, became friendly with Comte, for at one point during this period Comte begged him to tell him what was going on at a meeting at Blanqui's that he could not attend. David Albert Griffiths, *Jean Reynaud: Encyclopédiste de l'époque romantique* (Paris: Marcel Rivière, 1965), 67; Reynaud to Comte, n.d., MAC. See also [Henri-Joseph] Gisquet, *Mémoires*, 4 vols. (Paris, 1840), 3:394; Blanc, *Révolution française*, 4:403, 585; Jeannine Charon-Bordas, *Archives Nationales. Cours des Pairs. Procès Politiques*, vol. 2, *La Monarchie de Juillet: 1830–1835* (Paris: Archives Nationales, 1983), 17; "Relations d'Auguste Comte avec Armand Marrast," ed. Laffitte, 168, 173; Warrant for Marrast's arrest, April 13, 1834, in dossier of Marrast, CC 590, AN; Tchernoff, *Parti Républicain*, 302n3; Les Membres du Comité de défense to Comte, March 1835, in "Matériaux pour servir à la biographie d'Auguste Comte: Relations avec Armand Marrast (Suite et fin)," ed. Pierre Laffitte, *RO* 10 (May 1, 1883): 299–302.

[151] Lonchampt, *Précis*, 55; Comte to Marrast, January 7, 1832, *CG*, 1:231.

[152] Blanc, *Révolution française*, 4:590.

and said, "Oh, well, Sir, we are really in full anarchy."[153] Lamennais sorrowfully agreed.

The republicans' plans proved futile because the government had no intention of allowing the trial to be exploited. On March 20, 1835, the president of the Chamber of Peers decreed that the defenders would not be allowed to appear in court because they were not lawyers and, furthermore, the court would appoint lawyers for the accused men. Marrast and two other *accusés* were sent to protest this decision. When the huge trial opened on May 5, the *accusés* repeated their demand to choose their own counsel, and thirteen of the most active defenders asked to be recognized, including Voyer d'Argenson, Carrel, Reynaud, Lamennais, Ulysse Trélat, Raspail, Carnot, and Leroux. The fact that Comte's name did not appear on this list suggests that he did not play a leading part in the "republican congress."[154]

When the government persisted in barring the defenders from the trial, about thirty of them, led by the distinguished lawyer Michel de Bourges, wrote the accused an inflammatory letter, encouraging them to persevere in defense of the people's rights: "The infamy of the judge makes for the glory of the accused."[155] Bourges and his colleagues signed the names of all the other defenders without their knowledge and had it published in *La Tribune* and Raspail's journal, *Le Réformateur*, on May 11, 1835.

The letter quickly became an object of scandal and controversy. When the president of the Chamber of Peers demanded that those who had signed it appear before that body to face the charge of having insulted it, Comte was one of the first to object to what Michel de Bourges had done.[156] He had already experienced the adverse effects of government action when he was dismissed from the Ecole Polytechnique in 1816 and did not want to incur its wrath again for something he did not do. Though accused of cowardice, Carrel agreed with Comte and proposed that the defenders disavow the letter and let Michel de Bourges and Trélat take responsibility for it. On May 29, the day the trial regarding this letter opened, the defenders therefore repudiated the letter. The Chamber evidently

---

[153] Comte, quoted in "Variétés: Relations d'Auguste Comte avec l'abbé de Lamennais," ed. Laffitte, 246.

[154] Blanc, *Révolution française*, 4: vi, 404, 555, 590–3; Les Membres du Comité de défense to Comte, March 1835, in "Relations avec Armand Marrast (Suite et fin)," ed. Laffitte, 298–9; Perreux, *Sociétés secrètes*, 334, 337; *Histoire impartiale du procès des accusés d'avril* (Paris, 1835), 3.

[155] Letter reprinted in Blanc, *Révolution française*, 4:413.

[156] "Relations d'Auguste Comte avec Armand Marrast," ed. Laffitte, 174; Perreux, *Sociétés secrètes*, 344; Blanc, *Révolution française*, 4:426–8.

did not consider Comte a threat, for it had not bothered to gather information on him as it had on many of the others. Because it did not know even his address, he was not notified to appear at the trial. Worried, Comte wrote the president of the Chamber that he had "neither signed nor published this incriminating letter nor contributed in any manner to its publication."[157] He was told to be in court June 1. On that day he quickly denied participating in the affair.[158] The following day, Michel de Bourges, Trélat, and seven other men were sentenced to prison and fined. Comte was found "not guilty."[159]

Comte's activities after this point are unknown. On August 4 he received a letter from Marrast begging him to attend a meeting of the defenders the next day. The letter gives the impression, however, that Comte had lost interest in the whole affair.[160] At the trial's end in January 1836, Marrast found himself condemned to one of the strictest sentences: deportation. When he returned to France, he and Comte were on bad terms. Possibly because of political differences, Comte distrusted him.

As for the others associated with these events, Comte kept up with Armand Carrel until he was killed in a duel in July 1836, a tragedy that greatly saddened him.[161] According to Deroisin, the legendary conspirator Blanqui became acquainted with Comte during the trial and was so fascinated by his ideas that he proposed his legislative candidacy as a philosopher in 1848.[162] Later Comte would carry on a short correspondence with another of the conspirators that he met at this time – Barbès.

Comte's respect for Lamennais lessened as the priest abandoned his ultramontane position and sought to reconcile Catholicism with nineteenth-century liberalism and democracy. The *Paroles d'un croyant*, which appeared in April 1834, marked Lamennais's conversion to leftist politics.[163] While on vacation in Lyons, Massin read it. Laughing at Lamennais's ideas, she wrote to Comte, "Moreover, revolt is preached openly. Provided that it puts the cross on its banner, it is sure of absolution." Unable to forgive Lamennais for

---

[157] Comte to the President of the Chamber of Peers, May 1835, *CG*, 1:250. See also Report on trial, May 29, 1835, dossier 3, CC 670, AN.

[158] Letter of Convocation, with an addition by the bailiff, to Comte, June 1, 1835, MAC. See also Report on trial, June 1, 1835, dossier 4, CC 670, AN.

[159] Report on trial, June 2, 1835, dossier 5, CC 670, AN.

[160] Marrast to Comte, June 1, 1835, in "Relations d'Auguste Comte avec Armand Marrast," ed. Laffitte, 185–6.

[161] Carrel to Comte, June 6, 1836, MAC. For the rest of his life, Comte kept the issue of *Le National* that described the circumstances of the fatal duel and contained his friend's obituary. See the obituary of Armand Carrel, *Le National*, July 26, 1836.

[162] Deroisin, *Notes sur Auguste Comte*, 30.

[163] Latreille and Rémond, *Histoire du catholicisme*, 290.

having tried to put Comte in a religious institution during his illness, she gloated that the priest was "finished": "There is no great harm in that according to me. Amen."[164] Apparently agreeing with her, Comte found Lamennais's change of position abnormal, illogical, and even dishonest. Whereas he had previously considered Lamennais an "estimable adversary," he complained during the trial that he was a "disgraceful ally."[165] He accused him of becoming "blindly hostile to the positive doctrine as he degenerated into a revolutionary ranter."[166] Preferring to fight Catholicism in its pure, archaic state, Comte could not imagine the possibility that this religion might evolve. Like Pope Gregory XVI, he thus condemned Lamennais's efforts to adapt Catholicism to the modern age.[167]

After the trial, the republicans became demoralized, and the movement was taken over by extremists seeking violent revolution.[168] Comte maintained some interest in their activities but admitted his "personal influence" was "very remote."[169] He found the republicans to be a "mob," a group of "show-offs."[170] He disapproved of their disunity, their unrealistic and vague goals, their lengthy debates, and their preoccupation with political power and insurrection. Their opponents seemed at times to have a "more real, although very narrow, tendency toward truly progressive measures." Since he believed that the transformation of society would come about by the establishment of a spiritual power and the proper education of the people, he felt, in short, little kinship with the republicans, who were led by "discredited" procurators and lawyers.[171] He found himself as alienated from the world of politics as he did from the world of science, for both had rejected his ideas.

CAREER POSSIBILITIES AT THE ECOLE POLYTECHNIQUE

Comte's desire not to appear a troublemaker during the tumultuous trial may be partly explained by his academic ambitions. Notwithstanding his failure in 1831 to become professor of analysis and mechanics at the Ecole Polytechnique, he still hoped to advance in that institution.

Comte was not having any trouble being reelected adjunct *répétiteur*

---

[164] Caroline Massin to Auguste Comte, May 8, 1834, MAC.
[165] Comte to Mill, May 15, 1845, *CG*, 3:10.   [166] *Système*, vol. 4, "Appendice," iv.
[167] Latreille and Rémond, *Histoire du catholicisme*, 290. See also Comte's condemnation of Lamennais's "scandalous revolutionary conversion" in *Cours*, 2:613–14.
[168] Tchernoff, *Parti républicain*, 305.
[169] Comte to Mme Auguste Comte, August 27, 1838, *CG*, 1:294.
[170] Ibid.; Comte to Mme Auguste Comte, September 3, 1838, *CG*, 1:297.
[171] Comte to Mme Auguste Comte, September 3, 1838, *CG*, 1:297.

every year. The only criticism was that he was too severe. Although warned in 1834 by the Conseil d'Instruction that his grades were too low, he paid no attention.[172] An opportunity to improve his position appeared in the summer of 1835 when his former teacher and employer Reynaud became sick and required a temporary replacement as admissions examiner to the school.[173] Comte turned for help to his old patron General Bernard, who had come back to Paris. Assuring Comte that he was an illustrious thinker, Bernard recommended him as he "would recommend a brother" to General de Tholozé, head of the Ecole Polytechnique and president of the Conseil d'Instruction.[174] A committee formed of Navier, Claude-Louis Mathieu (the other professor of analysis and mechanics), and Pierre-Louis Dulong (the director of studies) presented to the Conseil d'Instruction a list of five candidates, among whom Comte was number two.[175] The position was finally awarded to the first candidate, Joseph Liouville, whose "merit and qualifications" were judged superior.[176] "Shocked" that his "rights" to this position had been neglected, Comte protested that he was a better mathematician and teacher than Liouville, whom he likened to his former professor Cauchy – a "detestable professor."[177] Although he prided himself on being devoted to the philosophy of the sciences, not to the various specialties, his ego could not bear the suggestion that he was inferior to another mathematician. Yet in 1839 he would show his respect for Liouville by strongly advising Blainville to support his candidacy to the Academy of Sciences.[178]

Comte was also deeply bitter about Liouville's success because another ill examiner had just been replaced by Comte's good friend

---

[172] In May 1834 the Conseil d'Instruction, comparing the average grades given in Navier's course, found that Coriolis's grades averaged 14.71 (out of 20.00), those of Navier 13.25, and Comte's 9.75. Meeting of May 9, 1834, Registre: Procès-Verbal du Conseil d'Instruction, vol. 7, EP. See also Meetings of October 31, 1834, July 13, 1835, July 1, 1836, and July 11, 1837, Registre: Procès-Verbal du Conseil d'Instruction, vol. 7, EP.

[173] Dossier of Reynaud, EP. Gouhier and Arnaud are mistaken when they say that Comte was trying to become professor of geometry. Gouhier, *Vie*, 146; Arnaud, Note 53, *CG*, 1:410.

[174] Bernard to Comte, July 16, 1835, MAC. See also *Almanach royal pour l'an 1836*, 681; Bernard to Comte, August 1, 1835, MAC.

[175] Meeting of July 17, 1835, Registre: Procès-Verbal du Conseil d'Instruction, vol. 7, EP.

[176] Tholozé to Bernard, July 18, 1835, MAC. See also Comte to Valat, November 21, 1837, *CG*, 1:284; Dossier of Liouville, EP.

[177] Comte to Navier, July 23, 1835, *CG*, 1:252, 253. Cauchy was Comte's professor of analysis in late 1815 to April 1816. When Comte once asked him for a job, Cauchy, who was known as a conservative, tried to prove the existence of God by showing that the series of prime numbers was infinite. This episode may have been the source of Comte's aversion for this famous scientist. See "Relations d'Auguste Comte avec Poinsot," ed. Laffitte, 148n1; Laffitte's comment in "Bibliothèque d'Auguste Comte," ed. Laffitte, 119.

[178] Comte to Blainville, May 29, 1839, *CG*, 1:307.

Duhamel, who, like Liouville, was a regular *répétiteur*. The Conseil d'Instruction had never even considered Comte for this job, although it was similar to the one he was being considered for two days later. It seems that Comte had told Navier of his desire to be nominated, but that he had never specifically asked him to propose him or made a formal declaration.[179] Dulong apologized, claiming he was unaware that Comte wanted the position, a comment that must have seemed disingenuous.[180]

Comte felt betrayed. He concluded that his attack on conventional doctrines in the *Cours* had made him "ardent enemies" who were acting against him in the school administration.[181] To get revenge, he threatened to write a polemic against the scientists. But Navier tried to dissuade him, explaining that his failure was due to the fact that he had never made a contribution to the "progress of the sciences by new research." His dissertation on cosmogony was insufficient, and his *Cours* did not represent purely scientific work. Furthermore, Navier warned Comte that he was not "gifted naturally in the spirit of intrigue and coterie" and therefore needed the help of others to advance his cause. Writing against scientists would only harm him.[182] Although more than ever convinced that the "spirit of intrigue and coterie" had pushed people to vote against him, Comte agreed to wait until he experienced another "injustice." Claiming that his actions would not be motivated by "inordinate ambition" or "envy," he further declared that he had a right to judge the scientists since he was devoted to elevating their "social condition" and knew "the strong and the weak in science and among scientists better than any other person today." Rebuffed by the Academy and the Ecole Polytechnique, he was already in 1835 relishing the thought of the "grave reverberation" that his judgments would produce.[183]

Comte experienced more setbacks in 1836. When Reynaud became sick again in the summer, the Conseil d'Instruction voted once again to replace him with Liouville, who had just become *docteur ès sciences mathématiques* and was successfully developing his own mathematics journal.[184] Comte also lost his "only really zealous friend" on the Conseil d'Instruction when Navier died in July.[185]

---

[179] Navier to Comte, July 14, 1835, MAC.   [180] Dulong to Comte, July 17, 1835, MAC.
[181] Comte to Navier, July 23, 1835, *CG*, 1:252. See also Barbot de Chement to Laffitte, July 27, 1886, MAC.
[182] Navier to Comte, July 20, 1835, MAC.   [183] Comte to Navier, July 23, 1835, *CG*, 1:251.
[184] Meeting of July 8, 1836, Registre: Procès-Verbal du Conseil d'Instruction, vol. 7, EP. On Liouville's career, see Jesper Lutzen, *Joseph Liouville, 1809–1882: Master of Pure and Applied Mathematics* (Berlin: Springer, 1990), 43.
[185] Comte to Dulong, August 31, 1836, *CG*, 1:257.

Navier's death, however, left the chair in analysis and mechanics vacant. As Navier's teaching assistant, Comte decided to apply for the position, although he assumed that Coriolis, who was the regular *répétiteur* for the analysis course, would be appointed. Yet when Coriolis declined to apply because of poor health, Comte felt he had a good chance of winning.[186] His chief rivals were Liouville and especially his good friend Duhamel. At this point, the latter had published a *Cours d'analyse* and a *Cours de mécanique*, read several papers at the Academy of Sciences, and worked since 1830 as a *répétiteur* at the Ecole Polytechnique.[187] Comte highly respected him; he had encouraged Blainville to vote for his admission to the Academy of Sciences in 1833 and praised him in the *Cours* for making the only substantial contribution to Fourier's theories.[188]

Knowing his rivals' stature and more aware of the rules of the game, which he had neglected in 1835, Comte tried to gather support for his case by writing a series of letters to prominent people, such as Dulong, Coriolis, Flourens, Poinsot, General Bernard, Blainville, and Paul Dubois. (Dubois had helped found the original *Le Globe* and had recently started teaching literature at the Ecole Polytechnique.)[189]

In a letter to General de Tholozé, Comte explained that philosophical works, such as his, were a far better guarantee of didactic talent than academic studies, whose specialization was incompatible with the "spirit of the whole" that had to dominate in "rational instruction."[190] It must be said that Comte had not endeared himself to the general. Several months before, when the general had invited Comte to dinner, Comte had caustically declined, claiming the general had deliberately left him out of his earlier soirées. Tholozé had angrily denied it.[191]

[186] Meeting of October 7, Registre: Procès-Verbal du Conseil d'Instruction, vol. 7, EP; *Almanach royal pour l'an 1836*, 682; Comte to Poinsot, September 18, 1836, *CG*, 1:261; Comte to Blainville, September 24, 1836, *CG*, 1:271.

[187] Dossier of Duhamel, EP.

[188] Comte to Blainville, March 17, 1833, *CG*, 1:243; Comte to Poinsot, September 18, 1836, *CG*, 1:261; "Carrière Polytechnique d'Auguste Comte," ed. Laffitte, 319; *Cours*, 1:511.

[189] Comte to Coriolis, September 13, 1836, *CG*, 1:258; Comte to Flourens, September 18, 1836, *CG*, 1:259–60; Comte to Poinsot, September 18, 1836, *CG*, 1:260–3; Comte to the Président de l'Académie des Sciences, September 19, 1836, *CG*, 1:263–6; Comte to General Bernard, September 20, 1836, *CG*, 1:267–8; Comte to General de Tholozé, September 21 and 23, 1836, *CG*, 1:268–70; Comte to Blainville, September 24, 1836, *CG*, 1:270–2; Comte to Paul Dubois, September 25, 1836, *CG*, 1:272–3. Dubois promised to "weigh" Comte's "rights." Paul Dubois to Comte, September 27, 1836, MAC. On Dubois, see Paul Gerbod, *Paul-François Dubois: Universitaire, journaliste et homme politique* (Paris: C. Klincksieck, 1967), 152.

[190] Comte to General de Tholozé, September 21, 1836, *CG*, 1:269.

[191] Comte to General de Tholozé, January 14, 1836, *CG*, 1:255; Tholozé to Comte, January 15, 1836, MAC.

Comte explained to his old protector Poinsot that the post of adjunct *répétiteur* could never be the "terminating point" of his "ambition" because he wanted the chance to reform the teaching of mathematics at the school. Most important, he could not resign himself to his "miserable" job because it meant he had to give private lessons and work at a preparatory school, the Institut Laville, to supplement his income; teaching five or six hours a day exhausted him. Reminding Poinsot that he had waited twenty years for such an opportunity, Comte demanded that he make up his mind immediately whether he would support him or his other former student Duhamel.[192]

Finally, Comte wrote a long letter to the president of the Academy of Sciences in which he claimed that its members were qualified to judge the merits of scientists, not professors. His own concentration on philosophy had precluded him from making any contributions to the sciences, but twenty years of teaching experience and the *Cours* made him a superior candidate. He also pleaded with the nonmathematicians in the Academy to come to his aid to ensure that he would not be rudely passed over again as he had been in 1831 because of the mathematicians' "prejudices" against him.[193]

To obtain the support of the nonmathematicians, Comte begged Flourens, the permanent secretary, to read this provocative letter aloud to the Academy.[194] When Flourens refused, Comte turned to Poinsot but without success. Dulong finally asked the Academy to listen to it.[195] The letter was also published in the *Journal des débats* and *Le National*, both of which favored Comte's interest in educational reforms and his promotion of grand philosophical ideas.[196] Comte rejoiced that his letter was "very warmly welcomed."[197] And he was further encouraged by the fact that Bernard was now minister of war, for he assumed he would support him.

Despite his energetic campaign, Comte received only two votes during the first round of voting at the Academy of Sciences on October 24, 1836. Duhamel received twenty, while Liouville obtained nineteen. There was one abstention.[198] It seems that only

---

[192] Comte to Poinsot, September 18, 1836, *CG*, 1:262–3.

[193] Comte to the Président de l'Académie des Sciences, September 19, 1836, *CG*, 1:265–6.

[194] Comte to Flourens, September 18, 1836, *CG*, 1:259.

[195] Comte to Poinsot, September 18, 1836, *CG*, 1:262; Comte to Blainville, September 24, 1836, *CG*, 1:271.

[196] "D & G," "Académie des Sciences: Séance du 28 septembre," *Le National*, September 28, 1836, 3; Al. D., Review of meeting of Academy of Sciences of September 19, *Journal des débats*, September 24, 1836, 3.

[197] Comte to Blainville, September 24, 1836, *CG*, 1:271.

[198] *Comptes rendus hebdomadaires des séances de l'Académie des Sciences* 3 (July–December 1836): 488. In making its recommendation to the Academy, the geometry section, composed of Puissant, Biot, Poinsot, Lacroix, Libri, and Ampère, had put Duhamel and Liouville in

Poinsot and the mathematician F. Lacroix voted for Comte.[199] On the second round of voting, Duhamel received twenty-three votes, and Liouville, supported by Poisson and his clique, obtained twenty.[200] In spite of the vote, the Conseil d'Instruction, following the advice of its own special committee, nominated Liouville as the most qualified applicant.[201]

Comte was very bitter that he had failed once again to acquire "his" chair. His outrage intensified several weeks later when the new school year began and he was told to teach analysis because no one had yet been officially appointed to the chair and Coriolis was ill.[202] On November 19 the Conseil d'Instruction was informed that Comte was doing an excellent job and that his lectures were a great success.[203] Comte was delighted. Less than a week later, however, General Bernard went against the school's nomination of Liouville and appointed Duhamel to the position.[204] Besides being scandalous, this decision was a blow to Comte, who now was to become the assistant *répétiteur* for a course run by his good friend. Comte's students were so pleased with his teaching that when Duhamel was

first place and Comte in second. It had thus left the final decision up to the entire Academy, most of whose members did not know how to evaluate mathematicians. Lutzen, *Liouville*, 44.

[199] Noting their similar interests, Lacroix had thanked Comte in 1833 for sending him the first volume of the *Cours* and sent him an autographed copy of his own *Essais sur l'enseignement en général* in 1838. Lacroix to Comte, March 1, 1833, MAC. Perhaps realizing that Comte had no chance of being chosen, Blainville did not return from the country to vote for him. See also Comte to Blainville, September 24, 1836, CG, 1:272.

[200] *Comptes rendus hebdomadaires des séances de l'Académie des Sciences* 3 (July–December 1836): 488; "Carrière Polytechnique d'Auguste Comte," ed. Laffitte, 319, 355–6; Comte to Poinsot, September 18, 1836, CG, 1:261. On Liouville and Poisson, see Lützen, *Liouville*, 35, 43.

[201] Meetings of October 7 and 14, 1836, Registre: Procès-Verbal du Conseil d'Instruction, vol. 7, EP. The members of the committee were Dulong, Mathieu, Savary, Leroy, and Lamé. They recommended Liouville first, then Duhamel, and finally Comte. See also Lützen, *Liouville*, 43–4.

[202] Dulong to Comte, November 6, 1836, MAC; Meeting of November 19, 1836, Registre: Procès-Verbal du Conseil d'Instruction, vol. 7, EP; Duhamel, "Cours d'Analyse," in Registre de l'Instruction, 1836–1837, EP. The dates and contents of Comte's lectures are all listed in this register. A more detailed, slightly modified synopsis of these twenty lessons on differential calculus and its applications was later printed at the end of Comte's *Traité élémentaire de géométrie analytique* in 1843. See "Programme du cours de calcul différentiel," in Auguste Comte, *Traité élémentaire de géométrie analytique* (Paris, 1843) (hereafter, *Traité de géométrie*), 590–5. See also lithographed brochure *Programme du cours de calcul différentiel professé à l'Ecole Polytechnique en 1836 par Mr. Ate. Comte*, MAC.

[203] Meeting of November 19, 1836, Registre: Procès-Verbal du Conseil d'Instruction, vol. 7, EP.

[204] Minister of War to the General of the Ecole Polytechnique, November 24, 1836, in dossier of Duhamel, EP.

ready to take over, they rushed to Arago, the leading member of the Conseil de Perfectionnement, to beg him to let Comte finish the course.[205] But their pleas were in vain. It was also galling that when a school administrator tried to pay Comte four hundred francs for doing such a good job, Bernard, his supposed friend, complained about not having been properly consulted and reduced his compensation to two hundred francs.[206]

It appears that Comte's teaching gift consisted in clarifying mathematics to such an extent that students found it "a hundred times less difficult than before."[207] Dulong was so impressed with Comte's teaching that he diligently followed the lectures Comte gave while substituting for Duhamel.[208] James Hamilton, an Englishman who was one of Comte's private students, described the manner in which Comte gave lessons in 1836:

> Daily as the clock struck eight on the *horloge* of the Luxembourg, . . . the door of my room opened, and then entered a man, short, rather stout, almost what one might call sleek, freshly shaven, without vestige of whisker or moustache. He was invariably dressed in a suit of the most spotless black, as if going to a dinner-party; his white neckcloth was fresh from the laundress's hands, and his hat shining like a racer's coat. He advanced to the arm-chair prepared for him in the centre of the writing-table, laid his hat on the left-hand corner, his snuff-box was deposited on the same side, beside the quire of paper placed in readiness for his use.

Comte did not speak until he began giving the lesson and then carefully guided Hamilton through the problems. At the stroke of nine, he brushed off the "shower of superfluous snuff that had fallen" on his clothes with the "little finger of the right hand" and left "as silently as when he came in." Hamilton said that he did not feel repelled by Comte, although this would have been the normal feeling of a pupil faced with "such a teacher, gliding in and out like a piece of clock-work, without an interchange of any of the gentle courtesies of life." He tried in vain to get beyond Comte's "frigid mask" and the "coldness' of their relations, but gradually the "intellectual giant" won Hamilton's "love."

[205] For a list of the Conseil's members, see Registre: Le Conseil de Perfectionnement, vol. 6, EP. See also Georges Audiffrent, *Centenaire de la fondation de l'Ecole Polytechnique: Auguste Comte, sa plus puissante émanation. Notice sur sa vie et sa doctrine* (Paris, 1894), 41.

[206] General Bernard to M. le Maréchal de Camp, commandant de l'Ecole Polytechnique, February 10, March 18, 1837, Dossier of Comte, EP.

[207] Louis de Troismonts to Comte, September 16, 1833, MAC.

[208] *Cours*, 2:474; "Carrière Polytechnique d'Auguste Comte," ed. Laffitte, 320. Comte often praised Dulong's work. See *Cours*, 1:493, 603.

I could not feel . . . his greatness; but I acquired an interest in the dry science he taught me; and had I continued under his charge I might have become a mathematician. I had been taught to fear, not to revere my masters; if I had a liking for any, it had been in proportion to his laxness; and I now found myself half unconsciously, and quite unaccountably, gliding into a sort of affection for the most unapproachable, the most uncongenial of them all.

Hamilton insisted that this love for Comte did not arise from the "sway of reason" over his mind but "from an instinctive perception of the smothered kindliness which entered so largely into his composition."[209] An opposing view was voiced by the scientist Joseph Bertrand, who was examined for admission to the Ecole Polytechnique by Comte in 1839, became one of his students, and later taught at the school.[210] He claimed that Comte had not studied mathematics since his dismissal from the Ecole Polytechnique, and that he created a minor scandal by teaching the students divergent series, a mathematical subject generally considered a "heresy."[211] When Duhamel contradicted Comte during the first lesson, most students sided with Comte. Although Comte was very proud of his triumphant success, many other professors were furious and did not welcome his future demands for a higher post. An idea of what the administration thought of Comte can be adduced from the comments of General Louis-Pierre-Jean-Mammès Cosseron de Villenoisy, who later wrote this short description of Comte:

We had for him a respect mixed with terror. . . . [W]e feared his coldness and the singularity of the questions that he asked without ever coming to the help of a troubled or intimidated student. Extremely myopic, he kept his head bent over his table, without looking at the board, and we heard only two words leave his mouth: "Erase!" or "That is enough!" He was for us a singular example of mathematical rigor and exactitude, and also of ignorance of real life. Knowing his profound incredulity in matters of faith, we said of him: "Accustomed to formulas, old man COMTE has put GOD in an equation and he has found for him only imaginary roots."[212]

---

[209] James Hamilton, *Personal Recollections of Auguste Comte* (London, 1897), 4–9. This article was originally published in *Chambers' Journal*, June 19, 1858.
[210] See Comte's examination of Bertrand, "Examinations: 1839," MAC.
[211] Bertrand, "Souvenirs académiques," 536.
[212] Villenoisy, "Comte," in *Ecole Polytechnique: Livre du centenaire*, 3:461.

ADMISSIONS EXAMINER

In July 1837 Reynaud finally resigned as admissions examiner, and Comte and a young man named Monferrand were presented as the candidates to fill in for him for the year.[213] Comte was worried not only because Navier had warned him before that Monferrand was a "redoubtable rival"[214] but also because his application to become examiner at the Ecole Saint-Cyr, a prestigious military school, had just been rejected.[215] But thanks to the support of Dulong, who stressed his "merit," Comte was nominated for the post of examiner as compensation for his failure the previous year.[216] General Bernard quickly approved of the decision.[217] The following year, in June 1838, Comte was elected to be the regular admissions examiner.[218] Unfortunately, because of new rules, his appointment as examiner, like that of assistant *répétiteur*, had to be reviewed yearly, a provision that aggravated Comte from the beginning.[219]

His new position brought him another 3,000 francs a year, which, when added to the 1,200 that he was making as assistant *répétiteur*, gave him an annual salary of 4,200 francs.[220] This increased in November 1838, when Comte became a full *répétiteur*, earning 2,000 francs a year.[221] Since 1836, Comte had also been working at the Institut Laville, which paid him 3,000 francs a year to give students daily lessons preparing them for the Ecole Polytechnique and other

[213] The committee who nominated the two candidates was composed of Dulong, Mathieu, and Savary. See Meeting of July 11, 1837, Registre: Procès-Verbal du Conseil d'Instruction, vol. 7, EP.

[214] Navier to Comte, July 20, 1835, MAC.

[215] The director of Saint-Cyr informed Comte that he was not eligible because he taught at a preparatory school. Director of Saint-Cyr to Comte, June 20, 1837, MAC;

[216] Menjaud to Comte, July 11, 1837, MAC; Dulong to Comte, July 12, 1837, MAC; Littré, *Auguste Comte*, 235; Meeting of July 11, Registre: Procès-Verbal du Conseil d'Instruction, vol. 7, EP.

[217] Général Bernard to M. le Maréchal de Camp, Commandant, July 18, 1838, in Dossier of Reynaud, EP.

[218] Dossier of Comte, EP. In the dossier is written the following statement about Comte: "Designated to replace Mr. REYNAUD, Admissions Examiner from July 1, 1836, to July 1, 1837. Named temporary Admissions Examiner by the ministerial decision of July 8, 1838." Also see Bouttier to the Minister of War, June 25, 1838, in Comte's dossier; Général Bernard to M. le Maréchal de Camp, July 18, 1837, in Reynaud's dossier, EP.

[219] Meeting of July 11, 1837, Registre: Procès-Verbal du Conseil d'Instruction, vol. 7, EP; Comte to Valat, November 21, 1837, CG, 1:284.

[220] Peronnier to Comte, September 8, 1837, MAC. Gouhier is mistaken when he suggests that Comte at this time earned two thousand francs a year as a *répétiteur*. Gouhier, *Vie*, 146.

[221] See the official report concerning Comte's pension, 1851, in Comte's dossier, EP.

schools.[222] (Comte disliked the school, for he found it too Catholic and reactionary.)[223] His annual income from these three posts and his private lessons, which often earned him as much as 3,000 francs a year, exceeded 10,000 francs.[224] This was a considerable sum, considering that an average hotel room cost 2 or 3 francs a night, a dinner at a hotel restaurant came to about 4 francs, and a professor at the Ecole Polytechnique usually made 5,000 francs a year, which he supplemented with income from other appointments.[225] Successful academics in the sciences made around 13,000 francs, although major ones made as much as 60,000.[226]

Starting in January 1837, Massin began maintaining two notebooks to keep abreast of expenses. Apparently, she was far more interested in saving than Comte was.[227] One notebook was a day-to-day rough draft; the other followed routine accounting procedures.[228] Extremely detailed, the latter showed monthly expenses as follows: 25 francs for a maid, 150 to 200 francs for food, and 20 francs for laundry. Annual rent varied between 980 and 1,100 francs but went up to 1,600 francs beginning in 1841, when Comte moved to his last apartment at 10, rue Monsieur le Prince.[229] Yet by this time, he earned an additional 500 francs per year giving examinations for the Ecole Royale Forestière. Thus every year the Comtes usually managed to save 1,000 francs. With his money worries over,

---

[222] Adolphe Daguenet to Comte, July 27, 1838, MAC; Comte to Pouzin, October 4, 1839, *CG*, 1:324; lithographed brochure, *Institution Laville: Programme du cours de Mr. Ate. Comte,* 1836, MAC; Comte to Mill, July 22, 1842, *CG*, 2:60.

[223] Comte to Mill, May 16, 1843, *CG*, 2:152.

[224] In 1837 he made 3,230 francs giving private lessons. One of his students was François Delessert's son. See the seven letters from Delessert to Comte and Caroline Massin's formal notebook, "Recettes et dépenses janvier 1837 à décembre 1841," MAC; Comte to Mill, July 22, 1842, *CG*, 2:60.

[225] For information on salaries, see the dossiers of Navier, Bertrand, Chasles, and Savary, EP. Also see the packet containing receipts from Comte's hotels and restaurants, MAC.

[226] Robert Fox, "Science, the University, and the State in Nineteenth-Century France," in *Professions and the French State, 1700–1900*, ed. Gerald L. Geison (Philadelphia: University of Pennsylvania Press, 1984), 85, 129n66.

[227] Comte to Mill, May 16, 1843, *CG*, 2:151; Comte to Blainville, May 28, 1844, *CG*, 2:255; Massin to Comte, December 23, 1842, MAC.

[228] See these two notebooks, MAC. The rough draft is called "Recettes et dépenses janvier 1837 à juillet 1842." (The notebook does not cover all of 1842 because Comte and Massin separated in August.) The notebook that is the final copy is called "Recettes et dépenses janvier 1837 à décembre 1841."

[229] The Comtes lived at 9, rue de Vaugirard from 1835 to 1837; 18, rue des Francs Bourgeois (then near the place Saint-Michel) from 1837 to 1838; and 5, rue d'Ulm from 1838 to 1841. See Contrat de location entre Crapelet et Comte, October 3, 1834, MAC; Contrat de location, January 28, 1837, in packet "A. Bayen, Proprietaire," MAC; Quittances de Loyer, MAC.

Comte now could reduce his private lessons and devote more time to his philosophy.

Comte was one of four examiners required to give approximately one-hour oral tests to candidates throughout France. Once the Parisian students were examined in late July and early August, Comte traveled with his colleague Bourdon until mid-October either to the west and south of France or to the east and north.[230] He had to prepare the questions, grade the 200 to 300 students whom he tested, classify them in order of excellence, and decide whom he would recommend for admission. To help him remember the students' responses and rank them, he devised a peculiar system of notation in English.[231] Bourdon examined and ranked the same boys. The final decision was made by the admissions committee, which usually admitted 125 new students.[232]

Since Comte believed the Ecole Polytechnique was almost a prototype of the spiritual power, choosing its members was to him a vocation that required much devotion.[233] By all accounts, he excelled as an examiner. Even Bertrand, who did not respect him as a professor, admitted that he was a "faultless examiner" and gave tests that were "legendary" and cited as a "model of wisdom and finesse." With great patience and goodwill, Comte would ask questions simple enough for everyone to answer but sufficiently difficult to permit advanced students to display their superiority. Only the best students were able to avoid the traps that Comte "ingeniously" laid for those who thought in a routine fashion.[234] He wrote careful notes about the candidates, which indicate that he believed intelligent thinking to be far more important than the ability to do mechanical calculations.[235] His examination rooms were always full because all types of people, including professors, came to witness the dramatic scenes that he produced. One colonel even followed him to another town to see him perform again.[236]

---

[230] See packet labeled "Examinations: 1841," MAC; Comte to Mill, July 22, 1842, *CG*, 2:57–8.

[231] He established a scale of twenty grades, each of which corresponded to an English expression. "Perfectly" was the highest score, and "extremely badly" the lowest. Some of the other grades that fell in between were "enough well," "near about well," "indifferently," and "extremely weakly." See the examination packets in MAC, especially "Examinations: 1839."

[232] Tholozé to Comte, November 9, 1837, MAC.

[233] Comte to Mill, July 22, 1842, *CG*, 2:58.

[234] Bertrand, "Souvenirs académiques," 536, 537.

[235] See Comte's comments on Harle, Pellicot, and Kreyselle, "Examinations: 1837," MAC; Deroisin, *Notes sur Auguste Comte*, 32n1.

[236] Joseph Bertrand, Review of *Auguste Comte, fondateur du positivisme, sa vie, sa doctrine*, by R. P. Gruber, trans. P. Mazoyer, *Journal des savants* (August 1892): 688; Comte to Mme Auguste Comte, September 13, 1837, *CG*, 1:278.

Comte's position gave him a great deal of personal satisfaction, for he became convinced that his influence on the educational system was greater than that of a simple professor. After only four months, he felt that he had begun to alter the "miserably artful and narrow habits of the scholastic routine" encouraged by the mediocre schools.[237] He hoped to increase his influence, and soon, Bertrand noted, mathematics teachers throughout France used Comte's questions in their classes to train their students to think less mechanically so that they could resolve the unusual problems their future examiner would give them.[238]

Comte enjoyed much prestige and power as an examiner for one of the most illustrious schools in France, and he now found himself cultivated and courted by all those who wanted to influence the destiny of a young man important to them in some way. Dozens of prominent people wrote him on behalf of favorite candidates. Even Marrast did not let his republican principles prevent him from asking Comte twice to do him a favor.[239] Yet Comte's "impartiality" was well known, and these requests did not seem to affect him.[240]

Now that he had resolved his material problems and was more self-confident, he began to think about renewing old friendships. In the eleven years since his bout with madness, his paranoia had disrupted his life and prevented him from forming close personal ties. He had broken with his old friends because he felt they were not interested enough in what he was doing.[241] Yet now he recognized that the "ties of these first years of youth" were the most important because he had experienced the "sad fragility of the majority of other liaisons whose origin could not go back to a trust that is as pure and innocent."[242] Although Valat was away when he passed through Bordeaux in 1837, they finally renewed their correspondence. (Valat had passed the *agrégation* and was teaching at a secondary school there.)[243] Valat did not hesitate to describe the pain Comte had caused him:

[237] Comte to Valat, November 21, 1837, *CG*, 1:286.

[238] Bertrand, Review of Gruber, *Auguste Comte*, 688.

[239] Marrast to Comte, October 21, 1841, and July 22, 1843, MAC. Pierre Laffitte was not completely honest in omitting the first letter and the relevant section of the second letter from the collection of letters that he published between Comte and Marrast in "Relations d'Auguste Comte avec Armand Marrast" and "Relations avec Armand Marrast (Suite et fin)," ed. Laffitte.

[240] Laville to Comte, October 2, 1839, MAC. See also Baron Bourgeois to Comte, September 4, 1839, MAC; Comte's examination of Bourgeois, "Examinations: 1839," MAC.

[241] Valat to Comte, September 28, 1839, MAC.

[242] Comte to Valat, November 21, 1837, *CG*, 1:284.

[243] Comte to Valat, September 28, 1837, *CG*, 1:279; Arnaud, Note 99, *CG*, 1:414; Valat to Comte, November 4, 1837, and September 28, 1839, MAC.

I was unable to console myself for no longer receiving your personal secrets [*confidences*]. I did not miss the scholar because I was sure that he was fulfilling his destiny; I pitied the friend whom I challenged to find a soul that responded to his and knew how to appreciate him.[244]

Comte also occasionally corresponded with d'Eichthal, who sent him the books he had written. But Comte was careful to keep his distance, reminding him of the "disappointments" he had caused him.[245]

At first, the two-month circuit of the provinces suited Comte. He enjoyed the museums and monuments as well as the warm welcome he received at the homes of former students and friends. Yet despite its pleasant aspects, Comte found his job too demanding. During the school year, he was able to squeeze work on the *Cours* into his few moments of free time, but in the summer, when he was traveling to give examinations, this was impossible.[246] With no time or energy left for the *Cours*, he soon decided that his position was a "horrible burden."[247] Accustomed to going to bed at nine o'clock, he also hated the sleepless nights spent journeying from town to town.[248] To escape dull local notables, he began to eat simple meals alone at his hotels, which in his usual systematic fashion he rated to avoid returning to the bad ones.[249] When in 1837 he was back in the Midi after a ten-year absence, he was offended by the abundance of priests, the "extremely crude patois" of the people, and the "noisy strolling about." He wrote to his wife: "All in all, the more one sees the provinces, the less one regrets the exclusive supremacy of Paris."[250]

A VISIT TO MONTPELLIER

Comte's mother had died in March 1837 without having seen him in ten years, and he found her death to be a "cruel" loss – a loss that

---

[244] Valat to Comte, February 14, 1838, MAC. See also Valat's letter of September 28, 1839, which describes his past efforts to renew his friendship with Comte and his bitterness.

[245] Comte to G. d'Eichthal, August 5, 1839, *CG*, 1:308. See also Comte to G. d'Eichthal, October 23, 1836, *CG*, 1:275.

[246] Comte to Mme Auguste Comte, September 13, 1837, *CG*, 1:277; Comte to Valat, November 21, 1837, *CG*, 1:286; Comte to General Vaillant, August 19, 1839, *CG*, 1:311.

[247] Comte to Mme Auguste Comte, September 18, 1838, *CG*, 1:300.

[248] Comte to Mme Auguste Comte, September 13, 1837, *CG*, 1:278; Comte to Mme Auguste Comte, August 27, 1838, *CG*, 1:294.

[249] See packet of bills from hotels and restaurants, MAC; Comte to Mme Auguste Comte, September 13, October 6, 1837, and August 27, 1838, *CG*, 1:278, 280, 294.

[250] Comte to Mme Auguste Comte, October 6, 1837, *CG*, 1:280-1.

made him reflect on his own mortality.[251] Seeking a reconciliation with the remainder of his family, he told them he would take advantage of his first examination circuit to visit them for a few days. When he heard the news, Comte's father was overjoyed that he would at last get to see his son before he died.[252]

Yet just as Louis Comte was often angry that his son failed to mention his sister, Comte was furious that his father did not write a word about Massin.[253] When Comte threatened to stay in a hotel, his father relented and told him he would welcome Massin to his home if she came to Montpellier.[254] Still dissatisfied, Comte consulted with Massin, who gave him permission to go without her: "You can be very sure that it is . . . a great pleasure for me that you can be with your family."[255] Yet, in reality, the prospect of their "possessing" her husband for "several days" made her extremely jealous.[256] When he was there, she wrote him several letters reminding him of the "great pain" she felt at his being with the "people who have done me so much harm and would do more if they could."[257] To exact a measure of revenge, she asked Comte to announce that she was coming to Montpellier the following year and to make sure that everyone in the town gossiped about it. Comte was impressed with her "truly feminine ingenuity."[258]

Comte's visit to Montpellier was not as pleasant as he had hoped. He enjoyed giving his examinations in his old *lycée* but was bored by the "very pronounced intellectual and moral apathy" of the Montpelliérains. At home, he found "all the good and bad passions

[251] Comte to Valat, November 21, 1837, *CG*, 1:286. See also Louis Comte to Auguste Comte, March 12, April 10, 1837, "Lettres de Louis Comte," ed. Laffitte, 14, 15.

[252] Louis Comte to Auguste Comte, July 22, 1837, "Lettres de Louis Comte," ed. Laffitte, 16.

[253] Louis Comte to Auguste Comte, March 12, 1837, "Lettres de Louis Comte," ed. Laffitte, 14; Comte to Mme Auguste Comte, September 20, 1837, *CG*, 1:278. Massin later complained to Comte that three times since 1826 Louis Comte had refused to allow her to visit because of his hatred for her. Caroline Massin to Comte, April 20, late October, 1843, MAC.

[254] Comte to Mme Auguste Comte, September 30, 1837, *CG*, 1:279. See also Comte to Mme Auguste Comte, October 13, 1837, *CG*, 1:283; Louis Comte to Auguste Comte, October 1, 1837, "Lettres de Louis Comte," ed. Laffitte, 16–17.

[255] Caroline Massin to Comte, September 23, 1837, MAC. See also Comte to Mme Auguste Comte, September 20, 1837, *CG*, 1:278; Caroline Massin to Comte, October 20, 1837, MAC. Although Alix Comte accused her sister-in-law of preventing a reconciliation, Caroline had begged her husband for years to visit his parents and was in fact very proud of her kindness in this respect. Caroline Massin to Comte, September 13, 1839, MAC.

[256] Caroline Massin to Comte, September 23, 1837, MAC.

[257] Caroline Massin to Comte, October 11, 1837, MAC. See also Caroline Massin to Comte, October 20, 1837, MAC.

[258] Comte to Mme Auguste Comte, September 30, 1837, *CG*, 1:279.

considerably weakened," lamented the "deplorable state of infirmity" of his almost blind and toothless father, and deeply missed his mother, whom he now perceived to have been the "most passionate" member of the family.[259] When he left, he hoped all would be well between him and his family, but he wanted a "year of proofs" to convince himself of the "sincerity" of their affections for him – and for Caroline, who still felt they were trying to get rid of her, that is, "butcher" her.[260]

THE BITTERSWEET NATURE OF HIS MARRIAGE IN 1837

The letters exchanged by Comte and Massin during his examination tours demonstrate their mutual affection. While he would reproach her for not writing, she would complain about her boredom and loneliness without him and beg him to be warmer in his letters. Although he repeatedly asked her to accompany him, she felt it was a waste of money. Upon returning to Paris, he usually gave her a gift of several hundred francs to make amends for his absence.[261]

Despite these marks of devotion, the letters also reveal signs of strain. In addressing each other, they had again moved from the informal *tu* to the formal *vous*, as in 1833. A constantly recurring word in their correspondence was "reproach." After Comte reacted to Massin's complaints about her rheumatism by saying he hoped she was feeling healthy, she retorted, "I do not care for formulas [of politeness]; you know that very well."[262] In turn, when she reminded him that sleepless nights on the road were dangerous to his health, Comte responded in an annoyed manner, prompting her to write, "You must want to reproach me very much, judging by what such a singular occasion furnished you." Although Comte and his disciples accused her of making him overwork, she actually told him that she did not want him to ruin himself just to improve their material life:

> I believe and I feel that a change of position at this price would cost too much. I think you need to take care of yourself because you worked [hard when you were] young, and if I am wrong and you feel

[259] Comte to Mme Auguste Comte, October 13, 1837, *CG*, 1:282–3; Comte to Valat, November 21, 1837, *CG*, 1:286.

[260] Comte to Mme Auguste Comte, October 20, 1837, *CG*, 1:283; Caroline Massin to Comte, October 10, 1837, MAC.

[261] Comte to Mme Auguste Comte, September 13, October 6, October 20, 1837, *CG*, 1:277–8, 281, 283; Caroline Massin to Comte, September 23, September 28, September 30, October 10, 1837, MAC; "Examinations: 1837," MAC.

[262] Caroline Massin to Comte, September 15, 1837, MAC.

that you have nothing to fear from a great deal of stimulation, it is not a reason to write me harsh words that I do not deserve.

She concluded sadly:

If everything that comes from me is so painful to you, I will limit myself to telling you from now on that the house is in its place and that I am not dead. . . . I desire infinitely your letters, and when I have them, they pain me.[263]

Tensions rose in November when Massin had a mysterious quarrel with one of Auguste's friends, Gondinet. Massin accused him of acting against her husband's interests and insisted on an apology. Gondinet refused, claiming that he had been trying to do Comte a favor and that the fuss was over "bagatelles." He was tired of being accused of "treachery" and treated like a "domestic."[264] Comte was furious, especially because Gondinet had complained about Massin to Menjaud. After receiving an insulting letter from Comte, Gondinet justified his actions by citing Massin's "strange behavior" and "outrageous words." Upset about the threats to the "long relationship of friendship and intimacy" he had had with Comte, he warned him, "Henceforth I will be with you what you will be with me."[265] Once again Comte had come to his wife's defense, but in so doing broke off one of his few close relationships.

However, Comte resented Massin's lack of gratitude for his loyal support and accused her of not sufficiently valuing his work. Toward the end of his life, he claimed that in 1837 Massin had "dared" to declare before two witnesses that she found Armand Marrast to be superior to him because he, unlike her husband, combined the practical spirit and the theoretical spirit.[266] Massin vehemently denied this accusation:

Is it possible that you had the courage to say that I put Mr. A. Marrast above you? So much as to call me "The Ember of Hell"? I do not put anyone above you, not even next to you. Is it possible that you believe me so stupid? Oh God, what a blow to the head![267]

Comte apparently magnified a statement made by Massin in September 13, 1839. At that time, Comte wanted to know her opinion as to whether thinkers or men of action were more important in regenerating society, perhaps because of some argument he had had

---

[263] Caroline Massin to Comte, September 23, 1837, MAC.
[264] Gondinet to Comte, n.d., MAC.   [265] Gondinet to Comte, November 8, 1837, MAC.
[266] Comte to Littré, April 28, 1851, *CG*, 6:65. See also Laffitte's comments in "Notes sur la seconde du mercredi 2 juin 1847" in packet entitled "Notes sur les confessions annuelles d'Auguste Comte," MAC.
[267] Caroline Massin to Comte, August 1849, MAC.

with Marrast over this issue. She evasively replied that men of action and men of reason were equals and had to work together. She added, "If the thinker believes he is the stronger, he must prove it by putting aside this spirit of antagonism. It is up to the supreme one to be generous."[268] In the next breath, she expressed her regret that her plan to reconcile Marrast and Comte had failed. This suggested that her husband, the thinker, had not been generous and that Marrast was supreme. This taunt truly rankled Comte, who was evidently jealous of her relationship with Marrast.[269] It did not escape his notice that she always took up the "cudgels" on Marrast's behalf.[270]

It is possible that a basic cause of tension between Comte and Massin was their different ideas as to what direction he should take intellectually. Comte claimed to prefer devoting himself to the *Cours* even if it failed to bring him instant fame. He rather fancied the role of martyr, expecting someday, nevertheless, to attain great influence and prestige. But Caroline argued that if he worked for two or three years on more specialized works, he would have the high position he deserved and she would have the "pleasure of seeing the eccentric man beat them [the people who derided him]."[271] When Comte accused his wife of respecting Marrast more than himself, he was revealing his profound irritation at her disappointment in him.

DIFFICULTIES COMPLETING VOLUME 3 OF THE *COURS*

As soon as Comte got back to Paris in the fall of 1837, he returned to the third volume of the *Cours*, which he had started two years before, in September 1835. From September 7 to October 9, 1835, he had written the five lessons that made up the section on chemistry (lessons 35 through 39).[272] This was one lesson less than he had planned because he reduced the chapters on organic chemistry – a subject he disliked – from two to one. Both physics and chemistry thus received less space than he had originally intended, for he decided they were not as positive as he had thought at first.[273] (What was also undoubtedly a factor was that he did not know them as well as the other sciences.) On December 29, 1835, Comte had begun the section on biology, which he hoped to finish in time for

---

[268] Caroline Massin to Comte, September 13, 1839, MAC.
[269] Comte to Mme Auguste Comte, December 3, 1842, *CG*, 2:114.
[270] Caroline Massin to Comte, January 21, 1843, MAC.
[271] Caroline Massin to Comte, August 30, 1838, MAC.
[272] "Tableau du nombre de jours," in "Du temps dans le travail intellectuel," ed. Laffitte, 437.
[273] *Cours*, 1:589.

his book to be published by April 1836.[274] He wrote lesson 40 – "Considérations philosophiques sur l'ensemble de la science biologique" – quite easily from December 29, 1835, to January 28, 1836. One of the most important chapters of the *Cours*, this introductory lesson was also one of the longest, more than two hundred pages, which he justified by pointing out the need to define biology carefully since it was a new science.[275] Then as if to recover from this tremendous exertion, he wrote nothing for seven months, attributing the delay to physical and emotional problems. Also, a fire at the Dépôt de Livres required Bachelier to reprint some older books instead of working on new ones, and he therefore did not pressure Comte to finish.[276] Only in early August 1836 did Comte begin the next two lessons on anatomy and biotaxy, which he completed in two weeks. But the next subject – vegetative or organic life – took him almost a year to cover, for he was interrupted by his battle for the analysis chair at the Ecole Polytechnique, the teaching of Duhamel's course, his mother's death, a move from one apartment to another, and his first examination tour. When he wanted to resume his work two weeks after his return from his tour in 1837, Massin and Gondinet's argument distracted him.

Finally, Comte was able to regain his composure and write the last three lessons quickly from November 26 to December 31, 1837.[277] Pestered by Bachelier to finish and pressed for space, he had to reduce the chapters on vegetative life from two to one, those on animal life from three to one, and those on the intellectual and affective functions from four to one.[278] Although he covered the same material on biology as he had planned, he compressed it into six lessons instead of the original twelve.

Comte gave the volume containing the eleven lessons to Bachelier on January 2, 1838, and it was printed two months later in March – almost three years after volume 2.[279] Eight years after he had begun his great work, Comte had finally finished all of the chapters relating to the natural sciences. As usual, he naively expected to complete the next volume in a year.

---

[274] Comte to Barbot de Chement, January 15, 1836, CG, 1:255.

[275] *Cours*, 1:746. See also *Cours de philosophie positive* (1830–42), 3:269–486.

[276] "Tableau du nombre de jours," in "Du temps dans le travail intellectuel," ed. Laffitte, 437–8; Comte to Barbot de Chement, October 7,1836, CG, 1:274; Felkay, "Libraires de l'époque romantique," 38. Comte had been under the care of Dr. Félix Pinel-Grandchamps (a former member of the Société des Amis du Peuple) from January 25 to May 21. Pinel-Grandchamps to Comte, October 20, 1836, MAC.

[277] "Tableau du nombre de jours," in "Du temps dans le travail intellectuel," ed. Laffitte, 438.

[278] The crucial lesson on the intellectual and affective functions was less than eighty-five pages in the original volume. *Cours de philosophie positive* (1830–42), 3:761–845.

[279] Comte to Valat, May 15, 1838, CG, 1:291.

Chapter 11

Comte's Changing Psyche and Aberrant Behavior, 1838–1840

In finishing this volume [volume 5], . . . I will not forget to warn you that I will not respond to any criticism whatsoever that is not made from the same point of view that I have adopted; this will . . . free me, no doubt, from all philosophical polemics, considering how few people are able and disposed to fulfill this indispensable condition, without which discussions can really produce no useful insights.

Comte to Valat, 1840

THE CRISIS OF 1838: A SECOND ATTACK OF MADNESS AND A THIRD SEPARATION

Buoyed by having completed volume 3, Comte began in April 1838 to tackle the science he wished to establish: social physics. For eight years he had devoted himself to the natural sciences, a subject he felt he knew well. Now he realized more fully that this part of the *Cours* was but the preamble to his philosophy. The time had come to create the new science of social physics, the science that would definitively establish his philosophy. The dimension of the task daunted him. Since his youth, he had considered the emotions of utmost importance in enriching one's existence, but now that he was about to write on society, he knew he would have to devote more attention to them. He wondered whether he had developed within himself the sentiments he would need to discuss society properly.[1] When he had approached the subject of social physics in the course he was giving at home in 1826, he had suffered an attack of insanity. Now in 1838, as he took up the same subject, he went through an "intense" and "prolonged" period of mental illness.[2] Comte described it as an "intermediary crisis," not as intense as his previous attack but of the "same nature."[3] Again he suffered alternating periods of melancholy and excitation marked by paranoia.

As in 1826 his physical and mental problems were combined with a "moral" difficulty, and he once more assigned the blame to Massin.

---

[1] Comte to Clotilde de Vaux, August 5, 1845, *CG*, 3:82.
[2] Comte to Valat, May 15, 1838, *CG*, 1:291.
[3] Comte to Clotilde de Vaux, August 5, 1845, *CG*, 3:82.

He accused her of "sinful visits," as he had in 1826 and 1829.[4] On May 3, 1838, they separated for the third time. The break seemed definitive this time since it involved a financial settlement of more than three thousand francs and her move to a new apartment.[5] Also, having decided that Massin had an "undisciplinable nature," Comte had resolved to take a firmer, more punitive approach toward his wife's behavior. For the first time, he did not beg her to return home. It was she who appeared one day at the door, asking that they resume their life together. Although he gave in, he warned her that her next departure would be "irrevocable."[6]

To reinforce his new austerity and control, he began on May 23, 1838, to keep a very detailed notebook recording his income and their expenses, a move that seems to indicate a lack of confidence in Massin, who already kept two such notebooks.[7] As if to remind her of the Napoleonic Code, which reinforced French patriarchalism by legalizing the wife's obedience to her husband, he demanded that she accept her subservient role and respect his "conjugal authority."[8] Unquestioned obedience was the key to stable, peaceful government, whether that government be of the household or of society. He wished to regulate her just as he did society.

Curiously, the letters that Comte and Massin exchanged during his examination circuit of 1838 do not reveal the same degree of tension as in 1837. They addressed each other more often as "my dear friend" and rebuked each other kindly for neglecting their health. Comte reminded Massin to keep her regular habits, which were crucial for her well-being: "I hope my insistence in this area does not weary you; for you know how important it is to me."[9] When he stayed at the same hotel in Avignon where they had spent the night thirteen years before, Comte told her he was deeply moved by the memory of the "mutual satisfaction" they had achieved that evening.[10] To counter his charges that she had a "sad and touchy character," she tried to be her old witty self.[11] When Comte told her of his invitation to dine with local notables and made predictions concerning

---

[4] Comte to Littré, April 28, 1851, *CG*, 6:63.
[5] See notebook of expenses, which runs through 1838 in the packet "Examinations: 1837," MAC; Entry for July 1838, in Massin's notebook entitled "Recettes et dépenses janvier 1837 à décembre 1841," MAC. This entry shows that she paid 280 francs for rent for an apartment on the rue Saint-Hyacinthe (not far from their first apartment) in addition to their regular payment of 250 francs for their apartment on the rue d'Ulm.
[6] Comte to Littré, April 28, 1851, *CG*, 6:64.
[7] See Comte's notebook "Recettes et dépenses courantes," MAC.
[8] Comte to Littré, April 28, 1851, *CG*, 6:64.
[9] Comte to Mme Auguste Comte, September 3, 1838, *CG*, 1:295.
[10] Comte to Mme Auguste Comte, September 26, 1838, *CG*, 1:301.
[11] Caroline Massin to Comte, September 13, 1838, MAC.

various movements in France, Massin congratulated him on being "decidedly a great person" and a "prophet."[12] He did not even get angry when she reminded him that he had not yet reached the position in life that he deserved. He simply explained that the posts he held at the moment were important "stepping stones," necessary to "consolidate and extend" his "great future influence."[13] Upon his return to Paris in October he gave her a present of 243 francs.[14]

Despite the expressions of warmth, Comte's new attitude toward his inner feelings worried Massin. When he told her at one point that his "social affections" were sufficient and that he no longer needed people close to him, she was dumbfounded, for she found her own life of isolation to be a crushing burden.[15] Taunting him for feeling so "happy" in his solitude, she said that at least their cat needed her: "I like it when someone needs me."[16] Realizing that he had hurt her, he talked in subsequent letters about how he was suffering from not having anyone to talk to and how much he wished they could afford her company on his circuit.[17] Although he may have felt that his love for humanity was growing and would be satisfying in itself, he was still not entirely sure he could do without his wife. After all, he had taken her in again after their third separation.

A SEPARATION FROM HIS FAMILY

Comte may have been forgiving with Massin, but he was not with his family. Again his paranoia seems to have played a large role. At the end of March 1838, he had decided to spend some time with his father and sister in Montpellier. Massin tried to get out of this visit by telling his father that she did not want to travel alone. Louis Comte then had Alix write her to beg her to join her husband in Lyon, from where they could easily travel together to Montpellier.[18] Alix's letter, which has since disappeared, evidently incensed the

---

[12] Caroline Massin to Comte, August 30, 1838, MAC.

[13] Comte to Mme Auguste Comte, September 3, 1838, CG, 1:296.

[14] Comte's notebook, "Recettes et dépenses courantes," MAC.

[15] Caroline Massin to Comte, September 21, 1838, MAC.

[16] Caroline Massin to Comte, September 7, 1838, MAC. The portion of the letter in which Comte wrote about the social affections was left out of the copy of the letter that appears in CG, 1:295–7. Doctor Félix Pinel-Grandchamp gave Caroline the cat. Littré, *Auguste Comte*, 487nl.

[17] Comte to Mme Auguste Comte, September 10, 1838, CG, 1:297–8.

[18] Alix Comte to Auguste Comte, March 30, 1838, "Lettres d'Alix Comte," ed. Laffitte: 84; Louis Comte to Auguste Comte, August 19, 1838, "Lettres de Louis Comte," ed. Laffitte, 17.

already suspicious Massin as well as the mentally unstable Comte. A friend of the family intervened, claiming that Comte was too touchy, had a "cruel and unjust prejudice" against his family, and had "misread" Alix's letter.[19] Nevertheless, sure that his family did not want Massin to come, Comte told his father that he no longer wanted to communicate with him. His father replied in utter astonishment:

> I fell from the clouds in reading your letter of the 13th of this month [August], and I am vainly seeking to explain to myself its contents. . . . I do not see in this plan what there is to provoke your anger to the point of insulting your sister as you did in your letter.

Weary of his son's demands, he acknowledged the rupture. "It is undoubtedly very painful for me to break with my son, but what tempers my pain a little in this regard is that it is you who are throwing down the gauntlet."[20]

Auguste was surprised and pained by the "dryness" and "bitterness" of his father's letter.[21] Issalène wrote that he should not be; even if his mother were still living, the separation would have occurred anyway, considering Alix's character and the fact that Louis Comte never had much of a will and now was "almost a mummy."[22] Massin was convinced that Louis Comte was using her as a pretext to keep his distance from his son, whom he intended to disinherit, and that Alix was turning his affections against Auguste for her own profit. Massin told Auguste that his father was "*in all respects* a mediocre man" who could never forgive him for choosing the path of a scholar instead of that of a bureaucrat.[23] Comte agreed with her and decided that the separation would be "irrevocable" until his family treated her better.[24]

Making Massin the "sole legitimate judge" of his family's behavior, he did not seek to communicate again with his father and sister for eight years and did not attempt a reconciliation until 1848.[25] This decision was particularly painful because for five years in a row his

[19] Eulalie Carquet to Auguste Comte, September 6, 1838, in "Matériaux pour servir à la biographie d'Auguste Comte," ed. Pierre Laffitte, *RO*, 3d ser., 2 (May 1, 1911): 131, 133.

[20] Louis Comte to Auguste Comte, August 19, 1838, "Lettres de Louis Comte," ed. Laffitte, 17–18.

[21] Comte to Mme Auguste Comte, August 27, 1838, *CG*, 1:295.

[22] Issalène to Comte, September 24, 1838, MAC.

[23] Caroline Massin to Comte, August 30, 1838, MAC.

[24] Comte to Mme Auguste Comte, August 27, 1838, *CG*, 1:295. See also Comte to Mme Auguste Comte, September 3, 1838, *CG*, 1:297; Comte to Valat, October 22, 1839, *CG*, 1:323.

[25] Comte to Valat, October 13, 1840, *CG*, 1:364. See also Comte to Louis Comte, June 2, 1846, *CG*, 4:15; Comte to Alix Comte, March 8, 1848, *CG*, 4:140–1.

examination tour took him to Montpellier, where he stayed at hotels or with friends. He got most of the information about his family from Issalène, who informed him at one point that Alix was devoted to the relics of Saint Roch and had become very fat: "The whole town is in admiration of this marvel."[26] He made similar unkind remarks about Louis Comte, who he said never asked about his son because he was a "used-up" old man whose heart was petrifying with age.[27] On a visit to Montpellier in 1843, Auguste was startled by the sudden appearance of Alix at his hotel. She threw herself around his neck to embrace him. But he thrust her away, demanding that she seek Massin's pardon and respect her. When she refused, Comte ordered her from the room. Since he was separated from Massin at this point, Alix found his behavior aberrant.[28]

THE "AESTHETIC REVOLUTION"

Besides causing more disruptions in his relationships with his family and his wife, Comte's crisis of 1838 marked an important turning point in other respects. One of his "little philosophical secrets" was that in order to "strengthen and facilitate every intellectual or affective improvement, it is very important to connect it with some physical improvement." Seeking a physical and concrete sign of his "spiritual" progress, he stopped smoking, just as in 1826 he had given up coffee.[29]

Comte also realized that he needed new stimuli, emotional and intellectual. To improve his mental health and to get relief from his boring examination tours, he sought some form of distraction. Most important, he understood that he had to develop his own feelings to deepen his comprehension of society. He insisted, as he had in the 1820s, that the "needs of the heart" had to be in harmony with the "most sublime flights of the mind."[30] But he realized that his "unhappy domestic situation" could not meet these needs.[31] His frustration with his stagnant emotional life was compounded by his feeling of being at a loss intellectually; having completed the part of the *Cours* covering the natural sciences, he no longer felt compelled to study them. To avoid stagnation and to prove to himself that he

[26] Issalène to Comte, May 24, 1839, MAC.   [27] Issalène to Comte, May 22, 1840, MAC.

[28] Alix Comte to Robinet, March 26, 1860, MAC; Alix Comte to Audiffrent, August 19, 1868, MAC.

[29] Comte to Clotilde de Vaux, August 5, 1845, *CG*, 3:83.

[30] Comte to Valat, July 10, 1840, *CG*, 1:344. See also Comte to Mill, May 15, 1845, *CG*, 3:9; Comte to Mme Auguste Comte, September 4, 1839, *CG*, 1:315.

[31] Comte to Clotilde de Vaux, August 5, 1845, *CG*, 3:82.

was still in a "state of development," he experienced in 1838 what he called an "aesthetic revolution." It led him to develop a new interest in all the beaux arts, especially poetry and music.[32] He would use his new grasp of the arts to improve his description of the "aesthetic evolution of Humanity."[33] Although admittedly a "feeble equivalent" to familial affections, his aesthetic emotions, he hoped, would further his mental development.[34]

Comte's new attitude toward the feelings and the arts appears to confirm the criticism of Saint-Simon and his disciples that he had been a cold rational being without appreciation for the emotional and the beautiful. But although he was in a way following in their footsteps, he had in fact always been convinced that people's emotional lives were vital to their existence. His letters of the 1820s often referred to his "needs of the heart." Now, in 1838, after having laid the groundwork for the scientific organization of society, he intended to examine and discuss the emotional aspects of humanity more systematically. He realized the time had come to turn his attention to the affections and the arts. And just as the Saint-Simonians had criticized his disregard of aesthetics, he now brought the same accusation against the scientists.[35] Henceforth, with the example of the Saint-Simonian success in front of him, he seemed to appropriate different aspects of their discourse.

Although "romanticism" was reaching its heights in the 1830s, Comte showed no interest in this movement in France. Never do the names Victor Hugo, Charles Nodier, Honoré de Balzac, or Stendhal appear in his books or letters. Comte had isolated himself from society to such an extent that he did not seem to know what was going on. But it is also true that, at the beginning, romanticism was connected with reactionary politics and eclecticism. Marrast, Andrieux,[36] Destutt de Tracy, and other Idéologues had come out strongly against the new movement, which they regarded as obscure and inimical to a rational society.[37] Hostile to "littérateurs," whose political meddling and social criticism interfered with social regeneration, Comte had always insisted that scientifically trained philosophers, not artists, were to direct society.[38] Chateaubriand was the only nineteenth-century French writer represented in the Positivist Library and then only by a comparatively minor work – *Les*

---

[32] Comte to Valat, May 1, 1842, *CG*, 2:9. See also Comte to Valat, May 10, 1840, *CG*, 1:336.

[33] Comte to Clotilde de Vaux, August 5, 1845, *CG*, 3:83.

[34] Comte to Valat, July 10, 1840, *CG*, 1:344.   [35] *Cours*, 2:635.

[36] According to one of Comte's friends, Andrieux did not like romanticism because it seemed to "make a great deal of noise about nothing." Langlade to Tabarié, January 29, 1822, MAC.

[37] Welch, *Liberty and Utility*, 164–8.

[38] Christian Cherfils, *L'Esthéthique positiviste* (Paris: A. Messein, 1909), 29.

Martyrs.[39] A book depicting people dying for their faith naturally appealed to the dejected founder of positivism.[40]

Just as in the 1820s he had studied Scottish and German philosophy, Comte sought his inspiration mainly abroad – in English, Italian, Spanish, and German literature. Having learned English in preparation for his emigration to the United States, he began to read Milton, Shakespeare, Fielding, Defoe, Goldsmith, and Byron. But his favorite author was Sir Walter Scott, whose works began to be translated into French in 1816 and were extremely popular, especially in liberal circles.[41] Sharing his taste for the Middle Ages, Comte believed Scott to be the greatest writer of the time, and when he made up his list of the 150 volumes to be included in the Positivist Library, 7 of them were by Scott.[42] As for Spanish and German writers, the works of Lope de Vega, Calderón, Cervantes, Schiller, and Goethe figure in his personal library.[43]

In August 1839 Comte bought an Italian grammar book and a volume of Dante's works – the *Opere poetiche* – which included the *Divine Comedy.*[44] Aided by his powerful memory, he easily learned Italian, whose lyricism delighted him.[45] Dante, Boccaccio, Petrarch, Ariosto, Cellini, and Tasso became his favorite authors.[46]

On his examination tour of 1839, Comte read Alessandro Manzoni's *I Promessi Sposi*, which he praised for its "gracefulness" and "charming details," especially of Catholic culture. He claimed that "Manzoni is certainly, after W. Scott, the greatest poet of the age. We have nothing even approximately equivalent in France."[47]

---

[39] *Système*, 4:558.

[40] There were very few works by nineteenth-century French writers in Comte's personal library. The only ones that can be found there are *Delphine* by Madame de Staël (an 1839 edition), *Adolphe* by Benjamin Constant (an 1824 edition), and volume 15 – *Mélanges* – of the *Oeuvres complètes* of George Sand (published in 1843). Comte lent Sand's work to Clotilde de Vaux. See "Liste des livres figurant dans la bibliothèque d'Auguste Comte à son décès et prêtés par celui-ci à Clotilde de Vaux," MAC.

[41] Max Milner and Claude Pichois, *Littérature française*, vol. 7, *De Chateaubriand à Baudelaire* (Paris: Arthaud, 1985), 65, 199.

[42] *Système*, 4:558. Comte kept *Ivanhoe, Kenilworth, Quentin Durward*, and four other of Scott's novels in the bookcase that he referred to most often. Another bookcase held eighteen volumes of Scott's *Vie de Napoléon Buonaparte, Empereur des Français*, but only the pages of the first volume are cut. See the Bibliothèque Usuel and the Bibliothèque Superflue at the Maison d'Auguste Comte.

[43] Comte never learned German but began to study Spanish in 1842. He read the Spanish works in the original.

[44] Bill of August 7, 1839, from a store owned by Vabois, in packet called "Factures," MAC.

[45] Comte to Valat, May 1, 1842, *CG*, 2:9.

[46] See Comte's library at the Maison d'Auguste Comte and the books in the Positivist Library, *Système*, 4:557–61.

[47] Comte to Mme Auguste Comte, September 4, 1839, *CG*, 1:315.

What he liked in both Scott and Manzoni was that they wrote historical epics, a genre he believed would renovate art and was the "best adapted to modern civilization." The epic represented a wonderful "alliance of private life, which heretofore had been only abstractly envisaged, and public life, which in every social age necessarily modifies . . . [private life's] basic character."[48] Moreover, both Manzoni and Scott seemed to epitomize the power of the artist to enchant and ennoble.[49] In depicting the past and delineating their protagonists' strong emotions, they had not sought to direct destructive criticisms against contemporary society as French writers seemed to do. Thus, though disdainful of the social novel, Comte was attracted to at least two aspects of "romanticism" – the medieval revival and the study of the passions and private life.

Comte also showed a greater interest in music, which he had always liked thanks to Ernestine de Goy and Pauline, but had neglected. In 1838 Massin, knowing he had a beautiful voice, tried to get him to relax by listening to music, particularly operatic works.[50] The following year, he began to attend performances of Italian operas at the Théâtre Royal Italien located at the Odéon, practically at his doorstep.[51] Delighted with these operas, which also appealed to his new fondness for the Italian language, he paid more than two hundred francs to go every Thursday during the 1840–1 season. And because he was so nearsighted, he insisted on sitting in the center of the front row of the orchestra.[52] As a true opera lover, he carefully studied the librettos of his favorites, such as *The Barber of Seville*, *Semiramide*, and *The Puritans*, and replayed the arias in his mind as he worked.

As Comte withdrew more and more from society, the opera became his only distraction from his labors. It also served as a refuge from his battles with Massin, who was annoyed that he preferred a good seat in the orchestra to two seats in the balcony, which would have allowed her to accompany him.[53] Fleeing in this manner from the reality of his daily life became vital to his mental well-being. During the 1841–2 season and the following one, he subscribed to the Théâtre Royal Italien three times a week at a cost of 690 francs.[54]

---

[48] *Cours*, 2:621.   [49] Cherfils, *L'Esthétique Positiviste*, 41.   [50] Littré, *Auguste Comte*, 257.

[51] Comte to Valat, May 10, 1840, *CG*, 1:335–6. In the summer of 1841, the theater relocated to the rue Monsigny on the Right Bank. Théâtre Royal Italien to Comte, August 12, 1841, MAC.

[52] Comte to the Director of the Théâtre Royal Italien, April 7, 1841, *CG*, 2:3. For information about Comte's subscriptions, see "Documents: Théâtre Royal Italien," MAC.

[53] Caroline Massin to Comte, September 15, 1840, MAC.

[54] Théâtre Royal Italien to Comte, August 10, 1842, MAC. See also "Documents: Théâtre Royal Italien," MAC.

His passion, which he admitted was "singular," had become a true – and expensive – obsession.[55]

The final and most important result of Comte's bout with mental instability in 1838 was his adoption of a new intellectual regime, which he called "cerebral hygiene."[56] Exasperated by the Saint-Simonians' and journalists' attacks on his creativity, he decided that he needed to preserve his "characteristic originality." Henceforth, he abstained from reading newspapers, books, and journals, except the weekly bulletins of the Academy of Sciences, which he only glanced through irregularly. To relax, he did permit himself, however, to read the "great poets of every age and nation."[57]

In his eagerness to favor his "aesthetic revolution," Comte seemed to be rejecting the sciences, which heretofore had been his main preoccupation.[58] For a person aspiring to become a member of the Academy of Sciences and a professor at the Ecole Polytechnique and the Collège de France, this systematic cultivation of ignorance seems inappropriate. It appears to have been a repudiation of scientific observation, intellectual and social progress, and education, the cornerstones of his philosophy. In adopting this position, he may have been influenced by the example of Saint-Simon, who had insisted on reading nothing but novels, since it was important "to have thought a great deal and to have read very little to produce really new ideas."[59] Moreover, because Comte had been severely criticized by the Saint-Simonians for neglecting the inspired, creative genius, perhaps they helped to stimulate not only his new appreciation of the arts but his new emphasis on an originality that came from within oneself. These two themes were also common in this age of romanticism, when the writer was assuming the mantle of the spiritual leader of society.[60] But given the fact that Comte was more familiar with the doctrine of the Saint-Simonians than with this literary movement, it seems that they introduced him to many of the leading trends of the times.

Comte's sudden adoption of the regime of "cerebral hygiene" may also have been an outgrowth of his attempt to shield himself more effectively from the contemporary world, which he

---

[55] Comte to Valat, May 10, 1840, *CG*, 1:336. [56] *Cours*, 2:479.
[57] Comte to Valat, May 10, 1840, *CG*, 1:336. See also Comte to Maximilien Marie, July 4, 1841, *CG*, 2:12; *Cours*, 2:480.
[58] Comte to Valat, May 1, 1842, *CG*, 2:9.
[59] Saint-Simon, "Correspondance avec M. de Redern," in *Oeuvres*, 1.1:110. See also Léon Halévy, "Souvenirs de Saint-Simon," 535. [60] Bénichou, *Sacre de l'écrivain*, 17, 470.

increasingly denounced as "pretentious," "superficial," and "vulgar."[61] This world presented him, moreover, with certain dangers. His sense of self-preservation may have told him that cerebral hygiene was essential to his mental health, which required calm and the absence of controversy. By not reading periodicals and other works, he could avoid encountering attacks on his system as well as reminders that his books had not achieved the renown he felt they deserved. He claimed his isolation would allow him to attain "more general views," "purer and more impartial sentiments," and more "homogeneity" and "consistency" in his doctrines.[62] By systematically blocking out the world around him, he could, in a sense, rise above the scientific, social, and political developments of his time, free himself from debilitating distractions and criticisms, and concentrate solely on the grand outlines of the history he had already formulated sixteen years before. He alone held the key to progress, and nothing new could change his mind about the proper way to create social change. In short, Comte's cerebral hygiene represented an effort to protect his ego by turning his back on the contemporary world that he felt was neglecting, if not persecuting, him.

THE MONTGÉRY AFFAIR

Comte's interest in preserving his mental health was reinforced by a curious series of events. He had an old friend, Captain Jacques-Philippe Mérigon de Montgéry, who was a famous military technologist. Comte may have met him through Saint-Simon, with whom Montgéry liked to discuss his military schemes.[63] Montgéry had a deep respect for Comte, derived from having attended the opening of his course in 1826 and 1829 and reading the *Cours*.[64] When Montgéry informed him in January 1838 that he was suffering from an attack of madness, Comte was shocked.[65]

Comte and his wife took an unprecedented interest in Montgéry's affairs. Massin visited him often, although she knew that Montgéry reproached Comte for wasting his time with her. Comte lent him

[61] Comte to Valat, May 1, 1842, *CG*, 2:8; Comte to Mill, November 20, 1841, *CG*, 2:20.

[62] Comte to Mill, November 20, 1841, *CG*, 2:20; *Cours*, 2:479.

[63] Montgéry was also a friend of Mellet and Issalène, had shown some interest in the Saint-Simonians, and had sent Comte two essays that he had written for the *Revue encyclopédique* in 1824. On Montgéry, see Manuel, *Saint-Simon*, 328; Frank H. Winter, "Montgéry, Jacques-Philippe Mérigon de," in *Dictionary of Scientific Biography*, ed. Gillispie; Littré, *Auguste Comte*, 36–7.

[64] Caroline Massin to Comte, October 5, 1838, MAC; Montgéry to Comte, May 18, 1838, MAC.

[65] Montgéry to Comte, January 28, 1838, MAC.

money and even became deeply involved in the problems between him and his working-class mistress, whom Massin detested and banned from their apartment. With great reluctance, Comte met with Montgéry for seven or eight hours in an insane asylum in Marseille during his examination circuit of 1838, a visit that revived unpleasant memories and prevented him from sleeping that night. Traumatized, he remembered with gratitude that Massin had rescued him from his own asylum and cured him many years before. Montgéry was not so fortunate. From him and his doctor, Comte received a steady stream of news for months about his deep depression, violence, paranoia, and intellectual incoherence. And this was during the time that Comte himself did not feel well mentally. Finally after Montgéry tried to hang himself, Comte prevailed upon the minister of the navy to free him from the hospital and arranged for his own doctor, Félix Pinel-Grandchamp, to care for him. Yet Montgéry died soon afterward, in late 1839.[66]

Comte's involvement in his friend's affair did not end with his death, however, because for almost ten years he was involved in all sorts of negotiations with the government and Montgéry's mistress about Pinel-Grandchamp's fees, the care and education of Montgéry's illegitimate daughter, and the fate of his papers. In this case at least, his "social affections" do seem to have developed, for he had never before taken such an interest in anyone. Perhaps he was stimulated by his awareness that without Caroline he might have suffered a similar fate.

CONFRONTING SOCIAL PHYSICS: WRITING VOLUME 4
OF THE *COURS*

Comte's efforts to maintain his mental and physical well-being absorbed so much energy that he was unable to work on the *Cours* for about a year. It was not until December 23, 1838, that he began writing the next volume, presumably his last. He completed the 200-page introduction to social physics on April 6, 1839. Then in four days he wrote the 60 pages of the next chapter, which covered

[66] Caroline Massin to Comte, September 7 and 8, 1838, and November 9, 1842, MAC; Zédé to Comte, February 6, 18, and 28, November 18, 1839, MAC; Comte to Anna Barbazon, November 11, 1829, CG, 1:325; Montgéry to Comte, January 28, October 9, 1838, and April 5, 1839; Anna Barbazon to Comte, November 11, 1839, MAC; Comte to Mme Auguste Comte, October 2, 1838, CG, 1:301; Dr. Mercurin to Comte, July 21, September 3, October 3, 1838, MAC; Comte to Amiral de Rosamel, October 17, 1838, CG, 1:304; Issalène to Comte, September 21, 1839, MAC; Ministère de la Marine et des Colonies to Comte, October 15, 1839, MAC; Pinel-Grandchamp to Comte, January 15, 1840, MAC.

the work of his predecessors and derived from his early essays. During the following three months, he had to squeeze work on the *Cours* into his busy teaching and examination schedule. Going to bed by nine o'clock, he worked every day from four in the morning to dinner. In this way, he managed to write another 450 pages (lessons 48 to 51) describing social physics.[67]

At this point, Comte became aware of a severe problem: he had already written more than 700 pages but had discussed only the "dogmatic" part of his social philosophy.[68] Although ten years had elapsed, he had not finished his project, which he had insisted would be completed by 1840 at the latest. Imagining that his readers were impatient to read the climax of his great work, he persuaded Bachelier to publish immediately the portion on social physics that he had just written. It became volume 4, part 1. The fifth volume would cover the historical component of the new science. Remembering the sting of Benjamin Constant's criticisms of his unfinished articles for *Le Producteur*, Comte worried about separating his subject matter in this fashion. He had already refused to read a critique made by Blainville of volume 4 because he felt "discussion is very inopportune during production."[69] He therefore had Bachelier write an "Avis de l'Editeur," begging the readers to suspend their final judgment until they read both volumes relating to social physics.

The fourth volume appeared on July 25, 1839, and six weeks later Comte went on his examination tour. In Angers he met the famous leftist Joseph Rey, who was working on his own version of socialism, blending the ideas of the Idéologues, Charles Fourier, and Robert Owen.[70] Comte was demoralized to discover that Rey, who shared his interest in the science of society, had not even heard of the *Cours*. Moreover, Comte could not get over the fact that throughout France people still referred to him only as "Mr. Examiner."[71] The erratic publication of the various volumes of the *Cours* had clearly reduced the impact of his ideas. The public's neglect especially galled him now that he prided himself on having just laid the groundwork for a new science.

At this point, Comte had only two or three self-proclaimed

[67] "Tableau du nombre de jours," 438–9; Comte to Valat, May 10, 1840, *CG*, 1:336. Comte was exaggerating slightly when he told Valat that he had written the whole volume of 736 pages in four months.

[68] Bachelier, "Avis de l'Editeur," July 24, 1839, *Cours*, 2:11. See also Comte, "L'Avertissement de l'Auteur," 8.

[69] Comte to Valat, September 17, 1842, *CG*, 2:85. See also Comte to Valat, July 10, 1840, *CG*, 1:344.

[70] Comte to Mme Auguste Comte, Auguste 23, 1839, *CG*, 1:314; Spitzer, *French Generation*, 55; Welch, *Liberty and Utility*, 178–85.

[71] Comte to Mme Auguste Comte, September 4, 1839, *CG*, 1:316.

disciples. One was the elderly, minor republican publicist Charles Bonnin, who became friendly with Comte after reading his article on Broussais.[72] Another was a former student, Jean Lefoullon, who went to New Orleans in 1836 to open a rural primary school based on the "positivism of everyday life."[73] In 1840 Auguste Francelle, a working-class auditor in Comte's astronomy course, would become attracted to the positive system because of its antitheological and scientific basis. His zeal for Comte's "sublime philosophy" was so strong that he persuaded twelve other young men to audit this course.[74]

These minor figures did not provide Comte with the public recognition he felt his work deserved. He therefore sent copies of his work to many of the foremost scientists and public figures in France as well as to various institutions, including the Academy of Sciences in Berlin.[75] At the end of December, he also gave a copy of his work to Emile Littré, an important journalist and editor of the complete works of Hippocrates. After a common friend also lent Littré the fundamental opuscule, which completely "captivated" him, he and Comte met for the first time in 1840 and quickly became friends.[76] Their relationship would later have a large impact on the development of the positive movement.

TENSIONS WITHIN THE COMTE HOUSEHOLD

The six months of intense work on the *Cours*, followed by three weeks of examinations in Paris, completely exhausted Comte and strained his marriage. Even on Sundays, his only "free" day, he had given astronomy lessons to workers and called on people he felt obliged to see. Consequently, Massin felt neglected. Yet Comte was tired of her complaints and wanted to get away from her. He was,

[72] Bonnin to Comte, December 10, 1829, and September 14, 1838, MAC.

[73] Jean Lefoullon to Comte, May 26, 1838, MAC. See also Jean Lefoullon to Comte, December 16, 1837, MAC.

[74] Francelle to Comte, July 30, 1842, MAC. See also Francelle to Comte, June 14, July 2, December 20, 1840, MAC.

[75] Comte sent his work to the scientists Poinsot, Blainville, Arago, Lacroix, Duhamel, and Lamé, as well as to people who had or still admired his work: Guizot, Dunoyer, Humboldt, Bernard, the Duc de Montebello, Armand Marrast, and Gondinet. The institutions who received it included the Academy of Sciences, the Ecole Polytechnique, the Ecole de Médecine in Montpellier, and the newly created Academy of Moral and Political Sciences. See Comte's list of people to whom he sent the *Cours*, MAC.

[76] Littré, *Auguste Comte*, i. See also Caroline Massin to Comte, September 3, 1840, MAC. On Littré, consult Alain Rey, *Littré: L'Humaniste et les mots* (Paris: Gallimard, 1970), and Jean-François Six, *Littré devant Dieu* (Paris: Seuil, 1962).

moreover, worried about his physical and mental health. Thus after completing the *Cours*, he decided to take a small vacation by leaving early on his examination tour.[77]

Massin proposed to accompany him for several days, but Comte, certain she wanted to stay the whole tour, bluntly refused. In response, she bitterly complained about the "bad treatment" she had received from him all year and the fact that he still harbored suspicions against her. Dismayed by his odd departure, she now saw more clearly his new approach to their marriage, which he had first taken in 1838 but followed more assiduously in 1839, the year he embraced the motto "all or nothing." Comte's demand for her complete submission was leading to a "true war," which made them both unhappy and created a "desperate situation."[78] She pleaded with him to stop placing all the blame for the malaise in their marriage on her and to recognize that what he chose was what always suited *him*.

Massin thought she knew the cause of their troubles. In describing her anxiety, she wrote to Blainville: "My husband's change with regard to me derives from physical causes that I would dare not write or even say to a doctor, and yet our position is the inevitable and irreparable consequence of it."[79] What were these "physical causes"?

According to d'Eichthal, Massin had told Comte before their marriage that she could not have children. But Comte did not seem upset by his childless state.[80] Moreover, this type of physical problem would not be one that Massin would be reluctant to mention to a doctor.

What Massin seemed to be implying was that Comte had developed sexual problems. Toward the end of his life, he admitted to a close disciple that beginning in puberty he had been "very bothered" by his strong "sexual instinct," but when he reached thirty, that is, around the time of his first attack of madness, he "finally surmounted" it "in a complete manner despite its pronounced energy in my natural constitution."[81] Thus to show how virtuous he was, he was suggesting that he used exceptional willpower to overcome his powerful sexual urges, which were indeed evident in his frequent recourse to prostitutes in his youth. Yet there remains a grave suspicion that he

---

[77] Comte to Valat, August 11, 1839, and May 10, 1840, *CG*, 1:309, 337; Comte to Mme Auguste Comte, August 27, 1838, and August 23, September 4, 1839, *CG*, 1:294, 313, 316; Lefoullon to Comte, January 19, 1840, MAC; Comte to Général Vaillant, August 19, 1839, *CG*, 1:311; Caroline Massin to Comte, August 28, 1839, MAC.

[78] Caroline Massin to Comte, September 7, 1839, MAC. See also Caroline Massin to Comte, August 28, 1839.

[79] Caroline Massin to Blainville, December 20, 1839, MAC.

[80] Deroisin, *Notes sur Auguste Comte*, 22n1.   [81] Comte to Edger, March 27, 1856, *CG*, 8:236.

became, in fact, impotent. Comte told Clotilde that his sexual relations with Massin stopped completely in 1834, that is, about a year after he again experienced mental problems and separated for a short while from his wife.[82] Since his sexual relations with Massin seem to have been satisfactory at the beginning of their marriage, it is possible that when she sought financial help from Cerclet in return perhaps for some sexual favors, Comte began to lose his self-confidence. Also, manic-depression often causes a marked decrease in sexual interest.[83] Massin herself hinted at his impotence by her embarrassment in the above-mentioned quotation. His frustration and lack of confidence in this realm may have led him to accuse her repeatedly of sleeping with other men, especially since she was considered to be beautiful. Her letters in 1839 give the same impression that there was something wrong sexually, for she begged him to stop taking out his "malaise" on her, to cease being so defensive, and to abandon his habit of treating her as an enemy.[84] She sadly wrote:

> I have always thought that all that is lost between us should make what may remain more precious to us; this is not your opinion. I cannot alone regulate our situation. If you wanted to use in this respect a little of this elevated reason that you make such good use of elsewhere, you would feel the justice of what I am telling you here. I alone cannot change our position. We have lost a great deal, and you place us in the situation of poor castaways who thrust away to the sea the few pieces of debris that they should hurry to gather.[85]

Although she did not specify what they had "lost," it seems clear that their lack of a sexual life was the problem when she said that they should learn to "live as brothers" or "friends." She tried to reassure her husband that she felt a "very deep friendship" for him and that in fact she still loved him: "You have occupied in my heart a place that never could . . . be taken by anyone else."[86] Was it, moreover, sheer coincidence that the only time Comte referred to their sexual life in his letters was when he nostalgically recalled the "mutual satisfaction" that they had enjoyed in a hotel room thirteen years before?[87] Now they no longer even slept in the same room and

---

[82] Comte to Clotilde de Vaux, December 5, 1845, *CG*, 3:219.

[83] Goodwin and Jamison, *Manic-Depressive Illness*, 44, 310–11.

[84] Caroline Massin to Comte, September 7, 1839, MAC.

[85] Caroline Massin to Comte, August 28, 1839, MAC.

[86] Caroline Massin to Comte, September 7, 1839, MAC.

[87] Comte to M[me] Auguste Comte, September 26, 1838, *CG*, 1:301.

had almost separate apartments.[88] It is significant that in discussing the relationship between men and women in the fourth volume of the *Cours* (written in 1839), Comte proclaimed the sexual instinct the "original source of the sweetest harmony" in marriage.[89] The implication is that the cause of the disharmony in Comte's own marriage was the absence of sex.

Comte's examination tour did not raise his spirits. Besides being disappointed that no one considered him a famous person, he grew depressed when he reached Montpellier and had to stay with Issalène. His family made no attempt to get in touch with him. Even his old friend Pouzin, whom he had not seen since 1827, gave him only a few minutes for a visit. Montgéry's death was another blow.[90]

By the end of the year, Comte's melancholy alarmed Massin. Although later he claimed that his attack of insanity was confined to a short period in 1838, it is clear that he had not recovered. A sure sign was his failure to resume his usual practice of working on the *Cours* upon his return to Paris. On December 20, 1839, Massin confided her worries to Blainville, for she was sure her husband was on the verge of another attack, similar to the one in 1826. Within the past year, there had appeared the "same rude reproaches, hard words, acts of violence all out of proportion to what determines them, [and] puerile and meticulous attention to prove and emphasize the power of the breadwinner in the family."[91] Moreover, these signs of mental disorder had recently become worse.

Massin was at her wits' end. She did not know what to do. Comte's confidence and trust in her had brought about the miracle of 1826. Now, however, his lack of "affection" for her prevented her from exerting any beneficial influence on him. If he became completely insane again, she feared he would be "lost" forever. She could not turn to Comte's friends, because she knew they disliked her and even curried favor with Comte by insulting her. Proclaiming her devotion to Comte and her willingness to sacrifice everything for him, she begged Blainville, who had always been kind to her, to come to her husband's rescue.[92] When Comte suddenly disappeared, she wrote to Blainville again, expressing her alarm more forcefully:

Monsieur is very sad and for a long time has been impervious to all distraction. He does not relax from the work that earns him a

---

[88] Caroline Massin to Comte, September 23 and 30, 1837, MAC; Bill from the locksmith, alluding to Massin's separate apartment and bedroom, August 14, 1841, in a packet on rue Monsieur le Prince, MAC.

[89] *Cours*, 2:184.

[90] Comte to Mme Auguste Comte, September 4, 1839, CG, 1:316; Comte to Valat, September 25, October 22, 1839, CG, 1:318–19, 323.

[91] Caroline Massin to Blainville, December 20, 1839, MAC.   [92] Ibid.

livelihood except to take up his special studies. If I did not believe that there was still time, I would not trouble you today, but it is very essential to find him and to prescribe for him a severe physical and intellectual regime that will save him because I believe he is in danger. . . . I repeat that it is because I feel I will be able to do nothing more that I fear everything.[93]

This time Blainville intervened. Comte finally realized that he needed a period of rest for his "mental reinstallation" and agreed to take a longer break than usual from the *Cours*.[94] It was not until April 1840 that he began to write again, pushing back a publication date one more time. As in the past, the *Cours* had to give way to his health problems. In May he bought *L'Art de prolonger la vie*.[95]

AN ENCOUNTER WITH THE GROTES

Comte's increasingly truculent behavior manifested itself in a singular fashion in January. Arago had written Comte a letter asking him to meet George Grote. The heir of a rich Tory banker, Grote had been introduced by his friend David Ricardo to James Mill, who had encouraged him to become actively involved in radical politics.[96] Arago explained to Comte that Grote and his friend William Molesworth had become very interested in the *Cours* while working on a new edition of Hobbes. Asked by Grote to arrange a meeting with the author, Arago wrote to Comte, "I hope I was not mistaken in assuring Mr. and Mrs. Grote that you would have the goodness of paying them a visit."[97]

Comte refused under any circumstances to take the "first steps." Explaining to Arago why he would not visit the Grotes in their hotel, Comte wrote that he did not want to encourage English aristocratic habits or give them any reason to think he was socially inferior. Insisting on maintaining his "speculative dignity," he said that if the Grotes wished to meet him, they could visit *him* at *his* apartment.[98] This episode lends credence to Massin's suggestion that

[93] Caroline Massin to Blainville, n.d., MAC. This letter follows logically from the one before.

[94] Comte to Valat, May 10, 1840, *CG*, 1:337.

[95] See Bill of May 10, 1840, from a store owned by Vabois, in "Factures," MAC.

[96] John Stuart Mill, *Autobiography and Literary Essays*, ed. John M. Robson and Jack Stillinger, vol. 1 of the *Collected Works of John Stuart Mill* (Toronto: University of Toronto Press and Routledge & Kegan Paul, 1981), 75, 205; Michael St. John Packe, *The Life of John Stuart Mill* (London: Secker & Warburg, 1954), 68.

[97] Arago to Comte, January 1, 1840, MAC.

[98] Comte to Arago, January 2, 1840, *CG*, 1:329.

Comte was becoming more sensitive about his own position and increasingly insulting. Moreover, although at first glance Comte's reaction appears to have been aimed at the aristocratic foreigner, he may well have also been directing his assertion of self-importance against Arago, who was a prominent figure in the scientific community and had gratuitously assumed that Comte would be willing to make the first call.

Despite Comte's rudeness, Grote admired his "great philosophical range" to such an extent that he did visit Comte in late January.[99] Comte was very pleased to learn that the *Cours* was making a greater "sensation" in England than in France. When Grote later sent him an article in the July 1838 issue of the prestigious Whig journal *Edinburgh Review*, Comte decided that out of "decency" he should make an exception to his regime of cerebral hygiene, and he read it with "satisfaction."[100]

A CRITIQUE OF THE *COURS* IN THE *EDINBURGH REVIEW*

The article was a thirty-seven-page review of the first two volumes of the *Cours*.[101] Although it was unsigned, Comte was right in assuming that it was written by the "illustrious" physicist David Brewster. Comte found it "serious" and "truly conscientious."[102] In fact, it was the first, longest, and most complete synopsis of his work that had appeared in any journal. Comte felt sure it would help others appreciate what he was doing.[103]

Brewster introduced Comte as one of the two best historians of science. Comte was, in fact, better than the other one, William Whewell, whose *History of the Inductive Sciences* was full of vague conceptions and misinformation. Except for a superficial review of optics, Comte's history – especially that of astronomy – was marked by "eloquence," "accuracy," "honesty," and "absolute freedom from all personal and national feelings."[104] Brewster praised the objectives of Comte's course, the law of three stages, the classification of the sciences, and his support for pure scientific research. Most of all, he appreciated Comte's approach to the formation and use of hypotheses.

[99] Grote to Comte, January 17, 1840, MAC.
[100] Comte to Valat, May 10, 1840, *CG*, 1:338.
[101] [David Brewster,] Review of *Cours de philosophie positive*, by Auguste Comte, in *Edinburgh Review*, 67 (July 1838): 271–308.
[102] Comte to Valat, May 10, 1840, *CG*, 1:338. See also *Cours*, 2:473.
[103] Comte to Valat, July 10, 1840, *CG*, 1:344.
[104] [Brewster,] Review of *Cours*, 292, 305.

Though very favorable, Brewster's article disappointed Comte because it condemned his antitheological arguments as "groundless." Brewster considered Comte's atheism a "stumbling block" and congratulated his countrymen on preventing such men from teaching in schools, where they reveled in "poisoning the springs of moral and religious instruction."[105] Indignant, Comte was sure that Brewster had missed the whole point of the *Cours* and felt that his remarks confirmed the "well-known" inferiority of English philosophers. Because France more readily accepted criticisms of religion, it would experience a "spiritual and moral regeneration" first, despite England's "secondary political advantages."[106] He seemed willing to overlook the fact that his advanced compatriots had scarcely even acknowledged the existence of the *Cours*.

ANOTHER EFFORT TO ACQUIRE THE CHAIR OF ANALYSIS
AND MECHANICS

In the spring of 1840, after a ten-month hiatus, Comte felt well enough to start writing on social physics again. But whereas previously he had tried to juggle teaching and writing on a daily basis, he found that he could more easily protect his sanity by alternating long stretches of intense work with extended periods of rest.[107] Between April 21 and July 2, he wrote five hundred pages, lessons 52 through 54, which covered the theological period of history. After this tremendous effort, he stopped.[108] His examinations were about to begin in Paris, and he began to prepare himself again for the next battle for his chair at the Ecole Polytechnique.

In 1840 Comte's former professor Poisson died. Never one of Comte's favorites, Poisson had opposed Comte's candidacy for the chair of analysis and mechanics in 1836. Although Poisson was the most important mathematician in France, Comte had denounced him as "disloyal" and "affected" and boldly proclaimed that his "destiny" was "to make war" against him "in all forms."[109] Comte disliked him for his belief in the universal application of the calculus

[105] Ibid., 275–8, 291. See also Comte to Valat, May 10, 1840, *CG*, 1:338.

[106] Comte to Valat, July 10, 1840, *CG*, 1:345.

[107] Comte to Valat, May 10, 1840, *CG*, 1:335; May 1, 1841, *CG*, 2:9; Comte to Mme Auguste Comte, August 23, 1839, *CG*, 1:313; November 4, 1842, *CG*, 2:102.

[108] *Cours de philosophie positive* (1830–42), 5:1–491; "Tableau du nombre de jours," in "Du temps dans le travail intellectuel," ed. Laffitte, 439–40.

[109] Comte to Poinsot, September 18, 1836, *CG*, 1:261; Comte to Mme Auguste Comte, September 3, 1838, *CG*, 1:296; Comte to Blainville, May 29, 1839, *CG*, 1:308.

of probabilities, his previous intimacy with Saint-Simon, his enmity toward two of Comte's most loyal friends, Fourier and Poinsot, his blatant use of patronage, and his easy accommodation to every political regime, including that of Napoleon.[110] In his notorious "Personal Preface" to the sixth volume of the *Cours*, Comte openly accused Poisson of resenting him and of using his attack of madness to discredit him in 1838 so that Liouville could obtain the chair of analysis. (Comte had not bothered to apply.)[111]

At Poisson's death, Duhamel replaced him as examiner of the graduating students and vacated his position as professor of analysis. Comte decided to try for the third time to acquire this chair, and he was certain this time he would succeed. Issalène expressed the general feeling among his friends when he immediately wrote to him, "Undoubtedly you are a professor since Poisson is dead."[112] Comte's situation was better than before because he had become the regular (or senior) *répétiteur* for Duhamel's analysis course on November 20, 1838, after Coriolis, who had previously held this post, replaced Dulong as director of studies.[113] Comte was so sure of obtaining his "definitive position" that he did not launch a campaign, as he had in 1836.[114] Absorbed in the fifth volume of the *Cours*, he wanted to maintain his "philosophical serenity" so that he could continue to write.[115] Besides, he felt that visits to well-known scientists to drum up support were humiliating and useless.

Taking a nonchalant approach as he had in 1835, Comte simply wrote a letter announcing his candidacy to General Jean-Baptiste-Philibert Vaillant, the head of the school.[116] To prevent sabotage, he insisted that his letter be read to the whole Council of Instruction, not just to the committee composed of Coriolis, Savary,

---

[110] Comte to Blainville, March 17, 1833, *CG*, 1:243; Comte to Poinsot, September 18, 1836, *CG*, 1:261; Comte to Mme Auguste Comte, September 3, 1838, *CG*, 1:296; Comte to Blainville, May 29, 1839, *CG*, 1:308; Gouhier, *Jeunesse*, 1:145; Pierre Costabel, "Poisson, Siméon-Denis," in *Dictionary of Scientific Biography*, ed. Gillispie.

[111] *Cours*, 2:468; Comte to Vaillant, August 19, 1839, *CG*, 1:310.

[112] Issalène to Comte, May 22, 1840, MAC. See also Chavelet to Comte, September 8, 1838, MAC; Hippolyte Colard to Comte, May 20, 1840, MAC; Comte to Valat, May 10, 1840, *CG*, 1:339. On the Comtes' eagerness for Poisson to die or retire, see Comte to Mme Auguste Comte, August 23, 1839, *CG*, 1:314; Caroline Massin to Comte, September 30, 1837, MAC.

[113] His salary was raised to two thousand francs. See dossier of Comte (especially report on Comte's pension in 1851); dossier of Coriolis and Dulong, EP.

[114] Comte to Valat, October 22, 1839, *CG*, 1:323.

[115] Comte to Valat, July 10, 1840, *CG*, 1:341.

[116] Comte to Valat, May 10, 1840, *CG*, 1:337. See also Comte to Général Vaillant, August 19, 1839, *CG*, 1:310–12 (this letter was sent in June 1840); Comte to Mme Auguste Comte, *CG*, 1:314; *Almanach royal pour l'an 1840*, 668; "Carrière Polytechnique d'Auguste Comte," ed. Laffitte, 359.

and Liouville, which had been designated to draw up the list of candidates. Vaillant was a "little embarrassed" by this demand.[117]

Comte's rival for the position was Charles-François Sturm, a famous geometer with a theorem named after him and also a member of the Academy of Sciences. Sturm had very strong connections; he was a former tutor to the son of Madame de Staël, a good friend of Victor de Broglie, and a close colleague of many scientists, including Arago and Liouville.[118] But Comte scorned him; he considered his work a useless extension of Fourier's theories. And besides, Sturm had been a *répétiteur* only since 1838. Comte was certain that even his opponents in the Council recognized that he would make a far better professor.[119]

Comte had faith especially in the support of the "noble" and "generous" students of the Ecole Polytechnique, who, he said, would accept no other choice.[120] With great pride, Comte asserted that the lessons he had given four years before in Duhamel's place had become a legend, touching even the present students. In late June these students did in fact send two delegates to each member of the Council to express their wish that Comte become professor, an unprecedented event. The professors, however, gave the delegates unsatisfactory answers, alluding to Comte's estrangement from the intellectual world of the other mathematicians.[121] Deeply moved by the students' action, Comte cried when he recounted these events to Valat.

Although in public Comte tried to affect a serene attitude, in private he was seething with anger and bitterness, displaying the same bellicose behavior that had alarmed Massin. In his letters, he continually insulted the scientists, whom he called his "enemies." If they "forced" him "to war," they would feel a "little too late" that he could make it "very difficult." He even threatened to resort to "illegal" action to get his way and imagined turning the students against them. As a "true philosopher" who represented the "sole present basis of the salvation of Humanity," Comte was ready "for everything."[122]

---

[117] Vaillant to Comte, June 4, 1840, MAC. See also Vaillant to Comte, June 5, 1840, MAC.

[118] Pierre Speziali, "Sturm, Charles-François," in *Dictionary of Scientific Biography*, ed. Gillispie.

[119] Comte to Valat, July 10, 1840, *CG*, 1:341; May 1, 1841, *CG*, 2:10; [Bertrand,] Review of *Cours*, 691; Audiffrent, *Réponse à Bertrand*, 29; "Carrière Polytechnique d'Auguste Comte," ed. Laffitte, 323.

[120] Comte to Valat, July 10, 1840, *CG*, 1:342. See also Comte to Valat, May 10, 1840, *CG*, 1:339.

[121] Comte to Valat, July 10, 1840, *CG*, 1:342; *Cours*, 2:474; Bertrand, "Souvenirs académiques," 537; Testimony of Mr. Barral, a chemist, who was a student at the school in 1840, in Audiffrent, *Centenaire de la fondation de l'Ecole Polytechnique*, 44–5. Barral's testimony is also in Littré, *Auguste Comte*, 249–50.

[122] Comte to Valat, July 10, October 13, 1840, *CG*, 1:343–4, 365.

By July he was plainly nervous. When the Council canceled some of its meetings, he began to think he was the victim of a plot.[123] For the third time since 1831, he presented his case in a letter to the president of the Academy of Sciences. He again made the point that his study of the *philosophy* of the sciences and his 1836 lectures more than qualified him for the position, that the mathematicians in the Academy were unfairly prejudiced against him, and that the teaching of mathematics at the Ecole Polytechnique needed to be reformed. He warned: "I will never renounce a chair that has been . . . a constant goal of [my] daily efforts for twenty-four years."[124]

Comte was so pleased with his "terrible epistle" that he had it printed and distributed to his friends.[125] Asked by Comte to read it aloud at the meeting of the Academy, Poinsot refused: "Stick to all the social norms as much as possible. . . . Always bear in mind that assemblies are very touchy. One word too much is all that is necessary to spoil the best affair."[126] Comte then asked Arago, the permanent secretary of the Academy of Sciences, but he too warned him about the possible effects of his tactlessness. Comte accused the two scientists of treating him as if he were "only twenty-five years old."[127] He refused to accept advice, which, in his eyes, always smacked of paternalism.

On July 26 Comte begged Blainville to ask the Academy to have his five-page letter read, and he agreed to do it at the meeting of August 3.[128] When the other permanent secretary, Flourens, started reading it, he was interrupted by the curses of Thenard, one of Comte's former professors, who demanded that he stop because the Academy did not have time to listen to it.[129] Alexandre Brongniart seconded Thenard's motion, for he wanted the Academy to begin its scheduled closed session, where he intended to nominate a new candidate to the mineralogy section.[130] Blainville appealed in vain to Poncelet, the president of the Academy. Poinsot remained silent and

---

[123] Comte to Blainville, July 30, 1840, *CG*, 1:352. See also Comte to Valat, July 10, 1840, *CG*, 1:341.

[124] Comte to the Président de l'Académie des Sciences, July 13, 1840, *CG*, 1:350.

[125] Comte to Blainville, July 30, 1830, *CG*, 1:352. See also Comte to Valat, August 26, 1840, *CG*, 1:354.

[126] Poinsot to Comte, received by Comte on July 24, 1840, in "Relations d'Auguste Comte avec Poinsot," ed. Laffitte, 156.

[127] Comte to Blainville, July 30, 1840, *CG*, 1:352.

[128] Comte to Blainville, July 26, and 27, 1830, *CG*, 1:350-1.

[129] *Cours*, 2:632; Dr. Al. Donne, "Académie des Sciences: Séance du 3 août," *Journal des débats*, August 6, 1840, 3; Article on meeting of August 3, 1840, *Comptes rendus hebdomadaires des séances de l'Académie des Sciences*, vol. 11, *Juillet–décembre 1840* (Paris, 1841): 210; Audiffrent, *Réponse à Bertrand*, 10.

[130] See the report on the meeting of August 3, 1840, Archives of the Academy of Sciences.

incurred the wrath of Comte, who in the last volume of the *Cours* accused him of breaking his promise to support him.[131] The majority of the Academy then voted to suppress Comte's letter.[132] Yet even Comte admitted that the letter was very much like the one that the Academy had listened to four years before.[133] When Blainville later paid a personal call on each of his colleagues to protest what he considered their unjust action and to tell them of Comte's precarious financial position, one of them told him that the Academy of Sciences was not a welfare office.[134]

Again, Comte blamed his failure on the antipathy of the mathematicians. He was sure the opposition had been led by someone whose son he had rejected for the Ecole Polytechnique. Although he did not name him, the culprit must have been Thenard. Comte had examined his son the year before, and he and Bourdon had agreed on giving him a poor mark, which prevented him from being admitted.[135]

On August 4, the day after the meeting, the very influential *Journal des débats* offered Comte the opportunity to respond to the Academy.[136] The newspaper published an article describing Comte favorably as an "eccentric spirit" whose "original character" was "even more remarkable since it rests on very solid and profound knowledge." His letter was simply a "plea in favor of the opinions of his whole life." According to the article, the Academicians, not wanting to be insulted, had violated his "right" to be heard, for any person could have a letter read if a member requested it.[137]

Grateful for the newspaper's offer, Comte simply asked that his letter of August 4 be published. He appended a short note accusing the Academy of favoring its own members (such as Sturm) over outsiders, monopolizing scientific posts, and violating its own rules. He also appealed to the judgment of the "impartial and enlightened public," whose feelings were "superior to the passions and prejudices of scientific coteries."[138] Such a statement sounds odd coming

---

[131] *Cours*, 2:632.
[132] "Carrière Polytechnique d'Auguste Comte," ed. Laffitte, 360. Donne, the journalist for the *Journal des débats*, said that at most ten members participated in the vote. Donne, "Séance du 3 août," 3. See also *Cours*, 2:475.
[133] *Cours*, 2:632.   [134] Audiffrent, *Réponse à Bertrand*, 10–11.
[135] *Cours*, 2:475; Comte to Valat, August 26, 1840, *CG*, 1:354. See "Examinations: 1839." There is no Thenard listed as a student at the Ecole Polytechnique in the 1830s or 1840s. Marielle, *Répertoire de l'Ecole Impériale Polytechnique*, 211.
[136] Comte to Blainville, August 6, 1840, *CG*, 1:352; Comte to Valat, August 26, 1840, *CG*, 1:354.
[137] Donne, "Séance du 3 août," 3.
[138] Note, August 4, 1840, appended to Comte's letter published in the *Journal des débats*, August 6, 1840, 3. This letter is reproduced in *CG*, 1:429.

from a man who had always insisted that only judgments of a suitably educated elite were correct.

After the publication of his letter, Comte noted happily – and naively – that the Academy felt "very ashamed" of its actions against him.[139] It did not occur to him that he had antagonized it, especially by using the *Journal des débats* to further his cause, for this periodical was generally considered conservative and pro-government. To many, it was the very symbol of the Orleanist haute bourgeoisie.[140] Undoubtedly, it had used Comte to attack the Ecole Polytechnique, whose support for the regime was at best lukewarm. Arago and Liouville, for example, were known for their leftist positions. The year before, the journal had, in fact, published several scandalous articles against the school, causing a great uproar among the students and administration.[141] Comte had unwisely politicized his battle for the chair.

One purpose of the Academy's dismissal of Comte's letter was, of course, to advise the Council of Instruction of the Ecole Polytechnique of its position. Comte believed that the Council was intimidated by the Academy but nevertheless recognized the brilliance of his 1836 lectures. Yet many of the professors were still annoyed by the scandal that had occurred when Duhamel had tried to assume his functions.[142] On August 14 the committee of Coriolis, Savary, and Liouville recommended to the Council of Instruction that Sturm be selected over Comte. According to the official transcript of the meeting, the person in the committee who made the report stated:

> It is not sufficient for a professor of analysis at the Ecole Polytechnique to have ease of elocution and to give agreeable lessons. It is necessary that he thoroughly know the science that he is teaching, that he establish it on rigorous demonstrations, and that he be able to respond to all the students' problems – those regarding not only the course materials but all parts of mathematics.

Sturm's "fine papers," which had led to his membership in the Academy of Sciences, and his lectures, which were "clear" and "easy to follow," proved his deep knowledge of mathematics. Comte's lectures in 1836 reflected "much talent," but that was the "limit of his qualifications in his favor." The *Cours* contained "only rather vague generalities about mathematics," indicated a superficial "knowledge of the more difficult parts," and proved he could not

[139] Comte to Valat, August 26, 1840, *CG*, 1:354.   [140] Collingham, *July Monarchy*, 178–9.
[141] René Taton, "Liouville, Joseph," in *Dictionary of Scientific Biography*, ed. Gillispie; Roger Hahn, "Arago, Dominique François Jean," in ibid.; Callot, *Histoire de l'Ecole Polytechnique*, 80–91.
[142] *Cours*, 2:475; Bertrand, "Souvenirs académiques," 536.

"enlighten the students on the obscure points of the science." The committee member concluded, "It is necessary to give to the Ecole [Polytechnique] a professor who has a solid mind and sound judgment; these qualities must prevail over the brilliance of his elocution and the extent of his general knowledge."[143] Here he was not only rejecting Comte's arguments that his teaching abilities and his philosophical work made him the better candidate, but questioning his good sense.

One committee member in support of the report's conclusion insisted that the school's reputation demanded the appointment of the "most distinguished and well-known" scholars. The third member dismissed Comte's ability as a teacher, claiming his lectures had more "form" than content.[144] Only one member of the Council of Instruction, perhaps Poinsot, replied to these criticisms, pointing out that Comte's philosophical and political works were widely acclaimed and appreciated in Germany and that his lectures were excellent and most enjoyable. The other members reminded him that regardless of the merit of Comte's philosophical works, they had no bearing on the question of who would make the best analysis professor. The meeting adjourned on that note.[145]

On August 21 the Council met again, nominating Sturm instead of Comte for the post.[146] Bertrand claimed that even Poinsot voted for Sturm.[147] Comte was further scandalized that at the Academy the committee of mathematicians put down only Sturm's name on its list of recommended candidates.[148] In the voting session that followed on October 12, 1840, Sturm received thirty-six votes and Comte three.[149] Sturm was officially appointed to the chair in late October.[150]

Comte was sure his failure was the result of a conspiracy supported by the "jesuitical character of the principal polytechnical ringleader of this iniquity."[151] Although he did not mention the culprit's name, he later stated that the success of his rival was due to Coriolis, the director of studies.[152] And in this he was not entirely wrong. In a letter written in 1842 to a cousin, Coriolis explained that he felt no animosity against Comte, who had a "deep grasp of

---

[143] Meeting of August 14, 1840, Registre: Procès-Verbal du Conseil d'Instruction, vol. 8, EP.

[144] Ibid.   [145] Ibid. See also Comte to Blainville, July 27, 1840, *CG*, 1:351.

[146] Comte to Valat, August 26, 1840, *CG*, 1:355.

[147] Bertrand, "Souvenirs académiques," 542.   [148] *Cours*, 2:475.

[149] Article on meeting of October 12, 1840, *Comptes rendus hebdomadaires des séances de l'Académie des Sciences*, 11:606.

[150] Meeting of October 23, 1840, Registre: Procès-Verbal du Conseil d'Instruction, vol. 8, EP.

[151] Comte to Valat, September 22, 1840, *CG*, 1:361.

[152] Comte to Valat, May 1, 1841, *CG*, 2:9, *Almanach royal pour l'an 1840*, 669.

the sciences" and was perhaps the best educated man in Europe. But he had not favored him for the job because of his obscurity as a mathematician and especially his atheism. Although not stemming from any essential "depravity" on his part, Comte's philosophy was a "little materialistic" and thus "dangerous . . . for young people": it was "hardly suitable to put him in a chair in our school."[153] Comte was partly right when he maintained that he was being penalized because the *Cours* posed a threat to religion and therefore to society.

Claiming that his chair had been "usurped" and finding himself the *répétiteur* once again for a man who had triumphed over him, Comte fantasized for almost a year that the students would be so outraged by Sturm's "radical incapacity" to teach that they would chase him from the classroom.[154] Heartened by every report critical of Sturm's teaching, he was supposedly told by Coriolis that he would not vote for Sturm again since he had never heard such a "*schoolboyish* course."[155] Yet despite the fact that the students did eventually send Comte a delegation to express their disappointment, he waited in vain for their revolt against his "vile enemies."[156] Comte wrongly believed his "philosophical regimen" protected him from "personal illusions."[157]

These battles against the Academy left their mark on Comte's development. From the beginning, he took a philosophical approach to the sciences whereby the "spirit of the whole" was more important than the "spirit of detail."[158] He thought he was the only person who combined the scientific spirit with the philosophical spirit; it was precisely this synthesis that made him feel certain he was the savior of humanity. However, this intellectual predilection as well as the arrogance that it engendered in him made the Academy of Sciences and the Ecole Polytechnique turn against him whenever he applied for a purely scientific position. In reaction, he began increasingly to consider himself a "pure philosopher," destined to fight against the "scientific spirit" that was becoming too specialized and tainted by industrialism.[159] He would eliminate the "merchants of detail," who easily made "huge scientific fortunes with very

[153] Coriolis to Madame Benoist, written from August 26 to August 31, 1842, MAC.

[154] Comte to Valat, August 26, 1840, *CG*, 1:355–6.

[155] Comte to Valat, May 1, 1841, *CG*, 2:10.

[156] Comte to Valat, August 26, 1840, *CG*, 1:356. See also Comte to Valat, September 22, 1840, *CG*, 1:361; Testimony of Barral, in Audiffrent, *Centenaire de la fondation de l'Ecole Polytechnique*, 44 (also in Littré, *Auguste Comte*, 250).

[157] Comte to Valat, August 26, 1840, *CG*, 1:358.

[158] Comte to the Président de l'Académie des Sciences, July 13, 1840, *CG*, 1:346.

[159] Comte to Valat, July 10, 1840, *CG*, 1:344. See also Comte to Valat, August 26, 1840, *CG*, 1:355.

frivolous materials."[160] Although Comte is always remembered as a spokesman for the scientific age, he spent most of the 1830s and 1840s fighting against the triumph of allegedly degenerate "scientific coteries."

Comte admitted that his "pronounced character," "independent intelligence," and "isolated" and "eccentric" life had alienated the important people of his time – especially the scientists – but he claimed their dislike of him stemmed from "egoism and envy."[161] Their lack of appreciation was further proof that his epoch was "pretentious," "superficial," and irrational. Already practicing cerebral hygiene, Comte decided that henceforth he would limit his "voluntary contacts" with his century to his evenings at the Théâtre Italien. By further removing himself from the contemporary world, he could better devote himself to anticipating the future – the only activity "suitable for a reasonable man."[162]

Comte's disputes with the scientists exacerbated his troubles at home, for Massin was convinced that if he had made the concessions she had advised, he would have obtained the coveted chair, the "desire of my life," as she put it.[163] Irritated by her reproaches and constant complaints of odd, mysterious illnesses, Comte concluded that she was in a "sad valetudinarian state" resulting from the "very hazardous crisis that characterizes feminine maturity."[164] As usual, he urged her to take a separate vacation, this time with Madame Littré, a good friend of theirs. But the idea of a vacation without her husband struck her as unappealing and socially unacceptable.[165] She realized that she relied on her husband, whereas he depended on no one and did not love her.

THE COMPLETION OF VOLUME 5 OF THE *COURS*

Three months after his return from his examination circuit, Comte began lesson 55, which reviewed the metaphysical stage of history through the eighteenth century. Although he decided to forgo writing in the evenings to save his eyes, he still managed to devote five or six hours a day before dinner to the *Cours*. In doing so, he was

[160] Comte to Valat, May 1, 1841, *CG*, 2:8.
[161] Comte to Maximilien Marie, July 4, 1841, *CG*, 2:13.
[162] Comte to Valat, May 1, 1841, *CG*, 2:8.
[163] Caroline Massin to Comte, September 3, 1840, MAC.
[164] Comte to Valat, May 1, 1841, *CG*, 2:6. See also Comte to Valat, January 5, August 26, 1840, *CG*, 1:334, 358; Caroline Massin to Comte, August 28, 1839, MAC.
[165] Caroline Massin to Comte, September 3, 1840, MAC.

able to write the entire chapter from January 10 to February 26, 1841.[166]

When he had finished, he was, as usual, surprised at how much he had written. "Chapter" 55 alone came to almost three hundred pages.[167] Although he thought he wrote concisely, this volume already ran to almost eight hundred pages, and he had yet to begin to describe the modern development of the positive movement. The *Cours* "seems to grow under my pen," he told Valat in exasperated tones.[168] Originally, social physics was to have taken one volume, but he now found it needed three. His philosophy of history was extending his work, for it was the subject of the last two volumes. It was also the part on which he prided himself the most.

The fifth volume finally appeared in May 1841 – two years after volume 4. To justify the "inconveniences" of the uneven manner of publication, Comte claimed that in this age of "dispersive" specialties, his readers were better off dealing with each new aspect of his philosophy separately, because they would not immediately understand the spirit of the whole anyway.[169] Some of them, however, agonized over the slow publication of the *Cours*. One former student, depressed by the fifth volume's description of the growing disorganization of modern life, begged Comte to send him the draft of his next volume to find the reassurance he needed to "face the storms that surround us on all sides."[170]

One of the people to whom Comte sent this volume was Armand Marrast, back from exile in England. He was "happy and proud" that Comte had remembered him. Although he had not yet read the fifth volume, he had found the ideas of the fourth to be far superior to those of Leroux, Buchez, and Lamennais. But in addition to expressing his impatience with Comte's slowness in finishing the *Cours*, he expressed his disagreement with his politics: "I cannot agree with . . . your appreciation of the ideas of *liberty*, equality, and popular sovereignty, and I fear that the rectitude of your mind, which is so positive, has been twisted."[171] Marrast's ambivalent letter reminded Comte of his alienation from republican circles.

---

[166] Comte to Valat, May 1, 1841, *CG*, 2:9; "Tableau du nombre de jours," in "Du temps dans le travail intellectuel," ed. Laffitte, 440.

[167] *Cours de philosophie positive* (1830–42), 5:492–775.

[168] Comte to Valat, May 1, 1841, *CG*, 2:6.   [169] Ibid., 7.

[170] Barbot de Chement to Comte, August 24, 1841, MAC. This young man graduated from the Ecole Polytechnique in 1836.

[171] Marrast to Comte, June 7, 1841, in "Relations d'Auguste Comte avec Armand Marrast," ed. Laffitte, 187. See also Marrast to Comte, May 22, 1842, in ibid., 189.

Chapter 12

The Encounter between Two Luminaries: Comte and Mill

In the middle of the still more complete isolation that results from my new domestic situation, I attach more and more value to the intimate sympathy – both intellectual and affectionate – that has so happily developed between us.

Comte to Mill, 1842

WORK ON VOLUME 6 OF THE *COURS* AND PROBLEMS AT SCHOOL

Comte's recent battle with the scientists reaffirmed his tendency to view history as a struggle between specialists and generalists. He was eager to delineate this conflict in the *Cours*. As soon as the fifth volume appeared, he started lesson 56 of the next volume. Although this chapter came to 344 pages and was the longest of all, he completed it in a month, on June 17, 1841. It covered the development of the positive stage of history and demonstrated the provisional nature of the contemporary period, which he aptly named the "age of specialization."[1] During the following month, he wrote the first half of lesson 57, another 300-page chapter. It dealt with the organic tendencies of the positive age and the inevitable triumph of the "spirit of generalization."[2]

These reveries about the future were interrupted, however, by his examination tour, which began July 14. He found it more onerous than usual, for he and other examiners were given the additional task of evaluating almost fifty candidates for the Ecole Royale Forestière.[3] What made matters worse was that the forestry school soon complained about his examination methods and grading practices.[4]

---

[1] *Cours*, 2:484. See also "Tableau du nombre de jours," in "Du temps danus le travail intellectuel," ed. Laffitte, 440; *Cours de philosophie positive* (1830–42): 6:1–344.

[2] *Cours*, 2:584. See also *Cours de philosophie positive* (1830–42): 6:344–45.

[3] For this work, Comte was paid an extra five hundred francs. Administration des Forêts to Comte, July 15, 1841, MAC; Entry, December 1841, in Caroline's formal notebook, "Recettes et dépenses janvier 1837 à décembre 1841," MAC; "Examinations: 1841," MAC.

[4] Administration de l'Ecole des Forêts to Comte, August 26, September 17, September 24, 1841, MAC.

Comte also received criticisms from others, who had been perhaps provoked by his recent condemnation of scientists and French mathematical education. The administrators of the Ecole Polytechnique felt his examinations were unfair.[5] In June, Coriolis informed him that the Council of Instruction had voted unanimously to warn Comte to ask "very simple problems closely related to the required theorems."[6] Two months later, an important administrator at the Ecole Saint-Cyr accused Comte of personal bias when he gave his son a poor grade.[7] Laville warned Comte that many preparatory school teachers were also turning against him. They claimed that because Comte used the same questions throughout his examination tour, the students whom he tested last, namely those in the provinces, had the unfair advantage of knowing the problems in advance.[8]

Not wanting to be bothered, Comte paid little attention to Coriolis's and Laville's admonitions. He took pride in asking complex and obscure questions to force candidates to think and was sure his techniques were improving mathematical instruction.[9] Instead of yielding, Comte nursed a plan of revenge, which he intended to execute in the final volume of the *Cours*. With great trepidation, Massin wrote to her husband, "Go ahead, dear friend, because all that I could tell you would accomplish nothing. I will wait unhappily, very persuaded that you have not known how to make yourself strong enough to be feared."[10]

THE FIRST STEP TOWARD FRIENDSHIP

Soon after Comte returned from his controversial examination circuit, he received on October 21, 1841, a note from Marrast, who wished to talk to him "in the name of several of my friends in London who have read your book, admire it, and asked me to tell you so."[11] Three weeks later, on November 12, Comte received a letter written in French from an Englishman:

> I do not know, Sir, if it is permitted for a man who is totally unknown to you to occupy a few moments of time as precious as yours, in talking to you of himself and of the great intellectual obligations that he owes to you; but encouraged by my friend M. Marrast, and

[5] Meeting of June 11, 1841, Registre: Procès-Verbal du Conseil d'Instruction de l'Ecole Polytechnique, vol. 8, EP.
[6] Coriolis to Comte, June 28, 1841, MAC.   [7] Lambert to Comte, August 12, 1841, MAC.
[8] Laville to Comte, August 11, 1841, MAC.
[9] Comte to Mill, July 22, 1842, *CG*, 2:57; Comte to Valat, August 26, 1840, *CG*, 1:358.
[10] Caroline Massin to Comte, September 20, 1841, MAC.
[11] Marrast to Comte, October 18, 1841, MAC.

thinking that maybe in the middle of your great philosophical works you would not be completely indifferent to receiving from a foreign land marks of sympathy and of adhesion, I dare to hope that you will not find my present step improper.[12]

It was with these humble words that the most important English thinker of the nineteenth century, John Stuart Mill, introduced himself to Comte. This note of November was the first of many that Mill and Comte would exchange over the next six years. Expressing deep sentiments of friendship and intellectual communion, the correspondence between these two very different men was one of the most remarkable of the century.

Mill had first become aware of Comte's works many years before, in 1828, when one of his close friends had brought a young Frenchman named Gustave d'Eichthal to a meeting of the London Debating Society. D'Eichthal was much taken with Mill's debating skills, and they soon became friends. D'Eichthal quickly understood the reason for their mutual attraction: "What brought us together was not abstract ideas but our character and our desire to be apostles."[13] At that time, d'Eichthal was still attached to Comte and asked him to send him several copies of his *Plan des travaux scientifiques*, one of which he gave to Mill.[14]

MILL'S BACKGROUND: BENTHAMISM

Mill's reaction to the fundamental opuscule had much to do with his background. Born in 1806, he was brought up in the heart of philosophical radicalism. James Mill was the friend and disciple of Jeremy Bentham, and it was expected that his son John would become the head of the utilitarian movement. Since James Mill believed a person was the product of his environment, John's education was of utmost importance, so much so that he himself undertook the task. Under his father's strict discipline, John by age twelve could read Latin and Greek with ease and perused treatises on chemistry and Ferguson's history books for amusement. Like Comte, he was an early unbeliever, chiefly because his father was one.[15]

Mill did have, however, a secular faith. In the winter of 1821, after reading *Traités de législation civile et pénale*, Etienne Dumont's edition

[12] Mill to Comte, November 8, 1841, *CG*, 2:345–6.
[13] Gustave d'Eichthal, Journal, quoted in introduction to John Stuart Mill, *Correspondance inédite avec Gustave d'Eichthal*, ed. Eugène d'Eichthal (Paris, 1898), ix.
[14] Gustave d'Eichthal to Comte, October 17, 1828, "Correspondance de Comte et d'Eichthal (Suite)," ed. Laffitte, 361; Mill to Gustave d'Eichthal, May 15, 1829, in *Earlier Letters*, 12:34; Eugène d'Eichthal, Introduction to Mill, *Correspondance inédite*, x.
[15] Mill, *Autobiography*, 7–33, 45, 55.

of Bentham's manuscripts, he experienced a revelation. Despite his Benthamite education and his own friendship with Bentham, Mill had not fully comprehended the essence of his philosophy until he read Dumont's work. Now he understood that the principle of the greatest happiness of the greatest number, used by Bentham to judge the morality of actions, put an end to the unreliability of all other moralists, who hid their feelings and prejudices behind the rhetoric of natural laws and right reason. Bentham's analysis of the consequences of actions according to their production of pain or pleasure and his classification of offenses seemed clear, scientific, and objective. With the help of such a tool in the creation of laws, the proper reform of society appeared promising. For Mill, the principle of utility explained the entire world and became the "keystone" that held together his beliefs and knowledge. Proclaiming that Bentham had opened up a "new era in thought," Mill expressed his conversion to his system in clearly spiritual terms:

> When I laid down the last volume of the *Traité* I had become a different being. . . . I now had opinions; a creed, a doctrine, a philosophy; in one among the best senses of the word, a religion; the inculcation and diffusion of which could be made the principal outward purpose of a life.[16]

In the 1820s, Mill propagated Bentham and his father's ideas with zeal. He joined such clubs as the Utilitarian Society and the London Debating Society; met friends several times a week at George Grote's house to discuss problems of political economy, logic, and psychology; and wrote articles for various periodicals, many of which had Benthamite inclinations. To support himself, he accepted a position at the East India Company that his father obtained for him. This job provided him with a living for the next thirty-five years, thus freeing him from the financial problems that beset Comte.[17]

Despite the even tenor of his life, Mill experienced an attack of mental illness in 1826, the same year as Comte. In the autumn of that year, he became increasingly depressed. Not only did he lose his enthusiasm for reforming the world, but he could find no reason at all for living. In an age emphasizing the emotions, he suddenly saw that his eighteenth-century philosophy was limited and weak. It dawned on him that he was not the incarnation of Benthamism: a "dry, hard, logical machine." Realizing that his father had starved his emotions, especially by his lack of tenderness, he, like Comte,

---

[16] Ibid., 67, 69.
[17] Ibid., 81–111; Packe, *John Stuart Mill*, 66–74; Alexander Bain, *John Stuart Mill: A Criticism with Personal Recollections* (London: Longmans, Green, 1882), 30–1, 40–1.

blamed his education for having isolated him and retarded the development of his feelings. He denounced "analytic habits" for being a "perpetual worm at the root both of the passions and of the virtues." They undermined "all desires, and all pleasures, which are the effects of association." His father's Benthamite association of pleasure and goodness now seemed to him too rational, too cold, too forced – in short, artificial. And if people's feelings were overlooked, it would not be possible to reform society by instituting legal means to recompense and punish its members. Henceforth, Mill would stress the importance of the internal cultivation of the individual to correct the defects of analysis. Like Comte, Mill came to the realization that poetry and music were crucial to the "cultivation of the feelings," which became "one of the cardinal points" in his "ethical and philosophical creed."[18] When he began to cry upon reading the *Mémoires d'un père* of Jean-François Marmontel, he realized that he was a man of feeling after all.

After his recovery, Mill continued to be in full revolt against Benthamism and his father, for the two were inseparable. In this respect, he was again similar to Comte, who had also reacted against his paternal mentor, Saint-Simon, and wanted to reform his philosophy. Although hesitant about becoming a fanatic once again, Mill explained to d'Eichthal his enthusiasm for new ideas: "The times are very favorable for starting new opinions, and especially any that hold out sufficient hopes of extensive good, to enlist in their behalf that enthusiasm and *dévouement*, which are now wandering about the world seeking an object worthy of them."[19] Just as Comte after his rupture with Saint-Simon had sought inspiration in the works of conservative thinkers, Mill began to be influenced by writers who represented the "reaction of the nineteenth century against the eighteenth." Coleridge, Carlyle, and Goethe became important sources of stimulation, but it was Comte and the Saint-Simonians who gave him a "new mode of political thinking."[20]

MILL'S INITIAL REACTION TO COMTE

Mill first referred to Comte's fundamental opuscule in October 1829, when he discussed with d'Eichthal another work that he had given him, the *Opinions littéraires, philosophiques, et industrielles* by Saint-Simon and his disciples.[21] By this time, d'Eichthal was a fervent

---

[18] Mill, *Autobiography*, 110, 143, 147.

[19] Mill to Gustave d'Eichthal, November 7, 1829, *Earlier Letters*, 12:39.

[20] Mill, *Autobiography*, 169, 171.

[21] In his first letter to Comte, Mill said he read the fundamental opuscule in 1828, but later he gave d'Eichthal the impression that he had read it in September or October 1829. Mill

Saint-Simonian and was trying to convert Mill to his new creed. Mill resisted, however. He not only wanted to avoid the sectarian spirit that he had abandoned three years before, but was "perfectly astonished at the shallowness" and crudeness of the *Opinions*. Even though he thought Comte was a Saint-Simonian because he had stated in the *Plan* that he was Saint-Simon's student, Mill made a very clear distinction between his writings and those of the Saint-Simonians. He told d'Eichthal that he found the fundamental opuscule to be far more impressive: "I was no longer surprised at the high opinion which I had heard you express of the book, & the writer, and was even seduced by the plausibility of his manner."[22]

To Mill, Comte incarnated the superior qualities of French thought, the "power of systematizing, of tracing a principle to its remotest consequences, and that power of clear and consecutive exposition which generally accompanies it." The most compelling part of Comte's work was the "partie critique," where he demonstrated that the revolutionary era was a period of transition marked by intellectual confusion and anarchy.[23] Comte's argument that people were lost in an era of "criticism and argumentation," which threatened the social fabric, appealed directly to Mill, who three years before had discovered that habits of analysis were ultimately destructive. Having rejected Benthamism, he too felt disoriented. He seemed to agree with Comte's demand for a new doctrine that would satisfy two apparently contradictory conditions: "the abandonment of the old system, and the establishment of a regular and stable order."[24] However, the solution – the creation of a new science of society – created problems for Mill, who wrote, "I find the same fault with his philosophy, that he does with the philosophy of the eighteenth century[;] it is only the *partie critique* which appears to me sound, the *partie organique* appears to me liable to a hundred objections."[25]

Mill did not find Comte's philosophy original, especially because his father and Bentham had also tried to create a scientific philosophy of society that would avoid abstract principles, such as the social contract and natural rights. Benthamism and the positive philosophy had not only the same goal of unifying theory and practice,

to Comte, November 8, 1841, CG, 2:346; Mill to Gustave d'Eichthal, May 15, 1829, *Earlier Letters*, 12:34.

[22] Mill to Gustave d'Eichthal, October 8, 1829, *Earlier Letters*, 12:35. An early draft of his *Autobiography* confirms this first reaction. Here Mill stated: "At the time of which I am now speaking, the only very strong impression which I received from anything connected with St. Simonism was derived from an early writing of Auguste Comte." Mill, *Autobiography*, 615.

[23] Mill to Gustave d'Eichthal, October 8, 1829, *Earlier Letters*, 12:35.

[24] *Système*, vol. 4, "Appendice," 58, 112.

[25] Mill to Gustave d'Eichthal, October 8, 1829, *Earlier Letters*, 12:35.

where the former must precede and guide the latter, but the same emphasis on the real, the useful, the concrete, and the certain. Comte himself at the outset of his career had endorsed Bentham's doctrine, which he believed was the "most eminent derivation" of political economy, one of the incomplete sciences of society that had preceded his own.[26] One reason utilitarianism and the positive philosophy were similar was that both were strongly influenced by David Hume.[27] At first glance, therefore, Comte's system seemed to Mill to be a reincarnation of the system he had just rejected.

Furthermore, Mill thought Comte was wrong to "suppose that a few striking and original observations, are sufficient to form the foundation of a *science positive*." He found the law of three stages and the classification of the sciences absurd and simplistic. Comte's historical perspective had been "distorted by the necessity of proving that civilization has but one law, & that a law of progressive advancement."[28] Since Mill shared his father's view that a person was a product of his environment, he rejected the idea of a particular and fixed order of intellectual and material development. To him, Comte debased human nature by making the history of the species a reflection of instinct – even if it was the instinct for perfection – because instinct was the law of the lower animals. Moreover, in Mill's view, there was no necessary progress. In each period, humanity advanced in some areas but often fell backward in others. Finally, Comte's social analysis struck him as limited, for it seemed inapplicable to England.

Mill generally disliked Comte's political opinions. Comte's idea that the government should direct its energies to the one end of production overlooked what should be its most important consideration: the moral and intellectual development of the individual. Living in a more industrialized country, Mill felt, in fact, that the current preoccupation with production was already threatening intellectual and moral advancement. Also, since he recognized the harmful effects of his own single-minded efforts to reform society, he argued that the government should never limit itself to one goal because "men do not come into the world to fulfill one single end, and there is no single end which if fulfilled even in the most

[26] Comte to Mill, November 20, 1841, *CG*, 2:22. See also *Ecrits*, 86.
[27] Bentham had also been profoundly marked by Hume's empiricism, his critique of natural rights and of the social contract, and his ethic that all virtue resides in utility. Hume was, in effect, the father of both positivism and utilitarianism. See John Plamenatz, *The English Utilitarians* (Oxford: Basil Blackwell, 1949), 22, 66–7, 145; R. P. Anschutz, *The Philosophy of J. S. Mill* (Oxford, Clarendon Press, 1953), 8–9; Kolakowski, *The Alienation of Reason*, 32.
[28] Mill to Gustave d'Eichthal, October 8, 1829, *Earlier Letters*, 12:35, 37.

complete manner would make them happy."[29] Mill's criticisms of Comte were partly in reaction to his new attitude toward Benthamism. In proclaiming that each man was an egoist seeking to maximize his pleasure, Bentham, according to Mill, had also neglected the totality of the individual.[30]

As for Comte's concept of the separation of powers, Mill disagreed completely with his choice of scientists as the most competent men to create a new spiritual power. To him, they were the "most remarkable for a narrow & bigoted understanding, & a sordid & contracted disposition as respects all things wider than their business or families."[31]

In sum, Mill considered Comte too narrow-minded, systematic, and dogmatic. Although charmed by his style and manner of arguing his points, he suspected that he was too eager to sacrifice truth to clarity and reasoning. Comte shared not only the virtues but also the faults of his compatriots:

> They [French thinkers] are so well satisfied with the clearness with which their conclusions flow from their premises, that they do not stop to compare the conclusions themselves with the fact. . . . They deduce politics like mathematics from a set of axioms & definitions, forgetting that in mathematics there is no danger of partial views.[32]

Mill implied that Comte had failed to establish an altogether scientific and positive doctrine of society because his deductive analysis, which derived from his mathematical training, neglected conflicting facts and other points of view. In arguing that Comte was wrong to deduce an entire system from a few simple, "scientific" premises, Mill was also reflecting his dissatisfaction with Benthamism, which was based on the greatest happiness principle. His appraisal was, in many respects, similar to the vicious critique that Macaulay had just made of James Mill's ideas in the *Edinburgh Review*.[33]

It is thus evident that in October 1829 Mill had made a severe and almost complete denunciation of Comte's philosophy, including his doctrine of social science, his method, his concept of spiritual power, and his theory of government. What was left? Mill most admired the critical part of Comte's philosophy, but this section represented a critique of individualism and liberty, two ideals that Mill strongly

---

[29] Ibid., 36.　　[30] Anschutz, *Philosophy of J. S. Mill*, 14.
[31] Mill to Gustave d'Eichthal, October 8, 1829, *Earlier Letters*, 12:37.　　[32] Ibid., 35–6.
[33] John Clive, *Macaulay: The Shaping of the Historian* (1973; New York: Random House, Vintage Books, 1975), 126–33; Gertrude Himmelfarb, *On Liberty and Liberalism: The Case of John Stuart Mill* (New York: Knopf, 1974), 9. See also Jack Lively and John Rees, *Utilitarian Logic and Politics: James Mill's "Essay on Government," and Macaulay's Critique and the Ensuing Debate* (Oxford: Clarendon Press, 1978).

defended. As a result, he seemed somewhat ambivalent. Although he believed that the anarchical crisis of his time was an evil, he could not agree with Comte on the need to create a unifying doctrine. Yet a month later he would change his mind.

In a letter to d'Eichthal on November 7, Mill apologized for his first judgment of Comte and the Saint-Simonians: "I am rather afraid that my former letter may have left an impression on your mind, that I do not think as highly of them as I do."[34] Wanting to demonstrate how much he did "admire . . . this school," Mill praised a part of the "Saint-Simonian" doctrine that he had previously condemned: the idea of the necessity of a spiritual power. Mill decided that he did, after all, share the view that humanity was advancing toward a state where

> the body of the people, i.e., the uninstructed, shall entertain the same feelings of deference & submission to the authority of the instructed, in morals and politics, as they at present do in the physical sciences. This, I am persuaded, is the only wholesome state of the human mind.

By agreeing with Comte's objection to unlimited liberty of conscience, Mill was showing himself to be more open to authoritarian ideas than in his first letter. He further asserted that the doctrine of the spiritual power would guard against the errors of the eighteenth-century philosophes, including their belief that "the diffusion of knowledge among the laboring classes & the consequent improvement of their intellects is to be the grand instrument of the regeneration of mankind."[35] In saying this, Mill was rejecting the central idea of Bentham and his father that education had unlimited potential for elevating the intellectual and moral level of man.[36]

Mill later suggested in his *Autobiography* that he was much impressed by Comte's idea of history and the link between history and politics:

> The writers by whom, more than by any others, a new mode of political thinking was brought home to me, were those of the St. Simonian school in France. . . . I was greatly struck with the connected view which they for the first time presented to me, of the

---

[34] The remarks that Mill was making refer to the Saint-Simonians, but the ideas he discussed derived chiefly from Comte. He still believed that Comte was a Saint-Simonian. Mill to Gustave d'Eichthal, November 7, 1829, *Earlier Letters*, 12:40.

[35] Ibid. [36] Mill, *Autobiography*, 111.

natural order of human progress; and especially with their division of all history into organic periods and critical periods.

Mill only mentioned one "Saint-Simonian": Auguste Comte. He could not restrain his admiration for the style and dogmatism that he had criticized in October 1829:

> Among their [the Saint-Simonians'] publications . . . there was one which seemed to be far superior to the rest; in which the general idea was matured into something much more definite and instructive. This was an early work of Auguste Comte.[37]

Mill was evidently far more attracted to Comte than he was willing to admit at the outset. At first, Comte's ideas had shocked him, but then they proved useful to him in his new state of mind. The profound influence Comte had on his intellectual development is evident in the first letter he wrote to Comte in November 1841. Addressing Comte in French as he would do for the next six years, Mill wrote:

> It was in the year 1828, Sir, that I read for the first time your treatise of *Politique Positive*; and this reading gave to all my ideas a strong jolt, which along with other causes, but much more than they, brought about my definitive exit from the Benthamist section of the revolutionary school, in which I was brought up and I can almost even say in which I was born.[38]

Now instead of criticizing positivism for being unoriginal, Mill decided that its similarity to utilitarianism made it respectable. In an early draft of his *Autobiography*, he wrote, "This doctrine harmonized very well with my existing notions; I already regarded the methods of physical science as the proper models for political."[39] He told Comte that Benthamism was the "best *preparation*" for the more advanced doctrine of positivism because of its "tight logic" and opposition to "ridiculous metaphysical entities."[40]

In full revolt against his father and his philosophy, Mill thus discovered in the positive system what had been lacking in Benthamism: a philosophy of history. This philosophy gave him a better understanding of the confusing events of his time and the role of his generation. It also became a useful tool against his father and the doctrine of his youth.

In discussing progress, Comte had attacked eighteenth-century philosophers and their successors for being excessively critical, that is, indifferent to organicism, and for relying too much on practical

[37] Ibid., 171, 173.   [38] Mill to Comte, November 8, 1841, *CG*, 2:346.
[39] Mill, *Autobiography*, 615.   [40] Mill to Comte, November 8, 1841, *CG*, 2:346.

and immediate reforms; he partly attributed these failures to the "legists." This analysis appealed to Mill, who had discovered in Benthamism that too much questioning could indeed be "fatal" and who now yearned for a solid, coherent, all-encompassing theory. Moreover, he no longer agreed with Bentham's faith in legislators to enact practical reforms leading to the greatest happiness of the greatest number. In fact, Mill now seemed to reject the entire Benthamite program of refashioning institutions and the environment in general to effect change: "I ceased to attach almost exclusive importance to the ordering of outward circumstances, and the training of the human being for speculation and for action."[41] The effect of Comte's interpretation of history is evident in Mill's famous 1838 essay on Bentham and Coleridge. Referring to the eighteenth century as a period of "negative or destructive philosophers," he wrote:

> To Bentham more than to any other source might be traced the questioning spirit, the disposition to demand the *why of everything*, which had gained so much ground and was producing such important consequences in these times . . . he is the great *subversive*, or, in the language of continental philosophers, the great *critical* thinker of his age and country.[42]

Later, when Mill mentioned in his *Autobiography* that during a certain period of his life he had underestimated the eighteenth century, he was perhaps referring to these years, when he was under Comte's influence.[43]

One of the most important ideas that Mill appropriated from Comte as well as from the Saint-Simonians, who reinforced it, was that their epoch was an age of transition. This realization that the anarchy of moral and intellectual opinions was an abnormal state led him to envision a very different future, one in which liberty and permanent beliefs could coexist. In 1831, when Mill incorporated these ideas in a series of articles for the *Examiner* entitled "The Spirit of the Age," Thomas Carlyle called him a "new Mystic" and sought to meet him.[44]

Under the sway of Carlyle, Coleridge, Goethe, and especially

---

[41] Mill, *Autobiography*, 147. See also John Robson, "Moralist," chap. in *The Improvement of Mankind: The Social and Political Thought of John Stuart Mill* (Toronto: University of Toronto Press, 1968), 117–59; Anschutz, *Philosophy of J. S. Mill*, 11.

[42] John Stuart Mill, "Bentham," chap. in *Essays on Ethics, Religion and Society*, ed. J. M. Robson, vol. 10 of *The Collected Works of John Stuart Mill* (Toronto: University of Toronto Press and Routledge & Kegan Paul, 1969), 78–9.

[43] Mill, *Autobiography*, 169.

[44] Carlyle, quoted in Mill, *Autobiography*, 181. See also ibid., 173, 179; Robson, *Improvement of Mankind*, 77; Packe, *John Stuart Mill*, 98.

Comte, whose exposition seemed the most remarkable to him, Mill learned that "all questions of political institutions are relative, not absolute, and that different states of human progress not only *will* have, but *ought* to have, different institutions."[45] Although apparently contradicting his first letter concerning Comte, Mill said in his *Autobiography* that the Saint-Simonians had convinced him that the progress of the human mind had a certain order that could not be altered by government legislation.[46] Comte's works had shown that a truly effective political philosophy must rest on a theory of progress, that is, a philosophy of history. Without such a theory, Bentham seemed to work in vain to create laws that corresponded to an abstract and absolute idea of man and civilization, and he overlooked the fact that even evil institutions could help advance humanity. Mill seemed to be attacking Bentham when he wrote in a letter to d'Eichthal about the need for each person to stop applying present-day standards to the past and to adopt a relativistic position:

> And yet, he who does not do this, will judge the present as ill as the past. For surely at every *present* epoch there are many things which would be good for that epoch, though not good for the being Man, at every epoch, nor perhaps at any other than that one: & whoever does not make this distinction must be a bad practical philosopher.[47]

Comte's philosophy of history encouraged Mill to devote himself to a new mission of construction. Shortly after reading the fundamental opuscule, he proudly declared that he was "completely . . . cured of those *habitudes critiques*" so common "among educated Englishmen and Frenchmen," and he vowed to "contribute to the formation of a better spirit."[48] But at the same time, he would not adopt a new "system of political philosophy" to replace the one he had "abandoned." He had

> only a conviction, that the true system was something much more complex and many sided than I had previously had any idea of, and that its office was to supply, not a set of model institutions, but principles from which the institutions suitable to any given circumstances might be deduced.[49]

---

[45] Mill, *Autobiography*, 169. See also Mill to Gustave d'Eichthal, November 7, 1829, *Earlier Letters*, 12:41.

[46] Mill, *Autobiography*, 169, 171.

[47] Mill to Gustave d'Eichthal, November 7, 1829, *Earlier Letters*, 12:41.

[48] Mill to Gustave d'Eichthal, February 9, 1830, *Earlier Letters*, 12:45. See also Mill to Gustave d'Eichthal, November 7, 1829, *Earlier Letters*, 12:42.

[49] Mill, *Autobiography*, 169.

Thus instead of creating an entire new system, Mill followed Comte's concept of relativity to the extreme.[50]

Mill sought to be constructive by taking what was valuable from different opinions, even those that might seem disreputable. This was the method that Comte had used in evaluating the contributions made by the Catholic Church, the monarchy, and other institutions to civilization. Also, when Comte had combined the revolutionaries' principle of progress with the reactionaries' principle of order, he had shown him the efficacy of synthesis. Mill decided that "substituting one fragment of the truth for another is not what is wanted, but combining them together so as to obtain as large a portion as possible of the whole."[51] From the late 1820s, he began to join the fragments of truth from the eighteenth century with those of the nineteenth century, just as Comte had done. After his first encounter with Comte's thought, he wrote: "I looked forward, through the present age of loud disputes but generally weak convictions, to a future which shall unite the best qualities of the critical with the best qualities of the organic periods."[52] This receptivity to all parts of the truth soon marked Mill's work and gave him much pride. He referred to it, in fact, on the very first page of his *Autobiography*, where he explained in Comtean terms why he wrote the book:

> It has also seemed to me that in an *age of transition in opinions*, there may be somewhat both of interest and of benefit in noting the *successive phases of any mind which was always pressing forward*, equally ready to learn and to unlearn either from its own thoughts or from those of others.[53]

In sum, Mill made a virtue of his eclecticism and even of the inconsistencies of his nonsystem.

In order to develop the principles that would direct the construction of a new era, Mill sought in particular to combine the intellectual liberty of the eighteenth century with convictions suitable to the

[50] This concept became even more important to him because it was strengthened by what he had discovered at the same time: Coleridge's observations on the dangers of half-truths and Goethe's notion of "many-sidedness." Mill, *Autobiography*, 171. See also Mill to Gustave d'Eichthal, November 7, 1829, *Earlier Letters*, 12:42.

[51] Mill to Gustave d'Eichthal, October 8, 1829, *Earlier Letters*, 12:38. See also Mill to Gustave d'Eichthal, November 7, 1829, and February 9, 1830, *Earlier Letters*, 12:41, 45–6.

[52] Mill, *Autobiography*, 173. Mill's effort to be receptive to all aspects of truth was a tendency he shared with Eyton Tooke, who explained to d'Eichthal after a conversation with Mill, "What I acknowledge, I say, is that we need . . . a *general doctrine*, . . . an *eclectic doctrine*. – I owe this conviction to the work of A. Comte." Eyton Tooke to G. d'Eichthal, January 19, 1830, in Mill, *Correspondance inédite*, 100.

[53] Mill, *Autobiography*, 5 (my emphasis).

nineteenth. Although reluctant to admit it, however, he increasingly directed his attention toward the second part of this task, that is, toward establishing the strong beliefs that characterized an organic era, for after his mental crisis, he was more aware of their importance. Also partly because of Comte's influence, Mill understood the necessity of

> convictions as to what is right and wrong, useful and pernicious, deeply engraven on the feelings by early education and general unanimity of sentiments, and so firmly grounded in reason and in the true exigencies of life, that they shall not, like all former and present creeds, religious, ethical, and political, require to be periodically thrown off and replaced by others.[54]

In fact, he was tempted by a type of elitism that ill suited his own Benthamite upbringing: the spiritual power of Comte. It was an idea he knew well because besides Comte's fundamental opuscule, he had read his articles for *Le Producteur*.[55] But he was not eager to express his attraction to it.

Mill's hesitation to pronounce his real opinion of Comte is evident not only in his letters to d'Eichthal but in his *Autobiography*. The new edition, published in 1981, shows that in the final draft he omitted several significant pages that he had written on Comte.[56] These pages reveal that Mill was far more influenced by Comte than he cared to admit publicly, probably because they detracted from the rhetoric of liberty to which he was attached.[57] At one point, in referring to Comte's comparison in the fundamental opuscule between the methods of the physical sciences and those of political science, Mill said that it had never occurred to him that in "mathematics and physics what is called the liberty of conscience, or the right of private judgment, is merely nominal," for "those who have not studied these sciences take their conclusions on trust from those who have." Comte showed "that the case would be the same in the moral, social, and political branches of speculation if they were equally advanced with the physical." Until he read Comte, he had always supposed that "deference to authority" was identical to "mental slavery and the repression of individual thought." He now realized that such deference was the "means by which adherence to opinions is enforced."[58]

These passages, which Mill subsequently eliminated out of

---

[54] Ibid., 173.   [55] Mill to Gustave d'Eichthal, February 9, 1830, *Earlier Letters*, 12:47.

[56] Mill, "Appendix G," *Autobiography*, 615–16.

[57] On Mill's attachment to the rhetoric of liberty, see Maurice Cowling, *Mill and Liberalism* (Cambridge: Cambridge University Press, 1963), 98.

[58] Mill, *Autobiography*, 615.

embarrassment, demonstrate that his Benthamism was challenged not only by Comte's philosophy of history but, more important, by his concept of a directing scientific elite. Bentham and James Mill had taught him that each individual was the best judge of his proper interests, authority should be distrusted, and education held the key to progress owing to its ability to improve the people's judgment.[59] They would have dismissed as dangerous the idea of an educated elite dictating the opinions of others.

Comte's fundamental opuscule changed Mill's attitude toward education and elitism. Although previously he had believed that progress would come from the "reason of the multitude, improved as . . . it might be by education," he now "saw that this was not the best, and not even a reasonable, hope." The multitude could never become competent judges in political matters. One could look forward only to their becoming sufficiently educated "to rely . . . on the knowledge of the more highly instructed." In effect, Mill believed that the best way to advance was to create a spiritual power consisting of experts on social science:

> From this time my hopes of improvement rested less on the reason of the multitude, than on the possibility of effecting such an improvement in the methods of political and social philosophy, as should enable all thinking and instructed persons . . . to be so nearly of one mind on these subjects as to carry the multitude with them by their united authority.[60]

Thus political truths enunciated by a spiritual power would inevitably create accord among the members of a society.[61]

Mill seemed to agree with Comte that a certain amount of intellectual repression was necessary to maintain a consensus and put an end to their era of transition. This idea was a far cry from democracy and liberalism. He himself admitted that it created a revolution in his own development, serving "still further to widen the distance between my present mode of thinking, and that which I had learnt from Bentham and my father."[62]

In sum, Mill's encounter with Comte occurred at a critical moment of his development, when he was in full rebellion against his father and Benthamism. Historians and philosophers often tend to include Comte's influence with that of the Saint-Simonians, probably because Mill did so in his *Autobiography*. However, in the rejected draft of the *Autobiography* and letters to d'Eichthal, he made

[59] Ibid., 615–16. See also Packe, *John Stuart Mill*, 98.　[60] Mill, *Autobiography*, 615–16.

[61] Mill to Gustave d'Eichthal, February 9, 1830, *Earlier Letters*, 12:46, 48.

[62] Mill, *Autobiography*, 616. See also John Stuart Mill, *Auguste Comte and Positivism* (1865; Ann Arbor: University of Michigan Press, Ann Arbor Paperbacks, 1961), 77.

a very clear distinction between the Saint-Simonians and Comte and suggested that the latter helped him to reconstitute his thought first and in a different manner. Mill acknowledged Comte's impact when, in his first letter to him, he wrote of the *Plan* that "the seeds thrown out by this opuscule did not rest sterile in my mind."[63] Comte's ideas on the age of transition, relativity, and the spiritual power became part of Mill's mind-set.[64]

An interesting example of Comte's influence can be seen in Mill's essay "Corporation and Church Property," in which he advocated replacing Christian ministers with a new national clergy composed of teachers. These educated men would exhort the masses to perform their duties and would be more effective than political institutions in removing the evils of society, which came from ignorance.[65] Although Mill's effort to outline a reformed Establishment was supposedly also written under the influence of Samuel Taylor Coleridge, who advocated the establishment of a clerisy devoted to general cultivation, the scholar Karl Britton attests that Mill included "too much of Comte and too little of Coleridge."[66]

COMTE'S INFLUENCE ON MILL FROM 1829 TO 1841

From 1829 to 1837, Mill lost all contact with Comte. D'Eichthal warned Mill in late 1829 that Comte and the other members of the sect had quarreled and that his excessively scientific ideas were "far from representing all the present doctrines of the school."[67] Comte's name then disappeared from the letters they exchanged. Although Mill and his new friend Carlyle watched with amazement and regret the bizarre behavior of the Saint-Simonians as they turned into religious fanatics, he had no news of Comte, who was increasingly withdrawing from society.[68]

[63] Mill to Comte, November 8, 1841, *CG*, 2:346.
[64] See Mill, "Remarks on Bentham's Philosophy," in *Essays on Ethics, Religion and Society*, 16.
[65] Mill, "Corporation and Church Property," in *Essays on Economy and Society*, ed. J. M. Robson, vol. 4 of *The Collected Works of John Stuart Mill* (Toronto: University of Toronto Press and Routledge & Kegan Paul, 1967), 213, 220. See also Mill to John Sterling, October 20–2, 1831, *Earlier Letters*, 12:76.
[66] Karl Britton, *John Stuart Mill* (Harmondsworth: Penguin Books, 1953), 110. On Coleridge, see Raymond Williams, *Culture and Society, 1780–1950* (1958; New York: Harper & Row, Harper Torchbooks, 1966), 63–4.
[67] Gustave d'Eichthal to Mill, November 23, 1829, in Mill, *Correspondance inédite*, 62.
[68] Thomas Carlyle to Gustave d'Eichthal, August 9, 1830, in "Carlyle et le Saint-Simonisme: Lettres à Gustave d'Eichthal," trans. and ed. Eugène d'Eichthal, *La Revue historique*, 82 (May–June 1903): 292–306; Carlyle to Mill, October 16, 1832, in *Letters of Thomas Carlyle to John Stuart Mill, John Sterling and Robert Browning*, ed. Alexander Carlyle (London: T. Fisher Unwin, 1923), 19; Mill to Thomas Carlyle, May 29, 1832, April 11 and 13, 1833, and September 17, 1842, *Earlier Letters*, 12:106, 120, 150.

In 1837 the scientist Sir Charles Wheatstone brought to England the first two volumes of the *Cours de philosophie positive*.[69] When Mill heard some scientists discussing this work, he hurried to read the volumes of the man who had changed his way of thinking almost ten years before. With great enthusiasm, he wrote to a friend on December 21, 1837:

> Meanwhile, have you read a book termed *Cours de Philosophie Positive* by Auguste Comte, the same Comte whose *Traité de Politique Positive* you have among the earlier of the St. Simonian tracts . . . ? This said book is, I think one of the most profound books ever written on the philosophy of the sciences; and that of the higher branches it appears to me to have *created* . . . I shall be much astonished if this book of Comte's does not strike you more than any logical speculations of our time.[70]

Because the *Cours* was less political than Comte's earlier essays, dealt with the logical laws of the mind, and used a single, unified method, the positive one, to create a "homogeneous doctrine," it had a special appeal to Mill.[71] At the time, Mill was working on his first book, *A System of Logic*, which shared the aim of the *Cours*, that of understanding the practice, not the theory, of logic. Like Comte, Mill believed differences in doctrine could be reduced to differences in method. His famous articles on Bentham and Coleridge suggested that progressive people emphasized experimentation, while conservatives tended to believe in intuition. In Mill's view, this fundamental epistemological and political division could be eliminated only by the "science of science itself, the science of investigation – of method," which would establish firm political principles and "forward that alliance among the most advanced intellects & characters of the age"– an alliance that he was most interested in promoting.[72] Thus both the *Cours* and *A System of Logic* were efforts to discover methods that could lead to a consensus. Comte's union of generalists – or the spiritual power – was not far from Mill's alliance of intellectuals. Mill could hardly wait to read volumes 3 and 4 of the *Cours* to see how Comte would develop his ideas.

Encouraged by Marrast, who had become his good friend while in exile in England after the trial of 1835, Mill sent his first letter to

---

[69] W. M. Simon, *European Positivism in the Nineteenth Century: An Essay in Intellectual History* (Ithaca, N.Y.: Cornell University Press, 1963), 173; Bain, *John Stuart Mill*, 70.

[70] Mill to John Pringle Nichol, December 21, 1837, *Earlier Letters*, 12:363.

[71] *Cours*, 1:41.

[72] Mill to John Sterling, October 20–2, 1831, *Earlier Letters*, 12:78–9. See also Mill to Carlyle, August 2, 1833, *Earlier Letters*, 12:173; Mill to John Sterling, October 20–2, 1831, ibid., 12:79; Mill, "Bentham," 77–8; Mill, "Coleridge," 119–31; Anschutz, *Philosophy of J. S. Mill*, 65.

Comte in November 1841 to tell him of his enthusiasm for the *Cours*. Mill was eager to begin building the intellectual alliance that both he and Comte called for in their respective books. Yet at the same time, he seemed to place himself in an inferior position vis-à-vis Comte because he carefully addressed him in diffident tones as if he were writing to the heroes of his youth, the French philosophes.[73]

THE EARLY CORRESPONDENCE BETWEEN COMTE AND MILL

In the first sentence of his letter, Mill offered Comte his "adhesion" and proceeded to give him the distinct impression that he was already his disciple. Describing how he had read each volume of the *Cours* several times with a "true intellectual passion," he declared that Comte was the "individual among the great intellects of our time whom I look upon with the greatest esteem and admiration." He hoped to be accepted as Comte's student so that they could have an "immediate intellectual relationship." And for this, he presented his qualifications: his immersion in the antimetaphysical spirit of Benthamism, his knowledge of all the sciences, and his keen interest in method. In short, Mill was declaring that he possessed the qualifications of the generalists, whom Comte now regarded as the new clergy. Furthermore, he told Comte that he had already been his student for the past thirteen years, ever since he had read the fundamental opuscule:

> I can say that I had already entered in a path very close to yours, especially by the impetus which your preceding work [the fundamental opuscule] had given me; but I still had many things of primary importance to learn from you, and I hope to give you shortly the proof that I learned them well.[74]

In brief, Mill did not hesitate to say that his Benthamite beliefs and his intellectual development as a whole had been significantly influenced by positive philosophy.

Another reason Mill wrote to Comte was to clarify some positive principles that were troubling him. He admitted at the outset that he disagreed with a few of Comte's opinions, but he reassured him that the questions he wished to ask him were only of a "secondary order." He was sure that a "profound discussion" would change his ideas if they were wrong.[75] Giving Comte the distinct impression

---

[73] Mill, *Autobiography*, 111.   [74] Mill to Comte, November 8, 1841, CG, 2:346–7.
[75] Ibid., 346.

that he would yield if necessary, Mill was submissive from the start.

The only substantial part of Mill's letter, covering the issue of religion in England, showed that he had a complete grasp of the spiritual goal of the *Cours*. Ever since his childhood, when his father forbade him to speak about his atheism in public, Mill had been wary of the force of religious opinions and longed for more freedom of discussion in this area. The recent revival of the religious spirit, manifested especially by the Oxford Movement, had alarmed him. He had always looked with hope to France, where Christianity's hold over the people seemed weaker and there was, consequently, more liberty. Yet since the Revolution of 1830, when he observed the egoism of the liberals, he had become discouraged by developments there. Tocqueville's warnings about the dangers of popular sovereignty and the opinions of the majority had also lessened his enthusiasm for democracy.[76] Worried about the death of progressivism in all arenas, Mill therefore supported Comte, who seemed to direct all his energies to the heart of the problem, that is, religion. He wrote to Comte:

> You know, Sir, that religious opinions have up to now more roots in our country than in all the other countries of Europe although they have lost for a long time, here as elsewhere, their former civilizing value: and it is, I believe, to be regretted for us that the revolutionary philosophy, which was still in full activity twelve years ago [1830], has today fallen into decrepitude before finishing its task.

What was crucial, Mill insisted, was to spread the doctrines of the *Cours* – "this great monument of the true modern philosophy" – so that the positive system would finally replace the feeble revolutionary one. English scientists, who in greater numbers were joining the positivist camp, offered more hope for change than politicians, whose "enervating and discouraging skepticism" made them as weak as their French counterparts.[77] He himself, having recognized the need for a new doctrine, was a wholehearted convert to positivism. He now agreed with Comte that an intellectual regeneration had to precede all efforts to achieve social progress. One of Mill's friends, noting his abandonment of his former "belief that politics and social

---

[76] Mill, *Autobiography*, 45, 88, 199–201; Mill to Gustave d'Eichthal, December 27, 1839, *Earlier Letters*, 12:415; Mill to Comte, March 22, 1842, *CG*, 2:353; Mill to John Sterling, October 20–2, 1831, *Earlier Letters*, 12:76; Robson, *Improvement of Mankind*, 108–14; Iris Wessel Mueller, *John Stuart Mill and French Thought* (Urbana: University of Illinois Press, 1956), 46–7.

[77] Mill to Comte, November 8, 1841, *CG*, 2:346.

institutions were everything," claimed that Mill would rather be a "private in the army of Truth" than the "undoubted leader of a powerful political party."[78]

Almost a recluse, Comte knew next to nothing about this Englishman who had written him such an enthusiastic letter, and he asked Marrast for information. Marrast told him that Mill was a "man of remarkable intelligence, who exercises in England a powerful influence on all men seriously occupied with philosophical and political ideas."[79] Mill's letter then raised Comte's spirits, for he had been depressed by his recent failures and the press's continuing neglect of the *Cours*. He responded enthusiastically on November 20, saying he was profoundly grateful for the letter, whose value Mill could never imagine.[80] Mill was, after all, the first important nonscientist who had voiced his approval; he was one of the "eminent" thinkers for whom Comte had always insisted he had written the *Cours*. For the first time, Comte felt his pains were justified.

Mill's letter also arrived at a time when Comte was becoming increasingly annoyed with Valat, who, he felt, did not care about his career problems at the Ecole Polytechnique and unkindly continued to criticize the *Cours*. Valat had recently condemned its "irrational" recommendation "to neglect all more or less advanced [social] series in order to take into consideration only the most perfect [societies]."[81] Reprimanding Valat for being too "analytical" and overly concerned about details, Comte had concluded that further discussion with him would be "necessarily unfruitful," since it "could only augment natural divergences."[82] He had also decided that "perfect convergences" between two men were impossible, "especially in our time."[83] But now with Mill, he could again dream of the possibility of arriving at a complete understanding with a contemporary.

Mill offered him great encouragement. Comte had just finished writing about the need to establish a commission of thirty representatives from all the advanced countries to direct the regeneration of the West, and Mill seemed to be offering himself as the first member of this "reunion of the elite."[84] In his second letter to Mill,

---

[78] John Sterling's opinion, summarized in Caroline Fox, *Memories of Old Friends: Being Extracts from the Journals and Letters of Caroline Fox – from 1835 to 1871*, 2d ed., ed. Horace N. Pym (Philadelphia: Lippincott, 1883), 196.

[79] Marrast to Comte, received by Comte, December 17, 1841, in "Relations d'Auguste Comte avec Armand Marrast," ed. Laffitte, 188. See also Comte to Mill, January 17, 1842, *CG*, 2:30.

[80] Comte to Mill, November 20, 1841, *CG*, 2:20.

[81] Valat to Comte, September 8, 1841, MAC. See also Comte to Valat, September 22, 1840, *CG*, 1:360.

[82] Comte to Valat, October 5, 1841, *CG*, 2:20.   [83] Comte to Valat, May 1, 1841, *CG*, 2:6.

[84] Comte to Mill, November 20, 1841, *CG*, 2:23.

Comte warmly welcomed him as a collaborator, explaining that "my extremely solitary life . . . makes me attach a very special price to such a relationship with every philosopher of true value," especially "because of the difficulty of finding minds that converge with mine." Already he sensed that a complete "intellectual and moral sympathy" existed between them.[85]

THE COLLABORATION

In the years that followed, Comte and Mill tried to put into practice their vision of an intellectual elite, that is, a new spiritual power. They wrote each other eighty-nine letters, almost one a month during the first years of their correspondence. (Mill wrote altogether forty-four, Comte forty-five.) They attached great importance to this correspondence because it represented the form of intellectual harmony they both hoped to achieve someday on a larger scale among all men.

In their eyes, their relationship contributed not only to their own individual development but to the progress of humanity itself. Each saw himself as a key figure of the times. Seven months after buying the complete works of Descartes, Comte boasted to Mill that the *Cours* was "equivalent" to the *Discours de la méthode*.[86] He was convinced that he had completed the "philosophical revolution that Descartes began."[87]

Mill too felt more self-confident. While previously he had been viewed as a "sort of political man belonging to the moderate revolutionary party," the reprinting of some of his best writings (i.e., "Some Unanswered Questions on Political Economy") and the imminent publication of *A System of Logic* provided him with "moral authority" and a place "among recognized intellectual superiorities." As a "sociological philosopher," he hoped to be able finally to influence the "spiritual movement," which was reaching a pivotal point in its development.[88] In effect, Mill sought Comte's advice on how to proceed as a missionary of the new science of society. Comte, in turn, exclaimed that Mill's letter made him "feel directly that the most advanced minds are vibrating essentially in

[85] Comte to Mill, January 17, 1842, *CG*, 2:30.
[86] Comte to Mill, June 19, 1842, *CG*, 2:52. See also the bill from the Librairie de Sauvaignat, November 30, 1841, in packet labeled "Factures," MAC.
[87] Comte to Valat, September 17, 1842, *CG*, 2:86. See also Comte to Mme Auguste Comte, September 13, 1842, *CG*, 2:83.
[88] Mill to Comte, February 25, 1842, *CG*, 2:351.

union with my own."[89] Although both men celebrated the harmony of their views and their collaboration, their enthusiasm would shortly lead to a series of misunderstandings.

Comte's very first letter should have warned Mill. Comte gave him an idea of his inflexibility when he told him immediately of his regime of cerebral hygiene. Moreover, his political views were evident in his argument that Mill should not listen to his friends' advice to run for Parliament, because immediate political action was futile, day-to-day affairs were distracting, and the discussion of individual rights was "as vain as it is stormy." Instead of lamenting recent political changes, especially the growth of reactionary (e.g., Catholic) ideas, as Mill did, Comte welcomed them as an indication of the death of metaphysical doctrines, which would no longer confuse and prolong the present situation. The final battle between counterrevolutionary ideas and positivism was thus more imminent than he thought and would be "clear and decisive." With great urgency, Comte insisted that Mill join with him to organize "broad philosophical action, outside of all political action."[90]

In sum, in this first letter Comte was very clear as to the outlines of his social philosophy, which, as he said, combined order with progress. His antiparliamentary and antiliberal sentiments were as obvious as his hatred of the old regime. His quietism regarding questions of government, his desire to replace the demand for individual rights by "the examination . . . of the proper *duties* of the diverse classes," and his enthusiasm about the elimination of so-called metaphysical ideas seemed far from the liberal spirit of Mill.[91] Even in the most extreme moments of hesitation and inconsistency, Mill had never denied the supreme importance of individual rights.

Despite these ominous signs of disagreement, Mill in his next letter greeted the "exchange of philosophical ideas in which I intend to find for the rest of my life such a precious source of both instruction and intellectual stimulation." He was amazed by how much he still had to learn from Comte, whose philosophical conceptions showed a "more complete maturity." Whenever he and Comte differed, Mill presented himself as a less advanced thinker, suffering from the backward situation in England. He maintained, for example, that he still used metaphysical words and avoided antireligious arguments for fear of losing his readers and his "social position."[92] Likewise, he explained that he wanted to contribute to political life

[89] Comte to Mill, November 20, 1841, *CG*, 2:21.
[90] Ibid., 23–4. See also Comte to Mill, January 17, 1842, *CG*, 2:34.
[91] Comte to Mill, November 20, 1841, *CG*, 2:23.
[92] Mill to Comte, December 18, 1841, *CG*, 2:347–8.

because the English respected only those who had proved themselves in the active arena. In justifying his differences with Comte,
Mill was using the concept of which his master was so proud – that
of relativity.

Mill's great respect for France played an important role in preserving his relationship with Comte. He had liked France ever since
he had spent a year there with Bentham's brother in 1820–1. While
in Paris, he had met Say, Ternaux, Dunoyer, and Saint-Simon
himself, the very circle that Comte had joined. He disapproved of
England's commercial and materialistic spirit, and although he often
criticized the French for disregarding the practical, he found them
generally less egotistical and more high-minded than his compatriots. Considering their mentality more compatible with his own,
Mill became the most renowned English expert on French life.[93]
Comte shared Mill's prejudices; he also thought England was philosophically inferior and too practical-minded and materialistic.[94] In fact,
in the *Cours*, Comte wrote that England, with its Protestant spirit of
individualism and excessive criticism, would be the fourth positivist
country – after France, Italy, and Germany (where a part of the
country was Catholic).[95] Whenever Mill disagreed with Comte, he
politely avoided conflict by arguing that he, like his country, was
merely less advanced. Yet in many respects, he believed in the truth
of his alibi.

THE "PERFECT" ACCORD

Because of the great pride they took in being linked by their intellectual, that is, religious, vocation, the principal topic that Comte
and Mill discussed, at least in the beginning, was spiritual: Comte's
concept of the "separation of powers." This was the idea that had
first attracted Mill to Comte twelve years before, for he considered
it the key to understanding history – especially the antagonism
"indispensable" to social progress. He was no longer tempted by
"utopian" thinkers like the Saint-Simonians, who dreamed of a
government of "philosophers," or by liberals, who wished to give
the direction of state affairs to men of "high intellectual capacity."
Mill now agreed with Comte that the "speculative class" must act

---

[93] Mill to Gustave d'Eichthal, May 15, 1829, *Earlier Letters*, 12:30–1; Mill to James Mill,
August 27–8, 1830, *Earlier Letters*, 12:63; Mill to John Sterling, October 20–2, 1831, *Earlier
Letters*, 12:78.
[94] Comte to Valat, July 10, 1840, *CG*, 1:345.   [95] *Cours*, 2:693–5.

only in areas that were not governmental because political power corrupted the moral and intellectual habits of learned men; once in government, these individuals, who as a rule had unoriginal, plodding minds, refused to listen to more advanced thinkers and ultimately became an obstacle to progress. A government of intellectuals, such as the mandarin system in China, represented what Mill called a *"pedantocracy."*[96]

Mill's appreciation profoundly touched Comte, who felt he was the first to recognize fully that the separation of powers was "perhaps the most delicate and . . . decisive" point of his political philosophy. Mill understood, unlike Constant, that he did *not* intend to create a theocracy, a political system that was both "dangerous" and "chimerical." Mill's accord with Comte on this issue surpassed all his hopes, "completely" proving their "philosophical sympathy." They were now ready, in Comte's view, to take the "most difficult" step of philosophical regeneration – the "real union of *two* truly original intellects."[97]

Because Comte believed the dream of the rule of reason constituted the "greatest obstacle to a true harmony between theoreticians and practical people in politics," he was grateful for Mill's invention of the word "pedantocracy" and immediately adopted it to use against his enemies.[98] He accused Guizot, for example, of belonging to the "pedantocracy."[99] Later, in mid-1842, while writing the last part of the *Cours*, Comte asked Mill's permission to use the term and attribute it to him. In so doing, he wanted not only to publicize their association but also to use his support to "wound profoundly the pride and ambition of the speculative mob."[100] Although Mill gladly obliged, he was surprised that "pedantocracy" was the only idea that Comte wished to take from him.[101]

As for Mill's favorable attitude toward the active life, Comte reassured him that their "secondary divergences" on this issue were "more apparent than real." He conceded that the abnormality and confusion of their era permitted philosophers to participate directly in political life in exceptional circumstances, though they had to be aware of the dangers.

Instead of further exploring the question of whether Mill should run for Parliament, Comte stated that the combination of the French and English spirits seemed the "most suitable and decisive"

---

[96] Mill to Comte, February 25, 1842, *CG*, 2:349–50.
[97] Comte to Mill, March 4, 1842, *CG*, 2:35–7.
[98] Comte to Mill, May 29, 1842, *CG*, 2:47. See also Comte to Mill, June 19, 1842, *CG*, 2:51.
[99] Comte to Mill, April 5, 1842, *CG*, 2:43.   [100] Comte to Mill, May 29, 1842, *CG*, 2:47.
[101] Mill to Comte, June 9, 1842, *CG*, 2:356.

association that could be demanded by the "new European synergy of the five great occidental populations."[102] Encouraged by Mill's example and conveniently overlooking David Brewster's religious scruples, he added that English scholars seemed more favorable to positivism than did any other European intellectuals – including the French.

Mill was delighted with Comte's response. He too was careful to stress their areas of agreement, which he said were "not limited to fundamental principles" but extended even to "secondary questions." Their "philosophical sympathy" could only grow deeper.[103] He also believed in the necessity of combining the French spirit, known for its generality, and the English spirit, characterized by its precision and practicality. Thus both he and Comte felt that their association had large consequences, one that pointed the way to the creation of a significant international alliance in the near future.

Besides the issues of positive philosophy's religious function and the spiritual power, Mill brought up the question of methodology. In his *System of Logic*, he was analyzing intellectual methods without connecting them to any doctrine, an approach that had been condemned by Comte, who believed logical processes could not be understood apart from their use in the sciences.[104] In fact, he was sure Comte would find his work imperfect. Mill timidly explained that he had been forced to make "concessions" to the "dominant spirit" of the English, who would have rejected a purely scientific and antireligious discussion, such as the one developed by Comte in the *Cours*. Mill defended the *System of Logic* by claiming that it had at least "transitory value" for his countrymen.[105] Agreeing to break his rule of cerebral hygiene to read it when it appeared, Comte tried to reassure Mill that it did not seem "metaphysical" to him and that it would give him a better idea of their "philosophical convergence."[106] But in spite of the efforts of the two men to paper over their differences, a misunderstanding arose that created tension between them.

While Mill was explaining which ideas in *A System of Logic* might strike Comte as too metaphysical, he added as an afterthought that he believed in the possibility of a "positive psychology."[107] He defended it by arguing that his version was close to Comte's phrenological analysis of intellectual and affective faculties. In this fashion,

---

[102] Comte to Mill, March 4, 1842, CG, 2:36–7.
[103] Mill to Comte, March 22, 1842, CG, 2:352. [104] *Cours*, 1:35, 2:101.
[105] Mill to Comte, December 18, 1841, CG, 2:347–8. See also Mill to Carlyle, August 2, 1833, *Earlier Letters*, 12:173; *Cours*, 1:35, 2:101.
[106] Comte to Mill, January 17, 1842, CG, 2:35.
[107] Mill to Comte, December 18, 1841, CG, 2:348.

he gave Comte the impression that *A System of Logic* was a discussion of psychology from a scientific perspective. Though gently rebuking him for overlooking anatomy in his analysis of the faculties, Comte was enthusiastic about Mill's endeavor.[108] Mill then had to explain to Comte that *A System of Logic* covered only "method," that is, "intellectual acts," but that in the future he might write about "our mental faculties and our moral tendencies." To prepare himself, he asked Comte to recommend some books on phrenology, a subject that in England was cultivated only "by men of an intellect less than mediocre," certainly not by a "true thinker."[109]

Claiming that Gall's doctrines were so widespread in France that only metaphysicians ignored them, Comte recommended the six volumes of his *Sur les functions du cerveau*.[110] But Gall's work failed to convince Mill of the truth of phrenology. Mill objected that he had seen stupid men with large heads and that he himself had a pronounced "organ of constructiveness" but completely lacked the corresponding faculty of manual dexterity. There was no anatomical proof of the tripartite division of the brain into organs corresponding to animal, moral, and intellectual faculties. Moreover, Gall's idea of primordial instincts seemed too vague and intuitive.[111] In sum, Mill rejected as deterministic Gall's and Comte's belief that each person had organic dispositions and was ruled by biological laws.

Mill's objections ultimately reflected the lingering allegiance that he felt to his father, whose principal book, *Analysis of the Phenomena of the Human Mind*, was a discussion of the psychology of associationism of Locke, Condillac, and Helvétius. Going back to his father's belief that a person was a tabula rasa formed by outside circumstances, Mill praised Helvétius's "exaggerations" for having given an impulse to education, whose importance he felt Gall had grossly underestimated. Gall's idea that the character of individuals and even nations simply reflected an inherent difference of physical organization seemed too "facile" an explanation and led to a deadening conservatism.[112] Mill argued that a science of the formation of individual character had to be created to provide social science with a truly solid basis.[113]

The importance of the divergence between Comte and Mill on

---

[108] Comte to Mill, January 17, 1842, *CG*, 2:35.
[109] Mill to Comte, February 25, 1842, *CG*, 2:351.
[110] Comte to Mill, June 19, 1842, *CG*, 2:54–5.
[111] Mill to Comte, June 9, 1842, *CG*, 2:356–7.   [112] Ibid.
[113] John Stuart Mill, *A System of Logic Ratiocinative and Inductive: Being a Connected View of the Principles of Evidence and the Methods of Scientific Investigation*, ed. J. M. Robson, vols. 7 and 8 of *The Collected Works of John Stuart Mill* (Toronto: University of Toronto Press and Routledge & Kegan Paul, 1974), 8:861–76.

the subject of psychology and phrenology can scarcely be exaggerated, for Comte had given Gall a prominent place in the *Cours* and considered him an "indispensable" predecessor.[114] Gall had systematized biology, the science of man, which had to be founded before the science of society. Most important, Comte used his deterministic phrenology to reinforce the concept of social order and the constraints on liberty in the positivist system. Mill, however, would write his *Autobiography* to prove the impact of education on a human being; he believed education was crucial to the functioning of a representative and reformist government.

Although the differences between the two men touched the very essence of their being, they continued to play the game of concord. Mill claimed the "difficulties" that he had with Gall were merely "questions," not objections.[115] Hoping that he had not given Comte an "exaggerated idea" of his distance from Gall's doctrine, he even claimed that the more he familiarized himself with it, the closer he felt to it.[116] For his part, Comte agreed with many of Mill's criticisms of Gall's localizations and felt his new disciple had admirably understood the biologist's "anti-ontological doctrine." Their "spontaneous" agreement on this issue was "just about as complete" as it was on all other matters.[117]

From this point on, the relationship between the two thinkers became increasingly personal, reflecting their need to cultivate their emotions. Both men blamed their childhood experiences for having left them emotionally crippled; Comte bemoaned his isolation in the *lycée*, Mill, his father's lack of affection. Sensing the inadequacy of purely cerebral associations, they gradually extended their relationship into a friendship. Curiously, this new aspect of their correspondence began within the context of a discussion of pedantocracy and Guizot. Angry at not having been appointed to a chair at the Collège de France, Comte told Mill that Guizot was "an arrogant pedant and an ambitious vulgarian" who "oscillates between the vulgar philosophical utopia that you have so happily qualified 'pedantocracy' . . . and the anti-French dream of a new 1688."[118] As hypocritical as other Protestants from Geneva, Guizot had devised his theory of self-enrichment merely to conceal his desire to sanction the system of corruption. These criticisms surprised Mill, especially since Guizot had spoken well of Comte during a stay in England. Pained to learn that Guizot had lacked "magnanimity toward a philosopher who never lacked it in regard to anyone," Mill did not hesitate to side

---

[114] Comte to Mill, May 29, 1842, *CG*, 2:49. See also *Catéchisme positiviste*, 32.
[115] Mill to Comte, June 9, 1842, *CG*, 2:357.   [116] Mill to Comte, July 11, 1842, *CG*, 2:359.
[117] Comte to Mill, July 22, 1842, *CG*, 2:60.
[118] Comte to Mill, April 5, 1842, *CG*, 2:42–3.

with Comte.[119] Comte in turn was grateful for an understanding that was not only "intellectual" but also "affective."[120] In his response of June 9, 1842, Mill agreed that his sympathy with Comte had become "personal."[121]

From that point on, Comte confided his problems with his family and wife to Mill. Less than a year after their first letters, Comte openly called Mill "one of my best friends" and referred to their "fraternal" relationship.[122] Mill was clearly replacing Valat as the source of the "sincere affections" that were so important to Comte.[123]

For almost ten months, from October 1841 to July 1842, Comte and Valat had not corresponded. Valat was sure this rift between them was his fault, because he had failed to call on Massin when he went to Paris while Comte was away on his examination tour. Comte denied, however, having been insulted and explained that since he had always been the one to break a long silence in the past, he was simply waiting for Valat to do so this time.[124] Comte was evidently testing Valat's friendship.

Soon afterward, in late August 1842, Valat expressed his reactions to volume 6 of the Cours. He asserted that Comte's cold, impartial historical exposition seemed to lack a goal, his discussions presenting the pros and cons of an issue often failed to reach a conclusion, and his numerous long digressions taxed his readers' attention span. Most of all, Valat attacked Comte for refusing to acknowledge the value of psychology and for neglecting the importance of epistemology, which was vital to scientific verification.[125] These imperfections, Valat maintained, caused scholars and politicians to neglect the book.

Already disappointed by Valat's objections to volume 5, Comte was truly "pained" by these new criticisms, which he felt lacked all foundation and appreciation of his work. Refusing to be troubled by his friends any more than by his enemies, Comte declared that he was "not running after proselytes" and had already formed his "mental system," which he had no intention of ever changing: "I have neither the time nor the desire to be converted or corrected." Convinced that he could get along only with those who had completed or almost completed the evolution from theology to positivism, he warned Valat in the future to discuss "other things"

---

[119] Mill to Comte, May 6, 1842, *CG*, 2:355.   [120] Comte to Mill, May 29, 1842, *CG*, 2:48.
[121] Mill to Comte, May 6, 1842, *CG*, 2:355.
[122] Comte to Valat, September 23, 1842, *CG*, 2:89; Comte to Mill, September 30, 1842, *CG*, 2:95.
[123] Comte to Valat, September 17, 1842, *CG*, 2:87.
[124] Comte to Valat, August 1, 1842, *CG*, 2:63.
[125] Valat to Comte, August 25, 1842, MAC; Comte to Valat, October 5, 1841, *CG*, 2:20.

besides philosophy. He suggested that their correspondence should concentrate instead on their emotional understanding.[126] Cerebral hygiene had extended to his friends, even to his best friend.

Valat was dumbfounded that his objections had "alarmed" Comte to such an extent and cautioned him that a refusal to discuss criticism "would be a cruel condemnation of your entire doctrine."[127] Comte replied that the "age of discussion" was over for him.[128] Conversation was to be replaced by a professorial monologue. Comte seemed to be endorsing Maistre's concept that a spiritual leader had to be considered infallible.

On the verge of a break with Valat, Comte turned with relief to Mill. He explained to him that he felt closer to him than to Valat "due to a more perfect organic conformity, leading to more intimate philosophical convergences."[129] When soon afterward he separated from Massin, Comte told Mill that he attached "more and more value to the intimate sympathy, both intellectual and moral, that has so happily developed between us."[130] Most scholars concentrate on Clotilde de Vaux as the source of Comte's revived emotional life, but it is clear that Mill also played a significant role in this aspect of his development. Their relationship would encourage him to expound on the importance of sentiment in the *Système de politique positive*.

Although touched by these outbursts of emotion and signs of profound friendship, Mill at first seemed embarrassed and reserved. He too had financial worries and problems relating to the woman closest to him, but he did not air his concerns as Comte did. He preferred to describe his physical troubles and melancholy in more general terms.[131] Stricken often by depression himself, Comte enjoyed giving him advice.[132] However, Mill's friend Alexander Bain claimed that Mill was far more open and frank with Comte than with most of his other friends and that the *Autobiography* did not sufficiently express the "influence in detail, nor the warmth of esteem and affection displayed in the years of their correspondence."[133] In many respects, Comte represented the perfect friend that Mill had been seeking for years. Lamenting his solitude, Mill wrote at one point that he yearned for a friendship where there would be the

---

[126] Comte to Valat, August 29, 1842, CG, 2:79–80.
[127] Valat to Comte, September 11, 1842, MAC.
[128] Comte to Valat, September 17, 1842, CG, 2:86.
[129] Comte to Mill, September 30, 1842, CG, 2:93.
[130] Comte to Mill, November 5, 1842, CG, 2:103.
[131] Mill to Comte, June 15, 1843, CG, 2:387.
[132] Comte to Mill, June 29, 1843, CG, 2:168–9.
[133] Bain, *John Stuart Mill*, 70–1.

"feeling of being engaged in the pursuit of a common object, and of mutually cheering one another on, and helping one another in an arduous undertaking. This . . . is one of the strongest ties of sympathy."[134]

The ties between the two men were strengthened by the discovery of a remarkable coincidence. When Mill learned of Comte's origins, he told him that in the winter of 1820-1 he had spent the "six happiest months" of his youth in Montpellier, studying at the Faculty of Sciences.[135] For the first time in his life he had made a friend, Balard, who was not chosen for him by his family.[136] Comte had heard of Balard because he was an associate of Roméo Pouzin, who had actually tried unsuccessfully to have Comte meet him in 1839.[137] Comte was therefore able to give Mill the information that he wanted about Balard.[138] It turned out that Mill had also been a close friend of Pouzin and another childhood friend of Comte's, Emile Guillaume.[139] They remembered Mill with great fondness.[140] Pouzin told Comte that he had recognized Mill's "superior nature" even at that young age.[141]

The high point of their apparently growing harmony came in October 1842, when Mill read the last volume of the *Cours*, for which he had been waiting for months. He found a "sort of intellectual voluptuousness [*volupté*] in the idea of savoring this last volume."[142] His friend Bain described their excitement about this last part, whose errors they agreed "were mostly of the kind that could be remedied by ordinary men better informed on special points than Comte."[143] Mill told Comte that their "differences of opinion of minor importance" had "notably diminished."[144]

In describing his reaction to this work, Mill used almost the same terms that he had employed when he expressed his feelings after having read Dumont's version of Bentham: "This volume has worthily completed a work necessarily unique in the development of humanity." Comte was the "founder of the true sociological

---

[134] Mill to John Sterling, April 15, 1829, *Earlier Letters*, 12:30.

[135] Mill to Comte, August 12, 1842, *CG*, 2:363. See also *John Mill's Boyhood Visit to France: Being a Journal and Notebook Written by John Stuart Mill in France, 1820–1821*, ed. Anna Jean Mill (Toronto: University of Toronto Press, 1960).

[136] Mill to Comte, August 12, 1842, *CG*, 2:363.

[137] Comte to Pouzin, October 4, 1839, *CG*, 1:321.

[138] Comte to Mill, August 24, September 30, November 5, December 30, 1842, and March 25, 1843, *CG*, 2:75, 94, 108, 127, 147; Mill to Comte, September 10, 1842, *CG*, 2:368.

[139] Comte to Mill, December 30, 1842, *CG*, 2:127. Both Pouzin and Guillaume were doctors.

[140] Comte to Mill, November 5, 1842, *CG*, 2:109.

[141] Pouzin to Comte, August 3, 1843, MAC.   [142] Mill to Comte, July 11, 1842, *CG*, 2:358.

[143] Bain, *John Stuart Mill*, 71.   [144] Mill to Comte, October 23, 1842, *CG*, 2:369.

method . . . and consequently that of the definitive systematization of human knowledge." It is clear that Mill had experienced another revelation. He wrote to Comte:

> Once I felt there this sort of shock that your works have often made me experience and that results from the sudden perception of a great luminous and new idea. It is in the place where you speak of the high social qualities that one will finally find in industrial life in spite of the essentially egoistic moving power that almost exclusively directs it today.[145]

Mill was referring to Comte's belief that progress was equivalent to the growth of order because it created greater "solidarity." One of the themes of volume 6 was that the individual (and society) would grow less animalistic and more human as the intellect increasingly dominated the "inclinations" and the sympathies prevailed over the instinct of self-interest.[146]

Mill was deeply attracted to Comte's social vision – a vision totally opposed to Bentham's. Whereas Bentham saw man as an egoist living in an increasingly atomistic society, Comte visualized him as a sociable being who lived at least ideally in an organic society. Mill appreciated Comte's view, for he feared the antisocial tendencies of industrial society resulting from the egoism of its members.[147]

Positivism again seemed to fill the gap created by Mill's rejection of Benthamism. Mill described his spiritual existence in a very important passage, which shows that he had completely understood the religious claims of positivism:

> Since I had the very rare destiny in my country of not ever having believed in God, even in my childhood, I always regarded the creation of a true social philosophy as the only possible foundation of a general regeneration of human morality, and the idea of Humanity as the only [concept] that could replace that of God.

Having repudiated Benthamism as insufficient, especially with regard to the affections, Mill experienced a moral "crisis" in reading the last part of the *Cours*. He realized that positivism was the type of religion he had been seeking since his depression of 1826. Proudly, he told Comte:

> I believe that what is presently happening in me is a first special verification of the great general conclusion of your Treatise, the aptitude of positive philosophy, once organized in its totality, to take

[145] Ibid.   [146] *Cours*, 2:768–9.   [147] Mill to Comte, October 23, 1842, *CG*, 2:370.

full possession of the high social attributions that up to now have been very imperfectly filled only by religions.[148]

Mill now understood more fully the important role that positivism was destined to play, for it alone could create the "speculative revolution" that had to precede practical reforms. He agreed that the spiritual power would impose a better morality "by consent or by force."[149] Liberals like Dunoyer were "truly too naive to believe today that simple liberty of discussion" would ever suffice to create a "system of common opinions that would be accepted as authoritative."[150] The *Cours* produced, in effect, Mill's second spiritual conversion. For his part, Comte thanked Mill for "completely" adhering to his doctrine; this allegiance amounted to the "principal compensation" of his entire spiritual life.[151]

After having read the sixth volume and reread the fourth and fifth volumes of the *Cours*, Mill completely revised the last section of *A System of Logic* to give "much more space to the new doctrine" and to make his work harmonize better with his present way of thinking.[152] Acknowledging that the *Cours* was exerting a "great influence" on him, Mill was relieved that he had written the first three sections before he had made contact with Comte so that he could show at least some "originality."[153] He admitted that *A System of Logic* was not as brilliant as the *Cours*, but he justified its metaphysical ideas by claiming that it was the "most advanced work that my country is yet capable of receiving."[154] Moreover, because of its attachment to the school of Hobbes and Locke, it would at least present the first "rude" shock to the German school of Kant, Hegel, and Schelling, which was dominant in England.[155] Thus Mill was convinced that *A System of Logic* would serve as valuable "work of propaganda" for Comte's doctrine. Since he had mentioned Comte as the source of many of his important ideas, he hoped his readers would come to adhere to the "sole way of studying social phenomena that is today at the level of the intellectual state of humanity."[156]

[148] Mill to Comte, December 15, 1842, *CG*, 2:374.
[149] Mill to Comte, October 23, 1842, *CG*, 2:370.
[150] Mill to Comte, April 26, 1845, *CG*, 3:387.
[151] Comte to Mill, December 30, 1842, *CG*, 2:124.
[152] Mill to Comte, January 28, 1843, *CG*, 2:378. See also David Lewisohn, "Mill and Comte on the Methods of Social Science," *Journal of the History of Ideas* 33 (April–June 1972): 317–18.
[153] Mill to Comte, March 13, 1843, *CG*, 2:380.
[154] Mill to Comte, January 28, 1843, *CG*, 2:378.
[155] Mill to Comte, July 11, 1842, *CG*, 2:358. See also Mill to Comte, March 22, 1842, *CG*, 2:352.
[156] Mill to Comte, May 6, 1842, *CG*, 2:354.

Mill considered *A System of Logic* his most important work, and many scholars agree with him.[157] It is also the one in which Comte's influence is most evident; in the first edition Mill made almost a hundred references to him.[158] Most of the textual changes were in the sixth book, which treated the question of the possibility of creating a moral and political science. In this part, Mill often cited very long passages of the *Cours* in which Comte underlined the necessity of dividing sociology into two sections, social statics and social dynamics.[159] Mill was showing that he agreed with Comte's view that the study of order and consensus, on the one hand, and the study of history and progress, on the other, were essential components of a science of society.

Mill referred to another important passage from the *Cours*, in which Comte declared that institutional reforms could be only "provisional" and that the positive philosophy was the "only social basis of social reorganization which must terminate the state of crisis," because it alone reunited "individual intellects" by "a common social doctrine."[160] Mill here demonstrated that the attraction of positivism lay in its ability to produce a consensus based on a doctrine. Positivism's religious function still appealed to him the most.

At great length, Mill also praised Comte's historical method, which he called the "Inverse Deductive Method."[161] Whereas in 1829 Mill had vehemently criticized Comte's argument that the study of society had to begin with a priori arguments, which it had to verify by a posteriori reasoning, now he wrote:

> The only thinker who, with a competent knowledge of scientific methods in general, has attempted to characterize the method of Sociology, M. Comte, considers this inverse order as inseparably inherent in the nature of sociological speculation. He looks upon the social science as essentially consisting of generalizations from history, verified, not originally suggested, by deduction from the laws of human nature.[162]

Mill considered Comte's method superior to Bentham's, which, instead of grounding itself in historical facts, began with an abstract, static image of human nature – the idea that all people are governed by pleasure. Comte impressed Mill because he alone among the new historians connected the laws of history with those of human nature. Based on the law of the three stages, the positivist philosophy

---

[157] R. F. McRae, Introduction to Mill, *A System of Logic*, 7:xxi.

[158] John M. Robson, "Textual Introduction," in Mill, *A System of Logic*, 7:lxxxiii. See also the list of references to Comte, ibid., 8:1187.

[159] Mill, *A System of Logic*, 8:915–19.   [160] Comte, quoted in ibid., 8:832.

[161] Mill, *A System of Logic*, 8:911.   [162] Ibid., 897.

of history was for Mill, as it was for Comte, the foundation of sociology.[163]

In view of all these citations from the *Cours* in *A System of Logic*, scholars of Mill seem misled when they try to minimize Comte's impact on his thought.[164] Durkheim was far closer to the truth when he said, "Mill, it is true, was preoccupied by this question [of the methodology of sociology] for a rather long time; but he only sifted what Comte had said about it into his dialectics without adding anything truly personal."[165] It seems clear that Mill accepted the essential points of Comte's social science: his law of three stages, classification of the sciences, scientific and historical methods, idea of relativism, concept of progress (with its stress on intellectual development), and distinction between social dynamics and social statics. Moreover, Mill agreed with Comte's idea of the separation of powers, which was essential to the fulfillment of the regenerative, that is, religious, role positivism was to play in Western civilization.

Comte recognized Mill's almost complete adherence to his doctrine. When he read *A System of Logic* in the spring of 1843, he was highly satisfied with what Mill had said – especially about the "indispensable intervention of the deductive step." He could find no divergences, or he banished them from his mind by reminding himself of the immature state of Mill's philosophy and that of his country. Comte wrote to Mill:

> As for points of discord, I am happy to declare to you that I have searched there vainly for the numerous indications that your letters seemed to announce to me. I must first discard totally, according to the spirit of this great work, all that results essentially from a transitory and now completed phase in the spontaneous evolution of your own understanding.[166]

[163] Ibid., 915, 928–9.
[164] Mueller, *Mill and French Thought*, 129.
[165] Emile Durkheim, *Les Règles de la méthode sociologique* (Paris, 1895), 1.
[166] Comte to Mill, May 16, 1843, *CG*, 2:155.

Chapter 13

1842: A Turning Point

The preface ... will make my friends afraid without making my enemies laugh.

Comte, 1842

PRAISES AND ATTACKS

Other Englishmen from Mill's circle began to pay homage to Comte in 1842. When the Grotes came to Paris to attend the reception of their friend Alexis de Tocqueville at the Académie Française, Mrs. Grote found time to pay Comte a visit, informing him that many English statesmen had read his works with "pleasure" and "instruction." Sir William Molesworth, the founder of the *London Review* and an important leader of the Philosophic Radicals, thought so well of the *Cours* that he was reading it for the third time.[1] In 1842 Marrast put Comte in contact with another admirer, George Lewes, who was also a young friend of Mill. Though disappointed that Lewes was "still imperfectly cured of the psychological illness," Comte would later become enchanted with him.[2]

While enjoying praises from England, Comte faced growing troubles at home. In spite of having expressed pleasure at the success of the reactionary movement, he found himself suddenly under attack by a Catholic journal. This incident, according to Comte, followed an unfortunate set of events. On January 16, 1842, he had awakened early to write the conclusion of lesson 57 of his *Cours*, in which he claimed to have "laid the foundations of truly stable new convictions."[3] Yet this stability did not extend to his private life, for as he was finishing the last page, he had a "horrible domestic

---

[1] Mrs. Grote to Comte, April 15, 1842, MAC. See also Comte to Mill, August 24, 1842, *CG*, 2:73; Mill, *Autobiography*, 207–9; Packe, *John Stuart Mill*, 195.

[2] Comte to Mill, May 29, 1842, *CG*, 2:49. See also Packe, *John Stuart Mill*, 291; Marrast to Comte, May 22, 1842, in "Relations d'Auguste Comte avec Armand Marrast," ed. Laffitte, 189; Mill to Comte, June 9, 1842, *CG*, 2:357.

[3] *Cours*, 2:697. See also "Tableau du nombre de jours," 440–1; Comte to Mill, February 27, 1843, *CG*, 2:139. There is a slight discrepancy in these accounts. Comte recorded that he finished this chapter on January 15, but he told Mill that he completed it on January 16.

quarrel," which lasted two hours. This squabble took up all the time
he had planned to devote to preparing for his course on astronomy,
which he was about to begin for the twelfth time.[4] When he arrived,
completely disconcerted, at the city hall of the third arrondissement,
he found four hundred people eagerly waiting to hear what he had
to say.[5] Although he was supposed to confine his remarks to astronomy, it had been his custom in the opening lessons to speak out
against theological habits and propagate the positive spirit. Comte
prided himself on being the only philosopher willing to risk speaking freely because he had no political ambitions. On this particular
occasion, he was carried away in his attacks on religion by the optimistic conclusion of his chapter and the memory of his vitupera-
tive fight with Massin. Even he admitted his opening lecture was
"volatile and acerbic."[6]

Although for years Comte had suffered no ill effects from his bold
opening remarks, this time some of his Catholic listeners complained.
One auditor went so far as to accuse him of ruining morality and
religion and inciting the dangerous lower classes.[7] A Catholic periodical, L'Ami de la religion: Journal ecclésiastique, politique et littéraire,
took advantage of the occasion to demand greater freedom of religious instruction. On January 27, it published a long article
objecting to the government's authorization of Comte's "course of
invectives against what is most sacred in the world." The article
reproduced parts of Comte's discourse in which he supposedly told
the proletarians that people no longer believed in the devil; the upper
class found religious morality useless for itself but wanted the lower
classes to adopt it; the government neglected to give morality "a
more SOLID BASIS" in a "science of duties"; and the July Monarchy
was not really interested in liberty but in a "universal laissez-faire,"
which it would support as long as there was "tranquillity" on the
streets. The government took very seriously the article's warning
that the people might adopt Comte's "convenient" and dangerous
doctrine.[8] The day after it appeared, Abel-François Villemain, the
minister of public instruction, asked Comte Charles-Marie-Tanneguy
Duchâtelet, the minister of the interior, to look into the matter.[9]

---

[4] Comte to Mill, February 27, 1843, CG, 2:139.

[5] Comte to Mill, January 17, 1842, CG, 2:34.

[6] Comte to Mill, February 27, 1843, CG, 2:140. See also Littré, Auguste Comte, 254; "Cours
d'Astronomie 10me Année: 1840," MAC. The latter is Comte's handwritten outline of the
contents of his course.

[7] An auditor of the course on astronomy to Comte, n.d., MAC.

[8] "Qu'il importe, plus que jamais, de réclamer la liberté de l'enseignement," L'Ami de la
religion: Journal ecclésiastique, politique et littéraire 112 (January 27, 1842): 180–1.

[9] Ministre de l'Instruction Publique to Ministre de l'Intérieur, January 28, 1842, F17 6676, AN;
Almanach royale pour l'an 1842, 148, 194.

The scientist Isidore Geoffroy Saint-Hilaire was sent to spy on Comte's course. In his second report of February 20, 1842, Geoffroy Saint-Hilaire wrote that even though "the lesson lasted *almost two and a half hours*," it presented "exclusively scientific" material and was not a cause for worry.[10] Yet he was told to continue his surveillance because of the gravity of the charges.[11] Although Comte was not supposed to know that he was the subject of an inquiry, he was evidently aware of it, for he was pleased to discover that the scientist was writing only "favorable" reports.[12]

Comte admitted that the whole affair had really been his own fault, but he inveighed against the "theological ranters" who had the nerve to demand his "destitution."[13] He vowed to insist even more strongly the following year on the antitheological bias of positivism. Nothing could deter him from using every means available to proclaim the imminent victory of his philosophy. When he discovered in March 1842 that the *Cours* was on the Index, he was more than ever convinced of the imminence of the final battle between positivism and Catholicism.[14]

PROBLEMS AGAIN WITH THE *COURS*

Despite his enthusiasm and resolve, Comte could not face writing the last three chapters of his *Cours*, which would correlate the various ideas of the entire work. Having been preoccupied by the science of society for the past three years, he decided he needed a three-month rest to grasp again the "true spirit of the whole."[15] He then extended this break to five months owing to an "indisposition," which he blamed on atmospheric changes.[16] Finally, on May 17, 1842, he began lesson 58 on the positive method and finished it a month later. Worried about not completing the work before the

---

[10] He added that the course "seemed to interest the audience very much" and presented "science in all its rigor and austerity." Report of Isidore Geoffroy Saint-Hilaire, February 20, 1842, F^{17} 6676, AN.

[11] Inspecteur Général Chargé de l'Administration de l'Académie de Paris to the Ministre de l'Instruction Publique, February 21, 1842, F^{17} 6676, AN; Ministre de l'Instruction Publique to the Inspecteur Général Chargé de l'Administration de l'Académie de Paris, February 24, 1842, F^{17} 6676, AN.

[12] Comte to Mme Auguste Comte, December 3 and 12, 1842, *CG*, 2:114, 115.

[13] Comte to Mme Auguste Comte, December 3, 1842, *CG*, 2:114. See also Comte to Mill, February 27, 1843, *CG*, 2:139.

[14] Comte to Mill, March 4, 1842, *CG*, 2:38.

[15] Comte to Mill, January 17, 1842, *CG*, 2:29. See also Comte to Valat, May 1, 1841, *CG*, 2:8.

[16] Comte to Mill, May 29, 1842, *CG*, 2:45.

start of his examination tour, he began to harass his printer and to work "without interruption" and with an "extraordinary intensity."[17] The result was that he completed the next lesson on positive doctrine in five days and the lesson on the future of positive philosophy in four. The latter was especially difficult because he had to discuss the influence of positivism "without falling into a utopia."[18]

Comte's excitement about the end of his twelve-year ordeal was evident when he wrote, "60th and last lesson!" on his work sheet recording his daily progress. On the same sheet, he wrote in Latin next to July 13, the day he finished this chapter, "The cost of the effort does not matter if something better results from it." He also wrote and underlined twice the word *exegi*, referring probably to Horace's very famous statement "Exegi monumentum aere perennius," which means "I have finished a monument more lasting than bronze."[19] Comte was promising his work – and himself – similar immortality.

Although the speed with which Comte tackled the last chapters may give the impression that his task was easy, the opposite was true. He suffered from stomach pains and distressing "moments of melancholy," which he admitted to Mill came often when he embarked on projects requiring "deep, very prolonged cerebral intensity."[20] Again, the tension caused by his work resulted in physical and emotional problems and would lead to accusations against Massin.

THE FINAL SEPARATION

Since the quarrel of January 16, the Comtes had experienced serious marital difficulties. These were aggravated when Comte, still smarting from his rejection at the Ecole Polytechnique, decided in March to devote part of lesson 57 to a critical analysis of scientific specialization, the "principal obstacle to the great philosophical movement

---

[17] Comte to Bachelier, June 7, 1842, *CG*, 2:50; Comte to Mill, June 19, 1842, *CG*, 2:52.
[18] Comte to Mill, May 29, 1842, *CG*, 2:46.
[19] Comte wrote, "*Le 13 exegi (5,6,) 28!* Nil reputans actum si quid superesset agendum." The term "(5,6) 28" refers to the pages Comte completed. Comte repeated the single word "(*Exegi!*)" when he finished his preface on July 19. See his original work sheet called "Temps du Travail," MAC. Laffitte's reproduction of this work sheet is full of errors. See "Tableau du nombre de jours," in "Du temps dans le travail intellectuel," ed. Laffitte, 441. See also Horace, *The Odes and Epodes*, trans. C. E. Bennett (Cambridge, Mass.: Harvard University Press, 1968), 278–9. Two volumes of Horace's works can be found in Comte's library at the Maison d'Auguste Comte.
[20] Comte to Mill, May 29, 1842, *CG*, 2:46–7. See also Comte to Mill, June 19, 1842, *CG*, 2:52; Caroline Massin to Comte, August 24, November 9, 1842, MAC.

of the nineteenth century."[21] He realized that his attack could be dangerous, but as his provocative lecture in January indicated, he seemed more heedless of risks to his hard-fought financial security.

Encouraged by Mill's growing sympathy, Comte told him of his plan and received the following response:

> It is certainly in order that philosophers today are persecuted by scientists, as they were previously by priests, as they will be probably one day by industrialists. . . . But it is to be hoped that you at least will not be the victim [of persecutions] and that even if you experienced from the wounded self-love of a scholarly body the infamous injustice that does not seem impossible to you, this [persecution] would inspire in all impartial persons an opposite feeling, [one] that could exercise a more than equivalent influence, even on your material position.[22]

Mill had convinced Comte that he and others would help him financially if necessary. Bolstered by these assurances, Comte decided to write a personal preface to the *Cours* in which he would place himself "directly under the formal protection of the European public" and show how contemporary scientists were trying to prevent his success. Boasting about being "perhaps the first philosopher" to tell the whole truth, he explained that it would be "strange" if, after having "openly defied the most powerful beliefs," he retreated before scientific "prejudices," especially because "the natural course of my subject leads me inevitably to . . . [such a bold step]."[23] He was ready to follow Saint-Simon's principle that society had an obligation to support philosophers.[24]

If Comte was enchanted with the prospect of defying the scientific elite and suffering martyrdom, Massin was not. She was unconvinced that the European public would support her husband, and she feared a return to the hand-to-mouth existence of the past, which would have devastating effects on their health. Reminding Comte that it had taken him ten painful years to establish his position, she asked, "You no longer have the same stomach, and then what resource will we find for old age?"[25] For months, she begged him not to attack scientists at the Academy and Ecole Polytechnique. She warned him that he would lose such a war.[26] But Comte was adamant in his resolve to carry out the threat that he had already voiced to Navier in 1835.[27] He accused her of trying to demoralize him, of

---

[21] Comte to Mill, March 4, 1842, *CG*, 2:39.

[22] Mill to Comte, March 22, 1842, *CG*, 2:353.

[23] Comte to Mill, April 5, 1842, *CG*, 2:41–2.   [24] Littré, *Auguste Comte*, 502.

[25] Caroline Massin to Comte, December 23, 1842, MAC. See also Caroline Massin to Comte, September 9, 1842, MAC.

[26] Littré, *Auguste Comte*, 500–2.   [27] Comte to Navier, July 23, 1835, *CG*, 1:251.

having joined his enemies. When she objected, he shouted, "Leave me alone; get away from me."[28] Constantly rebuffing her, he demanded peace to finish his last chapters. After weeks of conflict, Massin decided to live apart; she ate her meals in her room and saw Comte only to discuss bills.

After two months of this solitary existence, Massin threatened to leave, although she secretly believed he could not live without her. Comte warned her, as he had in May 1838, that he would not take her back again; the fourth separation would be the last. (The other separations had taken place in 1826, 1833, and 1838.) But her threats upset him, for he had learned from previous experience – in 1826, when he began the *Cours*, and in 1838, when he created "sociology" – that he could not face domestic problems and intense intellectual challenges at the same time. And the strain of concluding the *Cours* had already precipitated a "great intellectual crisis."[29]

When Massin suddenly announced on June 15, 1842, that she had found another apartment and was leaving, he was stunned: "This day was terrible for me, and I felt ready to fall back in 1842 into the ghastly cerebral episode of 1826 by an analogous coincidence of disturbing influences."[30] To prevent such an outcome, he refused to give her any money and thus forced her to stay until he finished. She accused him of being a tyrant;[31] he charged her with being "despotic."[32]

Thus in the summer of 1842, Comte defied not only the scientists but his wife. She left on August 5, about two weeks after the completion of the preface. She moved far away to a peaceful area of the ninth arrondissement.[33] Blaming her "stupid pride," Comte claimed that he had not "provoked" her departure, and his disciples maintained that she had "voluntarily abandoned" him.[34] She reminded him, however, that after having done everything to avoid a separation, she had left only "after I had heard for *several years* that I tired you, that you wished only to be alone and tranquil, and that I was only staying to torment you."[35] She was compelled to leave because

---

[28] Comte, quoted in Littré, *Auguste Comte*, 501.

[29] Comte to Littré, April 28, 1851, *CG*, 6:64. See also "De quelques documents relatifs à la crise cérébrale," ed. Laffitte, 437.

[30] Comte to Littré, April 28, 1851, *CG*, 6:64.   [31] Ibid.

[32] Comte to Mill, August 24, 1842, *CG*, 2:76.

[33] She resided at 37, rue Rochechouart, close to where they had lived during Comte's mental breakdown of 1826. See also ibid., 77; Lonchampt, *Précis*, 67.

[34] Comte to Mme Comte, January 10, 1847, *CG*, 4:95; Comte to Clotilde de Vaux, August 5, 1845, *CG*, 3:82; Audiffrent, *Centenaire de la fondation de l'Ecole Polytechnique*, 54. Robinet used the same words as Audiffrent. Robinet, *Notice*, 192.

[35] Caroline Massin to Comte, September 20, 1842, MAC.

she felt "more dead than alive" when she was with him.[36] However, even if divorce were still legal, she would not consent to it.[37] (Divorce was abolished in 1816.)

Out of his annual income of around ten thousand francs, Comte agreed to pay her three thousand francs a year. No price, he said, was too high to attain "peace."[38] Although he and his disciples liked to portray Massin as a woman driven by cupidity, she insisted that she had not stayed with him for eighteen years as a way of "investing funds" to assure herself "some bread."[39] She did not like being dependent on him but saw no other way of maintaining herself. Her dilemma was typical of most nineteenth-century women, who were often forced to rely on the earning power of men close to them (i.e., their fathers, husbands, brothers, or sons) to survive because their own ability to make a living was limited.

One reason Comte decided at this point to confront his wife was that he blamed her for having delayed the completion of the *Cours*. He reassured himself that, without domestic strife, he would have written it in eight years instead of twelve.[40] His friend Charles Bonnin agreed that Comte had lacked the necessary tranquillity for writing because of Massin's "domineering character."[41] Massin, too, recognized the problems caused by their bitter struggle for power. She considered herself, however, not domineering, but assertive:

> I have always been devoted to you, but I was not at all submissive. If there had been less real devotion and more submission, things would have been better between us. Many times you were basically right, but you asked me to yield in the name of your authority, and I stood up to you when I should have submitted. Really, I did not know how to be submissive, but *even so*, I did love you. You know that very well.[42]

She demanded a marriage based on equality. "My great crime was to see in you a husband, not a master. I know very well that you are superior to me in many respects, and besides, this comparison has always seemed to me . . . most absurd. We did not do the same things."[43] Rejecting her position, Comte felt he had a duty to humanity to forbid this disobedient, unruly woman to return to his

[36] Caroline Massin to Comte, October 1, 1842, MAC.
[37] Caroline Massin to Comte, October 25, 1842, MAC.
[38] Comte to Mill, August 24, 1842, CG, 2:76.
[39] Caroline Massin to Comte, October 1, 1842, MAC.
[40] Comte to Littré, April 28, 1851, CG, 6:65; Comte to Mill, August 24, 1842, CG, 2:71.
[41] Bonnin to Comte, September 22, 1842, MAC.
[42] Caroline Massin to Comte, January 17, 1850, MAC.
[43] Caroline Massin to Comte, May 28, 1843, MAC.

apartment, and he even had a friend deliver her allowance so that he could avoid seeing her.[44]

Yet Comte's feelings were not as clear as he pretended. In describing their separation to Mill, he said that Massin was "gifted with a rare moral and intellectual elevation" and that her "high value" was diminished only by the "mistakes of her character and education." Her main crime was that she did not love him enough. She failed to understand that woman's role was to respond to man's needs for affection, needs that Comte felt "very sharply."[45] The "affectionate domestic care" she gave him during his crisis of 1826 still evoked words of gratitude in his "Personal Preface."[46]

After their separation, Massin expressed her sadness in every letter she wrote to him and begged him not to make a complete break. She even reminded him of the care she had given him during the seventeen years of their marriage – the "most beautiful years" of their lives. She attributed their problems partially to Comte's obsession with his work: "A man is not only in this world to write volumes on behalf of posterity, . . . [and] if there had been less science at home, there would have been far more happiness."[47] Thus she resented having been forced to play such a small role in his life. And despite this small role, it appeared that he still "feared" her "devoted influence."[48] In a sense, by separating from his wife and freeing himself from a disturbing influence, Comte was applying cerebral hygiene in another domain. She pleaded with him not to repeat the pattern of behavior that was well established in all his other social relationships, especially because "only Monsieur de Blainville . . . is really interested in you."[49] When Comte failed to give her news about his examination circuit, she wrote in words reminiscent of those of Michel Chevalier in his article of 1832: "You have greatly hurt me; are you happier for it?"[50]

By October she came to realize that he never intended to see her again. When she told him that she desperately needed to see him, he angrily accused her of scheming and threatening him. With great anxiety, she exclaimed, "I know that with your character the position that you are going to take will be eternal."[51] She was right. Like

[44] Caroline Massin to Comte, August 26, November 9, 1842, MAC; "Documents: Pension"; Comte's notebook, "Recettes et dépenses," MAC.
[45] Comte to Mill, August 24, 1842, CG, 2:76.   [46] Cours, 2:468.
[47] Caroline Massin to Comte, November 9, 1842, MAC.
[48] Caroline Massin to Comte, October 25, 1842, MAC.
[49] Caroline Massin to Comte, September 9, 1842, MAC. See also Caroline Massin to Comte, August 26, 1842, MAC.
[50] Caroline Massin to Comte, September 9, 1842, MAC. See also Caroline Massin to Comte, October 28, 1842, MAC.
[51] Caroline Massin to Comte, October 25, 1842, MAC.

his views of his other "enemies," such as Saint-Simon, Arago, and the Academicians, Comte's low opinion of Caroline Massin would resonate throughout his system.

THE "PERSONAL PREFACE"

The immediate cause of their separation, the "Personal Preface" to the sixth volume of the *Cours*, was written in three days, from July 17 to July 19, 1842. Though as brash and antagonistic as his opening discourse to his astronomy course, the preface was thoroughly premeditated. Already in July 1840, Comte boasted that he alone had succeeded in uniting the opposing spirits of philosophy and science and, in so doing, had become the savior of humanity. Even before his defeat by Sturm, he had been preparing to disgrace the scientists. Then he was convinced by Mill's warnings about the force of religion, the Catholic journal's attack, and the inclusion of the *Cours* in the Index that his last volume would cause a scandal and stimulate animosity against him. He resolved to attack first.[52] Thus the "Personal Preface" was a deliberately provocative manifesto that did not totally escape the pathological – despite some scholars' assertions to the contrary.[53] Overcome by the humiliation, discouragement, and bitterness caused by the failure to acquire his chair in 1840, Comte decided to exact his final revenge against those members of the "pedantocracy" who had persecuted him. He wanted to relieve his anxiety by creating a crisis that would in some way settle his life once and for all.

In the preface, Comte felt he had to provide a personal explanation of why the *Cours* took twelve years to write instead of the six that it should have required. The preface was thus important for demonstrating his belief in the unity of his life and work. Because he closely identified with his philosophy, his problems could not be separated from those of his doctrine. The public had a right to know his entire intellectual development as well as "his individual position," not only because his work was "destined to mark an important epoch in the general development of human reason" but because his personal life was intimately bound up with the "general state of human reason in the nineteenth century."[54] Equally important, Comte wanted to open his heart to his readers in the hope of acquiring

---

[52] "Tableau du nombre de jours," in "Du temps dans le travail intellectuel," ed. Laffitte, 441; Comte to Valat, July 10, 1840, *CG*, 1:343–4; Comte to Valat, August 1, 1842, *CG*, 2:64; *Cours*, 2:468.

[53] See, e.ġ., Arbousse-Bastide, *Doctrine d'éducation*, 1:130.

[54] Comte to Mme Auguste Comte, December 29, 1842, *CG*, 2:122; *Cours*, 2:466.

more sympathy for his plight from them than from those around him. Here again, he was following the example of Saint-Simon, who had written an autobiographical preface to the *Lettres au Bureau de Longitudes* to justify his life and work.

In his autobiographical preface, Comte described his family background and education, early renunciation of God, first articles, devotion to the teaching of mathematics, and career at the Ecole Polytechnique. He showed that each stage in his development and in the growth of his philosophy reflected his reaction to the cultural environment of his time. Following the tenets of his doctrine, he thus connected his own evolution with that of society at large. His enterprise was similar to the analyses of the interrelationship between a protagonist and the objective world that constituted the heart of the *roman d'éducation*, the literary genre that arose with the new urban society.[55] Like the novelists, Comte seemed to be searching for a way to express more effectively the powerful impact of new social forces. He apparently felt imprisoned by the textual constraints of the *Cours*, which was organized into lessons as if to serve as an introductory textbook to the science of society. Moreover, his decision to insert an autoportrait, which seems at odds with the tenor of the rest of the *Cours*, reflects his deep desire to discuss his personal problems and emotions. In fact, in calling attention to his own individuality, he almost subverted his main text, whose whole purpose was to highlight the primacy of society.

Although Comte discreetly avoided mentioning his wife's role in delaying the *Cours*, he brought up his "deadly liaison" with the "very superficial" thinker Saint-Simon. He criticized the Saint-Simonians for introducing in Saint-Simon's name "shameful ephemeral aberrations" that their master would never have espoused. Their efforts to found a church certainly went beyond the "vague religiosity" exhibited by Saint-Simon in his declining years. Comte wished to publicize his detachment from this "subversive" group.[56]

With great frankness, he also provided his readers with details about his attack of madness of 1826. Although at first hesitant about including this episode, he followed the advice of Charles Bonnin, who warned him that if he did not discuss it, his cowardly enemies would use his illness as a "weapon" against his "superiority."[57] Bolstered by Bonnin, Comte therefore explained in the preface that he wanted to protect himself in advance against the "infamous insinuations" that his enemies might make against him to discredit

---

[55] Richard Terdiman, *Discourse/Counter-Discourse: The Theory and Practice of Symbolic Resistance in Nineteenth-Century France* (Ithaca, N.Y.: Cornell University Press, 1985), 85–9.

[56] *Cours*, 2:466–7.

[57] Bonnin to Comte, July 12, 1842, MAC.

him after they read his sixth volume. He wrote in a particularly
vindictive fashion:

> This accurate prediction already rests on the shameful use of similar
> machinations, which in 1838 a powerful scientific personage, whose
> name must finally figure here in *deserved punishment*, . . . vainly re-
> sorted to in order to satisfy [his] ignoble private feelings of resent-
> ment against me – the famous geometer Poisson.[58]

Such language does not bear the marks of sanity.

The main part of the preface dealt with the three groups that
shared the "intellectual empire" of the period – the theological,
metaphysical, and scientific. Comte showed how each group was
persecuting him because his "installation of the true modern philosophy" threatened its power.[59]

The theologians were responsible for dismissing him from the
Ecole Polytechnique in 1816, preventing him from teaching in the
University, and trying to censure him with the Index and their
journals.

The metaphysicians were more "dangerous" to him because they
were more powerful and supple.[60] One of the most menacing in his
eyes was Guizot. Angry at not being a member of the Collège de
France, Comte accused him of nepotism, and he condemned him for
having revived the Academy of Moral and Political Sciences, which
also refused to admit him. Besides attacking the academies, Comte
condemned the press. Its neglect of his books reflected the attitude
of the metaphysicians, who feared that the establishment of the positive philosophers would destroy their own power.

Ironically, the main target of Comte's ravings was the agent of
positivism, the scientific class. The scientists represented his "intellectual family" since they were the "very imperfect but direct germ
of the true modern spirituality." But his "official lords" were also
the real cause of his delays and personal troubles because they were
the people who ensured his material existence. In control of the
Conseil d'Instruction, the mathematicians were his nemesis; they
realized that the positive regime would put an end to their powerful
domination of the sciences. At least the biologists, such as Blainville,
favored his cause, for they knew his triumph would free them from
the "oppression of the geometers."[61] Yet they had no influence on
his livelihood.

Comte tediously described his efforts to acquire the chair of analysis
at the Ecole Polytechnique, a position he felt he needed to give him
time to develop his philosophy. He did not fail to mention his

---

[58] *Cours*, 2:468 (my emphasis).   [59] Ibid., 472.   [60] Ibid.   [61] Ibid., 471, 473–4.

"memorable lessons" of 1836, Dulong's admiration for him, or his students' support. What made this part even more bizarre was that he had covered much of the same ground in lesson 57. Carried away by a personal vendetta ill-suited to a philosophical work, he inveighed against the scientists, the Academy of Sciences, and even the "absurd" Conseil d'Instruction. In a section that was soon to become notorious, Comte declared:

> Every well-informed person knows even now that the irrational and oppressive dispositions adopted during the past ten years at the Ecole Polytechnique derive especially from the disastrous influence exercised by M. Arago, the faithful spontaneous organ of the passions and aberrations proper to the class that he so deplorably dominates today.[62]

Arago, who had headed the reorganization of the Ecole Polytechnique after the Revolution of 1830, was the man whom Comte decided to blame ultimately for his failures at the school.[63]

Comte also complained that he had to be reelected every year to his two sensitive posts of *répétiteur* and examiner. Although he was indeed the only examiner subject to annual reevaluation, the system was not, in truth, directed against him personally. In 1832 the administrators, frustrated by their inability to fire his predecessor Reynaud, who had held the job for the past sixteen years, had changed the rules so that examiners had to be reappointed annually. So far, the reappointment process had been a mere formality. But to Comte, the only new appointee, the yearly election was a severe trial, especially because of his paranoia. Each year he was driven to despair by the thought that he would be rejected.[64] The letters from important people seeking to influence his judgment and the pressure from his superiors to persuade him to change his methods indicate that his fears were not entirely groundless. As scientific antipathy toward him grew with the appearance of each new volume of the *Cours*, the yearly routine grew more painful. Expressing his desperate need for relief, he wrote "It is in order to get out of . . . this intolerable situation that I thought obliged by this preface to provoke with respect to me, a decisive crisis, whose peril . . . is in my eyes less deadly than the continual perspective of an imminent [act of] oppression."[65]

---

[62] Ibid., 470, 474, 631–2.   [63] Callot, *Histoire de l'Ecole Polytechnique*, 78.

[64] *Cours*, 2:471; Audiffrent, *Réponse à Bertrand*, 26; Reynaud's Dossier, Archives of the Ecole Polytechnique; Bertrand, Review of *Cours*, 687; Bertrand, "Souvenirs académiques," 543; Meetings of July 11, 1837, and February 22, 1838, Registre: Procès-Verbal du Conseil d'Instruction, vol. 7, EP; Comte to Valat, November 21, 1837, *CG*, 1:284; Comte to Mme Auguste Comte, October 6, 1837, *CG*, 1:281.

[65] *Cours*, 2:471.

In this fashion, Comte was forcing the Ecole Polytechnique to take a position on the issue of reelection. He was, in effect, telling the administration not to reappoint him if he was not to be henceforth guaranteed a position as permanent examiner.[66]

In sum, Comte wrote this "unprecedented" preface to put himself "under the noble patronage of public opinion" throughout Europe.[67] He thought that with the publication of the *Cours*, he would win such influence over his "great friend the public" that his tormenters would not dare act against him.[68] Since his earliest writings, he had expressed the view, born in the turmoil of the eighteenth century, that public opinion was the ultimate tribunal; now he invoked public opinion once again to appeal to a supposedly impartial judge beyond the passions aroused by politics.[69] By making the people, instead of individuals, like Arago, his "patron," he rebelled against the powerful patronage network that was still dominant and prided himself on preserving his sincerity and autonomy.[70] His position was paradoxical. Unable to find an individual or group powerful enough to protect him, he was forced to call on the people to obtain their support for a basically elitist, authoritarian system.

Comte's growing faith in his power partly explains his increasing boldness. Eagerly awaiting the crisis that he knew his preface was bound to provoke, Comte maintained – somewhat naively, as Littré pointed out – that if the next annual elections confirmed his position at the Ecole Polytechnique, he could rest assured that "this formality" was no longer dangerous for him and the scientists would no longer harass him.[71] His intellectual and social regeneration of humanity could then proceed in the calm he required. If, however, he failed to achieve his goal, he knew what to do to ensure his survival and that of his system. Thanks to Mill's encouraging words, he was beginning to devise what became known as the "Positivist Subsidy," a fund that Littré later helped to establish to support Comte.

Comte claimed that he would not allow the ensuing controversy to trouble his philosophical work, but events took a startling turn that forced him into action. He expected his volume to be published by the end of July, about two weeks after he handed his "Personal Preface" to his printer, Bachelier.[72] As the weeks passed and his volume did not appear, Comte began to suspect that Bachelier was deliberately delaying the publication so that he could secretly give

[66] Bertrand, Review of *Cours*, 687; Audiffrent, *Réponse à Bertrand*, 26.
[67] *Cours*, 2:478. [68] Comte to Mme Auguste Comte, December 3, 1842, *CG*, 2:115.
[69] Baker, *Inventing the French Revolution*, 168, 198.
[70] On the importance of patronage, see Dorinda Outram, "Politics and Vocation: French Science, 1793–1830," *British Journal for the History of Science* 13 (March 1980): 27–43.
[71] *Cours*, 2:479. See also Littré, *Auguste Comte*, 315.
[72] Comte to Valat, August 1, 1842, *CG*, 2:64.

the manuscript of the preface to his "enemies."[73] Many of Bachelier's customers were connected with the Ecole Polytechnique and frequented his shop. Comte therefore demanded the return of the manuscript if it was not printed immediately. Despite assurances that Bachelier was an honest printer, Comte soon discovered that he was indeed delaying the project in order to consult Arago, who had been campaigning in the south for reelection to the Chamber of Deputies and had not yet returned to Paris.[74]

After consulting Arago, Bachelier begged Comte on August 11 to remove the one sentence denouncing Arago's influence at the Ecole Polytechnique. Evidently Arago had censured this passage. Bachelier was in an uncomfortable position. He published Arago's works as well as the *Annuaire du Bureau des Longitudes*, the official yearbook of the Observatory, which Arago headed. In addition, Bachelier was hoping to persuade Arago to let him reprint a work of Laplace, which would bring him fifty thousand francs.[75] But Comte refused to eliminate the sentence, contending that he alone had to fear the animosity of the "Sultan of the Observatory."[76] He had not yielded to anyone since his disputes with Saint-Simon and was not about to do so again.

When Bachelier refused to publish the volume, Comte reminded him of their contract, in which the "adoration of M. Arago was never obligatory." Yet to avoid further delay and the inconvenience of bringing legal action against his publisher, he said that if Bachelier wanted to avoid offending "his boss," he could append a statement declaring that he did not agree with Comte's assertions and had tried to persuade him to modify or delete them.[77]

Bachelier finally published the *Cours* on August 18, 1842, and attached to the inside front cover the following notice:

> At the moment of printing the Preface to this volume, I perceived that the author was hurting M. Arago. Those who know how much gratitude I owe to the secretary of the Academy of Sciences and the

[73] Comte to Bachelier, August 3, 1842, CG, 2:65.

[74] Bailleul to Comte, August 6, 1842, MAC; Comte's speech at the trial, quoted in "Justice civile," *Gazette des Tribunaux: Journal de jurisprudence et des débats judiciaires*, December 17, 1842, 205.

[75] Comte to Mill, August 24, 1842, CG, 2:74.

[76] Comte to Bachelier, August 11, 1842, CG, 2:67. Comte borrowed this expression from the navigator Admiral Dumont d'Urville, who was not a friend of Arago either. It was probably a reference to an incident when Arago was caught in a war between Spain and France and had to travel from the west coast of Africa through Algeria disguised as a bedouin. Arago had been appointed to the Observatory in 1805 and became "directeur des observations" in 1834. Suzanne Debarbat, Solange Grillot, and Jacques Lévy, *L'Observatoire de Paris: Son Histoire* (Paris: Observatoire de Paris, 1984), 28–9.

[77] Comte to Bachelier, August 11, 1842, CG, 2:66. See also "Justice civile," 205.

Bureau des Longitudes will understand that I had demanded *categorically* the suppression of a passage that wounded all of my feelings. M. Comte *refused*. From this moment, I had only one position to take, that of not lending my cooperation to the publication of this sixth volume. M. Arago, to whom I communicated this resolution, forced me to renounce it. "Do not worry," he told me, "about the attacks of M. Comte; if they are worth the effort, I will respond to them. The portion of the public that is interested in these discussions knows, moreover, very well that the bad humor of the *philosopher* dates exactly from the period when M. Sturm was nominated professor of analysis at the Ecole Polytechnique. Now, counselling the limited circle of my influence to prefer an illustrious geometer to a rival in whom I saw no mathematical qualifications of any sort, neither great nor small, is an act in my life that I could never regret." Despite such liberal incitements of M. Arago, I believed I should publish this work only by adding a note explaining the debate that arose between M. Comte and myself.[78]

When Comte arrived home, he was shocked to open the box containing his copies. He had never given Bachelier permission to publish this kind of editorial note and regarded his "literary violence" as "scandalous."[79] It reminded him all too clearly of the time when Saint-Simon had surreptitiously inserted a disapproving introduction to his *Plan*. Comte was in a quandary, for although he would have liked to find another publisher, he was bound to Bachelier by their contract. His only means of escape was to bring Bachelier to trial before the Tribunal of Commerce.

Although he boasted of being "decent," "rational," and self-controlled, Comte aggravated his situation a short time later when, on August 21, he sent volume 6 and an irate letter to his former protector and Arago's colleague, Poinsot.[80] Comte pointed out that in lesson 57 he had denounced Poinsot's silence during the 1840 session of the Academy of Sciences (regarding Comte's candidacy) as "cowardly" and asserted that his character was inferior to his intellect.[81] Calling Poinsot a "dreamer without importance," Comte formally announced he was ending their twenty-five-year relationship.[82] Any possibility of Poinsot's support in Comte's battle against his enemies was brusquely dismissed.

Yet several scientists showed sympathy for Comte. Coriolis

---

[78] Bachelier, "Avis de l'Editeur," *Cours de philosophie positive* (1830–42), 6:iii. It is also reproduced in Littré, *Auguste Comte*, 323.

[79] Comte to Mill, August 24, 1842, CG, 2:74–5.

[80] Comte to Bachelier, August 11, 1842, CG, 2:67.   [81] *Cours*, 2:632.

[82] Comte to Poinsot, August 21, 1842, CG, 2:69.

explained to his cousin that although he had voted for Sturm, he valued Comte for his "honesty," conscientiousness, and refusal to compromise in matters of duty. He also admired his willingness to express his feelings even at the risk of offending others. Comte's only fault was his "extreme vanity," which made him think that he was a "great philosopher" when he was, in truth, only a "very erudite man in all the sciences."[83] Seeking Comte's esteem, Coriolis told him that he was hurt to be included among his enemies because he respected him as a philosopher.[84] Kind words also came from Comte's old friend Gabriel Lamé, who told him that the *Cours* would certainly be very influential. Although it was stimulating the scientists' "active and passionate opposition," it would soon prove its "utility," especially because Comte was the "oracle" and "guide" of the "rising generation."[85]

These letters convinced Comte that the "wind" was blowing favorably for him at the Ecole Polytechnique, despite his preface and denunciation of Poinsot.[86] He went so far as to think that the professors were treating him better out of fear and that there was still a chance to get the chair of analysis, which was soon to be vacated by Liouville or Sturm. He even boasted that for the third time the students were clamoring for his appointment as professor.

Upon his return from his examination tour, Comte decided to push for the "public punishment" of Bachelier, who he thought was deliberately trying to curtail the volume's circulation in the provinces and abroad.[87] He would seek the suppression of Bachelier's editorial notice on all the remaining copies, the cancellation of the contract, and damages amounting to ten thousand francs, which he intended to donate to charity in order not to be "sullied" by money obtained in this fashion.[88] He added the third condition because he feared Bachelier might agree to the first two. In this way, he was guaranteed a public hearing at the Tribunal. Comte first met with his lawyer, Bordeaux, in mid-November to discuss his case, and the

[83] Coriolis also spoke in amazement of having discovered in the preface that Comte had not read anything in four years: "He has not even read a *newspaper*; now that is a *phenomenon*." Coriolis to Madame Benoist, written from August 26 to August 31, 1842, MAC.

[84] Coriolis also defended himself by saying that he was sick the day the Academy voted to suspend the reading of Comte's letter and that he would not have supported such an unjust action. Coriolis to Comte, August 19, 1842, MAC.

[85] Lamé to Comte, Ocotber 19, 1842, MAC.

[86] Comte to Mme Auguste Comte, September 13, 1842, *CG*, 2:83.

[87] Comte to Valat, October 27, 1842, *CG*, 2:99. See also Comte to Bachelier, October 8, 1842, *CG*, 2:96.

[88] Comte to Valat, October 27, 1842, *CG*, 2:100. See also Comte to Mill, November 5, 1842, *CG*, 2:104–5; Chamonard to Comte, November 9, 1842, MAC.

public hearing at the Tribunal of Commerce was scheduled for the following month.[89]

As time passed, Comte increasingly focused on Arago as his chief enemy. He called him superficial and avid for power and popularity.[90] Arago seemed to personify the scientific establishment, the group Comte held responsible for his failures. He was part of the governing body of the Ecole Polytechnique, the head of the Observatory (and the Bureau des Longitudes), a member of numerous scientific committees, and the permanent secretary of the mathematical section of the Academy. In fact, he was the dominant figure in the Academy, because the presidency was only a one-year honorific position. Arago used his position to introduce many changes, such as founding the *Comptes rendus*, which publicized the Academy's proceedings. His combative, flamboyant style made him the "star" of the institution. Furthermore, as a liberal politician, he had worked to secure the election of many republican scientists to the Academy, including Savary, Sturm, and Liouville.[91] His principal enemy was Comte's royalist friend Blainville.[92] Comte was not exempt from the rivalry among coteries. After all, his dislike of Poisson had stemmed partly from the fact that Poisson was at odds with two of Comte's protectors – Fourier and Poinsot.

One of Comte's future disciples, Georges Audiffrent, claimed that Arago resented Comte's criticisms of mathematics and his desire to make the organic sciences dominant. He led the "campaign of hatred and persecution" against Comte to deprive him of his livelihood and thereby silence him.[93] Yet this dramatic account probably derived from Comte and is not entirely credible. Arago was certainly the patron of the republican scientist Sturm; having already furthered Sturm's career on several occasions, Arago no doubt voted with the majority in the Academy for his appointment as professor at the Ecole Polytechnique.[94] And Arago's republican principles, which were similar to those of Marrast, unquestionably did not coincide with Comte's. But there is no evidence of any personal animus against Comte. In fact, in the 1820s Arago had supported Comte's

[89] Collard to Comte, November 11, 1842; Bordeaux to Comte, November 17, 1842, MAC. Bordeaux must have persuaded Comte to lower the damages from ten to six thousand francs because the latter was the sum that Bordeaux demanded during the trial itself. See "Justice civile," 205.

[90] Comte to Mill, August 24, 1842, *CG*, 2:74–5.

[91] Horace Chauvet, *François Arago et son temps* (Perpignan: Edition des "Amis de François Arago," 1954), 37, 47; Crosland, *Science under Control*, xvn6, 119–20, 188–9, 288; Robert Fox, "Science, the University, and the State," 78, 82–3.

[92] Audiffrent, *Réponse à Bertrand*; idem, *A propos du centenaire de la naissance d'un maître vénéré* (Paris, 1898), 4; Deroisin, *Notes sur Auguste Comte*, 32.

[93] Audiffrent, *Réponse à Bertrand*, 10, 11.   [94] Speziali, "Sturm."

experiments relating to air pressure and his candidacy for inspector of commerce, and in 1840 he had been kind enough to tell him of the Grotes' admiration. Massin also reminded him of how "friendly" Arago had always been to him.[95]

Arago's opinion of Comte after the publication of the *Cours* is clearer. Laffitte found Arago's copy of volume 6, which is full of the scientist's annotations, especially on the "Personal Preface." At one point, Arago wrote in the margin that he rejected "with all the forces of my soul the title of enemy. Mr. Comte inspires in me compassion and not hatred." Arago may not have hated Comte, but his notes ridiculing his statements indicate his utter contempt for him. Next to a passage where Comte said that he did Guizot the honor of asking him to create a chair for him (Comte) at the Collège de France, Arago scribbled, "*I did him the honor!* The expression would be fine if it were not here in the mouth of a personage without any real qualifications and without any fame." When Comte declared that his private situation had a correlation with the state of the intellectual world, Arago called this "incredible buffoonery."[96]

Eager for revenge, Comte hoped the results of the trial would echo throughout all of Europe.[97] Describing in great detail his various maneuvers to Mill, he was chiefly worried that Arago and his "vast and powerful coterie" would stifle the publicity in the press.[98] He was convinced that Arago would use any means – except "assassination" – to stop him.[99] Indeed, Arago's brother-in-law, Claude Mathieu, who held the post of *examinateur permanent* at the school, told Marrast that he would make sure Comte lost his post as examiner if he so much as mentioned Arago's name at the trial. But Comte failed to enlist the support of Marrast, who backed Arago's leadership of the republican opposition in the Chamber of Deputies. Appalling Massin, Comte then turned to more conservative journals, such as the *Journal des débats*, to come to his aid, but with no success.[100]

Motivated by his dislike of lawyers and his overweening

[95] Caroline Massin to Comte, February 10, 1843, MAC.
[96] Notes of Arago, in "Quelques remarques de François Arago sur Auguste Comte," ed. Pierre Laffitte, *RO* 10 (May 1883): 306–8.
[97] Comte to Valat, December 13, 1842, *CG*, 2:116.
[98] Comte to Mill, November 5, 1842, *CG*, 2:105.
[99] Comte to Valat, December 13, 1842, *CG*, 2:117. During the trial, Arago was on a trip in Spain. *CG*, 2:389n.
[100] Caroline Massin to Comte, December 8, 1842, MAC; Mathieu's Dossier, EP; Comte to Mill, November 5, December 30, 1842, *CG*, 2:105, 123–4; Comte to Mme Auguste Comte, December 3, 1842, *CG*, 2:114; Audiffrent, *Réponse à Bertrand*, 11; Comte to Bordeaux, November 28, 1842, *CG*, 2:113; A. Dame to Comte, November 27, 1842, MAC; Littré, *Auguste Comte*, 326, 326n1.

self-confidence, he decided to plead his own case. He claimed that because of his uncompromising stances and sacrifices in the past as well as all the "painful duties" he had performed, he had developed a "moral force" that his "ignoble" enemies could not know and would not be able to defeat.[101] In volume 4 of the *Cours*, he had implied that a great intellectual had to be a model of virtue.[102] The trial thus gave him the opportunity to demonstrate that his "moral energy" was on the same level as his intellectual power and that he was "more complete than any of the personages who have up to now occupied the revolutionary scene."[103] This statement suggests that he believed that the so-called completeness of his character, which he had been carefully cultivating since his crisis of 1838, made him superior morally and intellectually to the other republicans of his era and therefore most qualified to save humanity. This sentiment of moral purity was one Comte shared with another republican *régénérateur* who defied Christianity and sought legitimacy as a leader – Robespierre.[104]

After months of waiting, Comte finally prepared to present his case on December 15, 1842. He had a friend listen to his forty-five-minute speech to make sure it was not only incisive but moderate. The three nights before the trial, he could hardly sleep because of the extreme "agitation" and "uncertainty" aroused by his "first battle."[105] When he began his speech, he was disconcerted by the noise, the interruptions, and the generally hostile atmosphere. Convinced that Arago was at the head of the conspiracy against him, he suspected the scientist of having sent his "emissaries" to tell everyone a "madman" was talking.[106] Behind him, he supposedly overheard two "leaders" of the liberal party whispering about his wife's background as a prostitute, which he thought was known only to Lamennais.[107] Despite his bewilderment, Comte persevered and was proud of his "eloquence."[108] Disregarding Marrast's advice to concentrate on Bachelier, Comte emphasized the turpitude of Arago and other scientists. When at one point he insinuated that Arago would make a poor candidate for public office because he did not believe in freedom of the press, the president of the Tribunal cut him off: "M. Arago is not in question. He is not here to defend himself, and you cannot attack him. Stick to the facts of the case." Comte, though startled, refused to listen and replied that Arago was

[101] Comte to Valat, December 13, 1842, *CG*, 2:118.   [102] *Cours*, 2:181–2.
[103] Comte to Mme Auguste Comte, December 3, 1842, *CG*, 2:114.
[104] Blum, *Rousseau*, 150–2.
[105] Comte to Mme Auguste Comte, December 17, 1842, *CG*, 2:121.
[106] Comte to Mill, February 27, 1843, *CG*, 2:138.   [107] *Testament*, 31.
[108] Comte to Mme Auguste Comte, December 17, 1842, *CG*, 2:120.

his "real adversary." Thoroughly annoyed by this tirade, the president again interrupted Comte: "I am calling you back once more to the facts of the trial."[109] After complaining about not being able to continue, Comte limited himself to his case against Bachelier, only at the end mentioning Mathieu's threats and the possibility of losing his job. Though disappointed that the president had "mutilated" his discourse and shown his partiality, Comte told his wife, who, though separated from him, had been supportive throughout the trial, that he had at least displayed his "insurmountable energy, and that was the essential [issue]." Now he could walk with his head high, "full of confidence in the future."[110]

In his reply, Bachelier complained that Comte had used him and had not held to the contract. Instead of four volumes, Comte had written six, each one selling more poorly than the previous one. The sixth was the worst of all. Comte gave Bachelier half of it and then made him wait six months for the other half, and instead of 560 pages, which was supposed to be the upper limit, it came to 936 pages in small print. Comte's verbosity had cost him not only more work but an extra thousand francs.[111] Bachelier's records reveal that in November 1842 there remained 398 copies of the first volume, 560 of the second, 602 of the third, 669 of the fourth, and 871 of the fifth. By November 20 only 40 copies of the sixth had been sold. Having spent around 16,000 francs on printing the volumes plus another 2,250 francs for Comte's compensation, Bachelier was very worried about his returns on the project.[112] (Comte's dream of a second edition, whereby all the volumes would be published together and would attract more attention, was never to be realized.)[113]

---

[109] President of the Tribunal, quoted in "Justice civile," 205–6. See also Littré, *Auguste Comte*, 330.

[110] Comte to Mme Auguste Comte, December 17, 1842, *CG*, 2:120–1. See also Caroline Massin to Comte, December 15, 1842, MAC.

[111] Durmont (Bachelier's lawyer), quoted in "Justice civile," 206; Comte to Valat, November 29, 1840, *CG*, 1:368; Statement of Bachelier, n.d., MAC; Bachelier, "Compte d'impression," MAC.

[112] Bachelier's statement and records, especially "Etat des exemplaires du *Cours de philosophie* par M. Comte au magasin le 20 novembre 1842"; "Justice civile," 206; Bachelier, "Compte d'impression déboursé," MAC. Bachelier paid Comte 1,500 francs in 1833 plus another 750 francs when 750 volumes were sold. After beginning legal action, Comte was paid the final 750 francs that Bachelier owed him in July 1851. See notarized statement of the court bailiff, Auguste Jean Toussaint, June 19, 1851, MAC; Comte's note to Bachelier, July 4, 1851, MAC. In this note, Comte acknowledges having received 750 francs.

[113] Comte to Valat, January 5, 1840, *CG*, 1:333; Comte to Chamonard, November 8, 1842, *CG*, 2:110. As of November 11, 1850, Bachelier's warehouse still held eleven copies of volume 1, 158 copies of volume 2, 178 copies of volume 3, 284 copies of volume 4, 340 copies of volume 5, and 397 copies of volume 6. See Bachelier to Comte, "Nombre

What Bachelier found most appalling, according to his lawyer, was the "spirit of denigration and calumny that impelled the author." Since Comte sullied every page with the "most crude insults," directed at Laplace, Poisson, Poinsot, Thenard, Brongniart, the Ecole Polytechnique, and the Academy of Sciences, Bachelier feared a libel suit. He also claimed that Comte had given him permission to publish the "Avis" – a contention so hotly denied by Comte that everyone present laughed. To Comte's charge of incompetence, Bachelier maintained that he had advertised the *Cours* in hundreds of catalogs and several newspapers.[114]

On December 29 the Tribunal issued its verdict. Bachelier had been wrong not to limit himself to a disclaimer in his notice. His addition of "inconvenient expressions" and his failure to obtain Comte's formal consent to the "Avis" beforehand were therefore punishable.[115] In addition to annulling the contract, the court ordered Bachelier to remove the offending notice from the remaining copies and pay the cost of both the trial and the registration of the judgment. (On February 23, 1843, Bachelier paid Comte 37 francs, 65 centimes.)[116] Though disappointed not to have received the ten thousand francs in damages, Comte was angrier that he did not get the publicity he craved, for the trial had been covered only by the *Gazette des Tribunaux*, which he thought favored Arago. To spread the news of the "cowardly violence" that had been committed against him and his philosophy, he had two hundred copies made of the judgment and sent them to all his friends.[117]

This episode marked the end of the twelve-year saga of the publication of the *Cours de philosophie positive*. Comte had written 4,712 pages in all – at least twice as many as he had planned.[118] The price he paid for his twelve years of intense effort to lay the scientific basis of his philosophy was a lonely retreat from the outside world. He had withdrawn because he not only felt obliged to concentrate all his resources on his mission but resented the neglect of journalists and scholars. Their indifference can be attributed partly to the numerous delays in the publication of the *Cours*, its overwhelming length,

d'exemplaires de chaque volume du *Cours de Philosophie positive* par Monsieur Auguste Comte restants au magasin le 11 novembre 1850," MAC.

[114] "Justice civile," 206; statement of Bachelier, MAC.

[115] "Extrait du jugement rendu le 29 décembre 1842 par le Tribunal de Commerce de Paris," MAC. This is reprinted in Littré, *Auguste Comte*, 330–1. Also see the text of the judgment in "Chronique," *Gazette des Tribunaux*, December 30, 1842, 277.

[116] Bachelier to Comte, February 23, 1843, MAC.

[117] Comte to Mill, December 30, 1842, *CG*, 2:124. See also Comte to Mill, February 27, 1843, *CG*, 2:138; Comte to Bordeaux, January 3, 1843, *CG*, 2:133; Comte's handwritten copy of the judgment, June 19, 1843, MAC.

[118] *Cours*, 2:465, 480.

Comte's forbidding, almost grotesque style, and the abstruseness of his subject matter. Furthermore, many people were devoting their energies to political and industrial pursuits during the July Monarchy and had little interest in abstract scientific theory. Scientists, for their part, did not view the *Cours* as a contribution to their fields. Even Comte admitted that it was not a work likely to be treasured by specialists.

Comte interpreted the public's reaction to his masterpiece as a "conspiracy of silence."[119] The plot against him began to extend through every facet of his life as he became increasingly disillusioned and paranoid. His article on Broussais was his last venture in journalism. His disappointment with the Revolution of 1830 and his vain appeals to Guizot had estranged him from the world of politics. His defeats at the Academy of Sciences and the Ecole Polytechnique had alienated him from the scientific community – the very group on which he had counted for the regeneration of society. His rupture with Saint-Simon, his family, his wife, and many friends, including Valat, completed his isolation. This emotional and professional isolation was matched by the intellectual detachment of his cerebral hygiene.

Propelled, however, by his "aesthetic revolution," Comte was convinced that he alone was fired by the moral and intellectual energy needed to rescue humanity. He alone was complete. But he fell deeper and deeper into obscurity. In fact, he had been better known under the Restoration than under the July Monarchy.[120] The *Cours de philosophie positive* would later even strike him as a "parenthesis" in his life.[121]

---

[119] Robinet, *Notice*, 190; Deroisin, *Notes sur Auguste Comte*, 26.
[120] "Un Document pour servir à l'histoire d'Auguste Comte," ed. Pierre Laffitte, *RO* 5 (November 1, 1880): 425.
[121] Comte, quoted in ibid.

Chapter 14

Cours de philosophie positive:
Positivism and the Natural Sciences

Let us not forget that in almost all minds, even the most elevated, ideas usually remain connected following the order of their first acquisition and that it is, consequently, a failing, which is most often irremediable, not to have begun by the beginning. Each century allows only a very small number of capable thinkers at the time of their maturity, like Bacon, Descartes, and Leibniz, to make a true tabula rasa in order to reconstruct from top to bottom the entire system of their acquired ideas.

Comte, 1830

AN INTRODUCTION TO POSITIVE PHILOSOPHY

Comte dedicated the *Cours* to Joseph Fourier and Blainville, both of whom had been a source of personal encouragement and exemplified the positive spirit in the inorganic and organic sciences respectively. In Comte's view, Fourier's mathematical theory of heat was the most valuable scientific contribution since Newton's law of gravity.[1] Blainville's work was admirable for its synthetic and systematic character and use of classification and hierarchy. His theory that every living being should be studied from two points of view – the static (its conditions) and the dynamic (its actions) – was used throughout the *Cours*, for Comte believed it could be applied to *all* phenomena "without exception."[2] Although he would later harshly criticize the Academy of Sciences, Comte now sought to enhance the validity and respectability of his project by claiming Blainville, a member of the Academy of Sciences, and Fourier, its permanent secretary, as his "illustrious friends."[3]

---

[1] Fourier had twice attended Comte's course, recommended him to the post of inspector of commerce, and invited him to soirées. One can still find in Comte's library Fourier's *Théorie analytique de la chaleur* and his *Remarques générales sur l'application des principes de l'analyse algébrique aux équations transcendantes*, as well as the book he wrote with Lagrange, *Traité de la résolution des équations numériques de tous les degrés*.

[2] *Cours*, 1:739. See also Florence Khodoss, Introduction to *Cours de philosophie positive: Première et Deuxième Leçons*, by Auguste Comte (Paris: Hatier, 1982), 39; Comte, "Discours prononcé aux funérailles de Blainville," in *Système*, vol. 1, "Appendice," 737–46; Gouhier, "La Philosophie 'positiviste' et 'chrétienne' de D. de Blainville," 46.

[3] *Cours*, 1: dedication page.

562   Cours de philosophie positive: *Positivism*

In the two introductory lessons to volume 1, Comte outlined his main ideas clearly and systematically. The first lesson discussed the importance of "positive philosophy." Without mentioning that he took his definition from Saint-Simon, Comte explained that the term "positive" meant "this special manner of philosophizing that consists of envisaging the theories in any order of ideas as having for their object the coordination of observed facts."[4] Positive philosophy thus represented a way of reasoning that could be applied to all subjects. Comte did not explain what he meant by "observation" or by "fact," although these terms were crucial to his definition.

Instead, he took a historicist approach to his own philosophy, using the past to justify it. Because, to him, no conception whatsoever could be understood without grasping its history, he explained positive philosophy by means of the law of three stages, which showed its development. He had propounded this theory in his fundamental opuscule of 1824, and here he elaborated it further, explaining that the theological, metaphysical, and positive stages represented different methods of philosophizing and thus different ways of looking at the world. The existence of each stage could be verified by considering not only the historical epochs of the human species but the different phases of individual development. In a famous passage, chiefly reflecting his own experience, Comte wrote, "Now each one of us, in contemplating his own history, does he not remember that he has been successively, in terms of his most important notions, a *theologian* in his childhood, a *metaphysician* in his youth, and a *natural philosopher* [*physicien*] in his virility?"[5]

Each stage in the evolution of knowledge was characterized by a drive for perfection because human understanding was systematic by nature; it always sought to consolidate its methods and make its doctrines homogeneous. The apogee of the theological system was monotheism, in which one God replaced numerous independent supernatural agents. The metaphysical system reached its height when it considered nature, instead of numerous different forces, to be the source of all phenomena. The positive philosophy's quest for perfection consisted of connecting all phenomena by relations of succession and resemblance and subjecting them to a decreasing number of invariable natural laws. Rejecting other philosophers' search for a "vague and absurd unity," Comte insisted that a single explanatory law would remain impossible to attain.[6] As the last and definitive stage of human intellectual development, the positive era would

---

[4] Foreword to *Cours de philosophie positive* (1830–42), 1:vii. The foreword is not in the Hermann edition.
[5] *Cours*, 1:22.   [6] Ibid., 874.

seek unity not in one entity, principle, or law, but in one method. In espousing a revolution based on a new method, Comte was following the example set by Bacon and Descartes.

He further explained the diversity of these three stages by referring to the problems encountered by the human mind in understanding the world. The human mind was always torn between the "necessity of observing to form real theories and the necessity, not any less imperious, of creating some theories in order to devote oneself to coherent observations."[7] The nature of human understanding had compelled primitive man to begin with the theological system, for he could escape the vicious circle between fact and theory only by creating hypotheses, that is, myths, to explain the universe. The theological system stimulated social activity and development by giving him the illusion that the universe was made for him and that he had some control over it. The positive system grew out of this provisional system and reflected man's humbling realization that the causes and nature of phenomena and the origin and purpose of the universe were mysteries beyond his reach. But man's reason was now sufficiently mature for him to be stimulated solely by his intellectual desire to understand the laws of phenomena. Because the positive outlook was so radically opposed to the theological, Comte claimed that the metaphysical state had acted as a necessary transition between the two and partook of enough of their respective characteristics to ensure some degree of continuity in mankind's development.

Though he described three distinct stages, Comte maintained that history was a gradual development; elements of each stage had been growing since the beginning of civilization. For example, although the positive "revolution" had begun in the seventeenth century with the work of Bacon, Descartes, and Galileo, positive philosophy had, in reality, existed since Aristotle.[8] Again, Comte's approach was paradoxical. He wished to justify the future by looking toward the past. To satisfy conservatives afraid of risk, he sought to make his enterprise legitimate by appealing to tradition, but at the same time he hoped to appease those on the Left by giving the past a revolutionary cast. He took his approach from biology, where germs and embryos were preexisting objects that developed in time.[9]

The first and "special" aim of the *Cours* was to establish social physics, which would extend the positive method to the last group of phenomena still under the theological and metaphysical regimes.

---

[7] Ibid., 23.   [8] Ibid., 27.
[9] Johan Heilbron, "Auguste Comte and Modern Epistemology," *Sociological Theory* 8 (Fall 1990): 159.

The creation of this last science was, according to Comte, the "greatest and most pressing need of our intelligence."[10] By finally making all our conceptions homogeneous, he would realize the positive revolution.

Yet Comte had already fallen into an intellectual trap. As Lévy-Bruhl pointed out, Comte began the *Cours* with the law of three stages to demonstrate that the coming of social physics was inevitable. However, the law proved at the same time that the science of society *already* existed because this was the main law of sociology.[11] In using universal sociological laws to verify sociology, Comte was making sociology legitimize itself – a questionable procedure.

Comte's second and "general" aim was pedagogical: to give a course in positive philosophy as a whole.[12] Since social physics now was completing the system of natural sciences, it was possible and necessary to review the positive state of scientific knowledge in its entirety. Not aimed at specialists, the *Cours* would examine each of the five fundamental positive sciences – astronomy, physics, chemistry, physiology, and social physics – in terms of its relation to the whole positive system, especially to see how it developed the logical procedures of the positive method, which could not be understood apart from its application. This review of the individual sciences was important not only for revealing the method and tendencies of the new philosophy, but also for laying the groundwork for social physics, which required a firm grasp of the various scientific methods as well as the laws of the more simple phenomena that influenced society. Therefore, Comte's two aims in writing the *Cours* were inseparable.

Finally, this overview of the sciences was necessary to combat specialization, one of the main characteristics of the positive age. Comte believed that increased specialization was a crucial component of progress, but he condemned this tendency to become isolated and lost in detail as the great weakness of positive philosophy. To diminish its impact, Comte urged the formation of a class of learned men, the positive philosophers, who would specialize in the "study of scientific generalities."[13] Other scientists would study the work of these generalists so that their own specialties would profit from the knowledge of the whole. In this way, positive philosophy would ensure the unity of human knowledge.

Comte believed his course on positive philosophy had four advantages. The first was that, because scientific theories were products of man's intellectual faculties and showed the mind in action,

---

[10] *Cours*, 1:29.   [11] Lévy-Bruhl, *Philosophie d'Auguste Comte*, 44.   [12] *Cours*, 1:29.
[13] Ibid., 31.

studying these theories would lead to a firm grasp of the logical laws of the human mind. One of the main themes of the *Cours*, whose importance was recognized by Mill, was that the logical and scientific points of view were indivisible because logical education coincided with scientific education. The way to understand logic was to study the history of science. Like Hegel, Comte was concerned with studying the mind in action, that is, the way it manifested itself throughout history and in society.[14] Rejecting abstract, static studies of logic and of the individual, he sought to substitute positive philosophy for psychology, which he called the "last transformation of theology."[15] Unlike the members of Cousin's school, who disagreed among themselves due to the looseness of their speculations about the mind's observation of itself, positive philosophers would agree on how the mind functioned and could lay the basis of social consensus.[16]

The second main advantage of the establishment of positive philosophy would be the reorganization of the educational system to make it more responsive to the "needs of modern civilization." Objecting to the confused curriculum of traditional schools and to premature specialization, Comte felt that positive philosophy – the study of the spirit, results, and method of every science – must not be a monopoly of the scientists but had to become the basis of the education of even the "popular masses." After all, science's "true point of departure" always consisted of ideas held by the common people about the "subjects under consideration."[17] Comte's animus against the scientific elite and the populist strain in his thought, which had been apparent in his earliest writings, could not have been clearer.

The third advantage of the positive philosophy would be the reform of the sciences. Arguing that the divisions among the sciences were ultimately artificial, he hoped he could encourage a more interdisciplinary approach to the solution of problems, which would lead to more rapid progress.

The fourth advantage of this new philosophy would be the most important: the reorganization of the social system, which would end the state of crisis that had existed since the French Revolution. Although Comte was frequently accused of materialism, he believed that "ideas govern and overturn the world, or in other words, that the entire social mechanism rests ultimately on opinions." The "intellectual anarchy" that was at the root of the present social disorder

---

[14] Macherey, *Comte: La Philosophie*, 54.
[15] *Cours*, 1:33. See also Macherey, *Comte: La Philosophie*, 50.
[16] Khodoss, Introduction to *Cours*, 34. [17] *Cours*, 1:35, 36, 523.

was caused by the simultaneous use of theological, metaphysical, and positive ways of thinking. With the inevitable extension of the positive method to social phenomena, human knowledge would become homogeneous, and there would emerge the intellectual consensus necessary for society to return to "normal." Thus in his first "lesson" of the *Cours*, Comte made it clear that he was advocating a "general revolution of the human mind" and that its ultimate object was practical and political: the completion of the social revolution.[18] Although not directly involved in politics, he aimed in an indirect and profound fashion to shape the world of action.

The first lesson summed up the important results of Comte's lifework. It did not introduce any new material or reflect any radical changes in his opinions since his fundamental opuscule. Most of the significant themes of positivism were developed in a concise and austere manner: the importance of ending the revolutionary crisis by a philosophy of the sciences, the law of three stages, the theory of hypotheses, the necessity of raising politics to a positive science, the reorganization of the educational system, the interdisciplinary approach to intellectual problems, and the condemnation of psychology, reductionism (in terms of both reducing one science to another and reducing scientific knowledge to one law), and excessive specialization.

Lesson 2, the complement of lesson 1, dealt with the classification of the sciences. He argued that this classification was possible only at the current time because social physics, which ensured the uniformity of our knowledge, was becoming a positive science. Moreover, botanists and zoologists had only recently provided a model of classification based on observation. Comte made it clear that he was not seeking to classify and unify *all* of human knowledge as the Encyclopedists endeavored to do, for this was impossible. The *Cours* was concerned only with theoretical knowledge, above all, the laws of nature, which led to action. Even he admitted that his classification of this knowledge was ultimately "arbitrary" and "artificial."[19]

One of Comte's favorite aphorisms was "*from science comes prediction; from prediction comes action.*"[20] The aim of each science was therefore prediction. Prediction to Comte meant going not only from the present to the future, but from the known to the unknown. "Scientific prevision . . . consists . . . in knowing a fact independently of its direct exploration in virtue of its relations with others already given."[21] Larry Laudan has pointed out that Comte

---

[18] Ibid., 38–9.   [19] Ibid., 50, 53.   [20] Ibid., 45.
[21] *Traité philosophique d'astronomie populaire*, 31.

departed in a significant way from traditional criteria of what made knowledge scientific. Up to this point, scientists insisted on the certainty and infallibility of their knowledge. But with his relativism, which outlawed appeals to truth, Comte declared that knowledge was scientific if it displayed predictive power. He thus could avoid the problem of dictating one means of scientific investigation. According to Laudan, Comte was influential in the philosophy of science because he believed that "a statement is scientific so long as it makes *general* claims about how nature behaves, which are capable of being put to experimental test."[22] Scientific propositions were thus different from nonscientific ones if they were general and capable of being tested.

In lesson 28, Comte clarified this novel and important methodological approach in his famous theory of hypotheses, to which he had previously alluded in the third and fourth opuscules and the first lesson of the *Cours*.[23] He agreed with Bacon that knowledge must rest on facts, but rejecting his empiricism, he maintained that facts could not even be perceived or retained without the guidance of an a priori theory. At the beginning of the scientific investigation of a subject, a "provisional supposition" – a hypothesis – was "indispensable" for aiding the discovery of natural laws.[24] The scientist was not a passive, mechanical observer as the empiricists believed; he first had to use his imagination and come up with an explanatory theory simply to be able to make an observation:

> If, in contemplating phenomena, we did not immediately attach them to some principles, not only would it be impossible for us to connect these isolated observations, and, consequently, to draw something from them, but also we would even be entirely incapable of remembering them; and facts would most often remain imperceptible before our very eyes.[25]

Although geometers had devised the artifice of a theory, Comte asserted that no one had yet discussed the fundamental condition that legitimized its usage:

> This condition . . . consists of imagining only hypotheses [that are] susceptible . . . of a positive verification, more or less in the future, but always clearly inevitable, and whose degree of precision is exactly in harmony with that which the study of the corresponding phenomena comprises. In other words, truly philosophical hypotheses must

---

[22] Larry Laudan, "Towards a Reassessment of Comte's 'Méthode Positive,'" *Philosophy of Science* 38 (March 1971): 37; see also 38.
[23] See esp. *Système*, vol. 4, "Appendice," 103–4, 140–2; *Cours*, 1:23.　　[24] *Cours*, 1:457.
[25] Ibid., 23. See also Laudan, "Reassessment," 41.

constantly present the character of simple anticipations of that which experiment and reason would have revealed immediately, if the circumstances of the problem had been more favorable.

Once a hypothesis that was in harmony with already determined data was conceived, the science could freely develop and would explore new consequences that would confirm or negate the conjecture. Hypotheses could not be considered scientific theories until they were verified by induction ("the immediate analysis" of the movement of a phenomenon) and deduction (the analysis of the relation of a phenomenon to a previously established law).[26] Thus one reason Comte insisted upon prediction as a criterion of scientific knowledge was that he wished to avoid having to base this knowledge solely on induction, as empiricists did. Scientific investigation rested on the use of both induction and deduction. His predilection is revealed in a comment he later made to a disciple:

> I consider Descartes and even Leibniz infinitely superior to Bacon. The latter, who wrote so much on deduction, never made a single inductive discovery of any value, . . . while Descartes, who . . . philosophically appreciated only deduction, made important advances in mathematics and elsewhere by means of induction.[27]

In volume 3, Comte also introduced the "art" of "scientific fictions," which he acknowledged derived from the "poetic imagination." Whereas the art of hypothesis related fictions to the solution of a problem, this other art applied them to the problem itself by inventing a series of purely hypothetical cases. One example of the possible use of this new method in biology would be to place "purely fictive organisms," which one hoped to discover later, between already known organisms in order to make the biological series more homogeneous, continuous, and regular.[28]

Like his theory of hypothesis, this art of scientific fiction showed that Comte was not a slave to his belief in the supreme importance of observation. Despite the criticism of the Saint-Simonians, he always gave a large role to imagination in the scientific process.[29] And to avoid giving reason too much importance in scientific research, he deliberately refused to offer elaborate, ahistorical rules of scientific procedure and proof.[30]

Comte's attitude toward the use of hypotheses and "scientific fictions" resembled his view of the manipulation of mathematical

[26] *Cours*, 1:457.   [27] Comte to George Frederick Holmes, November 28, 1852, *CG*, 8:433.
[28] *Cours*, 1:728.   [29] Lévy-Bruhl, *Philosophie d'Auguste Comte*, 75.
[30] Scharff, "Positivism," 256–8.

principles because they all offered man the ability to do scientific exploration in an indirect manner whenever direct investigation was impossible.[31] In proclaiming the utility and advantages of such conjectures and fictions, which were not exact representations of reality, Comte was stressing the relativity of knowledge while trying to save man from total skepticism or empiricism.

At the same time, he carefully limited the range of this indirect means of investigation. Hypotheses, for example, could pertain only to the laws of phenomena, that is, to their "constant relations of succession or of similitude." They could not be used to solve problems concerning the causes or nature of phenomena, which were beyond our means of observation and reasoning and thus "necessarily insoluble."[32] Thus, as Warren Schmaus has pointed out, Comte did not insist that hypotheses be formulated in the "language of observation." They could use theoretical terms as long as they did not refer to "unobservable *entities*, especially causal entities."[33] The molecule was, for example, a theoretical term whose use Comte permitted, although he did not think this "artifice" pertained to "reality."[34] But theories about God, for example, could never be affirmed or refuted. And isolated facts were not scientific either because they had no predictive capability.[35]

The majority of early-nineteenth-century methodologists still believed that scientific theories could be constructed simply on the basis of induction or analogy, without recourse to conjectures. Although Comte did not spell out the rules of verification, his explanation of hypotheses as useful, convenient, and respectable devices that served a crucial function in scientific discovery was a novel theory, one that became very influential. It foreshadowed the later work of Hans Vaihinger and Henri Poincaré and may have also influenced Claude Bernard, Marcelin Berthelot, Paul Janet, Ernst Mach, Wilhelm Ostwald, and Pierre Duhem. The logical positivists took up a similar approach to the problems of ascertaining meaningfulness, distinguishing scientific from nonscientific knowledge, and using verifiability to criticize metaphysicians.[36]

To Comte, prediction was important in itself as a way of demar-

---

[31] Serres, ed., in *Cours*, 1:457n16.   [32] *Cours*, 1:457.

[33] Warren Schmaus, "Hypotheses and Historical Analysis in Durkheim's Sociological Methodology: A Comtean Tradition," *Studies in History and Philosophy of Science* 16 (March 1985): 8.

[34] *Cours*, 2:736.   [35] Laudan, "Reassessment," 39–40.

[36] Ibid., 40, 47; André Lalande, *Les Théories de l'induction et de l'expérimentation* (Paris: Boivin, 1929), 138; Serres, ed., in *Cours*, 1:542n14, 372n9; Ivan Lins, "L'Oeuvre d'Auguste Comte et sa signification scientifique et philosophique au XIXᵉ siècle," Extract from the *Journal of World History* 11.4 (1969), 15.

cating scientific knowledge, but it was also crucial because it enabled man to act more effectively. Despite the determinism of the law of three stages and his stress on the limitations of human knowledge and operations, Comte retained an activist conception of man. Like Marx, he believed man must use his intellect to discover scientific laws enabling him to modify the universe "to his advantage . . . despite the obstacles of his condition."[37] Comte never lost sight of the practical goal of his *Cours*. His scientific exposition was always subordinated to his social goal; philosophy had to be realized in politics.[38]

While emphasizing that theoretical knowledge had a utilitarian end, he argued, nevertheless, that it had to be pursued in a separate domain without regard to its practical application. He rejected the new, materialistic trend to make the sciences the handmaidens of industry, for to him, they had a "more elevated destination, that of satisfying the fundamental need felt by our intelligence to know the laws of phenomena."[39] This innate desire to put facts into order and to arrive at simple, general conceptions was more important than practical needs in stimulating scientific research and thus intellectual progress.

Comte upheld a philosophical, historicist approach to the sciences. Influenced by Blainville, he maintained that the philosophy of a science could not be studied apart from the "intellectual history" of that science and vice versa.[40] (This consideration of a science in terms of either its ideas or its history corresponded to the dichotomy between statics and dynamics, i.e., order and progress.) As Johan Heilbron has suggested, Comte's epistemology rejected the traditional approach of grounding the sciences on universal principles and showed that scientific knowledge itself had to be considered a historical process.[41]

This process was complex. According to Comte, the history of a particular science could not be studied in isolation because the progress of each science was connected to the simultaneous development of the other sciences, to the arts (practical applications), and to society as a whole. In other words, one could not understand how the ideas and theories of a single science changed without studying the entire history of humanity. Comte was thus one of the first thinkers to point out that the history of science was the "most important" and "neglected" part of the development of humanity and, moreover,

---

[37] *Cours*, 1:361. See also Serres, ed., in ibid., 361n14.
[38] Lévy-Bruhl, *Philosophie d'Auguste Comte*, 3, 6.   [39] *Cours*, 1:45.
[40] Comte to Maximilien Marie, April 15, 1841, *CG*, 2:4.
[41] Heilbron, "Auguste Comte and Modern Epistemology," 155.

had to be interdisciplinary in scope.[42] His analysis later had a large impact in France, where scholars such as Bachelard and Canguilhem sought to approach the formation of concepts and theories from a historical, instead of a logical, perspective.[43]

Comte's basic rules for classifying the sciences elaborated on the principles that he had announced in his fundamental opuscule. The sciences devoted to the most simple and thus the most general phenomena came first in the hierarchy. Influencing all other phenomena without in turn being influenced by them, these simple, abstract phenomena were also the most independent and the farthest away from man. The later, more complicated sciences studied phenomena that were increasingly complex, particular (specialized), and concrete. These phenomena were closer to man and more dependent on the phenomena studied by the previous sciences in the hierarchy. In sum, because the classification of the sciences reflected the dependence that existed among their corresponding natural phenomena, each science was founded on the knowledge of the principal laws of the preceding one and became, in turn, the foundation of the one that came after it. Therefore, each science depended on its antecedents but had its own peculiarities that prevented it from being reduced to the science preceding it. Likewise, each science could influence only the sciences that followed it in the hierarchy.

According to Heilbron, Comte's important "differential theory of science" reflected his profound grasp of the new kind of disciplinary battles raging in the age of specialization. At this time, the spokesmen for the mathematico-mechanical disciplines were fighting the representatives of the life sciences; each group claimed universal validity for its models and methods. Comte's theory was effective in destroying the illusions of such monism.[44]

Concerned with differentiating the sciences in terms of their history and ideas, Comte argued that the organic sciences were more complex and more particular than the inorganic ones and thus came after them in the hierarchy. The inorganic sciences were divided into those dealing with celestial phenomena – astronomy – and those dealing with terrestrial phenomena – physics and chemistry. The organic sciences were divided into the science of the individual – physiology – and that of the species – social physics. The most difficult science of all, social physics, dealt with the most particular, complex, and concrete phenomena – those closest to man. It depended on all of the other sciences but could not influence them.

---

[42] *Cours*, 1:53. See also Georges Gusdorf, *De l'histoire des sciences à l'histoire de la pensée* (Paris: Payot, 1977), 97.

[43] Heilbron, "Auguste Comte and Modern Epistemology," 161.   [44] Ibid., 156–7.

Beside these five sciences, natural philosophy included a sixth –
mathematics – which was its "true fundamental basis." Mathematics
was more significant to Comte as a method, that is, as a "means of
investigation in the study of other natural phenomena," than as a
doctrine. It constituted the "most powerful instrument that the human
mind can use in the search for the laws of natural phenomena." It
was the most perfect science as well as the oldest, and because it
served as the foundation of the other five sciences, it came first in his
classification. Comte was making the science that was his own
specialty the "head of positive philosophy."[45] At the opposite end of
the hierarchy, he placed the other science to which he was most
attached – social physics. It too represented the point of departure
and the head of positive philosophy but in a different sense that
would become clearer later on.

Comte declared that his classification of the sciences not only reflected the divisions that had grown up spontaneously among them
but also accorded with their development in history. His classification verified the law of the three stages by showing why the diverse
branches of our knowledge were often at different stages of development. Because the simplest sciences were studied first and thus
matured quickly, they were the first to reach the positive state. The
more complex sciences took longer to reach that stage, for they
depended on the knowledge of the simpler sciences and could not
make any real progress until the preceding sciences did.

Moreover, the classification marked the "relative perfection" of
the diverse sciences. Throughout the *Cours* Comte defined perfection in terms of unity, abstraction, simplicity, universality, precision, and coordination of facts, which made predictions more exact.
Yet at the same time, he stressed the limitations of knowledge – as
he had done when he prohibited man from trying to uncover first
causes and the destiny of the universe and when he showed the
necessity of using hypotheses because of the feebleness of the mind.
Now he declared that whereas astronomy was fairly precise and
tightly organized, the sciences of organic phenomena (especially social phenomena) could never be very exact or systematic. However,
although physiology and social physics might even be extremely
imprecise, Comte maintained somewhat dogmatically that they were
as certain as the other sciences, for "everything that is positive, that
is, founded on well-observed facts, is certain."[46] He did not revel in
the torments of doubt.[47]

The most important property of the classification of the sciences
was that it presented the general outlines of a rational scientific

[45] *Cours*, 1:63, 64, 307.   [46] Ibid., 59, 60.   [47] Khodoss, Introduction to *Cours*, 50.

education. To learn what constituted a scientific law, a positive conception, or a valid observation, one first needed to study the simpler sciences, which were easiest to understand. Otherwise, one would not be able to comprehend the more complex sciences. Moreover, the simpler sciences should be studied first because their greater distance from man meant they did not generate passions and prejudices. (This distance and objectivity also helped make them more precise than the science of society, whose phenomena were so close to man and defied exactitude.) Comte insisted, furthermore, that this order of study was important for both the scientist and layperson. He was thinking not only of Guizot and other brilliant men who had disappointed him because they lacked scientific knowledge, but also of scientists themselves, who had neglected to start "at the beginning" and thus lacked a "rational education."[48] Most of all, he was worried that without a grasp of all the sciences, people undertaking the study of society would not know how to relate society to natural phenomena or apply the positive method to social phenomena.

Composed of these two lessons, the "Exposition" of the *Cours* was a remarkably clear discussion of most of the main points of Comte's doctrine. It has, in fact, become a classic text of nineteenth-century French philosophy.[49] Arguing his points well, he anticipated criticisms and added numerous nuances, which made the tone of his discourse much less dogmatic than many of his other writings. His theory of hypotheses showed that he did not believe that scientific discoveries could proceed by the observation of facts alone. His concern with the practical side of the sciences was balanced by his warning that considerations of pure utility would stifle the sciences. His attraction to the law of gravity as one unifying principle was offset by his realization that the sciences were too complex to be reduced in this fashion. His classification of the sciences according to their ideas was modified by his assertion that this classification was consistent with their historical development. Although he repeatedly emphasized the necessity of establishing a science of society, he did not attempt to hide the fact that its findings would not always be as precise as one would like. In brief, despite his many peremptory statements and his often gross assumptions, Comte revealed himself to be a complex thinker.

The "Exposition" is perhaps most striking by what it left out. The passion of his earlier opuscules was replaced by a cool, dry, "objective" tone suitable to a scientific treatise. Absent from the lessons is any reference to the separation of powers, especially to the

---

[48] *Cours*, 1:61.   [49] Khodoss, Introduction to *Cours*, 5; Macherey, *Comte: La Philosophie*, 6.

new spiritual power controlling the educational system and advising the government. Such questions were reserved for the last volumes. Comte may have decided to keep his vehemently anticlerical and anti-Catholic opinions temporarily to himself so as not to estrange his readers before they read even a hundred pages.

He was also being true to the decision that he had made just before his mental breakdown of 1826, when he suddenly recognized the necessity of establishing positive philosophy before positive politics. Realizing that intellectual supremacy had to precede political dominion, Comte believed that only positive philosophy could give validity and authority to positive politics, which completed it. He felt that what distinguished him from reactionaries, revolutionaries, and liberals was his creation of a philosophy supplying the *scientific* basis of the reorganization of society.[50] His first volumes did initially appear "scientistic" and "materialistic," for he did nothing but discuss the sciences. But as he explained later to Mill, he was trying to systematize ideas without which social regeneration would fall "into a sort of more or less vague mysticism." Emphasizing the threat of mysticism, which would come from basing a reorganization first on feelings, he continued:

> This is why my fundamental work [the *Cours*] had to address itself almost exclusively to the intellect: this had to be a work of research, and even incidentally of discussion, destined to discover and constitute true universal principles by climbing by hierarchical degrees from the most simple scientific questions to the highest social speculations.[51]

Only when these "highest social speculations" came up at the end of the *Cours* could Comte logically develop his ideas of a spiritual power and spiritual doctrine. Once these views of spiritual reorganization were established at the end of the *Cours*, he could then turn his attention to systematizing the feelings. Broaching these subjects at the beginning would have ruined the scientific impressions of his enterprise, which were initially most important to impart to his readers.

MATHEMATICS

Except for the two introductory lessons, volume 1 was devoted to mathematics. It developed ideas that had first appeared in Comte's

---

[50] Lévy-Bruhl, *Philosophie d'Auguste Comte*, 4–6; Serres, ed., Introduction to *Cours*, 1:1; Angèle Kremer-Marietti, "Une Science politique conçue comme science de la consistance agrégative," *Les Etudes philosophiques*, no. 3 (July–December 1974): 340.

[51] Comte to Mill, July 14, 1845, *CG*, 3:61.

incomplete essays of 1818 to 1820. Whereas at that time he had not been sure about the proper way to begin intellectual reform, he now decided it must start with mathematics. In fact, he inserted a long critique of French mathematical education, whose defects he blamed on the "extreme inferiority" of the majority of teachers. They did not fully appreciate Descartes's "fundamental revolution," lacked a grasp of the whole of their subject, and failed especially to give their students a solid understanding of geometry, which was important for showing the relationship between the abstract and the concrete.[52] Comte's disparagement of his fellow professors and of the Ecole Polytechnique would not win him many friends in the future and was undiplomatic considering his current attempts to find a position. But it shows that he had a poor opinion of these scientists even before they created problems for him. His later difficulties merely confirmed what he had already thought and dared to write.[53]

In these lessons, Comte's highest praises went to Descartes, Leibniz, Newton, and Lagrange. Greatly inspired by Lagrange, a former professor at the Ecole Polytechnique, Comte relied heavily on several of his books, going so far as to paraphrase whole sections of them.[54] Much of the text of the *Cours* is plainly derivative.

As he would do with the other five sciences, Comte first treated mathematics as a whole. He considered its aim, subject matter, composition, theories, discoveries, methods, relationships with the other sciences, limitations, and possibilities for future development. He then broke the science down into different divisions, which he further subdivided and characterized, revealing his passion for classifications and definitions. Dividing and labeling in this fashion gave him a feeling of power, a feeling that he was in control of his subject. Disregarding his criticism of scientists for creating specialized languages, he also often tried to imprint an original character on his reflections by simply giving a new name of his own to old terms.[55]

Throughout the *Cours*, Comte aimed to show how each science incorporated the positive method and contributed to the positive system. He believed mathematics represented the origin of positive

---

[52] *Cours*, 1:199–200.   [53] Boudot, "De l'usurpation géométrique," 394.

[54] To Comte, Lagrange was as important in mechanics as Descartes was in geometry. See *Cours*, 1:243. While describing the resolution of algebraic equations in lesson 5, Comte took almost textually a section of Lagrange's *Réflexions sur la résolution algébrique des équations*. And according to Michel Serres, lesson 8 on the calculus of variations came entirely from Lagrange's main works. Serres, ed., in ibid., 98n7, 129n4, 135n15, 141 ("Remarque"). On Lagrange's influence on Comte, see Craig G. Fraser, "Lagrange's Analytical Mathematics, Its Cartesian Origins and Reception in Comte's Positive Philosophy," *Studies in History and Philosophy of Science* 21 (June 1990): 243–56.

[55] For example, he called synthetic geometry "special geometry," and analytical geometry "general geometry." *Cours*, 1:167.

philosophy. Only by studying this quintessential science could one arrive at a "correct and deep idea" of what a science was in general.[56] One learned that positive laws must show relationships between independent and even apparently isolated phenomena, which enabled the scientist to make predictions. Indifferent to the search for causes or substances, mathematics was, in short, the science of invariable relationships and best demonstrated the positive method.

Thanks especially to the work of Descartes in geometry, mathematics exhibited the interrelationship of the abstract and concrete realms. Comte argued that intellectual development was synonymous with the growth of abstraction; the consideration of increasingly abstract ideas allowed people to solve more concrete problems. As the most abstract science, mathematics first stimulated this intellectual development. Thus its translation of concrete facts into abstract ideas was necessary for scientific advancement.

Deeply influenced by Descartes, Comte asserted that the range of mathematics could be extended indefinitely; its deductive logic was universal. In fact, he hoped to replace formal logic, which was too abstract and ontological, with mathematics, which would then become the "normal basis of all healthy logical education."[57] Ideally, each science would be one day as rigorously deductive and rational as mathematics:

> One can even say generally that *science* is essentially destined to dispense with all direct observation – as much as the diverse phenomena allow – by making it possible to deduce from the smallest possible number of immediate data the greatest possible number of results.[58]

Comte was thus no simple inductivist. He believed science must aim at constructing laws and theories that would do away with the tedious task of observing facts and enable one to go beyond direct evidence.[59]

Yet although very loyal to Descartes and deduction, Comte distrusted pure abstraction. Trained in the synthetic or realist school of geometry of Monge, he maintained that positive theories had to be ultimately founded on the observation of a real, concrete body. To prevent an "abuse of pure reasoning" that would lead to "sterile" works, even the most rational science had to remember its experiential roots, for there was no a priori knowledge.[60]

Comte rejected Descartes's effort to make mathematics the uni-

---

[56] Ibid., 71.   [57] Ibid., 2:742.   [58] Ibid., 1:71.   [59] Laudan, "Reassessment," 43, 46.

[60] *Cours*, 2:704. See also ibid., 1:23, 174–5; Lévy-Bruhl, *Philosophie d'Auguste Comte*, 156; Boudot, "De l'usurpation géométrique," 402; Lorraine J. Daston, "The Physicalist Tradition in Early Nineteenth-Century French Geometry," *Studies in History and Philosophy of Science* 17 (September 1986): 275–7, 294.

versal science by reducing every problem in natural philosophy to a question of numbers. He argued that the human mind could represent mathematically only the least complicated and most general inorganic phenomena, those whose properties were fairly fixed. Complex inorganic phenomena and all organic phenomena would always remain closed to mathematical analysis because they exhibited "extreme numerical variability" and were affected by so many factors that no two cases were alike.[61] This criticism of the abuse of statistics, particularly in biology and the science of society, reflected Comte's effort to preserve the autonomy and individuality of each science.

In sum, although Comte praised mathematics for being the most universal and most applicable of all the sciences, he warned his contemporaries not to continue to exaggerate its power. Mathematicians, who were dominant in early-nineteenth-century France, could not, in his eyes, continue to pretend to monopolize the scientific realm.[62] A certain realism about the range of the human mind and consequently a certain humility characterized Comte's approach to the science that occupied his daily life. Indeed, one of the main principles of the *Cours* was the deficiency of our knowledge even in the limited realm of what was understandable. Comte insisted that

> it was necessary to recognize that by an indisputable law of human nature, our means for conceiving new questions . . . [are] much more powerful than our resources for solving them, or in other words the human mind . . . [is] far more capable of imagining than of reasoning.[63]

Although one could not determine with precision the boundaries of the power of the mind, their existence was undeniable.[64] Comte reveled in the fruitfulness of the sciences, but he never declared them to be all-powerful. His arguments were far more complex than those who accused him of scientism admit.

ASTRONOMY

The first part of the second volume was devoted to astronomy, which Comte considered to be the first "direct" natural science and a model for the "true study of nature."[65] It best demonstrated that

---

[61] *Cours*, 1:78.   [62] Heilbron, "Auguste Comte and Modern Epistemology," 158–9.
[63] *Cours*, 1:99.   [64] Ibid., 139.
[65] Ibid., 307, 456. Much of the philosophical and historical material that he used derived from his former teacher Delambre. Laplace and Poinsot were other influences.

a science consisted of laws, not isolated facts, and predictions. New-ton's law of gravity brought astronomy to the "highest philosophi-cal perfection" that any science could hope to achieve.[66] This theory proved the importance not only of reducing phenomena to a single law but also of using hypotheses to advance one's understanding, especially when concrete, observed facts were missing. Pointing out that even this model of a positive explanation could conceivably be superseded one day by another hypothesis, Comte did not fail to stress the relativity of knowledge even in the most precise and cer-tain science.

He also placed astronomy at the head of the natural sciences be-cause its laws represented the foundation of our whole system of knowledge. Astronomical phenomena influenced physical, chemi-cal, physiological, and social phenomena but could not be influenced by them in turn. Subsequent research, however, proved him wrong.

One of Comte's scientific laws was that "as the phenomena to be studied become more complex, they are at the same time sus-ceptible . . . of more extensive and varied means of exploration." Since astronomical phenomena were the simplest, astronomy had only one means of exploration, observation, which it introduced into the positive system. Here Comte explained that the art of observation consisted of three methods: the direct observation of concrete objects (which led to induction), experimentation, and comparison. He thus restricted astronomical research to "simple visual observations."[67] Again, later developments regarding dark stars and black holes would invalidate his position. Furthermore, he unwisely limited the range of astronomy to the solar system. His rejection of sidereal astronomy was based on his assumption that it was impos-sible to arrive at a true conception of the universe of stars. More-over, he believed man did not need to know about this universe, which did not affect him. To Comte, man should always ask what he needed to know, not what he could know.[68]

This optimistic assumption that a basic harmony existed between man's needs and the scope of his knowledge would run throughout the *Cours*. Instead of being frustrated by the restrictions of know-ledge, Comte simply dismissed them as irrelevant. His engineering mind-set was evident in the supposition that science could solve the practical problems of man's existence. Although worried about the enslavement of theory to practice, he was not always in favor of scientific curiosity for its own sake and sometimes adopted a more utilitarian approach.

Astronomy was also an important science because it showed the

---

[66] Ibid., 308.   [67] Ibid., 301, 305.   [68] Arnaud, *Pour connaître la pensée de Comte*, 83.

importance of combining induction and deduction. Given that astral bodies were distant and hard to observe, astronomy had to make recourse to mathematics, which it used to represent its simple objects and make deductions. Comte considered astronomy the most perfect science and a model for all the others precisely because its method was primarily mathematical and abstract and consequently the most free of theological and metaphysical influences.

However, once again, he condemned the calculus of probabilities. He believed the notion of "evaluated probability" could never regulate human conduct. Often contradicting common sense, it would lead people to "absurd consequences," such as rejecting "as numerically unlikely events that are, nevertheless, going to happen."[69] Comte therefore denied a place for probabilities in any of the sciences – especially the science of society, where he felt that its repercussions could be especially damaging. Here again, Comte proved to be conservative about scientific innovations. Despite his faith in the predictive power of scientific thought and his law of three stages, his projections about the future direction of scientific development often missed the mark.

Comte argued that the two extremes of natural philosophy – astronomy and physiology – had the most beneficial impact on intellectual progress because questions concerning the world and man had always attracted the most attention. As the most scientific of all the sciences, astronomy was the most opposed to theology. It had not only freed the human mind of its "absurd prejudices" and "superstitious terrors," but also hurt the doctrine of final causes, the keystone of the theological system. The heliocentric theory humiliated man, who had thought he was the center of the universe, and it stripped providential action of any intelligible aim. Challenging the theological argument by design and arguing that man was more intelligent than nature, Comte maintained, moreover, that the elements of the solar system were *not* arranged in the best manner as theologians liked to imagine; science could "easily" conceive of a better one.[70] Inspired by Laplace, he argued that astronomers presented a much more ordered universe than did theologians, who believed all things were governed by the will of one or several supreme beings and were thus irregular. To Comte, order was "necessary and spontaneous" and not dependent on outside agents.[71]

In these chapters on astronomy, he repeatedly stressed the harmony,

[69] *Cours*, 1:435.
[70] Ibid., 310–11. See also G. W. Lewes, *Comte's Philosophy of the Sciences: Being an Exposition of the Principles of the "Cours de Philosophie Positive" of Auguste Comte* (London: Henry C. Bohn, 1853), 91.
[71] *Cours*, 1:440.

regularity, and stability of the solar system, which were reflected in the precision, rationality, and invariability of astronomical laws. Although he wrote in a cold, dry style, he could hardly contain his passion for the order incarnated in the solar system and in the science that explored it. It is evident that he found more certainty, consistency, and reassurance in a world explained by the sciences than in a world ruled by a god. This love of stability, which would pervade the remaining lessons of the *Cours*, seemed discordant with his activist image of human nature.

PHYSICS

After considering the laws of the heavens, Comte turned his attention in volume 2 to the laws of the earth, studied by physics and chemistry. As the second natural science, dealing with more complex phenomena, physics was more backward than astronomy. Whereas astronomy had been positive (at least in its geometrical aspect) ever since the foundation of the School of Alexandria, physics had reached this stage only with Galileo. Instead of the "perfect mathematical harmony" that characterized astronomy, physics was, moreover, marked by disunity; it was composed of numerous branches that had little relation to each other, and its theories were not well coordinated.[72]

Physics demonstrated Comte's law that as one ascended the scale of the sciences, prediction became more imperfect and the power of man to modify phenomena increased. There was therefore an inverse relation between prediction and human intervention. In physics, where prediction was not as wide-ranging or exact as it was in astronomy, natural phenomena began for the first time to be modified by human intervention. Comte argued that this ability to modify phenomena proved that phenomena were not under the control of the gods.

Because of its imperfections, physics was still pervaded by metaphysical habits, which were absent in astronomy. It was in the context of contrasting astronomy with physics that Comte appeared to use the term "positivism" for the first time:

> In astronomy the discussion [among people supporting the positive spirit and those maintaining metaphysics] was less marked, and positivism triumphed almost spontaneously, except on the subject of the earth's movement.[73]

[72] Ibid., 455.   [73] Ibid., 454.

Up to this point, Comte had usually referred to his system as the "positive philosophy." Occasionally, he had used the word "positivity."[74] In general, he was very careful about the fabrication of new terms, which he thought often served to "hide the real emptiness of ideas."[75] Nevertheless, he liked to use neologisms, such as "positivity," and conscientiously explained their background.[76] Because this time he did not claim to have invented the term "positivism," it seems probable that Comte adopted it from someone else, perhaps from Bazard, who had used the word during the summer of 1829.[77] Comte later made a virtue of having "spontaneously" chosen this word, pointing out that his philosophy, unlike all others, such as Christianity and Fourierism, was the "only one" that had a name different from that of its author.[78]

Comte believed that the complicated nature of physical phenomena meant that physics would never be as perfect as astronomy, but this complexity gave it more methods of exploration. Physics introduced and fully developed the art of experimentation – the second method of observation – thanks to the possibility of modifying physical bodies almost without restriction. The emphasis on experimentation meant that induction was more important in physics than in astronomy and that deduction was no longer dominant. Yet once again, Comte argued for the simultaneous use of deduction and induction, lamenting that the "art of closely combining analysis and experimentation, without subordinating one to the other, is still almost unknown."[79]

Although he urged that mathematical analysis be used to a greater extent in physics, where it could connect isolated facts and make experiments more rational, he warned against its misapplication, which would lead to "useless hypotheses" and "entirely chimerical conceptions."[80] Therefore, mathematicians, who despised experimentation and liked excessive abstraction, should not be allowed to dominate in physics. But this fear of the possible abuse of mathematics led Comte to make imprudent statements. For example, his assertion that physics, not chemistry, was the last field where purely

---

[74] Comte to G. d'Eichthal, December 9, 1828, *CG*, 1:202. The word "positivist" appears in a letter written by Comte on June 6, 1824, to Gustave d'Eichthal, but it seems to be a misprint. *CG*, 1:98. The original letter is missing.

[75] *Cours*, 1:466. Comte was also wary of the way mathematical formulations were used to disguise superficial concepts and prevent the spread of ideas, particularly to the common people. He criticized scholars who tried to appear intellectually superior or improve a science merely by creating an esoteric language. See ibid., 2:629.

[76] Comte to G. d'Eichthal, December 9, 1828, *CG*, 1:202. See also *Cours*, 1:466, 567. Comte also made a verb out of positivism: "positiver." Ibid., 1:736.

[77] *Doctrine de Saint-Simon, première année, 1829*, 416.

[78] Comte to Mill, November 14, 1843, *CG*, 2:212.   [79] *Cours*, 1:450.   [80] Ibid., 535.

mathematical analysis was effective showed his ignorance of stoichiometry, which covers the quantitative expressions of chemical reactions.[81]

Comte used his doctrine of hypotheses to warn physicists not to resort to the metaphysical theories of universal ethers and imaginary fluids that were popular in his era as a means of explaining the phenomena of heat, light, electricity, and magnetism.[82] These ethers and fluids, he said, were like angels and genies: their existence could be neither negated nor affirmed, and they explained nothing. He also unwisely treated all questions of light in the same manner. To him, both the corpuscular and undulatory theories of light were "antiscientific" because they simply piled one mystery on top of another. They also connected optics too closely with mechanics and acoustics.[83]

It seems clear that Comte's goals were occasionally problematical. On the one hand, he was eager to unify the sciences as much as possible through the discovery of their interrelationships. On the other hand, he wished to keep each science (or branch of science) distinct by avoiding the temptation of reducing one to another.[84] Yet he carried his antireductionist tendencies too far when he wrote, "Despite all arbitrary assumptions, luminous phenomena will always constitute one sui generis category necessarily irreducible to any other: a light will be eternally heterogeneous to a movement or to a sound."[85] Such an absolutist position went against scientific progress.

CHEMISTRY

The subject of the first half of the third volume was chemistry, a science that had been developing rapidly since the late eighteenth and early nineteenth centuries. Based to a large extent on the works of Claude-Louis Berthollet, a former professor at the Ecole Polytechnique, Comte's exposition centered on what prevented chemistry from becoming a true science consisting of uniform laws. Instead of urging chemists to find new facts, Comte encouraged them to systematize the knowledge they already had in order to make one homogeneous doctrine. They should particularly take advantage of the comparative method, the third scientific means of observation, which chemistry introduced into the positive system, for it would at least allow them to classify chemical phenomena according to their natural families.

---

[81] Ibid., 578; see also François Dagognet, comment, 578n9.   [82] *Cours*, 1:458, 713.
[83] Ibid., 531.   [84] Serres, ed., in *Cours*, 1:534n8.   [85] *Cours*, 1:534.

Comte's objective in the lessons on chemistry was to stress its distinctiveness as a science, for he saw many threats to the validity of its findings and to its independence. For example, he strongly criticized Lorenz Oken, the leader of German *Naturphilosophen*, for trying to reduce all substances to four elements. Oken, according to Comte, had carried the search for simplification to such an extreme that he had disregarded the "reality" of natural phenomena.[86] When Comte turned to the relationship of chemistry to physics and physiology, which was one of the leading questions of the day, he concluded that chemistry had an ambiguous but nevertheless independent position between these two sciences. He insisted that the separate identities of all three sciences should be preserved and that scientists should not completely take over the work of a less developed science. Condemning reductionism, he warned physicists not to include chemical phenomena in their science. He also reprimanded chemists for trying to deal with organic phenomena, because he said they lacked an understanding of the whole of physiology. In fact, he argued against the existence of organic chemistry as a separate science. Precluded from dealing with the phenomena of life, all of chemistry should be inorganic. Despite his stress on the need to preserve a place for chemistry in the positive hierarchy, Comte seemed most interested in saving physiology from its encroachments. His restrictions on the realm of direct chemical investigation would be unacceptable today.[87]

Comte argued that verification of the results of chemical research could occur by the double process of analysis and synthesis, terms that he suggested had been abused by the Saint-Simonians and other metaphysicians.[88] Properly confined to chemistry, analysis pertained to decomposition, and synthesis to composition. To verify a chemical demonstration, a substance that was decomposed should be able to be recomposed exactly. Comte criticized chemists for using their analytical faculties far more than their synthetic ones. Just as he encouraged both induction and deduction, he was arguing for the use of both analysis and synthesis in scientific investigation in order to maximize possibilities in research.

Comte claimed that chemistry had an important impact on intellectual development, especially on humanity's liberation from theology and metaphysics. The ability to transform chemical phenomena improved the "human condition" and represented the "principal source" of people's power to effect change in general. The "positive

---

[86] Ibid., 2:592. Despite these criticisms, Comte was an admirer of many of Oken's biological concepts. See ibid., 2:628, 764.

[87] Dagognet, Comment, *Cours*, 1:646n5.   [88] *Cours*, 1:575.

notions of decomposition and recomposition" and the "necessarily indefinite perpetuity of all matter" replaced the theological dogma of "absolute destructions and creations."[89] Also, by showing that transformations in living bodies obeyed the laws of chemical phenomena, chemistry put an end to the theological dogma that organic matter was radically different from inorganic matter.

In sum, Comte's five lessons on chemistry are remarkable for their reformist spirit. Although the rapid changes in chemistry caused most of his specific suggestions for improvement to become outdated, his demand for homogeneity, systematization, predictive laws, and clearer hypotheses remained valid and encouraged the science to develop to a higher stage of "positivity."[90]

EVALUATION OF COMTE'S LESSONS ON
THE INORGANIC SCIENCES

The last lesson on chemistry marked the end of Comte's discussion of the inorganic sciences. Many scientists and philosophers from Comte's time to the present have judged these thirty-nine lessons in an unfavorable light. As mentioned previously, Comte's rigid approach to the classification of the sciences – particularly his infatuation with the vague term "complexity of phenomena" – often led him to make untenable, if not absurd, predictions about their development. At times, he also appears to have made errors in discussing certain laws or discoveries. Comte's contemporary Joseph Bertrand even accused him of making significant errors in his discussion of mathematics, the very subject he taught.[91] In a recent article, Craig Fraser points out that Comte's personal animosity toward Cauchy and Poisson prevented him from taking seriously their important work, which showed the weaknesses of Lagrange's mathematics.[92]

The renowned philosopher Michel Serres has also demonstrated that Comte's knowledge of purely mathematical developments was remarkably poor.[93] Serres goes so far as to say that Comte's

---

[89] Ibid., 586–7.   [90] Ibid., 567; see also Dagognet, Introduction to lessons 35 to 39, 565.

[91] For example, Bertrand stated that Comte misunderstood d'Alembert's principle of dynamics when he (Comte) asserted that it confirmed and developed Newton's law of the equivalence of reaction and action. Bertrand also claimed that Comte erred in declaring that Kepler's theories foreshadowed Newton's second principle of dynamics. Bertrand, "Souvenirs académiques," 537–41. Positivists, such as Dr. Georges Audiffrent and the engineer Luis Lagarrigue, refuted Bertrand. See Audiffrent, *Réponse à Bertrand*, 38. An extract from Luis Lagarrigue's letter to Bertrand can be found in the same book, 49–72.

[92] Fraser, "Lagrange's Analytical Mathematics," 255–6.

[93] Serres, ed., in *Cours*, 1:427 ("Remarque"), 245n3, 87n6, 107 ("Remarque"), 117n15, 171n26, 172 ("Remarque"), 186n3; Michel Serres, *La Traduction*, vol. 3 of *Hermès* (Paris: Minuit, 1974), 159.

mathematical knowledge stopped with Lagrange, who died in 1813, and that he consequently neglected the "great mathematical revolution of his time" – the rebirth of formalism and abstraction that was occurring in the early nineteenth century with Gauss, Abel, and Jacobi.[94] Comte was therefore partly responsible for the backwardness of French mathematical instruction in the nineteenth and twentieth centuries. Although Serres praises Comte's explanation of astronomy as "clear" and "definitive" for his time, he suggests that his Cartesian conception of this science was likewise turned toward the past and totally missed the trends toward thermodynamics and astrophysics.[95] Serres caustically calls the entire *Cours* a "monument" of the times:

> His encyclopedia of the exact sciences was . . . dead the first day of its birth. Let us not speak of the errors, which are especially notable in mathematics. It was dead for two reasons, two praises: because it *recapitulates*, and the exhaustive knowledge of the author is rarely in the wrong: whence the best general survey of a present and its past: because it *prohibits* what, for us, became its future, and the wisdom of the author is unsurpassable: he perceives in a dazzling manner what will be, only to cross it out immediately.[96]

Presenting its own static "decisive model of the universe," the *Cours* thus ironically tried to prevent the development of the modern scientific spirit, which was occurring at the very moment Comte was writing.[97]

Paul Tannery, a famous historian of the sciences who was Comte's disciple, claimed that at the very least the *Cours* was a historical document that faithfully reflected the state of the sciences in the early nineteenth century. Yet he had to admit that Comte was not at all informed about the new developments in the mathematical and physical sciences. As a result, scientists even of Comte's time did not take him seriously.[98] It seems, then, that in his knowledge of the sciences, Comte had not gone much beyond what he had learned as an adolescent at the Ecole Polytechnique.

Pierre Arnaud points out that these criticisms of Comte's know-

---

[94] Serres, ed., in *Cours*, 1:36n14.

[95] Ibid., 36n14, 66n2, 379n1, 427 ("Remarque"); Serres, *La Traduction*, 167.

[96] Serres, *La Traduction*, 159. See the chapter "Auguste Comte auto-traduit dans l'encyclopédie," 159–85.

[97] Ibid., see also 166.

[98] Paul Tannery, "Auguste Comte et l'histoire des sciences," *Revue générale des sciences pures et appliquées* 16.9 (1905): 411. On Tannery, see Lins, "L'Oeuvre d'Auguste Comte," 22. See also George Sarton on Comte's superficial knowledge of the history of science: *The Life of Science: Essays in the History of Civilization* (New York: Henry Schuman, 1948), 30–2, 122.

ledge of mathematics and the other sciences are irrelevant because he was not a specialist and was not trying to write on the sciences per se but on philosophy.[99] Yet most of the lessons in the *Cours* deal with specific scientific questions. Comte spoke with confidence and authority, even proposing reforms and fruitful areas of research to scientific specialists.[100] His lack of credibility on some of these issues – especially in the first volume on mathematics and astronomy – may have hindered the reception of the positive philosophy. His audience was probably less sympathetic to these problems, given the fact that the science of society, which would put all the other sciences in perspective philosophically, was merely a distant prospect. The general reader, who had great difficulty wading through the long volumes on the sciences with no relief in sight, was no happier than the scientist, who was offended by Comte's scientific errors and criticisms.

Comte was repeatedly advised to discuss at the beginning the main principles of social science, but he angrily rejected this counsel as illogical. Discussing social science first would have "ruined in advance the fundamental principles of the scientific hierarchy," which "best" characterized his philosophy.[101] After all, one of the points of the *Cours* was that the education of each individual had to start at the beginning and go through the whole history of knowledge. And this history ended with the science of society.[102] Moreover, by following such advice, Comte would have deprived himself of the scientific foundation necessary for the establishment of a social theory. The *Cours* was a learning process not only for his readers but, more important, for himself.

COMTE'S STYLE

Besides finding it difficult to follow a work published in pieces over a period of twelve years, both the layperson and the scientist had one other hurdle to face: Comte's poor writing. Comte's method of composing the *Cours* had a significant effect on the work. He always had to think first about his subject matter for a very long time in order to formulate a complete outline in his mind. Without taking a single note, he ordered the main ideas, the secondary points, and then the mass of supporting details. Before he was ready to write, the chapter had to be already composed in his head. Then it almost

[99] Arnaud, *Pour connaître la pensée d'Auguste Comte*, 71.
[100] John Morley, "Comte, Auguste [Isidore Auguste Marie François Xavier]," *Encyclopaedia Britannica*, 11th ed., 29 vols. (New York: Encyclopaedia Britannica, 1910–11), 6:819.
[101] *Cours*, 2:8.   [102] Ibid., 1:51. See also Gusdorf, *De l'histoire des sciences*, 97.

poured forth onto the page as he scribbled away at a furious pace. Comte was so pressed for time to finish the *Cours* and to realize his many projects and so confident that he had not forgotten anything in what he had just written that he immediately gave the finished pages to his publisher. The manuscript of the *Cours* shows that he indeed made very few corrections. He crossed out on average only three to seven words a page.[103] As a result, the *Cours* is basically a rapidly executed first draft, one that Comte never even reread.[104]

His method of composition is reflected in his atrocious style. Valat had attacked him for his use of a dry scientific language in 1824, and many other readers criticized him throughout the years as well. But in defending his mode of discourse, Comte suggested that he sought precisely to avoid literary and rhetorical devices that would have made reading his works more pleasant, because he sought to differentiate himself from the *littérateurs*, or metaphysicians, who spoke in dangerous abstractions.[105] To mark the uniqueness of his approach, he chose another style, a difficult "scientific style" that made his study of society seem scientific and objective and thus more worthy of respect. Boasting about the direct, spontaneous nature of his writing, one not marred by artistic conventions, he added:

> I write under the inspiration of my thought and . . . I have the profound conviction that it would be absolutely impossible for me to write in any other manner than that which the moment dictates to me. . . . [S]*tyle is the man himself*, and the one cannot be remade any more than the other.[106]

Very much an individualist when questions of his own development arose, Comte viewed his style as a means of self-expression – a position in keeping with the romantic age in which he lived. Yet he sought to disprove the romantic writers' conviction that scientists could not be creative.[107] Refusing to be manipulated by the marketplace, with its demands for pleasure, Comte wished to display his originality and maintain his purity.[108]

The result, however, is that the *Cours* is almost unreadable. Its

---

[103] Manuscript of the *Cours de philosophie positive*, N.a.fr. 17903 through 17908, BN. The Maison d'Auguste Comte gave the manuscript to the Bibliothèque Nationale. Lessons 10 through 18 – the second half of the volume on mathematics – are missing.

[104] Comte defended himself by claiming that it would have taken him another five or six years to write the *Cours* if he had rewritten it. *Cours*, 2:465; Comte to de Tholouze; January 4, 1856, *CG*, 8:181; *Système*, 1:7.

[105] Comte to Valat, September 8, 1824, *CG*, 1:130.

[106] Ibid., 130–1. See also Comte to Valat, December 25, 1824, *CG*, 1:147.

[107] On the rivalry between scientific and literary groups, see Dhombres and Dhombres, *Naissance d'un pouvoir*, 313–17, 614.

[108] Kofman, *Aberrations*, 15, 24.

sentences are far too long and convoluted, littered with too many adjectives, adverbs, and parenthetical phrases. The reader's attention span is further taxed by Comte's repetitions, digressions, and numerous empty formulas, such as the "nature of things." One professor wrote to Littré in despair:

> You told me that reading it [the *Cours*] once cannot suffice. In fact, from reading it once, I retained almost nothing. . . . Reading Comte's book is tiring. The sentences are so long that one has trouble remembering the beginning when one gets to the end. Now one must remember in order to understand, and one must understand in order to remember. It is a vicious circle. The essence and the form are, for the reader, two causes of serious difficulties.[109]

Especially in France, where style is highly prized, Comte's graceless, heavy prose undoubtedly worked against him and was another factor reinforcing his isolation.[110]

BIOLOGY

Although Comte's review of the inorganic sciences was open to criticism, there was one natural science that he covered in an extraordinarily insightful manner: biology. Having studied this science since 1816, when he enrolled in the famous Ecole de Médecine in Montpellier, he recognized that it was in an important and exciting period of development.[111] By classifying biology as one of the five major sciences, instead of a division of terrestrial physics as Lamarck and others did, Comte ensured its new significance.[112]

Although the medical school in Montpellier had taught Comte much about biology, especially about the popular theories of vitalism, it was Blainville who most influenced his views and made him a strong opponent of mechanism.[113] From 1829 through 1832, Comte had followed Blainville's lectures on general and comparative

---

[109] Rigolage to Littré, July 31, 1876, in "Correspondance de M. E. Rigolage avec M. Littré et Mme Comte," ed. Pierre Laffitte, *RO*, 2d ser., 23 (March 1, 1901), 263. See also Littré, *Auguste Comte*, 259.

[110] Kofman, *Aberrations*, 15. Kofman argues that Comte's "masculine" writing style reflected his fears about his sexual virility. Ibid., 11–44.

[111] Roland Mourgue, "La Philosophie biologique d'Auguste Comte," parts 1, 2, *Archives de l'anthropologie criminelle de médecine légale et de psychologie normal et pathologique* 24.190–1, 192 (October–November, December 1909): 829; *Cours*, 2:623.

[112] Lois N. Magner, *A History of the Life Sciences* (New York: Dekker, 1979), 341–2. Comte considered the founders of biology to be Bichat, Lamarck, Cabanis, Gall, and Broussais. See *Cours*, 2:764; "Discours prononcé aux funérailles de Blainville," *Système*, 1:738.

[113] Comte never tried to conceal the fact that most of his own concepts about this science derived directly from Blainville. Comte, "Discours prononcé aux funérailles de Blainville,"

physiology at the Faculty of Sciences. He considered this course to be the "most perfect example of the most advanced state of present biology."[114] Therefore, thanks to Blainville, Comte knew the latest ideas in this nascent science far better than those in the other sciences. Moreover, because biology was the "immediate point of departure" for the science of society and had to be established first, he exercised greater care in discussing it.[115] His efforts to unify and systematize biology's new theories and to make it an independent science would have a decisive impact on its development.[116]

What first strikes the reader of these lessons in volume 3 is Comte's use of the term "biology" rather than the usual word, "physiology." He adopted the expression "biology" from Blainville, whom he wrongly credited with inventing it. (Lamarck actually introduced the term "biology" into France in 1802 to denote theories relating to the vegetal and animal series.)[117] Comte adopted Blainville's idea that to understand all the phenomena of life, biology had to cover the study of man as an individual (physiology) as well as that of animals and plants. Comte's influence in this instance was such that henceforth people referred to the study of the phenomena of life as "biology" instead of "physiology."[118]

Comte was convinced that only the positive philosophy could establish biology on a solid basis. Because theology and metaphysics studied man, then nature, they tended to explain all phenomena from man's standpoint, attributed an arbitrary will to these phenomena, and thus ultimately neglected nature. Positivism used the inverse method. It subordinated the conception of man to that of the external world, made the concept of "natural laws" of primary importance, and opened up the possibility of extending such laws to man and society.

On the basis of this difference in methodology, Comte criticized vitalism. He rejected such notions as the "soul" of Stahl, the "vital principle" of Barthez, and the "vital forces" of the "great Bichat himself."[119] He felt all three vitalists were metaphysicians because there was no evidence for their theory of an independent life force, which resembled a first cause.[120] He disapproved of their studying

739; *Cours*, 1:602, 665. See also Gouhier, "La Philosophie 'positiviste' et 'chrétienne' de D. de Blainville," 54.

[114] *Cours*, 1:665. The 1829 edition of Blainville's *Cours de physiologie générale et comparée* can still be found in Comte's library.

[115] Ibid., 708.   [116] Mourgue, "Philosophie biologique," 833.   [117] Ibid., 829–30.

[118] Ibid., 829n3. See also ibid., 839; Coleman, *Biology*, 1.

[119] *Cours*, 1:667, 719, 806. Bichat was not entirely a vitalist, however. See Sinaceur, ed., in *Cours*, 1:668n4.

[120] Michael A. McCormick, "Tissue Theory in Auguste Comte's Positive Biology," *Texas Reports on Biology and Medicine* 32.1 (1974): 83.

man in isolation from nature and their neglect of general laws, especially those of chemistry.[121] They did not see that the study of man had to rest on the inorganic sciences. Above all, Comte was preoccupied with linking the two great subjects of philosophical speculation – man and the universe.

Besides vitalism, the other great enemy of biology was, in Comte's eyes, the mechanism of Boerhaave, which was particularly strong in the medical school in Paris. Although Boerhaave had introduced the "fundamental link between inorganic philosophy and biological philosophy," making all of natural philosophy "one homogeneous and continuous system," he had gone too far.[122] Whereas vitalism exaggerated the independence of vital phenomena, mechanism denied it altogether by reducing biology to physics.

Comte argued that the true nature of biology lay somewhere between the two extremes of vitalism and materialism, whose disputes he blamed for making the science eclectic and disorderly.[123] Although he appreciated the fact that Boerhaave had demonstrated the importance of physico-chemical phenomena, Comte was also favorable, if not more so, to the vitalists, because he continually defended the idea of the distinctiveness of life and said that they at least recognized physiology as a separate science.[124] His views were influenced by Jacques Lordat, a renowned expert on Barthez and one of the professors at the Montpellier Ecole de Médecine who had befriended him. Thanks to Lordat, Barthez, along with Bichat, had a large impact on Comte.[125]

Comte also wanted to free biology from medicine. Now that it was becoming a science in its own right, biology required speculative freedom to develop and thus had to separate itself from its corresponding practical science of application, that is, medicine. It needed scientists exclusively devoted to it and a place in formal scientific bodies, such as academies. Comte recognized that the proper

---

[121] *Cours*, 1:667. See also Sinaceur, ed., in ibid., 667n3; Gouhier, "La Philosophie 'positiviste' et 'chrétienne' de D. de Blainville," 44.

[122] *Cours*, 1:806, 822.

[123] Reflecting his understanding that scientific positions had political implications, Comte connected vitalism and materialism respectively to the reactionary and revolutionary parties that were fighting to take over the direction of society.

[124] See also Comte's criticism of Blainville for being too materialistic. Comte to G. d'Eichthal, August 5, 1824, *CG*, 1:109.

[125] Georges Canguilhem, "L'Ecole de Montpellier jugée par Auguste Comte," *Bulletin et mémoires de la Société Internationale d'Histoire de la Médecine*, n.s., 6, special issue (1959): 47. Comte's esteem for the vitalists is reflected in the fact that the Positivist Library includes two books by Bichat and two by Barthez. Comte also gave the name "Bichat" to the thirteenth month of the Positivist Calendar, that of modern science. *Système*, 4:559, 561, Table B'.

organization of the scientific division of labor was a necessary element in the progress of science itself.[126]

In discussing the nature of biology, Comte objected to the widely held definition of life originally proposed by Bichat. To combat mechanism and to separate organic from inorganic phenomena, Bichat had defined life as the totality of functions opposed to death. But having learned from Cabanis, Lamarck, and especially Blainville of the environment's strong influence on the living organism, Comte argued there could be no such absolute antagonism between "living nature" and "dead nature"; living bodies were so fragile that they could not exist if their surroundings tended to destroy them.[127] Thus life depended on matter, and the fundamental condition of life was a "harmony between the living being and the corresponding milieu." Comte expanded the definition of the word "milieu" to include the "total ensemble of all types of external circumstances that are necessary for the existence of each determined organism."[128] In this way, he encouraged interest in the relationship between man and his environment, which was already being stimulated by the industrial revolution.[129] Inspired by Blainville and German *Naturphilosophen*, Comte also urged biologists to create a special general theory clarifying the influence of milieus on organisms. In a sense, he was promoting the importance of ecology.

In searching for the correct definition of life, Comte criticized contemporary German philosophy (*Naturphilosophie*) for equating life with spontaneous activity. He argued that this definition failed to relate the idea of life to inorganic laws and made life lose all significance because all natural bodies were active.[130] Instead, he adopted Blainville's definition of life as the "double internal movement, both general and continuous, of composition and decomposition."[131] Comte was therefore close to the mechanists in arguing that organic life was characterized by chemical and physical activity.[132] In fact,

---

[126] Sinaceur, ed., in *Cours*, 1:674n9.

[127] *Cours*, 1:676. Comte's library at the Maison d'Auguste Comte contains Lamarck's *Philosophie zoologique* and his *Système analytique des connaissances positives de l'homme*. See also Mourgue, "Philosophie biologique," 840–1; Lévy-Bruhl, *La Philosophie d'Auguste Comte*, 227; Lessertisseur and Jouffroy, "L'Idée de série," 40; Bernard Balon, "L'Organisation, organisme, économie et milieu chez Henri Ducrotay de Blainville," *Revue d'histoire des sciences* 32.1 (1979): 5–24; Gouhier, "La Philosophie 'positiviste' et 'chrétienne' de D. de Blainville," 45; Sinaceur, ed., in *Cours*, 1:675n10, 676n11; *Cours*, 1:685; *Système*, 4:559.

[128] *Cours*, 1:676, 682.

[129] Sinaceur, ed., in ibid., 682n19; McLaren, "A Prehistory of the Social Sciences," 13.

[130] *Cours*, 1:710. See also Mourgue, "Philosophie biologique," 841–2.

[131] *Cours*, 1:680. On the importance of Blainville in this respect, see Balon, "L'Organisation," 21.

[132] McCormick, "Tissue Theory," 85. McCormick exaggerates when he asserts that Comte was a "firm anti-vitalist." Ibid., 86.

according to Paul Tannery, Comte's conception of the chemical foundation of life had a significant impact on nineteenth-century biological research.[133] But Comte also reproached Blainville for not having emphasized in his definition that the organism had to exist in a proper milieu. A biological phenomenon could be understood only in relation to other phenomena in the living body and to the outside world.[134] Life was, in effect, this dualism between the milieu and the organism.

Thanks to Blainville, Comte also maintained that one of the key differences between the organic and the inorganic was that only the former was characterized by organization. Without organization, there was no life.[135] Therefore, biology could not be reduced to chemistry because vital phenomena were influenced not only by laws of composition and decomposition but by their organization, that is, their anatomical structure. The chemical transformations in living organisms were different from those in inorganic bodies in that they were continuous and dependent on the anatomical organization of the living bodies in question. Comte did not endeavor to define the essence of life but insisted that it could not be summed up in chemical reactions.[136]

Influenced again by Blainville, Comte criticized biologists for separating the static state (the anatomical point of view) and the dynamic state (the physiological point of view).[137] He argued that this division would disappear only when the whole biological system derived from his principle that the concept of life was inseparable from that of organization. Biologists would then see that there could be no organ without a function and no function without an organ. (Function designated the "action" of the organism when influenced by the milieu.) They would accept the principle that when an organism was "placed in a given system of external circumstances," it must act in a "determined manner."[138] Such determinism was necessary for biology to fulfill the primary aim of all positive

---

[133] Tannery, "Auguste Comte," 411.

[134] Lévy-Bruhl, *Philosophie d'Auguste Comte*, 199–200.

[135] Gouhier, "La Philosophie 'positiviste' et 'chrétienne' de D. de Blainville," 54.

[136] Mourgue, "Philosophie biologique," 860, 930. F. Pillon overlooks the complexity of Comte's argument when he claims that Comte had a narrow materialistic and mechanistic conception of life. F. Pillon, "Claude Bernard: Sa Conception de la vie comparée à celle de l'Ecole Positiviste," *La Critique philosophique, politique, scientifique, littéraire* 7.4 (1878): 54, 56.

[137] *Cours*, 1:699, 739. See also Lessertisseur and Jouffroy, "L'Idée de série," 40; Sinaceur, ed., in *Cours*, 1:684n22; Mourgue, "Philosophie biologique," 845n1; F. Pillon, "La Biologie selon Auguste Comte et selon Claude Bernard," *La Critique philosophique, politique, scientifique, littéraire* 7.5 (1878): 75.

[138] *Cours*, 1:683.

sciences, that of prediction. By insisting on determinism, Comte opposed the vitalists and made a significant contribution to the development of biology in the nineteenth century. Thanks to Claude Bernard, determinism became one of the leading principles of this new science.[139]

Comte's theory of organization and milieu was one of the most important and original points of the entire *Cours*. It enabled him to create a theory of life totally distinct from that of death. On the one hand, in proclaiming the originality and autonomy of life and the specificity of biology, he avoided taking a purely empirical or materialistic position. His stress on organization as one of the conditions of life allowed him to avoid the reductionism of the physico-chemical school. On the other hand, his insistence that the second condition of life was a suitable milieu eliminated the mystical or vitalist notion that life was universally diffused throughout nature and could be produced spontaneously. Thanks to the efforts of the Société de Biologie, founded by his disciples, Comte's theory of milieu had an enormous impact on French biology.[140] The term "milieu" would later be applied to historical circumstances by the historian Hippolyte Taine.[141]

In discussing methodology, Comte declared, as he had in 1824, that in contrast to the inorganic sciences, the study of life should begin with the best known phenomena, which were the most particular and complex (i.e., human beings), and proceed gradually to the least known phenomena, which were the most general and simplest. Since life was characterized above all by solidarity and consensus, the whole had to be grasped before the details could be comprehended. Epistemologically, biology was, therefore, a synthetic science.[142]

Because it dealt with more complex phenomena than the sciences that preceded it, its means of investigation were greater. Direct observations made by the natural senses could be improved by artificial apparatuses, such as the microscope. However, reflecting the fears of Bichat and Blainville, Comte had some reservations about its use, because he feared it could lead to illusions.[143]

---

[139] Mourgue, "Philosophie biologique," 843–4.

[140] Sinaceur, ed., Introduction, to *Cours*, 1:660, 663–4; Mourgue, "Philosophie biologique," 860.

[141] Sinaceur, ed., in *Cours*, 1:682n19.

[142] F. Pillon, "La Méthode en biologie: Cuvier, Blainville, Auguste Comte," *La Critique philosophique: Politique, scientifique, littéraire* 7.9 (1878): 134; *Cours*, 1:746; Sinaceur, ed., in ibid., 745n98; idem, Introduction to *Cours*, 1:651–3; Lévy-Bruhl, *Philosophie d'Auguste Comte*, 199–201.

[143] Sinaceur, ed., in *Cours*, 1:688n25.

Like Cuvier and Blainville, he was also wary of experimentation, the second means of investigation. Since each organism was very complex, depended on many interconnected external and internal influences, and formed an indivisible system, it was impossible to isolate phenomena sufficiently to make experimentation as effective as it was in the inorganic sciences.[144] Comte particularly protested against the increasing use of vivisection, for he believed it disturbed the organism too much and led to a "deplorable levity" and "habits of cruelty," which were intellectually and morally detrimental to the scientist.[145] The only experimentation that Comte endorsed was the introduction of disturbances into the milieu – a much less "violent" procedure than vivisection.[146] He also believed the study of disease was like experimentation in that the biologist learned about normal physiological conditions by investigating a variation of the normal state. Comte credited Broussais with this idea and unwisely attacked the "incompetent judges" at the Academy of Sciences for rejecting his candidacy.[147]

Impressed by Blainville's use of the comparative method in anatomy, Comte declared that this third general mode of investigation would blossom in biology because of the fundamental resemblance of organic phenomena. Relying on classification for organizing distinct but analogous beings, the comparative method was the most important means of investigating living bodies. His recommendation of a wide use of this method in physiology was one of the original points of the *Cours*.[148]

Comte believed that biology was the most intellectually demanding natural science because it depended on a preliminary mastery of the methods and laws of all the other sciences preceding it in the hierarchy. Though critical of Bichat's vitalism, Comte did agree with his prohibition of the excessive use of mathematics in biology.[149] Like chemical phenomena, biological phenomena were too complicated, varied, and diverse to permit numerical calculations. Comte's views on this subject were shortsighted.

Comte claimed that biology had a strong impact on the "eman-

[144] Mourgue, "Philosophie biologique," 853n2; Sinaceur, ed., in *Cours*, 1:690n31, 692n34; Pillon, "La Méthode en biologie," 129, 138; *Cours*, 1:692, 798.

[145] *Cours*, 1:692. See also Mourgue, "Philosophie biologique," 847.   [146] *Cours*, 1:693.

[147] Ibid., 695. See also Sinaceur, ed., in ibid., 696n38; Pillon, "La Méthode en biologie," 132, 137. Broussais's reputation had suffered because of his disastrous treatment of cholera victims in 1832. See Braunstein, *Broussais*, 19–20. Comte also condemned the Academy for closing its doors to Bichat and Gall. *Cours*, 1:869.

[148] Mourgue, "Philosophie biologique," 855.

[149] Blainville had also condemned the use of mathematics in biology. Remnants of this hostility to mathematics can be seen in Claude Bernard. Ibid., 864–65, 925.

cipation of human reason."[150] By proving that the organic world was regulated by natural laws and that organisms and the environment could be modified by human intervention, it actively combated "theological fictions" and "metaphysical entities."[151] In terms of method or logic, biology contributed to the positive system of knowledge by developing two of man's most basic powers, those of comparison and classification.[152] Biology had taught Comte himself that he could unify the sciences by classifying them in a hierarchy and that subordination was one of the characteristics of order.

Comte expressed reservations about several recent developments in biology. He rejected nascent cell theory because he felt cells were an absurd and incomprehensible imitation of molecules and tissue theory already established anatomy on a solid scientific base.[153] Microscopic research, which supported the "metaphysical" cellular theory, was in his eyes much too vague and unreliable. Comte's views on cell theory, microscopic research, and vivisection meant that he failed to put himself in the forefront of biological research, and they proved embarrassing to some of his disciples.[154]

Following Blainville's lead, Comte also took a conservative approach in rejecting Lamarck's new theories of evolution. It is clear that Comte greatly admired Lamarck's linear approach to the chain of being, his investigations into the influence of the milieu on the organism, his concept of the heredity of acquired characteristics, and his theory of habit, whereby habit was "one of the principal bases of the gradual perfectibility of animals and especially of man."[155] Yet he considered Lamarck's concept of the variation of the species to be a farfetched exaggeration. Repeating Cuvier's argument, Comte maintained that observation could not verify Lamarck's theory that needs created organs.[156] Moreover, if, as Lamarck asserted, different species could transform themselves into others owing to external influences, the idea of "species" would be deprived of meaning, classification would become almost impossible, and the science of biology itself would become muddled. Lamarck's suggestion that

---

[150] *Cours*, 1:731. [151] Ibid., 736.

[152] Sinaceur, ed., Introduction to *Cours*, 1:656; Mourgue, "Philosophie biologique," 930.

[153] Comte also criticized cellular theory because he felt it was connected with Oken and Schelling's *Naturphilosophie*, which promulgated the idea that a single, universal force of life animated the moral and physical universes and did not maintain "any distinction between the organic and inorganic." *Cours*, 1:764–5. See also ibid., 445; Lévy-Bruhl, *Philosophie d'Auguste Comte*, 215.

[154] Arnaud, *Pour connaître la pensée d'Auguste Comte*, 100; Lewes, *Comte's Philosophy*, 189; Sinaceur, ed., in *Cours*, 1:761n29, and Introduction, 659.

[155] *Cours*, 1:839. See Lessertisseur and Jouffroy, "L'Idée de série," 40; Mourgue, "Philosophie biologique," 934.

[156] *Cours*, 1:777. See also Sinaceur, ed., in ibid., 778n12.

the organism was completely determined by its milieu threatened the unity and distinctiveness of the living organism.[157] Whereas earlier in these lessons on biology Comte seemed closer to Lamarck in insisting on the effect of the milieu on the organism, he now stressed that the influence of the milieu on the species was limited to nonessential changes, and he seemed to increase the power of the organism to modify its environment.[158]

Instead of Lamarck's transformism, Comte maintained the old doctrine of the fixity of the species. Just as he admired the stability of the celestial world, he insisted upon the unchanging order of the world of vital phenomena. Although he referred to the adaptation of the organism to its milieu and even to the "perfectibility" of the animal and human species, his conception of biology neglected the significance of time and was ultimately more static than dynamic. Comte's position is paradoxical, considering that he is regarded as the philosopher of progress. He apparently wished to empower individuals so that they could transform their world in an advantageous manner, but reflecting the strains of the postrevolutionary era, he seemed basically more concerned about the disruptive consequences of change.

The last chapter of volume 3 was devoted to the biological study of cerebral phenomena.[159] By extending the positive method to these phenomena, Comte claimed to complete the scientific revolution begun by Descartes. Comte believed that Descartes had erred when he separated the study of man from that of the animals, thereby giving new life to the theological and metaphysical philosophies. But thanks to the work of Gall, intellectual and moral phenomena, which represented the last stronghold of the theological and metaphysical philosophies, now could be made a subject of scientific investigations. In denying the separation of matter and spirit, phrenology thus strengthened Comte's stance against Cartesian dualism.[160]

Much of Comte's discussion was motivated by his dislike of metaphysical theories of psychology, which he divided into three schools. First there was the Scottish school, which he most admired.

---

[157] Canguilhem, "L'Ecole de Montpellier," 49.   [158] Sinaceur, ed., in *Cours*, 1:777n11.

[159] Originally, Comte had planned to cover this topic in greater depth by devoting two chapters to old theories and two chapters to new theories. But evidently he had run out of time and space, because Bachelier was pressing him to finish and he had already written 760 pages before even embarking on this subject. Thus these 70 pages constituted a very condensed version of his analysis. "Tableau synoptique du *Cours de philosophie positive* de M. Auguste Comte," *Cours de philosophie positive* (1830–42), 1:ix.

[160] Anne Marie Wettley, "Les Idées d'instinct d'Auguste Comte dans sa philosophie positive," *Bulletin et mémoires de la Société Internationale d'Histoire de la Médecine*, n.s., 6, special issue (1959): 51.

Then there was the French school of the Idéologues and their predecessors, the sensationalists Condillac and Helvétius, which he felt was the clearest and most systematic. Finally there was the German school, which included the French eclectics, such as the "famous sophist" Cousin, whom he accused of inspiring in French youth the "deplorable psychological mania." These three schools based their theories on the unscientific notion of "interior observation."[161] Because the mind could not be studied apart from nature, as the psychologists claimed, the study of the mind, according to Comte, had to be a physical science based on the other, more simple sciences.

Psychologists, fond of referring to "purely nominal entities," such as the soul, the will, and the ego, also neglected the fact that every function had an organ and vice versa.[162] "Phrenological physiology" was superior to psychology because it determined intellectual and affective functions by considering the organs on which they depended in the brain.[163] Phrenology showed that intellectual and moral phenomena depended in a *concrete* fashion on organization, that is, on anatomical structure.

At this point, Comte added another criticism of the psychologists and Idéologues, which sheds light on his concept of human nature. In his private letters, he had often mentioned that he had strong emotional needs that directed the way he lived. Now backed by Gall, he criticized psychology and Idéologie for neglecting the affections and wrongly subordinating them to the intellect. As if directing his attack against Hegel and Cousin, Comte denounced the exclusive attention given to the "mind" (*l'esprit*). "Daily experience" shows that "the affections, penchants, [and] passions constitute the principal motives of human action." Arising spontaneously and independently from the intellect, they stimulate the "first awakening and the continuous development of the different intellectual faculties" because they give them a "permanent goal," without which these faculties would remain "dull." Comte added, "It is even only too certain that the least noble and the most animalistic penchants are habitually the most energetic, and consequently, the most influential." Because the psychologists and Idéologues vaguely attached the affections to some unifying principle, such as sympathy or egoism, which was supposedly directed by the intellect, they portrayed man "against all evidence as an essentially reasoning being,

---

[161] *Cours*, 1:854. Tracy, whom Comte called the metaphysician closest to the positive spirit partly because of his critique of psychology, recognized this problem when he stated that "*ideology is a part of zoology.*" But he was wrong when he stated that this science of ideology was independent of all the other sciences and should direct them. Ibid., 854–5.

[162] Ibid., 855. See also Sinaceur, ed., in ibid., 855n26. [163] *Cours*, 1:851.

executing continually, without his knowledge, a multitude of imperceptible calculations with almost no spontaneity of action, even from the most tender age of childhood."[164] Attacking one of the bases of Enlightenment and liberal theory, Comte insisted, furthermore, that it was wrong to argue that man could be changed and improved by his intelligence. Stressing the limits of rationalism, Comte was not only responding to the criticisms that the Saint-Simonians had made of him but contributing in his own fashion to the cult of the emotions that was having an impact on literature and the arts at the time.[165]

Comte was convinced that the psychologists' unified ego represented a "purely fictive state," one designed to preserve artificially the separation between men and animals and to maintain the theological idea of a unified soul. In reality, human nature was "essentially multiple, that is, prompted almost always by several very distinct and fully independent powers, between which equilibrium is established very painfully." Influenced by Barthez and Broussais, Comte argued that the only real unity was physical; it was the "fundamental unity of the animal organism," which resulted from an "exact harmony among [its] diverse principal functions," that is, from the association of the animal's different organs.[166] This primarily physical sense of equilibrium among the faculties constituted health and determined the "general feeling of the self [*le moi*]."[167] Moreover, the sentiment of personal harmony was extremely unstable and complex and could not be the basis of a philosophy, despite Cousin's assertions to the contrary. As Lévy-Bruhl indicates, Comte was here speaking as a successor of Hume and Cabanis.[168] In sum, by stating that the ego was merely the "universal consensus of the whole of the organism," Comte was arguing, in contrast to the psychologists, that both men and animals had a feeling of the ego because this feeling was mainly physical.[169] He was, in effect, placing man and the animals on the same level, reaffirming the unity of living beings and attacking theologians and metaphysicians for painting a more noble picture of man than was scientifically admissible.

To combat Descartes's original, fatal distinction between intelligence and instinct that was used by the psychologists and Idéologues to separate human from animal nature, Comte praised Gall's view

---

[164] Ibid., 856.
[165] Schenk, "Reaction against Rationalism," chap. in *The Mind of the European Romantics*, 3–8.
[166] *Cours*, 1:841, 857. See also Canguilhem, "L'Ecole de Montpellier," 48.
[167] *Cours*, 1:841.   [168] Lévy-Bruhl, *Philosophie d'Auguste Comte*, 226.   [169] *Cours*, 1:858.

that instinct and intelligence were not opposites.[170] Instinct was not confined to animals any more than intelligence was to humans. Instinct, defined as "any spontaneous impulse toward a determined direction," could be applied to any faculty, including intelligence. One could have an instinct for mathematics or music, and people had at least as many instincts as animals. Furthermore, since intelligence was the "aptitude for modifying one's conduct in conformity to the circumstances of each case," animals, like people, were obviously intelligent because they could transform their behavior if necessary. The usual theological and metaphysical definition of man as a "rational animal" was, therefore, "nonsense," for animals themselves had to act in a reasonable manner in order to survive.[171] People were different from animals only because they developed the intellectual and affective faculties more fully. This difference was one of degree, not of kind. Comte's stress on the affective and intellectual attributes of animals helps explain his antivivisectionism. Denying once again that man was the center of the universe, Comte found theologians' and metaphysicians' worries about degrading human nature a barrier to scientific progress. Although he himself opposed theories of evolution, his predilection for placing animals and humans on the same continuum pointed the way toward Darwinism.

Comte's purely "naturalistic" approach to man made him vulnerable to accusations of materialism. Yet he distanced himself from the sensationalists, such as Locke, Condillac, and Helvétius, who were considered the leading exponents of materialism, for he believed that they grossly exaggerated the power of intellectual faculties and the environment's influence on man. He particularly criticized Helvétius for suggesting not only that all men had similar senses and were equal intellectually but also that "egoism" should be the sole moral principle.[172] These dangerous ideas led to the "most absurd exaggerations about the unlimited power of education" to make improvements. They also reduced social relations to "ignoble coalitions of private interests."[173] Again, Comte was criticizing Enlightenment and liberal philosophy, which he held partly

---

[170] Gall claimed that animals and men shared nineteen of the twenty-seven faculties. Wettley, "Les Idées d'instinct," 50. Comte enlisted Blainville and Georges Leroy, a leading expert on animal life, to support his position. Comte included the first volume of Blainville's *Sur l'organisation des animaux* and Leroy's *Lettres sur les animaux* in the Positivist Library. *Système*, 4:559, 561. Both of these books are in Comte's library at the Maison d'Auguste Comte.

[171] *Cours*, 1:858–9.

[172] Ibid., 862. Comte also ridiculed Condillac's idea of "transformed sensation," which made every intellectual act identical and consequently eliminated all the differences that exist among animal species and also among individuals. See Comte's comment about the "strange" *Traité des Systèmes*. Ibid., 456–7.

[173] Ibid., 862.

responsible for the destructive political movements since the French Revolution.

Comte praised German philosophy (German idealism) for trying to refute the errors of the French school, but he felt that it was hindered by the "vague Absolute of its unintelligible doctrines."[174] Thinking, probably of Fichte's ego, Comte argued that because the German philosophers claimed the ego to be characterized by "vagabond liberty," they made it "essentially ungovernable" and free from all laws. This approach ran counter to Comte's basic principle that all phenomena were subject to natural laws. Kant's and Fichte's notions of the categorical imperative seemed equally false. Condemning the Germans' tendency toward "universal mystification," Comte criticized their idea of allowing "each individual to direct exclusively his conduct according to the abstract idea of duty." Acting in the name of an abstract metaphysical entity "would lead ultimately to the exploitation of the species by a small number of clever charlatans."[175] Thus the errors of German philosophy had social and political consequences as dangerous as the French school's.

The school of psychology that Comte found the "least absurd of all" was the Scottish. Although their doctrines suffered from a lack of clarity, unity, and widespread influence, Hume, Smith, and Ferguson offered the best metaphysical rebuttal to the philosophy of sensationalism because they recognized that sympathy was at least as powerful a force in man as egoism.[176]

Despite Comte's admiration for the Scots, he was still most enthusiastic about Gall's doctrine, which he believed was the clearest and most scientific refutation of metaphysical theories, especially sensationalism. Although Comte claimed to be a relativist, he argued that two of Gall's principles of human nature would remain forever unchanged. Indeed, since they provided Comte with the basis for his social and political philosophy, his own system would fall if they one day proved false.

The first principle was the innateness of fundamental intellectual and emotional dispositions. Because it asserted that people were born with different characteristics, this principle put an end to the sensationalists' insistence on equality and their optimistic approach to the effects of environment.

The second principle involved the plurality of distinct, independent faculties. Far from being one organ, the brain was an apparatus

---

[174] Ibid., 861. This reference to the "vague Absolute" may pertain to Hegel, whose concept of the "Spirit" Comte had criticized in 1824. Comte to G. d'Eichthal, December 10, 1824, *CG*, 1:144.

[175] *Cours*, 1:862. See also Sinaceur, ed., in ibid., 861n38.   [176] *Cours*, 1:853.

composed of different organs that corresponded to these faculties or dispositions. Comte rejected Gall's view that each action was linked to a faculty and that there were "organs" of theft, murder, music, poetry, and so forth. He preferred Spurzheim's theory that action depended on the *association* of certain faculties (or "organs") and the corresponding circumstances, especially because he believed this theory could be verified anatomically and applied to both human beings and animals.[177] Comte commended both Gall and Spurzheim for having eliminated the sensationalist and metaphysical theory that sensation, memory, imagination, and judgment were fundamental, separate faculties of abstraction, invariable in all human beings. Instead, these abilities were related to each phrenological function and varied from one person (and animal) to the next, according to how much they were exercised. Eliminating the idea that everyone had a similar intellectual makeup, this second principle also showed the absurdity of the notion of human equality.

Most important, Gall's principles provided scientific confirmation for the Scottish philosophers' theory that sympathy was an innate disposition in man. Arguing in favor of the predominance of the affective faculties in human and animal nature, Gall placed the affective faculties in the back and middle part of the brain and the intellectual faculties in the front part, where they constituted merely a quarter or a sixth of the encephalic mass. This anatomical discovery destroyed the basis of psychology and Idéologie, which insisted on the preeminence of man's intellect. By placing the affections directly in the brain, Gall disproved Cabanis's and Bichat's theories that the brain was one organ composed solely of the intellect and that the passions were located in other organs such as the heart or the liver. Comte was delighted to have this "proof" of the human being's inherent sociability because it demonstrated man's natural tendency to form a group without resorting to the old theories of the social contract and utility, which were ultimately based on individualism.[178]

Comte admitted that Gall's and Spurzheim's efforts to localize the diverse cerebral functions were full of errors. So far, there was no conclusive theory about the "type, number, range, and reciprocal influence of the organs" that could be assigned to the intellectual and

---

[177] The faculties characteristic of man were found in the least developed and most anterior part of the brain, whereas those of animals were located in the most voluminous and most posterior part. Comte believed it was likely that the highest animals also shared the most eminent intellectual aptitudes of man. The only reason their aptitudes were not more developed was that men had repressed animals for the benefit of human progress. *Cours*, 1:865. See also Sinaceur, ed., in ibid., 865n47.

[178] McLaren, "A Prehistory of the Social Sciences," 19.

affective functions.[179] Nevertheless, Comte did accept phrenology's main subdivisions. What were traditionally called the heart, character, and mind could be found respectively in the back, middle, and front parts of the brain.[180] Comte denied that this schematic presentation of the brain meant that all human action was predetermined. Since moral and intellectual phenomena were more complex than other phenomena, they could be modified more easily. Also, the faculties could be exercised and strengthened. In particular, the intellectual faculties, which affected an animal's or a person's behavior, could significantly alter the influence of all the other faculties. Yet although Comte claimed that Gall upheld human freedom and responsibility, what appealed most to him was clearly Gall's principle of the innateness of certain dispositions, which challenged not only the German philosophers' insistence on the unlimited power of the ego to transform one's moral nature, but also the French philosophers' belief in the unlimited ability of institutions to change the individual.

Comte maintained that Gall's theories demonstrated that people could not be improved through education unless they had the requisite predispositions. He fully accepted the phrenological principle that people, for the most part, were "essentially mediocre" both intellectually and emotionally. Each person possessed all the penchants, sentiments, and elementary aptitudes, but usually none of these faculties dominated the others. Although education could improve people, it would never allow them to overcome their essential mediocrity, which in fact was necessary for "good social harmony."[181] It seems that Comte's years of teaching had discouraged him and left him with a certain bitterness that was strikingly different from the enthusiasm of his youth. But even in his youth he had once said to Valat that a friend of theirs had disappointed him by displaying an "odious trait":

> I thought I could consider that man one of the people who came to virtue through instruction, and I see that I must erase him from my list. In truth, I am beginning to discover that the more one examines

---

[179] *Système*, vol. 4, "Appendice," 159.

[180] Gall and Spurzheim divided the affective faculties into penchants (the basic drives of the individual for self-preservation) and sentiments (the social affections) and located them respectively in the posterior and middle parts of the brain. Intellectual faculties were divided into those of perception, which made up the spirit of observation, and those of reflection, which involved comparison and coordination. Located in the anterior, superior part of the frontal region, these faculties of reflection constituted the "principal characteristic attribute of human nature." *Cours*, 1:867.

[181] Ibid., 870.

men, the less one finds within their interior anything that gains in being seen.[182]

Nevertheless, Comte's views on the limitations of instruction seem incongruous considering that the purpose of the *Cours* was to effect an educational revolution leading to the regeneration of humanity.

Despite his enthusiasm for Gall and Spurzheim, Comte criticized them and other phrenologists for their arbitrary localizations, their superficial grasp of the association of the different faculties, and their excessive multiplication of "organs" and functions. (Gall claimed there were twenty-seven faculties, and Spurzheim, thirty-five.) He insisted that phrenology's analysis of the brain had to be "entirely" redone, especially with the help of anatomical studies, in order to avoid the base charlatanism that was now endangering its credibility.[183] Once corrected, this new science would be useful politically and socially because it would improve the "difficult art of judging men according to incontestable signs."[184]

Like many other of his scientific forecasts, Comte's prediction that cerebral physiology would become one of the most important scientific developments of the nineteenth century proved erroneous. Nevertheless, his criticism of the vagueness and limited views of the psychological schools of his day as well as his insistence that psychology be considered a part of biology instead of epistemology proved valid. Lévy-Bruhl pointed out that Comte's dislike of "psychology" referred mainly to the "science of the soul obtained by the introspective method," a method that would be unacceptable to many modern psychologists. He avoided the use of the term "psychology" to denote the study of cerebral phenomena because he did not want to be confused with Cousin's metaphysical school. Lévy-Bruhl was right to insist that "it is inexact to say that there is no psychology in Comte."[185] Comte's animosity toward scholars who speculated in an a priori manner about the nature of the mind foreshadowed the position of twentieth-century behaviorists.[186] B. F. Skinner and other behavioral psychologists still contend that one cannot directly observe the processes of the mind itself and challenge the Freudian interest in the unconscious. Furthermore, Comte's vision of man as an emotional being not entirely governed by reason and his insistence that human equilibrium was very fragile would not be denied by later psychologists. Like him, they have stressed the importance of studying animal behavior, insanity, and more respectable forms of "cerebral localization" as a means of deepening one's understanding

---

[182] Comte to Valat, October 29, 1816, *CG*, 1:15.   [183] *Cours*, 1:876.   [184] Ibid., 848.
[185] Lévy-Bruhl, *Philosophie d'Auguste Comte*, 219–20.
[186] Timasheff and Theodorson, *Sociological Theory*, 19.

of human nature. In recent years, there seems to have been a revival of Comte's ideas that there are physiological bases for mental illness, that parts of the brain control certain actions, and that the brain has "functions."[187] Thus, although Comte's enthusiasm for phrenology seems singularly unscientific, at least some of his views remain worthy of attention.

[187] Young, *Mind, Brain and Adaptation*, 22–3.

Chapter 15

Cours de philosophie positive: *Sociology*

Considered from the static and dynamic points of view, man properly speaking is at heart a pure abstraction; there is nothing real except humanity, especially in the intellectual and moral order.

Comte, *Cours de philosophie positive*

POLITICAL ARGUMENTS SHOWING THE NECESSITY AND TIMELINESS OF THE SCIENCE OF SOCIETY

When Comte turned to the science of society, he had just isolated himself intellectually by adopting the regime of "cerebral hygiene" and was obsessed by his own originality. Whereas heretofore he had merely evaluated and systematized the natural sciences, now he was establishing an entirely new "order of scientific conceptions."[1] He inveighed against those who had employed and misused the terms "social physics" and "positive philosophy," which he claimed to have coined seventeen years before. Overlooking the fact that Saint-Simon had used the term "positive philosophy" in his essays written during the Empire, Comte vaguely accused him and his disciples of taking ideas from "his writings, his lessons, and . . . his conversations."[2] Comte claimed that his superiority to these and other transgressors was due to his scientific education, which had permitted him to discover the "fundamental principle and rational system" of the doctrine that would solve the philosophical dilemma of the day.[3]

---

[1] *Cours*, 2:13. See also Comte to Valat, January 5, 1840, *CG*, 1:333.

[2] Saint-Simon, "Correspondance avec M. de Redern," in *Oeuvres*, 1.1:109; *Cours*, 2:8. See the accusations Comte made against the Saint-Simonians in the foreword to the *Cours de philosophie* (1830–42), 1:vi. The foreword is not in the Hermann edition. Comte also charged a Belgian thinker with seizing his expression "social physics" and using it as the title of a book that applied statistics to the study of society, a perversion of its meaning. This scholar was Lambert-Adolphe-Jacques Quételet, whose *Sur l'homme et le développement de ses facultés, ou Essai de physique sociale* had been published by Bachelier at the same time as the second volume of the *Cours*. See Bachelier's dossier, F[18] 44, AN.

[3] *Cours*, 2:9.

To prove his originality and consistency, he had planned to append to volume 4 of the *Cours* some of his early essays, in which he had first outlined his ideas. But problems of length made him postpone this project until the *Système de politique positive*. Thus even before he was accused of betraying his principles and constructing a religion, Comte insisted that he had not changed direction. The transition from the natural sciences to social science appeared to him as logical as his future switch from social theory to religious theory. Once again Comte was engaged in a covert dialogue with the Saint-Simonians, who had charged him with having abandoned his early principles.

Comte emphasized that his goal in these lessons was purely theoretical because the main problem of social reorganization was one of logic. The primary need of his era was for a rational, coherent theory that could become the basis of a moral reorganization, which would then direct the political reorganization. Thus despite his denials, Comte was thoroughly preoccupied by politics in these lessons. His activist, radical purpose is evident in his statement that positive philosophy aimed to "seize finally the spiritual government of humanity" in order to create social and political harmony.[4] His revival of the word "spiritual," a term that had disappeared from his preceding, purely scientific volumes, shows that he was returning to the "first inspirations" of his "youth."[5]

The main principle of Comte's social physics was that order and progress were inseparable. "Real order" could not be established unless it was "fully compatible with progress," and "great progress" could not occur unless it led to the "evident consolidation of order." He based his argument on a biological analogy: "Order and progress must be as rigorously indivisible in social physics as the ideas of organization and life are in biology, whence . . . they obviously derive." Assuming that society was similar to an organism, Comte thus extended Blainville's biological distinction between statics and dynamics to society in order to give his principle a scientific aura. Throughout the last three volumes on the science of society, he sought to emphasize the scientific tone of his commentary by using biological terms, such as "social illness," "pathological case," and "chronic epidemic," to characterize French society.[6] Since 1822, when he wrote the fundamental opuscule, Comte had prided himself on having united the scientific and political points of view.

Comte also used both scientific and political arguments to bolster his case for the opportuneness of his new philosophy. The first three volumes of the *Cours* had demonstrated the scientific conditions for

[4] Ibid., 15.   [5] Ibid., 8.   [6] Ibid., 16, 48, 50.

positivism's triumph. Now he examined contemporary politics to show that positive philosophy held the key to social regeneration.

His discussion focused exclusively on France, for he believed it was there that the revolutionary movement was most advanced and positivism would first triumph. He felt the country was torn between the reactionary and revolutionary parties, each of which was favored according to whether events made people fear more the oppressive "despotism" of the old system or an "undefinable and imminent anarchy."[7] The Revolution of 1830, the almost yearly change of ministries, and the compromises made by each party served merely to reconfirm the schematic view that he had adopted twenty years before. Yet there was one change: his attention was drawn more to the "social question," the primary problem of the 1830s and 1840s.

As he had done in the fundamental opuscule, Comte criticized both political schools for their logical inconsistencies, which epitomized their incapacity to manage society. The reactionary party, or theological school, betrayed its fundamental commitment to order by making concessions to the modern trends favoring the sciences, industry, and fine arts – the very factors causing the decay of the Catholic and feudal system that it was trying to reestablish. The revolutionary party, or metaphysical school, espoused doctrines that, though useful in destroying theology, could not be the basis of a stable government.

Comte wrote a sweeping critique of the revolutionary school. He explained that its most important doctrine, the idea of freedom of conscience, was crucial in a period of transition because it facilitated the communication of ideas by means of the press and education. But it could not be a permanent principle since human reason needed fixed ideas to spur its efforts. As if remembering the distressing consequences of his own bout with incertitude in 1826, Comte wrote that the skepticism produced by the passage from "one dogmatism to another" constituted a "sort of sick perturbation, which could not be prolonged without grave dangers. . . . To examine always without ever deciding would almost be called madness in private conduct." Action, not contemplation, was the call of the "mass of men." Convinced that human beings were mediocre and egoistic, Comte maintained that freedom of conscience was also harmful because it catered to the "pride" of individuals, who were, for the most part, too "incompetent and badly prepared" to settle obscure and difficult questions "without any real control." If each individual tried to judge for himself the "general maxims indispensable to the good direction

[7] Ibid., 64.

of his personal activity," society would collapse because its very foundation would constantly be challenged in "indefinite discussion." Social order and individual liberty were, in short, "necessarily incompatible."[8] In the positive regime, the right of inquiry would be strictly limited. The elitism and contempt for human nature that had been implicit in such early writings as the "Séparation générale entre les opinions et les désirs" now became more evident.

Comte argued that the idea of liberty of conscience had three dangerous corollary doctrines. The first, the doctrine of equality, had been useful in destroying the old social hierarchy but now was hindering the establishment of a new social classification. People were intellectually and morally different and did not have the same rights. A person had only the right to fulfill the conditions necessary for his personal dignity and for the "normal free development of his personal activity once it was suitably directed." Comte did not clarify these conditions. The second offshoot of liberty of conscience was the doctrine of the sovereignty of the people, a concept that opposed the installation of any permanent and regular government by condemning "superiors to an arbitrary dependence on the multitude of their inferiors." Whereas the reactionaries unwisely encouraged the upper classes to separate themselves from the lower by depicting the "proletarians as savages ready to invade them," the revolutionaries foolishly persuaded the "masses" to rebel "blindly" against their "natural chiefs."[9] The third doctrine was that of national independence, which Comte disliked because it impeded any kind of international association.

Comte's severe criticism of freedom of conscience, individual liberty, the idea of rights, equality, popular sovereignty, and the rising sentiments of nationalism shows the extent of his disillusionment with most of the basic tenets of liberalism. Liberalism no longer appeared to him to be the correct prescription for the future. Its illogical ideas, such as an ideal state of nature, which encouraged regression, and a natural religion, which was nothing but a "vague and powerless theism," proved that the metaphysical school did not fulfill the conditions for progress any more than the theological school fulfilled those for order.[10]

Although in his fundamental opuscule Comte had favored the third party, the center party, he now was more critical of it, especially because it managed to dominate the July Monarchy. He felt it combined the vices of the other two parties. The mere fact that this "stationary" school sought to combine the monarchy with the parliamentary system indicated its lack of moral principles and new

---

[8] Ibid., 29, 30, 63, 64; see also 504.   [9] Ibid., 32, 63.   [10] Ibid., 36.

ideas.[11] The results of its incompetence were materialism, favoritism, censorship, unfair voting rights, and more class conflict.

In discussing the most dangerous problems facing French society, Comte emphasized that intellectual anarchy was causing moral anarchy, which was in turn creating political anarchy. Intellectual anarchy came from each individual's habit of voicing his opinion on any subject, while moral anarchy was epitomized by the absence of any sense of public good and by contemporary attacks on the family. "The true nature of the social malady" was not "exclusively physical" but was "above all, moral."[12]

For the first time, Comte derided social reformers and "utopian" thinkers of his day. He denounced their proposals to suppress the use of money and the death penalty, destroy the great capitals as centers of social corruption, establish a minimum daily wage, and pay everyone equal wages. Their attacks on private property and marriage struck him as equally reckless. He was as opposed to the back-to-nature movement as he was to the socialist or communist plans of economic cooperation and social justice. Many of these reforms, he believed, were too materialistic and were attractive only because they could be immediately implemented.

Comte's most acerbic comments were directed against "demented sects" who, with their "superb mediocrity," were trying to reorganize society by suppressing the two bases of family life – inheritance and marriage. Taking aim at the Saint-Simonians and their chief, Enfantin, he referred to the way "one ephemeral sect" tried to realize "its futile projects of regeneration, or rather universal domination," by strangely blending the "most licentious anarchy with the most degrading despotism." He ridiculed their revival of the "Egyptian or Hebraic theocracy, founded on a true fetishism, vainly hidden under the name of pantheism." But he was no more favorable to Charles Fourier and his disciples. Comte thought their plan to have people pursue many different occupations would abolish the division of labor, a key ingredient of progress. Moreover, Fourier's encouragement of the passions had led to the situation where now people prided themselves on having "the most disordered, the most animal" emotions.[13] Although Comte had praised phrenology for recognizing the predominance of the passions and criticized psychologists for believing they could be repressed, he insisted that the emotions should not exert excessive control over reason.[14]

Political anarchy was especially evident in the spread of political

---

[11] Ibid., 43. Saint-Simon had used the term "stationary" to define the middle party in his *Lettres de Saint-Simon à un Américain*, 169.

[12] Ibid., 59.   [13] Ibid., 35, 51–2; see also 49, 59, 85, 194, 609.

[14] M. J. Hawkins, "Reason and Sense Perception," 158.

corruption, which derived from the absence of general ideas and convictions. Writing this section after a very crooked electoral campaign, Comte was more convinced than ever that individual interests ruled both personal and governmental affairs and that mediocre political leaders were maintaining material discipline and order only by means of systematic corruption. The problem was that the abolition of the old class barriers enabled ambitious individuals to rise ever higher by exploiting the nation. Comte seemed to have in mind Guizot and Thiers, whose ambitions and political opportunism were well known.

The reason Comte criticized the metaphysical school more than the theological one was that he took the former's challenge more seriously, especially because it presented the "appearance of a new system." Whereas he firmly believed the reactionary doctrine could not appeal to any intelligent person, he knew that the new positive society could be established only with the help of metaphysical principles. Freedom of conscience was needed in the transitional period so that people could determine the principles of social reorganization and then give them their "voluntary and unanimous approval."[15] Equality and popular sovereignty reminded the new powers and social classes of the duty of devoting themselves to the public interest. So convinced was he of the need for revolutionary principles that he feared the decline of progressive ideas among the young and the weakening of the revolutionary movement after the riots of 1831–4. Thus Comte wanted to use liberalism to arrive at the positive regime. Yet because he, like Maistre, now strongly believed in the importance of faith in one's superiors, he no longer maintained, as he had in his youth, that this regime itself would be liberal.

Significantly, he blamed the stationary and reactionary parties more than the revolutionary party for the intellectual and moral anarchy that was at the heart of contemporary problems. The stationary school, that is, the center party, denied the need to search for new principles, while the reactionary school wanted to revive the "same vain principles whose inevitable decrepitude led originally to this anarchy." Unlike these two politically corrupt schools, the revolutionaries had at least "true convictions" and were not completely egotistical.[16] The revolutionary party was more qualified than the conservative party to reorganize society because it sought to establish the conditions necessary for social reconstruction. In this section of the *Cours*, Comte was evidently trying to temper his antirevolutionary statements, which he realized had previously estranged readers in 1822.

[15] *Cours*, 1:26, 41.   [16] Ibid., 47, 50.

Comte insisted on positivism's inevitable triumph over all current political doctrines. In the first three volumes of the *Cours*, he had shown that it would prevail due to the fact that it embodied a scientific and logical method. Now he affirmed that because positivism had satisfactorily reorganized all other areas of human knowledge during the last three centuries, it would inevitably unify social ideas in the same logical manner. It would make these ideas rational, coherent, consistent, homogeneous, and harmonious.

Positive philosophy would create harmony in social ideas by finding the connections among all aspects of contemporary society and also by linking this society to the past. One of the causes of the present chaos was a lack of appreciation for history. While the theological school rejected social development since the sixteenth century, the metaphysical school condemned prerevolutionary history. In contrast, positive philosophy would appreciate all of the past. It would show how contemporary society derived from the past by subordinating "humanity to an identical fundamental law of continuous development."[17]

Positive philosophy would also demonstrate its coherence and homogeneity by introducing ideas about society into all of natural philosophy. Because positivism was an "organic operation" that considered each concept in relation to the whole, all categories of ideas would be more interconnected than before. Belying his claims to be relativistic, Comte maintained that the resultant intellectual unity would be "permanent and definitive."[18]

Comte believed that positivism's all-encompassing character would enable it to appeal to all parties and classes. It would triumph because it would present a doctrine that was "more organic than the theological doctrine and more progressive than the metaphysical doctrine."[19]

To promote social order and gain the approval of the Right, positivism would oppose anarchy with its scientific spirit. It would reserve complex social questions for an elite, whose scientific training and resultant objectivity and freedom from political prejudices would help them to avoid making arbitrary pronouncements. The common people, whose voice in government was the main cause of disorder, would be excluded from the political process. Positivism would, in fact, teach all people to accept the limits of progress and resign themselves to incurable ills. It is not clear how the parties of the Left to which Comte also sought to appeal would react to such elitism and quietism.

Nevertheless, he believed the progressive aspects of positive politics

[17] Ibid., 66. [18] Ibid. [19] Ibid., 40.

were clearer and less controversial than those relating to order. To him, progress was a "continuous development with an inevitable and permanent tendency toward a determined goal," an end that was never to be fully realized, however. Positive politics would save society from its "vague" and "floating" state by revealing its true objective and the steps to approach it. Because positivism was more logical and scientific than the metaphysical school, it would also completely eliminate the lingering remains of the old theological order. Furthermore, positivism's view of liberty was superior. Whereas the metaphysical school advocated the "gradual growth of human faculties" in a negative sense because it sought to destroy whatever constrained this development, positivism asserted that "true liberty" involved a "rational submission" to the "fundamental laws of nature."[20] It would thus free society from the arbitrary commands of persons or political assemblies, which pretended to represent the popular will. Although Comte's idea of liberty was repressive, he felt being oppressed by one's fellow man was more intolerable than being subjugated by nature, which he believed was less erratic and thus less tyrannical.

Finally, he claimed that positive political philosophy was progressive because it sought to improve the miserable conditions of the lower classes. He derided the metaphysical school's solution of upward mobility, which simply unleashed popular ambitions. Because most people were destined to live precariously from the fruits of their labor, the "true social problem consists . . . in ameliorating the fundamental condition of this immense majority without destroying the class system or disturbing the general economy." He proposed to unite the spiritual power and proletarians, both of whose "legitimate rights" were unrecognized. As an "independent" and "enlightened" intermediary between the industrial leaders and the lower class, the spiritual power would equitably resolve their conflicts.[21] Thus like Marx, Comte favored an alliance of the proletarians and a special category of intellectuals. Yet unlike him, he believed that the social conflict could be resolved peacefully by improving the conditions of the lower classes without destroying the class structure. Marx would have labeled this approach utopian.

Despite his authoritarianism, elitism, social conservatism, antiparliamentary spirit, narrow conception of liberty, and recommendation of passive obedience, Comte ended this introductory chapter with a stirring appeal to the revolutionary school to support his politics. He argued that his doctrine embodied their main progressive principles while eschewing their anarchical tendencies.

In a way, Comte had to look to the Left, his former colleagues,

---

[20] Ibid., 71; see also 83.   [21] Ibid., 73.

for support because he had nowhere else to turn. The reactionaries would not have approved of a philosophy that denied God, while the center party, with its allegiance to the parliamentary system, its materialistic interests, and its politically dominant ideology, would have seen no gain in embracing positivism. Although positivism called on the "scientific spirit to regenerate the political world," Comte's "long personal experience" – his fights with the Academy and the Ecole Polytechnique – led him to abandon his earlier appeals to the scientists. He felt that their narrow specialization and egoism made them politically and socially indifferent. Priding himself on his "habitual frankness," Comte embarked on a tirade against the scientists, who, he said, were mediocrities fearful of positive philosophy because it would rob them of prestigious posts.[22] His diatribe was hardly calculated to win their approval.[23]

THE HISTORICAL INEVITABILITY OF "SOCIOLOGY":
THE REVIEW OF HIS PREDECESSORS

After having shown that positive politics was the only doctrine capable of satisfying contemporary needs for order and progress, Comte demonstrated in the next chapter that its triumph was historically inevitable. His arguments, which derived chiefly from the writings of his youth, developed one of his earliest and most interesting ideas – that the science of society was a "modern institution," for it could not have emerged without the idea of progress.[24] Whereas people had previously viewed history in terms of "oscillatory or circular movements" and at most discerned scientific progress, the French Revolution revealed for the first time the possibility of social and political progress. But only positive politics would show that the "previous transformations of humanity" in both politics and science followed a necessary and "spontaneous development" determined by natural laws. Yet when Comte stated that the positive idea of progress would eliminate metaphysical sophisms equating "continuous growth" with "unlimited growth," he seemed to contradict his own insistence on

---

[22] Ibid., 76.

[23] Comte believed that the only members of the scholarly world who would show any interest in him would be students studying scientific generalities in schools of medicine, and especially the Ecole Polytechnique. In effect, he was placing his faith in young people who had the same education he had, mainly because they appeared to be practically his only supporters at the Ecole Polytechnique.

[24] Ibid., 85. The chapter derived from the unpublished essay that Comte wrote in 1819 ("Considérations sur les tentatives qui ont été faites pour fonder la science sociale sur la physiologie et sur quelques autres sciences") and from the last part of his fundamental opuscule of 1822.

continuity.[25] Like Marx's rule of the proletariat, positivism was to be the last stage of history.

The rest of the chapter repeated what Comte had said in his fundamental opuscule about Montesquieu and Condorcet. He now considered Montesquieu to have been more profound than Condorcet, who, he suggested for the first time, had been too taken with Turgot's theory of human perfectibility.[26] Reflecting his own impatience with his contemporaries' proclamations of unlimited growth, Comte condemned more harshly than before Condorcet's "concepts of indefinite perfectibility" as "vague and irrational." His position seems to reflect his growing conservatism, despite his appeals to the Left. This tendency is exhibited in his praise of Bossuet's *Discours sur l'histoire universelle*, which, in spite of its theological argument, he found to be an "imposing model" of social thought because it linked all human events according to a single design – a teleological approach missing from Condorcet's *Esquisse*.[27]

Comte then turned to political economy, a science he once thought would be the basis of the science of society but now considered merely the last indispensable part of metaphysical philosophy. It was important because it had discredited the old economic system, stressed the development of human industry, and demonstrated the possibility of reconciling everyone's material interests. However, Comte criticized its opposition to industrial regulation, which prevented the resolution of important social questions; when a worker was replaced by a machine, it was scant consolation to tell him that everyone would be better off in the long run. Comte also rejected political economists' claim to offer a scientific model of social thought.[28] To him, they were mere metaphysicians who studied the economy in isolation, without regard to the intellectual and moral state of society or its history.[29] He implied that his philosophy would be not only

---

[25] Ibid., 83, 84.   [26] Ibid., 89.

[27] Ibid., 90, 97; see also 574. Comte later admitted that his ideas on polytheism were derived partly from Bossuet. He also went so far as to say that Bossuet was "perhaps the most powerful mind of modern times, after Descartes and Leibniz." Ibid., 411. The Positivist Library would include *Le Discours sur l'histoire universelle*, which was to precede Condorcet's *Esquisse*, as well as four other works by Bossuet: *L'Abrégé de l'histoire de France, Politique sacré* (which was to precede Maistre's *Du pape*), *Exposition de la doctrine catholique*, and *L'Histoire des variations protestantes*.

[28] *Cours*, 2:92. Comte particularly condemned the government's creation of special professorships to propagate this new "science." His bitterness may have been caused by the fact that Guizot had preferred the economist Pellegrino Rossi to him for a chair at the Collège de France.

[29] The only two thinkers who escaped Comte's censure were Adam Smith and Destutt de Tracy. According to him, the former never pretended to found a separate science of political economy, while the latter recognized its metaphysical nature. Ibid., 94.

more scientific and logical but more concerned with "human ques-tions" and more active.[30] But it is not clear what steps Comte's future interventionist state would take. His radical tone is hard to reconcile with his stress on the need for resignation and his denunciation of contemporary social reforms.[31]

In sum, in this chapter, lesson 47, Comte showed that society required a science of its own. He now replaced the term "social physics" with a new one of his own invention – "sociology."[32] He wrote and underlined the word in his manuscript on April 27, 1839.[33] Though embarrassed by coining another neologism, especially after he had strongly criticized political economists for creating a special-ized, scientific-sounding language, he defended himself by saying he had a "legitimate right" to invent terms.[34] In doing so, he was fol-lowing the example of Saint-Simon, who had also felt compelled to coin terms such as *industriel* and *industrielisme* to refer to new devel-opments.[35] Creating the word "sociology" was Comte's way of stak-ing a claim to originality; to him, it was proof that he had invented a new science.

THE MAIN CHARACTERISTICS OF SOCIOLOGY

Sociology referred to the "positive study of all the fundamental laws pertaining to social phenomena." It was therefore the "science of social development" and the "new political philosophy." Comte defined its method, doctrine, and aim, continually contrasting it to the "theological-metaphysical state," which was "ideal in its proce-dure, absolute in its conception, and arbitrary in its application."[36]

Sociology's method would subordinate imagination to the obser-vation of facts so that, in the future, reason would take over the "reins of human government." Yet sociology would offer imagina-tion the "most vast and fertile" field for discovering and coordinat-ing facts.[37]

By replacing the theologians' and metaphysicians' search for causes

---

[30] Ibid., 96.   [31] Arnaud, *Le "Nouveau Dieu,"* 58.   [32] *Cours,* 2:88.

[33] See the manuscript of volume 4 of the *Cours de philosophie positive,* N.a.fr. 17906, fol. 15, BN; "Tableau du nombre de jours," in "Du temps dans le travail intellectuel," ed. Laffitte, 438.

[34] *Cours,* 2:88. On Comte's ambivalence toward the use of neologisms, see also Comte to Valat, December 25, 1824, *CG,* 1:150.

[35] Saint-Simon, "Aux Anglais et aux français qui sont zélés pour le bien public," in Taylor, *Saint-Simon (1760–1825),* 145. See also ibid., 307n47; Manuel, *Saint-Simon,* 189. Comte describes his problems coming up with new terms in Comte to Mme Auguste Comte, November 4, 1842, *CG,* 2:102.

[36] *Cours,* 2:88, 101, 102, 122.   [37] Ibid., 102, 279.

with the discovery of laws, the sociological doctrine would be relative instead of absolute. "Exact reality can never, in any way, be perfectly unveiled." Yet Comte was unwilling to accept the skeptical attitude implied by relativism. He argued that scientific ideas would acquire a new "solidity" and "stability," which would be "very superior to their original vague immutability."[38] There would be no uncertainty or disagreement, for he assumed that everyone would agree on the validity of these laws.

As for its aim, sociology would show the necessity of recognizing the limits of political power. Comte claimed that the main intellectual cause of the present political upheaval was the theological and metaphysical parties' assertion that it was within human power to construct an "immutable type of government." In fact, although social phenomena were the most complex and therefore the most modifiable, they were subject to natural laws. Change was possible only if it accorded with the state of civilization. Sociology, Comte felt, was more favorable to human dignity because it did not treat people like passive, machine-like creatures directed by a supreme authority. Rather, it required that they simply assume the role ascribed to them by nature. To him, the "principal tendencies of humanity" had an "imposing character of authority" that had to be respected by all legislators.

Adopting Condorcet's useful "artifice" and assuming that all societies underwent the same fixed evolution, he defined humanity as a "single people to whom one could refer all the successive social modifications really observed in distinct populations."[39] Already in 1839 he seemed ready to make humanity the centerpiece of his social theory. Instead of being directed by a legislator as in previous theories, individuals would be subordinated to humanity. Thus, despite his criticism of metaphysical entities, Comte gave authority to a new abstraction.

He tried to reinforce his ideas of relativism and the limitation of political action by stressing the importance of predicting social developments. Once all social phenomena were subject to natural laws, he assumed sociology would be able to make forecasts. If the course of events could be changed by a legislator or a genius, prediction would be impossible, and there would be no "scientific security."[40] It was this ability to make predictions that made sociology most scientific and useful.

To distinguish sociology's subject matter and to guarantee its scientific character, Comte borrowed the terms "statics" and "dynamics," which he had employed in discussing the other sciences,

---

[38] Ibid., 103–4. [39] Ibid., 123. [40] Ibid., 108.

especially biology. Just as biology was divided into the study of organization (anatomy) and life (physiology), sociology would have two parts: the analysis of the conditions of existence and the study of the laws of continuous movement. It would thus observe every social phenomenon according to its relationships with other, coexisting phenomena and to its connection with the past and future of human development. "Social statics" would be devoted to the first point of view, which was ultimately the study of order, while "social dynamics" would be consecrated to the second, which was essentially the analysis of progress.[41] Adopting Hume's definition of law as the study of the relations of similitude or affiliation through time, Comte said that social statics studied the laws of "coexistence" of social phenomena, while social dynamics revealed the laws of their "succession."[42] These two areas of study were as inseparable in sociology as they were in biology. In effect, Comte was warning that the sociologist could not discover the source or nature of society; he could explain only the way its phenomena were related in space and time.

Social statics was the foundation of Comte's political philosophy. It assumed that social phenomena were intimately related:

> It is clear, in effect, that not only political institutions and social customs, on the one hand, and morals and ideas, on the other, must be always interdependent, but also that this whole is always attached by its nature to the corresponding state of the integral development of humanity, considered in all its diverse modes of activity – intellectual, moral, and physical.[43]

Thus no aspect of society could be analyzed apart from the whole; the entire social organism had to be studied first, like a living organism in biology. In fact, because social phenomena were the most complex, they displayed more solidarity and harmony than any other phenomena. Social statics would thus study the "actions and reactions" of the different parts of the social system. Just as biological anatomy deduced organs from functions and vice versa, social statics, that is, "social anatomy," would deduce the characteristics of one part of the social system from those of the others.[44] Social consensus was the keystone of social statics and therefore of Comte's political theory.

Since all parts of the "social organism" were intimately connected,

---

[41] Ibid., 110. Comte also argued that the laws of social statics corresponded to man's intellectual instinct for order and harmony, while the laws of social dynamics accorded with his "irresistible tendency" to believe in the "perpetuity of recurrences that have already been observed." Ibid., 736–7.

[42] Ibid., 123. [43] Ibid., 114. [44] Ibid., 111.

political institutions were related not only to one another but to social conditions, with which they had to be in harmony. As a result, the political regime played an important role in maintaining and improving social consensus. Moreover, political authority was held by the most powerful members of society, an idea shared by Marx, who felt the state was run for the benefit of the ruling class. And when Comte claimed that reigning ideas were always closely associated with the interests of the most powerful social group, he was not far from Marx's idea of superstructure. To take an example, Comte asserted that Galileo's "intellectual revolution" transformed not only the religious system but also the social system, because the idea that the earth was the center of the universe had been connected with the "system of controlling opinions" manipulated by the dominant social classes.[45]

The idea of social interdependence provided Comte with another argument against exaggerated claims for the power of political systems to effect change. An effective, strong political power was one that followed the main inclinations of society and was in harmony with the corresponding state of civilization. Ultimately, it was limited to improving the "natural and involuntary order" toward which all human societies were tending. Aware of the conservative tenor of his argument, Comte denied that his doctrine displayed an inappropriate "optimism," "social tepidness," or "political indifference."[46] Though insistent that social phenomena were the most easily modified, he gave no concrete examples and failed to support the political activism that he felt was at the heart of his doctrine. His ideas seemed closer to the liberals' noninterventionist principles than he would have cared to admit.

The most striking weakness of Comte's discussion was his failure to define precisely what he meant by "social." Moreover, because everything was interdependent and no aspect of society could be studied in isolation, sociology encompassed all realms of thought and activity, thereby losing its meaning.

Although the foundation of sociology was social statics, its main object was social dynamics. Social dynamics was based on and verified the laws of social statics because "the laws of existence are manifested especially in movement."[47] It also highlighted the solidarity among social phenomena, for when one part of the social organism changed, so did the other parts.

Social dynamics was the source of the idea of progress, which, Comte believed, gave sociology its most distinctive character. He did not, however, equate progress with perfection. He insisted that

---

[45] Ibid., 1:360.   [46] Ibid., 2:117–18.   [47] Ibid., 149.

positivism would never be able to create the perfect society because the moral and mental weaknesses of man would never disappear. Social abuses in the positive age would also arise from the scientists' inveterate charlatanism, the intellectuals' tendency to oppress the people, and the temporal power's efforts to usurp the authority of the spiritual power. Comte did not want to be accused of utopianism and went so far as to say that society would inevitably experience a "spontaneous decline."[48] Progress was not to be confused with the growth of human happiness, a metaphysical concept that was too vague to be admitted into the positive system.[49] Thus, to him, progress meant "development," a biological term free of moral connotations. Biological studies of an organism at different ages simply verified that "development" took place.[50] Historical studies would do the same for society.

The main theme of social dynamics was continuous, necessary, orderly, and limited development. Each social state grew out of the preceding one and was the requisite motor of the next. Intellectual evolution – especially scientific development – was the most incontestable and advanced form of progress, serving as the "fundamental guide" for progress as a whole. Almost in Hegelian terms, Comte declared that even "men of genius" were only "organs of a predetermined movement."[51] He seemed to feel that this argument enhanced his authority by making him the agent of progress.

Throughout evolution, the physical, intellectual, and moral conditions of man improved as did human nature. Referring to Lamarck's theory, Comte argued that man developed his physical, moral, and intellectual faculties by employing them. Thus through exercise, the unique characteristics of the human species – intelligence and sociability – would eventually become more dominant within both the individual and society.

Man's moral, that is, social, sentiments would develop to the highest possible degree once the new science of society achieved its goal of showing that the "mass of the human species" constitutes in "space and time" an enormous "eternal social unity," whose members cooperate in the "fundamental evolution of humanity." This "truly capital and very modern conception" of the solidarity and evolution of humanity would "later" become the "principal rational

---

[48] Ibid., 774.
[49] To Comte, happiness depended not so much on progress as on the harmony between the development of one's faculties and the surrounding circumstances. Since these circumstances differed from individual to individual and could not be compared, questions of happiness were irresolvable.
[50] Ibid., 124.   [51] Ibid., 125.

basis of positive morality."[52] Here one can see the roots of Comte's Religion of Humanity.

He defined the development of humanity as a "simple spontaneous growth that is maintained by a suitable cultivation of the fundamental faculties" of human nature.[53] The improvement of human nature was thus both a cause and an effect of the development of humanity. Yet although the faculties would improve, Comte rejected Lamarck's theory that species created new faculties as they developed new needs. The basic characteristics of the faculties and their relationships would not change. As in his discussion of progress, Comte put certain limits on the improvement of human nature, going so far as to claim that human nature was invariable. It is therefore unclear to what extent he thought human nature could actually change.[54]

In spite of Comte's claim to have eliminated the word "cause" from positive philosophy, he maintained that the "causes" of the variations in the evolution of humanity were race, climate, and political action.[55] Only the latter involved human intervention. Yet people, constrained by their physical, intellectual, and moral environment, could not govern phenomena. They could only modify humanity's spontaneous development in terms of intensity and speed. (The speed of progress was affected by such factors as the driving force of ennui, urbanization, and population growth leading to a high proportion of young people, who represented the spirit of innovation.) Ultimately, people had to support the dominant tendencies of the period, which would enable them to lessen or shorten crises.

Comte's vague theory of human intervention was characterized by a mixture of fatalism in the face of crisis and optimism in regard to the general movement of history. Convinced that the individual had limited influence, he went so far as to claim that Julian the Apostate, Philip II, and Napoleon had left "no profound trace" on human development because their efforts went against the progressive movement of civilization. But considering that Comte himself had witnessed the Empire's impact on all aspects of French life, it is difficult to understand how he could have maintained that Napoleon had not affected history. Also, in arguing that the "fundamental march" of social development was "attached to the essence" of

---

[52] Ibid., 136.   [53] Ibid., 129.

[54] An amusing example of his arbitrariness was his criticism of Gall for asserting that military tendencies were a fixed part of human nature. Since Comte wanted positivism to be a pacifist doctrine, he maintained that the warrior spirit would decrease with the development of civilization. His views on the progress of human nature were more idealistic than scientific.

[55] Ibid., 131.

society, which could never be changed by progress, he seemed close to the metaphysicians.[56] In effect, he was reifying society and making it an all-powerful entity whose "nature" was its driving force. Although he pointed out that the assumption of the uniformity of progress was necessary for sociology to be a science, that did not mean the assumption was true.

THE THREE METHODS OF SOCIOLOGY: OBSERVATION, EXPERIMENTATION, AND COMPARISON

Since sociology was the most complex science, it had more methods of investigation than the other sciences. Observation was the first scientific method. Comte maintained that, contrary to general assumptions, social facts were not the easiest to perceive. Mundane social phenomena, which were the most important of all, were particularly difficult to discern because when one was in society, it was hard to notice the commonplace. A scientist of society needed at least a provisional social theory to connect discrete facts and to place himself outside of society so that he could examine it. Also, a theory enabled him to be more impartial in regard to social phenomena, which normally provoked the most intense prejudices. Comte's suggestion that scientific objectivity was an unattainable ideal in sociology was one of the most original ideas in the *Cours*.

Since every aspect of society had multiple connections when the whole was kept in mind, Comte believed the means of sociological observation would be so extensive that they would include the study of commonplace events, apparently insignificant customs, diverse types of monuments, languages, and other incidents of social life. Comte's prediction has been verified by recent social and cultural history, which has brought to light the significance of different aspects of everyday life, stressed the importance of studying ordinary texts to understand society at large, and looked for interconnections among all forms of discourse.

Yet going against important nineteenth-century innovations, Comte condemned social statistics, that is, the application of the calculus of probabilities to social phenomena, and he challenged biblical critics who cast doubt on the validity of historical documents. Sociologists, he said, had to use other people's testimony just as other scientists needed to have faith in the work of their predecessors.

As for experimentation, the second means of scientific investigation, Comte felt its use was as problematic in sociology as it was in biology. Because a disturbance in any single social element affected

[56] Ibid., 134, 165.

all the others, it was impossible to isolate sufficiently any of the circumstances surrounding a phenomenon or the consequences of its actions. Instead, as in biology, one must study pathological cases, which provided the scientist with a type of indirect experimentation. When one studied a sick social organism, such as society during the Revolution, one could acquire a better understanding of the laws of social harmony and history by examining how they were troubled by accidental or temporary causes. Here Comte was applying Broussais's principle to society to show that, in cases of social disorder, natural laws were still at work and phenomena were being modified in their "diverse degrees," but not in their nature or their relationships. The scientific analysis of these modifications could deepen the "positive theory of normal existence" because the pathological was simply a variation of the normal.[57]

Comparison was sociology's third method of scientific investigation, as it was in biology. In sociology, there would be three types of comparison. The first would be that between human and animal societies and would further the study of social interconnections. The second would be basically anthropological, comparing the different existing states of human society, that is, savage and civilized peoples. Comte thought that all the various phases of evolution were represented on the earth and that because human nature was the same everywhere, human development was the same too. The third method, the historical method, would consist of comparing consecutive social states and would be sociology's chief means of scientific investigation.

Comte claimed that history was a "real science" in itself. Based on the example of the animal series in biology, it would establish the social series. This series was the "appreciation of the diverse stages of humanity," showing "the continued growth of every disposition – physical, intellectual, moral, or political – and the indefinite decrease of the opposite disposition."[58] The study of history would enable one to foresee the rise and fall of these various dispositions and thus guide political action. The historical method would also help develop social sentiments because it would demonstrate that the actions of previous generations affected present civilization. A new sense of human unity would emerge from seeing the social solidarity among not only individuals and peoples, but also generations. The feeling of solidarity was thus both synchronic and diachronic. This appreciation of the past, lacking in both the theological and metaphysical philosophies, would spread downward from the elite to everyone.

The historical method would make a major contribution to the

---

[57] Ibid., 143.   [58] Ibid., 150–1.

positive method itself. The idea of progress distinguished sociology from biology and prevented the former from being reduced to the latter. The establishment of sociology would lead to the historical consideration of every science, for in terms of logic the historical method perfected and completed the positive method. Moreover, because all social phenomena were interrelated and society had to be studied as a whole, the history of one science, including pure political history, would make no sense unless it were attached to the study of the general progress of all of humanity. In short, Comte was suggesting that the positive theory of social evolution had to be the basis of the study of all the various sciences. Although sociology was the last science, it would dominate all the others.

THE RELATION OF SOCIOLOGY TO THE OTHER SCIENCES

One of the main points of the *Cours* was that in order for the science of society to be productive and convincing, it had to rest on knowledge of the sciences preceding it in the hierarchy. By studying the positive method in the other, simpler sciences, sociologists would learn "what constitutes the real explanation of any phenomena, the invariable conditions of a truly rational exploration whether by pure observation or by experimentation, and . . . the use of scientific hypotheses."[59] The reason the theological and metaphysical philosophies were unable to solve social questions was that they did not require this rigorous scientific training.

Sociologists had to learn the laws of society's physical environment, that is, the external conditions of human existence, from inorganic philosophy. Knowledge of inorganic philosophy was necessary because astronomical, physical, and chemical conditions (along with human action) determined the *speed* of progress. Moreover, man's growing action on the exterior world was one of the motors of progress and was based on knowledge of physical laws, especially chemical laws. Thus a grasp of these laws was essential to an understanding of the material basis of social development. Like the improvement of human nature, the growing action of man on nature was, to Comte, both a cause and an effect of progress.

Biology, particularly the study of moral and intellectual phenomena, was crucial to sociology because it revealed the laws of human nature. Moreover, biology established the organic conditions of human sociability. Comte claimed that the theory of the conditions of existence would replace the old dogma of final causes. Sociology would use this new principle to present as "inevitable" that which

[59] Ibid., 167.

first seemed "indispensable" and vice versa. He claimed there was always a "necessary harmony . . . between the possible and the indispensable." Expressing his optimism, determinism, and faith in the natural order, Comte fully adopted Maistre's aphorism: "*Everything that is necessary exists.*"[60] Again, Comte seemed very close to Hegel on this point.[61]

Although sociology would depend on the other sciences, it would introduce to them its own special methodology and superior means of investigation: the study of history. It would show that each scientific discovery was a "true social phenomenon," one that was an integral part of the development of humanity. Sociology would also lead to the first valid history of the sciences – the "theory of the real connection among the principal discoveries."[62] Knowledge of that history was necessary to understand sociology and would help scientific progress by systematizing and directing research.

In conclusion, Comte asserted that once sociology was established, it would make the cultivation of the other sciences more rational. All of them would be considered "distinct branches" of a "single trunk." This trunk – sociology – would always dominate the other specialties and would solve the problem of the narrowing, isolating effects of the scientific division of labor. Sociology would connect the sciences by showing their mutual relations and by subordinating all scientific work to the theory of human development. Sociology would thus intervene "in all the possible orders of human speculations" to make the consideration of the social state prevail.[63] It would, in effect, absorb all the other sciences.

What did the dominance of sociology mean to the individual scientist? Comte made it clear that the scientist would not be able to create his own path; even his choice of subject would be controlled by the sociologist. And he would not be able to pride himself on his discoveries, for they would be considered a social product, not the result of his own efforts. It is not surprising that the members of the Academy of Sciences found Comte's doctrine uncongenial.

THE PRINCIPLES OF SOCIAL STATICS

Lesson 50, covering social statics, was written in the old tradition of moral philosophy and is surprisingly unscientific and banal. It

---

[60] Ibid., 162, 164.   [61] Enthoven, ed., in ibid., 162n7.

[62] *Cours*, 2:171. Lagrange's works, especially his "sublime chapters" on the development of mechanics in *Mécanique analytique*, were the model for Comte's historical approach to the sciences. Ibid., 174.

[63] Ibid., 170.

confirms Comte's statement that social dynamics was more interesting than social statics and thus better understood. He discussed three subjects, each more complex and specialized than the preceding one: first the individual, then the family, and finally society (the whole human species).

Relying on Gall, Comte argued that individuals were inherently sociable and were not originally driven to live in society by rational calculations about the utility of joining forces to fulfill their needs. Here he seemed to be making use of Adam Ferguson's ideas in order to counter social contract theory, utilitarianism, and liberalism. Above all, he wished to show that prevailing ideas of individualism could not explain the formation and maintenance of society and thus could not be the foundation of a valid social theory. In Comte's view, people could not even perceive how their own interests would be satisfied in society until after social evolution was already fairly advanced.

Two aspects of human nature determined the character of social existence. The first was that man's affections were stronger than his intellect. Although the intellect was man's primary characteristic and responsible for social development, it was the least energetic of all faculties. The use of the intellect caused fatigue, and man was naturally lazy. The affections, less noble but more energetic, were necessary to stimulate the intellect. Comte did not find this domination of the affections over the intellect regrettable, and he insisted that it would never change. Although the intellectual faculties would become stronger with the advance of civilization, they would still need the superior power of the affections to rouse them from their habitual torpor, give them direction, and subject them to the control of reality. Comte pointed to the example of mystics, who in their effort to become pure intellects found themselves in a state of "transcendental idiocy," where they were "eternally absorbed by an essentially futile and almost stupid contemplation of the divine majesty."[64] Thus before Clotilde de Vaux entered his life, he knew from his own experience that emotional life was crucial to a sane and productive existence and that the affective faculties took precedence over the intellectual ones. Despite his indifference to the contemporary romantic movement, he shared its novelists' preoccupation with the role of the passions in dictating human behavior and enriching existence.

The second main characteristic of human nature was that within the realm of man's affections, his egoistic, personal instincts were stronger than his noble, social ones. The superior power of these

---

[64] Ibid., 179.

personal instincts gave an aim, direction, and impulse to action. They were also the basis of morality, for man could wish for others only what he wished for himself. Repressing all personal interests would only lead to a "vague and sterile charity."[65] Comte therefore adopted the Christian maxim Love thy neighbor as thyself. At the same time, he criticized the eighteenth-century metaphysicians' belief that man was entirely selfish. To Comte, the social instincts were vitally important because they represented the basis of society and the source of man's happiness. Although they would never become dominant, they would be strengthened as civilization developed.

In conclusion, the main motor of existence was the personal instinct, moderated by intellectual activity and the social instinct. The development of these two moderating influences within human nature would constitute the essence of positive morality.

In fact, Comte believed that proper intellectual development increased the "sentiments of general sympathy" by "dismissing egoistic impulses" and "inspiring a wise . . . predilection for the fundamental order." Comte went so far as to assert that "no great intellect" could develop "in a suitable manner without a certain amount of universal benevolence," which alone could give him a lofty goal. In asserting that great thinkers were models of morality with strong feelings of "natural benevolence," Comte was reflecting the great need that he felt in his personal life to develop his "social affections."[66] Despite his problems with his friends and loved ones, Comte was increasingly convinced that he was becoming a morally superior being. He was already certain that he was intellectually exceptional.

The second division of social statics was the family, composed of at least the couple, who married to satisfy and contain the "most energetic instinct of our animality" – the sexual instinct.[67] The family was the primary unit of society, for the individual had to learn to live with at least one other person. Domestic life thus represented a transitional period, preparing the individual for society by first stimulating his sympathies.

Despite his own marital difficulties, Comte had a very traditional view of the family and was horrified by contemporary reformers who attacked it. Positivism, he said, would lead to its regeneration and would recognize that the family, like all associations, rested on inequalities. The "perfect intimacy" of the family had to derive from a common goal and from the "natural" and "indispensable" dual

[65] Ibid., 181. [66] Ibid., 181-2.
[67] Overlooking the loose behavior of his youth, he added that in marriage the sexual instinct became the "source of the sweetest harmony instead of troubling the world by its impetuous excesses." This passage is significant because it shows that at this point Comte was not advocating chastity. Ibid., 184.

subordination that was necessary to achieve this goal.[68] This subordination consisted of that of the sexes, which was the origin of the family, and that of the generations, which maintained it. Because progress made each social element fulfill its function in the general harmony, it developed and accentuated sexual and generational inequalities, in fact, all the disparities that existed in society. Comte's position is markedly different from that of Condorcet, who believed that with progress inequalities would diminish.

Comte's principal point in discussing the sexes was to show that marriage demanded the "inevitable natural subordination of woman to man." Arguing against the contemporary movement for the equality between the sexes, Comte declared that woman was man's inferior. Always in a "state of continued infancy," she was far from the "ideal type of the race."[69] And to prove his point, Comte created a stereotypical image of woman, which reflected nineteenth-century prejudices, including the idea that biology is destiny. As Londa Schiebinger and Thomas Laqueur have recently shown, writers beginning in the late eighteenth century were increasingly interested in delineating the differences between men and women to reinforce the political subordination of the latter, and they sought to found these differences on biological distinctions. One important book connecting physical and social differences was Rousseau's *Emile*, which Comte owned and had read as early as 1818. Another popular book was Pierre Roussel's *Système physique et moral de la femme*. A doctor and Idéologue who had influenced Cabanis, Roussel showed that women's differences extended throughout the bodily organs. These differences were not only skeletal but moral and intellectual, because the mind and spirit were physical organs.[70] Comte also owned this book, which he kept in his most important bookcase, and he subscribed to similar views.

According to Comte, woman's reason was weak and her character imperfect. More sensitive physically and morally than man, woman was unable to think abstractly or in a concentrated fashion and thus could not govern either the family or the state. Although women were intellectually inferior to men, they were superior in terms of their sympathies and sociability. Their function was to stimulate the "social instinct" and thereby modify the "general direction" of

---

[68] Ibid., 183.   [69] Ibid., 185–6.

[70] Pierre Roussel, *Système physique et moral de la femme* . . . (Paris, 1775); Thomas Laqueur, *Making Sex: Body and Gender from the Greeks to Freud* (Cambridge, Mass.: Harvard University Press, 1990), 5–6; Londa Schiebinger, *The Mind Has No Sex? Women in the Origins of Modern Science* (Cambridge, Mass.: Harvard University Press, 1989), 220–2. On Roussel, see also Staum, *Cabanis*, 215. Having read *Emile*, Comte had mentioned Rousseau's advice on breast feeding in a letter to Valat, November 17, 1818, *CG*, 1:46.

society, which stemmed from the "excessively cold or unrefined reason that characterizes . . . the preponderant sex." Comte felt that it was the strength of the intellectual faculties and the greater energy of the social affections that separated humans from animals. The former was the "most essential" attribute and justified the necessary domination of men, while the latter characterized the moderating influence of women.[71] Therefore, as early as 1839, Comte was upholding a sexual division of labor whereby men and women were opposites and to a certain extent complemented each other, despite their inequalities.[72] Important to social harmony, the female sex had the task of developing the sympathies and injecting a warmth and refinement into the male-dominated society. Referring to the "feminine genius," Comte also began in 1840 to exalt the complementary role women would play as aides to the spiritual power; their feelings would soften the dominant material activity of society, while the spiritual power's intelligence would modify it.[73] The association between the intellectuals and women in the political sphere corresponded to the cooperation of the intellectual and moral tendencies in the biological sphere.[74] Even before meeting Clotilde de Vaux, Comte was dreaming about the type of woman who could help him in his mission.

Comte's discussion of the sexes reflects not only the increasingly dominant ideology of the separation of spheres but his relationship to his wife, who was the opposite of the ideal woman he described. He repeatedly complained about her desire to control him and her failure to love him. In one passage emphasizing man's need to develop his affections within the family, Comte seemed to be describing his own plight:

> Even the most eminent men who succeed in turning . . . their sympathetic instincts toward the whole of the [human] species or society, are almost always pushed to this by the moral disappointments of a domestic life that has failed to achieve its goal . . . and no matter how sweet the imperfect compensation may be to them, the abstract love of the species can never include this full satisfaction of our affectionate dispositions, which can be obtained only by a very close attachment, especially to an individual.[75]

Here Comte appeared to be acknowledging that he had turned to humanity because his life with Caroline was a disaster.

---

[71] *Cours*, 2:186–7.
[72] On the notion of "complementarity," see Schiebinger, *The Mind Has No Sex?* 214–27.
[73] *Cours*, 2:300.   [74] Vernon, "The Political Self," 272.   [75] *Cours*, 2:192.

The second type of subordination within the family was that of children to their parents. Taking a very conservative stance, Comte maintained that since the family was a model of society, obedience and command were properly learned at home. Submission in society at large should be as respectful, complete, and spontaneous as that of children, while authority should be as absolute, affectionate, devoted, and protective as that of parents. Comte attacked reformers who undermined parental authority by exaggerating the influence of education on society and preaching the abolition of inheritance.

Society, which was composed of families, was the third and last division of social statics. Comte emphasized that society was superior to the individual especially because of the greater diversity of its functions. Society presented a "marvelous spectacle" of a great number of distinct individuals working in separate tasks but, nevertheless, cooperating to further a common goal, one that connected them with their predecessors and descendants.[76] In fact, society could not exist without this division of labor, which extended to all individuals, classes, and nations. As the division of labor and social cooperation developed, so did society.

Whereas social instincts, that is, the affections, dominated family life, which did not rely heavily on a highly developed division of labor, the intellect presided over social life. Social ties were more intellectual than affectionate because people's common interests and opinions kept them together. But the social contract theory was wrong when it claimed that this cooperation produced society in the first place. Comte insisted that society derived from the alliance of families motivated by their social or sympathetic instincts, and it had to exist *before* cooperation could begin.

Once society was constituted, a division of labor to make people interdependent was required for its continued existence. The division of labor became the main cause of the development and extension of society. But it ironically threatened the continued growth of civilization. As people grew more specialized, their intellect and social affections narrowed. Comte borrowed Adam Smith's example of the worker devoting his life to making pinheads and compared him to the scholar who was exclusively preoccupied with resolving a few equations or classifying a couple of insects; both epitomized indifference to human affairs. Like Marx, Comte condemned the "sort of human automatism" that the progress of civilization produced.[77] But unlike Marx, he did not want to challenge it, for he felt it was crucial to social stability and development.

Instead, Comte counted on the state to restrain the particularism

[76] Ibid., 191.   [77] Ibid., 196.

of society, which was reflected in the dispersion of ideas, sentiments, and interests. It must connect the individual with society and intervene in all activities to maintain the idea of the whole and the feeling of solidarity. To make society prevail over the individual, it should have supreme power in all domains, including the intellectual and moral.

He felt the state would have to assume a new intellectual and moral role because as people grew more specialized, they would have to rely increasingly on unfamiliar intellectual and moral superiors whose aptitudes were becoming more developed. With the growth of moral and intellectual inequalities, these superiors would become more dominant. Since the government arose spontaneously from the heart of society itself, it would become more moral and intellectual. In this way, Comte demonstrated that the positive state required both a spiritual and a temporal government. But at the same time, he gave the state the potential to become a dangerously strong power, one completely at odds with liberal theory and his own distrust of politics.

He believed that this state would be easily established because he assumed there existed in "the majority of men a . . . disposition to obedience" and a natural respect for "every superiority." Criticizing the current "universal thirst for command," he claimed that people could recognize "how sweet it is to obey" when they had "wise and worthy guides" who would free them from the "heavy responsibility" of directing their own conduct.[78] In Comte's mind, there was no need for a violent revolution to achieve his state; it would come about simply because men were inherently submissive and intellectually and morally mediocre. Based on the Maistre-like assumption that men had to be dominated by an all-pervasive government to counter their own weakness, positivism could scarcely be called a noble, uplifting creed.

A simplistic, tripartite approach pervaded all of sociology. The schema of social statics derived from Gall's phrenology, which asserted that there were three parts to the brain: the basic penchants or instincts, located in the back, the social sentiments in the middle, and the intellectual faculties in the front. The individual was associated with the simple penchants, the family with the more complex social sentiments, and society with the even more complex intellectual faculties. Morality also had three corresponding parts. First it was personal, disciplining the individual's drive toward self-preservation. Then it was domestic, for it involved subordinating as much as possible egoism to the sympathies. Finally, morality was social,

[78] Ibid., 200.

focusing all the penchants and faculties on the social economy and making sure that the "general love of humanity" prevailed.[79] Comte was already preoccupied with the idea of directing all of man's activities to the improvement of "humanity," which represented the "whole" that had to dominate.

THE PRINCIPLES OF SOCIAL DYNAMICS

In the last lesson of the fourth volume of the *Cours*, Comte covered the basic principles of social dynamics, a subject that would take up all of volume 5 and more than half of volume 6. History was the field of sociology he was most eager to develop.

Social development consisted of the growth of the faculties that distinguished man from the animals. Contrary to Rousseau, Comte argued that advanced civilization was a fulfillment of nature, because human faculties grew only in the mature state of social life for which they were destined. People's intellectual and moral faculties could not develop if they had no sense of security, which derived from their successful action on nature. The "ideal type" of progress for both the individual and society involved not only "subordinating as much as possible" the personal instincts to the social ones, but also "subjugating" the passions to the "increasingly preponderant intellect so that the individual is increasingly identified with the species."[80]

In terms of the pattern of progress, intellectual evolution was the predominant element and came first, for history was the story of the "emancipation of human reason." Provoked by the appetites, passions, and sentiments, the intellect regularly and continuously stimulated the other aspects of social development, which in turn influenced its own evolution:

One has always recognized . . . the history of society as being dominated above all by the history of the human mind. It follows . . . that in this intellectual history, we should always attach ourselves to the predominant considerations of the most general and most abstract conceptions. . . . It is, . . . in short, the general history of *philosophy* . . . that must necessarily preside over . . . our historical analysis.[81]

In particular, the most complex moral and social ideas determined the intellectual state of each period. For Comte, as for Hegel, the history of the mind reflected history in general.

Both histories reflected the law of three stages. This law was the

[79] Ibid., 297.   [80] Ibid., 204.   [81] Ibid., 210, 379.

great law of sociology because it encompassed the whole history of civilization; it was applicable to the intellectual realm as well as to the moral, social, material, and political realms, for they were all interrelated.

In reviewing the law of three stages, Comte repeated what he had said before, but for the first time in the *Cours*, he used more boldly the words "spiritual" and "temporal," which he admitted borrowing from Catholicism.[82] The spiritual power referred to the speculative or moral authority, which regulated thoughts and inclinations, while the temporal power referred to the active or strictly political power, which had jurisdiction over actions. Spiritual evolution (intellectual, moral, and social progress) was inseparable from temporal, or material, development.

Intellectually, the theological stage was characterized by man's effort to explain the essence and causes of phenomena by relating them to his own nature, which he knew best. Early man's idea that phenomena had a life of their own and that there was an invisible world of superhuman beings in complete control was the theory he needed to link facts. Comte emphasized that in this stage man considered himself the center and ruler of the world, for he sought to stress positivism's recognition of the limits of human power. Morally, the theological stage was characterized by supernatural agents, which man called upon to help him modify his environment. Socially, theology furnished the first social organization because it offered a system of shared intellectual opinions. It also established a special class, that of the priests, who devoted themselves only to speculation and thus created the first permanent division between theory and practice, an important political improvement. In the material realm, militarism dominated the theological stage because it represented the only action that primitive man could sustain. It promoted habits of regularity and discipline and associated isolated families for war or defense. The military and theological powers depended on each other politically and, despite their rivalry, had a deep affinity. The military needed theological consecration to enforce subordination and maintain its power, while theologians required the military to consolidate and extend their authority. Both were also united by a common antipathy to the sciences and industry.

Once the theological system had fulfilled its destiny and was challenged by positive philosophy, it began to decline. By arguing that from the outset man subjected the most common and simplest facts, such as weight, to laws, Comte sought to prove that the positive philosophy existed, even if only faintly, as early as the theological

[82] Ibid., 228.

stage. Intellectual progress represented a slow gradual evolution from a simple beginning.

Theology declined as it was challenged by the scientific spirit, which fulfilled people's needs much more effectively. Theology sought to maintain its position by repressing the mind and ruling by "an oppressive terror and an apathetic languor."[83] As its beliefs grew controversial, social divisions arose.

A transitory period, the metaphysical stage, soon appeared. Intellectually, its methods and doctrines were only modifications of the theological stage, from which it derived. The substitution of absurd entities for divinities reflected the same search for a rigorous supreme unity. Socially, its critical spirit prevented the organization of human beings. In the material realm, the metaphysical spirit was as vague and equivocal as it was in the spiritual because society was partly military and partly industrial. The spiritual power, that is, the metaphysicians, and the temporal power, namely the lawyers, were political allies. The philosophical ascendancy of the former depended on the political preponderance of the latter and vice versa.

The positive stage was superior to the other two stages because it developed in man "an unshakable vigor and a deliberate steadfastness which derived directly from human nature and did not depend on any external assistance of illusory obstacle."[84] Only its conceptions could establish a true intellectual community. Positivism would reunite, direct, and stimulate mankind to create a new, industrial, and pacific society in which the industrialists would be united with the scientists because of their natural affinity for one another.

In sum, Comte was sure that his fundamental law of sociology, like all scientific theories, was correct because it confirmed the "ordinary instinct of public reason." Common sense already divided the past into the ancient world, the Middle Ages, and the modern world, with the intermediate period separating and reuniting the other two. Sociology imprinted this "vague" and "sterile" conception with rationality and fruitfulness.[85] Its ability to extend common sense was, for Comte, one more proof of its validity.

HISTORY

The fifth volume of the *Cours* marked the beginning of Comte's exposition of the past according to the law of three stages, which he felt epitomized his "philosophy of history." He concentrated on the most general, familiar phenomena and followed Bossuet's example

[83] Ibid., 221. [84] Ibid. [85] Ibid., 234.

by confining himself to Western Europe. Reflecting a Eurocentric mentality, he assumed non-Western countries would follow the pattern of development of the "great occidental republic" because its evolution was the most advanced, complete, and representative.[86]

He first covered the history of religion, of which he naively claimed to have a "rational," objective view because he was free from religious prejudice. He highlighted the beneficial role that religion had played in social development, pointing out the way it strengthened people's feelings and ideas. One reason religion was always influential was that its vague beliefs could be easily adapted to changing political and social requirements. Unlike some of the philosophes, Comte did not think that religious leaders were dishonest when they made useful changes. As if anticipating the need to justify his own espousal of the Religion of Humanity, he wrote, "A truly superior man has never been able to exert a big influence on his fellow men without first of all being entirely convinced himself."[87]

FETISHISM

The historical exposition began with fetishism, the first stage of the theological philosophy. Comte had first mentioned this stage along with the next two, polytheism and monotheism, in his "Considérations philosophiques sur les sciences et les savants." These three phases corresponded to the theological, metaphysical, and positive periods in the theological stage itself. Now for the first time, he began to explain the significance of these phases.

He wanted to inspire a "sort of intellectual sympathy" for fetishism by showing that it corresponded to man's unchanging moral and intellectual nature.[88] Attacking modern man's pride, he maintained that everyone was a fetishist in his early childhood. And by stressing the fetishist origin of theology, he struck a blow at Christianity, which claimed to have its origins in divine revelation.

Fetishism came first because it satisfied the needs of the human mind in its infancy. It was the "free and direct growth of our primitive tendency to conceive all external bodies . . . as animated by a life essentially analogous to ours."[89] The specificity, materialism, and

---

[86] The "European republic" was composed of France, Italy, Spain, Germany, England, and their "natural appendages." The "natural appendages" of England, for example, were Scotland, Ireland, and the United States. Comte promised that his big treatise on political philosophy (the future *Système de politique positive*) would deal in detail with civilization as a whole, suggesting that he still did not feel capable of writing the more wide-ranging history that he had planned since 1822. Ibid., 235, 491, 520, 537, 692.

[87] Ibid., 250, 258.   [88] Ibid., 268.   [89] Ibid., 244.

incoherence of man's early observations were reproduced in fetishism, where gods were concrete, crude, and particular. Instead of being an aberration, fetishism was the most spontaneous and natural form of theology.

Fetishism also satisfied primitive man's emotional needs. At a time when the affective dominated the intellectual, it was natural for man to personify the phenomena around him and endow them with his own strong passions.

In no other period did religion exert such a dominant and complete influence on the intellect, for man understood everything through the lens of fetishism. Unchallenged by metaphysics, or positivism, fetishism was the most intense form of theology. Thus in Comte's mind, fetishism, not Christianity, represented theology's intellectual apogee.

One of Comte's points was that the three stages of his sociological law represented not only historical periods but different ways of thinking that could coexist in any era, despite the dominance of one of them. Modern fetishism differed from the primitive version only because it referred to abstract and collective beings rather than concrete and individual beings. When metaphysicians sought to "penetrate the mystery of the essential production of any phenomena . . . whose laws they did not know," they were thinking like fetish worshipers. Comte specifically criticized the "tenebrous pantheism" rampant in Germany, although later he would fall into this way of thinking.[90] Modern intellectuals, he said, also reverted to fetishism to satisfy their emotional needs. When they were hopeful or fearful, they tended to personify and deify inert objects that attracted their affections. Comte was thus one of the first thinkers to point out that fetishism did not belong exclusively to the primitive age and did not always represent a type of false consciousness or prelogical mindset.[91] Marx also showed the continuity of this way of thinking when he referred to commodities as fetishes, but he thought commodity fetishism represented a type of perverse alienation. Comte was more sympathetic to this way of thinking.

However, he did not think fetishism was an effective instrument of civilization, for its influence was weak in social and political matters. Since most fetishes were personal and domestic, there were neither general beliefs to unify people nor priests to direct society. Comte asserted that the social weakness of fetishism belied the common assumption that only religious beliefs could serve as the basis of social ties, for when religion was at its height, it had no unifying power. Here Comte was suggesting that nonreligious, universally

---

[90] Ibid., 246–7.   [91] Enthoven, ed., in ibid., 235 ("Remarque"), 252n7.

held beliefs, such as those of positivism, could replace religion in unifying society.

Despite its weakness as a social force, Comte believed fetishism had contributed to human progress and should be considered the first motor of the positive philosophy of history.[92] It wrested the mind from its original torpor and provided a way to link ideas. Its stimulation of the imagination encouraged the fine arts, whose development began in this period. Because it gave man confidence that with the assistance of supernatural agents he could be supreme in nature, he began to conquer the earth, tame animals, engage in commerce, and hunt in groups. Thus it stimulated material development. Even some social progress was made, for man's basic natural impulses were countered by increased sociability and social discipline. For example, religious prescriptions led to hygiene, the use of clothes, and the spirit of property (by the institution of taboos). And since a fixed residence was needed to worship certain objects, fetishism facilitated the transition from nomadic to agricultural life. Political powers also emerged at this time. Hunters and warriors displayed military qualities, such as force, courage, and prudence, which became the basis of temporal authority. Old people, the transmitters of tribal traditions and experience, acquired a certain advisory authority, which became the foundation of the spiritual power. Women turned out to be the spiritual power's domestic auxiliary because their feelings modified the preponderant material activity.

True to his principle of relativism, Comte was one of the first philosophers to view fetishism in an approving manner, for he believed that in the history of the mind there were no "real differences [among periods] other than those of maturity and gradually developed experience." Understanding fetishism enabled one to grasp the principles of uniformity and continuity, both essential concepts of sociological theory. As an admirer of fetishism's emotional and intellectual power, Comte was not entirely free from a certain nostalgia for the primitive. In a sense, positivism would be the realization of fetishism because the "spontaneous germs of all the great ulterior establishments," including the separation of the spiritual and temporal powers, were already present in this period.[93] Comte did not have to seek causes of development, since everything was created all at once in the beginning. What interested him was blossoming and fulfillment. In re-creating the coherence and stability of the first stage of history, positivism represented, in a sense, the rebirth of theology, especially its first, purest phase, that of fetishism.

[92] Ibid., 252n7.   [93] *Cours*, 2:265, 286.

THE TRANSITION TO POLYTHEISM

The transition from fetishism to the next religious stage, polytheism, was due to the natural development of reason, that is, man's innate "ability to compare, abstract, generalize, and foresee."[94] Thanks to the theory of fetishism, which enabled him to connect facts, he began to make more observations and inductions, saw that his facts differed from his principles, and changed his philosophy. This discordance between facts and principles was, to Comte, the impulse behind all scientific revolutions. As primitive man observed more similarities among phenomena, he replaced his particular, specialized gods, which animated matter, with more general, abstract, and invisible ones, each of which administered a category of phenomena, not just one object. Matter was now considered inert and subject to the arbitrary will of an *external* divine agent.

This transformation began with the stars as the most general, independent, and universally influential phenomena. With its nascent priesthood, "astrolatry" – the worship of the stars – was the highest form of fetishism and the only part incorporated into polytheism. Instead of animating external phenomena, man began to engage in pure speculation, the distinguishing mark of the human species. Although phenomena were still ruled by divine wills, many of them were no longer divine or living and thus could be examined by the scientific spirit, which henceforth increasingly pervaded man's intellectual system and prepared him for the concept of natural laws.

Curiously, at the end of the discussion, Comte attributed this transitional period to metaphysics, whereas he had been saying before that it was caused by the development of reason or the scientific spirit. Now he maintained that the transition reflected the historical origin of metaphysics as a "distinct nuance of the purely theological philosophy."[95] Polytheism was metaphysical because a single living god was a personified abstraction, reflecting the typical confusion between the abstract and concrete. Therefore, at this time, the theological and the metaphysical spirits became rivals. As the latter increased in power, the former would decrease until positivism would triumph over both. Yet Comte's introduction of the metaphysical spirit seemed forced and imposed. He clearly sought to prove that the germs of the metaphysical stage were present at the first age of humanity and to sustain his principle that all of history had its origins in this period.

[94] Ibid., 264.   [95] Ibid., 267.

POLYTHEISM

Comte believed that the main form of theology was polytheism, the middle term between fetishism, which marked the inception of the religious spirit, and monotheism, which marked its decline and end. Polytheism had less dominance intellectually and more influence on society than fetishism, while it had less social influence but more intellectual power than monotheism. Although aware that this contention would shock his readers, Comte maintained that polytheism was the period when theology was in its most durable and complete form because it constituted the height not only of the theological system but of the military regime as well. Polytheists were more devout than monotheists because of their more detailed theological explanations for everything. The social system was more homogeneous and closely knit than at any other time and produced the most complete men that the world had ever seen. In saying this, Comte was reflecting his early, classical education and admiration for the ancient world.

During the polytheistic stage of history, there was some progress in all spheres. The scientific spirit grew as it was applied to the secondary details of phenomena, which were no longer considered divine. Since matter was no longer godly and could now be altered, industrial activity also increased. To communicate with the new invisible and inaccessible gods, there was established a priesthood, which worked for the consolidation of society, polytheism's main achievement. Once the community was organized, polytheism exercised its civilizing function through military activity, which further disciplined and extended societies. The authority and unity needed to wage war led to the merger of the two emerging political powers, the sacerdotal and the military. But since the political system's main goal was war, morality suffered. However, to maintain his principle that progress was continuous in all areas, Comte claimed that polytheism encouraged morality by fostering monogamy, patriotism, and respect for the old.

The main contribution of polytheism was aesthetic, for the fine arts had more social influence in this period than ever before or since. Hoping to reproduce this power in the positive era, Comte for the first time celebrated the arts as one of the main elements of human progress.[96] Whereas in the past he had considered the art of the ancient world to be superior to that of the Moderns, he now sided with the Moderns, declaring aesthetic progress to be

---

[96] As in the sciences, the most general arts developed first. The order was poetry, music, painting, sculpture, and architecture.

continuous. He did concede, however, that this progress was most stimulated in the polytheistic period, that of antiquity, when the arts were valued more highly by everyone.

In recognizing the key role of the arts, Comte was coming around to the opinion voiced by the Saint-Simonians ten years before. In fact, his neglect of the artists' role had been one cause of his dispute with Saint-Simon in 1824. Comte was also reflecting his own recent "aesthetic revolution," which stemmed from his mental crisis of 1838. This passage from the *Cours*, which obviously pertains to him, helps to explain why he now found the arts to be of supreme importance:

> In the very small number of eminent human beings in whom mental life becomes preponderant, especially following a long, continued, and almost exclusive exercise, the influence of the fine arts tends to remind them of moral life, which they had too often forgotten or scorned.[97]

Recognizing the moral value of the arts, Comte decided at this point to develop his own aesthetic theory. Whereas he had previously divided the brain into the affective faculties (the penchants and the sentiments) and the intellectual faculties, he now added a third section between them for the aesthetic faculties. Intellectual progress now had three parts as well: scientific, industrial, and aesthetic. Comte's concept of the aesthetic faculties was evidently new, given the fact that his volume on biology, written in 1837, did not mention it.

Comte claimed that by their aims the aesthetic faculties were attached to the moral faculties, while by their means they were connected with the intellectual faculties. Because the development of the aesthetic faculties simultaneously influenced the mind and the heart, it was "one of the most powerful" stimuli of "intellectual or moral education that we can conceive." There was a natural tendency that united the "sentiment of the beautiful" with the "taste for the truth" and the "love of the good." Beauty was the "instinct of perfection rapidly appreciated." For the ordinary man, whose affective life absorbed his intellect, the arts were the only stimulus of mental activity besides sheer necessity. Thus, to Comte, popular interest in the arts perfected a "true birth of spiritual life."[98]

On the surface, the sciences and the arts seemed fundamentally different, since the former studied the external world and was analytical and abstract, whereas the latter analyzed the influence of this world on man and was synthetic and concrete. Yet in reply to the

[97] Ibid., 279.   [98] Ibid., 279, 283, 785.

Saint-Simonians, who had exalted artists and criticized him for being too scientific and cold, Comte denied that there was a strict
distinction between the sciences and the arts. In reality, they had a
"secret affinity," for they used the same cerebral faculties, sought to
observe with exactitude, and often came up with identical ideas.[99]

Although the scientific, or purely intellectual, spirit was superior,
its activity prepared the way for the growth of the aesthetic spirit.
In all periods, artistic development depended on a preexisting, generally accepted philosophy. Comte therefore denounced contemporary writers who claimed that their ignorance of science and
philosophy made them original. (His own regime of cerebral
hygiene, however, was not so different.) According to Comte, the
greatest writers and artists were thoroughly conversant in the most
advanced philosophy of the time. Thus the faculties of expression
never dominated the faculties of conception. Yet Comte seemed to
be contradicting himself, for in a previous chapter he had explained
that "the positive growth of the human faculties had to begin op-
erating first by the faculties of expression in order to accelerate
gradually the later evolution of the superior and less pronounced
faculties."[100] It was not clear how the faculties of expression evolved
before the faculties of conception if they could not develop without
the previous establishment of a philosophical system.

Comte's idea of the arts was generally moralistic and utilitarian.
He believed that for the arts to flourish, society had to have a strong
character, which could be easily idealized, and much stability, allowing for the expression of common ideas and feelings. The arts had
a social function, which was to give an idealized portrayal of the
"personal, domestic, and social sentiments" and to embellish and
improve the "general conduct of our life." Comte thus agreed with
the Saint-Simonians that art should always strive to be popular among
the masses. The arts provided the people with a source of moral
inspiration, encouraged social ties, and strengthened the reigning
philosophical system. Comte's conception of art was, in short, very
limited and was reminiscent of the revolutionaries' insistence on
making the artist a propagandist. Because Comte was most concerned with their "popular efficacy" – the "true criterion of the fine
arts" – he considered the new idea of art for art's sake, which Victor
Hugo claimed to have invented, completely unacceptable.[101]

Returning to polytheism, Comte explained its aesthetic superiority. Because it was the most popular form of religion, it gave the
fine arts a dominant system of common and familiar opinions with

[99] Ibid., 280.   [100] Ibid., 255.
[101] Ibid., 280, 527, 536. See also Hemmings, *Culture and Society*, 249, 256.

which to work. As a result, in no other era was art so well understood and socially influential. Moreover, giving a concrete character to each abstract divinity, imagination played a more important part in polytheism than in fetishism, whose divinities were already concrete, or in monotheism, in which it was reduced to helping with worship and propagation.

Having covered the general outlines of polytheism, Comte broke it down into three forms, which were reflected in the three historical phases of antiquity and also occurred in other nations at different times. First, there was "theocratic polytheism," that is, the "Egyptian mode," in which geographical location favored intellectual development instead of military conquest, and the sacerdotal caste had a monopoly of power and knowledge. Comte recognized that the main problem of a theocracy was that its intellectual stability was excessive and worked against progress.

The second form of polytheism was "military polytheism," in which the strong spirit of conquest prevented the development of a theocracy and the temporal power was stronger than the spiritual. Military polytheism had two phases, first the Greek and then the Roman.

The "Greek mode" developed the intellectual side of military polytheism. Because military activity did not absorb everyone's faculties, intellectual life flourished. A new independent class of nonsacerdotal thinkers emerged and became the "organ of the main mental development of the elite of humanity."[102] The first clear signs of positivism emerged when a rudimentary conception of natural law evolved in mathematics and astronomy. As the sciences developed, metaphysics began transforming polytheism into monotheism.[103] Although at first the sciences, arts, and philosophy were cultivated simultaneously by the same thinkers, a division of labor took place with the establishment of the museum at Alexandria. At that time, the scientists separated themselves from the philosophers and devoted themselves to natural philosophy. Henceforth, the philosophers became metaphysicians, advancing moral philosophy and remaining independent of both the theologians and the scientists. The philosophers' incapacity to organize mental and social life was epitomized by the increasing importance of doubt in the thought of Socrates, Pyrrho, and Epicurus. This schism between the natural and moral philosophies was very important to Comte because it marked the end of the mental unity that had been established

---

[102] *Cours*, 2:309.
[103] Comte particularly admired the "vast encyclopedic conception" of Aristotle, who was able to appreciate equally with a "profound wisdom" the sciences and fine arts. Yet Comte was intolerant of Plato, whose philosophy seemed full of "daydreams." Ibid., 85, 312.

by theology. Henceforth, the antagonism among the theological, metaphysical, and positive schools would worsen until positivism reestablished unity and thus resolved the problem of Western civilization.

The third type of polytheism – the "Roman mode" – developed the social and political side of military polytheism. All aspects of life were organized around the goal of universal empire. Comte greatly admired Roman society for its single-mindedness, consistency, homogeneity, and solidarity. But he felt it began to decay as soon as it stopped expanding and lost its unifying goal.

MONOTHEISM

Monotheism gradually evolved from the intellectual development of Greek polytheism and the social development of Roman polytheism. Weary of their disorderly, capricious gods, the Greeks reduced the supernatural assembly to one monotheistic center, who absorbed the attributes of the other divinities. Rome recognized the need for replacing its numerous sterile cults with one homogeneous, general religion that could appeal to its diverse subject populations.

The temporal organization of monotheism was the feudal system, which differed from the military system of antiquity because it was more defensive, required smaller territorial units, and replaced slavery with serfdom. These three changes were inevitable and spontaneous, given the nature of the Roman system. Comte believed nothing was accidental in history, for everything followed a certain predetermined design and evolved from a previous institution, practice, or belief. Influenced by Sir Walter Scott, Comte added that these three characteristics of the medieval temporal organization could be summed up in chivalry, which encouraged sociability and protected individuals at a time when the central political power was still weak. Because of these three changes and chivalry, he argued that the feudal system was the "necessary cradle of modern societies." By lessening the importance of war, forcing the barbarians to civilize themselves, making agricultural exploitation a primary concern, and eventually freeing the serfs, feudalism transformed "military life into industrial life."[104] The people, however, did not consciously strive toward this goal. "Society" in Comte's system seemed to have a life of its own and simply obeyed the laws of history.

His interpretation of monotheism was idiosyncratic. Neglecting other religions, he concentrated almost exclusively on Catholicism.

[104] Ibid., 356.

At the same time, he argued that Catholicism did not represent the apogee of theology, but a decadent, transitional period between pure theology and positivism. As the concept of the divine became more generalized, the religious spirit paradoxically declined.[105] Furthermore, in Comte's view, Jesus was not the founder of Christianity and was not divine. Instead it was Saint Paul who conceived the general spirit of Christianity. It is possible that David Strauss's *Life of Jesus*, which Littré had translated and sent to Comte six months before he wrote this chapter, influenced his opinion.[106] Yet Strauss's doubts about the scriptural testimony regarding Christ probably only reconfirmed what Comte had already heard from Saint-Simon, who in his *Introduction aux travaux scientifiques* maintained that because Jesus was too uncultivated to formulate the Christian doctrine, Paul, with his knowledge of Platonism, was responsible.

Reflecting Maistre's influence, Comte maintained, moreover, that Catholicism was chiefly a political system whose moral efficacy derived more from the power of the clergy than from its religious doctrine. In fact, he believed that monotheism was stronger socially and politically than polytheism. Its principal political attribute was the separation of the spiritual and temporal powers, which occurred because monotheistic beliefs were sufficiently uniform to be disseminated to different peoples not united under one government.

Comte paused here to add a long and important aside, in which he emphasized that he did not wish to be numbered among those philosophers who dreamed of total dominion. Creating an "absolute reign of the intellectual capacity," as the Greek philosophers tried to do, was absurd because it ran counter to nature. Weak and lethargic, the mind required constant stimulation from human needs and "obstacles" in order to grow. It would atrophy if it began to fulfill its desire to rule the material realm, for it would simply admire the order it created. Eventually, the mind would seek only to reconfirm its "monstrous domination" and would destroy speculative advancement, the source of progress.[107]

In short, contrary to common belief, Comte did not actively support the idea of a government of philosophers, for he recognized that the "reign of the mind" was a "chimerical utopia." Eminent thinkers, lost in abstraction, were too misunderstood and unappreciated to attract popular admiration and "gratitude." Moreover, the rule of the intellect would result in a "very dangerous" reactionary

---

[105] Enthoven, ed., in ibid., 340n7.
[106] Feldman and Richardson, *Modern Mythology*, 450. Littré autographed Strauss's work on December 21, 1839. Comte seems to have read the book, for all the pages are cut. See Comte's library at the Maison d'Auguste Comte.
[107] *Cours*, 2:328–30.

regime. Although the speculative class wanted "instinctively" to govern humanity, it was not interested in "present, detailed reality" and was thus incapable of directing daily social affairs.[108] Its point of view was so narrow that it could not see the whole. Like his appeals to revolutionaries, Comte's stance against intellectual theocracy represented an attempt to disarm critics suspicious of his intentions. It also represented a repudiation of the program of the Idéologues, who gave priority to the intellect and dreamed of an elite of intellectuals dominating the government.[109]

To bolster his case, he argued that the best antidote to a government of intellectuals was the separation of powers, for it would give men of thought and men of action different roles that suited their nature. Each group would be sovereign in its own sphere and act as a consultant in the other sphere. To Comte, this system was the "political masterpiece of human wisdom."[110]

The separation of powers was the main reason for the superiority of modern over antique politics. Independent of any centralized temporal power, the Catholic Church was able to expand its membership indefinitely, promote international harmony, and create a powerful intellectual and moral class. Most important, it did not subordinate morality to political considerations.

The establishment of universal morality, which improved human sociability, was indeed the main purpose and achievement of Catholicism. Since positivism offered no afterlife, Comte was forced to deny that Catholicism's success was due to its doctrine of faraway rewards and punishments – a doctrine he found vague and incoherent. Instead, influenced by Maistre and Bossuet, he attributed its moral success to its organization; the independent spiritual power made morality more important than politics and constantly intervened in individual and social affairs to make sure morality prevailed. It forced even the government and the upper classes to obey the "rigorous maxims of universal morality."[111]

Critical of the moral principle of enlightened self-interest, Comte emphasized that Catholicism prepared the way for "modern sociability" because its principle of "universal love" was "far more important than the intellect itself in ... our individual or social existence." The reason was that "love utilizes spontaneously even the lowest mental faculties for the profit of each and of all, while egoism distorts or paralyzes the most eminent dispositions." Thus as it became obvious that humanity's needs were mainly moral, the intellectual faculties were subordinated to morality, which became the guide and controller of all action. Comte's basic distrust of the

[108] Ibid., 306, 327, 330.   [109] Kofman, *Aberrations*, 279.   [110] *Cours*, 2:332.   [111] Ibid., 333.

reign of the intellect emerged again when he declared that the mind must be limited to improving forecasts and understanding and satisfying individual and social needs. He added that geniuses had to be controlled by moral goals to discourage their "unsociable vanity" and their "absurd pretensions to dominate the world in the name of capacity."[112]

Comte's awareness of the need for the intellect to be subordinated to morality reflected his own self-understanding. He had been interested in moral codes and self-restraint ever since he read Franklin as a young man. His "aesthetic revolution," the completion of the scientific volumes of the *Cours*, and his recent battles with the Academy of Sciences had confirmed his misgivings about the rule of reason and the intellectuals. In fact, his opinions on this subject were not far from those of Saint-Simon and the Saint-Simonians, who had criticized him for being too concerned with rationality. Thus already in 1840, Comte was claiming that positivism would once again make universal love the supreme social principle.

Catholicism also influenced morality by instituting "moral types," who by their exaggerated and idealistic behavior, served as guides to people's conceptions in the same way scientific and artistic models did. Catholic philosophers made Christ perfect to use him as the model of conduct for both the weak and the strong. Christ's divinity and infinite goodness were thus parts of a useful social fiction. The idea of Christ was completed by that of the Virgin Mary, "an even more ideal conception that represented for women the happiest mystical reconciliation of purity and maternity."[113] It is clear that this combination of qualities impressed Comte *before* he met Clotilde de Vaux. He recognized the importance of hagiography and would seek to resurrect it in the Religion of Humanity, with its Cult of the Virgin Mother.

Comte then turned to the conditions that led to monotheism's success. He explained that after a thousand years of trials, Catholicism finally established itself as head of the European system in the eleventh century. Its period of splendor lasted until the thirteenth century, when it began to decline rapidly. The main "dynamic" condition for its success was its promotion of a system of continuous moral and intellectual education that touched all classes. Education was the most important function of the Church and the basis of all its other operations. From the "static" point of view, Comte attributed the Church's success to clerical celibacy, a temporal principality, papal election by qualified electors, papal infallibility, monasteries, and the ecclesiastical hierarchy, which led to stability,

[112] Ibid., 362, 644. [113] Ibid., 363.

mobility, and unity. Most of all, he emphasized the importance of the special education of the clergy, which produced a large number of distinguished minds capable of placing themselves at the "true point of view of all human affairs."[114] In a sense, the *Cours* was an imitation of the training that the Catholic clergy received, for the positive clergy would assume their responsibility of maintaining a system of education for all members of society.

Although he denied that he was influenced by his own upbringing in the Catholic religion, Comte was remarkably uncritical of it. He believed that all its elements, no matter how apparently irrational, had an important social function. For example, the various dogmas, such as the Fall, the divinity of Christ, and transubstantiation, were rationalizations, useful to the social and political efficacy of the ecclesiastical hierarchy. Catholic worship also had an important role, for at every phase of life, a person was reminded by the sacraments of the spirit of Catholicism. Taking a swipe at Protestantism, Comte argued that all the facets of Catholicism were so interdependent that the elimination of one of them weakened Christianity as a whole. In sum, it was not the mystical qualities of Catholicism that impressed Comte, but the brilliance of its organization – an organization he hoped to re-create.

Comte vigorously defended Catholicism's contributions to progress, especially in the intellectual realm. Instead of being the Dark Ages, as the Protestants claimed, the Middle Ages were, to him, the cradle of civilization. With only one god, Catholicism allowed science more freedom in dealing with phenomena that were no longer sacred. To encourage the scientific spirit, which it hoped would lead to greater admiration for the divine plan, the Church promoted education among the masses, made intellectual merit a key factor in the clerical hierarchy, and championed intellectual activity.

Catholicism also improved the morality of the individual, the family, and society. In terms of the virtues of the individual, it correctly encouraged the subordination of his passions to reason – the source of moral improvement. In contrast to Marx and Nietzsche, Comte also found the Catholic stress on humility to be a "capital prescription," for it countered pride and vanity, which could never be sufficiently repressed. In fact, by showing the weakness of human reason, positivism would extend humility to intellectual affairs. Moreover, Comte praised Catholicism for condemning suicide as an "antisocial practice." Positivism would condemn suicide to prevent an individual from having the "dangerous freedom of canceling" the

---

[114] Ibid., 339.

influence society exerted on him.[115] In his condemnation of pride and suicide, Comte displayed a remarkable lack of self-awareness.

As for domestic morality, positivism could do no better than to "consolidate and complete" the improvements already instituted by Catholicism. Despite his own problems with the moral code, his attitude toward it was entirely conventional. For example, he praised paternal authority, and he objected to divorce, which he worried would encourage sexual promiscuity. Although he himself could not become accustomed to his wife's ways, he supported the sanctity of marriage by claiming that people underestimated the human ability to adapt to "every truly immutable situation." This emphasis on adaptability resembled his stress on resignation to the laws of nature and history; both contributed to the conservative, almost fatalistic tenor of positivism. His attitude toward individual liberty emerged when he stated that most people were happier doing what was prescribed, for "our chief moral felicity relates to situations that have not been chosen, like those, for example, of father and son."[116] One could hardly say that Comte's difficulties with his own father were a source of happiness or that he had succeeded in adapting to them.

Comte's conventional outlook extended to his attitude toward women. Reflecting the nineteenth-century cult of domesticity, he praised Catholicism for having restricted women to the domestic realm. He even made women's increasing detachment from all nondomestic activities a "general law of social evolution."[117] His model was the nonworking bourgeois woman who was a devoted wife and mother. Clearly, Comte's "sociological law" reflected his own prejudices and those of his times.

As for social morality, Catholicism modified the "savage patriotism" of the ancients by stressing the "more elevated sentiment of humanity or universal brotherhood." Besides promoting social solidarity, Catholicism encouraged the feeling of perpetuity, especially through its commemorative system of beatification. Positivism would perfect this system by extending it to all activities, eras, and places in order to "recognize and glorify" every person who contributed to human evolution.[118] The germs of the Positivist Calendar were already sown.

Comte was so respectful of the "immense moral regeneration" produced by Catholicism that he could not conceive of any fundamental changes that positivism could introduce. He merely stated that positivism, a "more real and stable philosophy," would defend Catholic principles better than Catholicism itself did.[119]

Catholicism began to decline as soon as it established itself, that

[115] Ibid., 364. [116] Ibid., 365. [117] Ibid., 366. [118] Ibid., 367. [119] Ibid., 367, 377.

is, in the eleventh century. An almost dialectical process was at work. Just as Hegel felt that everything contained the seeds of its own destruction, Comte believed that the "least equivocal sign" of the demise of secular and spiritual institutions was the "sight of their turning spontaneously against their original goal."[120] These paradoxical situations were marks of extinction because they reflected logical inconsistencies – the point of damnation in Comte's mind. Comte's argument was thus original in that he claimed that Catholicism was undermined by its own progressive aspects. First, owing to the Church's encouragement of intellectual progress, the growth of reason went beyond its control, and conceptions and habits were gradually freed from the yoke of theology. As a result, the reconciliation between religion and science ended; Catholicism grew antagonistic toward metaphysical philosophy, which tried to restrict the realm of divine inspiration. The religious spirit lost its hold over the people. The moral progress stimulated by Catholicism also worked against theology. Once people adopted Christian moral precepts, they came to understand the true motives behind them. They then appealed to the authority of human reason rather than to theology, whose sanctions seemed superfluous. Intellectual and moral decadence was followed by the decay of the social system. Once feudalism fulfilled its main function of defense and stopped the barbarian invasions, military activity became obsolete, the fiefdoms gave way to centralized government, and the serfs became emancipated.

In Comte's eyes, what mainly perished in Catholicism was the Church's doctrine, not its splendid organization. Reconstructed by positivism on a more extensive and stable intellectual foundation, this organization would preside over the spiritual rebirth of modern society. It is clear that positivism would be the modern incarnation of Catholicism. The switch from Catholicism to positivism would not, in Comte's eyes, represent a rupture. The organization and the moral system of the positive regime would be basically the same as Catholicism's but would be founded on a different intellectual basis, one that would end the division between natural and moral philosophy.

Comte hoped to see a dialogue between Catholics and positivists, who, he said, shared a "common feeling . . . of the real needs of Humanity." He wanted both camps to agree on eliminating Protestant metaphysics, which engendered only "sterile and interminable controversies."[121] Although in 1840 Comte had small hopes for this project, he would actively pursue this alliance in the 1850s.

---

[120] Ibid., 405.   [121] Ibid., 332, 428.

THE METAPHYSICAL STAGE OF HISTORY

To Comte, modern history began in the fourteenth century, when there emerged two almost inseparable movements that would characterize the five-hundred-year period following the theological stage of history: the movement of disorganization, that is, metaphysics, and the movement of reorganization, that is, positivism. Each profoundly influenced the other. On the one hand, the metaphysical system cleared the way for the development of a new industrial and scientific system. On the other hand, the growth of positivism buttressed the revolutionary action against theology, whose decline was hastened.

While the positive stage was the subject of volume 6, the metaphysical stage was covered in lesson 55, the last and longest chapter of volume 5. Written in haste in five weeks, it was repetitious, unorganized, and poorly written.[122] Comte acknowledged that his exposition of history grew more complex and vague at this point but merely suggested that anyone with problems should read it a second time.

His basic thoughts about the metaphysical period had not changed much. As with the theological era, he chiefly refined his schema by stressing the dialectical process at work in history and by simply dividing the period into different phases. The metaphysical period had two phases: the fourteenth and fifteenth centuries, on the one hand, and the sixteenth, seventeenth, and eighteenth centuries, on the other.

In the first phase, which was the most important period, the metaphysical movement was "spontaneous and involuntary" and the theological regime began to decay from within, a victim of its own success.[123] As Catholicism's philosophical weaknesses became more apparent, people found themselves at odds with it because they wanted the freedom to pursue their own intellectual goals. Moreover, it turned out that the separation of powers, the foundation of monotheism, had been established prematurely. The military and theological authorities became equally despotic as each sought exclusive rule. The temporal power finally prevailed, destroying the separation of powers. The Church then became reactionary, and the feudal order decayed more rapidly. Inherently unstable, the old system was on its way to extinction even before the critical doctrine became influential.

---

[122] Comte wrote this chapter between January 10 and February 26, 1841. See "Tableau du nombre de jours," 440. For an example of the way in which Comte goes back and forth in his discussion, see *Cours*, 2:396–7, 402.

[123] *Cours*, 2:387.

In this first phase, two new groups, the metaphysicians and the lawyers, emerged as the representatives of the revolutionary movement. The former were academic scholars and literary men who exerted their influence through the universities. Preferring Aristotelianism to Platonism, they came to rely on the scientific approach. They influenced scholasticism, which in submitting the action of God to invariable laws caused theology to decay. The other group, the lawyers and judges, who exercised their power through parliaments, had absorbed the metaphysical spirit when they studied at the universities run by the Aristotelians. They were hostile to Catholic power, which threatened royal and seigneurial authority. Although both critical forces, the metaphysicians and legists, sought political supremacy, they aimed only to reform, not destroy, the old regime, for they knew that their existence would end with its death.

In the second period, stretching from the sixteenth through the eighteenth century, the critical or revolutionary doctrine became important and helped to complete the destruction of the old system. To Comte, however, it simply prolonged the theological point of view because its theory of self-interest focused entirely on personal salvation.

Comte divided this second metaphysical period – that of systematic decay – into two phases: Protestantism (from the sixteenth to the mid-seventeenth century) and deism (from the mid-seventeenth to the nineteenth century). Unitarianism served as the transition from the first to the second phase.

Protestantism, with its doctrine of freedom of thought and action, became the foundation of the negative doctrine of metaphysics. Confirming theology's growing disorganization, it was an inevitable consequence of the fact that Catholicism had been granting more and more freedom of examination in secondary matters. Comte went to some effort to show, not altogether convincingly, that Protestantism did not represent a sudden change and was *not* influenced by positivism, which was still weak. Because of his hatred of Protestantism, he wanted to minimize its connections with positivism.

There were three stages in Protestantism's systematic dissolution of Catholicism: Lutheranism, Calvinism, and the antitrinitarianism of Socianism (Unitarianism). They represented the fundamental paradox of Protestantism: while pretending to reform Christianity, they actually destroyed the fundamental conditions of its existence – the separation of powers, the Church hierarchy, and Catholic dogma.

Protestantism embraced four principles of freedom to bolster morality and protect the weak members of society. The idea of popular sovereignty promoted the common good; liberty of conscience supported the old Catholic idea that only spiritual means should be employed to strengthen opinions; the concept of equality stressed the dignity of human nature; and the doctrine of national independence offered small states a measure of security after the breakup of the Catholic system. In this way, the metaphysical doctrine encouraged individualism and personal development, which Comte recognized were crucial to the establishment of new social elements and progress.

Threatened by this movement of emancipation, the Catholic clergy allied itself with the royal power and eventually became a mere instrument of the king's reactionary authority. As its doctrines and institutions became increasingly "repugnant," Catholicism completely lost its influence. The result was a "temporal dictatorship," which tried in vain to maintain the old regime.[124] The coalition of the spiritual and temporal powers led paradoxically to the ruination of each of them.

The "two great anomalies" that issued from the movement of decomposition – the reactionary, temporal dictatorship and the revolutionary doctrine – were inseparable. In fact, their antagonism helped to preserve society. The temporal dictatorship maintained order, while the revolutionary doctrine of Protestantism, with its stress on emancipation, allowed for progress by restraining the temporal dictatorship. Yet weakened by the changes caused by the critical doctrine, the government eventually fell apart. Growing mental and moral anarchy forced it to give up the direction of society and concentrate solely on maintaining material order. The revolutionary doctrine endorsed this political situation and viewed it wrongly, in Comte's view, as a "normal state."[125]

Because of this situation, Protestantism became aberrant. It scorned the Middle Ages, wanted to fuse the moral and political powers, tried to effect reform by changing institutions, and allowed individuals to make decisions on important subjects. Beginning in the sixteenth century, religious beliefs even began promoting hatred. To Comte, this degeneration proved that morality required a more solid intellectual basis outside of theology.

Like most movements in Comte's history, Protestantism gradually turned against itself in an almost dialectical fashion. Having gained power, it abandoned the critical principles it had adopted to gain authority and joined the Catholics in opposing progress. Both Protestant and Catholic kings arrogated to themselves a "vain and ridiculous spiritual supremacy." Yet Comte revealed his own prejudices when he asserted that Catholicism became regressive only because it

[124] Ibid., 409, 426. [125] Ibid., 426–7.

was controlled by the temporal power, whereas Protestantism demanded from the start the subjection of the spiritual power to the
temporal and had an innate "despotic spirit."[126] Against advancing
the decomposition that it had originally fostered, Protestantism lost
the progressive mission that it had taken from Catholicism.

Deism assumed this mission and became the second and final stage
of the metaphysical doctrine. It further developed the revolutionary
doctrine, reflecting the fact that the mind was naturally disposed to
emancipate itself from theology. In a way, Comte tended to reify
freedom of inquiry, which he believed could not be confined. In his
view, it eventually went beyond the boundaries of Christianity. At
that point, deism itself became increasingly antitheological and represented a sort of revolution against Protestantism.

For the first time, positivism emerged from the obscure scientific
research to which it had been devoted. It had played no role in
Protestantism because it rejected beliefs that could not be demonstrated. But in the sixteenth and early seventeenth centuries, positivism began to exert an influence and strengthened the antitheological
bias of deism. Bacon and Descartes, both founders of positivism,
unwittingly aided the negative, metaphysical movement by recommending the emancipation of human reason. (Again one sees the
Hegelian idea of the cunning of reason.) The persecution of Galileo,
the third founder of positivism, caused many people to lose their
faith. Henceforth, theology was increasingly considered incompatible with science. Though equally hostile to metaphysics and
theology, positivism began to ally itself with the former against the
latter.

Comte divided deism into three periods, a division that reflected
his assumption that philosophical changes preceded political transformations. The negative doctrine was systematized in the mid-
seventeenth century, propagated in the early eighteenth century, and
applied to politics in the second half of the eighteenth century. Thus
philosophical emancipation led to political emancipation.

For the first time, Comte praised Hobbes, who was active in
deism's beginnings. He called him the "true father of this revolutionary philosophy" and one of the "principal precursors of true
positive politics."[127] The first to apply the scientific method to society, Hobbes emphasized the importance of self-interest, the social
contract theory, the warlike nature of primitive society, and the
preponderance of material influences in society. He recognized that

---

[126] Ibid., 408, 412; see also 440.

[127] Ibid., 445. Comte's opinion of Hobbes may have been influenced by the utilitarians and
by Destutt de Tracy, who modified Hobbes's theory of the origins of society in volume
4 of the *Elémens d'idéologie*. See also Kennedy, *A Philosophe*, 167–8.

to maintain order in his period there had to be a temporal dictatorship that combined political power with spiritual liberty. Comte was sure that Hobbes always meant the dictatorship to be temporary.

A significant transformation occurred in the second phase of deism. Because universities and courts of justice began to support the reactionary system, scholars and judges were replaced by men of letters and lawyers as the leaders of the revolutionary movement. Comte criticized the men of letters, or "littérateurs," and the lawyers for not having any convictions or goals but commended them, nevertheless, for spreading the views of Hobbes, Bayle, Spinoza, and the other "more rational minds" of the first phase of deism.[128]

The philosophes in particular were not deep thinkers, but mere propagators, clearing the way for "mental emancipation."[129] One of the best propagandists, in Comte's opinion, was Voltaire. Although his youthful admiration for Voltaire had faded, Comte still felt that he had an enormous impact on his century.[130] Nevertheless, he criticized him for not having attacked the temporal power and failing to push theological emancipation beyond deism.

Another eighteenth-century metaphysical leader whom Comte admired was Diderot.[131] Comte credited him with saving the metaphysical philosophy by unifying the different intellectual tendencies of the day in the *Encyclopédie*, which gave them an appearance of a system. Yet because the *Encyclopédie* rested on a "powerless" metaphysics, only positivism could realize this "great project," which had originally been conceived by Bacon.[132]

Still another eighteenth-century thinker whom Comte held worthy of consideration was Rousseau, who became the leader of the metaphysical movement after the school of Voltaire had sufficiently fostered spiritual decadence and "mental emancipation." As a young man, Comte had greatly admired Rousseau.[133] But after 1818 he had

---

[128] *Cours*, 2:451.   [129] Ibid.

[130] Comte later included some of Voltaire's plays in the Positivist Library and reserved a day for him in the Positivist Calendar in the section called "Modern Drama." *Système*, 4: Table B', 539. In the bookcase that Comte used most often, there are four volumes of Voltaire's *Oeuvres poétiques, philosophiques, historiques, et correspondance*, which were published in 1827, 1828, and 1829. See Comte's library at the Maison d'Auguste Comte.

[131] Comte gave Diderot an important place in the Positivist Calendar in the section called "Modern Philosophy" and included his *Interprétation de la nature*, *Essai sur le beau*, and "double dissertation" – *Sur les sourds* and *Sur les aveugles* – in the Positivist Library. *Système*, 4: Table B', 560-1. Comte also respected other eighteenth-century figures, such as Montesquieu, Condorcet, Vauvenargues, and Madame de Staël, but he did not regard them as leaders of the metaphysical deistic school that he was discussing here.

[132] *Cours*, 2: 453-4.

[133] Ibid., 596. Comte owned *Du contrat social*, *Les Confessions*, and *Emile*. See Comte's library at the Maison d'Auguste Comte.

grown increasingly disillusioned with him and now felt that his school had "fewer truly new ideas, even negative ones" than Voltaire's school.[134] He also blamed Rousseau for appealing too much to the passions, which had disastrous social consequences, especially during the Revolution. This criticism was tempered, however, by Comte's claim that without Rousseau the deistic movement might have imitated Protestantism by becoming reconciled to the reactionary temporal dictatorship. It was Rousseau who saw that "moral and political regeneration," not "sterile mental agitation," was the real "goal of the philosophical turmoil." Yet although his radical political ideas were absolutely necessary to direct men against the evils of the old society, they negated society itself and led to "anarchical utopias." Only positivism could resolve this "fundamental paradox."[135]

The political economists were the last eighteenth-century "political sect" to play a role in the disorganization of the old social system.[136] Having shown that the government was incompetent to direct industrial growth, they eliminated its main function when they deprived it of its last excuse for war – the commercial interest of the country. Because they disliked government and favored individualism, they were basically anarchical.

Atheism was the last and most extreme form of deism. Comte had an ambivalent attitude toward it. Admitting that atheism was the last "indispensable" preparation for positivism, he criticized, nevertheless, "superficial and malicious" people who equated it with the positive philosophy. Unlike positivism, atheism was a completely "negative philosophy," with no appreciation for the "contribution of religious beliefs to the general evolution of humanity." Moreover, atheists often believed in a "sort of metaphysical pantheism" far from the spirit of positivism.[137] Although Comte himself was an atheist, atheism had such a poor connotation in his time that he was anxious to distance it from positivism.

In conclusion, deism aggravated the evils produced by the Protestant phase, for the "new spiritual guides" had even less conviction and logical consistency than their predecessors. Voltaire's school had no respect for profound philosophical work, while Rousseau's school led to moral difficulties since it called on the passions to settle problems. These two rival schools also intensified other troublesome trends of the age: hostility to the division of the two powers, contempt for the Middle Ages, aversion to Catholicism, nostalgia for the polytheism of antiquity, efforts to revive a metaphysical theocracy, exclusive preoccupation with practical reforms, and insistence

[134] *Cours*, 2: 456. See also Comte to Valat, May 15, 1818, *CG*, 1:37.   [135] *Cours*, 2:457.
[136] Ibid., 458.   [137] Ibid., 394, 446.

on individual conscience. For these ills, Comte held Rousseau more accountable than Voltaire, for he believed Rousseau pushed the aberrations of negative philosophy to the extreme. Though personally licentious, Rousseau "dared" to make his behavior a model for humanity and was responsible for the "brutal preponderance of the passions over reason" that Comte found spreading rapidly around him.[138] Yet Comte was not as free from Rousseau's influence as he imagined, for he too respected nature, the primitive, religion, and the emotions. He also sought to make himself a model of virtue for the new era of regeneration.

THE POSITIVE STAGE OF HISTORY

Volume 6 of the *Cours* covered the progress of positivism, which Comte showed was inseparable from the decline of the old system. "Continuity" and "interrelatedness" were the key words of his discourse. Beginning in the fourteenth century, the metaphysical and positive movements started to develop rapidly because the Catholic and feudal system had fulfilled its mission and began to decay. In the temporal sphere, the energies that were once directed toward war went into industry, while in the spiritual realm, intelligent people turned to science and art rather than to theology. The new social leaders united to destroy the old regime. They used the struggle among the obsolete powers to advance themselves and to move society closer to the positive state.

From the point of view of statics, the modern positive civilization that was born in the fourteenth century consisted of industry, science, and art – Saint-Simon's famous triad. The industrial element corresponded to the temporal order, while the scientific and aesthetic elements related to the spiritual. Comte sought to confirm this triad by referring to his biological theory of human nature. He explained that these three elements satisfied universal needs and aptitudes; impelled by the predominance of their emotions, people generally evaluated every subject according to first its goodness (or utility), then its beauty, and finally its truth. Reflecting the whole range of human activities, these three elements also corresponded to the three parts of the brain. In the rear were the instincts, which were concerned with utility and reflected industrial operations. In the middle were the social sentiments, including the aesthetic sense, which made people think about "ideal perfection."[139] In the front were the intellectual faculties, which corresponded to scientific operations.

[138] Ibid., 460, 463.   [139] Ibid., 488.

Philosophy was another, temporary component of modern civilization but would lose its separate status as soon as it was reunited with science. The *Cours* would in fact join them, giving to philosophy the "positivity" it lacked and to science the "generality" that it needed.[140]

The four orders of modern civilization had always coexisted but developed at unequal rates. Industry came first in the modern period and helped to energize the others, first the arts, then the sciences, and finally philosophy. The belief that industry was the foundation of modern civilization reflects the impact of political economy on Comte's thinking. This materialistic position seems at odds with his insistence that ideas and feelings ruled the universe and that the negative movement of history was stimulated by freedom of inquiry and intellectual speculation. Yet he asserted that industry developed first because it involved the easiest, most concrete, and most certain activity and thus attracted the attention of the majority of people, who were generally motivated by the lowest and most energetic penchants, those relating to material, practical needs. Philosophy was the last to develop because it dealt with the most general, abstract subjects that always interested the fewest people. The scientific or philosophical faculties, which established the basis of man's system of ideas, ultimately ruled human progress indirectly.

Industrialization was not only the "most fundamental" change that "humanity" ever experienced, but the distinctive mark of modern society.[141] It improved human intelligence and sociability (the two qualities separating man from the animals), encouraged discipline and cooperation, connected private and public interests, and created a more just society by making superiority rest on wealth acquired through work, not birth. Comte's position reflected the liberalism of his youth.

Industrialization was not accidental; it was a spontaneous, natural evolution, and like the other elements of modern civilization, it emerged from and was aided at the outset by the Catholic and feudal system itself. Industry developed during the Middle Ages, when it was closely connected with the movement for emancipation, which resulted in the abolition of slavery and serfdom and the establishment of the communes and guilds. As each man sought to develop his own industrial activity, he developed the "characteristic passion of the moderns" for liberty.[142]

From the fourteenth to the eighteenth century, industry went through three periods, corresponding to and confirming the three phases of the metaphysical movement. In the fourteenth and fifteenth

---

[140] Ibid., 548.   [141] Ibid., 493.   [142] Ibid., 506.

centuries, as the old system decayed, the industrial system emerged and came to rival the military. In the second period, the era of Protestant ascendancy in the sixteenth to the mid-seventeenth century, the industrial movement became more systematic as it was encouraged by the government as a means of political and military supremacy.[143] In the third period, that of deism, which lasted until the nineteenth century, industrial development finally triumphed over military interests and became the state's primary objective. Guided by scientific laws, industry encouraged "humanity's systematic action on the external world."[144] Already antimilitary, industry became antitheological since it denied there was a perfect divine order. The main problem with industry was that it encouraged egoism and the profits of the few at the expense of the whole community.

During these five hundred years, the intellectual aspect of the positive movement grew slowly, confined as it was to a small, powerless group. Art evolved first because the aesthetic faculties could develop as soon as material needs were met and they were the only faculties that most people were capable of enjoying. Thus the arts were destined above all for the masses.

Comte claimed that industry and the arts had a close, mutually beneficial relationship. On the one hand, industry helped to popularize the arts; it stimulated the common people's mental activity so that they could understand them, and it provided the ease and security necessary for enjoying them. On the other hand, the arts served as a corrective to the shameful narrowness of industrial activity by encouraging more disinterested mental activity and awakening benevolent affections through vivid, collective means of enjoyment. Because religion was weak and science and philosophy were too tiring for the masses to enjoy, the arts maintained speculative activity and prevented the triumph of materialism.

No doubt influenced by his "aesthetic revolution," Comte for the first time stressed the arts' spiritual role. He now believed that man's spiritual existence was not only philosophical (or scientific) but aesthetic. Yet he did not explain how artists were to share spiritual power with the philosophers. Although not well developed, his position had grown closer to that of the Saint-Simonians.

Comte maintained that aesthetic growth also confirmed the three metaphysical phases. The arts started in a spontaneous fashion. They

---

[143] Comte showed, for example, that the establishment of the colonial system stimulated industry and helped to extend the positive movement throughout the world. But it did so at the cost of setting up a system of slavery, which he called a "regressive" and "monstrous social aberration." Here Comte seemed to ally himself with the antislavery movement – the only reforming crusade that he appeared to favor. Ibid., 521.

[144] Ibid., 526.

were then patronized by political and religious rulers, who sought glory and popularity. In the third phase, the development of the arts became an important goal of the modern state, which had to encourage them to satisfy the public. As the arts became indispensable to society, artists and poets grew increasingly independent, powerful, and critical. They soon became the "spiritual chiefs of the modern populations" against the regressive system.[145] But when literary men took control of the spiritual movement, they prolonged the revolutionary transition just to maintain their position, to the detriment of both society and the arts.

Comte traced the beginning of the modern aesthetic evolution to the Middle Ages and praised the "present romantic school" for recognizing the splendors of that period.[146] He argued that the medieval arts were the source of the originality and popularity of the modern arts. For example, medieval poems about chivalry and domestic life inspired modern literature's celebration of private life.

Although he criticized the romantics for exaggerating the aesthetic decline after the Middle Ages, Comte himself was ambivalent about aesthetic progress. He criticized medieval artists for imitating the works of antiquity and pointed out that such regressive imitations became even more widespread during the classical revival of the Renaissance and the sixteenth and seventeenth centuries. He believed the buildings of this early modern period were inferior to the medieval cathedrals. He thus blamed medieval art for contributing to the "vague and indecisive character inherent in modern art."[147]

Although his theory of continual progress in every field required him to maintain that the arts were always improving, at heart he still seemed convinced that they were superior during antiquity. According to his theory of art, an individual artist could not create works of genius representing social life if his own society were weak, confused, and unstable because he would lack social direction and purpose. And since modern societies were shaky and inharmonious, artists could not find anything to idealize. Moreover, the "universal sympathies," on which their art should rest, had disappeared. Finding no "fixed sociability" in their own era, which they criticized as degenerate, they often looked to antiquity, failed to perform their function of uplifting the people, and sought simply to entertain. Lacking a social purpose, they thus deprived modern civilization of a constructive artistic movement of its own. Although Comte continued to assert that the works of art since the beginning of the Middle Ages were comparable, if not superior, to those of antiquity, it is difficult to escape the impression that he was manipulating the

---

[145] Ibid., 547.   [146] Ibid., 539.   [147] Ibid.

data to fit his theory of continuous progress. His examples of great artists of the past five hundred years were the builders of the medieval cathedrals, the writers of the Renaissance and early modern times, some modern German and Italian composers, and a very few contemporary novelists, such as Manzoni and Scott, whom he considered to be independent of the "sterile" literary (romantic) movement.[148] Scorning the artistic achievements of his own time but critical of classicism, he looked to positivism to regenerate the arts, especially in terms of their social influence, the main criterion for judging them.

The last faculties that Comte examined were those of the sciences and philosophy, whose modern development also began in the Middle Ages. He first concentrated on the sciences, for he believed they had a decisive impact on philosophy. Whereas in the first three volumes of the *Cours* he had discussed their methods and subject matter, now it was their history that most concerned him.

The history of the sciences in the transitional period followed the three phases of the evolution of industry and the arts. Beginning in the fourteenth century, the sciences developed spontaneously. In the second phase, the sixteenth and seventeenth centuries, they advanced rapidly, thanks to the support of the government and the work of Galileo, Descartes, and Bacon, Comte's so-called scientific predecessors.[149] At that time, mathematics, astronomy, and some simple theories of physics became positive. Science began to separate itself from the old metaphysical philosophy but could not yet become the basis of a new philosophy. In the third phase of the transitional period, the encouragement of the sciences became a major duty of the government. All scientists were behind the emerging positive movement, whose antitheological character suited their spirit. Chemistry became a positive science, and the growth of academies encouraged scientific specialization.

As for the development of modern philosophy, Comte declared that it increasingly depended on scientific development. In the first

---

[148] Ibid., 621. Comte greatly enjoyed the epics of Scott and Manzoni, which depicted faraway historical periods. He felt both novelists were improving the type of art that characterized the modern period: the "portrayal of private morals and manners [*moeurs*]." They also showed the historical connections between private life and public life, especially by revealing how the latter modified the former.

[149] Galileo helped to show in a concrete fashion that the positive principle of the invariability of physical laws was incompatible with theological doctrines. Persecuted for showing the movement of the earth, he was, in fact, the first modern scientist to clash with "the old [theological-metaphysical] philosophy." After Galileo, even the people would not accept doctrines that blatantly contradicted science. Descartes refined analytical geometry and organized the relations between the abstract and the concrete. He and Bacon also defined the positive spirit, especially in opposition to theology and metaphysics. Ibid., 559.

phase of the transitional period, the sciences (natural philosophy) and theology (moral philosophy), which had split apart in Greece during antiquity, were provisionally united by scholasticism. In accepting "reason's dangerous help," scholasticism favored metaphysics, which still dominated the sciences. Metaphysics, however, gradually extended its domain from the inorganic world to the social and moral world and challenged theology with such entities as "Nature." The incoherent, unstable doctrine of "natural theology" represented an effort to fuse faith and reason.[150] But demonstration became more important than permanent revelation, while Nature became more interesting than God. Consequently, theology declined. With its critical spirit, metaphysics also supported the temporal power's attacks against the Church. At this time, positivism was still in an incipient stage, gathering observations under the inspiration of astrology and alchemy and spreading the idea of invariable natural laws regulating all phenomena. It worked with metaphysics until they attained their common goal of triumphing over monotheism. Yet signs of the fundamental enmity between metaphysics and positivism were evident in the scholastic controversy between the Realists and the Nominalists.

In the second phase of the transitional period, the divergence between the metaphysical and positive spirits became greater. Metaphysics seized control of the spiritual power through Protestantism and became authoritarian. Positivism, with its discoveries in astronomy, clashed with theology and metaphysics, both of which now opposed the further growth of the sciences. To wage the battle against the older philosophical movements, England, Italy, and France each contributed an eminent thinker – Bacon, Galileo, and Descartes – who were the "first founders of positive philosophy."[151] The

---

[150] Ibid., 568.

[151] Ibid., 570. Pointing out that Galileo was more a scientist than a philosopher, Comte called Bacon and Descartes the "two eternal and original legislators of positive philosophy." Like Saint-Simon, Comte commended them for insisting that specialization (the spirit of analysis), which was important for developing the sciences, should not be overvalued; it was merely part of the preparation for the future general synthesis – a new philosophical system. Yet in evaluating these two scientists, Comte found Bacon to be "less rational" and "less eminent in all respects" than Descartes. Bacon's ideas floated between metaphysics and a sterile empiricism, whereas Descartes had a far more profound sense of "positivity" since he had learned it at its source – mathematics. And even though Bacon, unlike Descartes, had tried to extend the positive method to the study of man and society, his efforts were premature. Descartes had made a "provisional compromise" between metaphysics and positivism by abandoning moral and social studies to the former and giving the latter full reign over the inorganic sciences. In his Positivist Calendar, Comte thus assigned the name "Descartes" to the eleventh month, which was devoted to modern philosophy. He gave Bacon's name only to the second Sunday in that same month. Ibid., 570, 626, 640; *Système*, 4: Table B'.

supremacy of metaphysics was overturned thanks to Bacon and especially Descartes, whom Comte considered the superior thinker. It now ruled only morality, while positivism controlled natural philosophy.[152] This compromise thus reestablished the original division between moral philosophy and natural philosophy that had prevailed before scholasticism.

The third phase of the transitional period was a prolongation of the second one. Because of the Scottish philosophers, especially Hume and Adam Smith, moral studies advanced. The new interest in history and the new idea of progress, which derived from scientific development, stimulated political studies.[153] Nevertheless, philosophy was still cultivated in too much isolation.

Comte concluded that in order for the final regeneration to occur, these four partial evolutions – the industrial, aesthetic, scientific, and philosophical – had to be interconnected, for each of them was in a disorganized state. Positivism would emerge from and overcome this chaotic situation.

THE RECENT AND FUTURE DEVELOPMENT OF POSITIVISM

The anarchy in human affairs, according to Comte, culminated in the French Revolution, the "most decisive crisis of human evolution."[154] Positivism was the unavoidable, natural response to this revolution, a revolution that to him had not yet ended.

Comte believed the "salutary explosion" of 1789 was the climax of the movement of decomposition that had been going on since the fourteenth century.[155] The inevitability of the Revolution was a favorite argument of liberal historians of the Restoration, who sought to make it respectable and absolve it of its crimes.[156] In Comte's view, the Revolution took place because the negative, that is, the metaphysical, progression had outpaced the positive one, making reorganization imperative. The Terror showed that the critical principles could not reconstruct society. Even the lawyers and literary men who directed the Revolution lacked "real and stable convictions."[157]

---

[152] Comte pointed out that three great men strove to destroy the hold of metaphysics on morality: Machiavelli, Hobbes, and Bossuet.

[153] Comte explained that this idea of progress originated with Pascal, was firmly established by Fontenelle in the quarrel between the Ancients and Moderns, and then was refined by Turgot, Condorcet, and Montesquieu.

[154] *Cours*, 2:697.   [155] Ibid., 584.   [156] Mellon, *Political Uses of History*, 17, 27.

[157] *Cours*, 2:588. Compare Comte's view with that of Tocqueville. Tocqueville, "How Toward the Middle of the Eighteenth Century Men of Letters Took the Lead in Politics and the Consequences of This New Development," part 3, chap. 1, in *The Old Regime and the French Revolution*, 138–48.

But the positive movement had not yet reached the point where it could conceptualize the necessary reorganization. There was therefore a disparity between the Revolution's goal, which was organic, and its means, which were critical.

Comte scorned the first period of the Revolution, that of the Constituent Assembly, and the third period, that of the Directory, because they sought to introduce the unsuitable English constitution into France.[158] He most admired the period of the Convention because it displayed a "memorable progressive instinct." To save the Revolution from the coalition aligned against it, the Convention wisely delayed implementing the metaphysical Constitution of 1793 and created instead a "vast temporal dictatorship." Always intended to be provisional, this dictatorship was "perfectly adapted to the eminently transitory nature of the corresponding social milieu." In vanquishing the Girondins in order to establish the highly centralized state essential to national unity, the Convention was the *only* government since 1789 that understood its proper role in history and tried to introduce progressive but always provisional institutions. Distinctly less critical of this "great revolutionary dictatorship" than in 1820, when in his "Sommaire appréciation de l'ensemble du passé moderne," he had denounced the premature removal of the king, Comte now claimed that the monarchy had to be abolished for social regeneration to begin.[159] And although in his "Réflexions" of 1816, he had condemned the anarchy and tyranny of 1793–4, he now minimized them, maintaining that their horrors were offset by such beneficial developments as the suppression of Christianity. The "grave aberrations" that occurred were the fault of metaphysicians, not the early leaders of the Convention or the "masses," both of whom Comte considered to be eminently moral.[160] The Convention's power to make the people submit completely to its leaders to effect social reorganization clearly enthralled Comte. The Convention

---

[158] Whereas in England the nobility was more powerful than the monarch, in France the aristocracy had been decaying since the Middle Ages, while the king had been growing stronger. Thus, in Comte's eyes, it made no sense to make the decadent aristocracy the basis of the government in France. Moreover, the Constituent Assembly's effort to unite monarchical authority and popular power struck him as illogical and utopian. *Cours*, 2:589, 604.

[159] Ibid., 594–6, 686, 688.

[160] Ibid., 594–6. Comte particularly applauded the Jacobin Club, though he was careful not to mention it by name and referred to it only as a "celebrated voluntary association." He argued that when the Jacobins were independent of the government, they were able to provide it with "luminous" insights and acted as a rudimentary moral or spiritual government. Ibid., 595. See also Comte to John Stuart Mill, January 17, March 4, 1842, CG, 2:32, 37.

represented, in effect, his model of enlightened dictatorship, for he regarded it as a popular, temporary dictatorship, one that was morally uplifting and perfectly suited to the times. Its example later inspired his support of Napoleon III as a means of establishing positivism.

Of the two eighteenth-century schools of metaphysics, that of Voltaire and that of Rousseau, Comte preferred the former. According to Comte, Voltaire's school, led by Georges Danton and Camille Desmoulins, was in charge of the Convention at the beginning and recognized the negativity inherent in their metaphysics as well as the temporary nature of their republican dictatorship. Like Michelet and other romantics, Comte greatly admired Danton and was, in fact, the first to resurrect Danton's reputation.[161]

Comte blamed Robespierre, the spokesman for Rousseau, for unnecessarily prolonging and perverting the temporary dictatorship. Robespierre, he insisted, was the one who tried to base social reorganization on metaphysical principles, a move that was particularly reactionary because it stemmed from a desire to imitate antiquity in some vague fashion. Comte did not think that looking for models in the past – ancient Greek republicanism – was any more effective than seeking foreign models in the present – English constitutionalism. Unlike those who claimed that the "great regressive reaction" began with Thermidor, Comte attributed it to the triumph of Robespierre and his effort to organize a legal deism. Comte thought the Cult of the Supreme Being led to the domination of the passions, and he accused Robespierre – the "bloody ranter" – of making himself the "sovereign pontiff of this strange religious restoration" and of murdering Danton and Desmoulins. Saint-Just's only fault was his devotion to this "ambitious sophist."[162] Thus Robespierre was solely responsible for the Terror, and the Thermidorean reaction, directed by Danton's friends, was "indispensable."[163]

The revolutionary period profoundly inspired Comte. He favored the Convention and the regenerative aspect of the Terror and could not contain his enthusiasm for Danton, Desmoulins, and "the people." His views differed from those of many liberal historians, who hated the Terror and praised the events of 1789 and the role

---

[161] J. McManners, "The Historiography of the French Revolution," in *The New Modern Cambridge History*, ed. George Clark, vol. 8, *The American and French Revolutions: 1763–93*, ed. A. Goodwin (Cambridge: Cambridge University Press, 1965), 629. McManners wrongly states that Comte attributed the religion of reason to Danton. For an evaluation of Comte's view of Danton and that of the romantics, see Ozouf, "Danton," 213–22.

[162] *Cours*, 2:597–8. Comte owned a copy of Saint-Just's *Fragments sur les institutions républicaines*.

[163] Having been encouraged early in his career by Lazare Carnot, Comte was pleased that the "great Carnot" had managed to escape the bloodbath. Ibid., 598.

of the middle class.[164] Although his loyalties made him much closer to the radical or "socialist" tradition in France, he maintained his distance from the extreme Left by his denunciation of Rousseau and Robespierre. Comte's rehabilitation of the Convention by praising Danton, not Robespierre, represented a new perspective in French historical thinking.[165]

He also disagreed with some contemporary liberals, such as Thiers, who were trying to rehabilitate Napoleon. Napoleon remained, in Comte's eyes, the Revolution's "most dangerous enemy."[166]

Comte was very critical of the two regimes established since the Empire, both of which again erred by introducing a constitutional monarchy modeled on that of England. The constant antagonism between the king and the Legislative Assembly left France without any leadership or direction. The Bourbon Restoration was inherently contradictory – reactionary in its attempt to revive the monarchy and religion, progressive in its encouragement of industrialization and intellectual progress. The July Monarchy, a materialistic, repressive regime, was even worse. Comte derided liberals for not recognizing that this regime could never realize their "irrational hopes for social reform."[167] The simple fact, according to Comte, was that a liberal regime had to be corrupt to stay in power.

Because the government failed to fulfill its function of regulating the intellectual and moral realm, journalists had taken over this job. But influenced by the dangerous anarchical ideas of Rousseau and Robespierre and close to "ephemeral sects," namely the Saint-Simonians, they promoted the "most absurd utopias." Recognizing the power of the press, Comte considered the journalists his rivals for control of social reorganization, and as always when confronted with his enemies, he condemned them for their inadequate education and irrationality.[168]

Comte was convinced that both the revolutionary and reactionary schools had finally come to realize the need for intellectual and moral regeneration. The negative movement had gone as far as it could. During the past fifty years, the metaphysical regime had become antiprogressive, while the military and theological system had declined to the point where all serious wars were about to be banned and Catholicism – an "imposing historical ruin" – had become

---

[164] Jean Touchard, *La Gauche en France depuis 1900* (Paris: Seuil, 1977), 19, 24, 39; McManners, "Historiography of the French Revolution," 628; Girard, *Libéraux français*, 95; Gérard, *Révolution française*, 35.

[165] McManners, "Historiography of the French Revolution," 628–9; Gérard, *Révolution française*, 39.

[166] *Cours*, 2:603. See also Jardin and Tudesq, *Notables*, 1:152.   [167] *Cours*, 2:608.

[168] Ibid., 609.

"extraneous to present society."[169] This statement reveals not only Comte's naïveté but his blindness to the significance of the religious revivals of his era.

During the fifty years since the Revolution, the four aspects of the positive movement had also advanced as far as they could under the present system. Industrial development had destroyed the old hierarchy and made wealth the basis of civil influence. Yet Comte argued that the isolation of backward agricultural areas and especially the opposition between entrepreneurs and workers showed the need for central planning. The class struggle was due not to the workers but to the "political incapacity, social indifference, and especially blind egoism of the entrepreneurs." The wages, working conditions, and morals of the workers were worse than they had been in the Middle Ages. The class antagonism was not being regulated fairly because "the legislation forbade to one of them the coalitions that they permitted or tolerated among the other."[170] It is clear that Comte had not lost his sympathy for the workers. He felt positivism would resolve the class conflict, just as Marx thought his system would. Both philosophers believed the workers would be their natural supporters.

As for recent developments in the arts, Comte praised Scott, Manzoni, and Byron, the only romantic writers later included in the Positivist Calendar. Byron, the "most eminent poet of our century," best understood the transitional, "negative," and "floating" character of modern civilization and focused, wisely, on human achievements. But generally, the romantics struck Comte as superficial. Completely ignoring Stendhal's *Le Rouge et Le Noir* and Hugo's *Notre Dame de Paris*, which had appeared in the 1830s, he declared that the romantic movement, especially in France, had not yet produced "any truly durable work."[171] At the same time, he joined other contemporaries, such as Stendhal, in denouncing the excessively classical tendencies of the arts of the last fifty years.[172] He argued that the arts needed clearer philosophical principles and a social goal.

As for the sciences since the Revolution, Comte felt that they were becoming better integrated into society, and he praised most of all the development of biology as a science. Reflecting his greater preoccupation with the danger of specialization, he argued that biology prepared the way for the science of society by helping the

---

[169] Ibid., 613.   [170] Ibid., 620.

[171] Ibid., 621, 786. Yet not all of Byron's works pleased Comte. In his description of the Positivist Library, he recommended Byron's selected works, which he said must not include the controversial, irreverent *Don Juan*. *Système*, 4:558.

[172] Albert Thibaudet, *Histoire de la littérature française de Chateaubriand à Valéry* (1936; Verviers, Belgium: Marabout, 1981), 204.

"synthetic spirit" prevail over the "analytical spirit."[173] As soon as the organic sciences of biology and sociology were fully established, the spirit of the whole would triumph and the political crisis would end.

Comte's increasing preoccupation with the whole was due partly to his disastrous fight with the Academy of Sciences over "his" chair at the Ecole Polytechnique in 1840. Following Saint-Simon's example in the *Projet d'encyclopédie*, he blamed scientists for being so specialized that they lacked sound judgment and did not understand him. In Comte's view, the "didactic capacity" was linked to the spirit of the whole, whereas the "academic capacity" was one of pure specialization.[174]

To show the damage done by scientific specialization, Comte inserted in lesson 57 a long digression on his fight to attain his mathematics chair in 1840 and the general problems of scientists. Far more contentious than what he had already said about them in lesson 46, written in 1839, it foreshadowed his infamous "Personal Preface." He believed he had a duty to discuss the scientists' unethical treatment of him in order to demonstrate that the class that was supposed to be the organ of the regenerating doctrine was so egotistical that it could not fulfill its "great philosophical mission." He compared himself to the "great" Hildebrand, who sought to effect a "difficult spiritual reformation" but was opposed by the same clergy that he was trying to place at the head of society.[175]

Comte grew so angry at the scientists that the establishment of the spirit of the whole became one of the main objectives of the remainder of the *Cours*. He made the spirit of the whole (the tendency toward generalization, synthesis, and coordination) and the spirit of analysis (the tendency toward specialization, detail, and division) into historical forces. He thus adopted Saint-Simon's view that analysis and synthesis represented two distinct intellectual mindsets, which alternated in dominating mental evolution according to the needs of each age.

Analysis and synthesis were equally important in scientific speculations. Analysis, which first prevailed in the sixteenth century, reached its high point in the seventeenth and eighteenth centuries. But then, instead of ceding to the spirit of generality, it prolonged its own dominance and hampered scientific progress by promoting "blind and childish research." Comte now disliked research, because he had failed to get his chair for lack of doing any. As specialists, scientists did not want to make full use of the positive method and extend it to social and moral phenomena. He accused them of

---

[173] *Cours*, 2:624.   [174] Ibid., 631.   [175] Ibid., 625.

preferring the old theological and metaphysical philosophy, which maintained their superiority. Especially blameworthy were the mathematicians, who sought to extend their analysis to all phenomena, assuming there was a "scientific unity" founded on "one of the metaphysical fluids."[176] The mathematicians were not only Comte's main opponents in the Academy but his rivals in the contest to unify and dominate knowledge. He praised instead the biologists, who, he believed, were most favorable to positivism.[177] In this shift of interest from the inorganic to the organic sciences, Comte was following the general movement of his age.

Though theoretically opposed to practical reform, Comte suggested that the way to improve the Academy of Sciences, which he believed discouraged the establishment of biology, was to add a section devoted to social physics and positive philosophy. This section would furnish the president and perpetual secretary of the Academy and thus dominate the organization, dictating in which direction it should go. But rather than contemplating the reform of the Academy, Comte preferred to dream about reproducing the revolutionaries' momentous action, that of eliminating it altogether.

Comte's hatred of the scientists was so intense that he began to fantasize about other ways of destroying their power. To facilitate industrialization, he imagined making most of them engineers who would not be allowed the pleasure of intellectual speculation but would instead be limited to directing man's action on the exterior world. The most talented scientists would become positive philosophers. The scientists who refused to become engineers would become intermediaries between the engineers, who would be specialized and socially useful, and the positive philosophers, who would be the pure abstract thinkers. In his previous plans, the engineers were the intermediary class. Comte changed the scientists' position to obliterate their "strange current preponderance": "equivocal beings," like the scientists, would be excluded from "every regular hierarchy" in the positivist state.[178] These ideas, as well as his scheme to reorganize the Academy, show that Comte was already making detailed and

---

[176] Ibid., 628, 650. Comte was also disgusted that the "antisocial utopias" that were arising from the spiritual anarchy of his time had attracted many active members amid the "classes that were the most dominated by a mathematical education." He again seemed to be referring to the Saint-Simonians, whose members included numerous graduates of the Ecole Polytechnique. Ibid., 744.

[177] No doubt Blainville's support influenced his opinion. Comte maintained that the establishment of biology had threatened the Academy of Sciences to such an extent that it had rejected Bichat as a member, supported Napoleon's persecution of Gall, overlooked the value of Broussais, and let the "brilliant but superficial Cuvier" repress the theories of Lamarck and Blainville. Ibid., 628. See also ibid., 1:829.

[178] Ibid., 2:634.

grandiose plans to reform the world and falling into utopian schemes to get his revenge.

As for philosophy, the fourth element of civilization, Comte pointed out that because it considered man to be independent of the exterior world, it was limited to producing vague moral and social theories. The "last modern philosopher" to have grasped the spirit of the whole was the "great Leibniz." Kant was too specialized philosophically, and Maistre too reactionary.[179] Included in the various versions of the Positivist Calendar in the month of "Descartes," which was devoted to "modern philosophy," were only the following nineteenth-century thinkers: Cabanis, Destutt de Tracy, Dunoyer, Sophie Germain, Maistre, Bonald, Fichte, Hegel, and Oken.[180] Comte also ridiculed Guizot's 1832 creation – the Academy of Moral and Political Sciences – as an impediment to philosophical progress. Although he claimed the Academy was irrational, its main defect seems to have been its failure to make him a member.

In conclusion, Comte maintained that all the different political and intellectual tendencies of the past fifty years were preparing for the "spiritual reorganization." The Revolution had discredited the theological and metaphysical philosophies and their corresponding social systems. People now were sufficiently free to create a new philosophy, and science had proved its ability to serve as its foundation. The only missing element was an "indispensable philosophical initiative," an initiative now provided by the *Cours*.[181] It would resolve the crisis that had been growing worse since 1789.

Comte reminded his readers of the *longue durée*, for ultimately all of history since the Greeks was converging on this spiritual reorganization. The problem was a logical one, relating to the mind's need to "replace the philosophical method suited for its infancy by one appropriate to its maturity." By establishing sociology, which finally extended natural philosophy to morality and politics, Comte claimed that he was achieving the "great system of philosophical works first outlined by Aristotle in radical opposition to the Platonic system."[182] In resolving age-old problems, the *Cours* was the endpoint of history.

Comte now had completed the long historical exposition begun in lesson 52 and had shown that beneath the "confusion" and "incoherence" of the past, there was "a perfect unity and a rigorous continuity." This exposition had thus established sociology as the last branch of natural philosophy, especially by verifying the law of

---

[179] Ibid., 636.   [180] Comte, *Calendrier positiviste*, 33; *Catéchisme positiviste*, 270.
[181] *Cours*, 2:611.   [182] Ibid., 375, 651.

three stages, which was now "as fully demonstrated" as any other natural law.[183]

This law had successfully coordinated the different elements of positive life – first, the intellectual, then the moral, and finally the political. Intellectually, the law created "harmony in the total system of our understanding" and thereby made the spirit of the whole and the sense of duty prevail. Intellectual regeneration would lead to the renovation of moral or social doctrines, and these would in turn give rise to a "new spiritual authority" that would discipline minds, reconstruct morals, and then become the basis of the final political regime of "humanity."[184] Comte was getting very close to his Religion of Humanity.

Although Comte maintained that his law of three stages was the "abstract expression of general reality," he introduced no data that would have contested his theory.[185] Comte's law presented a very schematic view of history. It is all too evident that he had imposed this law on the past and had sought only developments confirming it. He had, for example, vastly overestimated the decline of religion and the military spirit. And when he claimed that the government had completely abandoned the intellectual and moral realm, he overlooked the censorship to which he himself was subject as well as the governmental regulations about the educational system that had prevented him from becoming part of the University. Much of Comte's theory derived from wishful thinking.

The utopian nature of Comte's thought is evident in the way he used the law of three stages to predict the future. The positive state would first establish the separation of powers, the social expression of the relation between theory and practice. Comte was sure that contemplative life required its own culture and direction and that there had to be an independent power solely responsible for assuring the supremacy of morality in society. With the idea of subsidizing geniuses firmly planted in his mind, he maintained that to guide progress, society should favor the "exceptional intelligences," who consecrate their lives to "thinking for the whole species" and represent the "most important wealth" of the human race. Never denying that he was reviving the "social office of the Catholic clergy," he maintained that the spiritual power's main function would be to direct education and to serve as a consultant in the realm of action, where it would bring to bear its moral principles to influence practical decision makers.[186] The temporal power would be supreme in matters of action and only advisory in the educational realm, where it could at most ask for a revision of principles harmful to practice.

[183] Ibid., 650.   [184] Ibid., 650–1.   [185] Ibid., 650.   [186] Ibid., 328, 660.

Although he did not say which power was superior, Comte seemed to favor the spiritual power. Since ideas ruled the world and were ultimately more important than practice, he argued that thinkers had an indirect, "final efficacy," which was superior to that of practical men and would increase with the growing influence of intelligence on society. Furthermore, he believed that the reorganization of society depended on the reform of the spiritual power, which would lead to the transformation of the temporal power. Toward the end of the *Cours*, his emphasis on moral reform grew stronger. He wrote that "the growth of our sociability tends . . . to make human government more and more moral and less and less political." When he described the need for the spiritual power to remind the industrial classes of moral precepts, he declared that "legitimate social supremacy does not belong . . . to force or to reason but to morality, dominating equally the acts of the latter and the advice of the former." These comments suggest that in his mind the temporal power would almost wither away. Yet he implied the contrary when he said in lesson 60 that the "positive organism" would become "more and more moral and less and less political without the practical power ever being able to lose its preponderant activity."[187] Thus Comte seemed to oscillate between materialism and idealism. On the one hand, he felt that though active, practical life would be more subject to speculative life, it would always remain dominant because most people were naturally actors and their fundamental needs had to be satisfied. On the other hand, he dreamed of the superiority of the spiritual authority – especially in the area of morality. This tension in his thought remained unresolved.

It is clear, however, that Comte increasingly referred to the spiritual power as a "new moral power." Its "characteristic mission" was to make "universal morality prevail in the whole social movement."[188] Positive morality would be more charitable than metaphysical morality, which was essentially egotistical. In 1841 Comte seemed already prepared to make morality the seventh science in control of all the rest. It was usurping the role just established for sociology. In fact, in this entire section on spiritual reorganization, Comte made no mention of sociology and focused his whole attention on moral philosophy. Perhaps after failing to obtain his chair, he had lost his enthusiasm not only for scientists, but for science as well. The *Système* would further develop his idea that morality, not the intellect or force, would be the true source of power in the positive era.[189]

In the *Cours*, Comte was not specific about the makeup of the

---

[187] Ibid., 655, 657, 782–3.   [188] Ibid., 659, 680.   [189] Kofman, *Aberrations*, 284.

new spiritual power. He explained that it would arise spontaneously and would consist of an "entirely new class without analogy to any of those who exist." At least at the outset, the members of this class would come from all walks of life and all social classes. Although the most talented scientists would become positive philosophers, the scientific contingent would probably not even be dominant. Scientists who did join would have to be philosophical. This new spiritual "European corporation" would also attract philosophers who had returned to science. By this time, science would be fully united with philosophy, and therefore the spiritual corporation could be considered either scientific or philosophical. Here Comte was trying to assure his readers that he was *not* trying to make the scientific community the new spiritual power. He would welcome all sorts of disciples, who would spontaneously become the new spiritual power once they obtained uniform views and common goals through courses in general education.[190]

The separation of powers would restore social harmony by satisfying the demands of the "masses" and the "most active minds," both of whom had legitimate complaints against the present system. Comte maintained that the needs of the masses were moral, not political, and would be fulfilled by the positive spiritual organization, which would make all classes accept their "moral duties." In this way, positivism would replace the "vague and stormy discussion of *rights*," which were basically negative and individualistic, by the "calm and rigorous determination of respective *duties*," which were positive and social.[191] The intellectuals would be pleased to have a consultative and educational role, which would suit their nature and make them more influential.

Yet his system would not please the "majority of thinkers preoccupied by social questions," who wanted the mind to govern the world by the "so-called right of capacity." Giving in to them would lead to a "degrading immobility analogous to that of theocracies." Comte claimed that his ideas on this subject had won the approval of "one of the most eminent and most independent thinkers" in England – John Stuart Mill – who had invented a new term, "pedantocracy," to describe the "profoundly oppressive domination . . . of ambitious mediocrities." By recommending the use of this term and describing the "happy epistolary commerce" between himself and Mill, Comte was at the same time cleverly announcing the latter's support for his philosophy.[192]

Throughout the *Cours*, Comte sought to allay his readers' fears

---

[190] *Cours*, 2:652, 662.   [191] Ibid., 658–9.
[192] Ibid., 655–7. Comte used the term "pedantocracy" again on page 779.

that he wanted to establish a scientific or intellectual dictatorship. Here he wished to stress his disagreement with liberals, who sought to give control of both the "speculative and active" government to those endowed with the "highest mental capacities."[193] He had in mind particularly Guizot, the notoriously ambitious minister who believed that the "capacity" of acting according to some transcendent notion of reason conferred the right to govern.[194] Comte also wished to distance himself once again from the Saint-Simonians – the "pernicious sect" that formulated "with the most ignoble exaggeration the dream [of the reign of the mind] cultivated by almost all ambitious thinkers." To Comte, a government of philosophers was an "illusion." Who were these philosophers? They were men with only a "vain erudition."[195] A good government was one in which morality, not reason or force, was supreme. Comte recognized that intellectuals were not necessarily moral. They were certainly no more moral by nature than businessmen, politicians, or other men involved in the public sphere. What made someone moral, in Comte's mind, was his devotion to the whole, that is, society. And this devotion to society came from having a general education and general activities.

To stress the nondictatorial nature of his state, Comte insisted that the moral government would not encroach upon the political government and that assent to positive principles would come logically, not by force. Moreover, positive authority would be *relative* because no one could know everything and there would be no absolute authority. Using the terminology of the reform movements of the 1840s, Comte declared that positivism would lead to the "emancipation" of mankind, whose dignity and energy would then grow freely.[196] But it does not seem that Comte's doctrine of the separation of powers went far enough in dispelling the dangers of conservatism, authoritarianism, and intellectual megalomania that he recognized were inherent in his system.

As already mentioned, education was to be the primary concern of the spiritual power. This was consistent with Comte's own role as a teacher and his goal to make the positive doctrine the basis of the educational system. With homogeneous scientific principles, positive philosophy would give human understanding a basic foundation and would ensure the triumph of the spirit of the whole to strengthen modern sociability. To become part of a common doctrine, the sciences would be condensed and better coordinated. In this way, the scientific spirit would grow more general and philosophical.

---

[193] Ibid., 657.   [194] On Guizot's idea of capacity, see Rosanvallon, *Le Moment Guizot*, 95–104.
[195] *Cours*, 2:656–7.   [196] Ibid., 657.

The new system of education would be "not only intellectual but also and especially moral." Making use of Lamarck's theory of the development of the faculties through exercise, Comte declared that people would be taught at an early age the habits that stimulate social feelings. Positivism's deep understanding of human nature ensured that it alone would systematically develop the social sentiments, the basis of morality. Whereas theology made egoism inherent in all moral action and metaphysics imitated theology by stressing self-interest, positive morality would appeal to and develop people's "generous instincts," especially by honestly proclaiming that the only reward for benevolence was "interior satisfaction."[197]

The purpose of education was to unify individuals, classes, nations, and generations, in short, to ensure social harmony. Positive education would be a permanent feature in the life of every person throughout the European republic and, with minor exceptions, would be identical for all classes. To stimulate the feeling of social solidarity, it would also imitate the Catholic system of commemoration by glorifying the phases of human evolution and the main promoters of the progress of each phase. Comte would later create the Positivist Calendar to incorporate this system. Reflecting the liberalism of his youth, Comte asserted that education would, moreover, ensure social mobility by allowing each person to achieve a position that "best suited his aptitudes in whatever rank his birth had thrown him."[198] Here he seemed to contradict his previous stress on the need to maintain a rigid social hierarchy.

In its advisory role, the spiritual power would be consulted in personal matters and in public affairs, especially in international relations, where finding an objective, nonaligned temporal power was impossible. It would become the supreme arbiter in all disputes, because everyone would have been educated in the positive system and would therefore trust the judgments of their teachers in all domains. Whereas the temporal authority depended on its material force or wealth, which was often repugnant, the spiritual authority rested on confidence freely given to "intellectual and moral superiority." Positive faith did not rest on revelation, which precluded popular participation, but on a "true demonstration whose examination is permitted to everyone under determined conditions."[199] Comte did not explain these "determined conditions." He seemed to be generalizing from the respect he felt his students had for him and the esteem he had for his own teachers – Encontre, Poinsot, Saint-Simon, and Blainville. But even he did not always trust the judgment of at least the last three.

---

[197] Ibid., 660, 664.   [198] Ibid., 679.   [199] Ibid., 668.

Ultimately, Comte's rhetoric regarding science seemed influenced by liberal discourse. Although, like Maistre, he believed in the importance of faith in one's superiors, he also emphasized, in an almost democratic fashion, that scientific laws, especially about society, would have to prove their superiority to old theological and metaphysical theories and secure the public's "unanimous and durable approval."[200] Still influenced by the Enlightenment principles of his youth, Comte did not completely subscribe to the irrational or wholeheartedly support authoritarianism, as Maistre did. One reason is that he did not share Maistre's belief that people were totally evil.

For example, to solve social ills, Comte relied not only on education, the chief panacea of eighteenth-century philosophers, but also on the critical spirit that he so frequently disparaged. He asserted that as soon as this critical spirit was subordinated to the organic positive state, it would no longer be subversive and could eliminate abuses. All members of the spiritual power would have to fulfill strict intellectual and moral qualifications guaranteeing their rationality and benevolence. The former Catholic "right" to criticize "any authority who violated public obligations, without excepting even the spiritual authority" would be revived; everything would be debatable "under suitable conditions."[201]

But again Comte left these conditions obscure. For someone who prided himself on his lucidity and candor, he was remarkably vague about the new role of the critical spirit. If it was supposed to uphold the system, how could it be critical? How could Comte now speak of rights when he said that they were to be replaced by duties?

Turning his attention to the temporal sphere, he emphasized that once the new fields of industry and science became socially acceptable, each person's activity would have social value as it did under Catholicism. Here Comte went against one of the essential tenets of liberalism when he asserted that there would no longer be any line dividing the private and public spheres. Whereas liberals, like Constant, wished to preserve a realm of private action, where the individual would be free from the state, Comte foreshadowed modern totalitarianism by insisting that every person would be considered a public functionary, a contributor to the whole social economy. Unlike Smith, who argued that entrepreneurs unconsciously contributed to society, Comte sought to impose a "certain systematic discipline" to force people to think about the whole.[202] Presumably, no part of their lives would be free from some type of control by the temporal or spiritual power.

Applying to society his idea of classifying the animals according

[200] Ibid., 104.   [201] Ibid., 669.   [202] Ibid., 672.

to their proximity to man, he argued that the most important classes would be those that had the most developed human characteristics. For example, the speculative class was superior to the masses because it developed the "faculties of generalization and of abstraction that distinguish human nature." But Comte could not assert that the speculative class was superior to the active class without weakening his theory of the separation of powers. Thus he declared that power and respect were criteria of classification and were distributed according to different laws. The speculative class represented the highest social class in terms of gaining people's respect, while the active class was superior in terms of power because it exerted the most influence on society's actions. "The natural opposition of these two types of supremacy" would lead to a "normal state of rivalry between the two powers," which would be "incompatible with the prolonged despotism of either of them."[203] Yet Comte believed that the spiritual power's dependence on the temporal power would aggravate the tension between them, and the people would have to regulate the conflict. Here he seemed to be trying to set up a system of checks and balances à la Montesquieu. But it is not clear that the people would sufficiently respect the positive philosophers or have the requisite force to counterbalance the temporal power.

Comte classified social groups according to the general, abstract nature of their activity, which indicated whether or not they kept the importance of the whole in mind. The speculative class was divided into scientists or philosophers (whom he viewed as equivalent) and artists and poets. The first group was superior because its powers of "abstraction, generalization, and coordination" were more developed. The aesthetic class handled more concrete, specialized matters.[204] Within the practical class there were four divisions. Bankers were first, merchants second, manufacturers third, and agriculturalists fourth. Agreeing with Saint-Simon and the Saint-Simonians, Comte made bankers the leaders of the temporal realm. Because bankers' work was abstract and wide-ranging, they had the best sense of the whole and the finest political aptitudes.

Comte naively assumed that he could end the class conflict by demonstrating the natural relations of subordination in society; each class would understand and respect the superiority of the classes above it because the same conditions of growing abstraction and generality determined its own superiority to the classes below it. Workers, for example, would understand that their subordination did not rest on an "abuse of force or wealth," but on the fact that their employers had more abstract and general functions. They would

[203] Ibid., 674–5.   [204] Ibid., 675.

not be disheartened by "necessary inequalities," for they would enjoy their carefree, secure lives and the sentiment of being socially useful in a concrete, immediate sense. The upper classes could never experience such pleasures.[205] Comte seemed oblivious to the workers' genuine feelings of envy, frustration, and insecurity. But at the same time, he assumed that these very feelings would lead the workers to support the spiritual power against the temporal one.

In fact, reflecting the influence of the social question of the 1840s, Comte stressed that one of the main purposes of the positive regime would be to incorporate the workers into society. Unless their demands were met, the social point of view could not predominate. Moreover, the triumph of positivism required the common people's help in supporting the speculative class. He appealed to them by arguing that the spiritual power, although supposedly impartial, would protect them against the upper classes. The positive philosophers and the people could, in fact, satisfy their ambitions only if they joined their respective intellectual and active forces. In saying that the spiritual power and the masses were naturally linked because of their monetary problems and oppression by the temporal power, Comte was speaking to some extent from his own experience.

This political alliance was complemented by an intellectual one, for positive speculations agreed with and extended the common sense of the people. Unlike theologians or metaphysicians, who pretended to have superhuman powers and kept aloof from the masses, positive philosophers would resemble the masses in that they would deal with the same "common facts," rooted in experience, and employ the same routine "logical procedures" of connecting and foreseeing.[206] Moreover, the reason of the common people, which was at the origin of all positive ideas, must continue to define the field and goal of scientific exploration so that research would be useful and meet the demands of society as a whole. In short, in order to emphasize that positivism would recognize the social value of the masses, Comte showed that the intellectual interests of the positive philosophers and the people were as close as their political concerns.

Here Comte was laying claim to the heritage of the "great republican assembly," the Convention, which had made the cause of the people the "essential goal of true revolutionary politics."[207] He intended to complete the work of the Revolution and surpass the man who was its traitor – Napoleon. Like Marx and Lenin, Comte was a déclassé who sought to become a leader of the masses.

Generalizing from his personal experience of teaching astronomy to the workers, he asserted, moreover, that the speculative class

[205] Ibid., 676–7.   [206] Ibid., 721.   [207] Ibid., 686.

would be effective among the people especially because it would be most devoted to their education. The positive philosophers would teach the workers the futility of political solutions, the indispensability of moral reforms, and the importance of allowing the industrial leaders to accumulate large sums so that they could use it in the interest of society. Such indoctrination would repress anarchical activity and deprive the "jugglers" (Saint-Simonians) and utopian thinkers of the opportunity to foment social chaos.[208] The upper classes would then have no more pretexts to delay large-scale social reform. In fact, by its control over morality, the spiritual power would compel the upper class to use its capital for the common good, especially by providing education and a job for everyone. It is evident that in Comte's system, change would come from the top, not from the bottom.

His plans for reorganizing society were confusing and contradictory. But it seems that he meant them to be ambiguous, for he sought the approval of the parties on the Left, who promoted progress, as well as those on the Right, who sought order. Appealing to the revolutionaries, he claimed that positive politics took up the people's cause, made better use of the critical spirit, and was more progressive than their own doctrines, which were reviving religion and militarism. He promised an intellectual and temporal reorganization that would be more extensive than any previous one. But carefully avoiding labeling this reorganization a "revolution," he argued that the conservative parties' desires would also be satisfied, for positivism was more organic than their doctrines. As the spirit of the whole and the feeling of duty came to dominate, the moral solutions to present problems would become more evident. Influenced by relativism, people would be persuaded that the present state of affairs was a "necessary" result of all of the past. Positivism would also ensure that only those who were scientifically and logically qualified could engage in social research. These arguments showing the orderly nature of positive political philosophy demonstrated that there were "partial, but very important points of contact" between positivism and the stationary and reactionary schools. They would surely appreciate his praise of the Middle Ages. Yet they would have to give up their dreams of restoring or keeping a "rotten" social system, including God and the king.[209] By asking the conservatives to abandon their most cherished principles, Comte still seemed to be tilting more toward the Left than the Right.

He proposed a plan to establish positivism throughout Western Europe, a practical project reminiscent of Saint-Simon. He called

[208] Ibid., 682.   [209] Ibid., 687–8, 691.

on the French, Italians, Germans, English, and Spanish to form the "Occidental Positive Committee" (Comité positif occidental), with headquarters in Paris. Because he believed that positivism could "reconcile everything without compromising anything," he hoped to draw disciples from each social group, including the clergy, which would join because of his stress on spiritual authority, and the military, which would like his idea that armies had to maintain material order during the time of transition. This council would initiate the positive reorganization by systematizing intellectual and moral life, applying positive precepts to political and social conflicts, and creating a new type of scientific and aesthetic education to propagate positivist ideas. Comte regarded this association as the "permanent council of the Positive Church."[210]

Thus long before he met Clotilde de Vaux or began the *Système*, Comte wanted to establish a church. Founding a positivist religion was the next logical step, especially because throughout this chapter (lesson 57) the discussion had taken on an increasingly moral tone and he had shown that positivism was to replace Catholicism in all its functions. Now that Comte was turning his attention to the political triumph of positivism, he realized it required an institution to represent it and carry it forward. The example of Catholicism showed that morality was weak without an organization and a creed. As his interest in the Right continued to grow, especially as a potential source of followers, the idea of establishing a church to lure the conservatives became ever more appealing. His decision to create a new church in an era of religious revival and utopian sects was understandable, if not original. The Saint-Simonians had already paved the way.

A REEVALUATION OF THE POSITIVE METHOD

Reviewing the positive method, doctrine, and future, the last three chapters of the *Cours* presented Comte's conclusions about all six sciences and about the philosophy he had just founded. He made it clear that his philosophy was to be the "basis of the spiritual regime of humanity," an idea that had been his original aim in writing the *Cours* but had been lost amid the scientific themes of the first volumes.[211] Now that he had established the scientific foundation of his reorganization, he no longer feared accusations of mysticism or metaphysics. He freely referred to his philosophy as a spiritual doctrine and even criticized "positivity."

[210] Ibid., 691, 696.   [211] Ibid., 699.

The first and most important conclusion was that since sociology rested on all the other sciences, it provided the connection among all positive ideas and therefore the philosophical unity that was the first condition of intellectual and moral reorganization. Yet Comte had suggested in his classification of the sciences that mathematics had intellectual preeminence and was the foundation of positive philosophy. His demotion of mathematics reflected his disillusionment with this science and his greater confidence in the "true positivity" of sociology. Using for the first time the word "sociologists" (*sociologistes*), he considered their triumph over mathematicians a personal victory. Now he talked freely of the "government of the sociologists."[212]

Reviewing his hierarchy from his new point of view, Comte divided the sciences into three groups according to the law of three stages and his conviction that man, especially in the current period, had two competing needs, generality and positivity. Mathematics and astronomy represented the origin of positivism, biology and sociology the endpoint, and physics and chemistry the intermediate group. Reflecting his own problems with mathematicians, Comte saw an inevitable conflict between the first group, with its scientific or positive spirit, which went from nature to man, and the last group, representing the philosophical or generalizing spirit, which went from man to external nature. Because he was deeply attached to both science and philosophy, the conflict between them raged within him too. (He even suggested, for the first time, that "positivity" was linked to specialization.) Yet he thought sociology would reconcile philosophy and science by incorporating what was legitimate and permanent in each. It would extend the *positivity* of external nature to the moral and social realm, while upholding the *generality* of the human point of view. With the preeminence of sociology, the synthetic spirit of the science of society would prevail over the analytical spirit of mathematics. Consequently, sociology would solve the main political difficulty, which involved reconciling order and progress, both of which depended on positivity and generality. Just as he was becoming more interested in morality than sociology, Comte now seemed more attracted to philosophy than science.

In his new view of mathematics, Comte saw the study of it as useful training in scientific logic, rationality, and "durable positivity." But whereas in the first volume of the *Cours* he had praised its abstraction, universality, and simplicity, he now found it insufficiently

---

[212] Ibid., 701, 703, 712. Curiously, the French dropped Comte's term *sociologiste* and use the word *sociologue*.

general and complex. Its deductive logic was too often a "sort of technical mechanism," substituting "argumentation for observation." Although heretofore it had been the sole science that offered guarantees of positivity, he now criticized it for failing to form a universal philosophy or to grasp the positive method. Its problem was that it did not rest on the other sciences and did not know their laws. Lacking familiarity with the art of observation and the historical and comparative methods, it was imbued with the absolute instead of the relative spirit and frequently aimed to dominate the other sciences. Thus sociology had "legitimate rights" to prevail; it would henceforth direct the development of mankind's intellectual life.[213] With the completion of the *Cours*, which consolidated modern intellectual evolution, people could cultivate generality, that is, the spirit of the whole, instead of positivity, that is, the specialized, scientific spirit. Comte seemed to imply that not only mankind but he himself had been too preoccupied with positivity. By reviewing the sciences, he had learned that positivity alone was an inadequate guide to intellectual and moral life.

The main reason sociology could claim philosophical supremacy was that it established the only truly universal standpoint – the human point of view, which, to Comte, was always social, not individual. The metaphysicians' concentration on the individual, which began with Descartes, was immoral and egotistical, for the evolution of the individual could unveil no important laws. In a famous passage reminiscent of Bonald, Comte declared that man was not real, for only humanity was.[214] In fact, owing to the development of intelligence and "sociability," the human species was being transformed into a "single individual, immense and eternal."[215] Comte's reification of society and rejection of the liberal philosophy of individualism could not be clearer.

The law of three stages, the basis of the positive method and of sociology, took into account the fact that the development of society, or humanity, was the only evolution that was "real and complete enough to manifest sufficiently the true march of our intelligence." Moreover, since the human intellect could grow only within an association, this law demonstrated the "simultaneous march of the human mind and society." And because all conceptions could be considered from a historical point of view, this law was universally applicable. In a sense, Comte was substituting the law of three stages for Saint-Simon's scientific law of gravity. To him, "scientific progress" consisted of "diminishing gradually the number of . . . laws while extending . . . the connections between them."[216]

[213] Ibid., 701, 703, 707.   [214] Ibid., 715.   [215] Ibid., 1:681.   [216] Ibid., 2:707, 716, 720.

Instead of basing the unity of knowledge on a single principle as Saint-Simon had tried to do with the theory of gravity, Comte thus attempted to achieve this harmony in two other ways. One was through the positive method, which would make all ideas homogeneous. The other, more important way was through a global scientific discipline based on one philosophical principle, which was more reductionist than he cared to admit.

He believed that sociology could use the law of history to create the unity that had forever eluded mathematics, for all of the sciences could be referred to it. He was aware that he was shocking his readers and making sociology far more influential and powerful than he had intended at the beginning:

> From this moment, readers . . . must appreciate . . . the new light that this new universal spirit, spontaneously constituted by the creation of sociology, can immediately cast on each of the anterior sciences – much beyond, I dare say, the initial promises formulated twelve years ago in my two first chapters.[217]

In sum, Comte made sociology the universal science because he felt its influence on the other sciences would unify his philosophical system. Sociology would ensure that all of the sciences kept in mind the social point of view, the spirit of the whole.

The change in Comte's approach to sociology is evident. Previously he had said that the law of human development would never be perfect and that it would be "chimerical" to imagine that the scientific hierarchy could be inverted. Now he asserted that the "ascending order" of growing complexity and specialization, which were the criteria he had used to classify the sciences, would switch to a "descending order" with the founding of sociology.[218] Although in his original classification of the sciences, sociology dealt with the most specific phenomena, Comte argued that once established it would become the first and most general science with control over all the others. Sociology, which was based on all the other sciences, would become their foundation. In effect, they would all become parts of sociology. The mathematicians' oppressive 300-year reign would come to an end. While Marx was turning Hegel's system upside down, Comte was doing the same with his own philosophy. It seemed that he was projecting his own megalomania onto his science to make it supreme.

The same sort of inversion or circular return that made sociology the first and, in truth, the only science would take place in the development of civilization and society. As the least abstract science

---

[217] Ibid., 708.   [218] Ibid., 170, 492.

and the one that was most concerned with the human point of view, sociology would favor not only the sciences but the arts. It would reconcile the aesthetic and scientific points of view, while making sure that the feeling of the beautiful or "ideality" did not overrule the "knowledge of the truth" or "reality."[219] Sociology would do more for the flowering of the arts than the theological and metaphysical philosophies had done. It would also improve industry by making man's action on nature more systematic and socially beneficial. In short, the future evolution of humanity would be the opposite of what it had been during the metaphysical transition; first the sciences would progress, then the arts, and finally industry. This was a return to the order that had prevailed in the primitive stage of history, in which intellectual activity developed first because of civilization's close ties to the theocratic principle, and the arts then blossomed because of their close connection with theocracy. Positivism was thus the endpoint in the ascending direction of progress. Once established, it would become the point of departure in the descending direction of human progress and would determine the development of the other realms of human activity. The future history of humanity represented, paradoxically, a return to the past.

Sociology's domination would end the contradiction between intellectual progress and moral development. By giving priority to morality, not the mind, it would accomplish the unfulfilled mission of medieval Catholicism. The supremacy of morality would improve the intellectual system not only by making scholars more sincere and generous but by giving intellectual progress a social goal. In one of the most important passages of the *Cours*, Comte wrote:

> The moral properties inherent in the great conception of God could not be suitably replaced by those included in the vague entity of nature; but they are, on the contrary, necessarily inferior in intensity and in stability to those which characterize the inalterable notion of humanity, which is finally presiding . . . over the satisfaction of all our intellectual and social needs in the full maturity of our collective organism.[220]

Here, for the first time, Comte suggested that the positive philosophy would replace the notion of God with the concept of humanity. The superiority of morality and its corollary, the supremacy of humanity, represented the "essence of positive philosophy." Criticizing the theological concept of God as well as the metaphysical idea of Nature, Comte claimed that the main result of history was

[219] Ibid., 738–9.   [220] Ibid., 715.

the "spontaneous convergence of all modern conceptions toward the great notion of humanity, whose . . . final preponderance must in every sense replace the old theological–metaphysical coordination." The idea of humanity would thus lead to a "new mental unity," which would be "necessarily more complete and durable than any other," and a new moral unity.[221] Although Comte had criticized theology for having made man the center of the universe, in a sense he was returning to this approach by substituting society (or humanity) for man. He was also falling back into metaphysical thinking by replacing nature with humanity. Whereas throughout the *Cours* he had condemned the search for unity by means of a principle or concept, at the end he seemed to repeat the same mistake.

Comte also reevaluated the use of observation and rationalism, equated respectively with induction and deduction. He reiterated his position that scientists had to create hypotheses to connect facts and that the positive spirit would "enlarge as much as possible the rational domain at the expense of the experiential domain." But whereas in the early chapters of the *Cours* he had suggested that the lower sciences, especially mathematics, were primarily deductive, he now asserted that the complex sciences also had many deductive ideas, which it borrowed from the simple ones. Reflecting his new animus against mathematicians and his greater emphasis on the deductive side of positivism, he went so far as to state that because sociology rested on all the other sciences and its phenomena were more interconnected, it was the "most rational of the sciences" and used more "a priori considerations" than any other science, including, presumably, mathematics. A single theory – the law of three stages – allowed the social scientist to *deduce* a wide range of the "most difficult speculations."[222] Comte thus made sociology, instead of mathematics, the model of the deductive science.

However, Comte still warned that rationality, if used alone, led to "mysticism" or to an "absurd metaphysical utopia."[223] To have a basis in reality, a priori reasoning had to derive ultimately from observation. Yet again he did not clarify at which point deduction could legitimately be used instead of induction.

Comte's appreciation of the principle of relativism deepened, for he extended it from politics to epistemology. Referring to Kant's theories for support, Comte argued that it was impossible to know external reality. Man's ideas about the inorganic world were relative because he could be only a spectator of phenomena that were essentially independent of him. Moreover, his own milieu (environment) and organism (body) shaped his "impressions and thoughts" in ways

---

[221] Ibid., 715, 785.   [222] Ibid., 720, 748.   [223] Ibid., 719, 727.

that could not be determined. Nevertheless, although Comte did not use Kant's expression "categories," he assumed that people's conceptions about the world were ultimately very similar because their "understandings" were homogeneous.[224]

Criticizing Kant for not understanding historical relativism, Comte also argued that the intellect changed and evolved throughout time. Although positivism could never completely attain "truth," a word that indeed hardly ever appears in the *Cours*, its theories would come closer and closer to reality because it would lead to a greater harmony between man's conceptions and observations. Positivism would, in fact, subordinate conceptions to "reality." Comte evidently did believe in the existence of an independent reality that could be approximated, although never completely grasped. Yet he neither examined the ways this reality was to be approached nor explained the limits of our knowledge. As Valat tried to tell him, his philosophy lacked a crucial element: a solid epistemological foundation.

Despite his vagueness regarding epistemology, Comte argued that the positive method was the source of mental harmony and logical coherence both in the individual and in society. Its ability to connect and extend ideas satisfied the human need not only for order, which was related to connection, but for progress, which derived from extension. For the first time, Comte suggested that order was more important than progress, especially because intellectual order, or "logical coherence," was our closest approximation to truth and reality.[225] Moreover, order was the basis of progress, for without intellectual harmony, it would be impossible to make predictions – the essence of scientific thought and a principal source of progress – or to maintain society itself.

Another advantage of sociology would be its ability to connect more closely theory and practice. Comte insisted that speculation had to be favored over practice because the mental need to know and link phenomena favored progress and the positive spirit. Yet practice had a beneficial effect on theory. Practical needs had stimulated the growth of positivism in the first place by activating and directing a normally sluggish intellect. With the impact of these needs growing steadily stronger, positivism would bring practical activity and science even closer together. Under positivism, scholars would be subjected to a "wise philosophical discipline," or "repression," so that they would be forced to work on the most pressing problems of their time, ones that affected humanity in some way. Therefore, scholars would not be permitted to analyze subjects in a very detailed fashion or explore certain topics merely to "satisfy a

[224] Ibid., 727–9.   [225] Ibid., 731.

vain curiosity."[226] Objecting both to excessive specialization and to a complete disregard of practice, Comte wanted to encourage scholars to work for the improvement of society. In so doing, he risked interfering with their freedom to conduct exhaustive research.

Just as speculation and practice would become closer, so would the sciences and arts. The scientists would give the artists a philosophical foundation, and in return the artists would provide them with the "most precious mental diversion and the sweetest moral stimulation." In forming hypotheses, scientists would legitimately use their aesthetic preferences to make their scientific thoughts more beautiful without detracting from the reality of their conceptions. Comte's appreciation of the aesthetic element in the formation of scientific hypotheses is strikingly modern, foreshadowing the work of Thomas Kuhn.

At the end of this chapter, Comte discussed the five main phases of the evolution of the positive method: the mathematical (which still remained the basis of logical education since it taught deduction), the astronomical (which developed observation), the physico-chemical (which generated experimentation), the biological (which produced the comparative method), and the sociological (which was the source of the historical method).[227] In each phase, the scientific spirit was raised a little closer to the philosophical spirit. Comte felt that each individual and each society should experience this historical evolution as he had done.

He concluded that his discussion of the positive method was "equivalent to the initial discourse of Descartes on method." He maintained that Descartes's masterpiece had laid the groundwork for "rational positivity," although it had overlooked Bacon's social objectives.[228] Because Comte believed that the correct scientific method had developed to a greater extent than the "sound" philosophy and that logical needs were more important than scientific ones, he was convinced that his final institution of the positive method was the crucial first step toward the triumph of the new philosophy. Thus he had no qualms in claiming to be Descartes's successor.

[226] Ibid., 734–5, 751. Comte's articles for *Le Producteur* seemed to stress to a greater extent the necessary independence of the scientist.

[227] Curiously, Comte made the development of physics and chemistry one phase because logically (not scientifically) they were similar in using the same method of exploration: experimentation. Both also used the same logical device, that of corpuscular or atomistic theory.

[228] Ibid., 703, 749.

A REASSESSMENT OF THE POSITIVE DOCTRINE

From the positive method, Comte turned to the positive doctrine. Previously he had said that his system of knowledge consisted of the inorganic and organic sciences. Now, more convinced that positivism was limited to the knowledge of phenomena that could influence the human species in some fashion, he changed his terminology slightly, asserting that the positive system comprised two main elements: "humanity" and the "general milieu." These two terms foreshadowed the "Great-Being" and the "Great-Milieu," which together with the "Great-Fetish" would constitute the "religious triumvirate" of the *Synthèse subjective*.[229]

The "milieu" comprised three "modes": the mathematical or astronomical, the physical, and the chemical. They were studied by the three inorganic sciences. "Humanity" had two "modes": the individual and society, studied by biology and sociology.[230] These five "modes," or steps, of the scientific series corresponded to the five phases of the logical evolution described in the preceding chapter. Essentially Comte was saying that the subordination of the study of humanity to the study of the milieu was both logical and scientific. Logically, one first had to study the positive method in the simpler sciences where it originated. Scientifically, one first had to examine the "conditions of existence" on which humanity depended. The positive system was thus united both scientifically and logically.

Comte seemed to be getting lost in a useless accumulation of details. He appeared to be playing with his system, rearranging the parts, redefining his terms, and creating schema after schema for no apparent reason. His intellectual games suggest that his hold on reality was slipping.

Curiously, however, he claimed that the sciences grew not only in complexity but in "reality." As their phenomena grew more complex, they were linked more to the other parts of natural philosophy, and this "close connection" constituted "their more pronounced reality."[231] He again implied that humanity was the most fundamental component of reality.

The entire *Cours* reflected Comte's basic allegiance to order and its corollaries: unity, interdependence, and harmony. This fascination is reflected in his admiration for the sciences. He praised mathematics for inculcating the ideas of order and harmony, and astronomy

---

[229] *Synthèse*, 107.

[230] *Cours*, 2:751. Having combined physics and chemistry into one methodological phase, Comte now joined mathematics and astronomy together in his scientific doctrine.

[231] Ibid., 753.

for teaching resignation to an unchangeable order. In fact, he now argued that the "ideas of order and harmony had to derive originally from inorganic studies because of their greater simplicity." He hoped one day that these laws of order would explain the nature of progress.[232] The "highest manifestation" of the ideas of order and harmony would, however, be the concepts of classification and hierarchy, which derived from biology and would be extended to society. Sociology would then "send them back everywhere with an irresistible energy."[233]

In sum, sociology, now called the "study of humanity," had two functions. Intellectually, it made a true system out of human knowledge by subjecting it to a hierarchy and to a law of evolution. Morally, it showed that individual and social progress consisted in the development of "our humanity over our animality, according to the double supremacy of the intellect over the penchants [especially in the growth of abstraction and generalization] and the sympathetic instinct over the personal instinct."[234] To make morality dominant, sociology made the social point of view, that is, the idea of the whole, supreme and developed the feelings of social solidarity and continuity. In this way, Comte presented his new science as an antidote to the egoism and indifference inherent in the scientific spirit and in modern life in general.

THE FUTURE CONSEQUENCES OF THE POSITIVE PHILOSOPHY

The final lesson of the *Cours* reviewed the regeneration that positive philosophy would effect once it triumphed. In terms of the intellect, positivism would lead to the "entire renovation of human reason."[235] Intellectual harmony would be greater than ever, because all conceptions would be positive and therefore homogeneous. Positivism would represent the final triumph of the wisdom of the people, who were avid to know the fundamental laws of phenomena, not their first causes. Its relativism would renew reason by showing that rational theories could only approximate an always elusive reality. This logical appreciation would accord with man's scientific knowledge that there was a natural order independent of his action, whose influence was very limited. Positivism would unite and improve all the sciences by subjecting them to the same method, giving them

---

[232] Ibid., 762. He pointed out that certain scientific laws were universal because human knowledge had a "scientific unity" that converged with its "logical unity." One example was Kepler's law of inertia, which was reflected in the "stubborn tendency of every political system to perpetuate itself spontaneously." Ibid., 753.

[233] Ibid., 764.   [234] Ibid., 748, 769.   [235] Ibid., 771.

the same goal, and subordinating them to the same evolutionary law. Finally, positivism would give the human intellect more liberty than absolutist theories, thereby accelerating progress.

The triumph of positive philosophy would result in a moral regeneration because it would extend the predominance of the view of the whole – the social point of view – from science and logic to morality and politics. As a result, the antagonism between intellectual and moral needs would finally end. By teaching individuals to value the present instead of seeking future rewards and by showing them that their behavior was a matter of public concern, positive morality would make their conduct more practical and force them to improve their personal lives as well as collective existence. Once they understood that the brutal penchants at first predominate, they would repress these animalistic inclinations and cultivate their affective and intellectual qualities, the marks of the human being. Although never able to attain perfection, they would become increasingly noble. Here Comte, in contrast to Maistre, for example, seemed to suggest that an individual could fundamentally change his nature by exercising great self-discipline.

According to Comte, positivism was the only philosophy that could make social morality prevail, because it alone believed strongly in the existence of purely benevolent and disinterested affections. It would encourage their development by emphasizing human solidarity and human perpetuity. This concept of the association of all people, or humanity, was an inspiring force that he felt was missing from religious systems. He argued, moreover, that individuals could best satisfy their natural "need for eternity" and attain happiness not by resorting to traditional religions but by contributing daily to the progress of humanity, especially through "benevolent actions" and "sympathetic emotions."[236] Although Comte did not yet declare that positivism was a religion, he was in the process of defining its religious characteristics.

The political regeneration of society was still positivism's "main destination." After all, one of the primary goals of the *Cours* was to constitute "directly" the new spiritual power – the "first social condition of the final regeneration."[237] Because of its ability to create mental harmony, positivism would lead to a worldwide spiritual association that would be larger, more complete, and more stable than that created by religions. Nations would become more interconnected, political repression would be reduced, and liberty and order would be assured. The crisis of the French Revolution would finally come to an end.

---

[236] Ibid., 778.   [237] Ibid., 779, 782.

This renovation of the social system would also come about because of the alliance between positivism's philosophical tendencies and the "popular impulses" at large. Since everyone would recognize the "mental supremacy of common reason," they would realize the corresponding importance of satisfying "true popular needs." Moreover, the problems of the common people would attract the most attention because of the "universal ascendancy of morality, dominating at the same time scientific inspirations and political determinations."[238]

Positivism would also regenerate the arts, making them finally correspond to modern civilization by freeing them from the influence of antiquity and devoting them to the glorification of peace, industrialism, and human sociability. By idealizing positive society in this fashion, artists would be inspired not only by the private realm but by public life as well. The idea of humanity would be a far more powerful stimulant than the theological concept of God or the metaphysical idea of perfect Nature, both of which detracted from man's achievements. Works of art would also become more popular than ever before because they would be in harmony with the widespread noble feeling of human superiority and with rational conceptions. Their political role would be to create and propagate intellectual and moral ideal types necessary to the spiritual organization. Comte would later develop this idea of using "fictional beings" as a source of inspiration in the Religion of Humanity.[239] In sum, the arts under positivism would improve human character far more effectively than ever before.

The mental, social, and aesthetic regeneration brought about by positivism would lead to the regime that best conformed to human nature. Able to develop freely, human attributes would be strengthened and harmonized. The social system would "greatly surpass in homogeneity, extension, and stability everything that the past had ever been able to offer." Instead of stressing the limitations of human activity and the need to resign oneself to one's condition, Comte ended the *Cours* on a very optimistic and, indeed, inspiring note. He called man the "supreme chief of the natural economy, which he modifies ceaselessly for his advantage with a wise boldness that is entirely free from every useless scruple and oppressive terror."[240]

Finally, Comte argued that because of the similarity between individual and collective minds, "any philosophy that can constitute a true logical coherence within one single mind proves by this fact alone that it can later rally the entire mass of thinkers." "Great philosophical geniuses," who were the "intellectual guides of humanity,"

---

[238] Ibid., 783.   [239] Ibid., 786.   [240] Ibid., 783, 785.

should not forget that all men were "collaborators" in the discovery of truth and that isolating themselves from the public would be "irrational" and "immoral." A genius always had to be under the "control of public reason," which would strengthen and correct his "adventurous" course until he obtained "universal assent, the final object of his works." In effect, Comte was claiming that because positivism had created intellectual order in his own mind, it would inevitably spread to all thinkers, who would then convert the masses. Yet with his regime of cerebral hygiene, he cultivated his isolation. And he himself was not checked by "public reason," because every time he was criticized, he accused his critic of a lack of understanding, poor education, or moral corruption. Nevertheless, Comte had not lost his youthful ideal of persuading all thinkers to collaborate in a new *Encyclopédie*. He still hoped that his own example of having reached the positive state would attract "all energetic thinkers to construct in common the final systematization of modern reason."[241] He boasted that "the complete and organic school, that of Diderot, Hume and Condorcet, relives in me. What they pursued at that time in a confused manner through the *Encyclopédie* is spontaneously realized in positivism."[242]

He also proclaimed that "true philosophers" had to present an example of the moral attributes of positivism, for they were the "natural precursors of humanity." Their personal, domestic, and social conduct had to be exemplary in order to prove to others that a sense of morality could exist solely on human grounds. Comte was repelled by the "pernicious metaphysical maxim" that forbade "any public appreciation of private life."[243] The conception of the positivist clergy and its obligation to live openly, without any real private life, was germinating in Comte's mind. Already with the "Personal Preface," his own private life was invading his philosophy – with devastating consequences.

---

[241] Ibid., 732, 788. [242] Comte to M'Clintock, August 7, 1852, *CG*, 6:325.
[243] *Cours*, 2:779.

Conclusion

In the 1860s, when Mill was contemplating his work on Comte, Gustave d'Eichthal asked him if he intended to include an exposition of the philosopher's life. Without hesitation, Mill replied, "In this work, a biography of Comte will count for very little, even more so since those who dispute around his tomb are in such disagreement as to the facts that I despair of arriving at the truth."[1] This book has attempted to accept the challenging task of tracing what Comte significantly termed his "original evolution."[2] It has focused on his demanding family, his regimented education, his volatile relations with friends and important figures of the period, his intense rivalry with the Saint-Simonians, his struggle against insanity, his enigmatic marriage, and the vicissitudes of his career. It has tied this personal story to the development of his thought and set both within the historical context. Comte's intellectual evolution is examined within the framework of the French Revolution and its aftermath, when the French were debating the advantages and disadvantages of both liberalism and nascent industrial capitalism.

Although the story of the last fifteen years of Comte's life remains to be told, I have maintained that there was no sudden break in his life in 1842. Particularly in the *Cours*, one can see that the seeds of the Religion of Humanity, the Positivist Society (together with the Positivist Subsidy), and his establishment of morality as the seventh science had already been planted. Moreover, Comte's search for a woman who could satisfy his demands for love and purity had already begun – at least in his mind. Clotilde de Vaux would become the realization of Comte's ideal woman of the positivist era. She did not inspire the model of the chaste, loving auxiliary of the spiritual power; she only enabled Comte to fill in the details.

The picture of Comte that emerges from this study is that of a man of strong convictions. Many of his decisions were, in fact, dictated by his strong fear of losing his independence and integrity. His anxiety was intensified by his paranoid character. Consequently,

---

[1] Mill to Gustave d'Eichthal, March 30, 1864, *Later Letters*, 15:931. The work that Mill was about to write was *Auguste Comte and Positivism* (1865).

[2] *Cours*, 2:749.

any relationship based on equality was impossible for him to bear. His contemporaries rightly pointed out that Comte appeared annoyingly stubborn and self-assured, if not arrogant. The high moral and intellectual standards that he set for himself, his friends, and his colleagues tended to alienate those around him. People close to him, such as the members of his family, Caroline Massin, Valat, d'Eichthal, Tabarié, Saint-Simon, Guizot, and professors at the Ecole Polytechnique, found him difficult to please. Gradually, Comte retreated more and more to his own world, set up a regime of "cerebral hygiene," and reveled in his eccentricity.

Unable to establish a truly loving relationship with his family or wife, Comte finally chose to find gratification in a love for humanity, which permitted him to avoid the difficulties inherent in personal associations. To his philosophical system, Comte brought a compulsive interest in integration, unity, and harmony, which were absent in the contemporary society, in his family, and, at least at the beginning of his career, in himself. Unity and coherence were, to Comte, the signs of mental health and normality.[3] The consensus for which he and his family members yearned was finally to be realized in society. Always a rebel, he prided himself on being the victim of his philosophy and then the savior of humanity. It is paradoxical that the founder of sociology – the science that specializes in the study of social relations – was a man who felt so ill at ease in the most basic human associations.

Though cold on the outside, Comte was sentimental and emotional within. As this book has demonstrated, he was convinced at an early age, before he met Clotilde de Vaux, that the emotions played a more significant role than the intellect in a person's life. They were responsible for an individual's intellectual activity and happiness. Comte was acutely aware of their importance because of his constant struggle against manic-depression. In his stress on the passions, he resembled many of the figures in the literary and artistic movement of his day. Yet he did not share their irrationalism, for he believed that individual and social development consisted of the growth of reason and of its influence on the emotions. The emotions could not change themselves; they had to be guided by ideas. At the same time, he never maintained that the emotional part of the individual should be eliminated or that its value should be lessened.

As Barbara Skarga has pointed out, Comte's effort to resolve the conflict between reason and emotion was one of the sources of the positive philosophy.[4] Disturbed by the social dislocations, the plethora of ineffective political experiments, and the growing

[3] Kofman, *Aberrations*, 206.   [4] Skarga, "Le Coeur et la raison," 385.

skepticism and secularization of the postrevolutionary period, he sought a synthesis to provide his contemporaries with new beliefs, that is, a new faith. The disappearance of divine right did not give rise immediately to another universally recognized unifying principle of legitimacy, and the absence of such a principle was a recurring problem throughout the nineteenth century. When, therefore, Comte spoke of the desperate need for a system of beliefs that would appeal to all classes, he was responding to a need felt by most of the leaders of society. This synthesis was particularly challenging because he believed it had to satisfy the demands of both the heart and the mind. Only if it were rational and emotional could it bring about the social consensus necessary to destroy the materialism and egoism of modern society.

Brought up in an era when the sciences seemed to be not only the source of certitude and change but the means of subverting the old regime, Comte naturally looked to them for the basis of his synthesis. Inspired by Bacon's dictum that knowledge was power, Comte devoted himself to uncovering the moral and political implications of scientific knowledge. Although remembered as a scientistic thinker, Comte was above all a moral and political philosopher. He never glorified the sciences for their own sake but considered them an instrument for improving social welfare. He intended to use them to create the new mental outlook required for the emerging modern industrial society. This intellectual revolution, he insisted, would lead to a transformation in morality and then to political and social reconstruction.

Montesquieu, Saint-Simon, Herder, and Hegel had shown Comte that society ultimately represented an application of ideas, particularly moral principles, because people were united by a common worldview. Politics and morality had to change just as the reigning philosophy did. As the nineteenth-century mind-set was growing more and more scientific, Comte assumed that politics and morality could also become scientific, since all aspects of knowledge were interrelated and the mind felt naturally compelled to make all of its ideas homogeneous. The way to create a unified system of knowledge was by applying the "positive method" to society – the last theological and metaphysical stronghold.

In his *Discours sur l'esprit positif* of 1844, Comte stated that the "positive" designated the real, the useful, the certain, the precise, the constructive (as opposed to the "negative"), and the relative.[5] He banished the theological and metaphysical search for first causes and

---

[5] Auguste Comte, *Discours sur l'esprit positif* (1844; Paris: Union générale d'éditions, 1963), 126–30.

essences because it involved insoluble questions and thus could not lead to conclusions useful to society. Inspired by Hume, Comte limited positive knowledge to the discovery of descriptive laws. These laws would express the relationships of succession and resemblance among phenomena. They would explain how, not why, phenomena existed. They would also allow science to perform its main function – that of making predictions about the future. Comte made it very clear that he was interested in the way facts were *connected* and organized into laws.

The term "positivism" that Comte created to describe his philosophy was so influential that by the late nineteenth century it was already a common word, recognized officially by the Académie Française in 1878.[6] But as the term became established, its meaning changed. It has come to mean today a "philosophical doctrine contending that sense perceptions are the only admissible basis of human knowledge and precise thought."[7] Gertrud Lenzer gives another definition:

> The triumph of the positive spirit consists in the reduction of quality to quantity in all realms of existence – in the realm of society and man as well as in the realm of nature – and the further reduction of quantity to ever larger and more abstract formulations of the relations that obtain between abstract quantities.[8]

Yet Comte would hardly recognize his version of positivism in these two definitions. They represent in fact the very approaches to which he was opposed.

In his criticisms of political economists, the philosophers of sensationalism (Locke, Helvétius, and Condillac), and the Idéologues, Comte denounced the pursuit of sensory observations as pure empiricism. Although observed facts were crucial to the establishment and verification of scientific laws, the accumulation of discrete facts struck him as unsystematic, even anarchical. He believed that empiricists neglected general laws and consequently failed to provide useful or real knowledge. Comte frequently linked this empirical approach to modern egoism, specialization, and pseudoimpartiality. In opposition to eighteenth-century sensationalism, he was, moreover, convinced that observation itself required more than experiencing sense impressions; facts could not be observed without the

---

[6] Kremer-Marietti, *Le Concept*, 22.

[7] "Positivism," in *The American Heritage Dictionary of the English Language*, ed. William Morris (1969; Boston: Houghton Mifflin, 1981).

[8] Lenzer, Introduction to *Auguste Comte*, xxi. For a similar definition of positivism, see Richard J. Bernstein, *The Restructuring of Social and Political Theory* (New York: Harcourt Brace Jovanovich, 1976), 207.

guidance of an a priori theory.[9] Observations and theories had to exist simultaneously, especially in the study of society, whose facts were among the hardest to perceive. Because one was within society, it was difficult to notice what was ordinary, yet the familiar social phenomena were the most important of all facts. Only a social theory relating to the *whole* could help the observer to place himself outside of society in order to examine the details of social life. Also, a theory enabled the observer to be more objective in regard to social phenomena, which normally provoked the deepest biases.

Contrary to empiricists, Comte therefore stressed the role of the mind and emphasized throughout his writings that imagination and subjectivity were crucial in the scientific process because they allowed one to form the hypotheses necessary to link facts. Lesson 58 of the *Cours* reveals that Comte even appreciated the aesthetic element in the construction of theories. His emphasis on the utility of scientific hypotheses as convenient, provisional devices for approximating reality and fulfilling our needs was an attempt to save individuals from pure empiricism. Comte's ideas were remarkably similar to the twentieth-century concept of a scientific theory as "*metaphor*."[10]

Yet at the same time, Comte was not an advocate of pure rationalism, because he felt that hypotheses had to be formed with the help of experience and that the concrete world must not be overlooked. Pure rationalism was as useless, vague, and unreal as pure empiricism. Comte's positivism suffered from a lack of attention to epistemology, which would have clarified his position. Nevertheless, his warning that observation had to be balanced by reasoning in the discovery of natural laws demonstrates that he did not reduce science to the purely experiential as Don Martindale and other scholars have argued.[11] Thus Comte's philosophy is marked by the effort to unite rationalism and empiricism, that is, induction and deduction, in order to take advantage of the contributions that each method made to scientific progress. He believed that as more and more observations were made, rationalism and deduction would become increasingly important.

Moreover, Comte did not refuse to call value judgments positive knowledge, though it is commonly assumed that positivism's empiricism made it opposed to normative statements.[12] As shown in his criticism of Montesquieu and the political economists, he

[9] Robert C. Scharff, "Mill's Misreading of Comte on 'Interior Observation'," *Journal of the History of Philosophy* 27 (October 1989): 565.

[10] Barry Barnes, *Scientific Knowledge and Sociological Theory* (London: Routledge & Kegan Paul, 1974), 49.

[11] Martindale, *Nature and Types*, 56.   [12] Kolakowski, *Alienation*, 7–8.

demanded that a social theory depict a better society. He suggested that it should not rest idle in vain objectivity. Furthermore, he implied that scientific objectivity was unattainable, especially in the science of society, whose phenomena were so close to man, but he never explicitly stated his position. Despite his vagueness, he urged sociological observation to embrace the goal of creating a unified society bound together by the natural sympathy that each person had for the other members of the community. The primary task of his sociologists was to instill moral principles. The main problem with Comte's approach was that he did not set forth the criteria for such principles. He was the first to admit that his principles basically derived from the Christian idea of universal love. Although his attacks on God destroyed its legitimacy, he extended this idea to promote the "liberal" idea – liberal in the original sense of generous – that people must devote themselves to the general good of the whole society. He argued that positivist principles would be more credible and effective because they would eliminate not only the theologians' advocacy of the egotistical search for salvation in another world, but the metaphysicians' stress on self-interest as the key to human motivation. However, his conviction that people would find sufficient personal satisfaction in simply following the precepts of positivist morality seems unfounded.

Comte was even more adamantly opposed to the other definition of positivism – the reduction of questions of quality to those of quantity. He berated those who contended that mathematics offered the only certain knowledge. Inspired by Bichat, Blainville, Poinsot, and Destutt de Tracy, Comte repeatedly denounced the extension of mathematics to all realms of knowledge. He warned of the abuse of the calculus of probability – statistics – in physics, chemistry, biology, and sociology. The complexity, diversity, and variability of biological and especially social phenomena precluded their ever being expressed in mathematical equations. Throughout the *Cours*, he insisted upon the autonomy and individuality of each science and pointed out that one could not be reduced to another or completely encompassed by another. Each science had to observe its own distinctive phenomena. Partly because of his attraction to vitalism, he stressed the unique characteristics of life and the organicism of living creatures in order to ensure that biology, as well as sociology, would not be reduced to the physical sciences.

In fact, much of the animus behind the *Cours*, particularly the last volumes, came from Comte's desire to overturn the dominance of mathematicians in the sciences. According to him, mathematics was too abstract, too simplistic, and too specialized. Instead of remaining a means of scientific investigation, it tended to dominate all research, though it had no understanding of the other sciences. Mathematicians, Comte believed, liked to use purely mathematical analysis to support whatever hypothesis pleased them. They were inclined to create their own special language for their own self-aggrandizement and for differentiating themselves from the people. Throughout the *Cours*, Comte denounced such abstruse languages and stressed that positive philosophers would extend, not suppress, the notions of common sense. Knowledge must not be used to create yet another set of privileges. Concerned with utility and concrete reality, the people would remind the sociologists to direct their attention to the problems of daily life. Thus positivism was not set up to oppose commonsense reflection as is often assumed.[13] Despite its elitist tendencies, it had a democratic strain that reflected Comte's loyalty to the revolutionaries' ideal of the republic as a government devoted to the people. He gave this social and political ideal an epistemological basis.

In sum, Comte would not recognize the mutilated version of positivism that exists today. Already in his own time, he was exasperated, countering those who were trying to make positivism something he felt it was not and should never be. In some respects, it seems that Littré, Mill, and other disciples of Comte made positivism a manifesto for the scientific age by removing many of the nuances of his thought. Their attitude is epitomized by Mill's response to Richard Congreve, one of the English positivists who objected to his manipulation of the master's doctrine:

> It is precisely because I consider M. Comte to have been a great thinker, that I regard it as a duty to balance the strong & deeply felt admiration which I express for what I deem the fundamental parts of his philosophy by an equally emphatic expression of the opposite feeling I entertain towards other parts. It is M. Comte himself, who, in my judgement, has thrown ridicule on his own philosophy by the extravagances of his later writings; & since he has done so, I conceive that the mischief can only be corrected if those who desire to separate the first from the last, shew that they are as much alive to the ridiculous side of his character & speculations as those are who are unable to appreciate his greatness.[14]

Comte would have sympathized with Marx, whose early humanistic and idealistic tendencies were obscured by Lenin and other followers who were trying to transform his philosophy into a more mechanistic, voluntaristic ideology that would satisfy the demands of

---

[13] Szacki, *History of Sociological Thought*, 174.
[14] Mill to Richard Congreve, August 8, 1865, *Later Letters*, 16:1085.

militancy.[15] Comte would have found the reductionist, mechanistic, empiricist, statistical, and materialist elements in modern positivism equally crude. Much like the appellation "romanticism," positivism has become a convenient term to designate a complex movement.[16] In the process, all of the rich ambiguities of Comte's thought have been lost.

Sociology, Comte's other great contribution to modern intellectual life, has undergone a different type of transformation. Sociology arose from a basic paradox deep within Comte. As Lamennais implied, Comte experienced a religious calling but suffered from the fact that he did not believe in God. He rejected atheism as too negative and scornful of the religious sentiment. Endeavoring to respond to the demands of the heart and mind, he chose to create an intellectual system based on science that would satisfy man's need for faith and for dogmatism, which he assumed was the natural mental state of humanity – the state that ensured the sanity of the individual and the community. By creating a new set of respectable beliefs, it would establish the intellectual, social, and political consensus that was the salient characteristic of a religious system.

Sociology, which was based on the positive philosophy and was its crowning achievement, would reflect the growth of reason. Comte assumed that reason was the driving force of human evolution because the development of abstraction and generalization encapsulated the essence of human as opposed to animal nature.

Sociology would combine features of Comte's two golden ages: the fetishist stage of human development and the Middle Ages. Comte admired the fetishist stage because it represented the period when religious beliefs were most intense and dominated all aspects of an individual's life. During this time, people's emotions were also the strongest. Moreover, Comte respected fetishism for its overriding concern with concrete reality. Because of these different factors, it also stimulated the arts. Comte envisioned the day when sociology would be as intellectually dominant and would turn the attention of all the members of the community to a single concrete reality – that of humanity. In the *Système de politique positive*, he would describe the "Great-Fetish," rituals, and positivist culture that would rejuvenate people's emotional life, bring them back into contact with the concrete, and stimulate the arts. This work represents the logical

---

[15] Avineri, *Karl Marx*, 257–8.

[16] On the problems of the term "romantic," see Arthur O. Lovejoy, "On the Discrimination of Romanticisms," chap. in *Essays in the History of Ideas* (Baltimore: Johns Hopkins University Press, 1948), 228–53.

result of Comte's fervent desire to effect a return to fetishism in a way suitable to modern society.

Just as fetishism was important to Comte for its intellectual and emotional aspects, the Middle Ages presented the model of moral, social, and political life. It was the era in which social harmony had reached its height. Encouraged by his reading of Joseph de Maistre, Comte realized that the key to the triumph of sociability, that is, morality, lay in an effective institutional structure. The example of the success of Catholicism gave him the idea of the "separation of powers," which corresponded to the distinction between theory and practice in the sciences. The establishment of the spiritual power as an indispensable complement to the temporal power became one of Comte's primary interests. Like the Catholic clergy, it would be responsible for spreading a unitary doctrine – the new "gospel" – and directing the opinions and morals of the people.

The *Cours de philosophie positive* was intended to lay the basis of the doctrine that the spiritual power would teach. It also represented his clergy's necessary training. It traced the methodology and principles of the physical sciences, biology, and sociology. Yet underneath this exposition lay another stratum. It is often forgotten that the *Cours* was also a compendium of seventeenth-, eighteenth-, and early-nineteenth-century philosophies. With his wide-ranging mind, Comte presented a critique of Bacon, Galileo, Descartes, the philosophes (especially Montesquieu and Condorcet), the Scottish philosophers of the Enlightenment, the Idéologues, the liberals, the counterrevolutionaries, the political economists, Saint-Simon and the Saint-Simonians, Gall, and the German idealists. Each of these people or groups of thinkers had had an impact on his formation. Comte placed their isolated ideas into a system that gave each of them a particular value. By giving their concepts a function in his program, he in some ways ensured their continued influence.

Tracing the scientific and philosophical developments of the previous two hundred years as well as his battles against the scientists of his day, the *Cours* essentially recapitulated Comte's own education and reinforced it by bringing all the strands of his thought together. Similar to a bildungsroman, it was the story of his learning process – a process that he wanted everyone to share. The *Cours* had almost a cathartic effect. Comte's cerebral hygiene, his aesthetic revolution of 1838, and his antiscientific manifesto embodied in the "Personal Preface" indicate his growing frustration with the realm of pure intellect. By the sixth volume, it is clear that Comte himself was ready to proceed to the next stage of his mission and turn his attention to emotional and moral existence. As Anthony Giddens points out, Comte recognized that "science cannot, after all, provide its own commitment."[17]

The key to the learning process illustrated in the *Cours* lay in the law of three stages, along with its complement, the classification of the sciences. This law enabled Comte to fuse his interest in mathematics and the sciences and his concern with philosophy and politics. Yet given the fact that the grand theories of history that were popular in the nineteenth century seem highly questionable and hopelessly obsolete today, Comte's law strikes the modern reader as far too schematic, if not "metaphysical." As F. Rochberg has recently pointed out, historians of science have erred in assuming that there is a "necessary historical pattern of unidirectional linear progress" beginning with the Greeks.[18] The law of three stages is, above all, a reflection of the development of nineteenth-century historicism. Comte and other thinkers of his period assumed that to comprehend and solve the crisis of the postrevolutionary world, one had to understand its evolution and the driving forces of civilization.

The law of three stages thus represents Comte's attempt to grasp the whole of history. It was based on the so-called progress of the mind, for, like Hegel, Comte saw history as the story of intellectual emancipation. Freedom of inquiry, self-improvement, and the realization of human nature became the motor, that is, the "cause," of historical development.[19] People could gain a certain, albeit limited, control of their destiny by reliving the past, increasing their self-consciousness, and predicting the future course of human evolution on the basis of the laws of society. Although Comte stressed the importance of ideas, he did not believe that intellectual evolution could be separated from material development. Because a person's basic, strong, practical needs stimulated the intellectual faculties, industry developed first in the modern period and was the basis of the movement of recomposition. Comte recognized that practical enterprises would always remain most dominant in society because most men were suited to the active life and their needs would continue to demand gratification. His interpretation of history was novel in the prominence it gave to the role of the "industrial" classes, the conflict between the workers and their employers, and the social question. Thus Comte's idealism was balanced to a certain extent by his materialist tendencies.

---

[17] Giddens believes that Comte's awareness of the unfulfilling nature of science is evident in the *Système*. But Comte's frustration is already apparent in the last volumes of the *Cours*. Anthony Giddens, "Positivism and Its Critics," in *A History of Sociological Analysis*, ed. Tom Bottomore and Robert Nisbet (New York: Basic Books, 1978), 242.

[18] Rochberg, "Introduction," 553.

[19] Giddens, "Positivism and Its Critics," 245.

Contrary to scholars' assumptions about Comte, he did not advocate the rule of scientists. Although he did incline in this direction in his early writings for Saint-Simon, he became increasingly convinced that scientists were among the least capable people to assume the direction of society. He recognized that the "vague and arbitrary" methods that were required to deal with social questions did not appeal to the scientists' preoccupation with "perfect rationality." More important, his personal battles against the Academy of Sciences and his colleagues at the Ecole Polytechnique reinforced his opinion that scientists were too egotistical, too proud, and too involved in their own specialties. Their inability to make generalizations and to understand the whole was reflected in their "monstrous" political indifference.[20] They were, in short, entirely neglectful of society.

Perhaps, too, Comte lost faith in his own scientific abilities as he was rejected for one scientific position after another. In the early nineteenth century, the pattern of career making in the sciences was in a state of transition. The old system of patronage was still in place, which meant that scientists made up a powerful elite bound by ties of friendship and family. Yet this system was being challenged by the professionalization of scholarship and science with its impersonal system of rules for advancement.[21] Comte found that he could not make the patronage system work for him without compromising his integrity. Nor could he meet the new professional standards that required specialization and research publications without sacrificing his mission. Frustrated and alienated, he rechanneled his energies into his philosophic mission. Increasingly considering himself a philosopher, he bitterly dismissed the importance of his former colleagues' aptitudes.

Comte was in a paradoxical situation of which he was fully aware. He was calling for a social philosophy based on the sciences, which were reaching the apogee of their influence, but he deeply distrusted the ability of the purely scientific spirit to regenerate the political and social world. Comte's disillusionment is evident in the closing sentence of the *Cours*, which condemned the "prejudices and passions of our deplorable scientific regime."[22] The *Cours*, an apparently scientistic tract, was meant to contain the scientific spirit.

Although Marxists and other social thinkers consider Comte an apologist for the modern era, he was in fact extremely critical of the

---

[20] *Cours*, 2:76.
[21] Robert Fox, "Science, University, and the State," 66–7, 73; Crosland, *Science under Control*, 28–30.
[22] *Cours*, 2:791.

coming reign of industrialists and scientists.[23] He viewed both of these elites as avaricious, mediocre, and unconcerned with social problems, particularly the anomie of the new society and the conflict between the classes.[24] Instead of arguing in favor of their autonomy, he firmly believed in the need for them to be controlled.

To make scientists and industrialists accountable to the public, Comte intended for his spiritual power to be constituted of generalists with a firm grasp of the whole. Although he wanted them to have an understanding of the sciences, he preferred to include men who were "entirely unfamiliar with science" than to admit pure scientists themselves, who were too preoccupied by the details of their research.[25] Comte assumed that having a general formation gave a person wider views and thus more sympathy. Comte's picture of the spiritual power was much closer to Coleridge's idea of clerisy than has been acknowledged.

Comte was very aware of the theocratic tendencies of his thought. Benjamin Constant, Saint-Simon, Michel Chevalier, the Saint-Simonians, and his friends had often criticized him on this point. In the *Cours*, his appeals to the revolutionaries and his constant denunciation of the reign of the mind reveal that their comments did not fall on deaf ears, as is commonly assumed. Comte maintained that a government of philosophers, or intellectuals, was a dangerous utopia because it would effectively hinder all progress and thus create a static society. The mind needed to be stimulated by the active life. Men of the intellect should never be given full authority because they would seek complete control over humanity, would lose all motivation once they had power over the material realm, and would only admire the society that they had produced. Comte argued, or tried to argue, that the separation of powers would eliminate this peril in the new society. The temporal power would be in charge of man's active and practical life, which would always remain dominant in any society, while the spiritual power would be responsible

[23] David Frisby, "The Frankfurt School: Critical Theory and Positivism," in *Approaches to Sociology: An Introduction to Major Trends in British Sociology*, ed. John Rex (London: Routledge & Kegan Paul, 1974), 209, 220–2; Jürgen Habermas, *Knowledge and Human Interests*, trans. Jeremy J. Shapiro (Boston: Beacon Press, 1971), 71, 76, 80; Georges Balandier, "Entretien sur les problèmes actuels de la sociologie," *L'Homme et la société* 3 (January–March, 1967): 48.

[24] Lenzer says, for example, that in Comte's system "the sole function allowed to reason was for it to become an instrument of computation and logic in the service of the existing order." Lenzer, Introduction to *Auguste Comte*, xlix. Herbert Marcuse argued that "the conceptual interest of the positive sociology is to be apologetic and justificatory. . . . It arrives at an ideological defense of middle-class society." Marcuse, *Reason and Revolution: Hegel and the Rise of Social Theory*, 2d ed. (Boston: Beacon Press, 1960), 341–2.

[25] *Cours*, 2:77.

for preserving and vivifying his moral, emotional, and intellectual life. The spiritual power had to be kept separate from the material and political realms in order to retain its moral purity. Moreover, Comte limited the spiritual power to an advisory position. It would share authority with the temporal power by guiding its decisions to ensure that they were in the interest of the "whole." It would also take over the education of all the members of the community, including adults. The aim of this education was to instill common principles throughout society so that everyone would have the same basic ideas, opinions, and moral principles and would therefore find themselves in complete agreement. Produced by "socialization," this form of social consensus was Comte's answer to the problem of disputations over questions of politics, which he believed caused extreme disharmony and acrimony.

The sociologists would attract the trust of the people because they would be intellectually and morally superior. Comte was convinced that the people's faith in their decisions would be no different from their confidence in the natural scientists. And he found this faith more honorable than that of theological faith because the demonstrations of the sociologists could ultimately be "proved." People were thus not relinquishing their reason.

Because Comte showed that control over ideas was the key to power in modern society, he laid himself open to the charge that he was espousing a technocratic society, that is, a society ruled exclusively by scientific experts.[26] But such a monist government was far from his intentions. To him, putting experts or intellectuals in charge of the government went against human nature, for the emotions would always be stronger and more energetic than the intellect. Moreover, he advocated a system of universal education that would benefit the proletariat and prevent savants from monopolizing knowledge. Because he limited the spiritual power's hegemony and forbade it to exercise practical or political power, it is not entirely fair to assert that he sought to erect a technocratic or theocratic society.[27]

Nevertheless, by restricting the individual's ability to criticize the social scientists, Comte did not go far enough in dispelling the

---

[26] Edward Shils, "The Calling of Sociology," in *Theories of Society: Foundation of Modern Sociological Theory*, vol. 2, ed. Talcott Parsons et al. (Glencoe, Ill.: Free Press, 1961), 1419–22; George A. Kelly, "The Expert as Historical Actor," *Daedalus* 92.3 (1963): 540.

[27] Both Macherey and Kofman show that Comte's thought is more complex than such criticisms imply. See Macherey, *Comte: La Philosophie*, 68; Kofman, *Aberrations*, 206–13, 279–85. On Comte's desire to make scientific knowledge a "public thing," see Bernadette Bensaude-Vincent, "L'Astronomie populaire: Priorité philosophique et projet politique," *Revue de synthèse* 112 (January–March 1991): 59.

suspicion that he was, in fact, setting up an authoritarian, blandly uniform regime devoted to the indoctrination of the people. He never satisfactorily reconciled the authority of the state and the freedom of the individual.[28] Comte believed that individuals would flourish in the positivist society because they would be fulfilling their destiny, that of acting on the world of nature to modify it for their own advantage. To him, liberty was freedom from arbitrary political measures. Yet when he ignored the need to preserve the individual's private sphere of activity, he opened up the way to arbitrary authority. He never regarded liberty as the independence of the individual to develop as he or she desired even if his or her actions did not tend toward the stability of the social system.

Comte's failure to appreciate the flowering of the individual was due at least partly to his poor image of human nature. Comte viewed people as essentially mediocre, irrational, selfish, unreflective, and docile creatures in need of direction and authority in order to render their sympathetic instincts more salient. People had to perform "duties," instead of demanding their rights. But considering Comte's low opinion of human nature, it is hard to believe that he thought people would fulfill their duties without being compelled to do so. Coercion and the "arbitrary" were clearly latent in his theory of the separation of powers, despite his denials. Another reason for Comte's deprecation of freedom of choice is that such liberty would threaten the uniform laws of behavior, which make scientific prediction possible.

In a sense, Comte derived his utopia partly from two sources within himself. First, it came from his own nature. Because of his problems with mental health, he required peace and could brook no disagreement or controversy of any kind. So insistent was he on the need for total harmony that he sacrificed first his family, then his wife, and then one friend after another to achieve it. Sensing, therefore, the absolute necessity for total accord in his own life, he prescribed the same thing for society itself. Thus the kind of society he envisioned consisted not of groups of warring and competing factions, but of a regime supervised by a spiritual power that would educate and inspire people to agree with one set of views. The other source of his vision came from his religion. Since he was brought up in a deeply religious household and city, Catholicism had a strong impact on him. He wished to re-create in the modern world the kind of government that prevailed during the High Middle Ages, the period of papal ascendancy, when spiritual leadership was considered infallible.

---

[28] See, e.g., Eugene J. Roesch, "Reflections on the Philosophy of Scientism and Its Notion of Tolerance," *Contemporary Review* 17 (October 1965): 173.

Comte's system was marked by the search for a synthesis.[29] He sought the middle way between the extremes in all realms. He hoped to balance the needs of the heart and those of the mind, order and progress, rationalism and empiricism, materialism and idealism, theory and practice, the abstract and the concrete, the spiritual power and the temporal power, the whole and the parts, religion and science, objectivity and subjectivity, synthesis and analysis, determinism and voluntarism, the sciences and the arts, and the ideas of the Left and the doctrines of the Right. To reduce Comtism to one side of the equation is to neglect the complexities of his thought.

Comte tried to effect a synthesis in order to appeal to all parties and thereby conclude the Revolution. His effort to found a science of society derived from the liberal tradition of Condorcet and the Idéologues, who rejected the legitimizing principle of divine right and sought to reconstruct politics and society on a rational basis. He always remained committed to the revolutionary "cause of reason and Humanity" that he had espoused in 1815.[30] Moreover, he retained the liberal concept that political authority must derive from people's "explicit or implicit" consent.[31] And like the liberal thinkers of the period, he broke new ground by showing the interactions between the political and social realms and pointing out the problems of mass society.[32] He was, therefore, convinced that the Left would be attracted by his stance against the Church and established religions, his republicanism, his faith in reason, relativism, and progress, his stress on the importance of freedom of discussion to change the world, his ideas of social reconstruction, his concern for the working class, and his vision of a new industrial and secular order.

Yet, encouraged by both the organicism of the counter-revolutionaries and the model of a Christian moral community espoused by many working-class leaders and bourgeois intellectuals, Comte found liberalism, based on self-interest, morally bankrupt.[33] Its individualism had been discredited during the Revolution. And though he agreed with the liberals in favoring the new industrial, capitalist system, he joined the Right in reacting against its abuses. He thus believed that the reactionaries would approve of his support for traditional values, his emphasis on a strong spiritual power, duties, hierarchy, order, and stability, and his opposition to equality, popular sovereignty, and individualism.

Comte could not, however, escape the conflict between rationalism

---

[29] Skarga, "Le Coeur et la raison," 385–9.   [30] Comte to Valat, January 2, 1815, *CG*, 1:8.
[31] *Cours*, 2:115.   [32] Siedentop, "Two Liberal Traditions," 172–4.
[33] Edward Berenson, *Populist Religion and Left-Wing Politics in France, 1830–1852* (Princeton, N.J.: Princeton University Press, 1984), 38.

Conclusion

and traditionalism that characterized his era.[34] Despite his ambitious scheme to achieve consensus by having all social groups sacrifice their desires for the good of the whole, the conflicting elements of his doctrine ended by alienating many potential supporters.

The Right did not approve of his antireligious, antimonarchical views. In reacting against commercial self-interest as a motive for human action, Comte glorified society, not God, the monarchy, or the state itself. A new secular abstraction, humanity became the vague source of legitimacy in the Comtean system and had little appeal to the Right at this time.

The failure of Comte's appeal to the Left, which he believed would support him, was particularly disappointing to him. He shared leftists' belief in the idea of social justice, which was at the heart of the liberal tradition of the Revolution: the authorities had to arrange the state for the common good. Yet ironically, though he placed the people at the center of his state, he disempowered them. Rejecting any representative system, Comte gave the people almost no role in politics. According to him, they were too incompetent to rule; they would "naturally" consent to the authorities because they were inherently inclined toward obedience and would recognize the authorities' superiority. Thus Comte seemed to displace the political realm as a site where conflict was worked out. He pushed the limitations of the temporal power too far. His insistence on restricting political power to realizing the "natural order" seemed too quietist for an age of reform.[35] And he seemed to give too much authority to the spiritual power, when he put it in charge of moral education, a subject that was anathema to other liberals, like Constant, reacting against the political paradigm of Rousseau and Robespierre.[36]

In a sense, Comte took Jacobin principles to the extreme. His spiritual power reflected the legacy of the Jacobins, who profoundly distrusted political power, considered political institutions to be inherently corrupt, and sought to make the state rise above party disputes and enforce the interests of the whole community.[37] Comte essentially inherited their concept of "liberty," which tended to promote, as Ozouf has shown, "virtuous actions" in the interest of society rather than a "free association of independent individuals." The Jacobins were attracted to Rousseau's idea that liberty came from a "unity based on identical rights and general rules," not from diversity, and they promoted a system of continuous moral

---

[34] Lefebvre, *French Revolution*, 2:298.   [35] *Cours*, 2:118.
[36] Holmes, *Benjamin Constant*, 100.
[37] Anne Sa'adah, *The Shaping of Liberal Politics in Revolutionary France: A Comparative Perspective* (Princeton, N.J.: Princeton University Press, 1990), 17–18, 191.

education to achieve this end.[38] In a sense, Rousseau's Legislator lived on in Comte's spiritual power. Annie Petit is right to point out the paradox that Comte was an "antirevolutionary" because he was an "ultrarevolutionary," one who was eager for France to continue its regenerative mission.[39]

The tensions in Comte's thought reflect the contradictory era in which he lived. As Anne Sa'adah has recently pointed out, the French Revolution's failure to redefine "political community around a new conception of legitimacy" led to political divisions complicating the "problem of cohesion in a liberal society." As a result, most Frenchmen, from traditional Catholics to republicans, had an "enduring nostalgia for moral unanimity and a deep-seated aversion to politics." In their ideal society, politics would have a minor role and individuals would be "like-minded" and would celebrate community. It seems, then, that Comte articulated their dreams, but in an extreme fashion. The republicans at least added the concepts of diversity, individual autonomy, and competition as afterthoughts.[40] Yet he was not drawn to this liberal solution, which seemed weak to him and to many of his contemporaries. He and others rejected liberal attempts to limit political authority through representative institutions because it appeared to encourage further fragmentation and instability.

Comte's solution was to place his trust in the authority of a new professoriate consisting of general social scientists endowed with encyclopedic knowledge and benevolent feelings.[41] Yet these men were untested and unconnected with any existing power or class. Comte's failure to show how a particular group would especially benefit from the positive state is in marked contrast to Marx, who won a following by appealing to the proletarians, and to Saint-Simon, who won the support of the industrialists. Comte's ruling group was so idiosyncratic that it had no potential for widespread appeal. But the main problem with Comte's scheme (as with Marx's and Saint-Simon's) was that there was no guarantee that his new elite would have any interest beyond self-aggrandizement.

Thus although Comte sought to preserve some of the progressive liberal values, he eventually reconstituted them in an ultimately illiberal system, one that betrayed the leading liberal principle, individual freedom, and its foundation, pluralism.[42] He had traveled

[38] Mona Ozouf, "Liberty," in *A Critical Dictionary*, ed. Furet and Ozouf, 718, 725.

[39] Annie Petit, "La Révolution occidentale selon Auguste Comte: Entre l'histoire et l'utopie," *Revue de synthèse* 112 (January–March 1991): 22.

[40] Sa'adah, *Shaping of Liberal Politics*, 14, 18.   [41] Macherey, *Comte: La Philosophie*, 60.

[42] Steven Seidman, *Liberalism and the Origins of European Social Theory* (Berkeley and Los Angeles: University of California Press, 1983), 15.

far from the liberalism of his youth, when he had stated that the government must be the people's agent, not their director: "Between the man who directs and the man who is directed, what morality can there be? The one must command, the other must obey, that is all."[43] By once again sacrificing freedom to social control, Comte seemed to exacerbate, rather than solve, the leading problem of the times, that of the abuse of power.

Nevertheless, Comte's effort to cure society of its ills has remained a central objective of the science of society. He gave sociology not only a name and a scientific basis, but a mission: to solve the problem of the spiritual anarchy of the industrial age by achieving consensus, that is, "integration."[44] In their attempt to formulate "social policy," bureaucrats, politicians, sociologists, and other social scientists have in many ways become the consultants that Comte envisioned.[45] Moreover, his effort to make sociology the queen of the sciences has had an immense effect on many disciplines, such as history, law, psychology, and political economy, which are now pervaded by an overriding concern with the social origins of their phenomena.[46] Social science has achieved a respectability within the university that would no doubt please Comte.

Yet sociologists tend to overlook their founding father. Many of their problems can be traced, however, to the vagueness and unresolved tensions in Comte's ideas. He set the program and method of sociology but was not completely clear about the contents of his new science. To him, sociology was all-encompassing because no single aspect of social life could be studied in isolation. Consequently, the undefined boundaries of this discipline derive from the fact that Comte's sociology was a mixture of history, moral philosophy, political economy, political theory, anthropology, aesthetics, religion, international relations, philosophy of science, biology, and the inorganic sciences.[47]

---

[43] *Ecrits*, 93.

[44] Talcott Parsons, "The General Interpretation of Action," in *Theories of Society: Foundation of Modern Sociological Theory*, vol. 1, ed. Talcott Parsons et al. (Glencoe, Ill.: Free Press, 1961), 92.

[45] Robert E. Lane, "The Decline of Politics and Ideology in a Knowledgeable Society," *American Sociological Review* 31.5 (1966): 649–63; Charles E. Lindblom and David K. Cohen, *Usable Knowledge: Social Science and Social Problem Solving* (New Haven, Conn.: Yale University Press, 1979), 8, 73, 91, 101.

[46] Robert Marjolin, "French Sociology – Comte and Durkheim," *American Journal of Sociology* 42 (1936): 693–702; Claude Lévi-Strauss, "French Sociology," in *Twentieth-Century Sociology*, ed. Georges Gurvitch and Wilbert E. Moore (New York: Philosophical Library, 1945), 504–6.

[47] On the problems of the boundaries of sociology, see Bernard Lacroix, "La Vocation originelle d'Emile Durkheim," *Revue française de sociologie* 17.2 (1976): 214; Ralf Dahrendorf, *Essays*

Furthermore, sociology is uncomfortable with the conflict in Comte's thought between science and religion. Sociology, to Comte, was a calling akin to that of a religious vocation. Modern sociology still aspires to effect social reform, but does so by neglecting the prescriptions of its founder and overemphasizing the scientific, technical, and objective character of their subject. Like positivism, sociology has succumbed to the "positivity" of the scientific age against which Comte warned in the last sections of the *Cours*. It has become increasingly empirical and fearful of abstraction and generalization. To appear scientific, it has created its own jargon and neologisms, which obscure its commonsense roots. It is too preoccupied by the model of the physical sciences to which it seeks to reduce social science. Seeking to verify ideas through mathematics, sociologists are enamored of statistics and the quantification of their research.[48] Their search for certainty has occurred at the very moment when the physical sciences, due in part to Einstein and Heisenberg, have themselves recognized and tried to adjust to the unpredictability and irregularity of the universe. Functionalists and structuralists have embraced Comte's "social statics," but his interest in "social dynamics" – history – has been too often forgotten.[49] Moreover, sociology has become riddled with specializations, such as criminology, race relations, and family sociology.[50] The bitter debates among structural-functionalists, poststructuralists, existential sociologists, social interaction theorists, ethnomethodologists, proponents of critical theory, and advocates of hermeneutics reveal that the certitude and consensus that Comte assumed would exist at least

---

in the Theory of Society (Stanford, Calif.: Stanford University Press, 1968), 22; Raymond Aron, "La Sociologie," in *Les Sciences sociales en France: Enseignement et recherche* (Paris: Centre d'Etudes de Politique Etrangère, n.d.), 34.

[48] Hans Gerth and Saul Landau, "The Relevance of History to the Sociological Ethos," in *Sociology on Trial*, ed. Maurice Stein and Arthur Vidich (Englewood Cliffs, N.J.: Prentice-Hall, 1963), 30–1; Pierre L. Van Den Berghe, *Man in Society: A Biosocial View* (New York: Elsevier, 1975), 3–4; Maurice R. Stein, "The Poetic Metaphors of Sociology," in *Sociology on Trial*, ed. Stein and Vidich, 177; Pitirim A. Sorokin, *Fads and Foibles in Modern Sociology and Related Sciences* (Chicago: Henry Regnery, 1956), 22, 30, 283, 304.

[49] Gerth and Landau, "Relevance of History," 32; MacRae, *Ideology and Society*, 48; Barrington Moore, "Strategy in Social Science," in *Sociology on Trial*, ed. Stein and Vidich, 73–5; Alvin Boskoff, "From Social Thought to Sociological Theory," in *Modern Sociological Theory in Continuity and Change*, ed. Howard Becker and Alvin Boskoff (New York: Dryden Press, 1957), 262; John Lewis Gaddis, "The Cold War's End Dramatizes the Failure of Political Theory," *Chronicle of Higher Education*, July 22, 1992, 44; Peter T. Manicas, *A History and Philosophy of the Social Sciences* (Oxford: Basil Blackwell, 1987), 281.

[50] Gerth and Landau, "Relevance of History," 30; Charles W. Lachenmeyer, *The Language of Sociology* (New York: Columbia University Press, 1971), 2.

in his new discipline remain increasingly elusive.[51] They neglect
Comte's conviction that a variety of theories were needed to embrace the whole and that reality itself may never be fully comprehended, especially in the most complex science, that of society.[52]
Finally, many modern social scientists have been upbraided by their
own colleagues for neglecting the artistic and subjective side of human
existence. These critics have emphasized the connections between
sociology and art because they feel that a sociologist, like a novelist
or a poet, interprets the life of society and makes value judgments
about social problems, the relations among the members of the
community, and the human condition.[53] In a moment of luminosity
in one of his first essays for Saint-Simon, Comte himself recognized
that to a certain extent social scientists were merely novelists constructing narratives that perhaps revealed more about themselves
and their own condition than the real world: "Each [political writer]
gives himself his own theme; each takes off from his own ideas, his
own system, and his own theory, and often his ideas are prejudices,
his system is a novel, and his theory a chimera."[54]

---

[51] Stanislav Andreski, *Social Science as Sorcery* (London: André Deutsch, 1972), 235–7. For
a description of the different schools of sociology, see Stephen Mennell, *Sociological Theory:
Uses and Unities* (New York: Praeger, 1974); Anthony Giddens and Jonathan H. Turner,
Introduction to *Social Theory Today* (Cambridge: Polity Press, 1987), 1–10.

[52] MacRae, *Ideology and Society*, 43.

[53] C. Wright Mills, *The Sociological Imagination* (New York: Oxford University Press, 1959),
18, 120, 196; Stein, "Poetic Metaphors," 173–82; Morroe Berger, *Real and Imagined Worlds:
The Novel and Social Science* (Cambridge, Mass.: Harvard University Press, 1977), 6, 14,
216; Richard Harvey Brown, *A Poetic for Sociology: Toward a Logic of Discovery for the
Human Sciences* (Cambridge: Cambridge University Press, 1977), 3–4, 7; Lewis A. Coser,
ed., Introduction to *Sociology through Literature: An Introductory Reader* (Englewood Cliffs,
N.J.: Prentice-Hall, 1963), 2–4; Lindblom and Cohen, *Usable Knowledge*, 84; Robert Nisbet,
Sociology as an Art Form (Oxford: Oxford University Press, 1976); Audrey Borenstein,
Redeeming the Sin: Social Science and Literature (New York: Columbia University Press, 1978),
ix, 37, 59, 215; Gaddis, "Cold War's End," 44; Alice Templeton and Stephen B. Groce,
"Sociology and Literature: Theoretical Considerations," *Sociological Inquiry* 60 (Winter 1990):
34–46. An excellent discussion of the emergence of sociology as a mixture of the scientific
and literary traditions can be found in Wolf Lepenies, *Between Literature and Science: The
Rise of Sociology*, trans. R. J. Hollingdale (Cambridge: Cambridge University Press, 1988).

[54] *Ecrits*, 64.

Bibliography

PRIMARY SOURCES

Works by Auguste Comte

Ecrits de jeunesse, 1816–1828: Suivis du Mémoire sur la cosmogonie de Laplace, 1835. Edited by Paulo E. de Berrêdo Carneiro and Pierre Arnaud. Paris: Ecole Pratique des Hautes Etudes, 1970.

Prospectus des travaux nécessaires pour réorganiser la société. In *Suite des travaux ayant pour object de fonder le système industriel: Du contrat social.* By Henri Saint-Simon. Paris, 1822.

Système de politique positive: Tome premier, première partie. Paris, 1824.

Cours de philosophie positive. 6 vols. Paris, 1830–42. Most of the references to this work are to the recent edition: *Cours de philosophie positive.* Edited by Michel Serres, François Dagognet, Allal Sinaceur, and Jean-Paul Enthoven. 2 vols. Paris: Hermann, 1975.

Traité élémentaire de géométrie analytique à deux et à trois dimensions. Paris, 1843.

Traité philosophique d'astronomie populaire. Paris, 1844. The citations are from the edition published in Paris by Fayard in 1985.

Discours sur l'esprit positif. Paris, 1844. The citations are from the edition published in Paris by the Union Générale d'Editions, 1963.

Discours sur l'ensemble du positivisme, ou Exposition sommaire de la doctrine philosophique et sociale propre à la grande république occidentale composée des cinq populations avancées, française, italienne, germanique, britannique et espagnole. Paris, 1848.

Calendrier positiviste ou Système générale de commémoration publique. . . . Paris, 1849.

Système de politique positive ou Traité du sociologie instituant la religion de l'Humanité. 4 vols. Paris, 1851–4; 5th ed., identical to the first, Paris: Au Siège de la Société Positiviste, 1929.

Catéchisme positiviste, ou Sommaire exposition de la religion universelle en treize entretiens systématiques entre une femme et un prêtre de l'humanité. Paris, 1852. The citations are from the recent edition, published in Paris by Garnier-Flammarion in 1966.

Appel aux Conservateurs. Paris, 1855.

Synthèse subjective ou Système universel des conceptions propres à l'état normal de l'humanité, vol. 1. Paris, 1856.

Testament d'Auguste Comte avec les documents qui s'y rapportent: Pièces justificatives, prières quotidiennes, confessions annuelles, correspondance avec Mme de Vaux. Paris, 1884. The citations are from the second edition of 1896, which contains the "Addition secrète."

Letters of Auguste Comte

Correspondance inédite d'Auguste Comte. 4 vols. Paris: Au Siège de la Société Positiviste, 1903.
Auguste Comte: Correspondance générale et confessions. Edited by Paulo E. de Berrêdo Carneiro, Pierre Arnaud, Paul Arbousse-Bastide, and Angèle Kremer-Marietti. 8 vols. Paris: Ecole des Hautes Etudes en Sciences Sociales, 1973–90.

Archives

L'Académie de Médecine
Archives Départementales de l'Hérault (Montpellier)
Archives Générales du Département de la Côte d'Or et de l'Ancienne Province de Bourgogne (Dijon)
Archives of Madame Sybil de Azevedo
Archives Nationales
Archives de Paris (Archives Départementales de la Seine)
Bibliothèque de l'Arsenal
Bibliothèque Historique de la Ville de Paris
Bibliothèque Nationale
Bibliothèque Thiers (attached to the Institut de France)
Collège de France
Ecole Polytechnique
Institut de France
La Maison d'Auguste Comte
La Maison Charavay
L'Observatoire

Contemporary Newspapers and Journals

L'Ami de la religion: Journal ecclésiastique, politique et littéraire. 1842.
Archives philosophiques, politiques, et littéraires. 1817–18.
Le Censeur européen. 1819.
Comptes rendus hebdomadaires des séances de l'Académie des Sciences. 1830–42.
Le Constitutionnel: Journal politique et littéraire. 1817.
Gazette des Tribunaux: Journal de jurisprudence et des débats judiciaires. 1842, 1870.
Le Globe. 1828.
Le Globe: Journal de la religion Saint-Simonienne. 1832.
Journal des débats. 1817, 1836, 1840.
Journal du génie civil, des sciences et des arts. 1830.
Journal de la Société Phrénologique de Paris. 1832.
Leipziger Literatur-Zeitung. 1824.
Le Lycée: Journal de l'instruction publique de la littérature, des sciences et des arts. 1831.
Le Mémorial Catholique. 1826.
Le Mercure du 19ᵉ siècle. 1823.
Le Nain jaune, ou Journal des arts, des sciences, et de la littérature. 1815.
Le Nain jaune refugié. Brussels, 1816.
Le National. 1833, 1836.

Le Nouveau Journal de Paris et des départements: Feuille administrative, commerciale, industrielle, et littéraire. 1827–8.

Le Politique. 1819.

Le Producteur: Journal de l'industrie, des sciences et des beaux arts. 1825–6.

Revue encyclopédique, ou Analyses et annonces raisonnées des productions les plus remarquables dans la littérature, les sciences, et les arts. 1824, 1827, 1829–30.

Revue française. 1830.

La Revue occidentale. Published under the direction of Pierre Laffitte, 1878–1914.

Revue de Paris. 1830.

La Société des Amis du Peuple. Brochures 1–14.

La Tribune politique et littéraire. 1831–3.

Other Primary Sources

Almanach royal. Paris, 1709–.

Andrieux, François-Guillaume-Jean-Stanislas. *Oeuvres de François-Guillaume-Jean-Stanislas Andrieux.* 4 vols. Paris, 1818–23.

L'Annuaire: L'Académie royale de médecine. Paris, 1824.

Association Polytechnique. *Compte rendu 1832.* Paris, 1832.

Association Polytechnique. *Compte rendu trimestriel, Janvier 1833.* Paris, 1833.

Association Polytechnique. *Documents pour servir à l'histoire de cette association, 1830–1855.* Paris, n.d.

Athénée. *Programme pour l'an 1829.* Paris, 1829.

Programme pour l'an 1832. Paris, 1832.

Programme pour l'an 1835. Paris, 1835.

Audiffrent, Georges. *A propos du centenaire de la naissance d'un maître vénéré.* Paris, 1898.

Centenaire de la fondation de l'Ecole Polytechnique: Auguste Comte, sa plus puissante émanation. Notice sur sa vie et sa doctrine. Paris, 1894.

Une Conversation avec Auguste Comte. Lyon: A. Storck, 1908.

Réponse à M. J. Bertrand. Paris, 1897.

Bacon, Francis. *The Works of Francis Bacon.* Edited by James Spedding, Robert Leslie Ellis, and Douglas Denon Heath. 14 vols. London, 1857–74.

Bain, Alexander. *John Stuart Mill: A Criticism with Personal Recollections.* London: Longmans, Green, 1882.

Barthez, P. J. *Nouveaux Eléments de la science de l'homme.* 1778. 2 vols. Paris, 1858.

Bentham, Jeremy. *The Works of Jeremy Bentham.* Edited by John Bowring. 11 vols. Edinburgh, 1843.

Bertrand, Joseph. Review of *Auguste Comte, fondateur du positivisme, sa vie, sa doctrine,* by R. P. Gruber. *Journal des savants* (August 1892): 685–95.

"Souvenirs académiques: Auguste Comte et l'Ecole Polytechnique." *Revue des deux mondes* 138 (December 1896): 528–48.

Blanc, Louis. *Révolution française: Histoire de dix ans, 1830–1840.* 5 vols. Paris, 1841–4.

Bonald, M. de. *Oeuvres complètes de M. de Bonald.* Edited by Migne. 3 vols. Paris, 1859–64.

[Brewster, David.] Review of the *Cours de philosophie positive. Edinburgh Review* 67 (July 1838): 271–308.

Broussais, F. J. V. *De l'irritation et de la folie.* Paris, 1828.

Cabanis, Pierre-Jean-Georges. *Oeuvres complètes de Cabanis.* 5 vols. Paris, 1823–5.
    Oeuvres philosophiques de Cabanis. Edited by Claude Lehec and Jean Cazeneuve.
    2 vols. Paris: Presses Universitaires de France, 1956.
    Rapports du physique et du moral de l'homme. 3d ed. Paris, 1815.
Carlyle, Thomas. *Letters of Thomas Carlyle to John Stuart Mill, John Sterling and*
    Robert Browning. Edited by Alexander Carlyle. London: T. Fisher Unwin, 1923.
Chateaubriand, François. *Essai sur les révolutions; Génie du christianisme.* Edited by
    Maurice Regard. Paris: Gallimard, 1978.
    Le Génie du christianisme. 1802. Paris: Garnier-Flammarion, 1966.
    Les Martyrs. 1809. Paris: Firmin Didot Frères, 1850.
Comte, [Louis]. *Mémoire justificatif.* Paris, 1846.
Condorcet, [Marie-Jean-Antoine-Nicolas Caritat de]. *Esquisse d'un tableau historique*
    des progrès de l'esprit humain. Paris, 1797.
    Oeuvres complètes de Condorcet. Edited by Mme Condorcet et al. 21 vols. Paris,
    1804.
    Vie de Monsieur Turgot. Paris, 1787.
Constant, Benjamin. *Collection complètes des ouvrages.* 4 vols. Paris, 1818.
    De la religion considérée dans sa source, ses formes, et ses développements. 5 vols. Paris,
    1824–31.
    Mélanges de littérature et de politique. Paris, 1829.
    Oeuvres. Edited by Alfred Roulin. Paris: Gallimard, 1957.
Cours des Pairs de France. Affaire du mois d'avril 1834. Procès verbal des séances relatives
    au jugement de cette affaire. 2 vols. Paris, 1835.
Cousin, Victor. *Cours de philosophie professé à la Faculté des Lettres pendant l'année*
    1818. Paris, 1836.
    Fragmens philosophiques. 2d ed. Paris, 1833.
Deroisin, [Hippolyte Philémon]. *Notes sur Auguste Comte par un de ses disciples.* Paris,
    1909.
Destutt de Tracy, [Antoine-Louis Claude de]. "De la métaphysique de Kant." In
    Mémoires de l'Institut National des Sciences et Arts: Sciences morales et politiques. 5
    vols. 4:544–606. Paris, Year VI–Year XII.
    Elémens d'idéologie. 2d and 3d eds. 4 vols. Paris, 1817–18.
    Principes logiques ou Recueil de faits relatifs à l'intelligence humaine. Paris, 1817.
    Quels sont les moyens de fonder la morale chez un peuple? Paris, Year VI.
Doctrine de Saint-Simon: Exposition, première année, 1829. 2d ed. Paris, 1830.
Doctrine de Saint-Simon: Exposition, deuxième année, 1829–1830. Paris, 1830.
Dumas, Alexandre, père. *Mes Mémoires.* 2 vols. Poissy, 1866.
Dunoyer, Charles-Barthélemy. *De la liberté du travail ou Simple Exposé des conditions*
    dans lesquelles les forces humaines s'exercent avec le plus de puissance. 3 vols. Paris,
    1845.
    L'Industrie et la morale considérées dans leurs rapports avec la liberté. Paris, 1825.
    Oeuvres de Charles Dunoyer. 3 vols. Paris, 1886.
Dupuis, Charles. *Abrégé de l'Origine de tous les cultes.* Paris, 1836.
Eichthal, Eugène d', ed. and trans. "Carlyle et le Saint-Simonisme: Lettres à
    Gustave d'Eichthal." *La Revue historique* 82 (May–June 1903): 292–306.
Eichthal, Gustave d'. *La Langue grecque.* With an introduction by the Marquis de
    Queux de Saint-Hilaire. Paris, 1887.
Esquirol, Jean-Etienne Dominique. *Aliénation mentale.* Paris, 1832.

Des maladies mentales considérées sous les rapports médical, hygiénique, et médico-légal. 2 vols. Paris, 1838.

Des passions considerées comme causes, symptômes et moyens curatifs de l'aliénation mentale. With a preface by Marcel Gauchet and Gladys Swain. Paris: Librairie des Deux Mondes, 1980.

Fauvety, C. "Nécrologie: Auguste Comte." *Revue philosophique et religieuse* 8.31 (1857): 467–80.

Ferguson, Adam. *An Essay on the History of Civil Society.* Basel, 1789.

Principles of Moral and Political Science. 2 vols. Edinburgh, 1792.

Fourcy, A. *Histoire de l'Ecole Polytechnique.* Paris, 1828.

Fournel, Henri. *Bibliographie Saint-Simonienne: De 1802 au 31 décembre 1832.* Paris, 1833.

Fox, Caroline. *Memories of Old Friends: Being Extracts from the Journals and Letters of Caroline Fox – From 1835 to 1871.* 2d ed., edited by Horace N. Pym. Philadelphia, 1883.

Franklin, Benjamin. *The Autobiography of Benjamin Franklin.* Edited by Leonard W. Labaree et al. New Haven, Conn.: Yale University Press, 1964.

Gans, Edouard. Preface to *Leçons sur la philosophie de l'histoire.* By G. W. Hegel. 3d ed., translated by J. Gibelin. Paris: J. Vrin, 1970.

Gerbet, P. *Les Doctrines philosophiques sur la certitude dans leurs rapports avec les fondements de la théologie.* Paris, 1826.

Gisquet, [Henri-Joseph]. *Mémoires.* 4 vols. Paris, 1840.

Guizot, François. *Des moyens de gouvernement et d'opposition dans l'état actuel de la France.* 2d ed. Paris, 1821.

Du gouvernement de la France depuis la Restauration et du ministère actuel. 3d ed. Paris, 1820.

Du gouvernement représentatif et de l'état actuel de la France. Paris, 1816.

Histoire des origines du gouvernement représentatif en Europe. 2 vols. Paris, 1851.

Méditations sur l'état actuel de la religion chrétienne. Paris, 1866.

Mémoires pour servir à l'histoire de mon temps. 8 vols. Paris, 1858–67.

Hachette, [Jean-Nicolas-Pierre]. *Second supplément de la Géométrie descriptive suivi de l'Analyse géometrique de M. John Leslie.* Paris, 1818.

Halévy, Léon. "Souvenirs de Saint-Simon." *La France littéraire,* lst ser., 1.3 (1832): 521–46.

Hamilton, James. *Personal Recollections of Auguste Comte.* London, 1897. (Extract from *Chambers' Journal,* June 19, 1858.)

Hegel, [Georg Wilhelm Friedrich]. *Briefe von und an Hegel.* Edited by Johannes Hoffmeister. 4 vols. Hamburg: Felix Meinen, 1969–81.

Philosophie der Geschichte. Vol. 9 of *Werke: Vollständige Ausgabe durch einen Verein von Freunden des Verewigten.* 2d ed., edited by D. P. Marheineke et al. Berlin, 1837.

Herder, Johann Gottfried. *Idées pour la philosophie de l'histoire de l'humanité.* Edited and translated by Max Rouché. Paris: Aubier-Montaigne, 1962.

Histoire impartiale du procès des accusés d'avril. Paris, 1835.

Un Homme de Rien. *Galerie des contemporains illustres: Littérateurs français.* Paris, n.d.

Horace. *The Odes and Epodes.* Translated by C. E. Bennett. Cambridge, Mass.: Harvard University Press, 1968.

Hume, David. *Enquiries Concerning the Human Understanding and Concerning the Prin-*

ciples of Morals. 2d ed., edited by L. A. Selby-Bigge. Oxford: Clarendon Press, 1902.

The History of England from the Invasion of Julius Caesar to the Accession of Henry VII. 2 vols. London, 1762.

A Treatise of Human Nature. Edited by L. A. Selby-Bigge. Oxford, 1846.

Huxley, Thomas Henry. *Lay Sermons, Addresses and Reviews.* New York, 1871.

Kant, Immanuel. *Critique of Pure Reason.* Translated by F. Max Müller. Garden City, N.Y.: Doubleday, Anchor Books, 1966.

Kritik der Reinen Vernunft. 1781. 2d ed. With an introduction by Benno Erdmann. Leipzig, 1880.

On History. Edited by Lewis White Beck. Translated by Lewis White Beck, Robert E. Anchor, and Emil L. Fackenheim. Indianapolis, Ind.: Bobbs-Merrill, 1963.

Lamennais, Felicité de. *Correspondance générale.* Edited by Louis Le Guillou. 8 vols. Paris: Armand Colin, 1971–81.

De la religion considérée dans ses rapports avec l'ordre politique et civil. 2 vols. Paris, 1825–6.

Nouveaux mélanges, vol. 1. Paris, 1826.

Oeuvres complètes. 12 vols. Paris, 1836–7.

Lessing, Gotthold Ephraïm. *L'Education du genre humain de Lessing.* Translated by Eugène Rodrigues. Paris, 1830.

Lewes, G. W. *Comte's Philosophy of the Sciences: Being an Exposition of the Principles of the "Cours de philosophie positive" of Auguste Comte.* London: Hency C. Bohn, 1853.

Littré, Emile. *Auguste Comte et la philosophie positive.* 2d ed. Paris, 1864.

De la philosophie positive. Paris, 1845.

Lonchampt, Joseph. *Epitome de vida e dos escritos de Auguste Comte.* 2d ed., edited by Miguel Lemos. Rio de Janeiro: Sede Central da Igreja Positivista do Brazil, Templo da Humanidade, 1959.

Précis de la vie et des écrits d'Auguste Comte. Paris, 1889. (Extract from the *Revue occidentale.*)

Louvet de Couvray, [Jean-Baptiste]. *Les Amours du chevalier de Faublas.* 1787–89. With an introduction by Michel Crouzet. Paris: Bibliothèque 1018, 1966.

Maistre, Joseph de. *Considérations sur la France.* 2d ed. Paris, 1814.

Du pape. 2d ed. 2 vols. Paris, 1821.

Soirées de Saint-Petersbourg (les six premiers entretiens). Vol. 4 of *Oeuvres complètes de J. de Maistre.* New ed. 14 vols. Paris, 1884–6.

Martineau, Harriet, ed. and trans. *The Positive Philosophy of Auguste Comte.* 2 vols. London: J. Chapman, 1853.

Mill, John Stuart. *Auguste Comte and Positivism.* 1865. Ann Arbor, University of Michigan Press, Ann Arbor Paperbacks, 1961.

Autobiography and Literary Essays. Edited by John M. Robson and Jack Stillinger. Vol. 1 of *The Collected Works of John Stuart Mill.* Toronto: University of Toronto Press and Routledge & Kegan Paul, 1981.

Correspondance inédite avec Gustave d'Eichthal. Edited by Eugène d'Eichthal. Paris, 1898.

The Earlier Letters of John Stuart Mill, 1812–1848. Edited by Francis E. Mineka. Vols. 12 and 13 of *The Collected Works of John Stuart Mill,* ed. John M. Robson. Toronto: University of Toronto Press and Routledge & Kegan Paul, 1963.

Essays on Economy and Society. Edited by J. M. Robson. Vol. 4 of *The Collected Works of John Stuart Mill*, ed. John M. Robson. Toronto: University of Toronto Press and Routledge & Kegan Paul, 1967.

Essays on Ethics, Religion and Society. Edited by J. M. Robson. Vol. 10 of *The Collected Works of John Stuart Mill*. Toronto: University of Toronto Press and Routledge & Kegan Paul, 1969.

John Mill's Boyhood Visit to France: Being a Journal and Notebook Written by John Stuart Mill in France, 1820–1821. Edited by Anna Jean Mill. Toronto: University of Toronto Press, 1960.

The Later Letters: 1849–1873. Edited by Francis E. Mineka and Dwight N. Lindley. 4 vols. Vols. 14–17 of *The Collected Works of John Stuart Mill*. Toronto: University of Toronto Press and Routledge & Kegan Paul, 1972.

A System of Logic Ratiocinative and Inductive: Being a Connected View of the Principles of Evidence and the Methods of Scientific Investigation. Edited by J. M. Robson. Vols. 7 and 8 of *The Collected Works of John Stuart Mill*. Toronto: University of Toronto Press and Routledge & Kegan Paul, 1974.

Montesquieu, [Charles de]. *De l'esprit des lois*. 1748. 2 Vols. Paris: Garnier, 1973.

Nouvelle Biographie générale depuis les temps les plus reculés jusqu'à nos jours, avec les renseignements bibliographiques et l'indication des sources à consulter. 46 vols. Paris: Firmin-Didot, 1852–66.

Parent-Duchâtelet, Alexandre. *La Prostitution à Paris au XIXe siècle, 1836*. Edited by Alain Corbin. Paris: Seuil, 1981.

Pereire, Alfred. *Autour de Saint-Simon: Documents originaux*. Paris: Honoré Champion, 1912.

Perry, E. "A Morning with Auguste Comte." *Nineteenth Century* (November 1877): 621–31.

Précis analytique des travaux de l'Académie Royale des Sciences, Belles-lettres, et Arts de Rouen pendant l'année 1835. Rouen, 1835.

Rabbe, A., and Vieilh de Boisjoslin, eds. *Biographie universelle et portative des contemporains ou Dictionnaire historique des hommes vivants et des hommes morts depuis 1788 jusqu'à nos jours*. 4 vols. Paris, 1830.

Rabbe, A., Vieilh de Boisjoslin, and Saint Preuve, eds. *Biographie universelle et portative des contemporains ou Dictionnaire historique des hommes vivants et des hommes morts depuis 1788 jusqu'à nos jours*. 2d ed. 5 vols. Paris, 1834.

Religion Saint-Simonienne. Morale. Réunion générale de la famille. Enseignements du père suprème. Les Trois Familles. Paris, 1832.

Religion Saint-Simonienne. Receuil de prédications. 2 vols. Paris, 1832.

Rémusat, Charles de. *Mémoires de ma vie*. Vol. 2, 1820–1832. Edited by Charles H. Pouthas. Paris: Plon, 1959.

Richerand, Anthelme. *Nouveaux élémens de physiologie*. 2d ed. 2 vols. Paris, 1802.

Robertson, William. *The History of Charles V*. 1769. Paris, 1828.

Robespierre, [Maximilien-François-Marie-Isidore de]. *Oeuvres de Robespierre*. 2d ed., edited by A. Vermorel. Paris, 1867.

Robinet, [Jean-François Eugène]. *Notice sur l'oeuvre et la vie d'Auguste Comte*. 1860. Paris, 1891.

Roussel, Pierre. *Système physique et moral de la femme. . . .* Paris, 1775.

Saint-Paul, P. de. *La Vie du Général Campredon*. Montpellier, 1837.

Saint-Simon, Henri-Claude de. *Catéchisme des industriels: Troisième Cahier*. Paris, 1824.

Henri Saint-Simon (1760–1825): Selected Writings on Science, Industry and Social Organisation. Edited and translated by Keith Taylor. London: Croom Helm, 1975.

Lettre de Henri Saint-Simon à Messieurs les Publicistes. Paris, [1817].

Lettres d'un habitant de Genève à ses contemporains [1803], réimprimées conformément à l'édition originale et suivies de deux documents inédits – Lettres aux Européens [Essai sur l'organisation sociale]. Edited by Alfred Pereire. Paris: Félix Alcan, 1925.

Oeuvres choisies de C. H. de Saint-Simon, précédées d'un essai sur sa doctrine. Edited by [Charles] Lemonnier. 3 vols. Brussels, 1859.

Oeuvres de Claude-Henri de Saint-Simon. 6 vols. Paris: Anthropos, 1966.

Oeuvres de Saint-Simon: Lettres, brochures, articles de journaux, pièces diverses, 1802–1824. Compiled by Henri Fournel. Paris, 1833. This book contains published material compiled by Henri Fournel and can be found in the Bibliothèque Nationale in Paris. The call number is 8° Z8086 (1–16).

Quelques idées soumises par M. de Saint-Simon à l'Assemblée Générale de la Société d'Instruction Primaire. Paris, [1816].

Suite des travaux ayant pour objet de fonder le système industriel: Du contrat social. Paris, 1822.

Saint-Simon, Henri de, and Prosper Enfantin. *Oeuvres de Saint-Simon et d'Enfantin*. 47 vols. Paris, 1865–78.

Saint-Simon, [Henri-Claude de], et al. *Opinions littéraires, philosophiques et industrielles*. Paris, 1825.

Say, Jean-Baptiste. *Traité d'économie politique*. 3d ed. 2 vols. Paris, 1817.

Sieyès, Emmanuel. *Qu'est-ce que le tiers-état?* 1789. Edited by Roberto Zapperi. Geneva: Droz, 1970.

Smith, Adam. *Essays on Philosophical Subjects*. With an introduction by Dugald Stewart. London, 1795.

An Inquiry into the Nature and Causes of the Wealth of Nations. 1776. New ed., rev. Edinburgh, 1870.

Staël, Madame de. *Considérations sur les principaux événements de la Révolution française*. 3 vols. Paris, 1818.

De la littérature considérée dans ses rapports avec les institutions sociales, suivi de L'Influence des passions sur le bonheur, des individus et des nations. 1800. Paris, 1842.

Des circonstances actuelles qui peuvent terminer la Révolution et des principes qui doivent fonder la république en France. 1906. Edited by Lucia Omacini. Paris: Droz, 1979.

Thierry, Augustin. *Dix Ans d'études historiques*. 5th ed. Paris, 1846.

Tocqueville, Alexis de. *Democracy in America*. 1835. Translated and edited by Phillips Bradley. 2 vols. New York: Random House, Vintage Books, 1945.

The Old Regime and the French Revolution. 1856. Translated by Stuart Gilbert. Garden City, N.Y.: Doubleday, Anchor Books, 1955.

Turgot, [Anne Robert Jacques]. *Oeuvres de Turgot et documents le concernant*. Edited by Gustave Schelle. 5 vols. Paris: Félix Alcan, 1913–23.

Valat, P. "Auguste Comte." *Revue bordelaise: Scientifique et littéraire* 2 (1880): 211, 241–6, 268–71, 303–5, 336–8, 353–4, 445–7, 431–2; 3 (1881): 54–5, 103–5, 180–2.

"Document historique sur Guizot et Aug. Comte." *Actes de l'Académie Nationale* de Sciences, Belles-Lettres et Arts de Bordeaux: *1874*, 3d ser. (Paris, 1875): 15–27.

Wollstonecraft, Mary. *A Vindication of the Rights of Woman*. 1792. 2d. ed., edited by Carol H. Poston. New York: Norton, 1988.

Secondary Sources

Ackerknecht, Erwin. *Medicine at the Paris Hospital, 1794–1848*. Baltimore, Md.: Johns Hopkins University Press, 1967.

Acton, H. B. "Hegel, George Wilhelm Friedrich." In *The Encyclopedia of Philosophy*, edited by Paul Edwards. 8 vols. 1967. Reprint. New York: Macmillan, 1972.

Adorno, Theodor W., et al., eds. *The Positivist Dispute in German Sociology*. Translated by Glyn Adey and David Frisby. New York: Harper Torchbooks, 1976.

Alain [Emile Chartier]. *Idées: Introduction à la philosophie – Platon, Descartes, Hegel, Comte*. N.p.: Paul Hartmann, 1939; Paris: Flammarion, 1983.

Alfaric, Prosper. *Laromiguière et son école*. Paris: Les Belles Lettres, 1929.

Allemagne, Henri-René d'. *Les Saint-Simoniens, 1827–1837*. Paris: Gründ, 1930.

Allen, James Smith. "Le Commerce du livre romantique à Paris (1820–1843)." *Revue française d'histoire du livre*, n.s., 26 (January–February 1980): 69–95.

———. *Popular French Romanticism: Authors, Readers, and Books in the Nineteenth Century*. Syracuse, N.Y.: Syracuse University Press, 1981.

Allix, Edgard. "La Méthode et la conception de l'économie politique dan l'oeuvre de J.-B. Say." *Revue d'histoire des doctrines économiques et sociales* 4 (1911): 321–60.

Althusser, Louis. *Montesquieu, Rousseau, Marx: Politics and History*. Translated by Ben Brewster. London: NLB, 1972; London: Verso, 1982.

Andreski, Stanislav. Introduction to *The Essential Comte: Selected from "Cours de Philosophie Positive*," edited by Andreski, translated by Margaret Clarke, 7–18. New York: Harper & Row, Barnes & Noble, 1974.

———. *Social Science as Sorcery*. London: André Deutsch, 1972.

Ansart, Pierre. *Marx et l'anarchisme: Essai sur les sociologies de Saint-Simon, Proudhon et Marx*. Paris: Presses Universitaires de France, 1969.

———. *Sociologie de Saint-Simon*. Paris: Presses Universitaires de France, 1970.

Anschutz, R. P. *The Philosophy of J. S. Mill*. Oxford: Clarendon Press, 1953.

Arbousse-Bastide, Paul. *Auguste Comte*. Paris: Presses Universitaires de France, 1968.

———. "Auguste Comte et la folie." In *Les Sciences de la folie*, 47–72. Paris: Mouton, 1972.

———. *La Doctrine d'éducation universelle dans la philosophie d'Auguste Comte*. 2 vols. Paris: Presses Universitaires de France, 1957.

Ariès, Philippe. *Centuries of Childhood: A Social History of Family Life*. Translated by Robert Baldick. New York: Knopf, 1962.

Arieti, S. Ivano. "Psychoses." In *The New Encyclopaedia Britannica: Macropaedia*. 15th ed. 30 vols. Chicago: Encyclopaedia Britannica, 1981.

Arnaud, Pierre. "Auguste Comte: Républicain hérétique." In *L'Esprit Républicain: Colloque d'Orléans, 4 & 5 septembre 1970*, edited by Jacques Viard, 227–30. Paris: Klincksieck, 1972.

Introduction to *Catéchisme positiviste*, by Auguste Comte, 15–24. Paris: Garnier-Flammarion, 1966.

Introduction to *Du pouvoir spirituel*, by Auguste Comte, 21–72. Paris: Le Livre de Poche, 1978.

"La Maladie occidentale: Un Diagnostic toujours actuel d'Auguste Comte." *L'Année sociologique*, 3rd ser., 23 (1972): 9–70.

Le *"Nouveau Dieu": Préliminaires à la politique positive*. Paris: J. Vrin, 1973.

Politique d'Auguste Comte. Paris: Armand Colin, 1965.

Pour connaître la pensée de A. Comte. Paris: Bordas, 1969.

"Saint-Simon, le Saint-Simonism, et les Saint-Simoniens vus par Auguste Comte." *Economies et Sociétés* 6 (June 1970): 1050–68.

Sociologie de Comte. Paris: Presses Universitaires de France, 1969.

Aron, Raymond. *Les Grandes Doctrines de sociologie historique: Les Cours de Sorbonne*. Paris: Centre de Documentation Universitaire, 1965.

Main Currents in Sociological Thought. Translated by Richard Howard and Helen Weaver. 2 vols. New York: Basic Books, 1965; Garden City, N.Y.: Doubleday, Anchor Books, 1968.

"La Sociologie." In *Les Sciences sociales en France: Enseignement et Recherche*. Paris: Centre d'Etudes de Politique Etrangère, n.d.

Artz, Frederick B. *The Development of Technical Education in France, 1500–1850*. Cambridge: MIT Press, 1966.

Auerbach, Nina. *Woman and the Demon: The Life of a Victorian Myth*. Cambridge, Mass.: Harvard University Press, 1982.

Augustin-Thierry, A. *Augustin Thierry (1795–1856) d'après sa correspondance et ses papiers de famille*. Paris: Plon, 1922.

Aulard, F. A. *Napoléon et le monopole universitaire: Origines et fonctionnement de l'Université impériale*. Paris: Armand Colin, 1911.

Preface to *Mémoires de Louvet de Couvrai sur la Révolution française*, by [Jean-Baptiste] Louvet de Couvrai, i–xxviii. 2 vols. Paris, 1889.

Auriol, C. *Le Lieutenant Général de Campredon*. Montpellier, 1894.

Avineri, Shlomo. *The Social and Political Thought of Karl Marx*. Cambridge: Cambridge University Press, 1968.

Bagge, Dominique. *Le Conflit des idées politiques en France sous la Restauration*. Paris: Presses Universitaires de France, 1952.

Baker, Keith Michael. "Closing the French Revolution: Saint-Simon and Comte." In *The French Revolution and the Creation of Modern Political Culture*. Vol. 3, *The Transformation of Political Culture, 1789–1848*, edited by François Furet and Mona Ozouf, 323–39. Oxford: Pergamon Press, 1989.

Condorcet: From Natural Philosophy to Social Mathematics. Chicago: University of Chicago Press, 1975.

Introduction to *Condorcet: Selected Writings*, edited and translated by Baker, vii–xxxviii. Indianapolis, Ind.: Bobbs-Merrill, 1976.

Inventing the French Revolution: Essays on French Political Culture in the Eighteenth Century. Cambridge: Cambridge University Press, 1990.

"Politics and Social Science in Eighteenth-Century France: The Société de 1789."

In *French Government and Society, 1500–1850*, edited by J. F. Bosher, 208–31. London: University of London, Athlone Press, 1973.

"Sovereignty." In *A Critical Dictionary of the French Revolution*. See Furet and Ozouf, 844–59.

Balandier, Georges. "Entretien sur les problèmes actuels de la sociologie." *L'Homme et la société* 3 (January–March, 1967): 47–53.

Balon, Bernard. "L'Organisation, organisme, économie et milieu chez Henri Ducrotay de Blainville." *Revue d'histoire des sciences* 32.1 (1979): 5–24.

Barbour, Ian G. *Issues in Science and Religion*. Englewood Cliffs, N.J.: Prentice-Hall, 1966; New York: Harper Torchbooks, 1971.

Barnard, F. M. *Herder's Social and Political Thought*. Oxford: Clarendon Press, 1965.

Barnard, H. C. *Education and the French Revolution*. Cambridge: Cambridge University Press, 1969.

Barnes, Barry. *Scientific Knowledge and Sociological Theory*. London: Routledge & Kegan Paul, 1974.

Barnes, Harry Elmer. "Social Thought in Early Modern Times." In *An Introduction to the History of Sociology*, abridged ed., edited by Barnes, 29–78. Chicago: University of Chicago Press, 1948.

Barrett, William. *The Illusion of Technique: The Search for Meaning in a Technological Civilization*. Garden City, N.Y.: Doubleday, Anchor Press, 1978; Garden City, N.Y.: Doubleday, Anchor Books, 1979.

Baumer, Franklin L. *Modern European Thought: Continuity and Change in Ideas, 1600–1950*. New York: Macmillan, 1977.

Beecher, Jonathan. *Charles Fourier: The Visionary and His World*. Berkeley and Los Angeles: University of California Press, 1986.

Bell, Susan Groag, and Karen M. Offen, *Women, the Family, and Freedom: The Debate in Documents*. 2 vols. Stanford, Calif.: Stanford University Press, 1983.

Bénichou, Paul. *Le Sacre de l'écrivain, 1750–1830: Essai sur l'avènement d'un pouvoir spirituel laïque dans la France moderne*. 2d ed. Paris: José Corti, 1973; Paris: José Corti, 1985.

Le Temps des prophètes: Doctrines de l'âge romantique. Paris: Gallimard, 1977.

Bensaude-Vincent, Bernadette. "L'Astronomie populaire: Priorité philosophique et projet politique." *Revue de synthèse* 112 (January–March 1991): 49–59.

Berenson, Edward. "A New Religion of the Left: Christianity and Social Radicalism in France, 1815–1848." In *The French Revolution and the Creation of Modern Political Culture*. Vol. 3, *The Transformation of Political Culture, 1789–1848*, edited by François Furet and Mona Ozouf, 543–60. Oxford: Pergamon Press, 1989.

Populist Religion and Left-Wing Politics in France, 1830–1852. Princeton, N.J.: Princeton University Press, 1984.

Berger, Morroe. *Real and Imagined Worlds: The Novel and Social Science*. Cambridge, Mass.: Harvard University Press, 1977.

Bergeron, Louis. *France under Napoleon*. Translated by R. R. Palmer. 1972. Princeton, N.J.: Princeton University Press, 1981.

Berlin, Isaiah. *The Crooked Timber of Humanity: Chapters in the History of Ideas*. Edited by Henry Hardy. London: John Murray, 1990; New York: Random House, Vintage Books, 1992.

Vico and Herder: Two Studies in the History of Ideas. New York: Viking Press, 1976; New York: Random House, Vintage Books, 1977.

Bernheimer, Charles. *Figures of Ill Repute: Representing Prostitution in Nineteenth-Century France.* Cambridge, Mass.: Harvard University Press, 1989.

Bernstein, Richard J. *The Restructuring of Social and Political Theory.* New York: Harcourt Brace Jovanovich, 1976.

Bertier de Sauvigny, Guillaume de. *The Bourbon Restoration.* Translated by Lynn M. Case. Philadelphia: University of Pennsylvania Press, 1966.

"French Politics, 1814–1847." In *The New Cambridge Modern History.* Vol. 9, *War and Peace in an Age of Upheaval, 1793–1830,* edited by C. W. Crawley, 337–66. Cambridge: Cambridge University Press, 1965.

Nouvelle Histoire de Paris: La Restauration, 1815–1830. Paris: Hachette, 1977.

"Science et politique sous la Restauration." *Revue des sciences morales et politiques* 139 (1984): 453–66.

Bierstedt, Robert. "Sociological Thought in the Eighteenth Century." In *A History of Sociological Analysis,* edited by Tom Bottomore and Robert Nisbet, 3–38. New York: Basic Books, 1978.

Blum, Carol. *Rousseau and the Republic of Virtue: The Language of Politics in the French Revolution.* Ithaca, N.Y.: Cornell University Press, 1986.

Boas, George. *French Philosophies of the Romantic Period.* Baltimore, Md.: Johns Hopkins Press, 1925.

"Maistre, Comte Joseph de." In *The Encyclopedia of Philosophy,* edited by Paul Edwards. 8 vols. 1967. Reprint. New York: Macmillan, 1972.

Bock, Kenneth. "Theories of Progress, Development, Evolution." In *A History of Sociological Analysis,* edited by Tom Bottomore and Robert Nisbet, 39–79. New York: Basic Books, 1978.

Boffa, Massimo. "La Contre-Révolution, Joseph de Maistre." In *The French Revolution and the Creation of Modern Political Culture.* Vol. 3, *The Transformation of Political Culture, 1789–1848,* edited by François Furet and Mona Ozouf, 291–308. Oxford: Pergamon Press, 1989.

Boiron, N. M. *La Prostitution dans l'histoire, devant le droit, devant l'opinion.* Paris: Berger-Levrault, 1926.

Boissard, Henri. *Théophile Foisset.* Paris, 1891.

Borenstein, Audrey. *Redeeming the Sin: Social Science and Literature.* New York: Columbia University Press, 1978.

Boskoff, Alvin. "From Social Thought to Sociological Theory." In *Modern Sociological Theory in Continuity and Change,* edited by Howard Becker and Alvin Boskoff, 3–35. New York: Dryden Press, 1957.

Boudot, Maurice. "De l'usurpation géométrique." *Revue philosophique de France et de l'étranger,* no. 4 (1985): 397–402.

Bourchenin, Daniel. *Daniel Encontre.* Paris, 1877.

Boutard, Charles. *Lamennais: Sa vie et ses doctrines.* Vol. 2, *Le Catholicisme libéral.* Paris, 1908.

Boutroux, Emile. *De l'influence de la philosophie écossaise sur la philosophie moderne.* Edinburgh, 1897. (Extract from the *Revue française d'Edimbourg.*)

Etudes d'histoire de la philosophie. Paris, 1897.

Boyer de Sainte Suzanne, R. de *Essai sur la pensée religieuse d'Auguste Comte.* Paris: Emile Nourry, 1923.

Braunstein, Jean-François. *Broussais et le matérialisme: Médecine et philosophie au XIXe siècle.* Paris: Méridiens Klincksieck, 1986.

Bréhier, Emile. *The History of Philosophy*. Translated by Joseph Thomas (vol. 1) and Wade Baskin (vols. 2–7). 7 vols. Chicago: University of Chicago Press, 1963–9.

Briscoe, James Bland. "Saint-Simonism and the Origins of Socialism in France, 1816–1832." Ph.D. diss., Columbia University, 1980.

Britton, Karl. *John Stuart Mill*. Harmondsworth: Penguin Books, 1953.

Brooker, B. "Mania" and "Manic-Depressive Psychosis." In *Encyclopedia of Psychology*, vol. 2, edited by H. J. Eysenck, W. Arnold, and R. Meili. New York: Herder & Herder, 1972.

Brown, Richard Harvey. *A Poetic for Sociology: Toward a Logic of Discovery for the Human Sciences*. Cambridge: Cambridge University Press, 1977.

"Symbolic Realism and Sociological Thought: Beyond the Positivist–Romantic Debate." In *Structure, Consciousness, and History*, edited by Richard Harvey Brown and Stanford M. Lyman, 13–37. Cambridge: Cambridge University Press, 1978.

Bryson, Gladys. *Man and Society: The Scottish Inquiry of the Eighteenth Century*. Princeton, N.J.: Princeton University Press, 1945.

Buis, Gérard. "Le Projet de réorganisation sociale dans les oeuvres de jeunesse d'Auguste Comte." Chap. in *Régénération et reconstruction sociale entre 1780 et 1848*, by A. Amiot et al., 133–48. Paris: J. Vrin, 1978.

Burrow, J. W. *Evolution and Society: A Study in Victorian Social Theory*. Cambridge: Cambridge University Press, 1966.

Butler, E. M. *The Saint-Simonian Religion in Germany: A Study of the Young German Movement*. 1926. New York: Howard Fertig, 1968.

Buzon, Frédéric de. "Auguste Comte, le *Cogito* et la modernité." *Revue de synthèse* 112 (January–March 1991): 61–73.

Caird, Edward. *The Social Philosophy and Religion of Comte*. Glasgow: James Maclehose, 1885.

Calippe, Charles. "Les Relations d'Auguste Comte avec Lamennais." *Revue du clergé français* 96 (1918): 17–28.

Callot, Jean-Pierre. *Histoire de l'Ecole Polytechnique*. Paris: Charles Lavauzelle, 1982.

Canguilhem, Georges. "Bichat, Marie-François-Xavier." In *Dictionary of Scientific Biography*. See Gillispie.

"L'Ecole de Montpellier jugée par Auguste Comte." *Bulletin et mémoires de la Société Internationale d'Histoire de la Médecine.*, n.s., 6, special issue (1959): 46–49.

"Histoire de l'homme et nature des choses selon Auguste Comte dans le *Plan des travaux scientifiques nécessaires pour réorganiser la société*, 1822." *Les Etudes philosophiques* 3 (July–September, 1974): 293–7.

"L'Histoire des sciences de l'organisation de Blainville et L'Abbé Maupied." *Revue d'histoire des sciences* 32.1 (1979): 73–91.

Le Normal et le pathologique. 5th ed. 1966. Paris: Quadrige-Presses Universitaires de France, 1984.

Carlisle, Robert B. *The Proffered Crown: Saint-Simonianism and the Doctrine of Hope*. Baltimore, Md.: Johns Hopkins University Press, 1987.

Carroll, Kiernan Joseph. *Some Aspects of the Historical Thought of Augustin Thierry*. Washington, D.C.: Catholic University of America, 1971.

Cassirer, Ernst. *The Philosophy of the Enlightenment*. Translated by Fritz C. A. Koelln and James P. Pettegrove. Princeton, N.J.: Princeton University Press, 1951; Boston: Beacon Press, 1955.

The Problem of Knowledge: Philosophy, Science, and History since Hegel. Translated by William H. Woglom and Charles W. Hendel. New Haven, Conn.: Yale University Press, 1950.

Catton, William R., Jr. *From Animistic to Naturalistic Sociology.* New York: McGraw-Hill, 1966.

Cazeneuve, Jean. "Saint-Simon et la mutation religieuse." *Economies et Sociétés* 4 (April 1970): 731–42.

Chabert, Pierre. "Pinel, Philippe." *Dictionary of Scientific Biography.* See Gillispie.

Charléty, Sebastien. *Histoire du Saint-Simonisme, 1825–1864.* Paris, 1896.

Charlton, D. G. *Positivist Thought in France during the Second Empire, 1852–1870.* Oxford: Clarendon Press, 1959.

Secular Religions in France, 1815–1870. London: Oxford University Press, 1963.

Charon-Bordas, Jeannine. *Archives Nationales. Cours des Pairs. Procès politiques.* Vol. 2, *La Monarchie de Juillet, 1830–1835.* Paris: Archives Nationales, 1983.

Chauvet, Horace. *François Arago et son temps.* Perpignan: Edition des "Amis de François Arago," 1954.

Cherfils, Christian. *L'Esthéthique positiviste.* Paris: A. Messein, 1909.

Chevalier, Louis. *Labouring Classes and Dangerous Classes in Paris During the First Half of the Nineteenth Century.* Translated by Frank Jellinek. London: Routledge & Kegan Paul, 1973.

Chobaut, H. "La Pétition du Club de Montpellier en faveur de la république (28 juin 1791)." *Annales historiques de la Révoluton française* 4 (January–December 1927): 547–63.

Clark, Robert T., Jr. *Herder: His Life and Thought.* Berkeley and Los Angeles: University of California Press, 1967.

Clavel, Marcel. *Le Centenaire d'Auguste Comte et la nouvelle constitution française.* Fontenay-sous-Bois (Seine): Fédération Humaniste Française, 1958.

Clive, John. *Macaulay: The Shaping of the Historian.* 1973. New York: Random House, Vintage Books, 1975.

Cobb, Richard. *Les Armées révolutionnaires des départements du Midi (automne et hiver de 1793, printemps de 1794).* Cahiers de l'Association Marc Bloch de Toulouse, Etudes d'histoire méridionale, no. 1. Toulouse: Soubiron, 1955.

Cohen, I. Bernard. "Delambre, Jean-Baptiste Joseph." In *Dictionary of Scientific Biography.* See Gillispie.

Coleman, William. *Biology in the Nineteenth Century: Problems of Form, Function, and Transformation.* New York: Wiley, 1971.

"Blainville, Henri Marie Ducrotay de." In *Dictionary of Scientific Biography.* See Gillispie.

Collingham, H. A. C. *The July Monarchy: A Political History of France, 1830–1848.* Edited by R. S. Alexander. London: Longman Group, 1988.

Collins, Irene. *The Government and the Newspaper Press in France, 1814–1881.* Oxford: Oxford University Press, 1959.

Copleston, Frederick. *Modern Philosophy: The British Philosophers – Hobbes to Paley.* Vol. 4, part 1, of *A History of Philosophy.* Garden City, N.Y.: Doubleday, Image Books, 1964.

Modern Philosophy: The French Enlightenment to Kant. Vol. 6, part 1 of *A History of Philosophy.* Garden City, N.Y.: Doubleday, Image Books, 1964.

Corbin, A. *Les Filles de noce: Misère sexuelle et prostitution (19ᵉ siècle).* Paris: Aubier Montaigne, 1978; Paris: Flammarion, 1982.

Corra, Emile. *Centenaire de l'essor du génie d'Auguste Comte.* Paris, n.d.

    La Naissance du génie d'Auguste Comte: Sa Vie jusqu'en 1819. Paris: Revue Positiviste Internationale, 1918.

    La Naissance du génie d'Auguste Comte II: Sa Vie, son oeuvre en 1820. Paris: Revue Positiviste Internationale, 1920.

    La Naissance du génie d'Auguste Comte III: L'Eclosion définitive – L'Opuscule de 1822. Paris: Revue Positiviste Internationale, 1922.

Coser, Lewis A. *Masters of Sociological Thought: Ideas in Historical and Social Context.* New York: Harcourt Brace Jovanovich, 1971.

Coser, Lewis A., ed. *Sociology through Literature: An Introductory Reader.* Englewood Cliffs, N.J.: Prentice-Hall, 1963.

Costabel, Pierre. "Poisson, Siméon-Denis." In *Dictionary of Scientific Biography.* See Gillispie.

Cotter, R. J. "Phrenology: The Provocation of Progress." *History of Science* 14 (1976): 211–34.

Cowling, Maurice. *Mill and Liberalism.* Cambridge: Cambridge University Press, 1963.

Crocker, L. G. "Cabanis, Pierre-Jean Georges." In *The Encyclopedia of Philosophy,* edited by Paul Edwards. 8 vols. 1967. Reprint. New York: Macmillan, 1972.

Crosland, Maurice P. "Chaptal, Jean Antoine." In *Dictionary of Scientific Biography.* See Gillispie.

    "The Development of a Professional Career in Science in France." In *The Emergence of Science in Western Europe,* edited by Crosland, 139–59. London: Macmillan Press, 1975.

    Science under Control: The French Academy of Sciences, 1795–1914. Cambridge: Cambridge University Press, 1992.

Dagognet, François. "D'une certaine unité de la pensée d'Auguste Comte: Science et religion inséparables?" *Revue philosophique de la France et de l'étranger,* no. 4, (1985): 403–22.

Dahrendorf, Ralf. *Essays in the Theory of Society.* Stanford, Calif.: Stanford University Press, 1968.

Darnton, Robert. *Mesmerism and the End of the Enlightenment in France.* Cambridge, Mass.: Harvard University Press, 1968; New York: Schocken Books, 1970.

Daston, Lorraine J. "The Physicalist Tradition in Early Nineteenth-Century French Geometry." *Studies in History and Philosophy of Science* 17 (September 1986): 269–95.

Daumard, Adeline. *Les Bourgeois de Paris au XIXᵉ siècle.* Paris: Flammarion, 1970.

Dautry, Jean. "Sur un imprimé retrouvé du Comte de Saint-Simon." *Annales historiques de la Révolution française* 20 (1948): 289–321.

Debarbat, Suzanne, Solange Grillot, and Jacques Levy. *L'Observatoire de Paris: Son histoire.* Paris: Observatoire de Paris, 1984.

Dejob, Charles. *De l'établissement connu sous le nom de Lycée et d'Athénée et de quelques établissements analogues.* (Extract from the *Revue internationale de l'enseignement,* July 15, 1889.) Paris, 1889.

Delamarre, Alexandre J.-L. "Le Pouvoir spirituel et la ruine de la constitution catholique chez Joseph de Maistre et Auguste Comte." *Revue philosophique de la France et de l'étranger*, no. 4 (1986): 423–60.

Delvolvé, Jean. *Réflexions sur la pensée Comtienne*. Paris: Félix Alcan, 1932.

Derré, Jean-René. *Le Renouvellement de la pensée religieuse en France de 1824 à 1834: Essai sur les origines et la signification du Mennaisisme*. Paris: C. Klincksieck, 1962.

Deschiens. *Collection de matériaux pour l'histoire de la Révolution de France depuis 1787 jusqu'à ce jour: Bibliographie des journaux*. Paris, 1829.

Descombes, Vincent. "A propos des crises cérébrales d'Auguste Comte." *Revue philosophique de la France et de l'étranger*, no. 1 (1979): 67–81.

Des Granges, C. M. *La Presse littéraire sous la Restauration, 1815–1830*. Paris: Société du Mercure de France, 1907.

Dheur, P. *La Maison de santé d'Esquirol*. Paris, 1898.

Dhombres, Nicole, and Jean Dhombres, *Naissance d'un pouvoir: Sciences et savants en France (1793–1824)*. Paris: Payot, 1989.

Dostrovsky, Sigalia. "Duhamel, Jean-Marie Constant." In *Dictionary of Scientific Biography*. See Gillispie.

Douglas, Jack D. "Understanding Everyday Life." In *Understanding Everyday Life: Toward the Reconstruction of Sociological Knowledge*, edited by Douglas, 3–44. Chicago: Aldine, 1970.

Dubuisson, Paul. *Comte et Saint-Simon: Comte n'est il que le disciple de Saint-Simon?* Paris: Au Siège de la Société Positiviste Internationale, 1906.

Ducassé, Pierre. *Auguste Comte et Gaspard Monge*. Paris. (Extract from *Revue positiviste internationale*, 1937.)

Essai sur les origines intuitives du positivisme. Paris: Félix Alcan, 1939.

Méthode et intuition chez Auguste Comte. Paris: Félix Alcan, 1939.

La Méthode positive et l'intuition comtienne. Paris: Félix Alcan, 1939 (bibliography).

Dumas, Georges. *Psychologie de deux messies positivistes*. Paris: Félix Alcan, 1905.

"Saint-Simon, père du positivisme." Parts 1, 2. *Revue philosophique* 57 (1904): 136–57, 263–87.

Dumas, Monique. "Etienne Esquirol: Sa famille, ses origines, ses années de formation." Ph.D. diss., Université Paul Sabatier-Toulouse, 1971.

Dupeux, Georges. *French Society, 1789–1970*. Translated by Peter Wait. London: Methuen, 1976.

Dupont, Paul. *Histoire de l'imprimerie*. 2 vols. Paris, 1854.

Durkheim, Emile. "Cours de science sociale: Leçon d'ouverture." *Revue internationale de l'enseignement* 15 (January–June 1888): 23–48.

"Les Etudes de science sociale." *Revue philosophique de la France et de l'étranger* 22 (July–December 1886): 61–80.

"Lettre de M. Durkheim." *Revue néo-scolastique* 14 (1907): 606–7, 612–14.

Montesquieu and Rousseau: Forerunners of Sociology. Translated by Ralph Manheim. 1960. Ann Arbor: University of Michigan Press, Ann Arbor Paperbacks, 1965.

Les Règles de la méthode sociologique. Paris, 1895.

"Saint-Simon, fondateur du positivisme et de la sociologie: Extrait d'un cours d'histoire du socialisme." *Revue philosophique* 99 (1925): 321–41.

Socialism and Saint-Simon. Edited by Alvin Gouldner. Translated by Charlotte Sattler. Yellow Springs, Ohio: Antioch Press, 1958.

Durkheim, Emile, and P. Fauconnet. "Sociologie et sciences sociales." *Revue philosophique de la France et de l'étranger* 55 (May 1903): 465–97.

Duval-Jouve, J. *Montpellier pendant la Révolution.* 2 vols. Montpellier, 1879–1881.

Ecole Polytechnique. *Livre du centenaire, 1794–1894.* 3 vols. Paris, 1894–7.

Evans, David Owen. *Social Romanticism in France, 1830–1848.* Oxford: Clarendon Press, 1951.

Evans-Pritchard, E. E. *The Sociology of Comte: An Appreciation.* Manchester: Manchester University Press, 1970.

Faguet, Emile. *Politiques et moralistes du dix-neuvième siècle.* 3 vols. Paris, 1891–9.

Farrington, Benjamin. *Francis Bacon: Philosopher of Industrial Science.* New York: Henry Schuman, 1949.

Fauchois, Yann. "Centralization." In *A Critical Dictionary of the French Revolution.* See Furet and Ozouf, 629–39.

Feldman, Burton, and Robert D. Richardson, eds. *The Rise of Modern Mythology, 1680–1860.* Bloomington: Indiana University Press, 1972.

Felkay, Nicole. "Les Libraires de l'époque romantique d'après des documents inédits." *Revue française d'histoire du livre,* n.s., 5.9 (1975): 31–87.

Fletcher, Ronald. *Auguste Comte and the Making of Sociology.* Auguste Comte Memorial Trust Lecture. London: University of London, Athlone, 1966.

"Evolutionary and Developmental Sociology." In *Approaches to Sociology: An Introduction to Major Trends in British Sociology,* edited by John Rex, 39–69. London: Routledge & Kegan Paul, 1974.

The Making of Sociology: A Study of Sociological Theory. 2 vols. London: Michael Joseph, 1971.

Fontana, Biancamaria. *Benjamin Constant and the Post-Revolutionary Mind.* New Haven, Conn.: Yale University Press, 1991.

Forbes, Duncan. *Hume's Philosophical Politics.* Cambridge: Cambridge University Press, 1975.

Foucault, Michel. *Histoire de la folie à l'âge classique.* Paris: Gallimard, 1972.

Naissance de la clinique. Paris: Presses Universitaires de France, 1963.

Fox, Robert. "Science, the University, and the State in Nineteenth-Century France." In *Professions and the French State, 1700–1900,* edited by Gerald L. Geison, 66–145. Philadelphia: University of Pennsylvania Press, 1984.

France, Anatole. "Le Positivisme au Collège de France." *Le Temps,* February 7, 1892.

Fraser, Craig G. "Lagrange's Analytical Mathematics, Its Cartesian Origins and Reception in Comte's Positive Philosophy." *Studies in History and Philosophy of Science* 21 (June 1990): 243–56.

Frick, Jean-Paul. "Le Problème du pouvoir chez A. Comte et la signification de sa philosophie positive." *Revue philosophique de la France et de l'étranger,* no. 3 (1988): 273–301.

Frisby, David. "The Frankfurt School: Critical Theory and Positivism." In *Approaches to Sociology: An Introduction to Major Trends in British Sociology,* edited by John Rex, 205–29. London: Routledge & Kegan Paul, 1974.

Furet, François. *Interpreting the French Revolution.* Translated by Elborg Forster. Cambridge: Cambridge University Press, 1981.

"Jacobinism." In *A Critical Dictionary of the French Revolution.* See Furet and Ozouf, 704–15.

Furet, François, and Mona Ozouf, eds. *A Critical Dictionary of the French Revolution.*

Translated by Arthur Goldhammer. Cambridge, Mass.: Harvard University Press, Belknap Press, 1989.

Gaddis, John Lewis. "The Cold War's End Dramatizes the Failure of Political Theory." *Chronicle of Higher Education*, July 22, 1992, 44.

Galston, William, A. *Kant and the Problem of History*. Chicago: University of Chicago Press, 1975.

Gauchet, Marcel. "Constant." In *A Critical Dictionary of the French Revolution*. See Furet and Ozouf, 924–32.

Gay, Peter. *The Enlightenment: An Interpretation*. 2 vols. New York: Knopf, 1966–9; New York: Norton, The Norton Library, 1977.

Gellner, Ernst. *Cause and Meaning in the Social Sciences*. London: Routledge & Kegan Paul, 1973.

Gentile, Francesco. "La trasformazione dell'idea di progresso da Condorcet a Saint-Simon." *Revue internationale de philosophie* 14 (1960): 417–44.

Gérard, Alice. *La Révolution française: Mythes et interprétations (1789–1970)*. Paris: Flammarion, 1970.

Gerbod, Paul. *Paul-François Dubois: Universitaire, journaliste et homme politique*. Paris: C. Klincksieck, 1967.

La Vie quotidienne dans les lycées et collèges au XIXᵉ siècle. Paris: Hachette, 1968.

Gerth, Hans, and Saul Landau. "The Relevance of History to the Sociological Ethos." In *Sociology on Trial*, edited by Maurice Stein and Arthur Vidich, 26–35. Englewood Cliffs, N.J.: Prentice-Hall, 1963.

Ghio, Michelangelo. "Condorcet." *Filosofia* 6.1 (1955): 227–63.

Giddens, Anthony, ed. "Positivism and Its Critics." In *A History of Sociological Analysis*, edited by Tom Bottomore and Robert Nisbet, 237–86. New York: Basic Books, 1978.

Positivism and Sociology. London: Heinemann, 1974.

Giddens, Anthony. *Studies in Social and Political Theory*. New York: Basic Books, 1977.

Giddens, Anthony, and Jonathan H. Turner, eds. *Social Theory Today*. Cambridge: Polity Press, 1987.

Gide, Charles, and Charles Rist. *A History of Economic Doctrines from the Time of the Physiocrats to the Present Day*. 2d English ed., translated by R. Richards. London: George G. Harrap, 1948.

Gillies, A. *Herder*. Oxford: Basil Blackwell, 1945.

Gillispie, Charles Coulston, ed. *Dictionary of Scientific Biography*. 16 vols. New York: Scribners, 1970–80.

"Science in the French Revolution." In *The Sociology of Science*, edited by Bernard Barber and Walter Hirsch, 89–97. New York: Free Press, 1962.

"Science and Technology." In *The New Cambridge Modern History*, ed. George Clark, Vol. 9, *War and Peace in an Age of Upheaval, 1793–1830*, edited by C. W. Crawley, 118–45. Cambridge: Cambridge University Press, 1965.

Girard, Louis. *Les Libéraux français: 1814–1875*. Paris: Aubier, 1985.

Godechot, Jacques. *The Counter-Revolution: Doctrine and Action, 1789–1804*. Translated by Salvator Attanasio. New York: Fertig, 1971; Princeton, N.J.: Princeton University Press, 1981.

Gohau, Gabriel. "L'Unité de création chez Blainville." *Revue d'histoire des sciences* 32.1 (1979): 43–58.

Goldstein, Jan. *Console and Classify: The French Psychiatric Profession in the Nineteenth Century*. 1987. Reprint. Cambridge: Cambridge University Press, 1990.

Gooch, C. P. *History and Historians in the Nineteenth Century*. New York: Longmans, Green, 1913.

Goodwin, Frederick K., and Kay Redfield Jamison. *Manic-Depressive Illness*. New York: Oxford University Press, 1990.

Gossman, Lionel. "Augustin Thierry and Liberal Historiography." *History and Theory* 15, no. 4 (1976): 3–83.

Gouhier, Henri. "Une Année de la jeunesse d'Auguste Comte: Juillet 1816–juillet 1817." *Revue philosophique* 110 (July–December 1930): 108–25.

"Blainville et Auguste Comte." *Revue d'histoire des sciences* 32.1 (1979): 59–72.

Introduction to *Auguste Comte: Oeuvres Choisies*, edited by Gouhier, 5–46. Paris: Aubier-Montaigne, 1943.

La Jeunesse d'Auguste Comte et la formation du positivisme. 3 vols. Paris: J. Vrin, 1933–41.

"Lettres inédites de Saint-Simon à Blainville." *Revue philosophique de la France et de l'étranger* 131.1–2 (1941): 70–80.

"L'Opuscule fondamental." *Les Etudes philosophiques*, no. 3 (1974): 325–37.

"La Philosophie 'positiviste' et 'chrétienne' de D. de Blainville." *Revue philosophique de la France et de l'étranger* 131.1–2 (1941): 38–69.

La Vie d'Auguste Comte. 2d ed. Paris: J. Vrin, 1965.

Gould, F. J. *Auguste Comte*. London: Watts, 1920.

Gould, Julius. "Auguste Comte." In *The Founding Fathers of Social Science*, edited by Timothy Raison, 35–43. Harmondsworth: Penguin Books, 1969.

Gouldner, Alvin W. *The Coming Crisis of Western Sociology*. New York: Basic Books, 1970.

The Dialectic of Ideology and Technology: The Origins, Grammar, and Future of Ideology. New York: Seabury Press, 1976; New York: Oxford University Press, 1982.

Goyau, Georges. *La Pensée religieuse de Joseph de Maistre*. Paris: Perrin, 1921.

Grana, César. *Modernity and Its Discontents: French Society and the French Man of Letters in the Nineteenth Century*. 2d ed. New York: Harper & Row, 1967. Originally published as *Bohemian vs. Bourgeois: French Society and the French Man of Letters in the Nineteenth Century* (New York: Basic Books, 1964).

Grasset, Joseph. *Un Demifou de génie: Auguste Comte, déséquilibré constant et fou intermittent*. Montpellier: Roumégous et Déhan, 1911.

Grave, S. A. *The Scottish Philosophy of Common Sense*. Oxford: Clarendon Press, 1960.

Griffiths, David Albert. *Jean Reynaud: Encyclopédiste de l'époque romantique*. Paris: Marcel Rivière, 1965.

Gruber, R. P. *Auguste Comte Fondateur du positivisme: Sa vie. Sa doctrine*. Translated by P. Mazoyer. Paris, 1892.

Guitard, Thierry. *La Querelle des infiniments petits à l'Ecole Polytechnique au XIXe siècle*. Japan: History of Science Society of Japan, 1986. (Extract from *Historian Scientiarum*, 1986, no. 30.)

Gurvitch, Georges. *Traité de Sociologie*, vol. 1. Paris: Presses Universitaires de France, 1955.

Gusdorf, Georges. *L'Avènement des sciences humaines au siècle des lumières*. Paris: Payot, 1973.

La Conscience révolutionnaire: Les Idéologues. Paris: Payot, 1978.

De l'histoire des sciences à l'histoire de la pensée. Paris: Payot, 1977.

Introduction aux sciences humaines: Essai critique sur leurs origines et leur développement. Paris: Les Belles Lettres, 1960.

Habermas, Jürgen. *Knowledge and Human Interests*. Translated by Jeremy J. Shapiro. Boston: Beacon Press, 1971.

Hahn, Roger. *The Anatomy of a Scientific Institution: The Paris Academy of Sciences, 1666–1803*. Berkeley and Los Angeles: University of California Press, 1971.

"Arago, Dominique François Jean." In *Dictionary of Scientific Biography*. See Gillispie.

Haines, Barbara. "The Inter-Relations between Social, Biological, and Medical Thought, 1750–1850: Saint-Simon and Comte." *British Journal for the History of Science* 11 (March 1978): 19–35.

Halbwachs, Maurice. *Les Causes du suicide*. Paris: Félix Alcan, 1930.

Halévy, Elie. *The Era of Tyrannies*. Translated by R. K. Webb. Garden City, N.Y.: Doubleday, Anchor Books, 1965.

The Growth of Philosophic Radicalism. 3d ed., translated by Mary Morris. London: Faber & Faber, 1972.

Hampshire, Stuart. Introduction to *Sketch for a Historical Picture of the Progress of the Human Mind*, by Antoine-Nicolas de Condorcet, translated by June Barraclough, vii–xii. New York: Noonday, 1955.

Hampson, Norman. *The Enlightenment*. Harmondsworth, Penguin Books, 1968.

A Social History of the French Revolution. Toronto: University of Toronto Press, 1963.

Harpaz, Ephraim. "*Le Censeur européen*: Histoire d'un journal industrialiste." *Revue d'histoire économique et sociale* 37 (1959), 185–218, 328–57.

Harrington, Anne. *Medicine, Mind, and the Double Brain: A Study in Nineteenth-Century Thought*. Princeton, N.J.: Princeton University Press, 1987.

Harrison, Royden. *Before the Socialists: Studies in Labour and Politics, 1861–1881*. London: Routledge & Kegan Paul, 1965.

Harsin, Jill. *Policing Prostitution in Nineteenth-Century Paris*. Princeton, N.J.: Princeton University Press, 1985.

Hawkins, M. J. "Reason and Sense Perception in Comte's Theory of Mind." *History of European Ideas* 5 (1984): 149–63.

Hawkins, Richard Laurin. *Auguste Comte and the United States (1816–1853)*. Cambridge, Mass.: Harvard University Press, 1936.

Positivism in the United States (1853–1861). Cambridge, Mass.: Harvard University Press, 1938.

Hayek, F. A. *The Counter-Revolution of Science: Studies on the Abuse of Reason*. Glencoe, Ill.: The Free Press, 1952.

New Studies in Philosophy, Politics, Economics and the History of Ideas. London: Routledge & Kegan Paul, 1978.

Hayward, Jack. *After the Revolution: Six Critics of Democracy and Nationalism*. New York: New York University Press, 1991.

Head, Brian W. *Ideology and Social Science: Destutt de Tracy and French Liberalism*. Dordrecht: Martinus Nijhoff, 1985.

"The Origins of 'La Science Sociale' in France, 1770–1800." *Australian Journal of French Studies* 9 (January–April 1982): 124.

Heilbron, Johan. "Auguste Comte and Modern Epistemology." *Sociological Theory* 8 (Fall 1990): 153–62.

Hemmings, F. W. J. *Culture and Society in France, 1789–1848*. Leicester: Leicester University Press, 1987.

Himmelfarb, Gertrude. *On Liberty and Liberalism: The Case of John Stuart Mill*. New York: Knopf, 1974.

Hodde, Lucien de la. *Histoire des sociétés secrètes et du parti républicain de 1830 à 1848*. Paris, 1850.

Hoffmann, Stanley. "Paradoxes of the French Political Community." In *In Search of France: The Economy, Society, and Political System in the Twentieth Century*, by Hoffmann et al. Cambridge, Mass.: Harvard University Press, 1963; New York: Harper & Row, Harper Torchbooks, 1965.

Holmes, Stephen. *Benjamin Constant and the Making of Modern Liberalism*. New Haven, Conn.: Yale University Press, 1984.

Horowitz, Irving Louis. *Professing Sociology: Studies in the Life Cycle of Social Science*. Chicago: Aldine, 1968.

Hourdin, George. *Lamennais: Prophète et combattant pour la liberté*. Paris: Perrin, 1982.

Huard, Pierre. "Broussais, François-Joseph Victor." In *Dictionary of Scientific Biography*. See Gillispie.

Huard, Pierre, and M. J. Imbault-Huart. "Vicq d'Azyr, Félix." In *Dictionary of Scientific Biography*. See Gillispie.

Hubbard, G. *Saint-Simon: Sa Vie et ses travaux*. Paris, 1857.

Hubert, René. *Les Sciences sociales dans l'Encyclopédie*. Paris: Alcan, 1923. Reprint. Geneva: Slatkine Reprints, 1970.

Hunt, Lynn. *Politics, Culture, and Class in the French Revolution*. Berkeley and Los Angeles: University of California Press, 1984.

Iggers, Georg. *The Cult of Authority: The Political Philosophy of the Saint–Simonians – A Chapter in the Intellectual History of Totalitarianism*. The Hague: Martinus Nijhoff, 1958.

Itard, Jean. "Lagrange, Joseph Louis." In *Dictionary of Scientific Biography*. See Gillispie.

James, Michael. "Pierre-Louis Roederer, Jean-Baptiste Say, and the Concept of *industrie*." *History of Political Economy* 9.4 (1977): 455–75.

Janet, Paul. "Les Origines de la philosophie d'Auguste Comte." *Revue des deux mondes* 82.3 (1887): 593–629.

Jardin, A., and A. J. Tudesq. *La France des notables*. 2 vols. Paris: Seuil, 1973.

Jaume, Lucien. *Le Discours Jacobin et la démocratie*. Paris: Fayard, 1989.

Johnson, Douglas. *Guizot: Aspects of French History, 1787–1874*. London: Routledge & Kegan Paul, 1963.

Johnson, Hubert C. *The Midi in Revolution: A Study of Regional Political Diversity, 1789–1793*. Princeton, N.J.: Princeton University Press, 1986.

Jones, Colin. *Charity and Bienfaisance: The Treatment of the Poor in the Montpellier Region, 1740–1815*. Cambridge: Cambridge University Press, 1982.

Judt, Tony. *Marxism and the French Left: Studies on Labour and Politics in France, 1830–1981*. Oxford: Oxford University Press, 1986.

Kaiser, Thomas E. "Politics and Political Economy in the Thought of the Idéologues." *History of Political Economy* 12.2 (1980): 141–60.

Keller, E. *Le Général de Lamoricière: Sa Vie militaire, politique, et religieuse.* 2 vols. Paris: Librairie Militaire de J. Dumaine, 1974.

Kelley, Donald R. *Historians and the Law in Postrevolutionary France.* Princeton, N.J.: Princeton University Press, 1984.

Kelly, George Armstrong. "The Expert as Historical Actor." *Daedalus* 92.3 (1963): 529–48.

——— *The Humane Comedy: Constant, Tocqueville and French Liberalism.* Cambridge: Cambridge University Press, 1992.

Kennedy, Emmet. *A Philosophe in the Age of Revolution: Destutt de Tracy and the Origins of "Ideology."* Philadelphia: American Philosophical Society, 1978.

Keohane, Nannerl O. *Philosophy and the State in France: The Renaissance to the Enlightenment.* Princeton, N.J.: Princeton University Press, 1980.

Khodoss, Florence. Introduction to *Cours de philosophie positive: Première et deuxième leçons,* by Auguste Comte, 5–57. Paris: Hatier, 1982.

Knight, David. *The Age of Science: The Scientific World-view in the Nineteenth Century.* Oxford: Basil Blackwell, 1986.

Kofman, Sarah. *Aberrations: Le Devenir-femme d'Auguste Comte.* Paris: Aubier-Flammarion, 1978.

Kolakowski, Leszek. *The Alienation of Reason: A History of Positivist Thought.* Translated by Norbert Guterman. Garden City, N.Y.: Doubleday, Anchor Books, 1969.

Körner, S. *Kant.* Harmondsworth: Penguin Books, 1955.

Koyré, Alexander. "Condorcet." *Journal of the History of Ideas* 9 (1948): 131–52.

Kremer-Marietti, Angèle. "L'Accomplissement du positivisme: A propos de la thèse de P. Arnaud." *Les Etudes philosophiques,* no. 3 (1974): 395–403.

——— *L'Anthropologie positiviste d'Auguste Comte.* Diss., University of Paris IV, 1977; Lille: Atelier, 1980.

——— *Auguste Comte et la théorie sociale du positivisme.* Paris: Seghers, 1970.

——— "Comte et le retour à une rhétorique originelle." *Romantisme* 21–2 (1978): 89–103.

——— *Le Concept de science positive: Ses Tenants et ses aboutissants dans les structures anthropologiques du positivisme.* Paris: Klincksieck, 1983.

——— *Entre le Signe et l'Histoire: L'Anthropologie positiviste d'Auguste Comte.* Paris: Klincksieck, 1982.

——— Introduction to *Auguste Comte: Sommaire appréciation de l'ensemble du passé moderne.* Paris: Aubier Montaigne, 1971.

——— Introduction to *Comte: Plan des travaux scientifiques nécessaires pour réorganiser la société.* Paris: Aubier, 1970.

——— Introduction to *La Science sociale,* by Auguste Comte, edited by Kremer-Marietti, 7–34. Paris: Gallimard, 1972.

——— *Le Positivisme.* Paris: Presses Universitaires de France, 1982.

——— *Le Projet anthropologique d'Auguste Comte.* Paris: Société d'Edition d'Enseignement Supérieur, 1980.

——— "Une Science politique conçue comme science de la consistance agrégative." *Les Etudes philosophiques,* no. 3 (1974): 290–353.

Lachenmeyer, Charles W. *The Language of Sociology.* New York: Columbia University Press, 1971.

Lacroix, Bernard. "La Vocation originelle d'Emile Durkheim." *Revue française de sociologie* 17.2 (1976): 213–47.

Lacroix, Jean. "Les Idées religieuses et esthétiques de Saint-Simon." *Economies et Sociétés* 4 (April 1970): 693–713.

La Sociologie d'Auguste Comte. 2d ed. Paris: Presses Universitaires de France, 1961.

Lalande, André. *Les Théories de l'induction et de l'expérimentation.* Paris: Boivin, 1929.

Landes, Joan B. *Women and the Public Sphere in the Age of the French Revolution.* Ithaca, N.Y.: Cornell University Press, 1988.

Lane, Robert E. "The Decline of Politics and Ideology in a Knowledgeable Society." *American Sociological Review* 31.5 (1966): 649–63.

Laqueur, Thomas. *Making Sex: Body and Gender from the Greeks to Freud.* Cambridge, Mass.: Harvard University Press, 1990.

Larousse, P. *Le Grand Dictionnaire universel du XIXe siècle.* 15 vols. Paris: Larousse, 1866–70.

Latreille, A., and René Rémond. *Histoire du catholicisme en France: La Période contemporaine.* 2d ed. Paris: Spes, 1962.

Laudan, Larry. "Towards a Reassessment of Comte's 'Méthode Positive.' " *Philosophy of Science* 38 (March 1971): 35–53.

Lazerges, Paul. *Lamennais: Essais sur l'unité de sa pensée.* Montauban, 1895.

Lebrun, Jean. *Lamennais ou l'Inquiétude de la liberté.* Paris: Fayard, 1981.

Lebrun, Richard Allen. *Throne and Altar: The Political and Religious Thought of Joseph de Maistre.* Ottawa: University of Ottawa Press, 1965.

Ledré, Charles. *La Presse à l'assaut de la monarchie, 1815–1848.* Paris: Armand Colin, 1960.

"La Presse nationale sous la Restauration et la Monarchie de Juillet." In *Histoire générale de la presse française*, edited by Claude Bellanger et al. Vol. 2, *De 1815– 1871*, 29–146. Paris: Presses Universitaires de France, 1969.

Leduc, Gaston. "Say, Jean Baptiste." In *International Encyclopedia of the Social Sciences*, edited by David Sills. 18 vols. New York: Macmillan, 1968–79.

Leenhardt, Albert. "La Maison natale d'Auguste Comte?" *Revue de l'Automobile-Club de l'Hérault et de l'Aveyron*, no. 62 (March–April 1940): 12–17.

Vieux Hôtels Montpelliérains. Ballegarde: SADAG, 1935.

Lefebvre, Georges. *The Directory.* Translated by Robert Baldick. New York: Random House, 1964; New York: Random House, Vintage Books, 1967.

The French Revolution. Translated by Elizabeth Moss Evanson. 2 vols. New York: Columbia University Press, 1962.

Le Febvre, Yves. *Le Génie du christianisme.* Paris: Edgar Mayère, 1929.

Le Guillou, Louis. *L'Evolution de la pensée religieuse de Félicité Lamennais.* Paris: Armand Colin, 1966.

Lenzer, Gertrud. Introduction to *Auguste Comte and Positivism: The Essential Writings*, edited by Gertrud Lenzer, xvii–lxviii. New York: Harper & Row, Harper Torchbooks, 1975.

Lepenies, Wolf. *Between Literature and Science: The Rise of Sociology.* Translated by R. J. Hollingdale. Cambridge: Cambridge University Press, 1988.

Das Ende der Naturgeschichte: Wandel kultureller Selbstverständlichkeiten in den Wissenschaften des 18. und 19. Jahrhunderts. Munich: C. Hanser, 1976.

Leroy, Maxime. *Histoire des idées sociales en France.* 2d ed. 3 vols. Paris: Gallimard, 1950.

La Vie véritable du Comte Henri de Saint-Simon (1760–1825). Paris: Bernard Grasset, 1925.

Le Roy Ladurie, Emmanuel. *The Peasants of Languedoc*. Translated by John Day. Urbana: University of Illinois, 1974.

Lessertisseur, J., and F. K. Jouffroy. "L'Idée de série chez Blainville." *Revue d'histoire des sciences* 32.1 (1979): 25–42.

Lévi-Strauss, Claude. "French Sociology." In *Twentieth-Century Sociology*, edited by Georges Gurvitch and Wilbert E. Moore, 503–37. New York: Philosophical Library, 1945.

Lévy-Bruhl, Lucien. *La Philosophie d'Auguste Comte*. Paris: Lacan, 1900.

Lewisohn, David. "Mill and Comte on the Methods of Social Science." *Journal of the History of Ideas* 33 (April–June 1972): 315–24.

Liard, Louis. *L'Enseignement supérieur en France, 1789–1893*. 2 vols. Paris, 1888–94.

Lindblom, Charles E., and David K. Cohen. *Usable Knowledge: Social Science and Social Problem Solving*. New Haven, Conn.: Yale University Press, 1979.

Lindemann, Albert S. *A History of European Socialism*. New Haven, Conn.: Yale University Press, 1983.

Lins, Ivan. "L'Oeuvre d'Auguste Comte et sa signification scientifique et philosophique au XIXᵉ siècle." Extract from the *Journal of World History* 11.4 (1969).

Lively, Jack. Introduction to *The Works of Joseph de Maistre*, edited by Lively. New York: Macmillan, 1965; New York: Schocken Books, 1971.

Lively, Jack, and John Rees. *Utilitarian Logic and Politics: James Mill's "Essay on Government," and Macaulay's Critique and the Ensuing Debate*. Oxford: Clarendon Press, 1978.

Livois, René de. *Histoire de la presse française*. Vol. 1, *Des origines à 1881*. Lausanne: Spes, 1965.

Lolli, Mirella Larizza. *Il Sansimonismo (1825–1830): Un ideologia per lo sviluppo industriale*. Torino: Giappichelli, 1976.

Lovejoy, Arthur O. *Essays in the History of Ideas*. Baltimore, Md.: Johns Hopkins University Press, 1948.

Lukacs, George. *The Young Hegel: Studies in the Relation between Dialectics and Economics*. Translated by Rodney Livingstone. 1966. Cambridge: MIT Press, 1976.

Lukes, Steven. *Essays in Social Theory*. London: Macmillan Press, 1977.

"Saint-Simon." In *The Founding Fathers of Social Science*, edited by Timothy Raison, 27–35. Harmondsworth: Penguin Books, 1969.

Lützen, Jesper. *Joseph Liouville, 1809–1882: Master of Pure and Applied Mathematics*. Berlin: Springer, 1990.

Lyons, Martyn. *France under the Directory*. Cambridge: Cambridge University Press, 1975.

Macherey, Pierre. *Comte: La Philosophie et les sciences*. Paris: Presses Universitaires de France, 1989.

"Le Positivisme entre la Révolution et la Contre-Révolution: Comte et Maistre." *Revue de synthèse* 112 (January–March 1991): 41–47.

MacRae, Donald G. "Adam Ferguson." In *The Founding Fathers of Social Science*, edited by Timothy Raison, 17–27. Harmondsworth: Penguin Books, 1969.

Ideology and Society: Papers in Sociology and Politics. London: Heinemann, 1961.

MacRae, Duncan, Jr. *The Social Function of Social Science*. New Haven, Conn.: Yale University Press, 1976.

Magner, Lois N. *A History of the Life Sciences.* New York: Dekker, 1979.

Magraw, Roger. *France, 1815–1914: The Bourgeois Century.* London: William Collins, 1983. Reprint. New York: Oxford University Press, 1986.

Mahoudeau, Jessie, and Jacques Fabre de Morlhon. *Montpellier révélé.* Albi: A.P.O.S.J., 1966.

"Les Maisons d'Auguste Comte." *La Vie montpelliéraine* 35.1790 (December 15, 1928): 28.

Mandelbaum, Maurice. *History, Man, and Reason: A Study in Nineteenth-Century Thought.* 1971. Baltimore, Md.: Johns Hopkins University Press, 1974.

Manicas, Peter T. *A History and Philosophy of the Social Sciences.* Oxford: Basil Blackwell, 1987.

Manuel, Frank E. *The Eighteenth Century Confronts the Gods.* Cambridge, Mass.: Harvard University Press, 1959.

Introduction to *Reflections on the Philosophy of the History of Mankind,* by Johann Gottfried von Herder, edited by Manuel, ix–xxv. Chicago: University of Chicago Press, 1968.

The New World of Henri Saint-Simon. Cambridge, Mass.: Harvard University Press, 1956.

The Prophets of Paris. Cambridge, Mass.: Harvard University Press, 1962; New York: Harper Torchbooks, 1965.

Manuel, Frank E., and Fritzie P. Manuel. *Utopian Thought in the Western World.* Cambridge, Mass.: Harvard University Press, Belknap Press, 1979.

Marcuse, Herbert. *Reason and Revolution: Hegel and the Rise of Social Theory.* 2d ed. New York: Oxford University Press, 1941; Boston: Beacon Press, 1960.

Maréchal, Christian. *La Jeunesse de Lamennais: Contribution à l'étude des origines du romantisme religieux en France au XIXe siècle.* Paris: Perrin, 1913.

Marès, J. "Maniaque dépressive ou maniaco-dépressive (psychose)." In *Dictionnaire encyclopédique de psychologie.* Paris: Bordas, 1980.

Marielle, C. P. *Répertoire de l'Ecole Impériale Polytechnique ou Reseignements sur les élèves qui ont fait partie de l'institution depuis l'époque de sa création en 1794 jusqu'en 1853 inclusivement.* Paris, 1855.

Marjolin, Robert. "French Sociology: Comte and Durkheim." *American Journal of Sociology* 42 (1936): 693–704.

Markham, Felix. Introduction to *Social Organization, the Science of Man and Other Writings,* by Henri de Saint-Simon, edited and translated by Markham, xi–xlix. Oxford: Basil Blackwell, 1952; New York: Harper Torchbooks, 1964.

Martindale, Don. *The Nature and Types of Sociological Theory.* Boston: Houghton Mifflin, 1960.

"Social Disorganization: The Conflict of Normative and Empirical Approaches." In *Modern Sociological Theory in Continuity and Change,* edited by Howard Becker and Alvin Boskoff, 340–67. New York: Dryden Press, 1957.

Marvin, F. S. *Comte: The Founder of Sociology.* London: Chapman & Hall, 1936; New York: Russell & Russell, 1965.

Mathiez, Albert. *La Révolution et l'Eglise.* Paris: Armand Colin, 1910.

Mauduit, Roger. *Auguste Comte et la science économique.* Paris: Félix Alcan, 1929.

Mazet, Henri. Introduction to *Six Lettres inédites à Roméo Pouzin,* 5–7. Paris: Crès, 1914.

Mazlish, Bruce. "The Idea of Progress." *Daedalus* 92.3 (1963): 447–61.

McCormick, Michael A. "Tissue Theory in Auguste Comte's Positive Biology." *Texas Reports on Biology and Medicine* 32.1 (1974): 75–87.

McHugh, Peter. "On the Failure of Positivism." In *Understanding Everyday Life: Towards the Reconstruction of Sociological Knowledge*, edited by Jack D. Douglas, 320–35. Chicago: Aldine, 1970.

McLaren, Angus. "Culture and Politics During the July Monarchy: The Case of the *National*." *Journal of European Studies* 10.2 (1980): 93–110.

"Phrenology: Medium and Message." *Journal of Modern History* 46.1 (1974): 86–97.

"A Prehistory of the Social Sciences: Phrenology in France." *Comparative Studies in Society and History* 23.1 (1981): 3–22.

McLellan, David. *Karl Marx: His Life and Thought*. New York: Harper & Row, 1973; New York: Harper Colophon Books, 1977.

McManners, John. "The Historiography of the French Revolution." In *The New Modern Cambridge History*, edited by George Clark. Vol. 8, *The American and French Revolutions: 1763–93*, edited by A. Goodwin, 618–52. Cambridge: Cambridge University Press, 1965.

Meek, Ronald. *Economics, Ideology and Other Essays: Studies in the Development of Economic Thought*. London: Chapman & Hall, 1967.

Mellon, Stanley. *The Political Uses of History: A Study of Historians in the French Restoration*. Stanford, Calif.: Stanford University Press, 1958.

Mennell, Stephen. *Sociological Theory: Uses and Unities*. New York: Praeger, 1974.

Mills, C. Wright. *The Sociological Imagination*. New York: Oxford University Press, 1959.

Milner, Max, and Claude Pichois. *Littérature française*. Vol. 7, *De Chateaubriand à Baudelaire*. Paris: Arthaud, 1985.

Monroe, D. H. "Bentham, Jeremy." In *The Encyclopedia of Philosophy*, edited by Paul Edwards. 8 vols. 1967. Reprint. New York: Macmillan, 1972.

Moore, Barrington. "Strategy in Social Science." In *Sociology on Trial*, edited by Maurice Stein and Arthur Vidich, 66–96. Englewood Cliffs, N.J.: Prentice-Hall, 1963.

Moravia, Sergio. *Il pensiero degli idéologues: Scienza e filosofia in Francia (1780–1815)*. Florence: La Nuova Italia, 1974.

Morley, John. "Comte, Auguste [Isidore Auguste Marie François Xavier]." In *Encyclopaedia Britannica*, 11th ed. 29 vols. New York: Encyclopaedia Britannica, 1910–11.

Mortier, Roland. "Madame de Staël et l'héritage des Lumières." In *Madame de Staël et l'Europe: Colloque de Coppet (18–24 juillet 1966)*. Paris: Klincksieck, 1970.

Moses, Claire Goldberg. *French Feminism in the Nineteenth Century*. Albany: State University of New York Press, 1984.

Moss, Bernard H. "Parisian Workers and the Origins of Republican Socialism, 1830–1833." In *1830 in France*, edited by John M. Merriman, 203–21. New York: Franklin Watts, New Viewpoints, 1975.

Mouliné, Henri. *De Bonald*. Paris: Félix Alcan, 1916.

Mourge, Roland. "La Philosophie biologique d'Auguste Comte." Parts 1, 2. *Archives de l'anthropologie criminelle de médecine légale et de psychologie normal et pathologique* 24.190–1, 192 (October–November, December 1909): 829–70, 911–45.

Mueller, Iris Wessel. *John Stuart Mill and French Thought.* Urbana: University of Illinois Press, 1956.

Negri, Antimo. "A. Comte, cent cinquante ans après." *Les Etudes Philosophiques,* no. 3 (1974): 367–79.

Auguste Comte et l'umanesimo positivistico. Rome: Armando Armando, 1971.

Nicard, Pol. *Etude sur la vie et les travaux de M. Ducrotay Blainville.* Paris, 1890.

Nicolet, Claude. *L'Idée républicaine en France (1789–1924): Essai d'histoire critique.* Paris: Gallimard, 1982.

Nisbet, H. B. *Herder and the Philosophy and History of Science.* Cambridge: Modern Humanities Research Association, 1970.

Nisbet, Robert. "Conservatism." In *A History of Sociological Analysis,* edited by Tom Bottomore and Robert Nisbet, 80–117. New York: Basic Books, 1978.

"Conservatism and Sociology." *American Journal of Sociology* 58 (1952): 167–75.

"De Bonald and the Concept of the Social Group." *Journal of the History of Ideas* 5 (1944): 315–31.

"The French Revolution and the Rise of Sociology in France." *American Journal of Sociology* 49 (1943): 156–65.

History of the Idea of Progress. New York: Basic Books, 1980.

The Sociological Tradition. New York: Basic Books, 1966.

Sociology as an Art Form. Oxford: Oxford University Press, 1976.

Nora, Pierre. "Republic." In *A Critical Dictionary of the French Revolution.* See Furet and Ozouf, 792–805.

Notice sur les ouvrages imprimés du Docteur Esquirol. Paris, 1832.

Nouveau Drouot, Salle No. 4, *Lettres, autographes, manuscrits, documents.* May 7, 8, 1981.

O'Boyle, Lenore. "The Problem of an Excess of Educated Men in Western Europe, 1800–1850." *Journal of Modern History* 42 (December 1970): 471–95.

Orr, Linda. *Headless History: Nineteenth-Century French Historiography of the Revolution.* Ithaca, N.Y.: Cornell University Press, 1990.

Outram, Dorinda. "Politics and Vocation: French Science, 1793–1830." *British Journal for the History of Science,* 13 (March 1980): 27–43.

Ouy, Achille. "La Jeunesse d'Auguste Comte d'après des lettres inédites." *Mercure de France* 302.1014 (1948): 256–61.

Ozouf, Mona. "Danton"; "Liberty"; "Public Spirit." In *A Critical Dictionary of the French Revolution.* See Furet and Ozouf, 213–23, 716–27, 771–80.

"La Révolution française et l'idée de l'homme nouveau." In *The French Revolution and the Creation of Modern Political Culture.* Vol. 2, *The Political Culture of the French Revolution,* edited by Colin Lucas, 213–32. Oxford: Pergamon Press, 1988.

Packe, Michael St. John. *The Life of John Stuart Mill.* London: Secker & Warburg, 1954.

Papillon, Fernand. "David Hume, précurseur d'Auguste Comte." *La Philosophie positive* 3 (September–October 1868): 292–308.

Parent-Lardeur, Françoise. *Les Cabinets de lecture: La Lecture publique à Paris sous la Restauration.* Paris: Payot, 1982.

Parsons, Talcott. *Essays in Sociological Theory.* 2d ed. Glencoe, Ill.: Free Press, 1954.

"The General Interpretation of Action." In *Theories of Society: Foundations of Modern Sociological Theory,* edited by Talcott Parsons et al., 1:85–97. New York: Free Press, 1961.

Parsons, Talcott. *Social Systems and the Evolution of Action Theory*. New York: Free Press, 1977.

Pélissier, Léon J. "Montpellier." *La Grande Encyclopédie*. 31 vols. Paris, 1885–1902.

Perreux, Gabriel. *Au temps des sociétés secrètes*. Paris: Hachette, 1931.

Petit, Annie. "La Révolution occidentale selon Auguste Comte: Entre l'histoire et l'utopie." *Revue de synthèse* 112 (January–March 1991): 21–40.

Peyre, Henri. *What Is Romanticism?* Translated by Roda Roberts. University: University of Alabama Press, 1977.

Philips, Edith. *Les Réfugiés Bonapartistes en Amérique (1815–1830)*. Paris, n.d.

La Philosophie positive. Published under the direction of Emile Littré and Grégoire Wyrouboff. 1867–83.

Picavet, Fr. *Les Idéologues: Essai sur l'histoire des idées et des théories scientifiques, philosophiques, religieuses, etc. en France depuis 1789*. Paris, 1891.

Pickering, Mary Barbara. "Auguste Comte: His Life and Works (1798–1842)." Ph.D. diss., Harvard University, 1988.

"New Evidence of the Link between Comte and German Philosophy." *Journal of the History of Ideas* 50 (July–September 1989): 443–63.

Pillon, F. "La Biologie selon Auguste Comte et selon Claude Bernard." *La Critique philosophique, politique, scientifique, littéraire* 7.5 (1878): 72–7.

"Claude Bernard: Sa conception de la vie comparée à celle de l'Ecole Positiviste." *La Critique philosophique, politique, scientifique, littéraire* 7.4 (1878): 54–64.

"La Méthode en biologie: Cuvier, Blainville, Auguste Comte." *La Critique philosophique, politique, scientifique, littéraire* 7.9 (1878): 129–38.

Pinet, G. *Histoire de l'Ecole Polytechnique*. Paris, 1887.

Pinkney, David H. *The French Revolution of 1830*. Princeton, N.J.: Princeton University Press, 1972.

Plamenatz, John. *The English Utilitarians*. Oxford: Basil Blackwell, 1949.

Man and Society: Political and Social Theory. 2 vols. New York: McGraw-Hill, 1963.

The Revolutionary Movement in France, 1815–1871. London: Longmans, Green, 1952.

Pledge, H. T. *Science Since 1500*. London: His Majesty's Stationery Office, 1939.

Poirier, Jean. "Lycéens d'il y a cent ans: 1814–1815." *Revue internationale de l'enseignement* 67 (1914): 175–88.

"Lycéens impériaux (1814–1815)." *La Revue de Paris* 3 (1921): 380–401.

Ponteil, Félix. *Histoire de l'enseignement en France: Les Grandes Étapes, 1789–1964*. Paris: Sirey, 1966.

Poovey, Mary. *Uneven Developments: The Ideological Work of Gender in Mid-Victorian England*. Chicago: University of Chicago Press, 1988.

Popper, Karl R. *The Poverty of Historicism*. 3d ed. London: Rouledge & Kegan Paul, 1957. Reprint. New York: Harper Torchbooks, 1964.

Pouthas, Charles. *Essai critique sur les sources et la bibliographie de Guizot pendant la Restauration*. Paris: Plon, 1923.

Guizot pendant la Restauration: Préparation de l'homme d'état (1814–1830) Paris: Plon, 1923.

Prost, Antoine. *Histoire de l'enseignement en France, 1800–1967*. Paris: Armand Colin, 1968.

Rader, Daniel L. *The Journalists and the July Revolution in France: The Role of the Political Press in the Overthrow of the Bourbon Restoration, 1827–1830*. The Hague: Martinus Nijhoff, 1973.

Ratcliffe, Barrie M., and W. H. Chalone, eds. and trans. *A French Sociologist Looks at Britain: Gustave d'Eichthal and British Society in 1828.* Manchester: University of Manchester, 1977.

Reardon, Bernard. *Liberalism and Tradition: Aspects of Catholic Thought in Nineteenth Century France.* Cambridge: Cambridge University Press, 1975.

Rearick, Charles. *Beyond the Enlightenment: Historians and Folklore in Nineteenth-Century France.* Bloomington: Indiana University Press, 1974.

Réizov, Boris. *L'Historiographie romantique française, 1815–1830.* Moscow: Editions en Langues Etrangères, n.d.

Rémond, René. *Les Droites en France.* 4th ed. Paris: Aubier Montaigne, 1982.

——. *Les Etats-Unis devant l'opinion française, 1815–1852.* 2 vols. Paris: Armand Colin, 1962.

Revue internationale de philosophie 14, nos. 53–4 (1960). Articles devoted to Saint-Simon.

Revue positiviste internationale. Published under the direction of Emile Corra, 1905–39.

Rex, John. *Discovering Sociology: Studies in Sociological Theory and Method.* London: Routledge & Kegan Paul, 1973.

Rey, Alain. *Littré: L'Humaniste et les mots.* Paris: Gallimard, 1970.

Rivers, John. *Louvet: Revolutionist and Romance Writer.* New York: Brentano's, 1911.

Roach, John. "Education and Public Opinion." In *The New Cambridge Modern History*, edited by George Clark. Vol. 9, *War and Peace in an Age of Upheaval, 1793–1830*, edited by C. W. Crawley, 179–208. Cambridge: Cambridge University Press, 1965.

Robson, John. *The Improvement of Mankind: The Social and Political Thought of John Stuart Mill.* Toronto: University of Toronto Press, 1968.

Rochberg, F. Introduction to "The Cultures or Ancient Science: Some Historical Reflections," *Isis* 83.4 (1992): 547–53.

Roesch, Eugene J. "Reflections on the Philosophy of Scientism and Its Notion of Tolerance." *Contemporary Review* 17 (October 1965): 169–75.

Rosanvallon, Pierre. "Les Doctrinaires et la question du gouvernement représentatif." In *The French Revolution and the Creation of Modern Political Culture.* Vol. 3, *The Transformation of Political Culture, 1789–1848*, edited by François Furet and Mona Ozouf, 411–31. Oxford: Pergamon Press, 1989.

——. *Le Moment Guizot.* Paris: Gallimard, 1985.

Rouvre, Charles de. *L'Amoureuse histoire d'Auguste Comte et Clotilde de Vaux.* Paris: Calmann-Levy, 1917.

Runciman, W. G. *Sociology in Its Place and Other Essays.* Cambridge: Cambridge University Press, 1970.

Russett, Cynthia Eagle. *Sexual Science: The Victorian Construction of Womanhood.* Cambridge, Mass.: Harvard University Press, 1989.

Rutten, Christian. *Essai sur la morale d'Auguste Comte.* Paris: Les Belles Lettres, 1972.

Sa'adah, Anne. *The Shaping of Liberal Politics in Revolutionary France: A Comparative Perspective.* Princeton, N.J.: Princeton University Press, 1990.

St. Paul, P. de. *La Vie du Général Campredon.* Montpellier, 1837.

Salomon, Albert. "Adam Smith as Sociologist." *Social Research* 2 (1945): 22–42.

Sarton, George. *The Life of Science: Essays in the History of Civilization.* New York: Henry Schuman, 1948.

Saurel, F. *Histoire religieuse du département de l'Hérault pendant la Révolution, le Consulat, et les premières années de l'Empire*. 4 vols. Paris, 1894-6.

Scharff, Robert C. "Mill's Misreading of Comte on 'Interior Observation.'" *Journal of the History of Philosophy* 27 (October 1989): 559-72.

"Monitoring Self-Activity: The Status of Reflection before and after Comte." *Metaphilosophy* 22 (October 1991): 333-48.

"Positivism, Philosophy of Science, and Self-Understanding in Comte and Mill." *American Philosophical Quarterly* 26 (October 1989): 253-68.

Schenk, H. G. *The Mind of the European Romantics*. Oxford: Oxford University Press, 1979.

Schiebinger, Londa. *The Mind Has No Sex? Women in the Origins of Modern Science*. Cambridge, Mass.: Harvard University Press, 1989.

Schmaus, Warren. "Hypotheses and Historical Analysis in Durkheim's Sociological Methodology: A Comtean Tradition." *Studies in History and Philosophy of Science* 16 (March 1985): 1-30.

"A Reappraisal of Comte's Three-State Law." *History and Theory* 21.2 (1982): 248-66.

Schweber, Silvan S. "Auguste Comte and the Nebular Hypothesis." In *In the Presence of the Past: Essays in Honor of Frank Manuel*, edited by Richard T. Bienvenu and Mordechai Feingold, 131-91. Dordrecht: Kluwer, 1991.

Seidman, Steven. *Liberalism and the Origins of European Social Theory*. Berkeley and Los Angeles: University of California Press, 1983.

Serres, Michel. *Hermès*. Vol. 3, *La Traduction*. Paris: Minuit, 1974.

Sewell, William H., Jr. "Beyond 1793: Babeuf, Louis Blanc and the Genealogy of 'Social Revolution.' " In *The French Revolution and the Creation of Modern Political Culture*. Vol. 3, *The Transformation of Political Culture, 1789-1848*, edited by François Furet and Mona Ozouf, 509-526. Oxford: Pergamon Press, 1989.

Work and Revolution in France: The Language of Labor from the Old Regime to 1848. Cambridge: Cambridge University Press, 1980.

Shackleton, Robert. *Montesquieu: A Critical Biography*. Oxford: Oxford University Press, 1961.

Shattuck, Roger. *The Forbidden Experiment: The Story of the Wild Boy of Aveyron*. New York: Farrar, Straus, & Giroux, 1980.

Shils, Edward. "The Calling of Sociology." In *Theories of Society: Foundation of Modern Sociological Theory*, edited by Talcott Parsons et al., 2:1405-50. New York: Free Press, 1961.

Shinn, Terry. *L'Ecole Polytechnique: 1794-1914*. Paris: Presses de la Fondation Nationale des Sciences Politiques, 1980.

Siedentop, Larry. "Two Liberal Traditions." In *The Idea of Freedom: Essays in Honour of Isaiah Berlin*, edited by Alan Ryan, 153-74. Oxford: Oxford University Press, 1979.

Simon, W. M. *European Positivism in the Nineteenth Century: An Essay in Intellectual History*. Ithaca, N.Y.: Cornell University Press, 1963.

"The 'Two Cultures' in Nineteenth-Century France: Victor Cousin and Auguste Comte." *Journal of the History of Ideas* 26 (January-March 1965): 45-58.

Simpson, George. *Auguste Comte: Sire of Sociology*. New York: Crowell, 1969.

Six, Georges. *Dictionnaire biographique des généraux et amiraux français de la Révolution et de l'Empire (1792-1824)*. 2 vols. Paris: Georges Saffroy, 1934.

Six, Jean-François. *Littré devant Dieu*. Paris: Seuil, 1962.

Skarga, Barbara. "Le Coeur et la raison, ou Les Antinomies du système de Comte." *Les Etudes philosophiques*, no. 3 (1974): 383–90.

Smith, Bonnie G. *Changing Lives: Women in European History since 1700*. Lexington, Mass.: Heath, 1989.

Smithson, Rulon Nephi. *Augustin Thierry: Social and Political Consciousness in the Evolution of a Historical Method*. Geneva: Droz, 1972.

Sokoloff, Boris. *The "Mad" Philosopher Auguste Comte*. New York: Vantage Press, 1961.

Soltau, Roger Henry. *French Political Thought in the Nineteenth Century*. New York: Russell & Russell, 1959.

Sorokin, Pitirim A. *Fads and Foibles in Modern Sociology and Related Sciences*. Chicago: Henry Regnery, 1956.

Speziali, Pierre. "Sturm, Charles-François." In *Dictionary of Scientific Biography*. See Gillispie.

Spitzer, Alan B. *The French Generation of 1820*. Princeton, N.J.: Princeton University Press, 1987.

Standley, Arline Reilein. *Auguste Comte*. Boston: Twayne, 1981.

Stark, Werner. "Saint-Simon as a Realist." *Journal of Economic History* 3.1 (1943): 42–55.

Staum, Martin S. *Cabanis: Enlightenment and Medical Philosophy in the French Revolution*. Princeton, N.J.: Princeton University Press, 1980.

　"Cabanis and the Science of Man." *Journal of the Behavioral Sciences* 10.1 (1974): 135–43.

　"The Class of Moral and Political Sciences, 1795–1803." *French Historical Studies* 11.3 (1980): 371–97.

Stein, Maurice R. "The Poetic Metaphors of Sociology." In *Sociology on Trial*, edited by Maurice Stein and Arthur Vidich, 173–82. Englewood Cliffs, N.J.: Prentice-Hall, 1963.

Sterns, Peter N. *Priest and Revolutionary: Lamennais and the Dilemma of French Catholicism*. New York: Harper & Row, 1967.

Stewart, John Hall. *The Restoration Era in France, 1814–1830*. Princeton, N.J.: Van Nostrand, 1968.

Swart, Koenraad W. *The Sense of Decadence in Nineteenth-Century France*. The Hague: Martinus Nijhoff, 1964.

Swingewood, Alan William. "Origins of Sociology: The Case of the Scottish Enlightenment." *British Journal of Sociology* 21.2 (1970): 165–80.

Szacki, Jerzy. *History of Sociological Thought*. Westport, Conn.: Greenwood Press, 1979.

Talmon, J. L. *The Origins of Totalitarianism*. New York: Praeger, 1960.

　Political Messianism: The Romantic Phase. New York: Praeger, 1960.

　Romanticism and Revolt: Europe, 1815–1848. 1967. New York: Harcourt, Brace & World, 1970.

Tannery, Paul. "Auguste Comte et l'histoire des sciences." *Revue générale des sciences pures et appliquées* 16.9 (1905): 410–17.

Taton, René. "Hachette, Jean Nicolas Pierre"; "Liouville, Joseph"; "Monge, Gaspard." In *Dictionary of Scientific Biography*. See Gillispie.

Tchernoff, I. *Le Parti républicain sous la Monarchie de Juillet*. Paris: A. Pedone, 1901.

Teixeira Mendes, R., ed. *Auguste Comte: Evolution originale*. Vol. 1, *1798–1820*. Rio de Janeiro: Au Siège Central de l'Eglise Positiviste de Brésil, 1913.

Templeton, Alice, and Stephen B. Groce. "Sociology and Literature: Theoretical Considerations." *Sociological Inquiry* 60 (Winter 1990): 34–46.

Terdiman, Richard. *Discourse/Counter-Discourse: The Theory and Practice of Symbolic Resistance in Nineteenth-Century France*. Ithaca, N.Y.: Cornell University Press, 1985.

Terrou, Fernand. "Le Cadre juridique." In *Histoire générale de la presse française*, edited by Claude Bellanger et al. Vol. 2, *De 1815–1871*, 3–13. Paris: Presses Universitaires de France, 1969.

Thibaudet, Albert. *Histoire de la littérature française de Chateaubriand à Valéry*. 1936. Verviers, Belgium: Marabout, 1981.

Thomas, Louis J. *Montpellier: Ville marchande – Histoire économique et sociale de Montpellier des origines à 1870*. Montpellier: Valat, n.d.

Thompson, Kenneth. *Auguste Comte: The Foundation of Sociology*. The Making of Sociology Series. New York: Wiley, Halsted, 1975.

Thureau-Dangin, Paul. *Histoire de la Monarchie de Juillet*. 7 vols. Paris, 1884.

Timasheff, Nicholas S., and George A. Theodorson. *Sociological Theory: Its Nature and Growth*. 4th ed. New York: Random House, 1976.

Timbal, Louis. *Un Grand Médecin français: Etienne Esquirol (1772–1840)*. (Extract from the *Toulouse Médical*, July 1 and 15, 1938.)

Touchard, Jean. *La Gauche en France depuis 1900*. 1977. Paris: Seuil, 1981.

Tourneux, Maurice. "Andrieux." In *La Grande Encyclopédie*. 31 vols. Paris, 1885–1902.

Tribunal de Première Instance de la Seine. Audience du 11 février 1870. Affaire Auguste Comte. Nullité du Testament. Plaidoirie de Me Allou pour les Exécuteurs Testamentaires. Paris, 1870.

Tronchon, Henri. *La Fortune intellectuelle de Herder en France*. Paris: Rieder, 1920.

Turner, Jonathan H. *The Structure of Sociological Theory*. Homewood, Ill.: Dorsey Press, 1975.

Vallois, Maximilien. *La Formation de l'influence Kantienne en France*. Paris: Félix Alcan, 1932.

Van Den Berghe, Pierre L. *Man in Society: A Biosocial View*. New York: Elsevier, 1975.

Van Duzer, Charles Hunter. *Contribution of the Ideologues to French Revolutionary Thought*. Baltimore, Md.: Johns Hopkins University Press, 1935.

Varney, Mecca M. *L'Influence des femmes sur Auguste Comte*. Paris: Presses Universitaires de France, 1931.

Vartanian, Aram. *Diderot and Descartes: A Study of Scientific Naturalism in the Enlightenment*. Princeton, N.J.: Princeton University Press, 1953.

Vaughan, Michalina, and Margaret Scotford Archer. *Social Conflict and Educational Change in England and France, 1789–1848*. Cambridge: Cambridge University Press, 1971.

Vernon, Richard. "Auguste Comte and 'Development': A Note." *History and Theory* 17.3 (1978): 323–6.

"The Political Self: Auguste Comte and Phrenology." *History of European Ideas* 7 (1986): 271–86.

Vidal, Enrico. *La scienza politica nell'opuscule fondamental del Comte.* Milan: Dott. A. Giuffrè, 1968.

Vidler, Alec. *Prophecy and Papacy: A Study of Lamennais, the Church and the Revolution.* The Birkbeck Lectures, 1952–3. New York: Scribners', 1954.

Voegelin, Eric. *From Enlightenment to Revolution.* Edited by John H. Hallowell. Durham, N.C.: Duke University Press, 1975.

Vyverberg, Henry. *Historical Pessimism in the French Enlightenment.* Cambridge, Mass.: Harvard University Press, 1958.

Walch, Jean. *Bibliographie du Saint-Simonism.* Paris: J. Vrin, 1967.

    Les Maîtres de l'histoire, 1815–1850: Augustin Thierry, Mignet, Guizot, Thiers, Michelet, Edgard Quinet. Paris: Editions Slatkine, 1986.

    Michel Chevalier: Economiste Saint-Simonien, 1806–1879. Paris: J. Vrin, 1975.

    "Qu'est-ce-que le Saint-Simonism: Vues actuelles sur le Saint-Simonism du XIXe siècle." *Economies et sociétés* 4 (April 1970): 613–29.

Walsh, John. "Religion: Church and State in Europe and the Americas." In *The New Cambridge Modern History,* edited by George Clark. Vol. 9, *War and Peace in an Age of Upheaval,* edited by C. W. Crawley, 146–78. Cambridge: Cambridge University Press, 1965.

Weill, Georges. *L'Ecole Saint-Simonienne: Son Histoire, son influence jusqu'à nos jours.* Paris, 1896.

    Histoire de l'enseignement secondaire en France, 1802–1920. Paris: Payot, 1921.

    Un Précurseur du socialisme: Saint-Simon et son oeuvre. Paris, 1894.

Weinburg, Mark. "The Social Analysis of Three Early Nineteenth-Century French Liberals: Say, Comte, and Dunoyer." *Journal of Libertarian Studies* 2.1 (1978): 45–61.

Welch, Cheryl B. *Liberty and Utility: The French Idéologues and the Transformation of Liberalism.* New York: Columbia University Press, 1984.

Wells, G. A. *Herder and After: A Study in the Development of Sociology.* The Hague: Mouton, 1959.

Wettley, Anne Marie. "Les Idées d'instinct d'Auguste Comte dans sa philosophie positive." *Bulletin et mémoires de la Société Internationale d'Histoire de la Médecine,* n.s., 6, special issue (1959): 50–2.

White, Hayden. *Metahistory: The Historical Imagination in Nineteenth-Century Europe.* Baltimore, Md.: Johns Hopkins University Press, 1973; Baltimore, Md.: Johns Hopkins University Press, 1975.

Williams, L. Pearce. "Science, Education, and Napoleon I." In *The Rise of Science in Relation to Society,* edited by Leonard M. Marsak, 80–91. New York: Macmillan, 1964.

Williams, Raymond. *Culture and Society, 1780–1950.* 1958. New York: Harper & Row, Harper Torchbooks, 1966.

Winter, Frank H. "Montgéry, Jacques-Philippe Mérigon de." In *Dictionary of Scientific Biography.* See Gillispie.

Wolff, Maurice. "Le Ménage d'Auguste Comte." *Mercure de France* 226.786 (1931): 557–605.

    "Le Ménage d'un philosophe: Auguste Comte et sa femme." In *Séances et travaux de l'Académie des Sciences Morales et Politiques,* edited by C. Lyon-Caen, 511–21. Paris: Félix Alcan, 1930.

Wokler, Robert. "Saint-Simon and the Passage from Political to Social Science." In

The Languages of Political Theory in Early-Modern Europe, edited by Anthony Pagden, 325–38. Cambridge: Cambridge University Press, 1987.

Wood, Gordon S. *The Creation of the American Republic, 1776–1787.* Chapel Hill: University of North Carolina Press, 1969; New York: Norton, 1972.

Woronoff, Denis. *La République bourgeoise de Thermidor à Brumaire, 1794–1799.* Paris: Seuil, 1972.

Wright, Gordon. *France in Modern Times: From the Enlightenment to the Present.* 4th ed. Chicago: Rand McNally, 1960; New York: Norton, 1987.

Wright, T. R. *The Religion of Humanity: The Impact of Comtean Positivism on Victorian Britain.* Cambridge: Cambridge University Press, 1986.

Wrong, Dennis W. "The Oversocialized Conception of Man in Modern Sociology." *American Sociological Review* 26.2 (1961): 183–93.

Young, Robert M. "Gall, Franz Joseph." In *Dictionary of Scientific Biography.* See Gillispie.

Mind, Brain, and Adaptation in the Nineteenth Century. Oxford: Clarendon Press, 1970.

Zeitlin, Irving M. *Ideology and the Development of Sociological Theory.* Englewood Cliffs, N.J.: Prentice-Hall.

Rethinking Sociology: A Critique of Contemporary Theory. Englewood Cliffs, N.J.: Prentice-Hall, 1973.

Zeldin, Theodore, ed. *Conflicts in French Society: Anticlericalism, Education, and Morals in the Nineteenth Century.* London: Allen & Unwin, 1970.

Zgismond, L. "Le Sort de l'héritage de Saint-Simon: La Manifestation de l'école Saint-Simonienne sous la direction d'Enfantin et Bazard, l'engagement de Comte pour élaborer le système scientifique du positivisme et de la sociologie." *Acta Historica* 24.3–4 (1978).

Index

147–58; Comte's early interest in, 46, 106; Condorcet's view of, 48–53; and the connection with the French Revolution, 49–50; Destutt de Tracy's concept of, 154; distinction of, from physiology, 151, 222; goals of, 210, 340; history as basis of, 37; and the Idéologues, 63, 156; as keystone of positivism, 4; and the law of three stages, 203; Montesquieu's view of, 46–8; and observation and experiment, 170; as part of classification of the sciences, 32, 149, 163; political effects of, 340; and the relationship to order, 10; and the relationship to social harmony, 10; Saint-Simon's view of, 80, 81, 90, 99, 242; as science of generalities, 22; Scottish Enlightenment's influence on, 307, 313; *see also Cours de philosophie positive*; politics; social physics; sociology

sciences: aim of, 566–7; and the arts, 639–40, 705; as basis of positivist synthesis, 693; and Comte's admiration for order, 686; Comte's general approach to, in *Cours*, 564, 570, 575, 578; Comte's interdisplinary approach to, 565, 566; Comte's knowledge of, 502–3, 585–6; Comte's reaction against, 481, 485, 699–700; Comte's study of, 185; conflict of, with philosophy, 679; development of, in Greece, 641; and the French revolutionaries, 19; future progression of, 682; Herder's attitude toward, 279–81; hierarchy of, 149; history of, 659; interrelationships of, 582; as key to understanding the mind, 159; limits of, in terms of propaganda, 213–14; and the *lycée* curriculum, 18; as model in modern sociology, 709; and modern civilization, 655; moral aspects of, 340; order of development of, 656; prestige of, in early-nineteenth-century France, 41; reality of, 686; reform of, 163; and relationship to common sense, 112–13; and religion, 705, 709; Saint-Simonians' attitude toward, 333; Saint-Simon's faith in, 67, 69–70, 75, 84–5, 423; and scientific fictions, 568–9; and the scientific method, 162; and the scientific revolution, 637; *see also* classification of the sciences; philosophy of science; scientists

scientific laws, 32, 33, 199, 206, 211, 223, 294, 336, 570, 573, 632, 637, 641, 673, 694; *see also* sciences

scientific method: as basis of all ideas in positivist system, 4; as basis of unity in positive system, 563; and Encontre, 22; espousal of, by Madame de Staël, 66; as essence of positive philosophy, 159–60; as source of improvement, 162, 185; and the use of a priori and a posteriori approaches, 161; *see also* positive method, sciences

scientism, 3, 32, 418, 424, 574, 577, 693, 701

scientists: allegiance of, to the French Revolution, 31; alliance of, with the people, 171; artists' relationship to, 685; attraction of, to positivism, 659; authority of, 142, 171; Comte's attack on, in *Cours*, 542–3, 550, 575, 613, 619, 666–8; Comte's early hopes for unity of, 107; Comte's general criticisms of, 106, 121, 461, 482, 497, 502–3, 549, 701, 702; education of, 573; *industriels*' relationship to, 109–10; limitations of, 214; as members of an intellectual elite, 37, 565, 675; Mill's view of, 512; as part of new spiritual power, 169; and problem of the dictatorship of, 172; qualifications of, to become spiritual power, 199; reference to, as savants, not scientists, 69n; and restrictions on their freedom in the positive state, 624, 684–5; as rivals of literary men, 31; Saint-Simon's view of, 66, 67, 76–7, 81, 92, 98, 99, 164; and the separation from philosophers in Greece, 641; support of Saint-Simon by, 94; *see also* spiritual power

scientists of society: and the artistic side of existence, 710; authority of, 142–3; Comte's coining of the term "sociologists," 679; Comte's development of his views of, in the fourth opuscule, 334; definition of, 220; vs. the *industriels*, 235–6; and knowledge of other sciences, 573, 623; and the need to come into contact with all types of people, 320; as novelists, 710; as positive philosophers, 366; problem with Comte's concept of, 707; problem of the education of, 366; *see also* positive philosophers; science of society; sociology; spiritual power

Scott, Walter, 392, 483–4, 642, 659, 665

DATE DUE

MFM